The Consumer Credit and Sales
Legal Practice Series

CONSUMER BANKRUPTCY LAW AND PRACTICE

SPECIAL GUIDE TO THE 2005 ACT

2005 Supplement

Henry J. Sommer and John Rao

Contributing Author: Susan A. Schneider

National Consumer Law Center
77 Summer Street, 10th Floor Boston, MA 02110 www.consumerlaw.org

About NCLC

The National Consumer Law Center, a nonprofit corporation founded in 1969, assists consumers, advocates, and public policy makers nationwide who use the powerful and complex tools of consumer law to ensure justice and fair treatment for all, particularly those whose poverty renders them powerless to demand accountability from the economic marketplace. For more information, go to www.consumerlaw.org.

Ordering NCLC Publications

Order securely online at www.consumerlaw.org, or contact Publications Department, National Consumer Law Center, 77 Summer Street, Boston, MA 02110, (617) 542-9595 x1, FAX: (617) 542-8028, e-mail: publications@nclc.org.

Training and Conferences

NCLC participates in numerous national, regional, and local consumer law trainings. Its annual fall conference is a forum for consumer rights attorneys from legal services programs, private practice, government, and nonprofit organizations to share insights into common problems and explore novel and tested approaches that promote consumer justice in the marketplace. Contact NCLC for more information or see our web site.

Case Consulting

Case analysis, consulting and co-counseling for lawyers representing vulnerable consumers are among NCLC's important activities. Administration on Aging funds allow us to provide free consulting to legal services advocates representing elderly consumers on many types of cases. Massachusetts Legal Assistance Corporation funds permit case assistance to advocates representing low-income Massachusetts consumers. Other funding may allow NCLC to provide very brief consultations to other advocates without charge. More comprehensive case analysis and research is available for a reasonable fee. See our web site for more information at www.consumerlaw.org.

Charitable Donations and Cy Pres *Awards*

NCLC's work depends in part on the support of private donors. Tax-deductible donations should be made payable to National Consumer Law Center, Inc. For more information, contact Suzanne Cutler of NCLC's Development Office at (617) 542-8010 or scutler@nclc.org. NCLC has also received generous court-approved *cy pres* awards arising from consumer class actions to advance the interests of class members. For more information, contact Robert Hobbs (rhobbs@nclc.org) or Rich Dubois (rdubois@nclc.org) at (617) 542-8010.

Comments and Corrections

Write to the above address to the attention of the Editorial Department or e-mail consumerlaw@nclc.org.

About This Volume

This is a Special Guide to the 2005 Act with a 2005 Companion CD-Rom. While it is the 2005 Supplement to *Consumer Bankruptcy Law and Practice* (7th ed. 2004), it can also be utilized as a stand-alone volume on the new Act. Retain the Seventh Edition, this Special Guide, and the 2005 CD-Rom. The 2004 CD-Rom can be discarded. Continuing developments can be found in periodic updates to this volume and in NCLC REPORTS, *Bankruptcy & Foreclosures Edition*.

Cite This Update As

National Consumer Law Center, Consumer Bankruptcy Law and Practice (Special Guide to 2005 Act). [When citing to the Seventh Edition and this update: National Consumer Law Center, Consumer Bankruptcy Law and Practice (7th ed. 2004 and 2005 Supp.).]

Attention

This publication is designed to provide authoritative information concerning the subject matter covered. Always use the most current edition and supplement, and use other sources for more recent developments or for special rules for individual jurisdictions. This publication cannot substitute for the independent judgment and skills of an attorney or other professional. Non-attorneys are cautioned against using these materials to conduct a lawsuit without advice from an attorney and are cautioned against engaging in the unauthorized practice of law.

Copyright

ISBN 1-931697-78-7 (this update)
ISBN 1-931697-74-4 (main volume)
ISBN 0-943116-10-4 (Series)

Library of Congress Control Number 2004114739

About the Authors

Henry J. Sommer is Supervising Attorney at the pro bono Consumer Bankruptcy Assistance Project in Philadelphia. Previously, he was the head of the Consumer Law Project at Community Legal Services in Philadelphia, where he worked for over 21 years. He has also served as a Lecturer-in-Law at the University of Pennsylvania Law School. He is Editor in Chief of *Collier on Bankruptcy* and the entire Collier line of bankruptcy publications published by Matthew Bender and Co. He is the author of *Consumer Bankruptcy Law and Practice* (7th ed. 2004) and *Consumer Bankruptcy: The Complete Guide to Chapter 7 and Chapter 13 Personal Bankruptcy* (John Wiley & Sons, 1994) as well as numerous articles on bankruptcy law. He is the co-author of *Collier Family Law and the Bankruptcy Code* (Matthew Bender). He is a former member of the Federal Judicial Conference Advisory Committee on Bankruptcy Rules and the Federal Reserve Board Consumer Advisory Council. He is a member of the National Bankruptcy Conference, a Fellow of the American College of Bankruptcy, and a member of the American Law Institute. He is also President of the National Association of Consumer Bankruptcy Attorneys, Vice President of the Coalition for Consumer Bankruptcy Debtor Education, and former Chairman of the Eastern District of Pennsylvania Bankruptcy Conference. He was the first recipient of the Vern Countryman Consumer Law Award.

John Rao is the editor and a contributing author to *Consumer Bankruptcy Law and Practice* (7th ed. 2004), and is an NCLC attorney with a focus on consumer bankruptcy, foreclosures, and credit law. He is the co-author of *Repossessions and Foreclosures* (5th ed. 2002), contributing author to *Student Loan Law* (2d ed. 2002), and head of NCLC's Advice and Assistance Project. He is also a contributing author to *Collier on Bankruptcy* and the *Collier Bankruptcy Practice Guide*. For 18 years, he had a bankruptcy and consumer law focus at Rhode Island Legal Services, and was a managing attorney there. He is a member of the board of directors for the National Association of Consumer Bankruptcy Attorneys and the American Bankruptcy Institute.

Susan A. Schneider, the contributing author for the family farmer bankruptcy chapter, is an Associate Professor of Law and Director of the Graduate Agricultural Law Program at the University of Arkansas School of Law. She has also taught at William Mitchell College of Law and at the Drake University Summer Agricultural Law Institute. Her private practice and consultation experience include agricultural law work with firms in Arkansas, Minnesota, North Dakota, and Washington, D.C. She served as a staff attorney at Farmer's Legal Action Group, Inc. and at the National Center for Agricultural Law Research and Information. She has published numerous articles on agricultural law subjects, served as the President of the American Agricultural Law Association (AALA) in 2004, and continues to serve on the AALA Board of Directors.

Acknowledgments: This book was supported in part by a grant from the Consumer Protection and Education Fund; we thank them for their assistance. We are particularly grateful to Eric Secoy for editorial supervision; Nathan Day for editorial assistance; Shannon Halbrook, Jon Sheldon, and Carolyn Carter for production assistance; Xylutions for typesetting services; and Neil Fogarty of Law Disks for developing the CD-Rom accompanying this volume, including Law Disks' Bankruptcy Forms.

What Your Library Should Contain

The Consumer Credit and Sales Legal Practice Series contains 16 titles, updated annually, arranged into four libraries, and designed to be an attorney's primary practice guide and legal resource in all 50 states. Each manual includes a CD-Rom allowing pinpoint searches and the pasting of text into a word processor.

Debtor Rights Library

2004 Seventh Edition, Special Guide to the 2005 Act, and 2005 CD-Rom, Including Law Disks' 2005 Bankruptcy Forms

Consumer Bankruptcy Law and Practice: the definitive personal bankruptcy manual, with step-by-step instructions from initial interview to final discharge, and including consumers' rights as creditors when a merchant or landlord files for bankruptcy. The Special Guide to the 2005 Act also includes numerous practice aids for use under the 2005 Act, including a redlined Code, Interim Rules, new forms, means test data, new pleadings, a new questionnaire, and a new client handout.

2004 Fifth Edition, 2005 Supplement, and 2005 CD-Rom

Fair Debt Collection: the basic reference in the field, covering the Fair Debt Collection Practices Act and common law, state statutory and other federal debt collection protections. Appendices and companion CD-Rom contain sample pleadings and discovery, the FTC's Official Staff Commentary, *all* FTC staff opinion letters, and summaries of reported and unreported cases.

2002 Fifth Edition, 2004 Supplement, and 2004 CD-Rom

Repossessions and Foreclosures: unique guide to VA, FHA and other types of home foreclosures, servicer obligations, motor vehicle and mobile home repossessions, threatened seizures of household goods, tax and other statutory liens, and automobile lease and rent-to-own default remedies. The CD-Rom reprints relevant UCC provisions and numerous key federal statutes, regulations, and agency letters, summarizes hundreds of state laws, and includes over 150 pleadings covering a wide variety of cases.

2002 Second Edition, 2004 Supplement, and 2004 CD-Rom

Student Loan Law: student loan debt collection and collection fees; discharges based on closed school, false certification, failure to refund, disability, and bankruptcy; tax intercepts, wage garnishment, and offset of social security benefits; repayment plans, consolidation loans, deferments, and non-payment of loan based on school fraud. CD-Rom and appendices contain numerous forms, pleadings, interpretation letters and regulations.

2004 Third Edition with CD-Rom

Access to Utility Service: the only examination of consumer rights when dealing with regulated, de-regulated, and unregulated utilities, including telecommunications, terminations, billing errors, low-income payment plans, utility allowances in subsidized housing, LIHEAP, and weatherization. Includes summaries of state utility regulations.

Credit and Banking Library

2003 Fifth Edition, 2004 Supplement, and 2004 CD-Rom

Truth in Lending: detailed analysis of *all* aspects of TILA, the Consumer Leasing Act, and the Home Ownership and Equity Protection Act (HOEPA). Appendices and the CD-Rom contain the Acts, Reg. Z, Reg. M, and their Official Staff Commentaries, numerous sample pleadings, rescission notices, and two programs to compute APRs.

2002 Fifth Edition, 2005 Supplement, and 2005 CD-Rom

Fair Credit Reporting: the key resource for handling any type of credit reporting issue, from cleaning up blemished credit records to suing reporting agencies and creditors for inaccurate reports. Covers credit scoring, privacy issues, identity theft, the FCRA, the new FACT Act, the Credit Repair Organizations Act, state credit reporting and repair statutes, and common law claims.

2005 Third Edition with CD-Rom

Consumer Banking and Payments Law: unique analysis of consumer law (and NACHA rules) as to checks, money orders, credit, debit, and stored value cards, and banker's right of setoff. Also extensive treatment of electronic records and signatures, electronic transfer of food stamps, and direct deposits of federal payments. The CD-Rom and appendices reprint relevant agency interpretations and pleadings.

2005 Third Edition with CD-Rom

The Cost of Credit: Regulation and Legal Challenges: a one-of-a-kind resource detailing state and federal regulation of consumer credit in all fifty states, federal usury preemption, explaining credit math, and how to challenge excessive credit charges and credit insurance. The CD-Rom includes a credit math program and hard-to-find agency interpretations.

2005 Fourth Edition with CD-Rom

Credit Discrimination: analysis of the Equal Credit Opportunity Act, Fair Housing Act, Civil Rights Acts, and state credit discrimination statutes, including reprints of all relevant federal interpretations, government enforcement actions, and numerous sample pleadings.

Consumer Litigation Library

2004 Fourth Edition with CD-Rom

Consumer Arbitration Agreements: numerous successful approaches to challenge the enforceability of a binding arbitration agreement, the interrelation of the Federal Arbitration Act and state law, class actions in arbitration, collections via arbitration, the right to discovery, and other topics. Appendices and CD-Rom include sample discovery, numerous briefs, arbitration service provider rules and affidavits as to arbitrator costs.

2002 Fifth Edition, 2005 Supplement, and 2005 CD-Rom

Consumer Class Actions: A Practical Litigation Guide: makes class action litigation manageable even for small offices, including numerous sample pleadings, class certification memoranda, discovery, class notices, settlement materials, and much more. Includes a detailed analysis of the Class Action Fairness Act of 2005, recent changes to Rule 23, and other contributions from seven of the most experienced consumer class action litigators around the country.

2004 CD-Rom with Index Guide: ALL pleadings from ALL NCLC Manuals, including Consumer Law Pleadings Numbers One through Ten

Consumer Law Pleadings on CD-Rom: Over 1000 notable recent pleadings from all types of consumer cases, including predatory lending, foreclosures, automobile fraud, lemon laws, debt collection, fair credit reporting, home improvement fraud, rent to own, student loans, and lender liability. Finding aids pinpoint the desired pleading in seconds, ready to paste into a word processing program.

Deception and Warranties Library

2004 Sixth Edition with CD-Rom

Unfair and Deceptive Acts and Practices: the only practice manual covering all aspects of a deceptive practices case in every state. Special sections on automobile sales, the federal racketeering (RICO) statute, unfair insurance practices, and the FTC Holder Rule.

2003 Second Edition, 2005 Supplement, and 2005 CD-Rom

Automobile Fraud: examination of title law, odometer tampering, lemon laundering, sale of salvage and wrecked cars, undisclosed prior use, prior damage to new cars, numerous sample pleadings, and title search techniques.

2001 Second Edition, 2005 Supplement, and 2005 CD-Rom

Consumer Warranty Law: comprehensive treatment of new and used car lemon laws, the Magnuson-Moss Warranty Act, UCC Articles 2 and 2A, mobile home, new home, and assistive device warranty laws, FTC Used Car Rule, tort theories, car repair and home improvement statutes, service contract and lease laws, with numerous sample pleadings.

NCLC's CD-Roms

Every NCLC manual comes with a companion CD-Rom featuring pop-up menus, PDF format, Internet-style navigation of appendices, indices, and bonus pleadings, hard-to-find agency interpretations and other practice aids. Documents can be copied into a word processing program. Of special note is *Consumer Law in a Box*:

July 2005 CD-Rom

Consumer Law in a Box: a CD-Rom combining *all* documents and software from 16 other NCLC CD-Roms. Quickly pinpoint a document from thousands found on the CD through keyword searches and Internet-style navigation, links, bookmarks, and other finding aids.

Other NCLC Publications for Lawyers

issued 24 times a year

NCLC REPORTS covers the latest developments and ideas in the practice of consumer law.

2003 First Edition with CD-Rom

The Practice of Consumer Law: Seeking Economic Justice: contains an essential overview to consumer law and explains how to get started in a private or legal services consumer practice. Packed with invaluable sample pleadings and practice pointers for even experienced consumer attorneys.

2002 First Edition with CD-Rom

STOP Predatory Lending: A Guide for Legal Advocates: provides a roadmap and practical legal strategy for litigating predatory lending abuses, from small loans to mortgage loans. The CD-Rom contains a credit math program, pleadings, legislative and administrative materials, and underwriting guidelines.

National Consumer Law Center Guide Series are books designed for consumers, counselors, and attorneys new to consumer law:

2005 Edition

NCLC Guide to Surviving Debt: a great overview of consumer law. Everything a paralegal, new attorney, or client needs to know about debt collectors, managing credit card debt, whether to refinance, credit card problems, home foreclosures, evictions, repossessions, credit reporting, utility terminations, student loans, budgeting, and bankruptcy.

2002 Edition

NCLC Guide to Mobile Homes: what consumers and their advocates need to know about mobile home dealer sales practices and an in-depth look at mobile home quality and defects, with 35 photographs and construction details.

2002 Edition

NCLC Guide to Consumer Rights for Immigrants: an introduction to many of the most critical consumer issues faced by immigrants, including international wires, check cashing and banking, *notario* and immigration consultant fraud, affidavits of support, telephones, utilities, credit history discrimination, high-cost credit, used car fraud, student loans and more.

2000 Edition

Return to Sender: Getting a Refund or Replacement for Your Lemon Car: Find how lemon laws work, what consumers and their lawyers should know to evaluate each other, investigative techniques and discovery tips, how to handle both informal dispute resolution and trials, and more.

Visit **www.consumerlaw.org** to order securely online or for more information on all NCLC manuals and CD-Roms, including the full tables of contents, indices, listings of CD-Rom contents, and **web-based searches of the manuals' full text**.

National Consumer Law Center ▪ 77 Summer Street ▪ 10th Floor ▪ Boston MA ▪ 02110
(617) 542-9595 ▪ FAX (617) 542-8028 ▪ publications@nclc.org
Order securely online at www.consumerlaw.org

Finding Aids and Search Tips

The Consumer Credit and Sales Legal Practice Series presently contains sixteen volumes, nine supplements, and sixteen companion CD-Roms—all constantly being updated. The Series includes over 10,000 pages, 100 chapters, 100 appendices, and over 1000 pleadings, as well as hundreds of documents found on the CD-Roms, but not found in the books. Here are a number of ways to pinpoint in seconds what you need from this array of materials.

Internet-Based Searches

www.consumerlaw.org

Electronically search every chapter and appendix of all sixteen manuals and their supplements: go to www.consumerlaw.org/keyword and enter a case name, regulation cite, or other search term. You are instantly given the book names and page numbers of any of the NCLC manuals containing that term, with those hits shown in context.

www.consumerlaw.org

Current indexes, tables of contents, and CD-Rom contents for all sixteen volumes are found at www.consumerlaw.org. Just click on *The Consumer Credit and Sales Legal Practice Series* and scroll down to the book you want. Then click on that volume's index, contents, or CD-Rom contents.

Finding Material on NCLC's CD-Roms

Consumer Law in a Box CD-Rom

Electronically search all sixteen NCLC CD-Roms, including thousands of agency interpretations, all NCLC appendices and almost 1000 pleadings: use Acrobat's search button* in NCLC's *Consumer Law in a Box CD-Rom* (this CD-Rom is free to set subscribers) to find every instance that a keyword appears on any of our sixteen CD-Roms. Then, with one click, go to that location to see the full text of the document.

CD-Rom accompanying this volume

Electronically search the CD-Rom accompanying this volume, including pleadings, agency interpretations, and regulations. Use Acrobat's search button* to find every instance that a keyword appears on the CD-Rom, and then, with one click, go to that location on the CD-Rom. Or just click on subject buttons until you navigate to the document you need.

Finding Pleadings

Consumer Law Pleadings on CD-Rom and Index Guide

Search five different ways for the right pleading from over 1000 choices: use the *Index Guide* accompanying *Consumer Law Pleadings on CD-Rom* to search for pleadings by type, subject, publication title, name of contributor, or contributor's jurisdiction. The guide also provides a summary of the pleading once the right pleading is located. *Consumer Law Pleadings on CD-Rom* and the *Consumer Law in a Box CD-Rom* also let you search for all pleadings electronically by subject, type of pleading, and by publication title, giving you instant access to the full pleading in Word and/or PDF format once you find the pleading you need.

Using This Volume to Find Material in All Sixteen Volumes

This volume

The Quick Reference at the back of this volume lets you pinpoint manual sections or appendices where over 1000 different subject areas are covered.

---

* Users of NCLC CD-Roms should become familiar with "search," a powerful Acrobat tool, distinguished from "find," another Acrobat feature that is less powerful than "search." The Acrobat 5 "search" icon is a pair of binoculars with paper in the background, while the "find" icon is a pair of binoculars without the paper. Acrobat 6 and 7 use one icon, a pair of binoculars, that opens a dialog box with several search options.

Contents

Chapter 3 Attorney Duties

Chapter 4 New Paperwork and Notice Requirements

Chapter 8 Exemption Provisions

Chapter 9 Domestic Support Obligations

Chapter 10 Discharge Provisions

Chapter 11 Changes to Chapter 12—Adjustment of Debts of a Family Farmer

Appendix A Bankruptcy Statutes

Appendix B Interim Bankruptcy Rules

Appendix C Bankruptcy Fees

Appendix D New and Amended Official Bankruptcy Forms

Appendix E Practice Aids

Appendix F Means Test Data

CD-Rom Contents

Bankruptcy Rules, Fees

Bankruptcy Forms Software

Bankruptcy Forms, Pleadings

Search This Manual

Search This Manual's Appendices, Plus All Other Documents on This CD-Rom
Limit Search Only to the Current File You Are Using on the CD-Rom
Search Chapters and Appendices of This Manual
Summary Contents of This Manual
Table of Contents of This Manual
Index of This Manual
CD-Rom Contents for This Manual
Contents of Other NCLC Manuals

Contents of NCLC Publications

Internet-Based Keyword Search of All NCLC Manuals
Detailed and Summary Tables of Contents for Each Manual
Short Description of Each Manual's Features with Link to Manual's Detailed Index
Short Index to Major Topics Covered in the 16-Volume Series
Descriptions of Other NCLC Books for Lawyers and Consumers
Features of *Consumer Law in a Box* (16 CD-Roms Combined into One Master CD-Rom)
Printer-Friendly 3-Page Description of All NCLC Publications, Latest Supplements
Printer-Friendly 25-Page Brochure Describing All NCLC Publications
Printer-Friendly Order Form for All NCLC Publications
Order Securely On-line

Consumer Education Brochures, Books

Legal and General Audience Books Available to Order from NCLC
- *The Practice of Consumer Law: Seeking Economic Justice*
- *STOP Predatory Lending: A Guide for Legal Advocates, with CD-Rom*
- *Return to Sender: Getting a Refund or Replacement for Your Lemon Car*
- *The NCLC Guide to Surviving Debt* (2005 Edition)
- *The NCLC Guide to Consumer Rights for Immigrants*
- *The NCLC Guide to Mobile Homes*
- Printer-Friendly Order Form
- Order Securely On-line

Brochures for Consumers on This CD-Rom
- General Consumer Education Brochures
- *Consumer Concerns for Older Americans*
- *Immigrant Justice in the Consumer Marketplace*

Order NCLC Publications, CD-Roms

new material

To Order This Publication
NCLC Manuals and CD-Roms
Order Publications On-line
Printer-Friendly Order Form
Consumer Law in a Box CD-Rom
Credit Math, Bankruptcy Forms Software
Printer-Friendly Publications Brochure
NCLC Newsletters
Case Assistance
Conferences, Training
Books for Lawyers, Consumers
Consumer Education Pamphlets
Consumer Web Links

Chapter 1 Using This Update

1.1 Can This Update Be Used As a Stand-Alone Guide?

While this update is the 2005 Supplement to NCLC's *Consumer Bankruptcy Law and Practice*,[1] experienced bankruptcy practitioners can also use it as a stand-alone guide to the 2005 amendments to the Bankruptcy Code. Subscribers to *Consumer Bankruptcy Law and Practice* will find this guide a convenient way to keep their existing volume current with the 2005 changes and related new practice aids: the appendices are organized similarly to the main volume, the text uses a similar format, there are numerous references to the main volume, and the CD-Rom accompanying this volume is cumulative, containing all the files on the 2004 CD-Rom, plus much new material.

Those not having access to *Consumer Bankruptcy Law and Practice* will still find this guide a useful and comprehensive resource to handling bankruptcies under the revised Act, as long as the practitioner has an understanding of existing bankruptcy practice. While not requiring the reader to refer to specific pages of *Consumer Bankruptcy Law and Practice*, this guide does presume knowledge of existing law. Those without that familiarity who wish to file a consumer bankruptcy case should utilize this guide in tandem with *Consumer Bankruptcy Law and Practice* or another consumer bankruptcy manual.

1.2 Overview of the 2005 Act

On April 20, 2005, the President signed the Bankruptcy Abuse Prevention and Consumer Protection Act of 2005 (the 2005 Act).[2] The Act, 512 pages in length, makes significant changes to the Bankruptcy Code and other bankruptcy statutes, and affects nearly every aspect of bankruptcy cases. The Act in general takes effect on October 17, 2005. Several provisions however became effective upon enactment, while other provisions have individualized effective dates.[3]

From its Orwellian title (the Act is clearly *not* a "Consumer Protection Act") to the last of its 512 pages, the 2005 Act presents numerous challenges to attorneys who represent consumer debtors. How such terrible legislation could be passed by Congress is a story of money, political mean-spiritedness, and intellectual dishonesty, as detailed in a number of media and law review articles.[4]

This guide focuses on the implications of this legislation for bankruptcy practitioners and debtors. There is no doubt that bankruptcy relief will be more expensive for almost all debtors, less effective for many debtors, and totally inaccessible for some debtors as a result of the new law. At the same time, other debtors, often the higher-income individuals whose "abuses" of bankruptcy the Act was ostensibly aimed at, will find themselves better off than before because of generous new exemptions for retirement and education savings accounts and a means test which can be turned to the debtor's advantage, in both chapters 7 and 13, by the careful planning that only higher income debtors can afford to do.

One of the chief problems that will be confronted is atrocious drafting, especially in many of the consumer provisions of the Act. In contrast to the 1978 legislation, which was crafted with extensive assistance from many of the finest minds in the bankruptcy world, the consumer provisions of the 2005 legislation were largely drafted by lobbyists with little knowledge of real-life consumer bankruptcy practice.[5] It is perhaps a credit to the bank-

1 (7th ed. 2004).

2 Pub. L. No. 109-08, 119 Stat. 23 (2005).

3 Most of the provisions affecting consumer bankruptcies take effect on or after October 17, 2005, except for several of the exemption changes discussed in Chapter 8, *infra*, which went into effect on April 20, 2005.

4 See Henry J. Sommer, *Causes of the Consumer Bankruptcy Explosion: Debtor Abuse or Easy Credit?*, 27 Hofstra L. Rev. 33 (1998) for some earlier views on this subject.

5 *See* Rehfeld, *Top Creditor Lobbyist Tassey Goes for Broke*, The Am. Banker, May 17, 2001, at 1 (lobbyist-produced report became framework for bill); McAllister, *Reopening Chapter 7*, Wash. Post, Jan. 1, 1998, at A23 (early version

ruptcy bar that no true expert in bankruptcy participated in drafting the consumer provisions sought by the financial services industry; apparently the industry did not trust any experienced bankruptcy attorneys, even creditor attorneys, to carry out its mission of defacing the Code. Or perhaps it is just an indication of the arrogance of the Act's drafters, who throughout the legislative process steadfastly resisted even the smallest technical corrections to their handiwork.

The silver lining is that the Act is so poorly drafted that it may not accomplish much of what its financial backers wanted to accomplish. It will be interesting to see whether courts that have been instructed to strictly follow the plain language of the statute adhere to that rule in interpreting the new provisions, leaving it to Congress to fix any mistakes.[6] Of course, some judges who profess to follow that method of statutory interpretation seem to do so only when it brings about the result they desire.[7]

Another redeeming fact is that the amendments will not be interpreted or implemented by those who wrote them, but rather by judges, trustees, United States trustees, and attorneys for both debtors and creditors, individuals who want to see the bankruptcy system work and serve its intended purposes, not come grinding to a halt. Some provisions may well be ignored due to their sheer silliness. Amended section 342(b)(1) of the Bankruptcy Code requires the clerk to give the debtor a notice[8] that another provision, new section 527(a)(1), seems to require attorneys and petition preparers to give to the debtor.[9] Section 528 requires many attorneys who solely represent creditors and landlords to advertise that they help debtors file bankruptcy cases.[10]

It is no secret that the Act's proponents sought to limit the discretion of bankruptcy judges who, they say, are "not real judges."[11] However, despite such efforts, there are many areas in which judicial discretion remains. In addition, one should never underestimate the inertia of local legal culture. After all, there still remain many districts where courts "require" chapter 13 plans to pay a minimum percentage to unsecured creditors, despite statutory amendments over twenty years ago and numerous appellate decisions making clear that the Code contains no such requirement.

There is no question that the provisions of the Bankruptcy Code have been changed in many significant respects. There is also no question that many debtors, especially those priced out of bankruptcy relief due to increased costs, will be adversely affected by those changes. And there is no question that some debtors will have to pay more to some creditors. However, debtors and creditors alike may be surprised to find that some of the supposedly pro-creditor changes in the Code could benefit some consumer debtors, that the credit industry has not accomplished all that it may have thought it did, and that practices may not change nearly as extensively as many people anticipate. If judges, attorneys, and trustees work together to try to make sense out of some of the bizarre language enacted by Congress, consumer bankruptcy will remain a lifeline, albeit a bit frayed, for most of the millions of families who so desperately need it.

1.3 Interim Rules and Forms

On August 22, 2005, the Judicial Conference of the United States released interim Rules of Bankruptcy Procedure and new and amended versions of the Official Forms required to file a bankruptcy. Because the Act goes into effect 180 days after passage, on October 17, 2005, there was not enough time to formally amend the Federal Rules of Bankruptcy Procedure to comply with the new requirements. Normally the rules amendment process takes several years to complete.

Consequently, the Judicial Conference of the United States urges bankruptcy courts to adopt the interim rules, which were approved by its Advisory Committee on Bankruptcy Rules and the Committee on Rules of Practice and Procedure. These interim rules are reprinted in Appendix B, *infra*, and are also found on the CD-Rom accompanying this volume.

The interim rules are expected to apply to bankruptcy cases from October 17, 2005, until final rules are pro-

of bankruptcy bill was "similar" to bill drafted by George J. Wallace for American Financial Services Association).

6 *See* Lamie v. United States Trustee, 540 U.S. 526, 124 S. Ct. 1023, 157 L. Ed. 2d 1024 (2004). One court has already adopted this plain meaning approach to the 2005 Act in reaching a holding apparently at odds with the drafter's intent. *See In re* McNabb, 326 B.R. 785 (Bankr. D. Ariz. 2005).

7 *See* BFP v. Resolution Trust Corp., 511 U.S. 531, 549, 114 S. Ct. 1757, 128 L. Ed. 2d 556 (1994) (Souter, J. dissenting) (noting that rejecting the holding of the majority opinion written by Justice Scalia that "value" means foreclosure sale price is as easy as plain language interpretation is likely to get).

8 A similar provision in existing section 342(b), requiring the clerk to give a notice to debtors (who rarely appear at the clerk's office) before the case is filed, is widely ignored.

9 *See* § 4.2.2, *infra*.

10 *See* § 3.5.3, *infra*.

11 Peter G. Gosselin, *Judges Say Overhaul Would Weaken Bankruptcy System*, L.A. Times, Mar 29, 2005, at A1 (quoting creditor lobbyist Jeff Tassey).

mulgated and effective under the regular Rules Enabling Act process. The Advisory Committee on Bankruptcy Rules and the Committee on Rules of Practice and Procedure expect to publish for public comment in August 2006 proposed new and amended Federal Rules of Bankruptcy Procedure, based "substantially in the form of the Interim Rules modified after considering input from the bench and bar as a result of the use of the Interim Rules."[12]

The Judicial Conference also released amended and new Official Forms to implement the new law on August 22, 2005. These forms, whose use is required to file a bankruptcy case, are reprinted in Appendix D, *infra*, and are also found on the CD-Rom accompanying this volume as Adobe Acrobat (PDF) files. In addition, the CD-Rom contains software which allows users to complete these new forms in either Microsoft Word or WordPerfect word processing programs. These files can then easily be converted to PDF format for electronic filing with the courts. Practitioners should keep in mind however that the Judicial Conference continues to review these forms and changes may continue to be made after the release of this guide. Practitioners should also review their district's local rules to determine whether any alterations were made to the interim rules and new and amended Official Forms when adopted by the local court.

1.4 Contents and Organization of This Guide

This guide is intended to analyze the significant changes to consumer bankruptcy practice under chapters 7, 12, and 13 due to the 2005 Act. The guide also suggests ways in which consumer bankruptcy practitioners can respond to these changes and still keep bankruptcy as a practical alternative for debtors and bankruptcy practice as a viable alternative for attorneys. In these regards, the guide is crammed with useful practice aids to facilitate the job of a bankruptcy attorney, both in the appendices and on the CD-Rom accompanying this volume.

The text is organized into eleven chapters. This first Chapter serves as an introduction to the guide. Chapters 2 through 4, *infra*, examine three of the most significant changes made by the Act for consumer bankruptcy practitioners—new limits on who may qualify to file for bankruptcy under chapter 7, new requirements placed on attorneys, and new paperwork and notice requirements. Other changes relevant to chapters 7, 13, and 12 filings are found in Chapters 5, 6, and 11, *infra*, respectively. Issues concerning repeat bankruptcy filings and also concerning automatic stay changes are set out in Chapter 7, *infra*. Chapters 8, 9, and 10, *infra*, examine changes concerning exemptions, domestic support obligations, and discharge provisions respectively.

The appendices contain a plethora of useful material. Appendix A, *infra*, reprints statutory material. Appendix A.1 is a red-lined version of the Bankruptcy Code, showing the 2005 changes. Appendix A.2 is a similar red-lined version of the changes made to Title 28 of the United States Code of particular relevance to consumer bankruptcies. Appendix A.3 reprints the entire 2005 Act, and Appendix A.4 includes selected materials from the Act's legislative history. All of this material can be easily searched and pasted into a word processing program using the CD-Rom accompanying this volume.

Appendix B, *infra*, reprints a red-lined version of the Bankruptcy Rules changes implemented by the interim rules just released by the Judicial Conference of the United States, to reflect the changes in bankruptcy practice required by the 2005 Act. The complete set of Bankruptcy Rules in effect prior to the proposal of the interim rules is found on the CD-Rom. Also on the CD-Rom are official changes to the Bankruptcy Rules that are scheduled to take effect in December of 2005, that were proposed and adopted independently of the 2005 Act.

Appendix C, *infra*, reprints changes to the bankruptcy fee schedules. Appendix C.1 indicates changes to filing fees that are scheduled to go into effect October 17, 2005. Appendix C.2 reprints the new miscellaneous fee schedule that went into effect earlier in 2005.

Appendix D, *infra*, reprints the new and amended Official Forms along with the Advisory Committee Notes explaining the changes made to the forms. These forms are also found on the CD-Rom and, more importantly, the CD-Rom also contains software which enables the user to complete these new and amended forms in either Microsoft Word or WordPerfect word processing programs.

Appendix E, *infra*, contains two useful practice aids. When filing a case under the 2005 Act, practitioners must now compute whether twenty-one pre-petition events occurred before or after a specified number of days from the date of the petition. The CD-Rom accompanying this guide contains a "Date Calculator" that performs this task quickly and simply, after the user merely types in the

---

12 *See* Memorandum from the Committee on Rules of Practice and Procedure to all Chief Judges, United States District Court Judges, and United States Bankruptcy Courts (August 22, 2005) (reprinted in Appx. B, *infra*).

expected petition filing date. An example of the results produced by this calculator, along with a detailed description of the twenty-one pre-petition events, is set out in Appendix E.1.

The 2005 Act also requires the debtor to produce tax records in certain situations, and such returns may not always be easy to obtain in a timely manner. Appendix E.2 provides advice and relevant Internal Revenue Service forms which may be used to expedite and simplify this process.

One of the major changes made by the 2005 Act is the addition of a means test used to determine a debtor's qualification to file under chapter 7. Whether the means test applies at all will depend on whether the debtor's income is above the applicable state's median income for a similar family size. The Executive Office of the United States Trustee has released the state median income figures for each family size for use in determining whether the means test applies to a particular bankruptcy filer. Appendix F.1, *infra*, reprints this official median income table for each state and family size (and also for United States territories).

If the means test applies, then the practitioner must compute allowable expenses in various categories. Appendix F.2, *infra*, contains Internal Revenue Service (IRS) standards for allowable expenses that can be utilized in this calculation, including material from the IRS manual and its national standards for allowable expenses. Separate standards are reprinted for Alaska, Hawaii, and Puerto Rico, and for transportation expenses for different areas of the country.

Appendix G, *infra*, reprints ten sample pleadings that are of special relevance to practitioners filing cases under the 2005 Act, including pleadings seeking an exemption from the credit counseling requirement, a statement of special circumstances rebutting the presumption of abuse created by the means test, a motion to excuse unavailable payment advices, and a motion for more time to fulfill the new paperwork requirements. Other pleadings relate to the automatic stay requirements and a pleading seeking reduction of a claim amount based on the creditor's refusal to negotiate a repayment plan.

These pleadings are also available in Microsoft Word format on the CD-Rom accompanying this volume, allowing them to be easily pasted into a word processing program for use in actual cases. In addition, the CD-Rom contains over 150 other sample pleadings to be used in consumer bankruptcy cases. These further pleadings were drafted prior to enactment of the 2005 amendments and may have to be adapted in some cases to meet the new requirements.

Appendix H, *infra*, is a detailed questionnaire to be filled out by the client to assist the practitioner in filing the case. This Appendix updates the questionnaire found in *Consumer Bankruptcy Law and Practice*[13] to reflect the new requirements created by the 2005 Act. The questionnaire is available in both Adobe Acrobat (PDF) and Microsoft Word format on the CD-Rom. Practitioners may use the PDF format to print the questionnaire out unchanged to hand to clients, and the Word version to adapt the questionnaire to their own requirements.

Appendix I, *infra*, is a client handout answering common bankruptcy questions. It is an adaptation of the handout found in the main volume, updated to reflect the changes made by the 2005 Act. As with the questionnaire, this handout is available on the CD-Rom in both PDF and Microsoft Word format, to facilitate use either in typeset form, or as adapted by an attorney using a word processing program.

1.5 The Companion CD-Rom

The CD-Rom accompanying this volume is cumulative to the CD-Rom accompanying *Consumer Bankruptcy Law and Practice*. It contains all material from the earlier CD-Rom that is still in effect, plus additional files and software to facilitate filings under the 2005 amendments. A detailed listing of the CD-Rom's contents is found just before this Chapter (and after the regular table of contents). In addition, directions on how to install and otherwise use the information on the CD-Rom is found in the last two pages of this guide, in a section called About the CD-Rom.

Key features included on the CD-Rom are the *Bankruptcy Forms* software which may be used to complete the Official Forms in Microsoft Word or WordPerfect format, and a Date Calculator that computes whether twenty-one pre-petition events occurred before or after a specified number of days from the date of the filing of the petition. This software comes with the guide at no additional charge. As such, it is generally unsupported, but it should be easy to use. The *Bankruptcy Forms* software creates Microsoft Word or WordPerfect files, which allows the user to fill in the blanks using either the Word or WordPerfect word processing programs and edit, print out, and save the form as a word processing document.

13 (7th ed. 2004).

The CD-Rom has all the material found in the appendices and much additional information in Adobe Acrobat (PDF) format, allowing Internet-style navigation, rapid key word searches, and also allowing material to be pasted into a word processing program. Sample pleadings, a questionnaire, and a client handout are also available on the CD-Rom in Word format, making it particularly easy to move those whole documents into a word processing program.

The CD-Rom also contains all relevant bankruptcy statutes—not just the Bankruptcy Code—and all the Federal Rules of Bankruptcy Procedure, with 2005 changes as applicable. Over 150 sample bankruptcy pleadings are also found on the CD-Rom, but these pleadings were drafted before enactment of the 2005 amendments, and should thus be reviewed carefully to insure that they are still correct. The CD-Rom also contains annotated, sample completed bankruptcy forms to aid a practitioner in completing the forms. While these completed forms utilize the old versions of the forms, they are still largely relevant to completing the amended forms reflecting the 2005 changes.

The CD-Rom is also packed with numerous consumer education brochures and client handouts covering many areas of concern to debtors and other consumers. Detailed information about other NCLC publications is also available on the CD-Rom.

1.6 Future Updates; Dedicated Weblink

Now, more than ever, practitioners will need to constantly keep current on changes to bankruptcy law and practice. There are numerous ambiguous or conflicting provisions of the 2005 Act that have yet to be interpreted by the courts. The Bankruptcy Rules will continue to be amended. Even as the Official Forms were released in late August, 2005, discussions were underway to revise them. Portions of the released forms indicate on the form itself that they are "under review." Means test data must be continually updated. Most importantly, bankruptcy courts and trustees have not yet begun to implement changes made by the 2005 Act in actual cases.

NCLC will keep readers current in four ways. **First, readers may visit www.consumerlaw.org/bankrupdate to find the latest changes to the forms, rules, means test data, analysis, and so forth (a weblink to this site may also be found on the CD-Rom accompanying this volume).** This dedicated website for readers of this guide will be kept current until NCLC produces its next update volume, as described below.

Second, for twenty-five years, NCLC has updated *Consumer Bankruptcy Law and Practice* each year by publishing either a cumulative supplement or a revised edition. The volume is now in its seventh edition. Clearly an eighth edition is not too far away, and NCLC will release at least one update in 2006.

In addition, our periodical publication NCLC REPORTS *Bankruptcy and Foreclosures Edition* keeps readers current on bankruptcy changes, six times a year. Finally, both authors of this guide frequently lecture and train on bankruptcy issues, particularly now with the 2005 amendments going into effect. For more information on NCLC publications and training, visit www.consumerlaw.org.

Chapter 2 Chapter 7 Dismissal, Means Testing, and Section 707(b) Motions

2.1 Introduction

The Bankruptcy Abuse Prevention and Consumer Protection Act of 2005 (2005 Act) changes the rules as to debtors' ability to proceed with a chapter 7 bankruptcy. A means test, added in section 707(b)(2) of the Bankruptcy Code, determines whether there is a presumption of abuse based on the debtor's ability to repay creditors. Importantly, this test does not apply to debtors whose income is below certain standards. This Chapter examines when a debtor's income is low enough to qualify for this safe harbor, and also looks at the formula to determine whether a presumption of abuse exists for purposes of dismissal under section 707(b). This Chapter also reviews the special circumstances which may rebut this presumption, and other changes made by the 2005 Act to the general grounds for dismissal or conversion of a chapter 7 case, which are now found in section 707(b)(1) of the Code.

2.2 Safe Harbor for Debtors with Incomes Below Median Income and Disabled Veterans

2.2.1 Limits on Section 707(b) Motions for Debtors with Incomes Below State's Median Income

Means testing to determine if a presumption of abuse exists for purposes of section 707(b) applies only to those debtors whose current monthly income is above the state median income. Section 707(b)(7) provides that a motion seeking to apply the means test under section 707(b)(2) may not be brought if the debtor's current monthly income multiplied by twelve is equal to or less than the highest median income figure for the debtor's state as reported by the Census Bureau. As stated in the 2005 Act's legislative history: "The Act's second safe harbor only pertains to a motion under section 707(b)(2), that is, a motion to dismiss based on a debtor's ability to repay. It does not allow a judge, United States trustee, bankruptcy administrator or party in interest to file such motion if the income of the debtor (including a veteran, as that term is defined in 38 U.S.C. § 101) and the debtor's spouse is less than certain monetary thresholds."[1]

This safe harbor should mean that an abuse motion based on *ability to repay* can not be brought against a debtor whose income is below the threshold, either under the means test in section 707(b)(2) or the general abuse provision found in section 707(b)(1). Otherwise, an entity pursuing such a motion under section 707(b)(1) would essentially be advancing a means test different than the bright line test set out by Congress precisely because it did not want vague and undefined determinations of ability to repay. Consequently, the bright line test set forth by Congress will protect some debtors who might have been subject to section 707(b) motions under the former law.

In addition, no section 707(b)(1) abuse motion may be brought against a debtor on other grounds, other than by a judge, United States trustee, or bankruptcy administrator, if the current monthly income of the debtor, or in a joint case of the debtor and the debtor's spouse, is below the state median income.[2] This provision is consistent with prior law, which explicitly stated that section 707(b) motions could be granted on the court's own motion or on the motion of the United States trustee, but not "at the request or suggestion of any party in interest." For debtors with incomes above the state median income, the 2005 Act now permits creditors and other parties in interest, including panel trustees, to file dismissal motions under the general abuse provisions of section 707(b)(1) and under the means test of section 707(b)(2).[3]

1 H.R. Rep. No. 109-31, at 51 (2005).

2 11 U.S.C. § 707(b)(6).

3 11 U.S.C. § 707(b)(1), (6), (7).

2.2.2 Determining the Debtor's Current Monthly Income

2.2.2.1 A Six-Month Average

"Current monthly income" is defined in section 101 of the Bankruptcy Code as the average of the last six months' income received from all sources by the debtor (or in a joint case, by the debtor and the debtor's spouse), with certain adjustments.[4] As a result, the debtor's actual income at the time the petition is filed may be significantly below or above "current monthly income," which is a six-month average.

The six-month period is defined as the six months ending on the last day of the month before the petition is filed. Thus the timing of filing the petition may determine whether a particular month puts the debtor over or under the median income safe harbor, that is, the amount that would create a presumption of abuse under the means test, or some other consequence. If a debtor's income has recently increased, the debtor may want to file quickly. If a debtor's income has gone down, waiting a few months would be preferable if no emergency requires an immediate filing.

All debtors whose debts are primarily consumer debts, all individual debtors in chapter 11, and all chapter 13 debtors are required to prepare and file a Statement of Current Monthly Income and Means Test Calculation, which is included in the interim rules and forms adopted by the Judicial Conference for implementation of the 2005 Act.[5] In Part II of the Statement, the debtor lists the income information used in calculating current monthly income for the section 707(b)(7) safe harbor. If this current monthly income amount is below the state median income, as reflected in Part III of the Statement, the debtor is not required to fill out the remaining means test calculations in Part IV through VI of the form.

2.2.2.2 Contributions Toward Household Expenses of Debtor or Dependents on a Regular Basis

Included in current monthly income is any amount paid by any entity *toward the household expenses* of the debtor or the debtor's dependents *on a regular basis*.[6] Presumably, amounts not used for such a purpose or not received on a regular basis are not included. For example, the definition would exclude child support received on a sporadic basis.[7]

2.2.2.3 Treatment of Spouse's Income

If a joint case is filed, current monthly income includes all income received by the debtor and the debtor's spouse. If a married debtor files alone and the debtor's non-debtor spouse is not a dependent, income received by the non-debtor spouse (or from some other entity) that is not used for the household expenses of the debtor and the debtor's dependents is not included in current monthly income for purposes of the means test under section 707(b)(2).[8] This exclusion may dictate consideration of whether or not to file a joint case, or perhaps two separate cases.

For purposes of the safe harbor from the means test the Advisory Committee on Bankruptcy Rules adopted a different position in regard to a non-debtor spouse's income, apparently based on the language in section 707(b)(7)(B). If a married debtor files alone the new form Statement of Current Monthly Income and Means Test Calculation provides that the non-debtor spouse's income is considered for purposes of the safe harbor test under section 707(b)(7). This provision ignores the fact that the definition of current monthly income clearly provides that one must be a bankruptcy debtor to have current monthly income. However, the income of a separated spouse is not counted in a case filed by only one spouse if the spouses are not living separately to evade the means test and the debtor files a sworn statement to that effect, and the debtor discloses payments from the non-debtor spouse that are included in current monthly income.[9]

2.2.2.4 Treatment of Business Income

The definition of current monthly income appears to include the debtor's gross business income, rather than net income, especially because in chapter 13 section 1325(b) explicitly provides for business expenses to be deducted from the debtor's current monthly income, while that is not so provided in the chapter 7 test. However, the forms adopted by the Judicial Conference count only net business income toward current monthly

4 11 U.S.C. § 101(10A).

5 *See* Form 22A, Appx. D.4, *infra*.

6 11 U.S.C. § 101(10A)(B).

7 Although current monthly income is used to determine disposable income in chapter 13 cases based on the amendments made to section 1325, child support payments are excluded from disposable income. *See* § 6.2.2.3, *infra*.

8 11 U.S.C. § 101(10A)(B).

9 11 U.S.C. § 707(b)(7)(B).

income.[10] If gross business income is used, a chapter 7 debtor who would be presumed abusive under the means test would have to argue that business expenses constituted special circumstances overcoming the presumption. However the presumption of abuse might not arise if the debtor is able to deduct the expenses from income under the means test formula.[11]

2.2.2.5 Treatment of Capital Gains and Losses

It is unclear whether income from capital gains is included in current monthly income and whether capital losses may be deducted from that income. The issue may turn on whether the income is received on a regular basis. If capital gains income is considered, the debtor may want to plan for sales of assets accordingly.

2.2.2.6 Explicit Statutory Exemptions from Current Monthly Income

Excluded from current monthly income are benefits received under the Social Security Act, and payments made to victims of war crimes, crimes against humanity, and international terrorism on account of such status.[12] This provision will bring many elderly and disabled debtors below median income thresholds. It would exclude from a debtor's current monthly income benefits paid to a disabled child.

The 2005 Act does not just exclude Social Security payments, but any benefits paid under the Social Security Act. Such benefits include Supplemental Security Income (SSI) for the elderly and disabled,[13] unemployment compensation,[14] public assistance under the Temporary Assistance for Needy Families (TANF) program,[15] and funds received through programs administered under block grants made to the states to provide social services.[16] However, the Advisory Committee on Bankruptcy Rules could not agree whether unemployment compensation is a "benefit received under the Social Security Act," and consequently the new form Statement of Current Monthly Income and Means Test Calculation takes no position on whether it should be excluded from current monthly income. Instead, the form provides an alternative in which the debtor can list unemployment compensation as countable income or list it separately and not countable if the debtor "contends" it is a benefit under the Social Security Act.[17]

2.2.3 *Measuring a State's Median Family Income*

The debtor's current monthly income (multiplied by twelve) is compared with the applicable state's median family income. "Median family income" is defined in section 101 of the Bankruptcy Code as the median family income calculated and reported by the Bureau of the Census in the then most recent year.[18] If no Census Bureau figure exists for a particular family size for the current year, then the most recent census figure is to be adjusted to reflect the change in the Consumer Price Index through the most recent year. Each August the Census Bureau publishes figures for families of two, three and four, as well as for one earner families, for the preceding year. The applicable state median income figures are available for review on the website of the Executive Office of the United States Trustee.[19]

The median income test looks at the median income for the "applicable" state. It is not clear whether the applicable state is the debtor's state of residence or the debtor's state of domicile, if the two are different. Military (or other) debtors temporarily stationed in a low median income state could be disadvantaged if the state of residence is used.

To determine the appropriate median family income for the safe harbor provisions found in section 707(b)(6) and (b)(7), these subsections specify that the *household* size of the debtor is to be used, which may include non-related individuals living in the household. The debtor's household size and figures are then compared to the Census figures for a *family* size of the same number, with certain exceptions. Household size appears to be determined as of the date of the filing of the petition.

For debtors in a one-person household, the Census figures for a "1 earner" family are to be used.[20] If the Census figures for state median income for two, three, or

10 *See* Forms 22A, 22A (Alt.), Appx. D.4, *infra*.

11 *See* § 2.3, *infra*.

12 11 U.S.C. § 101(10A)(B).

13 Subchapter XVI of the Social Security Act, 42 U.S.C. §§ 1381–1383f.

14 Subchapters III, XII, XIII, and XV of the Social Security Act, 42 U.S.C. §§ 501–504, 1321–1324.

15 Subchapter IV of the Social Security Act, 42 U.S.C. §§ 601–687.

16 Subchapter XX of the Social Security Act, 42 U.S.C. §§ 1397–1397f.

17 *See* Advisory Committee Note to Form 22A, Appx. D.3, *infra*; Form 22A, Appx. D.4, *infra*.

18 11 U.S.C. § 101(39A).

19 The median income figures are available at www.usdoj.gov/ust/bapcpa/meanstesting.htm.

20 11 U.S.C. § 707(b)(6), (7). The 2005 Act uses the phrase "1

four person families are lower than the Census figures for the median income for a smaller family, the figure for the smaller household is to be used. (In some states the median income for a family of three is higher than that for a family of four.)

In households larger than four members, for each additional family member $525 per month is added to the median income figure for a family of four.[21] This procedure permits a higher income to be utilized, even though in many states larger families have lower median incomes. This $525 per month amount will be periodically adjusted for inflation under section 104(b) of the Bankruptcy Code.

2.2.4 Safe Harbor for Disabled Veterans

The 2005 Act creates a separate safe harbor from the means test for debtors who are disabled veterans (as defined in 38 U.S.C. § 3741(1)), if their "indebtedness occurred primarily" during a period when they were on active duty or "performing a homeland defense activity."[22] The Act further provides that such debtors are not required to file a statement concerning the means test calculations. If the debtor meets the statutory qualifications for a disabled veteran, only Part I of the new Statement of Current Monthly Income and Means Test Calculation need be filled out.[23]

2.3 The Means Test Formula

2.3.1 Introduction

If the debtor is not protected by the median income safe harbor and has primarily consumer debts, a means test formula is then applied to determine whether a presumption of abuse exists. In general terms, the means test formula begins with the debtor's current monthly income, and deducts from that certain allowed expenses to come up with a monthly amount presumed to be available to general unsecured creditors. If the debtor's income exceeds expenses by a certain amount (in relation to the amount of unsecured debt), then there is a presumption of abuse. The means test formula is complex, and will be detailed in this section.

Section 707(b)(2)(A) of the Bankruptcy Code provides a list of the debtor's monthly expenses that are permitted to be deducted for purposes of the abuse analysis. For some items the amounts are determined based on the three categories of allowed expenses provided for in the Internal Revenue Service's collection guidelines: National Standards, Local Standards, and Other Necessary Expenses.[24] Other items may be an allowed expense based on the debtor's actual expenditures if they fall within one of the categories specifically referenced in the statute.

2.3.2 Deduction of IRS Expense Allowances

2.3.2.1 General

The debtor is allowed to deduct from current monthly income the total expenses allowed by the Internal Revenue Service (IRS) in its financial standards used in collecting taxes. These expenses are allowed for the debtor and the debtor's dependents, and for the debtor's spouse in a joint case. Expenses for a dependent are allowed even if the dependent is not in the same household. The allowance for certain expenses of a spouse only in a joint case may provide an incentive to file a joint case. Note that the non-allowance of some expenses for a spouse who does not file a joint case does not mesh with the inclusion of the spouse's circumstances in other provisions.

With some exceptions, the debtor is allowed to deduct the amounts specified in the IRS National and Local Standards, even if the debtor actually spends less. The debtor may spend more for one category and less for another, but the amounts listed for the category in the National and Local Standards are used. For expenses

earner" because the decennial census reports median family income in a data set that covers only two-person and larger families (for example: PCT118. Median Family Income In 1999 (Dollars) By Family Size). The Act therefore had to reference another Census Bureau data set that tracks median incomes for workers (for example: PCT115. Median Family Income In 1999 (Dollars) By Number Of Workers In Family In 1999). *See* Appx. F.1, *infra*.

21 11 U.S.C. § 707(b)(6), (7).

22 11 U.S.C. § 707(b)(2)(D).

23 *See* Form 22A, Appx. D, *infra*.

24 The Internal Revenue Service (IRS) developed these standards as guidelines for its own debt collectors, subject to individual collector's exercise of discretion and consideration of exceptions. The IRS Financial Analysis Handbook provides an overview of the collection standards and is reprinted in Appx. F.2.1, *infra*. Section 103 of the 2005 Act suggests as the "sense of Congress" that the IRS has authority to alter the standards to "accommodate their use under section 707(b)." Pub. L. No. 109-8, § 103, 119 Stat. 23 (2005)

under the categories listed in the IRS's Other Necessary Expenses, however, the debtor may deduct actual expense amounts.

The debtor may not deduct any payments for debts. Such payments are, however, deducted if they are for priority or secured debts, so this provision appears mainly designed to avoid double counting.[25] Although IRS standards allow debtors to deduct some unsecured debts, this provision overrides those standards, and unsecured debts are deductible only as allowed by other provisions (that is, as priority debts). In addition, the debtor can not deduct amounts for debts that are non-priority but non-dischargeable, unless the court finds that to be a special circumstance.

2.3.2.2 IRS National Standards for Food, Clothing, Housekeeping Supplies, Personal Care, and Miscellaneous Expenses

The IRS National Standards provide for the debtor's allowed living expenses in five categories: food, clothing and services, housekeeping supplies, personal care products and services, and miscellaneous items.[26] The amounts listed in the National Standards for these categories apply to debtors in every state, except Alaska and Hawaii. Separate standards are used for Alaska and Hawaii, and also for Puerto Rico.[27] Because the amounts allowed under these standards increase as family income increases, it should not be difficult for debtors to convince judges that special circumstances require them to pay an amount that would be allowed for a higher-income debtor.

The fact that the standards vary with income raises a number of as yet unresolved questions. Is current monthly income or actual income at the time of petition to be used? Is current monthly income or net business income (as used by the IRS) to be used? Are Social Security benefits and other exclusions from current monthly income included in income for this purpose?

The 2005 Act allows an upward adjustment of five percent in the allowable food and clothing expenses if these can be demonstrated to be reasonably necessary.[28] Certainly this standard should be possible to satisfy in urban or rural areas where food prices are higher. It should also be demonstrable when debtors have skimped on food and clothing due to their financial problems. Nevertheless, the amounts involved are not large, so the adjustment will be significant only for debtors very close to the presumption cut-off.

To claim the five percent adjustment in food and clothing expenses, the debtor may list the additional expense amount on a designated line item in Part V of the Statement of Current Monthly Income and Means Test Calculation.[29] The form indicates that the debtor must provide the trustee with documentation demonstrating that the additional amount claimed is reasonable and necessary.

2.3.2.3 IRS Local Standards for Transportation Expenses

The debtor may also claim transportation expenses under the regional IRS local standards for transportation, which differentiate between Ownership Costs, Operating Costs and Public Transportation Costs.[30] The Ownership Costs expense is provided as a national standard that is the same no matter where the debtor resides. Based on the updated 2005 figures, the debtor is permitted an ownership expense of $475 for the first car and $338 for the second car.[31]

The Operating Costs and Public Transportation costs sections of the IRS transportation standards are provided by Census Bureau region and metropolitan statistical area (MSA). A table provided by the IRS lists the states that are included within each Census Bureau region.[32] If the debtor lives within an MSA (MSAs are defined by county and city), the MSA standard is applicable. If the debtor does not reside in an MSA, the regional standard is used. A dollar amount is provided based on whether the debtor has no car, one car, or two cars. For example, if the debtor lives in the Midwest region and does not live in an MSA

25 Section § 707(b)(2)(A)(ii)(I) of the Bankruptcy Code provides that: "Notwithstanding any other provision of this clause, the monthly expenses of the debtor shall not include any payments for debts." However, payments on secured and priority debts are allowed expenses pursuant to provisions of other clauses of § 707(b)(2)(A). *See* §§ 2.3.3.2, 2.3.3.3, *infra*.

26 11 U.S.C. § 707(b)(2)(A)(ii)(I). The IRS National Standards are reprinted in Appx. F.2.2, *infra*.

27 The IRS National Standards for Alaska and Hawaii are reprinted in Appendices F.2.3 and F.2.4, *infra*. The relevant standards for Puerto Rico are reprinted in Appendix F.2.5, *infra*.

28 11 U.S.C. § 707(b)(2)(A)(ii)(I).

29 *See* Form 22A, Appx. D.4, *infra*.

30 11 U.S.C. § 707(b)(2)(A)(ii)(I). The IRS Allowable Living Expenses for Transportation are reprinted in Appx. F.2.6, *infra*.

31 The IRS standard for Ownership Costs does not include personal property taxes on a car, but such taxes may be deducted under the Other Expenses category. *See* § 2.3.2.5, *infra*.

32 The table is reprinted in Appx. F.2.6, *infra*.

such as Chicago or St. Louis, the debtor would be allowed (based on 2005 figures): $194 for public transportation costs if no car is owned, $251 for operating costs if one car is owned, and $345 if two cars are owned. If the debtor lives in the Chicago MSA, the allowances are $257 for public transportation costs, $329 for operating costs for one car, and $422 for two cars.

As discussed in § 2.3.3.2, *infra*, a separate expense deduction is permitted for payments on secured debts. There is some ambiguity about whether a debtor may deduct the IRS ownership allowance if the debtor's remaining car payments divided by sixty are less than the ownership allowance. The better view is that the IRS ownership allowance may be claimed, because the operative language in the means test merely states that the debtor may deduct the transportation allowance "specified" but the monthly expenses shall not include any payments for debts.[33] At most this language means that the car payments should not be double-counted, that is, they should not be added to the transportation expense.

A reading that did not allow IRS standards to be used whenever the debtor owed a debt for the expense involved would leave debtors unable to take any deduction for car or lease expenses, as liabilities for both are within the Code's definition of "debt." Thus a debtor might be left with an old car, bought used, with no way to replace it for five years. There is no reason to think Congress meant to allow debtors lower transportation expenses than the IRS allows.

The IRS transportation standards seem to assume that a household with a car does not use public transportation. In urban areas households for which this assumption is not valid may have to argue special circumstances in order to deduct public transportation expenses to get to school, work, or other locations.

2.3.2.4 IRS Local Standards for Housing and Utilities

The debtor may take as an expense deduction a housing allowance under the IRS Local Standards.[34] These allowances are specified for each county, dependent on family size, and include housing and utilities.

Mortgage payments that are separately deducted as payments on secured debt can not be added to the allowance. It appears the housing allowance should be deducted first, and then the mortgage payment, to the extent it would not be double counted.[35]

Most utility payments in addition to the mortgage are covered by a separate provision that allows an additional deduction for documented, reasonable, and necessary "home energy costs" in excess of the IRS standard.[36] Basic home maintenance in excess of the housing allowance could be considered an "other necessary" expense, as set out in § 2.3.2.5, *infra*. It would be hard to argue that plumbing or roof repairs are not necessary.

2.3.2.5 Other Necessary Expenses Allowed Under IRS Standards

Although most of the IRS collection standards do not consider a debtor's actual expenses, the debtor may deduct actual expense amounts for the categories specified by the IRS as Other Necessary Expenses.[37] It is unclear whether the expenses in these categories must meet the IRS qualification that they be necessary to health and welfare or the production of income.

The IRS list of Other Necessary Expenses is *nonexclusive*.[38] Therefore, it appears the court has discretion to determine whether other expenses necessary to a family's health and welfare may be deducted. Even if the court could not add to the Other Necessary Expenses categories, expenses necessary for family's health and welfare could be considered as special circumstances.[39]

The IRS list of Other Necessary Expenses includes:

- Child care;
- Court ordered payments, including alimony, support, and other court-ordered payments (like restitution);
- Expenses for the care of elderly, invalid, or handicapped individuals;
- Education required for employment or for special

33 *See* 11 U.S.C. § 707(b)(2)(A)(ii)(I).

34 11 U.S.C. § 707(b)(2)(A)(ii)(I). The IRS Local Standards for housing and utilities are available at: www.irs.gov/businesses/small/article/0,,id=104696,00.html (then search by state).

35 See § 2.3.3.2, *infra*, for a more complete discussion of the treatment of secured debts.

36 11 U.S.C. § 707(b)(2)(A)(ii)(V). The phrase "home energy costs" is not defined. The IRS Financial Analysis Handbook describes "utilities" as including "gas, electricity, water, fuel, oil, bottled gas, trash and garbage collection, wood and other fuels, septic cleaning, and telephone." Internal Revenue Service, Internal Revenue Manual, Financial Analysis Handbook § 5.15.1.9(1)(A).

37 11 U.S.C. § 707(b)(2)(A)(ii)(I). A description of the Other Necessary Expenses is contained in § 5.15.1.10 of the IRS Financial Analysis Handbook, which is reprinted in Appx. F.2.1, *infra*.

38 H.R. Rep. No. 109-31, at 14 n.66 (2005) (reprinted in Appx. A.4, *infra*).

39 *See* § 2.4.2, *infra*.

needs children if suitable education is not available from public schools;
- Necessary medical and dental expenses;
- Involuntary deductions from wages, including union dues, uniforms, and so forth;
- Term life insurance premiums;
- Taxes, including withholding taxes;
- Optional telephone services, such as cell phone, pager, and call waiting; and
- Internet service.

2.3.3 Other Expenses That May Be Deducted

2.3.3.1 General

In addition to expenses covered under the IRS guidelines, section 707(b) of the Code provides a list of expense items that may be deducted from the debtor's current monthly income in a range of categories, such as health insurance costs, expenses to maintain safety from domestic violence, certain expenses to care for others, costs necessary in a chapter 13 case, certain educational expenses, and charitable contributions. Some of these items are deductible under the IRS standards and presumably should not be double counted.

2.3.3.2 Deduction for Secured Debts

The debtor may also deduct the average monthly payments made on secured debts.[40] This amount is determined by taking the sum of (1) the total of all amounts "scheduled as contractually due" to secured creditors in each month of the sixty months following the date of the petition, and (2) any additional payments to secured creditors that would need to be paid under a chapter 13 plan as described below. This total is then divided by sixty to determine the monthly amount.

This provision clearly includes all regular mortgage and car loan payments regardless of how much they are, including any escrow payments. It would also include all payments to creditors secured by personal property, such as appliances, even if the appliance is worth little and its purchase price is a small portion of the debt. It would include payments contractually due to creditors holding liens that might be avoidable or on property the debtor may intend to surrender.

An issue that may arise is what the phrase "scheduled as contractually due" refers to when there is a minimum required payment, as on a credit card. When minimum payments include a high interest rate, they may add up to more than the amount of the debt. Similarly, when the total debt is contractually due immediately, as with a tax lien or other liens, can the debtor add the applicable interest over sixty months?

The deduction for secured debts can be taken in addition to the IRS standard deductions, as long as double counting is avoided. For example, a debtor may take as a deduction utilities and maintenance on a home plus necessary secured debt payments, even if the total exceeds the IRS housing and utilities allowance. To provide otherwise would lead to the nonsensical result of a debtor having no money in the budget to fix the plumbing or pay for other maintenance costs.[41]

The result should be same for cars, although the IRS transportation ownership allowance may exceed any remaining secured debt payments. In that case the larger of the two amounts should be allowed. The debtor's budget will need to include money toward replacement of the old car.

The debtor also may deduct any other payments to secured creditors that would be necessary in a chapter 13 case to maintain the debtor's possession of the debtor's primary residence, motor vehicle, or other property necessary for the support of the debtor or the debtor's dependents.[42] Again, the monthly amount is derived by taking all necessary payments over the next sixty months, and then dividing by sixty. Such payments would include:

- Any arrears, including charges and attorney fees, owed on mortgages;
- Arrears on car loans, plus fees;
- Amounts on cross-collateralized debts, for example, to credit unions;
- Any additional arrears on secured purchases of appliances or other property; and
- Arrearage payments on other liens on such property.

40 11 U.S.C. § 707(b)(2)(A)(iii). This section does not provide an allowance for payments on a car lease, so a deduction for lease payments should be taken as an Ownership Costs expense under the IRS transportation standard.

41 Even an Ernst and Young study used this methodology. *See* T. Neubig, et al., Ernst & Young, Chapter 7 Bankruptcy Petitioners' Ability to Repay: the National Perspective, 1997, (Mar. 1998); *cf.* Marianne B. Culhane & Michaela M. White, *Taking the New Consumer Bankruptcy Model for a Test Drive: Means-Testing Real Chapter 7 Debtors*, 7 Am. Bankr. Inst. L. Rev. 27 (1999).

42 11 U.S.C. § 707(b)(2)(A)(iii)(II).

2.3.3.3 Deduction for Priority Debts

The debtor may deduct as an allowed monthly expense payments on priority debts, which is calculated by finding the total amount of debts entitled to priority, and then dividing by sixty.[43] Such debts include priority taxes, child support (including the new priority for assigned support), and the new drunk driving debt priority.

There may be issues in determining whether domestic relations debts are in the nature of alimony and support and therefore priority, and also whether they are nondischargeable. Debtors may be estopped from claiming the debts are dischargeable if they claim the debts are in nature of support for purposes of the means test. However, because property settlement debts, including debts from hold harmless agreements, are no longer dischargeable in chapter 7, the debtor may have no great interest in claiming that such debts are not support.[44]

Similarly, debtors now have an incentive to have many tax debts treated as priority debts. If they have unfiled returns that would make the debts nondischargeable in both chapter 7 and chapter 13, it is in their interest to file a bankruptcy petition while the debts are priority debts, both to increase deductions under the means test and, in chapter 13, to separately classify them. These considerations suggest that attorneys may want to give different advice about what debts a debtor should prioritize for payment before bankruptcy.

2.3.3.4 Deduction for Health Insurance

The debtor may deduct reasonably necessary expenses for health insurance, disability insurance, and a health savings account for the debtor, the debtor's dependents, and the debtor's spouse.[45] For debtors who do not have such insurance, obtaining it can be an important step toward financial stability. In addition, it is a significant expense that can be deducted under the means test.

2.3.3.5 Deduction for Expenses to Maintain Safety from Domestic Violence

The debtor may also deduct reasonably necessary expenses to maintain the safety of the debtor and the family of the debtor from domestic violence, as identified under section 309 of the Family Violence Prevention and Services Act or other applicable federal law.[46] The debtor's use of this deduction must be kept confidential by the court, but it is unclear how this confidentiality provision will be implemented. As the court is to keep these expenses confidential, will the trustee, for example, be permitted to review them?

2.3.3.6 Deduction for Support of Elderly and Disabled Family Members

Other expenses that may be deducted include the "continuation of" actual, reasonable, and necessary expenses for the care and support of an elderly, chronically ill, or disabled household member or an immediate family member (parent, grandparent, sibling, child, grandchild, other dependent, or spouse in a joint case if not a dependent).[47] This deduction is broader than the similar IRS Other Necessary Expense category, as it is not limited to dependents. It also includes not simply care, but support, which may not be included in the IRS category.

2.3.3.7 Deduction for Administrative Expenses

If a debtor is eligible to file chapter 13, the debtor may deduct administrative expenses that would be incurred in a chapter 13 case in the district where the debtor resides, subject to a cap on such expenses of ten percent of projected plan payments.[48] This amount would include payments for attorney fees to debtor's counsel. If the debtor is not eligible to file chapter 13, the debtor can argue that chapter 11 administrative expenses should be deducted as a special circumstance.

The ability to deduct chapter 13 administrative expenses requires the debtor's counsel to construct a hypothetical chapter 13 plan, including calculation of amounts that would be paid to secured and priority creditors, and amounts that would be required to be paid unsecured creditors under the section 1325(b) application of the means test standards. If current monthly mortgage payments are paid through plan, they should be included in the calculation.

The Executive Office of the United States Trustee is to publish schedules of administrative expense percentages to be used in calculating the deduction for each district. Because administrative expenses include attorney fees, and chapter 13 trustees will have far more to do under the

43 11 U.S.C. § 707(b)(2)(A)(iv).

44 See Chapter 9, *infra*, for a discussion of the new family law changes.

45 11 U.S.C. § 707(b)(2)(A)(ii)(I).

46 11 U.S.C. § 707(b)(2)(A)(ii)(I).

47 11 U.S.C. § 707(b)(2)(A)(ii)(II).

48 11 U.S.C. § 707(b)(2)(A)(ii)(III).

2005 Act, it is hard to imagine any district where the percentage will not be ten percent.

2.3.3.8 Deduction for Education Expenses

The debtor may deduct actual public or private school educational expenses of up to $1500 per each child under eighteen years of age.[49] The debtor must provide documentation of such expenses and a detailed explanation of why such expenses are reasonable and necessary, and why such expenses are not already accounted for in the IRS National Standards, Local Standards, or Other Necessary Expenses. There is no explicit provision for a determination of whether the expenses are reasonable and necessary after the debtor supplies documentation stating they are.

This $1500 allowance is insufficient for virtually all parochial or private schools, and does not cover high school students over eighteen. To seek a deduction for a higher amount the debtor may be able to argue special circumstances, in that pulling children out of school in the middle of year is very disruptive.

2.3.3.9 Deduction for Charitable Contributions

Finally, section 707(b)(1) provides, as under current law, that the debtor may continue to make charitable and religious contributions.

2.4 Application of the Means Test Formula

2.4.1 Presumption of Abuse

A presumption of abuse arises under the means test if the debtor's current monthly income, after all monthly allowed expenses are deducted, multiplied by 60 is the lesser of $10,000 or 25% of non-priority unsecured debt, as long as that 25% is at least $6000.[50] For debtors with more than $40,000 in general unsecured debt, a presumption of abuse arises if the amount exceeds $10,000 ($166.67 per month). For debtors with less than $24,000 in general unsecured debt, a presumption of abuse arises if the amount exceeds $6000 ($100 per month). For debtors with $24,000 to $40,000 in general unsecured debt, the presumption of abuse arises if the amount is 25% or more of the unsecured debt.

49 11 U.S.C. § 707(b)(2)(A)(ii)(IV).

50 11 U.S.C. § 707(b)(2)(A)(i).

To determine the amount of non-priority unsecured debt, presumably, the court will look to the amount listed on the debtor's schedules. It is unclear whether the unsecured portion of an undersecured claim would be counted for this purpose, as it usually is under section 109(e) of the Bankruptcy Code.

2.4.2 Rebutting the Presumption of Abuse

To rebut the presumption of abuse if a motion to dismiss or convert is filed, new section 707(b)(2)(B)(i) of the Bankruptcy Code states that the debtor must demonstrate that "special circumstances" exist which would cause the debtor to fall below the presumed abuse tolerances set by the means test formula. The special circumstances must be those that "justify additional expenses or adjustments of current monthly income for which there is no reasonable alternative."[51] This standard is essentially a reasonableness test and significant discretion is vested in the court.

The debtor has a significant motive to show special circumstances, because debtors who lose means test motions are unlikely to be able to convert to chapter 13. Such debtors would be subjected to most of the same living expense standards as apply in chapter 7.[52] As they were not able to meet those living expense standards prior to filing a chapter 7 bankruptcy, they usually would not be able to meet them for the duration of a chapter 13 case.

Special circumstances must dictate an adjustment in income or expenses that changes the result of the means test formula sufficiently to eliminate the presumption of abuse. Examples that are given in the statute are a serious medical condition or a call to active duty in the armed forces. As mentioned in § 2.2.4, *supra*, there is also a complete safe harbor from the means test for disabled veterans whose debts were incurred primarily during active duty or homeland defense.

With respect to income, the most obvious special circumstance would be a reduction in income from the "current monthly income" based on income that the debtor is no longer actually receiving as of the petition date. A special circumstance with respect to expenses could be that the projected moving expenses and disruption to the debtor's children that would arise from a move to a lower-rent apartment would justify a higher rent than the IRS standards allow. There are many other possibilities, such as high commuting costs, increased price of gas, security costs in dangerous neighborhoods, and cost of infant formula and diapers.

51 11 U.S.C. § 707(b)(2)(B)(i)

52 *See* Ch. 5, *infra*.

The debtor must provide an itemization of expenses, "documentation" for the expense or adjustment to income, and a detailed explanation of why it is "necessary and reasonable," including a sworn statement as to accuracy.[53] It may be difficult to provide documentation for some expenses, especially cash expenses, such as gas for debtors who can no longer use credit cards. Debtors may have to keep records or the attorney may need to obtain a letter from the provider of a service or from some other source.

It is unclear where and when the documentation will be submitted. Section 707(b)(2)(B)(i) states that the debtor must demonstrate that the special circumstances exist in a proceeding under section 707(b). Consequently, if a motion to dismiss or convert is brought, it would be submitted in that proceeding. Nevertheless, the debtor may want to notify the United States trustee or panel trustee of the special circumstances before that time, to forestall such a proceeding.[54] United States trustees will presumably not be interested in bringing section 707(b) motions they are likely to lose. As the documentation requirements only apply in the section 707(b) proceeding itself, it does not appear necessary to provide documentation in the notice to the United States trustee.

2.5 Other Changes in the Abuse Standard Under Section 707(b)

2.5.1 *No Challenges Based on Ability to Pay for Debtors with Incomes Below Median Income*

With the new specific means testing provisions, debtors should not be subjected to section 707(b) motions based on ability to pay, if their incomes fall below the median income threshold. There are numerous statements in the legislative history that means testing applies only for debtors with incomes above the median income.[55] Congress has now set specific guidelines for who should be determined able to pay debts. This bright line test was intended not only to catch abusers, but also to protect other debtors. Provisions enacted to protect debtors can not be disregarded by a creditor or trustee in bringing an abuse motion, essentially by asserting some alternative means test other than that enacted by Congress. Even under current law, section 707(b) motions based on ability to pay were almost always filed against higher-income debtors.

2.5.2 *Substantial Abuse Standard Changed to Abuse Standard*

A case may now be dismissed under section 707(b) of the Code for "abuse," rather than for "substantial abuse."[56] This change is not likely to affect the result of section 707(b) motions, because few courts placed much weight on the requirement that the abuse be "substantial." This interpretation was probably due to the fact that the word "abuse" denotes conduct sufficiently deplorable that a court would not accept it.

2.5.3 *Elimination of Explicit Presumption Favoring the Debtor*

The 2005 Act also strikes the language in former section 707(b) that established a presumption in favor of granting a discharge to the debtor.[57] Congress had intended this presumption to limit the use of section 707(b) challenges only to egregious cases, but courts had largely ignored this presumption. It is not clear what the elimination of the language does, except in cases in which a presumption of abuse under the means test arises. The moving party will still have the burden of proof.

Even when a presumption of abuse arises under the means test, it is not clear what the elimination of the presumption in favor of discharge will have on the parties' evidentiary burdens. Does it just eliminate the burden of going forward on the motion? Once the presumption is overcome, is the bubble burst and does the burden of proof shift back to the moving party?

2.5.4 *Dismissal for Bad Faith or Based on a Totality of Circumstances Showing Abuse*

If the presumption of abuse is rebutted or does not arise, a court may still dismiss the case if the petition was filed in bad faith, or "the totality of the circumstances of the

53 11 U.S.C. § 707(b)(2)(B)(ii).

54 For an example of a Statement of Special Circumstances that may be submitted to a United States trustee prior to a proceeding, see Form 2, Appx. G, *infra*.

55 *See, e.g.*, H.R. Rep. No. 109-31, at 51 (2005).

56 11 U.S.C. § 707(b)(1).

57 Prior to the 2005 amendments section 707(b) contained the statement: "There shall be a presumption in favor of granting the relief requested by the debtor." Former 11 U.S.C. § 707(b).

debtor's financial situation demonstrates abuse."[58] This provision does not change the law in most circuits, where a bad faith filing was grounds for dismissal under section 707(a). A bad faith finding was the equivalent to finding the case was an "abuse," normally based on an examination of the totality of the underlying circumstances.[59]

By placing the bad faith dismissal provision in section 707(b), Congress eliminated the possibility of a party or trustee moving for dismissal based on bad faith or the totality of circumstances if the debtor's income is under the median income threshold.[60]

2.5.5 *Dismissal for an Abusive Rejection of an Executory Contract*

Section 707(b)(3) of the Code adds a new provision providing for dismissal based on a rejection of an executory personal services contract. Dismissal based on these grounds was a compromise reached by Congress on an issue related to recording contracts rejected by debtors. A case may be abusive if a contract is rejected for reasons other than the financial need of the debtor. This provision only applies in chapter 7, because section 103(a) of the Code limits the applicability of provisions in chapter 7 to chapter 7 cases.

2.6 Procedures for Means Testing Under Section 707(b)

The bankruptcy clerk must provide written notice to creditors within ten days of the petition date when the case is presumed to be abusive.[61] This determination will be based on the Statement of Current Monthly Income and Means Test Calculation, which requires the debtor to indicate whether a presumption of abuse arises.[62] Presumably this Statement may be amended if an initial rushed calculation in an emergency case proves to be incorrect.

New section 704(b)(1) of the Code establishes timeframes for the United States trustee or bankruptcy administrator to take certain actions relating to the means test. They must review all materials filed by debtors, and within ten days after the meeting of creditors file a statement as to whether a presumption of abuse arises. Presumably the ten days runs from the conclusion of the creditors meeting. Within five days of the filing of the trustee's statement, the bankruptcy court must provide a copy of the statement to all creditors. It would appear that the court can provide the statement electronically to the extent possible. Within thirty days after the filing of the statement by the United States trustee or bankruptcy administrator that a presumption of abuse arises, they must either file a motion to dismiss or convert under section 707(b) or file a new statement setting forth the reasons why such a motion is not appropriate. Creditors are no longer prohibited from communicating with United States trustee or bankruptcy administrator about section 707(b) motions or providing information to the court (except through improper *ex parte* contacts).[63]

2.7 New Section 707(c)—Dismissal Based on Certain Crimes

Section 707(c) of the Code provides that a voluntary chapter 7 case may be dismissed on the motion of a victim of a "crime of violence"[64] or a "drug trafficking crime."[65] Section 707(c)(2) makes clear that a conviction is required. Dismissal must also be in the "best interest of the victim." However, the court may not dismiss a case under this section if the debtor establishes by a preponderance of the evidence that the filing is necessary to satisfy a claim for a domestic support obligation.

This provision is not likely to see much use. A victim of a crime of violence would usually be better off bringing a nondischargeability action under section 523(a)(6) of the Code, because other debts would be discharged and the debtor would be in a better position to satisfy the debt owed to the victim post-discharge.[66] Moreover, most drug trafficking crimes probably do not have identifiable victims.

---

58 11 U.S.C. § 707(b)(3).

59 *See, e.g., In re* Green, 934 F.2d 568 (4th Cir. 1991); *see also* National Consumer Law Center, Consumer Bankruptcy Law and Practice § 13.9.2.2 (7th ed. 2004).

60 11 U.S.C. § 707(b)(6); *see* § 2.2.1, *supra*.

61 11 U.S.C. § 342(d). "Written notice" as provided under this section probably would encompass electronic notice.

62 *See* Form 22A, Appx. D.4, *infra*.

63 Section 102(e) of the 2005 Act states: "Nothing in this title shall limit the ability of a creditor to provide information to a judge (except for information communicated *ex parte*, unless otherwise permitted by applicable law), United States trustee (or bankruptcy administrator, if any), or trustee." Pub. L. No. 109-8, § 102(e), 119 Stat. 23 (2005). However, it does not appear that this language amends any section of the Code or that it will be codified as a Code provision.

64 The term "crime of violence" has the meaning given such term in 18 U.S.C. § 16.

65 The term "drug trafficking crime" has the meaning given such term in 18 U.S.C. § 924(c)(2).

66 This supposition may not be true, however, if federal exemptions were claimed by the debtor, as more property might be protected from execution than under state law.

Chapter 3 Attorney Duties

3.1 Introduction

Much concern has been expressed about the new provisions requiring additional duties and certifications of attorneys, referred to by some as the "attorney liability" provisions. A careful examination of these provisions reveals that many of the statements predicting impending doom for consumer bankruptcy attorneys are overblown, to say the least. Indeed, those most likely to innocently violate the provisions will be attorneys who do not regularly represent consumer debtors.

The first such set of these provisions is contained in section 707(b) of the Bankruptcy Code, enacted as part of the substantial changes made to that section by the 2005 Act, including the addition of the means test.[1] Because these provisions are found in section 707(b), they are therefore applicable only in chapter 7 cases.[2] The second such set of provisions is found in new sections 526 through 528 of the Code, and includes the requirements relating to "debt relief agencies."

3.2 New Provisions in Section 707(b)

3.2.1 Costs and Attorney Fees for Successful Section 707(b) Motions—Section 707(b)(4)(A)

Under new section 707(b)(4)(A) of the Bankruptcy Code, costs and attorney fees incurred in prosecuting a successful section 707(b) motion to dismiss the case may be assessed against the debtor's attorney, but only in certain circumstances—circumstances which would permit fees to be awarded under current law. Fees and costs may only be awarded if a debtor's attorney violates Rule 9011 of the Federal Rules of Bankruptcy Procedure in filing the bankruptcy case itself.[3] Moreover, the procedures contained in Bankruptcy Rule 9011 for awarding costs and fees must be followed.

1 See Chapter 2, *supra*, for a discussion of the means test.

2 11 U.S.C. § 103(b).

3 11 U.S.C. § 707(b)(4)(A).

In fact, the only real change brought about by this provision is that costs and fees may be awarded to the trustee even if a court initiates a proceeding to show cause.[4] However, this provision only applies to a motion brought by a trustee, not the United States trustee or bankruptcy administrator. As mentioned in Chapter 2, *supra*, this limitation means that a debtor's attorney may not be assessed liability under this provision if the debtor's income is below the state's median family income, because only the judge, United States trustee, or bankruptcy administrator may file a motion under section 707(b) in cases filed by a debtor whose income is below the median.[5]

The original purpose of the provision apparently was to give trustees an incentive to file section 707(b) motions, but since the provision was originally introduced[6] the standard under Section 707(b)(4)(A) was changed to the same standard as under Bankruptcy Rule 9011, which is unlikely to entice trustees to expend great efforts in litigating under the section.

3.2.2 Civil Penalties Under Bankruptcy Rule 9011—Section 707(b)(4)(B)

Under the 2005 Act, a court may also assess a civil penalty against a debtor's attorney who violates Bankruptcy Rule 9011.[7] But courts already possess the authority to assess civil penalties under Bankruptcy Rule 9011(c). The only difference is that this penalty, unlike the penalties under Bankruptcy Rule 9011, may be payable to the trustee, the United States trustee, or the bankruptcy administrator.[8]

4 Under Bankruptcy Rule 9011(c)(2), if the court initiates a proceeding the monetary sanction must be payable to the court.

5 *See* § 2.2.1, *supra*.

6 *See* S.625, 106th Cong. § 102 (1999) (as reported from the Senate Judiciary Committee).

7 11 U.S.C. § 707(b)(4)(B).

8 Bankruptcy Rule 9011 provides that a sanction imposed for violation of the rule may include "an order to pay a penalty

3.2.3 Attorney Certifications—Section 707(b)(4)(C)

Section 707(b)(4)(C) provides that the signature of an attorney on a petition, pleading, or written motion is a certification that the attorney has:

- Performed a reasonable investigation into the circumstances giving rise to the petition, pleading, or written motion;
- Determined that it is well-grounded in fact;
- Determined that it is warranted by existing law or a good faith argument for the extension, modification, or reversal of existing law; and
- Determined that it does not constitute an "abuse" under paragraph (707)(b)(1).[9]

This provision applies to all attorneys, not just those representing debtors, and is applicable to all motions and pleadings filed in chapter 7 cases. For example, it applies to frivolous motions for relief from the automatic stay filed in chapter 7 cases, and requires the attorney to reasonably investigate amounts asserted in such motions. On the other hand, the certification does not apply to schedules or statements.

The language of this provision is quite similar to the former language of Bankruptcy Rule 9011 and it is not clear that it adds anything to current Bankruptcy Rule 9011. One difference is the use of the phrase "reasonable investigation" rather than "reasonable inquiry." But it is unclear whether this change in wording makes any difference. The existing text of both *Moore's Federal Practice* when discussing Rule 11 of the Federal Rules of Civil Procedure and *Collier on Bankruptcy* when discussing Rule 9011 of the Federal Rules of Bankruptcy Procedure use the words "inquiry" and "investigation" interchangeably.[10] Moreover, in discussing the duty to investigate, *Moore's* states: "[a]n attorney may rely on objectively reasonable representations of his or her client."[11] It states further that "[a]ll *available* documents that are relevant to the case should be examined."[12] Such a standard would certainly include all documents in the possession of the client, but does not appear to require an attorney to obtain documents that are not easily accessible.

In view of this section's similarities to Bankruptcy Rule 9011, it is unlikely that courts will draw a distinction between the certification requirement under section 707(b)(4)(C) and Bankruptcy Rule 9011. Courts will likely, at most, use this section as an additional basis on which to sanction bad conduct that would have been punishable in any event.

Section 707(b)(4)(C) also provides that an attorney filing a petition certifies that the attorney has determined that the petition is not an abuse under section 707(b)(1). Based on its placement in the context of an attorney's "determination" with respect to other similar Bankruptcy Rule 9011 conclusions, courts are likely to look to analogous provisions in current and former Bankruptcy Rule 9011 and interpret this language to require a good faith determination, after reasonable inquiry under the circumstances. Importantly, the provision does not require an attorney to certify that the petition is not an abuse, but only that the attorney determined that it was not an abuse. In any event no remedies are provided for violations of this provision, which presumably means that the standards of Bankruptcy Rule 9011 would apply.

3.2.4 Attorney Certification As to Schedules—Section 707(b)(4)(D)

Section 707(b)(4)(D) provides that the signature of an attorney for the debtor also certifies that the attorney has no knowledge, after an inquiry, that the schedules are incorrect.[13] This standardis a pretty low one, requiring actual knowledge, not just a belief or suspicion, that the schedules are inaccurate. It requires an inquiry, which should be no greater than for other pleadings, perhaps less, because it does not use the word "reasonable."

Quite arguably this more specific, and less stringent, standard for schedules overrides any other standard. However, as with the other standards, courts are unlikely to look to the nuances of the language and simply continue to penalize those whom they believe to be engaged in seriously deficient conduct.

Finally, another provision of the 2005 Act expresses a "sense of Congress" that Bankruptcy Rule 9011 should be amended to provide that all papers (including schedules) submitted by debtors or attorneys for debtors be submitted only after reasonable inquiry to "verify" that the information contained in the documents is well-

into court," and reasonable attorney fees to a moving party if imposed on a motion. *See* Fed. R. Bankr. P. 9011(c)(2).

9 11 U.S.C. § 707(b)(4)(C).

10 2 Moore's Federal Practice § 11.11[2] (3d ed. 2004); 10 Collier on Bankruptcy ¶ 9011.04[2] (15th ed. rev.).

11 2 Moore's Federal Practice § 11.11[2] (3d ed. 2004).

12 2 Moore's Federal Practice § 11.11[2] (3d ed. 2004) (emphasis added).

13 11 U.S.C. § 707(b)(4)(D).

grounded in fact and warranted by existing law or a good faith argument for the extension, modification, or reversal of existing law.[14] This provision expressing the sense of Congress also adds to the arguments that the certifications required under current Bankruptcy Rule 9011 do not apply to the schedules. It seems unlikely that the Bankruptcy Rules Committee will follow Congress's suggestion, as it has only recently replaced very similar language in Rule 9011 in order to conform it to Federal Rule of Civil Procedure 11,[15] and the Committee should be loathe to impose a different standard on debtors' attorneys than on other attorneys.[16]

3.2.5 Penalties for Abusive Creditor Motions—Section 707(b)(5)

Section 707(b)(5) provides that the court may award the debtor reasonable costs and attorney fees in challenging a motion to dismiss under section 707(b) if (1) the motion is not granted and the position of the movant in filing the motion violated Bankruptcy Rule 9011,[17] or (2) the movant's attorney failed to perform a reasonable investigation, failed to determine that the motion was well grounded in fact and law (or possible modification of law), and the motion was filed solely to coerce the debtor into waiving bankruptcy rights.[18]

Like most fee-shifting provisions, this provision appears to authorize only an award of costs and fees against the actual movant, not the attorney for the movant. However the provision should not have any effect on the court's ability to sanction attorneys for such parties under Bankruptcy Rule 9011 or otherwise.

In addition, an award under this provision may not be assessed against a trustee, United States trustee, or bankruptcy administrator. The provision also exempts a "small business" that has a claim for an aggregate amount of less than $1000 from being assessed an award of costs and attorney fees if the position of the small business violated Bankruptcy Rule 9011.[19] This exemption does not protect a small business from the restrictions in section 707(b)(5)(A) that apply to the movant's attorney.

3.3 Definition of "Debt Relief Agency"

3.3.1 Applicability of Debt Relief Agency Provisions to Debtor's Attorney

More confusing, if not absurd, are the provisions setting out requirements for "debt relief agencies." These provisions, due to slipshod drafting, will apply to many attorneys who rarely, or never, represent consumer bankruptcy debtors. The determination of whether a person is a debt relief agency turns on the interrelated definitions in section 101 of the Bankruptcy Code of "assisted person," "bankruptcy assistance," and "debt relief agency."

An "assisted person" is defined in section 101 as any person whose debts are primarily consumer debts and whose non-exempt property is worth less than $150,000.[20] This definition encompasses the vast majority of consumers because there is no requirement that an assisted person be a bankruptcy debtor.

"Bankruptcy assistance" is defined as goods or services sold or otherwise provided to an "assisted person" with the purpose of providing advice, document preparation, or representation in a bankruptcy case or proceeding, regardless of the chapter.[21] The advice or representation need not be in connection with a case in which the assisted person is a debtor, nor need it be in connection with a consumer bankruptcy case.

A "debt relief agency" is defined as any person who provides bankruptcy assistance to an assisted person in return for compensation, or who is a bankruptcy petition preparer as defined in section 110 of the Code.[22] This definition includes attorneys who represent individual landlords or other mom and pop businesses that owe primarily consumer debts, as well as those who represent consumer creditors, or non-debtor spouses as creditors in title 11 cases.

Because "person" is defined to include partnerships and corporations, presumably the entire law firm is a debt

---

14 Pub. L. No. 109-8, § 319, 119 Stat. 23 (2005).

15 *See* Advisory Committee Note to Fed. R. Bankr. P. 9011 (1997).

16 No changes to Bankruptcy Rule 9011 have been proposed in the interim rules and forms adopted by the Judicial Conference to implement the 2005 Act.

17 *See* National Consumer Law Center, Consumer Bankruptcy Law and Practice § 15.5.5 (7th ed. 2004).

18 11 U.S.C. § 707(b)(5).

19 "Small business" is defined in § 707(b)(5)(C)(i) as: "an unincorporated business, partnership, corporation, association, or organization that has fewer than 25 full-time employees as determined on the date on which the motion is filed; and is engaged in commercial or business activity." Section 707(b)(5)(C)(ii) provides that the number of employees of a wholly-owned subsidiary of a corporation includes the employees of a parent corporation and any other subsidiary corporation of the parent corporation.

20 11 U.S.C. § 101(3).

21 11 U.S.C. § 101(4A).

22 11 U.S.C. § 101(12A).

relief agency, even if only one of the members handles bankruptcy matters or otherwise meets the definition for providing bankruptcy assistance. No time limit is established by the statute, so quite possibly representing one assisted person could make a firm a debt relief agency forever. On the other hand, as the definition is cast in the present tense, it could also be read to mean that a firm is a debt relief agency only if it is currently providing bankruptcy assistance to an assisted person. Under this interpretation, it could be difficult for a large firm which occasionally provides such services to keep track of whether it is a debt relief agency at any particular point in time. Some firms may cease representing individuals in title 11 cases for compensation to avoid the risk of becoming debt relief agencies.

It may be argued, also based on the present-tense language found in section 110(12A) of the Code, that a person is a debt relief agency only in those cases in which it is providing bankruptcy assistance to an assisted person for compensation. This interpretation would excuse an attorney that is a debt relief agency due to paid representation in other cases from complying with the debt relief agency provisions (many of which, such as the fee disclosures, have no relevance) in *pro bono* cases. However such an approach may be a risky strategy until this definition has been clarified either by case law or other interpretation.

3.3.2 *Persons Specifically Excluded from the Definition of Debt Relief Agency*

The definition of "debt relief agency" includes several specific exemptions. As mentioned above, a person is not a debt relief agency if the bankruptcy assistance provided is not "in return for the payment of money or other valuable assistance."[23] In addition, the following persons or entities are excluded from the definition:

- Any person who is an officer, employee, director, or agent of a debt relief agency or petition preparer;
- A nonprofit organization that is exempt from taxation under section 501(c)(3) of the Internal Revenue Code;
- A creditor of the assisted person to the extent the creditor is assisting the person in restructuring a debt owed to the creditor (this exemption would not include a new mortgage broker arranging a loan to pay off a chapter 13 case);
- A depository institution or credit union or affiliate or subsidiary thereof; and
- An author, publisher, distributor, or seller of copyrighted works, when acting in that capacity.[24]

By excluding officers, employees, directors, or agents of debt relief agencies or petition preparers, an attorney employed by a firm or by the attorney's own professional corporation (of which he is an officer), or by any entity providing bankruptcy assistance, is not a "debt relief agency" even though the attorney's employer is. This exclusion will seemingly allow thinly capitalized petition preparers and their officers, and perhaps thinly capitalized professional corporations or other entities employing attorneys, to escape liability under the remedy provision found in section 526(c) of the Code.

The exemption for nonprofit organizations will assist many legal services organizations and their attorneys by excluding them from the debt relief agency requirements. However, the exemption includes not only legitimate nonprofits but also operations masquerading as nonprofits, such as some of the new credit counseling agencies.

3.4 Restrictions on Debt Relief Agencies

Mostly the debt relief agency restrictions prohibit practices already considered improper, such as failing to perform services as promised, making untrue or misleading statements, or advising clients to make statements that an agency should know are misleading.[25] Although the latter restriction, by itself, might appear to be a strict liability provision for any untrue or misleading statements, the section's remedy provisions speak of negligence or intentional misconduct,[26] for which remedies exist under current law. Courts are unlikely to hold attorneys responsible for untruths they could not, with reasonable care, have discovered.

Section 526(a)(3) of the Code also prohibits debt relief agencies from misrepresenting the services to be provided to an assisted person or the benefits and risks of bankruptcy.[27] Again, these actions generally are improper under current law.

Section 526(a)(4) prohibits an attorney who is a debt relief agency from advising an assisted person to incur *more* debt in contemplation of filing a bankruptcy case or

23 11 U.S.C. § 101(12A).

24 11 U.S.C. § 101(12A).

25 11 U.S.C. § 526(a)(1), (2).

26 11 U.S.C. § 526(c); *see* § 3.8, *infra*.

27 11 U.S.C. § 526(a)(3).

in order to pay bankruptcy fees to an attorney or petition preparer.[28] This provision represents a departure from current law as it may be perfectly proper to advise a debtor to incur a debt that the debtor plans to pay. Indeed, the restriction on such lawful and proper advice could infringe on the First Amendment rights of attorneys and their clients.

3.5 Disclosures Required of Debt Relief Agencies

3.5.1 Relationship Between Section 527 and Section 342(b)(1) Disclosures

Section 527 of the Bankruptcy Code sets out a series of "disclosures" that debt relief agencies must make to all assisted persons being provided bankruptcy assistance (which would include creditors). Section 527(a)(1) also states that the agency must provide the assisted person with the written notice required by section 342(b)(1) of the Code, despite the fact that section 342 requires that the notice be given by the clerk of the court.[29] Confusingly, section 527(a)(1) only mentions a portion of the notice required under section 342, omitting the portion that section 342(b)(2) requires.[30]

3.5.2 Disclosures Concerning the Bankruptcy Process

To the extent not covered by the section 342(b)(1) notice, and within three days of when the agency first offers to provide bankruptcy assistance services to an assisted person (including a creditor or landlord), the agency must provide a clear and conspicuous notice that:

- All information provided in a bankruptcy case is required to be complete, accurate, and truthful;
- All assets and liabilities must be completely and accurately disclosed in documents filed to commence a case;
- Current monthly income, amounts for means test calculations and, in chapter 13 cases, disposable income must be stated after a reasonable inquiry; and
- Information provided in a case may be audited and failure to provide such information may lead to the case's dismissal or to sanctions, including criminal sanctions.[31]

In addition, the debtor must be informed that replacement value of each asset, as defined in section 506 of the Code, must be stated where requested in the "documents filed to commence the case" after reasonable inquiry to establish that value.[32] However, the document filed to commence the case is the petition, which requires no property valuation. Even if the provision is read to mean the schedules, those documents do not "request" replacement value[33] and it is not relevant to at least some purposes of the schedules. While the required statement may be misleading, few debtors will understand it anyway.

A debt relief agency must retain copies of the notices required under section 527(a) for two years after the date when the notices are given to an assisted person.[34]

3.5.3 Required Statement About Bankruptcy Assistance Services

A debt relief agency must also provide the assisted person with a statement about "bankruptcy assistance services."[35] This statement must be provided at the time the notice under section 527(a)(1) is given, but no time requirement is set in section 527(a)(1), which refers to the clerk's notice under section 342(b)(1). The clerk is required to give this notice before commencement of the case; so if a creditor, who is an assisted person, first consults an attorney after the commencement of the case, it may be impossible for the attorney to give timely notice to the creditor. This conundrum could lead attorneys to refuse to represent individual creditors because they can not comply with the notice provision's requirements.

The required statement must be clear and conspicuous and must be provided in a separate document. In addition

28 11 U.S.C. § 526(a)(4).

29 Section 342(b)(1) requires that the clerk of the court provide a notice containing: (1) a brief description of different chapters and their purpose, benefits, and costs, and (2) a brief description of the services provided by credit counseling agencies.

30 Section 342(b)(2) requires that the clerk of the court provide a notice containing: (1) a statement specifying that a person who knowingly and fraudulently conceals assets or makes a false oath or statement under penalty of perjury in a bankruptcy case shall be subject to fine and imprisonment, and (2) a statement specifying that all information supplied by a debtor in connection with a bankruptcy case is subject to examination by the attorney general.

31 11 U.S.C. § 527(a)(2).

32 11 U.S.C. § 527(a)(2)(B).

33 The information may be requested in the form chapter 13 plans used in some districts.

34 11 U.S.C. § 527(d).

35 11 U.S.C. § 527(b).

it must be given verbatim, or in substantially similar language to the extent applicable, even though it includes information that may be incorrect. For example, it states: "You will have to pay a filing fee to the bankruptcy court," which is not always true because the court may waive the fee,[36] or no fee may be charged for a particular proceeding. It also states: "The following information helps you understand what must be done in a routine bankruptcy case to help you evaluate how much service you need." In fact, the statement provides no such information. Finally, it proceeds to "inform" the assisted person that "you can hire an attorney to represent you, or you can get help in some localities from a bankruptcy petition preparer who is not an attorney," a statement that implies petition preparers are competent to help bankruptcy debtors and which may promote petition preparers' unauthorized practice of law.

Although much of the statement would be inapplicable to a creditor or landlord, some of it probably is applicable (for example, that the case may involve litigation and that the assisted person may choose to appear *pro se*). Many attorneys will probably give the statement verbatim to avoid possible issues in determining whether a substitute is "substantially similar" or "applicable" and, for debtors and creditors who read it, it will be basically useless. The full text of the statement is reprinted below.

Statement Required Under Section 527(b)

IMPORTANT INFORMATION ABOUT BANKRUPTCY ASSISTANCE SERVICES FROM AN ATTORNEY OR BANKRUPTCY PETITION PREPARER.

If you decide to seek bankruptcy relief, you can represent yourself, you can hire an attorney to represent you, or you can get help in some localities from a bankruptcy petition preparer who is not an attorney. THE LAW REQUIRES AN ATTORNEY OR BANKRUPTCY PETITION PREPARER TO GIVE YOU A WRITTEN CONTRACT SPECIFYING WHAT THE ATTORNEY OR BANKRUPTCY PETITION PREPARER WILL DO FOR YOU AND HOW MUCH IT WILL COST. Ask to see the contract before you hire anyone.

The following information helps you understand what must be done in a routine bankruptcy case to help you evaluate how much service you need. Although bankruptcy can be complex, many cases are routine.

Before filing a bankruptcy case, either you or your attorney should analyze your eligibility for different forms of debt relief available under the Bankruptcy Code and which form of relief is most likely to be beneficial for you. Be sure you understand the relief you can obtain and its limitations. To file a bankruptcy case, documents called a Petition, Schedules and Statement of Financial Affairs, as well as in some cases a Statement of Intention need to be prepared correctly and filed with the bankruptcy court. You will have to pay a filing fee to the bankruptcy court. Once your case starts, you will have to attend the required first meeting of creditors where you may be questioned by a court official called a 'trustee' and by creditors.

If you choose to file a chapter 7 case, you may be asked by a creditor to reaffirm a debt. You may want help deciding whether to do so. A creditor is not permitted to coerce you into reaffirming your debts.

If you choose to file a chapter 13 case in which you repay your creditors what you can afford over 3 to 5 years, you may also want help with preparing your chapter 13 plan and with the confirmation hearing on your plan which will be before a bankruptcy judge.

If you select another type of relief under the Bankruptcy Code other than chapter 7 or chapter 13, you will want to find out what should be done from someone familiar with that type of relief.

Your bankruptcy case may also involve litigation. You are generally permitted to represent yourself in litigation in bankruptcy court, but only attorneys, not bankruptcy petition preparers, can give you legal advice.

3.5.4 Disclosures Required of Non-Attorney Agencies That Prepare Bankruptcy Documents

Debt relief agencies, but not attorneys who prepare bankruptcy petitions, schedules, and statements for debtors, are required to provide clear and conspicuous written notice to an assisted person giving "reasonably sufficient information" on how to provide the information required to file for bankruptcy.[37] To the extent that the debt relief agency does not provide the required information itself, the notice must explain such unsettled questions of law as:

- How to determine replacement value of assets;
- How to determine current monthly income and per-

36 *See* 28 U.S.C. § 1930(f).

37 11 U.S.C. § 527(c).

form means test calculations;
- How to determine disposable income in a chapter 13 case;
- How to list creditors, determine the amount owed, and determine the proper address for the creditor; and
- How to determine what property is exempt and to value exempt property at replacement value as defined in section 506 of the Code (which has nothing to do with valuing property for exemption purposes).

A debt relief agency may give this information only to the extent allowed by applicable non-bankruptcy law. As all of these subjects constitute legal advice about very complicated issues no petition preparer can properly give such advice and the provision is essentially applicable to no one, or it will compel petition preparers to engage in the unauthorized practice of law.[38]

3.6 Written Contract Under Section 528(a)

A debt relief agency must execute a written contract with an assisted person within five days after the date the agency first provides bankruptcy assistance to the assisted person, and prior to filing a petition.[39] Fulfilling this obligation may be impossible because the assisted person may not wish to sign a contract, and obviously there is no way to force the assisted person to sign. In such cases, the debt relief agency's obligation should be satisfied by tendering the contract. Alternatively, a debt relief agency, even before rendering any advice or providing a free consultation, could tender a contract that states the services that would be provided if the debtor chooses to pursue a case, but gives the debtor the option to pursue a case or not, with little or no fee for services if the debtor chooses not to proceed.

In light of this requirement, attorneys may have to be careful not to give advice in an initial telephone call, which is probably good practice in any event. Telephone tape recordings and other general information provided to the public probably would not be considered bankruptcy assistance, because it is not provided "in a case or proceeding on behalf of another," especially in light of other provisions regulating advertising.[40]

The written contract must explain, clearly and conspicuously, the services that will be provided and the fees, charges, and terms of payment.[41] The assisted person must be provided a copy of the executed and completed contract.[42] These requirements apply to all attorneys who are debt relief agencies with respect to all assisted persons, even if the assisted person is a creditor or landlord.

3.7 Advertising Requirements Under Section 528(a)

If a debt relief agency advertises bankruptcy assistance services or the benefits of bankruptcy, it must disclose that the services or benefits are with respect to bankruptcy relief under title 11.[43] The agency must also clearly and conspicuously use the following statement, or a substantially similar statement, in such advertisements: "We are a debt relief agency. We help people file for relief under the Bankruptcy Code."[44]

Advertising is defined to include "general media, seminars, mailings, telephonic or electronic messages," but only if directed to the general public.[45] It appears that mailings to particular individuals facing foreclosure may not be included, if they are not sent to the general public. The term advertising is also defined to include:

- Descriptions of bankruptcy assistance in chapter 13, whether or not chapter 13 is mentioned in the advertisement;
- Statements such as "federally supervised repayment plans," or "federal debt restructuring help," or other similar statements that might lead a consumer to believe credit counseling is being offered when, in fact, bankruptcy services are being offered; and
- Advertisements to the general public indicating that a debt relief agency provides assistance with respect to credit defaults, mortgage foreclosures, evictions, excessive debt, debt collection pressure, or the in-

38 *See, e.g.*, Taub v. Weber, 366 F.3d 966 (9th Cir. 2004) (petition preparer's advice regarding the meaning of terms "market value" and "secured claim or exemption" was unauthorized practice of law); *In re* Doser, 292 B.R. 652 (D. Idaho 2003) (giving debtors an incomplete and inaccurate "bankruptcy overview" prepared by franchisor "We the People," and telling the debtors that it was reliable, constituted the practice of law); *see also* National Consumer Law Center, Consumer Bankruptcy Law and Practice § 15.6 (7th ed. 2004).

39 11 U.S.C. § 528(a)(1).

40 *See* 11 U.S.C. § 528(a)(3); § 3.7, *infra*.

41 11 U.S.C. § 528(a)(1)(A), (B).

42 11 U.S.C. § 528(a)(2).

43 11 U.S.C. § 528(a)(3).

44 11 U.S.C. § 528(a)(4).

45 11 U.S.C. § 528(a)(3).

ability to pay consumer debts.[46]

The advertising requirements apply to any advertisement offering assistance with respect to credit defaults, mortgage foreclosures, or evictions. They thus apply to attorneys offering services to creditors and landlords, who may never help people file for relief under the Bankruptcy Code, thus requiring them to engage in false advertising, not to mention advertising that will deter their desired clients from choosing to retain them. The requirements also blur the distinction between attorneys and petition preparers, which will cause more people to fall prey to petition preparers.

It is unclear how much leeway is given by the right to use "substantially similar" language. May an attorney omit the phrase "debt relief agency" if the attorney makes clear that bankruptcy services are offered? This change should be allowed, as the supposed purpose of the requirement is to prevent attorneys from "luring" clients in by not mentioning that the service they offer is bankruptcy. May attorneys for creditors and landlords omit the language stating they help people file bankruptcy petitions if, in fact, that is not true? Absent such leeway the provision may well be unconstitutional, requiring certain speech which may not even be truthful.

3.8 Remedies for Failure to Comply with Debt Relief Agency Provisions

The 2005 Act specifies remedies for failure to comply with the debt relief provisions. Contracts not complying with the requirements in sections 527 or 528 of the Code are void, and may not be enforced by any court or any other person, other than the assisted person (though it is unclear how even the assisted person can enforce a void contract, especially if a court can not enforce it).[47] Any waiver by an assisted person of rights under section 526 is not enforceable against the debtor.[48]

A debt relief agency is liable to an assisted person for any fees or charges in connection with bankruptcy assistance, plus actual damages, attorney fees, and costs, if the debt relief agency:

- Intentionally or negligently failed to comply with any provision of sections 526, 527, or 528 with respect to a bankruptcy case for such assisted person;
- Provided bankruptcy assistance in a case dismissed or converted to another chapter because of agency's intentional or negligent failure to file documents; or
- Intentionally or negligently disregarded material requirements of the Code or the Bankruptcy Rules applicable to the agency.[49]

The main effect of these provisions is to add statutory damages (in the amount of the fees paid to the agency), to the extent they exceed actual damages, and attorney fees, to the amount that could be recovered in malpractice and unfair and deceptive practices claims that already exist.

State attorneys general are given authority to enforce the provisions in state or federal court, and to seek injunctive relief, actual damages for assisted persons, and attorney fees.[50] In addition, the bankruptcy court on its own motion may enjoin and sanction debt relief agencies that intentionally violate or engage in a pattern of violating section 526.[51]

Nothing in sections 526, 527, or 528 exempts any person from complying with state law, except to the extent state law is inconsistent.[52] State regulations on lawyer advertising, however, may be preempted by these provisions. In addition, nothing in sections 526, 527, or 528 limits the ability of a state or federal court to enforce qualifications for the practice of law.[53]

3.9 Conclusion

Consumer bankruptcy attorneys will learn to cope with these new requirements, adding to the mounds of paper they give to their clients. The main impact, especially when combined with the many additional paperwork requirements imposed elsewhere in the 2005 Act,[54] will probably be to drive general practitioners out of bankruptcy practice. Such an exodus could create additional access problems for debtors in small towns and rural areas.

46 11 U.S.C. § 528(b)(1), (2).
47 11 U.S.C. § 526(c)(1).
48 11 U.S.C. § 526(b).
49 11 U.S.C. § 526(c)(2).
50 11 U.S.C. § 526(c)(3).
51 11 U.S.C. § 526(c)(5).
52 11 U.S.C. § 526(d).
53 11 U.S.C. § 526(d)(2).
54 *See* Ch. 4, *infra*.

Chapter 4 New Paperwork and Notice Requirements

4.1 Introduction

The most substantial increases in fees and expenses for consumer debtors will result from the numerous new document production requirements that will be imposed upon those debtors. For those who are subject to the means test, as discussed in Chapter 2, *supra*, not only will there be a requirement to complete a detailed and complicated means test calculation, but various of the expenses involved in the calculation must be documented in order to be allowed. In addition, there will be a number of new documents required of all debtors which will be discussed in this Chapter.

4.2 Additional Documents Required by Section 521(a)(1)(B) to Be Filed with Court

4.2.1 Introduction

Section 521(a)(1)(B) of the Bankruptcy Code is amended by the 2005 Act to require several new documents to be filed as part of the debtor's duties. These new documents are required to be filed unless the court orders otherwise.[1]

4.2.2 Certificate That Section 342(b) Notice Delivered

To the extent not covered by the section 342(b)(1) notice provided by the court, and within three days of when an attorney (debt relief agency) first offers to provide bankruptcy assistance services to the debtor (assisted person), the attorney must provide a clear and conspicuous notice to the debtor containing disclosures about the bankruptcy process.[2] If section 342(b) is applicable (that is, if the debtor is an individual with primarily consumer debts), the debtor's attorney must file a certificate that the section 342(b) notice was delivered by the attorney to the debtor.[3] The certification is to be made by signing the box marked Exhibit B on the bankruptcy petition.

4.2.3 Copies of Recent Payment Advices

The debtor is required to file copies of all "payment advices" received within sixty days before the petition from any employer of the debtor.[4] Few debtors retain pay stubs or other similar documents for the entire sixty-day period, so attorneys will have additional work involved in contacting the employer to obtain a statement which can be evidence of payment, or in filing a motion to excuse the filing.[5]

It is not clear from the amendments to the Code when the payment advices need to be filed. The only deadline in the legislation is forty-five days after the petition, at which point the case can be dismissed if they are not filed.[6] The suggested interim rules implement this requirement by adding Rule 1007 (b)(1)(E).[7] Interim Bankruptcy Rule 1007(c) provides that the payment advices are to be filed within fifteen days of the petition unless the court extends the time.[8]

Due to privacy concerns, the debtor's attorney should also review these documents because they usually include the debtor's full Social Security number. Interim Bankruptcy Rule 1007(b)(1)(E) provides that the debtor should redact all but the last four digits of the debtor's

1 *See* § 4.2.5, *infra*.

2 *See* 11 U.S.C. § 527(a)(2); § 3.5.2, *supra*.

3 11 U.S.C. § 521(a)(1)(B)(iii)(I).

4 11 U.S.C. § 521(a)(1)(B)(iv).

5 For a sample Motion to Excuse Filing of Lost or Unavailable Payment Advices, see Form 4, Appx. G, *infra*.

6 11 U.S.C. § 521(i)(1); *see* § 4.5, *infra*.

7 *See* Appx. B, *infra*.

8 Bankruptcy Rule 4002 was also amended to provide that the debtor shall bring evidence of current income, such as the most recent payment advice, to the meeting of creditors. *See* Interim Bankruptcy Rule 4002(b)(2)(A) (reprinted in Appx. B, *infra*).

Social Security number on the payment advices.[9] Debtors may also wish to prevent disclosure of these documents on the Internet by filing a form motion in every case under section 107(c) of the Code,[10] or seek a general order or local rule under that section preventing these documents from being made publicly available.

4.2.4 Statement of Monthly Net Income

The 2005 Act also requires that the debtor file a statement of "monthly net income," itemized to show how it was calculated,[11] and a statement disclosing any increases in income or expenditures reasonably anticipated by the debtor in the twelve months after the petition is filed.[12] Curiously, the provisions do not require disclosure of anticipated *decreases* in income or expenditures.

As the provision requiring Schedules I and J of Official Form 6 remains in the statute, this provision probably is referring to current monthly income which, under section 707(b), is one of the filings to be included under section 521.[13] However, the revised Official Form 6, Schedule J, calls the difference between Schedules I and J "monthly net income," although the Code never otherwise uses that term.[14] The number itself may be relevant to the feasibility of a chapter 13 plan in some cases. In addition, interim Bankruptcy Rule 1007(b)(6) provides that the debtor in a chapter 13 case must file a statement of current monthly income on the appropriate Official Form, and a calculation of the debtor's disposable income if the debtor's income is above the median family income.[15]

4.2.5 Documents Required Unless Court Orders Otherwise

The above documents are all required by section 521(a)(1)(B) and therefore must be filed "unless the court orders otherwise." When all payment advices for the past sixty days are not readily available, the debtor could file a motion to excuse the filing.[16] For example, a debtor may have been terminated by an employer who refuses to cooperate and provide the documents. It is unlikely that such a motion would be opposed, especially if a year-to-date figure is available on a recent pay stub.

A court may also adopt a local rule to this effect, perhaps "ordering otherwise and excusing production" upon a certification of why the documents can not be provided, after other parties have an opportunity to object. There is precedent for such a rule in situations in which the court can "order otherwise." Under Bankruptcy Rule 9014, before it was recently amended, no answer was required to a motion unless the court ordered otherwise, and many courts adopted local rules requiring such an answer.

4.3 Other Documents Required by Section 521 to Be Filed with Court

4.3.1 Certificate from Credit Counseling Agency

4.3.1.1 Filing Requirements

The debtor must file a certificate from an approved credit counseling agency that the debtor received the briefing required by section 109(h) of the Bankruptcy Code and, if a debt repayment plan was developed through the counseling, a copy of that plan.[17] The certificate and debt repayment plan, if any, must be filed with the petition in any voluntary case filed by an individual debtor.[18] The Voluntary Petition (Official Form 1) has also been modified to permit the debtor to certify that she has received the credit counseling briefing within 180 days of the bankruptcy filing.[19] Obviously, the requirement to obtain such counseling is yet another barrier, financial and otherwise, to bankruptcy relief.[20]

---

9 *See* Appx. B, *infra*.

10 Section 107(c) provides that the bankruptcy court, for cause, may protect an individual with respect to certain types of information to the extent the court finds that disclosure of such information would create an undue risk of identity theft or other unlawful injury to the individual or the individual's property. 11 U.S.C. § 107(c).

11 11 U.S.C. § 521(a)(1)(B)(v).

12 11 U.S.C. § 521(a)(1)(B)(vi).

13 *See* § 2.2.2.1, *supra*; Statement of Current Monthly Income and Means Test Calculation, Form 22A, Appx. D, *infra*.

14 The schedules also ask for both anticipated increases and decreases in expenses.

15 *See* Ch. 6, *infra*.

16 For a sample Motion to Excuse Filing of Lost or Unavailable Payment Advices, see Form 4, Appx. G, *infra*.

17 11 U.S.C. § 521(b); *see also* Interim Bankruptcy Rule 1007(b)(3) (reprinted in Appx. B, *infra*).

18 Interim Bankruptcy Rule 1007(c) (reprinted in Appx. B, *infra*).

19 Official Form 1, as amended, is reprinted in Appx. D.4, *infra*. *See also* 11 U.S.C. § 109(h)(1).

20 This new requirement is being imposed at a time when credit counseling is in turmoil based on a number of serious problems in the industry. *See* National Consumer Law Center & Consumer Federation of America, Credit Counseling

4.3.1.2 Content of Briefing

Section 109(h)(1) states that the debtor must receive from an approved counseling agency an individual or group briefing that outlines the opportunities for available credit counseling and assists the debtor in performing a budget-related analysis. The United States trustee is given authority under the 2005 Act to approve counseling agencies.[21] In developing application forms and related instructions for agency applicants, the United States trustee has stated that the agencies shall at a minimum provide "adequate briefings, budget analysis, and credit counseling services to clients which include consideration of all alternatives to resolve a client's credit problems, an analysis of the client's current financial condition, discussion of the factors that caused such financial condition, and how the client can develop a plan to respond to the problems without incurring negative amortization of debt."[22] The United States trustee has determined that the average length of a pre-filing "briefing" should be ninety minutes.[23]

The 2005 Act provides that counseling may be received by telephone or over the Internet.[24] Counseling must also be offered by approved agencies without regard to ability to pay.[25] The bankruptcy clerk is required to maintain a list of all approved counseling agencies,[26] and it is expected that a similar list, with perhaps additional information about the individual agencies, will be available on the Unites States trustee's website.[27]

4.3.1.3 Waiver or Deferral of Counseling Requirement

There is a limited exception to the counseling requirement provided for the disabled, the incapacitated, and those on active military duty in a combat zone. If the court determines, after notice and a hearing, that the debtor falls within one of these categories, the counseling requirement does not apply.[28] However, waivers of the counseling requirement may be infrequently granted under this provision based on the narrow definition provided for "incapacity" and "disability."[29]

The counseling requirement does not apply to debtors in a particular district if the United States trustee or bankruptcy administrator determines that the approved counseling agencies for such district are not reasonably able to provide adequate services.[30] It is not expected that the United States trustee will invoke this provision.

The 2005 Act also has a limited provision for deferral of the counseling requirement if the debtor needs to file a petition in an emergency, such as to stop a foreclosure sale.[31] The amended Voluntary Petition (Official Form 1) contains a box that the debtor may check if requesting a waiver of the counseling requirement.[32] To invoke this provision, the debtor must also submit a certification (1) describing the "exigent circumstances" that merit a waiver of the requirement and (2) stating that the debtor requested counseling services from an approved agency but was unable to obtain the services during the five-day period following the request.[33] It is not clear from the statutory language whether the deferral is to be allowed if the counseling is available within five days of the request.

Although section 109(h)(3)(A) of the Code refers to the certification as relating to a "waiver" or "exemption" from the requirements of section 109(h)(1), the certification provides only a deferral of the requirement as the debtor must still obtain counseling within thirty

in Crisis: The Impact on Consumers of Funding Cuts, Higher Fees and Aggressive New Market Entrants (Apr. 2003).

21 11 U.S.C. § 111(b).

22 Instructions for Application as a Nonprofit Budget and Credit Counseling Agency § 4(1), *available at* www.usdoj.gov/ust/bapcpa/ccde.htm. These additional guidelines for the counseling sessions are apparently based on new section 111(c)(1) of the Code, but it is not clear that the "all alternatives" requirement is supported by that section's language.

23 *See* Instructions for Application as a Nonprofit Budget and Credit Counseling Agency § 4(1), *available at* www.usdoj.gov/ust/bapcpa/ccde.htm.

24 11 U.S.C. § 109(h)(1).

25 11 U.S.C. § 111(c)(2)(B).

26 11 U.S.C. § 111(a). A similar list of approved financial education courses must also be maintained. *See* § 4.4.4, *infra*.

27 The website is located at www.usdoj.gov/ust.

28 11 U.S.C. § 109(h)(4).

29 *See* 11 U.S.C. § 109(h)(4). For a sample motion for exemption from the credit counseling and financial education requirements based on incapacity, disability, or active military duty, see Motion to Exempt Debtor from Credit Counseling and Financial Education Requirement Based on Incapacity, Disability, or Active Military Duty, Form 3, Appx. G, *infra*.

30 11 U.S.C. § 109(h)(2).

31 11 U.S.C. § 109(h)(3)(A).

32 Amended Official Form 1 is reprinted in Appx. D.4, *infra*.

33 For a sample Debtor's Certification in Support of Waiver of Credit Counseling Requirement Based on Exigent Circumstances, see Form 1, Appx. G, *infra*.

days of the petition date.[34] The court may, for cause, extend this period by an additional fifteen days.

4.3.2 Record of Debtor's Interest in Certain Educational Savings Programs

The debtor is required to file a "record" of any interest the debtor has in an education individual retirement account (IRA) or section 529 tuition program.[35] This requirement can be met by listing such interests in Item 11 on Schedule B of the revised Official Form 6.[36] In addition to the new exemption rights for retirement funds described in Chapter 8, *infra*, the 2005 Act provides that funds placed in an education IRA, as defined in section 530(b)(1) of the Internal Revenue Code, before the filing of the petition and funds contributed to a tuition program, as defined in section 529(b)(1) of the Internal Revenue Code, may be excluded from property of the estate if certain specified conditions are met.[37]

4.3.3 Production of Tax Returns or Transcripts

4.3.3.1 Filing Tax Returns or Transcripts with the Court

The 2005 Act requires that the debtor file tax returns or transcripts with the court.[38] At the request of the court, the United States trustee, or a party in interest, an individual debtor must file with the court:

- A copy of the debtor's federal income tax return (or at the election of the debtor a transcript of the return) for a tax year ending during the time the case is pending, at the same time it is filed with the taxing authority;
- A copy of any tax return (or transcript) that had not been filed with the taxing authority before the commencement of the case but was subsequently filed for a tax year ending in the three years before the petition, at the same time it is filed with the taxing authority; and
- A copy of any amendments to such returns.

It is unclear what will happen if the case has already been closed when such returns are filed with a taxing authority. The bankruptcy court is not likely to accept them for filing as documents for filing are not normally accepted in closed cases. And what would the remedy be if they were not filed with the court, once a discharge has already been entered?

4.3.3.2 Providing Tax Records to Trustee and Creditors

At least seven days before the section 341 meeting, the debtor must provide the trustee with a copy of the debtor's federal income tax return (or tax transcript thereof) required under applicable law for the most recent tax year ending immediately before the commencement of the case and for which a federal income tax return was filed.[39]

This language is somewhat unclear, because it appears to require a tax return or transcript only for the most recent year, and not require it if no return was required in that year. If read to require a return or transcript for the most recent tax year in which a return was required, it could require a return or transcript from twenty or thirty years before the case, which might be impossible to obtain. Interim Bankruptcy Rule 4002(b)(3) implements this requirement by providing that the debtor shall provide the tax return for the most recent tax year "ending immediately before the commencement of the case and for which a return was filed."[40]

At the same time as the return or transcript is provided to the trustee, it must be provided to any creditor that timely requests it.[41] By the plain words of the statute, if the return has already been provided to the trustee, a request from a creditor is not timely. Nevertheless, interim Bankruptcy Rule 4002(b)(4) provides that the debtor must comply with a creditor's request if the request is made at least fifteen days before the first date set for the section 341 meeting.[42]

If the debtor fails to provide a required return or transcript to the trustee or to a creditor that timely requests it, the case must be dismissed, unless the debtor

---

34 11 U.S.C. § 109(h)(3)(B).

35 11 U.S.C. § 521(c); *see also* Interim Bankruptcy Rule 1007(b)(1)(F) (reprinted in Appx. B, *infra*).

36 Schedule B of amended Official Form 6 is reprinted in Appx. D.4, *infra*.

37 11 U.S.C. § 541(b)(5), (6).

38 11 U.S.C. § 521(f)(1)–(3).

39 11 U.S.C. § 521(e)(2)(A).

40 *See* Appx. B, *infra*.

41 11 U.S.C. § 521(e)(2)(A)(ii).

42 *See* Appx. B, *infra*. Interim Bankruptcy Rule 4002(b)(4) also provides that the debtor may provide at least seven days before the first date set for the section 341 meeting a written statement that the tax documentation does not exist.

shows that such failure is due to circumstances beyond the debtor's control.[43] The most likely qualifying circumstance, in a case in which the debtor has counsel, would be the debtor's inability to timely obtain a copy of a return or transcript from the Internal Revenue Service (IRS), if the debtor has not retained a copy of the return.[44] The IRS is likely to be deluged with additional requests for returns or transcripts and it is unclear how quickly it can respond. A debtor with an emergency bankruptcy case may not be able to obtain the transcript in time. In such a case the debtor may wish to send a copy of the debtor's request for the return or transcript to the United States trustee at the time it is made so that the United States trustee knows the return is not being provided for reasons beyond the debtor's control. Similarly, a copy of such a request might also be sent to the trustee and any requesting creditor. If this procedure is followed, a motion to dismiss filed by a United States trustee or creditor with such knowledge and without reasonable inquiry into whether the request has been fulfilled might be deemed to be a sanctionable abuse, as the motion would not be well grounded in fact or law.

4.3.3.3 Privacy Concerns and Safeguards

Obviously, the requirement of filing tax returns with the court and the disclosure of those tax returns to the court and interested parties raises enormous privacy concerns. The new tax return requirements will be subject to procedures to be established by the federal Judicial Conference to safeguard the confidentiality of tax information, including restrictions on creditor access to the information.[45] The Judicial Conference should require a showing of cause before a creditor can request tax information, and should prohibit further disclosure of tax information by any entity that receives it. In addition, courts should not permit tax returns to be accessible to the public.

To prevent further invasion of the debtor's privacy, debtors may wish to provide or file tax transcripts, rather than tax returns, because transcripts generally include less personal identifying information. Typically, transcripts are also quicker and easier to obtain than tax returns.[46] There are several different types of tax transcripts that can be requested from the Internal Revenue Service, and section 521 does not specify which type of transcript is to be used. Due primarily to privacy concerns in most cases the preferred transcript will be the MFTRA-X, which is the simplest one.[47]

4.3.4 Annual Statements of Income and Expenditures in Chapter 13 Cases

The 2005 Act requires that annual statements of income and expenditures be filed in chapter 13 cases, if requested by the court, the United States trustee, or a party in interest.[48] The statements must be filed beginning one year after the case is filed or ninety days after the end of "such tax year," whichever is later, and annually after the plan is confirmed (at least forty-five days before the anniversary of confirmation). It is somewhat unclear which tax year is referred to by "such tax year" as the preceding paragraphs refer to multiple tax years. Presumably, as the language applies only before confirmation, the reference is to the first tax year that ends after the case is commenced.

The sworn statement required by this subsection must disclose:

- The debtor's income and expenditures in the preceding tax year and the monthly income of the debtor, showing how those numbers are calculated;
- The amounts and sources of income of the debtor;
- The identity of any person responsible with the debtor for support of any dependent of the debtor; and
- The identity of any person who contributes to the household in which the debtor resides, and the amounts contributed.[49]

The statement is to be available to the United States trustee, bankruptcy administrator, trustee, or any party in

43 11 U.S.C. § 521(e)(2)(B).

44 Interim Bankruptcy Rule 4002(b)(3) also provides that the debtor may provide at the section 341 meeting a written statement that the tax documentation does not exist. *See* Appx. B, *infra*.

45 Section 315(c) of the 2005 Act requires that the Administrative Office of the United States Courts "shall establish procedures for safeguarding the confidentiality of any tax information provided," which "shall include restrictions on creditor access." Pub. L. No. 109-8, § 315(c), 119 Stat. 23 (2005). These procedures must be in place within 180 days of the October 17, 2005 enactment date.

46 For information about requesting tax returns and transcripts, and copies of the relevant Internal Revenue Service forms, see Appx. E.2, *infra*.

47 Other transcripts, such as the IMF MCC SPECIFIC or the TXMOD, contain more tax information.

48 11 U.S.C. § 521(f)(4).

49 11 U.S.C. § 521(f)(4), (g)(1).

interest, subject to the confidentiality safeguards to be implemented by the federal Judicial Conference.[50]

It is too soon to tell whether all chapter 13 trustees will make a practice in every case of requesting annual tax returns and income and expense statements. If they do so, they presumably will then review all of them, which will require a great deal of additional resources. Likewise, a chapter 13 debtor's attorney will have to devote a great deal of resources to assembling these materials every year, which will lead to larger attorney fees for an annual consultation with the debtor and the preparation of the documents. Ultimately, in most cases, these administrative costs will come from the pockets of unsecured creditors, raising a serious question about whether they will increase or decrease the distributions to those creditors.

4.3.5 Providing Proof of Identity

If requested by the trustee or the United States trustee, the debtor shall provide proof of the debtor's identity, presumably at the section 341 meeting.[51] The debtor must provide a document that establishes the debtor's identity, including a driver's license, passport or other document containing the debtor's photograph, *or* other personal identifying information that establishes the identity of the debtor. This provision appears to be more liberal than the demands of some trustees prior to the 2005 Act, who had required that debtors provide photographic identification in every case.

Interim Bankruptcy Rule 4002(b)(1)(A) and (B), as approved by the Judicial Conference of the United States, require the debtor to bring to the section 341 meeting a picture identification issued by a governmental unit or other personal identifying information that establishes the debtor's identity, and evidence of Social Security number (or a written statement that such documentation of Social Security number does not exist).[52]

4.4 Other Document Requirements

4.4.1 Filing of Tax Returns with Taxing Authorities in Chapter 13 Cases

Chapter 13 debtors are required to file with the appropriate taxing authorities, by the day before the first scheduled section 341 meeting, all tax returns that the debtor was required to file for all taxable periods ending in the four years before the petition.[53] If the debtor was not required to file a return, no return need be filed. Presumably this provision includes only returns that were not already filed, although it does not say so.

If returns are not filed by this deadline, the trustee may hold the section 341 meeting open for a period of up to 120 days or, for a return that was not past due on the petition date, until the latest automatic extension date.[54] The debtor may also move for an extension of time to file returns beyond the time established by the trustee, but not more than thirty days after the trustee's deadline or, if a return was not past due on the petition date, beyond the latest automatic extension date. The debtor must demonstrate that the failure to file returns as required by this section is for reasons beyond the debtor's control.[55]

Section 1307(e) of the Bankruptcy Code provides a new ground for dismissal or conversion of a chapter 13 case if the debtor does not file the tax returns required by section 1308. As a practical matter chapter 13 debtors will often have to expend funds to have tax returns prepared in order to qualify for chapter 13 relief, even if they do not owe any taxes, further increasing the cost of bankruptcy. Again, if the returns are prepared after the petition is filed, such funds should be either an administrative expense (if prepared by the debtor's attorney) or an "other necessary expense" to be deducted in the disposable income test[56]—so the expenses will often reduce payments to unsecured creditors.

4.4.2 Statement of Current Monthly Income

Section 707(b)(2)(c) of the Bankruptcy Code requires the debtor to file, as part of the statement of current income and expenditures, a statement of the debtor's current monthly income, as defined in section 101, and the calculations showing whether a presumption of abuse arises. As discussed more fully in Chapter 2, *supra*, this requirement has been implemented through the addition of an Official Form called the Statement of Current Monthly Income and Means Test Calculation, which has been adopted by the Judicial Conference for implementation of the 2005 Act.[57]

50 11 U.S.C. § 521(g)(2); Pub. L. No. 109-8, § 315(c), 119 Stat 23 (2005).

51 11 U.S.C. § 521(h).

52 *See* Appx. B, *infra*.

53 11 U.S.C. § 1308(a).

54 11 U.S.C. § 1308(b)(1).

55 11 U.S.C. § 1308(b)(2).

56 *See* §§ 2.3.2.5, 2.3.3.7, *supra*.

57 *See* § 2.2.2, *supra*; Form 22A, Appx. D.4, *infra*.

4.4.3 Bank Statements

Although not required by the 2005 Act, interim Bankruptcy Rule 4002(b)(2)(B) provides that unless the trustee or the United States trustee instructs otherwise, the debtor shall bring to the section 341 meeting statements for each of the debtor's bank accounts, including checking accounts, savings accounts, money market accounts, mutual funds, and brokerage accounts, for the time period that includes the date of the petition.[58] The Advisory Committee Note to this rule states that "the rule does not require that the debtor create documents or obtain documents from third parties; rather, the debtor's obligation is to bring to the meeting of creditors under section 341 the documents which the debtor possesses."[59]

Now that Congress has added extensive new document production requirements for debtors by amending section 521 of the Code, and did not provide for the production of bank statements, the legal authority for interim Bankruptcy Rule 4002(b)(2)(B) is questionable. Debtor's counsel who participate in local rules committees may wish to recommend that local courts not adopt this provision of the interim rules.

4.4.4 Proof of Completion of a Financial Education Course

To receive a discharge in a chapter 7 or chapter 13 case, the debtor must submit proof of completion of an instructional course concerning financial management.[60] The interim Bankruptcy Rules provide that the certification of course completion will be submitted by the debtor using new Official Form 23.[61] This certification must be filed within forty-five days after the first date set for the section 341 meeting in a chapter 7 case, and no later than the date of the last payment made by the debtor as required by the plan or the date of filing of a motion for hardship discharge in a chapter 13 case.[62] Similar to the credit counseling requirement, there are limited exceptions for debtors with a disability or incapacity, or who are on active military duty, or if the courses are not available in the debtor's district.[63]

The Unites States trustee must approve courses, based on the vague statutory criteria provided in section 111(d) of the Code. In the application forms and related instructions developed by the United States trustee for those seeking approval of an instructional course, the United States trustee has stated that the agencies shall provide, at a minimum, written information and instruction on the following topics: budget development, money management, wise use of credit, and consumer information.[64] The United States trustee has also determined that the course should be a minimum of two hours in length.[65] The course may be taken by telephone or over the Internet.[66] If a fee is charged for an approved course, the entity providing the course must provide services without regard to ability to pay.[67]

Interim Bankruptcy Rule 4004(c)(1)(H) provides that the discharge will not be entered if the debtor has not filed a statement regarding completion of the required course.[68] The Advisory Committee Note to this Rule states that the clerk will close the case without entry of a discharge if the debtor fails to file the required statement. A court would probably reopen a bankruptcy to grant a discharge if a course was subsequently taken.

4.5 Consequences of Failing to Provide Documents

Failure to provide documents required by section 521(a)(1) of the Code, but not the other subsections, may lead to dismissal. Under section 521(i)(1), a case is to be "automatically dismissed" if the debtor does not file the information required by section 521(a)(1) within forty-five days of filing the petition. However, section 521(i)(2) provides that in such circumstances the case is to be dismissed on request of a party of interest within five days of the request.

If the debtor, within forty-five days of filing the petition, requests additional time, the court may allow up to forty-five additional days for the debtor to file the re-

---

58 *See* Appx. B, *infra*.

59 *See* Appx. B, *infra*.

60 11 U.S.C. §§ 727(a)(11), 1328(g).

61 *See* Interim Bankruptcy Rule 1007(b)(7) (reprinted in Appx. B, *infra*); Form 23, Appx. D.4, *infra*.

62 Interim Bankruptcy Rule 1007(c) (reprinted in Appx. B, *infra*).

63 *See* § 4.3.1.3, *supra*.

64 *See* Instructions for Application for Approval as a Provider of a Personal Financial Instructional Management Course § 4(2), *available at* www.usdoj.gov/ust/bapcpa/ccde.htm.

65 *Id.* § 4(3).

66 11 U.S.C. § 111(d)(1)(C).

67 11 U.S.C. § 111(d)(1)(E).

68 *See* Appx. B, *infra*.

quired documents.[69] The 2005 Act does not address the issue of how the court will deal with a request entered shortly before the forty-fifth day that has not been acted upon before "automatic dismissal" or a request for dismissal by a party. Hopefully, the court will determine whether a request for extension has been filed and rule upon it before dismissing a case.

One important issue is whether the new section 521(i)(1) overrides the right of the United States trustee to move for dismissal at an earlier time. The provision states that it applies notwithstanding section 707(a) of the Code. It certainly should override local court practices that automatically dismiss a case at an earlier time for not filing required documents.

If the trustee requests, the court may decline to dismiss the case if the debtor attempted in good faith to file the payment advices required by section 521(a)(1)(B)(iv) and the best interests of creditors are served by administration of the estate.[70] Presumably, because almost all of the documents required by section 521(a)(1) must be provided only if the court does not order otherwise, the debtor could still avoid dismissal if the court entered an order that the missing documents were not required.

4.6 Audits

The 2005 Act provides for audits to determine the accuracy, veracity, and completeness of debtors' petitions, schedules, and other information required by sections 521 and 1322 of the Code, beginning eighteen months after enactment.[71] The audits shall be conducted in random chapter 7 and chapter 13 cases, except that not less than one out of every 250 cases in each judicial district shall be selected for audit. There are to be other targeted audits of the schedules of income and expenses for those with unusually high income or expenses.

The procedures for conducting the audits are unknown at this time, but debtors may be required to provide additional documentation. The United States attorney general (in districts served by United States trustees) and the Judicial Conference of the United States (in districts served by bankruptcy administrators) shall establish these procedures. The failure of the debtor to satisfactorily explain a material misstatement in an audit or a failure to make papers or property available for inspection can be grounds for revocation of a discharge under section 727(d)(4) of the Code. There is no similar provision in chapter 13, perhaps because the audit will be completed before discharge.

69 11 U.S.C. § 521(a)(i)(3). For a sample Motion for Additional Time to Comply with Requirements under Section 521(a)(1), see Form 5, Appx. G, *infra*.

70 11 U.S.C. § 521(a)(i)(4).

71 *See* Pub. L. No. 109-8, § 603(a), 119 Stat. 23 (2005); 28 U.S.C. § 586(f).

4.7 New Notice Requirements

4.7.1 In General

The 2005 Act adds complicated and confusing notice requirements through amendments to section 342 of the Bankruptcy Code, with which both debtors' counsel and the courts must comply. While some of the new language is terribly drafted and confusing, the amendments to section 342 are likely to have little practical effect.

4.7.2 Deletion of the Safe Harbor from Section 342(c)

Section 342(c)(1) of the Code, as renumbered, is amended to delete language which had stated that the failure to provide a debtors' name, address and taxpayer identification (Social Security) number (now only the last four digits) does not invalidate the legal effect of a notice. It is unclear what deletion of this language means. Presumably, the effectiveness of the notice will be determined by otherwise applicable law. However, this subsection only applies to notices that the debtor is required to give by statute, rule or order of court, which are primarily notices of motions, amendments of schedules, and similar events.

4.7.3 Requirements on How Notice Shall Be Given

4.7.3.1 Scope

More significantly, the amendments to section 342 add new requirements regarding how notice "shall" be given. These requirements appear to override Bankruptcy Rule 7004, as incorporated in Bankruptcy Rule 9014, with respect to notices to governmental officers, governmental agencies, and insured depository institutions.[72] It is not clear whether a summons in an adversary proceeding is considered notice, as it is service of process but, if this

72 *See* National Consumer Law Center, Consumer Bankruptcy Law and Practice § 13.3.2.1 (7th ed. 2004).

provision applies, it also overrides Rule 7004 with respect to service of process on such entities.

4.7.3.2 Creditor Notice Request Given Pre-Petition

New section 342(c)(2) of the Code requires notice from a debtor to a creditor to be sent to an address specified by the creditor for receipt of correspondence, and to include the account number, but only if the creditor has supplied both the address request and the account number in at least two communications sent to the debtor in the ninety days before filing of the petition.

This subsection leaves open the question as to what is a creditor request to receive correspondence under this provision. Language such as "Send billing error notice to . . ." would not appear to be a request for correspondence.[73] Presumably the provision would not apply to communications from collection agencies, who are not "the creditor." And the use of the word "sent" precludes oral requests. Moreover, if only the address is supplied, or only an account number, the provision is not satisfied.

If the creditor was precluded by law from sending any communications to the debtor in the ninety days before the petition, the provision would apply to the last two communications, no matter when they were sent.[74] This prohibition might occur if the creditor had knowledge that the debtor was represented by an attorney or had been subject to the automatic stay in a prior case. For this exception to apply, the creditor must have been precluded from sending communications for the entire ninety-day period.

Importantly, the requirements of section 342(c)(2) only apply to notices the debtor is required to send by title 11 of the United States Code itself. This provision has no relation to addresses to be used on schedules, as those addresses are not used in notices that the debtor is required to send the creditor. However, if a debtor sends notice of the addition of a creditor to the schedules, the notice to the creditor must include the full taxpayer identification (Social Security) number, though it should not be included in the copy filed with the court.[75]

73 Such language is routinely found in monthly statements sent on credit card accounts in order to comply with the billing error notification requirements found in the Truth in Lending Act. *See* 15 U.S.C. § 1637(a)(7).

74 11 U.S.C. § 342(c)(2)(B).

75 11 U.S.C. § 342(c)(2).

4.7.3.3 Notice Request in Particular Case

New section 342(e) of the Code allows a creditor to file with the court and serve on the debtor an address which it wants used for notices in a particular chapter 7 or chapter 13 case. Any notice provided by the court or by the debtor more than five days after such an address request is made must use the requested address. This provision appears to override the more general address provisions of section 342(c)(2), though it does not expressly so state. This provision also neglects to include any coverage of notices from other parties, such as the trustee, United States trustee, or other creditors. Apparently, these parties, and participants in chapter 9, 11, and 12 cases, to which the provision does not apply, do not have to follow the dictates of this subsection. In any event, with the advent of electronic filing and noticing, most notices will soon be made electronically and available to any creditor in a particular case.

An entity may also file with any bankruptcy court an address request that is to be used by all bankruptcy courts or by particular bankruptcy courts, as specified by the entity, to provide notice in chapter 7 and chapter 13 cases.[76] This already occurs to the extent the Bankruptcy Noticing Center uses address matching software to send notices. All notices required to be sent by the court more than thirty days after such a request must be sent to the requested address, unless a request is made under section 342(e) by a creditor in a particular case for use of a different address.[77] Courts may wish to require creditors to file requests specifying the address they want used, to ensure that they give effective notice as defined by section 342(g).

4.7.4 Consequences of Lack of "Effective" Notice

The import of these new notice provisions is dictated by new section 342(g) of the Code, which provides that notice provided to a creditor other than in accordance with section 342 is not "effective notice" unless "brought to the attention of" the creditor. The first question raised by this provision is when is it applicable? Many notices given by a debtor, especially early in the case, do not come within the ambit of section 342(c) because they are not notices that are required by the Code, rules, court order, or other applicable laws. For example, notice from a debtor to a creditor that a case has

76 11 U.S.C. § 342(f).

77 11 U.S.C. § 342(f)(2).

been filed, intended to prevent an imminent foreclosure or repossession, is not required by any rule or Code provision.[78] Thus, such a notice is not provided in accordance with section 342 because the section does not set any particular requirements for this type of notice unless a creditor has requested use of a particular address in a particular case under section 342(e), which is unlikely to have happened in the first few days a case is pending. Read any other way, section 342 would not provide any way for such notice to a creditor to be given in accordance with section 342, as the section simply does not apply to such notices. It is almost inconceivable that courts would adopt a reading that makes it impossible for debtors to effectively notify creditors about the automatic stay. So for purposes of notifying creditors of the automatic stay, the provision in section 342(c)(2) regarding the address at which a creditor requests correspondence is irrelevant.

The next question concerns the language "brought to the attention of" the creditor, which is not defined, except by exclusion. Under section 342(g)(1), if a creditor has established reasonable procedures to deliver notices to a responsible person or department, then notice is not considered "brought to the attention of such creditor" until it reaches that person or department. This provision will provide fertile ground for discovery into a creditor's "reasonable procedures," including whether the creditor has given an address to the Bankruptcy Noticing Center for notices, whether it uses BANKO (an on-line service that notifies creditors of bankruptcy filings)[79] to check on filings, whether the creditor receives notices of case events electronically, and what mechanisms are in place to transmit timely notices to appropriate departments. If a debtor gives reasonable notice, a creditor should have procedures that transmit it almost instantly. It is hard to imagine how a creditor that does not have a procedure for immediate transmission of notices received by its attorneys, collection staff, repossession agents, and collection agents could be deemed to have reasonable procedures. And presumably, by negative implication, if such reasonable procedures do not exist, any actual notice given to a creditor should be deemed brought to the creditor's attention. So, in the end, any reasonable notice should be sufficient to be effective notice for purposes of section 342(g).

In any event, the only apparent relevance of lack of "effective notice," a term not used elsewhere in the Code, is that no monetary penalty can be imposed on a creditor for violation of the section 362 automatic stay or the sections 542 and 543 turnover requirements if the creditor has not received "effective notice" of the order for relief.[80] Section 342(g) does not affect the discharge of a debt or violations of the discharge injunction. Nor does it preclude other remedies, such as claims for actual damages and attorneys fees, or remedies against other entities, such as a creditor's attorney.[81]

---

78 *See* National Consumer Law Center, Consumer Bankruptcy Law and Practice, Form 23, Appx. G.4 (7th ed. 2004).

79 Information on BANKO is available at www.banko.com.

80 11 U.S.C. § 342(g)(2).

81 *See* § 7.4, *infra*.

Chapter 5 # Changes to Chapter 7 Bankruptcy

5.1 Introduction

The 2005 Act makes extensive changes to chapter 7 bankruptcy, many of which are discussed in other chapters of this guide. For example, changes which deal with means testing and abuse motions are discussed in Chapter 2, *supra*. In addition, issues relating to the new document production requirements are discussed in Chapter 4, *supra*, changes to the automatic stay provisions are discussed in Chapter 7, *infra*, and changes in the dischargeability of debts and reaffirmations are discussed in Chapter 10, *infra*.

This Chapter will discuss the changes made to the Code section dealing with the effect of conversion from a chapter 13 case to a chapter 7 case. It will also cover the new provisions dealing with the statement of intention with respect to property securing consumer debts. Finally, this Chapter will review the changes to the debtor's redemption rights under section 722 of the Code, to the lease assumptions in chapter 7 cases, and filing fee increases and waivers.

5.2 Conversion from Chapter 13

5.2.1 *Valuation of Property*

The 1994 amendments to the Code added section 348(f)(1)(B), which had provided that any valuations of property and of allowed secured claims made in a chapter 13 case were binding in the converted case.[1] The 2005 Act amends section 348(f)(1)(B) by providing that such valuations apply only in a case converted to chapter 11 or 12, but not in a case converted to chapter 7.

The 2005 Act also adds new section 348(f)(1)(C), which applies to conversions from chapter 13 to chapter 7. This subsection provides that, with respect to cases converted from chapter 13, the claim of any creditor holding security shall continue to be secured by that security unless the full amount of such claim determined under applicable non-bankruptcy law has been paid in full as of the date of conversion, notwithstanding any valuation or determination of the amount of the allowed secured claim made for purposes of the case under chapter 13.[2]

This language raises a number of questions. The language does not conflict with the first portion of section 348(f)(1)(B), as it contains no dictate concerning the valuation of property. However, for cases converted to chapter 7, this change means that the valuation of property must be determined by reference to some other source of law, because section 348(f)(1)(B) is made explicitly inapplicable to cases converted to chapter 7. This change may be advantageous to debtors who have converted to chapter 7 because, at least with respect to personal property, the property's value is likely to have gone down during the pendency of the chapter 13 case. For these debtors the valuation of the property should be determined under section 506(a)(2) of the Code, which provides that with respect to personal property acquired for personal, family, or household purposes, replacement value shall be determined "*considering the age and condition of the property at the time value is determined.*"[3] This provision would apply to a redemption proceeding under section 722 of the Code in the converted case, which could occur several years after the chapter 13 valuation and after significant depreciation of the property has occurred.[4]

5.2.2 *Cure of Pre-Bankruptcy Defaults*

Another amendment to section 348 provides that unless a pre-bankruptcy default has been fully cured under a chapter 13 plan at the time of the conversion, in any proceeding under title 11 or otherwise, the default will have the effect it has under applicable non-bankruptcy

1 *See* National Consumer Law Center, Consumer Bankruptcy Law and Practice § 8.7.4.4 (7th ed. 2004).

2 11 U.S.C. § 348(f)(1)(C)(i).

3 11 U.S.C. § 506(a)(2) (*emphasis added*).

4 *See* § 5.4.2, *infra*.

law.[5] The import of this provision is not entirely clear. The provision does not identify the effects of default to which it refers.

What does seem clear from the language is that the determination of whether the default has been cured is made by reference to the chapter 13 plan. If the terms of the plan provide that a default is cured upon certain payments, then a debtor who has made those payments has cured the default. In addition, based on the language of this provision, the debtor may have "otherwise" cured the default, perhaps under a foreclosure loss mitigation agreement with the lender independent of the bankruptcy.

When a debtor has not made such plan payments or otherwise cured the default, under the law prior to the 2005 amendments, no one would have argued that a default had been cured. This provision therefore seems to make no significant change, except perhaps to clarify that a cure under a chapter 13 plan continues to be effective even if the plan is not completed.

5.3 Statement of Intention

5.3.1 Stay Relief Based on Noncompliance with Statement of Intention

5.3.1.1 Overview

Section 521(a)(2) of the Bankruptcy Code requires that the debtor file a statement specifying certain intentions at the debtor with respect to property securing consumer debts. Prior to the enactment of the 2005 amendments, there was no sanction provided for failing to carry through on the intentions stated on the form, which reflected the view that the statement of intention was designed primarily as a notice provision for secured creditors. Thus, court decisions prior to the 2005 amendments held that a debtor's failure to follow through on a stated intention at best gave the secured creditor an additional argument in seeking relief from the automatic stay.[6] A series of overlapping and conflicting provisions in the 2005 Act codifies these cases and provides that relief from the stay is the proper remedy for a variety of violations relating to the statement of intention.

5.3.1.2 Stay Relief Under Section 362(h)

The first amendment dealing with the automatic stay and the statement of intention is found in section 521(a)(2)(C). This section was amended to add an exception for relief from the stay as permitted by section 362(h) of the Code. That subsection terminates the automatic stay with respect to personal property of the estate securing a claim, and renders that property no longer property of the estate, if the debtor fails to timely file a statement of intention, or fails to state an intention to surrender the property, to redeem the property, to enter into a reaffirmation agreement with respect to the underlying claim, or to assume an unexpired lease on the property.[7] The stay is also terminated if the debtor fails to take timely action to carry out the stated intention.[8]

This provision does not affect the debtor's substantive rights vis-a-vis the creditor, but merely creates a possible early termination of the automatic stay. The 2005 Act reinforces this conclusion by adding, as the sole exception to section 521(a)(2)(C), language making clear that the only effect of failing to take certain actions under the provision is relief from the automatic stay in some cases slightly earlier than would ordinarily occur without the application of section 362(h). Congress did not in any other way change the savings clause found in section 521(a)(2)(C) that courts have relied upon in interpreting the provision and in finding that the statement of intention primarily serves a notice function.[9]

It appears that if a debtor is willing to reaffirm any part of a debt secured by the property, perhaps equal to the value of the property, the debtor may state an intention to reaffirm and avoid termination of the stay under section

5 11 U.S.C. § 348(f)(1)(C)(ii).

6 *In re* Rathbun, 275 B.R. 434 (Bankr. D.R.I. 2001) (adopting opinion in *Donnell*); *In re* Donnell, 234 B.R. 567 (Bankr. D.N.H. 1999) (denying injunctive relief to enforce security interest and refusing to deny discharge of debt or dismiss case); *In re* Weir, 173 B.R. 682 (Bankr. E.D. Cal. 1994) (no implied cause of action or other remedy, except possibly relief from stay if debtors are in monetary default on obligation, if creditor believes debtors have not filed adequate statement of intentions); *see also* National Consumer Law Center, Consumer Bankruptcy Law and Practice § 11.4 (7th ed. 2004).

7 The Statement of Intention (Official Form 8) was amended by adding a section covering unexpired leases and an option labeled "lease will be assumed pursuant to 11 U.S.C. 362(h)(1)(A)." *See* § 5.5.2, *infra*.

8 If a creditor violates the stay based on a good faith belief that the stay had been terminated as to the debtor under section 362(h), section 362(k)(2) provides that the recovery under section 362(k)(1) shall be limited to actual damages. *See* § 7.4, *infra*.

9 *E.g., In re* Price, 370 F.3d 362 (3d Cir. 2004); *In re* Parker, 139 F.3d 668 (9th Cir. 1998); Capital Communications Fed. Credit Union v. Boodrow, 126 F.3d 43 (2d Cir. 1997); *see also* National Consumer Law Center, Consumer Bankruptcy Law and Practice § 11.4 (7th ed. 2004).

362(h) for failing to state an intention to reaffirm. This conclusion is supported by the fact that section 362(h)(1)(B) speaks of a particular type of reaffirmation and section 362(h)(1)(A) does not.

Section 362(h)(1)(B) provides that the stay of section 362(a) is terminated if the debtor does not take the action specified in the statement of intention in a timely manner, unless the statement states an intention to reaffirm the debt on its original terms and the creditor refuses to agree to such reaffirmation. Under section 521(a)(2)(B) of the Code, the debtor's action is timely if taken within thirty days after the first date set for the meeting of creditors, or such additional time fixed by the court within such thirty-day period. But it may not always be clear what taking timely action means in a particular instance. For example, is it sufficient to initiate a redemption proceeding? As a practical matter, it may be difficult to obtain a hearing on a contested valuation in a redemption proceeding within the time specified. Nothing in the 2005 amendments sets a deadline for the debtor's redemption.

The provision concerning reaffirmation on the original contract terms also creates uncertainty. There may be a question as to what the original contract terms were or how much is owed on the contract. Does "original contract terms" mean that any default rates, late charges, or other fees that have been assessed due to events subsequent to the contract, or other subsequent modifications in terms, should be eliminated? If there is a dispute regarding the current balance, a debtor may maintain that the creditor has refused to reaffirm on the original contract terms. If a creditor fails to provide a debtor sufficient information to determine the precise balance, the debtor may be able to take the position that she is willing to reaffirm on the original terms but has not been given sufficient information to be able to do so.

5.3.1.3 Stay Relief Under Section 521(a)(6)

The second new provision relating to the automatic stay and the statement of intention is section 521(a)(6). This provision is somewhat similar to section 362(h), so similar issues arise.

Section 521(a)(6) provides that the debtor shall not retain possession of personal property as to which a creditor has an allowed secured claim for the purchase price secured by that personal property, unless the debtor, not later than forty-five days after the section 341(a) meeting of creditors, enters into a reaffirmation agreement or redeems the property. If the debtor fails to "so act," the stay under section 362(a) is terminated and the property is no longer property of the estate. The creditor may then take whatever action is permitted with respect to the property under applicable non-bankruptcy law. However, such creditor action is not permitted if the court determines (on a motion filed by the trustee before the forty-five-day period expires and after notice and a hearing) that the property is of consequential value or benefit to the estate and further orders adequate protection of the creditor's interest and delivery of any "collateral" to the trustee's possession.[10]

Section 521(a)(6) raises a host of issues in addition to those raised by section 362(h). First, the time period stated is inconsistent with that allowed under section 521(a)(2)(B). That section requires the debtor to perform the stated intention within thirty days of the first date set for the meeting of creditors.[11] Section 521(a)(6), on the other hand, sets a period for reaffirmation or redemption of forty-five days after the meeting of creditors, which not only is a different length of time but probably should run from the conclusion of the meeting, which could be well after the first date set for the meeting. However, the time period set by section 521(a)(6) is not a deadline for such acts. It is simply a time period after which the property is no longer property of the estate protected by the section 362(a) stay. Because, as discussed below, this provision applies to a more specific category of secured debts, the forty-five-day time period may override the shorter thirty-day time period incorporated in section 362(h).

Second, the scope of section 521(a)(6) is more limited than the scope of section 521(a)(2). Section 521(a)(6) applies only to allowed claims and only to purchase money security interests, while the latter applies to any secured debt or lease covered by the statement of intention. Generally in order for a claim to be allowed it must be filed in accordance with section 501.[12] Few creditors file proofs of claim in chapter 7 no asset cases. Whether they will begin to do so to come within the ambit of section 521(a)(6) remains to be seen. Even if a creditor files a proof of claim in a no asset chapter 7 case, the debtor may file an objection to the claim and it is then not allowed unless the court overrules the objection.

Third, section 521(a)(6) only applies if the debtor has not entered into a reaffirmation agreement within the forty-five-day period. It does not state that it becomes inapplicable if the debtor later exercises the right to rescind the agreement. Of course, by the time the rescis-

10 11 U.S.C. § 362(h)(2).

11 11 U.S.C. § 521(a)(2)(B).

12 11 U.S.C. § 502(A).

sion period has run in most chapter 7 cases the case will be over, and the property will no longer be property of the estate protected by the stay in any event.

Fourth, the provision does not authorize a creditor to repossess property. It leaves that issue to applicable non-bankruptcy law. There are likely to be serious questions under non-bankruptcy law about whether repossession from a debtor who is current in payments is in good faith, whether a creditor has waived a default by accepting later payments, or whether other provisions of state law would prohibit repossession.

In any event the ultimate effect of section 521(a)(6), in most cases in which it applies and in which the debtor has neither entered into a reaffirmation agreement or redeemed the property, is to terminate the section 362(a) stay with respect to the property approximately fifteen days earlier than it would otherwise be terminated. In most chapter 7 cases, the court promptly closes the case once the sixty-day deadline for making objections to discharge has run.[13]

5.3.2 Ipso Facto *Clauses*

Section 521(d) of the Bankruptcy Code provides that if a debtor fails to take timely action as specified in section 521(a)(6) or section 362(h)(1) and (2) with respect to property as to which a creditor holds a security interest not otherwise avoidable under sections 522(f), 544, 545, 547, 548, or 549, nothing in title 11 shall limit the operation of an *ipso facto* clause in the credit agreement that makes bankruptcy or insolvency a default under the agreement. It contains similar language with respect to leases of personal property.

Even in those cases in which an *ipso facto* clause is not made inoperable due to the effect of section 521(d) it may be, or may become, inoperable due to non-bankruptcy law. A creditor who accepts payments after the debtor's bankruptcy or insolvency may be deemed to have waived the right to claim a default based on such events. Repossession from a debtor who is current in their payments may violate state law in other respects.

5.3.3 The Effect of the 2005 Act on the Keep and Pay Alternative

Prior to the 2005 Act, a number of courts held that the debtor was not limited to the choices listed on the statement of intention form that section 521(2) required.[14] These courts held that the debtor could opt to continue paying on the secured debt without either redeeming or reaffirming the debt. Although some of the proponents of the 2005 Act may have assumed that the 2005 amendments to section 521 overruled those cases, it is doubtful that this result has been achieved.

The 2005 Act did not change the basic language of section 521(2) (now redesignated as section 521(a)(2)). The language added to section 521(a)(2)(C), if anything, further undermines the reasoning of cases which had held that a debtor must redeem, reaffirm, or surrender. The Code now states with specificity that the general rule is that nothing in the statement of intention requirements affects the debtor's substantive rights with regard to the property, and that the only exception is the termination of the section 362(a) stay in certain circumstances described in section 362(h).[15]

Similarly, section 524(j) of the Code, also enacted in 2005, would not make sense if section 521(a)(2) required a debtor who retained property to redeem it or reaffirm the underlying debt in every case. Section 524(j) provides that certain actions of creditors holding security interests in real property of the debtor, such as seeking periodic payments in a ride-through situation, do not violate the discharge injunction.[16] If every debtor were required by section 521(a)(2) to surrender property in every case in which there was no reaffirmation or redemption, the situation contemplated by section 524(j) could never occur. Either the property would have been surrendered or would have been redeemed from the lien, in which case the creditor would have no claim after bankruptcy, or the debt would have been reaffirmed, in which case the discharge injunction would not be applicable in the first place.

13 Bankruptcy Rule 4004(c) requires the court to normally grant a discharge forthwith after the deadline for objections to discharge (sixty days after the first date set for the meeting of creditors) has run. Unless there are assets to administer the case is then closed and the automatic stay ends.

14 *E.g.*, *In re* Price, 370 F.3d 362 (3d Cir. 2004); *In re* Parker, 139 F.3d 668 (9th Cir. 1998); Capital Communications Fed. Credit Union v. Boodrow, 126 F.3d 43 (2d Cir. 1997); *see also* National Consumer Law Center, Consumer Bankruptcy Law and Practice § 11.4 (7th ed. 2004).

15 11 U.S.C. § 521(a)(2)(C).

16 *See* § 10.5, *infra*.

5.4 Right of Redemption in Chapter 7 Cases

5.4.1 Redemption by Payment in Installments

The 2005 Act amends section 722 of the Code by providing that the redemption amount must be paid to the secured creditor "in full at the time of redemption," thus making clear that section 722 does not give the debtor the right to pay the amount of the allowed secured claim in installments. This clarification is not a significant change from prior practice, as most courts had held that unless the creditor agrees otherwise, the debtor must redeem through cash payment of the redemption amount, and that neither the debtor nor the court can impose an installment arrangement upon the creditor.[17]

For a debtor who can not afford to pay the entire allowed secured claim in cash and is unwilling or unable to negotiate a reaffirmation agreement, one solution may be to request under section 521(a)(2)(B) that the court grant additional time for the debtor to perform an intended redemption. Nothing in the 2005 amendments sets a deadline for the debtor's redemption or limits the court's authority under section 521(a)(2)(B) to extend the time for the debtor to perform a stated intention. Also, the debtor and the creditor are not precluded from agreeing to installment payments, with or without reaffirmation.

5.4.2 Replacement Value Used for Determining Redemption Amount

Prior to the 2005 amendments, the majority of courts had held that, as a creditor has no risk of depreciation or destruction of collateral when redemption is made in a lump sum, the creditor should be compensated based on the liquidation value of the property rather than its replacement value.[18] The 2005 Act overrules these cases by adding new section 506(a)(2) to the Bankruptcy Code, which provides that value with respect to personal property securing an allowed claim shall be determined based on the replacement value of such property as of the date of the petition without deduction for sale costs or marketing. For property acquired for personal, family, or household purposes, section 506(a)(2) also provides that replacement value shall be determined "considering the age and condition of the property at the time value is determined." At least for items of personal property that depreciate rapidly, such as home appliances and furniture, this latter provision should help to reduce redemption values. With the expansion of on-line retailing, comparable values for used items not sold in most stores might be obtained from on-line auction sites such as ebay.com.

5.5 Assumption and Rejection of Personal Property Leases in Chapter 7

5.5.1 Effect of Lease Rejection

Section 365(d)(1) of the Bankruptcy Code provides that if the trustee does not assume or reject an unexpired lease of personal property within sixty days after the filing of the petition, or such longer time as the court orders, the lease is deemed rejected. Under the Code prior to the 2005 Act, if the lease was rejected and the lessor of personal property wanted to take action against the property before the case was closed, the lessor was required to seek relief from the stay. New section 365(p)(1) provides that the leased property is no longer property of the estate and the stay under section 362(a) is automatically terminated once an unexpired lease is rejected or not timely assumed.

5.5.2 Lease Assumption by the Debtor in a Chapter 7 Case

Prior to the 2005 Act, the power to assume or reject an unexpired lease was given only to the trustee in chapter 7 cases.[19] Under the 2005 Act, the debtor is given the right to assume a lease of personal property in a chapter 7 case.[20] Under section 365(p)(2) of the Code the debtor may notify the lessor in writing that the debtor desires to

17 *See* National Consumer Law Center, Consumer Bankruptcy Law and Practice § 11.5.3 (7th ed. 2004).

18 *See, e.g.*, *In re* Weathington, 254 B.R. 895 (B.A.P. 6th Cir. 2000) (liquidation value for automobile redemption); *see also* National Consumer Law Center, Consumer Bankruptcy Law and Practice § 11.5.5 (7th ed. 2004).

19 This power is given to debtors in chapter 13 cases. 11 U.S.C. § 1322(b)(7); *see also* National Consumer Law Center, Consumer Bankruptcy Law and Practice § 12.9.1 (7th ed. 2004).

20 Although not stated in section 365(p)(2), the negotiation of a lease assumption by the debtor and lessor presumably would occur only if the trustee decides not to assume the lease. Section 362(h)(1)(A) notes that the debtor may indicate on the statement of intention that the debtor shall

assume the lease.[21] Upon being notified the lessor may, at its option, notify the debtor that it is willing to have the lease assumed, and the lessor may condition the assumption on a cure of any default, on the terms set by the contract. Within thirty days after the section 365(p)(2)(A) notice is provided, the debtor may notify the lessor in writing that the lease is assumed.[22] Although the provisions give the lessor the right to condition the assumption on cure of an outstanding default, as is the case when the trustee chooses to make an assumption, there is no provision permitting a lessor to prohibit an assumption.

Section 365(p)(2)(B) provides that if the debtor gives notice that the lease is assumed liability under the lease is assumed by the debtor, and not by the estate. It is not clear what this provision means because the 2005 amendments do not provide any exception to the discharge injunction under section 524 for collection efforts on an assumed lease.[23] Therefore, assumption of a lease would not reinstate the debtor's personal liability on the lease unless the debtor also reaffirmed the debt, which section 365(p)(2) does not require.

assume an unexpired lease under section 365(p) "if the trustee does not do so."

21 This decision may also be stated as the debtor's intention on the Statement of Intention (Official Form 8), which was amended by adding a section covering unexpired leases and an option labeled "lease will be assumed pursuant to 11 U.S.C. 362(h)(1)(A)." Although the Advisory Committee Notes indicate that the form change was made to "conform to § 521(a)(6)," no mention of lease assumption is made in section 521(a)(6). The Statement of Intention is reprinted in Appx. D.4, *infra*.

22 Section 365(p)(2)(B) does not specify which of the two notices in section 365(p)(2)(A) it is referring to in setting this time limit. However it probably makes little difference. If the creditor has not given its optional notice stating conditions for cure, the only notice is the debtor's notice; if the creditor does give the notice of conditions for cure the time may run from that later notice, giving the debtor time to meet those conditions.

23 Section 365(p)(2)(C) states that the stay under section 362 and the injunction under section 524(a)(2) are not violated by notification of the debtor and negotiation of cure under the subsection, but these limited exceptions do not extend to actions to enforce the assumed lease as a personal liability of the debtor.

5.6 Chapter 7 Filing Fees

5.6.1 Chapter 7 Filing Fee Increase

The 2005 Act initially provided for an increase of the base chapter 7 filing fee from $155 to $200.[24] However, a separate bill, enacted on May 11, 2005, amended the fee increase provided in the 2005 Act and changed the base chapter 7 filing fee to $220.[25] Thus, for cases filed on or after October 17, 2005, the total filing fee for a chapter 7 case will be $274.[26] Unlike this substantial increase in the chapter 7 filing fee, the total filing fee for a chapter 13 case has been reduced to $189.

5.6.2 Waiver of Filing Fee

In an important positive change from prior law,[27] and in a step that should help blunt the effect of the chapter 7 filing fee increase for some debtors, the 2005 Act provides for the waiver of chapter 7 filing fees for debtors with incomes less than 150% of the applicable official poverty line based on family size.[28] In addition to the income test the debtor must be unable to pay the filing fee in installments.

The interim rules adopted by the Judicial Conference implement the fee waiver provision by adding Rule 1006(c).[29] The new rule provides that a voluntary chapter 7 petition shall be accepted for filing if accompanied by a debtor's application requesting a fee waiver prepared using Official Form 3B.[30]

The new fee waiver provision does not rule out the possibility that a court could grant a waiver if the attorney representing the debtor is being paid. In fact, some fee

24 *See* Pub. L. No. 109-8, § 325, 119 Stat. 23 (2005).

25 Pub. L. No. 109-13, 119 Stat. 231 (2005).

26 In addition to the $220 filing fee provided by amended 28 U.S.C. § 1930(a), an additional noticing fee of $39 in connection with all chapter 7 and chapter 13 filings is assessed pursuant to 28 U.S.C. § 1930(b), and another $15 fee is charged in chapter 7 cases to provide additional compensation to chapter 7 trustees as mandated by 11 U.S.C. § 330(b)(2). *See* Appx C.1, *infra*.

27 *See* former 28 U.S.C. § 1930(a) (codifying United States v. Kras, 409 U.S. 434, 93 S. Ct. 631, 34 L. Ed. 2d 626 (1973)).

28 28 U.S.C. § 1930(f)(1). The poverty line figures used are those provided by the Office of Management and Budget, and revised annually in accordance with section 673(2) of the Omnibus Budget Reconciliation Act of 1981. The current poverty figures can be found at www.census.gov/hhes/poverty/threshld/thresh00.html.

29 *See* Appx. B, *infra*.

30 A copy of Official Form 3B is reprinted in Appx. D.4, *infra*.

waivers were granted in cases in which attorneys had been paid, often on a reduced fee basis, during the three-year fee waiver pilot program that was conducted prior to the 2005 Act.[31] Part D of the Application for Waiver (Official Form 3B) requests that the debtor list all payments that have been made or promised to an attorney or petition preparer.[32]

31 In 1993, Congress authorized a three-year pilot program in six judicial districts in which fee waivers were allowed, and also directed the Judicial Conference to conduct a study on the pilot program. *See* Pub. L. No. 103-121, § 111, 107 Stat. 1153 (1993). In 1998, the Federal Judicial Center submitted a comprehensive report in which it found that a relatively small number of debtors sought fee waivers (under five percent) and most of the waivers were granted. The report also found that there were no increases in abusive filings and the cost to the system was modest. A copy of the report, Implementing and Evaluating the Chapter 7 Filing Fee Waiver Program, is available at: www.fjc.gov/public/pdf.nsf/lookup/IFPRepor.pdf/$file/IFPRepor.pdf.

32 *See* Form 3B, Appx. D.4, *infra*.

Chapter 6 Changes to Chapter 13 Bankruptcy

6.1 Introduction

The 2005 Act makes numerous changes to chapter 13, almost every one of which will make filing for bankruptcy under chapter 13 more difficult and more expensive, as well as much less effective, for debtors who want to try to repay some debts rather than file under chapter 7. Despite suggestions to the contrary by the Act's proponents, the real goal of the legislation was not to encourage more debtors to file chapter 13, but rather to make bankruptcy of all types more difficult for debtors who need it. It seems quite likely that the number of chapter 13 cases filed will decrease, rather than increase, as a percentage of bankruptcy filings.

This Chapter will address most of the chapter 13 changes, but some are discussed in other chapters of this guide. For example, issues related to the treatment of domestic support obligations in a chapter 13 case are discussed in Chapter 9, *infra*, changes made to the "superdischarge" are covered in Chapter 10, *infra*, and the new document filing requirements are discussed in Chapter 4, *supra*. Two topics that will receive particular attention in this Chapter have caused a great deal of confusion and consternation for debtors' attorneys and trustees—the new requirements for the disposable income test under section 1325(b) of the Code and the new requirement of pre-confirmation adequate protection payments to certain secured creditors.

6.2 Disposable Income Test—Section 1325(b)

6.2.1 Use of "Current Monthly Income"

Under section 1325(b) of the Bankruptcy Code, a chapter 13 plan that does not commit all of the debtor's disposable income for a three-to-five-year period can not be confirmed over an objection from the trustee or the holder of an allowed unsecured claim.[1] The first major change in the disposable income test under section 1325(b) is the use of "current monthly income" as the basis for determining disposable income. For all debtors, disposable income is based on "current monthly income," which is defined in section 101 of the Code as the average of the last six months income received from all sources by the debtor (or, in a joint case, by the debtor and the debtor's spouse), with certain adjustments.[2]

"Current monthly income" is defined to exclude benefits received under the Social Security Act and certain other payments.[3] The definition also makes clear that the income of other household members, including a non-debtor spouse, can only be considered to the extent that it is regularly contributed to household expenses.[4]

The use of prior income numbers in the definition of "current monthly income" directly contradicts language in section 1325(b)(1)(B), which refers to the debtor's "projected disposable income." This contradiction creates immediate interpretive difficulties because the confirmation of the plan may be denied only if all of the debtor's "projected disposable income" is not committed to the plan for the applicable time period. A projection of future income would seem to be something that could be quite different than an average of monthly income in the past. To the extent that courts give any meaning to the word "projected"—and courts are supposed to give meaning to every word in a statute—they may have to disregard the debtor's prior income if circumstances have changed.

If the word "projected" is disregarded, use of "current monthly income" will help some debtors whose income has increased, and could harm those whose income has decreased, as there is no explicit provision for adjusting income for such changes. If the debtor's income has increased, the trustee or unsecured creditors may not be

1 *See* National Consumer Law Center, Consumer Bankruptcy Law and Practice § 12.3.3 (7th ed. 2004).

2 *See* § 2.2.2, *supra*.

3 11 U.S.C. § 101(10)(B); *see* § 2.2.2.6, *supra*.

4 11 U.S.C. § 101(10)(B); *see* §§ 2.2.2.2, 2.2.2.3, *supra*.

able to tap all of it for plan payments. Even for a plan modification, if section 1325(b) is applicable, the disposable income standard remains based on current monthly income, which never changes because it is based on the six months prior to the filing of the petition.

To the extent current monthly income is determinative without regard to the debtor's actual income at the time the petition is filed or the plan is confirmed, it will put a premium on the timing of the bankruptcy. When possible, it will benefit debtors if they file at a time that will minimize current monthly income. For example, a debtor whose income has recently decreased significantly might decide to wait a few months before filing, so that the six-month average more accurately reflects the debtor's true income.

If the debtor's income has decreased at the time the petition is filed, and is unlikely to change, a trustee should not file an objection under section 1325(b) if the debtor is paying all disposable income as defined prior to the 2005 amendments. Trustees have no legitimate interest in objecting to plans when debtors are paying all that they can truly afford. Thus, unless an unsecured creditor objects, a reasonable plan based on the debtor's true income may be confirmed, because section 1325(b), by its own terms, comes into play only if an objection is filed. Even unsecured creditors are not likely to object. Unsecured creditors rarely have an interest in forcing debtors into chapter 7, which would be the usual result of an objection, especially if debtors are below median income and therefore not subject to the new means test.[5]

6.2.2 New Exclusions from Disposable Income

6.2.2.1 Overview

The 2005 Act also creates new exclusions from disposable income. As discussed above, there are exclusions in the definition of "current monthly income" for benefits under the Social Security Act and certain other payments. The definition also makes clear that the income of other household members, including a non-debtor spouse, can be considered only to the extent that it is regularly contributed to household expenses.[6] There are additional exclusions from current monthly income, discussed below, that are applicable only in chapter 13 cases.

5 *See* § 2.2.1, *supra*.

6 11 U.S.C. § 101(10A).

6.2.2.2 Child Support, Foster Care, and Similar Payments

The definition of disposable income excludes child support payments, foster care payments, or disability payments received for a dependent child to the extent reasonably necessary to be expended for the child.[7] It is not clear what effect this exclusion will have. If courts exclude these payments, which may well go to expenses for the debtor's dependents, the debtor's income will be reduced. But courts might exclude expenses for the child to the extent they are covered by these payments. If so, the provision would be rendered almost meaningless. Its main remaining effect would occur only if the payments exceed the child's pro-rata share of family expenses. Then the result would be that payments meant for the child would not be diverted to pay debts or imputed to the expenses of other household members. And courts could not exclude the expenses of the child if the debtor's current monthly income is over the median income, because expenses would be determined under the rigid means test formula, based on household size, as discussed below.[8]

6.2.2.3 Payments on Domestic Support Obligations

Payments made on domestic support obligations by the debtor that are first payable after the petition is filed are excluded from the definition of disposable income.[9] This amendment simply gives effective priority to current support payments, which were ordinarily deducted from the debtor's budget under pre-2005 Act law.

6.2.2.4 Repayments of Pension Loans and Pension Contributions

Another important exclusion from disposable income consists of funds used for repayments of pension loans. New section 1322(f) of the Code provides that amounts required to repay loans described in section 362(b)(19) of the Code, which are generally loans from qualified pension plans,[10] shall not constitute disposable income under section 1325(b) of the Code. This amendment reverses the holdings of most courts prior to the 2005 amend-

7 11 U.S.C. § 1325(b)(2).

8 *See* § 6.2.3, *infra*.

9 11 U.S.C. § 1325(b)(2)(A)(i).

10 *See* § 7.3.4.1, *infra*.

ments.[11] It is consistent with the increased protections given by the 2005 Act to retirement savings[12] and the fact that continued collection of such loans (usually through wage withholding) is permitted by section 362(b)(19) of the Code.[13] It also may be a recognition that debtors have often incurred such loans in attempts to pay other debts, so that repayment of the loans is really repaying an obligation incurred to pay other creditors.

Certain pension or benefit contributions withheld from the debtor's wages by an employer, or received by the debtor from an employer, are also not disposable income.[14] This provision does not distinguish between voluntary and involuntary contributions, so it appears to encompass both. The contribution must be to either an Employee Retirement Income Security Act (ERISA) plan, an employee benefit plan which is a governmental plan under section 414(d) of Internal Revenue Code (IRC), a deferred compensation plan under section 457 of the IRC, or a tax-deferred annuity under section 403(b) of the IRC.[15]

6.2.3 *Use of Means Test Expense Calculations for Debtors with Incomes Above Median Income*

Perhaps the most dramatic change in the disposable income test is the use of the section 707(b) means test expense calculations for some debtors. New section 1325(b)(3) of the Code provides that for debtors whose current monthly income is above the state median income for family size, reasonably necessary expenses are to be calculated using the means test formula in section 707(b)(2)(A) and (B) of the Code in order to determine payments to unsecured creditors. Because this provision is based on the backward-looking "current monthly income" standard rather than actual income, it may apply to debtors with actual income well below the state median income at the time they file the bankruptcy petition and throughout the plan. The trustee is not compelled to object to a plan that does not meet this standard, and a trustee should not object to a plan, or a later modification of a plan, if it pays all the debtor can truly afford.[16]

At the same time, this provision permits debtors to deduct amounts allowed by the means test, even if they seem excessive to a trustee or creditor. Secured debt payments are deductible, no matter how high.[17] Moreover, secured debt payments due under the contract are deductible in the full scheduled amount even if the debtor will have to pay less in a chapter 13 plan because the debt can be crammed down under section 1325(a)(5) of the Code. As a result, this calculation gives the debtor a cushion equal to the difference between the amount owing on a secured debt (or the Internal Revenue Service's National Standard, if higher)[18] and the amount payable on the debt in the chapter 13 case. It may also provide some leeway from the strictures of the Internal Revenue Service standards for other expenses. Other expenses that were sometimes not allowed under the law prior to the 2005 amendments, such as a limited amount for private school education, are also permitted.[19]

In addition the provisions of the means test permitting the court to adjust expenses for special circumstances are among those incorporated under this provision, so if there are other expenses for which there is no reasonable alternative, the court can take those facts into account.[20] Ultimately, the special circumstances test is not very different than the reasonably necessary test used prior to the 2005 amendments.[21] It is not completely clear, however, that adjustments to income are possible. Although section 707(b)(2)(B), referenced in section 1325(b)(3), allows for adjustment of income, section 1325(b)(3) speaks only of "amounts reasonably necessary to be expended."

6.2.4 *Administrative Expenses*

As a result of poor drafting, it is not crystal clear how administrative expenses are to be paid in a chapter 13 case. There has been some concern that the provisions incorporated from section 707(b) would limit the debtor's administrative expenses to the ten percent cap found in

11 *See, e.g.*, *In re* Anes, 195 F.3d 177 (3d Cir. 1999).

12 *See, e.g.*, 11 U.S.C. § 522(b)(3)(C), 522(d)(12); § 8.3, *infra*; *see also* H.R. Rep. No. 109-31, at 63–64 (2005) (reprinted in Appx. A.4, *infra*).

13 *See* § 7.3.4.1, *infra*.

14 11 U.S.C. § 541(b)(7).

15 11 U.S.C. § 541(b)(7)(A), (B).

16 *See* § 6.2.1, *supra*.

17 11 U.S.C. § 707(b)(2)(A)(iii); *see* § 2.3.3.2, *supra*. Some secured debt payments, such as payments on arrears, may be deducted if necessary in a chapter 13 case to maintain the debtor's possession of the debtor's primary residence, motor vehicle, or other property necessary for the support of the debtor or the debtor's dependents. *See* 11 U.S.C. § 707(b)(2)(A)(iii)(II).

18 *See* § 2.3.3.2, *supra*.

19 *See* § 2.3.3.8, *supra*.

20 11 U.S.C. § 707(b)(2)(B)(i); *see* § 2.4.2, *supra*.

21 *See* National Consumer Law Center, Consumer Bankruptcy Law and Practice § 12.3.3.4 (7th ed. 2004).

those provisions.[22] Such a limit would render almost every chapter 13 case impossible, because the expenses necessary to administer the case almost always exceed ten percent. Trustees will presumably not file such objections if their effect would be to put themselves out of business. Indeed, if the administrative expenses were limited to ten percent, trustees would share those funds pro rata with other administrative claimants and could not recover their full percentage payment.[23] However, unlike in the section 707(b) means test, in which the ten percent cap applies to hypothetical administrative expenses, the administrative expenses in chapter 13 are real priority claims that should be counted as such.

Alternatively, if an objection is filed, courts should recognize that an administrative expense is an unsecured claim and section 1325(b) requires disposable income remaining after the means test deductions to be paid to "unsecured creditors," not just non-priority creditors.[24] "Creditor" is defined as an entity holding a pre-petition claim.[25] Normally, the debtor's attorney seeking payment of fees is seeking payment of primarily pre-petition fees. Moreover, the provision merely states that unsecured creditors are the entities to be paid from disposable income. It does not limit the payments to payments on pre-petition claims. In addition, interpreting section 1325(b) to preclude payment of administrative expenses would place it in direct conflict with section 1326(b), which requires payment of "any unpaid claim" under section 507(a)(2), which provides for administrative claim priority. In light of all these issues, it seems very unlikely courts will adopt a reading of the statute that precludes payment of the expenses necessary to administer the case.

The same reasoning should apply for debtors whose income falls below the state median income, so that payments to "unsecured creditors" under section 1325(b) can include payments of administrative expenses to the debtor's attorney who is a creditor. If a creditor raises an objection, the trustee could argue that other provisions like section 1326 and 28 U.S.C. § 586 provide for payment of trustee's fees, and section 1325(b) should not be read in a way that would contradict those sections. Alternatively, debtors with incomes both above or below state median income may argue that because administrative expenses are reasonable and necessary legal expenses, the administrative claims should be allowed in chapter 13 as Other Necessary Expenses under the Internal Revenue Service standards.[26]

6.2.5 Payment to Secured Creditors by Debtors with Incomes Below Median Income

Because of poor drafting it is also unclear how secured creditors are to be paid by debtors whose incomes fall below state median income. Section 1325(b)(1)(B) uses language that was found in the subsection prior to the 2005 amendments to describe how much is to be paid into the plan for all creditors, but now states that this amount is to be paid to "unsecured creditors." This phrasing creates a possible interpretation that debtors below median income can not pay any money to secured creditors. In light of the fact that section 1325(b)(3) now considers payments to secured creditors a part of the "amounts reasonably necessary to be expended" for support of the debtor and dependents with respect to debtors over median income, it would be consistent to read the requirements for debtors below median income the same way, allowing necessary secured debt payments to be considered as reasonably necessary expenses. Some courts have implicitly done so in applying the pre-2005 Act version of section 1325(b)(1)(B), disallowing large secured debt payments made by debtors on items such as luxury automobiles as expenses that are not reasonably necessary.[27] Again, trustees are not likely to raise such an objection, as it would eliminate most of their cases. It is also absurd to think that the 2005 Act somehow makes one of the most fundamental and often used provisions of the Code, the right to cure a mortgage default under section 1325(b)(5), available only to debtors whose income falls above median income.

---

22 *See* 11 U.S.C. § 707(b)(2)(A)(ii)(III); § 2.3.3.7, *supra*.

23 *See* 11 U.S.C. § 1326(b).

24 The Official Forms appear to take this position. *See* Advisory Committee Note to Official Forms 22A–C (reprinted in Appx. D.3, *infra*). The confusion is compounded because section 707(b)(2)(A)(iv) allows the deduction of priority claims in the means test calculation, in addition to the chapter 13 administrative expenses of up to ten percent allowed by section 707(b)(2)(A)(ii)(III). Then, section 1325(b) requires the disposable income remaining after the calculation to be paid to unsecured creditors generally, presumably including priority claims. It is doubtful that any court would allow the double-counting, or even triple-counting, of administrative expenses that this language suggests.

25 *See* 11 U.S.C. § 101(10).

26 *See* 11 U.S.C. § 707(b)(2)(A)(ii)(I); § 2.3.2.5, *supra*.

27 *E.g.*, *In re* Rogers, 65 B.R. 1018 (Bankr. E.D. Mich. 1986); *see also* National Consumer Law Center, Consumer Bankruptcy Law and Practice § 12.3.3.4 (7th ed. 2004).

6.2.6 Length of Plan Payments

Another very significant change in the disposable income test is the duration of the plan payments which must be proposed if an objection is raised. New section 1325(b)(4) of the Code sets an "applicable commitment period" for section 1325(b) objections. The applicable commitment period, similar to prior law, is three years if the current monthly income of the "debtor and the debtor's spouse combined" is below the applicable state median income, but is five years if the current monthly income of the debtor and the debtor's spouse combined is above the applicable state median income.

One immediate issue in interpreting this provision is that a non-debtor spouse does not have any current monthly income, because "current monthly income" is defined as income received by the debtor (or in a joint case by the debtor and the debtor's spouse).[28] Thus, by definition, income of a non-debtor spouse that is not paid toward the debtor's expenses does not constitute current monthly income. This statutory language should be given effect because Congress must be assumed to know that its definitions will be used, and the definition itself makes clear the limited circumstances in which a spouse's income is current monthly income. The provision would still serve an important purpose under this interpretation, preventing two spouses from avoiding the five-year commitment period by filing separate cases, because in that situation the debtor's spouse, being a bankruptcy debtor also, would have current monthly income.

A contrary interpretation would mean that the income of a separated spouse would be included, even if that spouse contributed nothing to the household.[29] The debtor may not even know what a separated spouse's income is, so it may be hard to base an objection on it. In addition, the household size of the debtor for calculating the median income level would not be increased to take into account the members of the non-debtor spouse's household. For these reasons, including a separated spouse's total income makes no policy sense. It is hoped that trustees will not invoke section 1325(b) to demand a five-year plan based on income that in reality is unavailable to the debtor.

Because current monthly income does not change during the case—it remains the average income for the six months before the petition was filed[30]—the debtor can not be forced to change the commitment period if the debtor's income later changes from below the median income to above the median income.

If the current monthly income of the debtor and the debtor's spouse is above the state median income, the applicable commitment period is five years.[31] This requirement will discourage some debtors who might otherwise have filed under chapter 13. It will also make plans more likely to fail, because there will be sixty-six percent more time for an unexpected drop in income or an emergency expense to occur. The trustee is not compelled to demand a five-year plan from the debtor, however. This five-year requirement is only applicable when an objection to confirmation is filed.

It is important to note that the changes to section 1325(b) do not restrict the length of the plan itself. Rather, the amendments require the debtor to commit all of the debtor's projected disposable income for a three-to-five-year period. Section 1322(d), which controls the length of the plan, was amended by the 2005 Act to say only that a plan for a debtor above median can not be *longer* than five years.[32] Thus, although the test requires payment into the plan of the amount of disposable income that a debtor whose income is above the median income is projected to have over the five-year post-petition period, that amount may be paid over a shorter period of time if the debtor chooses to do so. In most cases, the better strategy for the debtor will probably be to propose a five-year plan in this situation and then, if the debtor desires, simply complete plan payments before the five years elapses.

Another limitation on the five-year commitment period requirement is that it does not appear to apply to modification of plans. Section 1329 of the Code was amended only to say that a modified plan can not be *longer* than the applicable commitment period unless the court approves, with a five-year maximum. Although there had been some dispute under current law as to whether section 1325(b) applies to modifications, this specific reference seems to make clear that this part of section 1325(b), at least, does not apply. Without a modification, the only resolution for a debtor's inability to complete a plan, even after three years, would be conversion, dismissal, or a hardship discharge.

---

28 11 U.S.C. § 101(10)(B); *see* § 2.2.2.3, *supra*.

29 In contrast with section 1325(b)(4), the safe harbor median income test has a provision permitting the income of a separated spouse to be disregarded. *See* 11 U.S.C. § 707(b)(7)(B); § 2.2.2.3, *supra*.

30 11 U.S.C. § 101(10)(A); *see* § 2.2.2.1, *supra*.

31 11 U.S.C. § 1325(b)(4).

32 11 U.S.C. § 1322(d)(1).

6.3 Payments and Distributions to Creditors

6.3.1 Commencement of Payments

Chapter 13 plan payments must now commence within thirty days after the filing of the plan or the order for relief, whichever is earlier.[33] Although this requirement is not well drafted, the thirty-day period presumably applies to both the filing of the plan and the order for relief. As the plan will never be filed before the order for relief, the payments must begin within thirty-day period of the order for relief, a change from existing law under which the thirty-day period ran from the filing of the plan.

If the plan is not confirmed, the trustee must return to the debtor any payments to the trustee "not previously paid and not yet due and owing to creditors under [section 1326(a)(3)]."[34] This language is hard to decipher. To whom were the payments not yet paid? Unless the court has ordered otherwise, the trustee would not have been paying the adequate protection payments, at least with respect to creditors secured by personal property who are to be paid directly by the debtor.[35] The payments returned to the debtor must also be not yet due and owing under section 1326(a)(3).[36] However, the trustee may have no way to know what payments are due and owing. There is no indication of what the trustee is to do with the money not returned to the debtor after paying administrative expenses. There is no authorization to distribute it to anyone else. To deal with these ambiguities, trustees may seek comfort orders authorizing them to return funds to the debtor.

6.3.2 Adequate Protection Payments

6.3.2.1 Extent of New Requirements

New section 1326(a)(1)(C) of the Code requires a chapter 13 debtor to make adequate protection payments directly to a creditor holding an allowed claim secured by personal property to the extent it is "attributable to the purchase of such property by the debtor for that portion of the obligation that becomes due after the order for relief." These payments are to commence within thirty days after the filing of the plan or the order for relief, whichever is earlier.[37] Plan payments are to be reduced by the amount of the adequate protection payments and the trustee is to be provided evidence of payments made, including the amounts and dates of the payments.[38] This new requirement promises bookkeeping headaches for the debtor, debtor's attorney, and chapter 13 trustee, who must keep track of this separate set of payments and integrate the amounts with the plan's payment requirements.

Adequate protection payments under section 1326(a)(1)(C) need only be provided for the portion of the claim that becomes due after the order for relief.[39] This limitation should mean that no adequate protection payments need to be provided for any arrears portion of a claim. In addition, adequate protection payments need be made only to the extent an obligation is purchase money and the property was purchased by the debtor.[40] If the property was originally titled in the name of another, such as a non-debtor spouse, it probably was not purchased by the debtor. And adequate protection payments need only be paid on an allowed claim. Under section 502(a) of the Code, a claim is deemed allowed when a proof of claim is filed, but only if no objection to the proof of claim is made, so adequate protection payments should not be due until the creditor files a proof of claim to which no objection is filed.

The adequate protection provision was obviously designed primarily for car lenders. As a practical matter, although it technically applies to appliance and furniture creditors, it is unlikely they will do much to enforce these provisions because any adequate protection payments they would receive would be minimal, and these creditors generally do not want the property back if they can collect anything on secured claims.

6.3.2.2 Determining the Amount and Timing of Adequate Protection Payments

The amount of the adequate protection payments presumably will initially be set by the debtor and be based on the rate of the collateral's depreciation. The rate of depreciation can be calculated for a vehicle by looking at the change in industry guide values over the previous few months. However, if the claim is substantially oversecured, and will remain oversecured, there should be no need for adequate protection payments, or they should be

33 11 U.S.C. § 1326(a)(1).

34 11 U.S.C. § 1326(a)(2).

35 *See* § 6.3.2, *infra*.

36 Section 1326(a)(3) provides that the court may, upon notice and hearing, modify, increase, or reduce the payments required pending confirmation of the plan.

37 11 U.S.C. § 1326(a)(1).

38 11 U.S.C. § 1326(a)(1)(C).

39 11 U.S.C. § 1326(a)(1)(C).

40 11 U.S.C. § 1326(a)(1)(C).

nominal.[41] In addition, the amount of the payments can be modified by order of the court "pending confirmation of a plan,"[42] which suggests that the plan will govern thereafter.

The court may "modify, increase, or reduce" the payments required upon notice and a hearing.[43] Some courts or trustees may wish to use this section to route payments through the trustee in order to ease the bookkeeping nightmare the payments will otherwise create if they are made directly by the debtor to the secured creditor. A local rule or practice could provide a default procedure providing notice and a hearing in every case regarding such a modification, which would be an opportunity for a creditor to object.

There is no requirement that the adequate protection payments be made at any particular time interval. For ease of administration, the debtor's attorney may wish to make one payment, directly through the attorney's office, to facilitate bookkeeping and provide evidence to the trustee. There would appear to be no downside when such a payment for the pre-confirmation period is less than a full plan payment (as will usually be the case), as the amount paid will be deducted from the plan payments due.[44]

The statute does not specifically state whether adequate protection payments end as of plan confirmation. There is nothing in the provision that gives an ending date. However, the plan is required by new language in section 1325(a)(5) of the Code to provide that payments on allowed secured claims under the plan be sufficient to provide adequate protection, and the plan can certainly provide that adequate protection shall be provided by the post-confirmation plan payments.

6.3.2.3 Remedy for Failure to Make Adequate Protection Payments

The remedy for failure to make adequate protection payments is likely to be relief from the automatic stay, the same remedy existing under prior law for failure to provide adequate protection. The main difference is that prior law in effect placed the burden on the creditor to demand adequate protection, usually by filing a motion. But a creditor will still have to file a motion for relief from the stay if adequate protection payments have not been provided, and the court may well allow a debtor to cure such a default in payments. Theoretically, failure to make payments required by section 1326 could be grounds for dismissal, but a creditor will usually prefer stay relief and the trustee will have no reason to seek dismissal of an otherwise viable plan.

6.3.3 Payments to Personal Property Lessors

Debtors are required to make scheduled lease payments to personal property lessors for the portion of the obligation that becomes due after the order for relief.[45] The debtor shall deduct such payments from the plan payments to the trustee and provide evidence of the lease payments to the trustee, including dates and amounts.[46] Although this provision was undoubtedly meant to protect auto lessors, it applies to all personal property leases. Such leases are not common for other types of property, but this provision could bring to a head disputes about whether rent-to-own contracts are leases.[47]

Generally, chapter 13 debtors make current auto lease payments to lessors if they assume the lease under section 1322(b)(7) of the Code. A debtor who does not wish to assume the lease does not make payments. Section 1326(a)(1)(B) should not be read to require lease payments from a debtor who does not wish to assume the lease. In such a situation, the lessor can seek relief from the automatic stay, if the stay with respect to the particular property has not terminated.[48] There is no indication the provision was intended to affect the right to assume or reject a lease.[49]

6.3.4 Payments to Former Chapter 7 Trustees

A chapter 7 trustee who is allowed compensation due to a previous dismissal or conversion of a case under section 707(b) of the Code is to be paid such compensation in monthly payments prorated over the entire term of

41 *See* National Consumer Law Center, Consumer Bankruptcy Law and Practice § 9.7.3.2.2 (7th ed. 2004).

42 11 U.S.C. § 1326(a)(3).

43 11 U.S.C. § 1326(a)(3).

44 Section 1326(a)(1)(C) provides that the plan payments are to be reduced by the amount of the adequate protection payments.

45 11 U.S.C. § 1326(a)(1)(B).

46 11 U.S.C. § 1326(a)(1)(B).

47 *See* National Consumer Law Center, Consumer Bankruptcy Law and Practice § 11.8 (7th ed. 2004).

48 *See* 11 U.S.C. § 362(h); § 5.3.1.2, *supra*; *see also* 11 U.S.C. § 365(p)(1); § 5.5.1, *supra*.

49 The title of this provision of the 2005 Act which amended section 1326 is "Adequate Protection of Lessors and Purchase Money Secured Creditors." *See* Pub. L. No. 109-8, § 309(c), 119 Stat. 23 (2005) (reprinted in Appx. A.3, *infra*).

the chapter 13 plan.[50] Monthly payments can not exceed the greater of $25 per month or five percent of the total to be paid to unsecured non-priority creditors, divided by the number of months in the plan.[51] In most cases, this limitation means that the payment amount under this provision will be no more than $25 per month (or $1500 over a five-year plan), because most chapter 13 plans do not pay more than $500 per month to unsecured non-priority creditors.

6.4 Proof of Insurance

Under the 2005 Act, a debtor who is retaining personal property subject to a lease or securing a purchase money claim is required to provide the lessor or creditor reasonable evidence of the maintenance of any required insurance coverage.[52] Normally, such creditors or lessors already know if insurance lapses, as they are named as loss payees in the policy. Only when insurance has lapsed will such evidence be important to creditors or lessors. If insurance is in force, the creditor is not likely to move for relief from the stay because it has not been notified of facts it already knows.

The debtor is required to continue to provide evidence of coverage "for as long as the debtor retains possession of the property."[53] This provision does not specify how often such evidence should be provided. Should it be annually, monthly, hourly? Creditors and lessors will not really have a concern, because they are notified if insurance lapses.

6.5 Plan Modification for Purchase of Health Insurance

The debtor may move to modify the plan to reduce the plan payments in order to purchase health insurance for the debtor and any dependent who does not have health insurance.[54] The debtor must demonstrate that the expense is reasonable and necessary and not more than necessary to maintain a previously lapsed policy if the debtor had one. Upon request of a party in interest the debtor must provide proof that health insurance was purchased.

50 11 U.S.C. § 1326(b)(3).

51 11 U.S.C. § 1326(b)(3)(B).

52 11 U.S.C. § 1326(a)(4).

53 11 U.S.C. § 1326(a)(4).

54 11 U.S.C. § 1329(a)(4).

6.6 Scheduling of the Confirmation Hearing

The confirmation hearing must be held between twenty and forty-five days after the section 341 meeting, unless the court finds that it would be in the best interests of creditors and the estate to hold it earlier and no party objects.[55] Although not stated, the deadline presumably runs from the conclusion of the section 341 meeting. It would make no sense to have a confirmation hearing before the section 341 meeting was concluded.

The new provision does not state that the confirmation hearing must be concluded between twenty and forty-five days after the section 341 meeting. It may be impossible to conclude the hearing simply because the hearing would take too long. More often, there is a need to continue the hearing to another date for any of a myriad of reasons.

This new scheduling requirement will be a significant change in districts where the confirmation hearing is not held until after the claims bar date. Those districts will now also face the problem of confirmation being decided before the court knows the amounts of the claims. Courts have never come up with a very satisfactory solution for the problem of secured and priority claims that exceed amounts provided for them in the confirmed plan. These districts are more likely to adopt the position that the amounts provided for in the confirmed plan are binding on creditors.[56] Because creditors have a specific statutory right under section 521(e)(3) of the Code to obtain a copy of the plan, it will be harder for them to argue lack of notice of clear plan provisions affecting their rights.[57]

6.7 Chapter 13 Cramdown and Other Changes Affecting Treatment of Secured Claims

6.7.1 Restrictions on Applicability of Section 1325(a)(5)

Perhaps the greatest powers to affect the rights of secured creditors are found in the provisions of chapter

55 11 U.S.C. § 1324(b).

56 *See* National Consumer Law Center, Consumer Bankruptcy Law and Practice § 12.11 (7th ed. 2004).

57 Section 521(e)(3) may obviate the need for the debtor to serve the plan on creditors. Creditors also have easy electronic access to the plan via the bankruptcy court's PACER system.

13 that give the debtor the right to limit the enforceability or change the terms of a creditor's contract over the creditor's objection. Section 1325(a)(5) of the Bankruptcy Code generally permits a debtor to pay only the allowed secured claim of a creditor, to modify payment terms and interest rates, and to treat the unsecured portion of an undersecured claim as an unsecured claim in the chapter 13 plan.[58] The 2005 amendments attempt to limit these cramdown rights by adding language at the end of section 1325(a) that removes certain claims from the protections of section 1325(a)(5).[59] This new language states that for purposes of section 1325(a)(5), section 506 of the Code shall not apply to certain claims. Those claims, therefore, can not be determined to be allowed secured claims under section 506(a) and are not within the ambit of section 1325(a)(5).

Claims covered by this new language may still be modified under section 1322(b)(2) of the Code, which allows modification of the rights of holders of secured claims, with certain exceptions, but the restrictions on modification that apply to allowed secured claims under section 1325(a)(5) do not apply. A debtor is presumably bound only by the dictates of good faith and the other provisions of the Code in determining how such claims may be modified. A number of courts have held that a secured creditor who does not object to a plan may be deemed to have accepted it for purposes of section 1325(a)(5)(A).[60] Some courts, understandably, may look to prior law for guidance regarding what modifications are equitable.[61]

The claims encompassed in this language at the end of section 1325(a) are two types of purchase money security interests. The first type is a purchase money security interest for a debt incurred within 910 days preceding the filing of the petition, if the collateral for that debt "consists of" a motor vehicle, as defined in section 30102 of title 49 of the United States Code, which was acquired for the personal use of the debtor. This language would not include a mobile home, because mobile homes do not fit within the definition found in 49 U.S.C. § 30102.[62] It also does not include a vehicle purchased for business use or for the use of someone other than the debtor, such as a child of the debtor. The language "the collateral consists" suggests that if there is any other collateral for the debt, the paragraph is inapplicable.

The second type of claim encompassed by this new language is a purchase money security interest for a debt incurred within one year preceding the filing of the petition, if the collateral consists of any other thing of value. Because the singular includes the plural in the Bankruptcy Code, this provision would include collateral that consists of multiple things of value as well.[63] Although this language could potentially include a purchase money mortgage on real property, such claims are often not subject to modification based on the limitations in section 1322(b)(2). In any event, the new language does not limit the debtor's right to cure a default on a purchase money mortgage under section 1322(b)(3) and section 1322(b)(5), or to modify a mortgage under section 1322(b)(2) (to the extent that the limitation in that subsection for home secured loans is not applicable).[64]

Some believe that the language added at the end of section 1325(a) was intended to prohibit the use of section 506(a) to bifurcate a secured claim into an allowed secured claim and an allowed unsecured claim as part of the cramdown permitted by section 1325(a)(5)(B). However, because the language instead renders section 506(a) inoperable as to certain creditors, that is, it classifies those creditors as no longer holders of allowed secured claims, it does not carry out such an intent, if that indeed was the intent. In fact, earlier versions of the 2005 bankruptcy legislation had contained language which eliminated only the section 506(a) bifurcation of certain claims into secured and unsecured claims based on the value of the property, but did not eliminate their status as allowed secured claims.[65] However, that language was not retained. Courts are required to implement the language of the statute and not what they think Congress might have intended instead.[66]

---

58 *See* National Consumer Law Center, Consumer Bankruptcy Law and Practice § 11.6 (7th ed. 2004).

59 This new provision was not given a section number designation by the 2005 Act.

60 *E.g.*, *In re* Andrews, 49 F.3d 1404, 1409 (9th Cir. 1995); *In re* Szostek, 886 F.2d 1405 (3d Cir. 1989); *see also* National Consumer Law Center, Consumer Bankruptcy Law and Practice § 11.6.1.3.2 (7th ed. 2004).

61 *See* National Consumer Law Center, Consumer Bankruptcy Law and Practice § 11.6.1 (7th ed. 2004).

62 Under 49 U.S.C. § 30102(a)(6): " 'motor vehicle' means a vehicle driven or drawn by mechanical power and manufactured primarily for use on public streets, roads, and highways, but does not include a vehicle operated only on a rail line."

63 *See* 11 U.S.C. § 102(7).

64 *See* § 6.8, *infra*; National Consumer Law Center, Consumer Bankruptcy Law and Practice § 11.6.1.2 (7th ed. 2004).

65 *See, e.g.*, H.R. 833, 106th Cong. § 122 (1999).

66 Among the many issues created by this new provision, an oversecured creditor who is not the holder of an allowed secured claim by operation of this language is not entitled to pre-confirmation interest and reasonable attorney fees based on section 506(b).

It is important to note that for an allowed secured claim, the 2005 amendments do not change the method of determining payments required under the plan to compensate the secured creditor for the present value of its claim.[67] This issue was not addressed by the Act and therefore the Supreme Court decision in *Till v. SCS Credit Corp.*,[68] which held that a formula method is to be used, with the prime rate of interest as the starting point, as adjusted by a factor for risk, remains good law.

6.7.2 Lien Retention During Plan

Section 1325(a) of the Bankruptcy Code provides that a court shall approve a plan if certain standards are met.[69] The 2005 Act adds new language to section 1325(a)(5)(B)(I), providing that to meet the lien retention standard the plan must permit the holder of an allowed secured claim to retain its lien until the earlier of the payment of the underlying debt determined under non-bankruptcy law or a discharge under section 1328 of the Code. New language in this provision also states that the plan must provide that if the case is dismissed or converted without completion of the plan, the lien will also be retained to the extent recognized by applicable non-bankruptcy law.[70]

This amendment is apparently an attempt to overrule cases under the prior language that required elimination of the creditor's lien when the allowed secured claim had been paid.[71] For debtors who can not complete a plan but who have completely paid an allowed secured claim, it makes more attractive the options of a hardship discharge or a modification that allows plan completion, so that a discharge is entered and the lien can be eliminated. It is important to note that the fact that a lien is retained to the extent recognized by applicable non-bankruptcy law if the case is converted does not affect the amount that may be necessary to redeem the property in a chapter 7 case. That amount is determined by sections 722 and 348(f)(1)(B) of the Code.[72]

6.7.3 Property to Be Distributed in Equal Monthly Payments

The 2005 Act provides that if property to be distributed to the holder of an allowed secured claim is to be in the form of periodic payments, such payments shall be in equal monthly amounts.[73] It is important to note that this provision refers to the distributions to the holder of the allowed secured claim and not to the debtor's plan payments. As long as the plan provides that the trustee's distributions to the holder of the allowed secured claim be made in equal monthly amounts, the debtor's plan payments need not be.

There also does not seem to be any requirement that the equal monthly amounts extend throughout the plan. A debtor may, for example, provide for equal monthly amounts to be distributed to a particular secured creditor for the first twenty-four months of a thirty-six-month plan or, if the requirement of providing adequate protection is met, the last twenty-four months of a thirty-six-month plan. Theoretically this provision requires that when a debtor makes a lump sum payment to the trustee, the trustee would have to defer the payments to a secured creditor into at least two equal monthly payments, but it is hard to imagine a creditor objecting to a plan that provided for payment of the entire lump sum in the first month.

6.7.4 Payments Must Be Sufficient to Provide Adequate Protection

Section 1325(a)(5)(B)(iii)(II) of the Code as amended by the 2005 Act simply codifies once more the right of the holder of an allowed secured claim to receive payments during the plan that are sufficient to provide adequate protection to the creditor's interest in the property, as was already provided by sections 362 and 363 of the Code. For the period prior to plan confirmation, section 1326(a)(1)(C) of the Code similarly provides for payments sufficient to provide adequate protection to creditors with security in personal property, to be made directly to the creditor unless the court orders otherwise.[74]

Decisions under prior law held that a creditor may not, after confirmation, seek relief from the stay based on a lack of adequate protection because the issue of adequate protection should have been raised before confirmation, and confirmation of the plan is res judicata on the issue

67 11 U.S.C. § 1325(a)(5)(B)(ii); *see* National Consumer Law Center, Consumer Bankruptcy Law and Practice § 11.6.1.3.3.5 (7th ed. 2004).

68 541 U.S. 465, 124 S. Ct. 1951, 158 L. Ed. 2d 787 (2004).

69 *See* National Consumer Law Center, Consumer Bankruptcy Law and Practice § 11.6.1.3 (7th ed. 2004).

70 11 U.S.C. § 1325(a)(5)(B)(II).

71 *E.g.*, *In re* Campbell, 180 B.R. 686 (M.D. Fla. 1995); *see* National Consumer Law Center, Consumer Bankruptcy Law and Practice § 11.6.1.3.3.1 (7th ed. 2004).

72 *See* §§ 5.2.1, 5.4.2, *supra*.

73 11 U.S.C. § 1325(a)(5)(B)(iii)(I).

74 *See* § 6.3.2, *supra*.

of adequate protection.[75] The fact that provision of adequate protection has now been explicitly included in the standards for plan confirmation further buttresses those cases.

6.7.5 *Valuation of Property*

In *Associates Commercial Corp. v. Rash*,[76] the Supreme Court held that the value of personal property under section 506(a) of the Code is the replacement value of the property, without deduction of the costs of sale or marketing.[77] The 2005 amendments to section 506(a) codify the *Rash* approach. Section 506(a)(2), as amended, provides that with respect to property acquired for personal, family, or household purposes, replacement value shall mean the price a retail merchant would charge for property of that kind, considering the age and condition of the property. Like the *Rash* decision, this standard requires the court to take into account what the debtor is not receiving, such as reconditioning and warranties.

The 2005 Act also clarifies when valuation is to occur. Section 506(a)(2) provides that the valuation of property acquired for personal, family, or household purposes should consider the age and condition of the property *at the time value is determined*, which would normally be the date of the confirmation hearing. For other personal property, section 506(a)(2) provides for valuation as of the date of the petition.

6.8 Debts Secured by Debtor's Principal Residence

6.8.1 *Definition of Principal Residence*

Under the 2005 Act, the "debtor's principal residence" is defined to mean a residential structure, without regard to whether it is attached to real property.[78] It includes an individual condominium or cooperative unit, as well as a mobile or manufactured home, or a trailer. It also includes "incidental property," which is separately defined in section 101(27B) of the Code.

The new definition for "debtor's principal residence" may have been intended to resolve some of the disputes about when creditors holding secured claims are protected from modification of their claims by a chapter 13 or chapter 11 plan based on section 1322(b)(2) of the Code. Under prior law it was clear that a lien secured by real estate upon which a mobile home was situated was not secured solely by real property that was the debtor's principal residence if the mobile home did not constitute real property under applicable non-bankruptcy law.[79] However, the new definition does not appear to change this result, because no change was made to section 1322(b)(2). While a mobile home may be the debtor's principal residence under the new definition, it would still be personal property under applicable non-bankruptcy law and therefore the debt would not be secured "only by a security interest in real property" that is the debtor's principal residence.[80] Only if a mobile home or cooperative is real property under applicable non-bankruptcy law would the limitations on modification apply, even though the mobile home or cooperative is considered the debtor's principal residence.

Although the definition itself says nothing about the residential structure being the principal residence of the debtor, that limitation should be implied. Otherwise, a 500 unit apartment house owned by a corporate chapter 11 debtor headquartered 3000 miles away could be considered the corporate debtor's principal residence, and a debtor could have an unlimited number of principal residences. In fact, the definition does not even explicitly state that the debtor must own the residential structure. There is no indication that Congress intended such nonsensical results and they can be avoided by acknowledging that the term "debtor's principal residence" also means that the residential structure must indeed be the principal residence of the debtor.

6.8.2 *Incidental Property*

The definition of "incidental property" added by the 2005 Act to section 101 of the Bankruptcy Code is intended to further elaborate on the definition of "debtor's principal residence," as discussed above. The definition of debtor's principal residence means "a residential structure, *including incidental property*."[81] Although the definition of debtor's principal residence refers to a structure, the definition of "incidental property" refers to property rights going beyond the ownership of the struc-

75 *See* National Consumer Law Center, Consumer Bankruptcy Law and Practice § 11.6.1.4 (7th ed. 2004).

76 520 U.S. 953, 117 S. Ct. 1879, 138 L. Ed. 2d 148 (1997).

77 *See* National Consumer Law Center, Consumer Bankruptcy Law and Practice § 11.2.2.3 (7th ed. 2004).

78 11 U.S.C. § 101(13A).

79 *See, e.g., In re* Thompson, 217 B.R. 375 (B.A.P. 2d Cir. 1998) (mobile home is personalty under New York law); *see also* National Consumer Law Center, Consumer Bankruptcy Law and Practice § 11.6.1.2.4 (7th ed. 2004).

80 11 U.S.C. § 1322(b)(2).

81 11 U.S.C. § 101(13A)(A).

ture. The rights included, apparently along with the structure, are rights to "property commonly conveyed with a principal residence in the area where the property is located, easements, rights, appurtenances, fixtures, rents, royalties, mineral rights, oil or gas rights, profits, water rights, escrow funds, or insurance proceeds," as well as all replacements or additions.[82]

The purpose of this amendment appears to be to further define debtor's principal residence, which is used in section 1322(b)(2). Courts had differed regarding whether some of the rights enumerated in the definition of incidental property were additional collateral which removed a secured claim from the protection against modification in section 1322(b)(2), a protection limited to debts secured only by a security interest in real property that is the debtor's principal residence.[83] The specificity in the new definition of incidental property clarifies that security interests in types of property not enumerated, such as appliances, furniture, bank accounts, motor vehicles, or property of entities other than the debtor, are sufficient to deny the protection against modification. Indeed, an additional security interest in any type of property not commonly conveyed with a principal residence in the area where the property is located should have that effect.

6.8.3 Other Exceptions to Anti-Modification Provision Remain Unchanged

Many courts have held that the holding in *Nobelman v. American Savings Bank*[84] does not apply in cases in which a junior mortgage is totally undersecured due to the fact that senior liens equal or exceed the value of the property. In *Nobelman* the Supreme Court rested its holding on the fact that the creditor, after bifurcation of its claim under section 506(a), had a secured claim as well as an unsecured claim, and therefore was a "holder of a secured claim."[85] When the creditor, after bifurcation, holds only an unsecured claim, it is not a "holder of secured claim" and does not come within the ambit of section 1322(b)(2).[86] Importantly, nothing in the 2005 Act overrules or otherwise undermines these decisions.

In addition section 1322(c)(2) provides that *notwithstanding section 1322(b)(2)*, in a case in which the last payment on the original payment schedule for a claim secured only by a mortgage on the debtor's principal residence is due before the due date of the final plan payment, the plan may modify the creditor's rights pursuant to section 1325(a)(5). Thus, debtors are permitted to modify many short term mortgages, mortgages on which the debtor's payments are nearly complete, and mortgages with balloon payments falling due before the end of the chapter 13 plan.[87] The 2005 Act did not amend section 1322(c)(2) or limit the modification rights under that subsection.

6.9 Objections to Claims

The 2005 Act includes a provision that permits the debtor to seek a reduction of an unsecured creditor's claim if the creditor unreasonably refused to negotiate, prior to the filing of the bankruptcy, a "reasonable alternative repayment schedule."[88] The debtor must attempt to negotiate the repayment plan through an approved nonprofit budgeting and credit counseling agency.[89] If the creditor unreasonably refuses to negotiate such a plan, a debtor who later files bankruptcy may bring a motion or objection to claim requesting that the court reduce the creditor's claim by no more than twenty percent of the claim amount.[90]

For this provision to apply, the debtor's repayment offer must be made at least sixty days before the petition is filed and it must provide for payment of at least sixty percent of the amount of the outstanding debt, over a period not to exceed the debt's repayment period.[91] The debtor has the burden of proving that the creditor unrea-

82 11 U.S.C. § 101(27B).

83 *See* National Consumer Law Center, Consumer Bankruptcy Law and Practice § 11.6.1.2.2 (7th ed. 2004).

84 508 U.S. 324, 113 S. Ct. 2106, 124 L. Ed. 2d 228 (1993); *see* National Consumer Law Center, Consumer Bankruptcy Law and Practice § 11.6.1.2.1 (7th ed. 2004).

85 508 U.S. at 328–329.

86 *In re* Zimmer, 313 F.3d 1220 (9th Cir. 2003); *In re* Lane, 280 F.3d 663 (6th Cir. 2002); *In re* Pond, 252 F.3d 122 (2d Cir. 2001); *In re* Dickerson, 222 F.3d 924 (11th Cir. 2000); *In re* Tanner, 217 F.3d 1357 (11th Cir. 2000); *In re* Bartee, 212 F.3d 277 (5th Cir. 2000); *In re* McDonald, 205 F.3d 606 (3d Cir. 2000); *In re* Mann, 249 B.R. 831 (B.A.P. 1st Cir. 2000).

87 *In re* Paschen, 296 F.3d 1203 (11th Cir. 2002) (statutory exception to Code's anti-modification provision permits debtors to bifurcate and cram down undersecured, short-term home mortgages); *In re* Eubanks, 219 B.R. 468 (B.A.P. 6th Cir. 1998) (short term mortgage modifiable); *In re* Mattson, 210 B.R. 157 (Bankr. D. Minn. 1997) (section 1322(b)(2) protections did not apply to loans maturing before end of plan).

88 11 U.S.C. § 502(k).

89 *See* § 4.3.1, *supra*.

90 For a sample Objection to Claim Seeking Reduction of Claim Amount Pursuant to Section 502(k), see Form 10, Appx. G, *infra*.

91 11 U.S.C. § 502(k)(1)(B).

sonably refused to consider the debtor's proposal and that the proposal was made at least sixty days before the petition was filed.[92]

While this provision is not likely to be used in many cases, debtors considering the filing of a chapter 13 case in which a 100% chapter 13 plan must be proposed based on the best interest of creditors test or some other reason might attempt to invoke this provision.

92 11 U.S.C. § 502(k)(2).

Chapter 7

Repeat Bankruptcy Filings and Automatic Stay Changes

7.1 Introduction

The 2005 Act imposes a number of new restrictions on repeat bankruptcy filings. Section 7.2, *infra*, analyzes the restrictions placed on the debtor's ability to obtain a discharge following a discharge in a prior case. Section 7.3, *infra*, reviews amendments that affect the application of the automatic stay based on certain repeat filings and other grounds.

7.2 Successive Bankruptcy Discharges

7.2.1 New Chapter 7 Case After Prior Bankruptcy Discharge

Prior to the 2005 amendments, a debtor could not obtain a discharge in a new chapter 7 case until six years had passed from the filing of a prior chapter 7 case in which a discharge had been granted.[1] The 2005 Act increases this period to eight years.[2] As under prior law, the bar against a successive discharge applies only when the prior case is one in which a discharge was granted. If the prior bankruptcy case was terminated without a discharge, by a dismissal for example, this objection to discharge may not be raised. In addition, the eight-year period runs from the date the earlier bankruptcy case was commenced, not from the date of the discharge.

The 2005 Act does not, however, make a corresponding amendment to the six-year waiting period after most prior chapter 13 discharges.[3] Thus, a debtor may obtain a discharge in a new chapter 7 case as long as six years have passed since the filing of a prior chapter 13 case in which a discharge had been granted. In addition, there is no time restriction on obtaining a discharge in a new chapter 7 case after a prior chapter 13 case in which a discharge was granted if one-hundred percent of the allowed unsecured claims were paid, or in which the actual payments under the previous chapter 13 plan comprised at least seventy percent of the allowed unsecured claims in that case, and the court finds that the plan was proposed by the debtor in good faith and was the debtor's "best effort."[4]

7.2.2 New Chapter 13 Case After Prior Bankruptcy Discharge

Under prior law there was no bar on the ability of the debtor to obtain a chapter 13 discharge after a prior discharge. There is still no restriction on the *filing* of a chapter 13 case after a prior discharge, but the 2005 amendments impose a time limit on obtaining a chapter 13 *discharge* after a prior discharge. A discharge can not be entered in a chapter 13 case if the debtor received a discharge in a prior chapter 7, 11, or 12 case that was filed within four years before the date of the chapter 13 order for relief.[5]

In addition, under the 2005 Act, a discharge can not be entered in a chapter 13 case if the debtor received a discharge in a prior chapter 13 case that was filed within two years before the date of the chapter 13 order for relief.[6] As a discharge in most chapter 13 cases will not enter until at least three years after the case is filed, this means that a prior chapter 13 case will almost never be a bar to a second chapter 13 discharge. Some have suggested that this interpretation can not be correct because the provision would almost never be applicable. However, the plain meaning of the statutory language compels this result. In addition, the alternative interpretation advanced—that the two years runs from the prior dis-

1 *See* National Consumer Law Center, Consumer Bankruptcy Law and Practice § 14.2.2.8 (7th ed. 2004).

2 11 U.S.C. § 727(a)(8)

3 11 U.S.C. § 727(a)(9).

4 *See* National Consumer Law Center, Consumer Bankruptcy Law and Practice § 14.2.2.9 (7th ed. 2004).

5 11 U.S.C. § 1328(f)(1).

6 11 U.S.C. § 1328(f)(2).

charge—would make no sense in terms of policy. Because a chapter 7 discharge is usually entered a few months after the filing of the petition, that interpretation would allow a chapter 13 discharge in less time after a prior chapter 7 discharge than after a prior chapter 13 discharge. In cases in which the debtor completed a five-year chapter 13 plan, it would also mean that the debtor could file a chapter 7 case and receive a discharge but not file a chapter 13 case and receive a discharge if the new case was filed one year after the prior discharge.

7.2.3 Determining Whether a Prior Discharge Was Under Chapter 7 or Chapter 13

Because the time periods restricting a subsequent discharge differ depending on whether the prior discharge was under chapter 7 or under chapter 13, it is important to be able to distinguish between the two. The language of section 1328(f) of the Bankruptcy Code, taken literally, seems to look to the chapter under which the case was originally "filed," rather than the chapter under which the discharge was granted. Thus, if a case was originally filed under chapter 13 and then converted to chapter 7, a debtor can argue that the two-year limit should apply.

For example, a debtor in a failing chapter 13 case might convert the case to chapter 7 and obtain a discharge, and then need to file a new chapter 13 case less than four years after the original chapter 13 case was filed. Under section 1328(f)(1), the debtor can not receive a chapter 13 discharge after receiving a discharge in a chapter 7 case that was filed within four years before the date of the chapter 13 order for relief. In this situation the debtor can argue that the new chapter 13 case can result in discharge because the prior discharge was received in a case filed under chapter 13.

7.2.4 Repeat Filing Still Permissible Even If Discharge Unavailable

It is important to recognize that it is still possible for a debtor to file a case even if a discharge can not be granted. There are a number of circumstances in which a bankruptcy filing can be useful to a debtor even though a discharge can not be granted. For example, a debtor may file a chapter 13 bankruptcy case to cure a mortgage default or other default. Subject to various limitations, the automatic stay can stop collection activity, foreclosure, or repossession, and may make a bankruptcy case valuable even without a discharge being available.[7] A chapter 7 or chapter 13 case can be used to protect exempt property from creditors, often more so than would be permitted under state law, based on the application of section 522(c) of the Code, which applies regardless of whether a discharge is granted.[8]

There is no indication in the 2005 amendments that the filing of a case in which no discharge can be granted tolls the time periods between discharges. Thus, for example, consider a debtor who obtained a discharge in a chapter 7 case, then filed a chapter 13 case too soon after the chapter 7 case to qualify for a discharge. The debtor should still be eligible for another chapter 7 discharge eight years after the filing of the first chapter 7 case. Nothing in the amended Bankruptcy Code indicates that the filing of the intervening chapter 13 case, in which no discharge was granted, should have any effect on the running of the eight-year period.

7.3 Automatic Stay Changes

7.3.1 Overview

The 2005 amendments create a number of new exceptions to the automatic stay. The exceptions or limitations are primarily applicable to repeat filers[9] and to tenants involved in landlord-tenant evictions.[10] The 2005 Act also amends the automatic stay provisions regarding certain post-petition transfers, the setoff of tax refunds, and the withholding of wages to repay loans from retirement funds.[11] The Act also makes relatively minor changes in the timetable for the bankruptcy court to resolve a motion for relief from the stay.[12]

Several other amendments affecting the application of the stay are discussed in other chapters. An amendment which provides for the termination of the automatic stay regarding personal property if the debtor fails to file a statement of intention regarding that property or fails to follow through on the stated intention is discussed in Chapter 5, *supra*. In addition, changes that affect the automatic stay in family law matters are discussed in Chapter 9, *infra*.

7 See also § 7.3, *infra*, for a discussion of limitations on the automatic stay imposed by the 2005 amendments.

8 *See* National Consumer Law Center, Consumer Bankruptcy Law and Practice § 10.5 (7th ed. 2004).

9 *See* § 7.3.2, *infra*.

10 *See* § 7.3.3, *infra*.

11 *See* § 7.3.4, *infra*.

12 *See* § 7.3.5, *infra*.

7.3.2 Limitations on the Automatic Stay in Repeat Filings

7.3.2.1 Prior Case Dismissed Within Previous Year—Section 362(c)(3)

7.3.2.1.1 General application

Section 362(c)(3) of the Bankruptcy Code, added by the 2005 Act, limits the stay under section 362(a) of the Code in an individual chapter 7, 11, or 13 case if the individual was a debtor in a case dismissed within the year before the petition. For debtors covered by this new restriction, the automatic stay under section 362(a) expires thirty days after the petition is filed, unless it is extended by the court upon a showing by the debtor that the case was filed in good faith.

This provision does not apply if the prior case was dismissed under section 707(b) of the Code and the new case is not a chapter 7 case. Because the stay terminates under this provision only as to actions taken in relation to a debt or property securing such a debt, or to a lease, the automatic stay provided under section 362(a) of the Code continues to apply in the later case to property of the estate, other than property securing a debt of the debtor. In addition, section 362(c)(3) does not prevent the application of the codebtor stay provided under section 1301 of the Code.[13] Finally, this stay limitation does not apply in a case brought by a family farmer under chapter 12.

7.3.2.1.2 Demonstrating good faith for extension of stay past thirty days

On the motion of a party in interest, after notice and a hearing held before the thirty-day period expires, the court may extend the stay as to all or some creditors upon a showing that the case was filed in good faith.[14] If the court extends the stay, it may impose conditions or limitations on it. The 2005 Act does not define good faith for purposes of this stay limitation, but good faith with respect to the filing of a case has been given a recognized meaning by existing case law.[15] Most cases should be found to have been filed in good faith under this standard.

The 2005 amendments, while not defining good faith, set forth several circumstances in which a case is presumed not to be filed in good faith.[16] A case is presumptively not filed in good faith, as to all creditors in the case, if any of the following is true:

- More than one prior case involving the debtor was pending in the year preceding filing of the petition.
- A case dismissed within the preceding year was dismissed after failure to file required documents without substantial excuse. The subsection specifies that inadvertence or negligence of the debtor is not such an excuse, but negligence of the debtor's attorney can be a substantial excuse.[17]
- The debtor failed to provide adequate protection as ordered by the court. This provision would not include adequate protection payments made under section 1326 unless the court ordered them.[18] This provision should not affect many debtors, as failure to provide adequate protection had not been a common problem or cause for plan failure under prior law.
- The debtor failed to comply with the terms of a confirmed plan. This provision does not apply if the debtor defaulted before confirmation of the plan, but it will apply to the common case of a debtor who, well into the plan period, suffers an interruption in income or a large unexpected expense. It should not be difficult, however, to overcome the presumption in such a case.
- There has not been a substantial change in circumstances or some other reason to expect that the new case will be successfully concluded with a discharge or with a confirmed plan that will be fully performed.

In addition, a case is presumptively not filed in good faith as to a particular creditor in the case if the creditor's request for relief from the automatic stay in a prior case was still pending when the case was dismissed or the request was resolved with an order terminating, conditioning, or limiting the stay.[19] If the presumption under this subsection as to a particular creditor is not rebutted and section 362(c)(3) is otherwise applicable, the stay would terminate only as to the creditor who had sought relief from the stay in the prior case.

There can be no presumption that a case was not filed in good faith if the prior case was dismissed due to the creation of a "debt repayment plan," often referred to as

13 *See* § 7.3.2.4, *infra*.
14 11 U.S.C. § 362(c)(3)(B).
15 *See* National Consumer Law Center, Consumer Bankruptcy Law and Practice §§ 9.7.3.1.5, 12.3.2, 12.3.3, 12.10 (7th ed. 2004).
16 11 U.S.C. § 362(c)(3)(C).
17 11 U.S.C. § 362(c)(3)(C)(i)(II)(aa).
18 *See* 11 U.S.C. § 1326(a)(1)(C); § 6.3.2, *supra*.
19 11 U.S.C. § 362(c)(3)(C)(ii).

a debt management plan.[20] Unlike the pre-petition credit counseling requirement found in section 109(h) of the Code, or the claim reduction provision found in section 502(k) of the Code, section 362(i) does not require that the debt repayment plan be proposed or negotiated by an approved nonprofit budgeting and credit counseling agency.[21] This provision also does not require that the debtor successfully complete the debt repayment plan.

7.3.2.1.3 Overcoming the presumption that case was not filed in good faith

A presumption that a case was not filed in good faith can be overcome by clear and convincing evidence.[22] There is no reason to think that the evidence required to show good faith under the 2005 amendments should be any different than that necessary to show good faith under current law. Under the existing body of law defining "good faith" in the bankruptcy context, an honest debtor making a second attempt to save a home or obtain other bankruptcy relief would be considered to have filed in good faith by most courts.[23]

It does not appear that the standard for allowing a stay in a second case filed after a prior dismissal within a year of the filing is necessarily changed significantly, except for the burden placed on the debtor to initiate a proceeding to have the stay extended beyond the initial thirty days. Presumably the debtor's motion to extend the automatic stay should be filed with the petition or immediately thereafter.[24] If courts make clear their intentions about how such issues will be resolved, most such motions to extend the automatic stay should not be contested. It is hoped that courts will allow uncontested motions to be granted without a hearing, or establish other procedures through standing orders or local rule that would help debtors avoid unnecessary added expenses in seeking extensions of the stay.

If the court does not extend the stay, it expires at the end of the thirty-day period. Nothing in the 2005 Act, however, prevents the court from granting a section 105 injunction reimposing the stay after the thirty-day period.[25]

7.3.2.2 Two or More Cases Dismissed Within Previous Year—Section 362(c)(4)

If an individual debtor has had two or more cases dismissed within the year before the petition is filed, section 362(c)(4) of the Code provides that the automatic stay under section 362(a) does not go into effect upon the filing of any case, other than a case refiled under section 707(b).[26] On a motion filed by a party in interest within thirty days after the filing of the later case, and after notice and a hearing, the court may order the stay to take effect as to all or some creditors, subject to such conditions or limitations as the court may impose.[27] The movant must demonstrate that the case has been filed in good faith as to the creditors whose actions are to be stayed.

If the debtor or another party in interest seeks an order imposing a stay, a presumption may arise that the case was not filed in good faith based on circumstances similar to those that apply to a debtor who had a single case dismissed in the previous year.[28] This presumption is subject to rebuttal by clear and convincing evidence to the contrary.

7.3.2.3 Order Confirming Stay Termination

Section 362(j) of the Code provides that, on request of a party in interest, the court shall issue an order under section 362(c) confirming that the automatic stay has been terminated. A similar provision is found in section 362(c)(4)(A)(ii), stating that the court shall promptly enter an order confirming that no stay is in effect as a

20 11 U.S.C. § 362(i).

21 *See* 11 U.S.C. § 111.

22 11 U.S.C. § 362(c)(3)(C).

23 *See In re* Metz, 820 F.2d 1495 (9th Cir. 1987) (filing of successive bankruptcies does not necessarily show bad faith and may be perfectly proper); *In re* Smith, 43 B.R. 319 (Bankr. E.D.N.C. 1984) (plan confirmed, with conditions, even though there had been three prior unsuccessful chapter 13 cases); National Consumer Law Center, Consumer Bankruptcy Law and Practice §§ 9.7.3.1.5, 12.3.2, 12.3.3, 12.10 (7th ed. 2004).

24 For a sample Motion for Continuation of Automatic Stay in Case Filed After Prior Dismissal Within Year of Filing, see Form 7, Appx. G, *infra*.

25 *See* National Consumer Law Center, Consumer Bankruptcy Law and Practice § 9.4.6 (7th ed. 2004).

26 The phrase "other than a case refiled under § 707(b)" was probably intended to mean, as under section 362(c)(3), that the stay limitation does not apply in a case other than chapter 7 following the dismissal of a prior chapter 7 case under section 707(b). In addition, when section 362(c)(3) and (c)(4) are read together, it should also mean that in counting whether there has been two or more prior dismissed cases, a prior dismissed case that was filed under chapter 11, 12, or 13 following a chapter 7 dismissal under section 707(b) should not be considered.

27 For a sample Motion to Invoke Automatic Stay in Case Filed after Two Prior Dismissals Within Year of Filing, see Form 6, Appx. G, *infra*.

28 11 U.S.C. § 362(c)(4)(D); *see* § 7.3.2.1.2, *supra*.

result of the application of section 362(c)(4). These provisions do not require the order to enter upon notice and a hearing, but local court rules may require that the request be made by motion to ensure that the court has sufficient information to determine whether the stay has been terminated or is not in effect based on the conditions set forth in section 362(c).

7.3.2.4 Codebtor Stay Still Applicable

The 2005 Act did not amend any of the provisions of section 1301 of the Code, and no mention of the codebtor stay is made in the revised versions of subsections 362(c)(3) or (c)(4). Thus, the stay limitations under these subsections discussed above do not prevent the application of the stay provided under section 1301 as to any actions taken against a codebtor on a consumer debt of the debtor. This arrangement suggests that, unless there is a compelling reason to file a joint case, it may be advisable for one spouse of a debtor couple to file an individual case, especially in the common situation in which a chapter 13 case is filed in order to cure a default on a joint mortgage. By proceeding in this way no issue will arise under section 362(c)(3) or (c)(4) about the application of the stay if the first case fails and circumstances later compel the filing of another case by the other spouse. Section 362(c) also would not prevent the codebtor stay from arising if the first case was a joint case and the second case was filed by only one spouse.

7.3.2.5 Filings in Violation of Section 109(g) or a Prior Court Order—Section 362(b)(21)

Another provision of the 2005 Act affects the automatic stay for two subcategories of repeat filers, but only as to the enforcement of real property liens. Section 362(b)(21) of the Code renders the automatic stay inapplicable to enforcement of a lien on, or security interest in, real property when the debtor is ineligible for relief under section 109(g) of the Code or has filed the case in violation of a prior court order limiting new bankruptcy case filings.

If there are codebtors on a real estate secured debt, this stay exception would not apply in a case filed by one of the codebtors if that codebtor is not ineligible under section 109(g) or was not named in the prior court order, and the stay under section 1301 would protect the interest of the non-filing codebtor.[29] In a joint case this provision would apply as to real property jointly held by both debtors only if both debtors are ineligible under section 109(g) or subject to the prior court order.[30] In addition, this provision does not affect the codebtor stay under section 1301 in a case in which only one of two codebtors files a case.

Under section 109(g) a debtor is not eligible for relief under the Code if, within 180 days before the filing of the petition, the debtor had a prior case dismissed for willful failure to abide by orders of the court or to prosecute the case, or the debtor requested and obtained the voluntary dismissal of the case following the filing of a request for relief from the automatic stay.[31] However, it is often not clear whether section 109(g) was invoked in the prior case. Courts rarely make express findings that the debtor willfully failed to prosecute the case or willfully failed to obey a court order. If the court did not make such an express finding in dismissing the prior case, the clerk normally accepts the petition filed in the later case because no determination has been made that the debtor is ineligible under section 109(g).

Thus it is not likely that real estate secured creditors will rely upon this stay exception if the debtor's filing status is unclear. A creditor who proceeds with enforcement of a real property lien in reliance on the exception based on section 109(g) may act at its peril. There may be factual or legal disputes about whether the debtor is eligible for relief and whether section 109(g) applies. If the debtor prevails the creditor's action is likely to be found a willful violation of the stay, as a mistake does not vitiate the willfulness of an action in violation of the stay.[32]

7.3.2.6 *In Rem* Stay Relief—Section 362(b)(20)

Another provision added by the 2005 Act allows creditors with claims secured by real property to seek *in rem* stay relief in certain limited circumstances.[33] If the court enters an *in rem* order under new section 362(d)(4) of the Code, and the order is properly recorded, section 362(b)(20) provides that the stay does not apply with

29 *See* § 7.3.2.4, *supra*.

30 Section 362(b)(21) should be compared with the refiling provision in section 362(c)(3), which expressly states that the provision is applicable in a single or joint case filed by an individual debtor.

31 *See* National Consumer Law Center, Consumer Bankruptcy Law and Practice §§ 3.2.12, 9.7.3.1.5 (7th ed. 2004).

32 *See* National Consumer Law Center, Consumer Bankruptcy Law and Practice § 9.6 (7th ed. 2004).

33 11 U.S.C. § 362(d)(4).

respect to the property in a later case filed within two years after the date of the order.[34]

An *in rem* order may be granted if the secured creditor proves that:

- The filing of the petition was part of a scheme to hinder, delay, or defraud creditors; *and*
- The scheme involved either (1) transfer of full or partial interests in the property without creditor or court approval, *or* (2) multiple bankruptcy filings involving the same property.[35]

If an *in rem* order is sought based on the provision regarding multiple filings involving the same property, the order can not be imposed during the first bankruptcy filing involving the property, given the "multiple" filing requirement. However, the new filing could be used as the basis for an order if a spouse, co-owner, or former owner of the property had recently filed for bankruptcy. A filing in the more distant past would not likely be considered a part of a scheme to hinder, delay, or defraud creditors.

For the exception to the automatic stay to be binding in a later case, section 362(d)(4) requires that the *in rem* order from the prior case be recorded in compliance with state laws for recording liens or interests in property.[36] It is not clear whether the order must be recorded before the later case is filed. If it need not be, the purpose of recording would seem to be defeated and an innocent purchaser may be unable to file a bankruptcy case to protect the property.

While section 362(b)(20), which creates the exception to the automatic stay, does not mention the recording requirement, if courts do not read the recording requirement into section 362(b)(20) then the recording requirement of 362(d)(4) would be mere surplusage.

Another potential problem is that the new *in rem* orders do not appear to be limited in scope to the creditor that sought the order in the first place. Thus, a predatory lender who extended credit after the order was recorded could take advantage of it. Nothing in section 362(d)(4) or section 362(b)(20), however, prevents the court from limiting application of the order to the creditor who requested it.

A debtor in a later case may move for relief from the order based on changed circumstances or other good cause.[37]

As the Code now sets a bright line rule for *in rem* stay relief, courts should not grant such orders in other circumstances.[38] Certainly, such an order should not be granted in the first bankruptcy filing involving a property. Nor should such an order be granted in a later bankruptcy case unless the case meets the requirement of being part of a scheme to hinder, delay, or defraud creditors.

The stay exception in section 362(b)(20) also does not affect the applicability of the section 1301 codebtor stay.

7.3.3 *Exceptions to Stay of Residential Tenant Evictions*

7.3.3.1 Overview

The 2005 Act creates two new limitations on the automatic stay in landlord-tenant matters. These are likely to cause hardship to some tenants seeking to avoid homelessness by curing rent arrearages through chapter 13 bankruptcy. They are also likely to cause confusion among landlords and lead to violations of the automatic stay.

The first limitation applies when the lessor has obtained a pre-petition judgment in an eviction, unlawful detainer, or similar action for possession of the residential real property where the debtor resides.[39] The second limitation applies if the landlord files a certification regarding illegal use of controlled substances or endangerment of the property.[40]

7.3.3.2 Pre-Petition Judgment for Possession

Under section 362(b)(22) of the Code, an eviction of a debtor from residential property is not stayed by section 362(a)(3) of the Code if the lessor has obtained a judgment for possession prior to the filing of the bankruptcy petition, unless the debtor meets certain conditions. If a pre-petition judgment for possession has been obtained

---

34 11 U.S.C. § 362(b)(20).

35 11 U.S.C. § 362(d)(4).

36 Section 362(d)(4) of the Code provides that federal, state, or local governmental units that accept notices of interests or liens in real property shall accept for indexing and recording any certified copy of an order entered under the subsection.

37 11 U.S.C. § 362(d)(4). For a sample Motion for Relief from *In Rem* Order Entered in Prior Case, see Form 9, Appx. G, *infra*.

38 Some of the grounds used to justify such orders in decisions prior to the 2005 amendments may no longer be valid. *See* National Consumer Law Center, Consumer Bankruptcy Law and Practice § 9.7.3.1.5 (7th ed. 2004).

39 *See* § 7.3.3.2, *infra*.

40 *See* § 7.3.3.3, *infra*.

for property in which the debtor resides, the debtor must so indicate on the bankruptcy petition, and state the name and address of the lessor.[41]

This stay exception is limited to the continuation of proceedings stayed under section 362(a)(3), which are actions seeking to obtain possession of property of the estate or of property from the estate, or to exercise control over property of the estate. If the lessor has obtained a judgment for possession that includes a money judgment against the debtor for back rent owed, the lessor must still seek relief from the stay under section 362(a)(6) of the Code in order to enforce the judgment against the debtor, or at least the portion of the judgment representing the claim for back rent. Section 362(b)(22) also does not apply to judicial actions stayed under section 362(a)(1) to recover a pre-petition claim against the debtor, including further proceedings that may be necessary to enforce the judgment for possession.

Notwithstanding the stay exception under new section 362(b)(22), the debtor may obtain an automatic stay for a period of thirty days by filing and serving on the lessor a certification under penalty of perjury that:

- The debtor has a right to cure the monetary default under applicable non-bankruptcy law; and
- The debtor, or an adult dependent of the debtor, has deposited with the clerk of the bankruptcy court all rent that would become due during the thirty days after the filing of the petition.[42]

If no certification is filed with the petition, the clerk must "immediately" serve on the debtor and the lessor a certified copy of the docket indicating the lack of a certification and the applicability of the exception to the stay.[43] If the debtor files a certification with the petition and makes the required deposit with the clerk, the clerk is to promptly transmit the deposit to the lessor.[44]

The debtor may obtain a stay under section 362(a)(3) beyond the initial thirty days if the debtor files, within thirty days after the petition, a further certification that the monetary default upon which the eviction is being sought has been completely cured.[45]

The lessor has the right to contest either the initial certification seeking a thirty-day stay or the certification that the monetary default has been cured.[46] If the lessor files an objection to either certification and serves it on the debtor, the court must hold a hearing within ten days to determine if the certification is true.[47]

7.3.3.3 Illegal Use of Controlled Substances or Endangerment to the Property

A second new exception to the automatic stay under section 362(a)(3) applies if the lessor files and serves on the debtor a certification under penalty of perjury that:

- An eviction has been commenced based on endangerment of the property or illegal use of controlled substances on the property; or
- The debtor has within thirty days before the certification either endangered the property or illegally used or allowed to be used controlled substances at the property.[48]

If the landlord files such a certification the debtor has fifteen days to file and serve on the lessor an objection to the truth or legal sufficiency of the lessor's certification before the stay exception goes into effect.[49] If the debtor files an objection challenging the truth or legal sufficiency of the lessor's certification the exception to the stay does not go into effect, if at all, until after the court rules on it. The court must hold a hearing within ten days of the filing of the debtor's objection to determine whether the circumstances described in the lessor's certification existed or have been remedied.[50] It is not clear when the debtor may remedy the circumstances, but presumably it may occur at any time prior to the hearing. If the court rules in favor of the debtor, the stay under section 362(a)(3) remains in effect.

If no objection to the lessor's certification is filed, or if the court rules against the debtor, the clerk must "immediately" serve a certified copy of the docket on the lessor and the debtor, indicating the failure to object or the court's order.[51]

It appears that if the certification is based on the commencement of an eviction action, the eviction must specifically have been based at least in part on the endangerment of the property or illegal use of controlled substances. In addition, because this stay exception is

41 11 U.S.C. § 362(*l*)(5).

42 11 U.S.C. § 362(*l*)(1). The form petition, Official Form 1, has been modified to include a Statement that contains the required certification. *See* Appx. D.4, *infra*.

43 11 U.S.C. § 362(*l*)(4)(A).

44 11 U.S.C. § 362(*l*)(5)(D).

45 11 U.S.C. § 362(*l*)(2).

46 11 U.S.C. § 362(*l*)(3).

47 11 U.S.C. § 362(*l*)(3)(A).

48 11 U.S.C. § 362(b)(23).

49 11 U.S.C. § 362(m).

50 11 U.S.C. § 362(m)(2)(A), (B).

51 11 U.S.C. § 362(m)(2)(D), 362(m)(3).

limited to the stay provided under section 362(a)(3), the lessor may not proceed with any eviction that seeks to recover on a pre-petition claim against the debtor, such as a property damages claim, without obtaining relief from the stay provided under section 362(a)(6), or with any judicial action that could have been commenced prior to the petition, without obtaining relief from the stay under section 362(a)(1).

7.3.4 Other New Exceptions to the Automatic Stay

7.3.4.1 Continued Withholding of Income for Loans from Retirement Funds

Another new exception to the automatic stay authorizes the continued withholding of wages for repayment of retirement fund loans.[52] The wage withholding must be for repayment of a loan from a plan under section 408(b)(1) of the Employee Retirement Income Security Act (ERISA) or that is subject to section 72(p) of the Internal Revenue Code, or from a thrift savings plan in the Federal Employee's Retirement System.

This provision is part of the enhanced protection of retirement accounts provided by the 2005 Act,[53] and dovetails with the new section 1322(f) provision which states that funds used for such loan repayments are not part of disposable income in a chapter 13 case.[54] By permitting wage withholding without interruption this stay exception will prevent the triggering of tax penalties through default on such loans.

7.3.4.2 Transfers Not Avoidable Under Section 549

Another new provision creates an exception from the automatic stay for post-petition transfers that are not avoidable under sections 544 and 549 of the Bankruptcy Code.[55] Generally, section 549 allows avoidance of involuntary post-petition transfers, absent authorization of the transfer by the court. The safe harbor found in section 549(c)[56] is limited to voluntary transfers because section 549(c) concerns transfers to "a good faith purchaser," and "purchaser" is defined in section 101(43) of the Code to mean transferee of a voluntary transfer. The 2005 Act also amends the definition of the term "transfer" in section 101(54) to make clear that the creation of a lien is a transfer for purposes of the Bankruptcy Code.[57]

7.3.4.3 Setoff of Tax Refunds

Section 362(b)(26) of the Bankruptcy Code permits taxing authorities to set off tax refunds for pre-petition tax periods against pre-petition tax debts. If there is a pending action to determine tax liability, the taxing authority may hold the refund pending the outcome of the action. However, on motion by the trustee and after notice and a hearing, the court may order turnover of the refund, but only if the taxing authority is granted adequate assurance for any secured claim it has under section 506(a) of the Code based on its setoff rights. Moreover, the setoff may still be prevented by the provisions of a confirmed chapter 13 plan.[58]

7.3.5 Timetable for Motions for Relief from Stay

If a party in interest files a motion for relief from the automatic stay, the 2005 amendments provide that the stay automatically terminates sixty days after the motion is filed, unless:

- The court decides the motion before that time; or
- The time period is extended by agreement of the parties or by the court for a specific period of time

52 11 U.S.C. § 362(b)(19). This provision also states that nothing in section 362(b)(19) may be construed to provide that either a loan made under a governmental plan under section 414(d) of the Internal Revenue Code, or a contract or account under section 403(b) of the Internal Revenue Code, constitutes a claim or a debt for purposes of a bankruptcy proceeding.

53 *See, e.g.*, 11 U.S.C. §§ 522(b)(3)(C),(d)(12); *see also* H.R. Rep. No. 109-31, at 63–64 (2005) (reprinted in Appx. A.4, *infra*); § 8.3, *infra*.

54 Section 1322(f) of the Bankruptcy Code also provides that a chapter 13 plan may not alter the terms of a pension loan described in section 362(b)(19).

55 11 U.S.C. § 362(b)(24).

56 Section 549(c) protects the transfer of real property to a good faith purchaser who pays present fair equivalent value and lacks knowledge of the bankruptcy case, unless a copy of the petition was recorded in the land records office.

57 The legislative history indicates that the stay exception in section 362(b)(24) and the amendment to the definition of "transfer" in section 101(54) were intended to respond to the outcome in Thompson v. Margen (*In re* McConville), 84 F.3d 340 (9th Cir. 1996). *See* H.R. Rep. No. 109-31, at 75–76 (2005) (reprinted in Appx. A.4, *infra*).

58 *See* National Consumer Law Center, Consumer Bankruptcy Law and Practice § 12.11 (7th ed. 2004).

for good cause based on findings of the court.[59]

It is unlikely that this provision will significantly change practice with respect to stay relief motions. Under pre-2005 Act practice, stay motions were normally decided within sixty days. In the few cases in which they were not, the delay beyond sixty days was usually based either on an agreement of the parties or for good cause. However, attorneys should be careful not to allow the sixty-day period to run through inadvertence.

7.4 Remedies for Stay Violations

Several amendments made by the 2005 Act limit the relief available for violations of the stay under section 362(k)(1) of the Code (formerly section 362(h)). If a creditor violates the stay based on a good faith belief that the stay had been terminated as to the debtor under section 362(h),[60] section 362(k)(2) provides that the recovery under section 362(k)(1) shall be limited to actual damages. As provided in section 362(k)(1), actual damages may include an award of attorney fees and costs. The majority of courts have also held that emotional distress damages may be recovered in an award of actual damages under section 362(k)(1).[61]

In addition, new section 342(g)(2) of the Code provides that a "monetary penalty" may not be imposed on a creditor under section 362(k) for violation of the stay if the creditor has not received "effective notice" of the order for relief as provided under section 342.[62] This provision appears to preclude only the recovery of punitive damages under section 362(k)(1), so actual damages or other relief that is not a monetary penalty should still be recoverable. This limitation also applies only to a creditor who has not received effective notice, not to others who may have violated the stay, such as the creditor's attorney.

59 11 U.S.C. § 362(e)(2).

60 Section 362(h) provides for the termination of the stay as to personal property based on the debtor's failure to take certain actions related to the statement of intention under section 521(a)(2) of the Code. *See* Ch. 5, *supra*.

61 *E.g.*, *In re* Dawson, 390 F.3d 1139, 1148 (9th Cir. 2004); Fleet Mortgage Group, Inc. v. Kaneb, 196 F.3d 265 (1st Cir. 1999). *But see* Aiello v. Providian Fin. Corp., 239 F.3d 876 (7th Cir. 2001). For a general discussion of this issue see National Consumer Law Center, Consumer Bankruptcy Law and Practice § 9.6 (7th ed. 2004).

62 11 U.S.C. § 342(g)(2); *see* § 4.7, *supra*.

Chapter 8 Exemption Provisions

8.1 Introduction

The 2005 Act makes a number of changes regarding the exemptions debtors may claim in a bankruptcy case. First, for debtors who have not lived in the same state for a full 730 days prior to filing, the new law changes the rules about which state's exemption laws may apply. These new rules are discussed in section 8.2, *infra*. Second, the 2005 Act creates generous new exemptions for retirement funds, discussed in section 8.3, *infra*, and for certain educational and pension funds, discussed in section 8.4, *infra*.

Third, while Congress rejected attempts to cap the unlimited homestead exemptions some states allow, it did restrict the use of state homestead exemptions in several circumstances, discussed in section 8.5, *infra*. Finally, the new law attempts to narrow the lien avoidance provision under section 522(f) of the Code for nonpossessory, nonpurchase money security interests in any exempt household goods, which is discussed in section 8.6, *infra*.

Although most provisions of the 2005 amendments affecting consumer bankruptcies take effect on or after October 17, 2005, several of the exemption changes went into effect on April 20, 2005, and those provisions with the earlier effective date will be noted when discussed in this Chapter.

8.2 Longer Period for Determining Debtor's Domicile

In an apparent attempt to discourage debtors from moving to states with more generous exemption laws before filing bankruptcy, the 2005 Act substantially changes the domiciliary provision found in former section 522(b)(2)(A) of the Code. The new requirements are found in section 522(b)(3)(A).

If the debtor elects or is required to claim exemptions under state law, the state exemption law that applies is determined by the state in which the debtor's domicile has been located for the 730 days immediately preceding the petition filing date, rather than the 180-day period adopted under former law. If the debtor's domicile has not been located in a single state for the 730-day period, the applicable state exemption law is that of the state in which the debtor was domiciled for the 180 days immediately preceding the 730-day period or in which the debtor was domiciled for the longer portion of such 180-day period than in any other place.[1]

If the effect of section 522(b)(3)(A) is to render the debtor ineligible for any exemption, the debtor may elect to exempt property as specified under section 522(d).[2] The debtor is therefore permitted to exempt property under the federal exemption scheme in this situation even if the state of the debtor's domicile as determined by section 522(b)(3)(A) is an opt-out state. This situation could arise if the exemption law of the state deemed to be the debtor's domicile requires the debtor to reside within the state to claim exemption rights or if the law does not permit an exemption to be taken on property located outside the state.

The amendments to section 522(b) are certain to produce many court decisions on the extraterritorial application of state exemption laws. Courts are currently divided on this issue when state exemption law is silent as to its extraterritorial effect.[3]

The longer look-back period will mean that debtors who have moved between states within the two years

1 11 U.S.C. § 522(b)(3)(A).

2 11 U.S.C. § 522(b)(3). This provision is found in the last sentence of section 522(b)(3) and appears to be a separate clause that probably should have been designated as section 522(b)(3)(D).

3 *Compare In re* Drenttel, 403 F.3d 611 (8th Cir. 2005) (debtors who moved to Arizona but whose domiciliary state was Minnesota permitted to claim Minnesota homestead exemption on property purchased in Arizona); *In re* Arrol, 170 F.3d 934 (9th Cir. 1999) (debtor domiciled in California entitled to claim California homestead exemption on residence located in Michigan) *with In re* Sipka, 149 B.R. 181 (D. Kan. 1992); *In re* Ginther, 282 B.R. 16 (Bankr. D. Kan. 2002) (relying upon state court decisions holding that Kansas exemption laws do not have effect in other states, court held that debtor may not exempt Colorado property under Kansas homestead exemption).

before an anticipated bankruptcy filing may want to delay or speed up a filing, if possible, in order to maximize the debtor's available exemptions.[4] It will also require bankruptcy attorneys to become familiar with the exemption laws in states other than where they practice.[5]

8.3 New Category of Exempt Property: Retirement Funds

8.3.1 Federal Exemption for Retirement Funds

The 2005 amendments add a broad new category of property that may be claimed as exempt when the debtor claims exemptions under either the state or federal bankruptcy exemption scheme. Sections 522(b)(3)(C) and 522(d)(12) of the Bankruptcy Code permit the debtor to exempt retirement funds to the extent they are in a fund or account that is exempt from taxation under sections 401, 403, 408, 408A, 414, 457, or 501(a) of the Internal Revenue Code.[6] These sections of the Internal Revenue Code deal with pension, profit-sharing, and stock bonus plans; employee annuities; individual retirement accounts (including Roth IRAs); deferred compensation plans of state and local governments, and tax-exempt organizations; and certain trusts.

The exemption for retirement funds found in new section 522(b)(3)(C) may be claimed by the debtor even if the debtor's state has opted out of the federal exemption scheme, and may be chosen as an alternative to less generous retirement fund exemptions available under state law. In addition, as this exemption is derived under federal bankruptcy law, it preempts state laws that prohibit the exemption of retirement funds or provide less protection.

The equivalent exemption for retirement funds found in new section 522(d)(12) may be claimed if the debtor elects exemptions under the federal scheme.[7] This exemption right is apparently intended to supplement similar rights found in section 522(d)(10)(E) of the Code, because Congress did not amend section 522(d)(10) when this new category of exempt funds was added by the 2005 Act. One significant advantage of exempting retirement funds under section 522(d)(12), as compared to section 522(d)(10)(E), is that the debtor does not have to prove that such funds are necessary for the support of the debtor and the debtor's dependents.[8] However, section 522(d)(10)(E) still remains important as it permits the debtor to exempt payments from retirement plans that do not qualify for tax-exempt status under the Internal Revenue Code, subject to the exception in section 522(d)(10)(E)(i) for plans established by an insider that employed the debtor.[9]

Both section 522(b)(3)(C) and section 522(d)(12) were intended by Congress to expand the protection of certain tax-exempt retirement plans that would not otherwise be protected as property excluded from the debtor's estate under section 541(c)(2) of the Code.[10]

8.3.2 Guidelines for Exempting Retirement Funds

If the debtor's funds are in a retirement fund that has received a favorable tax determination (under section 7805 of the Internal Revenue Code), and that determination is in effect when the debtor's petition is filed, the funds are presumed to be exempt for purposes of section 522(d)(12) and section 522(b)(3)(C).[11] If such funds are in a retirement fund that has not received a favorable tax determination, they are exempt if the debtor demonstrates that:

- No prior unfavorable determination has been made by a court or the Internal Revenue Service (IRS); and

---

4 The CD-Rom accompanying this guide contains a Date Calculator program that performs the task of computing the 730 and 180 day periods, after the user types in the expected petition filing date. A detailed description of the program and twenty-one other date-sensitive pre-petition events that it can compute is set out in Appx. E.1, *infra*.

5 For a summary of state exemption laws, see National Consumer Law Center, Fair Debt Collection Appx. F (5th ed. 2004 and Supp.).

6 26 U.S.C. §§ 401, 403, 408, 408A, 414, 457, 501(a).

7 *See* 11 U.S.C. § 522(b)(2).

8 Another point of comparison relates to the scope of the exemptions. Although courts have generally held that section 522(d)(10) permits the debtor to exempt not only the right to distributions from a retirement plan but also the funds in the plan itself (see, for example, *In re* Carmichael, 100 F.3d 375 (5th Cir. 1996)), section 522(d)(12) resolves this issue by making clear that funds held in the account for future distribution are exempt. *See* National Consumer Law Center, Consumer Bankruptcy Law and Practice § 10.2.2.11 (7th ed. 2004).

9 *See* National Consumer Law Center, Consumer Bankruptcy Law and Practice § 10.2.2.11 (7th ed. 2004).

10 *See* H.R. Rep. No. 109-31, at 63–64 (2005). New section 1322(f) of the Code also provides that amounts required to repay loans from qualified pension plans shall not constitute disposable income under section 1325(b). *See* § 6.2.2.4, *supra*.

11 11 U.S.C. § 522(b)(4)(A).

- The retirement fund is either in substantial compliance with applicable IRS requirements or the debtor is not materially responsible for any failure of the retirement fund to be in substantial compliance with applicable IRS requirements.[12]

In addition, retirement funds continue to qualify for exemption under section 522(d)(12) and section 522(b)(3)(C) if they are directly transferred from a tax-exempt fund or account into another qualifying fund or account.[13] The debtor's exemption rights under these sections also continue to apply if there has been a distribution that qualifies as an eligible rollover distribution within the meaning of section 402(c) of the Internal Revenue Code, or is a distribution from a fund or account that is exempt from taxation and is deposited to the extent allowed in such fund or account not later than sixty days after the distribution.[14]

New section 522(n) of the Bankruptcy Code imposes a $1 million[15] cap on the value of an individual debtor's aggregate interest that may be exempted under either section 522(b)(3)(C) or section 522(d)(12) in IRAs established under section 408 or 408A of the Internal Revenue Code, other than a simplified employee pension account under section 408(k) or a simple retirement account under section 408(p) of the Internal Revenue Code. The limit does not apply to amounts attributable to rollover contributions, and any earnings thereon, made under sections 402(c), 402(e)(6), 403(a)(4), 403(a)(5), and 403(b)(8) of the Internal Revenue Code. Although this dollar limit is set quite high and should protect most debtors' IRAs, section 522(n) also provides that the cap may be increased "if the interests of justice so require."

8.4 New Exclusions from Property of the Debtor's Estate

In addition to the new exemption rights for retirement funds, the 2005 Act also provides that funds placed before the filing of the petition in an education individual retirement account, as defined in section 530(b)(1) of the Internal Revenue Code, and funds contributed to a tuition program, as defined in section 529(b)(1) of the Internal Revenue Code, may be excluded from property of the estate if the conditions described in section 541(b) of the Bankruptcy Code are satisfied.[16]

Certain pension or benefit contributions withheld from the debtor's wages by an employer, or received by the debtor from an employer, are also not property of the debtor's estate.[17] This provision does not distinguish between voluntary and involuntary contributions, so it appears to encompass both. The contribution must be to an Employee Retirement Income Security Act (ERISA) plan, an employee benefit plan which is a governmental plan under section 414(d) of Internal Revenue Code, a deferred compensation plan under section 457 of the Internal Revenue Code, or a tax-deferred annuity under section 403(b) of the Internal Revenue Code.[18]

8.5 Limitations on State Homestead Exemptions

8.5.1 Introduction

The 2005 Act adds three new subsections to section 522 of the Bankruptcy Code that prevent the debtor from taking full advantage of state homestead exemptions in certain circumstances. These provisions deal with the pre-petition conversion of nonexempt property with fraudulent intent (section 522(o)), the acquisition of homestead property within 1215 days of the bankruptcy filing (section 522(p)), and the commission of certain bad acts by the debtor (section 522(q)). Unlike many other provisions in the 2005 Act that have a delayed effective date, these homestead limitations took effect for cases filed on or after April 20, 2005.[19]

8.5.2 Scope of the New Restrictions

All three subsections apply only to homestead property of a kind similar to that described in section 522(d)(1) of the Code. The property interest must fall within one of the following four categories:

- Real or personal property that the debtor or a dependent of the debtor uses as a residence;
- A cooperative that owns property that the debtor or a dependent of the debtor uses as a residence;
- A burial plot for the debtor or a dependent of the debtor; or

12 11 U.S.C. § 522(b)(4)(B).
13 11 U.S.C. § 522(b)(4)(C).
14 11 U.S.C. § 522(b)(4)(D).
15 This amount will be periodically adjusted pursuant to section 104 of the Bankruptcy Code to reflect changes in the Consumer Price Index.
16 11 U.S.C. § 541(b)(5), (6).
17 11 U.S.C. § 541(b)(7).
18 11 U.S.C. § 541(b)(7)(A), (B).
19 *See* Pub. L. No. 109-8, § 1501(b), 119 Stat. 23 (2005).

- Real or personal property that the debtor or a dependent of the debtor claims as a homestead.

Subsections 522(o), (p) and (q) apply only when the debtor seeks to exempt homestead property under section 522(b)(3)(A)[20] by claiming an exemption under state law or federal law other than section 522(d). The new homestead limitations therefore do not restrict the ability of the debtor to exempt homestead property under section 522(b)(2)[21] by making use of the federal homestead exemption found in section 522(d)(1), or to exempt homestead property under section 522(b)(3)(B)[22] held as a tenant by the entirety or by joint tenancy to the extent that the interest is exempt from process under non-bankruptcy law.

It is important to note that both section 522(p) and section 522(q) use language different than what is found in section 522(o) in describing when the limitations apply. Sections 522(p) and (q), unlike section 522(o), state that the provisions apply only "as a result of electing under subsection (b)(3)(A) to exempt property under State or local law." Thus, in order to give meaning to the plain words of the phrase "as a result of electing," one court has held that section 522(p) and section 522(q) are applicable only in states which have not opted out of the federal exemption scheme, because non-opt out states are the only states where such an election is available.[23]

8.5.3 Homestead Limitation Based on Fraudulent Conversion of Nonexempt Property

Section 522(o) provides that the value of the debtor's interest in certain homestead property shall be reduced to the extent that it is attributable to any nonexempt property that the debtor disposed of within ten years before the filing of the petition with the intent to hinder, delay, or defraud a creditor. This restriction on the debtor's homestead exemption is therefore limited to the conversion of nonexempt property into exempt homestead property with fraudulent intent.

The language of section 522(o) requires the court to look at whether the converted property could be exempted "if on such date the debtor had held the property so disposed of." Because the only other date in the subsection that could be referenced by the phrase "on such date" is the "10-year period ending on the date of the filing of the petition," it is the petition date that controls the determination of whether the interest is exemptible. This interpretation also gives meaning to the remaining words in the phrase "if . . . the debtor had held the property so disposed of," as there would be no need to include this language if the relevant timeframe was the time of disposition, which is a time when the debtor would hold the property. Thus, if the property converted within the ten-year look-back period could be exempted under any applicable provision of section 522(b) at the time the petition is filed, then the debtor's exemptible interest in the homestead should not be reduced under this provision.

The statutory language also requires that the debtor intended to hinder, delay, or defraud some creditor at the time the property was disposed of. Because the language section 522(o) uses is identical to the "intent to hinder, delay or defraud a creditor" language found in section 727(a)(2) of the Code, courts may construe the required intent in a similar manner. Thus, a party in interest objecting to the debtor's homestead exemption should have to prove that the conversion of nonexempt property was done with a specific intent on the part of the debtor to defraud a creditor, and this intent must involve actual rather than constructive intent.[24]

Another question raised by the provision is whether section 522(o) would be applicable if no creditor who may have been hindered, delayed, or defrauded is a "creditor" of the debtor at the time the petition is filed. Because "creditor" is defined in section 101(10) of the Code as an entity that has a claim against the debtor or the debtor's estate, a trustee or other party in interest should not prevail on an exemption objection under section 522(o) if the debts of the defrauded creditors have been satisfied pre-petition. This interpretation is consistent with the apparent purpose of the provision, which is to protect the ability of defrauded creditors to recover on their claims.

Prior to the enactment of the 2005 amendments, courts had uniformly held that the scope of an exemption created under state law and claimed in a bankruptcy proceeding was determined by state law.[25] This rule of interpretation meant that, depending upon the applicable

20 Prior to the 2005 amendments, the right to claim exemptions under state law or non-bankruptcy federal law was provided for in section 522(b)(2)(A).

21 11 U.S.C. § 522(b)(2) (formerly designated as section 522(b)(1)).

22 11 U.S.C. § 522(b)(3)(B) (formerly designated as section 522(b)(2)(B)).

23 *In re* McNabb, 326 B.R. 785 (Bankr. D. Ariz. 2005).

24 *See* National Consumer Law Center, Consumer Bankruptcy Law and Practice § 14.2.2.2 (7th ed. 2004).

25 *E.g.*, *In re* Johnson, 880 F.2d 78 (8th Cir. 1989).

state law, the issue of conversion with fraudulent intent could not be asserted in some bankruptcy cases. For example, the Florida Supreme Court concluded, on a question certified to it by the Eleventh Circuit in a bankruptcy case,[26] that conversion of nonexempt assets into an exempt homestead with the intent to hinder, delay, or defraud creditors does not defeat the unlimited Florida homestead exemption because such a transfer is not an exception provided for in the Florida Constitution.[27] New section 522(o) overrules the outcome in the Florida *Havoco* case and permits the issue of fraudulent conversion to be raised despite contrary state law.

8.5.4 Cap on Homestead Property Acquired During 1215-Day Period Before Filing

Under new section 522(p)(1), the debtor may not exempt "any amount of interest that was acquired" in homestead property by the debtor during the 1215-day period before the filing of the petition which exceeds the amount of $125,000.[28] The monetary cap imposed by section 522(p)(1) does not apply to any interest transferred from a debtor's previous principal residence to the debtor's current principal residence, if the debtor's previous residence was acquired before the 1215-day period and both the previous and current residences are located in the same state.[29] In addition, the limitation does not apply to an exemption claimed on a principal residence by a family farmer.[30]

A significant question to be decided by the courts will be how the phrase "interest that was acquired" should be interpreted. Given that the apparent legislative intent for enacting section 522(p) was to discourage pre-bankruptcy exemption planning in which some debtors have taken advantage of unlimited or substantial homestead exemption laws, it would seem that the phrase should be construed as applying to homestead property interests that the debtor gains though her own affirmative actions or efforts. Under this view, section 522(p) should not apply to an interest attributable solely to an increase in the market value of the debtor's homestead during the 1215-day period, because that is not an interest "acquired" by the debtor, but rather an increase in the value of the debtor's existing interest. Similarly, this provision should not prevent the debtor from claiming as exempt an interest in a homestead property resulting from the application of mortgage payments, unless the debtor makes unscheduled, lump-sum payments that reduce the principal during the 1215-day period by more than $125,000.

26 Havoco of Am., Ltd. v. Hill, 255 F.3d 1321 (11th Cir. 2001)

27 Havoco of Am., Ltd. v. Hill, 790 So. 2d 1018 (Fla. 2001).

28 This amount will be periodically adjusted pursuant to section 104 of the Bankruptcy Code to reflect changes in the Consumer Price Index.

29 11 U.S.C. § 522(p)(2)(B).

30 11 U.S.C. § 522(p)(2)(A).

8.5.5 Homestead Cap Based on Certain Criminal or Wrongful Conduct

8.5.5.1 Introduction

The final new restriction on homestead exemptions imposed by the 2005 Act applies to debtors who have been convicted of felonies or who owe debts arising from certain unlawful conduct.[31]

8.5.5.2 Felony Conviction

The debtor may not exempt an interest in homestead property that exceeds $125,000 if the debtor has been convicted of certain criminal conduct. Under new section 522(q)(1)(A) of the Code, the cap would apply if the court determines, after notice and a hearing on an objection to the exemption, that the debtor has been convicted of a felony (as defined by 18 U.S.C. § 3156),[32] "which under the circumstances, demonstrates that the filing of the case was an abuse" of the bankruptcy provisions. Based on the language of the provision, the felony conviction must occur prior to the filing of the petition, and any criminal activity of the debtor that takes place post-petition, such as during the three to five year pendency of a chapter 13 case, can not provide the basis for an objection to a homestead exemption under section 522(q)(1)(A).

Although the statutory language is not clear, it would seem that the objecting party would need to prove a connection between the felony conviction and the bankruptcy filing such that the filing would be deemed an abuse. This connection might be shown with proof that the debtor is attempting discharge a civil liability owing to victims of the crime, or that the bankruptcy filing may affect the debtor's obligation to pay restitution related to the felony.

31 11 U.S.C. § 522(q)(1).

32 The term "felony" is defined as an "offense punishable by a maximum term of imprisonment of more than one year." 18 U.S.C. § 3156.

8.5.5.3 Debts Arising from Certain Wrongful Conduct

A $125,000 cap on the debtor's exemptible homestead interest may also be invoked under new section 522(q)(1)(B) if the debtor owes a debt arising from certain wrongful conduct. The debt must arise from one of the four specified categories:

- Any violation of state or federal securities laws (as defined in section 3(a)(47) of the Securities Exchange Act)[33] or any regulation or order issued under state or federal securities laws;
- Fraud, deceit, or manipulation in a fiduciary capacity or in connection with the purchase or sale of any security registered under section 12 or 15(d) of the Securities Exchange Act of 1934 or under section 6 of the Securities Act of 1933;
- Any civil remedy under the Racketeer Influenced and Corrupt Organizations (RICO) Act[34]; or
- Any criminal act, intentional tort, or willful or reckless misconduct that caused serious physical injury or death to another individual in the preceding five years.

8.5.5.4 Standing to Bring Exemption Objection

Section 522(q)(1) does not specify who has standing to initiate a proceeding under the subsection, so presumably it would include any party in interest who timely files an objection to the debtor's exemption based on the procedures in Federal Rule of Bankruptcy Procedure 4003(b) and (c).[35] However, a creditor or other party having no direct involvement in the felony conviction may have a difficult time proving that the bankruptcy filing was an "abuse," particularly if the crime victim has not objected to the debtor's exemption claim. In fact, a crime victim who has a related civil judgment or claim against the debtor may oppose an objection to the debtor's homestead exemption, preferring instead to pursue a nondischargeability action.[36] Similar standing and proof problems might exist if a party other than the creditor who is owed a debt listed in section 522(q)(1)(B) asserts an exemption objection, particularly if the debt is unliquidated and the debtor offers defenses to owing the debt.

A related question is whether a court has jurisdiction in chapter 13 cases, before the completion of the plan, to adjudicate an exemption objection based on a debt owing under section 522(q)(1)(B), if the debtor is proposing to pay the debt in full as part of the chapter 13 plan.[37] This could create problems for courts which follow the majority view that the time to object to a claimed exemption under Federal Rule of Bankruptcy Procedure 4003(b) does not recommence if a chapter 13 case is converted to a chapter 7 case.[38] The suggested interim rules avoid this issue by providing in revised Rule 4003(b)(2) that an objection to a claim of exemption based on section 522(q) may be filed at any time before the closing of the case.[39]

8.5.5.5 No Cap If Homestead Reasonably Necessary for Support

Section 522(q)(2) provides that the $125,000 limit contained in section 522(q)(1) shall not apply to the extent that the amount of any interest in homestead property is reasonably necessary for the support of the debtor and any dependent of the debtor.[40] This exception would permit the court to deny application of the $125,000 cap on the debtor's exemptible interest based on a reasonably necessary test similar to that found in other subsections of section 522,[41] and other sections of

33 The term "securities laws" means the Securities Act of 1933 (15 U.S.C. §§ 77a *et seq.*), Securities Exchange Act of 1934 (15 U.S.C. §§ 78a *et seq.*), Sarbanes-Oxley Act of 2002, Public Utility Holding Company Act of 1935 (15 U.S.C. §§ 79a *et seq.*), Trust Indenture Act of 1939 (15 U.S.C. §§ 77aaa *et seq.*), Investment Company Act of 1940 (15 U.S.C. §§ 80a-1 *et seq.*), Investment Advisers Act of 1940 (15 U.S.C. §§ 80b-1 *et seq.*), and the Securities Investor Protection Act of 1970 (15 U.S.C. §§ 78aaa *et seq.*). *See* 15 U.S.C. § 78c(a)(47).

34 *See* 18 U.S.C. § 1964.

35 *See* Interim Bankruptcy Rule 4003(b)(2) (reprinted in Appx. B, *infra*).

36 The crime victim might prefer that the debtor keep her homestead, even though it is protected from seizure under section 522(c), so as to leave the debtor in a better financial position to satisfy the nondischargeable debt.

37 *See, e.g., In re* Campbell, 313 B.R. 313 (B.A.P. 10th Cir. 2004).

38 *See, e.g., In re* Rogers, 278 B.R. 201 (Bankr. D. Nev. 2002); *In re* Ferretti, 230 B.R. 883 (Bankr. S.D. Fla. 1999), *aff'd sub nom.* Dibraccio v. Ferretti, 268 F.3d 1065 (11th Cir. 2001) (table); *see also In re* Bell, 225 F.3d 203 (2d Cir. 2000) (conversion from chapter 11 to chapter 7). *But see In re* Campbell, 313 B.R. 313 (B.A.P. 10th Cir. 2004).

39 *See* Interim Bankruptcy Rule 4003(b)(2) (reprinted in Appx. B, *infra*).

40 Section 522(a)(1) defines "dependent" as including the debtor's spouse, whether or not actually dependent. This definition is ordinarily not relevant to the application of state exemption laws. However, it should apply in any consideration of whether section 522(q)(2) prevents the application of the $125,000 cap on a state homestead exemption.

41 *E.g.*, 11 U.S.C. § 522(d)(10), (11).

the Code.[42] For no apparent reason this exemption from the homestead cap may be asserted by the debtor only in response to an objection to a claim of exemption based on section 522(q) and not to an objection based on section 522(p). Congress was apparently more sympathetic to a debtor who commits securities fraud or criminal acts causing serious personal injury than to a debtor who may have innocently acquired homestead property within 1215 days of filing the petition.[43]

Based on court interpretations of identical language found in other provisions of section 522 (such as section 522(d)(10)) a determination as to whether the homestead interest in question is reasonably necessary would require the court to consider the debtor's (and dependents') age, health, earning capacity, present and future financial needs and ability, other assets, future financial obligations such as alimony and child support, and any special needs of the debtor and dependents.[44] In the context of the debtor's potential loss of homestead property if the monetary cap were applied, the debtor may wish to present additional evidence on matters such as any potential difficulty the debtor may have in finding suitable and affordable replacement housing, the length of time the debtor has lived in the community, the costs of relocation, the safety of the debtor's current neighborhood as compared to potential replacement housing, and the impact relocation may have on the debtor's future income and the education of the debtor's children.

8.5.5.6 Delay of Discharge

The 2005 Act adds new subsections 727(a)(12), 1141(d)(5)(C), 1228(f) and 1328(h) to the Code, which provide that the entry of the debtor's discharge in a chapter 7, 11, 12 or 13 case respectively may be delayed pending the outcome of any criminal and civil proceedings against the debtor referred to in section 522(q)(1). If a motion to delay or postpone discharge is filed under these sections,[45] and after notice and a hearing held ten days before the date that discharge would otherwise enter, the court shall not grant the discharge if it finds that there is reasonable cause to believe that (1) section 522(q)(1) may be applicable, and (2) there is a pending proceeding in which the debtor may be found guilty of a felony described in section 522(q)(1)(A) or liable for a debt described in section 522(q)(1)(B). These provisions are not intended to provide grounds for the denial of a discharge, but simply to provide a procedural mechanism for delaying the entry of discharge until the events that could trigger a potential exemption objection under section 522(q) are resolved.[46]

These delay of discharge provisions only come into play if section 522(q)(1) is applicable, so a debtor's discharge may not be delayed if the debtor is not claiming homestead property as exempt, the debtor does not claim a homestead interest in excess of $125,000 as exempt, or the debtor is claiming homestead property as exempt under section 522(b)(2) or (b)(3)(B).[47] In addition, there shall be no delay of discharge if the potential felony conviction did not cause the debtor's bankruptcy filing to be abusive, the debt alleged to be owed is not of the type described in section 522(q)(1), or the homestead property is reasonably necessary for the support of the debtor and any dependent of the debtor.[48]

The second condition requires the court, if a motion to delay is filed, to have reasonable cause to believe that one of the identified types of proceedings is pending against the debtor and that the debtor may be found guilty or liable in such proceeding. The debtor should therefore have the right to be heard on any claims or defenses asserted in the proceeding that would establish that the debtor may not be guilty or liable. However, to avoid the possibility of the debtor making self-incriminating statements, such a defense would not likely occur if a criminal proceeding is pending. Moreover, even as to a pending civil matter, the bankruptcy court may prefer to abstain and permit the court in which the proceeding is pending to determine the underlying debt. In such a case the entry of the debtor's discharge will be delayed until resolution of the criminal or civil proceeding.

A problem with the drafting of these new delay in discharge provisions is that they conflict with the language used in section 522(q) with regards to a criminal conviction. Section 522(q)(1)(A) provides that the homestead cap may apply if "the debtor *has been convicted* of

42 *E.g.*, 11 U.S.C. § 1325(b)(2)(A).

43 *See* § 8.5.4, *supra*.

44 *See, e.g.*, *In re* Cramer, 281 B.R. 193 (Bankr. E.D. Pa. 2002); *In re* Mann, 201 B.R. 910 (Bankr. E.D. Mich. 1996); *see also* National Consumer Law Center, Consumer Bankruptcy Law and Practice § 12.3.3 (7th ed. 2004).

45 *See* Interim Rule Bankruptcy Rule 4004(I) (reprinted in Appx. B, *infra*).

46 These provisions originate in section 330 of S.256, which is entitled: "Delay of Discharge During Pendency of Certain Proceedings." Presumably Congress sought to include these provisions because of the implications under section 522(c) that the entry of a discharge would have if the discharge occurred before a section 522(q) exemption objection was resolved.

47 *See* § 8.5.2, *supra*.

48 *See* §§ 8.5.5.2, 8.5.5.3, 8.5.5.5, *supra*.

a felony." Because exemptions are determined as of the date the petition is filed,[49] this language should mean that no objection may be brought under section 522(q) if the debtor has not been convicted of a felony prior to the filing of the petition. However the delay in discharge provisions, as in section 727(a)(12) for example, provide that the discharge may be delayed if there is a pending proceeding in which "the debtor *may be found guilty* of a felony," suggesting that the conviction could occur post-petition. Given the conflict between these provisions, and because section 522(q) is the more specific provision which controls a debtor's substantive rights under the Code relating to exemptions, rather than procedural matters relating to the timing of the entry of discharge, section 522(q) probably should control. Thus, the discharge should not be delayed if the debtor had not been convicted of a felony prior to the filing of the petition.

The new potential barrier to the granting of a discharge under these provisions could mean that some debtors will have to wait months or even years before their bankruptcy cases are concluded and they get a discharge. This result is particularly troublesome in chapter 7 cases in which debtors ordinarily are granted a discharge approximately three to four months after the filing of the petition. The delay could place some debtors in an extended period of uncertainty about their financial situation, during which time they will be effectively locked out the financial marketplace and denied a fresh start. While courts are generally not inclined to grant a motion for voluntary dismissal of a chapter 7 case in response to an exemption objection, courts may be more willing to do so under these circumstances.

8.5.6 Application of Homestead Caps in Joint Cases

If the homestead cap under section 522(p) (for property acquired within the 1215-day period before filing) or section 522(q) (for certain criminal or wrongful conduct) is imposed, it is applicable to interests that exceed "in the aggregate" $125,000 in value in homestead property. The use of the word "aggregate" in referring to the debtor's interest, consistent with its application in other subsections (such as section 522(d)(6)[50]) suggests that Congress intended the dollar limit to be applied to the combined interests of the debtor in the various forms of property listed in subsections 522(p)(1)(A) through (D). It is not intended to impose an overall $125,000 cap on the amount both debtors in a joint case may exempt in a homestead under a state exemption law. This construction is supported by the fact that the 2005 Act did not amend section 522(m) of the Code, which states that section 522 applies separately with respect to each debtor in a joint case.

Thus, the dollar limit in section 522(p) or (q), if applicable, should apply separately to each debtor's homestead interest and exemption claim. Section 522(p) or (q), if applicable, will not prevent each debtor in a joint case from claiming as exempt a homestead interest up to the amount of $125,000. For example, if the cap under section 522(q) were imposed in a joint case as to each debtor's homestead interest, the debtors could claim as exempt their total interest in homestead property up to the amount of $250,000 or, if less, the amount state law provides that the joint debtors may exempt in homestead property.

In addition, the dollar limit in sections 522(p) or (q) would not apply to both debtors' homestead interests in a joint case if only one of the debtors has been convicted of a felony or is liable on a debt specified in section 522(q)(1)(B).

8.6 Lien Avoidance on Household Goods

The debtor may avoid certain nonpossessory, nonpurchase-money security interests in exempt household furnishings, household goods, wearing apparel, appliances, books, animals, crops, musical instruments or jewelry that are held primarily for the personal, family, or household use of the debtor or a dependent of a debtor.[51] Prior to the 2005 amendments, the Bankruptcy Code did not define "household goods" for purposes of section 522(f) lien avoidance, though most courts held that that it included certain basic items of personal property "kept in or around the home and used to facilitate the day to day living of the debtor and the debtor's dependents."[52] Courts often rejected application of the restrictive defi-

49 *E.g.*, Lowe v. Sandoval (*In re* Sandoval), 103 F.3d 20 (5th Cir. 1997).

50 Section 522(d)(6) provides that a debtor who elects federal exemptions may exempt "[t]he debtor's aggregate interest, not to exceed $1500 in value, in any implements, professional books, or tools, of the trade of the debtor or the trade of a dependent of the debtor." 11 U.S.C. § 522(d)(6).

51 11 U.S.C. § 522(f)(1)(B)(i); *see also* National Consumer Law Center, Consumer Bankruptcy Law and Practice § 10.4.2.4 (7th ed. 2004).

52 *See, e.g.*, *In re* McGreevy, 955 F.2d 957, 960 (4th Cir. 1992).

nition of household goods found in the Federal Trade Commission's Credit Practices Rule.[53]

New section 522(f)(4) of the Code adds a narrow definition of "household goods," similar to that found in the FTC Rule, which is applicable in section 522(f)(1) lien avoidance proceedings. Section 522(f)(4)(A) provides that the term "household goods" means:

- Clothing;
- Furniture;
- Appliances;
- One radio;
- One television;
- One VCR;
- Linens;
- China, crockery, and kitchenware;
- Educational materials and educational equipment primarily for the use of minor dependent children of the debtor;
- Medical equipment and supplies;
- Furniture exclusively for the use of minor children, or elderly or disabled dependents of the debtor;
- Personal effects (including the toys and hobby equipment of minor dependent children and wedding rings) of the debtor and the dependents of the debtor; and
- One personal computer and related equipment.

Section 522(f)(4)(B) provides that the term "household goods" does not include:

- Works of art (unless by or of the debtor, or any relative of the debtor);
- Electronic entertainment equipment with a fair market value of more than $500 in the aggregate (except one television, one radio, and one VCR);
- Items acquired as antiques with a fair market value of more than $500 in the aggregate;[54]
- Jewelry with a fair market value of more than $500 in the aggregate (except wedding rings); and
- A computer (except as provided for in section 522(f)(4)(A)), motor vehicle (including a tractor or lawn tractor), boat, or a motorized recreational device, conveyance, vehicle, watercraft, or aircraft.

53 16 C.F.R. § 444.1(i); *see In re* Reid, 121 B.R. 875 (Bankr. D.N.M. 1990).

54 The wording of this provision would appear not to include items that become an antique after being acquired by the debtor.

One problem with the dollar limits used in this subsection is that finance companies which make loans secured by personal property often have consumers sign a personal property list that includes inflated values. While such lenders often currently engage in this practice to support the charging of higher premiums on personal property insurance sold in connection with these loans, they will now have another reason to do so.

Like many provisions of the 2005 Act that were drafted years ago when the first bankruptcy "reform" bill was introduced, and which were not amended or updated prior to passage, this subsection refers to a VCR even though many consumers have replaced this item with a DVD player. Of course, this highlights the problem of having a laundry list of items in a statutory provision as that list will inevitably become obsolete. Hopefully, courts will expand the list to include reasonable substitutes for the listed items.

However, the new definition should not pose much of a problem because no other changes were made to section 522(f)(1)(B). Some of the categories of items that continue to be listed in section 522(f)(1)(B) are broad and provide for overlapping coverage. To the extent that an item is excluded from the household goods category based on the definition in section 522(f)(4), the debtor should still be able to avoid a nonpossessory, nonpurchase-money lien on the item if it falls within another category listed in section 522(f)(1)(B), such as "appliances" or "household furnishings."

8.7 Other Exemption Provisions

The 2005 Act expands the exception to the judicial lien avoidance power in section 522(f)(1)(A) of the Code for domestic support obligations, and amends section 522(c)(1) of the Code by providing that a domestic support creditor may proceed against exempt property even if such action would be prohibited under state law. These provisions are discussed in Chapter 9, *infra*.[55]

55 *See* § 9.6, *infra*.

Chapter 9

Domestic Support Obligations

9.1 Definition of Domestic Support Obligation

The 2005 Act provides a new definition in section 101(14A) of the Bankruptcy Code for "domestic support obligation" that encompasses what was considered alimony, maintenance, or support under former section 523(a)(5), but is broader in several respects. The definition includes both pre-petition and post-petition obligations, and it includes interest that accrues on a debt under applicable non-bankruptcy law, "notwithstanding any other provision of this title."[1] It also includes obligations owed to or recoverable by a spouse, former spouse, or child of the debtor, by a child's parent, legal guardian, or responsible relative, or by a governmental unit. Also included in the definition are obligations established or subject to establishment before, on, or after the date of the order for relief, and obligations assigned to non-governmental units if voluntarily assigned for purposes of collection.

9.2 Priority of Domestic Support Obligations

All domestic support obligations are now "first" priority under section 507(a)(1) of the Code. However, within the category of domestic support obligations, those owed to a spouse, former spouse, child of debtor, or child's parent, legal guardian or responsible relative, or recoverable by a governmental unit on their behalf, are first among the first priority debts.[2]

Second among the first priority debts are those domestic support obligations assigned to a governmental unit (other than for purposes of collection) or owed directly to a governmental unit under applicable non-bankruptcy law.[3] And given higher priority than each of these categories are the administrative expenses of a trustee to administer the assets for such claims.[4] The biggest change made by these amendments is that support obligations owed or assigned to governmental units are now priority debts.

9.3 Changes in Chapter 13

Section 1307(c) of the Bankruptcy Code is amended to make the failure to pay post-petition support a grounds for dismissal. In addition, new section 1322(a)(4) of the Code provides that, although support owed to the government is now a priority debt, it need not be paid in full if the debtor proposes a five-year plan committing all the debtor's disposable income and the debtor can not pay the support obligation in full. This provision is intended to prevent large government support debts from making a mortgage cure and other chapter 13 remedies unavailable. Unpaid support will, of course, not be discharged, as is true under existing law.[5] The fact that support owed to the government is now a priority debt should make clear that it can be separately classified and paid before general unsecured debts.[6]

New section 1325(a)(8) of the Code makes payment of post-petition support one of the standards for chapter 13 plan confirmation. Section 1328(a) of the Code likewise is amended to require a debtor, in order to obtain a discharge, to certify that all post-petition support and all support required to be paid by the plan has been paid. However, this certification is not required for a hardship discharge.[7] Debtors who can not make the certification or obtain a hardship discharge may have to convert to chapter 7. The net result of all these amendments is to give domestic support creditors much more power in chapter 13 cases, and the ability to scuttle the plan if they are not paid.

---

1 11 U.S.C. § 101(14A).
2 11 U.S.C. § 507(a)(1)(A).
3 11 U.S.C. § 507(a)(1)(B).
4 11 U.S.C. § 507(a)(1)(C).
5 11 U.S.C. § 523(a)(5); *see* National Consumer Law Center, Consumer Bankruptcy Law and Practice § 14.4.3.5 (7th ed. 2004).
6 *See* National Consumer Law Center, Consumer Bankruptcy Law and Practice § 12.4.3 (7th ed. 2004).
7 *See* 11 U.S.C. § 1328(b).

9.4 Automatic Stay Changes

The 2005 Act adds new exceptions to the automatic stay provisions for proceedings concerning child custody, visitation rights, domestic violence, and divorce (to the extent the divorce proceeding does not seek to divide property of the estate).[8] These exceptions are commonsense corrections for proceedings that do not have an impact on bankruptcy. Many people had probably assumed they were not stayed, though in fact they usually were, as legal proceedings that could have been commenced prior to petition. There will be fewer void divorces and technically bigamous marriages.

Section 362(b)(2) of the Code was also amended to provide an exception to the stay for the commencement or continuation of a proceeding with respect to the withholding of income from property of the estate or property of the debtor for payment of a domestic support obligation.[9] In addition, the following methods of enforcement of support obligations authorized under the Social Security Act or comparable state laws are now excepted from the stay:

- The withholding, suspension, or restriction under state law of a driver's license, a professional or occupational license, or a recreational license, as provided in 42 U.S.C. § 666(a)(16);
- The reporting of overdue support owed by a parent to any consumer reporting agency, as provided in 42 U.S.C. § 666(a)(7):
- The interception of tax refunds, as provided in 42 U.S.C. §§ 664 and 666(a)(3), or under analogous state law; and
- The enforcement of medical obligations, as provided in 42 U.S.C. §§ 601–687.[10]

These new provisions largely give support creditors the ability to ignore the automatic stay and render the bankruptcy court process subservient to proceedings concerning support in the state courts. However, a support creditor remains bound by a confirmed plan, at least as long as current support is being paid and the debtor is performing under the plan.[11] Even then, a support creditor may, as under former law, seek to modify current support. But presumably, the support creditor could not seek to collect additional monies for past support by an income withholding or tax intercept.

8 11 U.S.C. § 362(b)(2).

9 11 U.S.C. § 362(b)(2)(C).

10 11 U.S.C. § 362(b)(2)(D), (E), (F), (G).

11 *See* National Consumer Law Center, Consumer Bankruptcy Law and Practice § 12.11 (7th ed. 2004).

9.5 Dischargeability Changes

Section 523(a)(5) of the Code now makes all domestic support obligations nondischargeable in all chapters. But, with the prior enactment of amendments to the Social Security Act and section 523(a)(18) of the Code, this result had been pretty much accomplished under prior law.[12] Section 523(a)(18) was deleted by the 2005 amendments as no longer necessary.

In addition, all property settlement debts owed to a spouse, former spouse, or child of the debtor are made nondischargeable in chapter 7.[13] The ability to pay and balancing tests[14] are eliminated from section 523(a)(15) of the Code. Section 523(c) of the Code is amended to no longer require that a dischargeability proceeding involving a property settlement be brought in the bankruptcy court. These debts remain dischargeable in chapter 13.[15] The result in most cases will be to saddle debtors with debts they can not afford to pay with no benefit to the non-debtor spouse. Because there may be advantages to having greater priority debts in chapter 7 for purposes of the means test,[16] or to assist a former spouse in chapter 13 by paying hold harmless debts, debtors in some cases may have an incentive to argue that debts labeled as property settlement are actually for the purpose of support.

9.6 Exemption Changes

Section 522(c)(1) of the Bankruptcy Code is amended to allow domestic support creditors to proceed against exempt property, including property exempted under state law. This amendment overrules the result in *In re Davis*,[17] which held that filing a bankruptcy case did not render property covered by a Texas homestead declaration liable for support debts it would not have been liable for outside of bankruptcy. This change means that a debtor filing a bankruptcy case who owes support debts will subject property exempt from such debts under state law to possible execution.

12 *See* National Consumer Law Center, Consumer Bankruptcy Law and Practice §§ 14.4.3.5, 14.4.3.17 (7th ed. 2004).

13 11 U.S.C. § 523(a)(15).

14 *See* National Consumer Law Center, Consumer Bankruptcy Law and Practice §§ 14.4.3.5, 14.4.3.14 (7th ed. 2004).

15 *See* § 10.1.7, *infra*.

16 *See* § 2.3.3.3, *supra*.

17 170 F.3d 475 (5th Cir. 1999) (en banc).

Section 522(f) of the Code is amended to prevent avoidance of a judicial lien for domestic support obligations.[18] The main effect of this change is to include debts assigned or owed to the government among those protected from lien avoidance.[19] The amendment also corrects a drafting error in prior language.

9.7 Preference Change

Section 547 of the Code is amended to protect all bona fide payments on domestic support obligations from preference avoidance.[20] The main effect of this amendment, based on the definition of a domestic support obligation in section 101(14A), is to add protection for payments on obligations assigned or owed to governments.

9.8 New Trustee Duties

Trustees in every chapter must now give notice to holders of domestic support obligations of the services provided by the state child support enforcement agency and the right to use such agency's services to collect child support during and after the bankruptcy case.[21] Trustees must also send notice of the claim to the state child support enforcement agency, which presumably could be combined with the notice to the holder of the claim.[22]

Another notice must be sent to the holder of the claim and the state child support enforcement agency when a discharge is granted.[23] This notice must contain the last known address of the debtor and the debtor's employer. It must also contain the name of each creditor holding a claim that was not discharged under section 523(a)(2), (4), or (14A) of the Code, or that was reaffirmed under section 524(c) of the Code. A potential problem, though, is that the trustee may not have this information at the time of discharge.

Domestic support creditors may also request that a creditor disclose the debtor's last known address.[24] There is no requirement that the creditor answer the request. If a creditor does answer, the creditor is protected from liability for the disclosure.

18 11 U.S.C. § 522(f)(1)(A).

19 The 1994 amendments to former section 522(f)(1)(A)(ii)(I) permitted the debtor to avoid a lien that secured a debt for alimony, maintenance, and support if the debt had been assigned to another entity. *See* National Consumer Law Center, Consumer Bankruptcy Law and Practice § 10.4.2.3.2 (7th ed. 2004).

20 11 U.S.C. § 547(c)(7).

21 *See* 11 U.S.C. §§ 704(c)(1), 1106((c)(1), 1202(c)(1), 1302(d)(1).

22 *See* 11 U.S.C. §§ 704(c)(1), 1106((c)(1), 1202(c)(1), 1302(d)(1).

23 *See* 11 U.S.C. §§ 704(c)(1), 1106((c)(1), 1202(c)(1), 1302(d)(1).

24 *See* 11 U.S.C. §§ 704(c)(1), 1106((c)(1), 1202(c)(1), 1302(d)(1).

Chapter 10 Discharge Provisions

10.1 Changes to Nondischargeability Provisions in Section 523(a)

10.1.1 Taxes—Section 523(a)(1)

A discharge is now barred if a tax return *or an equivalent report or notice* is not filed *or given* during the two years prior to the filing of the petition.[1] This new language may broaden nondischargeability to situations in which the debtor was required to give a notice to a taxing authority, such as perhaps after some event giving rise to tax liability.

This provision may have been an attempt to overrule the result in *In re Jackson*,[2] which held that a required report to a state after the Internal Revenue Service (IRS) reassessed taxes was not a "return" that restarted the two-year period. However, it is not clear that the new language accomplishes this result. The *Jackson* decision was based not only on the holding that a "return" did not mean a "report," but also on the principle that once a debtor has filed a return for a particular year, that person has satisfied the requirement of filing a return. The court quoted an earlier decision: "Once a debtor has filed 'a return' for a tax which is 'required' to be so reported that provision [section 523(a)(1)(B)(i)] has been met. . . . Once a requirement has been satisfied, it does not become 'unsatisfied' because some new requirement has been superadded."[3]

A paragraph added at the end of section 523(a) of the Bankruptcy Code defines "return" as "a return that satisfies the requirements of applicable non-bankruptcy law (including applicable filing requirements)," and includes returns filed under Internal Revenue Code section 6020(a) or equivalent state or local law, or stipulated judgments or orders, but does not include returns made pursuant to Internal Revenue Code section 6020(b) (service-filed returns) or equivalent state or local law. Returns filed under Internal Revenue Code section 6020(a) are generally prepared by the taxing authority with the debtor's assistance based on information and documentation provided by the debtor, whereas a return filed under Internal Revenue Code section 6020(b) is not done with the debtor's cooperation and is based on information the taxing authority has obtained on its own. This definition generally codifies the law that when a debtor participates in or signs off on a return, it is considered a return, but when the debtor does not participate in the taxing authority's creation of a return, it is not.[4]

The language requiring a return to satisfy "applicable filing requirements" could be troublesome. What requirements are included? If timeliness were included, it would render the timeliness language in section 523(a)(1)(B)(ii) superfluous.

10.1.2 Debts Incurred Through Fraud or False Pretenses—Section 523(a)(2)

The 2005 amendments change the time periods and amounts for the presumption of fraud relating to debts incurred through fraud or false pretenses under section 523(a)(2) of the Code.[5] For "luxury goods or services," a debt is presumed fraudulent if $500 is incurred to a single creditor within ninety days before bankruptcy.[6] For cash advances on an open-end credit plan, fraud is presumed if $750 is taken within seventy days before bankruptcy.[7]

The luxury goods and services definition is changed by replacing the words "reasonably acquired" with "reasonably necessary," so that the definition now reads that "luxury goods and services" do not include goods or services reasonably necessary for the support or mainte-

1 11 U.S.C. § 523(a)(1)(B); *see also* National Consumer Law Center, Consumer Bankruptcy Law and Practice § 14.4.3.1.1 (7th ed. 2004).

2 184 F.3d 1046 (9th Cir. 1999).

3 *In re* Dyer, 158 B.R. 904, 906 (Bankr. W.D.N.Y. 1993).

4 *See also* National Consumer Law Center, Consumer Bankruptcy Law and Practice § 14.4.3.1.1 (7th ed. 2004).

5 *See* National Consumer Law Center, Consumer Bankruptcy Law and Practice § 14.4.32.3.2 (7th ed. 2004).

6 11 U.S.C. § 523(a)(2)(C)(i)(I).

7 11 U.S.C. § 523(a)(2)(C)(i)(II).

nance of the debtor or a dependent of the debtor.[8] It could be argued that this change may benefit debtors in some cases. "Reasonably acquired" may have contemplated whether the debtor had an expectation of repayment when the debt was incurred, while "reasonably necessary" does not. It is not likely that this change will have much effect, however, in that courts will probably continue to determine what goods and services are "luxuries" without reliance upon the statutory definition.

Another minor change to the definition should not have any effect on the provision's interpretation. This change makes clear that the terms "consumer," "credit," and "open end credit plan" as used in section 523(a)(2)(C) have the same meaning as those terms have under section 103 of the Truth in Lending Act.[9] Prior to this amendment, the subsection stated that these terms were defined as under the Consumer Credit Protection Act.

10.1.3 Domestic Support Obligations—Section 523(a)(5) and 523(a)(18)

The 2005 amendments to section 523(a)(5) and 523(a)(18) of the Code are discussed in Chapter 9, *supra.* A new definition in section 101(14A) of the Code is provided for a "domestic support obligation," which encompasses what was considered alimony, maintenance, or support under former section 523(a)(5), but is broader in several respects.[10] Section 523(a)(5) now makes all domestic support obligations nondischargeable in all chapters of the Code. Section 523(a)(18) is deleted as no longer necessary.

10.1.4 Student Loans—Section 523(a)(8)

Although the general principle that student loans are nondischargeable unless the borrower can prove undue hardship remains unchanged, the 2005 Act expands the category of debts that may be excepted from discharge as student loans to include loans from for-profit lenders if they are qualified education loans as defined in section 221(d)(1) of the Internal Revenue Code.[11] The term "qualified education loan" is defined in section 221(d)(1) of the Internal Revenue Code to mean any indebtedness incurred by the taxpayer *solely* to pay qualified higher education expenses.[12] Debtors who have incurred debt for education and other purposes may argue the debt was not incurred solely to pay higher education expenses and therefore is not subject to the nondischargeability provision of section 523(a)(8) of the Bankruptcy Code.

The Internal Revenue Code also provides that the qualified higher education expenses must also be incurred on behalf of the taxpayer, the taxpayer's spouse, or any dependent of the taxpayer, and must be paid or incurred within a reasonable period of time before or after the indebtedness is incurred and attributable to education furnished during a period when the recipient was an eligible student.[13]

Thus, in order to be considered a qualified education loan, the loan must be incurred to pay expenses for education furnished during a period when the recipient was an eligible student.[14] There are circumstances in which a student may take out a loan to attend school, but not necessarily be an eligible student. For example, aggressive proprietary schools in some cases enroll non-high-school graduates without properly administering the required "ability to benefit test."[15] Student debtors improperly enrolled in this way are eligible for a cancellation of their loans and should also be categorized as "ineligible" students for purposes of whether the loan was a qualified education loan under section 523(a)(8).

In addition, a loan is a "qualified education loan" only if it is incurred solely to pay qualified higher education expenses. The term "qualified higher education expenses" means items and services considered to be "the cost of attendance," which is broadly defined in section 472 of the Higher Education Act.[16] If an indebtedness was incurred for any purpose other than for such expenses, it is not within the exception. Nondischargeabil-

8 11 U.S.C. § 523(a)(2)(C)(ii)(II).

9 15 U.S.C. § 1602; *see also* National Consumer Law Center, Truth in Lending Chs. 2, 5 (5th ed. 2003 and Supp.).

10 *See* § 9.1, *supra.*

11 11 U.S.C. § 523(a)(8).

12 26 U.S.C. § 221(d).

13 26 U.S.C. § 221(d)(1).

14 26 U.S.C. § 221(d)(1)(C).

15 *See* National Consumer Law Center, Student Loan Law § 6.3.2 (2d ed. 2002 and Supp.).

16 Expenses for "cost of attendance" include:

> (1) tuition and fees normally assessed a student carrying the same academic workload as determined by the institution, and including costs for rental or purchase of any equipment, materials, or supplies required of all students in the same course of study;
>
> (2) an allowance for books, supplies, transportation, and miscellaneous personal expenses, including a reasonable allowance for the documented rental or purchase of a personal computer, for a student attending the institution on at least a half-time basis, as determined by the institution;
>
> (3) an allowance (as determined by the institution) for room and board costs incurred by the student which—

ity is intended to be limited to education loans, and not extend to other debts incurred by students.

The expenses must also be for attendance at an "eligible education institution."[17] "Eligible institutions" are defined as institutions that are eligible to participate in a Title IV program, which refers to the title of the Higher Education Act that governs federal financial assistance programs.[18] Most, but not all schools, are eligible to participate in these programs. For example, numerous unaccredited schools have gone in and out of business in recent years. These unaccredited schools are not eligible to participate in the Title IV programs.[19] Other scam programs such as "diploma mills" are also not eligible to participate in Title IV programs. Borrowers with student loans from these schools should be able to discharge the loans without having to prove hardship.

10.1.5 Debts Incurred to Pay Nondischargeable State or Local Taxes—Section 523(a)(14A)

The 2005 amendments add to the list of nondischargeable debts under section 523(a) those debts which are incurred to pay nondischargeable state or local taxes.[20] This provision is in addition to section 523(a)(14) of the Code, which covers debts incurred to pay nondischargeable federal taxes. This new exception to discharge is likely primarily to catch debtors who innocently pay their taxes with their credit cards.

More crafty debtors will obtain cash advances or, alternatively, make a balance transfer so the creditor does not know how the debt was incurred. The provision, to the extent used, may present accounting nightmares in determining how much of the nondischargeable debt has been repaid, when, for example, payments are made on a credit card account balance which includes other charges.

(A) shall be an allowance determined by the institution for a student without dependents residing at home with parents;

(B) for students without dependents residing in institutionally owned or operated housing, shall be a standard allowance determined by the institution based on the amount normally assessed most of its residents for room and board; and

(C) for all other students shall be an allowance based on the expenses reasonably incurred by such students for room and board;

(4) for less than half-time students (as determined by the institution) tuition and fees and an allowance for only books, supplies, and transportation (as determined by the institution) and dependent care expenses (in accordance with paragraph (8));

(5) for a student engaged in a program of study by correspondence, only tuition and fees and, if required, books and supplies, travel, and room and board costs incurred specifically in fulfilling a required period of residential training;

(6) for incarcerated students only tuition and fees and, if required, books and supplies;

(7) for a student enrolled in an academic program in a program of study abroad approved for credit by the student's home institution, reasonable costs associated with such study (as determined by the institution at which such student is enrolled);

(8) for a student with one or more dependents, an allowance based on the estimated actual expenses incurred for such dependent care, based on the number and age of such dependents, except that—

(A) such allowance shall not exceed the reasonable cost in the community in which such student resides for the kind of care provided; and

(B) the period for which dependent care is required includes, but is not limited to, class-time, study-time, field work, internships, and commuting time;

(9) for a student with a disability, an allowance (as determined by the institution) for those expenses related to the student's disability, including special services, personal assistance, transportation, equipment, and supplies that are reasonably incurred and not provided for by other assisting agencies;

(10) for a student receiving all or part of the student's instruction by means of telecommunications technology, no distinction shall be made with respect to the mode of instruction in determining costs;

(11) for a student engaged in a work experience under a cooperative education program, an allowance for reasonable costs associated with such employment (as determined by the institution); and

(12) for a student who receives a loan under this or any other Federal law, or, at the option of the institution, a conventional student loan incurred by the student to cover a student's cost of attendance at the institution, an allowance for the actual cost of any loan fee, origination fee, or insurance premium charged to such student or such parent on such loan, or the average cost of any such fee or premium charged by the Secretary, lender, or guaranty agency making or insuring such loan, as the case may be.

See 20 U.S.C. § 1087*ll*.

17 26 U.S.C. § 221(d)(2).

18 26 U.S.C. § 221(d)(2) (referring to 26 U.S.C. § 25A(f)(2)(B)).

19 *See* National Consumer Law Center, Student Loan Law Ch. 9 (2d ed. 2002 and Supp.).

20 11 U.S.C. § 523(a)(14A).

10.1.6 Federal Election Law Fines and Penalties—Section 523(a)(14B)

Debts incurred to pay federal election law fines and penalties are now nondischargeable in chapters 7, 11, and 12.[21] This provision is not likely to affect many consumer debtors.

10.1.7 Property Settlement Debts—Section 523(a)(15)

The 2005 Act's amendment to section 523(a)(15) of the Code is discussed in Chapter 9, *supra*. Section 523(a)(15) is amended to make all property settlement debts owed to a spouse, former spouse, or child of the debtor nondischargeable in chapter 7, and the ability to pay and balancing tests are eliminated.[22] These debts remain dischargeable in chapter 13.[23]

10.1.8 Condominium and Homeowner Association Fees—Section 523(a)(16)

The 2005 Act amends the language in section 523(a)(16) of the Code so that fees incurred due to a debtor's ownership interest in a lot in a homeowner association are included in the exception to discharge.[24] In addition, the prior standard limiting fees to those incurred during a period that the debtor occupied the dwelling has now been changed to "for as long as the debtor or the trustee has a legal, equitable, or possessory ownership interest" in the property.

Under a literal reading of the new language, a discharge does not discharge the debtor from a debt for such fees "for as long as the debtor or the trustee has a legal, equitable, or possessory ownership interest" in the property. Once the debtor no longer has such an interest, the fees are discharged. Congress changed the language so that it no longer refers to fees incurred during a particular period, and this change must be assumed to have meaning.

10.1.9 Court Costs and Fees Incurred by Prisoners—Section 523(a)(17)

The 2005 Act contains a technical amendment, which clarifies that the exception to discharge applies only to costs and fees imposed on prisoners.[25] Most courts had found that this result was the intent of the provision, in any event.[26]

10.1.10 Pension Loans—Section 523(a)(18)

A new provision makes loans from pension funds and from section 403(b) and section 401(k) plans nondischargeable.[27] The debt must be owed to a pension, profit-sharing, stock bonus, or other plan established under sections 401, 403, 408, 408A, 414, 457, or 501(c) of the Internal Revenue Code, under a loan permitted under section 408(b)(1) of the Employee Retirement Income Security Act (ERISA) or subject to section 72(p) of the Internal Revenue Code, or a loan from a thrift savings plan that satisfies the requirements of 5 U.S.C. § 8433(g).

Few debtors had ever contended that such loans, which are essentially secured by a pension account, were eliminated by bankruptcy. Curiously, new section 523(a)(18) of the Bankruptcy Code also provides that nothing in the provision is to be construed to imply that the loans are debts that would be subject to discharge in the first place.[28]

10.1.11 Debts Arising from Securities Violations—Section 523(a)(19).

The 2005 Act clarifies that the provision excepting debts arising from securities violations is not limited to cases in which judgments were entered pre-petition. This provision does not have much applicability to consumer cases.

---

21 11 U.S.C. § 523(a)(14B).

22 *See* § 9.5, *supra*.

23 *See* § 10.6, *infra*.

24 11 U.S.C. § 523(a)(16).

25 11 U.S.C. § 523(a)(17).

26 *See* National Consumer Law Center, Consumer Bankruptcy Law and Practice § 14.4.3.16 (7th ed. 2004).

27 11 U.S.C. § 523(a)(18).

28 This reference to a loan not being construed as a debt applies to a loan made under a governmental plan under § 414(d) of the Internal Revenue Code, or a contract or account under § 403(b) of the Internal Revenue Code. A similar provision is found in new § 362(b)(19) of the Bankruptcy Code. These provisions may have been an attempt to overrule the result in *In re* Buchferer, 216 B.R. 332 (Bankr. E.D.N.Y. 1997) (pension loan found to be non-recourse secured claim), and to codify the result in New York City Employees Retirement Sys. v. Villarie, 648 F.2d 810 (2d Cir. 1981).

10.2 Denial and Revocation of Discharge

The debtor may be denied a discharge in a chapter 7 or chapter 13 case if the debtor does not submit proof of the completion of an instructional course concerning financial management.[29]

The failure of the debtor to explain satisfactorily either a material misstatement in an audit or a failure to make papers or property available for inspection[30] can be grounds for the revocation of a discharge in a chapter 7 case.[31] There is no similar provision in chapter 13, perhaps because any audit would be completed before discharge.

10.3 Reaffirmation Agreements—Section 524

10.3.1 New Disclosures—Section 524(k)

The 2005 amendments require new disclosures concerning reaffirmation agreements. According to section 524(k)(1) of the Code, the disclosures consist of a combination of the disclosure statement described in section 524(k)(3), completed as required by that section, and the agreement, statement, declaration, motion, and order described in sections 524(k)(4)–(8). Unless all of these documents conform to statutory requirements, the disclosures required by section 524(c)(2) have not been given. Section 524(k)(1) also provides that these are the only disclosures that are required.[32]

The disclosures required by section 524(k)(3), designated as "Part A," are in some ways similar to those required for consumer credit transactions under the Truth in Lending Act, and incorporate certain concepts from that law. They require the use of particular terms and phrases, including "Amount Reaffirmed" and "Annual Percentage Rate," as well as standardized statements.[33] However, creditors are given latitude in how the disclosures are to be made, limiting the amount of useful information provided to debtors and making it difficult to prove inaccuracies. For example, the amount reaffirmed is described as including the total of any fees and costs that have accrued prior to the disclosure, but the creditor is not compelled to itemize the separate charges.[34] A repayment schedule may be provided "at the election of the creditor," and if provided the creditor need only describe the repayment obligation with "reasonable specificity to the extent then known by the disclosing party."[35] Despite the well-known abuses by department store creditors in coercing reaffirmations based on inflated values for secured household goods,[36] the new disclosure form does not require creditors to disclose the current value of the secured property.[37] The form only requires a listing of the items and "their original purchase price" for a purchase-money security interest, or the "original amount of the loan" for a nonpurchase-money security interest.[38]

The required disclosures are far more lengthy and confusing than the form promulgated by the Administrative Office of the Courts that was previously used in many courts. It is likely that many debtors will not understand the new disclosures, and it is also likely that many law firms will be hired to draft forms that comply with these complicated new provisions. There is also a potential for much litigation, similar to that under the Truth in Lending Act, if creditors do not strictly comply with the disclosure requirements.

10.3.2 The Reaffirmation Agreement

The 2005 amendments establish requirements as to the form of a reaffirmation agreement, designated as "Part B," as dictated by section 524(k)(4). The agreement must include a brief description of the credit agreement, a task

---

29 11 U.S.C. §§ 727(a)(11), 1328(g); *see also* § 4.4.4, *supra*.

30 *See* § 4.6, *supra*.

31 11 U.S.C. § 727(d)(4).

32 Prior local rules and standing court orders concerning reaffirmation agreements may no longer be enforceable to the extent that they require disclosures that are inconsistent with new section 524(k). *See, e.g., In re* Kamps, 217 B.R. 836 (Bankr. C.D. Cal. 1998); *In re* Bruzzese, 214 B.R. 444 (Bankr. E.D.N.Y. 1997).

33 The "Amount Reaffirmed" and "Annual Percentage Rate" must be disclosed more conspicuously than other terms. 11 U.S.C. § 524(k)(2). Several of the disclosures, such as the "Annual Percentage Rate," seem to assume that the terms of the underlying credit contract will not be renegotiated and will remain in effect upon reaffirmation.

34 11 U.S.C. § 524(k)(3)(C).

35 11 U.S.C. § 524(k)(3)(H).

36 *See* National Consumer Law Center, Consumer Bankruptcy Law and Practice § 14.5.2.1 (7th ed. 2004).

37 By comparison, the reaffirmation form promulgated by the Administrative Office of the Courts that was previously used in many courts required, for secured debts, a disclosure of the value of the collateral, the basis or source of the valuation, the current location and use of the collateral, and the expected future use of the collateral. *See* National Consumer Law Center, Consumer Bankruptcy Law and Practice Appx. E.10 (7th ed. 2004).

38 11 U.S.C. § 524(k)(3)(G).

that may not be easy in light of the complicated agreements utilized by consumer creditors. The creditor and the debtor(s) must both sign and date the agreement.

The debtor must also sign a form statement, designated "Part D." This form requires the debtor to compute whether the debtor has sufficient disposable income to make the payments required under the reaffirmation agreement and, if not, to explain how the debtor can afford to make the payments and identify additional sources of income the debtor will use to make the payments.[39] However, this computation and the explanation is not required if the debtor is represented by an attorney and the creditor is a credit union.[40]

If an attorney signs a declaration in support of the reaffirmation, designated "Part C," and the debtor's budget, as reflected in Part D, does not demonstrate adequate income to make the payments required by the reaffirmation agreement, the declaration must also state that in the attorney's opinion the debtor is able to make those payments (unless the creditor is a credit union).[41]

10.3.3 Court's Option to Disapprove Agreement—Section 524(m)

The court may disapprove certain reaffirmation agreements, although a hearing is not required in every such case. If the debtor's declaration shows a budget insufficient to make payments under the agreement, a presumption arises that the reaffirmation agreement is an undue hardship, and the court is required to review the matter. An unrepresented debtor must complete "Part E" of the reaffirmation agreement, which is a "Motion for Court Approval."[42]

The debtor may submit a written explanation of how additional funds will be obtained to make the payments in order to rebut the presumption. If the presumption is not rebutted, the court "may" disapprove the agreement after notice to the debtor and creditor and a hearing concluded before the discharge.[43]

However, the standard for approval of a reaffirmation agreement remains unchanged in section 524(c)(6)(A) of the Code.[44] The agreement must not impose an undue hardship on the debtor and must be in the debtor's best interest, which suggests that the court should never approve an agreement when the presumption of undue hardship has not been satisfactorily rebutted.

In order to fully review all agreements in which the presumption arises, courts may have to delay the discharge in many cases. Suggested interim Rule 4004(c)(1)(J) provides that the discharge shall be delayed if a presumption of undue hardship has arisen. Nothing prevents a court from requiring additional information in order to evaluate whether an agreement should be approved. But these presumption of abuse provisions do not apply if the creditor is a credit union and in such cases court review is required only if the debtor is not represented by an attorney.

10.3.4 Creditor Protections

Section 524(*l*) of the Code permits creditors to accept payments made by debtors in connection with reaffirmation agreements. A creditor may accept a voluntary payment by the debtor either before or after the filing of a reaffirmation agreement with the court.

However, the authorization to accept payments is limited to an agreement that a creditor believes in good faith to be effective. Thus, for example, if the creditor knows, or should with reasonable diligence know, that the agreement does not meet the requirements for a valid reaffirmation, the creditor is not permitted to accept payments.

Section 524(*l*)(3) provides that the disclosure requirements of section 524(c)(2) and (k) are satisfied if the required disclosures are made in good faith. This provision, too, appears to be a limitation on creditors' actions to undermine the reaffirmation requirements. If the required disclosures are made, but are not made in good faith, perhaps because the creditor has added excessive charges to the agreement or plans to change the credit terms immediately, there is no protection. The provision does not excuse a creditor from making the required disclosures simply because the creditor has acted in good faith. It operates only if the creditor has made the disclosures that are required.

10.4 Proper Crediting of Plan Payments—Section 524(i)

Under a new provision, the creditor's willful failure to credit payments received under a confirmed plan in accordance with the plan constitutes a violation of the injunction in section 524(a) of the Code.[45] Although

39 11 U.S.C. § 524(k)(4).

40 11 U.S.C. § 524(m)(2).

41 11 U.S.C. § 524(k)(4).

42 11 U.S.C. § 524(k)(3)(J)(i), 524(k)(4).

43 11 U.S.C. § 524(m)(1).

44 *See* National Consumer Law Center, Consumer Bankruptcy Law and Practice § 14.5.2.2 (7th ed. 2004).

45 11 U.S.C. § 524(i).

section 524(a) previously was limited to violations of the discharge order, section 524(i) is not limited to acts occurring after discharge.

The section does not apply, however, if confirmation of the plan has been revoked, the plan is in default, or the creditor has not received the plan payments as required by the plan. The provision is also limited to cases in which the failure to credit the payments has caused material injury to the debtor.

Presumably this provision is a response to decisions in which courts questioned whether they had the ability to remedy a creditor's failure to credit payments properly. For example, it provides a remedy that the Court of Appeals for the Eleventh Circuit found missing in *Telfair v. First Union Mortgage Corp.*,[46] when a chapter 13 debtor challenged a creditor's application of plan payments to charges not contemplated by the plan. It also makes clear that a failure to properly credit plan payments that results in a post-discharge assertion that the debtor is in default is not simply a matter for state courts to resolve, but rather a critical issue that must be resolved by the bankruptcy court to ensure that the provisions and purposes of a plan are effectuated.

The willfulness requirement of section 524(i) should not be a significant obstacle for debtors. As in section 362(k)(1) of the Code, willfulness should be interpreted to mean simply that the creditor intended to commit the act, that is, credit the payment in the manner it did; the debtor should not need to prove that the creditor intended to violate the Code or the plan provisions.[47] Absent a creditor's proof that the improper crediting was a mistake in conflict with the creditor's normal procedures, the creditor should be presumed to have intended its acts.

The material injury requirement will be met in virtually every case involving a secured creditor. The failure to properly credit payments will almost always result in a higher payoff balance for the debtor and therefore a larger lien on the debtor's property than if the payments were credited properly. A creditor that has collected the payments made by the debtor under the plan and credited them in a manner leading to a higher balance remaining on a debt has caused a material injury to the debtor. Similarly, a creditor who has reported negative information on the debtor's credit report about nonpayment or collection efforts with respect to fees resulting from the improper crediting of payments has caused a material injury to the debtor.

46 216 F.3d 1333 (11th Cir. 2000).

47 *See* National Consumer Law Center, Consumer Bankruptcy Law and Practice § 9.6 (7th ed. 2004).

A common example of such an injury is the assessment of post-petition charges to the debtor that are not in accordance with the terms of the confirmed plan. If a creditor could subvert the terms of a plan simply by adding such charges, the cure of a default under the plan would be meaningless. As with other aspects of the injunction under section 524(a), a court can hold a creditor in contempt for violating section 524(i).[48]

10.5 Creditor Protection for Collection on Ride-Through Mortgages—Section 522(j)

Section 524(j) of the Code provides that certain actions of creditors holding security interests in real property of the debtor, such as seeking periodic payments in a ride-through situation, do not violate the discharge injunction. The lien retained by the creditor must be on real property that is the debtor's principal residence.[49]

The exception to the discharge injunction created by this provision applies to creditor acts that are in the ordinary course of business between the creditor and the debtor.[50] The acts must also be limited to seeking or obtaining periodic payments on a valid lien "in lieu of pursuit of *in rem* relief to enforce the lien."[51] This provision is consistent with court opinions in ride-through jurisdictions that have found section 524(a)(2) is not violated if the creditor does not attempt to collect on the discharged debt as a personal liability of the debtor, and if the collection efforts do not involve coercion or harassment by the creditor.[52]

10.6 Dischargeability of Debts in Chapter 13

One of the most significant changes to the discharge provisions is the elimination of the chapter 13 "super-discharge" for certain debts.[53] The following debts are now nondischargeable in chapter 13 cases:

48 *See* National Consumer Law Center, Consumer Bankruptcy Law and Practice § 14.5.1.4 (7th ed. 2004).

49 11 U.S.C. § 522(j)(1).

50 11 U.S.C. § 522(j)(2).

51 11 U.S.C. § 522(j)(3).

52 *In re* Garske, 287 B.R. 537 (B.A.P. 9th Cir. 2002) (telephone calls from secured creditor about whether debtor intended to continue payments in a ride-through jurisdiction did not violate discharge injunction); *In re* Ramirez, 280 B.R. 252 (C.D. Cal. 2002). *But see In re* Henry, 266 B.R. 457 (Bankr. C.D. Cal. 2001).

53 11 U.S.C. § 1328(a)(2); *see also* National Consumer Law

- Withheld taxes described in section 507(a)(8)(C);
- Unfiled or late-filed taxes, as provided under section 523(a)(1)(B);
- Fraudulently filed taxes, as provided under section 523(a)(1)(C);
- Debts incurred by fraud, as provided under section 523(a)(2) and (a)(4); and
- Unscheduled debts, as provided under section 523(a)(3).

With respect to the elimination of the chapter 13 discharge for debts incurred by fraud based on section 523(a)(2) and (a)(4), interim Rule 4007(c) provides that the same time limits that are applicable to other chapters are applicable in chapter 13 cases.[54] Thus a complaint objecting to dischargeability under section 523(a)(2) and (a)(4) in a chapter 13 case must be filed no later than sixty days after the first date set for the section 341 meeting.[55]

In addition, section 1328(a)(4) of the Code creates a new type of chapter 13 nondischargeability for an award of restitution or damages in a civil action against the debtor, based on willful or malicious injury by the debtor that caused personal injury or death of an individual. Willful and malicious injury to property, or to an individual who has not been awarded restitution or damages, continue to be dischargeable in chapter 13.[56] It is not clear whether the "willful *or* malicious" requirement in the new provision will be much different than the "willful *and* malicious" test under current section 523(a)(6) of the Code.[57]

It is important to note that section 1328(a)(2) continues to permit the discharge in chapter 13 cases of other debts that are nondischargeable in chapter 7. The following debts remain dischargeable in chapter 13 cases:

- Debts for willful and malicious injury to property (and to individuals to the extent that section 1328(a)(4) does not apply), as provided under section 523(a)(6);
- Debts incurred to pay nondischargeable tax obligations, as provided under section 523(a)(14) and (14A); and
- Debts arising from property settlements in divorce or separation proceedings, as provided under section 523(a)(15).

Center, Consumer Bankruptcy Law and Practice § 14.4.1 (7th ed. 2004).

54 *See* Appx. B, *infra*.

55 *See also* National Consumer Law Center, Consumer Bankruptcy Law and Practice § 14.4.2 (7th ed. 2004).

56 11 U.S.C. § 523(a)(6); *see also* National Consumer Law Center, Consumer Bankruptcy Law and Practice § 14.4.1 (7th ed. 2004).

57 *See* Kawaauhau v. Geiger, 523 U.S. 57, 118 S. Ct. 974, 140 L. Ed. 2d 90 (1998).

Chapter 11

Changes to Chapter 12—Adjustment of Debts of a Family Farmer[1]

11.1 Chapter 12 Now Permanent

Chapter 12 was first enacted in 1986 as a temporary provision that expired on October 1, 1993.[2] It was renewed numerous times, each time as another temporary extension.[3] Renewals, however, sometimes came months after chapter 12 had expired, creating frustrating gaps in its availability.[4] The Bankruptcy Abuse Prevention and Consumer Protection Act of 2005 (the Act) finally remedies this problem by making chapter 12 a permanent part of the Bankruptcy Code.[5] This provision of the Act took effect on July 1, 2005, replacing the final temporary extension, which expired on June 30, 2005.[6]

11.2 Expansion of Chapter 12 Eligibility

11.2.1 General

There are specific eligibility criteria for chapter 12 relief. When chapter 12 was enacted, only a "family farmer" who had "regular annual income" was eligible for chapter 12 relief.[7] The Bankruptcy Code defines "family farmer" and only farmers who fit within this definition have been eligible for chapter 12 relief. The 2005 Act amends these eligibility standards by expanding the definition of "family farmer"[8] and by extending eligibility to "family fishermen." Each of these changes will become effective on October 17, 2005.[9]

11.2.2 Increase in Maximum Debt

The statutory maximum for the amount of debt that a "family farmer" can have is increased from $1,500,000 to $3,237,000.[10] This amount is the maximum total of aggregate debts that a debtor can have and still be eligible for chapter 12 relief. In addition to this immediate increase, the 2005 Act also provides that the maximum amount will be periodicallly adjusted to reflect increases in the Consumer Price Index.[11]

11.2.3 Lowering of Percentage of Debt That Must Arise from Farming

The 2005 Act amends the requirement that at least eighty percent of the farmer's "aggregate, non-contingent, liquidated debts" must arise out of the debtor's farming operation.[12] Now not less than fifty percent of the

1 This Chapter was written by Susan A. Schneider, Associate Professor and Director, Graduate Program in Agricultural Law, University of Arkansas School of Law.

2 Bankruptcy Judges, United States Trustees, and Family Bankruptcy Act of 1986, Pub. L. No. 99-554, § 302(f), 10 Stat. 3103.

3 *See* Jerome M. Stam & Bruce L. Dixon, *Farmer Bankruptcies and Farm Exits in the United States, 1899–2002*, Econ. Research Serv., Agric. Info. Bull. No. AIB788, app. at 31–32 (Mar. 2004) (Legislative History of Chapter 12 Bankruptcy); National Consumer Law Center, Consumer Bankruptcy Law and Practice § 16.1.1.1 (7th ed. 2004); *see also* Susan A. Schneider, *History of Chapter 12 Bankruptcy: On Again, Off Again*, Agric. L. Update, Aug. 2001, at 1.

4 For example, chapter 12 expired on October 1, 2001 but was not reenacted until spring 2002. Bankruptcy—Chapter 12 Reenactment, Pub. L. No. 107-170, 116 Stat. 133 (2002).

5 Pub. L. No. 109-8, § 1001, 119 Stat. 23, 185–186 (2005).

6 Pub. L. No. 108-369, § 2(a), 118 Stat. 1749 (2004).

7 Former 11 U.S.C. § 109(f).

8 11 U.S.C. § 101(18).

9 Pub. L. No. 109-8, § 1501(a), 119 Stat. 23, 216 (2005).

10 11 U.S.C. § 101(18)(A), (B). The increase applies to both the eligibility requirements for an individual and for a family farm corporation or partnership.

11 11 U.S.C. § 104(b). The indexing applies to both the eligibility requirements for an individual and for a family farm corporation or partnership.

12 11 U.S.C. § 101(18). Under either the previous law or the new Act, the percentage is assessed as of the date the case is filed.

farmer's debt must arise out of the farming operation.[13] This amendment allows farmers with significant debt that is not associated with farming, such as medical expenses or other business expenses, to be eligible for chapter 12 relief.

11.2.4 Liberalized Test to Show That Fifty Percent of Income Arises from Farming

The farm income requirement is liberalized to expand eligibility. Since its origin chapter 12 has required that more than fifty percent of the farmer's income from the preceding taxable year must come from farming.[14] This eligibility requirement proved to be problematic for many farmers who tried to keep their operation afloat by taking on non-farm jobs or who were unable to obtain crop financing and rented out their land during the year prior to filing. The 2005 Act provides an alternative. Either the farmer can meet the fifty percent income requirement for the preceding taxable year or the farmer can meet it in each of the second and third taxable years preceding the filing.[15] This change will not assist farmers who have relied on non-farm income for an extended period of time, but it will allow those who relied on such income in only the year before filing bankruptcy to look back to prior years in order to maintain eligibility.

11.2.5 Family Fishermen Now Protected

"Family fisherman" is defined and those fishermen who qualify are afforded chapter 12 eligibility under the 2005 Act.[16] This definition mirrors the original requirements contained in the definition of family farmer. Family fishermen do not receive the expanded eligibility criteria that are afforded to family farmers, but remain subject to the pre-2005 income and debt standards for family farmers.[17] However, although allowable maximum aggregate debts are set at $1,500,000, this amount will be periodically adjusted to reflect increases in the Consumer Price Index.[18]

The definition of family fisherman applies to those "engaged in a commercial fishing operation."[19] A commercial fishing operation is defined as: "(A) the catching or harvesting of fish, shrimp, lobsters, urchins, seaweed, shellfish, or other aquatic species or products of such species; or (B) for purposes of section 109 and chapter 12, aquaculture activities consisting of raising for market any species or product described in subparagraph (A)."[20] Thus, catfish farmers who meet the family fisherman eligibility requirements will be eligible for chapter 12 relief as family fishermen. Under prior law, some courts assumed that they fit within the definition of family farmer under § 101(18), but it now appears that they will

13 11 U.S.C. § 101(18). In computing this percentage under either the previous law or the new Act, the debtor can exclude the debt for a "principal residence" unless that debt arises out of the farming operation. 11 U.S.C. § 101(18).

14 Former 11 U.S.C. § 101(18)(A). There is no comparable income requirement for family farm corporations or partnerships, although eighty percent of the value of the entity's assets must relate to the farming operation. 11 U.S.C. § 101(18)(B). No changes were made to this provision by the 2005 amendments.

15 11 U.S.C. § 101(18).

16 11 U.S.C. § 101(19A). A family fisherman is defined as:

> "(A) an individual or individual and spouse engaged in a commercial fishing operation—
>
> (i) whose aggregate debts do not exceed $1,500,000 and not less than 80 percent of whose aggregate noncontingent, liquidated debts (excluding a debt for the principal residence of such individual or such individual and spouse, unless such debt arises out of a commercial fishing operation), on the date the case is filed, arise out of a commercial fishing operation owned or operated by such individual or such individual and spouse; and
>
> (ii) who receive from such commercial fishing operation more than 50 percent of such individual's or such individual's and spouse's gross income for the taxable year preceding the taxable year in which the case concerning such individual or such individual and spouse was filed; or
>
> (B) a corporation or partnership—
>
> (i) in which more than 50 percent of the outstanding stock or equity is held by—(I) 1 family that conducts the commercial fishing operation; or (II) 1 family and the relatives of the members of such family, and such family or such relatives conduct the commercial fishing operation; and
>
> (ii)(I) more than 80 percent of the value of its assets consists of assets related to the commercial fishing operation; (II) its aggregate debts do not exceed $1,500,000 and not less than 80 percent of its aggregate noncontingent, liquidated debts (excluding a debt for 1 dwelling which is owned by such corporation or partnership and which a shareholder or partner maintains as a principal residence, unless such debt arises out of a commercial fishing operation), on the date the case is filed, arise out of a commercial fishing operation owned or operated by such corporation or such partnership; and (III) if such corporation issues stock, such stock is not publicly traded."

17 11 U.S.C. § 101(19A).

18 11 U.S.C. § 104.

19 11 U.S.C. § 101(19A).

20 11 U.S.C. § 101(7A).

be defined as fishermen instead of farmers, and will not benefit from the expanded eligibility provisions enacted for farmers.

11.3 Modified Priority of Certain Tax Obligations

The 2005 Act provides that certain tax claims will no longer be given priority status in a chapter 12 case.[21] A chapter 12 debtor is allowed to treat a claim that is "owed to a government unit" as a result of the sale or transfer of a farm asset as a nonpriority unsecured claim, provided that the debtor receives a discharge.[22] This type of tax claim will not be entitled to § 507 priority. Under prior law, taxes had priority status under § 507 and had to be paid in full. The new provision took effect on the date of the enactment of the 2005 amendments, April 20, 2005, but it does not apply with respect to cases commenced before that date.[23]

11.4 Prohibition on Retroactive Assessment of Disposable Income

Like chapter 13, chapter 12 sets forth different requirements for the treatment of secured and unsecured claims in the debtor's reorganization plan.[24] The disposable income requirement protects unsecured claim holders.[25] If either the trustee or an unsecured claim holder[26] objects to the debtor's proposed plan, that plan must either provide for full payment of unsecured claims or it must commit an amount of "projected disposable income" during the term of the plan to the payment of unsecured claims.[27] As it is generally unrealistic to consider payment of all unsecured claims, most plans will provide for the payment of an amount of projected disposable income over the term of the plan. If a creditor does not agree with the debtor's projection, that creditor can raise objections at confirmation.

Despite the fact that this disposable income provision is a confirmation requirement, courts have interpreted the chapter 12 "projected disposable income" requirement as allowing an unsecured creditor or the trustee to object to discharge on the basis that all "actual" disposable income was not paid to unsecured creditors, even though the projected amount was paid.[28] Courts addressing the same language under chapter 13 have interpreted the "projected" requirement literally, and have limited litigation to the confirmation stage, with plan modification actions available to deal with any significant changes to disposable income that occur during the course of the plan.[29]

Allowing creditors to object to the size of disposable income payments at discharge has been problematic for reorganizing debtors who hoped to successfully emerge from bankruptcy. It has forced farm debtors to go back and account for all income and expenses throughout the plan term, litigating a wide variety of issues, including whether expenses were actually "necessary for the continuation, preservation, and operation" of the farm.[30] As major undersecured creditors and the chapter 12 trustee[31] viewed discharge as their last chance to increase pay-

21 11 U.S.C. § 507.

22 11 U.S.C. § 507.

23 Pub. L. No. 109-8, § 1003(c), 119 Stat. 23, 186 (2005).

24 Former 11 U.S.C. § 1225(a)(5) (providing alternative requirements for the treatment of secured claims); former 11 U.S.C. § 1225(a)(4), (b); former § 1325(a)(4), (b) (providing for the treatment of unsecured claims).

25 Former 11 U.S.C. § 1225(b); *see also* former 11 U.S.C. § 1325(b). Unsecured claim holders are also protected by a liquidation test which requires that the plan must provide them with at least the value they would receive in a chapter 7 liquidation. Former 11 U.S.C. § 1225(a)(4).

26 This provision may provide little protection to the traditional unsecured creditor such as a tradesman or input supplier. Because the Bankruptcy Code provides for the bifurcation of obligations owed to creditors into secured and unsecured claims, in many cases a creditor who is secured, but whose security is insufficient in value to cover the debt, will be the largest unsecured creditor. *See* former 11 U.S.C. § 506.

27 Former 11 U.S.C. § 1225(b).

28 *See, e.g.*, Rowley v. Yarnall, 22 F.3d 190, 192–193 (8th Cir. 1994) (holding that a plain reading of the statutory language would yield "an absurd result" and reviewing the debtor's actual income and expenses throughout the plan in response to an objection to discharge).

29 *See, e.g.*, *In re* Anderson, 21 F.3d 355, 357–358 (9th Cir. 1994) (stating that the "language of the statute is clear" and holding that the debtor can not be forced to sign a promise to pay all actual disposable income as a confirmation requirement); *In re* Bass, 267 B.R. 812, 817–818 (Bankr. S.D. Ohio. 2001) (rejecting *Rowley* and stating that *Anderson* reflects the better statutory authority; holding that the debtor can not be required to commit all actual disposable income in order to obtain confirmation).

30 *See, e.g.*, *In re* Wood, 122 B.R. 107, 115 (Bankr. Idaho 1990) (holding that the disposable income test requires the court to conduct a subjective analysis of the debtor's expenditures to determine if they were reasonably necessary).

31 Chapter 12 is a self-funded system under which the trustee is compensated by taking a percentage of the payments that the debtor makes under the plan. A trustee may be entitled to up to ten percent of whatever can be recovered in an objection to discharge based on disposable income obligations. Former 28 U.S.C. § 586(e)(2).

ments from the debtor, aggressive investigations have been conducted.[32] Moreover, particularly harsh judicial rulings raised concerns that farmers' otherwise successful reorganizations would fail due to the imposition of significant obligations at the end of the plan term.[33] There was also concern that farmers were not being left with sufficient liquid assets to keep the farm operating after discharge.[34]

Section 1006 of the 2005 Act addresses these concerns.[35] It retains the "projected disposable income" language as part of the confirmation requirements and adds an additional alternative that the debtor can meet in order to achieve plan confirmation. The debtor's plan can provide that the "value of property distributed under the plan . . . is not less than the debtor's projected disposable income."[36]

Even more significantly, section 1006 of the Act amends section 1229 of the Bankruptcy Code (Modification of Plan after Confirmation) to restrict changes to the plan once it has been confirmed. The plan may not be modified to "increase the amount of any payment due before the plan as modified becomes the plan."[37] Under this new provision, modifications will be allowed only to create new, prospective obligations, capturing future income that is greater than that anticipated when the plan was originally confirmed.

Section 1006 also amends chapter 12 to provide that no one, but for the debtor, can call for any increase based on disposable income that would "increase the amount of payments to unsecured creditors required for a particular month so that the aggregate of such payments exceeds the debtor's disposable income for such month."[38] This provision seems to prevent a court from revisiting the debtor's past payments at a discharge hearing and imposing a new obligation that is greater than what the debtor can presently afford to pay from disposable income that month.

Finally, section 1006 provides that the plan may not be modified "in the last year of the plan by anyone except the debtor, to require payments that would leave the debtor with insufficient funds to carry on the farming operation after the plan is completed."[39] This provision emphasizes the importance of allowing the debtor sufficient income for the continuation of the farming operation, which is also anticipated by the current definition of disposable income which excludes expenditures necessary for the "continuation" and "preservation" of the farming operation from the definition of disposable income.[40]

These provisions appear to prohibit the type of retroactive accounting that courts have undertaken at discharge, attempting to reconcile early projections with what, through litigation at discharge, the trustee or creditors argue is "actual" disposable income.[41] Sometimes, at the insistence of the chapter 12 trustee, debtors may file a reorganization plan that requires the payment of actual disposable income. In such cases this plan provision will control despite the changes in the law. These changes to the disposable income and plan modification provisions will become effective on October 17, 2005 and will apply to cases filed on or after that date.[42]

---

32 *See, e.g.*, *In re* Wood, 122 B.R. 107, 116 (Bankr. Idaho 1990) (categorizing trustee's "microscopic examination" of debtor's records as "extreme" and finding that no disposable income was owed). In *Wood*, the trustee claimed that the debtor owed over $218,000 in disposable income. In reaching that sum, he included non-cash items such as depreciation deductions and a net operating loss carryover as items of income. *Id.*

33 *See, e.g.*, Hammrich v. Lovald (*In re* Hammrich), 98 F.3d 388, 389 (8th Cir. 1996) (debtors required to pay $95,885.86 in order to receive discharge); Broken Bow Ranch v. Farmers Home Admin. (*In re* Broken Bow), 33 F.3d 1005, 1007 (8th Cir. 1994) (debtors required to pay $81,862.00 in order to receive discharge).

34 *See, e.g.*, *Hammrich*, 98 F.3d at 390 (holding that the value of calves that were not yet ready for market were "marketable commodities" that should be included in disposable income calculations); *Broken Bow Ranch*, 33 F.3d at 1009 (holding that computation of disposable income can require debtor to obtain borrowed financing for crop input expenses).

35 Pub. L. No. 109-8, § 1006, 119 Stat. 23 (2005) (amending 11 U.S.C. § 1225(b)).

36 11 U.S.C. § 1225(b).

37 11 U.S.C. § 1225(b).

38 11 U.S.C. § 1225(b).

39 Pub. L. No. 109-8, § 1006, 119 Stat. 23 (2005).

40 11 U.S.C. § 1225(b)(2) (excluding from the definition of disposable income that "which is not reasonably necessary to be expended . . . for the payment of expenditures necessary for the continuation, preservation, and operation of the debtor's business").

41 This issue has been complicated by the proposal and confirmation of plans that require the debtor to pay actual disposable income. Although these plans have been the direct result of judicial interpretation of the disposable income requirement as requiring actual accounting at discharge, if the debtor's plan provides such a requirement, the debtor will be bound to its terms regardless of the statutory change.

42 Pub. L. No. 109-8, § 1501, 119 Stat. 23, 216 (2005).

11.5 Changes Relating to Domestic Support Obligations

The 2005 Act encourages payment of domestic support obligations, defined to include child support, alimony, and maintenance:[43]

- A new first priority status for prepetition unsecured claims for domestic support obligations is created. These obligations will receive top priority under section 507(a)(1)(B);[44]
- The debtor is not allowed to reduce the amount of a domestic support obligation that has section 507(a)(1)(B) priority, unless the debtor's plan commits to paying out all of the debtor's projected disposable income for a five-year period;[45]
- A new chapter 12 confirmation requirement is added, requiring that the debtor be current on all postpetition domestic support obligations;[46]
- Failure to pay a postpetition domestic support obligation will be grounds for dismissal of the bankruptcy;[47]
- A debtor who has a domestic support obligation will not be entitled to a discharge unless the debtor is current with respect to this obligation and files a certification of this fact. The obligations included within this requirement are all postpetition obligations and prepetition obligations, but only to the extent that they are provided for by the plan.[48]

A change made to section 1222 of the Bankruptcy Code permits a chapter 12 plan to "provide for the payment of interest accruing after the date of filing of the petition on unsecured claims that are nondischargeable under § 1228(a)."[49] A limitation is placed on this provision so that interest may be paid only to the extent that the debtor has disposable income available after providing for all allowed claims. Debts that are nondischargeable under section 1228(a) include domestic support obligations but also include debts provided for under section 1222(b)(5), section 1222(b)(9) or specified in section 523(a).[50]

11.6 Other Changes Affecting Chapter 12 Cases

In addition to amendments to chapter 12, the 2005 Act makes many changes to other chapters of the Bankruptcy Code that will have an impact on the filing or administration of a chapter 12 bankruptcy. Many of the changes discussed earlier in this volume may apply to chapter 12 filings as well, and this subsection only provides two examples of changes outside chapter 12 that affect chapter 12 filings.

A new requirement provides that "an individual may not be a debtor" under title 11 unless such individual has received a briefing from an approved credit counseling agency outlining the opportunities available for credit counseling and assisting in a budgetary analysis.[51] This requirement applies to chapter 12 to the same extent as to chapter 7 or 13 filings.

Another general change that affects chapter 12 debtors is the increase in the amount of information that it is the duty of of the debtor to provide. In addition to the bankruptcy schedules, an individual debtor will be required to provide additional financial information including:

- Payment advices or other evidence of payment from employers received within sixty days before the bankruptcy filing;
- An itemized statement of monthly net income; and,
- A statement disclosing any reasonably anticipated increase in income or expenditures during the next year.[52]

If requested by the United States trustee or the trustee, the debtor will be required to produce proof of identification.[53]

43 11 U.S.C. § 101(14A).
44 11 U.S.C. § 507(a)(1).
45 11 U.S.C. § 1222(b).
46 11 U.S.C. § 1225(a)(7).
47 11 U.S.C. § 1208(c)(8).
48 11 U.S.C. § 1228(a).
49 11 U.S.C. § 1222(b)(11).
50 11 U.S.C. § 1228(a).
51 11 U.S.C. § 109(h)(2). Credit counseling approval requirements are found at 11 U.S.C. § 111. *See* § 4.3.1, *supra.*
52 11 U.S.C. § 521(a).
53 11 U.S.C. § 521(h).

Appendix A

Bankruptcy Statutes

A.1 Selected Provisions of the Bankruptcy Code, 11 U.S.C. §§ 101–1532

Appendix A.1 contains a red-lined version of chapters 1, 3, and 5, subchapters I and II of chapter 7, subchapters I, II and III of chapter 11, and the complete text of chapters 12 and 13 of title 11 of the United States Code, marked to show the changes made to the statute by the Bankruptcy Abuse Prevention and Consumer Protection Act of 2005. See Appendix A.3, *infra*, for the text of that act. Most of the act's amendments to the Bankruptcy Code apply only to cases under title 11 commenced on or after October 17, 2005. Footnotes to the relevant redlined provisions note any amendments which have a different effective date. These laws may also be found on the CD-Rom accompanying this volume.

TITLE 11—BANKRUPTCY[1]

TABLE OF CONTENTS

CHAPTER 1—GENERAL PROVISIONS

CHAPTER 3—CASE ADMINISTRATION

Subchapter I—Commencement of a Case

Subchapter II—Officers

Subchapter III—Administration

1 This red-lined version was prepared with the aid of a similar version prepared by attorney Richard Levin of Skadden, Arps, Slate, Meagher & Flom LLP. NCLC wishes to thank Mr. Levin for his kind permission to utilize his version in our preparation of this Appendix.

§ 348. Effect of conversion
§ 349. Effect of dismissal
§ 350. Closing and reopening cases
§ 351. Disposal of patient records

Subchapter IV—Administrative Powers

§ 361. Adequate protection
§ 362. Automatic stay
§ 363. Use, sale, or lease of property
§ 364. Obtaining credit
§ 365. Executory contracts and unexpired leases
§ 366. Utility service

CHAPTER 5—CREDITORS, THE DEBTOR, AND THE ESTATE

Subchapter 1—Creditors and Claims

§ 501. Filing of proofs of claims or interests
§ 502. Allowance of claims or interests
§ 503. Allowance of administrative expenses
§ 504. Sharing of compensation
§ 505. Determination of tax liability
§ 506. Determination of secured status
§ 507. Priorities
§ 508. Effect of distribution other than under this title
§ 509. Claims of codebtors
§ 510. Subordination
§ 511. Rate of interest on tax claims

Subchapter II—Debtor's Duties and Benefits

§ 521. Debtor's duties
§ 522. Exemptions
§ 523. Exceptions to discharge
§ 524. Effect of discharge
§ 525. Protection against discriminatory treatment
§ 526. Restrictions on debt relief agencies
§ 527. Disclosures
§ 528. Requirements for debt relief agencies

Subchapter III—The Estate

§ 541. Property of the estate
§ 542. Turnover of property to the estate
§ 543. Turnover of property by a custodian
§ 544. Trustee as lien creditor and as successor to certain creditors and purchasers
§ 545. Statutory liens
§ 546. Limitations on avoiding powers
§ 547. Preferences
§ 548. Fraudulent transfers and obligations
§ 549. Postpetition transactions
§ 550. Liability of transferee of avoided transfer
§ 551. Automatic preservation of avoided transfer
§ 552. Postpetition effect of security interest
§ 553. Setoff
§ 554. Abandonment of property of the estate
§ 555. Contractual right to liquidate, terminate, or accelerate a securities contract
§ 556. Contractual right to liquidate, terminate, or accelerate a commodit~~y~~ ies contract or forward contract
§ 557. Expedited determination of interests in, and abandonment or other disposition of grain assets
§ 558. Defenses of the estate
§ 559. Contractual right to liquidate, terminate, or accelerate a repurchase agreement
§ 560. Contractual right to liquidate, terminate, or accelerate a swap agreement
§ 561. Contractual right to terminate, liquidate, accelerate, or offset under a master netting agreement and across contracts; proceedings under chapter 15
§ 562. Timing of damage measure in connection with swap agreements, securities contracts, forward contracts, commodity contracts, repurchase agreements, or master netting agreements

CHAPTER 7—LIQUIDATION

Subchapter I—Officers and Administration

§ 701. Interim trustee
§ 702. Election of trustee
§ 703. Successor trustee
§ 704. Duties of trustee
§ 705. Creditors' committee
§ 706. Conversion
§ 707. Dismissal of a case or conversion to a case under chapter 11 or 13

Subchapter II—Collection, Liquidation, and Distribution of the Estate

§ 721. Authorization to operate business
§ 722. Redemption
§ 723. Rights of partnership trustee against general partners
§ 724. Treatment of certain liens
§ 725. Disposition of certain property
§ 726. Distribution of property of the estate
§ 727. Discharge
~~§ 728. Special tax provisions~~

* * *

CHAPTER 11—REORGANIZATION

Subchapter I—Officers and Administration

§ 1101. Definitions for this chapter
§ 1102. Creditors' and equity security holders' committees
§ 1103. Powers and duties of committees

* * *

CHAPTER I

GENERAL PROVISIONS

§ 101. Definitions

In this title—the following definitions shall apply:

(1) The term "accountant" means accountant authorized under applicable law to practice public accounting, and includes professional accounting association, corporation, or partnership, if so authorized;.

(2) The term "affiliate" means—

(A) entity that directly or indirectly owns, controls, or holds with power to vote, 20 percent or more of the outstanding voting securities of the debtor, other than an entity that holds such securities—

(i) in a fiduciary or agency capacity without sole discretionary power to vote such securities; or

(ii) solely to secure a debt, if such entity has not in fact exercised such power to vote;

(B) corporation 20 percent or more of whose outstanding voting securities are directly or indirectly owned, controlled, or held with power to vote, by the debtor, or by an entity that directly or indirectly owns, controls, or holds with power to vote, 20 percent or more of the outstanding voting securities of the debtor, other than an entity that holds such securities—

(i) in a fiduciary or agency capacity without sole discretionary power to vote such securities; or

(ii) solely to secure a debt, if such entity has not in fact exercised such power to vote;

(C) person whose business is operated under a lease or operating agreement by a debtor, or person substantially all of whose property is operated under an operating agreement with the debtor; or

(D) entity that operates the business or substantially all of the property of the debtor under a lease or operating agreement;.

(3) The term "assisted person" means any person whose debts consist primarily of consumer debts and the value of whose nonexempt property is less than $150,000.

(4) The term "attorney" means attorney, professional law association, corporation, or partnership, authorized under applicable law to practice law;.

(4A) The term "bankruptcy" assistance means any goods or services sold or otherwise provided to an assisted person with the express or implied purpose of providing information, advice, counsel, document preparation, or filing, or attendance at a creditors' meeting or appearing in a case or proceeding on behalf of another or providing legal representation with respect to a case or proceeding under this title.

(5) The term "claim" means—

(A) right to payment, whether or not such right is reduced to judgment, liquidated, unliquidated, fixed, contingent, matured, unmatured, disputed, undisputed, legal, equitable, secured, or unsecured; or

(B) right to an equitable remedy for breach of performance if such breach gives rise to a right to payment, whether or not such right to an equitable remedy is reduced to judgment, fixed, contingent, matured, unmatured, disputed, undisputed, secured, or unsecured;.

(6) The term "commodity broker" means futures commission merchant, foreign futures commission merchant, clearing organization, leverage transaction merchant, or commodity options dealer, as defined in section 761 of this title, with respect to which there is a customer, as defined in section 761 of this title;.

(7) The term "community claim" means claim that arose before the commencement of the case concerning the debtor for which property of the kind specified in section 541(a)(2) of this title is liable, whether or not there is any such property at the time of the commencement of the case;.

(7A) The term "commercial fishing operation" means—

(A) the catching or harvesting of fish, shrimp, lobsters, urchins, seaweed, shellfish, or other aquatic species or products of such species; or

(B) for purposes of section 109 and chapter 12, aquaculture activities consisting of raising for market any species or product described in subparagraph (A).

(7B) The term "commercial fishing vessel" means a vessel used by a family fisherman to carry out a commercial fishing operation.

(8) The term "consumer debt" means debt incurred by an individual primarily for a personal, family, or household purpose;.

(9) The term "corporation"—

(A) includes—

(i) association having a power or privilege that a private corporation, but not an individual or a partnership, possesses;

(ii) partnership association organized under a law that makes only the capital subscribed responsible for the debts of such association;

(iii) joint-stock company;

(iv) unincorporated company or association; or

(v) business trust; but

(B) does not include limited partnership;.

(10) The term "creditor" means—

(A) entity that has a claim against the debtor that arose at the time of or before the order for relief concerning the debtor;

(B) entity that has a claim against the estate of a kind specified in section 348(d), 502(f), 502(g), 502(h) or 502(i) of this title; or

(C) entity that has a community claim;.

(10A) The term "current monthly income"—

(A) means the average monthly income from all sources that the debtor receives (or in a joint case the debtor and the debtor's spouse receive) without regard to whether such income is taxable income, derived during the 6-month period ending on—

(i) the last day of the calendar month immediately preceding the date of the commencement of the case if the debtor files the schedule of current income required by section 521(a)(1)(B)(ii); or

(ii) the date on which current income is determined by the court for purposes of this title if the debtor does not file the schedule of current income required by section 521(a)(1)(B)(ii); and

(B) includes any amount paid by any entity other than the debtor (or in a joint case the debtor and the debtor's spouse), on a regular basis for the household expenses of the debtor or the debtor's dependents (and in a joint case the debtor's spouse if not otherwise a dependent), but excludes benefits received under the Social Security Act, payments to victims of war crimes or crimes against humanity on account of their status as victims of such crimes, and payments to victims of international terrorism (as defined in section 2331 of title 18) or domestic terrorism (as defined in section 2331 of title 18) on account of their status as victims of such terrorism.

(11) The term "custodian" means—

(A) receiver or trustee of any of the property of the debtor, appointed in a case or proceeding not under this title;

(B) assignee under a general assignment for the benefit of the debtor's creditors; or

(C) trustee, receiver, or agent under applicable law, or under a contract, that is appointed or authorized to take charge of property of the debtor for the purpose of enforcing a lien against such property, or for the purpose of general administration of such property for the benefit of the debtor's creditors~~;~~.

(12) The term "debt" means liability on a claim~~;~~.

~~(12A) "debt for child support" means a debt of a kind specified in section 523(a)(5) of this title for maintenance or support of a child of the debtor;~~

(12A) The term "debt relief agency" means any person who provides any bankruptcy assistance to an assisted person in return for the payment of money or other valuable consideration, or who is a bankruptcy petition preparer under section 110, but does not include—

(A) any person who is an officer, director, employee, or agent of a person who provides such assistance or of the bankruptcy petition preparer;

(B) a nonprofit organization that is exempt from taxation under section 501(c)(3) of the Internal Revenue Code of 1986;

(C) a creditor of such assisted person, to the extent that the creditor is assisting such assisted person to restructure any debt owed by such assisted person to the creditor;

(D) a depository institution (as defined in section 3 of the Federal Deposit Insurance Act) or any Federal credit union or State credit union (as those terms are defined in section 101 of the Federal Credit Union Act), or any affiliate or subsidiary of such depository institution or credit union; or

(E) an author, publisher, distributor, or seller of works subject to copyright protection under title 17, when acting in such capacity.

(13) The term "debtor" means person or municipality concerning which a case under this title has been commenced~~;~~.

(13A) The term "debtor's principal residence"—

(A) means a residential structure, including incidental property, without regard to whether that structure is attached to real property; and

(B) includes an individual condominium or cooperative unit, a mobile or manufactured home, or trailer.

(14) The term "disinterested person" means a person that—

(A) is not a creditor, an equity security holder, or an insider;

~~(B) is not and was not an investment banker for any outstanding security of the debtor;~~

~~(C) has not been, within three years before the date of the filing of the petition, an investment banker for a security of the debtor, or an attorney for such an investment banker in connection with the offer, sale, or issuance of a security of the debtor;~~

(~~D~~B) is not and was not, within ~~two~~ 2 years before the date of the filing of the petition a director, officer or employee of the debtor ~~or of an investment banker specified in subparagraph (B) or (C) of this paragraph~~; and

(~~E~~C) does not have an interest materially adverse to the interest of the estate or of any class of creditors or equity security holders, by reason of any direct or indirect relationship to, connection with, or interest in, the debtor ~~or an investment banker specified in subparagraph (B) or (C) of this paragraph~~, or for any other reason~~;~~.

(14A) The term "domestic support obligation" means a debt that accrues before, on, or after the date of the order for relief in a case under this title, including interest that accrues on that debt as provided under applicable nonbankruptcy law notwithstanding any other provision of this title, that is—

(A) owed to or recoverable by—

(i) a spouse, former spouse, or child of the debtor or such child's parent, legal guardian, or responsible relative; or

(ii) a governmental unit;

(B) in the nature of alimony, maintenance, or support (including assistance provided by a governmental unit) of such spouse, former spouse, or child of the debtor or such child's parent, without regard to whether such debt is expressly so designated;

(C) established or subject to establishment before, on, or after the date of the order for relief in a case under this title, by reason of applicable provisions of—

(i) a separation agreement, divorce decree, or property settlement agreement;

(ii) an order of a court of record; or

(iii) a determination made in accordance with applicable nonbankruptcy law by a governmental unit; and

(D) not assigned to a nongovernmental entity, unless that obligation is assigned voluntarily by the spouse, former spouse, child of the debtor, or such child's parent, legal guardian, or responsible relative for the purpose of collecting the debt.

(15) The term "entity" includes person, estate, trust, governmental unit, and United States trustee~~;~~.

(16) The term "equity security" means—

(A) share in a corporation, whether or not transferable or denominated "stock," or similar security;

(B) interest of a limited partner in a limited partnership; or

(C) warrant or right, other than a right to convert, to purchase, sell, or subscribe to a share, security, or interest of a kind specified in subparagraph (A) or (B) of this paragraph~~;~~.

(17) The term "equity security holder" means holder of an equity security of the debtor~~;~~.

(18) The term "family farmer" means—

(A) individual or individual and spouse engaged in a farming operation whose aggregate debts do not exceed ~~$1,500,000~~ $3,237,000 and not less than ~~80~~ 50 percent of whose aggregate noncontingent, liquidated debts (excluding a debt for the principal residence of such individual or such individual and spouse unless such debt arises out of a farming operation), on the date the case is filed, arise out of a farming operation owned or operated by such individual or such individual and spouse, and such individual or such individual and spouse receive from such farming operation more than 50 percent of such individual's or such individual and spouse's gross income for—

(i) the taxable year preceding; or

(ii) each of the 2d and 3d taxable years preceding;

the taxable year in which the case concerning such individual or such individual and spouse was filed; or

(B) corporation or partnership in which more than 50 percent of the outstanding stock or equity is held by one family, or by one family and the relatives of the members of such family, and such family or such relatives conduct the farming operation, and

(i) more than 80 percent of the value of its assets consists of assets related to the farming operation;

(ii) its aggregate debts do not exceed ~~$1,500,000~~ $3,237,000 and not less than ~~80~~ 50 percent of its aggregate noncontingent, liquidated debts (excluding a debt for one dwelling which is owned by such corporation or partnership and which a shareholder or partner maintains as a principal residence, unless such debt arises out of a farming operation), on the date the case is filed, arise out of the farming operation owned or operated by such corporation or such partnership; and

(iii) if such corporation issues stock, such stock is not publicly traded~~;~~.

(19) The term "family farmer with regular annual income" means family farmer whose annual income is sufficiently stable and regular to enable such family farmer to make payments under a plan under chapter 12 of this title~~;~~.

(19A) The term "family fisherman" means—

(A) an individual or individual and spouse engaged in a commercial fishing operation—

(i) whose aggregate debts do not exceed $1,500,000 and not less than 80 percent of whose aggregate noncontingent, liquidated debts (excluding a debt for the principal residence of such individual or such individual and spouse, unless such debt arises out of a commercial fishing operation), on the date the case is filed, arise out of a commercial fishing operation owned or operated by such individual or such individual and spouse; and

(ii) who receive from such commercial fishing operation more than 50 percent of such individual's or such individual's and spouse's gross income for the taxable year preceding the taxable year in which the case concerning such individual or such individual and spouse was filed; or

(B) a corporation or partnership—

(i) in which more than 50 percent of the outstanding stock or equity is held by—

(I) 1 family that conducts the commercial fishing operation; or

(II) 1 family and the relatives of the members of such family, and such family or such relatives conduct the commercial fishing operation; and

(ii)(I) more than 80 percent of the value of its assets consists of assets related to the commercial fishing operation;

(II) its aggregate debts do not exceed $1,500,000 and not less than 80 percent of its aggregate noncontingent, liquidated debts (excluding a debt for 1 dwelling which is owned by such corporation or partnership and which a shareholder or partner maintains as a principal residence, unless such debt arises out of a commercial fishing operation), on the date the case is filed, arise out of a commercial fishing operation owned or operated by such corporation or such partnership; and

(III) if such corporation issues stock, such stock is not publicly traded.

(19B) The term "family fisherman with regular annual income" means a family fisherman whose annual income is sufficiently stable and regular to enable such family fisherman to make payments under a plan under chapter 12 of this title.

(20) The term "farmer" means (except when such term appears in the term "family farmer") person that received more than 80 percent of such person's gross income during the taxable year of such person immediately preceding the taxable year of such person during which the case under this title concerning such person was commenced from a farming operation owned or operated by such person~~;~~.

(21) The term "farming operation" includes farming, tillage of the soil, dairy farming, ranching, production or raising of crops, poultry, or livestock, and production of poultry or livestock products in an unmanufactured state~~;~~.

(21A) The term "farmout agreement" means a written agreement in which—

(A) the owner of a right to drill, produce, or operate liquid or gaseous hydrocarbons on property agrees or has agreed to transfer or assign all or a part of such right to another entity; and

(B) such other entity (either directly or through its agents or its assigns), as consideration, agrees to perform drilling, reworking, recompleting, testing, or similar or related operations, to develop or produce liquid or gaseous hydrocarbons on the property~~;~~.

(21B) The term "Federal depository institutions regulatory agency" means—

(A) with respect to an insured depository institution (as defined in section 3(c)(2) of the Federal Deposit Insurance Act) for which no conservator or receiver has been appointed, the appropriate Federal banking agency (as defined in section 3(q) of such Act);

(B) with respect to an insured credit union (including an insured credit union for which the National Credit Union Administration has been appointed conservator or liquidating agent), the National Credit Union Administration;

(C) with respect to any insured depository institution for which the Resolution Trust Corporation has been appointed conservator or receiver, the Resolution Trust Corporation; and

(D) with respect to any insured depository institution for which the Federal Deposit Insurance Corporation has been appointed conservator or receiver, the Federal Deposit Insurance Corporation~~;~~.

(22) The term "financial institution" ~~—(A)~~ means—

(~~i~~A) a Federal reserve bank or an entity (domestic or foreign) that is a commercial or savings bank, industrial savings bank, savings and loan association, trust company, federally-insured credit union, or receiver, liquidating agent, or conservator for such entity and, when any such Federal reserve bank, receiver, liquidating agent, conservator, or entity is acting as agent or custodian for a customer in connection with a securities contract~~,~~ (as defined in section 741 ~~of this title,~~) ~~the~~ such customer; or

(~~ii~~B) in connection with a securities contract~~,~~ (as defined in section 741) ~~of this title,~~ an investment company registered under the Investment Company Act of 1940; ~~and~~

~~(B) includes any person described in subparagraph (A) which operates, or operates as, a multilateral clearing organization pursuant to section 409 of the Federal Deposit Insurance Corporation Improvement Act of 1991;~~

(22A) The term "financial participant" means—

(A) an entity that, at the time it enters into a securities contract, commodity contract, swap agreement, repurchase agreement, or forward contract, or at the time of the date of the filing of the petition, has one or more agreements or transactions described in paragraph (1), (2), (3), (4), (5), or (6) of section 561(a) with the debtor or any other entity (other than an affiliate) of a total gross dollar value of not less than $1,000,000,000 in notional or actual principal amount outstanding on any day during the previous 15-month period, or has gross mark-to-market positions of not less than $100,000,000 (aggregated across counterparties) in one or more such agreements or transactions with the debtor or any other entity (other than an affiliate) on any day during the previous 15-month period; or

(B) a clearing organization (as defined in section 402 of the Federal Deposit Insurance Corporation Improvement Act of 1991).

(23) The term "foreign proceeding" means ~~proceeding, whether judicial or administrative and whether or not under bankruptcy law, in a foreign country in which the debtor's domicile, residence, principal place of business, or principal assets were located at the commencement of such proceeding, for the purpose of liquidating an estate, adjusting debts by composition, extension, or discharge, or effecting a reorganization~~ a collective judicial or administrative proceeding in a foreign country, including an interim proceeding, under a law relating to insolvency or adjustment of debt in which proceeding the assets and affairs of the debtor are subject to control or supervision by a foreign court, for the purpose of reorganization or liquidation~~;~~.

(24) The term "foreign representative" means ~~duly selected trustee, administrator, or other representative of an estate in a foreign proceeding~~ a person or body, including a person or body appointed on an interim basis, authorized in a foreign proceeding to administer the reorganization or the liquidation of the debtor's assets or affairs or to act as a representative of such foreign proceeding~~;~~.

(25) The term "forward contract" means—

(A) a contract (other than a commodity contract) for the purchase, sale, or transfer of a commodity, as defined in section 761(8) of this title, or any similar good, article, service, right, or interest which is presently or in the future becomes the subject of dealing in the forward contract trade, or product or byproduct thereof, with a maturity date more than two days after the date the contract is entered into, including, but not limited to, a repurchase transaction, reverse repurchase transaction, consignment, lease, swap, hedge transaction, deposit, loan, option, allocated transaction, unallocated transaction, or any ~~combination thereof or option thereon~~ other similar agreement;

(B) any combination of agreements or transactions referred to in subparagraphs (A) and (C);

(C) any option to enter into an agreement or transaction referred to in subparagraph (A) or (B);

(D) a master agreement that provides for an agreement or transaction referred to in subparagraph (A), (B), or (C), together with all supplements to any such master agreement, without regard to whether such master agreement provides for an agreement or transaction that is not a forward contract under this paragraph, except that such master agreement shall be considered to be a forward contract under this paragraph only with respect to each agreement or transaction under such master agreement that is referred to in subparagraph (A), (B), or (C); or

(E) any security agreement or arrangement, or other credit enhancement related to any agreement or transaction referred to in subparagraph (A), (B), (C), or (D), including any guarantee or reimbursement obligation by or to a forward contract merchant or financial participant in connection with any agreement or transaction referred to in any such subparagraph, but not to exceed the damages in connection with any such agreement or transaction, measured in accordance with section 562~~;~~.

(26) The term "forward contract merchant" means ~~a person whose business~~ a Federal reserve bank, or an entity the business of which consists in whole or in part of entering into forward contracts as or with merchants in a commodity~~,~~ (as defined in section 761~~(8)) of this title,~~ or any similar good, article, service, right, or interest which is presently or in the future becomes the subject of dealing in the forward contract trade~~;~~.

(27) The term "governmental unit" means United States; State; Commonwealth; District; Territory; municipality; foreign state; department, agency, or instrumentality of the United States (but not a United States trustee while serving as a trustee in a case under this title), a State, a Commonwealth, a District, a Territory, a municipality, or a foreign state; or other foreign or domestic government~~;~~.

(27A) The term "health care business"—

(A) means any public or private entity (without regard to whether that entity is organized for profit or not for profit) that is primarily engaged in offering to the general public facilities and services for—

(i) the diagnosis or treatment of injury, deformity, or disease; and

(ii) surgical, drug treatment, psychiatric, or obstetric care; and

(B) includes—

(i) any—

(I) general or specialized hospital;

(II) ancillary ambulatory, emergency, or surgical treatment facility;

(III) hospice;

(IV) home health agency; and

(V) other health care institution that is similar to an entity referred to in subclause (I), (II), (III), or (IV); and

(ii) any long-term care facility, including any—

(I) skilled nursing facility;

(II) intermediate care facility;

(III) assisted living facility;

(IV) home for the aged;

(V) domiciliary care facility; and

(VI) health care institution that is related to a facility referred to in subclause (I), (II), (III), (IV), or (V), if that institution is primarily engaged in offering room, board, laundry, or personal assistance with activities of daily living and incidentals to activities of daily living.

(27B) The term "incidental property" means, with respect to a debtor's principal residence—

(A) property commonly conveyed with a principal residence in the area where the real property is located;

(B) all easements, rights, appurtenances, fixtures, rents, royalties, mineral rights, oil or gas rights or profits, water rights, escrow funds, or insurance proceeds; and

(C) all replacements or additions.

(28) The term "indenture" means mortgage, deed of trust, or indenture, under which there is outstanding a security, other than a voting-trust certificate, constituting a claim against the debtor, a claim secured by a lien on any of the debtor's property, or an equity security of the debtor~~;~~.

(29) The term "indenture trustee" means trustee under an indenture~~;~~.

(30) The term "individual with regular income" means individual whose income is sufficiently stable and regular to enable such individual to make payments under a plan under chapter 13 of this title, other than a stockbroker or a commodity broker~~;~~.

(31) The term "insider" includes—

(A) if the debtor is an individual—

(i) relative of the debtor or of a general partner of the debtor;

(ii) partnership in which the debtor is a general partner;

(iii) general partner of the debtor; or

(iv) corporation of which the debtor is a director, officer, or person in control;

(B) if the debtor is a corporation—

(i) director of the debtor;

(ii) officer of the debtor;

(iii) person in control of the debtor;

(iv) partnership in which the debtor is a general partner;

(v) general partner of the debtor; or

(vi) relative of a general partner, director, officer, or person in control of the debtor;

(C) if the debtor is a partnership—

(i) general partner in the debtor;

(ii) relative of a general partner in, general partner of, or person in control of the debtor;

(iii) partnership in which the debtor is a general partner;

(iv) general partner of the debtor; or

(v) person in control of the debtor;

(D) if the debtor is a municipality, elected official of the debtor or relative of an elected official of the debtor;

(E) affiliate, or insider of an affiliate as if such affiliate were the debtor; and

(F) managing agent of the debtor~~;~~.

(32) The term "insolvent" means—

(A) with reference to an entity other than a partnership and a municipality, financial condition such that the sum of such entity's debts is greater than all of such entity's property, at a fair valuation, exclusive of—

(i) property transferred, concealed, or removed with intent to hinder, delay, or defraud such entity's creditors; and

(ii) property that may be exempted from property of the estate under section 522 of this title;

(B) with reference to a partnership, financial condition such that the sum of such partnership's debts is greater than the aggregate of, at a fair valuation—

(i) all of such partnership's property, exclusive of property of the kind specified in subparagraph (A)(i) of this paragraph; and

(ii) the sum of the excess of the value of each general partner's nonpartnership property, exclusive of property of the kind specified in subparagraph (A) of this paragraph, over such partner's nonpartnership debts; and

(C) with reference to a municipality, financial condition such that the municipality is—

(i) generally not paying its debts as they become due unless such debts are the subject of a bona fide dispute; or

(ii) unable to pay its debts as they become due~~;~~.

(33) The term "institution-affiliated party"—

(A) with respect to an insured depository institution (as defined in section 3(c)(2) of the Federal Deposit Insurance Act), has the meaning given it in section 3(u) of the Federal Deposit Insurance Act; and

(B) with respect to an insured credit union, has the meaning given it in section 206(r) of the Federal Credit Union Act~~;~~.

(34) The term "insured credit union" has the meaning given it in section 101(7) of the Federal Credit Union Act~~;~~.

(35) The term "insured depository institution"—

(A) has the meaning given it in section 3(c)(2) of the Federal Deposit Insurance Act; and

(B) includes an insured credit union (except in the case of paragraphs (~~21B~~23) and (~~33)(A~~35) of this subsection)~~;~~.

(35A) The term "intellectual property" means—

(A) trade secret;

(B) invention, process, design, or plant protected under title 35;

(C) patent application;

(D) plant variety;

(E) work of authorship protected under title 17; or

(F) mask work protected under chapter 9 of title 17;

to the extent protected by applicable nonbankruptcy law~~;~~. ~~and~~

(36) The term "judicial lien" means lien obtained by judgment, levy, sequestration, or other legal or equitable process or proceeding~~;~~.

(37) The term "lien" means charge against or interest in property to secure payment of a debt or performance of an obligation~~;~~.

(38) The term "margin payment" means, for purposes of the forward contract provisions of this title, payment or deposit of cash, a security or other property, that is commonly known in the forward contract trade as original margin, initial margin, maintenance margin, or variation margin, including mark-to-market payments, or variation payments~~;~~. ~~and~~

(38A) The term "master netting agreement"—

(A) means an agreement providing for the exercise of rights, including rights of netting, setoff, liquidation, termination, acceleration, or close out, under or in connection with one or more contracts that are described in any one or more of paragraphs (1) through (5) of section 561(a), or any security agreement or arrangement or other credit enhancement related to one or more of the foregoing, including any guarantee or reimbursement obligation related to 1 or more of the foregoing; and

(B) if the agreement contains provisions relating to agreements or transactions that are not contracts described in paragraphs (1) through (5) of section 561(a), shall be deemed to be a master netting agreement only with respect to those agreements or transactions that are described in any one or more of paragraphs (1) through (5) of section 561(a).

(38B) The term "master netting agreement participant" means an entity that, at any time before the date of the filing of the petition, is a party to an outstanding master netting agreement with the debtor.

(39) The term "mask work" has the meaning given it in section 901(a)(2) of title 17.

(39A) The term "median family income" means for any year—

(A) the median family income both calculated and reported by the Bureau of the Census in the then most recent year; and

(B) if not so calculated and reported in the then current year, adjusted annually after such most recent year until the next year in which median family income is both calculated and reported by the Bureau of the Census, to reflect the percentage change in the Consumer Price Index for All Urban Consumers during the period of years occurring after such most recent year and before such current year.

(40) The term "municipality" means political subdivision or public agency or instrumentality of a State~~;~~.

(40A) The term "patient" means any individual who obtains or receives services from a health care business.

(40B) The term "patient records" means any written document relating to a patient or a record recorded in a magnetic, optical, or other form of electronic medium.

(41) The term "person" includes individual, partnership, and corporation, but does not include governmental unit, except that a governmental unit that—

(A) acquires an asset from a person—

(i) as a result of the operation of a loan guarantee agreement; or

(ii) as receiver or liquidating agent of a person;

(B) is a guarantor of a pension benefit payable by or on behalf of the debtor or an affiliate of the debtor; or

(C) is the legal or beneficial owner of an asset of—

(i) an employee pension benefit plan that is a governmental plan, as defined in section 414(d) of the Internal Revenue Code of 1986; or

(ii) an eligible deferred compensation plan, as defined in section 457(b) of the Internal Revenue Code of 1986;

shall be considered, for purposes of section 1102 of this title, to be a person with respect to such asset or such benefit~~;~~.

(41A) The term "personally identifiable information" means—

(A) if provided by an individual to the debtor in connection with obtaining a product or a service from the debtor primarily for personal, family, or household purposes—

(i) the first name (or initial) and last name of such individual, whether given at birth or time of adoption, or resulting from a lawful change of name;

(ii) the geographical address of a physical place of residence of such individual;

(iii) an electronic address (including an e-mail address) of such individual;

(iv) a telephone number dedicated to contacting such individual at such physical place of residence;

(v) a social security account number issued to such individual; or

(vi) the account number of a credit card issued to such individual; or

(B) if identified in connection with 1 or more of the items of information specified in subparagraph (A)—

(i) a birth date, the number of a certificate of birth or adoption, or a place of birth; or

(ii) any other information concerning an identified individual that, if disclosed, will result in contacting or identifying such individual physically or electronically.

(42) The term "petition" means petition filed under section 301, 302, 303, or 304 of this title, as the case may be, commencing a case under this title~~;~~.

(42A) The term "production payment" means a term overriding royalty satisfiable in cash or in kind—

(A) contingent on the production of a liquid or gaseous hydrocarbon from particular real property; and

(B) from a specified volume, or a specified value, from the liquid or gaseous hydrocarbon produced from such property, and determined without regard to production costs~~;~~.

(43) The term "purchaser" means transferee of a voluntary transfer, and includes immediate or mediate transferee of such a transferee~~;~~.

(44) The term "railroad" means common carrier by railroad engaged in the transportation of individuals or property, or owner of trackage facilities leased by such a common carrier~~;~~.

(45) The term "relative" means individual related by affinity or consanguinity within the third degree as determined by the common law, or individual in a step or adoptive relationship within such third degree~~;~~.

(46) The term "repo participant" means an entity that, ~~on any day during the period beginning 90 days before the date of~~ at any time before the filing of the petition, has an outstanding repurchase agreement with the debtor~~;~~.

(47) The term "repurchase agreement" (which definition also applies to a reverse repurchase agreement)—

(A) means—

(i) an agreement, including related terms, which provides for the transfer of one or more certificates of deposit, mortgage related securities (as defined in section 3 of the Securities Exchange Act of 1934), mortgage loans, interests in mortgage related securities or mortgage loans, eligible bankers' acceptances, qualified foreign government securities (defined as a security that is a direct obligation of, or that is fully guaranteed by, the central government of a member of the Organization for Economic Cooperation and Development), or securities that are direct obligations of, or that are fully guaranteed ~~as to principal and interest~~ by, the United States or any agency of the United States against the transfer of funds by the transferee of such certificates of deposit, eligible bankers' acceptances, ~~or~~ securities, mortgage loans, or interests, with a simultaneous agreement by such transferee to transfer to the transferor thereof certificates of deposit, eligible bankers' acceptance~~s~~, ~~or~~ securities mortgage loans, or interests of the kind as described ~~above~~ in this clause, at a date certain not later than ~~one~~ 1 year after such transfer~~s~~ or on demand, against the transfer of funds;

(ii) any combination of agreements or transactions referred to in clauses (i) and (iii);

(iii) an option to enter into an agreement or transaction referred to in clause (i) or (ii);

(iv) a master agreement that provides for an agreement or transaction referred to in clause (i), (ii), or (iii), together with all supplements to any such master agreement, without regard to whether such master agreement provides for an agreement or transaction that is not a repurchase agreement under this paragraph, except that such master agreement shall be considered to be a repurchase agreement under this paragraph only with respect to each agreement or transaction under the master agreement that is referred to in clause (i), (ii), or (iii); or

(v) any security agreement or arrangement or other credit enhancement related to any agreement or transaction referred to in clause (i), (ii), (iii), or (iv), including any guarantee or reimbursement obligation by or to a repo participant or financial participant in connection with any agreement or transaction referred to in any such clause, but not to exceed the damages in connection with any such agreement or transaction, measured in accordance with section 562 of this title; and

(B) does not include a repurchase obligation under a participation in a commercial mortgage loan.

(48) The term "securities clearing agency" means person that is registered as a clearing agency under section 17A of the Securities Exchange Act of 1934 or exempt from such registration under such section pursuant to an order of the Securities and Exchange Commission, or whose business is confined to the performance of functions of a clearing agency with respect to exempted securities, as defined in section 3(a)(12) of such Act for the purposes of such section 17A~~;~~.

(48A) The term "securities self regulatory organization" means either a securities association registered with the Securities and Exchange Commission under section 15A of the Securities Exchange Act of 1934 or a national securities exchange registered with the Securities and Exchange Commission under section 6 of the Securities Exchange Act of 1934.

(49) The term "security"—

(A) includes—

(i) note;

(ii) stock;

(iii) treasury stock;

(iv) bond;

(v) debenture;

(vi) collateral trust certificate;

(vii) pre-organization certificate or subscription;

(viii) transferable share;

(ix) voting-trust certificate;

(x) certificate of deposit;

(xi) certificate of deposit for security;

(xii) investment contract or certificate of interest or participation in a profit-sharing agreement or in an oil, gas, or mineral royalty or lease, if such contract or interest is required to be the subject of a registration statement filed with the Securities and Exchange Commission under the provisions of the Securities Act of 1933, or is exempt under section 3(b) of such Act from the requirement to file such a statement;

(xiii) interest of a limited partner in a limited partnership;

(xiv) other claim or interest commonly known as "security"; and

(xv) certificate of interest or participation in, temporary or interim certificate for, receipt for, or warrant or right to subscribe to or purchase or sell, a security; but

(B) does not include—

(i) currency, check, draft, bill of exchange, or bank letter of credit;

(ii) leverage transaction, as defined in section 761 of this title;

(iii) commodity futures contract or forward contract;

(iv) option, warrant, or right to subscribe to or purchase or sell a commodity futures contract;

(v) option to purchase or sell a commodity;

(vi) contract or certificate of a kind specified in subparagraph A (xii) of this paragraph that is not required to be the subject of a registration statement filed with the Securities and Exchange Commission and is not exempt under section 3(b) of the Securities Act of 1933 from the requirement to file such a statement; or

(vii) debt or evidence of indebtedness for goods sold and delivered or services rendered~~;~~.

(50) The term "security agreement" means agreement that creates or provides for a security interest~~;~~.

(51) The term "security interest" means lien created by an agreement~~;~~.

(51A) The term "settlement payment" means, for purposes of the forward contract provisions of this title, a preliminary settlement payment, a partial settlement payment, an interim settlement payment, a settlement payment on account, a final settlement payment, a net settlement payment, or any other similar payment commonly used in the forward contract trade~~;~~.

(51B) The term "single asset real estate" means real property constituting a single property or project, other than residential real property with fewer than 4 residential units, which generates substantially all of the gross income of a debtor who is not a family farmer and on which no substantial business is being conducted by a debtor other than the business of operating the real property and activities incidental ~~thereto having aggregate noncontingent, liquidated secured debts in an amount no more than $4,000,000;~~.

(51C) The term "small business case" means a case filed under chapter 11 of this title in which the debtor is a small business debtor.

(51~~C~~D) The term "small business debtor"~~—~~

(A) subject to subparagraph (B), means a person engaged in commercial or business activities (including any affiliate of such person that is also a debtor under this title ~~but does not include~~ and excluding a person whose primary activity is the business of owning or operating real property ~~and~~ or activities incidental thereto) ~~whose~~ that has aggregate noncontingent liquidated secured and unsecured debts as of the date of the petition or the date of the order for relief ~~do not exceed~~ in an amount not more than $2,000,000 (excluding debts owed to 1 or more affiliates or insiders) for a case in which the United

States trustee has not appointed under section 1102(a)(1) a committee of unsecured creditors or where the court has determined that the committee of unsecured creditors is not sufficiently active and representative to provide effective oversight of the debtor; and

(B) does not include any member of a group of affiliated debtors that has aggregate noncontingent liquidated secured and unsecured debts in an amount greater than $2,000,000 (excluding debt owed to 1 or more affiliates or insiders).~~;~~

(52) The term "State" includes the District of Columbia and Puerto Rico, except for the purpose of defining who may be a debtor under chapter 9 of this title~~;~~.

(53) The term "statutory lien" means lien arising solely by force of a statute on specified circumstances or conditions, or lien of distress for rent, whether or not statutory, but does not include security interest or judicial lien, whether or not such interest or lien is provided by or is dependent on a statute and whether or not such interest or lien is made fully effective by statute~~;~~.

(53A) The term "stockbroker" means person—

(A) with respect to which there is a customer, as defined in section 741 of this title; and

(B) that is engaged in the business of effecting transactions in securities—

(i) for the account of others; or

(ii) with members of the general public, from or for such person's own account~~;~~.

(53B) The term "swap agreement"—

(A) means—

(~~A~~i) any agreement~~, (~~including the terms and conditions incorporated by reference ~~therein~~ in such agreement~~)~~, which is~~—a rate swap agreement, basis swap, forward rate agreement, commodity swap, interest rate option, forward foreign exchange agreement, spot foreign exchange agreement, rate cap agreement, rate floor agreement, rate collar agreement, currency swap agreement, cross-currency rate swap agreement, currency option, any other similar agreement (including any option to enter into any of the foregoing);~~

(I) an interest rate swap, option, future, or forward agreement, including a rate floor, rate cap, rate collar, cross-currency rate swap, and basis swap;

(II) a spot, same day-tomorrow, tomorrow-next, forward, or other foreign exchange or precious metals agreement;

(III) a currency swap, option, future, or forward agreement;

(IV) an equity index or equity swap, option, future, or forward agreement;

(V) a debt index or debt swap, option, future, or forward agreement;

(VI) a total return, credit spread or credit swap, option, future, or forward agreement;

(VII) a commodity index or a commodity swap, option, future, or forward agreement; or

(VIII) a weather swap, weather derivative, or weather option;

(ii) any agreement or transaction that is similar to any other agreement or transaction referred to in this paragraph and that—

(I) is of a type that has been, is presently, or in the future becomes, the subject of recurrent dealings in the swap markets (including terms and conditions incorporated by reference therein); and

(II) is a forward, swap, future, or option on one or more rates, currencies, commodities, equity securities, or other equity instruments, debt securities or other debt instruments, quantitative measures associated with an occurrence, extent of an occurrence, or contingency associated with a financial, commercial, or economic consequence, or economic or financial indices or measures of economic or financial risk or value;

(~~B~~iii) any combination of ~~the foregoing~~ agreements or transactions referred to in this subparagraph; ~~or~~

(iv) any option to enter into an agreement or transaction referred to in this subparagraph;

(~~C~~ v) a master agreement ~~for any of the foregoing~~ that provides for an agreement or transaction referred to in clause (i), (ii), (iii), or (iv), together with all supplements to any such master agreement, and without regard to whether the master agreement contains an agreement or transaction that is not a swap agreement under this paragraph, except that the master agreement shall be considered to be a swap agreement under this paragraph only with respect to each agreement or transaction under the master agreement that is referred to in clause (i), (ii), (iii), or (iv); or

(vi) any security agreement or arrangement or other credit enhancement related to any agreements or transactions referred to in clause (i) through (v), including any guarantee or reimbursement obligation by or to a swap participant or financial participant in connection with any agreement or transaction referred to in any such clause, but not to exceed the damages in connection with any such agreement or transaction, measured in accordance with section 562; and

(B) is applicable for purposes of this title only, and shall not be construed or applied so as to challenge or affect the characterization, definition, or treatment of any swap agreement under any other statute, regulation, or rule, including the Securities Act of 1933, the Securities Exchange Act of 1934, the Public Utility Holding Company Act of 1935, the Trust Indenture Act of 1939, the Investment Company Act of 1940, the Investment Advisers Act of 1940, the Securities Investor Protection Act of 1970, the Commodity Exchange Act, the Gramm-Leach-Bliley Act, and the Legal Certainty for Bank Products Act of 2000~~;~~.

(53C) The term "swap participant" means an entity that, at any time before the filing of the petition, has an outstanding swap agreement with the debtor~~;~~.

(56A)[2] The term "term overriding royalty" means an interest in liquid or gaseous hydrocarbons in place or to be produced from particular real property that entitles the owner thereof to a share of production, or the value thereof, for a term limited by time, quantity, or value realized;.

(53D) The term "timeshare plan" means and shall include that interest purchased in any arrangement, plan, scheme, or similar device, but not including exchange programs, whether by membership, agreement, tenancy in common, sale, lease, deed, rental agreement, license, right to use agreement, or by any other means, whereby a purchaser, in exchange for consideration, receives a right to use accommodations, facilities, or recreational sites, whether improved or unimproved, for a specific period of time less than a full year during any given year, but not necessarily for consecutive years, and which extends for a period of more than three years. A "timeshare interest" is that interest purchased in a timeshare plan which grants the purchaser the right to use and occupy accommodations, facilities, or recreational sites, whether improved or unimproved, pursuant to a timeshare plan;.

(54) The term "transfer" means—

(A) the creation of a lien;

(B) the retention of title as a security interest;

(C) the foreclosure of a debtor's equity of redemption; or

(D) ~~every~~ each mode, direct or indirect, absolute or conditional, voluntary or involuntary, of disposing of or parting with—

(i) property; or

(ii) ~~with~~ an interest in property~~, including retention of title as a security interest and foreclosure of the debtor's equity of redemption;~~.

(54A) ~~t~~ The term "uninsured State member bank" means a State member bank (as defined in section 3 of the Federal Deposit Insurance Act) the deposits of which are not insured by the Federal Deposit Insurance Corporation;. ~~and~~

(55) The term "United States," when used in a geographical sense, includes all locations where the judicial jurisdiction of the United States extends, including territories and possessions of the United States;.

§ 102. Rules of construction

In this title—

(1) "after notice and a hearing," or a similar phrase—

(A) means after such notice as is appropriate in the particular circumstances, and such opportunity for a hearing as is appropriate in the particular circumstances; but

(B) authorizes an act without an actual hearing if such notice is given properly and if—

(i) such a hearing is not requested timely by a party in interest; or

(ii) there is insufficient time for a hearing to be commenced before such act must be done, and the court authorizes such act;

(2) "claim against the debtor" includes claim against property of the debtor;

(3) "includes" and "including" are not limiting;

(4) "may not" is prohibitive, and not permissive;

(5) "or" is not exclusive;

(6) "order for relief" means entry of an order for relief;

(7) the singular includes the plural;

(8) a definition, contained in a section of this title that refers to another section of this title, does not, for the purpose of such reference, affect the meaning of a term used in such other section; and

(9) "United States trustee" includes a designee of the United States trustee.

§ 103. Applicability of chapters

(a) Except as provided in section 1161 of this title, chapters 1, 3, and 5 of this title apply in a case under chapter 7, 11, 12, or 13 of this title, and this chapter, sections 307, 362(n), 555 through 557, and 559 through 562 apply in a case under chapter 15.

(b) Subchapters I and II of chapter 7 of this title apply only in a case under such chapter.

(c) Subchapter III of chapter 7 of this title applies only in a case under such chapter concerning a stockbroker.

(d) Subchapter IV of chapter 7 of this title applies only in a case under such chapter concerning a commodity broker.

(e) Scope of Application.—Subchapter V of chapter 7 of this title shall apply only in a case under such chapter concerning the liquidation of an uninsured State member bank, or a corporation organized under section 25A of the Federal Reserve Act, which operates, or operates as, a multilateral clearing organization pursuant to section 409 of the Federal Deposit Insurance Corporation Improvement Act of 1991.

(f) Except as provided in section 901 of this title, only chapters 1 and 9 of this title apply in a case under such chapter 9.

(g) Except as provided in section 901 of this title, subchapters I, II, and III of chapter 11 of this title apply only in a case under such chapter.

(h) Subchapter IV of chapter 11 of this title applies only in a case under such chapter concerning a railroad.

(i) Chapter 13 of this title applies only in a case under such chapter.

(j) Chapter 12 of this title applies only in a case under such chapter.

(k) Chapter 15 applies only in a case under such chapter, except that—

2 *Editor's Note*: So in original. Paragraph (56A) was inserted between paragraphs (53C) and (53D).

(1) sections 1505, 1513, and 1514 apply in all cases under this title; and

(2) section 1509 applies whether or not a case under this title is pending.

§ 104. Adjustment of dollar amounts

(a) The Judicial Conference of the United States shall transmit to the Congress and to the President before May 1, 1985, and before May 1 of every sixth year after May 1, 1985, a recommendation for the uniform percentage adjustment of each dollar amount in this title and in section 1930 of title 28.

(b)(1) On April 1, 1998, and at each 3-year interval ending on April 1 thereafter, each dollar amount in effect under sections 101(3), 101(18), 101(19A), 101(51D), 109(e), 303(b), 507(a), 522(d), 522(f)(3) and (f)(4), 522(n), 522(p), 522(q), ~~and~~ 523(a)(2)(C), 541(b), 547(c)(9), 707(b), 1322(d), 1325(b), and 1326(b)(3) of this title and section 1409(b) of title 28[3] immediately before such April 1 shall be adjusted—

(A) to reflect the change in the Consumer Price Index for All Urban Consumers, published by the Department of Labor, for the most recent 3-year period ending immediately before January 1 preceding such April 1, and

(B) to round to the nearest $25 the dollar amount that represents such change.

(2) Not later than March 1, 1998, and at each 3-year interval ending on March 1 thereafter, the Judicial Conference of the United States shall publish in the Federal Register the dollar amounts that will become effective on such April 1 under sections 101(3), 101(18), 101(19A), 101(51D), 109(e), 303(b), 507(a), 522(d), 522(f)(3) and (f)(4), 522(n), 522(p), 522(q), ~~and~~ 523(a)(2)(C), 541(b), 547(c)(9), 707(b), 1322(d), 1325(b), and 1326(b)(3) of this title and section 1409(b) of title 28.[4]

(3) Adjustments made in accordance with paragraph (1) shall not apply with respect to cases commenced before the date of such adjustments.

§ 105. Power of court

(a) The court may issue any order, process, or judgment that is necessary or appropriate to carry out the provisions of this title. No provision of this title providing for the raising of an issue by a party in interest shall be construed to preclude the court from, sua sponte, taking any action or making any determination necessary or appropriate to enforce or implement court orders or rules, or to prevent an abuse of process.

(b) Notwithstanding subsection (a) of this section, a court may not appoint a receiver in a case under this title.

(c) The ability of any district judge or other officer or employee of a district court to exercise any of the authority or responsibilities conferred upon the court under this title shall be determined by reference to the provisions relating to such judge, officer, or employee set forth in title 28. This subsection shall not be interpreted to exclude bankruptcy judges and other officers or employees appointed pursuant to chapter 6 of title 28 from its operation.

(d) The court, on its own motion or on the request of a party in interest~~, may~~—

(1) shall hold ~~a~~ such status conferences ~~regarding any case or proceeding under this title after notice to the parties in interest~~ as are necessary to further the expeditious and economical resolution of the case; and

(2) unless inconsistent with another provision of this title or with applicable Federal Rules of Bankruptcy Procedure, issue an order at any such conference prescribing such limitations and conditions as the court deems appropriate to ensure that the case is handled expeditiously and economically, including an order that—

(A) sets the date by which the trustee must assume or reject an executory contract or unexpired lease; or

(B) in a case under chapter 11 of this title—

(i) sets a date by which the debtor, or trustee if one has been appointed, shall file a disclosure statement and plan;

(ii) sets a date by which the debtor, or trustee if one has been appointed, shall solicit acceptances of a plan;

(iii) sets the date by which a party in interest other than a debtor may file a plan;

(iv) sets a date by which a proponent of a plan, other than the debtor, shall solicit acceptances of such plan;

(v) fixes the scope and format of the notice to be provided regarding the hearing on approval of the disclosure statement; or

(vi) provides that the hearing on approval of the disclosure statement may be combined with the hearing on confirmation of the plan.

§ 106. Waiver of sovereign immunity

(a) Notwithstanding an assertion of sovereign immunity, sovereign immunity is abrogated as to a governmental unit to the extent set forth in this section with respect to the following:

(1) Sections 105, 106, 107, 108, 303, 346, 362, 363, 364, 365, 366, 502, 503, 505, 506, 510, 522, 523, 524, 525, 542, 543, 544, 545, 546, 547, 548, 549, 550, 551, 552, 553, 722, 724, 726, 728, 744, 749, 764, 901, 922, 926, 928, 929, 944, 1107, 1141, 1142, 1143, 1146, 1201, 1203, 1205, 1206, 1227, 1231, 1301, 1303, 1305, and 1327 of this title.

(2) The court may hear and determine any issue arising with respect to the application of such sections to governmental units.

(3) The court may issue against a governmental unit an order, process, or judgment under such sections or the Federal Rules of Bankruptcy Procedure, including an order or judgment awarding a money recovery, but not including an award of punitive damages. Such order or judgment for costs or fees

3 *Editor's Note*: These changes to section 104(b)(1) are effective for cases commenced under title 11 on or after April 20, 2005.

4 *Editor's Note*: These changes to section 104(b)(2) are effective for cases commenced under title 11 on or after April 20, 2005.

under this title or the Federal Rules of Bankruptcy Procedure against any governmental unit shall be consistent with the provisions and limitations of section 2412(d)(2)(A) of title 28.

(4) The enforcement of any such order, process, or judgment against any governmental unit shall be consistent with appropriate nonbankruptcy law applicable to such governmental unit and, in the case of a money judgment against the United States, shall be paid as if it is a judgment rendered by a district court of the United States.

(5) Nothing in this section shall create any substantive claim for relief or cause of action not otherwise existing under this title, the Federal Rules of Bankruptcy Procedure, or nonbankruptcy law.

(b) A governmental unit that has filed a proof of claim in the case is deemed to have waived sovereign immunity with respect to a claim against such governmental unit that is property of the estate and that arose out of the same transaction or occurrence out of which the claim of such governmental unit arose.

(c) Notwithstanding any assertion of sovereign immunity by a governmental unit, there shall be offset against a claim or interest of a governmental unit any claim against such governmental unit that is property of the estate.

§ 107. Public access to papers

(a) Except as provided in subsections (b) and (c) of this section and subject to section 112, a paper filed in a case under this title and the dockets of a bankruptcy court are public records and open to examination by an entity at reasonable times without charge.

(b) On request of a party in interest, the bankruptcy court shall, and on the bankruptcy court's own motion, the bankruptcy court may—

(1) protect an entity with respect to a trade secret or confidential research, development, or commercial information; or

(2) protect a person with respect to scandalous or defamatory matter contained in a paper filed in a case under this title.

(c)(1) The bankruptcy court, for cause, may protect an individual, with respect to the following types of information to the extent the court finds that disclosure of such information would create undue risk of identity theft or other unlawful injury to the individual or the individual's property:

(A) Any means of identification (as defined in section 1028(d) of title 18) contained in a paper filed, or to be filed, in a case under this title.

(B) Other information contained in a paper described in subparagraph (A).

(2) Upon ex parte application demonstrating cause, the court shall provide access to information protected pursuant to paragraph (1) to an entity acting pursuant to the police or regulatory power of a domestic governmental unit.

(3) The United States trustee, bankruptcy administrator, trustee, and any auditor serving under section 586(f) of title 28—

(A) shall have full access to all information contained in any paper filed or submitted in a case under this title; and

(B) shall not disclose information specifically protected by the court under this title.

§ 108. Extension of time

(a) If applicable nonbankruptcy law, an order entered in a nonbankruptcy proceeding, or an agreement fixes a period within which the debtor may commence an action, and such period has not expired before the date of the filing of the petition, the trustee may commence such action only before the later of—

(1) the end of such period, including any suspension of such period occurring on or after the commencement of the case; or

(2) two years after the order for relief.

(b) Except as provided in subsection (a) of this section, if applicable nonbankruptcy law, an order entered in a nonbankruptcy proceeding, or an agreement fixes a period within which the debtor or an individual protected under section 1201 or 1301 of this title may file any pleading, demand, notice, or proof of claim or loss, cure a default, or perform any other similar act, and such period has not expired before the date of the filing of the petition, the trustee may only file, cure, or perform, as the case may be, before the later of—

(1) the end of such period, including any suspension of such period occurring on or after the commencement of the case; or

(2) 60 days after the order for relief.

(c) Except as provided in section 524 of this title, if applicable nonbankruptcy law, an order entered in a nonbankruptcy proceeding, or an agreement fixes a period for commencing or continuing a civil action in a court other than a bankruptcy court on a claim against the debtor, or against an individual with respect to which such individual is protected under section 1201 or 1301 of this title, and such period has not expired before the date of the filing of the petition, then such period does not expire until the later of—

(1) the end of such period, including any suspension of such period occurring on or after the commencement of the case; or

(2) 30 days after notice of the termination or expiration of the stay under section 362, 922, 1201, or 1301 of this title, as the case may be, with respect to such claim.

§ 109. Who may be a debtor

(a) Notwithstanding any other provision of this section, only a person that resides or has a domicile, a place of business, or property in the United States, or a municipality, may be a debtor under this title.

(b) A person may be a debtor under chapter 7 of this title only if such person is not—

(1) a railroad;

(2) a domestic insurance company, bank, savings bank, cooperative bank, savings and loan association, building and loan association, homestead association, a small business investment company licensed by the Small Business Administration under ~~subsection (c) or (d) of~~ section 301 of the Small Business

Investment Act of 1958, credit union, or industrial bank or similar institution which is an insured bank as defined in section 3(h) of the Federal Deposit Insurance Act, except that an uninsured State member bank, or a corporation organized under section 25A of the Federal Reserve Act, which operates, or operates as, a multilateral clearing organization pursuant to section 409 of the Federal Deposit Insurance Corporation Improvement Act of 1991 may be a debtor if a petition is filed at the direction of the Board of Governors of the Federal Reserve System; or

(3)(A) a foreign insurance company, engaged in such business in the United States; or

(B) a foreign bank, savings bank, cooperative bank, savings and loan association, building and loan association, ~~homestead association,~~ or credit union, ~~engaged in such business~~ that has a branch or agency (as defined in section 1(b) of the International Banking Act of 1978 in the United States.

(c) An entity may be a debtor under chapter 9 of this title if and only if such entity—

(1) is a municipality;

(2) is specifically authorized, in its capacity as a municipality or by name, to be a debtor under such chapter by State law, or by a governmental officer or organization empowered by State law to authorize such entity to be a debtor under such chapter;

(3) is insolvent;

(4) desires to effect a plan to adjust such debts; and

(5)(A) has obtained the agreement of creditors holding at least a majority in amount of the claims of each class that such entity intends to impair under a plan in a case under such chapter;

(B) has negotiated in good faith with creditors and has failed to obtain the agreement of creditors holding at least a majority in amount of the claims of each class that such entity intends to impair under a plan in a case under such chapter;

(C) is unable to negotiate with creditors because such negotiation is impracticable; or

(D) reasonably believes that a creditor may attempt to obtain a transfer that is avoidable under section 547 of this title.

(d) Only a railroad, a person that may be a debtor under chapter 7 of this title (except a stockbroker or a commodity broker), and an uninsured State member bank, or a corporation organized under section 25A of the Federal Reserve Act, which operates, or operates as, a multilateral clearing organization pursuant to section 409 of the Federal Deposit Insurance Corporation Improvement Act of 1991 may be a debtor under chapter 11 of this title.

(e) Only an individual with regular income that owes, on the date of the filing of the petition, noncontingent, liquidated, unsecured debts of less than $307,675[5] and noncontingent, liquidated, secured debts of less than $922,975,[6] or an individual with regular income and such individual's spouse, except a stockbroker or a commodity broker, that owe, on the date of the filing of the petition, noncontingent, liquidated, unsecured debts that aggregate less than $307,675[7] and noncontingent, liquidated, secured debts of less than $922,975[8] may be a debtor under chapter 13 of this title.

(f) Only a family farmer or family fisherman with regular annual income may be a debtor under chapter 12 of this title.

(g) Notwithstanding any other provision of this section, no individual or family farmer may be a debtor under this title who has been a debtor in a case pending under this title at any time in the preceding 180 days if—

(1) the case was dismissed by the court for willful failure of the debtor to abide by orders of the court, or to appear before the court in proper prosecution of the case; or

(2) the debtor requested and obtained the voluntary dismissal of the case following the filing of a request for relief from the automatic stay provided by section 362 of this title.

(h)(1) Subject to paragraphs (2) and (3), and notwithstanding any other provision of this section, an individual may not be a debtor under this title unless such individual has, during the 180-day period preceding the date of filing of the petition by such individual, received from an approved nonprofit budget and credit counseling agency described in section 111(a) an individual or group briefing (including a briefing conducted by telephone or on the Internet) that outlined the opportunities for available credit counseling and assisted such individual in performing a related budget analysis.

(2)(A) Paragraph (1) shall not apply with respect to a debtor who resides in a district for which the United States trustee (or the bankruptcy administrator, if any) determines that the approved nonprofit budget and credit counseling agencies for such district are not reasonably able to provide adequate services to the additional individuals who would otherwise seek credit counseling from such agencies by reason of the requirements of paragraph (1).

(B) The United States trustee (or the bankruptcy administrator, if any) who makes a determination described in subparagraph (A) shall review such determination not later than 1 year after the date of such determination, and not less frequently than annually thereafter. Notwithstanding the preceding sentence, a nonprofit budget and credit counseling agency may be disapproved by the United States trustee (or the bankruptcy administrator, if any) at any time.

(3)(A) Subject to subparagraph (B), the requirements of paragraph (1) shall not apply with respect to a debtor who submits to the court a certification that—

5 *Editor's Note*: This dollar amount reflects an inflationary adjustment, effective April 1, 2004. For cases commenced before April 1, 2004, the applicable dollar amount is $290,525.

6 *Editor's Note*: This dollar amount reflects an inflationary adjustment, effective April 1, 2004. For cases commenced before April 1, 2004, the applicable dollar amount is $871,550.

7 *Editor's Note*: This dollar amount reflects an inflationary adjustment, effective April 1, 2004. For cases commenced before April 1, 2004, the applicable dollar amount is $290,525.

8 *Editor's Note*: This dollar amount reflects an inflationary adjustment, effective April 1, 2004. For cases commenced before April 1, 2004, the applicable dollar amount is $871,550.

(i) describes exigent circumstances that merit a waiver of the requirements of paragraph (1);

(ii) states that the debtor requested credit counseling services from an approved nonprofit budget and credit counseling agency, but was unable to obtain the services referred to in paragraph (1) during the 5-day period beginning on the date on which the debtor made that request; and

(iii) is satisfactory to the court.

(B) With respect to a debtor, an exemption under subparagraph (A) shall cease to apply to that debtor on the date on which the debtor meets the requirements of paragraph (1), but in no case may the exemption apply to that debtor after the date that is 30 days after the debtor files a petition, except that the court, for cause, may order an additional 15 days.

(4) The requirements of paragraph (1) shall not apply with respect to a debtor whom the court determines, after notice and hearing, is unable to complete those requirements because of incapacity, disability, or active military duty in a military combat zone. For the purposes of this paragraph, incapacity means that the debtor is impaired by reason of mental illness or mental deficiency so that he is incapable of realizing and making rational decisions with respect to his financial responsibilities; and "disability" means that the debtor is so physically impaired as to be unable, after reasonable effort, to participate in an in person, telephone, or Internet briefing required under paragraph (1).

§ 110. Penalty for persons who negligently or fraudulently prepare bankruptcy petitions

(a) In this section—

(1) "bankruptcy petition preparer" means a person, other than an attorney ~~or an employee of an attorney~~ for the debtor or an employee of such attorney under the direct supervision of such attorney, who prepares for compensation a document for filing; and

(2) "document for filing" means a petition or any other document prepared for filing by a debtor in a United States bankruptcy court or a United States district court in connection with a case under this title.

(b)(1) A bankruptcy petition preparer who prepares a document for filing shall sign the document and print on the document the preparer's name and address. If a bankruptcy petition preparer is not an individual, then an officer, principal, responsible person, or partner of the bankruptcy petition preparer shall be required to—

(A) sign the document for filing; and

(B) print on the document the name and address of that officer, principal, responsible person or partner.

~~(2) A bankruptcy petition preparer who fails to comply with paragraph (1) may be fined not more than $500 for each such failure unless the failure is due to reasonable cause.~~

(2)(A) Before preparing any document for filing or accepting any fees from a debtor, the bankruptcy petition preparer shall provide to the debtor a written notice which shall be on an official form prescribed by the Judicial Conference of the United States in accordance with rule 9009 of the Federal Rules of Bankruptcy Procedure.

(B) The notice under subparagraph (A)—

(i) shall inform the debtor in simple language that a bankruptcy petition preparer is not an attorney and may not practice law or give legal advice;

(ii) may contain a description of examples of legal advice that a bankruptcy petition preparer is not authorized to give, in addition to any advice that the preparer may not give by reason of subsection (e)(2); and

(iii) shall—

(I) be signed by the debtor and, under penalty of perjury, by the bankruptcy petition preparer; and

(II) be filed with any document for filing.

(c)(1) A bankruptcy petition preparer who prepares a document for filing shall place on the document, after the preparer's signature, an identifying number that identifies individuals who prepared the document.

(2)(A) Subject to subparagraph (B), for ~~For~~ purposes of this section, the identifying number of a bankruptcy petition preparer shall be the Social Security account number of each individual who prepared the document or assisted in its preparation.

(B) If a bankruptcy petition preparer is not an individual, the identifying number of the bankruptcy petition preparer shall be the Social Security account number of the officer, principal, responsible person, or partner of the bankruptcy petition preparer.

~~(3) A bankruptcy petition preparer who fails to comply with paragraph (1) may be fined not more than $500 for each such failure unless the failure is due to reasonable cause.~~

(d)~~(1)~~ A bankruptcy petition preparer shall, not later than the time at which a document for filing is presented for the debtor's signature, furnish to the debtor a copy of the document.

~~(2) A bankruptcy petition preparer who fails to comply with paragraph (1) may be fined not more than $500 for each such failure unless the failure is due to reasonable cause.~~

(e)(1) A bankruptcy petition preparer shall not execute any document on behalf of a debtor.

(2)(A) A bankruptcy petition preparer may not offer a potential bankruptcy debtor any legal advice, including any legal advice described in subparagraph (B).

(B) The legal advice referred to in subparagraph (A) includes advising the debtor—

(i) whether—

(I) to file a petition under this title; or

(II) commencing a case under chapter 7, 11, 12, or 13 is appropriate;

(ii) whether the debtor's debts will be discharged in a case under this title;

(iii) whether the debtor will be able to retain the debtor's home, car, or other property after commencing a case under this title;

(iv) concerning—

(I) the tax consequences of a case brought under this title; or

(II) the dischargeability of tax claims;

(v) whether the debtor may or should promise to repay debts to a creditor or enter into a reaffirmation agreement with a creditor to reaffirm a debt;

(vi) concerning how to characterize the nature of the debtor's interests in property or the debtor's debts; or

(vii) concerning bankruptcy procedures and rights.

~~(2) A bankruptcy petition preparer may be fined not more than $500 for each document executed in violation of paragraph (1).~~

(f)~~(1)~~ A bankruptcy petition preparer shall not use the word "legal" or any similar term in any advertisements, or advertise under any category that includes the word "legal" or any similar term.

~~(2) A bankruptcy petition preparer shall be fined not more than $500 for each violation of paragraph (1).~~

(g)~~(1)~~ A bankruptcy petition preparer shall not collect or receive any payment from the debtor or on behalf of the debtor for the court fees in connection with filing the petition.

~~(2) A bankruptcy petition preparer shall be fined not more than $500 for each violation of paragraph (1).~~

(h)(1) The Supreme Court may promulgate rules under section 2075 of title 28, or the Judicial Conference of the United States may prescribe guidelines, for setting a maximum allowable fee chargeable by a bankruptcy petition preparer.A bankruptcy petition preparer shall notify the debtor of any such maximum amount before preparing any document for filing for a debtor or accepting any fee from the debtor.

(~~1~~2) ~~Within 10 days after the date of the filing of a petition, a bankruptcy petition preparer shall file a~~ A declaration under penalty of perjury by the bankruptcy petition preparer shall be filed together with the petition, disclosing any fee received from or on behalf of the debtor within 12 months immediately prior to the filing of the case, and any unpaid fee charged to the debtor. If rules or guidelines setting a maximum fee for services have been promulgated or prescribed under paragraph (1), the declaration under this paragraph shall include a certification that the bankruptcy petition preparer complied with the notification requirement under paragraph (1).

(~~2~~3)(A) The court shall disallow and order the immediate turnover to the bankruptcy trustee ~~of~~ any fee referred to in paragraph (~~1~~2) found to be in excess of the value of any services ~~rendered for the documents prepared.~~

(i) rendered by the bankruptcy petition preparer during the 12-month period immediately preceding the date of the filing of the petition; or

(ii) found to be in violation of any rule or guideline promulgated or prescribed under paragraph (1).

(B) All fees charged by a bankruptcy petition preparer may be forfeited in any case in which the bankruptcy petition preparer fails to comply with this subsection or subsection (b), (c), (d), (e), (f), or (g).

(C) An individual ~~debtor~~ may exempt any funds ~~so~~ recovered under this paragraph under section 522(b).

(~~3~~4) The debtor, the trustee, a creditor, ~~or~~ the United States trustee (or the bankruptcy administrator, if any) or the court, on the initiative of the court, may file a motion for an order under paragraph (2).

(~~4~~5) A bankruptcy petition preparer shall be fined not more than $500 for each failure to comply with a court order to turn over funds within 30 days of service of such order.

(i)(1) If ~~a bankruptcy case or related proceeding is dismissed because of the failure to file bankruptcy papers, including papers specified in section 521(1) of this title, the negligence or intentional disregard of this title or the Federal Rules of Bankruptcy Procedure by a bankruptcy petition preparer, or if~~ a bankruptcy petition preparer violates this section or commits any act that the court finds to be fraudulent, unfair, or deceptive ~~act~~, ~~the bankruptcy court shall certify that fact to the district court, and the district court,~~ on motion of the debtor, ~~the~~ trustee, ~~or a creditor~~ United States trustee (or the bankruptcy administrator, if any), and after a hearing, the court shall order the bankruptcy petition preparer to pay to the debtor—

(A) the debtor's actual damages;

(B) the greater of—

(i) $2,000; or

(ii) twice the amount paid by the debtor to the bankruptcy petition preparer for the preparer's services; and

(C) reasonable attorneys' fees and costs in moving for damages under this subsection.

(2) If the trustee or creditor moves for damages on behalf of the debtor under this subsection, the bankruptcy petition preparer shall be ordered to pay the movant the additional amount of $1,000 plus reasonable attorneys' fees and costs incurred.

(j)(1) A debtor for whom a bankruptcy petition preparer has prepared a document for filing, the trustee, a creditor, or the United States trustee in the district in which the bankruptcy petition preparer resides, has conducted business, or the United States trustee in any other district in which the debtor resides may bring a civil action to enjoin a bankruptcy petition preparer from engaging in any conduct in violation of this section or from further acting as a bankruptcy petition preparer.

(2)(A) In an action under paragraph (1), if the court finds that—

(i) a bankruptcy petition preparer has—

(I) engaged in conduct in violation of this section or of any provision of this title ~~a violation of which subjects a person to criminal penalty~~;

(II) misrepresented the preparer's experience or education as a bankruptcy petition preparer; or

(III) engaged in any other fraudulent, unfair, or deceptive conduct; and

(ii) injunctive relief is appropriate to prevent the recurrence of such conduct,

the court may enjoin the bankruptcy petition preparer from engaging in such conduct.

(B) If the court finds that a bankruptcy petition preparer has continually engaged in conduct described in subclause (I), (II), or (III) of clause (i) and that an injunction prohibiting such conduct would not be sufficient to prevent such person's interference with the proper administration of this title, ~~or~~ has not paid a penalty imposed under this section, or failed to disgorge all fees ordered by the court the court may enjoin the person from acting as a bankruptcy petition preparer.

(3) The court, as part of its contempt power, may enjoin a bankruptcy petition preparer that has failed to comply with a previous order issued under this section.The injunction under this paragraph may be issued on the motion of the court, the trustee, or the United States trustee (or the bankruptcy administrator, if any).

(~~3~~4) The court shall award to a debtor, trustee, or creditor that brings a successful action under this subsection reasonable attorney's fees and costs of the action, to be paid by the bankruptcy petition preparer.

(k) Nothing in this section shall be construed to permit activities that are otherwise prohibited by law, including rules and laws that prohibit the unauthorized practice of law.

(*l*)(1) A bankruptcy petition preparer who fails to comply with any provision of subsection (b), (c), (d), (e), (f), (g), or (h) may be fined not more than $500 for each such failure.

(2) The court shall triple the amount of a fine assessed under paragraph (1) in any case in which the court finds that a bankruptcy petition preparer—

(A) advised the debtor to exclude assets or income that should have been included on applicable schedules;

(B) advised the debtor to use a false Social Security account number;

(C) failed to inform the debtor that the debtor was filing for relief under this title; or

(D) prepared a document for filing in a manner that failed to disclose the identity of the bankruptcy petition preparer.

(3) A debtor, trustee, creditor, or United States trustee (or the bankruptcy administrator, if any) may file a motion for an order imposing a fine on the bankruptcy petition preparer for any violation of this section.

(4)(A) Fines imposed under this subsection in judicial districts served by United States trustees shall be paid to the United States trustee, who shall deposit an amount equal to such fines in a special account of the United States Trustee System Fund referred to in section 586(e)(2) of title 28.Amounts deposited under this subparagraph shall be available to fund the enforcement of this section on a national basis.

(B) Fines imposed under this subsection in judicial districts served by bankruptcy administrators shall be deposited as offsetting receipts to the fund established under section 1931 of title 28, and shall remain available until expended to reimburse any appropriation for the amount paid out of such appropriation for expenses of the operation and maintenance of the courts of the United States.

§ 111. Nonprofit budget and credit counseling agencies; financial management instructional courses

(a) The clerk shall maintain a publicly available list of—

(1) nonprofit budget and credit counseling agencies that provide 1 or more services described in section 109(h) currently approved by the United States trustee (or the bankruptcy administrator, if any); and

(2) instructional courses concerning personal financial management currently approved by the United States trustee (or the bankruptcy administrator, if any), as applicable.

(b) The United States trustee (or bankruptcy administrator, if any) shall only approve a nonprofit budget and credit counseling agency or an instructional course concerning personal financial management as follows:

(1) The United States trustee (or bankruptcy administrator, if any) shall have thoroughly reviewed the qualifications of the nonprofit budget and credit counseling agency or of the provider of the instructional course under the standards set forth in this section, and the services or instructional courses that will be offered by such agency or such provider, and may require such agency or such provider that has sought approval to provide information with respect to such review.

(2) The United States trustee (or bankruptcy administrator, if any) shall have determined that such agency or such instructional course fully satisfies the applicable standards set forth in this section.

(3) If a nonprofit budget and credit counseling agency or instructional course did not appear on the approved list for the district under subsection (a) immediately before approval under this section, approval under this subsection of such agency or such instructional course shall be for a probationary period not to exceed 6 months.

(4) At the conclusion of the applicable probationary period under paragraph (3), the United States trustee (or bankruptcy administrator, if any) may only approve for an additional 1-year period, and for successive 1-year periods thereafter, an agency or instructional course that has demonstrated during the probationary or applicable subsequent period of approval that such agency or instructional course—

(A) has met the standards set forth under this section during such period; and

(B) can satisfy such standards in the future.

(5) Not later than 30 days after any final decision under paragraph (4), an interested person may seek judicial review of such decision in the appropriate district court of the United States.

(c)(1) The United States trustee (or the bankruptcy administrator, if any) shall only approve a nonprofit budget and credit counseling agency that demonstrates that it will provide qualified counselors, maintain adequate provision for safekeeping and payment of client funds, provide adequate counseling with respect to client credit problems, and deal responsibly and effectively with other matters relating to the quality, effectiveness, and financial security of the services it provides.

(2) To be approved by the United States trustee (or the bankruptcy administrator, if any) a nonprofit budget and credit counseling agency shall, at a minimum—

(A) have a board of directors the majority of which—

(i) are not employed by such agency; and

(ii) will not directly or indirectly benefit financially from the outcome of the counseling services provided by such agency;

(B) if a fee is charged for counseling services, charge a reasonable fee, and provide services without regard to ability to pay the fee;

(C) provide for safekeeping and payment of client funds, including an annual audit of the trust accounts and appropriate employee bonding;

(D) provide full disclosures to a client, including funding sources, counselor qualifications, possible impact on credit reports, and any costs of such program that will be paid by such client and how such costs will be paid;

(E) provide adequate counseling with respect to a client credit problems that includes an analysis of such client's current financial condition, factors that caused such financial condition, and how such client can develop a plan to respond to the problems without incurring negative amortization of debt;

(F) provide trained counselors who receive no commissions or bonuses based on the outcome of the counseling services provided by such agency, and who have adequate experience, and have been adequately trained to provide counseling services to individuals in financial difficulty, including the matters described in subparagraph (E);

(G) demonstrate adequate experience and background in providing credit counseling; and

(H) have adequate financial resources to provide continuing support services for budgeting plans over the life of any repayment plan.

(d) The United States trustee (or the bankruptcy administrator, if any) shall only approve an instructional course concerning personal financial management—

(1) for an initial probationary period under subsection (b)(3) if the course will provide at a minimum—

(A) trained personnel with adequate experience and training in providing effective instruction and services;

(B) learning materials and teaching methodologies designed to assist debtors in understanding personal financial management and that are consistent with stated objectives directly related to the goals of such instructional course;

(C) adequate facilities situated in reasonably convenient locations at which such instructional course is offered, except that such facilities may include the provision of such instructional course by telephone or through the Internet, if such instructional course is effective;

(D) the preparation and retention of reasonable records (which shall include the debtor's bankruptcy case number) to permit evaluation of the effectiveness of such instructional course, including any evaluation of satisfaction of instructional course requirements for each debtor attending such instructional course, which shall be available for inspection and evaluation by the Executive Office for United States Trustees, the United States trustee (or the bankruptcy administrator, if any), or the chief bankruptcy judge for the district in which such instructional course is offered; and

(E) if a fee is charged for the instructional course, charge a reasonable fee, and provide services without regard to ability to pay the fee.

(2) for any 1-year period if the provider thereof has demonstrated that the course meets the standards of paragraph (1) and, in addition—

(A) has been effective in assisting a substantial number of debtors to understand personal financial management; and

(B) is otherwise likely to increase substantially the debtor's understanding of personal financial management.

(e) The district court may, at any time, investigate the qualifications of a nonprofit budget and credit counseling agency referred to in subsection (a), and request production of documents to ensure the integrity and effectiveness of such agency. The district court may, at any time, remove from the approved list under subsection (a) a nonprofit budget and credit counseling agency upon finding such agency does not meet the qualifications of subsection (b).

(f) The United States trustee (or the bankruptcy administrator, if any) shall notify the clerk that a nonprofit budget and credit counseling agency or an instructional course is no longer approved, in which case the clerk shall remove it from the list maintained under subsection (a).

(g)(1) No nonprofit budget and credit counseling agency may provide to a credit reporting agency information concerning whether a debtor has received or sought instruction concerning personal financial management from such agency.

(2) A nonprofit budget and credit counseling agency that willfully or negligently fails to comply with any requirement under this title with respect to a debtor shall be liable for damages in an amount equal to the sum of—

(A) any actual damages sustained by the debtor as a result of the violation; and

(B) any court costs or reasonable attorneys' fees (as determined by the court) incurred in an action to recover those damages.

§ 112. Prohibition on disclosure of name of minor children

The debtor may be required to provide information regarding a minor child involved in matters under this title but may not be required to disclose in the public records in the case the name of such minor child. The debtor may be required to disclose the name of such minor child in a nonpublic record that is maintained by the court and made available by the court for examination by the United States trustee, the trustee, and the auditor (if any) serving under section 586(f) of title 28, in the case.The court, the United States trustee, the trustee, and such auditor shall not disclose the name of such minor child maintained in such nonpublic record.

CHAPTER 3

CASE ADMINISTRATION

Subchapter I—Commencement of a Case

§ 301. Voluntary cases

(a) A voluntary case under a chapter of this title is commenced by the filing with the bankruptcy court of a petition under such chapter by an entity that may be a debtor under such chapter.

(b) The commencement of a voluntary case under a chapter of this title constitutes an order for relief under such chapter.

§ 302. Joint cases

(a) A joint case under a chapter of this title is commenced by the filing with the bankruptcy court of a single petition under such chapter by an individual that may be a debtor under such chapter and such individual's spouse. The commencement of a joint case under a chapter of this title constitutes an order for relief under such chapter.

(b) After the commencement of a joint case, the court shall determine the extent, if any, to which the debtors' estates shall be consolidated.

§ 303. Involuntary cases

(a) An involuntary case may be commenced only under chapter 7 or 11 of this title, and only against a person, except a farmer, family farmer, or a corporation that is not a moneyed, business, or commercial corporation, that may be a debtor under the chapter under which such case is commenced.

(b) An involuntary case against a person is commenced by the filing with the bankruptcy court of a petition under chapter 7 or 11 of this title—

(1) by three or more entities, each of which is either a holder of a claim against such person that is not contingent as to liability or the subject of a bona fide dispute as to liability or amount, or an indenture trustee representing such a holder, if such noncontingent, undisputed[9] claims aggregate at least $12,300[10] more than the value of any lien on property of the debtor securing such claims held by the holders of such claims;

(2) if there are fewer than 12 such holders, excluding any employee or insider of such person and any transferee of a transfer that is voidable under section 544, 545, 547, 548, 549, or 724(a) of this title, by one or more of such holders that hold in the aggregate at least $12,300[11] of such claims;

(3) if such person is a partnership—

(A) by fewer than all of the general partners in such partnership; or

(B) if relief has been ordered under this title with respect to all of the general partners in such partnership, by a general partner in such partnership, the trustee of such a general partner, or a holder of a claim against such partnership; or

(4) by a foreign representative of the estate in a foreign proceeding concerning such person.

(c) After the filing of a petition under this section but before the case is dismissed or relief is ordered, a creditor holding an unsecured claim that is not contingent, other than a creditor filing under subsection (b) of this section, may join in the petition with the same effect as if such joining creditor were a petitioning creditor under subsection (b) of this section.

(d) The debtor, or a general partner in a partnership debtor that did not join in the petition, may file an answer to a petition under this section.

(e) After notice and a hearing, and for cause, the court may require the petitioners under this section to file a bond to indemnify the debtor for such amounts as the court may later allow under subsection (i) of this section.

(f) Notwithstanding section 363 of this title, except to the extent that the court orders otherwise, and until an order for relief in the case, any business of the debtor may continue to operate, and the debtor may continue to use, acquire, or dispose of property as if an involuntary case concerning the debtor had not been commenced.

(g) At any time after the commencement of an involuntary case under chapter 7 of this title but before an order for relief in the case, the court, on request of a party in interest, after notice to the debtor and a hearing, and if necessary to preserve the property of the estate

9 *Editor's Note*: These changes to section 303(b)(1) are effective for cases commenced under title 11 on or after April 20, 2005.

10 *Editor's Note*: This dollar amount reflects an inflationary adjustment, effective April 1, 2004. For cases commenced before April 1, 2004, the applicable dollar amount is $11,625.

11 *Editor's Note*: This dollar amount reflects an inflationary adjustment, effective April 1, 2004. For cases commenced before April 1, 2004, the applicable dollar amount is $11,625.

or to prevent loss to the estate, may order the United States trustee to appoint an interim trustee under section 701 of this title to take possession of the property of the estate and to operate any business of the debtor. Before an order for relief, the debtor may regain possession of property in the possession of a trustee ordered appointed under this subsection if the debtor files such bond as the court requires, conditioned on the debtor's accounting for and delivering to the trustee, if there is an order for relief in the case, such property, or the value, as of the date the debtor regains possession, of such property.

(h) If the petition is not timely controverted, the court shall order relief against the debtor in an involuntary case under the chapter under which the petition was filed. Otherwise, after trial, the court shall order relief against the debtor in an involuntary case under the chapter under which the petition was filed, only if—

(1) the debtor is generally not paying such debtor's debts as such debts become due unless such debts are the subject of a bona fide dispute as to liability or amount;[12] or

(2) within 120 days before the date of the filing of the petition, a custodian, other than a trustee, receiver, or agent appointed or authorized to take charge of less than substantially all of the property of the debtor for the purpose of enforcing a lien against such property, was appointed or took possession.

(i) If the court dismisses a petition under this section other than on consent of all petitioners and the debtor, and if the debtor does not waive the right to judgment under this subsection, the court may grant judgment—

(1) against the petitioners and in favor of the debtor for—

(A) costs; or

(B) a reasonable attorney's fee; or

(2) against any petitioner that filed the petition in bad faith, for—

(A) any damages proximately caused by such filing; or

(B) punitive damages.

(j) Only after notice to all creditors and a hearing may the court dismiss a petition filed under this section—

(1) on the motion of a petitioner;

(2) on consent of all petitioners and the debtor; or

(3) for want of prosecution.

~~(k) Notwithstanding subsection (a) of this section, an involuntary case may be commenced against a foreign bank that is not engaged in such business in the United States only under chapter 7 of this title and only if a foreign proceeding concerning such bank is pending.~~

(*l*)[13] (1) If—

(A) the petition under this section is false or contains any materially false, fictitious, or fraudulent statement;

(B) the debtor is an individual; and

(C) the court dismisses such petition,

the court, upon the motion of the debtor, shall seal all the records of the court relating to such petition, and all references to such petition.

(2) If the debtor is an individual and the court dismisses a petition under this section, the court may enter an order prohibiting all consumer reporting agencies (as defined in section 603(f) of the Fair Credit Reporting Act (15 U.S.C. 1681a(f)) from making any consumer report (as defined in section 603(d) of that Act) that contains any information relating to such petition or to the case commenced by the filing of such petition.

(3) Upon the expiration of the statute of limitations described in section 3282 of title 18, for a violation of section 152 or 157 of such title, the court, upon the motion of the debtor and for good cause, may expunge any records relating to a petition filed under this section.

12 *Editor's Note*: This change to section 303(h)(1) is effective for cases commenced under title 11 on or after April 20, 2005.

13 *Editor's Note*: So in original. Subsection (*l*) was added even though subsection (k) was repealed.

~~§ 304. Cases ancillary to foreign proceedings~~

~~(a) A case ancillary to a foreign proceeding is commenced by the filing with the bankruptcy court of a petition under this section by a foreign representative.~~

~~(b) Subject to the provisions of subsection (c) of this section, if a party in interest does not timely controvert the petition, or after trial, the court may—~~

~~(1) enjoin the commencement or continuation of—~~

~~(A) any action against—~~

~~(i) a debtor with respect to property involved in such foreign proceeding; or~~

~~(ii) such property; or~~

~~(B) the enforcement of any judgment against the debtor with respect to such property, or any act or the commencement or continuation of any judicial proceeding to create or enforce a lien against the property of such estate;~~

~~(2) order turnover of the property of such estate, or the proceeds of such property, to such foreign representative; or~~

~~(3) order other appropriate relief.~~

~~(c) In determining whether to grant relief under subsection (b) of this section, the court shall be guided by what will best assure an economical and expeditious administration of such estate, consistent with—~~

~~(1) just treatment of all holders of claims against or interests in such estate;~~

~~(2) protection of claim holders in the United States against prejudice and inconvenience in the processing of claims in such foreign proceeding;~~

~~(3) prevention of preferential or fraudulent dispositions of property of such estate;~~

~~(4) distribution of proceeds of such estate substantially in accordance with the order prescribed by this title;~~

~~(5) comity; and~~

~~(6) if appropriate, the provision of an opportunity for a fresh start for the individual that such foreign proceeding concerns.~~

§ 305. Abstention

(a) The court, after notice and a hearing, may dismiss a case under this title, or may suspend all proceedings in a case under this title, at any time if—

(1) the interests of creditors and the debtor would be better served by such dismissal or suspension; or

(2)(A) ~~there is pending a foreign proceeding~~ a petition under section 1515 for recognition of a foreign proceeding has been granted; and

(B) ~~the factors specified in section 304(c) of this title warrant~~ the purposes of chapter 15 of this title would be best served by such dismissal or suspension.

(b) A foreign representative may seek dismissal or suspension under subsection (a)(2) of this section.

(c) An order under subsection (a) of this section dismissing a case or suspending all proceedings in a case, or a decision not so to dismiss or suspend, is not reviewable by appeal or otherwise by the court of appeals under section 158(d), 1291, or 1292 of title 28 or by the Supreme Court of the United States under section 1254 of title 28.

§ 306. Limited appearance

An appearance in a bankruptcy court by a foreign representative in connection with a petition or request under section 303~~, 304,~~ or 305 of this title does not submit such foreign representative to the jurisdiction of any court in the United States for any other purpose, but the bankruptcy court may condition any order under section 303~~, 304,~~ or 305 of this title on compliance by such foreign representative with the orders of such bankruptcy court.

§ 307. United States trustee

The United States trustee may raise and may appear and be heard on any issue in any case or proceeding under this title but may not file a plan pursuant to section 1121(c) of this title.

§ 308. Debtor reporting requirements[14]

(a) For purposes of this section, the term "profitability" means, with respect to a debtor, the amount of money that the debtor has earned or lost during current and recent fiscal periods.

(b) A small business debtor shall file periodic financial and other reports containing information including—

(1) the debtor's profitability;

(2) reasonable approximations of the debtor's projected cash receipts and cash disbursements over a reasonable period;

(3) comparisons of actual cash receipts and disbursements with projections in prior reports;

(4)(A) whether the debtor is—

(i) in compliance in all material respects with postpetition requirements imposed by this title and the Federal Rules of Bankruptcy Procedure; and

(ii) timely filing tax returns and other required government filings and paying taxes and other administrative expenses when due;

(B) if the debtor is not in compliance with the requirements referred to in subparagraph (A)(i) or filing tax returns and other required government filings and making the payments referred to in subparagraph (A)(ii), what the failures are and how, at what cost, and when the debtor intends to remedy such failures; and

(C) such other matters as are in the best interests of the debtor and creditors, and in the public interest in fair and efficient procedures under chapter 11 of this title.

SUBCHAPTER II

Officers

§ 321. Eligibility to serve as trustee

(a) A person may serve as trustee in a case under this title only if such person is—

(1) an individual that is competent to perform the duties of trustee and, in a case under chapter 7, 12, or 13 of this title, resides or has an office in the judicial district within which the case is pending, or in any judicial district adjacent to such district; or

(2) a corporation authorized by such corporation's charter or bylaws to act as trustee, and, in a case under chapter 7, 12, or 13 of this title, having an office in at least one of such districts.

(b) A person that has served as an examiner in the case may not serve as trustee in the case.

(c) The United States trustee for the judicial district in which the case is pending is eligible to serve as trustee in the case if necessary.

§ 322. Qualification of trustee

(a) Except as provided in subsection (b)(1), a person selected under section 701, 702, 703, 1104, 1163, 1202, or 1302 of this title to serve as trustee in a case under this title qualifies if before five days after such selection, and before beginning official duties, such person has filed with the court a bond in favor of the United States conditioned on the faithful performance of such official duties.

(b)(1) The United States trustee qualifies wherever such trustee serves as trustee in a case under this title.

(2) The United States trustee shall determine—

(A) the amount of a bond required to be filed under subsection (a) of this section; and

(B) the sufficiency of the surety on such bond.

14 *Editor's Note*: This new section will take effect sixty days after the date on which forms are prescribed under 28 U.S.C. § 2075 for use in complying with the requirements of this section.

(c) A trustee is not liable personally or on such trustee's bond in favor of the United States for any penalty or forfeiture incurred by the debtor.

(d) A proceeding on a trustee's bond may not be commenced after two years after the date on which such trustee was discharged.

§ 323. Role and capacity of trustee

(a) The trustee in a case under this title is the representative of the estate.

(b) The trustee in a case under this title has capacity to sue and be sued.

§ 324. Removal of trustee or examiner

(a) The court, after notice and a hearing, may remove a trustee, other than the United States trustee, or an examiner, for cause.

(b) Whenever the court removes a trustee or examiner under subsection (a) in a case under this title, such trustee or examiner shall thereby be removed in all other cases under this title in which such trustee or examiner is then serving unless the court orders otherwise.

§ 325. Effect of vacancy

A vacancy in the office of trustee during a case does not abate any pending action or proceeding, and the successor trustee shall be substituted as a party in such action or proceeding.

§ 326. Limitation on compensation of trustee

(a) In a case under chapter 7 or 11, the court may allow reasonable compensation under section 330 of this title of the trustee for the trustee's services, payable after the trustee renders such services, not to exceed 25 percent on the first $5,000 or less, 10 percent on any amount in excess of $5,000 but not in excess of $50,000, 5 percent on any amount in excess of $50,000 but not in excess of $1,000,000, and reasonable compensation not to exceed 3 percent of such moneys in excess of $1,000,000, upon all moneys disbursed or turned over in the case by the trustee to parties in interest, excluding the debtor, but including holders of secured claims.

(b) In a case under chapter 12 or 13 of this title, the court may not allow compensation for services or reimbursement of expenses of the United States trustee or of a standing trustee appointed under section 586(b) of title 28, but may allow reasonable compensation under section 330 of this title of a trustee appointed under section 1202(a) or 1302(a) of this title for the trustee's services, payable after the trustee renders such services, not to exceed five percent upon all payments under the plan.

(c) If more than one person serves as trustee in the case, the aggregate compensation of such persons for such service may not exceed the maximum compensation prescribed for a single trustee by subsection (a) or (b) of this section, as the case may be.

(d) The court may deny allowance of compensation for services or reimbursement of expenses of the trustee if the trustee failed to make diligent inquiry into facts that would permit denial of allowance under section 328(c) of this title or, with knowledge of such facts, employed a professional person under section 327 of this title.

§ 327. Employment of professional persons

(a) Except as otherwise provided in this section, the trustee, with the court's approval, may employ one or more attorneys, accountants, appraisers, auctioneers, or other professional persons, that do not hold or represent an interest adverse to the estate, and that are disinterested persons, to represent or assist the trustee in carrying out the trustee's duties under this title.

(b) If the trustee is authorized to operate the business of the debtor under section 721, 1202, or 1108 of this title, and if the debtor has regularly employed attorneys, accountants, or other professional persons on salary, the trustee may retain or replace such professional persons if necessary in the operation of such business.

(c) In a case under chapter 7, 12, or 11 of this title, a person is not disqualified for employment under this section solely because of such person's employment by or representation of a creditor, unless there is objection by another creditor or the United States trustee, in which case the court shall disapprove such employment if there is an actual conflict of interest.

(d) The court may authorize the trustee to act as attorney or accountant for the estate if such authorization is in the best interest of the estate.

(e) The trustee, with the court's approval, may employ, for a specified special purpose, other than to represent the trustee in conducting the case, an attorney that has represented the debtor, if in the best interest of the estate, and if such attorney does not represent or hold any interest adverse to the debtor or to the estate with respect to the matter on which such attorney is to be employed.

(f) The trustee may not employ a person that has served as an examiner in the case.

§ 328. Limitation on compensation of professional persons

(a) The trustee, or a committee appointed under section 1102 of this title, with the court's approval, may employ or authorize the employment of a professional person under section 327 or 1103 of this title, as the case may be, on any reasonable terms and conditions of employment, including on a retainer, on an hourly basis, on a fixed or percentage fee basis, or on a contingent fee basis. Notwithstanding such terms and conditions, the court may allow compensation different from the compensation provided under such terms and conditions after the conclusion of such employment, if such terms and conditions prove to have been improvident in light of developments not capable of being anticipated at the time of the fixing of such terms and conditions.

(b) If the court has authorized a trustee to serve as an attorney or accountant for the estate under section 327(d) of this title, the court may allow compensation for the trustee's services as such attorney or accountant only to the extent that the trustee performed services as attorney or accountant for the estate and not for performance of any of the trustee's duties that are generally performed by a trustee without the assistance of an attorney or accountant for the estate.

(c) Except as provided in section 327(c), 327(e), or 1107(b) of this title, the court may deny allowance of compensation for services and reimbursement of expenses of a professional person employed under section 327 or 1103 of this title if, at any time during such professional person's employment under section 327 or 1103 of this title, such professional person is not a disinterested person, or represents or holds an interest adverse to the interest of the estate with respect to the matter on which such professional person is employed.

§ 329. Debtor's transactions with attorneys

(a) Any attorney representing a debtor in a case under this title, or in connection with such a case, whether or not such attorney applies for compensation under this title, shall file with the court a statement of the compensation paid or agreed to be paid, if such payment or agreement was made after one year before the date of the filing of the petition, for services rendered or to be rendered in contemplation of or in connection with the case by such attorney, and the source of such compensation.

(b) If such compensation exceeds the reasonable value of any such services, the court may cancel any such agreement, or order the return of any such payment, to the extent excessive, to—

(1) the estate, if the property transferred—

(A) would have been property of the estate; or

(B) was to be paid by or on behalf of the debtor under a plan under chapter 11, 12, or 13 of this title; or

(2) the entity that made such payment.

§ 330. Compensation of officers

(a)(1) After notice to the parties in interest and the United States trustee and a hearing, and subject to sections 326, 328, and 329, the court may award to a trustee, a consumer privacy ombudsman appointed under section 332, an examiner, an ombudsman appointed under section 333, or a professional person employed under section 327 or 1103—

(A) reasonable compensation for actual, necessary services rendered by the trustee, examiner, ombudsman, professional person, or attorney and by any paraprofessional person employed by any such person; and

(B) reimbursement for actual, necessary expenses.

(2) The court may, on its own motion or on the motion of the United States Trustee, the United States Trustee for the District or Region, the trustee for the estate, or any other party in interest, award compensation that is less than the amount of compensation that is requested.

(3)~~(A)~~ In determining the amount of reasonable compensation to be awarded to an examiner, trustee under chapter 11, or professional person, the court shall consider the nature, the extent, and the value of such services, taking into account all relevant factors, including—

(A) the time spent on such services;

(B) the rates charged for such services;

(C) whether the services were necessary to the administration of, or beneficial at the time at which the service was rendered toward the completion of, a case under this title;

(D) whether the services were performed within a reasonable amount of time commensurate with the complexity, importance, and nature of the problem, issue, or task addressed; ~~and~~

(E) with respect to a professional person, whether the person is board certified or otherwise has demonstrated skill and experience in the bankruptcy field; and

(~~E~~F) whether the compensation is reasonable based on the customary compensation charged by comparably skilled practitioners in cases other than cases under this title.

(4)(A) Except as provided in subparagraph (B), the court shall not allow compensation for—

(i) unnecessary duplication of services; or

(ii) services that were not—

(I) reasonably likely to benefit the debtor's estate; or

(II) necessary to the administration of the case.

(B) In a chapter 12 or chapter 13 case in which the debtor is an individual, the court may allow reasonable compensation to the debtor's attorney for representing the interests of the debtor in connection with the bankruptcy case based on a consideration of the benefit and necessity of such services to the debtor and the other factors set forth in this section.

(5) The court shall reduce the amount of compensation awarded under this section by the amount of any interim compensation awarded under section 331, and, if the amount of such interim compensation exceeds the amount of compensation awarded under this section, may order the return of the excess to the estate.

(6) Any compensation awarded for the preparation of a fee application shall be based on the level and skill reasonably required to prepare the application.

(7) In determining the amount of reasonable compensation to be awarded to a trustee, the court shall treat such compensation as a commission, based on section 326.

(b)(1) There shall be paid from the filing fee in a case under chapter 7 of this title $45 to the trustee serving in such case, after such trustee's services are rendered.

(2) The Judicial Conference of the United States—

(A) shall prescribe additional fees of the same kind as prescribed under section 1914(b) of title 28; and

(B) may prescribe notice of appearance fees and fees charged against distributions in cases under this title;

to pay $15 to trustees serving in cases after such trustees' services are rendered. Beginning 1 year after the date of the enactment of the Bankruptcy Reform Act of 1994, such $15 shall be paid in addition to the amount paid under paragraph (1).

(c) Unless the court orders otherwise, in a case under chapter 12 or 13 of this title the compensation paid to the trustee serving in the case shall not be less than $5 per month from any distribution under the plan during the administration of the plan.

(d) In a case in which the United States trustee serves as trustee, the compensation of the trustee under this section shall be paid to the clerk of the bankruptcy court and deposited by the clerk into the United States Trustee System Fund established by section 589a of title 28.

§ 331. Interim compensation

A trustee, an examiner, a debtor's attorney, or any professional person employed under section 327 or 1103 of this title may apply to the court not more than once every 120 days after an order for relief in a case under this title, or more often if the court permits, for such compensation for services rendered before the date of such an application or reimbursement for expenses incurred before such date as is provided under section 330 of this title. After notice and a hearing, the court may allow and disburse to such applicant such compensation or reimbursement.

§ 332. Consumer privacy ombudsman

(a) If a hearing is required under section 363(b)(1)(B), the court shall order the United States trustee to appoint, not later than 5 days before the commencement of the hearing, 1 disinterested person (other than the United States trustee) to serve as the consumer privacy ombudsman in the case and shall require that notice of such hearing be timely given to such ombudsman.

(b) The consumer privacy ombudsman may appear and be heard at such hearing and shall provide to the court information to assist the court in its consideration of the facts, circumstances, and conditions of the proposed sale or lease of personally identifiable information under section 363(b)(1)(B). Such information may include presentation of—

(1) the debtor's privacy policy;

(2) the potential losses or gains of privacy to consumers if such sale or such lease is approved by the court;

(3) the potential costs or benefits to consumers if such sale or such lease is approved by the court; and

(4) the potential alternatives that would mitigate potential privacy losses or potential costs to consumers.

(c) A consumer privacy ombudsman shall not disclose any personally identifiable information obtained by the ombudsman under this title.

§ 333. Appointment of patient care ombudsman

(a)(1) If the debtor in a case under chapter 7, 9, or 11 is a health care business, the court shall order, not later than 30 days after the commencement of the case, the appointment of an ombudsman to monitor the quality of patient care and to represent the interests of the patients of the health care business unless the court finds that the appointment of such ombudsman is not necessary for the protection of patients under the specific facts of the case.

(2)(A) If the court orders the appointment of an ombudsman under paragraph (1), the United States trustee shall appoint 1 disinterested person (other than the United States trustee) to serve as such ombudsman.

(B) If the debtor is a health care business that provides long-term care, then the United States trustee may appoint the State Long-Term Care Ombudsman appointed under the Older Americans Act of 1965 for the State in which the case is pending to serve as the ombudsman required by paragraph (1).

(C) If the United States trustee does not appoint a State Long-Term Care Ombudsman under subparagraph (B), the court shall notify the State Long-Term Care Ombudsman appointed under the Older Americans Act of 1965 for the State in which the case is pending, of the name and address of the person who is appointed under subparagraph (A).

(b) An ombudsman appointed under subsection (a) shall—

(1) monitor the quality of patient care provided to patients of the debtor, to the extent necessary under the circumstances, including interviewing patients and physicians;

(2) not later than 60 days after the date of appointment, and not less frequently than at 60-day intervals thereafter, report to the court after notice to the parties in interest, at a hearing or in writing, regarding the quality of patient care provided to patients of the debtor; and

(3) if such ombudsman determines that the quality of patient care provided to patients of the debtor is declining significantly or is otherwise being materially compromised, file with the court a motion or a written report, with notice to the parties in interest immediately upon making such determination.

(c)(1) An ombudsman appointed under subsection (a) shall maintain any information obtained by such ombudsman under this section that relates to patients (including information relating to patient records) as confidential information. Such ombudsman may not review confidential patient records unless the court approves such review in advance and imposes restrictions on such ombudsman to protect the confidentiality of such records.

(2) An ombudsman appointed under subsection (a)(2)(B) shall have access to patient records consistent with authority of such ombudsman under the Older Americans Act of 1965 and under non-Federal laws governing the State Long-Term Care Ombudsman program.

SUBCHAPTER III

Administration

§ 341. Meetings of creditors and equity security holders

(a) Within a reasonable time after the order for relief in a case under this title, the United States trustee shall convene and preside at a meeting of creditors.

(b) The United States trustee may convene a meeting of any equity security holders.

(c) The court may not preside at, and may not attend, any meeting under this section including any final meeting of creditors. Notwithstanding any local court rule, provision of a State constitution, any otherwise applicable nonbankruptcy law, or any other requirement that representation at the meeting of creditors under subsection (a) be by an attorney, a creditor holding a consumer debt or any representative of the creditor (which may include an entity or an employee of an entity and may be a representative for more than 1 creditor) shall be permitted to appear at and participate in the meeting of creditors in a case under chapter 7 or 13, either alone or in conjunction with an attorney for the creditor.Nothing in this subsection shall be construed to require any creditor to be represented by an attorney at any meeting of creditors.

(d) Prior to the conclusion of the meeting of creditors or equity security holders, the trustee shall orally examine the debtor to ensure that the debtor in a case under chapter 7 of this title is aware of—

(1) the potential consequences of seeking a discharge in bankruptcy, including the effects on credit history;

(2) the debtor's ability to file a petition under a different chapter of this title;

(3) the effect of receiving a discharge of debts under this title; and

(4) the effect of reaffirming a debt, including the debtor's knowledge of the provisions of section 524(d) of this title.

(e) Notwithstanding subsections (a) and (b), the court, on the request of a party in interest and after notice and a hearing, for cause may order that the United States trustee not convene a meeting of creditors or equity security holders if the debtor has filed a plan as to which the debtor solicited acceptances prior to the commencement of the case.

§ 342. Notice

(a) There shall be given such notice as is appropriate, including notice to any holder of a community claim, of an order for relief in a case under this title.

(b) ~~Prior to~~ Before the commencement of a case under this title by an individual whose debts are primarily consumer debts, the clerk shall give to such individual written notice ~~to such individual that indicates each chapter of this title under which such individual may proceed.~~ containing—

(1) a brief description of—

(A) chapters 7, 11, 12, and 13 and the general purpose, benefits, and costs of proceeding under each of those chapters; and

(B) the types of services available from credit counseling agencies; and

(2) statements specifying that—

(A) a person who knowingly and fraudulently conceals assets or makes a false oath or statement under penalty of perjury in connection with a case under this title shall be subject to fine, imprisonment, or both; and

(B) all information supplied by a debtor in connection with a case under this title is subject to examination by the Attorney General.

(c)(1) If notice is required to be given by the debtor to a creditor under this title, any rule, any applicable law, or any order of the court, such notice shall contain the name, address, and last 4 digits of the taxpayer identification number of the debtor~~, but the failure of such notice to contain such information shall not invalidate the legal effect of such notice~~.

(2)(A) If, within the 90 days before the commencement of a voluntary case, a creditor supplies the debtor in at least 2 communications sent to the debtor with the current account number of the debtor and the address at which such creditor requests to receive correspondence, then any notice required by this title to be sent by the debtor to such creditor shall be sent to such address and shall include such account number.

(B) If a creditor would be in violation of applicable nonbankruptcy law by sending any such communication within such 90-day period and if such creditor supplies the debtor in the last 2 communications with the current account number of the debtor and the address at which such creditor requests to receive correspondence, then any notice required by this title to be sent by the debtor to such creditor shall be sent to such address and shall include such account number.

If the notice concerns an amendment that adds a creditor to the schedules of assets and liabilities, the debtor shall include the full taxpayer identification number in the notice sent to that creditor, but the debtor shall include only the last 4 digits of the taxpayer identification number in the copy of the notice filed with the court.

(d) In a case under chapter 7 of this title in which the debtor is an individual and in which the presumption of abuse arises under section 707(b), the clerk shall give written notice to all creditors not later than 10 days after the date of the filing of the petition that the presumption of abuse has arisen.

(e)(1) In a case under chapter 7 or 13 of this title of a debtor who is an individual, a creditor at any time may both file with the court and serve on the debtor a notice of address to be used to provide notice in such case to such creditor.

(2) Any notice in such case required to be provided to such creditor by the debtor or the court later than 5 days after the court and the debtor receive such creditor's notice of address, shall be provided to such address.

(f)(1) An entity may file with any bankruptcy court a notice of address to be used by all the bankruptcy courts or by particular bankruptcy courts, as so specified by such entity at the time such notice is filed, to provide notice to such entity in all cases under chapters 7 and 13 pending in the courts with respect to which such notice is filed, in which such entity is a creditor.

(2) In any case filed under chapter 7 or 13, any notice required to be provided by a court with respect to which a notice is filed under paragraph (1), to such entity later than 30 days after the filing of such notice under paragraph (1) shall be provided to

such address unless with respect to a particular case a different address is specified in a notice filed and served in accordance with subsection (e).

(3) A notice filed under paragraph (1) may be withdrawn by such entity.

(g)(1) Notice provided to a creditor by the debtor or the court other than in accordance with this section (excluding this subsection) shall not be effective notice until such notice is brought to the attention of such creditor. If such creditor designates a person or an organizational subdivision of such creditor to be responsible for receiving notices under this title and establishes reasonable procedures so that such notices receivable by such creditor are to be delivered to such person or such subdivision, then a notice provided to such creditor other than in accordance with this section (excluding this subsection) shall not be considered to have been brought to the attention of such creditor until such notice is received by such person or such subdivision.

(2) A monetary penalty may not be imposed on a creditor for a violation of a stay in effect under section 362(a) (including a monetary penalty imposed under section 362(k)) or for failure to comply with section 542 or 543 unless the conduct that is the basis of such violation or of such failure occurs after such creditor receives notice effective under this section of the order for relief.

§ 343. Examination of the debtor

The debtor shall appear and submit to examination under oath at the meeting of creditors under section 341(a) of this title. Creditors, any indenture trustee, any trustee or examiner in the case, or the United States trustee may examine the debtor. The United States trustee may administer the oath required under this section.

§ 344. Self-incrimination; immunity

Immunity for persons required to submit to examination, to testify, or to provide information in a case under this title may be granted under part V of title 18.

§ 345. Money of estates

(a) A trustee in a case under this title may make such deposit or investment of the money of the estate for which such trustee serves as will yield the maximum reasonable net return on such money, taking into account the safety of such deposit or investment.

(b) Except with respect to a deposit or investment that is insured or guaranteed by the United States or by a department, agency, or instrumentality of the United States or backed by the full faith and credit of the United States, the trustee shall require from an entity with which such money is deposited or invested—

(1) a bond—

(A) in favor of the United States;

(B) secured by the undertaking of a corporate surety approved by the United States trustee for the district in which the case is pending; and

(C) conditioned on—

(i) a proper accounting for all money so deposited or invested and for any return on such money;

(ii) prompt repayment of such money and return; and

(iii) faithful performance of duties as a depository; or

(2) the deposit of securities of the kind specified in section 9303 of title 31;

unless the court for cause orders otherwise.

(c) An entity with which such moneys are deposited or invested is authorized to deposit or invest such moneys as may be required under this section.

~~§ 346. Special tax provisions~~

~~(a) Except to the extent otherwise provided in this section, subsections (b), (c), (d), (e), (g), (h), (i), and (j) of this section apply notwithstanding any State or local law imposing a tax, but subject to the Internal Revenue Code of 1986.~~

~~(b)(1) In a case under chapter 7, 12, or 11 of this title concerning an individual, any income of the estate may be taxed under a State or local law imposing a tax on or measured by income only to the estate, and may not be taxed to such individual. Except as provided in section 728 of this title, if such individual is a partner in a partnership, any gain or loss resulting from a distribution of property from such partnership, or any distributive share of income, gain, loss, deduction, or credit of such individual that is distributed, or considered distributed, from such partnership, after the commencement of the case is gain, loss, income, deduction, or credit, as the case may be, of the estate.~~

~~(2) Except as otherwise provided in this section and in section 728 of this title, any income of the estate in such a case, and any State or local tax on or measured by such income, shall be computed in the same manner as the income and the tax of an estate.~~

~~(3) The estate in such a case shall use the same accounting method as the debtor used immediately before the commencement of the case.~~

~~(c)(1) The commencement of a case under this title concerning a corporation or a partnership does not effect a change in the status of such corporation or partnership for the purposes of any State or local law imposing a tax on or measured by income. Except as otherwise provided in this section and in section 728 of this title, any income of the estate in such case may be taxed only as though such case had not been commenced.~~

~~(2) In such a case, except as provided in section 728 of this title, the trustee shall make any tax return otherwise required by State or local law to be filed by or on behalf of such corporation or partnership in the same manner and form as such corporation or partnership, as the case may be, is required to make such return.~~

(d) In a case under chapter 13 of this title, any income of the estate or the debtor may be taxed under a State or local law imposing a tax on or measured by income only to the debtor, and may not be taxed to the estate.

(e) A claim allowed under section 502(f) or 503 of this title, other than a claim for a tax that is not otherwise deductible or a capital expenditure that is not otherwise deductible, is deductible by the entity to which income of the estate is taxed unless such claim was deducted by another entity, and a deduction for such a claim is deemed to be a deduction attributable to a business.

(f) The trustee shall withhold from any payment of claims for wages, salaries, commissions, dividends, interest, or other payments, or collect, any amount required to be withheld or collected under applicable State or local tax law, and shall pay such withheld or collected amount to the appropriate governmental unit at the time and in the manner required by such tax law, and with the same priority as the claim from which such amount was withheld was paid.

(g)(1) Neither gain nor loss shall be recognized on a transfer—

(A) by operation of law, of property to the estate;

(B) other than a sale, of property from the estate to the debtor; or

(C) in a case under chapter 11 or 12 of this title concerning a corporation, of property from the estate to a corporation that is an affiliate participating in a joint plan with the debtor, or that is a successor to the debtor under the plan, except that gain or loss may be recognized to the same extent that such transfer results in the recognition of gain or loss under section 371 of the Internal Revenue Code of 1986.

(2) The transferee of a transfer of a kind specified in this subsection shall take the property transferred with the same character, and with the transferor's basis, as adjusted under subsection (j)(5) of this section, and holding period.

(h) Notwithstanding sections 728(a) and 1146(a) of this title, for the purpose of determining the number of taxable periods during which the debtor or the estate may use a loss carryover or a loss carryback, the taxable period of the debtor during which the case is commenced is deemed not to have been terminated by such commencement.

(i)(1) In a case under chapter 7, 12, or 11 of this title concerning an individual, the estate shall succeed to the debtor's tax attributes, including—

(A) any investment credit carryover;

(B) any recovery exclusion;

(C) any loss carryover;

(D) any foreign tax credit carryover;

(E) any capital loss carryover; and

(F) any claim of right.

(2) After such a case is closed or dismissed, the debtor shall succeed to any tax attribute to which the estate succeeded under paragraph (1) of this subsection but that was not utilized by the estate. The debtor may utilize such tax attributes as though any applicable time limitations on such utilization by the debtor were suspended during the time during which the case was pending.

(3) In such a case, the estate may carry back any loss of the estate to a taxable period of the debtor that ended before the order for relief under such chapter the same as the debtor could have carried back such loss had the debtor incurred such loss and the case under this title had not been commenced, but the debtor may not carry back any loss of the debtor from a taxable period that ends after such order to any taxable period of the debtor that ended before such order until after the case is closed.

(j)(1) Except as otherwise provided in this subsection, income is not realized by the estate, the debtor, or a successor to the debtor by reason of forgiveness or discharge of indebtedness in a case under this title.

(2) For the purposes of any State or local law imposing a tax on or measured by income, a deduction with respect to a liability may not be allowed for any taxable period during or after which such liability is forgiven or discharged under this title. In this paragraph, "a deduction with respect to a liability" includes a capital loss incurred on the disposition of a capital asset with respect to a liability that was incurred in connection with the acquisition of such asset.

(3) Except as provided in paragraph (4) of this subsection, for the purpose of any State or local law imposing a tax on or measured by income, any net operating loss of an individual or corporate debtor, including a net operating loss carryover to such debtor, shall be reduced by the amount of indebtedness forgiven or discharged in a case under this title, except to the extent that such forgiveness or discharge resulted in a disallowance under paragraph (2) of this subsection.

(4) A reduction of a net operating loss or a net operating loss carryover under paragraph (3) of this subsection or of basis under paragraph (5) of this subsection is not required to the extent that the indebtedness of an individual or corporate debtor forgiven or discharged—

(A) consisted of items of a deductible nature that were not deducted by such debtor; or

(B) resulted in an expired net operating loss carryover or other deduction that—

(i) did not offset income for any taxable period; and

(ii) did not contribute to a net operating loss in or a net operating loss carryover to the taxable period during or after which such indebtedness was discharged.

(5) For the purposes of a State or local law imposing a tax on or measured by income, the basis of the debtor's property or of property transferred to an entity required to use the debtor's basis in whole or in part shall be reduced by the lesser of—

(A)(i) the amount by which the indebtedness of the debtor has been forgiven or discharged in a case under this title; minus

~~(ii) the total amount of adjustments made under paragraphs (2) and (3) of this subsection; and~~

~~(B) the amount by which the total basis of the debtor's assets that were property of the estate before such forgiveness or discharge exceeds the debtor's total liabilities that were liabilities both before and after such forgiveness or discharge.~~

~~(6) Notwithstanding paragraph (5) of this subsection, basis is not required to be reduced to the extent that the debtor elects to treat as taxable income, of the taxable period in which indebtedness is forgiven or discharged, the amount of indebtedness forgiven or discharged that otherwise would be applied in reduction of basis under paragraph (5) of this subsection.~~

~~(7) For the purposes of this subsection, indebtedness with respect to which an equity security, other than an interest of a limited partner in a limited partnership, is issued to the creditor to whom such indebtedness was owed, or that is forgiven as a contribution to capital by an equity security holder other than a limited partner in the debtor, is not forgiven or discharged in a case under this title—~~

~~(A) to any extent that such indebtedness did not consist of items of a deductible nature; or~~

~~(B) if the issuance of such equity security has the same consequences under a law imposing a tax on or measured by income to such creditor as a payment in cash to such creditor in an amount equal to the fair market value of such equity security, then to the lesser of—~~

~~(i) the extent that such issuance has the same such consequences; and~~

~~(ii) the extent of such fair market value.~~

§ 346. Special provisions related to the treatment of State and local taxes

(a) Whenever the Internal Revenue Code of 1986 provides that a separate taxable estate or entity is created in a case concerning a debtor under this title, and the income, gain, loss, deductions, and credits of such estate shall be taxed to or claimed by the estate, a separate taxable estate is also created for purposes of any State and local law imposing a tax on or measured by income and such income, gain, loss, deductions, and credits shall be taxed to or claimed by the estate and may not be taxed to or claimed by the debtor. The preceding sentence shall not apply if the case is dismissed. The trustee shall make tax returns of income required under any such State or local law.

(b) Whenever the Internal Revenue Code of 1986 provides that no separate taxable estate shall be created in a case concerning a debtor under this title, and the income, gain, loss, deductions, and credits of an estate shall be taxed to or claimed by the debtor, such income, gain, loss, deductions, and credits shall be taxed to or claimed by the debtor under a State or local law imposing a tax on or measured by income and may not be taxed to or claimed by the estate. The trustee shall make such tax returns of income of corporations and of partnerships as are required under any State or local law, but with respect to partnerships, shall make such returns only to the extent such returns are also required to be made under such Code. The estate shall be liable for any tax imposed on such corporation or partnership, but not for any tax imposed on partners or members.

(c) With respect to a partnership or any entity treated as a partnership under a State or local law imposing a tax on or measured by income that is a debtor in a case under this title, any gain or loss resulting from a distribution of property from such partnership, or any distributive share of any income, gain, loss, deduction, or credit of a partner or member that is distributed, or considered distributed, from such partnership, after the commencement of the case, is gain, loss, income, deduction, or credit, as the case may be, of the partner or member, and if such partner or member is a debtor in a case under this title, shall be subject to tax in accordance with subsection (a) or (b).

(d) For purposes of any State or local law imposing a tax on or measured by income, the taxable period of a debtor in a case under this title shall terminate only if and to the extent that the taxable period of such debtor terminates under the Internal Revenue Code of 1986.

(e) The estate in any case described in subsection (a) shall use the same accounting method as the debtor used immediately before the commencement of the case, if such method of accounting complies with applicable nonbankruptcy tax law.

(f) For purposes of any State or local law imposing a tax on or measured by income, a transfer of property from the debtor to the estate or from the estate to the debtor shall not be treated as a disposition for purposes of any provision assigning tax consequences to a disposition, except to the extent that such transfer is treated as a disposition under the Internal Revenue Code of 1986.

(g) Whenever a tax is imposed pursuant to a State or local law imposing a tax on or measured by income pursuant to subsection (a) or (b), such tax shall be imposed at rates generally applicable to the same types of entities under such State or local law.

(h) The trustee shall withhold from any payment of claims for wages, salaries, commissions, dividends, interest, or other payments, or collect, any amount required to be withheld or collected under applicable State or local tax law, and shall pay such withheld or collected amount to the appropriate governmental unit at the time and in the manner required by such tax law, and with the same priority as the claim from which such amount was withheld or collected was paid.

(i)(1) To the extent that any State or local law imposing a tax on or measured by income provides for the carryover of any tax attribute from one taxable period to a subsequent taxable period, the estate shall succeed to such tax attribute in any case in which such estate is subject to tax under subsection (a).

(2) After such a case is closed or dismissed, the debtor shall succeed to any tax attribute to which the estate succeeded under paragraph (1) to the extent consistent with the Internal Revenue Code of 1986.

(3) The estate may carry back any loss or tax attribute to a taxable period of the debtor that ended before the date of the order for relief under this title to the extent that—

(A) applicable State or local tax law provides for a carryback in the case of the debtor; and

(B) the same or a similar tax attribute may be carried back by the estate to such a taxable period of the debtor under the Internal Revenue Code of 1986.

(j)(1) For purposes of any State or local law imposing a tax on or measured by income, income is not realized by the estate, the debtor, or a successor to the debtor by reason of discharge of indebtedness in a case under this title, except to the extent, if any, that such income is subject to tax under the Internal Revenue Code of 1986.

(2) Whenever the Internal Revenue Code of 1986 provides that the amount excluded from gross income in respect of the discharge of indebtedness in a case under this title shall be applied to reduce the tax attributes of the debtor or the estate, a similar reduction shall be made under any State or local law imposing a tax on or measured by income to the extent such State or local law recognizes such attributes. Such State or local law may also provide for the reduction of other attributes to the extent that the full amount of income from the discharge of indebtedness has not been applied.

(k)(1) Except as provided in this section and section 505, the time and manner of filing tax returns and the items of income, gain, loss, deduction, and credit of any taxpayer shall be determined under applicable nonbankruptcy law.

(2) For Federal tax purposes, the provisions of this section are subject to the Internal Revenue Code of 1986 and other applicable Federal nonbankruptcy law.

§ 347. Unclaimed property

(a) Ninety days after the final distribution under section 726, 1226, or 1326 of this title in a case under chapter 7, 12, or 13 of this title, as the case may be, the trustee shall stop payment on any check remaining unpaid, and any remaining property of the estate shall be paid into the court and disposed of under chapter 129 of title 28.

(b) Any security, money, or other property remaining unclaimed at the expiration of the time allowed in a case under chapter 9, 11, or 12 of this title for the presentation of a security or the performance of any other act as a condition to participation in the distribution under any plan confirmed under section 943(b), 1129, 1173, or 1225 of this title, as the case may be, becomes the property of the debtor or of the entity acquiring the assets of the debtor under the plan, as the case may be.

§ 348. Effect of conversion

(a) Conversion of a case from a case under one chapter of this title to a case under another chapter of this title constitutes an order for relief under the chapter to which the case is converted, but, except as provided in subsections (b) and (c) of this section, does not effect a change in the date of the filing of the petition, the commencement of the case, or the order for relief.

(b) Unless the court for cause orders otherwise, in sections 701(a), 727(a)(10), 727(b), 728(a), 728(b), 1102(a), 1110(a)(1), 1121(b), 1121(c), 1141(d)(4), 1146(a), 1146(b), 1201(a), 1221, 1228(a), 1301(a), and 1305(a) of this title, "the order for relief under this chapter" in a chapter to which a case has been converted under section 706, 1112, 1208, or 1307 of this title means the conversion of such case in such chapter.

(c) Sections 342 and 365(d) of this title apply in a case that has been converted under section 706, 1112, 1208, or 1307 of this title, as if the conversion order were the order for relief.

(d) A claim against the estate or the debtor that arises after the order for relief but before conversion in a case that is converted under section 1112, 1208, or 1307 of this title, other than a claim specified in section 503(b) of this title, shall be treated for all purposes as if such claim had arisen immediately before the date of the filing of the petition.

(e) Conversion of a case under section 706, 1112, 1208, or 1307 of this title terminates the service of any trustee or examiner that is serving in the case before such conversion.

(f)(1) Except as provided in paragraph (2), when a case under chapter 13 of this title is converted to a case under another chapter under this title—

(A) property of the estate in the converted case shall consist of property of the estate, as of the date of filing of the petition, that remains in the possession of or is under the control of the debtor on the date of conversion; ~~and~~

(B) valuations of property and of allowed secured claims in the chapter 13 case shall apply ~~in the converted case~~ only in a case converted to a case under chapter 11 or 12, but not in a case converted to a case under chapter 7, with allowed secured claims in cases under chapters 11 and 12 reduced to the extent that they have been paid in accordance with the chapter 13 plan~~.~~; and

(C) with respect to cases converted from chapter 13—

(i) the claim of any creditor holding security as of the date of the petition shall continue to be secured by that security unless the full amount of such claim determined under applicable nonbankruptcy law has been paid in full as of the date of conversion, notwithstanding any valuation or determination of the amount of an allowed secured claim made for the purposes of the case under chapter 13; and

(ii) unless a prebankruptcy default has been fully cured under the plan at the time of conversion, in any proceeding under this title or otherwise, the default shall have the effect given under applicable nonbankruptcy law.

(2) If the debtor converts a case under chapter 13 of this title to a case under another chapter under this title in bad faith, the property of the estate in the converted case shall consist of the property of the estate as of the date of conversion.

§ 349. Effect of dismissal

(a) Unless the court, for cause, orders otherwise, the dismissal of a case under this title does not bar the discharge, in a later case under this title, of debts that were dischargeable in the case dismissed; nor does the dismissal of a case under this title prejudice the debtor with regard to the filing of a subsequent petition under this title, except as provided in section 109(g) of this title.

(b) Unless the court, for cause, orders otherwise, a dismissal of a case other than under section 742 of this title—

(1) reinstates—

(A) any proceeding or custodianship superseded under section 543 of this title;

(B) any transfer avoided under section 522, 544, 545, 547, 548, 549, or 724(a) of this title, or preserved under section 510(c)(2), 522(i)(2), or 551 of this title; and

(C) any lien voided under section 506(d) of this title;

(2) vacates any order, judgment, or transfer ordered, under section 522(i)(1), 542, 550, or 553 of this title; and

(3) revests the property of the estate in the entity in which such property was vested immediately before the commencement of the case under this title.

§ 350. Closing and reopening cases

(a) After an estate is fully administered and the court has discharged the trustee, the court shall close the case.

(b) A case may be reopened in the court in which such case was closed to administer assets, to accord relief to the debtor, or for other cause.

§ 351. Disposal of patient records

If a health care business commences a case under chapter 7, 9, or 11, and the trustee does not have a sufficient amount of funds to pay for the storage of patient records in the manner required under applicable Federal or State law, the following requirements shall apply:

(1) The trustee shall—

(A) promptly publish notice, in 1 or more appropriate newspapers, that if patient records are not claimed by the patient or an insurance provider (if applicable law permits the insurance provider to make that claim) by the date that is 365 days after the date of that notification, the trustee will destroy the patient records; and

(B) during the first 180 days of the 365-day period described in subparagraph (A), promptly attempt to notify directly each patient that is the subject of the patient records and appropriate insurance carrier concerning the patient records by mailing to the most recent known address of that patient, or a family member or contact person for that patient, and to the appropriate insurance carrier an appropriate notice regarding the claiming or disposing of patient records.

(2) If, after providing the notification under paragraph (1), patient records are not claimed during the 365-day period described under that paragraph, the trustee shall mail, by certified mail, at the end of such 365-day period a written request to each appropriate Federal agency to request permission from that agency to deposit the patient records with that agency, except that no Federal agency is required to accept patient records under this paragraph.

(3) If, following the 365-day period described in paragraph (2) and after providing the notification under paragraph (1), patient records are not claimed by a patient or insurance provider, or request is not granted by a Federal agency to deposit such records with that agency, the trustee shall destroy those records by—

(A) if the records are written, shredding or burning the records; or

(B) if the records are magnetic, optical, or other electronic records, by otherwise destroying those records so that those records cannot be retrieved.

SUBCHAPTER IV

Administrative Powers

§ 361. Adequate protection

When adequate protection is required under section 362, 363, or 364 of this title of an interest of an entity in property, such adequate protection may be provided by—

(1) requiring the trustee to make a cash payment or periodic cash payments to such entity, to the extent that the stay under section 362 of this title, use, sale, or lease under section 363 of this title, or any grant of a lien under section 364 of this title results in a decrease in the value of such entity's interest in such property;

(2) providing to such entity an additional or replacement lien to the extent that such stay, use, sale, lease, or grant results in a decrease in the value of such entity's interest in such property; or

(3) granting such other relief, other than entitling such entity to compensation allowable under section 503(b)(1) of this title as an administrative expense, as will result in the realization by such entity of the indubitable equivalent of such entity's interest in such property.

§ 362. Automatic stay

(a) Except as provided in subsection (b) of this section, a petition filed under section 301, 302, or 303 of this title, or an application filed under section 5(a)(3) of the Securities Investor Protection Act of 1970, operates as a stay, applicable to all entities, of—

(1) the commencement or continuation, including the issuance or employment of process, of a judicial, administrative, or other action or proceeding against the debtor that was or could have been commenced before the commencement of the case under this title, or to recover a claim against the debtor that arose before the commencement of the case under this title;

(2) the enforcement, against the debtor or against property of the estate, of a judgment obtained before the commencement of the case under this title;

(3) any act to obtain possession of property of the estate or of property from the estate or to exercise control over property of the estate;

(4) any act to create, perfect, or enforce any lien against property of the estate;

(5) any act to create, perfect, or enforce against property of the debtor any lien to the extent that such lien secures a claim that arose before the commencement of the case under this title;

(6) any act to collect, assess, or recover a claim against the debtor that arose before the commencement of the case under this title;

(7) the setoff of any debt owing to the debtor that arose before the commencement of the case under this title against any claim against the debtor; and

(8) the commencement or continuation of a proceeding before the United States Tax Court concerning ~~the debtor~~ a corporate debtor's tax liability for a taxable period the bankruptcy court may determine or concerning the tax liability of a debtor who is an individual for a taxable period ending before the date of the order for relief under this title.

(b) The filing of a petition under section 301, 302, or 303 of this title, or of an application under section 5(a)(3) of the Securities Investor Protection Act of 1970, does not operate as a stay—

(1) under subsection (a) of this section, of the commencement or continuation of a criminal action or proceeding against the debtor;

(2) under subsection (a) ~~of this section—~~

(A) of the commencement or continuation of a~~-n~~ civil action or proceeding ~~for—~~

(i) for the establishment of paternity; ~~or~~

(ii) for the establishment or modification of an order for ~~alimony, maintenance, or support~~ domestic support obligations; ~~or~~

(iii) concerning child custody or visitation;

(iv) for the dissolution of a marriage, except to the extent that such proceeding seeks to determine the division of property that is property of the estate; or

(v) regarding domestic violence;

(B) of the collection of ~~alimony, maintenance, or support~~ a domestic support obligation from property that is not property of the estate;

(C) with respect to the withholding of income that is property of the estate or property of the debtor for payment of a domestic support obligation under a judicial or administrative order or a statute;

(D) of the withholding, suspension, or restriction of a driver's license, a professional or occupational license, or a recreational license under State law, as specified in section 466(a)(16) of the Social Security Act;

(E) of the reporting of overdue support owed by a parent to any consumer reporting agency as specified in section 466(a)(7) of the Social Security Act;

(F) of the interception of a tax refund, as specified in sections 464 and 466(a)(3) of the Social Security Act or under an analogous State law; or

(G) of the enforcement of a medical obligation as specified under title IV of the Social Security Act;

(3) under subsection (a) of this section, of any act to perfect, or to maintain or continue the perfection of, an interest in property to the extent that the trustee's rights and powers are subject to such perfection under section 546(b) of this title or to the extent that such act is accomplished within the period provided under section 547(e)(2)(A) of this title;

(4) under paragraph (1), (2), (3), or (6) of subsection (a) of this section, of the commencement or continuation of an action or proceeding by a governmental unit or any organization exercising authority under the Convention on the Prohibition of the Development, Production, Stockpiling and Use of Chemical Weapons and on Their Destruction, opened for signature on January 13, 1993, to enforce such governmental unit's or organization's police and regulatory power, including the enforcement of a judgment other than a money judgment, obtained in an action or proceeding by the governmental unit to enforce such governmental unit's or organization's police or regulatory power;

(5) [*Abrogated*].

(6) under subsection (a) of this section, of the setoff by a commodity broker, forward contract merchant, stockbroker, financial institution~~-s~~, financial participant, or securities clearing agency of any mutual debt and claim under or in connection with commodity contracts, as defined in section 761 of this title, forward contracts, or securities contracts, as defined in section 741 of this title, that constitutes the setoff of a claim against the debtor for a margin payment, as defined in section 101, 741, or 761 of this title, or settlement payment, as defined in section 101 or 741 of this title, arising out of commodity contracts, forward contracts, or securities contracts against cash, securities, or other property held by, pledged to, under the control of, or due from such commodity broker, forward contract merchant, stockbroker, financial institution~~-s~~, financial participant, or securities clearing agency to margin, guarantee, secure, or settle commodity contracts, forward contracts, or securities contracts;

(7) under subsection (a) of this section, of the setoff by a repo participant or financial participant, of any mutual debt and claim under or in connection with repurchase agreements that constitutes the setoff of a claim against the debtor for a margin payment, as defined in section 741 or 761 of this title, or settlement payment, as defined in section 741 of this title, arising out of repurchase agreements against cash, securities, or other property held by, pledged to, under the control of, or due from such repo participant or financial participant to margin, guarantee, secure or settle repurchase agreements;

(8) under subsection (a) of this section, of the commencement of any action by the Secretary of Housing and Urban Develop-

ment to foreclose a mortgage or deed of trust in any case in which the mortgage or deed of trust held by the Secretary is insured or was formerly insured under the National Housing Act and covers property, or combinations of property, consisting of five or more living units;

(9) under subsection (a), of—

(A) an audit by a governmental unit to determine tax liability;

(B) the issuance to the debtor by a governmental unit of a notice of tax deficiency;

(C) a demand for tax returns; or

(D) the making of an assessment for any tax and issuance of a notice and demand for payment of such an assessment (but any tax lien that would otherwise attach to property of the estate by reason of such an assessment shall not take effect unless such tax is a debt of the debtor that will not be discharged in the case and such property or its proceeds are transferred out of the estate to, or otherwise revested in, the debtor).

(10) under subsection (a) of this section, of any act by a lessor to the debtor under a lease of nonresidential real property that has terminated by the expiration of the stated term of the lease before the commencement of or during a case under this title to obtain possession of such property;

(11) under subsection (a) of this section, of the presentment of a negotiable instrument and the giving of notice of and protesting dishonor of such an instrument;

(12) under subsection (a) of this section, after the date which is 90 days after the filing of such petition, of the commencement or continuation, and conclusion to the entry of final judgment, of an action which involves a debtor subject to reorganization pursuant to chapter 11 of this title and which was brought by the Secretary of Transportation under section 31325 of title 46 (including distribution of any proceeds of sale) to foreclose a preferred ship or fleet mortgage, or a security interest in or relating to a vessel or vessel under construction, held by the Secretary of Transportation under section 207 or title XI of the Merchant Marine Act, 1936, or under applicable State law;

(13) under subsection (a) of this section, after the date which is 90 days after the filing of such petition, of the commencement or continuation, and conclusion to the entry of final judgment, of an action which involves a debtor subject to reorganization pursuant to chapter 11 of this title and which was brought by the Secretary of Commerce under section 31325 of title 46 (including distribution of any proceeds of sale) to foreclose a preferred ship or fleet mortgage in a vessel or a mortgage, deed of trust, or other security interest in a fishing facility held by the Secretary of Commerce under section 207 or title XI of the Merchant Marine Act, 1936;

(14) under subsection (a) of this section, of any action by an accrediting agency regarding the accreditation status of the debtor as an educational institution;

(15) under subsection (a) of this section, of any action by a State licensing body regarding the licensure of the debtor as an educational institution;

(16) under subsection (a) of this section, of any action by a guaranty agency, as defined in section 435(j) of the Higher Education Act of 1965 or the Secretary of Education regarding the eligibility of the debtor to participate in programs authorized under such Act;

(17) under subsection (a) ~~of this section~~, of the setoff by a swap participant or financial participant~~,~~ of a~~ny~~ mutual debt and claim under or in connection with ~~any~~ one or more swap agreements that constitutes the setoff of a claim against the debtor for any payment or other transfer of property due from the debtor under or in connection with any swap agreement against any payment due to the debtor from the swap participant or financial participant under or in connection with any swap agreement or against cash, securities, or other property ~~of the debtor~~ held by, pledged to, under the control of, or due from such swap participant or financial participant to margin, guarantee, secure or settle any swap agreement; ~~or~~

(18) under subsection (a) of the creation or perfection of a statutory lien for an ad valorem property tax, or a special tax or special assessment on real property whether or not ad valorem, imposed by ~~the District of Columbia, or a political subdivision of a State~~ a governmental unit, if such tax or assessment comes due after the date of the filing of the petition~~. The provisions of paragraphs (12) and (13) of this subsection shall apply with respect to any such petition filed on or before December 31, 1989.~~;

(19) under subsection (a), of withholding of income from a debtor's wages and collection of amounts withheld, under the debtor's agreement authorizing that withholding and collection for the benefit of a pension, profit-sharing, stock bonus, or other plan established under section 401, 403, 408, 408A, 414, 457, or 501(c) of the Internal Revenue Code of 1986, that is sponsored by the employer of the debtor, or an affiliate, successor, or predecessor of such employer—

(A) to the extent that the amounts withheld and collected are used solely for payments relating to a loan from a plan under section 408(b)(1) of the Employee Retirement Income Security Act of 1974 or is subject to section 72(p) of the Internal Revenue Code of 1986; or

(B) a loan from a thrift savings plan permitted under subchapter III of chapter 84 of title 5, that satisfies the requirements of section 8433(g) of such title; but nothing in this paragraph may be construed to provide that any loan made under a governmental plan under section 414(d), or a contract or account under section 403(b) of the Internal Revenue Code of 1986 constitutes a claim or a debt under this title;

(20) under subsection (a), of any act to enforce any lien against or security interest in real property following entry of the order under subsection (d)(4) as to such real property in any prior case under this title for a period of 2 years after the date of the entry of such an order, except that the debtor, in a subsequent case under this title, may move for relief from such order based upon changed circumstances or for other good cause shown, after notice and a hearing;

(21) under subsection (a), of any act to enforce any lien against or security interest in real property—

(A) if the debtor is ineligible under section 109(g) to be a debtor in a case under this title; or

(B) if the case under this title was filed in violation of a bankruptcy court order in a prior case under this title prohibiting the debtor from being a debtor in another case under this title;

(22) subject to subsection (*l*), under subsection (a)(3), of the continuation of any eviction, unlawful detainer action, or similar proceeding by a lessor against a debtor involving residential property in which the debtor resides as a tenant under a lease or rental agreement and with respect to which the lessor has obtained before the date of the filing of the bankruptcy petition, a judgment for possession of such property against the debtor;

(23) subject to subsection (m), under subsection (a)(3), of an eviction action that seeks possession of the residential property in which the debtor resides as a tenant under a lease or rental agreement based on endangerment of such property or the illegal use of controlled substances on such property, but only if the lessor files with the court, and serves upon the debtor, a certification under penalty of perjury that such an eviction action has been filed, or that the debtor, during the 30-day period preceding the date of the filing of the certification, has endangered property or illegally used or allowed to be used a controlled substance on the property;

(24) under subsection (a), of any transfer that is not avoidable under section 544 and that is not avoidable under section 549;

(25) under subsection (a), of—

(A) the commencement or continuation of an investigation or action by a securities self regulatory organization to enforce such organization's regulatory power;

(B) the enforcement of an order or decision, other than for monetary sanctions, obtained in an action by such securities self regulatory organization to enforce such organization's regulatory power; or

(C) any act taken by such securities self regulatory organization to delist, delete, or refuse to permit quotation of any stock that does not meet applicable regulatory requirements;

(26) under subsection (a), of the setoff under applicable nonbankruptcy law of an income tax refund, by a governmental unit, with respect to a taxable period that ended before the date of the order for relief against an income tax liability for a taxable period that also ended before the date of the order for relief, except that in any case in which the setoff of an income tax refund is not permitted under applicable nonbankruptcy law because of a pending action to determine the amount or legality of a tax liability, the governmental unit may hold the refund pending the resolution of the action, unless the court, on the motion of the trustee and after notice and a hearing, grants the taxing authority adequate protection (within the meaning of section 361) for the secured claim of such authority in the setoff under section 506(a);

(27) under subsection (a), of the setoff by a master netting agreement participant of a mutual debt and claim under or in connection with one or more master netting agreements or any contract or agreement subject to such agreements that constitutes the setoff of a claim against the debtor for any payment or other transfer of property due from the debtor under or in connection with such agreements or any contract or agreement subject to such agreements against any payment due to the debtor from such master netting agreement participant under or in connection with such agreements or any contract or agreement subject to such agreements or against cash, securities, or other property held by, pledged to, under the control of, or due from such master netting agreement participant to margin, guarantee, secure, or settle such agreements or any contract or agreement subject to such agreements, to the extent that such participant is eligible to exercise such offset rights under paragraph (6), (7), or (17) for each individual contract covered by the master netting agreement in issue; and

(28) under subsection (a), of the exclusion by the Secretary of Health and Human Services of the debtor from participation in the medicare program or any other Federal health care program (as defined in section 1128B(f) of the Social Security Act pursuant to title XI or XVIII of such Act.

(c) Except as provided in subsections (d), (e), ~~and~~ (f) and (h) of this section—

(1) the stay of an act against property of the estate under subsection (a) of this section continues until such property is no longer property of the estate; ~~and~~

(2) the stay of any other act under subsection (a) of this section continues until the earliest of—

(A) the time the case is closed;

(B) the time the case is dismissed; or

(C) if the case is a case under chapter 7 of this title concerning an individual or a case under chapter 9, 11, 12, or 13 of this title, the time a discharge is granted or denied~~.~~;

(3) if a single or joint case is filed by or against debtor who is an individual in a case under chapter 7, 11, or 13, and if a single or joint case of the debtor was pending within the preceding 1-year period but was dismissed, other than a case refiled under a chapter other than chapter 7 after dismissal under section 707(b)—

(A) the stay under subsection (a) with respect to any action taken with respect to a debt or property securing such debt or with respect to any lease shall terminate with respect to the debtor on the 30th day after the filing of the later case;

(B) on the motion of a party in interest for continuation of the automatic stay and upon notice and a hearing, the court may extend the stay in particular cases as to any or all creditors (subject to such conditions or limitations as the court may then impose) after notice and a hearing completed before the expiration of the 30-day period only if the party in interest demonstrates that the filing of the later case is in good faith as to the creditors to be stayed; and

(C) for purposes of subparagraph (B), a case is presumptively filed not in good faith (but such presumption may be rebutted by clear and convincing evidence to the contrary)—

(i) as to all creditors, if—

(I) more than 1 previous case under any of chapters 7, 11, and 13 in which the individual was a debtor was pending within the preceding 1-year period;

(II) a previous case under any of chapters 7, 11, and 13 in which the individual was a debtor was dismissed within such 1-year period, after the debtor failed to—

(aa) file or amend the petition or other documents as required by this title or the court without substantial excuse (but mere inadvertence or negligence shall not be a substantial excuse unless the dismissal was caused by the negligence of the debtor' s attorney);

(bb) provide adequate protection as ordered by the court; or

(cc) perform the terms of a plan confirmed by the court; or

(III) there has not been a substantial change in the financial or personal affairs of the debtor since the dismissal of the next most previous case under chapter 7, 11, or 13 or any other reason to conclude that the later case will be concluded—

(aa) if a case under chapter 7, with a discharge; or

(bb) if a case under chapter 11 or 13, with a confirmed plan that will be fully performed; and

(ii) as to any creditor that commenced an action under subsection (d) in a previous case in which the individual was a debtor if, as of the date of dismissal of such case, that action was still pending or had been resolved by terminating, conditioning, or limiting the stay as to actions of such creditor; and

(4)(A)(i) if a single or joint case is filed by or against a debtor who is an individual under this title, and if 2 or more single or joint cases of the debtor were pending within the previous year but were dismissed, other than a case refiled under section 707(b), the stay under subsection (a) shall not go into effect upon the filing of the later case; and

(ii) on request of a party in interest, the court shall promptly enter an order confirming that no stay is in effect;

(B) if, within 30 days after the filing of the later case, a party in interest requests the court may order the stay to take effect in the case as to any or all creditors (subject to such conditions or limitations as the court may impose), after notice and a hearing, only if the party in interest demonstrates that the filing of the later case is in good faith as to the creditors to be stayed;

(C) a stay imposed under subparagraph (B) shall be effective on the date of the entry of the order allowing the stay to go into effect; and

(D) for purposes of subparagraph (B), a case is presumptively filed not in good faith (but such presumption may be rebutted by clear and convincing evidence to the contrary)—

(i) as to all creditors if—

(I) 2 or more previous cases under this title in which the individual was a debtor were pending within the 1-year period;

(II) a previous case under this title in which the individual was a debtor was dismissed within the time period stated in this paragraph after the debtor failed to file or amend the petition or other documents as required by this title or the court without substantial excuse (but mere inadvertence or negligence shall not be substantial excuse unless the dismissal was caused by the negligence of the debtor's attorney), failed to provide adequate protection as ordered by the court, or failed to perform the terms of a plan confirmed by the court; or

(III) there has not been a substantial change in the financial or personal affairs of the debtor since the dismissal of the next most previous case under this title, or any other reason to conclude that the later case will not be concluded, if a case under chapter 7, with a discharge, and if a case under chapter 11 or 13, with a confirmed plan that will be fully performed; or

(ii) as to any creditor that commenced an action under subsection (d) in a previous case in which the individual was a debtor if, as of the date of dismissal of such case, such action was still pending or had been resolved by terminating, conditioning, or limiting the stay as to such action of such creditor.

(d) On request of a party in interest and after notice and a hearing, the court shall grant relief from the stay provided under subsection (a) of this section, such as by terminating, annulling, modifying, or conditioning such stay—

(1) for cause, including the lack of adequate protection of an interest in property of such party in interest;

(2) with respect to a stay of an act against property under subsection (a) of this section, if—

(A) the debtor does not have an equity in such property; and

(B) such property is not necessary to an effective reorganization; ~~or~~

(3) with respect to a stay of an act against single asset real estate under subsection (a), by a creditor whose claim is secured by an interest in such real estate, unless, not later than the date that is 90 days after the entry of the order for relief (or such later date as the court may determine for cause by order entered within that 90-day period) or 30 days after the court determines that the debtor is subject to this paragraph, whichever is later—

(A) the debtor has filed a plan of reorganization that has a reasonable possibility of being confirmed within a reasonable time; or

(B) the debtor has commenced monthly payments that—

(i) may, in the debtor's sole discretion, notwithstanding section 363(c)(2), be made from rents or other income generated before, on, or after the date of the commencement of the case by or from the property to each creditor whose claim is secured by such real estate (other than a claim secured by a judgment lien or by an unmatured statutory lien)~~,~~; and

(ii) ~~which payments~~ are in an amount equal to interest at ~~a current fair market rate~~ the then applicable nondefault contract rate of interest on the value of the creditor's interest in the real estate~~.~~; or

(4) with respect to a stay of an act against real property under subsection (a), by a creditor whose claim is secured by an interest in such real property, if the court finds that the filing of the petition was part of a scheme to delay, hinder, and defraud creditors that involved either—

(A) transfer of all or part ownership of, or other interest in, such real property without the consent of the secured creditor or court approval; or

(B) multiple bankruptcy filings affecting such real property.

If recorded in compliance with applicable State laws governing notices of interests or liens in real property, an order entered under paragraph (4) shall be binding in any other case under this title purporting to affect such real property filed not later than 2 years after the date of the entry of such order by the court, except that a debtor in a subsequent case under this title may move for relief from such order based upon changed circumstances or for good cause shown, after notice and a hearing. Any Federal, State, or local governmental unit that accepts notices of interests or liens in real property shall accept any certified copy of an order described in this subsection for indexing and recording.

(e) (1) Thirty days after a request under subsection (d) of this section for relief from the stay of any act against property of the estate under subsection (a) of this section, such stay is terminated with respect to the party in interest making such request, unless the court, after notice and a hearing, orders such stay continued in effect pending the conclusion of, or as a result of, a final hearing and determination under subsection (d) of this section. A hearing under this subsection may be a preliminary hearing, or may be consolidated with the final hearing under subsection (d) of this section. The court shall order such stay continued in effect pending the conclusion of the final hearing under subsection (d) of this section if there is a reasonable likelihood that the party opposing relief from such stay will prevail at the conclusion of such final hearing. If the hearing under this subsection is a preliminary hearing, then such final hearing shall be concluded not later than thirty days after the conclusion of such preliminary hearing, unless the 30-day period is extended with the consent of the parties in interest or for a specific time which the court finds is required by compelling circumstances.

(2) Notwithstanding paragraph (1), in a case under chapter 7, 11, or 13 in which the debtor is an individual, the stay under subsection (a) shall terminate on the date that is 60 days after a request is made by a party in interest under subsection (d), unless—

(A) a final decision is rendered by the court during the 60-day period beginning on the date of the request; or

(B) such 60-day period is extended—

(i) by agreement of all parties in interest; or

(ii) by the court for such specific period of time as the court finds is required for good cause, as described in findings made by the court.

(f) Upon request of a party in interest, the court, with or without a hearing, shall grant such relief from the stay provided under subsection (a) of this section as is necessary to prevent irreparable damage to the interest of an entity in property, if such interest will suffer such damage before there is an opportunity for notice and a hearing under subsection (d) or (e) of this section.

(g) In any hearing under subsection (d) or (e) of this section concerning relief from the stay of any act under subsection (a) of this section—

(1) the party requesting such relief has the burden of proof on the issue of the debtor's equity in property; and

(2) the party opposing such relief has the burden of proof on all other issues.

(h)(1) In a case in which the debtor is an individual, the stay provided by subsection (a) is terminated with respect to personal property of the estate or of the debtor securing in whole or in part a claim, or subject to an unexpired lease, and such personal property shall no longer be property of the estate if the debtor fails within the applicable time set by section 521(a)(2)—

(A) to file timely any statement of intention required under section 521(a)(2) with respect to such personal property or to indicate in such statement that the debtor will either surrender such personal property or retain it and, if retaining such personal property, either redeem such personal property pursuant to section 722, enter into an agreement of the kind specified in section 524(c) applicable to the debt secured by such personal property, or assume such unexpired lease pursuant to section 365(p) if the trustee does not do so, as applicable; and

(B) to take timely the action specified in such statement, as it may be amended before expiration of the period for taking action, unless such statement specifies the debtor's intention to reaffirm such debt on the original contract terms and the creditor refuses to agree to the reaffirmation on such terms.

(2) Paragraph (1) does not apply if the court determines, on the motion of the trustee filed before the expiration of the applicable time set by section 521(a)(2), after notice and a hearing,

that such personal property is of consequential value or benefit to the estate, and orders appropriate adequate protection of the creditor's interest, and orders the debtor to deliver any collateral in the debtor's possession to the trustee.If the court does not so determine, the stay provided by subsection (a) shall terminate upon the conclusion of the hearing on the motion.

(i) If a case commenced under chapter 7, 11, or 13 is dismissed due to the creation of a debt repayment plan, for purposes of subsection (c)(3), any subsequent case commenced by the debtor under any such chapter shall not be presumed to be filed not in good faith.

(j) On request of a party in interest, the court shall issue an order under subsection (c) confirming that the automatic stay has been terminated.

(~~h~~k)(1) Except as provided in paragraph (2), an ~~An~~ individual injured by any willful violation of a stay provided by this section shall recover actual damages, including costs and attorneys' fees, and, in appropriate circumstances, may recover punitive damages.

(2) If such violation is based on an action taken by an entity in the good faith belief that subsection (h) applies to the debtor, the recovery under paragraph (1) of this subsection against such entity shall be limited to actual damages.

(*l*)(1) Except as otherwise provided in this subsection, subsection (b)(22) shall apply on the date that is 30 days after the date on which the bankruptcy petition is filed, if the debtor files with the petition and serves upon the lessor a certification under penalty of perjury that—

(A) under nonbankruptcy law applicable in the jurisdiction, there are circumstances under which the debtor would be permitted to cure the entire monetary default that gave rise to the judgment for possession, after that judgment for possession was entered; and

(B) the debtor (or an adult dependent of the debtor) has deposited with the clerk of the court, any rent that would become due during the 30-day period after the filing of the bankruptcy petition.

(2) If, within the 30-day period after the filing of the bankruptcy petition, the debtor (or an adult dependent of the debtor) complies with paragraph (1) and files with the court and serves upon the lessor a further certification under penalty of perjury that the debtor (or an adult dependent of the debtor) has cured, under nonbankrupcty law applicable in the jurisdiction, the entire monetary default that gave rise to the judgment under which possession is sought by the lessor, subsection (b)(22) shall not apply, unless ordered to apply by the court under paragraph (3).

(3)(A) If the lessor files an objection to any certification filed by the debtor under paragraph (1) or (2), and serves such objection upon the debtor, the court shall hold a hearing within 10 days after the filing and service of such objection to determine if the certification filed by the debtor under paragraph (1) or (2) is true.

(B) If the court upholds the objection of the lessor filed under subparagraph (A)—

(i) subsection (b)(22) shall apply immediately and relief from the stay provided under subsection (a)(3) shall not be required to enable the lessor to complete the process to recover full possession of the property; and

(ii) the clerk of the court shall immediately serve upon the lessor and the debtor a certified copy of the court's order upholding the lessor's objection.

(4) If a debtor, in accordance with paragraph (5), indicates on the petition that there was a judgment for possession of the residential rental property in which the debtor resides and does not file a certification under paragraph (1) or (2)—

(A) subsection (b)(22) shall apply immediately upon failure to file such certification, and relief from the stay provided under subsection (a)(3) shall not be required to enable the lessor to complete the process to recover full possession of the property; and

(B) the clerk of the court shall immediately serve upon the lessor and the debtor a certified copy of the docket indicating the absence of a filed certification and the applicability of the exception to the stay under subsection (b)(22).

(5)(A) Where a judgment for possession of residential property in which the debtor resides as a tenant under a lease or rental agreement has been obtained by the lessor, the debtor shall so indicate on the bankruptcy petition and shall provide the name and address of the lessor that obtained that prepetition judgment on the petition and on any certification filed under this subsection.

(B) The form of certification filed with the petition, as specified in this subsection, shall provide for the debtor to certify, and the debtor shall certify—

(i) whether a judgment for possession of residential rental housing in which the debtor resides has been obtained against the debtor before the date of the filing of the petition; and

(ii) whether the debtor is claiming under paragraph (1) that under nonbankruptcy law applicable in the jurisdiction, there are circumstances under which the debtor would be permitted to cure the entire monetary default that gave rise to the judgment for possession, after that judgment of possession was entered, and has made the appropriate deposit with the court.

(C) The standard forms (electronic and otherwise) used in a bankruptcy proceeding shall be amended to reflect the requirements of this subsection.

(D) The clerk of the court shall arrange for the prompt transmittal of the rent deposited in accordance with paragraph (1)(B) to the lessor.

(m)(1) Except as otherwise provided in this subsection, subsection (b)(23) shall apply on the date that is 15 days after the date on which the lessor files and serves a certification described in subsection (b)(23).

(2)(A) If the debtor files with the court an objection to the truth or legal sufficiency of the certification described in subsection (b)(23) and serves such objection upon the lessor, subsection (b)(23) shall not apply, unless ordered to apply by the court under this subsection.

(B) If the debtor files and serves the objection under subparagraph (A), the court shall hold a hearing within 10 days after the filing and service of such objection to determine if the situation giving rise to the lessor's certification under paragraph (1) existed or has been remedied.

(C) If the debtor can demonstrate to the satisfaction of the court that the situation giving rise to the lessor's certification under paragraph (1) did not exist or has been remedied, the stay provided under subsection (a)(3) shall remain in effect until the termination of the stay under this section.

(D) If the debtor cannot demonstrate to the satisfaction of the court that the situation giving rise to the lessor's certification under paragraph (1) did not exist or has been remedied—

(i) relief from the stay provided under subsection (a)(3) shall not be required to enable the lessor to proceed with the eviction; and

(ii) the clerk of the court shall immediately serve upon the lessor and the debtor a certified copy of the court's order upholding the lessor's certification.

(3) If the debtor fails to file, within 15 days, an objection under paragraph (2)(A)—

(A) subsection (b)(23) shall apply immediately upon such failure and relief from the stay provided under subsection (a)(3) shall not be required to enable the lessor to complete the process to recover full possession of the property; and

(B) the clerk of the court shall immediately serve upon the lessor and the debtor a certified copy of the docket indicating such failure.

(n)(1) Except as provided in paragraph (2), subsection (a) does not apply in a case in which the debtor—

(A) is a debtor in a small business case pending at the time the petition is filed;

(B) was a debtor in a small business case that was dismissed for any reason by an order that became final in the 2-year period ending on the date of the order for relief entered with respect to the petition;

(C) was a debtor in a small business case in which a plan was confirmed in the 2-year period ending on the date of the order for relief entered with respect to the petition; or

(D) is an entity that has acquired substantially all of the assets or business of a small business debtor described in subparagraph (A), (B), or (C), unless such entity establishes by a preponderance of the evidence that such entity acquired substantially all of the assets or business of such small business debtor in good faith and not for the purpose of evading this paragraph.

(2) Paragraph (1) does not apply—

(A) to an involuntary case involving no collusion by the debtor with creditors; or

(B) to the filing of a petition if—

(i) the debtor proves by a preponderance of the evidence that the filing of the petition resulted from circumstances beyond the control of the debtor not foreseeable at the time the case then pending was filed; and

(ii) it is more likely than not that the court will confirm a feasible plan, but not a liquidating plan, within a reasonable period of time.

(*o*) The exercise of rights not subject to the stay arising under subsection (a) pursuant to paragraph (6), (7), (17), or (27) of subsection (b) shall not be stayed by any order of a court or administrative agency in any proceeding under this title.

§ 363. Use, sale, or lease of property

(a) In this section, "cash collateral" means cash, negotiable instruments, documents of title, securities, deposit accounts, or other cash equivalents whenever acquired in which the estate and an entity other than the estate have an interest and includes the proceeds, products, offspring, rents, or profits of property and the fees, charges, accounts or other payments for the use or occupancy of rooms and other public facilities in hotels, motels, or other lodging properties subject to a security interest as provided in section 552(b) of this title, whether existing before or after the commencement of a case under this title.

(b)(1) The trustee, after notice and a hearing, may use, sell, or lease, other than in the ordinary course of business, property of the estate, except that if the debtor in connection with offering a product or a service discloses to an individual a policy prohibiting the transfer of personally identifiable information about individuals to persons that are not affiliated with the debtor and if such policy is in effect on the date of the commencement of the case, then the trustee may not sell or lease personally identifiable information to any person unless—

(A) such sale or such lease is consistent with such policy; or

(B) after appointment of a consumer privacy ombudsman in accordance with section 332, and after notice and a hearing, the court approves such sale or such lease—

(i) giving due consideration to the facts, circumstances, and conditions of such sale or such lease; and

(ii) finding that no showing was made that such sale or such lease would violate applicable nonbankruptcy law.

(2) If notification is required under subsection (a) of section 7A of the Clayton Act in the case of a transaction under this subsection, then—

(A) notwithstanding subsection (a) of such section, the notification required by such subsection to be given by the debtor shall be given by the trustee; and

(B) notwithstanding subsection (b) of such section, the required waiting period shall end on the 15th day after the date of the receipt, by the Federal Trade Commission and the Assistant Attorney General in charge of the Antitrust Division of the Department of Justice, of the notification required under such subsection (a), unless such waiting period is extended—

(i) pursuant to subsection (e)(2) of such section, in the same manner as such subsection (e)(2) applies to a cash tender offer;

(ii) pursuant to subsection (g)(2) of such section; or

(iii) by the court after notice and a hearing.

(c)(1) If the business of the debtor is authorized to be operated under section 721, 1108, 1203, 1204, or 1304 of this title and unless the court orders otherwise, the trustee may enter into transactions, including the sale or lease of property of the estate, in the ordinary course of business, without notice or a hearing, and may use property of the estate in the ordinary course of business without notice or a hearing.

(2) The trustee may not use, sell, or lease cash collateral under paragraph (1) of this subsection unless—

(A) each entity that has an interest in such cash collateral consents; or

(B) the court, after notice and a hearing, authorizes such use, sale, or lease in accordance with the provisions of this section.

(3) Any hearing under paragraph (2)(B) of this subsection may be a preliminary hearing or may be consolidated with a hearing under subsection (c) of this section, but shall be scheduled in accordance with the needs of the debtor. If the hearing under paragraph (2)(B) of this subsection is a preliminary hearing, the court may authorize such use, sale, or lease only if there is a reasonable likelihood that the trustee will prevail at the final hearing under subsection (e) of this section. The court shall act promptly on any request for authorization under paragraph (2)(B) of this subsection.

(4) Except as provided in paragraph (2) of this subsection, the trustee shall segregate and account for any cash collateral in the trustee's possession, custody, or control.

(d) The trustee may use, sell, or lease property under subsection (b) or (c) of this section only—

(1) in accordance with applicable nonbankruptcy law that governs the transfer of property by a corporation or trust that is not a moneyed, business, or commercial corporation or trust;[15] and

(2) to the extent not inconsistent with any relief granted under subsection (c), (d), (e), or (f) of section 362~~(e), 362(d), 362(c), or 362(f) of this title~~.

(e) Notwithstanding any other provision of this section, at any time, on request of an entity that has an interest in property used, sold, or leased, or proposed to be used, sold, or leased, by the trustee, the court, with or without a hearing, shall prohibit or condition such use, sale, or lease as is necessary to provide adequate protection of such interest. This subsection also applies to property that is subject to any unexpired lease of personal property (to the exclusion of such property being subject to an order to grant relief from the stay under section 362).

(f) The trustee may sell property under subsection (b) or (c) of this section free and clear of any interest in such property of an entity other than the estate, only if—

(1) applicable nonbankruptcy law permits sale of such property free and clear of such interest;

(2) such entity consents;

(3) such interest is a lien and the price at which such property is to be sold is greater than the aggregate value of all liens on such property;

(4) such interest is in bona fide dispute; or

(5) such entity could be compelled, in a legal or equitable proceeding, to accept a money satisfaction of such interest.

(g) Notwithstanding subsection (f) of this section, the trustee may sell property under subsection (b) or (c) of this section free and clear of any vested or contingent right in the nature of dower or curtesy.

(h) Notwithstanding subsection (f) of this section, the trustee may sell both the estate's interest, under subsection (b) or (c) of this section, and the interest of any co-owner in property in which the debtor had, at the time of the commencement of the case, an undivided interest as a tenant in common, joint tenant, or tenant by the entirety, only if—

(1) partition in kind of such property among the estate and such co-owners is impracticable;

(2) sale of the estate's undivided interest in such property would realize significantly less for the estate than sale of such property free of the interests of such co-owners;

(3) the benefit to the estate of a sale of such property free of the interests of co-owners outweighs the detriment, if any, to such co-owners; and

(4) such property is not used in the production, transmission, or distribution, for sale, of electric energy or of natural or synthetic gas for heat, light, or power.

(i) Before the consummation of a sale of property to which subsection (g) or (h) of this section applies, or of property of the estate that was community property of the debtor and the debtor's spouse immediately before the commencement of the case, the debtor's spouse, or a co-owner of such property, as the case may be, may purchase such property at the price at which such sale is to be consummated.

15 *Editor's Note*: These changes to section 363(d)(1) apply to cases pending under title 11 on April 20, 2005 and to cases commenced on or after that date, except that a court shall not confirm a plan under chapter 11 of title 11 without considering whether these changes would substantially affect the rights of a party in interest who first acquired rights with respect to the debtor after the date of the petition.

(j) After a sale of property to which subsection (g) or (h) of this section applies, the trustee shall distribute to the debtor's spouse or the co-owners of such property, as the case may be, and to the estate, the proceeds of such sale, less the costs and expenses, not including any compensation of the trustee, of such sale, according to the interests of such spouse or co-owners, and of the estate.

(k) At a sale under subsection (b) of this section of property that is subject to a lien that secures an allowed claim, unless the court for cause orders otherwise the holder of such claim may bid at such sale, and, if the holder of such claim purchases such property, such holder may offset such claim against the purchase price of such property.

(*l*) Subject to the provisions of section 365, the trustee may use, sell, or lease property under subsection (b) or (c) of this section, or a plan under chapter 11, 12, or 13 of this title may provide for the use, sale, or lease of property, notwithstanding any provision in a contract, a lease, or applicable law that is conditioned on the insolvency or financial condition of the debtor, on the commencement of a case under this title concerning the debtor, or on the appointment of or the taking possession by a trustee in a case under this title or a custodian, and that effects, or gives an option to effect, a forfeiture, modification, or termination of the debtor's interest in such property.

(m) The reversal or modification on appeal of an authorization under subsection (b) or (c) of this section of a sale or lease of property does not affect the validity of a sale or lease under such authorization to an entity that purchased or leased such property in good faith, whether or not such entity knew of the pendency of the appeal, unless such authorization and such sale or lease were stayed pending appeal.

(n) The trustee may avoid a sale under this section if the sale price was controlled by an agreement among potential bidders at such sale, or may recover from a party to such agreement any amount by which the value of the property sold exceeds the price at which such sale was consummated, and may recover any costs, attorneys' fees, or expenses incurred in avoiding such sale or recovering such amount. In addition to any recovery under the preceding sentence, the court may grant judgment for punitive damages in favor of the estate and against any such party that entered into such an agreement in willful disregard of this subsection.

(*o*) Notwithstanding subsection (f), if a person purchases any interest in a consumer credit transaction that is subject to the Truth in Lending Act or any interest in a consumer credit contract (as defined in section 433.1 of title 16 of the Code of Federal Regulations (January 1, 2004), as amended from time to time), and if such interest is purchased through a sale under this section, then such person shall remain subject to all claims and defenses that are related to such consumer credit transaction or such consumer credit contract, to the same extent as such person would be subject to such claims and defenses of the consumer had such interest been purchased at a sale not under this section.

(~~o~~p) In any hearing under this section—

(1) the trustee has the burden of proof on the issue of adequate protection; and

(2) the entity asserting an interest in property has the burden of proof on the issue of the validity, priority, or extent of such interest.

§ 364. Obtaining credit

(a) If the trustee is authorized to operate the business of the debtor under section 721, 1108, 1203, 1204, or 1304 of this title, unless the court orders otherwise, the trustee may obtain unsecured credit and incur unsecured debt in the ordinary course of business allowable under section 503(b)(1) of this title as an administrative expense.

(b) The court, after notice and a hearing, may authorize the trustee to obtain unsecured credit or to incur unsecured debt other than under subsection (a) of this section, allowable under section 503(b)(1) of this title as an administrative expense.

(c) If the trustee is unable to obtain unsecured credit allowable under section 503(b)(1) of this title as an administrative expense, the court, after notice and a hearing, may authorize the obtaining of credit or the incurring of debt—

(1) with priority over any or all administrative expenses of the kind specified in section 503(b) or 507(b) of this title;

(2) secured by a lien on property of the estate that is not otherwise subject to a lien; or

(3) secured by a junior lien on property of the estate that is subject to a lien.

(d)(1) The court, after notice and a hearing, may authorize the obtaining of credit or the incurring of debt secured by a senior or equal lien on property of the estate that is subject to a lien only if—

(A) the trustee is unable to obtain such credit otherwise; and

(B) there is adequate protection of the interest of the holder of the lien on the property of the estate on which such senior or equal lien is proposed to be granted.

(2) In any hearing under this subsection, the trustee has the burden of proof on the issue of adequate protection.

(e) The reversal or modification on appeal of an authorization under this section to obtain credit or incur debt, or of a grant under this section of a priority or a lien, does not affect the validity of any debt so incurred, or any priority or lien so granted, to an entity that extended such credit in good faith, whether or not such entity knew of the pendency of the appeal, unless such authorization and the incurring of such debt, or the granting of such priority or lien, were stayed pending appeal.

(f) Except with respect to an entity that is an underwriter as defined in section 1145(b) of this title, section 5 of the Securities Act of 1933, the Trust Indenture Act of 1939, and any State or local law requiring registration for offer or sale of a security or registration or licensing of an issuer of, underwriter of, or broker or dealer in, a security does not apply to the offer or sale under this section of a security that is not an equity security.

§ 365. Executory contracts and unexpired leases

(a) Except as provided in sections 765 and 766 of this title and in subsections (b), (c), and (d) of this section, the trustee, subject to the court's approval, may assume or reject any executory contract or unexpired lease of the debtor.

(b)(1) If there has been a default in an executory contract or unexpired lease of the debtor, the trustee may not assume such contract or lease unless, at the time of assumption of such contract or lease, the trustee—

(A) cures, or provides adequate assurance that the trustee will promptly cure, such default other than a default that is a breach of a provision relating to the satisfaction of any provision (other than a penalty rate or penalty provision) relating to a default arising from any failure to perform nonmonetary obligations under an unexpired lease of real property, if it is impossible for the trustee to cure such default by performing nonmonetary acts at and after the time of assumption, except that if such default arises from a failure to operate in accordance with a nonresidential real property lease, then such default shall be cured by performance at and after the time of assumption in accordance with such lease, and pecuniary losses resulting from such default shall be compensated in accordance with the provisions of this paragraph;

(B) compensates, or provides adequate assurance that the trustee will promptly compensate, a party other than the debtor to such contract or lease, for any actual pecuniary loss to such party resulting from such default; and

(C) provides adequate assurance of future performance under such contract or lease.

(2) Paragraph (1) of this subsection does not apply to a default that is a breach of a provision relating to—

(A) the insolvency or financial condition of the debtor at any time before the closing of the case;

(B) the commencement of a case under this title;

(C) the appointment of or taking possession by a trustee in a case under this title or a custodian before such commencement; or

(D) the satisfaction of any penalty rate or penalty provision relating to a default arising from any failure by the debtor to perform nonmonetary obligations under the executory contract or unexpired lease.

(3) For the purposes of paragraph (1) of this subsection and paragraph (2)(B) of subsection (f), adequate assurance of future performance of a lease of real property in a shopping center includes adequate assurance—

(A) of the source of rent and other consideration due under such lease, and in the case of an assignment, that the financial condition and operating performance of the proposed assignee and its guarantors, if any, shall be similar to the financial condition and operating performance of the debtor and its guarantors, if any, as of the time the debtor became the lessee under the lease;

(B) that any percentage rent due under such lease will not decline substantially;

(C) that assumption or assignment of such lease is subject to all the provisions thereof, including (but not limited to) provisions such as a radius, location, use, or exclusivity provision, and will not breach any such provision contained in any other lease, financing agreement, or master agreement relating to such shopping center; and

(D) that assumption or assignment of such lease will not disrupt any tenant mix or balance in such shopping center.

(4) Notwithstanding any other provision of this section, if there has been a default in an unexpired lease of the debtor, other than a default of a kind specified in paragraph (2) of this subsection, the trustee may not require a lessor to provide services or supplies incidental to such lease before assumption of such lease unless the lessor is compensated under the terms of such lease for any services and supplies provided under such lease before assumption of such lease.

(c) The trustee may not assume or assign an executory contract or unexpired lease of the debtor, whether or not such contract or lease prohibits or restricts assignment of rights or delegation of duties, if—

(1)(A) applicable law excuses a party, other than the debtor, to such contract or lease from accepting performance from or rendering performance to an entity other than the debtor or the debtor in possession, whether or not such contract or lease prohibits or restricts assignment of rights or delegation of duties; and

(B) such party does not consent to such assumption or assignment; or

(2) such contract is a contract to make a loan, or extend other debt financing or financial accommodations, to or for the benefit of the debtor, or to issue a security of the debtor; or

(3) such lease is of nonresidential real property and has been terminated under applicable nonbankruptcy law prior to the order for relief~~; or~~

~~(4) such lease is of nonresidential real property under which the debtor is lessee of an aircraft terminal or aircraft gate at an airport at which the debtor is the lessee under one or more additional nonresidential leases of an aircraft terminal or aircraft gate and the trustee, in connection with such assumption or assignment, does not assume all such leases or does not assume and assign all of such leases to the same person, except that the trustee may assume or assign less than all of such leases with the airport operator's written consent~~.

(d)(1) In a case under chapter 7 of this title, if the trustee does not assume or reject an executory contract or unexpired lease of residential real property or of personal property of the debtor within 60 days after the order for relief, or within such additional time as the court, for cause, within such 60-day period, fixes, then such contract or lease is deemed rejected.

(2) In a case under chapter 9, 11, 12, or 13 of this title, the trustee may assume or reject an executory contract or unexpired lease of residential real property or of personal property of the debtor at any time before the confirmation of a plan but the court, on

request of any party to such contract or lease, may order the trustee to determine within a specified period of time whether to assume or reject such contract or lease.

(3) The trustee shall timely perform all the obligations of the debtor, except those specified in section 365(b)(2), arising from and after the order for relief under any unexpired lease of nonresidential real property, until such lease is assumed or rejected, notwithstanding section 503(b)(1) of this title. The court may extend, for cause, the time for performance of any such obligation that arises within 60 days after the date of the order for relief, but the time for performance shall not be extended beyond such 60-day period. This subsection shall not be deemed to affect the trustee's obligations under the provisions of subsection (b) or (f) of this section. Acceptance of any such performance does not constitute waiver or relinquishment of the lessor's rights under such lease or under this title.

(4)(A) ~~Notwithstanding paragraphs (1) and (2), in a case under any chapter of this title, if the trustee does not assume or reject an unexpired lease of nonresidential real property under which the debtor is the lessee within 60 days after the date of the order for relief, or within such additional time as the court, for cause, within such 60-day period, fixes, then such lease is~~ Subject to subparagraph (B), an unexpired lease of nonresidential real property under which the debtor is the lessee shall be deemed rejected, and the trustee shall immediately surrender ~~such~~ that nonresidential real property to the lessor, if the trustee does not assume or reject the unexpired lease by the earlier of—

(i) the date that is 120 days after the date of the order for relief; or

(ii) the date of the entry of an order confirming a plan.

(B)(i) The court may extend the period determined under subparagraph (A), prior to the expiration of the 120-day period, for 90 days on the motion of the trustee or lessor for cause.

(ii) If the court grants an extension under clause (i), the court may grant a subsequent extension only upon prior written consent of the lessor in each instance.

~~(5) Notwithstanding paragraphs (1) and (4) of this subsection, in a case under any chapter of this title, if the trustee does not assume or reject an unexpired lease of nonresidential real property under which the debtor is an affected air carrier that is the lessee of an aircraft terminal or aircraft gate before the occurrence of a termination event, then (unless the court orders the trustee to assume such unexpired leases within 5 days after the termination event), at the option of the airport operator, such lease is deemed rejected 5 days after the occurrence of a termination event and the trustee shall immediately surrender possession of the premises to the airport operator; except that the lease shall not be deemed to be rejected unless the airport operator first waives the right to damages related to the rejection. In the event that the lease is deemed to be rejected under this paragraph, the airport operator shall provide the affected air carrier adequate opportunity after the surrender of the premises to remove the fixtures and equipment installed by the affected air carrier.~~

~~(6) For the purposes of paragraph (5) of this subsection and paragraph (f)(1) of this section, the occurrence of a termination event means, with respect to a debtor which is an affected air carrier that is the lessee of an aircraft terminal or aircraft gate—~~

~~(A) the entry under section 301 or 302 of this title of an order for relief under chapter 7 of this title;~~

~~(B) the conversion of a case under any chapter of this title to a case under chapter 7 of this title; or~~

~~(C) the granting of relief from the stay provided under section 362(a) of this title with respect to aircraft, aircraft engines, propellers, appliances, or spare parts, as defined in section 40102(a) of title 49, except for property of the debtor found by the court not to be necessary to an effective reorganization.~~

~~(7) Any order entered by the court pursuant to paragraph (4) extending the period within which the trustee of an affected air carrier must assume or reject an unexpired lease of nonresidential real property shall be without prejudice to—~~

~~(A) the right of the trustee to seek further extensions within such additional time period granted by the court pursuant to paragraph (4); and~~

~~(B) the right of any lessor or any other party in interest to request, at any time, a shortening or termination of the period within which the trustee must assume or reject an unexpired lease of nonresidential real property.~~

~~(8) The burden of proof for establishing cause for an extension by an affected air carrier under paragraph (4) or the maintenance of a previously granted extension under paragraph (7)(A) and (B) shall at all times remain with the trustee.~~

~~(9) For purposes of determining cause under paragraph (7) with respect to an unexpired lease of nonresidential real property between the debtor that is an affected air carrier and an airport operator under which such debtor is the lessee of an airport terminal or an airport gate, the court shall consider, among other relevant factors, whether substantial harm will result to the airport operator or airline passengers as a result of the extension or the maintenance of a previously granted extension. In making the determination of substantial harm, the court shall consider, among other relevant factors, the level of actual use of the terminals or gates which are the subject of the lease, the public interest in actual use of such terminals or gates, the existence of competing demands for the use of such terminals or gates, the effect of the court's extension or termination of the period of time to assume or reject the lease on such debtor's ability to successfully reorganize under chapter 11 of this title, and whether the trustee of the affected air carrier is capable of continuing to comply with its obligations under section 365(d)(3) of this title.~~

(~~10~~5) The trustee shall timely perform all of the obligations of the debtor, except those specified in section 365(b)(2), first arising from or after 60 days after the order for relief in a case under chapter 11 of this title under an unexpired lease of personal property (other than personal property leased to an individual primarily for personal, family, or household purposes), until such lease is assumed or rejected notwithstanding section 503(b)(1) of this title, unless the court, after notice and a hearing and based on the equities of the case, orders otherwise with respect to the obligations or timely performance thereof. This subsection shall not be deemed to affect the trustee's obligations under the provisions of subsection (b) or (f). Acceptance of any such performance does not constitute waiver or relinquishment of the lessor's rights under such lease or under this title.

(e)(1) Notwithstanding a provision in an executory contract or unexpired lease, or in applicable law, an executory contract or unexpired lease of the debtor may not be terminated or modified, and any right or obligation under such contract or lease may not be terminated or modified, at any time after the commencement of the case solely because of a provision in such contract or lease that is conditioned on—

(A) the insolvency or financial condition of the debtor at any time before the closing of the case;

(B) the commencement of a case under this title; or

(C) the appointment of or taking possession by a trustee in a case under this title or a custodian before such commencement.

(2) Paragraph (1) of this subsection does not apply to an executory contract or unexpired lease of the debtor, whether or not such contract or lease prohibits or restricts assignment of rights or delegation of duties, if—

(A)(i) applicable law excuses a party, other than the debtor, to such contract or lease from accepting performance from or rendering performance to the trustee or to an assignee of such contract or lease, whether or not such contract or lease prohibits or restricts assignment of rights or delegation of duties; and

(ii) such party does not consent to such assumption or assignment; or

(B) such contract is a contract to make a loan, or extend other debt financing or financial accommodations, to or for the benefit of the debtor, or to issue a security of the debtor.

(f)(1) Except as provided in subsections (b) and (c) of this section, notwithstanding a provision in an executory contract or unexpired lease of the debtor, or in applicable law, that prohibits, restricts, or conditions the assignment of such contract or lease, the trustee may assign such contract or lease under paragraph (2) of this subsection~~; except that the trustee may not assign an unexpired lease of nonresidential real property under which the debtor is an affected air carrier that is the lessee of an aircraft terminal or aircraft gate if there has occurred a termination event~~.

(2) The trustee may assign an executory contract or unexpired lease of the debtor only if—

(A) the trustee assumes such contract or lease in accordance with the provisions of this section; and

(B) adequate assurance of future performance by the assignee of such contract or lease is provided, whether or not there has been a default in such contract or lease.

(3) Notwithstanding a provision in an executory contract or unexpired lease of the debtor, or in applicable law that terminates or modifies, or permits a party other than the debtor to terminate or modify, such contract or lease or a right or obligation under such contract or lease on account of an assignment of such contract or lease, such contract, lease, right, or obligation may not be terminated or modified under such provision because of the assumption or assignment of such contract or lease by the trustee.

(g) Except as provided in subsections (h)(2) and (i)(2) of this section, the rejection of an executory contract or unexpired lease of the debtor constitutes a breach of such contract or lease—

(1) if such contract or lease has not been assumed under this section or under a plan confirmed under chapter 9, 11, 12, or 13 of this title, immediately before the date of the filing of the petition; or

(2) if such contract or lease has been assumed under this section or under a plan confirmed under chapter 9, 11, 12, or 13 of this title—

(A) if before such rejection the case has not been converted under section 1112, 1208, or 1307 of this title, at the time of such rejection; or

(B) if before such rejection the case has been converted under section 1112, 1208, or 1307 of this title—

(i) immediately before the date of such conversion, if such contract or lease was assumed before such conversion; or

(ii) at the time of such rejection, if such contract or lease was assumed after such conversion.

(h)(1)(A) If the trustee rejects an unexpired lease of real property under which the debtor is the lessor and—

(i) if the rejection by the trustee amounts to such a breach as would entitle the lessee to treat such lease as terminated by virtue of its terms, applicable nonbankruptcy law, or any agreement made by the lessee, then the lessee under such lease may treat such lease as terminated by the rejection; or

(ii) if the term of such lease has commenced, the lessee may retain its rights under such lease (including rights such as those relating to the amount and timing of payment of rent and other amounts payable by the lessee and any right of use, possession, quiet enjoyment, subletting, assignment, or hypothecation) that are in or appurtenant to the real property for the balance of the term of such lease and for any renewal or extension of such rights to the extent that such rights are enforceable under applicable nonbankruptcy law.

(B) If the lessee retains its rights under subparagraph (A)(ii), the lessee may offset against the rent reserved under such lease for the balance of the term after the date of the rejection of such lease and for the term of any renewal or extension of such lease, the value of any damage caused by the nonperformance after the date of such rejection, of any obligation of the debtor under such lease, but the lessee shall not have any other right against the estate or the debtor on account of any damage occurring after such date caused by such nonperformance.

(C) The rejection of a lease of real property in a shopping center with respect to which the lessee elects to retain its rights under subparagraph (A)(ii) does not affect the enforceability under applicable nonbankruptcy law of any provision in the lease pertaining to radius, location, use, exclusivity, or tenant mix or balance.

(D) In this paragraph, "lessee" includes any successor, assign, or mortgagee permitted under the terms of such lease.

(2)(A) If the trustee rejects a timeshare interest under a timeshare plan under which the debtor is the timeshare interest seller and—

(i) if the rejection amounts to such a breach as would entitle the timeshare interest purchaser to treat the timeshare plan as terminated under its terms, applicable nonbankruptcy law, or any agreement made by timeshare interest purchaser, the timeshare interest purchaser under the timeshare plan may treat the timeshare plan as terminated by such rejection; or

(ii) if the term of such timeshare interest has commenced, then the timeshare interest purchaser may retain its rights in such timeshare interest for the balance of such term and for any term of renewal or extension of such timeshare interest to the extent that such rights are enforceable under applicable nonbankruptcy law.

(B) If the timeshare interest purchaser retains its rights under subparagraph (A), such timeshare interest purchaser may offset against the moneys due for such timeshare interest for the balance of the term after the date of the rejection of such timeshare interest, and the term of any renewal or extension of such timeshare interest, the value of any damage caused by the nonperformance after the date of such rejection, of any obligation of the debtor under such timeshare plan, but the timeshare interest purchaser shall not have any right against the estate or the debtor on account of any damage occurring after such date caused by such nonperformance.

(i)(1) If the trustee rejects an executory contract of the debtor for the sale of real property or for the sale of a timeshare interest under a timeshare plan, under which the purchaser is in possession, such purchaser may treat such contract as terminated, or, in the alternative, may remain in possession of such real property or timeshare interest.

(2) If such purchaser remains in possession—

(A) such purchaser shall continue to make all payments due under such contract, but may, offset against such payments any damages occurring after the date of the rejection of such contract caused by the non-performance of any obligation of the debtor after such date, but such purchaser does not have any rights against the estate on account of any damages arising after such date from such rejection, other than such offset; and

(B) the trustee shall deliver title to such purchaser in accordance with the provisions of such contract, but is relieved of all other obligations to perform under such contract.

(j) A purchaser that treats an executory contract as terminated under subsection (i) of this section, or a party whose executory contract to purchase real property from the debtor is rejected and under which such party is not in possession, has a lien on the interest of the debtor in such property for the recovery of any portion of the purchase price that such purchaser or party has paid.

(k) Assignment by the trustee to an entity of a contract or lease assumed under this section relieves the trustee and the estate from any liability for any breach of such contract or lease occurring after such assignment.

(*l*) If an unexpired lease under which the debtor is the lessee is assigned pursuant to this section, the lessor of the property may require a deposit or other security for the performance of the debtor's obligations under the lease substantially the same as would have been required by the landlord upon the initial leasing to a similar tenant.

(m) For purposes of this section 365 and sections 541(b)(2) and 362(b)(10), leases of real property shall include any rental agreement to use real property.

(n)(1) If the trustee rejects an executory contract under which the debtor is a licensor of a right to intellectual property, the licensee under such contract may elect—

(A) to treat such contract as terminated by such rejection if such rejection by the trustee amounts to such a breach as would entitle the licensee to treat such contract as terminated by virtue of its own terms, applicable nonbankruptcy law, or an agreement made by the licensee with another entity; or

(B) to retain its rights (including a right to enforce any exclusivity provision of such contract, but excluding any other right under applicable nonbankruptcy law to specific performance of such contract) under such contract and under any agreement supplementary to such contract, to such intellectual property (including any embodiment of such intellectual property to the extent protected by applicable nonbankruptcy law), as such rights existed immediately before the case commenced, for—

(i) the duration of such contract; and

(ii) any period for which such contract may be extended by the licensee as of right under applicable nonbankruptcy law.

(2) If the licensee elects to retain its rights, as described in paragraph (1)(B) of this subsection, under such contract—

(A) the trustee shall allow the licensee to exercise such rights;

(B) the licensee shall make all royalty payments due under such contract for the duration of such contract and for any period described in paragraph (1)(B) of this subsection for which the licensee extends such contract; and

(C) the licensee shall be deemed to waive—

(i) any right of setoff it may have with respect to such contract under this title or applicable nonbankruptcy law; and

(ii) any claim allowable under section 503(b) of this title arising from the performance of such contract.

(3) If the licensee elects to retain its rights, as described in paragraph (1)(B) of this subsection, then on the written request of the licensee the trustee shall—

(A) to the extent provided in such contract, or any agreement supplementary to such contract, provide to the licensee any intellectual property (including such embodiment) held by the trustee; and

(B) not interfere with the rights of the licensee as provided in such contract, or any agreement supplementary to such contract, to such intellectual property (including such embodiment) including any right to obtain such intellectual property (or such embodiment) from another entity.

(4) Unless and until the trustee rejects such contract, on the written request of the licensee the trustee shall—

(A) to the extent provided in such contract or any agreement supplementary to such contract—

(i) perform such contract; or

(ii) provide to the licensee such intellectual property (including any embodiment of such intellectual property to the extent protected by applicable nonbankruptcy law) held by the trustee; and

(B) not interfere with the rights of the licensee as provided in such contract, or any agreement supplementary to such contract, to such intellectual property (including such embodiment), including any right to obtain such intellectual property (or such embodiment) from another entity.

(*o*) In a case under chapter 11 of this title, the trustee shall be deemed to have assumed (consistent with the debtor's other obligations under section 507), and shall immediately cure any deficit under, any commitment by the debtor to a Federal depository institutions regulatory agency (or predecessor to such agency) to maintain the capital of an insured depository institution, and any claim for a subsequent breach of the obligations thereunder shall be entitled to priority under section 507. This subsection shall not extend any commitment that would otherwise be terminated by any act of such an agency.

(p)(1) If a lease of personal property is rejected or not timely assumed by the trustee under subsection (d), the leased property is no longer property of the estate and the stay under section 362(a) is automatically terminated.

(2)(A) If the debtor in a case under chapter 7 is an individual, the debtor may notify the creditor in writing that the debtor desires to assume the lease. Upon being so notified, the creditor may, at its option, notify the debtor that it is willing to have the lease assumed by the debtor and may condition such assumption on cure of any outstanding default on terms set by the contract.

(B) If, not later than 30 days after notice is provided under subparagraph (A), the debtor notifies the lessor in writing that the lease is assumed, the liability under the lease will be assumed by the debtor and not by the estate.

(C) The stay under section 362 and the injunction under section 524(a)(2) shall not be violated by notification of the debtor and negotiation of cure under this subsection.

(3) In a case under chapter 11 in which the debtor is an individual and in a case under chapter 13, if the debtor is the lessee with respect to personal property and the lease is not assumed in the plan confirmed by the court, the lease is deemed rejected as of the conclusion of the hearing on confirmation. If the lease is rejected, the stay under section 362 and any stay under section 1301 is automatically terminated with respect to the property subject to the lease.

§ 366. Utility service

(a) Except as provided in subsections (b) and (c) of this section, a utility may not alter, refuse, or discontinue service to, or discriminate against, the trustee or the debtor solely on the basis of the commencement of a case under this title or that a debt owed by the debtor to such utility for service rendered before the order for relief was not paid when due.

(b) Such utility may alter, refuse, or discontinue service if neither the trustee nor the debtor, within 20 days after the date of the order for relief, furnishes adequate assurance of payment, in the form of a deposit or other security, for service after such date. On request of a party in interest and after notice and a hearing, the court may order reasonable modification of the amount of the deposit or other security necessary to provide adequate assurance of payment.

(c)(1)(A) For purposes of this subsection, the term "assurance of payment" means—

(i) a cash deposit;

(ii) a letter of credit;

(iii) a certificate of deposit;

(iv) a surety bond;

(v) a prepayment of utility consumption; or

(vi) another form of security that is mutually agreed on between the utility and the debtor or the trustee.

(B) For purposes of this subsection an administrative expense priority shall not constitute an assurance of payment.

(2) Subject to paragraphs (3) and (4), with respect to a case filed under chapter 11, a utility referred to in subsection (a) may alter, refuse, or discontinue utility service, if during the 30-day period beginning on the date of the filing of the petition, the utility does not receive from the debtor or the trustee adequate assurance of payment for utility service that is satisfactory to the utility.

(3)(A) On request of a party in interest and after notice and a hearing, the court may order modification of the amount of an assurance of payment under paragraph (2).

(B) In making a determination under this paragraph whether an assurance of payment is adequate, the court may not consider—

(i) the absence of security before the date of the filing of the petition;

(ii) the payment by the debtor of charges for utility service in a timely manner before the date of the filing of the petition; or

(iii) the availability of an administrative expense priority.

(4) Notwithstanding any other provision of law, with respect to a case subject to this subsection, a utility may recover or set off against a security deposit provided to the utility by the debtor before the date of the filing of the petition without notice or order of the court.

CHAPTER 5

CREDITORS, THE DEBTOR, AND THE ESTATE

Subchapter I

Creditors and Claims

§ 501. Filing of proofs of claims or interests

(a) A creditor or an indenture trustee may file a proof of claim. An equity security holder may file a proof of interest.

(b) If a creditor does not timely file a proof of such creditor's claim, an entity that is liable to such creditor with the debtor, or that has secured such creditor, may file a proof of such claim.

(c) If a creditor does not timely file a proof of such creditor's claim, the debtor or the trustee may file a proof of such claim.

(d) A claim of a kind specified in section 502(e)(2), 502(f), 502(g), 502(h) or 502(i) of this title may be filed under subsection (a), (b), or (c) of this section the same as if such claim were a claim against the debtor and had arisen before the date of the filing of the petition.

(e) A claim arising from the liability of a debtor for fuel use tax assessed consistent with the requirements of section 31705 of title 49 may be filed by the base jurisdiction designated pursuant to the International Fuel Tax Agreement (as defined in section 31701 of title 49) and, if so filed, shall be allowed as a single claim.

§ 502. Allowance of claims or interests

(a) A claim or interest, proof of which is filed under section 501 of this title, is deemed allowed, unless a party in interest, including a creditor of a general partner in a partnership that is a debtor in a case under chapter 7 of this title, objects.

(b) Except as provided in subsections (e)(2), (f), (g), (h) and (i) of this section, if such objection to a claim is made, the court, after notice and a hearing, shall determine the amount of such claim in lawful currency of the United States as of the date of the filing of the petition, and shall allow such claim in such amount, except to the extent that—

(1) such claim is unenforceable against the debtor and property of the debtor, under any agreement or applicable law for a reason other than because such claim is contingent or unmatured;

(2) such claim is for unmatured interest;

(3) if such claim is for a tax assessed against property of the estate, such claim exceeds the value of the interest of the estate in such property;

(4) if such claim is for services of an insider or attorney of the debtor, such claim exceeds the reasonable value of such services;

(5) such claim is for a debt that is unmatured on the date of the filing of the petition and that is excepted from discharge under section 523(a)(5) of this title;

(6) if such claim is the claim of a lessor for damages resulting from the termination of a lease of real property, such claim exceeds—

(A) the rent reserved by such lease, without acceleration, for the greater of one year, or 15 percent, not to exceed three years, of the remaining term of such lease, following the earlier of—

(i) the date of the filing of the petition; and

(ii) the date on which such lessor repossessed, or the lessee surrendered, the leased property; plus

(B) any unpaid rent due under such lease, without acceleration, on the earlier of such dates;

(7) if such claim is the claim of an employee for damages resulting from the termination of an employment contract, such claim exceeds—

(A) the compensation provided by such contract, without acceleration, for one year following the earlier of—

(i) the date of the filing of the petition; or

(ii) the date on which the employer directed the employee to terminate, or such employee terminated, performance under such contract; plus

(B) any unpaid compensation due under such contract, without acceleration, on the earlier of such dates;

(8) such claim results from a reduction, due to late payment, in the amount of an otherwise applicable credit available to the debtor in connection with an employment tax on wages, salaries, or commissions earned from the debtor; or

(9) proof of such claim is not timely filed, except to the extent tardily filed as permitted under paragraph (1), (2), or (3) of section 726(a) of this title or under the Federal Rules of Bankruptcy Procedure, except that a claim of a governmental unit shall be timely filed if it is filed before 180 days after the date of the order for relief or such later time as the Federal Rules of Bankruptcy Procedure may provide, and except that in a case under chapter 13, a claim of a governmental unit for a tax with respect to a return filed under section 1308 shall be timely if the claim is filed on or before the date that is 60 days after the date on which such return was filed as required.

(c) There shall be estimated for purpose of allowance under this section—

(1) any contingent or unliquidated claim, the fixing or liquidation of which, as the case may be, would unduly delay the administration of the case; or

(2) any right to payment arising from a right to an equitable remedy for breach of performance.

(d) Notwithstanding subsections (a) and (b) of this section, the court shall disallow any claim of any entity from which property is recoverable under section 542, 543, 550, or 553 of this title or that is a transferee of a transfer avoidable under section 522(f), 522(h), 544, 545, 547, 548, 549, or 724(a) of this title, unless such entity or transferee has paid the amount, or turned over any such property, for which such entity or transferee is liable under section 522(i), 542, 543, 550, or 553 of this title.

(e)(1) Notwithstanding subsections (a), (b), and (c) of this section and paragraph (2) of this subsection, the court shall disallow any claim for reimbursement or contribution of an entity that is liable with the debtor on or has secured the claim of a creditor, to the extent that—

(A) such creditor's claim against the estate is disallowed;

(B) such claim for reimbursement or contribution is contingent as of the time of allowance or disallowance of such claim for reimbursement or contribution; or

(C) such entity asserts a right of subrogation to the rights of such creditor under section 509 of this title.

(2) A claim for reimbursement or contribution of such an entity that becomes fixed after the commencement of the case shall be determined, and shall be allowed under subsection (a), (b), or (c) of this section, or disallowed under subsection (d) of this section, the same as if such claim had become fixed before the date of the filing of the petition.

(f) In an involuntary case, a claim arising in the ordinary course of the debtor's business or financial affairs after the commencement of the case but before the earlier of the appointment of a trustee and the order for relief shall be determined as of the date such claim arises, and shall be allowed under subsection (a), (b), or (c) of this section or disallowed under subsection (d) or (e) of this section, the same as if such claim had arisen before the date of the filing of the petition.

(g) (1) A claim arising from the rejection, under section 365 of this title or under a plan under chapter 9, 11, 12, or 13 of this title, of an executory contract or unexpired lease of the debtor that has not been assumed shall be determined, and shall be allowed under subsection (a), (b), or (c) of this section or disallowed under subsection (d) or (e) of this section, the same as if such claim had arisen before the date of the filing of the petition.

(2) A claim for damages calculated in accordance with section 562 shall be allowed under subsection (a), (b), or (c), or disallowed under subsection (d) or (e), as if such claim had arisen before the date of the filing of the petition.

(h) A claim arising from the recovery of property under section 522, 550, or 553 of this title shall be determined, and shall be allowed under subsection (a), (b), or (c) of this section, or disallowed under subsection (d) or (e) of this section, the same as if such claim had arisen before the date of the filing of the petition.

(i) A claim that does not arise until after the commencement of the case for a tax entitled to priority under section 507(a)(8) of this title shall be determined, and shall be allowed under subsection (a), (b), or (c) of this section, or disallowed under subsection (d) or (e) of this section, the same as if such claim had arisen before the date of the filing of the petition.

(j) A claim that has been allowed or disallowed may be reconsidered for cause. A reconsidered claim may be allowed or disallowed according to the equities of the case. Reconsideration of a claim under this subsection does not affect the validity of any payment or transfer from the estate made to a holder of an allowed claim on account of such allowed claim that is not reconsidered, but if a reconsidered claim is allowed and is of the same class as such holder's claim, such holder may not receive any additional payment or transfer from the estate on account of such holder's allowed claim until the holder of such reconsidered and allowed claim receives payment on account of such claim proportionate in value to that already received by such other holder. This subsection does not alter or modify the trustee's right to recover from a creditor any excess payment or transfer made to such creditor.

(k)(1) The court, on the motion of the debtor and after a hearing, may reduce a claim filed under this section based in whole on an unsecured consumer debt by not more than 20 percent of the claim, if—

(A) the claim was filed by a creditor who unreasonably refused to negotiate a reasonable alternative repayment schedule proposed on behalf of the debtor by an approved nonprofit budgeting and credit counseling agency described in section 111;

(B) the offer of the debtor under subparagraph (A)—

(i) was made at least 60 days before the date of the filing of the petition; and

(ii) provided for payment of at least 60 percent of the amount of the debt over a period not to exceed the repayment period of the loan, or a reasonable extension thereof; and

(C) no part of the debt under the alternative repayment schedule is nondischargeable.

(2) The debtor shall have the burden of proving, by clear and convincing evidence, that—

(A) the creditor unreasonably refused to consider the debtor's proposal; and

(B) the proposed alternative repayment schedule was made prior to expiration of the 60-day period specified in paragraph (1)(B)(i).

§ 503. Allowance of administrative expenses

(a) An entity may timely file a request for payment of an administrative expense, or may tardily file such request if permitted by the court for cause.

(b) After notice and a hearing, there shall be allowed administrative expenses, other than claims allowed under section 502(f) of this title, including—

(1)(A) the actual, necessary costs and expenses of preserving the estate~~,~~ including~~—~~

(i) wages, salaries, and ~~or~~ commissions for services rendered after the commencement of the case; and

(ii) wages and benefits awarded pursuant to a judicial proceeding or a proceeding of the National Labor Relations Board as back pay attributable to any period of time occurring after commencement of the case under this title, as a result of a violation of Federal or State law by the debtor, without regard to the time of the occurrence of unlawful conduct on which such award is based or to whether any services were rendered, if the court determines that payment of wages and benefits by reason of the operation of this clause will not substantially increase the probability of layoff or termination of current employees, or of nonpayment of domestic support obligations, during the case under this title;

(B) any tax—

(i) incurred by the estate, whether secured or unsecured, including property taxes for which liability is in rem, in personam, or both, except a tax of a kind specified in section 507(a)(8) of this title; or

(ii) attributable to an excessive allowance of a tentative carryback adjustment that the estate received, whether the taxable year to which such adjustment relates ended before or after the commencement of the case; ~~and~~

(C) any fine, penalty, or reduction in credit relating to a tax of a kind specified in subparagraph (B) of this paragraph; and

(D) notwithstanding the requirements of subsection (a), a governmental unit shall not be required to file a request for the payment of an expense described in subparagraph (B) or (C), as a condition of its being an allowed administrative expense;

(2) compensation and reimbursement awarded under section 330(a) of this title;

(3) the actual, necessary expenses, other than compensation and reimbursement specified in paragraph (4) of this subsection, incurred by—

(A) a creditor that files a petition under section 303 of this title;

(B) a creditor that recovers, after the court's approval, for the benefit of the estate any property transferred or concealed by the debtor;

(C) a creditor in connection with the prosecution of a criminal offense relating to the case or to the business or property of the debtor;

(D) a creditor, an indenture trustee, an equity security holder, or committee representing creditors or equity security holders other than a committee appointed under section 1102 of this title, in making a substantial contribution in a case under chapter 9 or 11 of this title;

(E) a custodian superseded under section 543 of this title, and compensation for the services of such custodian; or

(F) a member of a committee appointed under section 1102 of this title, if such expenses are incurred in the performance of the duties of such committee;

(4) reasonable compensation for professional services rendered by an attorney or an accountant of an entity whose expense is allowable under subparagraph (A), (B), (C), (D), or (E) of paragraph (3) of this subsection, based on the time, the nature, the extent, and the value of such services, and the cost of comparable services other than in a case under this title, and reimbursement for actual, necessary expenses incurred by such attorney or accountant;

(5) reasonable compensation for services rendered by an indenture trustee in making a substantial contribution in a case under chapter 9 or 11 of this title, based on the time, the nature, the extent, and the value of such services, and the cost of comparable services other than in a case under this title; ~~and~~

(6) the fees and mileage payable under chapter 119 of title 28~~.~~;

(7) with respect to a nonresidential real property lease previously assumed under section 365, and subsequently rejected, a sum equal to all monetary obligations due, excluding those arising from or relating to a failure to operate or a penalty provision, for the period of 2 years following the later of the rejection date or the date of actual turnover of the premises, without reduction or setoff for any reason whatsoever except for sums actually received or to be received from an entity other than the debtor, and the claim for remaining sums due for the balance of the term of the lease shall be a claim under section 502(b)(6);

(8) the actual, necessary costs and expenses of closing a health care business incurred by a trustee or by a Federal agency (as defined in section 551(1) of title 5) or a department or agency of a State or political subdivision thereof, including any cost or expense incurred—

(A) in disposing of patient records in accordance with section 351; or

(B) in connection with transferring patients from the health care business that is in the process of being closed to another health care business; and

(9) the value of any goods received by the debtor within 20 days before the date of commencement of a case under this title in which the goods have been sold to the debtor in the ordinary course of such debtor's business.

(c) Notwithstanding subsection (b), there shall neither be allowed, nor paid—

(1) a transfer made to, or an obligation incurred for the benefit of, an insider of the debtor for the purpose of inducing such person

to remain with the debtor's business, absent a finding by the court based on evidence in the record that—

(A) the transfer or obligation is essential to retention of the person because the individual has a bona fide job offer from another business at the same or greater rate of compensation;

(B) the services provided by the person are essential to the survival of the business; and

(C) either—

(i) the amount of the transfer made to, or obligation incurred for the benefit of, the person is not greater than an amount equal to 10 times the amount of the mean transfer or obligation of a similar kind given to nonmanagement employees for any purpose during the calendar year in which the transfer is made or the obligation is incurred; or

(ii) if no such similar transfers were made to, or obligations were incurred for the benefit of, such nonmanagement employees during such calendar year, the amount of the transfer or obligation is not greater than an amount equal to 25 percent of the amount of any similar transfer or obligation made to or incurred for the benefit of such insider for any purpose during the calendar year before the year in which such transfer is made or obligation is incurred;

(2) a severance payment to an insider of the debtor, unless—

(A) the payment is part of a program that is generally applicable to all full-time employees; and

(B) the amount of the payment is not greater than 10 times the amount of the mean severance pay given to nonmanagement employees during the calendar year in which the payment is made; or

(3) other transfers or obligations that are outside the ordinary course of business and not justified by the facts and circumstances of the case, including transfers made to, or obligations incurred for the benefit of, officers, managers, or consultants hired after the date of the filing of the petition.

§ 504. Sharing of compensation

(a) Except as provided in subsection (b) of this section, a person receiving compensation or reimbursement under section 503(b)(2) or 503(b)(4) of this title may not share or agree to share—

(1) any such compensation or reimbursement with another person; or

(2) any compensation or reimbursement received by another person under such sections.

(b)(1) A member, partner, or regular associate in a professional association, corporation, or partnership may share compensation or reimbursement received under section 503(b)(2) or 503(b)(4) of this title with another member, partner, or regular associate in such association, corporation, or partnership, and may share in any compensation or reimbursement received under such sections by another member, partner, or regular associate in such association, corporation, or partnership.

(2) An attorney for a creditor that files a petition under section 303 of this title may share compensation and reimbursement received under section 503(b)(4) of this title with any other attorney contributing to the services rendered or expenses incurred by such creditor's attorney.

(c) This section shall not apply with respect to sharing, or agreeing to share, compensation with a bona fide public service attorney referral program that operates in accordance with non-Federal law regulating attorney referral services and with rules of professional responsibility applicable to attorney acceptance of referrals.

§ 505. Determination of tax liability

(a)(1) Except as provided in paragraph (2) of this subsection, the court may determine the amount or legality of any tax, any fine or penalty relating to a tax, or any addition to tax, whether or not previously assessed, whether or not paid, and whether or not contested before and adjudicated by a judicial or administrative tribunal of competent jurisdiction.

(2) The court may not so determine—

(A) the amount or legality of a tax, fine, penalty, or addition to tax if such amount or legality was contested before and adjudicated by a judicial or administrative tribunal of competent jurisdiction before the commencement of the case under this title; ~~or~~

(B) any right of the estate to a tax refund, before the earlier of—

(i) 120 days after the trustee properly requests such refund from the governmental unit from which such refund is claimed; or

(ii) a determination by such governmental unit of such request~~.~~; or

(C) the amount or legality of any amount arising in connection with an ad valorem tax on real or personal property of the estate, if the applicable period for contesting or redetermining that amount under any law (other than a bankruptcy law) has expired.

(b)(1)(A) The clerk shall maintain a list under which a Federal, State, or local governmental unit responsible for the collection of taxes within the district may—

(i) designate an address for service of requests under this subsection; and

(ii) describe where further information concerning additional requirements for filing such requests may be found.

(B) If such governmental unit does not designate an address and provide such address to the clerk under subparagraph (A), any request made under this subsection may be served at the address for the filing of a tax return or protest with the appropriate taxing authority of such governmental unit.

(~~b~~2) A trustee may request a determination of any unpaid liability of the estate for any tax incurred during the administration of the case by submitting a tax return for such tax and a request for such a determination to the governmental unit charged with responsibility for collection or determination of such tax at the address and in the manner designated in paragraph (1). Unless such return is fraudulent, or contains a material misrepresentation, the estate, the trustee, the debtor, and any successor to the debtor are discharged from any liability for such tax—

(~~1~~A) upon payment of the tax shown on such return, if—

(~~A~~i) such governmental unit does not notify the trustee, within 60 days after such request, that such return has been selected for examination; or

(~~B~~ii) such governmental unit does not complete such an examination and notify the trustee of any tax due, within 180 days after such request or within such additional time as the court, for cause, permits;

(~~2~~B) upon payment of the tax determined by the court, after notice and a hearing, after completion by such governmental unit of such examination; or

(~~3~~C) upon payment of the tax determined by such governmental unit to be due.

(c) Notwithstanding section 362 of this title, after determination by the court of a tax under this section, the governmental unit charged with responsibility for collection of such tax may assess such tax against the estate, the debtor, or a successor to the debtor, as the case may be, subject to any otherwise applicable law.

§ 506. Determination of secured status

(a) (1) An allowed claim of a creditor secured by a lien on property in which the estate has an interest, or that is subject to setoff under section 553 of this title, is a secured claim to the extent of the value of such creditor's interest in the estate's interest in such property, or to the extent of the amount subject to setoff, as the case may be, and is an unsecured claim to the extent that the value of such creditor's interest or the amount so subject to setoff is less than the amount of such allowed claim. Such value shall be determined in light of the purpose of the valuation and of the proposed disposition or use of such property, and in conjunction with any hearing on such disposition or use or on a plan affecting such creditor's interest.

(2) If the debtor is an individual in a case under chapter 7 or 13, such value with respect to personal property securing an allowed claim shall be determined based on the replacement value of such property as of the date of the filing of the petition without deduction for costs of sale or marketing. With respect to property acquired for personal, family, or household purposes, replacement value shall mean the price a retail merchant would charge for property of that kind considering the age and condition of the property at the time value is determined.

(b) To the extent that an allowed secured claim is secured by property the value of which, after any recovery under subsection (c) of this section, is greater than the amount of such claim, there shall be allowed to the holder of such claim, interest on such claim, and any reasonable fees, costs, or charges provided for under the agreement or State statute under which such claim arose.

(c) The trustee may recover from property securing an allowed secured claim the reasonable, necessary costs and expenses of preserving, or disposing of, such property to the extent of any benefit to the holder of such claim, including the payment of all ad valorem property taxes with respect to the property.

(d) To the extent that a lien secures a claim against the debtor that is not an allowed secured claim, such lien is void unless—

(1) such claim was disallowed only under section 502(b)(5) or 502(e) of this title; or

(2) such claim is not an allowed secured claim due only to the failure of any entity to file a proof of such claim under section 501 of this title.

§ 507. Priorities

(a) The following expenses and claims have priority in the following order:

(1) First:

(A) Allowed unsecured claims for domestic support obligations that, as of the date of the filing of the petition in a case under this title, are owed to or recoverable by a spouse, former spouse, or child of the debtor, or such child's parent, legal guardian, or responsible relative, without regard to whether the claim is filed by such person or is filed by a governmental unit on behalf of such person, on the condition that funds received under this paragraph by a governmental unit under this title after the date of the filing of the petition shall be applied and distributed in accordance with applicable nonbankruptcy law.

(B) Subject to claims under subparagraph (A), allowed unsecured claims for domestic support obligations that, as of the date of the filing of the petition are assigned by a spouse, former spouse, child of the debtor, or such child's parent, legal guardian, or responsible relative to a governmental unit (unless such obligation is assigned voluntarily by the spouse, former spouse, child, parent, legal guardian, or responsible relative of the child for the purpose of collecting the debt) or are owed directly to or recoverable by a governmental unit under applicable nonbankruptcy law, on the condition that funds received under this paragraph by a governmental unit under this title after the date of the filing of the petition be applied and distributed in accordance with applicable nonbankruptcy law.

(C) If a trustee is appointed or elected under section 701, 702, 703, 1104, 1202, or 1302, the administrative expenses of the trustee allowed under paragraphs (1)(A), (2), and (6) of section 503(b) shall be paid before payment of claims under subparagraphs (A) and (B), to the extent that the trustee administers assets that are otherwise available for the payment of such claims.

(~~1~~2) ~~First~~ Second, administrative expenses allowed under section 503(b) of this title, and any fees and charges assessed against the estate under chapter 123 of title 28.

(~~2~~3) ~~Second~~ Third, unsecured claims allowed under section 502(f) of this title.

(~~3~~4) ~~Third~~ Fourth, allowed unsecured claims, but only to the extent of ~~$4,925~~ $10,000[16] for each individual or corporation, as the case may be, earned within ~~90~~ 180 days before the date of the filing of the petition or the date of the cessation of the debtor's business, whichever occurs first, for—

(A) wages, salaries, or commissions, including vacation, severance, and sick leave pay earned by an individual; or

(B) sales commissions earned by an individual or by a corporation with only 1 employee, acting as an independent contractor in the sale of goods or services for the debtor in the ordinary course of the debtor's business if, and only if, during the 12 months preceding that date, at least 75 percent of the amount that the individual or corporation earned by acting as an independent contractor in the sale of goods or services was earned from the debtor~~;~~.

(~~4~~5) ~~Fourth~~ Fifth, allowed unsecured claims for contributions to an employee benefit plan—

(A) arising from services rendered within 180 days before the date of the filing of the petition or the date of the cessation of the debtor's business, whichever occurs first; but only

(B) for each such plan, to the extent of—

(i) the number of employees covered by each such plan multiplied by ~~$4,925~~ $10,000;[17] less

(ii) the aggregate amount paid to such employees under paragraph (~~3~~4) of this subsection, plus the aggregate amount paid by the estate on behalf of such employees to any other employee benefit plan.

(~~5~~6) ~~Fifth~~ Sixth, allowed unsecured claims of persons—

(A) engaged in the production or raising of grain, as defined in section 557(b) of this title, against a debtor who owns or operates a grain storage facility, as defined in section 557(b) of this title, for grain or the proceeds of grain, or

(B) engaged as a United States fisherman against a debtor who has acquired fish or fish produce from a fisherman through a sale or conversion, and who is engaged in operating a fish produce storage or processing facility—

but only to the extent of $4,925[18] for each such individual.

(~~6~~7) ~~Sixth~~ Seventh, allowed unsecured claims of individuals, to the extent of $2,225[19] for each such individual, arising from the deposit, before the commencement of the case, of money in connection with the purchase, lease, or rental of property, or the purchase of services, for the personal, family, or household use of such individuals, that were not delivered or provided.

~~(7) Seventh, allowed claims for debts to a spouse, former spouse, or child of the debtor, for alimony to, maintenance for, or support of such spouse or child, in connection with a separation agreement, divorce decree or other order of a court of record, determination made in accordance with State or territorial law by a governmental unit, or property settlement agreement, but not to the extent that such debt—~~

~~(A) is assigned to another entity, voluntarily, by operation of law, or otherwise; or~~

~~(B) includes a liability designated as alimony, maintenance, or support, unless such liability is actually in the nature of alimony, maintenance or support.~~

(8) Eighth, allowed unsecured claims of governmental units, only to the extent that such claims are for—

(A) a tax on or measured by income or gross receipts for a taxable year ending on or before the date of the filing of the petition—

(i) ~~for a taxable year ending on or before the date of the filing of the petition~~ for which a return, if required, is last due, including extensions, after three years before the date of the filing of the petition;

(ii) assessed within 240 days before the date of the filing of the petition, ~~plus any time plus 30 days during which an offer in compromise with respect to such tax that was made within 240 days after such assessment was pending, before the date of the filing of the petition; or~~ exclusive of—

(I) any time during which an offer in compromise with respect to that tax was pending or in effect during that 240-day period, plus 30 days; and

(II) any time during which a stay of proceedings against collections was in effect in a prior case under this title during that 240-day period, plus 90 days.

(iii) other than a tax of a kind specified in section 523(a)(1)(B) or 523(a)(1)(c) of this title, not assessed before, but assessable, under applicable law or by agreement, after, the commencement of the case;

---

16 *Editor's Note*: The former dollar amount of $4,925 reflects an inflationary adjustment, effective April 1, 2004. For cases commenced before April 1, 2004, the applicable dollar amount is $4,650. The amendment to section 507(a)(4) changing this dollar amount to $10,000 is effective for cases commenced under title 11 on or after April 20, 2005.

17 *Editor's Note*: The former dollar amount of $4,925 reflects an inflationary adjustment, effective April 1, 2004. For cases commenced before April 1, 2004, the applicable dollar amount is $4,650. The amendment to section 507(a)(5) changing this dollar amount to $10,000 is effective for cases commenced under title 11 on or after April 20, 2005.

18 *Editor's Note*: This dollar amount reflects an inflationary adjustment, effective April 1, 2004. For cases commenced before April 1, 2004, the applicable dollar amount is $4,650.

19 *Editor's Note*: This dollar amount reflects an inflationary adjustment, effective April 1, 2004. For cases commenced before April 1, 2004, the applicable dollar amount is $2,100.

(B) a property tax ~~assessed~~ incurred before the commencement of the case and last payable without penalty after one year before the date of the filing of the petition;

(C) a tax required to be collected or withheld and for which the debtor is liable in whatever capacity;

(D) an employment tax on a wage, salary, or commission of a kind specified in paragraph (3) of this subsection earned from the debtor before the date of the filing of the petition, whether or not actually paid before such date, for which a return is last due, under applicable law or under any extension, after three years before the date of the filing of the petition;

(E) an excise tax on—

(i) a transaction occurring before the date of the filing of the petition for which a return, if required, is last due, under applicable law or under any extension, after three years before the date of the filing of the petition; or

(ii) if a return is not required, a transaction occurring during the three years immediately preceding the date of the filing of the petition;

(F) a customs duty arising out of the importation of merchandise—

(i) entered for consumption within one year before the date of the filing of the petition;

(ii) covered by an entry liquidated or reliquidated within one year before the date of the filing of the petition; or

(iii) entered for consumption within four years before the date of the filing of the petition but unliquidated on such date, if the Secretary of the Treasury certifies that failure to liquidate such entry was due to an investigation pending on such date into assessment of antidumping or countervailing duties or fraud, or if information needed for the proper appraisement or classification of such merchandise was not available to the appropriate customs officer before such date; or

(G) a penalty related to a claim of a kind specified in this paragraph and in compensation for actual pecuniary loss.

An otherwise applicable time period specified in this paragraph shall be suspended for any period during which a governmental unit is prohibited under applicable nonbankruptcy law from collecting a tax as a result of a request by the debtor for a hearing and an appeal of any collection action taken or proposed against the debtor, plus 90 days; plus any time during which the stay of proceedings was in effect in a prior case under this title or during which collection was precluded by the existence of 1 or more confirmed plans under this title, plus 90 days.

(9) Ninth, allowed unsecured claims based upon any commitment by the debtor to a Federal depository institutions regulatory agency (or predecessor to such agency) to maintain the capital of an insured depository institution.

(10) Tenth, allowed claims for death or personal injuries resulting from the operation of a motor vehicle or vessel if such operation was unlawful because the debtor was intoxicated from using alcohol, a drug, or another substance.

(b) If the trustee, under section 362, 363, or 364 of this title, provides adequate protection of the interest of a holder of a claim secured by a lien on property of the debtor and if, notwithstanding such protection, such creditor has a claim allowable under subsection (a)(~~1~~2) of this section arising from the stay of action against such property under section 362 of this title, from the use, sale, or lease of such property under section 363 of this title, or from the granting of a lien under section 364(d) of this title, then such creditor's claim under such subsection shall have priority over every other claim under such subsection.

(c) For the purpose of subsection (a) of this section, a claim of a governmental unit arising from an erroneous refund or credit of a tax has the same priority as a claim for the tax to which such refund or credit relates.

(d) An entity that is subrogated to the rights of a holder of a claim of a kind specified in subsection (a)(~~3~~1), (a)(4), (a)(5), (a)(6), (a)(7), (a)(8), or (a)(9) of this section is not subrogated to the right of the holder of such claim to priority under such subsection.

§ 508. Effect of distribution other than under this title

~~(a) If a creditor receives, in a foreign proceeding, payment of, or a transfer of property on account of, a claim that is allowed under this title, such creditor may not receive any payment under this title on account of such claim until each of the other holders of claims on account of which such holders are entitled to share equally with such creditor under this title has received payment under this title equal in value to the consideration received by such creditor in such foreign proceeding.~~

~~(b)~~ If a creditor of a partnership debtor receives, from a general partner that is not a debtor in a case under chapter 7 of this title, payment of, or a transfer of property on account of, a claim that is allowed under this title and that is not secured by a lien on property of such partner, such creditor may not receive any payment under this title on account of such claim until each of the other holders of claims on account of which such holders are entitled to share equally with such creditor under this title has received payment under this title equal in value to the consideration received by such creditor from such general partner.

§ 509. Claims of codebtors

(a) Except as provided in subsection (b) or (c) of this section, an entity that is liable with the debtor on, or that has secured, a claim of a creditor against the debtor, and that pays such claim, is subrogated to the rights of such creditor to the extent of such payment.

(b) Such entity is not subrogated to the rights of such creditor to the extent that—

(1) a claim of such entity for reimbursement or contribution on account of such payment of such creditor's claim is—

(A) allowed under section 502 of this title;

(B) disallowed other than under section 502(e) of this title; or

(C) subordinated under section 510 of this title; or

(2) as between the debtor and such entity, such entity received the consideration for the claim held by such creditor.

(c) The court shall subordinate to the claim of a creditor and for the benefit of such creditor an allowed claim, by way of subrogation under this section, or for reimbursement or contribution, of an entity that is liable with the debtor on, or that has secured, such creditor's claim, until such creditor's claim is paid in full, either through payments under this title or otherwise.

§ 510. Subordination

(a) A subordination agreement is enforceable in a case under this title to the same extent that such agreement is enforceable under applicable nonbankruptcy law.

(b) For the purpose of distribution under this title, a claim arising from rescission of a purchase or sale of a security of the debtor or of an affiliate of the debtor, for damages arising from the purchase or sale of such a security, or for reimbursement or contribution allowed under section 502 on account of such a claim, shall be subordinated to all claims or interests that are senior to or equal the claim or interest represented by such security, except that if such security is common stock, such claim has the same priority as common stock.

(c) Notwithstanding subsections (a) and (b) of this section, after notice and a hearing, the court may—

(1) under principles of equitable subordination, subordinate for purposes of distribution all or part of an allowed claim to all or part of another allowed claim or all or part of an allowed interest to all or part of another allowed interest; or

(2) order that any lien securing such a subordinated claim be transferred to the estate.

§ 511. Rate of interest on tax claims

(a) If any provision of this title requires the payment of interest on a tax claim or on an administrative expense tax, or the payment of interest to enable a creditor to receive the present value of the allowed amount of a tax claim, the rate of interest shall be the rate determined under applicable nonbankruptcy law.

(b) In the case of taxes paid under a confirmed plan under this title, the rate of interest shall be determined as of the calendar month in which the plan is confirmed.

SUBCHAPTER II

Debtor's Duties and Benefits

§ 521. Debtor's duties

(a) The debtor shall—

(1) file—

(A) a list of creditors~~,~~; and

(B) unless the court orders otherwise~~,~~—

(i) a schedule of assets and liabilities~~,~~;

(ii) a schedule of current income and current expenditures~~,~~ ~~and~~;

(iii) a statement of the debtor's financial affairs and, if section 342(b) applies, a certificate—

(I) of an attorney whose name is indicated on the petition as the attorney for the debtor, or a bankruptcy petition preparer signing the petition under section 110(b)(1), indicating that such attorney or the bankruptcy petition preparer delivered to the debtor the notice required by section 342(b); or

(II) if no attorney is so indicated, and no bankruptcy petition preparer signed the petition, of the debtor that such notice was received and read by the debtor;

(iv) copies of all payment advices or other evidence of payment received within 60 days before the date of the filing of the petition, by the debtor from any employer of the debtor;

(v) a statement of the amount of monthly net income, itemized to show how the amount is calculated; and

(vi) a statement disclosing any reasonably anticipated increase in income or expenditures over the 12-month period following the date of the filing of the petition;

(2) if an individual debtor's schedule of assets and liabilities includes ~~consumer~~ debts which are secured by property of the estate—

(A) within thirty days after the date of the filing of a petition under chapter 7 of this title or on or before the date of the meeting of creditors, whichever is earlier, or within such additional time as the court, for cause, within such period fixes, the debtor shall file with the clerk a statement of his intention with respect to the retention or surrender of such property and, if applicable, specifying that such property is claimed as exempt, that the debtor intends to redeem such property, or that the debtor intends to reaffirm debts secured by such property;

(B) within ~~forty-five days after the filing of a notice of intent under this section~~ 30 days after the first date set for the meeting of creditors under section 341(a), or within such additional time as the court, for cause, within such ~~forty-five~~ 30- day period fixes, the debtor shall perform his intention with respect to such property, as specified by subparagraph (A) of this paragraph; and

(C) nothing in subparagraphs (A) and (B) of this paragraph shall alter the debtor's or the trustee's rights with regard to such property under this title, except as provided in section 362(h);

(3) if a trustee is serving in the case or an auditor serving under section 586(f) of title 28,[20] cooperate with the trustee as necessary to enable the trustee to perform the trustee's duties under this title;

(4) if a trustee is serving in the case or an auditor serving under section 586(f) of title 28,[21] surrender to the trustee all property

20 *Editor's Note*: This change to section 521(a)(3) is effective for cases commenced under title 11 on or after April 20, 2005.

21 *Editor's Note*: This change to section 521(a)(4) is effective for cases commenced under title 11 on or after April 20, 2005.

of the estate and any recorded information, including books, documents, records, and papers, relating to property of the estate, whether or not immunity is granted under section 344 of this title; ~~and~~

(5) appear at the hearing required under section 524(d) of this title;

(6) in a case under chapter 7 of this title in which the debtor is an individual, not retain possession of personal property as to which a creditor has an allowed claim for the purchase price secured in whole or in part by an interest in such personal property unless the debtor, not later than 45 days after the first meeting of creditors under section 341(a), either—

(A) enters into an agreement with the creditor pursuant to section 524(c) with respect to the claim secured by such property; or

(B) redeems such property from the security interest pursuant to section 722.

If the debtor fails to so act within the 45-day period referred to in paragraph (6), the stay under section 362(a) is terminated with respect to the personal property of the estate or of the debtor which is affected, such property shall no longer be property of the estate, and the creditor may take whatever action as to such property as is permitted by applicable nonbankruptcy law, unless the court determines on the motion of the trustee filed before the expiration of such 45-day period, and after notice and a hearing, that such property is of consequential value or benefit to the estate, orders appropriate adequate protection of the creditor's interest, and orders the debtor to deliver any collateral in the debtor's possession to the trustee; and

(7) unless a trustee is serving in the case, continue to perform the obligations required of the administrator (as defined in section 3 of the Employee Retirement Income Security Act of 1974) of an employee benefit plan if at the time of the commencement of the case the debtor (or any entity designated by the debtor) served as such administrator.

(b) In addition to the requirements under subsection (a), a debtor who is an individual shall file with the court—

(1) a certificate from the approved nonprofit budget and credit counseling agency that provided the debtor services under section 109(h) describing the services provided to the debtor; and

(2) a copy of the debt repayment plan, if any, developed under section 109(h) through the approved nonprofit budget and credit counseling agency referred to in paragraph (1).

(c) In addition to meeting the requirements under subsection (a), a debtor shall file with the court a record of any interest that a debtor has in an education individual retirement account (as defined in section 530(b)(1) of the Internal Revenue Code of 1986) or under a qualified State tuition program (as defined in section 529(b)(1) of such Code).

(d) If the debtor fails timely to take the action specified in subsection (a)(6) of this section, or in paragraphs (1) and (2) of section 362(h), with respect to property which a lessor or bailor owns and has leased, rented, or bailed to the debtor or as to which a creditor holds a security interest not otherwise voidable under section 522(f), 544, 545, 547, 548, or 549, nothing in this title shall prevent or limit the operation of a provision in the underlying lease or agreement that has the effect of placing the debtor in default under such lease or agreement by reason of the occurrence, pendency, or existence of a proceeding under this title or the insolvency of the debtor. Nothing in this subsection shall be deemed to justify limiting such a provision in any other circumstance.

(e)(1) If the debtor in a case under chapter 7 or 13 is an individual and if a creditor files with the court at any time a request to receive a copy of the petition, schedules, and statement of financial affairs filed by the debtor, then the court shall make such petition, such schedules, and such statement available to such creditor.

(2)(A) The debtor shall provide—

(i) not later than 7 days before the date first set for the first meeting of creditors, to the trustee a copy of the Federal income tax return required under applicable law (or at the election of the debtor, a transcript of such return) for the most recent tax year ending immediately before the commencement of the case and for which a Federal income tax return was filed; and

(ii) at the same time the debtor complies with clause (i), a copy of such return (or if elected under clause (i), such transcript) to any creditor that timely requests such copy.

(B) If the debtor fails to comply with clause (i) or (ii) of subparagraph (A), the court shall dismiss the case unless the debtor demonstrates that the failure to so comply is due to circumstances beyond the control of the debtor.

(C) If a creditor requests a copy of such tax return or such transcript and if the debtor fails to provide a copy of such tax return or such transcript to such creditor at the time the debtor provides such tax return or such transcript to the trustee, then the court shall dismiss the case unless the debtor demonstrates that the failure to provide a copy of such tax return or such transcript is due to circumstances beyond the control of the debtor.

(3) If a creditor in a case under chapter 13 files with the court at any time a request to receive a copy of the plan filed by the debtor, then the court shall make available to such creditor a copy of the plan—

(A) at a reasonable cost; and

(B) not later than 5 days after such request is filed.

(f) At the request of the court, the United States trustee, or any party in interest in a case under chapter 7, 11, or 13, a debtor who is an individual shall file with the court—

(1) at the same time filed with the taxing authority, a copy of each Federal income tax return required under applicable law (or at the election of the debtor, a transcript of such tax return) with respect to each tax year of the debtor ending while the case is pending under such chapter;

(2) at the same time filed with the taxing authority, each Federal income tax return required under applicable law (or at the election of the debtor, a transcript of such tax return) that had not been filed with such authority as of the date of the

commencement of the case and that was subsequently filed for any tax year of the debtor ending in the 3-year period ending on the date of the commencement of the case;

(3) a copy of each amendment to any Federal income tax return or transcript filed with the court under paragraph (1) or (2); and

(4) in a case under chapter 13—

(A) on the date that is either 90 days after the end of such tax year or 1 year after the date of the commencement of the case, whichever is later, if a plan is not confirmed before such later date; and

(B) annually after the plan is confirmed and until the case is closed, not later than the date that is 45 days before the anniversary of the confirmation of the plan; a statement, under penalty of perjury, of the income and expenditures of the debtor during the tax year of the debtor most recently concluded before such statement is filed under this paragraph, and of the monthly income of the debtor, that shows how income, expenditures, and monthly income are calculated.

(g)(1) A statement referred to in subsection (f)(4) shall disclose—

(A) the amount and sources of the income of the debtor;

(B) the identity of any person responsible with the debtor for the support of any dependent of the debtor; and

(C) the identity of any person who contributed, and the amount contributed, to the household in which the debtor resides.

(2) The tax returns, amendments, and statement of income and expenditures described in subsections (e)(2)(A) and (f) shall be available to the United States trustee (or the bankruptcy administrator, if any), the trustee, and any party in interest for inspection and copying, subject to the requirements of section 315(c) of the Bankruptcy Abuse Prevention and Consumer Protection Act of 2005.

(h) If requested by the United States trustee or by the trustee, the debtor shall provide—

(1) a document that establishes the identity of the debtor, including a driver's license, passport, or other document that contains a photograph of the debtor; or

(2) such other personal identifying information relating to the debtor that establishes the identity of the debtor.

(i)(1) Subject to paragraphs (2) and (4) and notwithstanding section 707(a), if an individual debtor in a voluntary case under chapter 7 or 13 fails to file all of the information required under subsection (a)(1) within 45 days after the date of the filing of the petition, the case shall be automatically dismissed effective on the 46th day after the date of the filing of the petition.

(2) Subject to paragraph (4) and with respect to a case described in paragraph (1), any party in interest may request the court to enter an order dismissing the case.If requested, the court shall enter an order of dismissal not later than 5 days after such request.

(3) Subject to paragraph (4) and upon request of the debtor made within 45 days after the date of the filing of the petition described in paragraph (1), the court may allow the debtor an additional period of not to exceed 45 days to file the information required under subsection (a)(1) if the court finds justification for extending the period for the filing.

(4) Notwithstanding any other provision of this subsection, on the motion of the trustee filed before the expiration of the applicable period of time specified in paragraph (1), (2), or (3), and after notice and a hearing, the court may decline to dismiss the case if the court finds that the debtor attempted in good faith to file all the information required by subsection (a)(1)(B)(iv) and that the best interests of creditors would be served by administration of the case.

(j)(1) Notwithstanding any other provision of this title, if the debtor fails to file a tax return that becomes due after the commencement of the case or to properly obtain an extension of the due date for filing such return, the taxing authority may request that the court enter an order converting or dismissing the case.

(2) If the debtor does not file the required return or obtain the extension referred to in paragraph (1) within 90 days after a request is filed by the taxing authority under that paragraph, the court shall convert or dismiss the case, whichever is in the best interests of creditors and the estate.

§ 522. Exemptions

(a) In this section—

(1) "dependent" includes spouse, whether or not actually dependent; and

(2) "value" means fair market value as of the date of the filing of the petition or, with respect to property that becomes property of the estate after such date, as of the date such property becomes property of the estate.

(b)(1) Notwithstanding section 541 of this title, an individual debtor may exempt from property of the estate the property listed in either paragraph (~~1~~2) or, in the alternative, paragraph (~~2~~3) of this subsection. In joint cases filed under section 302 of this title and individual cases filed under section 301 or 303 of this title by or against debtors who are husband and wife, and whose estates are ordered to be jointly administered under Rule 1015(b) of the Federal Rules of Bankruptcy Procedure, one debtor may not elect to exempt property listed in paragraph (~~1~~2) and the other debtor elect to exempt property listed in paragraph (~~2~~3) of this subsection. If the parties cannot agree on the alternative to be elected, they shall be deemed to elect paragraph (1), where such election is permitted under the law of the jurisdiction where the case is filed. ~~Such property is—~~

(~~1~~2) Property listed in this paragraph is property that is specified under subsection (d) ~~of this section~~, unless the State law that is applicable to the debtor under paragraph (~~2~~3)(A) ~~of this subsection~~ specifically does not so authorize.~~; or, in the alternative,~~

~~(2)(A)~~ (3) Property listed in this paragraph is—

(A) subject to subsections (o) and (p),[22] any property that is exempt under Federal law, other than subsection (d) of this section, or State or local law that is applicable on the date of the filing of the petition at the place in which the debtor's domicile has been located for the ~~180~~ 730 days immediately preceding the date of the filing of the petition~~,~~ or if the debtor's domicile has not been located at a single State for such 730-day period, the place in which the debtor's domicile was located for 180 days immediately preceding the 730-day period or for a longer portion of such 180-day period than in any other place; ~~and~~

(B) any interest in property in which the debtor had, immediately before the commencement of the case, an interest as a tenant by the entirety or joint tenant to the extent that such interest as a tenant by the entirety or joint tenant is exempt from process under applicable nonbankruptcy law~~.~~; and

(C) retirement funds to the extent that those funds are in a fund or account that is exempt from taxation under section 401, 403, 408, 408A, 414, 457, or 501(a) of the Internal Revenue Code of 1986.

If the effect of the domiciliary requirement under subparagraph (A) is to render the debtor ineligible for any exemption, the debtor may elect to exempt property that is specified under subsection (d).

(4) For purposes of paragraph (3)(C) and subsection (d)(12), the following shall apply:

(A) If the retirement funds are in a retirement fund that has received a favorable determination under section 7805 of the Internal Revenue Code of 1986, and that determination is in effect as of the date of the filing of the petition in a case under this title, those funds shall be presumed to be exempt from the estate.

(B) If the retirement funds are in a retirement fund that has not received a favorable determination under such section 7805, those funds are exempt from the estate if the debtor demonstrates that—

(i) no prior determination to the contrary has been made by a court or the Internal Revenue Service; and

(ii)(I) the retirement fund is in substantial compliance with the applicable requirements of the Internal Revenue Code of 1986; or

(II) the retirement fund fails to be in substantial compliance with the applicable requirements of the Internal Revenue Code of 1986 and the debtor is not materially responsible for that failure.

(C) A direct transfer of retirement funds from 1 fund or account that is exempt from taxation under section 401, 403, 408, 408A, 414, 457, or 501(a) of the Internal Revenue Code of 1986, under section 401(a)(31) of the Internal Revenue Code of 1986, or otherwise, shall not cease to qualify for exemption under paragraph (3)(C) or subsection (d)(12) by reason of such direct transfer.

(D)(i) Any distribution that qualifies as an eligible rollover distribution within the meaning of section 402(c) of the Internal Revenue Code of 1986 or that is described in clause (ii) shall not cease to qualify for exemption under paragraph (3)(C) or subsection (d)(12) by reason of such distribution.

(ii) A distribution described in this clause is an amount that—

(I) has been distributed from a fund or account that is exempt from taxation under section 401, 403, 408, 408A, 414, 457, or 501(a) of the Internal Revenue Code of 1986; and

(II) to the extent allowed by law, is deposited in such a fund or account not later than 60 days after the distribution of such amount.

(c) Unless the case is dismissed, property exempted under this section is not liable during or after the case for any debt of the debtor that arose, or that is determined under section 502 of this title as if such debt had arisen, before the commencement of the case, except—

(1) a debt of a kind specified in ~~section 523(a)(1) or 523(a)(5) of this title~~ paragraph (1) or (5) of section 523(a) (in which case, notwithstanding any provision of applicable nonbankruptcy law to the contrary, such property shall be liable for a debt of a kind specified in section 523(a)(5));

(2) a debt secured by a lien that is—

(A)(i) not avoided under subsection (f) or (g) of this section or under section 544, 545, 547, 548, 549, or 724(a) of this title; and

(ii) not void under section 506(d) of this title; or

(B) a tax lien, notice of which is properly filed;

(3) a debt of a kind specified in section 523(a)(4) or 523(a)(6) of this title owed by an institution-affiliated party of an insured depository institution to a Federal depository institutions regulatory agency acting in its capacity as conservator, receiver, or liquidating agent for such institution; or

(4) a debt in connection with fraud in the obtaining or providing of any scholarship, grant, loan, tuition, discount, award, or other financial assistance for purposes of financing an education at an institution of higher education (as that term is defined in section 101 of the Higher Education Act of 1965 (20 U.S.C. 1001)).

(d) The following property may be exempted under subsection (b)(~~1~~2) of this section:

(1) The debtor's aggregate interest, not to exceed $18,450[23] in value, in real property or personal property that the debtor or

22 *Editor's Note*: The introductory phrase added to section 522(b)(3)(A) is effective for cases commenced under title 11 on or after April 20, 2005.

23 *Editor's Note*: This dollar amount reflects an inflationary adjustment, effective April 1, 2004. For cases commenced before April 1, 2004, the applicable dollar amount is $17,425.

a dependent of the debtor uses as a residence, in a cooperative that owns property that the debtor or a dependent of the debtor uses as a residence, or in a burial plot for the debtor or a dependent of the debtor.

(2) The debtor's interest, not to exceed $2,950[24] in value, in one motor vehicle.

(3) The debtor's interest, not to exceed $475[25] in value in any particular item or $9,850[26] in aggregate value, in household furnishings, household goods, wearing apparel, appliances, books, animals, crops, or musical instruments, that are held primarily for the personal, family, or household use of the debtor or a dependent of the debtor.

(4) The debtor's aggregate interest, not to exceed $1,225[27] in value, in jewelry held primarily for the personal, family, or household use of the debtor or a dependent of the debtor.

(5) The debtor's aggregate interest in any property, not to exceed in value $975[28] plus up to $9,250[29] of any unused amount of the exemption provided under paragraph (1) of this subsection.

(6) The debtor's aggregate interest, not to exceed $1,850[30] in value, in any implements, professional books, or tools, of the trade of the debtor or the trade of a dependent of the debtor.

(7) Any unmatured life insurance contract owned by the debtor, other than a credit life insurance contract.

(8) The debtor's aggregate interest, not to exceed in value $9,850[31] less any amount of property of the estate transferred in the manner specified in section 542(d) of this title, in any accrued dividend or interest under, or loan value of, any unmatured life insurance contract owned by the debtor under which the insured is the debtor or an individual of whom the debtor is a dependent.

(9) Professionally prescribed health aids for the debtor or a dependent of the debtor.

(10) The debtor's right to receive—

(A) a social security benefit, unemployment compensation, or a local public assistance benefit;

(B) a veterans' benefit;

(C) a disability, illness, or unemployment benefit;

(D) alimony, support, or separate maintenance, to the extent reasonably necessary for the support of the debtor and any dependent of the debtor;

(E) a payment under a stock bonus, pension, profitsharing, annuity, or similar plan or contract on account of illness, disability, death, age, or length of service, to the extent reasonably necessary for the support of the debtor and any dependent of the debtor, unless—

(i) such plan or contract was established by or under the auspices of an insider that employed the debtor at the time the debtor's rights under such plan or contract arose;

(ii) such payment is on account of age or length of service; and

(iii) such plan or contract does not qualify under section 401(a), 403(a), 403(b), or 408 of the Internal Revenue Code of 1986.

(11) The debtor's right to receive, or property that is traceable to—

(A) an award under a crime victim's reparation law;

(B) a payment on account of the wrongful death of an individual of whom the debtor was a dependent, to the extent reasonably necessary for the support of the debtor and any dependent of the debtor;

(C) a payment under a life insurance contract that insured the life of an individual of whom the debtor was a dependent on the date of such individual's death, to the extent reasonably necessary for the support of the debtor and any dependent of the debtor;

(D) a payment, not to exceed $18,450,[32] on account of personal bodily injury, not including pain and suffering or compensation for actual pecuniary loss, of the debtor or an individual of whom the debtor is a dependent; or

(E) a payment in compensation of loss of future earnings of the debtor or an individual of whom the debtor is or was a dependent, to the extent reasonably necessary for the support of the debtor and any dependent of the debtor.

(12) Retirement funds to the extent that those funds are in a fund or account that is exempt from taxation under section 401,403, 408, 408A, 414, 457, or 501(a) of the Internal Revenue Code of 1986.

(e) A waiver of an exemption executed in favor of a creditor that holds an unsecured claim against the debtor is unenforceable in a

24 *Editor's Note*: This dollar amount reflects an inflationary adjustment, effective April 1, 2004. For cases commenced before April 1, 2004, the applicable dollar amount is $2,775.

25 *Editor's Note*: This dollar amount reflects an inflationary adjustment, effective April 1, 2004. For cases commenced before April 1, 2004, the applicable dollar amount is $450.

26 *Editor's Note*: This dollar amount reflects an inflationary adjustment, effective April 1, 2004. For cases commenced before April 1, 2004, the applicable dollar amount is $9,300.

27 *Editor's Note*: This dollar amount reflects an inflationary adjustment, effective April 1, 2004. For cases commenced before April 1, 2004, the applicable dollar amount is $1,150.

28 *Editor's Note*: This dollar amount reflects an inflationary adjustment, effective April 1, 2004. For cases commenced before April 1, 2004, the applicable dollar amount is $925.

29 *Editor's Note*: This dollar amount reflects an inflationary adjustment, effective April 1, 2004. For cases commenced before April 1, 2004, the applicable dollar amount is $8,725.

30 *Editor's Note*: This dollar amount reflects an inflationary adjustment, effective April 1, 2004. For cases commenced before April 1, 2004, the applicable dollar amount is $1,750.

31 *Editor's Note*: This dollar amount reflects an inflationary adjustment, effective April 1, 2004. For cases commenced before April 1, 2004, the applicable dollar amount is $9,300.

32 *Editor's Note*: This dollar amount reflects an inflationary adjustment, effective April 1, 2004. For cases commenced before April 1, 2004, the applicable dollar amount is $17,425.

case under this title with respect to such claim against property that the debtor may exempt under subsection (b) of this section. A waiver by the debtor of a power under subsection (f) or (h) of this section to avoid a transfer, under subsection (g) or (i) of this section to exempt property, or under subsection (i) of this section to recover property or to preserve a transfer, is unenforceable in a case under this title.

(f)(1) Notwithstanding any waiver of exemptions but subject to paragraph (3), the debtor may avoid the fixing of a lien on an interest of the debtor in property to the extent that such lien impairs an exemption to which the debtor would have been entitled under subsection (b) of this section, if such lien is—

(A) a judicial lien, other than a judicial lien that secures a debt of a kind that is specified in section 523(a)(5); or~~—~~

~~(i) to a spouse, former spouse, or child of the debtor, for alimony to, maintenance for, or support of such spouse or child, in connection with a separation agreement, divorce decree or other order of a court of record, determination made in accordance with State or territorial law by a governmental unit, or property settlement agreement; and~~

~~(ii) to the extent that such debt—~~

~~(I) is not assigned to another entity, voluntarily, by operation of law, or otherwise; and~~

~~(II) includes a liability designated as alimony, maintenance, or support, unless such liability is actually in the nature of alimony, maintenance or support. or~~

(B) a nonpossessory, nonpurchase-money security interest in any—

(i) household furnishings, household goods, wearing apparel, appliances, books, animals, crops, musical instruments, or jewelry that are held primarily for the personal, family, or household use of the debtor or a dependent of the debtor;

(ii) implements, professional books, or tools, of the trade of the debtor or the trade of a dependent of the debtor; or

(iii) professionally prescribed health aids for the debtor or a dependent of the debtor.

(2)(A) For the purposes of this subsection, a lien shall be considered to impair an exemption to the extent that the sum of—

(i) the lien,

(ii) all other liens on the property; and

(iii) the amount of the exemption that the debtor could claim if there were no liens on the property;

exceeds the value that the debtor's interest in the property would have in the absence of any liens.

(B) In the case of a property subject to more than 1 lien, a lien that has been avoided shall not be considered in making the calculation under subparagraph (A) with respect to other liens.

(C) This paragraph shall not apply with respect to a judgment arising out of a mortgage foreclosure.

(3) In a case in which State law that is applicable to the debtor—

(A) permits a person to voluntarily waive a right to claim exemptions under subsection (d) or prohibits a debtor from claiming exemptions under subsection (d); and

(B) either permits the debtor to claim exemptions under State law without limitation in amount, except to the extent that the debtor has permitted the fixing of a consensual lien on any property or prohibits avoidance of a consensual lien on property otherwise eligible to be claimed as exempt property;

the debtor may not avoid the fixing of a lien on an interest of the debtor or a dependent of the debtor in property if the lien is a nonpossessory, nonpurchase-money security interest in implements, professional books, or tools of the trade of the debtor or a dependent of the debtor or farm animals or crops of the debtor or a dependent of the debtor to the extent the value of such implements, professional books, tools of the trade, animals, and crops exceeds $5,000.

(4)(A) Subject to subparagraph (B), for purposes of paragraph (1)(B), the term "household goods" means—

(i) clothing;

(ii) furniture;

(iii) appliances;

(iv) 1 radio;

(v) 1 television;

(vi) 1 VCR;

(vii) linens;

(viii) china;

(ix) crockery;

(x) kitchenware;

(xi) educational materials and educational equipment primarily for the use of minor dependent children of the debtor;

(xii) medical equipment and supplies;

(xiii) furniture exclusively for the use of minor children, or elderly or disabled dependents of the debtor;

(xiv) personal effects (including the toys and hobby equipment of minor dependent children and wedding rings) of the debtor and the dependents of the debtor; and

(xv) 1 personal computer and related equipment.

(B) The term "household goods" does not include—

(i) works of art (unless by or of the debtor, or any relative of the debtor);

(ii) electronic entertainment equipment with a fair market value of more than $500 in the aggregate (except 1 television, 1 radio, and 1 VCR);

(iii) items acquired as antiques with a fair market value of more than $500 in the aggregate;

(iv) jewelry with a fair market value of more than $500 in the aggregate (except wedding rings); and

(v) a computer (except as otherwise provided for in this section), motor vehicle (including a tractor or lawn tractor), boat, or a motorized recreational device, conveyance, vehicle, watercraft, or aircraft.

(g) Notwithstanding sections 550 and 551 of this title, the debtor may exempt under subsection (b) of this section property that the trustee recovers under section 510(c)(2), 542, 543, 550, 551, or 553 of this title, to the extent that the debtor could have exempted such property under subsection (b) of this section if such property had not been transferred, if—

(1)(A) such transfer was not a voluntary transfer of such property by the debtor; and

(B) the debtor did not conceal such property; or

(2) the debtor could have avoided such transfer under subsection ~~(f)(2)~~ (f)(1)(B) of this section.

(h) The debtor may avoid a transfer of property of the debtor or recover a setoff to the extent that the debtor could have exempted such property under subsection (g)(1) of this section if the trustee had avoided such transfer, if—

(1) such transfer is avoidable by the trustee under section 544, 545, 547, 548, 549, or 724(a) of this title or recoverable by the trustee under section 553 of this title; and

(2) the trustee does not attempt to avoid such transfer.

(i)(1) If the debtor avoids a transfer or recovers a setoff under subsection (f) or (h) of this section, the debtor may recover in the manner prescribed by, and subject to the limitations of section 550 of this title, the same as if the trustee had avoided such transfer, and may exempt any property so recovered under subsection (b) of this section.

(2) Notwithstanding section 551 of this title, a transfer avoided under section 544, 545, 547, 548, 549, or 724(a) of this title, under subsection (f) or (h) of this section, or property recovered under section 553 of this title, may be preserved for the benefit of the debtor to the extent that the debtor may exempt such property under subsection (g) of this section or paragraph (1) of this subsection.

(j) Notwithstanding subsections (g) and (i) of this section, the debtor may exempt a particular kind of property under subsections (g) and (i) of this section only to the extent that the debtor has exempted less property in value of such kind than that to which the debtor is entitled under subsection (b) of this section.

(k) Property that the debtor exempts under this section is not liable for payment of any administrative expense except—

(1) the aliquot share of the costs and expenses of avoiding a transfer of property that the debtor exempts under subsection (g) of this section, or of recovery of such property, that is attributable to the value of the portion of such property exempted in relation to the value of the property recovered; and

(2) any costs and expenses of avoiding a transfer under subsection (f) or (h) of this section, or of recovery of property under subsection (i)(1) of this section, that the debtor has not paid.

(*l*) The debtor shall file a list of property that the debtor claims as exempt under subsection (b) of this section. If the debtor does not file such a list, a dependent of the debtor may file such a list, or may claim property as exempt from property of the estate on behalf of the debtor. Unless a party in interest objects, the property claimed as exempt on such list is exempt.

(m) Subject to the limitation in subsection (b), this section shall apply separately with respect to each debtor in a joint case.

(n) For assets in individual retirement accounts described in section 408 or 408A of the Internal Revenue Code of 1986, other than a simplified employee pension under section 408(k) of such Code or a simple retirement account under section 408(p) of such Code, the aggregate value of such assets exempted under this section, without regard to amounts attributable to rollover contributions under sections 402(c), 402(e)(6), 403(a)(4), 403(a)(5), and 403(b)(8) of the Internal Revenue Code of 1986, and earnings thereon, shall not exceed $1,000,000 in a case filed by a debtor who is an individual, except that such amount may be increased if the interests of justice so require.

(*o*) For purposes of subsection (b)(3)(A), and notwithstanding subsection (a), the value of an interest in—

(1) real or personal property that the debtor or a dependent of the debtor uses as a residence;

(2) a cooperative that owns property that the debtor or a dependent of the debtor uses as a residence;

(3) a burial plot for the debtor or a dependent of the debtor; or

(4) real or personal property that the debtor or a dependent of the debtor claims as a homestead; shall be reduced to the extent that such value is attributable to any portion of any property that the debtor disposed of in the 10-year period ending on the date of the filing of the petition with the intent to hinder, delay, or defraud a creditor and that the debtor could not exempt, or that portion that the debtor could not exempt, under subsection (b), if on such date the debtor had held the property so disposed of.[33]

(p)(1) Except as provided in paragraph (2) of this subsection and sections 544 and 548, as a result of electing under subsection (b)(3)(A) to exempt property under State or local law, a debtor may not exempt any amount of interest that was acquired by the debtor during the 1215-day period preceding the date of the filing of the petition that exceeds in the aggregate $125,000 in value in—

(A) real or personal property that the debtor or a dependent of the debtor uses as a residence;

---

33 *Editor's Note*: New subsection 522(*o*) is effective for cases commenced under title 11 on or after April 20, 2005.

(B) a cooperative that owns property that the debtor or a dependent of the debtor uses as a residence;

(C) a burial plot for the debtor or a dependent of the debtor; or

(D) real or personal property that the debtor or dependent of the debtor claims as a homestead.

(2)(A) The limitation under paragraph (1) shall not apply to an exemption claimed under subsection (b)(3)(A) by a family farmer for the principal residence of such farmer.

(B) For purposes of paragraph (1), any amount of such interest does not include any interest transferred from a debtor's previous principal residence (which was acquired prior to the beginning of such 1215-day period) into the debtor's current principal residence, if the debtor's previous and current residences are located in the same State.[34]

(q)(1) As a result of electing under subsection (b)(3)(A) to exempt property under State or local law, a debtor may not exempt any amount of an interest in property described in subparagraphs (A), (B), (C), and (D) of subsection (p)(1) which exceeds in the aggregate $125,000 if—

(A) the court determines, after notice and a hearing, that the debtor has been convicted of a felony (as defined in section 3156 of title 18), which under the circumstances, demonstrates that the filing of the case was an abuse of the provisions of this title; or

(B) the debtor owes a debt arising from—

(i) any violation of the Federal securities laws (as defined in section 3(a)(47) of the Securities Exchange Act of 1934), any State securities laws, or any regulation or order issued under Federal securities laws or State securities laws;

(ii) fraud, deceit, or manipulation in a fiduciary capacity or in connection with the purchase or sale of any security registered under section 12 or 15(d) of the Securities Exchange Act of 1934 or under section 6 of the Securities Act of 1933;

(iii) any civil remedy under section 1964 of title 18; or

(iv) any criminal act, intentional tort, or willful or reckless misconduct that caused serious physical injury or death to another individual in the preceding 5 years.

(2) Paragraph (1) shall not apply to the extent the amount of an interest in property described in subparagraphs (A), (B), (C), and (D) of subsection (p)(1) is reasonably necessary for the support of the debtor and any dependent of the debtor.[35]

§ 523. Exceptions to discharge

(a) A discharge under section 727, 1141, 1228(a), 1228(b), or 1328(b) of this title does not discharge an individual debtor from any debt—

(1) for a tax or a customs duty—

(A) of the kind and for the periods specified in section 507(a)(~~2~~3) or 507(a)(8) of this title, whether or not a claim for such tax was filed or allowed;

(B) with respect to which a return, or equivalent report or notice, if required—

(i) was not filed or given; or

(ii) was filed or given after the date on which such return, report, or notice was last due, under applicable law or under any extension, and after two years before the date of the filing of the petition; or

(C) with respect to which the debtor made a fraudulent return or willfully attempted in any manner to evade or defeat such tax;

(2) for money, property, services, or an extension, renewal, or refinancing of credit, to the extent obtained by—

(A) false pretenses, a false representation, or actual fraud, other than a statement respecting the debtor's or an insider's financial condition;

(B) use of a statement in writing—

(i) that is materially false;

(ii) respecting the debtor's or an insider's financial condition;

(iii) on which the creditor to whom the debtor is liable for such money, property, services, or credit reasonably relied; and

(iv) that the debtor caused to be made or published with intent to deceive; or

(C) (i) for purposes of subparagraph (A)~~ of this paragraph,—~~

(I) consumer debts owed to a single creditor and aggregating more than ~~$1,225~~ $500[36] for "luxury goods or services" incurred by an individual debtor on or within ~~60~~ 90 days before the order for relief under this title~~, or~~ are presumed to be nondischargeable; and

(II) cash advances aggregating more than ~~$1,225~~ $750[37] that are extensions of consumer credit under an open end credit plan obtained by an individual debtor on or within ~~60~~ 70 days before the order for relief under this title, are presumed to be nondischargeable; and

34 *Editor's Note*: New subsection 522(p) is effective for cases commenced under title 11 on or after April 20, 2005.

35 *Editor's Note*: New subsection 522(q) is effective for cases commenced under title 11 on or after April 20, 2005.

36 *Editor's Note*: The dollar amount of $1,225 reflects an inflationary adjustment, effective April 1, 2004. For cases commenced before April 1, 2004, the applicable dollar amount is $1,150. The amendment to section 523(a)(2)(C)(I) changing this dollar amount to $500 is effective for cases commenced under title 11 on or after October 17, 2005.

37 *Editor's Note*: The dollar amount of $1,225 reflects an inflationary adjustment, effective April 1, 2004. For cases commenced before April 1, 2004, the applicable dollar amount is $1,150. The amendment to section 523(a)(2)(C)(II) changing this dollar amount to $750 is effective for cases commenced under title 11 on or after October 17, 2005.

(ii) for purposes of this subparagraph—

(I) the terms "consumer", "credit", and "open end credit plan" have the same meanings as in section 103 of the Truth in Lending Act; and

(II) the term "luxury goods or services" does not include goods or services reasonably ~~acquired~~ necessary for the support or maintenance of the debtor or a dependent of the debtor; ~~an extension of consumer credit under an open end credit plan is to be defined for purposes of this subparagraph as it is defined in the Consumer Credit Protection Act;~~

(3) neither listed nor scheduled under section 521(1) of this title, with the name, if known to the debtor, of the creditor to whom such debt is owed, in time to permit—

(A) if such debt is not of a kind specified in paragraph (2), (4), or (6) of this subsection, timely filing of a proof of claim, unless such creditor had notice or actual knowledge of the case in time for such timely filing; or

(B) if such debt is of a kind specified in paragraph (2), (4), or (6) of this subsection, timely filing of a proof of claim and timely request for a determination of dischargeability of such debt under one of such paragraphs, unless such creditor had notice or actual knowledge of the case in time for such timely filing and request;

(4) for fraud or defalcation while acting in a fiduciary capacity, embezzlement, or larceny;

~~(5) to a spouse, former spouse, or child of the debtor, for alimony to, maintenance for, or support of such spouse or child, in connection with a separation agreement, divorce decree or other order of a court of record, determination made in accordance with State or territorial law by a governmental unit, or property settlement agreement, but not to the extent that—~~

~~(A) such debt is assigned to another entity, voluntarily, by operation of law, or otherwise (other than debts assigned pursuant to section 408(a)(3) of the Social Security Act, or any such debt which has been assigned to the Federal Government or to a State or any political subdivision of such State); or~~

~~(B) such debt includes a liability designated as alimony, maintenance, or support, unless such liability is actually in the nature of alimony, maintenance, or support;~~

(5) for a domestic support obligation;

(6) for willful and malicious injury by the debtor to another entity or to the property of another entity;

(7) to the extent such debt is for a fine, penalty, or forfeiture payable to and for the benefit of a governmental unit, and is not compensation for actual pecuniary loss, other than a tax penalty—

(A) relating to a tax of a kind not specified in paragraph (1) of this subsection; or

(B) imposed with respect to a transaction or event that occurred before three years before the date of the filing of the petition;

(8) unless excepting such debt from discharge under this paragraph would impose an undue hardship on the debtor and the debtor's dependents, for—

(A)(i) an educational benefit overpayment or loan made, insured or guaranteed by a governmental unit, or made under any program funded in whole or in part by a governmental unit or nonprofit institution, or

(ii) ~~for~~ an obligation to repay funds received as an educational benefit, scholarship or stipend; or

(B) any other educational loan that is a qualified education loan, as defined in section 221(d)(1) of the Internal Revenue Code of 1986, incurred by a debtor who is an individual; ~~, unless excepting such debt from discharge under this paragraph will impose an undue hardship on the debtor and the debtor's dependents;~~

(9) for death or personal injury caused by the debtor's operation of a motor vehicle, vessel, or aircraft if such operation was unlawful because the debtor was intoxicated from using alcohol, a drug, or another substance;

(10) that was or could have been listed or scheduled by the debtor in a prior case concerning the debtor under this title or under the Bankruptcy Act in which the debtor waived discharge, or was denied a discharge under section 727(a)(2), (3), (4), (5), (6), or (7) of this title, or under section 14c (1), (2), (3), (4), (6), or (7) of such Act;

(11) provided in any final judgment, unreviewable order, or consent order or decree entered in any court of the United States or of any State, issued by a Federal depository institutions regulatory agency, or contained in any settlement agreement entered into by the debtor, arising from any act of fraud or defalcation while acting in a fiduciary capacity committed with respect to any depository institution or insured credit union;

(12) for malicious or reckless failure to fulfill any commitment by the debtor to a Federal depository institutions regulatory agency to maintain the capital of an insured depository institution, except that this paragraph shall not extend any such commitment which would otherwise be terminated due to any act of such agency; or

(13) for any payment of an order of restitution issued under title 18, United States Code;

(14) incurred to pay a tax to the United States that would be nondischargeable pursuant to paragraph (1);

(14A) incurred to pay a tax to a governmental unit, other than the United States, that would be nondischargeable under paragraph (1);

(14B) incurred to pay fines or penalties imposed under Federal election law;

(15) to a spouse, former spouse, or child of the debtor and not of the kind described in paragraph (5) that is incurred by the debtor in the course of a divorce or separation or in connection with a separation agreement, divorce decree or other

order of a court of record, or a determination made in accordance with State or territorial law by a governmental unit; ~~unless—~~

~~(A) the debtor does not have the ability to pay such debt from income or property of the debtor not reasonably necessary to be expended for the maintenance or support of the debtor or a dependent of the debtor and, if the debtor is engaged in a business, for the payment of expenditures necessary for the continuation, preservation, and operation of such business; or~~

~~(B) discharging such debt would result in a benefit to the debtor that outweighs the detrimental consequences to a spouse, former spouse, or child of the debtor;~~

(16) for a fee or assessment that becomes due and payable after the order for relief to a membership association with respect to the debtor's interest in a ~~dwelling~~ unit that has condominium ownership~~, or~~ in a share of a cooperative ~~housing~~ corporation, ~~but only if such fee or assessment is payable for a period during which—~~

~~(A) the debtor physically occupied a dwelling unit in the condominium or cooperative project; or~~

~~(B) the debtor rented the dwelling unit to a tenant and received payments from the tenant for such period,~~

or a lot in a homeowners association, for as long as the debtor or the trustee has a legal, equitable, or possessory ownership interest in such unit, such corporation, or such lot, but nothing in this paragraph shall except from discharge the debt of a debtor for a membership association fee or assessment for a period arising before entry of the order for relief in a pending or subsequent bankruptcy case;

(17) for a fee imposed on a prisoner by any court for the filing of a case, motion, complaint, or appeal, or for other costs and expenses assessed with respect to such filing, regardless of an assertion of poverty by the debtor under subsection (b) or (f)(2) of section 1915~~(b) or (f)~~ of title 28 (or a similar non-Federal law), or the debtor's status as a prisoner, as defined in section 1915(h) of title 28 (or a similar non-Federal law);

~~(18) owed under State law to a State or municipality that is—~~

~~(A) in the nature of support, and~~

~~(B) enforceable under part D of title IV of the Social Security Act (42 U.S.C. 601 et seq.); or~~

(18) owed to a pension, profit-sharing, stock bonus, or other plan established under section 401, 403, 408, 408A, 414, 457, or 501(c) of the Internal Revenue Code of 1986, under—

(A) a loan permitted under section 408(b)(1) of the Employee Retirement Income Security Act of 1974, or subject to section 72(p) of the Internal Revenue Code of 1986; or

(B) a loan from a thrift savings plan permitted under subchapter III of chapter 84 of title 5, that satisfies the requirements of section 8433(g) of such title; but nothing in this paragraph may be construed to provide that any loan made under a governmental plan under section 414(d), or a contract or account under section 403(b), of the Internal Revenue Code of 1986 constitutes a claim or a debt under this title; or

(19) that—

(A) is for—

(i) the violation of any of the Federal securities laws (as that term is defined in section 3(a)(47) of the Securities Exchange Act of 1934), any of the State securities laws, or any regulation or order issued under such Federal or State securities laws; or

(ii) common law fraud, deceit, or manipulation in connection with the purchase or sale of any security; and

(B) results, before, on, or after the date on which the petition was filed, from—

(i) any judgment, order, consent order, or decree entered in any Federal or State judicial or administrative proceeding;

(ii) any settlement agreement entered into by the debtor; or

(iii) any court or administrative order for any damages, fine, penalty, citation, restitutionary payment, disgorgement payment, attorney fee, cost, or other payment owed by the debtor.

For purposes of this subsection, the term "return" means a return that satisfies the requirements of applicable nonbankruptcy law (including applicable filing requirements). Such term includes a return prepared pursuant to section 6020(a) of the Internal Revenue Code of 1986, or similar State or local law, or a written stipulation to a judgment or a final order entered by a nonbankruptcy tribunal, but does not include a return made pursuant to section 6020(b) of the Internal Revenue Code of 1986, or a similar State or local law.

(b) Notwithstanding subsection (a) of this section, a debt that was excepted from discharge under subsection (a)(1), (a)(3), or (a)(8) of this section, under section 17a(1), 17a(3), or 17a(5) of the Bankruptcy Act, under section 439A of the Higher Education Act of 1965, or under section 733(g) of the Public Health Service Act in a prior case concerning the debtor under this title, or under the Bankruptcy Act, is dischargeable in a case under this title unless, by the terms of subsection (a) of this section, such debt is not dischargeable in the case under this title.

(c)(1) Except as provided in subsection (a)(3)(B) of this section, the debtor shall be discharged from a debt of a kind specified in paragraph (2), (4), or (6)~~, or (15)~~ of subsection (a) of this section, unless, on request of the creditor to whom such debt is owed, and after notice and a hearing, the court determines such debt to be excepted from discharge under paragraph (2), (4), or (6)~~, or (15)~~ as the case may be, of subsection (a) of this section.

(2) Paragraph (1) shall not apply in the case of a Federal depository institutions regulatory agency seeking, in its capacity as conservator, receiver, or liquidating agent for an insured depository institution, to recover a debt described in subsection (a)(2), (a)(4), (a)(6), or (a)(11) owed to such institution by an institution-affiliated party unless the receiver, conservator, or liquidating agent was appointed in time to reasonably comply, or for a Federal depository institutions regulatory agency

acting in its corporate capacity as a successor to such receiver, conservator, or liquidating agent to reasonably comply, with subsection (a)(3)(B) as a creditor of such institution-affiliated party with respect to such debt.

(d) If a creditor requests a determination of dischargeability of a consumer debt under subsection (a)(2) of this section, and such debt is discharged, the court shall grant judgment in favor of the debtor for the costs of, and a reasonable attorney's fee for, the proceeding if the court finds that the position of the creditor was not substantially justified, except that the court shall not award such costs and fees if special circumstances would make the award unjust.

(e) Any institution-affiliated party of an insured depository institution shall be considered to be acting in a fiduciary capacity with respect to the purposes of subsection (a)(4) or (11).

§ 524. Effect of discharge

(a) A discharge in a case under this title—

(1) voids any judgment at any time obtained, to the extent that such judgment is a determination of the personal liability of the debtor with respect to any debt discharged under section 727, 944, 1141, 1228, or 1328 of this title, whether or not discharge of such debt is waived;

(2) operates as an injunction against the commencement or continuation of an action, the employment of process, or an act, to collect, recover or offset any such debt as a personal liability of the debtor, whether or not discharge of such debt is waived; and

(3) operates as an injunction against the commencement or continuation of an action, the employment of process, or an act, to collect or recover from, or offset against, property of the debtor of the kind specified in section 541(a)(2) of this title that is acquired after the commencement of the case, on account of any allowable community claim, except a community claim that is excepted from discharge under section 523, 1228(a)(1), or 1328(a)(1) ~~of this title~~, or that would be so excepted, determined in accordance with the provisions of sections 523(c) and 523(d) of this title, in a case concerning the debtor's spouse commenced on the date of the filing of the petition in the case concerning the debtor, whether or not discharge of the debt based on such community claim is waived.

(b) Subsection (a)(3) of this section does not apply if—

(1)(A) the debtor's spouse is a debtor in a case under this title, or a bankrupt or a debtor in a case under the Bankruptcy Act, commenced within six years of the date of the filing of the petition in the case concerning the debtor; and

(B) the court does not grant the debtor's spouse a discharge in such case concerning the debtor's spouse; or

(2)(A) the court would not grant the debtor's spouse a discharge in a case under chapter 7 of this title concerning such spouse commenced on the date of the filing of the petition in the case concerning the debtor; and

(B) a determination that the court would not so grant such discharge is made by the bankruptcy court within the time and in the manner provided for a determination under section 727 of this title of whether a debtor is granted a discharge.

(c) An agreement between a holder of a claim and the debtor, the consideration for which, in whole or in part, is based on a debt that is dischargeable in a case under this title is enforceable only to any extent enforceable under applicable nonbankruptcy law, whether or not discharge of such debt is waived, only if—

(1) such agreement was made before the granting of the discharge under section 727, 1141, 1228, or 1328 of this title;

~~(2)(A) such agreement contains a clear and conspicuous statement which advises the debtor that the agreement may be rescinded at any time prior to discharge or within sixty days after such agreement is filed with the court, whichever occurs later, by giving notice of rescission to the holder of such claim; and~~

~~(B) such agreement contains a clear and conspicuous statement which advises the debtor that such agreement is not required under this title, under nonbankruptcy law, or under any agreement not in accordance with the provisions of this subsection;~~

(2) the debtor received the disclosures described in subsection (k) at or before the time at which the debtor signed the agreement;

(3) such agreement has been filed with the court and, if applicable, accompanied by a declaration or an affidavit of the attorney that represented the debtor during the course of negotiating an agreement under this subsection, which states that—

(A) such agreement represents a fully informed and voluntary agreement by the debtor;

(B) such agreement does not impose an undue hardship on the debtor or a dependent of the debtor; and

(C) the attorney fully advised the debtor of the legal effect and consequences of—

(i) an agreement of the kind specified in this subsection; and

(ii) any default under such an agreement;

(4) the debtor has not rescinded such agreement at any time prior to discharge or within sixty days after such agreement is filed with the court, whichever occurs later, by giving notice of rescission to the holder of such claim;

(5) the provisions of subsection (d) of this section have been complied with; and

(6)(A) in a case concerning an individual who was not represented by an attorney during the course of negotiating an agreement under this subsection, the court approves such agreement as—

(i) not imposing an undue hardship on the debtor or a dependent of the debtor; and

(ii) in the best interest of the debtor.

(B) Subparagraph (A) shall not apply to the extent that such debt is a consumer debt secured by real property.

(d) In a case concerning an individual, when the court has determined whether to grant or not to grant a discharge under section 727, 1141, 1228, or 1328 of this title, the court may hold a hearing at which the debtor shall appear in person. At any such hearing, the court shall inform the debtor that a discharge has been granted or the reason why a discharge has not been granted. If a discharge has been granted and if the debtor desires to make an agreement of the kind specified in subsection (c) of this section and was not represented by an attorney during the course of negotiating such agreement, then the court shall hold a hearing at which the debtor shall appear in person and at any such hearing the court shall—

(1) inform the debtor—

(A) that such an agreement is not required under this title, under nonbankruptcy law, or under any agreement not made in accordance with the provisions of subsection (c) of this section; and

(B) of the legal effect and consequences of—

(i) an agreement of the kind specified in subsection (c) of this section; and

(ii) a default under such an agreement; and

(2) determine whether the agreement that the debtor desires to make complies with the requirements of subsection (c)(6) of this section, if the consideration for such agreement is based in whole or in part on a consumer debt that is not secured by real property of the debtor.

(e) Except as provided in subsection (a)(3) of this section, discharge of a debt of the debtor does not affect the liability of any other entity on, or the property of any other entity for, such debt.

(f) Nothing contained in subsection (c) or (d) of this section prevents a debtor from voluntarily repaying any debt.

(g)(1)(A) After notice and hearing, a court that enters an order confirming a plan of reorganization under chapter 11 may issue, in connection with such order, an injunction in accordance with this subsection to supplement the injunctive effect of a discharge under this section.

(B) An injunction may be issued under subparagraph (A) to enjoin entities from taking legal action for the purpose of directly or indirectly collecting, recovering, or receiving payment or recovery with respect to any claim or demand that, under a plan of reorganization, is to be paid in whole or in part by a trust described in paragraph (2)(B)(i), except such legal actions as are expressly allowed by the injunction, the confirmation order, or the plan of reorganization.

(2)(A) Subject to subsection (h), if the requirements of subparagraph (B) are met at the time an injunction described in paragraph (1) is entered, then after entry of such injunction, any proceeding that involves the validity, application, construction, or modification of such injunction, or of this subsection with respect to such injunction, may be commenced only in the district court in which such injunction was entered, and such court shall have exclusive jurisdiction over any such proceeding without regard to the amount in controversy.

(B) The requirements of this subparagraph are that—

(i) the injunction is to be implemented in connection with a trust that, pursuant to the plan of reorganization—

(I) is to assume the liabilities of a debtor which at the time of entry of the order for relief has been named as a defendant in personal injury, wrongful death, or property-damage actions seeking recovery for damages allegedly caused by the presence of, or exposure to, asbestos or asbestos-containing products;

(II) is to be funded in whole or in part by the securities of 1 or more debtors involved in such plan and by the obligation of such debtor or debtors to make future payments, including dividends;

(III) is to own, or by the exercise of rights granted under such plan would be entitled to own if specified contingencies occur, a majority of the voting shares of—

(aa) each such debtor;

(bb) the parent corporation of each such debtor; or

(cc) a subsidiary of each such debtor that is also a debtor; and

(IV) is to use its assets or income to pay claims and demands; and

(ii) subject to subsection (h), the court determines that—

(I) the debtor is likely to be subject to substantial future demands for payment arising out of the same or similar conduct or events that gave rise to the claims that are addressed by the injunction;

(II) the actual amounts, numbers, and timing of such future demands cannot be determined;

(III) pursuit of such demands outside the procedures prescribed by such plan is likely to threaten the plan's purpose to deal equitably with claims and future demands;

(IV) as part of the process of seeking confirmation of such plan—

(aa) the terms of the injunction proposed to be issued under paragraph (1)(A), including any provisions barring actions against third parties pursuant to paragraph (4)(A), are set out in such plan and in any disclosure statement supporting the plan; and

(bb) a separate class or classes of the claimants whose claims are to be addressed by a trust described in clause (i) is established and votes, by at least 75 percent of those voting, in favor of the plan; and

(V) subject to subsection (h), pursuant to court orders or otherwise, the trust will operate through mechanisms such as structured, periodic, or supplemental payments, pro rata distributions, matrices, or periodic review of estimates of the numbers and values of present claims and future demands, or other comparable mechanisms, that provide reasonable assurance that the trust will value, and be in a financial position to pay, present claims and future demands that involve similar claims in substantially the same manner.

(3)(A) If the requirements of paragraph (2)(B) are met and the order confirming the plan of reorganization was issued or affirmed by the district court that has jurisdiction over the reorganization case, then after the time for appeal of the order that issues or affirms the plan—

(i) the injunction shall be valid and enforceable and may not be revoked or modified by any court except through appeal in accordance with paragraph (6);

(ii) no entity that pursuant to such plan or thereafter becomes a direct or indirect transferee of, or successor to any assets of, a debtor or trust that is the subject of the injunction shall be liable with respect to any claim or demand made against such entity by reason of its becoming such a transferee or successor; and

(iii) no entity that pursuant to such plan or thereafter makes a loan to such a debtor or trust or to such a successor or transferee shall, by reason of making the loan, be liable with respect to any claim or demand made against such entity, nor shall any pledge of assets made in connection with such a loan be upset or impaired for that reason;

(B) Subparagraph (A) shall not be construed to—

(i) imply that an entity described in subparagraph (A) (ii) or (iii) would, if this paragraph were not applicable, necessarily be liable to any entity by reason of any of the acts described in subparagraph (A);

(ii) relieve any such entity of the duty to comply with, or of liability under, any Federal or State law regarding the making of a fraudulent conveyance in a transaction described in subparagraph (A) (ii) or (iii); or

(iii) relieve a debtor of the debtor's obligation to comply with the terms of the plan of reorganization, or affect the power of the court to exercise its authority under sections 1141 and 1142 to compel the debtor to do so.

(4)(A)(i) Subject to subparagraph (B), an injunction described in paragraph (1) shall be valid and enforceable against all entities that it addresses.

(ii) Notwithstanding the provisions of section 524(e), such an injunction may bar any action directed against a third party who is identifiable from the terms of such injunction (by name or as part of an identifiable group) and is alleged to be directly or indirectly liable for the conduct of, claims against, or demands on the debtor to the extent such alleged liability of such third party arises by reason of—

(I) the third party's ownership of a financial interest in the debtor, a past or present affiliate of the debtor, or a predecessor in interest of the debtor;

(II) the third party's involvement in the management of the debtor or a predecessor in interest of the debtor, or service as an officer, director or employee of the debtor or a related party;

(III) the third party's provision of insurance to the debtor or a related party; or

(IV) the third party's involvement in a transaction changing the corporate structure, or in a loan or other financial transaction affecting the financial condition, of the debtor or a related party, including but not limited to—

(aa) involvement in providing financing (debt or equity), or advice to an entity involved in such a transaction; or

(bb) acquiring or selling a financial interest in an entity as part of such a transaction.

(iii) As used in this subparagraph, the term "related party" means—

(I) a past or present affiliate of the debtor;

(II) a predecessor in interest of the debtor; or

(III) any entity that owned a financial interest in—

(aa) the debtor;

(bb) a past or present affiliate of the debtor; or

(cc) a predecessor in interest of the debtor.

(B) Subject to subsection (h), if, under a plan of reorganization, a kind of demand described in such plan is to be paid in whole or in part by a trust described in paragraph (2)(B)(i) in connection with which an injunction described in paragraph (1) is to be implemented, then such injunction shall be valid and enforceable with respect to a demand of such kind made, after such plan is confirmed, against the debtor or debtors involved, or against a third party described in subparagraph (A)(ii), if—

(i) as part of the proceedings leading to issuance of such injunction, the court appoints a legal representative for the purpose of protecting the rights of persons that might subsequently assert demands of such kind, and

(ii) the court determines, before entering the order confirming such plan, that identifying such debtor or debtors, or such third party (by name or as part of an identifiable group), in such injunction with respect to such demands for purposes of this subparagraph is fair and equitable with respect to the persons that might subsequently assert such demands, in light of the benefits provided, or to be provided, to such trust on behalf of such debtor or debtors or such third party.

(5) In this subsection, the term "demand" means a demand for payment, present or future, that—

(A) was not a claim during the proceedings leading to the confirmation of a plan of reorganization;

(B) arises out of the same or similar conduct or events that gave rise to the claims addressed by the injunction issued under paragraph (1); and

(C) pursuant to the plan, is to be paid by a trust described in paragraph (2)(B)(i).

(6) Paragraph (3)(A)(i) does not bar an action taken by or at the direction of an appellate court on appeal of an injunction issued under paragraph (1) or of the order of confirmation that relates to the injunction.

(7) This subsection does not affect the operation of section 1144 or the power of the district court to refer a proceeding under section 157 of title 28 or any reference of a proceeding made prior to the date of the enactment of this subsection.

(h) Application to existing injunctions. For purposes of subsection (g)—

(1) subject to paragraph (2), if an injunction of the kind described in subsection (g)(1)(B) was issued before the date of the enactment of this Act, as part of a plan of reorganization confirmed by an order entered before such date, then the injunction shall be considered to meet the requirements of subsection (g)(2)(B) for purposes of subsection (g)(2)(A), and to satisfy subsection (g)(4)(A)(ii), if—

(A) the court determined at the time the plan was confirmed that the plan was fair and equitable in accordance with the requirements of section 1129(b);

(B) as part of the proceedings leading to issuance of such injunction and confirmation of such plan, the court had appointed a legal representative for the purpose of protecting the rights of persons that might subsequently assert demands described in subsection (g)(4)(B) with respect to such plan; and

(C) such legal representative did not object to confirmation of such plan or issuance of such injunction; and

(2) for purposes of paragraph (1), if a trust described in subsection (g)(2)(B)(i) is subject to a court order on the date of the enactment of this Act staying such trust from settling or paying further claims—

(A) the requirements of subsection (g)(2)(B)(ii)(V) shall not apply with respect to such trust until such stay is lifted or dissolved; and

(B) if such trust meets such requirements on the date such stay is lifted or dissolved, such trust shall be considered to have met such requirements continuously from the date of the enactment of this Act.

(i) The willful failure of a creditor to credit payments received under a plan confirmed under this title, unless the order confirming the plan is revoked, the plan is in default, or the creditor has not received payments required to be made under the plan in the manner required by the plan (including crediting the amounts required under the plan), shall constitute a violation of an injunction under subsection (a)(2) if the act of the creditor to collect and failure to credit payments in the manner required by the plan caused material injury to the debtor.

(j) Subsection (a)(2) does not operate as an injunction against an act by a creditor that is the holder of a secured claim, if—

(1) such creditor retains a security interest in real property that is the principal residence of the debtor;

(2) such act is in the ordinary course of business between the creditor and the debtor; and

(3) such act is limited to seeking or obtaining periodic payments associated with a valid security interest in lieu of pursuit of in rem relief to enforce the lien.

(k)(1) The disclosures required under subsection (c)(2) shall consist of the disclosure statement described in paragraph (3), completed as required in that paragraph, together with the agreement specified in subsection (c), statement, declaration, motion and order described, respectively, in paragraphs (4) through (8), and shall be the only disclosures required in connection with entering into such agreement.

(2) Disclosures made under paragraph (1) shall be made clearly and conspicuously and in writing. The terms 'Amount Reaffirmed' and 'Annual Percentage Rate' shall be disclosed more conspicuously than other terms, data or information provided in connection with this disclosure, except that the phrases 'Before agreeing to reaffirm a debt, review these important disclosures' and 'Summary of Reaffirmation Agreement' may be equally conspicuous. Disclosures may be made in a different order and may use terminology different from that set forth in paragraphs (2) through (8), except that the terms 'Amount Reaffirmed' and 'Annual Percentage Rate' must be used where indicated.

(3) The disclosure statement required under this paragraph shall consist of the following:

(A) The statement: 'Part A: Before agreeing to reaffirm a debt, review these important disclosures:';

(B) Under the heading 'Summary of Reaffirmation Agreement', the statement: 'This Summary is made pursuant to the requirements of the Bankruptcy Code';

(C) The 'Amount Reaffirmed', using that term, which shall be—

(i) the total amount of debt that the debtor agrees to reaffirm by entering into an agreement of the kind specified in subsection (c), and

(ii) the total of any fees and costs accrued as of the date of the disclosure statement, related to such total amount.

(D) In conjunction with the disclosure of the 'Amount Reaffirmed', the statements—

(i) 'The amount of debt you have agreed to reaffirm'; and

(ii) 'Your credit agreement may obligate you to pay additional amounts which may come due after the date of this disclosure. Consult your credit agreement.'.

(E) The 'Annual Percentage Rate', using that term, which shall be disclosed as—

(i) if, at the time the petition is filed, the debt is an extension of credit under an open end credit plan, as the terms 'credit' and 'open end credit plan' are defined in section 103 of the Truth in Lending Act, then—

(I) the annual percentage rate determined under paragraphs (5) and 6) of section 127(b) of the Truth in Lending Act, as applicable, as disclosed to the debtor in the most recent periodic statement prior to entering into an agreement of the kind specified in subsection (c) or, if no such periodic statement has been given to the debtor during the prior 6 months, the annual percentage rate as it would have been so disclosed at the time the disclosure statement is given to the debtor, or to the extent this annual percentage rate is not readily available or not applicable, then

(II) the simple interest rate applicable to the amount reaffirmed as of the date the disclosure statement is given to the debtor, or if different simple interest rates apply to different balances, the simple interest rate applicable to each such balance, identifying the amount of each such balance included in the amount reaffirmed, or

(III) if the entity making the disclosure elects, to disclose the annual percentage rate under subclause (I) and the simple interest rate under subclause (II); or

(ii) if, at the time the petition is filed, the debt is an extension of credit other than under an open end credit plan, as the terms 'credit' and 'open end credit plan' are defined in section 103 of the Truth in Lending Act, then—

(I) the annual percentage rate under section 128(a)(4) of the Truth in Lending Act, as disclosed to the debtor in the most recent disclosure statement given to the debtor prior to the entering into an agreement of the kind specified in subsection (c) with respect to the debt, or, if no such disclosure statement was given to the debtor, the annual percentage rate as it would have been so disclosed at the time the disclosure statement is given to the debtor, or to the extent this annual percentage rate is not readily available or not applicable, then

(II) the simple interest rate applicable to the amount reaffirmed as of the date the disclosure statement is given to the debtor, or if different simple interest rates apply to different balances, the simple interest rate applicable to each such balance, identifying the amount of such balance included in the amount reaffirmed, or

(III) if the entity making the disclosure elects, to disclose the annual percentage rate under (I) and the simple interest rate under (II).

(F) If the underlying debt transaction was disclosed as a variable rate transaction on the most recent disclosure given under the Truth in Lending Act, by stating 'The interest rate on your loan may be a variable interest rate which changes from time to time, so that the annual percentage rate disclosed here may be higher or lower.'.

(G) If the debt is secured by a security interest which has not been waived in whole or in part or determined to be void by a final order of the court at the time of the disclosure, by disclosing that a security interest or lien in goods or property is asserted over some or all of the debts the debtor is reaffirming and listing the items and their original purchase price that are subject to the asserted security interest, or if not a purchase-money security interest then listing by items or types and the original amount of the loan.

(H) At the election of the creditor, a statement of the repayment schedule using 1 or a combination of the following—

(i) by making the statement: 'Your first payment in the amount of $ XXX is due on XXX but the future payment amount may be different. Consult your reaffirmation agreement or credit agreement, as applicable.', and stating the amount of the first payment and the due date of that payment in the places provided;

(ii) by making the statement: 'Your payment schedule will be:', and describing the repayment schedule with the number, amount and due dates or period of payments scheduled to repay the debts reaffirmed to the extent then known by the disclosing party; or

(iii) by describing the debtor's repayment obligations with reasonable specificity to the extent then known by the disclosing party.

(I) The following statement: 'Note: When this disclosure refers to what a creditor "may" do, it does not use the word "may" to give the creditor specific permission. The word "may" is used to tell you what might occur if the law permits the creditor to take the action.If you have questions about your reaffirming a debt or what the law requires, consult with the attorney who helped you negotiate this agreement reaffirming a debt. If you don' t have an attorney helping you, the judge will explain the effect of your reaffirming a debt when the hearing on the reaffirmation agreement is held.'.

(J)(i) The following additional statements:

"Reaffirming a debt is a serious financial decision.The law requires you to take certain steps to make sure the decision is in your best interest. If these steps are not completed, the reaffirmation agreement is not effective, even though you have signed it.

"1. Read the disclosures in this Part A carefully. Consider the decision to reaffirm carefully. Then, if you want to reaffirm, sign the reaffirmation agreement in Part B (or you may use a separate agreement you and your creditor agree on).

"2. Complete and sign Part D and be sure you can afford to make the payments you are agreeing to make and have received a copy of the disclosure statement and a completed and signed reaffirmation agreement.

"3. If you were represented by an attorney during the negotiation of your reaffirmation agreement, the attorney must have signed the certification in Part C.

"4. If you were not represented by an attorney during the negotiation of your reaffirmation agreement, you must have completed and signed Part E.

"5. The original of this disclosure must be filed with the court by you or your creditor.If a separate reaffirmation agreement (other than the one in Part B) has been signed, it must be attached.

"6. If you were represented by an attorney during the negotiation of your reaffirmation agreement, your reaffirmation agreement becomes effective upon filing with the court unless the reaffirmation is presumed to be an undue hardship as explained in Part D.

"7. If you were not represented by an attorney during the negotiation of your reaffirmation agreement, it will not be effective unless the court approves it. The court will notify you of the hearing on your reaffirmation agreement. You must attend this hearing in bankruptcy court where the judge will review your reaffirmation agreement. The bankruptcy court must approve your reaffirmation agreement as consistent with your best interests, except that no court approval is required if your reaffirmation agreement is for a consumer debt secured by a mortgage, deed of trust, security deed, or other lien on your real property, like your home.

"Your right to rescind (cancel) your reaffirmation agreement. You may rescind (cancel) your reaffirmation agreement at any time before the bankruptcy court enters a discharge order, or before the expiration of the 60-day period that begins on the date your reaffirmation agreement is filed with the court, whichever occurs later. To rescind (cancel) your reaffirmation agreement, you must notify the creditor that your reaffirmation agreement is rescinded (or canceled).

"What are your obligations if you reaffirm the debt? A reaffirmed debt remains your personal legal obligation. It is not discharged in your bankruptcy case.That means that if you default on your reaffirmed debt after your bankruptcy case is over, your creditor may be able to take your property or your wages. Otherwise, your obligations will be determined by the reaffirmation agreement which may have changed the terms of the original agreement. For example, if you are reaffirming an open end credit agreement, the creditor may be permitted by that agreement or applicable law to change the terms of that agreement in the future under certain conditions.

"Are you required to enter into a reaffirmation agreement by any law? No, you are not required to reaffirm a debt by any law. Only agree to reaffirm a debt if it is in your best interest. Be sure you can afford the payments you agree to make.

"What if your creditor has a security interest or lien? Your bankruptcy discharge does not eliminate any lien on your property. A 'lien' is often referred to as a security interest, deed of trust, mortgage or security deed. Even if you do not reaffirm and your personal liability on the debt is discharged, because of the lien your creditor may still have the right to take the security property if you do not pay the debt or default on it. If the lien is on an item of personal property that is exempt under your State's law or that the trustee has abandoned, you may be able to redeem the item rather than reaffirm the debt. To redeem, you make a single payment to the creditor equal to the current value of the security property, as agreed by the parties or determined by the court.".

(ii) In the case of a reaffirmation under subsection (m)(2), numbered paragraph 6 in the disclosures required by clause (i) of this subparagraph shall read as follows:

"6. If you were represented by an attorney during the negotiation of your reaffirmation agreement, your reaffirmation agreement becomes effective upon filing with the court.".

(4) The form of such agreement required under this paragraph shall consist of the following:

"Part B: Reaffirmation Agreement. I (we) agree to reaffirm the debts arising under the credit agreement described below.

"Brief description of credit agreement:

"Description of any changes to the credit agreement made as part of this reaffirmation agreement:

"Signature: Date:

"Borrower:

"Co-borrower, if also reaffirming these debts:

"Accepted by creditor:

"Date of creditor acceptance:".

(5) The declaration shall consist of the following:

(A) The following certification:

"Part C: Certification by Debtor's Attorney (If Any).

"I hereby certify that (1) this agreement represents a fully informed and voluntary agreement by the debtor; (2) this agreement does not impose an undue hardship on the debtor or any dependent of the debtor; and (3) I have fully advised the debtor of the legal effect and consequences of this agreement and any default under this agreement.

"Signature of Debtor's Attorney: Date:".

(B) If a presumption of undue hardship has been established with respect to such agreement, such certification shall state that in the opinion of the attorney, the debtor is able to make the payment.

(C) In the case of a reaffirmation agreement under subsection (m)(2), subparagraph (B) is not applicable.

(6)(A) The statement in support of such agreement, which the debtor shall sign and date prior to filing with the court, shall consist of the following:

"Part D: Debtor's Statement in Support of Reaffirmation Agreement.

"1. I believe this reaffirmation agreement will not impose an undue hardship on my dependents or me. I can afford to make the payments on the reaffirmed debt because my monthly income (take home pay plus any other income received) is $_____, and my actual current monthly expenses including monthly payments on post-bankruptcy debt and other reaffirmation agreements total $_____, leaving $____ to make the required payments on this reaffirmed debt. I understand that if my income less my monthly expenses does not leave enough to make the payments, this reaffirmation agreement is presumed to be an undue hardship on me and must be reviewed by the court.However, this presumption may be overcome if I explain to the satisfaction of the court how I can afford to make the payments here: _____.

"2. I received a copy of the Reaffirmation Disclosure Statement in Part A and a completed and signed reaffirmation agreement.".

(B) Where the debtor is represented by an attorney and is reaffirming a debt owed to a creditor defined in section 19(b)(1)(A)(iv) of the Federal Reserve Act, the statement of support of the reaffirmation agreement, which the debtor shall sign and date prior to filing with the court, shall consist of the following:

'I believe this reaffirmation agreement is in my financial interest. I can afford to make the payments on the reaffirmed debt. I received a copy of the Reaffirmation Disclosure Statement in Part A and a completed and signed reaffirmation agreement.'

(7) The motion that may be used if approval of such agreement by the court is required in order for it to be effective shall be signed and dated by the movant and shall consist of the following:

"Part E: Motion for Court Approval (To be completed only if the debtor is not represented by an attorney.). I (we), the debtor(s), affirm the following to be true and correct:

"I am not represented by an attorney in connection with this reaffirmation agreement.

"I believe this reaffirmation agreement is in my best interest based on the income and expenses I have disclosed in my Statement in Support of this reaffirmation agreement, and because (provide any additional relevant reasons the court should consider):

"Therefore, I ask the court for an order approving this reaffirmation agreement."

(8) The court order, which may be used to approve a such agreement, shall consist of the following:

"Court Order: The court grants the debtor's motion and approves the reaffirmation agreement described above."

(*l*) Notwithstanding any other provision of this title the following shall apply:

(1) A creditor may accept payments from a debtor before and after the filing of an agreement of the kind specified in subsection (c) with the court.

(2) A creditor may accept payments from a debtor under such agreement that the creditor believes in good faith to be effective.

(3) The requirements of subsections (c)(2) and (k) shall be satisfied if disclosures required under those subsections are given in good faith.

(m)(1) Until 60 days after an agreement of the kind specified in subsection (c) is filed with the court (or such additional period as the court, after notice and a hearing and for cause, orders before the expiration of such period), it shall be presumed that such agreement is an undue hardship on the debtor if the debtor's monthly income less the debtor's monthly expenses as shown on the debtor's completed and signed statement in support of such agreement required under subsection (k)(6)(A) is less than the scheduled payments on the reaffirmed debt. This presumption shall be reviewed by the court. The presumption may be rebutted in writing by the debtor if the statement includes an explanation that identifies additional sources of funds to make the payments as agreed upon under the terms of such agreement. If the presumption is not rebutted to the satisfaction of the court, the court may disapprove such agreement. No agreement shall be disapproved without notice and a hearing to the debtor and creditor and such hearing shall be concluded before the entry of the debtor's discharge.

(2) This subsection does not apply to reaffirmation agreements where the creditor is a credit union, as defined in section 19(b)(1)(A)(iv) of the Federal Reserve Act.

§ 525. Protection against discriminatory treatment

(a) Except as provided in the Perishable Agricultural Commodities Act, 1930, the Packers and Stockyards Act, 1921, and section 1 of the Act entitled "An Act making appropriations for the Department of Agriculture for the fiscal year ending June 30, 1944, and for other purposes," approved July 12, 1943, a governmental unit may not deny, revoke, suspend, or refuse to renew a license, permit, charter, franchise, or other similar grant to, condition such a grant to, discriminate with respect to such a grant against, deny employment to, terminate the employment of, or discriminate with respect to employment against, a person that is or has been a debtor under this title or a bankrupt or a debtor under the Bankruptcy Act, or another person with whom such bankrupt or debtor has been associated, solely because such bankrupt or debtor is or has been a debtor under this title or a bankrupt or debtor under the Bankruptcy Act, has been insolvent before the commencement of the case under this title, or during the case but before the debtor is granted or denied a discharge, or has not paid a debt that is dischargeable in the case under this title or that was discharged under the Bankruptcy Act.

(b) No private employer may terminate the employment of, or discriminate with respect to employment against, an individual who is or has been a debtor under this title, a debtor or bankrupt under the Bankruptcy Act, or an individual associated with such debtor or bankrupt, solely because such debtor or bankrupt—

(1) is or has been a debtor under this title or a debtor or bankrupt under the Bankruptcy Act;

(2) has been insolvent before the commencement of a case under this title or during the case but before the grant or denial of a discharge; or

(3) has not paid a debt that is dischargeable in a case under this title or that was discharged under the Bankruptcy Act.

(c)(1) A governmental unit that operates a student grant or loan program and a person engaged in a business that includes the making of loans guaranteed or insured under a student loan program may not deny a student grant, loan, loan guarantee, or loan insurance to a person that is or has been a debtor under this title or a bankrupt or debtor under the Bankruptcy Act, or another person with whom the debtor or bankrupt has been associated, because the debtor or bankrupt is or has been a debtor under this title or a bankrupt or debtor under the Bankruptcy Act, has been insolvent before the commencement of a case under this title or during the pendency of the case but before the debtor is granted or denied a discharge, or has not paid a debt that is dischargeable in the case under this title or that was discharged under the Bankruptcy Act.

(2) In this section, "student loan program" means ~~the~~ any program operated under ~~part B, D, or E of~~ title IV of the Higher Education Act of 1965 or a similar program operated under State or local law.

§ 526. Restrictions on debt relief agencies

(a) A debt relief agency shall not—

(1) fail to perform any service that such agency informed an assisted person or prospective assisted person it would provide in connection with a case or proceeding under this title;

(2) make any statement, or counsel or advise any assisted person or prospective assisted person to make a statement in a document filed in a case or proceeding under this title, that is untrue and misleading, or that upon the exercise of reasonable care, should have been known by such agency to be untrue or misleading;

(3) misrepresent to any assisted person or prospective assisted person, directly or indirectly, affirmatively or by material omission, with respect to—

(A) the services that such agency will provide to such person; or

(B) the benefits and risks that may result if such person becomes a debtor in a case under this title; or

(4) advise an assisted person or prospective assisted person to incur more debt in contemplation of such person filing a case under this title or to pay an attorney or bankruptcy petition preparer fee or charge for services performed as part of preparing for or representing a debtor in a case under this title.

(b) Any waiver by any assisted person of any protection or right provided under this section shall not be enforceable against the debtor by any Federal or State court or any other person, but may be enforced against a debt relief agency.

(c)(1) Any contract for bankruptcy assistance between a debt relief agency and an assisted person that does not comply with the material requirements of this section, section 527, or section 528 shall be void and may not be enforced by any Federal or State court or by any other person, other than such assisted person.

(2) Any debt relief agency shall be liable to an assisted person in the amount of any fees or charges in connection with providing bankruptcy assistance to such person that such debt relief agency has received, for actual damages, and for reasonable attorneys' fees and costs if such agency is found, after notice and a hearing, to have—

(A) intentionally or negligently failed to comply with any provision of this section, section 527, or section 528 with respect to a case or proceeding under this title for such assisted person;

(B) provided bankruptcy assistance to an assisted person in a case or proceeding under this title that is dismissed or converted to a case under another chapter of this title because of such agency's intentional or negligent failure to file any required document including those specified in section 521; or

(C) intentionally or negligently disregarded the material requirements of this title or the Federal Rules of Bankruptcy Procedure applicable to such agency.

(3) In addition to such other remedies as are provided under State law, whenever the chief law enforcement officer of a State, or an official or agency designated by a State, has reason to believe that any person has violated or is violating this section, the State—

(A) may bring an action to enjoin such violation;

(B) may bring an action on behalf of its residents to recover the actual damages of assisted persons arising from such violation, including any liability under paragraph (2); and

(C) in the case of any successful action under subparagraph (A) or (B), shall be awarded the costs of the action and reasonable attorneys' fees as determined by the court.

(4) The district courts of the United States for districts located in the State shall have concurrent jurisdiction of any action under subparagraph (A) or (B) of paragraph (3).

(5) Notwithstanding any other provision of Federal law and in addition to any other remedy provided under Federal or State law, if the court, on its own motion or on the motion of the United States trustee or the debtor, finds that a person intentionally violated this section, or engaged in a clear and consistent pattern or practice of violating this section, the court may—

(A) enjoin the violation of such section; or

(B) impose an appropriate civil penalty against such person.

(d) No provision of this section, section 527, or section 528 shall—

(1) annul, alter, affect, or exempt any person subject to such sections from complying with any law of any State except to the extent that such law is inconsistent with those sections, and then only to the extent of the inconsistency; or

(2) be deemed to limit or curtail the authority or ability—

(A) of a State or subdivision or instrumentality thereof, to determine and enforce qualifications for the practice of law under the laws of that State; or

(B) of a Federal court to determine and enforce the qualifications for the practice of law before that court.

§ 527. Disclosures

(a) A debt relief agency providing bankruptcy assistance to an assisted person shall provide—

(1) the written notice required under section 342(b)(1); and

(2) to the extent not covered in the written notice described in paragraph (1), and not later than 3 business days after the first date on which a debt relief agency first offers to provide any bankruptcy assistance services to an assisted person, a clear and conspicuous written notice advising assisted persons that—

(A) all information that the assisted person is required to provide with a petition and thereafter during a case under this title is required to be complete, accurate, and truthful;

(B) all assets and all liabilities are required to be completely and accurately disclosed in the documents filed to commence the case, and the replacement value of each asset as defined in section 506 must be stated in those documents where requested after reasonable inquiry to establish such value;

(C) current monthly income, the amounts specified in section 707(b)(2), and, in a case under chapter 13 of this title, disposable income (determined in accordance with section 707(b)(2), are required to be stated after reasonable inquiry; and

(D) information that an assisted person provides during their case may be audited pursuant to this title, and that failure to provide such information may result in dismissal of the case under this title or other sanction, including a criminal sanctions.

(b) A debt relief agency providing bankruptcy assistance to an assisted person shall provide each assisted person at the same time as the notices required under subsection (a)(1) the following statement, to the extent applicable, or one substantially similar.The statement shall be clear and conspicuous and shall be in a single document separate from other documents or notices provided to the assisted person:

"IMPORTANT INFORMATION ABOUT BANKRUPTCY ASSISTANCE SERVICES FROM AN ATTORNEY OR BANKRUPTCY PETITION PREPARER.

"If you decide to seek bankruptcy relief, you can represent yourself, you can hire an attorney to represent you, or you can get help in some localities from a bankruptcy petition preparer who is not an attorney. THE LAW REQUIRES AN ATTORNEY OR BANKRUPTCY PETITION PREPARER TO GIVE YOU A WRITTEN CONTRACT SPECIFYING WHAT THE ATTORNEY OR BANKRUPTCY PETITION PREPARER WILL DO FOR YOU AND HOW MUCH IT WILL COST. Ask to see the contract before you hire anyone.

"The following information helps you understand what must be done in a routine bankruptcy case to help you evaluate how much service you need. Although bankruptcy can be complex, many cases are routine.

"Before filing a bankruptcy case, either you or your attorney should analyze your eligibility for different forms of debt relief available under the Bankruptcy Code and which form of relief is most likely to be beneficial for you. Be sure you understand the relief you can obtain and its limitations.To file a bankruptcy case, documents called a Petition, Schedules and Statement of Financial Affairs, as well as in some cases a Statement of Intention need to be prepared correctly and filed with the bankruptcy court. You will have to pay a filing fee to the bankruptcy court. Once your case starts, you will have to attend the required first meeting of creditors where you may be questioned by a court official called a 'trustee' and by creditors.

"If you choose to file a chapter 7 case, you may be asked by a creditor to reaffirm a debt. You may want help deciding whether to do so. A creditor is not permitted to coerce you into reaffirming your debts.

"If you choose to file a chapter 13 case in which you repay your creditors what you can afford over 3 to 5 years, you may also want help with preparing your chapter 13 plan and with the confirmation hearing on your plan which will be before a bankruptcy judge.

"If you select another type of relief under the Bankruptcy Code other than chapter 7 or chapter 13, you will want to find out what should be done from someone familiar with that type of relief.

"Your bankruptcy case may also involve litigation. You are generally permitted to represent yourself in litigation in bankruptcy court, but only attorneys, not bankruptcy petition preparers, can give you legal advice.".

(c) Except to the extent the debt relief agency provides the required information itself after reasonably diligent inquiry of the assisted person or others so as to obtain such information reasonably accurately for inclusion on the petition, schedules or statement of financial affairs, a debt relief agency providing bankruptcy assistance to an assisted person, to the extent permitted by nonbankruptcy law, shall provide each assisted person at the time required for the notice required under subsection (a)(1) reasonably sufficient information (which shall be provided in a clear and conspicuous writing) to the assisted person on how to provide all the information the assisted person is required to provide under this title pursuant to section 521, including—

(1) how to value assets at replacement value, determine current monthly income, the amounts specified in section 707(b)(2) and, in a chapter 13 case, how to determine disposable income in accordance with section 707(b)(2) and related calculations;

(2) how to complete the list of creditors, including how to determine what amount is owed and what address for the creditor should be shown; and

(3) how to determine what property is exempt and how to value exempt property at replacement value as defined in section 506.

(d) A debt relief agency shall maintain a copy of the notices required under subsection (a) of this section for 2 years after the date on which the notice is given the assisted person.

§ 528. Requirements for debt relief agencies

(a) A debt relief agency shall—

(1) not later than 5 business days after the first date on which such agency provides any bankruptcy assistance services to an assisted person, but prior to such assisted person's petition under this title being filed, execute a written contract with such assisted person that explains clearly and conspicuously—

(A) the services such agency will provide to such assisted person; and

(B) the fees or charges for such services, and the terms of payment;

(2) provide the assisted person with a copy of the fully executed and completed contract;

(3) clearly and conspicuously disclose in any advertisement of bankruptcy assistance services or of the benefits of bankruptcy directed to the general public (whether in general media, seminars or specific mailings, telephonic or electronic messages, or otherwise) that the services or benefits are with respect to bankruptcy relief under this title; and

(4) clearly and conspicuously use the following statement in such advertisement: "We are a debt relief agency. We help people file for bankruptcy relief under the Bankruptcy Code." or a substantially similar statement.

(b)(1) An advertisement of bankruptcy assistance services or of the benefits of bankruptcy directed to the general public includes—

(A) descriptions of bankruptcy assistance in connection with a chapter 13 plan whether or not chapter 13 is specifically mentioned in such advertisement; and

(B) statements such as "federally supervised repayment plan" or "Federal debt restructuring help" or other similar statements that could lead a reasonable consumer to believe that debt counseling was being offered when in fact the services were directed to providing bankruptcy assistance with a chapter 13 plan or other form of bankruptcy relief under this title.

(2) An advertisement, directed to the general public, indicating that the debt relief agency provides assistance with respect to credit defaults, mortgage foreclosures, eviction proceedings, excessive debt, debt collection pressure, or inability to pay any consumer debt shall—

(A) disclose clearly and conspicuously in such advertisement that the assistance may involve bankruptcy relief under this title; and

(B) include the following statement: "We are a debt relief agency. We help people file for bankruptcy relief under the Bankruptcy Code." or a substantially similar statement.

Subchapter III

The Estate

§ 541. Property of the estate

(a) The commencement of a case under section 301, 302, or 303 of this title creates an estate. Such estate is comprised of all the following property, wherever located and by whomever held:

(1) Except as provided in subsections (b) and (c)(2) of this section, all legal or equitable interests of the debtor in property as of the commencement of the case.

(2) All interests of the debtor and the debtor's spouse in community property as of the commencement of the case that is—

(A) under the sole, equal, or joint management and control of the debtor; or

(B) liable for an allowable claim against the debtor, or for both an allowable claim against the debtor and an allowable claim against the debtor's spouse, to the extent that such interest is so liable.

(3) Any interest in property that the trustee recovers under section 329(b), 363(n), 543, 550, 553, or 723 of this title.

(4) Any interest in property preserved for the benefit of or ordered transferred to the estate under section 510(c) or 551 of this title.

(5) Any interest in property that would have been property of the estate if such interest had been an interest of the debtor on the date of the filing of the petition, and that the debtor acquires or becomes entitled to acquire within 180 days after such date—

(A) by bequest, devise, or inheritance;

(B) as a result of a property settlement agreement with debtor's spouse, or of an interlocutory or final divorce decree; or

(C) as beneficiary of a life insurance policy or of a death benefit plan.

(6) Proceeds, product, offspring, rents, or profits of or from property of the estate, except such as are earnings from services performed by an individual debtor after the commencement of the case.

(7) Any interest in property that the estate acquires after the commencement of the case.

(b) Property of the estate does not include—

(1) any power that the debtor may exercise solely for the benefit of an entity other than the debtor;

(2) any interest of the debtor as a lessee under a lease of nonresidential real property that has terminated at the expiration of the stated term of such lease before the commencement of the case under this title, and ceases to include any interest of the debtor as a lessee under a lease of nonresidential real property that has terminated at the expiration of the stated term of such lease during the case;

(3) any eligibility of the debtor to participate in programs authorized under the Higher Education Act of 1965 (20 U.S.C. 1001

et seq.; 42 U.S.C. 2751 *et seq.*), or any accreditation status or State licensure of the debtor as an educational institution;

(4) any interest of the debtor in liquid or gaseous hydrocarbons to the extent that—

(A)(i) the debtor has transferred or has agreed to transfer such interest pursuant to a farmout agreement or any written agreement directly related to a farmout agreement; and

(ii) but for the operation of this paragraph, the estate could include the interest referred to in clause (i) only by virtue of section 365 or 544(a)(3) of this title; or

(B)(i) the debtor has transferred such interest pursuant to a written conveyance of a production payment to an entity that does not participate in the operation of the property from which such production payment is transferred; and

(ii) but for the operation of this paragraph, the estate could include the interest referred to in clause (i) only by virtue of section 365 or 542 of this title; ~~or~~

(5) funds placed in an education individual retirement account (as defined in section 530(b)(1) of the Internal Revenue Code of 1986) not later than 365 days before the date of the filing of the petition in a case under this title, but—

(A) only if the designated beneficiary of such account was a child, stepchild, grandchild, or stepgrandchild of the debtor for the taxable year for which funds were placed in such account;

(B) only to the extent that such funds—

(i) are not pledged or promised to any entity in connection with any extension of credit; and

(ii) are not excess contributions (as described in section 4973(e) of the Internal Revenue Code of 1986); and

(C) in the case of funds placed in all such accounts having the same designated beneficiary not earlier than 720 days nor later than 365 days before such date, only so much of such funds as does not exceed $5,000;

(6) funds used to purchase a tuition credit or certificate or contributed to an account in accordance with section 529(b)(1)(A) of the Internal Revenue Code of 1986 under a qualified State tuition program (as defined in section 529(b)(1) of such Code) not later than 365 days before the date of the filing of the petition in a case under this title, but—

(A) only if the designated beneficiary of the amounts paid or contributed to such tuition program was a child, stepchild, grandchild, or stepgrandchild of the debtor for the taxable year for which funds were paid or contributed;

(B) with respect to the aggregate amount paid or contributed to such program having the same designated beneficiary, only so much of such amount as does not exceed the total contributions permitted under section 529(b)(7) of such Code with respect to such beneficiary, as adjusted beginning on the date of the filing of the petition in a case under this title by the annual increase or decrease (rounded to the nearest tenth of 1 percent) in the education expenditure category of the Consumer Price Index prepared by the Department of Labor; and

(C) in the case of funds paid or contributed to such program having the same designated beneficiary not earlier than 720 days nor later than 365 days before such date, only so much of such funds as does not exceed $5,000;

(7) any amount—

(A) withheld by an employer from the wages of employees for payment as contributions—

(i) to—

(I) an employee benefit plan that is subject to title I of the Employee Retirement Income Security Act of 1974 or under an employee benefit plan which is a governmental plan under section 414(d) of the Internal Revenue Code of 1986;

(II) a deferred compensation plan under section 457 of the Internal Revenue Code of 1986; or

(III) a tax-deferred annuity under section 403(b) of the Internal Revenue Code of 1986; except that such amount under this subparagraph shall not constitute disposable income, as defined in section 1325(b)(2); or

(ii) to a health insurance plan regulated by State law whether or not subject to such title; or

(B) received by an employer from employees for payment as contributions to—

(i) to—

(I) an employee benefit plan that is subject to title I of the Employee Retirement Income Security Act of 1974 or under an employee benefit plan which is a governmental plan under section 414(d) of the Internal Revenue Code of 1986;

(II) a deferred compensation plan under section 457 of the Internal Revenue Code of 1986; or

(III) a tax-deferred annuity under section 403(b) of the Internal Revenue Code of 1986; except that such amount under this subparagraph shall not constitute disposable income, as defined in section 1325(b)(2); or

(ii) to a health insurance plan regulated by State law whether or not subject to such title;

(8) subject to subchapter III of chapter 5, any interest of the debtor in property where the debtor pledged or sold tangible personal property (other than securities or written or printed evidences of indebtedness or title) as collateral for a loan or advance of money given by a person licensed under law to make such loans or advances, where—

(A) the tangible personal property is in the possession of the pledgee or transferee;

(B) the debtor has no obligation to repay the money, redeem the collateral, or buy back the property at a stipulated price; and

(C) neither the debtor nor the trustee have exercised any right to redeem provided under the contract or State law, in a timely manner as provided under State law and section 108(b); or

(59) any interest in cash or cash equivalents that constitute proceeds of a sale by the debtor of a money order that is made—

(A) on or after the date that is 14 days prior to the date on which the petition is filed; and

(B) under an agreement with a money order issuer that prohibits the commingling of such proceeds with property of the debtor (notwithstanding that, contrary to the agreement, the proceeds may have been commingled with property of the debtor),

unless the money order issuer had not taken action, prior to the filing of the petition, to require compliance with the prohibition.

Paragraph (4) shall not be construed to exclude from the estate any consideration the debtor retains, receives, or is entitled to receive for transferring an interest in liquid or gaseous hydrocarbons pursuant to a farmout agreement.

(c)(1) Except as provided in paragraph (2) of this subsection, an interest of the debtor in property becomes property of the estate under subsection (a)(1), (a)(2), or (a)(5) of this section notwithstanding any provision in an agreement, transfer instrument, or applicable nonbankruptcy law—

(A) that restricts or conditions transfer of such interest by the debtor; or

(B) that is conditioned on the insolvency or financial condition of the debtor, on the commencement of a case under this title, or on the appointment of or taking possession by a trustee in a case under this title or a custodian before such commencement, and that effects or gives an option to effect a forfeiture, modification, or termination of the debtor's interest in property.

(2) A restriction on the transfer of a beneficial interest of the debtor in a trust that is enforceable under applicable nonbankruptcy law is enforceable in a case under this title.

(d) Property in which the debtor holds, as of the commencement of the case, only legal title and not an equitable interest, such as a mortgage secured by real property, or an interest in such a mortgage, sold by the debtor but as to which the debtor retains legal title to service or supervise the servicing of such mortgage or interest, becomes property of the estate under subsection (a)(1) or (2) of this section only to the extent of the debtor's legal title to such property, but not to the extent of any equitable interest in such property that the debtor does not hold.

(e) In determining whether any of the relationships specified in paragraph (5)(A) or (6)(A) of subsection (b) exists, a legally adopted child of an individual (and a child who is a member of an individual's household, if placed with such individual by an authorized placement agency for legal adoption by such individual), or a foster child of an individual (if such child has as the child's principal place of abode the home of the debtor and is a member of the debtor's household) shall be treated as a child of such individual by blood.

(f) Notwithstanding any other provision of this title, property that is held by a debtor that is a corporation described in section 501(c)(3) of the Internal Revenue Code of 1986 and exempt from tax under section 501(a) of such Code may be transferred to an entity that is not such a corporation, but only under the same conditions as would apply if the debtor had not filed a case under this title.[38]

§ 542. Turnover of property to the estate

(a) Except as provided in subsection (c) or (d) of this section, an entity, other than a custodian, in possession, custody, or control, during the case, of property that the trustee may use, sell, or lease under section 363 of this title, or that the debtor may exempt under section 522 of this title, shall deliver to the trustee, and account for, such property or the value of such property, unless such property is of inconsequential value or benefit to the estate.

(b) Except as provided in subsection (c) or (d) of this section, an entity that owes a debt that is property of the estate and that is matured, payable on demand, or payable on order, shall pay such debt to, or on the order of, the trustee, except to the extent that such debt may be offset under section 553 of this title against a claim against the debtor.

(c) Except as provided in section 362(a)(7) of this title, an entity that has neither actual notice nor actual knowledge of the commencement of the case concerning the debtor may transfer property of the estate, or pay a debt owing to the debtor, in good faith and other than in the manner specified in subsection (d) of this section, to an entity other than the trustee, with the same effect as to the entity making such transfer or payment as if the case under this title concerning the debtor had not been commenced.

(d) A life insurance company may transfer property of the estate or property of the debtor to such company in good faith, with the same effect with respect to such company as if the case under this title concerning the debtor had not been commenced, if such transfer is to pay a premium or to carry out a nonforfeiture insurance option, and is required to be made automatically, under a life insurance contract with such company that was entered into before the date of the filing of the petition and that is property of the estate.

(e) Subject to any applicable privilege, after notice and a hearing, the court may order an attorney, accountant, or other person that holds recorded information, including books, documents, records, and papers, relating to the debtor's property or financial affairs, to turn over or disclose such recorded information to the trustee.

---

38 *Editor's Note*: New subsection 541(f) applies to cases pending under title 11 on April 20, 2005 and to cases commenced on or after that date, except that a court shall not confirm a plan under chapter 11 of title 11 without considering whether these changes would substantially affect the rights of a party in interest who first acquired rights with respect to the debtor after the date of the petition.

§ 543. Turnover of property by a custodian

(a) A custodian with knowledge of the commencement of a case under this title concerning the debtor may not make any disbursement from, or take any action in the administration of, property of the debtor, proceeds, product, offspring, rents, or profits of such property, or property of the estate, in the possession, custody, or control of such custodian, except such action as is necessary to preserve such property.

(b) A custodian shall—

(1) deliver to the trustee any property of the debtor held by or transferred to such custodian, or proceeds, product, offspring, rents, or profits of such property, that is in such custodian's possession, custody, or control on the date that such custodian acquires knowledge of the commencement of the case; and

(2) file an accounting of any property of the debtor, or proceeds, product, offspring, rents, or profits of such property that, at any time, came into the possession, custody, or control of such custodian.

(c) The court, after notice and a hearing, shall—

(1) protect all entities to which a custodian has become obligated with respect to such property or proceeds, product, offspring, rents, or profits of such property;

(2) provide for the payment of reasonable compensation for services rendered and costs and expenses incurred by such custodian; and

(3) surcharge such custodian, other than an assignee for the benefit of the debtor's creditors that was appointed or took possession more than 120 days before the date of the filing of the petition, for any improper or excessive disbursement, other than a disbursement that has been made in accordance with applicable law or that has been approved, after notice and a hearing, by a court of competent jurisdiction before the commencement of the case under this title.

(d) After notice and hearing, the bankruptcy court—

(1) may excuse compliance with subsection (a), (b), or (c) of this section if the interests of creditors and, if the debtor is not insolvent, of equity security holders would be better served by permitting a custodian to continue in possession, custody, or control of such property, and

(2) shall excuse compliance with subsections (a) and (b)(1) of this section if the custodian is an assignee for the benefit of the debtor's creditors that was appointed or took possession more than 120 days before the date of the filing of the petition, unless compliance with such subsections is necessary to prevent fraud or injustice.

§ 544. Trustee as lien creditor and as successor to certain creditors and purchasers

(a) The trustee shall have, as of the commencement of the case, and without regard to any knowledge of the trustee or of any creditor, the rights and powers of, or may avoid any transfer of property of the debtor or any obligation incurred by the debtor that is voidable by—

(1) a creditor that extends credit to the debtor at the time of the commencement of the case, and that obtains, at such time and with respect to such credit, a judicial lien on all property on which a creditor on a simple contract could have obtained such a judicial lien, whether or not such a creditor exists;

(2) a creditor that extends credit to the debtor at the time of the commencement of the case, and obtains, at such time and with respect to such credit, an execution against the debtor that is returned unsatisfied at such time, whether or not such a creditor exists; or

(3) a bona fide purchaser of real property, other than fixtures, from the debtor, against whom applicable law permits such transfer to be perfected, that obtains the status of a bona fide purchaser and has perfected such transfer at the time of the commencement of the case, whether or not such a purchaser exists.

(b)(1) Except as provided in paragraph (2), the trustee may avoid any transfer of an interest of the debtor in property or any obligation incurred by the debtor that is voidable under applicable law by a creditor holding an unsecured claim that is allowable under section 502 of this title or that is not allowable only under section 502(e) of this title.

(2) Paragraph (1) shall not apply to a transfer of a charitable contribution (as that term is defined in section 548(d)(3)) that is not covered under section 548(a)(1)(B), by reason of section 548(a)(2). Any claim by any person to recover a transferred contribution described in the preceding sentence under Federal or State law in a Federal or State court shall be preempted by the commencement of the case.

§ 545. Statutory liens

The trustee may avoid the fixing of a statutory lien on property of the debtor to the extent that such lien—

(1) first becomes effective against the debtor—

(A) when a case under this title concerning the debtor is commenced;

(B) when an insolvency proceeding other than under this title concerning the debtor is commenced;

(C) when a custodian is appointed or authorized to take possession;

(D) when the debtor becomes insolvent;

(E) when the debtor's financial condition fails to meet a specified standard; or

(F) at the time of an execution against property of the debtor levied at the instance of an entity other than the holder of such statutory lien;

(2) is not perfected or enforceable at the time of the commencement of the case against a bona fide purchaser that purchases such property at the time of the commencement of the case, whether or not such a purchaser exists, except in any case in which a purchaser is a purchaser described in section 6323 of the Internal Revenue Code of 1986, or in any other similar provision of State or local law;

(3) is for rent; or

(4) is a lien of distress for rent.

§ 546. Limitations on avoiding powers

(a) An action or proceeding under section 544, 545, 547, 548, or 553 of this title may not be commenced after the earlier of—

(1) the later of—

(A) 2 years after the entry of the order for relief; or

(B) 1 year after the appointment or election of the first trustee under section 702, 1104, 1163, 1202, or 1302 of this title if such appointment or such election occurs before the expiration of the period specified in subparagraph (A); or

(2) the time the case is closed or dismissed.

(b)(1) The rights and powers of a trustee under sections 544, 545, and 549 of this title are subject to any generally applicable law that—

(A) permits perfection of an interest in property to be effective against an entity that acquires rights in such property before the date of perfection; or

(B) provides for the maintenance or continuation of perfection of an interest in property to be effective against an entity that acquires rights in such property before the date on which action is taken to effect such maintenance or continuation.

(2) If—

(A) a law described in paragraph (1) requires seizure of such property or commencement of an action to accomplish such perfection, or maintenance or continuation of perfection of an interest in property; and

(B) such property has not been seized or such an action has not been commenced before the date of the filing of the petition;

such interest in such property shall be perfected, or perfection of such interest shall be maintained or continued, by giving notice within the time fixed by such law for such seizure or such commencement.

(c)(1) Except as provided in subsection (d) of this section and in section 507(c), and subject to the prior rights of a holder of a security interest in such goods or the proceeds thereof, the rights and powers of ~~a~~ the trustee under sections 544(a), 545, 547, and 549 ~~of this title~~ are subject to ~~any statutory or common-law~~ the right of a seller of goods that has sold goods to the debtor, in the ordinary course of such seller's business, to reclaim such goods if the debtor has received such goods while insolvent, within 45 days before the date of the commencement of a case under this title, but~~—(1)~~ such a seller may not reclaim ~~any~~ such goods unless such seller demands in writing reclamation of such goods—

(A) ~~before 10~~ not later than 45 days after the date of receipt of such goods by the debtor; or

(B) not later than 20 days after the date of commencement of the case, if ~~such 10-day~~ the 45-day period expires after the commencement of the case.~~, before 20 days after receipt of such goods by the debtor; and~~

(2) If a seller of goods fails to provide notice in the manner described in paragraph (1), the seller still may assert the rights contained in section 503(b)(9).

~~(2) the court may deny reclamation to a seller with such a right of reclamation that has made such a demand only if the court—~~

~~(A) grants the claim of such a seller priority as a claim of a kind specified in section 503(b) of this title; or~~

~~(B) secures such claim by a lien.~~

(d) In the case of a seller who is a producer of grain sold to a grain storage facility, owned or operated by the debtor, in the ordinary course of such seller's business (as such terms are defined in section 557 of this title) or in the case of a United States fisherman who has caught fish sold to a fish processing facility owned or operated by the debtor in the ordinary course of such fisherman's business, the rights and powers of the trustee under sections 544(a), 545, 547, and 549 of this title are subject to any statutory or common law right of such producer or fisherman to reclaim such grain or fish if the debtor has received such grain or fish while insolvent, but—

(1) such producer or fisherman may not reclaim any grain or fish unless such producer or fisherman demands, in writing, reclamation of such grain or fish before ten days after receipt thereof by the debtor; and

(2) the court may deny reclamation to such a producer or fisherman with a right of reclamation that has made such a demand only if the court secures such claim by a lien.

(e) Notwithstanding sections 544, 545, 547, 548(a)(1)(B), and 548(b) of this title, the trustee may not avoid a transfer that is a margin payment, as defined in section 101, 741, or 761 of this title, or settlement payment, as defined in section 101 or 741 of this title, made by or to a commodity broker, forward contract merchant, stockbroker, financial institution, financial participant, or securities clearing agency, that is made before the commencement of the case, except under section 548(a)(1)(A) of this title.

(f) Notwithstanding sections 544, 545, 547, 548(a)(1)(B), and 548(b) of this title, the trustee may not avoid a transfer that is a margin payment, as defined in section 741 or 761 of this title, or settlement payment, as defined in section 741 of this title, made by or to a repo participant or financial participant, in connection with a repurchase agreement and that is made before the commencement of the case, except under section 548(a)(1)(A) of this title.

(g) Notwithstanding sections 544, 545, 547, 548(a)(1)(B) and 548(b) of this title, the trustee may not avoid a transfer ~~under a swap agreement~~, made by or to a swap participant or financial participant, under or in connection with any swap agreement and that is made before the commencement of the case, except under section 548(a)(1)(A) of this title.

(gh)[39] Notwithstanding the rights and powers of a trustee under sections 544(a), 545, 547, 549, and 553, if the court determines on a motion by the trustee made not later than 120 days after the date of the order for relief in a case under chapter 11 of this title and after notice and a hearing, that a return is in the best interests of the estate, the debtor, with the consent of a creditor and subject to the prior rights of holders of security interests in such goods or the proceeds of such goods, may return goods shipped to the debtor by the creditor before the commencement of the case, and the creditor may offset the purchase price of such goods against any claim of the creditor against the debtor that arose before the commencement of the case.

(i)(1) Notwithstanding paragraphs (2) and (3) of section 545, the trustee may not avoid a warehouseman's lien for storage, transportation, or other costs incidental to the storage and handling of goods.

(2) The prohibition under paragraph (1) shall be applied in a manner consistent with any State statute applicable to such lien that is similar to section 7-209 of the Uniform Commercial Code, as in effect on the date of enactment of the Bankruptcy Abuse Prevention and Consumer Protection Act of 2005, or any successor to such section 7-209.

(j) Notwithstanding sections 544, 545, 547, 548(a)(1)(B), and 548(b) the trustee may not avoid a transfer made by or to a master netting agreement participant under or in connection with any master netting agreement or any individual contract covered thereby that is made before the commencement of the case, except under section 548(a)(1)(A) and except to the extent that the trustee could otherwise avoid such a transfer made under an individual contract covered by such master netting agreement.

§ 547. Preferences

(a) In this section—

(1) "inventory" means personal property leased or furnished, held for sale or lease, or to be furnished under a contract for service, raw materials, work in process, or materials used or consumed in a business, including farm products such as crops or livestock, held for sale or lease;

(2) "new value" means money or money's worth in goods, services, or new credit, or release by a transferee of property previously transferred to such transferee in a transaction that is neither void nor voidable by the debtor or the trustee under any applicable law, including proceeds of such property, but does not include an obligation substituted for an existing obligation;

(3) "receivable" means right to payment, whether or not such right has been earned by performance; and

(4) a debt for a tax is incurred on the day when such tax is last payable without penalty, including any extension.

(b) Except as provided in subsections (c) and (i) of this section, the trustee may avoid any transfer of an interest of the debtor in property—

(1) to or for the benefit of a creditor;

(2) for or on account of an antecedent debt owed by the debtor before such transfer was made;

(3) made while the debtor was insolvent;

(4) made—

(A) on or within 90 days before the date of the filing of the petition; or

(B) between 90 days and one year before the date of the filing of the petition, if such creditor at the time of such transfer was an insider; and

(5) that enables such creditor to receive more than such creditor would receive if—

(A) the case were a case under chapter 7 of this title;

(B) the transfer had not been made; and

(C) such creditor received payment of such debt to the extent provided by the provisions of this title.

(c) The trustee may not avoid under this section a transfer—

(1) to the extent that such transfer was—

(A) intended by the debtor and the creditor to or for whose benefit such transfer was made to be a contemporaneous exchange for new value given to the debtor; and

(B) in fact a substantially contemporaneous exchange;

(2) to the extent that such transfer was—(A) in payment of a debt incurred by the debtor in the ordinary course of business or financial affairs of the debtor and the transferee,; and such transfer was—

(BA) made in the ordinary course of business or financial affairs of the debtor and the transferee; and or

(CB) made according to ordinary business terms;

(3) that creates a security interest in property acquired by the debtor—

(A) to the extent such security interest secures new value that was—

(i) given at or after the signing of a security agreement that contains a description of such property as collateral;

(ii) given by or on behalf of the secured party under such agreement;

(iii) given to enable the debtor to acquire such property; and

(iv) in fact used by the debtor to acquire such property; and

(B) that is perfected on or before 20 30 days after the debtor receives possession of such property;

(4) to or for the benefit of a creditor, to the extent that, after such transfer, such creditor gave new value to or for the benefit of the debtor—

(A) not secured by an otherwise unavoidable security interest; and

39 *Editor's Note*: So in original. The 1994 Bankruptcy Reform Act added a second § 546(g). The 2005 bankruptcy amendments relettered the second § 546(g) as § 546(h).

(B) on account of which new value the debtor did not make an otherwise unavoidable transfer to or for the benefit of such creditor;

(5) that creates a perfected security interest in inventory or a receivable or the proceeds of either, except to the extent that the aggregate of all such transfers to the transferee caused a reduction, as of the date of the filing of the petition and to the prejudice of other creditors holding unsecured claims, of any amount by which the debt secured by such security interest exceeded the value of all security interests for such debt on the later of—

(A)(i) with respect to a transfer to which subsection (b)(4)(A) of this section applies, 90 days before the date of the filing of the petition; or

(ii) with respect to a transfer to which subsection (b)(4)(B) of this section applies, one year before the date of the filing of the petition; or

(B) the date on which new value was first given under the security agreement creating such security interest;

(6) that is the fixing of a statutory lien that is not avoidable under section 545 of this title;

(7) to the extent such transfer was a bona fide payment of a debt for a domestic support obligation; ~~to a spouse, former spouse, or child of the debtor, for alimony to, maintenance for, or support of such spouse or child, in connection with a separation agreement, divorce decree or other order of a court of record, determination made in accordance with State or territorial law by a governmental unit, or property settlement agreement, but not to the extent that such debt—~~

~~(A) is assigned to another entity, voluntarily, by operation of law, or otherwise; or~~

~~(B) includes a liability designated as alimony, maintenance, or support, unless such liability is actually in the nature of alimony, maintenance or support; or~~

(8) if, in a case filed by an individual debtor whose debts are primarily consumer debts, the aggregate value of all property that constitutes or is affected by such transfer is less than $600; or

(9) if, in a case filed by a debtor whose debts are not primarily consumer debts, the aggregate value of all property that constitutes or is affected by such transfer is less than $5,000.

(d) The trustee may avoid a transfer of an interest in property of the debtor transferred to or for the benefit of a surety to secure reimbursement of such a surety that furnished a bond or other obligation to dissolve a judicial lien that would have been avoidable by the trustee under subsection (b) of this section. The liability of such surety under such bond or obligation shall be discharged to the extent of the value of such property recovered by the trustee or the amount paid to the trustee.

(e)(1) For the purposes of this section—

(A) a transfer of real property other than fixtures, but including the interest of a seller or purchaser under a contract for the sale of real property, is perfected when a bona fide purchaser of such property from the debtor against whom applicable law permits such transfer to be perfected cannot acquire an interest that is superior to the interest of the transferee; and

(B) a transfer of a fixture or property other than real property is perfected when a creditor on a simple contract cannot acquire a judicial lien that is superior to the interest of the transferee.

(2) For the purposes of this section, except as provided in paragraph (3) of this subsection, a transfer is made—

(A) at the time such transfer takes effect between the transferor and the transferee, if such transfer is perfected at, or within ~~10~~ 30 days after, such time, except as provided in subsection (c)(3)(B);

(B) at the time such transfer is perfected, if such transfer is perfected after such ~~10~~ 30 days; or

(C) immediately before the date of the filing of the petition, if such transfer is not perfected at the later of—

(i) the commencement of the case; or

(ii) ~~10~~ 30 days after such transfer takes effect between the transferor and the transferee.

(3) For the purposes of this section, a transfer is not made until the debtor has acquired rights in the property transferred.

(f) For the purposes of this section, the debtor is presumed to have been insolvent on and during the 90 days immediately preceding the date of the filing of the petition.

(g) For the purposes of this section, the trustee has the burden of proving the avoidability of a transfer under subsection (b) of this section, and the creditor or party in interest against whom recovery or avoidance is sought has the burden of proving the nonavoidability of a transfer under subsection (c) of this section.

(h) The trustee may not avoid a transfer if such transfer was made as a part of an alternative repayment schedule between the debtor and any creditor of the debtor created by an approved nonprofit budgeting and credit counseling agency.

(i) If the trustee avoids under subsection (b) a transfer made between 90 days and 1 year before the date of the filing of the petition, by the debtor to an entity that is not an insider for the benefit of a creditor that is an insider, such transfer shall be considered to be avoided under this section only with respect to the creditor that is an insider.[40]

§ 548. Fraudulent transfers and obligations

(a)(1) The trustee may avoid any transfer (including any transfer to or for the benefit of an insider under an employment contract) of an interest of the debtor in property, or any obligation (including any obligation to or for the benefit of an insider under an employment contract) incurred by the debtor, that was made or incurred on or

40 *Editor's Note*: New subsection 547(i) applies to cases pending under title 11 on April 20, 2005 and to cases commenced on or after that date.

within ~~one~~ 2 years before the date of the filing of the petition, if the debtor voluntarily or involuntarily—

(A) made such transfer or incurred such obligation with actual intent to hinder, delay, or defraud any entity to which the debtor was or became, on or after the date that such transfer was made or such obligation was incurred, indebted; or

(B)(i) received less than a reasonably equivalent value in exchange for such transfer or obligation; and

(ii)(I) was insolvent on the date that such transfer was made or such obligation was incurred, or became insolvent as a result of such transfer or obligation;

(II) was engaged in business or a transaction, or was about to engage in business or a transaction, for which any property remaining with the debtor was an unreasonably small capital; ~~or~~

(III) intended to incur, or believed that the debtor would incur, debts that would be beyond the debtor's ability to pay as such debts matured; or

(IV) made such transfer to or for the benefit of an insider, or incurred such obligation to or for the benefit of an insider, under an employment contract and not in the ordinary course of business.[41]

(2) A transfer of a charitable contribution to a qualified religious or charitable entity or organization shall not be considered to be a transfer covered under paragraph (1)(B) in any case in which—

(A) the amount of that contribution does not exceed 15 percent of the gross annual income of the debtor for the year in which the transfer of the contribution is made; or

(B) the contribution made by a debtor exceeded the percentage amount of gross annual income specified in subparagraph (A), if the transfer was consistent with the practices of the debtor in making charitable contributions.

(b) The trustee of a partnership debtor may avoid any transfer of an interest of the debtor in property, or any obligation incurred by the debtor, that was made or incurred on or within ~~one~~ 2 years[42] before the date of the filing of the petition, to a general partner in the debtor, if the debtor was insolvent on the date such transfer was made or such obligation was incurred, or became insolvent as a result of such transfer or obligation.

(c) Except to the extent that a transfer or obligation voidable under this section is voidable under section 544, 545, or 547 of this title, a transferee or obligee of such a transfer or obligation that takes for value and in good faith has a lien on or may retain any interest transferred or may enforce any obligation incurred, as the case may be, to the extent that such transferee or obligee gave value to the debtor in exchange for such transfer or obligation.

(d)(1) For the purposes of this section, a transfer is made when such transfer is so perfected that a bona fide purchaser from the debtor against whom applicable law permits such transfer to be perfected cannot acquire an interest in the property transferred that is superior to the interest in such property of the transferee, but if such transfer is not so perfected before the commencement of the case, such transfer is made immediately before the date of the filing of the petition.

(2) In this section—

(A) "value" means property, or satisfaction or securing of a present or antecedent debt of the debtor, but does not include an unperformed promise to furnish support to the debtor or to a relative of the debtor;

(B) a commodity broker, forward contract merchant, stockbroker, financial institution, financial participant, or securities clearing agency that receives a margin payment, as defined in section 101, 741 or 761 of this title, or settlement payment, as defined in section 101 or 741 of this title, takes for value to the extent of such payment;

(C) a repo participant or financial participant that receives a margin payment, as defined in section 741 or 761 of this title, or settlement payment, as defined in section 741 of this title, in connection with a repurchase agreement, takes for value to the extent of such payment; ~~and~~

(D) a swap participant or financial participant that receives a transfer in connection with a swap agreement takes for value to the extent of such transfer; and

(E) a master netting agreement participant that receives a transfer in connection with a master netting agreement or any individual contract covered thereby takes for value to the extent of such transfer, except that, with respect to a transfer under any individual contract covered thereby, to the extent that such master netting agreement participant otherwise did not take (or is otherwise not deemed to have taken) such transfer for value.

(3) In this section, the term "charitable contribution" means a charitable contribution, as that term is defined in section 170(c) of the Internal Revenue Code of 1986, if that contribution—

(A) is made by a natural person; and

(B) consists of—

(i) a financial instrument (as that term is defined in section 731(c)(2)(C) of the Internal Revenue Code of 1986); or

(ii) cash.

(4) In this section, the term "qualified religious or charitable entity or organization" means—

(A) an entity described in section 170(c)(1) of the Internal Revenue Code of 1986; or

(B) an entity or organization described in section 170(c)(2) of the Internal Revenue Code of 1986.

(e)(1) In addition to any transfer that the trustee may otherwise avoid, the trustee may avoid any transfer of an interest of the debtor in property that was made on or within 10 years before the date of the filing of the petition if—

---

41 *Editor's Note*: These changes to section 548(a)(1) are effective for cases commenced under title 11 on or after April 20, 2005.

42 *Editor's Note*: This change to section 548(b) is effective for cases commenced under title 11 after April 20, 2006.

(A) such transfer was made to a self-settled trust or similar device;

(B) such transfer was by the debtor;

(C) the debtor is a beneficiary of such trust or similar device; and

(D) the debtor made such transfer with actual intent to hinder, delay, or defraud any entity to which the debtor was or became, on or after the date that such transfer was made, indebted.

(2) For the purposes of this subsection, a transfer includes a transfer made in anticipation of any money judgment, settlement, civil penalty, equitable order, or criminal fine incurred by, or which the debtor believed would be incurred by—

(A) any violation of the securities laws (as defined in section 3(a)(47) of the Securities Exchange Act of 1934 (15 U.S.C. 78c(a)(47))), any State securities laws, or any regulation or order issued under Federal securities laws of State securities laws; or

(B) fraud, deceit, or manipulation in a fiduciary capacity or in connection with the purchase or sale of any security registered under section 12 of 15(d) of the Securities Exchange Act of 1934 (15 U.S.C. 78l and 78o(d)) or under section 6 of the Securities Act of 1933 (15 U.S.C. 77f).[43]

§ 549. Postpetition transactions

(a) Except as provided in subsection (b) or (c) of this section, the trustee may avoid a transfer of property of the estate—

(1) that occurs after the commencement of the case; and

(2)(A) that is authorized only under section 303(f) or 542(c) of this title; or

(B) that is not authorized under this title or by the court.

(b) In an involuntary case, the trustee may not avoid under subsection (a) of this section a transfer made after the commencement of such case but before the order for relief to the extent any value, including services, but not including satisfaction or securing of a debt that arose before the commencement of the case, is given after the commencement of the case in exchange for such transfer, notwithstanding any notice or knowledge of the case that the transferee has.

(c) The trustee may not avoid under subsection (a) of this section a transfer of an interest in real property to a good faith purchaser without knowledge of the commencement of the case and for present fair equivalent value unless a copy or notice of the petition was filed, where a transfer of an interest in such real property may be recorded to perfect such transfer, before such transfer is so perfected that a bona fide purchaser of such real property, against whom applicable law permits such transfer to be perfected, could not acquire an interest that is superior to ~~the~~ such interest of such good faith purchaser. A good faith purchaser without knowledge of the commencement of the case and for less than present fair equivalent value has a lien on the property transferred to the extent of any present value given, unless a copy or notice of the petition was so filed before such transfer was so perfected.

(d) An action or proceeding under this section may not be commenced after the earlier of—

(1) two years after the date of the transfer sought to be avoided; or

(2) the time the case is closed or dismissed.

§ 550. Liability of transferee of avoided transfer

(a) Except as otherwise provided in this section, to the extent that a transfer is avoided under section 544, 545, 547, 548, 549, 553(b), or 724(a) of this title, the trustee may recover, for the benefit of the estate, the property transferred, or, if the court so orders, the value of such property, from—

(1) the initial transferee of such transfer or the entity for whose benefit such transfer was made; or

(2) any immediate or mediate transferee of such initial transferee.

(b) The trustee may not recover under section (a)(2) of this section from—

(1) a transferee that takes for value, including satisfaction or securing of a present or antecedent debt, in good faith, and without knowledge of the voidability of the transfer avoided; or

(2) any immediate or mediate good faith transferee of such transferee.

(c) If a transfer made between 90 days and one year before the filing of the petition—

(1) is avoided under section 547(b) of this title; and

(2) was made for the benefit of a creditor that at the time of such transfer was an insider;

the trustee may not recover under subsection (a) from a transferee that is not an insider.

(d) The trustee is entitled to only a single satisfaction under subsection (a) of this section.

(e)(1) A good faith transferee from whom the trustee may recover under subsection (a) of this section has a lien on the property recovered to secure the lesser of—

(A) the cost, to such transferee, of any improvement made after the transfer, less the amount of any profit realized by or accruing to such transferee from such property; and

(B) any increase in the value of such property as a result of such improvement, of the property transferred.

(2) In this subsection, "improvement" includes—

(A) physical additions or changes to the property transferred;

(B) repairs to such property;

(C) payment of any tax on such property;

(D) payment of any debt secured by a lien on such property that is superior or equal to the rights of the trustee; and

(E) preservation of such property.

43 *Editor's Note*: New subsection 548(e) is effective for cases commenced under title 11 on or after April 20, 2005.

(f) An action or proceeding under this section may not be commenced after the earlier of—

(1) one year after the avoidance of the transfer on account of which recovery under this section is sought; or

(2) the time the case is closed or dismissed.

§ 551. Automatic preservation of avoided transfer

Any transfer avoided under section 522, 544, 545, 547, 548, 549, or 724(a) of this title, or any lien void under section 506(d) of this title, is preserved for the benefit of the estate but only with respect to property of the estate.

§ 552. Postpetition effect of security interest

(a) Except as provided in subsection (b) of this section, property acquired by the estate or by the debtor after the commencement of the case is not subject to any lien resulting from any security agreement entered into by the debtor before the commencement of the case.

(b)(1) Except as provided in sections 363, 506(c), 522, 544, 545, 547, and 548 of this title, if the debtor and an entity entered into a security agreement before the commencement of the case and if the security interest created by such security agreement extends to property of the debtor acquired before the commencement of the case and to proceeds, products, offspring, or profits of such property, then such security interest extends to such proceeds, products, offspring, or profits acquired by the estate after the commencement of the case to the extent provided by such security agreement and by applicable nonbankruptcy law, except to any extent that the court, after notice and a hearing and based on the equities of the case, orders otherwise.

(2) Except as provided in sections 363, 506(c), 522, 544, 545, 547, and 548 of this title, and notwithstanding section 546(b) of this title, if the debtor and an entity entered into a security agreement before the commencement of the case and if the security interest created by such security agreement extends to property of the debtor acquired before the commencement of the case and to amounts paid as rents of such property or the fees, charges, accounts, or other payments for the use or occupancy of rooms and other public facilities in hotels, motels, or other lodging properties, then such security interest extends to such rents and such fees, charges, accounts, or other payments acquired by the estate after the commencement of the case to the extent provided in such security agreement, except to any extent that the court, after notice and a hearing and based on the equities of the case, orders otherwise.

§ 553. Setoff

(a) Except as otherwise provided in this section and in sections 362 and 363 of this title, this title does not affect any right of a creditor to offset a mutual debt owing by such creditor to the debtor that arose before the commencement of the case under this title against a claim of such creditor against the debtor that arose before the commencement of the case, except to the extent that—

(1) the claim of such creditor against the debtor is disallowed;

(2) such claim was transferred, by an entity other than the debtor, to such creditor—

(A) after the commencement of the case; or

(B)(i) after 90 days before the date of the filing of the petition; and

(ii) while the debtor was insolvent (except for a setoff of a kind described in section 362(b)(6), 362(b)(7), 362(b)(17), 362(b)(27), 555, 556, 559, 560, or 561); or

(3) the debt owed to the debtor by such creditor was incurred by such creditor—

(A) after 90 days before the date of the filing of the petition;

(B) while the debtor was insolvent; and

(C) for the purpose of obtaining a right of setoff against the debtor (except for a setoff of a kind described in section 362(b)(6), 362(b)(7), 362(b)(17), 362(b)(27), 555, 556, 559, 560, or 561).

(b)(1) Except with respect to a setoff of a kind described in sections 362(b)(6), 362(b)(7), ~~362(b)(14),~~ 362(b)(17), 362(b)(27), 555, 556, 559, 560, 561, 365(h), 546(h), or 365(i)(2), of this title, if a creditor offsets a mutual debt owing to the debtor against a claim against the debtor on or within 90 days before the date of the filing of the petition, then the trustee may recover from such creditor the amount so offset to the extent that any insufficiency on the date of such setoff is less than the insufficiency on the later of—

(A) 90 days before the date of the filing of the petition; and

(B) the first date during the 90 days immediately preceding the date of the filing of the petition on which there is an insufficiency.

(2) In this subsection, "insufficiency" means amount, if any, by which a claim against the debtor exceeds a mutual debt owing to the debtor by the holder of such claim.

(c) For the purposes of this section, the debtor is presumed to have been insolvent on and during the 90 days immediately preceding the date of the filing of the petition.

§ 554. Abandonment of property of the estate

(a) After notice and a hearing, the trustee may abandon any property of the estate that is burdensome to the estate or that is of inconsequential value and benefit to the estate.

(b) On request of a party in interest and after notice and a hearing, the court may order the trustee to abandon any property of the estate that is burdensome to the estate or that is of inconsequential value and benefit to the estate.

(c) Unless the court orders otherwise, any property scheduled under section 521(1) of this title not otherwise administered at the time of the closing of a case is abandoned to the debtor and administered for purposes of section 350 of this title.

(d) Unless the court orders otherwise, property of the estate that is not abandoned under this section and that is not administered in the case remains property of the estate.

§ 555. Contractual right to liquidate, terminate, or accelerate a securities contract

The exercise of a contractual right of a stockbroker, financial institution, financial participant, or securities clearing agency to cause the liquidation, termination, or acceleration of a securities contract, as defined in section 741 of this title, because of a condition of the kind specified in section 365(e)(1) of this title shall not be stayed, avoided, or otherwise limited by operation of any provision of this title or by order of a court or administrative agency in any proceeding under this title unless such order is authorized under the provisions of the Securities Investor Protection Act of 1970 or any statute administered by the Securities and Exchange Commission. As used in this section, the term "contractual right" includes a right set forth in a rule or bylaw of a derivatives clearing organization (as defined in the Commodity Exchange Act), a multilateral clearing organization (as defined in the Federal Deposit Insurance Corporation Improvement Act of 1991), a national securities exchange, a national securities association, ~~or~~ a securities clearing agency, a contract market designated under the Commodity Exchange Act, a derivatives transaction execution facility registered under the Commodity Exchange Act, or a board of trade (as defined in the Commodity Exchange Act), or in a resolution of the governing board thereof, and a right, whether or not in writing, arising under common law, under law merchant, or by reason of normal business practice.

§ 556. Contractual right to liquidate, terminate, or accelerate a commodities contract or forward contract

The contractual right of a commodity broker, financial participant, or forward contract merchant to cause the liquidation, termination, or acceleration of a commodity contract, as defined in section 761 of this title, or forward contract because of a condition of the kind specified in section 365(e)(1) of this title, and the right to a variation or maintenance margin payment received from a trustee with respect to open commodity contracts or forward contracts, shall not be stayed, avoided, or otherwise limited by operation of any provision of this title or by the order of a court in any proceeding under this title. As used in this section, the term "contractual right" includes a right set forth in a rule or bylaw of a derivatives clearing organization (as defined in the Commodity Exchange Act), a multilateral clearing organization (as defined in the Federal Deposit Insurance Corporation Improvement Act of 1991), a national securities exchange, a national securities association, a securities clearing agency, ~~or~~ a contract market designated under the Commodity Exchange Act, a derivatives transaction execution facility registered under the Commodity Exchange Act, or a board of trade (as defined in the Commodity Exchange Act) or in a resolution of the governing board thereof and a right, whether or not evidenced in writing, arising under common law, under law merchant or by reason of normal business practice.

§ 557. Expedited determination of interests in, and abandonment or other disposition of grain assets

(a) This section applies only in a case concerning a debtor that owns or operates a grain storage facility and only with respect to grain and the proceeds of grain. This section does not affect the application of any other section of this title to property other than grain and proceeds of grain.

(b) In this section—

(1) "grain" means wheat, corn, flaxseed, grain sorghum, barley, oats, rye, soybeans, other dry edible beans, or rice;

(2) "grain storage facility" means a site or physical structure regularly used to store grain for producers, or to store grain acquired from producers for resale; and

(3) "producer" means an entity which engages in the growing of grain.

(c)(1) Notwithstanding sections 362, 363, 365, and 554 of this title, on the court's own motion the court may, and on the request of the trustee or an entity that claims an interest in grain or the proceeds of grain the court shall, expedite the procedures for the determination of interests in and the disposition of grain and the proceeds of grain, by shortening to the greatest extent feasible such time periods as are otherwise applicable for such procedures and by establishing, by order, a timetable having a duration of not to exceed 120 days for the completion of the applicable procedure specified in subsection (d) of this section. Such time periods and such timetable may be modified by the court, for cause, in accordance with subsection (f) of this section.

(2) The court shall determine the extent to which such time periods shall be shortened, based upon—

(A) any need of an entity claiming an interest in such grain or the proceeds of grain for a prompt determination of such interest;

(B) any need of such entity for a prompt disposition of such grain;

(C) the market for such grain;

(D) the conditions under which such grain is stored;

(E) the costs of continued storage or disposition of such grain;

(F) the orderly administration of the estate;

(G) the appropriate opportunity for an entity to assert an interest in such grain; and

(H) such other considerations as are relevant to the need to expedite such procedures in the case.

(d) The procedures that may be expedited under subsection (c) of this section include—

(1) the filing of and response to—

(A) a claim of ownership;

(B) a proof of claim;

(C) a request for abandonment;

(D) a request for relief from the stay of action against property under section 362(a) of this title;

(E) a request for determination of secured status;

(F) a request for determination of whether such grain or the proceeds of grain—

(i) is property of the estate;

(ii) must be turned over to the estate; or

(iii) may be used, sold, or leased; and

(G) any other request for determination of an interest in such grain or the proceeds of grain;

(2) the disposition of such grain or the proceeds of grain, before or after determination of interests in such grain or the proceeds of grain, by way of—

(A) sale of such grain;

(B) abandonment;

(C) distribution; or

(D) such other method as is equitable in the case;

(3) subject to sections 701, 702, 703, 1104, 1202, and 1302 of this title, the appointment of a trustee or examiner and the retention and compensation of any professional person required to assist with respect to matters relevant to the determination of interests in or disposition of such grain or the proceeds of grain; and

(4) the determination of any dispute concerning a matter specified in paragraph (1), (2), or (3) of this subsection.

(e)(1) Any governmental unit that has regulatory jurisdiction over the operation or liquidation of the debtor or the debtor's business shall be given notice of any request made or order entered under subsection (c) of this section.

(2) Any such governmental unit may raise, and may appear and be heard on, any issue relating to grain or the proceeds of grain in a case in which a request is made, or an order is entered, under subsection (c) of this section.

(3) The trustee shall consult with such governmental unit before taking any action relating to the disposition of grain in the possession, custody, or control of the debtor or the estate.

(f) The court may extend the period for final disposition of grain or the proceeds of grain under this section beyond 120 days if the court finds that—

(1) the interests of justice so require in light of the complexity of the case; and

(2) the interests of those claimants entitled to distribution of grain or the proceeds of grain will not be materially injured by such additional delay.

(g) Unless an order establishing an expedited procedure under subsection (c) of this section, or determining any interest in or approving any disposition of grain or the proceeds of grain, is stayed pending appeal—

(1) the reversal or modification of such order on appeal does not affect the validity of any procedure, determination, or disposition that occurs before such reversal or modification, whether or not any entity knew of the pendency of the appeal; and

(2) neither the court nor the trustee may delay, due to the appeal of such order, any proceeding in the case in which such order is issued.

(h)(1) The trustee may recover from grain and the proceeds of grain the reasonable and necessary costs and expenses allowable under section 503(b) of this title attributable to preserving or disposing of grain or the proceeds of grain, but may not recover from such grain or the proceeds of grain any other costs or expenses.

(2) Notwithstanding section 326(a) of this title, the dollar amounts of money specified in such section include the value, as of the date of disposition, of any grain that the trustee distributes in kind.

(i) In all cases where the quantity of a specific type of grain held by a debtor operating a grain storage facility exceeds ten thousand bushels, such grain shall be sold by the trustee and the assets thereof distributed in accordance with the provisions of this section.

§ 558. Defenses of the estate

The estate shall have the benefit of any defense available to the debtor as against any entity other than the estate, including statutes of limitation, statutes of frauds, usury, and other personal defenses. A waiver of any such defense by the debtor after the commencement of the case does not bind the estate.

§ 559. Contractual right to liquidate, terminate, or accelerate a repurchase agreement

The exercise of a contractual right of a repo participant or financial participant to cause the liquidation, termination, or acceleration of a repurchase agreement because of a condition of the kind specified in section 365(e)(1) of this title shall not be stayed, avoided, or otherwise limited by operation of any provision of this title or by order of a court or administrative agency in any proceeding under this title, unless, where the debtor is a stockbroker or securities clearing agency, such order is authorized under the provisions of the Securities Investor Protection Act of 1970 or any statute administered by the Securities and Exchange Commission. In the event that a repo participant or financial participant liquidates one or more repurchase agreements with a debtor and under the terms of one or more such agreements has agreed to deliver assets subject to repurchase agreements to the debtor, any excess of the market prices received on liquidation of such assets (or if any such assets are not disposed of on the date of liquidation of such repurchase agreements, at the prices available at the time of liquidation of such repurchase agreements from a generally recognized source or the most recent closing bid quotation from such a source) over the sum of the stated repurchase prices and all expenses in connection with the liquidation of such repurchase agreements shall be deemed property of the estate, subject to the available rights of setoff. As used in this section, the term "contractual right" includes a right set forth in a rule or bylaw of ~~; applicable to each party to the repurchase agreement,~~ a derivatives clearing organization (as defined in the Commodity Exchange Act), a multilateral clearing organization (as defined in the Federal Deposit Insurance Corporation Improvement Act of 1991), a national securities exchange, a national securities association, ~~or~~ a securities clearing agency, a contract market designated under the Commodity Exchange Act, a derivatives transaction execution facility registered under the Commodity Exchange Act, or a board of trade (as defined in the Commodity Exchange Act) or in a resolution of the governing board thereof and a right, whether or not evidenced in writing, arising under common law, under law merchant or by reason of normal business practice.

§ 560. Contractual right to liquidate, terminate, or accelerate a swap agreement

The exercise of any contractual right of any swap participant or financial participant to cause the liquidation, termination, or acceleration of ~~a~~ one or more swap agreements because of a condition of the kind specified in section 365(e)(1) of this title or to offset or net out any termination values or payment amounts arising under or in connection with the termination, liquidation, or acceleration of one or more ~~any~~ swap agreement shall not be stayed, avoided, or otherwise limited by operation of any provision of this title or by order of a court or administrative agency in any proceeding under this title. As used in this section, the term "contractual right" includes a right set forth in a rule or bylaw of a derivatives clearing organization (as defined in the Commodity Exchange Act), a multilateral clearing organization (as defined in the Federal Deposit Insurance Corporation Improvement Act of 1991), a national securities exchange, a national securities association, a securities clearing agency, a contract market designated under the Commodity Exchange Act, a derivatives transaction execution facility registered under the Commodity Exchange Act, or a board of trade (as defined in the Commodity Exchange Act) or in a resolution of the governing board thereof and a right, whether or not evidenced in writing, arising under common law, under law merchant, or by reason of normal business practice.

§ 561. Contractual right to terminate, liquidate, accelerate, or offset under a master netting agreement and across contracts; proceedings under chapter 15

(a) Subject to subsection (b), the exercise of any contractual right, because of a condition of the kind specified in section 365(e)(1), to cause the termination, liquidation, or acceleration of or to offset or net termination values, payment amounts, or other transfer obligations arising under or in connection with one or more (or the termination, liquidation, or acceleration of one or more)—

(1) securities contracts, as defined in section 741(7);

(2) commodity contracts, as defined in section 761(4);

(3) forward contracts;

(4) repurchase agreements;

(5) swap agreements; or

(6) master netting agreements,

shall not be stayed, avoided, or otherwise limited by operation of any provision of this title or by any order of a court or administrative agency in any proceeding under this title.

(b)(1) A party may exercise a contractual right described in subsection (a) to terminate, liquidate, or accelerate only to the extent that such party could exercise such a right under section 555, 556, 559, or 560 for each individual contract covered by the master netting agreement in issue.

(2) If a debtor is a commodity broker subject to subchapter IV of chapter 7—

(A) a party may not net or offset an obligation to the debtor arising under, or in connection with, a commodity contract traded on or subject to the rules of a contract market designated under the Commodity Exchange Act or a derivatives transaction execution facility registered under the Commodity Exchange Act against any claim arising under, or in connection with, other instruments, contracts, or agreements listed in subsection (a) except to the extent that the party has positive net equity in the commodity accounts at the debtor, as calculated under such subchapter; and

(B) another commodity broker may not net or offset an obligation to the debtor arising under, or in connection with, a commodity contract entered into or held on behalf of a customer of the debtor and traded on or subject to the rules of a contract market designated under the Commodity Exchange Act or a derivatives transaction execution facility registered under the Commodity Exchange Act against any claim arising under, or in connection with, other instruments, contracts, or agreements listed in subsection (a).

(3) No provision of subparagraph (A) or (B) of paragraph (2) shall prohibit the offset of claims and obligations that arise under—

(A) a cross-margining agreement or similar arrangement that has been approved by the Commodity Futures Trading Commission or submitted to the Commodity Futures Trading Commission under paragraph (1) or (2) of section 5c(c) of the Commodity Exchange Act and has not been abrogated or rendered ineffective by the Commodity Futures Trading Commission; or

(B) any other netting agreement between a clearing organization (as defined in section 761) and another entity that has been approved by the Commodity Futures Trading Commission.

(c) As used in this section, the term "contractual right" includes a right set forth in a rule or bylaw of a derivatives clearing organization (as defined in the Commodity Exchange Act), a multilateral clearing organization (as defined in the Federal Deposit Insurance Corporation Improvement Act of 1991), a national securities exchange, a national securities association, a securities clearing agency, a contract market designated under the Commodity Exchange Act, a derivatives transaction execution facility registered under the Commodity Exchange Act, or a board of trade (as defined in the Commodity Exchange Act) or in a resolution of the governing board thereof, and a right, whether or not evidenced in writing, arising under common law, under law merchant, or by reason of normal business practice.

(d) Any provisions of this title relating to securities contracts, commodity contracts, forward contracts, repurchase agreements, swap agreements, or master netting agreements shall apply in a case under chapter 15, so that enforcement of contractual provisions of such contracts and agreements in accordance with their terms will not be stayed or otherwise limited by operation of any provision of this title or by order of a court in any case under this title, and to limit avoidance powers to the same extent as in a proceeding under chapter 7 or 11 of this title (such enforcement not to be limited based on the presence or absence of assets of the debtor in the United States).

§ 562. Timing of damage measurement in connection with swap agreements, securities contracts, forward contracts, commodity contracts, repurchase agreements, and master netting agreements

(a) If the trustee rejects a swap agreement, securities contract (as defined in section 741), forward contract, commodity contract (as defined in section 761), repurchase agreement, or master netting agreement pursuant to section 365(a), or if a forward contract merchant, stockbroker, financial institution, securities clearing agency, repo participant, financial participant, master netting agreement participant, or swap participant liquidates, terminates, or accelerates such contract or agreement, damages shall be measured as of the earlier of—

(1) the date of such rejection; or

(2) the date or dates of such liquidation, termination, or acceleration.

(b) If there are not any commercially reasonable determinants of value as of any date referred to in paragraph (1) or (2) of subsection (a), damages shall be measured as of the earliest subsequent date or dates on which there are commercially reasonable determinants of value.

(c) For the purposes of subsection (b), if damages are not measured as of the date or dates of rejection, liquidation, termination, or acceleration, and the forward contract merchant, stockbroker, financial institution, securities clearing agency, repo participant, financial participant, master netting agreement participant, or swap participant or the trustee objects to the timing of the measurement of damages—

(1) the trustee, in the case of an objection by a forward contract merchant, stockbroker, financial institution, securities clearing agency, repo participant, financial participant, master netting agreement participant, or swap participant; or

(2) the forward contract merchant, stockbroker, financial institution, securities clearing agency, repo participant, financial participant, master netting agreement participant, or swap participant, in the case of an objection by the trustee, has the burden of proving that there were no commercially reasonable determinants of value as of such date or dates.

CHAPTER 7

LIQUIDATION

Subchapter I—Officers and Administration

§ 701. Interim trustee

(a)(1) Promptly after the order for relief under this chapter, the United States trustee shall appoint one disinterested person that is a member of the panel of private trustees established under section 586(a)(1) of title 28 or that is serving as trustee in the case immediately before the order for relief under this chapter to serve as interim trustee in the case.

(2) If none of the members of such panel is willing to serve as interim trustee in the case, then the United States trustee may serve as interim trustee in the case.

(b) The service of an interim trustee under this section terminates when a trustee elected or designated under section 702 of this title to serve as trustee in the case qualifies under section 322 of this title.

(c) An interim trustee serving under this section is a trustee in a case under this title.

§ 702. Election of trustee

(a) A creditor may vote for a candidate for trustee only if such creditor—

(1) holds an allowable, undisputed, fixed, liquidated, unsecured claim of a kind entitled to distribution under sections 726(a)(2), 726(a)(3), 726(a)(4), 752(a), 766(h), or 766(i) of this title;

(2) does not have an interest materially adverse, other than an equity interest that is not substantial in relation to such creditor's interest as a creditor, to the interest of creditors entitled to such distribution; and

(3) is not an insider.

(b) At the meeting of creditors held under section 341 of this title, creditors may elect one person to serve as trustee in the case if election of a trustee is requested by creditors that may vote under subsection (a) of this section, and that hold at least 20 percent in amount of the claims specified in subsection (a)(1) of this section that are held by creditors that may vote under subsection (a) of this section.

(c) A candidate for trustee is elected trustee if—

(1) creditors holding at least 20 percent in amount of the claims of a kind specified in subsection (a)(1) of this section that are held by creditors that may vote under subsection (a) of this section vote; and

(2) such candidate receives the votes of creditors holding a majority in amount of claims specified in subsection (a)(1) of this section that are held by creditors that vote for a trustee.

(d) If a trustee is not elected under this section, then the interim trustee shall serve as trustee in the case.

§ 703. Successor trustee

(a) If a trustee dies or resigns during a case, fails to qualify under section 322 of this title, or is removed under section 324 of this title, creditors may elect, in the manner specified in section 702 of this title, a person to fill the vacancy in the office of trustee.

(b) Pending election of a trustee under subsection (a) of this section, if necessary to preserve or prevent loss to the estate, the United States trustee may appoint an interim trustee in the manner specified in section 701(a).

(c) If creditors do not elect a successor trustee under subsection (a) of this section or if a trustee is needed in a case reopened under section 350 of this title, then the United States trustee—

(1) shall appoint one disinterested person that is a member of the panel of private trustees established under section 586(a)(1) of title 28 to serve as trustee in the case; or

(2) may, if none of the disinterested members of such panel is willing to serve as trustee, serve as trustee in the case.

§ 704. Duties of trustee

(a) The trustee shall—

(1) collect and reduce to money the property of the estate for which such trustee serves, and close such estate as expeditiously as is compatible with the best interests of parties in interest;

(2) be accountable for all property received;

(3) ensure that the debtor shall perform his intention as specified in section 521(2)(B) of this title;

(4) investigate the financial affairs of the debtor;

(5) if a purpose would be served, examine proofs of claims and object to the allowance of any claim that is improper;

(6) if advisable, oppose the discharge of the debtor;

(7) unless the court orders otherwise, furnish such information concerning the estate and the estate's administration as is requested by a party in interest;

(8) if the business of the debtor is authorized to be operated, file with the court, with the United States trustee, and with any governmental unit charged with responsibility for collection or determination of any tax arising out of such operation, periodic reports and summaries of the operation of such business, including a statement of receipts and disbursements, and such other information as the United States trustee or the court requires; ~~and~~

(9) make a final report and file a final account of the administration of the estate with the court and with the United States trustee~~.~~;

(10) if with respect to the debtor there is a claim for a domestic support obligation, provide the applicable notice specified in subsection (c);

(11) if, at the time of the commencement of the case, the debtor (or any entity designated by the debtor) served as the administrator (as defined in section 3 of the Employee Retirement Income Security Act of 1974) of an employee benefit plan, continue to perform the obligations required of the administrator; and

(12) use all reasonable and best efforts to transfer patients from a health care business that is in the process of being closed to an appropriate health care business that—

(A) is in the vicinity of the health care business that is closing;

(B) provides the patient with services that are substantially similar to those provided by the health care business that is in the process of being closed; and

(C) maintains a reasonable quality of care.

(b)(1) With respect to a debtor who is an individual in a case under this chapter—

(A) the United States trustee (or the bankruptcy administrator, if any) shall review all materials filed by the debtor and, not later than 10 days after the date of the first meeting of creditors, file with the court a statement as to whether the debtor's case would be presumed to be an abuse under section 707(b); and

(B) not later than 5 days after receiving a statement under subparagraph (A), the court shall provide a copy of the statement to all creditors.

(2) The United States trustee (or bankruptcy administrator, if any) shall, not later than 30 days after the date of filing a statement under paragraph (1), either file a motion to dismiss or convert under section 707(b) or file a statement setting forth the reasons the United States trustee (or the bankruptcy administrator, if any) does not consider such a motion to be appropriate, if the United States trustee (or the bankruptcy administrator, if any) determines that the debtor's case should be presumed to be an abuse under section 707(b) and the product of the debtor's current monthly income, multiplied by 12 is not less than—

(A) in the case of a debtor in a household of 1 person, the median family income of the applicable State for 1 earner; or

(B) in the case of a debtor in a household of 2 or more individuals, the highest median family income of the applicable State for a family of the same number or fewer individuals.

(c)(1) In a case described in subsection (a)(10) to which subsection (a)(10) applies, the trustee shall—

(A)(i) provide written notice to the holder of the claim described in subsection (a)(10) of such claim and of the right of such holder to use the services of the State child support enforcement agency established under sections 464 and 466 of the Social Security Act for the State in which such holder resides, for assistance in collecting child support during and after the case under this title;

(ii) include in the notice provided under clause (i) the address and telephone number of such State child support enforcement agency; and

(iii) include in the notice provided under clause (i) an explanation of the rights of such holder to payment of such claim under this chapter;

(B)(i) provide written notice to such State child support enforcement agency of such claim; and

(ii) include in the notice provided under clause (i) the name, address, and telephone number of such holder; and

(C) at such time as the debtor is granted a discharge under section 727, provide written notice to such holder and to such State child support enforcement agency of—

(i) the granting of the discharge;

(ii) the last recent known address of the debtor;

(iii) the last recent known name and address of the debtor's employer; and

(iv) the name of each creditor that holds a claim that—

(I) is not discharged under paragraph (2), (4), or (14A) of section 523(a); or

(II) was reaffirmed by the debtor under section 524(c).

(2)(A) The holder of a claim described in subsection (a)(10) or the State child support enforcement agency of the State in which such holder resides may request from a creditor described in paragraph (1)(C)(iv) the last known address of the debtor.

(B) Notwithstanding any other provision of law, a creditor that makes a disclosure of a last known address of a debtor in connection with a request made under subparagraph (A) shall not be liable by reason of making such disclosure.

§ 705. Creditors' committee

(a) At the meeting under section 341(a) of this title, creditors that may vote for a trustee under section 702(a) of this title may elect a committee of not fewer than three, and not more than eleven, creditors, each of whom holds an allowable unsecured claim of a kind entitled to distribution under section 726(a)(2) of this title.

(b) A committee elected under subsection (a) of this section may consult with the trustee or the United States trustee in connection with the administration of the estate, make recommendations to the trustee or the United States trustee respecting the performance of the trustee's duties, and submit to the court or the United States trustee any question affecting the administration of the estate.

§ 706. Conversion

(a) The debtor may convert a case under this chapter to a case under chapter 11, 12, or 13 of this title at any time, if the case has not been converted under section 1112, 1208, or 1307 of this title. Any waiver of the right to convert a case under this subsection is unenforceable.

(b) On request of a party in interest and after notice and a hearing, the court may convert a case under this chapter to a case under chapter 11 of this title at any time.

(c) The court may not convert a case under this chapter to a case under chapter 12 or 13 of this title unless the debtor requests or consents to such conversion.

(d) Notwithstanding any other provision of this section, a case may not be converted to a case under another chapter of this title unless the debtor may be a debtor under such chapter.

§ 707. Dismissal of a case or conversion to a case under chapter 11 or 13

(a) The court may dismiss a case under this chapter only after notice and a hearing and only for cause, including—

(1) unreasonable delay by the debtor that is prejudicial to creditors;

(2) nonpayment of any fees or charges required under chapter 123 of title 28; and

(3) failure of the debtor in a voluntary case to file, within fifteen days or such additional time as the court may allow after the filing of the petition commencing such case, the information required by paragraph (1) of section 521, but only on a motion by the United States trustee.

(b) (1) After notice and a hearing, the court, on its own motion or on a motion by the United States trustee, ~~but not at the request or suggestion of~~ trustee (or bankruptcy administrator, if any), or any party in interest, may dismiss a case filed by an individual debtor under this chapter whose debts are primarily consumer debts, or, with the debtor's consent, convert such a case to a case under chapter 11 or 13 of this title, if it finds that the granting of relief would be an~~ substantial~~ abuse of the provisions of this chapter. ~~There shall be a presumption in favor of granting the relief requested by the debtor.~~ In making a determination whether to dismiss a case under this section, the court may not take into consideration whether a debtor has made, or continues to make, charitable contributions (that meet the definition of "charitable contribution" under section 548(d)(3)) to any qualified religious or charitable entity or organization (as that term is defined in section 548(d)(4)).

(2)(A)(i) In considering under paragraph (1) whether the granting of relief would be an abuse of the provisions of this chapter, the court shall presume abuse exists if the debtor's current monthly income reduced by the amounts determined under clauses (ii), (iii), and (iv), and multiplied by 60 is not less than the lesser of—

(I) 25 percent of the debtor's nonpriority unsecured claims in the case, or $6,000, whichever is greater; or

(II) $10,000.

(ii)(I) The debtor's monthly expenses shall be the debtor's applicable monthly expense amounts specified under the National Standards and Local Standards, and the debtor's actual monthly expenses for the categories specified as Other Necessary Expenses issued by the Internal Revenue Service for the area in which the debtor resides, as in effect on the date of the order for relief, for the debtor, the dependents of the debtor, and the spouse of the debtor in a joint case, if the spouse is not otherwise a dependent. Such expenses shall include reasonably necessary health insurance, disability insurance, and health savings account expenses for the debtor, the spouse of the debtor, or the dependents of the debtor. Notwithstanding any other provision of this clause, the monthly expenses of the debtor shall not include any payments for debts. In addition, the debtor's monthly expenses shall include the debtor's reasonably necessary expenses incurred to maintain the safety of the debtor and the family of the debtor from family violence as identified under section 309 of the Family Violence Prevention and Services Act, or other applicable Federal law. The expenses included in the debtor's monthly expenses described in the preceding sentence shall be kept confidential by the court. In addition, if it is demonstrated that it is reasonable and necessary, the debtor's monthly expenses may also include an additional allowance for food and clothing of up to 5 percent of the food and clothing categories as specified by the National Standards issued by the Internal Revenue Service.

(II) In addition, the debtor's monthly expenses may include, if applicable, the continuation of actual expenses paid by the debtor that are reasonable and necessary for care and support of an elderly, chronically ill, or disabled household member or member of the debtor's immediate family (including parents, grandparents, siblings, children, and grandchildren of the debtor, the dependents of the debtor, and the spouse of the debtor in a joint case who is not a dependent) and who is unable to pay for such reasonable and necessary expenses.

(III) In addition, for a debtor eligible for chapter 13, the debtor's monthly expenses may include the actual administrative expenses of administering a chapter 13 plan for the district in which the debtor resides, up to an amount of 10 percent of the projected plan payments, as determined under schedules issued by the Executive Office for United States Trustees.

(IV) In addition, the debtor's monthly expenses may include the actual expenses for each dependent child less than 18 years of age, not to exceed $1,500 per year per child, to attend a private or public elementary or secondary school if the debtor provides documentation of such expenses and a detailed explanation of why such expenses are reasonable and necessary, and why such expenses are not already accounted for in the National Standards, Local Standards, or Other Necessary Expenses referred to in subclause (I).

(V) In addition, the debtor's monthly expenses may include an allowance for housing and utilities, in excess of the allowance specified by the Local Standards for housing and utilities issued by the Internal Revenue Service, based on the actual expenses for home energy costs if the debtor provides documentation of such actual expenses and demonstrates that such actual expenses are reasonable and necessary.

(iii) The debtor's average monthly payments on account of secured debts shall be calculated as the sum of—

(I) the total of all amounts scheduled as contractually due to secured creditors in each month of the 60 months following the date of the petition; and

(II) any additional payments to secured creditors necessary for the debtor, in filing a plan under chapter 13 of this title, to maintain possession of the debtor's primary residence, motor vehicle, or other property necessary for the support of the debtor and the debtor's dependents, that serves as collateral for secured debts; divided by 60.

(iv) The debtor's expenses for payment of all priority claims (including priority child support and alimony claims) shall be calculated as the total amount of debts entitled to priority, divided by 60.

(B)(i) In any proceeding brought under this subsection, the presumption of abuse may only be rebutted by demonstrating special circumstances, such as a serious medical condition or a call or order to active duty in the Armed Forces, to the extent such special circumstances that justify additional expenses or adjustments of current monthly income for which there is no reasonable alternative.

(ii) In order to establish special circumstances, the debtor shall be required to itemize each additional expense or adjustment of income and to provide—

(I) documentation for such expense or adjustment to income; and

(II) a detailed explanation of the special circumstances that make such expenses or adjustment to income necessary and reasonable.

(iii) The debtor shall attest under oath to the accuracy of any information provided to demonstrate that additional expenses or adjustments to income are required.

(iv) The presumption of abuse may only be rebutted if the additional expenses or adjustments to income referred to in clause (i) cause the product of the debtor's current monthly income reduced by the amounts determined under clauses (ii), (iii), and (iv) of subparagraph (A) when multiplied by 60 to be less than the lesser of—

(I) 25 percent of the debtor's nonpriority unsecured claims, or $6,000, whichever is greater; or

(II) $10,000.

(C) As part of the schedule of current income and expenditures required under section 521, the debtor shall include a statement of the debtor's current monthly income, and the calculations that determine whether a presumption arises under subparagraph (A)(i), that show how each such amount is calculated.

(D) Subparagraphs (A) through (C) shall not apply, and the court may not dismiss or convert a case based on any form of means testing, if the debtor is a disabled veteran (as defined in section 3741(1) of title 38), and the indebtedness occurred primarily during a period during which he or she was—

(i) on active duty (as defined in section 101(d)(1) of title 10); or

(ii) performing a homeland defense activity (as defined in section 901(1) of title 32).

(3) In considering under paragraph (1) whether the granting of relief would be an abuse of the provisions of this chapter in a case in which the presumption in subparagraph (A)(i) of such paragraph does not arise or is rebutted, the court shall consider—

(A) whether the debtor filed the petition in bad faith; or

(B) the totality of the circumstances (including whether the debtor seeks to reject a personal services contract and the financial need for such rejection as sought by the debtor) of the debtor's financial situation demonstrates abuse.

(4)(A) The court, on its own initiative or on the motion of a party in interest, in accordance with the procedures described in rule 9011 of the Federal Rules of Bankruptcy Procedure, may order the attorney for the debtor to reimburse the trustee for all reasonable costs in prosecuting a motion filed under section 707(b), including reasonable attorneys' fees, if—

(i) a trustee files a motion for dismissal or conversion under this subsection; and

(ii) the court—

(I) grants such motion; and

(II) finds that the action of the attorney for the debtor in filing a case under this chapter violated rule 9011 of the Federal Rules of Bankruptcy Procedure.

(B) If the court finds that the attorney for the debtor violated rule 9011 of the Federal Rules of Bankruptcy Procedure, the court, on its own initiative or on the motion of a party in interest, in accordance with such procedures, may order—

(i) the assessment of an appropriate civil penalty against the attorney for the debtor; and

(ii) the payment of such civil penalty to the trustee, the United States trustee (or the bankruptcy administrator, if any).

(C) The signature of an attorney on a petition, pleading, or written motion shall constitute a certification that the attorney has—

(i) performed a reasonable investigation into the circumstances that gave rise to the petition, pleading, or written motion; and

(ii) determined that the petition, pleading, or written motion—

(I) is well grounded in fact; and

(II) is warranted by existing law or a good faith argument for the extension, modification, or reversal of existing law and does not constitute an abuse under paragraph (1).

(D) The signature of an attorney on the petition shall constitute a certification that the attorney has no knowledge after an inquiry that the information in the schedules filed with such petition is incorrect.

(5)(A) Except as provided in subparagraph (B) and subject to paragraph (6), the court, on its own initiative or on the motion of a party in interest, in accordance with the procedures described in rule 9011 of the Federal Rules of Bankruptcy Procedure, may award a debtor all reasonable costs (including reasonable attorneys' fees) in contesting a motion filed by a party in interest (other than a trustee or United States trustee, (or bankruptcy administrator, if any) under this subsection if—

(i) the court does not grant the motion; and

(ii) the court finds that—

(I) the position of the party that filed the motion violated rule 9011 of the Federal Rules of Bankruptcy Procedure; or

(II) the attorney (if any) who filed the motion did not comply with the requirements of clauses (i) and (ii) of paragraph (4)(C), and the motion was made solely for the purpose of coercing a debtor into waiving a right guaranteed to the debtor under this title.

(B) A small business that has a claim of an aggregate amount less than $1,000 shall not be subject to subparagraph (A)(ii)(I).

(C) For purposes of this paragraph—

(i) the term 'small business' means an unincorporated business, partnership, corporation, association, or organization that—

(I) has fewer than 25 full-time employees as determined on the date on which the motion is filed; and

(II) is engaged in commercial or business activity; and

(ii) the number of employees of a wholly owned subsidiary of a corporation includes the employees of—

(I) a parent corporation; and

(II) any other subsidiary corporation of the parent corporation.

(6) Only the judge or United States trustee (or bankruptcy administrator, if any) may file a motion under section 707(b), if the current monthly income of the debtor, or in a joint case, the debtor and the debtor's spouse, as of the date of the order for relief, when multiplied by 12, is equal to or less than—

(A) in the case of a debtor in a household of 1 person, the median family income of the applicable State for 1 earner;

(B) in the case of a debtor in a household of 2, 3, or 4 individuals, the highest median family income of the applicable State for a family of the same number or fewer individuals; or

(C) in the case of a debtor in a household exceeding 4 individuals, the highest median family income of the applicable State for a family of 4 or fewer individuals, plus $525 per month for each individual in excess of 4.

(7)(A) No judge, United States trustee (or bankruptcy administrator, if any), trustee, or other party in interest may file a motion under paragraph (2) if the current monthly income of the debtor, including a veteran (as that term is defined in section 101 of title 38), and the debtor's spouse combined, as of the date of the order for relief when multiplied by 12, is equal to or less than—

(i) in the case of a debtor in a household of 1 person, the median family income of the applicable State for 1 earner;

(ii) in the case of a debtor in a household of 2, 3, or 4 individuals, the highest median family income of the applicable State for a family of the same number or fewer individuals; or

(iii) in the case of a debtor in a household exceeding 4 individuals, the highest median family income of the applicable State for a family of 4 or fewer individuals, plus $525 per month for each individual in excess of 4.

(B) In a case that is not a joint case, current monthly income of the debtor's spouse shall not be considered for purposes of subparagraph (A) if—

(i)(I) the debtor and the debtor's spouse are separated under applicable nonbankruptcy law; or

(II) the debtor and the debtor's spouse are living separate and apart, other than for the purpose of evading subparagraph (A); and

(ii) the debtor files a statement under penalty of perjury—

(I) specifying that the debtor meets the requirement of subclause (I) or (II) of clause (i); and

(II) disclosing the aggregate, or best estimate of the aggregate, amount of any cash or money payments received from the debtor's spouse attributed to the debtor's current monthly income.

(c)(1) In this subsection—

(A) the term 'crime of violence' has the meaning given such term in section 16 of title 18; and

(B) the term 'drug trafficking crime' has the meaning given such term in section 924(c)(2) of title 18.

(2) Except as provided in paragraph (3), after notice and a hearing, the court, on a motion by the victim of a crime of violence or a drug trafficking crime, may when it is in the best interest of the victim dismiss a voluntary case filed under this chapter by a debtor who is an individual if such individual was convicted of such crime.

(3) The court may not dismiss a case under paragraph (2) if the debtor establishes by a preponderance of the evidence that the filing of a case under this chapter is necessary to satisfy a claim for a domestic support obligation.

Subchapter II—Collection, Liquidation, and Distribution of the Estate

§ 721. Authorization to operate business

The court may authorize the trustee to operate the business of the debtor for a limited period, if such operation is in the best interest of the estate and consistent with the orderly liquidation of the estate.

§ 722. Redemption

An individual debtor may, whether or not the debtor has waived the right to redeem under this section, redeem tangible personal property intended primarily for personal, family, or household use, from a lien securing a dischargeable consumer debt, if such property is exempted under section 522 of this title or has been abandoned under section 554 of this title, by paying the holder of such lien the amount of the allowed secured claim of such holder that is secured by such lien in full at the time of redemption.

§ 723. Rights of partnership trustee against general partners

(a) If there is a deficiency of property of the estate to pay in full all claims which are allowed in a case under this chapter concerning a partnership and with respect to which a general partner of the partnership is personally liable, the trustee shall have a claim against such general partner to the extent that under applicable nonbankruptcy law such general partner is personally liable for such deficiency.

(b) To the extent practicable, the trustee shall first seek recovery of such deficiency from any general partner in such partnership that is not a debtor in a case under this title. Pending determination of such deficiency, the court may order any such partner to provide the estate with indemnity for, or assurance of payment of, any deficiency recoverable from such partner, or not to dispose of property.

(c) Notwithstanding section 728(c) of this title, the trustee has a claim against the estate of each general partner in such partnership that is a debtor in a case under this title for the full amount of all claims of creditors allowed in the case concerning such partnership. Notwithstanding section 502 of this title, there shall not be allowed in such partner's case a claim against such partner on which both such partner and such partnership are liable, except to any extent that such claim is secured only by property of such partner and not by property of such partnership. The claim of the trustee under this subsection is entitled to distribution in such partner's case under section 726(a) of this title the same as any other claim of a kind specified in such section.

(d) If the aggregate that the trustee recovers from the estates of general partners under subsection (c) of this section is greater than any deficiency not recovered under subsection (b) of this section, the court, after notice and a hearing, shall determine an equitable distribution of the surplus so recovered, and the trustee shall distribute such surplus to the estates of the general partners in such partnership according to such determination.

§ 724. Treatment of certain liens

(a) The trustee may avoid a lien that secures a claim of a kind specified in section 726(a)(4) of this title.

(b) Property in which the estate has an interest and that is subject to a lien that is not avoidable under this title (other than to the extent that there is a properly perfected unavoidable tax lien arising in connection with an ad valorem tax on real or personal property of the estate) and that secures an allowed claim for a tax, or proceeds of such property, shall be distributed—

(1) first, to any holder of an allowed claim secured by a lien on such property that is not avoidable under this title and that is senior to such tax lien;

(2) second, to any holder of a claim of a kind specified in sections 507(a)(1) (except that such expenses, other than claims for wages, salaries, or commissions that arise after the date of the filing of the petition, shall be limited to expenses incurred under chapter 7 of this title and shall not include expenses incurred under chapter 11 of this title), 507(a)(2), 507(a)(3), 507(a)(4), 507(a)(5), or 507(a)(6), or 507(a)(7) of this title, to the extent of the amount of such allowed tax claim that is secured by such tax lien;

(3) third, to the holder of such tax lien, to any extent that such holder's allowed tax claim that is secured by such tax lien exceeds any amount distributed under paragraph (2) of this subsection;

(4) fourth, to any holder of an allowed claim secured by a lien on such property that is not avoidable under this title and that is junior to such tax lien;

(5) fifth, to the holder of such tax lien, to the extent that such holder's allowed claim secured by such tax lien is not paid under paragraph (3) of this subsection; and

(6) sixth, to the estate.

(c) If more than one holder of a claim is entitled to distribution under a particular paragraph of subsection (b) of this section, distribution to such holders under such paragraph shall be in the same order as distribution to such holders would have been other than under this section.

(d) A statutory lien the priority of which is determined in the same manner as the priority of a tax lien under section 6323 of the Internal Revenue Code of 1986 shall be treated under subsection (b) of this section the same as if such lien were a tax lien.

(e) Before subordinating a tax lien on real or personal property of the estate, the trustee shall—

(1) exhaust the unencumbered assets of the estate; and

(2) in a manner consistent with section 506(c), recover from property securing an allowed secured claim the reasonable, necessary costs and expenses of preserving or disposing of such property.

(f) Notwithstanding the exclusion of ad valorem tax liens under this section and subject to the requirements of subsection (e), the following may be paid from property of the estate which secures a tax lien, or the proceeds of such property:

(1) Claims for wages, salaries, and commissions that are entitled to priority under section 507(a)(4).

(2) Claims for contributions to an employee benefit plan entitled to priority under section 507(a)(5).

§ 725. Disposition of certain property

After the commencement of a case under this chapter, but before final distribution of property of the estate under section 726 of this title, the trustee, after notice and a hearing, shall dispose of any property in which an entity other than the estate has an interest, such as a lien, and that has not been disposed of under another section of this title.

§ 726. Distribution of property of the estate

(a) Except as provided in section 510 of this title, property of the estate shall be distributed—

(1) first, in payment of claims of the kind specified in, and in the order specified in, section 507 of this title, proof of which is timely filed under section 501 of this title or tardily filed on or before the earlier of—

(A) the date that is 10 days after the mailing to creditors of the summary of the trustee's final report; or

(B) the date on which the trustee commences final distribution under this section;

(2) second, in payment of any allowed unsecured claim, other than a claim of a kind specified in paragraph (1), (3), or (4) of this subsection, proof of which is—

(A) timely filed under section 501(a) of this title;

(B) timely filed under section 501(b) or 501(c) of this title; or

(C) tardily filed under section 501(a) of this title, if—

(i) the creditor that holds such claim did not have notice or actual knowledge of the case in time for timely filing of a proof of such claim under section 501(a) of this title; and

(ii) proof of such claim is filed in time to permit payment of such claim;

(3) third, in payment of any allowed unsecured claim proof of which is tardily filed under section 501(a) of this title, other than a claim of the kind specified in paragraph (2)(C) of this subsection;

(4) fourth, in payment of any allowed claim, whether secured or unsecured, for any fine, penalty, or forfeiture, or for multiple, exemplary, or punitive damages, arising before the earlier of the order for relief or the appointment of a trustee, to the extent that such fine, penalty, forfeiture, or damages are not compensation for actual pecuniary loss suffered by the holder of such claim;

(5) fifth, in payment of interest at the legal rate from the date of the filing of the petition, on any claim paid under paragraph (1), (2), (3), or (4) of this subsection; and

(6) sixth, to the debtor.

(b) Payment on claims of a kind specified in paragraph (1), (2), (3), (4), (5), (6), (7), or (8) of section 507(a) of this title, or in paragraph (2), (3), (4), or (5) of subsection (a) of this section, shall be made pro rata among claims of the kind specified in each such particular paragraph, except that in a case that has been converted to this chapter under section ~~1009,~~ 1112, 1208, or 1307 of this title, a claim allowed under section 503(b) of this title incurred under this chapter after such conversion has priority over a claim allowed under section 503(b) of this title incurred under any other chapter of this title or under this chapter before such conversion and over any expenses of a custodian superseded under section 543 of this title.

(c) Notwithstanding subsections (a) and (b) of this section, if there is property of the kind specified in section 541(a)(2) of this title, or proceeds of such property, in the estate, such property or proceeds shall be segregated from other property of the estate, and such property or proceeds and other property of the estate shall be distributed as follows:

(1) Claims allowed under section 503 of this title shall be paid either from property of the kind specified in section 541(a)(2) of this title, or from other property of the estate, as the interest of justice requires.

(2) Allowed claims, other than claims allowed under section 503 of this title, shall be paid in the order specified in subsection (a) of this section, and, with respect to claims of a kind specified in a particular paragraph of section 507(a) of this title or subsection (a) of this section, in the following order and manner:

(A) First, community claims against the debtor or the debtor's spouse shall be paid from property of the kind specified in section 541(a)(2) of this title, except to the extent that such property is solely liable for debts of the debtor.

(B) Second, to the extent that community claims against the debtor are not paid under subparagraph (A) of this paragraph, such community claims shall be paid from property of the kind specified in section 541 (a)(2) of this title that is solely liable for debts of the debtor.

(C) Third, to the extent that all claims against the debtor including community claims against the debtor are not paid under subparagraph (A) or (B) of this paragraph such claims shall be paid from property of the estate other than property of the kind specified in section 541(a)(2) of this title.

(D) Fourth, to the extent that community claims against the debtor or the debtor's spouse are not paid under subparagraph (A), (B), or (C) of this paragraph, such claims shall be paid from all remaining property of the estate.

§ 727. Discharge

(a) The court shall grant the debtor a discharge, unless—

(1) the debtor is not an individual;

(2) the debtor, with intent to hinder, delay, or defraud a creditor or an officer of the estate charged with custody of property under this title, has transferred, removed, destroyed, mutilated, or concealed, or has permitted to be transferred, removed, destroyed, mutilated, or concealed—

(A) property of the debtor, within one year before the date of the filing of the petition; or

(B) property of the estate, after the date of the filing of the petition;

(3) the debtor has concealed, destroyed, mutilated, falsified, or failed to keep or preserve any recorded information, including books, documents, records, and papers, from which the debtor's financial condition or business transactions might be ascertained, unless such act or failure to act was justified under all of the circumstances of the case;

(4) the debtor knowingly and fraudulently, in or in connection with the case—

(A) made a false oath or account;

(B) presented or used a false claim;

(C) gave, offered, received, or attempted to obtain money, property, or advantage, or a promise of money, property, or advantage, for acting or forbearing to act; or

(D) withheld from an officer of the estate entitled to possession under this title, any recorded information, including books, documents, records, and papers, relating to the debtor's property or financial affairs;

(5) the debtor has failed to explain satisfactorily, before determination of denial of discharge under this paragraph, any loss of assets or deficiency of assets to meet the debtor's liabilities;

(6) the debtor has refused, in the case—

(A) to obey any lawful order of the court, other than an order to respond to a material question or to testify;

(B) on the ground of privilege against self-incrimination, to respond to a material question approved by the court or to testify, after the debtor has been granted immunity with respect to the matter concerning which such privilege was invoked; or

(C) on a ground other than the properly invoked privilege against self-incrimination, to respond to a material question approved by the court or to testify;

(7) the debtor has committed any act specified in paragraph (2), (3), (4), (5), or (6) of this subsection, on or within one year before the date of the filing of the petition, or during the case, in connection with another case, under this title or under the Bankruptcy Act, concerning an insider;

(8) the debtor has been granted a discharge under this section, under section 1141 of this title, or under sections 14, 371, or 476 of the Bankruptcy Act, in a case commenced within ~~six~~ 8 years before the date of the filing of the petition;

(9) the debtor has been granted a discharge under sections 1228 or 1328 of this title, or under sections 660 or 661 of the Bankruptcy Act, in a case commenced within six years before the date of the filing of the petition, unless payments under the plan in such case totaled at least—

(A) 100 percent of the allowed unsecured claims in such case; or

(B) (i) 70 percent of such claims; and

(ii) the plan was proposed by the debtor in good faith, and was the debtor's best effort; ~~or~~

(10) the court approves a written waiver of discharge executed by the debtor after the order for relief under this chapter~~.~~;

(11) after filing the petition, the debtor failed to complete an instructional course concerning personal financial management described in section 111, except that this paragraph shall not apply with respect to a debtor who is a person described in section 109(h)(4) or who resides in a district for which the United States trustee (or the bankruptcy administrator, if any) determines that the approved instructional courses are not adequate to service the additional individuals who would otherwise be required to complete such instructional courses under this section (The United States trustee (or the bankruptcy administrator, if any) who makes a determination described in this paragraph shall review such determination not later than 1 year after the date of such determination, and not less frequently than annually thereafter.); or

(12) the court after notice and a hearing held not more than 10 days before the date of the entry of the order granting the discharge finds that there is reasonable cause to believe that—

(A) section 522(q)(1) may be applicable to the debtor; and

(B) there is pending any proceeding in which the debtor may be found guilty of a felony of the kind described in section 522(q)(1)(A) or liable for a debt of the kind described in section 522(q)(1)(B).[44]

(b) Except as provided in section 523 of this title, a discharge under subsection (a) of this section discharges the debtor from all debts that arose before the date of the order for relief under this chapter, and any liability on a claim that is determined under section 502 of this title as if such claim had arisen before the commencement of the case, whether or not a proof of claim based on any such debt or liability is filed under section 501 of this title, and whether or not a claim based on any such debt or liability is allowed under section 502 of this title.

(c)(1) The trustee, a creditor, or the United States trustee may object to the granting of a discharge under subsection (a) of this section.

(2) On request of a party in interest, the court may order the trustee to examine the acts and conduct of the debtor to determine whether a ground exists for denial of discharge.

(d) On request of the trustee, a creditor, or the United States trustee, and after notice and a hearing, the court shall revoke a discharge granted under subsection (a) of this section if—

(1) such discharge was obtained through the fraud of the debtor, and the requesting party did not know of such fraud until after the granting of such discharge;

(2) the debtor acquired property that is property of the estate, or became entitled to acquire property that would be property of the estate, and knowingly and fraudulently failed to report the acquisition of or entitlement to such property, or to deliver or surrender such property to the trustee; ~~or~~

(3) the debtor committed an act specified in subsection (a)(6) of this section~~.~~; or

(4) the debtor has failed to explain satisfactorily—

(A) a material misstatement in an audit referred to in section 586(f) of title 28; or

(B) a failure to make available for inspection all necessary accounts, papers, documents, financial records, files, and all other papers, things, or property belonging to the debtor that are requested for an audit referred to in section 586(f) of title 28.[45]

(e) The trustee, a creditor, or the United States trustee may request a revocation of a discharge—

(1) under subsection (d)(1) of this section within one year after such discharge is granted; or

(2) under subsection (d)(2) or (d)(3) of this section before the later of—

(A) one year after the granting of such discharge; and

(B) the date the case is closed.

~~§ 728. Special tax provisions~~

~~(a) For the purposes of any State or local law imposing a tax on or measured by income, the taxable period of a debtor that is an individual shall terminate on the date of the order for relief under this chapter, unless the case was converted under section 1112 or 1208 of this title.~~

~~(b) Notwithstanding any State or local law imposing a tax on or measured by income, the trustee shall make tax returns of income for the estate of an individual debtor in a case under this chapter or for a debtor that is a corporation in a case under this chapter only if such estate or corporation has net taxable income for the entire period after the order for relief under this chapter during which the case is pending. If such entity has such income, or if the debtor is a partnership, then the trustee shall make and file a return of income for each taxable period during which the case was pending after the order for relief under this chapter.~~

~~(c) If there are pending a case under this chapter concerning a partnership and a case under this chapter concerning a partner in such partnership, a governmental unit's claim for any unpaid liability of such partner for a State or local tax on or measured by income, to the extent that such liability arose from the inclusion in such partner' s taxable income of earnings of such partnership that were not withdrawn by such partner, is a claim only against such partnership.~~

~~(d) Notwithstanding section 541 of this title, if there are pending a case under this chapter concerning a partnership and a case under this chapter concerning a partner in such partnership, then any State or local tax refund or reduction of tax of such partner that would have otherwise been property of the estate of such partner under section 541 of this title—~~

44 *Editor's Note*: New subsection 727(a)(12) is effective for cases commenced under title 11 on or after April 20, 2005.

45 *Editor's Note*: The changes to subsection 727(d) are effective for cases commenced under title 11 on or after April 20, 2005.

~~(1) is property of the estate of such partnership to the extent that such tax refund or reduction of tax is fairly apportionable to losses sustained by such partnership and not reimbursed by such partner; and~~

~~(2) is otherwise property of the estate of such partner.~~

* * *

CHAPTER 11

REORGANIZATION

Subchapter 1—Officers and Administration

§ 1101. Definitions for this chapter

In this chapter—

(1) "debtor in possession" means debtor except when a person that has qualified under section 322 of this title is serving as trustee in the case;

(2) "substantial consummation" means—

(A) transfer of all or substantially all of the property proposed by the plan to be transferred;

(B) assumption by the debtor or by the successor to the debtor under the plan of the business or of the management of all or substantially all of the property dealt with by the plan; and

(C) commencement of distribution under the plan.

§ 1102. Creditors' and equity security holders' committees

(a)(1) Except as provided in paragraph (3), as soon as practicable after the order for relief under chapter 11 of this title, the United States trustee shall appoint a committee of creditors holding unsecured claims and may appoint additional committees of creditors or of equity security holders as the United States trustee deems appropriate.

(2) On request of a party in interest, the court may order the appointment of additional committees of creditors or of equity security holders if necessary to assure adequate representation of creditors or of equity security holders. The United States trustee shall appoint any such committee.

(3) On request of a party in interest in a case in which the debtor is a small business debtor and for cause, the court may order that a committee of creditors not be appointed.

(4) On request of a party in interest and after notice and a hearing, the court may order the United States trustee to change the membership of a committee appointed under this subsection, if the court determines that the change is necessary to ensure adequate representation of creditors or equity security holders. The court may order the United States trustee to increase the number of members of a committee to include a creditor that is a small business concern (as described in section 3(a)(1) of the Small Business Act), if the court determines that the creditor holds claims (of the kind represented by the committee) the aggregate amount of which, in comparison to the annual gross revenue of that creditor, is disproportionately large.

(b)(1) A committee of creditors appointed under subsection (a) of this section shall ordinarily consist of the persons, willing to serve, that hold the seven largest claims against the debtor of the kinds represented on such committee, or of the members of a committee organized by creditors before the commencement of the case under this chapter, if such committee was fairly chosen and is representative of the different kinds of claims to be represented.

(2) A committee of equity security holders appointed under subsection (a)(2) of this section shall ordinarily consist of the persons, willing to serve, that hold the seven largest amounts of equity securities of the debtor of the kinds represented on such committee.

(3) A committee appointed under subsection (a) shall—

(A) provide access to information for creditors who—

(i) hold claims of the kind represented by that committee; and

(ii) are not appointed to the committee;

(B) solicit and receive comments from the creditors described in subparagraph (A); and

(C) be subject to a court order that compels any additional report or disclosure to be made to the creditors described in subparagraph (A).

§ 1103. Powers and duties of committees

(a) At a scheduled meeting of a committee appointed under section 1102 of this title, at which a majority of the members of such committee are present, and with the court's approval, such committee may select and authorize the employment by such committee of one or more attorneys, accountants, or other agents, to represent or perform services for such committee.

(b) An attorney or accountant employed to represent a committee appointed under section 1102 of this title may not, while employed by such committee, represent any other entity having an adverse interest in connection with the case. Representation of one or more creditors of the same class as represented by the committee shall not per se constitute the representation of an adverse interest.

(c) A committee appointed under section 1102 of this title may—

(1) consult with the trustee or debtor in possession concerning the administration of the case;

(2) investigate the acts, conduct, assets, liabilities, and financial condition of the debtor, the operation of the debtor's business and the desirability of the continuance of such business, and any other matter relevant to the case or to the formulation of a plan;

(3) participate in the formulation of a plan, advise those represented by such committee of such committee's determinations as to any plan formulated, and collect and file with the court acceptances or rejections of a plan;

(4) request the appointment of a trustee or examiner under section 1104 of this title; and

(5) perform such other services as are in the interest of those represented.

(d) As soon as practicable after the appointment of a committee under section 1102 of this title, the trustee shall meet with such committee to transact such business as may be necessary and proper.

§ 1104. Appointment of trustee or examiner

(a) At any time after the commencement of the case but before confirmation of a plan, on request of a party in interest or the United States trustee, and after notice and a hearing, the court shall order the appointment of a trustee—

(1) for cause, including fraud, dishonesty, incompetence, or gross mismanagement of the affairs of the debtor by current management, either before or after the commencement of the case, or similar cause, but not including the number of holders of securities of the debtor or the amount of assets or liabilities of the debtor; ~~or~~

(2) if such appointment is in the interest of creditors, any equity security holders, and other interests of the estate, without regard to the number of holders of securities of the debtor or the amount of assets or liabilities of the debtor~~.~~; or

(3) if grounds exist to convert or dismiss the case under section 1112, but the court determines that the appointment of a trustee or an examiner is in the best interests of creditors and the estate.

(b) (1) Except as provided in section 1163 of this title, on the request of a party in interest made not later than 30 days after the court orders the appointment of a trustee under subsection (a), the United States trustee shall convene a meeting of creditors for the purpose of electing one disinterested person to serve as trustee in the case. The election of a trustee shall be conducted in the manner provided in subsections (a), (b), and (c) of section 702 of this title.

(2)(A) If an eligible, disinterested trustee is elected at a meeting of creditors under paragraph (1), the United States trustee shall file a report certifying that election.

(B) Upon the filing of a report under subparagraph (A)—

(i) the trustee elected under paragraph (1) shall be considered to have been selected and appointed for purposes of this section; and

(ii) the service of any trustee appointed under subsection (d) shall terminate.

(C) The court shall resolve any dispute arising out of an election described in subparagraph (A).

(c) If the court does not order the appointment of a trustee under this section, then at any time before the confirmation of a plan, on request of a party in interest, or the United States trustee, and after notice and a hearing, the court shall order the appointment of an examiner to conduct such an investigation of the debtor as is appropriate, including an investigation of any allegations of fraud, dishonesty, incompetence, misconduct, mismanagement, or irregularity in the management of the affairs of the debtor of or by current or former management of the debtor, if—

(1) such appointment is in the interests of creditors, any equity security holders, and other interests of the estate; or

(2) the debtor's fixed, liquidated, unsecured debts, other than debts for goods, services, or taxes, or owing to an insider, exceed $5,000,000.

(d) If the court orders the appointment of a trustee or examiner, if a trustee or an examiner dies or resigns during the case or is removed under section 324 of this title, or if a trustee fails to qualify under section 322 of this title, then the United States trustee, after consultation with parties in interest shall appoint, subject to the court's approval, one disinterested person other than the United States trustee to serve as trustee or examiner, as the case may be, in the case.

(e) The United States trustee shall move for the appointment of a trustee under subsection (a) if there are reasonable grounds to suspect that current members of the governing body of the debtor, the debtor's chief executive or chief financial officer, or members of the governing body who selected the debtor's chief executive or chief financial officer, participated in actual fraud, dishonesty, or criminal conduct in the management of the debtor or the debtor's public financial reporting.[46]

§ 1105. Termination of trustee's appointment

At any time before confirmation of a plan, on request of a party in interest or the United States trustee, and after notice and a hearing, the court may terminate the trustee's appointment and restore the debtor to possession and management of the property of the estate and of the operation of the debtor's business.

§ 1106. Duties of trustee and examiner

(a) A trustee shall—

(1) perform the duties of a trustee, as specified in paragraphs ~~sections 704~~ (2), ~~704~~ (5), ~~704~~ (7), ~~704~~ (8), ~~and 704~~ (9), (10), (11), and (12) of section 704 ~~of this title~~;

(2) if the debtor has not done so, file the list, schedule, and statement required under section 521(1) of this title;

(3) except to the extent that the court orders otherwise, investigate the acts, conduct, assets, liabilities, and financial condition of the debtor, the operation of the debtor's business and the desirability of the continuance of such business, and any other matter relevant to the case or to the formulation of a plan;

(4) as soon as practicable—

(A) file a statement of any investigation conducted under paragraph (3) of this subsection, including any fact ascertained pertaining to fraud, dishonesty, incompetence, misconduct, mismanagement, or irregularity in the management of the affairs of the debtor, or to a cause of action available to the estate; and

46 *Editor's Note*: New subsection 1104(e) is effective for cases commenced under title 11 on or after April 20, 2005.

(B) transmit a copy or a summary of any such statement to any creditors' committee or equity security holders' committee, to any indenture trustee, and to such other entity as the court designates;

(5) as soon as practicable, file a plan under section 1121 of this title, file a report of why the trustee will not file a plan, or recommend conversion of the case to a case under chapter 7, 12, or 13 of this title or dismissal of the case;

(6) for any year for which the debtor has not filed a tax return required by law, furnish, without personal liability, such information as may be required by the governmental unit with which such tax return was to be filed, in light of the condition of the debtor's books and records and the availability of such information; ~~and~~

(7) after confirmation of a plan, file such reports as are necessary or as the court orders~~.~~; and

(8) if with respect to the debtor there is a claim for a domestic support obligation, provide the applicable notice specified in subsection (c).

(b) An examiner appointed under section 1104(d) of this title shall perform the duties specified in paragraphs (3) and (4) of subsection (a) of this section, and, except to the extent that the court orders otherwise, any other duties of the trustee that the court orders the debtor in possession not to perform.

(c)(1) In a case described in subsection (a)(8) to which subsection (a)(8) applies, the trustee shall—

(A)(i) provide written notice to the holder of the claim described in subsection (a)(8) of such claim and of the right of such holder to use the services of the State child support enforcement agency established under sections 464 and 466 of the Social Security Act for the State in which such holder resides, for assistance in collecting child support during and after the case under this title; and

(ii) include in the notice required by clause (i) the address and telephone number of such State child support enforcement agency;

(B)(i) provide written notice to such State child support enforcement agency of such claim; and

(ii) include in the notice required by clause (i) the name, address, and telephone number of such holder; and

(C) at such time as the debtor is granted a discharge under section 1141, provide written notice to such holder and to such State child support enforcement agency of—

(i) the granting of the discharge;

(ii) the last recent known address of the debtor;

(iii) the last recent known name and address of the debtor's employer; and

(iv) the name of each creditor that holds a claim that—

(I) is not discharged under paragraph (2), (4), or (14A) of section 523(a); or

(II) was reaffirmed by the debtor under section 524(c).

(2)(A) The holder of a claim described in subsection (a)(8) or the State child enforcement support agency of the State in which such holder resides may request from a creditor described in paragraph (1)(C)(iv) the last known address of the debtor.

(B) Notwithstanding any other provision of law, a creditor that makes a disclosure of a last known address of a debtor in connection with a request made under subparagraph (A) shall not be liable by reason of making such disclosure.

§ 1107. Rights, powers, and duties of debtor in possession

(a) Subject to any limitations on a trustee serving in a case under this chapter, and to such limitations or conditions as the court prescribes, a debtor in possession shall have all the rights, other than the right to compensation under section 330 of this title, and powers, and shall perform all the functions and duties, except the duties specified in sections 1106(a)(2), (3), and (4) of this title, of a trustee serving in a case under this chapter.

(b) Notwithstanding section 327(a) of this title, a person is not disqualified for employment under section 327 of this title by a debtor in possession solely because of such person's employment by or representation of the debtor before the commencement of the case.

§ 1108. Authorization to operate business

Unless the court, on request of a party in interest and after notice and a hearing, orders otherwise, the trustee may operate the debtor's business.

§ 1109. Right to be heard

(a) The Securities and Exchange Commission may raise and may appear and be heard on any issue in a case under this chapter, but the Securities and Exchange Commission may not appeal from any judgment, order, or decree entered in the case.

(b) A party in interest, including the debtor, the trustee, a creditors' committee, an equity security holders' committee, a creditor, an equity security holder, or any indenture trustee, may raise and may appear and be heard on any issue in a case under this chapter.

§ 1110. Aircraft equipment and vessels

(a)(1) Except as provided in paragraph (2) and subject to subsection (b), the right of a secured party with a security interest in equipment described in paragraph (3), or of a lessor or conditional vendor of such equipment, to take possession of such equipment in compliance with a security agreement, lease, or conditional sale contract, and to enforce any of its other rights or remedies, under such security agreement, lease, or conditional sale contract, to sell, lease, or otherwise retain or dispose of such equipment, is not limited or otherwise affected by any other provision of this title or by any power of the court.

(2) The right to take possession and to enforce the other rights and remedies described in paragraph (1) shall be subject to section 362 if—

(A) before the date that is 60 days after the date of the order for relief under this chapter, the trustee, subject to the approval of the court, agrees to perform all obligations of the debtor under such security agreement, lease, or conditional sale contract; and

(B) any default, other than a default of a kind specified in section 365(b)(2), under such security agreement, lease, or conditional sale contract—

(i) that occurs before the date of the order is cured before the expiration of such 60-day period;

(ii) that occurs after the date of the order and before the expiration of such 60-day period is cured before the later of—

(I) the date that is 30 days after the date of the default; or

(II) the expiration of such 60-day period; and

(iii) that occurs on or after the expiration of such 60-day period is cured in compliance with the terms of such security agreement, lease, or conditional sale contract, if a cure is permitted under that agreement, lease, or contract.

(3) The equipment described in this paragraph—

(A) is—

(i) an aircraft, aircraft engine, propeller, appliance, or spare part (as defined in section 40102 of title 49) that is subject to a security interest granted by, leased to, or conditionally sold to a debtor that, at the time such transaction is entered into, holds an air carrier operating certificate issued pursuant to chapter 447 of title 49 for aircraft capable of carrying 10 or more individuals or 6,000 pounds or more of cargo; or

(ii) a documented vessel (as defined in section 30101(1) of title 46) that is subject to a security interest granted by, leased to, or conditionally sold to a debtor that is a water carrier that, at the time such transaction is entered into, holds a certificate of public convenience and necessity or permit issued by the Department of Transportation; and

(B) includes all records and documents relating to such equipment that are required, under the terms of the security agreement, lease, or conditional sale contract, to be surrendered or returned by the debtor in connection with the surrender or return of such equipment.

(4) Paragraph (1) applies to a secured party, lessor, or conditional vendor acting in its own behalf or acting as trustee or otherwise in behalf of another party.

(b) The trustee and the secured party, lessor, or conditional vendor whose right to take possession is protected under subsection (a) may agree, subject to the approval of the court, to extend the 60-day period specified in subsection (a)(1).

(c)(1) In any case under this chapter, the trustee shall immediately surrender and return to a secured party, lessor, or conditional vendor, described in subsection (a)(1), equipment described in subsection (a)(3), if at any time after the date of the order for relief under this chapter such secured party, lessor, or conditional vendor is entitled pursuant to subsection (a)(1) to take possession of such equipment and makes a written demand for such possession to the trustee.

(2) At such time as the trustee is required under paragraph (1) to surrender and return equipment described in subsection (a)(3), any lease of such equipment, and any security agreement or conditional sale contract relating to such equipment, if such security agreement or conditional sale contract is an executory contract, shall be deemed rejected.

(d) With respect to equipment first placed in service on or before October 22, 1994, for purposes of this section—

(1) the term "lease" includes any written agreement with respect to which the lessor and the debtor, as lessee, have expressed in the agreement or in a substantially contemporaneous writing that the agreement is to be treated as a lease for Federal income tax purposes; and

(2) the term "security interest" means a purchase-money equipment security interest.

§ 1111. Claims and interests

(a) A proof of claim or interest is deemed filed under section 501 of this title for any claim or interest that appears in the schedules filed under section 521(1) or 1106(a)(2) of this title, except a claim or interest that is scheduled as disputed, contingent, or unliquidated.

(b)(1)(A) A claim secured by a lien on property of the estate shall be allowed or disallowed under section 502 of this title the same as if the holder of such claim had recourse against the debtor on account of such claim, whether or not such holder has such recourse, unless—

(i) the class of which such claim is a part elects, by at least two-thirds in amount and more than half in number of allowed claims of such class, application of paragraph (2) of this subsection; or

(ii) such holder does not have such recourse and such property is sold under section 363 of this title or is to be sold under the plan.

(B) A class of claims may not elect application of paragraph (2) of this subsection if—

(i) the interest on account of such claims in such property is of inconsequential value; or

(ii) the holder of a claim of such class has recourse against the debtor on account of such claim and such property is sold under section 363 of this title or is to be sold under the plan.

(2) If such an election is made, then notwithstanding section 506(a) of this title, such claim is a secured claim to the extent

that such claim is allowed.

§ 1112. Conversion or dismissal

(a) The debtor may convert a case under this chapter to a case under chapter 7 of this title unless—

(1) the debtor is not a debtor in possession;

(2) the case originally was commenced as an involuntary case under this chapter; or

(3) the case was converted to a case under this chapter other than on the debtor's request.

(b) (1) Except as provided in paragraph (2) of this subsection, subsection (c) of this section, and section 1104(a)(3), on request of a party in interest or the United States trustee or bankruptcy administrator, and after notice and a hearing, absent unusual circumstances specifically identified by the court that establish that the requested conversion or dismissal is not in the best interests of the creditors and the estate, the court may shall convert a case under this chapter to a case under chapter 7 of this title or may dismiss a case under this chapter, whichever is in the best interests of creditors and the estate, for if the movant establishes cause, including.

(2) The relief provided in paragraph (1) shall not be granted absent unusual circumstances specifically identified by the court that establish that such relief is not in the best interests of creditors and the estate, if the debtor or another party in interest objects and establishes that—

(A) there is a reasonable likelihood that a plan will be confirmed within the timeframes established in sections 1121(e) and 1129(e) of this title, or if such sections do not apply, within a reasonable period of time; and

(B) the grounds for granting such relief include an act or omission of the debtor other than under paragraph (4)(A)—

(i) for which there exists a reasonable justification for the act or omission; and

(ii) that will be cured within a reasonable period of time fixed by the court.

(3) The court shall commence the hearing on a motion under this subsection not later than 30 days after filing of the motion, and shall decide the motion not later than 15 days after commencement of such hearing, unless the movant expressly consents to a continuance for a specific period of time or compelling circumstances prevent the court from meeting the time limits established by this paragraph.

(4) For purposes of this subsection, the term "cause" includes—

(1A) substantial or continuing loss to or diminution of the estate and the absence of a reasonable likelihood of rehabilitation;

(2) inability to effectuate a plan;

(3) unreasonable delay by the debtor that is prejudicial to creditors;

(B) gross mismanagement of the estate;

(C) failure to maintain appropriate insurance that poses a risk to the estate or to the public;

(D) unauthorized use of cash collateral substantially harmful to 1 or more creditors;

(E) failure to comply with an order of the court;

(F) unexcused failure to satisfy timely any filing or reporting requirement established by this title or by any rule applicable to a case under this chapter;

(G) failure to attend the meeting of creditors convened under section 341(a) or an examination ordered under rule 2004 of the Federal Rules of Bankruptcy Procedure without good cause shown by the debtor;

(H) failure timely to provide information or attend meetings reasonably requested by the United States trustee (or the bankruptcy administrator, if any);

(I) failure timely to pay taxes owed after the date of the order for relief or to file tax returns due after the date of the order for relief;

(4J) failure to file a disclosure statement, or to file or confirm propos e a plan, under section 1121 of this title within any the time fixed by this title or by order of the court;

(5) denial of confirmation of every proposed plan and denial of a request made for additional time for filing another plan or a modification of a plan;

(10K) nonpayment of failure to pay any fees or charges required under chapter 123 of title 28.

(6L) revocation of an order of confirmation under section 1144 of this title, and denial of confirmation of another plan or a modified plan under section 1129 of this title;

(7M) inability to effectuate substantial consummation of a confirmed plan;

(8N) material default by the debtor with respect to a confirmed plan;

(9O) termination of a confirmed plan by reason of the occurrence of a condition specified in the plan; or and

(P) failure of the debtor to pay any domestic support obligation that first becomes payable after the date of the filing of the petition.

(10) [*Moved to become (K).*]

(c) The court may not convert a case under this chapter to a case under chapter 7 of this title if the debtor is a farmer or a corporation that is not a moneyed, business, or commercial corporation, unless the debtor requests such conversion.

(d) The court may convert a case under this chapter to a case under chapter 12 or 13 of this title only if—

(1) the debtor requests such conversion;

(2) the debtor has not been discharged under section 1141(d) of this title; and

(3) if the debtor requests conversion to chapter 12 of this title, such conversion is equitable.

(e) Except as provided in subsections (c) and (f), the court, on request of the United States trustee, may convert a case under this chapter to a case under chapter 7 of this title or may dismiss a case under this chapter, whichever is in the best interest of creditors and the estate if the debtor in a voluntary case fails to file, within fifteen days after the filing of the petition commencing such case or such additional time as the court may allow, the information required by paragraph (1) of section 521, including a list containing the names and addresses of the holders of the twenty largest unsecured claims (or of all unsecured claims if there are fewer than twenty unsecured claims), and the approximate dollar amounts of each of such claims.

(f) Notwithstanding any other provision of this section, a case may not be converted to a case under another chapter of this title unless the debtor may be a debtor under such chapter.

§ 1113. Rejection of collective bargaining agreements

(a) The debtor in possession, or the trustee if one has been appointed under the provisions of this chapter, other than a trustee in a case covered by subchapter IV of this chapter and by title I of the Railway Labor Act, may assume or reject a collective bargaining agreement only in accordance with the provisions of this section.

(b)(1) Subsequent to filing a petition and prior to filing an application seeking rejection of a collective bargaining agreement, the debtor in possession or trustee (hereinafter in this section "trustee" shall include a debtor in possession), shall—

(A) make a proposal to the authorized representative of the employees covered by such agreement, based on the most complete and reliable information available at the time of such proposal, which provides for those necessary modifications in the employees benefits and protections that are necessary to permit the reorganization of the debtor and assures that all creditors, the debtor and all of the affected parties are treated fairly and equitably; and

(B) provide, subject to subsection (d)(3), the representative of the employees with such relevant information as is necessary to evaluate the proposal.

(2) During the period beginning on the date of the making of a proposal provided for in paragraph (1) and ending on the date of the hearing provided for in subsection (d)(1), the trustee shall meet, at reasonable times, with the authorized representative to confer in good faith in attempting to reach mutually satisfactory modifications of such agreement.

(c) The court shall approve an application for rejection of a collective bargaining agreement only if the court finds that—

(1) the trustee has, prior to the hearing, made a proposal that fulfills the requirements of subsection (b) (1);

(2) the authorized representative of the employees has refused to accept such proposal without good cause; and

(3) the balance of the equities clearly favors rejection of such agreement.

(d)(1) Upon the filing of an application for rejection the court shall schedule a hearing to be held not later than fourteen days after the date of the filing of such application. All interested parties may appear and be heard at such hearing. Adequate notice shall be provided to such parties at least ten days before the date of such hearing. The court may extend the time for the commencement of such hearing for a period not exceeding seven days where the circumstances of the case, and the interests of justice require such extension, or for additional periods of time to which the trustee and representative agree.

(2) The court shall rule on such application for rejection within thirty days after the date of the commencement of the hearing. In the interests of justice, the court may extend such time for ruling for such additional period as the trustee and the employees' representative may agree to. If the court does not rule on such application within thirty days after the date of the commencement of the hearing, or within such additional time as the trustee and the employees' representative may agree to, the trustee may terminate or alter any provisions of the collective bargaining agreement pending the ruling of the court on such application.

(3) The court may enter such protective orders, consistent with the need of the authorized representative of the employee to evaluate the trustee's proposal and the application for rejection, as may be necessary to prevent disclosure of information provided to such representative where such disclosure could compromise the position of the debtor with respect to its competitors in the industry in which it is engaged.

(e) If during a period when the collective bargaining agreement continues in effect, and if essential to the continuation of the debtor's business, or in order to avoid irreparable damage to the estate, the court, after notice and a hearing, may authorize the trustee to implement interim changes in the terms, conditions, wages, benefits, or work rules provided by a collective bargaining agreement. Any hearing under this paragraph shall be scheduled in accordance with the needs of the trustee. The implementation of such interim changes shall not render the application for rejection moot.

(f) No provision of this title shall be construed to permit a trustee to unilaterally terminate or alter any provisions of a collective bargaining agreement prior to compliance with the provisions of this section.

§ 1114. Payment of insurance benefits to retired employees

(a) For purposes of this section, the term "retiree benefits" means payments to any entity or person for the purpose of providing or reimbursing payments for retired employees and their spouses and dependents, for medical, surgical, or hospital care benefits, or benefits in the event of sickness, accident, disability, or death under any plan, fund, or program (through the purchase of insurance or otherwise) maintained or established in whole or in part by the debtor prior to filing a petition commencing a case under this title.

(b)(1) For purposes of this section, the term "authorized representative" means the authorized representative designated pursuant to subsection (c) for persons receiving any retiree benefits covered by a collective bargaining agreement or subsection (d) in the case of persons receiving retiree benefits not covered by such an agreement.

(2) Committees of retired employees appointed by the court pursuant to this section shall have the same rights, powers, and duties as committees appointed under sections 1102 and 1103 of this title for the purpose of carrying out the purposes of sections 1114 and 1129(a)(13) and, as permitted by the court, shall have the power to enforce the rights of persons under this title as they relate to retiree benefits.

(c)(1) A labor organization shall be, for purposes of this section, the authorized representative of those persons receiving any retiree benefits covered by any collective bargaining agreement to which that labor organization is signatory, unless (A) such labor organization elects not to serve as the authorized representative of such persons, or (B) the court, upon a motion by any party in interest, after notice and hearing, determines that different representation of such persons is appropriate.

(2) In cases where the labor organization referred to in paragraph (1) elects not to serve as the authorized representative of those persons receiving any retiree benefits covered by any collective bargaining agreement to which that labor organization is signatory, or in cases where the court, pursuant to paragraph (1) finds different representation of such persons appropriate, the court, upon a motion by any party in interest, and after notice and a hearing, shall appoint a committee of retired employees if the debtor seeks to modify or not pay the retiree benefits or if the court otherwise determines that it is appropriate, from among such persons, to serve as the authorized representative of such persons under this section.

(d) The court, upon a motion by any party in interest, and after notice and a hearing, shall ~~appoint~~ order the appointment of a committee of retired employees if the debtor seeks to modify or not pay the retiree benefits or if the court otherwise determines that it is appropriate, to serve as the authorized representative, under this section, of those persons receiving any retiree benefits not covered by a collective bargaining agreement. The United States trustee shall appoint any such committee.

(e)(1) Notwithstanding any other provision of this title, the debtor in possession, or the trustee if one has been appointed under the provisions of this chapter (hereinafter in this section "trustee" shall include a debtor in possession), shall timely pay and shall not modify any retiree benefits, except that—

(A) the court, on motion of the trustee or authorized representative, and after notice and a hearing, may order modification of such payments, pursuant to the provisions of subsections (g) and (h) of this section, or

(B) the trustee and the authorized representative of the recipients of those benefits may agree to modification of such payments,

after which such benefits as modified shall continue to be paid by the trustee.

(2) Any payment for retiree benefits required to be made before a plan confirmed under section 1129 of this title is effective has the status of an allowed administrative expense as provided in section 503 of this title.

(f)(1) Subsequent to filing a petition and prior to filing an application seeking modification of the retiree benefits, the trustee shall—

(A) make a proposal to the authorized representative of the retirees, based on the most complete and reliable information available at the time of such proposal, which provides for those necessary modifications in the retiree benefits that are necessary to permit the reorganization of the debtor and assures that all creditors, the debtor and all of the affected parties are treated fairly and equitably; and

(B) provide, subject to subsection (k)(3), the representative of the retirees with such relevant information as is necessary to evaluate the proposal.

(2) During the period beginning on the date of the making of a proposal provided for in paragraph (1), and ending on the date of the hearing provided for in subsection (k)(1), the trustee shall meet, at reasonable times, with the authorized representative to confer in good faith in attempting to reach mutually satisfactory modifications of such retiree benefits.

(g) The court shall enter an order providing for modification in the payment of retiree benefits if the court finds that—

(1) the trustee has, prior to the hearing, made a proposal that fulfills the requirements of subsection (f);

(2) the authorized representative of the retirees has refused to accept such proposal without good cause; and

(3) such modification is necessary to permit the reorganization of the debtor and assures that all creditors, the debtor, and all of the affected parties are treated fairly and equitably, and is clearly favored by the balance of the equities;

except that in no case shall the court enter an order providing for such modification which provides for a modification to a level lower than that proposed by the trustee in the proposal found by the court to have complied with the requirements of this subsection and subsection (f): *Provided, however*, That at any time after an order is entered providing for modification in the payment of retiree benefits, or at any time after an agreement modifying such benefits is made between the trustee and the authorized representative of the recipients of such benefits, the authorized representative may apply to the court for an order increasing those benefits which order shall be granted if the increase in retiree benefits sought is consistent with the standard set forth in paragraph (3); and: *Provided further*, That neither the trustee nor the authorized representative is precluded from making more than one motion for a modification order governed by this subsection.

(h)(1) Prior to a court issuing a final order under subsection (g) of this section, if essential to the continuation of the debtor's business, or in order to avoid irreparable damage to the estate, the court, after notice and a hearing, may authorize the trustee to implement interim modifications in retiree benefits.

(2) Any hearing under this subsection shall be scheduled in accordance with the needs of the trustee.

(3) The implementation of such interim changes does not render the motion for modification moot.

(i) No retiree benefits paid between the filing of the petition and the time a plan confirmed under section 1129 of this title becomes effective shall be deducted or offset from the amounts allowed as claims for any benefits which remain unpaid, or from the amounts to be paid under the plan with respect to such claims for unpaid benefits, whether such claims for unpaid benefits are based upon or arise from a right to future unpaid benefits or from any benefits not paid as a result of modifications allowed pursuant to this section.

(j) No claim for retiree benefits shall be limited by section 502(b)(7) of this title.

(k)(1) Upon the filing of an application for modifying retiree benefits, the court shall schedule a hearing to be held not later than fourteen days after the date of the filing of such application. All interested parties may appear and be heard at such hearing. Adequate notice shall be provided to such parties at least ten days before the date of such hearing. The court may extend the time for the commencement of such hearing for a period not exceeding seven days where the circumstances of the case, and the interests of justice require such extension, or for additional periods of time to which the trustee and the authorized representative agree.

(2) The court shall rule on such application for modification within 90 days after the date of the commencement of the hearing. In the interests of justice, the court may extend such time for ruling for such additional period as the trustee and the authorized representative may agree to. If the court does not rule on such application within 90 days after the date of the commencement of the hearing, or within such additional time as the trustee and the authorized representative may agree to, the trustee may implement the proposed modifications pending the ruling of the court on such application.

(3) The court may enter such protective orders, consistent with the need of the authorized representative of the retirees to evaluate the trustee's proposal and the application for modification, as may be necessary to prevent disclosure of information provided to such representative where such disclosure could compromise the position of the debtor with respect to its competitors in the industry in which it is engaged.

(*l*) If the debtor, during the 180-day period ending on the date of the filing of the petition—

(1) modified retiree benefits; and

(2) was insolvent on the date such benefits were modified;

the court, on motion of a party in interest, and after notice and a hearing, shall issue an order reinstating as of the date the modification was made, such benefits as in effect immediately before such date unless the court finds that the balance of the equities clearly favors such modification.[47]

(~~*l*~~m) This section shall not apply to any retiree, or the spouse or dependents of such retiree, if such retiree's gross income for the 12 months preceding the filing of the bankruptcy petition equals or exceeds $250,000, unless such retiree can demonstrate to the satisfaction of the court that he is unable to obtain health, medical, life, and disability coverage for himself, his spouse, and his dependents who would otherwise be covered by the employer's insurance plan, comparable to the coverage provided by the employer on the day before the filing of a petition under this title.

§ 1115. Property of the estate

(a) In a case in which the debtor is an individual, property of the estate includes, in addition to the property specified in section 541—

(1) all property of the kind specified in section 541 that the debtor acquires after the commencement of the case but before the case is closed, dismissed, or converted to a case under chapter 7, 12, or 13, whichever occurs first; and

(2) earnings from services performed by the debtor after the commencement of the case but before the case is closed, dismissed, or converted to a case under chapter 7, 12, or 13, whichever occurs first.

(b) Except as provided in section 1104 or a confirmed plan or order confirming a plan, the debtor shall remain in possession of all property of the estate.

§ 1116. Duties of trustee or debtor in possession in small business cases

In a small business case, a trustee or the debtor in possession, in addition to the duties provided in this title and as otherwise required by law, shall—

(1) append to the voluntary petition or, in an involuntary case, file not later than 7 days after the date of the order for relief—

(A) its most recent balance sheet, statement of operations, cash-flow statement, and Federal income tax return; or

(B) a statement made under penalty of perjury that no balance sheet, statement of operations, or cash-flow statement has been prepared and no Federal tax return has been filed; (2) attend, through its senior management personnel and counsel, meetings scheduled by the court or the United States trustee, including initial debtor interviews, scheduling conferences, and meetings of creditors convened under section 341 unless the court, after notice and a hearing, waives that requirement upon a finding of extraordinary and compelling circumstances;

(3) timely file all schedules and statements of financial affairs, unless the court, after notice and a hearing, grants an extension, which shall not extend such time period to a date later than 30 days after the date of the order for relief, absent extraordinary and compelling circumstances;

---

47 *Editor's Note*: New subsection 1114(*l*) is effective for cases commenced under title 11 on or after April 20, 2005.

(4) file all postpetition financial and other reports required by the Federal Rules of Bankruptcy Procedure or by local rule of the district court;

(5) subject to section 363(c)(2), maintain insurance customary and appropriate to the industry;

(6)(A) timely file tax returns and other required government filings; and

(B) subject to section 363(c)(2), timely pay all taxes entitled to administrative expense priority except those being contested by appropriate proceedings being diligently prosecuted; and

(7) allow the United States trustee, or a designated representative of the United States trustee, to inspect the debtor's business premises, books, and records at reasonable times, after reasonable prior written notice, unless notice is waived by the debtor.

Subchapter II—The Plan

§ 1121. Who may file a plan

(a) The debtor may file a plan with a petition commencing a voluntary case, or at any time in a voluntary case or an involuntary case.

(b) Except as otherwise provided in this section, only the debtor may file a plan until after 120 days after the date of the order for relief under this chapter.

(c) Any party in interest, including the debtor, the trustee, a creditors' committee, an equity security holders' committee, a creditor, an equity security holder, or any indenture trustee, may file a plan if and only if—

(1) a trustee has been appointed under this chapter;

(2) the debtor has not filed a plan before 120 days after the date of the order for relief under this chapter; or

(3) the debtor has not filed a plan that has been accepted, before 180 days after the date of the order for relief under this chapter, by each class of claims or interests that is impaired under the plan.

(d)(1) Subject to paragraph (2), on ~~On~~ request of a party in interest made within the respective periods specified in subsections (b) and (c) of this section and after notice and a hearing, the court may for cause reduce or increase the 120-day period or the 180-day period referred to in this section.

(2)(A) The 120-day period specified in paragraph (1) may not be extended beyond a date that is 18 months after the date of the order for relief under this chapter.

(B) The 180-day period specified in paragraph (1) may not be extended beyond a date that is 20 months after the date of the order for relief under this chapter.

(e) In ~~a case in which the debtor is a small business and elects to be considered~~ a small business case—

(1) only the debtor may file a plan until after ~~100~~ 180 days after the date of the order for relief, ~~under this chapter~~ unless that period is—

(A) extended as provided by this subsection, after notice and a hearing; or

(B) the court, for cause, orders otherwise;

~~(2) all plans shall be filed within 160 days after the date of the order for relief; and~~

~~(3) on request of a party in interest made within the respective periods specified in paragraphs (1) and (2) and after notice and a hearing, the court may—~~

~~(A) reduce the 100-day period or the 160-day period specified in paragraph (1) or (2) for cause; and~~

~~(B) increase the 100-day period specified in paragraph (1) if the debtor shows that the need for an increase is caused by circumstances for which the debtor should not be held accountable.~~

(2) the plan and a disclosure statement (if any) shall be filed not later than 300 days after the date of the order for relief; and

(3) the time periods specified in paragraphs (1) and (2), and the time fixed in section 1129(e) within which the plan shall be confirmed, may be extended only if—

(A) the debtor, after providing notice to parties in interest (including the United States trustee), demonstrates by a preponderance of the evidence that it is more likely than not that the court will confirm a plan within a reasonable period of time;

(B) a new deadline is imposed at the time the extension is granted; and

(C) the order extending time is signed before the existing deadline has expired.

§ 1122. Classification of claims or interests

(a) Except as provided in subsection (b) of this section, a plan may place a claim or an interest in a particular class only if such claim or interest is substantially similar to the other claims or interests of such class.

(b) A plan may designate a separate class of claims consisting only of every unsecured claim that is less than or reduced to an amount that the court approves as reasonable and necessary for administrative convenience.

§ 1123. Contents of plan

(a) Notwithstanding any otherwise applicable nonbankruptcy law, a plan shall—

(1) designate, subject to section 1122 of this title, classes of claims, other than claims of a kind specified in section 507(a)(~~1~~2), 507(a)(~~2~~3), or 507(a)(8) of this title, and classes of interests;

(2) specify any class of claims or interests that is not impaired under the plan;

(3) specify the treatment of any class of claims or interests that is impaired under the plan;

(4) provide the same treatment for each claim or interest of a particular class, unless the holder of a particular claim or interest agrees to a less favorable treatment of such particular claim or interest;

(5) provide adequate means for the plan's implementation such as—

(A) retention by the debtor of all or any part of the property of the estate;

(B) transfer of all or any part of the property of the estate to one or more entities, whether organized before or after the confirmation of such plan;

(C) merger or consolidation of the debtor with one or more persons;

(D) sale of all or any part of the property of the estate, either subject to or free of any lien, or the distribution of all or any part of the property of the estate among those having an interest in such property of the estate;

(E) satisfaction or modification of any lien;

(F) cancellation or modification of any indenture or similar instrument;

(G) curing or waiving of any default;

(H) extension of a maturity date or a change in an interest rate or other term of outstanding securities;

(I) amendment of the debtor's charter; or

(J) issuance of securities of the debtor, or of any entity referred to in subparagraph (B) or (C) of this paragraph, for cash, for property, for existing securities, or in exchange for claims or interests, or for any other appropriate purpose;

(6) provide for the inclusion in the charter of the debtor, if the debtor is a corporation, or of any corporation referred to in paragraph (5)(B) or (5)(C) of this subsection, of a provision prohibiting the issuance of nonvoting equity securities, and providing, as to the several classes of securities possessing voting power, an appropriate distribution of such power among such classes, including, in the case of any class of equity securities having a preference over another class of equity securities with respect to dividends, adequate provisions for the election of directors representing such preferred class in the event of default in the payment of such dividends; ~~and~~

(7) contain only provisions that are consistent with the interests of creditors and equity security holders and with public policy with respect to the manner of selection of any officer, director, or trustee under the plan and any successor to such officer, director, or trustee; and

(8) in a case in which the debtor is an individual, provide for the payment to creditors under the plan of all or such portion of earnings from personal services performed by the debtor after the commencement of the case or other future income of the debtor as is necessary for the execution of the plan.

(b) Subject to subsection (a) of this section, a plan may—

(1) impair or leave unimpaired any class of claims, secured or unsecured, or of interests;

(2) subject to section 365 of this title, provide for the assumption, rejection, or assignment of any executory contract or unexpired lease of the debtor not previously rejected under such section;

(3) provide for—

(A) the settlement or adjustment of any claim or interest belonging to the debtor or to the estate; or

(B) the retention and enforcement by the debtor, by the trustee, or by a representative of the estate appointed for such purpose, of any such claim or interest;

(4) provide for the sale of all or substantially all of the property of the estate, and the distribution of the proceeds of such sale among holders of claims or interests;

(5) modify the rights of holders of secured claims, other than a claim secured only by a security interest in real property that is the debtor's principal residence, or of holders of unsecured claims, or leave unaffected the rights of holders of any class of claims; and

(6) include any other appropriate provision not inconsistent with the applicable provisions of this title.

(c) In a case concerning an individual, a plan proposed by an entity other than the debtor may not provide for the use, sale, or lease of property exempted under section 522 of this title, unless the debtor consents to such use, sale, or lease.

(d) Notwithstanding subsection (a) of this section and sections 506(b), 1129(a)(7), and 1129(b) of this title, if it is proposed in a plan to cure a default the amount necessary to cure the default, shall be determined in accordance with the underlying agreement and applicable nonbankruptcy law.

§ 1124. Impairment of claims or interests

Except as provided in section 1123(a)(4) of this title, a class of claims or interests is impaired under a plan unless, with respect to each claim or interest of such class, the plan—

(1) leaves unaltered the legal, equitable, and contractual rights to which such claim or interest entitles the holder of such claim or interest; or

(2) notwithstanding any contractual provision or applicable law that entitles the holder of such claim or interest to demand or receive accelerated payment of such claim or interest after the occurrence of a default—

(A) cures any such default that occurred before or after the commencement of the case under this title or of a kind that section 365(b)(2) expressly does not require to be cured, other than a default of a kind specified in section 365(b)(2) of this title;

(B) reinstates the maturity of such claim or interest as such maturity existed before such default;

(C) compensates the holder of such claim or interest for any damages incurred as a result of any reasonable reliance by such holder on such contractual provision or such applicable law; and

(D) if such claim or such interest arises from any failure to perform a nonmonetary obligation, other than a default arising from failure to operate a nonresidential real property lease subject to section 365(b)(1)(A), compensates the holder of such claim or such interest (other than the debtor or an insider) for any actual pecuniary loss incurred by such holder as a result of such failure;

(~~D~~E) does not otherwise alter the legal, equitable, or contractual rights to which such claim or interest entitles the holder of such claim or interest.

§ 1125. Postpetition disclosure and solicitation

(a) In this section—

(1) "adequate information" means information of a kind, and in sufficient detail, as far as is reasonably practicable in light of the nature and history of the debtor and the condition of the debtor's books and records, including a discussion of the potential material Federal tax consequences of the plan to the debtor, any successor to the debtor, and a hypothetical investor typical of the holders of claims or interests in the case, that would enable such a hypothetical ~~reasonable~~ investor ~~typical of holders of claims or interests~~ of the relevant class to make an informed judgment about the plan, but adequate information need not include such information about any other possible or proposed plan and in determining whether a disclosure statement provides adequate information, the court shall consider the complexity of the case, the benefit of additional information to creditors and other parties in interest, and the cost of providing additional information; and

(2) "investor typical of holders of claims or interests of the relevant class" means investor having—

(A) a claim or interest of the relevant class;

(B) such a relationship with the debtor as the holders of other claims or interests of such class generally have; and

(C) such ability to obtain such information from sources other than the disclosure required by this section as holders of claims or interests in such class generally have.

(b) An acceptance or rejection of a plan may not be solicited after the commencement of the case under this title from a holder of a claim or interest with respect to such claim or interest unless, at the time of or before such solicitation, there is transmitted to such holder the plan or a summary of the plan, and a written disclosure statement approved, after notice and a hearing, by the court as containing adequate information. The court may approve a disclosure statement without a valuation of the debtor or an appraisal of the debtor's assets.

(c) The same disclosure statement shall be transmitted to each holder of a claim or interest of a particular class, but there may be transmitted different disclosure statements, differing in amount, detail, or kind of information, as between classes.

(d) Whether a disclosure statement required under subsection (b) of this section contains adequate information is not governed by any otherwise applicable non-bankruptcy law, rule, or regulation, but an agency or official whose duty is to administer or enforce such a law, rule, or regulation may be heard on the issue of whether a disclosure statement contains adequate information. Such an agency or official may not appeal from, or otherwise seek review of, an order approving a disclosure statement.

(e) A person that solicits acceptance or rejection of a plan, in good faith and in compliance with the applicable provisions of this title, or that participates, in good faith and in compliance with the applicable provisions of this title, in the offer, issuance, sale, or purchase of a security, offered or sold under the plan, of the debtor, of an affiliate participating in a joint plan with the debtor, or of a newly organized successor to the debtor under the plan, is not liable, on account of such solicitation or participation, for violation of any applicable law, rule, or regulation governing solicitation of acceptance or rejection of a plan or the offer, issuance, sale, or purchase of securities.

(f) Notwithstanding subsection (b), in a small business case ~~in which the debtor has elected under section 1121(e) to be considered a small business—~~

(1) the court may determine that the plan itself provides adequate information and that a separate disclosure statement is not necessary;

(2) the court may approve a disclosure statement submitted on standard forms approved by the court or adopted under section 2075 of title 28; and

(~~1~~3)(A) the court may conditionally approve a disclosure statement subject to final approval after notice and a hearing;

(~~2~~B) acceptances and rejections of a plan may be solicited based on a conditionally approved disclosure statement ~~as long as~~ if the debtor provides adequate information to each holder of a claim or interest that is solicited, but a conditionally approved disclosure statement shall be mailed ~~at least 10~~ not later than 25 days ~~prior to~~ before the date of the hearing on confirmation of the plan; and

(~~3~~C) ~~a~~ the hearing on the disclosure statement may be combined with ~~a~~ the hearing on confirmation of a plan.

(g) Notwithstanding subsection (b), an acceptance or rejection of the plan may be solicited from a holder of a claim or interest if such solicitation complies with applicable nonbankruptcy law and if such holder was solicited before the commencement of the case in a manner complying with applicable nonbankruptcy law.

§ 1126. Acceptance of plan

(a) The holder of a claim or interest allowed under section 502 of this title may accept or reject a plan. If the United States is a creditor or equity security holder, the Secretary of the Treasury may accept or reject the plan on behalf of the United States.

(b) For the purposes of subsections (c) and (d) of this section, a holder of a claim or interest that has accepted or rejected the plan before the commencement of the case under this title is deemed to have accepted or rejected such plan, as the case may be, if—

(1) the solicitation of such acceptance or rejection was in compliance with any applicable nonbankruptcy law, rule, or regulation governing the adequacy of disclosure in connection with such solicitation; or

(2) if there is not any such law, rule, or regulation, such acceptance or rejection was solicited after disclosure to such holder of adequate information, as defined in section 1125(a) of this title.

(c) A class of claims has accepted a plan if such plan has been accepted by creditors, other than any entity designated under subsection (e) of this section, that hold at least two-thirds in amount and more than one-half in number of the allowed claims of such class held by creditors, other than any entity designated under subsection (e) of this section, that have accepted or rejected such plan.

(d) A class of interests has accepted a plan if such plan has been accepted by holders of such interests, other than any entity designated under subsection (e) of this section, that hold at least two-thirds in amount of the allowed interests of such class held by holders of such interests, other than any entity designated under subsection (e) of this section, that have accepted or rejected such plan.

(e) On request of a party in interest, and after notice and a hearing, the court may designate any entity whose acceptance or rejection of such plan was not in good faith, or was not solicited or procured in good faith or in accordance with the provisions of this title.

(f) Notwithstanding any other provision of this section, a class that is not impaired under a plan, and each holder of a claim or interest of such class, are conclusively presumed to have accepted the plan, and solicitation of acceptances with respect to such class from the holders of claims or interests of such class is not required.

(g) Notwithstanding any other provision of this section, a class is deemed not to have accepted a plan if such plan provides that the claims or interests of such class do not entitle the holders of such claims or interests to receive or retain any property under the plan on account of such claims or interests.

§ 1127. Modification of plan

(a) The proponent of a plan may modify such plan at any time before confirmation, but may not modify such plan so that such plan as modified fails to meet the requirements of sections 1122 and 1123 of this title. After the proponent of a plan files a modification of such plan with the court, the plan as modified becomes the plan.

(b) The proponent of a plan or the reorganized debtor may modify such plan at any time after confirmation of such plan and before substantial consummation of such plan, but may not modify such plan so that such plan as modified fails to meet the requirements of sections 1122 and 1123 of this title. Such plan as modified under this subsection becomes the plan only if circumstances warrant such modification and the court, after notice and a hearing, confirms such plan as modified, under section 1129 of this title.

(c) The proponent of a modification shall comply with section 1125 of this title with respect to the plan as modified.

(d) Any holder of a claim or interest that has accepted or rejected a plan is deemed to have accepted or rejected, as the case may be, such plan as modified, unless, within the time fixed by the court, such holder changes such holder's previous acceptance or rejection.

(e) If the debtor is an individual, the plan may be modified at any time after confirmation of the plan but before the completion of payments under the plan, whether or not the plan has been substantially consummated, upon request of the debtor, the trustee, the United States trustee, or the holder of an allowed unsecured claim, to—

(1) increase or reduce the amount of payments on claims of a particular class provided for by the plan;

(2) extend or reduce the time period for such payments; or

(3) alter the amount of the distribution to a creditor whose claim is provided for by the plan to the extent necessary to take account of any payment of such claim made other than under the plan.

(f)(1) Sections 1121 through 1128 and the requirements of section 1129 apply to any modification under subsection (a).

(2) The plan, as modified, shall become the plan only after there has been disclosure under section 1125 as the court may direct, notice and a hearing, and such modification is approved.

§ 1128. Confirmation hearing

(a) After notice, the court shall hold a hearing on confirmation of a plan.

(b) A party in interest may object to confirmation of a plan.

§ 1129. Confirmation of plan

(a) The court shall confirm a plan only if all of the following requirements are met:

(1) The plan complies with the applicable provisions of this title.

(2) The proponent of the plan complies with the applicable provisions of this title.

(3) The plan has been proposed in good faith and not by any means forbidden by law.

(4) Any payment made or to be made by the proponent, by the debtor, or by a person issuing securities or acquiring property under the plan, for services or for costs and expenses in or in connection with the case, or in connection with the plan and incident to the case, has been approved by, or is subject to the approval of, the court as reasonable.

(5)(A)(i) The proponent of the plan has disclosed the identity and affiliations of any individual proposed to serve, after confirmation of the plan, as a director, officer, or voting trustee of the debtor, an affiliate of the debtor participating in a joint plan with the debtor, or a successor to the debtor under the plan; and

(ii) the appointment to, or continuance in, such office of such individual, is consistent with the interests of creditors and equity security holders and with public policy; and

(B) the proponent of the plan has disclosed the identity of any insider that will be employed or retained by the reorganized debtor, and the nature of any compensation for such insider.

(6) Any governmental regulatory commission with jurisdiction, after confirmation of the plan, over the rates of the debtor has approved any rate change provided for in the plan, or such rate change is expressly conditioned on such approval.

(7) With respect to each impaired class of claims or interests—

(A) each holder of a claim or interest of such class—

(i) has accepted the plan; or

(ii) will receive or retain under the plan on account of such claim or interest property of a value, as of the effective date of the plan, that is not less than the amount that such holder would so receive or retain if the debtor were liquidated under chapter 7 of this title on such date; or

(B) if section 1111(b)(2) of this title applies to the claims of such class, each holder of a claim of such class will receive or retain under the plan on account of such claim property of a value, as of the effective date of the plan, that is not less than the value of such holder's interest in the estate's interest in the property that secures such claims.

(8) With respect to each class of claims or interests—

(A) such class has accepted the plan; or

(B) such class is not impaired under the plan.

(9) Except to the extent that the holder of a particular claim has agreed to a different treatment of such claim, the plan provides that—

(A) with respect to a claim of a kind specified in section 507(a)(~~1~~2) or 507(a)(~~2~~3) of this title, on the effective date of the plan, the holder of such claim will receive on account of such claim cash equal to the allowed amount of such claim;

(B) with respect to a class of claims of a kind specified in section 507(a)(~~3~~1), 507(a)(4), 507(a)(5), 507(a)(6), or 507(a)(7) of this title, each holder of a claim of such class will receive—

(i) if such class has accepted the plan, deferred cash payments of a value, as of the effective date of the plan, equal to the allowed amount of such claim; or

(ii) if such class has not accepted the plan, cash on the effective date of the plan equal to the allowed amount of such claim; ~~and~~

(C) with respect to a claim of a kind specified in section 507(a)(8) of this title, the holder of such claim will receive on account of such claim ~~deferred cash~~ regular installment payments in cash, ~~over a period not exceeding six years after the date of assessment of such claim,~~

(i) of a total value, as of the effective date of the plan, equal to the allowed amount of such claim;

(ii) over a period ending not later than 5 years after the date of the order for relief under section 301, 302, or 303; and

(iii) in a manner not less favorable than the most favored nonpriority unsecured claim provided for by the plan (other than cash payments made to a class of creditors under section 1122(b)); and

(D) with respect to a secured claim which would otherwise meet the description of an unsecured claim of a governmental unit under section 507(a)(8), but for the secured status of that claim, the holder of that claim will receive on account of that claim, cash payments, in the same manner and over the same period, as prescribed in subparagraph (C).

(10) If a class of claims is impaired under the plan, at least one class of claims that is impaired under the plan has accepted the plan, determined without including any acceptance of the plan by any insider.

(11) Confirmation of the plan is not likely to be followed by the liquidation, or the need for further financial reorganization, of the debtor or any successor to the debtor under the plan, unless such liquidation or reorganization is proposed in the plan.

(12) All fees payable under section 1930 of title 28, as determined by the court at the hearing on confirmation of the plan, have been paid or the plan provides for the payment of all such fees on the effective date of the plan.

(13) The plan provides for the continuation after its effective date of payment of all retiree benefits, as that term is defined in section 1114 of this title, at the level established pursuant to subsection (e)(1)(B) or (g) of section 1114 of this title, at any time prior to confirmation of the plan, for the duration of the period the debtor has obligated itself to provide such benefits.

(14) If the debtor is required by a judicial or administrative order, or by statute, to pay a domestic support obligation, the debtor has paid all amounts payable under such order or such statute for such obligation that first become payable after the date of the filing of the petition.

(15) In a case in which the debtor is an individual and in which the holder of an allowed unsecured claim objects to the confirmation of the plan—

(A) the value, as of the effective date of the plan, of the property to be distributed under the plan on account of such claim is not less than the amount of such claim; or

(B) the value of the property to be distributed under the plan is not less than the projected disposable income of the debtor (as defined in section 1325(b)(2)) to be received during the 5-year period beginning on the date that the first payment is due under the plan, or during the period for which the plan provides payments, whichever is longer.

(16) All transfers of property of the plan shall be made in accordance with any applicable provisions of nonbankruptcy law

that govern the transfer of property by a corporation or trust that is not a moneyed, business, or commercial corporation or trust.[48]

(b)(1) Notwithstanding section 510(a) of this title, if all of the applicable requirements of subsection (a) of this section other than paragraph (8) are met with respect to a plan, the court, on request of the proponent of the plan, shall confirm the plan notwithstanding the requirements of such paragraph if the plan does not discriminate unfairly, and is fair and equitable, with respect to each class of claims or interests that is impaired under, and has not accepted, the plan.

(2) For the purpose of this subsection, the condition that a plan be fair and equitable with respect to a class includes the following requirements:

(A) With respect to a class of secured claims, the plan provides—

(i)(I) that the holders of such claims retain the liens securing such claims, whether the property subject to such liens is retained by the debtor or transferred to another entity, to the extent of the allowed amount of such claims; and

(II) that each holder of a claim of such class receive on account of such claim deferred cash payments totaling at least the allowed amount of such claim, of a value, as of the effective date of the plan, of at least the value of such holder's interest in the estate's interest in such property;

(ii) for the sale, subject to section 363(k) of this title, of any property that is subject to the liens securing such claims, free and clear of such liens, with such liens to attach to the proceeds of such sale, and the treatment of such liens on proceeds under clause (i) or (iii) of this subparagraph; or

(iii) for the realization by such holders of the indubitable equivalent of such claims.

(B) With respect to a class of unsecured claims—

(i) the plan provides that each holder of a claim of such class receive or retain on account of such claim property of a value, as of the effective date of the plan, equal to the allowed amount of such claim; or

(ii) the holder of any claim or interest that is junior to the claims of such class will not receive or retain under the plan on account of such junior claim or interest any property, except that in a case in which the debtor is an individual, the debtor may retain property included in the estate under section 1115, subject to the requirements of subsection (a)(14) of this section.

48 *Editor's Note*: New subsection 1129(a)(16) applies to cases pending under title 11 on April 20, 2005 and to cases commenced on or after that date, except that a court shall not confirm a plan under chapter 11 of title 11 without considering whether these changes would substantially affect the rights of a party in interest who first acquired rights with respect to the debtor after the date of the petition.

(C) With respect to a class of interests—

(i) the plan provides that each holder of an interest of such class receive or retain on account of such interest property of a value, as of the effective date of the plan, equal to the greatest of the allowed amount of any fixed liquidation preference to which such holder is entitled, any fixed redemption price to which such holder is entitled, or the value of such interest; or

(ii) the holder of any interest that is junior to the interests of such class will not receive or retain under the plan on account of such junior interest any property.

(c) Notwithstanding subsections (a) and (b) of this section and except as provided in section 1127(b) of this title, the court may confirm only one plan, unless the order of confirmation in the case has been revoked under section 1144 of this title. If the requirements of subsections (a) and (b) of this section are met with respect to more than one plan, the court shall consider the preferences of creditors and equity security holders in determining which plan to confirm.

(d) Notwithstanding any other provision of this section, on request of a party in interest that is a governmental unit, the court may not confirm a plan if the principal purpose of the plan is the avoidance of taxes or the avoidance of the application of section 5 of the Securities Act of 1933. In any hearing under this subsection, the governmental unit has the burden of proof on the issue of avoidance.

(e) In a small business case, the court shall confirm a plan that complies with the applicable provisions of this title and that is filed in accordance with section 1121(e) not later than 45 days after the plan is filed unless the time for confirmation is extended in accordance with section 1121(e)(3).

Subchapter III—Postconfirmation Matters

§ 1141. Effect of confirmation

(a) Except as provided in subsections (d)(2) and (d)(3) of this section, the provisions of a confirmed plan bind the debtor, any entity issuing securities under the plan, any entity acquiring property under the plan, and any creditor, equity security holder, or general partner in the debtor, whether or not the claim or interest of such creditor, equity security holder, or general partner is impaired under the plan and whether or not such creditor, equity security holder, or general partner has accepted the plan.

(b) Except as otherwise provided in the plan or the order confirming the plan, the confirmation of a plan vests all of the property of the estate in the debtor.

(c) Except as provided in subsections (d)(2) and (d)(3) of this section and except as otherwise provided in the plan or in the order confirming the plan, after confirmation of a plan, the property dealt with by the plan is free and clear of all claims and interests of creditors, equity security holders, and of general partners in the debtor.

(d)(1) Except as otherwise provided in this subsection, in the plan, or in the order confirming the plan, the confirmation of a plan—

(A) discharges the debtor from any debt that arose before the date of such confirmation, and any debt of a kind specified in section 502(g), 502(h) or 502(i) of this title, whether or not—

(i) a proof of the claim based on such debt is filed or deemed filed under section 501 of this title;

(ii) such claim is allowed under section 502 of this title; or

(iii) the holder of such claim has accepted the plan; and

(B) terminates all rights and interests of equity security holders and general partners provided for by the plan.

(2) ~~The confirmation of a plan does not~~ A discharge under this chapter does not discharge a debtor who is an individual ~~debtor~~ from any debt excepted from discharge under section 523 of this title.

(3) The confirmation of a plan does not discharge a debtor if-

(A) the plan provides for the liquidation of all or substantially all of the property of the estate;

(B) the debtor does not engage in business after consummation of the plan; and

(C) the debtor would be denied a discharge under section 727(a) of this title if the case were a case under chapter 7 of this title.

(4) The court may approve a written waiver of discharge executed by the debtor after the order for relief under this chapter.

(5) In a case in which the debtor is an individual—

(A) unless after notice and a hearing the court orders otherwise for cause, confirmation of the plan does not discharge any debt provided for in the plan until the court grants a discharge on completion of all payments under the plan;

(B) at any time after the confirmation of the plan, and after notice and a hearing, the court may grant a discharge to the debtor who has not completed payments under the plan if—

(i) the value, as of the effective date of the plan, of property actually distributed under the plan on account of each allowed unsecured claim is not less than the amount that would have been paid on such claim if the estate of the debtor had been liquidated under chapter 7 on such date; and

(ii) modification of the plan under section 1127 is not practicable; and

(C) unless after notice and a hearing held not more than 10 days before the date of the entry of the order granting the discharge, the court finds that there is no reasonable cause to believe that—

(i) section 522(q)(1) may be applicable to the debtor; and

(ii) there is pending any proceeding in which the debtor may be found guilty of a felony of the kind described in section 522(q)(1)(A) or liable for a debt of the kind described in section 522(q)(1)(B).[49]

(6) Notwithstanding paragraph (1), the confirmation of a plan does not discharge a debtor that is a corporation from any debt—

(A) of a kind specified in paragraph (2)(A) or (2)(B) of section 523(a) that is owed to a domestic governmental unit, or owed to a person as the result of an action filed under subchapter III of chapter 37 of title 31 or any similar State statute; or

(B) for a tax or customs duty with respect to which the debtor—

(i) made a fraudulent return; or

(ii) willfully attempted in any manner to evade or to defeat such tax or such customs duty.

§ 1142. Implementation of plan

(a) Notwithstanding any otherwise applicable nonbankruptcy law, rule, or regulation relating to financial condition, the debtor and any entity organized or to be organized for the purpose of carrying out the plan shall carry out the plan and shall comply with any orders of the court.

(b) The court may direct the debtor and any other necessary party to execute or deliver or to join in the execution or delivery of any instrument required to effect a transfer of property dealt with by a confirmed plan, and to perform any other act, including the satisfaction of any lien, that is necessary for the consummation of the plan.

§ 1143. Distribution

If a plan requires presentment or surrender of a security or the performance of any other act as a condition to participation in distribution under the plan, such action shall be taken not later than five years after the date of the entry of the order of confirmation. Any entity that has not within such time presented or surrendered such entity's security or taken any such other action that the plan requires may not participate in distribution under the plan.

§ 1144. Revocation of an order of confirmation

On request of a party in interest at any time before 180 days after the date of the entry of the order of confirmation, and after notice and a hearing, the court may revoke such order if and only if such order was procured by fraud. An order under this section revoking an order of confirmation shall—

(1) contain such provisions as are necessary to protect any entity acquiring rights in good faith reliance on the order of confirmation; and

(2) revoke the discharge of the debtor.

§ 1145. Exemption from securities laws

(a) Except with respect to an entity that is an underwriter as defined in subsection (b) of this section, section 5 of the Securities Act of 1933 and any State or local law requiring registration for offer or sale of a security or registration or licensing of an issuer of, underwriter of, or broker or dealer in, a security do not apply to-

---

49 *Editor's Note*: New subsection 1141(d)(5)(C) is effective for cases commenced under title 11 on or after April 20, 2005.

(1) the offer or sale under a plan of a security of the debtor, of an affiliate participating in a joint plan with the debtor, or of a successor to the debtor under the plan—

(A) in exchange for a claim against, an interest in, or a claim for an administrative expense in the case concerning, the debtor or such affiliate; or

(B) principally in such exchange and partly for cash or property;

(2) the offer of a security through any warrant, option, right to subscribe, or conversion privilege that was sold in the manner specified in paragraph (1) of this subsection, or the sale of a security upon the exercise of such a warrant, option, right, or privilege;

(3) the offer or sale, other than under a plan, of a security of an issuer other than the debtor or an affiliate, if—

(A) such security was owned by the debtor on the date of the filing of the petition;

(B) the issuer of such security is—

(i) required to file reports under section 13 or 15(d) of the Securities Exchange Act of 1934; and

(ii) in compliance with the disclosure and reporting provision of such applicable section; and

(C) such offer or sale is of securities that do not exceed—

(i) during the two-year period immediately following the date of the filing of the petition, four percent of the securities of such class outstanding on such date; and

(ii) during any 180-day period following such two-year period, one percent of the securities outstanding at the beginning of such 180-day period; or

(4) a transaction by a stockbroker in a security that is executed after a transaction of a kind specified in paragraph (1) or (2) of this subsection in such security and before the expiration of 40 days after the first date on which such security was bona fide offered to the public by the issuer or by or through an underwriter, if such stockbroker provides, at the time of or before such transaction by such stockbroker, a disclosure statement approved under section 1125 of this title, and, if the court orders, information supplementing such disclosure statement.

(b)(1) Except as provided in paragraph (2) of this subsection and except with respect to ordinary trading transactions of an entity that is not an issuer, an entity is an underwriter under section 2(11) of the Securities Act of 1933, if such entity—

(A) purchases a claim against, interest in, or claim for an administrative expense in the case concerning, the debtor, if such purchase is with a view to distribution of any security received or to be received in exchange for such a claim or interest;

(B) offers to sell securities offered or sold under the plan for the holders of such securities;

(C) offers to buy securities offered or sold under the plan from the holders of such securities, if such offer to buy is—

(i) with a view to distribution of such securities; and

(ii) under an agreement made in connection with the plan, with the consummation of the plan, or with the offer or sale of securities under the plan; or

(D) is an issuer, as used in such section 2(11), with respect to such securities.

(2) An entity is not an underwriter under section 2(11) of the Securities Act of 1933 or under paragraph (1) of this subsection with respect to an agreement that provides only for—

(A)(i) the matching or combining of fractional interests in securities offered or sold under the plan into whole interests; or

(ii) the purchase or sale of such fractional interests from or to entities receiving such fractional interests under the plan; or

(B) the purchase or sale for such entities of such fractional or whole interests as are necessary to adjust for any remaining fractional interests after such matching.

(3) An entity other than an entity of the kind specified in paragraph (1) of this subsection is not an underwriter under section 2(11) of the Securities Act of 1933 with respect to any securities offered or sold to such entity in the manner specified in subsection (a)(1) of this section.

(c) An offer or sale of securities of the kind and in the manner specified under subsection (a)(1) of this section is deemed to be a public offering.

(d) The Trust Indenture Act of 1939 does not apply to a note issued under the plan that matures not later than one year after the effective date of the plan.

§ 1146. Special tax provisions

~~(a) For the purposes of any State or local law imposing a tax on or measured by income, the taxable period of a debtor that is an individual shall terminate on the date of the order for relief under this chapter, unless the case was converted under section 706 of this title.~~

~~(b) The trustee shall make a State or local tax return of income for the estate of an individual debtor in a case under this chapter for each taxable period after the order for relief under this chapter during which the case is pending.~~

(~~c~~a) The issuance, transfer, or exchange of a security, or the making or delivery of an instrument of transfer under a plan confirmed under section 1129 of this title, may not be taxed under any law imposing a stamp tax or similar tax.

(~~d~~b) The court may authorize the proponent of a plan to request a determination, limited to questions of law, by a State or local governmental unit charged with responsibility for collection or determination of a tax on or measured by income, of the tax effects, under section 346 of this title and under the law imposing such tax, of the plan. In the event of an actual controversy, the court may declare such effects after the earlier of—

(1) the date on which such governmental unit responds to the request under this subsection; or

(2) 270 days after such request.

* * *

CHAPTER 12[50]

ADJUSTMENT OF DEBTS OF A FAMILY FARMER OR FISHERMAN WITH REGULAR ANNUAL INCOME

Subchapter I—Officers, Administration, and the Estate

§ 1201. Stay of action against codebtor

(a) Except as provided in subsections (b) and (c) of this section, after the order for relief under this chapter, a creditor may not act, or commence or continue any civil action, to collect all or any part of a consumer debt of the debtor from any individual that is liable on such debt with the debtor, or that secured such debt, unless—

(1) such individual became liable on or secured such debt in the ordinary course of such individual's business; or

(2) the case is closed, dismissed, or converted to a case under chapter 7 of this title.

(b) A creditor may present a negotiable instrument, and may give notice of dishonor of such an instrument.

(c) On request of a party in interest and after notice and a hearing, the court shall grant relief from the stay provided by subsection (a) of this section with respect to a creditor, to the extent that—

(1) as between the debtor and the individual protected under subsection (a) of this section, such individual received the consideration for the claim held by such creditor;

(2) the plan filed by the debtor proposes not to pay such claim; or

(3) such creditor's interest would be irreparably harmed by continuation of such stay.

(d) Twenty days after the filing of a request under subsection (c)(2) of this section for relief from the stay provided by subsection (a) of this section, such stay is terminated with respect to the party in interest making such request, unless the debtor or any individual that is liable on such debt with the debtor files and serves upon such party in interest a written objection to the taking of the proposed action.

§ 1202. Trustee

(a) If the United States trustee has appointed an individual under section 586(b) of title 28 to serve as standing trustee in cases under this chapter and if such individual qualifies as a trustee under section 322 of this title, then such individual shall serve as trustee in any case filed under this chapter. Otherwise, the United States trustee shall appoint one disinterested person to serve as trustee in the case or the United States trustee may serve as trustee in the case if necessary.

(b) The trustee shall—

(1) perform the duties specified in sections 704(2), 704(3), 704(5), 704(6), 704(7), and 704(9) of this title;

(2) perform the duties specified in section 1106(a)(3) and 1106(a)(4) of this title if the court, for cause and on request of a party in interest, the trustee, or the United States trustee, so orders;

(3) appear and be heard at any hearing that concerns—

(A) the value of property subject to a lien;

(B) confirmation of a plan;

(C) modification of the plan after confirmation; or

(D) the sale of property of the estate;

(4) ensure that the debtor commences making timely payments required by a confirmed plan; ~~and~~

(5) if the debtor ceases to be a debtor in possession, perform the duties specified in sections 704(8), 1106(a)(1), 1106(a)(2), 1106(a)(6), 1106(a)(7), and 1203~~.~~; and

(6) if with respect to the debtor there is a claim for a domestic support obligation, provide the applicable notice specified in subsection (c).

(c)(1) In a case described in subsection (b)(6) to which subsection (b)(6) applies, the trustee shall—

(A)(i) provide written notice to the holder of the claim described in subsection (b)(6) of such claim and of the right of such holder to use the services of the State child support enforcement agency established under sections 464 and 466 of the Social Security Act for the State in which such holder resides, for assistance in collecting child support during and after the case under this title; and

(ii) include in the notice provided under clause (i) the address and telephone number of such State child support enforcement agency;

(B)(i) provide written notice to such State child support enforcement agency of such claim; and

(ii) include in the notice provided under clause (i) the name, address, and telephone number of such holder; and

(C) at such time as the debtor is granted a discharge under section 1228, provide written notice to such holder and to such State child support enforcement agency of—

(i) the granting of the discharge;

(ii) the last recent known address of the debtor;

50 *Editor's Note*: Chapter 12 of the Bankruptcy Code expired on January 1, 2004. However, Pub. L. No. 108-369, 118 Stat. 1749 (2004), enacted October 25, 2004, extended chapter 12 through June 30, 2005, with a retroactive effective date of January 1, 2004. Pub. L. No. 109-8, 119 Stat. 23, enacted April 20, 2005, made the provisions of chapter 12 permanent. See § A.2.10, *infra*.

(iii) the last recent known name and address of the debtor's employer; and

(iv) the name of each creditor that holds a claim that—

(I) is not discharged under paragraph (2), (4), or (14A) of section 523(a); or

(II) was reaffirmed by the debtor under section 524(c).

(2)(A) The holder of a claim described in subsection (b)(6) or the State child support enforcement agency of the State in which such holder resides may request from a creditor described in paragraph (1)(C)(iv) the last known address of the debtor.

(B) Notwithstanding any other provision of law, a creditor that makes a disclosure of a last known address of a debtor in connection with a request made under subparagraph (A) shall not be liable by reason of making that disclosure.

§ 1203. Rights and powers of debtor

Subject to such limitations as the court may prescribe, a debtor in possession shall have all the rights, other than the right to compensation under section 330, and powers, and shall perform all the functions and duties, except the duties specified in paragraphs (3) and (4) of section 1106(a), of a trustee serving in a case under chapter 11, including operating the debtor's farm or commercial fishing operation.

§ 1204. Removal of debtor as debtor in possession

(a) On request of a party in interest, and after notice and a hearing, the court shall order that the debtor shall not be a debtor in possession for cause, including fraud, dishonesty, incompetence, or gross mismanagement of the affairs of the debtor, either before or after the commencement of the case.

(b) On request of a party in interest, and after notice and a hearing, the court may reinstate the debtor in possession.

§ 1205. Adequate protection

(a) Section 361 does not apply in a case under this chapter.

(b) In a case under this chapter, when adequate protection is required under section 362, 363, or 364 of this title of an interest of an entity in property, such adequate protection may be provided by—

(1) requiring the trustee to make a cash payment or periodic cash payments to such entity, to the extent that the stay under section 362 of this title, use, sale, or lease under section 363 of this title, or any grant of a lien under section 364 of this title results in a decrease in the value of property securing a claim or of an entity's ownership interest in property;

(2) providing to such entity an additional or replacement lien to the extent that such stay, use, sale, lease, or grant results in a decrease in the value of property securing a claim or of an entity's ownership interest in property;

(3) paying to such entity for the use of farmland the reasonable rent customary in the community where the property is located, based upon the rental value, net income, and earning capacity of the property; or

(4) granting such other relief, other than entitling such entity to compensation allowable under section 503(b)(1) of this title as an administrative expense, as will adequately protect the value of property securing a claim or of such entity's ownership interest in property.

§ 1206. Sales free of interests

After notice and a hearing, in addition to the authorization contained in section 363(f), the trustee in a case under this chapter may sell property under section 363(b) and (c) free and clear of any interest in such property of an entity other than the estate if the property is farmland, ~~or~~ farm equipment, or property used to carry out a commercial fishing operation (including a commercial fishing vessel), except that the proceeds of such sale shall be subject to such interest.

§ 1207. Property of the estate

(a) Property of the estate includes, in addition to the property specified in section 541 of this title—

(1) all property of the kind specified in such section that the debtor acquires after the commencement of the case but before the case is closed, dismissed, or converted to a case under chapter 7 of this title, whichever occurs first; and

(2) earnings from services performed by the debtor after the commencement of the case but before the case is closed, dismissed, or converted to a case under chapter 7 of this title, whichever occurs first.

(b) Except as provided in section 1204, a confirmed plan, or an order confirming a plan, the debtor shall remain in possession of all property of the estate.

§ 1208. Conversion or dismissal

(a) The debtor may convert a case under this chapter to a case under chapter 7 of this title at any time. Any waiver of the right to convert under this subsection is unenforceable.

(b) On request of the debtor at any time, if the case has not been converted under section 706 or 1112 of this title, the court shall dismiss a case under this chapter. Any waiver of the right to dismiss under this subsection is unenforceable.

(c) On request of a party in interest, and after notice and a hearing, the court may dismiss a case under this chapter for cause, including—

(1) unreasonable delay, or gross mismanagement, by the debtor that is prejudicial to creditors;

(2) nonpayment of any fees and charges required under chapter 123 of title 28;

(3) failure to file a plan timely under section 1221 of this title;

(4) failure to commence making timely payments required by a confirmed plan;

(5) denial of confirmation of a plan under section 1225 of this title and denial of a request made for additional time for filing

another plan or a modification of a plan;

(6) material default by the debtor with respect to a term of a confirmed plan;

(7) revocation of the order of confirmation under section 1230 of this title, and denial of confirmation of a modified plan under section 1229 of this title;

(8) termination of a confirmed plan by reason of the occurrence of a condition specified in the plan; ~~or~~

(9) continuing loss to or diminution of the estate and absence of a reasonable likelihood of rehabilitation~~.~~; and

(10) failure of the debtor to pay any domestic support obligation that first becomes payable after the date of the filing of the petition.

(d) On request of a party in interest, and after notice and a hearing, the court may dismiss a case under this chapter or convert a case under this chapter to a case under chapter 7 of this title upon a showing that the debtor has committed fraud in connection with the case.

(e) Notwithstanding any other provision of this section, a case may not be converted to a case under another chapter of this title unless the debtor may be a debtor under such chapter.

Subchapter II—The Plan

§ 1221. Filing of plan

The debtor shall file a plan not later than 90 days after the order for relief under this chapter, except that the court may extend such period if the need for an extension is attributable to circumstances for which the debtor should not justly be held accountable.

§ 1222. Contents of plan

(a) The plan shall—

(1) provide for the submission of all or such portion of future earnings or other future income of the debtor to the supervision and control of the trustee as is necessary for the execution of the plan;

(2) provide for the full payment, in deferred cash payments, of all claims entitled to priority under section 507 ~~of this title~~, unless—

(A) the claim is a claim owed to a governmental unit that arises as a result of the sale, transfer, exchange, or other disposition of any farm asset used in the debtor's farming operation, in which case the claim shall be treated as an unsecured claim that is not entitled to priority under section 507, but the debt shall be treated in such manner only if the debtor receives a discharge;[51] or

(B) the holder of a particular claim agrees to a different treatment of ~~such~~ that claim; ~~and~~

(3) if the plan classifies claims and interests, provide the same treatment for each claim or interest within a particular class unless the holder of a particular claim or interest agrees to less favorable treatment~~.~~; and

(4) notwithstanding any other provision of this section, a plan may provide for less than full payment of all amounts owed for a claim entitled to priority under section 507(a)(1)(B) only if the plan provides that all of the debtor's projected disposable income for a 5-year period beginning on the date that the first payment is due under the plan will be applied to make payments under the plan.

(b) Subject to subsections (a) and (c) of this section, the plan may—

(1) designate a class or classes of unsecured claims, as provided in section 1122 of this title, but may not discriminate unfairly against any class so designated; however, such plan may treat claims for a consumer debt of the debtor if an individual is liable on such consumer debt with the debtor differently than other unsecured claims;

(2) modify the rights of holders of secured claims, or of holders of unsecured claims, or leave unaffected the rights of holders of any class of claims;

(3) provide for the curing or waiving of any default;

(4) provide for payments on any unsecured claim to be made concurrently with payments on any secured claim or any other unsecured claim;

(5) provide for the curing of any default within a reasonable time and maintenance of payments while the case is pending on any unsecured claim or secured claim on which the last payment is due after the date on which the final payment under the plan is due;

(6) subject to section 365 of this title, provide for the assumption, rejection, or assignment of any executory contract or unexpired lease of the debtor not previously rejected under such section;

(7) provide for the payment of all or part of a claim against the debtor from property of the estate or property of the debtor;

(8) provide for the sale of all or any part of the property of the estate or the distribution of all or any part of the property of the estate among those having an interest in such property;

(9) provide for payment of allowed secured claims consistent with section 1225(a)(5) of this title, over a period exceeding the period permitted under section 1222(c);

(10) provide for the vesting of property of the estate, on confirmation of the plan or at a later time, in the debtor or in any other entity; ~~and~~

(11) provide for the payment of interest accruing after the date of the filing of the petition on unsecured claims that are nondischargeable under section 1228(a), except that such interest may be paid only to the extent that the debtor has disposable income available to pay such interest after making provision for full payment of all allowed claims; and

(~~11~~12) include any other appropriate provision not inconsistent with this title.

---

51 *Editor's Note*: New subsection 1222(a)(2)(A) is effective for cases commenced under title 11 on or after April 20, 2005.

(c) Except as provided in subsections (b)(5) and (b)(9), the plan may not provide for payments over a period that is longer than three years unless the court for cause approves a longer period, but the court may not approve a period that is longer than five years.

(d) Notwithstanding subsection (b)(2) of this section and sections 506(b) and 1225(a)(5) of this title, if it is proposed in a plan to cure a default, the amount necessary to cure the default, shall be determined in accordance with the underlying agreement and applicable nonbankruptcy law.

§ 1223. Modification of plan before confirmation

(a) The debtor may modify the plan at any time before confirmation, but may not modify the plan so that the plan as modified fails to meet the requirements of section 1222 of this title.

(b) After the debtor files a modification under this section, the plan as modified becomes the plan.

(c) Any holder of a secured claim that has accepted or rejected the plan is deemed to have accepted or rejected, as the case may be, the plan as modified, unless the modification provides for a change in the rights of such holder from what such rights were under the plan before modification, and such holder changes such holder's previous acceptance or rejection.

§ 1224. Confirmation hearing

After expedited notice, the court shall hold a hearing on confirmation of the plan. A party in interest, the trustee, or the United States trustee may object to the confirmation of the plan. Except for cause, the hearing shall be concluded not later than 45 days after the filing of the plan.

§ 1225. Confirmation of plan

(a) Except as provided in subsection (b), the court shall confirm a plan if—

(1) the plan complies with the provisions of this chapter and with the other applicable provisions of this title;

(2) any fee, charge, or amount required under chapter 123 of title 28, or by the plan, to be paid before confirmation, has been paid;

(3) the plan has been proposed in good faith and not by any means forbidden by law;

(4) the value, as of the effective date of the plan, of property to be distributed under the plan on account of each allowed unsecured claim is not less than the amount that would be paid on such claim if the estate of the debtor were liquidated under chapter 7 of this title on such date;

(5) with respect to each allowed secured claim provided for by the plan—

(A) the holder of such claim has accepted the plan;

(B)(i) the plan provides that the holder of such claim retain the lien securing such claim; and

(ii) the value, as of the effective date of the plan, of property to be distributed by the trustee or the debtor under the plan on account of such claim is not less than the allowed amount of such claim; or

(C) the debtor surrenders the property securing such claim to such holder; ~~and~~

(6) the debtor will be able to make all payments under the plan and to comply with the plan~~.~~; and

(7) the debtor has paid all amounts that are required to be paid under a domestic support obligation and that first become payable after the date of the filing of the petition if the debtor is required by a judicial or administrative order, or by statute, to pay such domestic support obligation.

(b)(1) If the trustee or the holder of an allowed unsecured claim objects to the confirmation of the plan, then the court may not approve the plan unless, as of the effective date of the plan—

(A) the value of the property to be distributed under the plan on account of such claim is not less than the amount of such claim; ~~or~~

(B) the plan provides that all of the debtor's projected disposable income to be received in the three-year period, or such longer period as the court may approve under section 1222(c), beginning on the date that the first payment is due under the plan will be applied to make payments under the plan; or

(C) the value of the property to be distributed under the plan in the 3-year period, or such longer period as the court may approve under section 1222(c), beginning on the date that the first distribution is due under the plan is not less than the debtor's projected disposable income for such period.

(2) For purposes of this subsection, "disposable income" means income which is received by the debtor and which is not reasonably necessary to be expended—

(A) for the maintenance or support of the debtor or a dependent of the debtor or for a domestic support obligation that first becomes payable after the date of the filing of the petition; or

(B) for the payment of expenditures necessary for the continuation, preservation, and operation of the debtor's business.

(c) After confirmation of a plan, the court may order any entity from whom the debtor receives income to pay all or any part of such income to the trustee.

§ 1226. Payments

(a) Payments and funds received by the trustee shall be retained by the trustee until confirmation or denial of confirmation of a plan. If a plan is confirmed, the trustee shall distribute any such payment in accordance with the plan. If a plan is not confirmed, the trustee shall return any such payments to the debtor, after deducting—

(1) any unpaid claim allowed under section 503(b) of this title; and

(2) if a standing trustee is serving in the case, the percentage fee fixed for such standing trustee.

(b) Before or at the time of each payment to creditors under the plan, there shall be paid—

(1) any unpaid claim of the kind specified in section 507(a)(~~1~~2) of this title; and

(2) if a standing trustee appointed under section 1202(c) of this title is serving in the case, the percentage fee fixed for such standing trustee under section 1202(d) of this title.

(c) Except as otherwise provided in the plan or in the order confirming the plan, the trustee shall make payments to creditors under the plan.

§ 1227. Effect of confirmation

(a) Except as provided in section 1228(a) of this title, the provisions of a confirmed plan bind the debtor, each creditor, each equity security holder, and each general partner in the debtor, whether or not the claim of such creditor, such equity security holder, or such general partner in the debtor is provided for by the plan, and whether or not such creditor, such equity security holder, or such general partner in the debtor has objected to, has accepted, or has rejected the plan.

(b) Except as otherwise provided in the plan or the order confirming the plan, the confirmation of a plan vests all of the property of the estate in the debtor.

(c) Except as provided in section 1228(a) of this title and except as otherwise provided in the plan or in the order confirming the plan, the property vesting in the debtor under subsection (b) of this section is free and clear of any claim or interest of any creditor provided for by the plan.

§ 1228. Discharge

(a) Subject to subsection (d), as ~~As~~ soon as practicable after completion by the debtor of all payments under the plan, and in the case of a debtor who is required by a judicial or administrative order, or by statute, to pay a domestic support obligation after such debtor certifies that all amounts payable under such order or such statute that are due on or before the date of the certification (including amounts due before the petition was filed, but only to the extent provided for by the plan) have been paid, other than payments to holders of allowed claims provided for under section 1222(b)(5) or 1222(b)(9) of this title, unless the court approves a written waiver of discharge executed by the debtor after the order for relief under this chapter, the court shall grant the debtor a discharge of all debts provided for by the plan allowed under section 503 of this title or disallowed under section 502 of this title, except any debt—

(1) provided for under section 1222(b)(5) or 1222(b)(9) of this title; or

(2) of the kind specified in section 523(a) of this title.

(b) Subject to subsection (d), at ~~At~~ any time after the confirmation of the plan and after notice and a hearing, the court may grant a discharge to a debtor that has not completed payments under the plan only if—

(1) the debtor's failure to complete such payments is due to circumstances for which the debtor should not justly be held accountable;

(2) the value, as of the effective date of the plan, of property actually distributed under the plan on account of each allowed unsecured claim is not less than the amount that would have been paid on such claim if the estate of the debtor had been liquidated under chapter 7 of this title on such date; and

(3) modification of the plan under section 1229 of this title is not practicable.

(c) A discharge granted under subsection (b) of this section discharges the debtor from all unsecured debts provided for by the plan or disallowed under section 502 of this title, except any debt—

(1) provided for under section 1222(b)(5) or 1222(b)(9) of this title; or

(2) of a kind specified in section 523(a) of this title.

(d) On request of a party in interest before one year after a discharge under this section is granted, and after notice and a hearing, the court may revoke such discharge only if—

(1) such discharge was obtained by the debtor through fraud; and

(2) the requesting party did not know of such fraud until after such discharge was granted.

(e) After the debtor is granted a discharge, the court shall terminate the services of any trustee serving in the case.

(f) The court may not grant a discharge under this chapter unless the court after notice and a hearing held not more than 10 days before the date of the entry of the order granting the discharge finds that there is no reasonable cause to believe that—

(1) section 522(q)(1) may be applicable to the debtor; and

(2) there is pending any proceeding in which the debtor may be found guilty of a felony of the kind described in section 522(q)(1)(A) or liable for a debt of the kind described in section 522(q)(1)(B).[52]

§ 1229. Modification of plan after confirmation

(a) At any time after confirmation of the plan but before the completion of payments under such plan, the plan may be modified, on request of the debtor, the trustee, or the holder of an allowed unsecured claim, to—

(1) increase or reduce the amount of payments on claims of a particular class provided for by the plan;

(2) extend or reduce the time for such payments; or

(3) alter the amount of the distribution to a creditor whose claim is provided for by the plan to the extent necessary to take account of any payment of such claim other than under the plan.

52 *Editor's Note*: New subsection 1228(f) is effective for cases commenced under title 11 on or after April 20, 2005.

(b)(1) Sections 1222(a), 1222(b), and 1223(c) of this title and the requirements of section 1225(a) of this title apply to any modification under subsection (a) of this section.

(2) The plan as modified becomes the plan unless, after notice and a hearing, such modification is disapproved.

(c) A plan modified under this section may not provide for payments over a period that expires after three years after the time that the first payment under the original confirmed plan was due, unless the court, for cause, approves a longer period, but the court may not approve a period that expires after five years after such time.

(d) A plan may not be modified under this section—

(1) to increase the amount of any payment due before the plan as modified becomes the plan;

(2) by anyone except the debtor, based on an increase in the debtor's disposable income, to increase the amount of payments to unsecured creditors required for a particular month so that the aggregate of such payments exceeds the debtor's disposable income for such month; or

(3) in the last year of the plan by anyone except the debtor, to require payments that would leave the debtor with insufficient funds to carry on the farming operation after the plan is completed.

§ 1230. Revocation of an order of confirmation

(a) On request of a party in interest at any time within 180 days after the date of the entry of an order of confirmation under section 1225 of this title, and after notice and a hearing, the court may revoke such order if such order was procured by fraud.

(b) If the court revokes an order of confirmation under subsection (a) of this section, the court shall dispose of the case under section 1207 of this title, unless, within the time fixed by the court, the debtor proposes and the court confirms a modification of the plan under section 1229 of this title.

§ 1231. Special tax provisions

~~(a) For the purpose of any State or local law imposing a tax on or measured by income, the taxable period of a debtor that is an individual shall terminate on the date of the order for relief under this chapter, unless the case was converted under section 706 of this title.~~

~~(b) The trustee shall make a State or local tax return of income for the estate of an individual debtor in a case under this chapter for each taxable period after the order for relief under this chapter during which the case is pending.~~

(~~c~~a) The issuance, transfer, or exchange of a security, or the making or delivery of an instrument of transfer under a plan confirmed under section 1225 of this title, may not be taxed under any law imposing a stamp tax or similar tax.

(~~d~~b) The court may authorize the proponent of a plan to request a determination, limited to questions of law, by any ~~State or local~~[53] governmental unit charged with responsibility for collection or determination of a tax on or measured by income, of the tax effects, under section 346 of this title and under the law imposing such tax, of the plan. In the event of an actual controversy, the court may declare such effects after the earlier of—

(1) the date on which such governmental unit responds to the request under this subsection; or

(2) 270 days after such request.

CHAPTER 13

ADJUSTMENT OF DEBTS OF AN INDIVIDUAL WITH REGULAR INCOME

Subchapter I—Officers, Administration, and the Estate

§ 1301. Stay of action against codebtor

(a) Except as provided in subsections (b) and (c) of this section, after the order for relief under this chapter, a creditor may not act, or commence or continue any civil action, to collect all or any part of a consumer debt of the debtor from any individual that is liable on such debt with the debtor, or that secured such debt, unless—

(1) such individual became liable on or secured such debt in the ordinary course of such individual's business; or

(2) the case is closed, dismissed, or converted to a case under chapter 7 or 11 of this title.

(b) A creditor may present a negotiable instrument, and may give notice of dishonor of such an instrument.

(c) On request of a party in interest and after notice and a hearing, the court shall grant relief from the stay provided by subsection (a) of this section with respect to a creditor, to the extent that—

(1) as between the debtor and the individual protected under subsection (a) of this section, such individual received the consideration for the claim held by such creditor;

(2) the plan filed by the debtor proposes not to pay such claim; or

(3) such creditor's interest would be irreparably harmed by continuation of such stay.

(d) Twenty days after the filing of a request under subsection (c)(2) of this section for relief from the stay provided by subsection (a) of this section, such stay is terminated with respect to the party in interest making such request, unless the debtor or any individual that is liable on such debt with the debtor files and serves upon such party in interest a written objection to the taking of the proposed action.

§ 1302. Trustee

(a) If the United States trustee appoints an individual under section 586(b) of title 28 to serve as standing trustee in cases under this chapter and if such individual qualifies under section 322 of this title, then such individual shall serve as trustee in the case. Otherwise, the United States trustee shall appoint one disinterested

53 *Editor's Note*: The change made to the text of subsection 1231(b) (formerly subsection 1231(d)) is effective for cases commenced under title 11 on or after April 20, 2005.

person to serve as trustee in the case or the United States trustee may serve as a trustee in the case.

(b) The trustee shall—

(1) perform the duties specified in sections 704(2), 704(3), 704(4), 704(5), 704(6), 704(7) and 704(9) of this title;

(2) appear and be heard at any hearing that concerns—

(A) the value of property subject to a lien;

(B) confirmation of a plan; or

(C) modification of the plan after confirmation;

(3) dispose of, under regulations issued by the Director of the Administrative Office of the United States Courts, moneys received or to be received in a case under chapter XIII of the Bankruptcy Act;

(4) advise, other than on legal matters, and assist the debtor in performance under the plan; ~~and~~

(5) ensure that the debtor commences making timely payments under section 1326 of this title~~.~~; and

(6) if with respect to the debtor there is a claim for a domestic support obligation, provide the applicable notice specified in subsection (d).

(c) If the debtor is engaged in business, then in addition to the duties specified in subsection (b) of this section, the trustee shall perform the duties specified in sections 1106(a)(3) and 1106(a)(4) of this title.

(d)(1) In a case described in subsection (b)(6) to which subsection (b)(6) applies, the trustee shall—

(A)(i) provide written notice to the holder of the claim described in subsection (b)(6) of such claim and of the right of such holder to use the services of the State child support enforcement agency established under sections 464 and 466 of the Social Security Act for the State in which such holder resides, for assistance in collecting child support during and after the case under this title; and

(ii) include in the notice provided under clause (i) the address and telephone number of such State child support enforcement agency;

(B)(i) provide written notice to such State child support enforcement agency of such claim; and

(ii) include in the notice provided under clause (i) the name, address, and telephone number of such holder; and

(C) at such time as the debtor is granted a discharge under section 1328, provide written notice to such holder and to such State child support enforcement agency of—

(i) the granting of the discharge;

(ii) the last recent known address of the debtor;

(iii) the last recent known name and address of the debtor's employer; and

(iv) the name of each creditor that holds a claim that—

(I) is not discharged under paragraph (2) or (4) of section 523(a); or

(II) was reaffirmed by the debtor under section 524(c).

(2)(A) The holder of a claim described in subsection (b)(6) or the State child support enforcement agency of the State in which such holder resides may request from a creditor described in paragraph (1)(C)(iv) the last known address of the debtor.

(B) Notwithstanding any other provision of law, a creditor that makes a disclosure of a last known address of a debtor in connection with a request made under subparagraph (A) shall not be liable by reason of making that disclosure.

§ 1303. Rights and powers of debtor

Subject to any limitations on a trustee under this chapter, the debtor shall have, exclusive of the trustee, the rights and powers of a trustee under sections 363(b), 363(d), 363(e), 363(f), and 363(*l*), of this title.

§ 1304. Debtor engaged in business

(a) A debtor that is self-employed and incurs trade credit in the production of income from such employment is engaged in business.

(b) Unless the court orders otherwise, a debtor engaged in business may operate the business of the debtor and, subject to any limitations on a trustee under sections 363(c) and 364 of this title and to such limitations or conditions as the court prescribes, shall have, exclusive of the trustee, the rights and powers of the trustee under such sections.

(c) A debtor engaged in business shall perform the duties of the trustee specified in section 704(8) of this title.

§ 1305. Filing and allowance of postpetition claims

(a) A proof of claim may be filed by any entity that holds a claim against the debtor—

(1) for taxes that become payable to a governmental unit while the case is pending; or

(2) that is a consumer debt, that arises after the date of the order for relief under this chapter, and that is for property or services necessary for the debtor's performance under the plan.

(b) Except as provided in subsection (c) of this section, a claim filed under subsection (a) of this section shall be allowed or disallowed under section 502 of this title, but shall be determined as of the date such claim arises, and shall be allowed under section 502(a), 502(b), or 502(c) of this title, or disallowed under section 502(d) or 502(e) of this title, the same as if such claim had arisen before the date of the filing of the petition.

(c) A claim filed under subsection (a)(2) of this section shall be disallowed if the holder of such claim knew or should have known that prior approval by the trustee of the debtor's incurring the obligation was practicable and was not obtained.

§ 1306. Property of the estate

(a) Property of the estate includes, in addition to the property specified in section 541 of this title—

(1) all property of the kind specified in such section that the debtor acquires after the commencement of the case but before the case is closed, dismissed, or converted to a case under chapter 7, 11, or 12 of this title whichever occurs first; and

(2) earnings from services performed by the debtor after the commencement of the case but before the case is closed, dismissed, or converted to a case under chapter 7, 11, or 12 of this title, whichever occurs first.

(b) Except as provided in a confirmed plan or order confirming a plan, the debtor shall remain in possession of all property of the estate.

§ 1307. Conversion or dismissal

(a) The debtor may convert a case under this chapter to a case under chapter 7 of this title at any time. Any waiver of the right to convert under this subsection is unenforceable.

(b) On request of the debtor at any time, if the case has not been converted under section 706, 1112, or 1208 of this title, the court shall dismiss a case under this chapter. Any waiver of the right to dismiss under this subsection is unenforceable.

(c) Except as provided in subsection (e) of this section, on request of a party in interest or the United States trustee and after notice and a hearing, the court may convert a case under this chapter to a case under chapter 7 of this title, or may dismiss a case under this chapter, whichever is in the best interests of creditors and the estate, for cause, including—

(1) unreasonable delay by the debtor that is prejudicial to creditors;

(2) nonpayment of any fees and charges required under chapter 123 of title 28;

(3) failure to file a plan timely under section 1321 of this title;

(4) failure to commence making timely payments under section 1326 of this title;

(5) denial of confirmation of a plan under section 1325 of this title and denial of a request made for additional time for filing another plan or a modification of a plan;

(6) material default by the debtor with respect to a term of a confirmed plan;

(7) revocation of the order of confirmation under section 1330 of this title, and denial of confirmation of a modified plan under section 1329 of this title;

(8) termination of a confirmed plan by reason of the occurrence of a condition specified in the plan other than completion of payments under the plan;

(9) only on request of the United States trustee, failure of the debtor to file, within fifteen days, or such additional time as the court may allow, after the filing of the petition commencing such case, the information required by paragraph (1) of section 521; ~~or~~

(10) only on request of the United States trustee, failure to timely file the information required by paragraph (2) of section 521~~.~~; or

(11) failure of the debtor to pay any domestic support obligation that first becomes payable after the date of the filing of the petition.

(d) Except as provided in subsection (e) of this section, at any time before the confirmation of a plan under section 1325 of this title, on request of a party in interest or the United States trustee and after notice and a hearing, the court may convert a case under this chapter to a case under chapter 11 or 12 of this title.

(e) Upon the failure of the debtor to file a tax return under section 1308, on request of a party in interest or the United States trustee and after notice and a hearing, the court shall dismiss a case or convert a case under this chapter to a case under chapter 7 of this title, whichever is in the best interest of the creditors and the estate.

(~~e~~f) The court may not convert a case under this chapter to a case under chapter 7, 11, or 12 of this title if the debtor is a farmer, unless the debtor requests such conversion.

(~~f~~g) Notwithstanding any other provision of this section, a case may not be converted to a case under another chapter of this title unless the debtor may be a debtor under such chapter.

§ 1308. Filing of prepetition tax returns

(a) Not later than the day before the date on which the meeting of the creditors is first scheduled to be held under section 341(a), if the debtor was required to file a tax return under applicable nonbankruptcy law, the debtor shall file with appropriate tax authorities all tax returns for all taxable periods ending during the 4-year period ending on the date of the filing of the petition.

(b)(1) Subject to paragraph (2), if the tax returns required by subsection (a) have not been filed by the date on which the meeting of creditors is first scheduled to be held under section 341(a), the trustee may hold open that meeting for a reasonable period of time to allow the debtor an additional period of time to file any unfiled returns, but such additional period of time shall not extend beyond—

(A) for any return that is past due as of the date of the filing of the petition, the date that is 120 days after the date of that meeting; or

(B) for any return that is not past due as of the date of the filing of the petition, the later of—

(i) the date that is 120 days after the date of that meeting; or

(ii) the date on which the return is due under the last automatic extension of time for filing that return to which the debtor is entitled, and for which request is timely made, in accordance with applicable nonbankruptcy law.

(2) After notice and a hearing, and order entered before the tolling of any applicable filing period determined under this subsection, if the debtor demonstrates by a preponderance of the evidence that the failure to file a return as required under this subsection is attributable to circumstances beyond the control

of the debtor, the court may extend the filing period established by the trustee under this subsection for—

(A) a period of not more than 30 days for returns described in paragraph (1); and

(B) a period not to extend after the applicable extended due date for a return described in paragraph (2).

(c) For purposes of this section, the term "return" includes a return prepared pursuant to subsection (a) or (b) of section 6020 of the Internal Revenue Code of 1986, or a similar State or local law, or a written stipulation to a judgment or a final order entered by a nonbankruptcy tribunal.

Subchapter II—The Plan

§ 1321. Filing of plan

The debtor shall file a plan.

§ 1322. Contents of plan

(a) The plan shall—

(1) provide for the submission of all or such portion of future earnings or other future income of the debtor to the supervision and control of the trustee as is necessary for the execution of the plan;

(2) provide for the full payment, in deferred cash payments, of all claims entitled to priority under section 507 of this title, unless the holder of a particular claim agrees to a different treatment of such claim; ~~and~~

(3) if the plan classifies claims, provide the same treatment for each claim within a particular class~~.~~; and

(4) notwithstanding any other provision of this section, a plan may provide for less than full payment of all amounts owed for a claim entitled to priority under section 507(a)(1)(B) only if the plan provides that all of the debtor's projected disposable income for a 5-year period beginning on the date that the first payment is due under the plan will be applied to make payments under the plan.

(b) Subject to subsections (a) and (c) of this section, the plan may—

(1) designate a class or classes of unsecured claims, as provided in section 1122 of this title, but may not discriminate unfairly against any class so designated; however, such plan may treat claims for a consumer debt of the debtor if an individual is liable on such consumer debt with the debtor differently than other unsecured claims;

(2) modify the rights of holders of secured claims, other than a claim secured only by a security interest in real property that is the debtor's principal residence, or of holders of unsecured claims, or leave unaffected the rights of holders of any class of claims;

(3) provide for the curing or waiving of any default;

(4) provide for payments on any unsecured claim to be made concurrently with payments on any secured claim or any other unsecured claim;

(5) notwithstanding paragraph (2) of this subsection, provide for the curing of any default within a reasonable time and maintenance of payments while the case is pending on any unsecured claim or secured claim on which the last payment is due after the date on which the final payment under the plan is due;

(6) provide for the payment of all or any part of any claim allowed under section 1305 of this title;

(7) subject to section 365 of this title, provide for the assumption, rejection, or assignment of any executory contract or unexpired lease of the debtor not previously rejected under such section;

(8) provide for the payment of all or part of a claim against the debtor from property of the estate or property of the debtor;

(9) provide for the vesting of property of the estate, on confirmation of the plan or at a later time, in the debtor or in any other entity; ~~and~~

(10) provide for the payment of interest accruing after the date of the filing of the petition on unsecured claims that are nondischargeable under section 1328(a), except that such interest may be paid only to the extent that the debtor has disposable income available to pay such interest after making provision for full payment of all allowed claims; and

(~~10~~11) include any other appropriate provision not inconsistent with this title.

(c) Notwithstanding subsection (b)(2) and applicable nonbankruptcy law—

(1) a default with respect to, or that gave rise to, a lien on the debtor's principal residence may be cured under paragraph (3) or (5) of subsection (b) until such residence is sold at a foreclosure sale that is conducted in accordance with applicable nonbankruptcy law; and

(2) in a case in which the last payment on the original payment schedule for a claim secured only by a security interest in real property that is the debtor's principal residence is due before the date on which the final payment under the plan is due, the plan may provide for the payment of the claim as modified pursuant to section 1325(a)(5) of this title.

(d)(1) If the current monthly income of the debtor and the debtor's spouse combined, when multiplied by 12, is not less than—

(A) in the case of a debtor in a household of 1 person, the median family income of the applicable State for 1 earner;

(B) in the case of a debtor in a household of 2, 3, or 4 individuals, the highest median family income of the applicable State for a family of the same number or fewer individuals; or

(C) in the case of a debtor in a household exceeding 4 individuals, the highest median family income of the applicable State for a family of 4 or fewer individuals, plus $525 per month for each individual in excess of 4,

the plan may not provide for payments over a period that is longer than 5 years.

(2) If the current monthly income of the debtor and the debtor's spouse combined, when multiplied by 12, is less than—

(A) in the case of a debtor in a household of 1 person, the median family income of the applicable State for 1 earner;

(B) in the case of a debtor in a household of 2, 3, or 4 individuals, the highest median family income of the applicable State for a family of the same number or fewer individuals; or

(C) in the case of a debtor in a household exceeding 4 individuals, the highest median family income of the applicable State for a family of 4 or fewer individuals, plus $525 per month for each individual in excess of 4,

~~T~~the plan may not provide for payments over a period that is longer than ~~three~~ 3 years, unless the court, for cause, approves a longer period, but the court may not approve a period that is longer than ~~five~~ 5 years.

(e) Notwithstanding subsection (b)(2) of this section and sections 506(b) and 1325(a)(5) of this title, if it is proposed in a plan to cure a default, the amount necessary to cure the default, shall be determined in accordance with the underlying agreement and applicable nonbankruptcy law.

(f) A plan may not materially alter the terms of a loan described in section 362(b)(19) and any amounts required to repay such loan shall not constitute "disposable income" under section 1325.

§ 1323. Modification of plan before confirmation

(a) The debtor may modify the plan at any time before confirmation, but may not modify the plan so that the plan as modified fails to meet the requirements of section 1322 of this title.

(b) After the debtor files a modification under this section, the plan as modified becomes the plan.

(c) Any holder of a secured claim that has accepted or rejected the plan is deemed to have accepted or rejected, as the case may be, the plan as modified, unless the modification provides for a change in the rights of such holder from what such rights were under the plan before modification, and such holder changes such holder's previous acceptance or rejection.

§ 1324. Confirmation hearing

(a) Except as provided in subsection (b) and ~~A~~ after notice, the court shall hold a hearing on confirmation of the plan. A party in interest may object to confirmation of the plan.

(b) The hearing on confirmation of the plan may be held not earlier than 20 days and not later than 45 days after the date of the meeting of creditors under section 341(a), unless the court determines that it would be in the best interests of the creditors and the estate to hold such hearing at an earlier date and there is no objection to such earlier date.

§ 1325. Confirmation of plan

(a) Except as provided in subsection (b), the court shall confirm a plan if—

(1) the plan complies with the provisions of this chapter and with the other applicable provisions of this title;

(2) any fee, charge, or amount required under chapter 123 of title 28, or by the plan, to be paid before confirmation, has been paid;

(3) the plan has been proposed in good faith and not by any means forbidden by law;

(4) the value, as of the effective date of the plan, of property to be distributed under the plan on account of each allowed unsecured claim is not less than the amount that would be paid on such claim if the estate of the debtor were liquidated under chapter 7 of this title on such date;

(5) with respect to each allowed secured claim provided for by the plan—

(A) the holder of such claim has accepted the plan;

(B)(i) the plan provides that— ~~the holder of such claim retain the lien securing such claim; and~~

(I) the holder of such claim retain the lien securing such claim until the earlier of—

(aa) the payment of the underlying debt determined under nonbankruptcy law; or

(bb) discharge under section 1328; and

(II) if the case under this chapter is dismissed or converted without completion of the plan, such lien shall also be retained by such holder to the extent recognized by applicable nonbankruptcy law; and

(ii) the value, as of the effective date of the plan, of property to be distributed under the plan on account of such claim is not less than the allowed amount of such claim; and

(iii) if—

(I) property to be distributed pursuant to this subsection is in the form of periodic payments, such payments shall be in equal monthly amounts; and

(II) the holder of the claim is secured by personal property, the amount of such payments shall not be less than an amount sufficient to provide to the holder of such claim adequate protection during the period of the plan; or

(C) the debtor surrenders the property securing such claim to such holder; ~~and~~

(6) the debtor will be able to make all payments under the plan and to comply with the plan~~.~~;

(7) the action of the debtor in filing the petition was in good faith;

(8) the debtor has paid all amounts that are required to be paid under a domestic support obligation, and that first become payable after the date of the filing of the petition if the debtor is required by a judicial or administrative order, or by statute, to pay such domestic support obligation; and

(9) the debtor has filed all applicable Federal, State, and local tax returns as required by section 1308.

For purposes of paragraph (5), section 506 shall not apply to a claim described in that paragraph if the creditor has a purchase money security interest securing the debt that is the subject of the claim, the debt was incurred within the 910-day[54] preceding the date of the filing of the petition, and the collateral for that debt consists of a motor vehicle (as defined in section 30102 of title 49) acquired for the personal use of the debtor, or if collateral for that debt consists of any other thing of value, if the debt was incurred during the 1-year period preceding that filing.

(b)(1) If the trustee or the holder of an allowed unsecured claim objects to the confirmation of the plan, then the court may not approve the plan unless, as of the effective date of the plan—

(A) the value of the property to be distributed under the plan on account of such claim is not less than the amount of such claim; or

(B) the plan provides that all of the debtor's projected disposable income to be received in the ~~three-year~~ applicable commitment period beginning on the date that the first payment is due under the plan will be applied to make payments to unsecured creditors under the plan.

(2) For purposes of this subsection, the term "disposable income" means current monthly income ~~which is~~ received by the debtor (other than child support payments, foster care payments, or disability payments for a dependent child made in accordance with applicable nonbankruptcy law to the extent reasonably necessary to be expended for such child) less amounts ~~and which is not~~ reasonably necessary to be expended—

(A)(i) for the maintenance or support of the debtor or a dependent of the debtor, or for a domestic support obligation, that first becomes payable after the date the petition is filed; and

(ii) for ~~including~~ charitable contributions (that meet the definition of "charitable contribution" under section 548(d)(3)) to a qualified religious or charitable entity or organization (as ~~that term is~~ defined in section 548(d)(4)) in an amount not to exceed 15 percent of ~~the~~ gross income of the debtor for the year in which the contributions are made; and

(B) if the debtor is engaged in business, for the payment of expenditures necessary for the continuation, preservation, and operation of such business.

(3) Amounts reasonably necessary to be expended under paragraph (2) shall be determined in accordance with subparagraphs (A) and (B) of section 707(b)(2), if the debtor has current monthly income, when multiplied by 12, greater than—

(A) in the case of a debtor in a household of 1 person, the median family income of the applicable State for 1 earner;

(B) in the case of a debtor in a household of 2, 3, or 4 individuals, the highest median family income of the applicable State for a family of the same number or fewer individuals; or

(C) in the case of a debtor in a household exceeding 4 individuals, the highest median family income of the applicable State for a family of 4 or fewer individuals, plus $525 per month for each individual in excess of 4.

(4) For purposes of this subsection, the "applicable commitment period"—

(A) subject to subparagraph (B), shall be—

(i) 3 years; or

(ii) not less than 5 years, if the current monthly income of the debtor and the debtor's spouse combined, when multiplied by 12, is not less than—

(I) in the case of a debtor in a household of 1 person, the median family income of the applicable State for 1 earner;

(II) in the case of a debtor in a household of 2, 3, or 4 individuals, the highest median family income of the applicable State for a family of the same number or fewer individuals; or

(III) in the case of a debtor in a household exceeding 4 individuals, the highest median family income of the applicable State for a family of 4 or fewer individuals, plus $525 per month for each individual in excess of 4; and

(B) may be less than 3 or 5 years, whichever is applicable under subparagraph (A), but only if the plan provides for payment in full of all allowed unsecured claims over a shorter period.

(c) After confirmation of a plan, the court may order any entity from whom the debtor receives income to pay all or any part of such income to the trustee.

§ 1326. Payments

(a)(1) Unless the court orders otherwise, the debtor shall commence making ~~the~~ payments ~~proposed by a plan within~~ not later than 30 days after ~~the plan is filed~~ the date of the filing of the plan or the order for relief, whichever is earlier, in the amount—

(A) proposed by the plan to the trustee;

(B) scheduled in a lease of personal property directly to the lessor for that portion of the obligation that becomes due after the order for relief, reducing the payments under subparagraph (A) by the amount so paid and providing the trustee with evidence of such payment, including the amount and date of payment; and

(C) that provides adequate protection directly to a creditor holding an allowed claim secured by personal property to the extent the claim is attributable to the purchase of such property by the debtor for that portion of the obligation that becomes due after the order for relief, reducing the payments under subparagraph (A) by the amount so paid and providing the trustee with evidence of such payment, including the amount and date of payment.

---

54 *Editor's Note*: So in original.

(2) A payment made under ~~this subsection~~ paragraph (1)(A) shall be retained by the trustee until confirmation or denial of confirmation ~~of a plan~~. If a plan is confirmed, the trustee shall distribute any such payment in accordance with the plan as soon as is practicable. If a plan is not confirmed, the trustee shall return any such payments not previously paid and not yet due and owing to creditors pursuant to paragraph (3) to the debtor, after deducting any unpaid claim allowed under section 503(b) ~~of this title~~.

(3) Subject to section 363, the court may, upon notice and a hearing, modify, increase, or reduce the payments required under this subsection pending confirmation of a plan.

(4) Not later than 60 days after the date of filing of a case under this chapter, a debtor retaining possession of personal property subject to a lease or securing a claim attributable in whole or in part to the purchase price of such property shall provide the lessor or secured creditor reasonable evidence of the maintenance of any required insurance coverage with respect to the use or ownership of such property and continue to do so for so long as the debtor retains possession of such property.

(b) Before or at the time of each payment to creditors under the plan, there shall be paid—

(1) any unpaid claim of the kind specified in section 507(a)(~~1~~ 2) of this title; ~~and~~

(2) if a standing trustee appointed under section 586(b) of title 28 is serving in the case, the percentage fee fixed for such standing trustee under section 586(e)(1)(B) of title 28~~.~~; and

(3) if a chapter 7 trustee has been allowed compensation due to the conversion or dismissal of the debtor's prior case pursuant to section 707(b), and some portion of that compensation remains unpaid in a case converted to this chapter or in the case dismissed under section 707(b) and refiled under this chapter, the amount of any such unpaid compensation, which shall be paid monthly—

(A) by prorating such amount over the remaining duration of the plan; and

(B) by monthly payments not to exceed the greater of—

(i) $25; or

(ii) the amount payable to unsecured nonpriority creditors, as provided by the plan, multiplied by 5 percent, and the result divided by the number of months in the plan.

(c) Except as otherwise provided in the plan or in the order confirming the plan, the trustee shall make payments to creditors under the plan.

(d) Notwithstanding any other provision of this title—

(1) compensation referred to in subsection (b)(3) is payable and may be collected by the trustee under that paragraph, even if such amount has been discharged in a prior case under this title; and

(2) such compensation is payable in a case under this chapter only to the extent permitted by subsection (b)(3).

§ 1327. Effect of confirmation

(a) The provisions of a confirmed plan bind the debtor and each creditor, whether or not the claim of such creditor is provided for by the plan, and whether or not such creditor has objected to, has accepted, or has rejected the plan.

(b) Except as otherwise provided in the plan or the order confirming the plan, the confirmation of a plan vests all of the property of the estate in the debtor.

(c) Except as otherwise provided in the plan or in the order confirming the plan, the property vesting in the debtor under subsection (b) of this section is free and clear of any claim or interest of any creditor provided for by the plan.

§ 1328. Discharge

(a) Subject to subsection (d),[55] as ~~As~~ soon as practicable after completion by the debtor of all payments under the plan, and in the case of a debtor who is required by a judicial or administrative order, or by statute, to pay a domestic support obligation, after such debtor certifies that all amounts payable under such order or such statute that are due on or before the date of the certification (including amounts due before the petition was filed, but only to the extent provided for by the plan) have been paid, unless the court approves a written waiver of discharge executed by the debtor after the order for relief under this chapter, the court shall grant the debtor a discharge of all debts provided for by the plan or disallowed under section 502 of this title, except any debt—

(1) provided for under section 1322(b)(5) ~~of this title~~;

(2) of the kind specified in section 507(a)(8)(C) or in paragraph (1)(B), (1)(C), (2), (3), (4), (5), (8) or (9) of section 523(a) ~~of this title~~; ~~or~~

(3) for restitution, or a criminal fine, included in a sentence on the debtor's conviction of a crime; or

(4) for restitution, or damages, awarded in a civil action against the debtor as a result of willful or malicious injury by the debtor that caused personal injury to an individual or the death of an individual.

(b) Subject to subsection (d),[56] at ~~At~~ any time after the confirmation of the plan and after notice and a hearing, the court may grant a discharge to a debtor that has not completed payments under the plan only if—

(1) the debtor's failure to complete such payments is due to circumstances for which the debtor should not justly be held accountable;

(2) the value, as of the effective date of the plan, of property actually distributed under the plan on account of each allowed unsecured claim is not less than the amount that would have been paid on such claim if the estate of the debtor had been liquidated under chapter 7 of this title on such date; and

---

55 *Editor's Note*: The introductory phrase added to section 1328(a) is effective for cases commenced under title 11 on or after April 20, 2005.

56 *Editor's Note*: The introductory phrase added to section 1328(b) is effective for cases commenced under title 11 on or after April 20, 2005.

(3) modification of the plan under section 1329 of this title is not practicable.

(c) A discharge granted under subsection (b) of this section discharges the debtor from all unsecured debts provided for by the plan or disallowed under section 502 of this title, except any debt—

(1) provided for under section 1322(b)(5) of this title; or

(2) of a kind specified in section 523(a) of this title.

(d) Notwithstanding any other provision of this section, a discharge granted under this section does not discharge the debtor from any debt based on an allowed claim filed under section 1305(a)(2) of this title if prior approval by the trustee of the debtor's incurring such debt was practicable and was not obtained.

(e) On request of a party in interest before one year after a discharge under this section is granted, and after notice and a hearing, the court may revoke such discharge only if—

(1) such discharge was obtained by the debtor through fraud; and

(2) the requesting party did not know of such fraud until after such discharge was granted.

(f) Notwithstanding subsections (a) and (b), the court shall not grant a discharge of all debts provided for in the plan or disallowed under section 502, if the debtor has received a discharge—

(1) in a case filed under chapter 7, 11, or 12 of this title during the 4-year period preceding the date of the order for relief under this chapter, or

(2) in a case filed under chapter 13 of this title during the 2-year period preceding the date of such order.

(g)(1) The court shall not grant a discharge under this section to a debtor unless after filing a petition the debtor has completed an instructional course concerning personal financial management described in section 111.

(2) Paragraph (1) shall not apply with respect to a debtor who is a person described in section 109(h)(4) or who resides in a district for which the United States trustee (or the bankruptcy administrator, if any) determines that the approved instructional courses are not adequate to service the additional individuals who would otherwise be required to complete such instructional course by reason of the requirements of paragraph (1).

(3) The United States trustee (or the bankruptcy administrator, if any) who makes a determination described in paragraph (2) shall review such determination not later than 1 year after the date of such determination, and not less frequently than annually thereafter.

(h) The court may not grant a discharge under this chapter unless the court after notice and a hearing held not more than 10 days before the date of the entry of the order granting the discharge finds that there is no reasonable cause to believe that—

(1) section 522(q)(1) may be applicable to the debtor; and

(2) there is pending any proceeding in which the debtor may be found guilty of a felony of the kind described in section 522(q)(1)(A) or liable for a debt of the kind described in section 522(q)(1)(B).[57]

§ 1329. Modification of plan after confirmation

(a) At any time after confirmation of the plan but before the completion of payments under such plan, the plan may be modified, upon request of the debtor, the trustee, or the holder of an allowed unsecured claim, to—

(1) increase or reduce the amount of payments on claims of a particular class provided for by the plan;

(2) extend or reduce the time for such payments; ~~or~~

(3) alter the amount of the distribution to a creditor whose claim is provided for by the plan to the extent necessary to take account of any payment of such claim other than under the plan~~.~~; or

(4) reduce amounts to be paid under the plan by the actual amount expended by the debtor to purchase health insurance for the debtor (and for any dependent of the debtor if such dependent does not otherwise have health insurance coverage) if the debtor documents the cost of such insurance and demonstrates that—

(A) such expenses are reasonable and necessary;

(B)(i) if the debtor previously paid for health insurance, the amount is not materially larger than the cost the debtor previously paid or the cost necessary to maintain the lapsed policy; or

(ii) if the debtor did not have health insurance, the amount is not materially larger than the reasonable cost that would be incurred by a debtor who purchases health insurance, who has similar income, expenses, age, and health status, and who lives in the same geographical location with the same number of dependents who do not otherwise have health insurance coverage; and

(C) the amount is not otherwise allowed for purposes of determining disposable income under section 1325(b) of this title;

and upon request of any party in interest, files proof that a health insurance policy was purchased.

(b)(1) Sections 1322(a), 1322(b), and 1323(c) of this title and the requirements of section 1325(a) of this title apply to any modification under subsection (a) of this section.

(2) The plan as modified becomes the plan unless, after notice and a hearing, such modification is disapproved.

(c) A plan modified under this section may not provide for payments over a period that expires after ~~three years~~ the applicable commitment period under section 1325(b)(1)(B) after the time that the first payment under the original confirmed plan was due, unless the court, for cause, approves a longer period, but the court may not approve a period that expires after five years after such time.

§ 1330. Revocation of an order of confirmation

(a) On request of a party in interest at any time within 180 days after the date of the entry of an order of confirmation under section

57 *Editor's Note*: New subsection 1328(h) is effective for cases commenced under title 11 on or after April 20, 2005.

1325 of this title, and after notice and a hearing, the court may revoke such order if such order was procured by fraud.

(b) If the court revokes an order of confirmation under subsection (a) of this section, the court shall dispose of the case under section 1307 of this title, unless, within the time fixed by the court, the debtor proposes and the court confirms a modification of the plan under section 1329 of this title.

* * *

A.2 Selected Provisions of Title 28 of the United States Code

TITLE 28—JUDICIARY AND JUDICIAL PROCEDURE

TABLE OF CONTENTS

28 U.S.C. § 151. Designation of bankruptcy courts

In each judicial district, the bankruptcy judges in regular active service shall constitute a unit of the district court to be known as the bankruptcy court for that district. Each bankruptcy judge, as a judicial officer of the district court, may exercise the authority conferred under this chapter with respect to any action, suit, or proceeding and may preside alone and hold a regular or special session of the court, except as otherwise provided by law or by rule or order of the district court.

28 U.S.C. § 152. Appointment of bankruptcy judges

(a)(1) ~~The United States court of appeals for the circuit shall appoint bankruptcy judges for the judicial districts established in paragraph (2) in such numbers as are established in such paragraph.~~ Each bankruptcy judge to be appointed for a judicial district, as provided in paragraph (2), shall be appointed by the court of appeals of the United States for the circuit in which such district is located.[58] Such appointments shall be made after considering the recommendations of the Judicial Conference submitted pursuant to subsection (b). Each bankruptcy judge shall be appointed for a term of fourteen years, subject to the provisions of subsection (e). However, upon the expiration of the term, a bankruptcy judge may, with the approval of the judicial council of the circuit, continue to perform the duties of the office until the earlier of the date which is 180 days after the expiration of the term or the date of the appointment of a successor. Bankruptcy judges shall serve as judicial officers of the United States district court established under Article III of the Constitution.

58 *Editor's Note*: These changes to subsection 152(a) are effective as of April 20, 2005.

(2) The bankruptcy judges appointed pursuant to this section shall be appointed for the several judicial districts as follows:

[*table omitted*]

(3) Whenever a majority of the judges of any court of appeals cannot agree upon the appointment of a bankruptcy judge, the chief judge of such court shall make such appointment.

(4) The judges of the district courts for the territories shall serve as the bankruptcy judges for such courts. The United States court of appeals for the circuit within which such a territorial district court is located may appoint bankruptcy judges under this chapter for such district if authorized to do so by the Congress of the United States under this section.

(b)(1) The Judicial Conference of the United States shall, from time to time, and after considering the recommendations submitted by the Director of the Administrative Office of the United States Courts after such Director has consulted with the judicial council of the circuit involved, determine the official duty stations of bankruptcy judges and places of holding court.

(2) The Judicial Conference shall, from time to time, submit recommendations to the Congress regarding the number of bankruptcy judges needed and the districts in which such judges are needed.

(3) Not later than December 31, 1994, and not later than the end of each 2-year period thereafter, the Judicial Conference of the United States shall conduct a comprehensive review of all judicial districts to assess the continuing need for the bankruptcy judges authorized by this section, and shall report to the Congress its findings and any recommendations for the elimination of any authorized position which can be eliminated when a vacancy exists by reason of resignation, retirement, removal, or death.

(c) Each bankruptcy judge may hold court at such places within the judicial district, in addition to the official duty station of such judge, as the business of the court may require.

(d) With the approval of the Judicial Conference and of each of the judicial councils involved, a bankruptcy judge may be designated to serve in any district adjacent to or near the district for which such bankruptcy judge was appointed.

(e) A bankruptcy judge may be removed during the term for which such bankruptcy judge is appointed, only for incompetence, misconduct, neglect of duty, or physical or mental disability and only by the judicial council of the circuit in which the judge's official duty station is located. Removal may not occur unless a majority of all of the judges of such council concur in the order of removal. Before any order of removal may be entered, a full specification of charges shall be furnished to such bankruptcy judge who shall be accorded an opportunity to be heard on such charges.

28 U.S.C. § 153. Salaries; character of service

(a) Each bankruptcy judge shall serve on a full-time basis and shall receive as full compensation for his services, a salary at an annual rate that is equal to 92 percent of the salary of a judge of the district court of the United States as determined pursuant to section 135, to be paid at such times as the Judicial Conference of the United States determines.

(b) A bankruptcy judge may not engage in the practice of law and may not engage in any other practice, business, occupation, or employment inconsistent with the expeditious, proper, and impartial performance of such bankruptcy judge's duties as a judicial officer. The Conference may promulgate appropriate rules and regulations to implement this subsection.

(c) Each individual appointed under this chapter shall take the oath or affirmation prescribed by section 453 of this title before performing the duties of the office of bankruptcy judge.

(d) A bankruptcy judge appointed under this chapter shall be exempt from the provisions of subchapter I of chapter 63 of title 5.

28 U.S.C. § 154. Division of businesses; chief judge

(a) Each bankruptcy court for a district having more than one bankruptcy judge shall by majority vote promulgate rules for the division of business among the bankruptcy judges to the extent that the division of business is not otherwise provided for by the rules of the district court.

(b) In each district court having more than one bankruptcy judge the district court shall designate one judge to serve as chief judge of such bankruptcy court. Whenever a majority of the judges of such district court cannot agree upon the designation as chief judge, the chief judge of such district court shall make such designation. The chief judge of the bankruptcy court shall ensure that the rules of the bankruptcy court and of the district court are observed and that the business of the bankruptcy court is handled effectively and expeditiously.

28 U.S.C. § 155. Temporary transfer of bankruptcy judges

(a) A bankruptcy judge may be transferred to serve temporarily as a bankruptcy judge in any judicial district other than the judicial district for which such bankruptcy judge was appointed upon the approval of the judicial council of each of the circuits involved.

(b) A bankruptcy judge who has retired may, upon consent, be recalled to serve as a bankruptcy judge in any judicial district by the judicial council of the circuit within which such district is located. Upon recall, a bankruptcy judge may receive a salary for such service in accordance with regulations promulgated by the Judicial Conference of the United States, subject to the restrictions on the payment of an annuity in section 377 of this title or in subchapter III of chapter 83, and chapter 84, of title 5 which are applicable to such judge.

28 U.S.C. § 156. Staff; expenses

(a) Each bankruptcy judge may appoint a secretary, a law clerk, and such additional assistants as the Director of the Administrative Office of the United States Courts determines to be necessary. A law clerk appointed under this section shall be exempt from the provisions of subchapter I of chapter 63 of title 5, unless specifically included by the appointing judge or by local rule of court.

(b) Upon certification to the judicial council of the circuit involved and to the Director of the Administrative Office of the United States Courts that the number of cases and proceedings pending within the jurisdiction under section 1334 of this title within a judicial district so warrants, the bankruptcy judges for such district may appoint an individual to serve as clerk of such bankruptcy court. The clerk may appoint, with the approval of such bankruptcy judges, and in such number as may be approved by the Director, necessary deputies, and may remove such deputies with the approval of such bankruptcy judges.

(c) Any court may utilize facilities or services, either on or off the court's premises, which pertain to the provision of notices, dockets, calendars, and other administrative information to parties in cases filed under the provisions of title 11, United States Code, where the costs of such facilities or services are paid for out of the assets of the estate and are not charged to the United States. The utilization of such facilities or services shall be subject to such conditions and limitations as the pertinent circuit council may prescribe.

(d) No office of the bankruptcy clerk of court may be consolidated with the district clerk of court office without the prior approval of the Judicial Conference and the Congress.

(e) In a judicial district where a bankruptcy clerk has been appointed pursuant to subsection (b), the bankruptcy clerk shall be the official custodian of the records and dockets of the bankruptcy court.

(f) For purposes of financial accountability in a district where a bankruptcy clerk has been certified, such clerk shall be accountable for and pay into the Treasury all fees, costs, and other monies collected by such clerk except uncollected fees not required by an Act of Congress to be prepaid. Such clerk shall make returns thereof to the Director of the Administrative Office of the United States Courts and the Director of the Executive Office For United States Trustees, under regulations prescribed by such Directors.

28 U.S.C. § 157. Procedures

(a) Each district court may provide that any or all cases under title 11 and any or all proceedings arising under title 11 or arising in or related to a case under title 11 shall be referred to the bankruptcy judges for the district.

(b)(1) Bankruptcy judges may hear and determine all cases under title 11 and all core proceedings arising under title 11 or arising in a case under title 11 referred under subsection (a) of this section, and may enter appropriate orders and judgments, subject to review under section 158 of this title.

(2) Core proceedings include, but are not limited to—

(A) matters concerning the administration of the estate;

(B) allowance or disallowance of claims against the estate or exemptions from property of the estate, and estimation of claims or interests for the purposes of confirming a plan under chapter 11, 12, or 13 of title 11 but not the liquidation or estimation of contingent or unliquidated personal injury tort or wrongful death claims against the estate for purposes of distribution in a case under title 11;

(C) counterclaims by the estate against persons filing claims against the estate;

(D) orders in respect to obtaining credit;

(E) orders to turn over property of the estate;

(F) proceedings to determine, avoid, or recover preferences;

(G) motions to terminate, annul, or modify the automatic stay;

(H) proceedings to determine, avoid, or recover fraudulent conveyances;

(I) determinations as to the dischargeability of particular debts;

(J) objections to discharges;

(K) determinations of the validity, extent, or priority of liens;

(L) confirmations of plans;

(M) orders approving the use or lease of property, including the use of cash collateral;

(N) orders approving the sale of property other than property resulting from claims brought by the estate against persons who have not filed claims against the estate; ~~and~~

(O) other proceedings affecting the liquidation of the assets of the estate or the adjustment of the debtor-creditor or the equity security holder relationship, except personal injury tort or wrongful death claims~~.~~; and

(P) recognition of foreign proceedings and other matters under chapter 15 of title 11.

(3) The bankruptcy judge shall determine, on the judge's own motion or on timely motion of a party, whether a proceeding is a core proceeding under this subsection or is a proceeding that is otherwise related to a case under title 11. A determination that a proceeding is not a core proceeding shall not be made solely on the basis that its resolution may be affected by State law.

(4) Non-core proceedings under section 157(b)(2)(B) of title 28, United States Code, shall not be subject to the mandatory abstention provisions of section 1334(c)(2).

(5) The district court shall order that personal injury tort and wrongful death claims shall be tried in the district court in which the bankruptcy case is pending, or in the district court in the district in which the claim arose, as determined by the district court in which the bankruptcy case is pending.

(c)(1) A bankruptcy judge may hear a proceeding that is not a core proceeding but that is otherwise related to a case under title 11. In such proceeding, the bankruptcy judge shall submit proposed findings of fact and conclusions of law to the district court, and any final order or judgment shall be entered by the district judge after considering the bankruptcy judge's proposed findings and conclusions and after reviewing de novo those matters to which any party has timely and specifically objected.

(2) Notwithstanding the provisions of paragraph (1) of this subsection, the district court, with the consent of all the parties to

the proceeding, may refer a proceeding related to a case under title 11 to a bankruptcy judge to hear and determine and to enter appropriate orders and judgments, subject to review under section 158 of this title.

(d) The district court may withdraw, in whole or in part, any case or proceeding referred under this section, on its own motion or on timely motion of any party, for cause shown. The district court shall, on timely motion of a party, so withdraw a proceeding if the court determines that resolution of the proceeding requires consideration of both title 11 and other laws of the United States regulating organizations or activities affecting interstate commerce.

(e) If the right to a jury trial applies in a proceeding that may be heard under this section by a bankruptcy judge, the bankruptcy judge may conduct the jury trial if specially designated to exercise such jurisdiction by the district court and with the express consent of all the parties.

28 U.S.C. § 158. Appeals

(a) The district courts of the United States shall have jurisdiction to hear appeals

(1) from final judgments, orders, and decrees;

(2) from interlocutory orders and decrees issued under section 1121(d) of title 11 increasing or reducing the time periods referred to in section 1121 of such title; and

(3) with leave of the court, from other interlocutory orders and decrees;

of bankruptcy judges entered in cases and proceedings referred to the bankruptcy judges under section 157 of this title. An appeal under this subsection shall be taken only to the district court for the judicial district in which the bankruptcy judge is serving.

(b)(1) The judicial council of a circuit shall establish a bankruptcy appellate panel service composed of bankruptcy judges of the districts in the circuit who are appointed by the judicial council in accordance with paragraph (3), to hear and determine, with the consent of all the parties, appeals under subsection (a) unless the judicial council finds that—

(A) there are insufficient judicial resources available in the circuit; or

(B) establishment of such service would result in undue delay or increased cost to parties in cases under title 11.

Not later than 90 days after making the finding, the judicial council shall submit to the Judicial Conference of the United States a report containing the factual basis of such finding.

(2)(A) a judicial council may reconsider, at any time, the finding described in paragraph (1).

(B) On the request of a majority of the district judges in a circuit for which a bankruptcy appellate panel service is established under paragraph (1), made after the expiration of the 1-year period beginning on the date such service is established, the judicial council of the circuit shall determine whether a circumstance specified in subparagraph (A) or (B) of such paragraph exists.

(C) On its own motion, after the expiration of the 3-year period beginning on the date a bankruptcy appellate panel service is established under paragraph (1), the judicial council of the circuit may determine whether a circumstance specified in subparagraph (A) or (B) of such paragraph exists.

(D) If the judicial council finds that either of such circumstances exists, the judicial council may provide for the completion of the appeals then pending before such service and the orderly termination of such service.

(3) Bankruptcy judges appointed under paragraph (1) shall be appointed and may be reappointed under such paragraph.

(4) If authorized by the Judicial Conference of the United States, the judicial councils of 2 or more circuits may establish a joint bankruptcy appellate panel comprised of bankruptcy judges from the districts within the circuits for which such panel is established, to hear and determine, upon the consent of all the parties, appeals under subsection (a) of this section.

(5) An appeal to be heard under this subsection shall be heard by a panel of 3 members of the bankruptcy appellate panel service, except that a member of such service may not hear an appeal originating in the district for which such member is appointed or designated under section 152 of this title.

(6) Appeals may not be heard under this subsection by a panel of the bankruptcy appellate panel service unless the district judges for the district in which the appeals occur, by majority vote, have authorized such service to hear and determine appeals originating in such district.

(c)(1) subject to subsections (b) and (d)(2), each appeal under subsection (a) shall be heard by a 3-judge panel of the bankruptcy appellate panel service established under subsection (b)(1) unless—

(A) the appellant elects at the time of filing the appeal; or

(B) any other party elects, not later than 30 days after service of notice of the appeal;

to have such appeal heard by the district court.

(2) An appeal under subsection (a) and (b) of this section shall be taken in the same manner as appeals in civil proceedings generally are taken to the courts of appeals from the district courts and in the time provided by Rule 8002 of the Bankruptcy Rules.

(d)(1) The courts of appeals shall have jurisdiction of appeals from all final decisions, judgments, orders, and decrees entered under subsections (a) and (b) of this section.

(2)(A) The appropriate court of appeals shall have jurisdiction of appeals described in the first sentence of subsection (a) if the bankruptcy court, the district court, or the bankruptcy appellate panel involved, acting on its own motion or on the request of a party to the judgment, order, or decree described in such first sentence, or all the appellants and appellees (if any) acting jointly, certify that—

(i) the judgment, order, or decree involves a question of law as to which there is no controlling decision of the court of appeals for the circuit or of the Supreme Court of the United States, or involves a matter of public importance;

(ii) the judgment, order, or decree involves a question of law requiring resolution of conflicting decisions; or

(iii) an immediate appeal from the judgment, order, or decree may materially advance the progress of the case or proceeding in which the appeal is taken;

and if the court of appeals authorizes the direct appeal of the judgment, order, or decree.

(B) If the bankruptcy court, the district court, or the bankruptcy appellate panel—

(i) on its own motion or on the request of a party, determines that a circumstance specified in clause (i), (ii), or (iii) of subparagraph (A) exists; or

(ii) receives a request made by a majority of the appellants and a majority of appellees (if any) to make the certification described in subparagraph (A); then the bankruptcy court, the district court, or the bankruptcy appellate panel shall make the certification described in subparagraph (A).

(C) The parties may supplement the certification with a short statement of the basis for the certification.

(D) An appeal under this paragraph does not stay any proceeding of the bankruptcy court, the district court, or the bankruptcy appellate panel from which the appeal is taken, unless the respective bankruptcy court, district court, or bankruptcy appellate panel, or the court of appeals in which the appeal in pending, issues a stay of such proceeding pending the appeal.

(E) Any request under subparagraph (B) for certification shall be made not later than 60 days after the entry of the judgment, order, or decree.

28 U.S.C. § 159. Bankruptcy statistics[59]

(a) The clerk of the district court, or the clerk of the bankruptcy court if one is certified pursuant to section 156(b) of this title, shall collect statistics regarding debtors who are individuals with primarily consumer debts seeking relief under chapters 7, 11, and 13 of title 11. Those statistics shall be in a standardized format prescribed by the Director of the Administrative Office of the United States Courts (referred to in this section as the "Director").

(b) The Director shall—

(1) compile the statistics referred to in subsection (a);

(2) make the statistics available to the public; and

(3) not later than June 1, 2008, and annually thereafter, prepare, and submit to Congress a report concerning the information collected under subsection (a) that contains an analysis of the information.

(c) The compilation required under subsection (b) shall—

(1) be itemized, by chapter, with respect to title 11;

(2) be presented in the aggregate and for each district; and

(3) include information concerning—

(A) the total assets and total liabilities of the debtors described in subsection (a), and in each category of assets and liabilities, as reported in the schedules prescribed pursuant to section 2075 of this title and filed by those debtors;

(B) the current monthly income, average income, and average expenses of those debtors as reported on the schedules and statements that each such debtor files under sections 521 and 1322 of title 11;

(C) the aggregate amount of debt discharged in cases filed during the reporting period, determined as the difference between the total amount of debt and obligations of a debtor reported on the schedules and the amount of such debt reported in categories which are predominantly nondischargeable;

(D) the average period of time between the filing of the petition and the closing of the case for cases closed during the reporting period;

(E) for cases closed during the reporting period—

(i) the number of cases in which a reaffirmation was filed; and

(ii)(I) the total number of reaffirmations filed;

(II) of those cases in which a reaffirmation was filed, the number of cases in which the debtor was not represented by an attorney; and

(III) of those cases in which a reaffirmation was filed, the number of cases in which the reaffirmation was approved by the court;

(F) with respect to cases filed under chapter 13 of title 11, for the reporting period—

(i)(I) the number of cases in which a final order was entered determining the value of property securing a claim in an amount less than the amount of the claim; and

(II) the number of final orders entered determining the value of property securing a claim;

(ii) the number of cases dismissed, the number of cases dismissed for failure to make payments under the plan, the number of cases refiled after dismissal, and the number of cases in which the plan was completed, separately itemized with respect to the number of modifications made before completion of the plan, if any; and

(iii) the number of cases in which the debtor filed another case during the 6-year period preceding the filing;

(G) the number of cases in which creditors were fined for misconduct and any amount of punitive damages awarded by the court for creditor misconduct; and

(H) the number of cases in which sanctions under rule 9011 of the Federal Rules of Bankruptcy Procedure were imposed

59 *Editor's Note*: New section 159 takes effect eighteen months after April 20, 2005.

against debtor's attorney or damages awarded under such Rule.

* * *

28 U.S.C. § 581. United States trustees

(a) The Attorney General shall appoint one United States trustee for each of the following regions composed of Federal judicial districts (without regard to section 451):

(1) The judicial districts established for the States of Maine, Massachusetts, New Hampshire, and Rhode Island.

(2) The judicial districts established for the States of Connecticut, New York, and Vermont.

(3) The judicial districts established for the States of Delaware, New Jersey, and Pennsylvania.

(4) The judicial districts established for the States of Maryland, North Carolina, South Carolina, Virginia, and West Virginia and for the District of Columbia.

(5) The judicial districts established for the States of Louisiana and Mississippi.

(6) The Northern District of Texas and the Eastern District of Texas.

(7) The Southern District of Texas and the Western District of Texas.

(8) The judicial districts established for the States of Kentucky and Tennessee.

(9) The judicial districts established for the States of Michigan and Ohio.

(10) The Central District of Illinois and the Southern District of Illinois; and the judicial districts established for the State of Indiana.

(11) The Northern District of Illinois; and the judicial districts established for the State of Wisconsin.

(12) The judicial districts established for the States of Minnesota, Iowa, North Dakota, and South Dakota.

(13) The judicial districts established for the States of Arkansas, Nebraska, and Missouri.

(14) The District of Arizona.

(15) The Southern District of California; and the judicial districts established for the State of Hawaii, and for Guam and the Commonwealth of the Northern Mariana Islands.

(16) The Central District of California.

(17) The Eastern District of California and the Northern District of California; and the judicial district established for the State of Nevada.

(18) The judicial districts established for the States of Alaska, Idaho (exclusive of Yellowstone National Park), Montana (exclusive of Yellowstone National Park), Oregon, and Washington.

(19) The judicial districts established for the States of Colorado, Utah, and Wyoming (including those portions of Yellowstone National Park situated in the States of Montana and Idaho).

(20) The judicial districts established for the States of Kansas, New Mexico, and Oklahoma.

(21) The judicial districts established for the States of Alabama, Florida, and Georgia and for the Commonwealth of Puerto Rico and the Virgin Islands of the United States.

(b) Each United States trustee shall be appointed for a term of five years. On the expiration of his term, a United States trustee shall continue to perform the duties of his office until his successor is appointed and qualifies.

(c) Each United States trustee is subject to removal by the Attorney General.

28 U.S.C. § 582. Assistant United States trustees

(a) The Attorney General may appoint one or more assistant United States trustees in any region when the public interest so requires.

(b) Each assistant United States trustee is subject to removal by the Attorney General.

28 U.S.C. § 583. Oath of Office

Each United States trustee and assistant United States trustee, before taking office, shall take an oath to execute faithfully his duties.

28 U.S.C. § 584. Official stations

The Attorney General may determine the official stations of the United States trustees and assistant United States trustees within the regions for which they were appointed.

28 U.S.C. § 585. Vacancies

(a) The Attorney General may appoint an acting United States trustee for a region in which the office of the United States trustee is vacant. The individual so appointed may serve until the date on which the vacancy is filled by appointment under section 581 of this title or by designation under subsection (b) of this section.

(b) The Attorney General may designate a United States trustee to serve in not more than two regions for such time as the public interest requires.

28 U.S.C. § 586. Duties; supervision by Attorney General

(a) Each United States trustee, within the region for which such United States trustee is appointed, shall—

(1) establish, maintain, and supervise a panel of private trustees that are eligible and available to serve as trustees in cases under chapter 7 of title 11;

(2) serve as and perform the duties of a trustee in a case under title 11 when required under title 11 to serve as trustee in such a case;

(3) supervise the administration of cases and trustees in cases under chapter 7, 11, 12 ~~or~~ 13, or 15 of title 11 by, whenever the United States trustee considers it to be appropriate—

(A)(i) reviewing, in accordance with procedural guidelines adopted by the Executive Office of the United States Trustee (which guidelines shall be applied uniformly by the United States Trustee except when circumstances warrant different treatment), applications filed for compensation and reimbursement under section 330 of title 11; and

(ii) filing with the court comments with respect to such application and, if the united states trustee considers it to be appropriate, objections to such application.

(B) monitoring plans and disclosure statements filed in cases under chapter 11 of title 11 and filing with the court, in connection with hearings under sections 1125 and 1128 of such title, comments with respect to such plans and disclosure statements;

(C) monitoring plans filed under chapters 12 and 13 of title 11 and filing with the court, in connection with hearings under sections 1224, 1229, 1324, and 1329 of such title, comments with respect to such plans;

(D) taking such action as the United States trustee deems to be appropriate to ensure that all reports, schedules, and fees required to be filed under title 11 and this title by the debtor are properly and timely filed;

(E) monitoring creditors' committees appointed under title 11;

(F) notifying the appropriate United States attorney of matters which relate to the occurrence of any action which may constitute a crime under the laws of the United States and, on the request of the United States attorney, assisting the United States attorney in carrying out prosecutions based on such action;

(G) monitoring the progress of cases under title 11 and taking such actions as the United States trustee deems to be appropriate to prevent undue delay in such progress;

(H) in small business cases (as defined in section 101 of title 11), performing the additional duties specified in title 11 pertaining to such cases; and

(~~H~~I) monitoring applications filed under section 327 of title 11 and, whenever the United States trustee deems it to be appropriate, filing with the court comments with respect to the approval of such applications;

(4) deposit or invest under section 345 of title 11 money received as trustee in cases under title 11;

(5) perform the duties prescribed for the United States trustee under title 11 and this title, and such duties consistent with title 11 and this title as the Attorney General may prescribe; ~~and~~

(6) make such reports as the Attorney General directs, including the results of audits performed under section 603(a) of the Bankruptcy Abuse Prevention and Consumer Protection Act of 2005;~~.~~

(7) in each of such small business cases—

(A) conduct an initial debtor interview as soon as practicable after the date of the order for relief but before the first meeting scheduled under section 341(a) of title 11, at which time the United States trustee shall—

(i) begin to investigate the debtor's viability;

(ii) inquire about the debtor's business plan;

(iii) explain the debtor's obligations to file monthly operating reports and other required reports;

(iv) attempt to develop an agreed scheduling order; and

(v) inform the debtor of other obligations;

(B) if determined to be appropriate and advisable, visit the appropriate business premises of the debtor, ascertain the state of the debtor's books and records, and verify that the debtor has filed its tax returns; and

(C) review and monitor diligently the debtor's activities, to identify as promptly as possible whether the debtor will be unable to confirm a plan; and

(8) in any case in which the United States trustee finds material grounds for any relief under section 1112 of title 11, the United States trustee shall apply promptly after making that finding to the court for relief.

(b) If the number of cases under chapter 12 or 13 of title 11 commenced in a particular region so warrants, the United States trustee for such region may, subject to the approval of the Attorney General, appoint one or more individuals to serve as standing trustee, or designate one or more assistant United States trustees to serve in cases under such chapter. The United States trustee for such region shall supervise any such individual appointed as standing trustee in the performance of the duties of standing trustee.

(c) Each United States trustee shall be under the general supervision of the Attorney General, who shall provide general coordination and assistance to the United States trustees.

(d)(1) The Attorney General shall prescribe by rule qualifications for membership on the panels established by United States trustees under paragraph (a)(1) of this section, and qualifications for appointment under subsection (b) of this section to serve as standing trustee in cases under chapter 12 or 13 of title 11. The Attorney General may not require that an individual be an attorney in order to qualify for appointment under subsection (b) of this section to serve as standing trustee in cases under chapter 12 or 13 of title 11.

(2) A trustee whose appointment under subsection (a)(1) or under subsection (b) is terminated or who ceases to be assigned to cases filed under title 11, United States Code, may obtain judicial review of the final agency decision by commencing an action in the district court of the United States for the district for which the panel to which the trustee is appointed under subsection (a)(1), or in the district court of the United States for the district in which the trustee is appointed under subsection (b) resides, after first exhausting all available administrative remedies, which if the trustee so elects, shall also include an administrative hearing on the record. Unless the trustee elects to have an administrative hearing on the record, the trustee shall be deemed to have exhausted all administrative

remedies for purposes of this paragraph if the agency fails to make a final agency decision within 90 days after the trustee requests administrative remedies. The Attorney General shall prescribe procedures to implement this paragraph. The decision of the agency shall be affirmed by the district court unless it is unreasonable and without cause based on the administrative record before the agency.

(e)(1) The Attorney General, after consultation with a United States trustee that has appointed an individual under subsection (b) of this section to serve as standing trustee in cases under chapter 12 or 13 of title 11, shall fix—

(A) a maximum annual compensation for such individual consisting of—

(i) an amount not to exceed the highest annual rate of basic pay in effect for level V of the Executive Schedule; and

(ii) the cash value of employment benefits comparable to the employment benefits provided by the United States to individuals who are employed by the United States at the same rate of basic pay to perform similar services during the same period of time; and

(B) a percentage fee not to exceed—

(i) in the case of a debtor who is not a family farmer, ten percent; or

(ii) in the case of a debtor who is a family farmer, the sum of—

(I) not to exceed ten percent of the payments made under the plan of such debtor, with respect to payments in an aggregate amount not to exceed $450,000; and

(II) three percent of payments made under the plan of such debtor, with respect to payments made after the aggregate amount of payments made under the plan exceeds $450,000;

based on such maximum annual compensation and the actual, necessary expenses incurred by such individual as standing trustee.

(2) Such individual shall collect such percentage fee from all payments received by such individual under plans in the cases under chapter 12 or 13 of title 11 for which such individual serves as standing trustee. Such individual shall pay to the United States trustee, and the United States trustee shall deposit in the United States Trustee System Fund—

(A) any amount by which the actual compensation of such individual exceeds 5 per centum upon all payments received under plans in cases under chapter 12 or 13 of title 11 for which such individual serves as standing trustee; and

(B) any amount by which the percentage for all such cases exceeds—

(i) such individual's actual compensation for such cases, as adjusted under subparagraph (A) of paragraph (1); plus

(ii) the actual, necessary expenses incurred by such individual as standing trustee in such cases. Subject to the approval of the Attorney General, any or all of the interest earned from the deposit of payments under plans by such individual may be utilized to pay actual, necessary expenses without regard to the percentage limitation contained in subparagraph (d)(1)(B) of this section.

(3) After first exhausting all available administrative remedies, an individual appointed under subsection (b) may obtain judicial review of final agency action to deny a claim of actual, necessary expenses under this subsection by commencing an action in the district court of the United States for the district where the individual resides. The decision of the agency shall be affirmed by the district court unless it is unreasonable and without cause based upon the administrative record before the agency.

(4) The Attorney General shall prescribe procedures to implement this subsection.

(f)[60](1) The United States trustee for each district is authorized to contract with auditors to perform audits in cases designated by the United States trustee, in accordance with the procedures established under section 603(a) of the Bankruptcy Abuse Prevention and Consumer Protection Act of 2005.

(2)(A) The report of each audit referred to in paragraph (1) shall be filed with the court and transmitted to the United States trustee. Each report shall clearly and conspicuously specify any material misstatement of income or expenditures or of assets identified by the person performing the audit. In any case in which a material misstatement of income or expenditures or of assets has been reported, the clerk of the district court (or the clerk of the bankruptcy court if one is certified under section 156(b) of this title) shall give notice of the misstatement to the creditors in the case.

(B) If a material misstatement of income or expenditures or of assets is reported, the United States trustee shall—

(i) report the material misstatement, if appropriate, to the United States Attorney pursuant to section 3057 of title 18; and

(ii) if advisable, take appropriate action, including but not limited to commencing an adversary proceeding to revoke the debtor's discharge pursuant to section 727(d) of title 11.

28 U.S.C. § 587. Salaries

Subject to sections 5315 through 5317 of title 5, the Attorney General shall fix the annual salaries of United States trustees and assistant United States trustees at rates of compensation not in excess of the rate of basic compensation provided for Executive Level IV of the Executive Schedule set forth in section 5315 of title 5, United States Code.

28 U.S.C. § 588. Expenses

Necessary office expenses of the United States trustee shall be allowed when authorized by the Attorney General.

60 *Editor's Note*: New subsection 586(f) takes effect eighteen months after April 20, 2005.

28 U.S.C. § 589. Staff and other employees

The United States trustee may employ staff and other employees on approval of the Attorney General.

28 U.S.C. § 589a. United States Trustee System Fund

(a) There is hereby established in the Treasury of the United States a special fund to be known as the "United States Trustee System Fund" (hereinafter in this section referred to as the "Fund"). Monies in the Fund shall be available to the Attorney General without fiscal year limitation in such amounts as may be specified in appropriations Acts for the following purposes in connection with the operations of United States trustees—

(1) salaries and related employee benefits;

(2) travel and transportation;

(3) rental of space;

(4) communication, utilities, and miscellaneous computer charges;

(5) security investigations and audits;

(6) supplies, books, and other materials for legal research;

(7) furniture and equipment;

(8) miscellaneous services, including those obtained by contract; and

(9) printing.

(b) There shall be deposited in the Fund—

(1)(A) ~~27.42~~ 40.46 per centum of the fees collected under section 1930(a)(1)(A) of this title; and

(B) 28.33 percent of the fees collected under section 1930(a)(1)(B);

(2) ~~one-half~~ 55%[61] of the fees collected under section 1930(a)(3) of this title;

(3) one-half of the fees collected under section 1930(a)(4) of this title;

(4) one-half of the fees collected under section 1930(a)(5);

(5) 100 percent of the fees collected under section 1930(a)(6) of this title until a reorganization plan is confirmed;

(6) three-fourths of the fees collected under the last sentence of section 1930(a) of this title;

(7) the compensation of trustees received under section 330(d) of title 11 by the clerks of the bankruptcy courts;

(8) excess fees collected under section 586(e)(2) of this title; and

(9) interest earned on Fund investment.

(c) Amounts in the Fund which are not concurrently needed for the purposes specified in subsection (a) shall be kept on deposit or invested in obligations of, or guaranteed by, the United States.

(d) The Attorney General shall transmit to the Congress, not later than 120 days after the end of each fiscal year, a detailed report on the amounts deposited in the Fund and a description of the expenditures made under this section.

(e) There are authorized to be appropriated to the Fund for any fiscal year such sums as may be necessary to supplement amounts deposited under subsection (b) for purposes specified in subsection (a).

28 U.S.C. § 589b. Bankruptcy data

(a) Rules.—The Attorney General shall, within a reasonable time after the effective date of this section, issue rules requiring uniform forms for (and from time to time thereafter to appropriately modify and approve)—

(1) final reports by trustees in cases under chapters 7, 12, and 13 of title 11; and

(2) periodic reports by debtors in possession or trustees in cases under chapter 11 of title 11.

(b) Reports.—Each report referred to in subsection (a) shall be designed (and the requirements as to place and manner of filing shall be established) so as to facilitate compilation of data and maximum possible access of the public, both by physical inspection at one or more central filing locations, and by electronic access through the Internet or other appropriate media.

(c) Required Information.—The information required to be filed in the reports referred to in subsection (b) shall be that which is in the best interests of debtors and creditors, and in the public interest in reasonable and adequate information to evaluate the efficiency and practicality of the Federal bankruptcy system. In issuing rules proposing the forms referred to in subsection (a), the Attorney General shall strike the best achievable practical balance between—

(1) the reasonable needs of the public for information about the operational results of the Federal bankruptcy system;

(2) economy, simplicity, and lack of undue burden on persons with a duty to file reports; and

(3) appropriate privacy concerns and safeguards.

(d) Final Reports.—The uniform forms for final reports required under subsection (a) for use by trustees under chapters 7, 12, and 13 of title 11 shall, in addition to such other matters as are required by law or as the Attorney General in the discretion of the Attorney General shall propose, include with respect to a case under such title—

(1) information about the length of time the case was pending;

(2) assets abandoned;

(3) assets exempted;

(4) receipts and disbursements of the estate;

(5) expenses of administration, including for use under section

61 *Editor's Note*: These changes to subsection 589a(b) were made by the Emergency Supplemental Appropriations Act for Defense, the Global War on Terror, and Tsunami Relief, 2005, Pub. L. No. 109-13, 119 Stat. 231, which was enacted on May 11, 2005. They supersede the changes made to this section by Pub. L. No. 109-8 on April 20, 2005.

707(b), actual costs of administering cases under chapter 13 of title 11;

(6) claims asserted;

(7) claims allowed; and

(8) distributions to claimants and claims discharged without payment, in each case by appropriate category and, in cases under chapters 12 and 13 of title 11, date of confirmation of the plan, each modification thereto, and defaults by the debtor in performance under the plan.

(e) Periodic Reports.—The uniform forms for periodic reports required under subsection (a) for use by trustees or debtors in possession under chapter 11 of title 11 shall, in addition to such other matters as are required by law or as the Attorney General in the discretion of the Attorney General shall propose, include—

(1) information about the industry classification, published by the Department of Commerce, for the businesses conducted by the debtor;

(2) length of time the case has been pending;

(3) number of full-time employees as of the date of the order for relief and at the end of each reporting period since the case was filed;

(4) cash receipts, cash disbursements and profitability of the debtor for the most recent period and cumulatively since the date of the order for relief;

(5) compliance with title 11, whether or not tax returns and tax payments since the date of the order for relief have been timely filed and made;

(6) all professional fees approved by the court in the case for the most recent period and cumulatively since the date of the order for relief (separately reported, for the professional fees incurred by or on behalf of the debtor, between those that would have been incurred absent a bankruptcy case and those not); and

(7) plans of reorganization filed and confirmed and, with respect thereto, by class, the recoveries of the holders, expressed in aggregate dollar values and, in the case of claims, as a percentage of total claims of the class allowed.

* * *

28 U.S.C. § 959. Trustees and receivers suable; management; State laws

(a) Trustees, receivers or managers of any property, including debtors in possession, may be sued, without leave of the court appointing them, with respect to any of their acts or transactions in carrying on business connected with such property. Such actions shall be subject to the general equity power of such court so far as the same may be necessary to the ends of justice, but this shall not deprive a litigant of his right to trial by jury.

(b) Except as provided in section 1166 of title 11, a trustee, receiver or manager appointed in any cause pending in any court of the United States, including a debtor in possession, shall manage and operate the property in his possession as such trustee, receiver or manager according to the requirements of the valid laws of the State in which such property is situated, in the same manner that the owner or possessor thereof would be bound to do if in possession thereof.

28 U.S.C. § 960. Tax liability

(a) Any officers and agents conducting any business under authority of a United States court shall be subject to all Federal, State and local taxes applicable to such business to the same extent as if it were conducted by an individual or corporation.

(b) A tax under subsection (a) shall be paid on or before the due date of the tax under applicable nonbankruptcy law, unless—

(1) the tax is a property tax secured by a lien against property that is abandoned within a reasonable period of time after the lien attaches by the trustee in a bankruptcy case under title 11; or

(2) payment of the tax is excused under a specific provision of title 11.

(c) In a case pending under chapter 7 of title 11, payment of a tax may be deferred until final distribution is made under section 726 of title 11, if—

(1) the tax was not incurred by a trustee duly appointed or elected under chapter 7 of title 11; or

(2) before the due date of the tax, an order of the court makes a finding of probable insufficiency of funds of the estate to pay in full the administrative expenses allowed under section 503(b) of title 11 that have the same priority in distribution under section 726(b) of title 11 as the priority of that tax.

* * *

28 U.S.C. § 1334. Bankruptcy cases and proceedings

(a) Except as provided in subsection (b) of this section, the district courts shall have original and exclusive jurisdiction of all cases under title 11.

(b) Except as provided in subsection (e)(2), and ~~N~~notwithstanding any Act of Congress that confers exclusive jurisdiction on a court or courts other than the district courts, the district courts shall have original but not exclusive jurisdiction of all civil proceedings arising under title 11, or arising in or related to cases under title 11.

(c)(1) Except with respect to a case under chapter 15 of title 11, ~~N~~nothing in this section prevents a district court in the interest of justice, or in the interest of comity with State courts or respect for State law, from abstaining from hearing a particular proceeding arising under title 11 or arising in or related to a case under title 11.

(2) Upon timely motion of a party in a proceeding based upon a State law claim or State law cause of action, related to a case under title 11 but not arising under title 11 or arising in a case under title 11, with respect to which an action could not have been commenced in a court of the United States absent jurisdiction under this section, the district court shall abstain from hearing such proceeding if an action is commenced, and can be timely adjudicated, in a State forum of appropriate jurisdiction.

(d) Any decision to abstain or not abstain made under ~~this~~ subsection (c) (other than a decision not to abstain in a proceeding described in subsection (c)(2)) is not reviewable by appeal or otherwise by the court of appeals under section 158(d), 1291, or 1292 of this title or by the supreme court of the united states under section 1254 of this title. Subsection (c) and ~~T~~this subsection shall not be construed to limit the applicability of the stay provided for by section 362 of title 11, United States Code, as such section applies to an action affecting the property of the estate in bankruptcy.

(e) The district court in which a case under title 11 is commenced or is pending shall have exclusive jurisdiction—

(1) of all of the property, wherever located, of the debtor as of the commencement of such case, and of property of the estate; and

(2) over all claims or causes of action that involve construction of section 327 of title 11, United States Code, or rules relating to disclosure requirements under section 327.[62]

* * *

28 U.S.C. § 1408. Venue of cases under title 11

Except as provided in section 1410 of this title, a case under title 11 may be commenced in the district court for the district—

(1) in which the domicile, residence, principal place of business in the United States, or principal assets in the United States, of the person or entity that is the subject of such case have been located for the one hundred and eighty days immediately preceding such commencement, or for a longer portion of such one-hundred-and-eighty-day period than the domicile, residence, or principal place of business, in the United States, or principal assets in the United States, of such person were located in any other district; or

(2) in which there is pending a case under title 11 concerning such person's affiliate, general partner, or partnership.

28 U.S.C. § 1409. Venue of proceedings arising under title 11 or arising in or related to cases under title 11

(a) Except as otherwise provided in subsections (b) and (d), a proceeding arising under title 11 or arising in or related to a case under title 11 may be commenced in the district court in which such case is pending.

(b) Except as provided in subsection (d) of this section, a trustee in a case under title 11 may commence a proceeding arising in or related to such case to recover a money judgment of or property worth less than $1,000 or a consumer debt of less than ~~$5,000~~ $15,000, or a debt (excluding a consumer debt) against a noninsider of less than $10,000, only in the district court for the district in which the defendant resides.

(c) Except as provided in subsection (b) of this section, a trustee in a case under title 11 may commence a proceeding arising in or related to such case as statutory successor to the debtor or creditors under section 541 or 544(b) of title 11 in the district court for the district where the State or Federal court sits in which, under applicable nonbankruptcy venue provisions, the debtor or creditors, as the case may be, may have commenced an action on which such proceeding is based if the case under title 11 had not been commenced.

(d) A trustee may commence a proceeding arising under title 11 or arising in or related to a case under title 11 based on a claim arising after the commencement of such case from the operation of the business of the debtor only in the district court for the district where a State or Federal court sits in which, under applicable nonbankruptcy venue provisions, an action on such claim may have been brought.

(e) A proceeding arising under title 11 or arising in or related to a case under title 11, based on a claim arising after the commencement of such case from the operation of the business of the debtor, may be commenced against the representative of the estate in such case in the district court for the district where the State or Federal court sits in which the party commencing such proceeding may, under applicable nonbankruptcy venue provisions, have brought an action on such claim, or in the district court in which such case is pending.

28 U.S.C. § 1410. Venue of cases ancillary to foreign proceedings

~~(a) A case under section 304 of title 11 to enjoin the commencement or continuation of an action or proceeding in a State or Federal court, or the enforcement of a judgment, may be commenced only in the district court for the district where the State or Federal court sits in which is pending the action or proceeding against which the injunction is sought.~~

~~(b) A case under section 304 of title 11 to enjoin the enforcement of a lien against a property, or to require the turnover of property of an estate, may be commenced only in the district court for the district in which such property is found.~~

~~(c) A case under section 304 of title 11, other than a case specified in subsection (a) or (b) of this section, may be commenced only in the district court for the district in which is located the principal place of business in the United States, or the principal assets in the United States, of the estate that is the subject of such case.~~

A case under chapter 15 of title 11 may be commenced in the district court of the United States for the district—

(1) in which the debtor has its principal place of business or principal assets in the United States;

(2) if the debtor does not have a place of business or assets in the United States, in which there is pending against the debtor an action or proceeding in a Federal or State court; or

(3) in a case other than those specified in paragraph (1) or (2), in which venue will be consistent with the interests of justice and the convenience of the parties, having regard to the relief sought by the foreign representative.

28 U.S.C. § 1411. Jury trials

(a) Except as provided in subsection (b) of this section, this chapter and title 11 do not affect any right to trial by jury that an individual has under applicable nonbankruptcy law with regard to a personal injury or wrongful death tort claim.

62 *Editor's Note*: The amendment adding subsection 1334(e)(2) takes effect Oct. 17, 2005 and is only applicable to cases filed after April 20, 2005.

(b) The district court may order the issues arising under section 303 of title 11 to be tried without a jury.

28 U.S.C. § 1412. Change of venue

A district court may transfer a case or proceeding under title 11 to a district court for another district, in the interest of justice or for the convenience of the parties.

* * *

28 U.S.C. § 1452. Removal of claims related to bankruptcy cases

(a) A party may remove any claim or cause of action in a civil action other than a proceeding before the United States Tax Court or a civil action by a governmental unit to enforce such governmental unit's police or regulatory power, to the district court for the district where such civil action is pending, if such district court has jurisdiction of such claim or cause of action under section 1334 of this title.

(b) The court to which such claim or cause of action is removed may remand such claim or cause of action on any equitable ground. An order entered under this subsection remanding a claim or cause of action, or a decision to not remand, is not reviewable by appeal or otherwise by the court of appeals under section 158(d), 1291, or 1292 of this title or by the Supreme Court of the United States under section 1254 of this title.

* * *

28 U.S.C. § 1927. Counsel's liability for excessive costs

Any attorney or other person admitted to conduct cases in any court of the United States or any Territory thereof who so multiplies the proceedings in any case unreasonably and vexatiously may be required by the court to satisfy personally the excess costs, expenses, and attorneys' fees reasonably incurred because of such conduct.

* * *

28 U.S.C. § 1930. Bankruptcy fees

(a) ~~Notwithstanding section 1915 of this title, the~~ The parties commencing a case under title 11 shall pay to the clerk of the district court or the clerk of the bankruptcy court, if one has been certified pursuant to section 156(b) of this title, the following filing fees:

(1) For a case commenced under—

(A) chapter 7 of title 11, $220; and ~~or~~

(B) chapter 13 of title 11, ~~$155~~ $150.[63]

(2) For a case commenced under chapter 9 of title 11, equal to the fee specified in paragraph (3) for filing a case under chapter 11 of title 11. The amount by which the fee payable under this paragraph exceeds $300 shall be deposited in the fund established under section 1931 of this title.

(3) For a case commenced under chapter 11 of title 11 that does not concern a railroad, as defined in section 101 of title 11, ~~$800~~ $1000.

(4) For a case commenced under chapter 11 of title 11 concerning a railroad, as so defined, $1,000.

(5) For a case commenced under chapter 12 of title 11, $200.

(6) In addition to the filing fee paid to the clerk, a quarterly fee shall be paid to the United States trustee, for deposit in the Treasury, in each case under chapter 11 of title 11 for each quarter (including any fraction thereof) until the case is converted or dismissed, whichever occurs first. The fee shall be $250 for each quarter in which disbursements total less than $15,000; $500 for each quarter in which disbursements total $15,000 or more but less than $75,000; $750 for each quarter in which disbursements total $75,000 or more but less than $150,000; $1,250 for each quarter in which disbursements total $150,000 or more but less than $225,000; $1,500 for each quarter in which disbursements total $225,000 or more but less than $300,000; $3,750 for each quarter in which disbursements total $300,000 or more but less than $1,000,000; $5,000 for each quarter in which disbursements total $1,000,000 or more but less than $2,000,000; $7,500 for each quarter in which disbursements total $2,000,000 or more but less than $3,000,000; $8,000 for each quarter in which disbursements total $3,000,000 or more but less than $5,000,000; $10,000 for each quarter in which disbursements total $5,000,000 or more. The fee shall be payable on the last day of the calendar month following the calendar quarter for which the fee is owed.

(7) In districts that are not part of a United States trustee region as defined in section 581 of this title, the Judicial Conference of the United States may require the debtor in a case under chapter 11 of title 11 to pay fees equal to those imposed by paragraph (6) of this subsection. Such fees shall be deposited as offsetting receipts to the fund established under section 1931 of this title and shall remain available until expended.

An individual commencing a voluntary case or a joint case under title 11 may pay such fee in installments. For converting, on request of the debtor, a case under chapter 7, or 13 of title 11, to a case under chapter 11 of title 11, the debtor shall pay to the clerk of the court a fee of the amount equal to the difference between the fee specified in paragraph (3) and the fee specified in paragraph (1).

(b) The Judicial Conference of the United States may prescribe additional fees in cases under title 11 of the same kind as the Judicial Conference prescribes under section 1914(b) of this title.

(c) Upon the filing of any separate or joint notice of appeal or application for appeal or upon the receipt of any order allowing, or notice of the allowance of, an appeal or a writ of certiorari $5 shall be paid to the clerk of the court, by the appellant or petitioner.

63 *Editor's Note*: These changes to subsection 1930(a) were made by the Emergency Supplemental Appropriations Act for Defense, the Global War on Terror, and Tsunami Relief, 2005, Pub. L. No. 109-13, 119 Stat. 231, which was enacted on May 11, 2005. They supersede the changes made to this section by Pub. L. No. 109-8 on April 20, 2005. The Administrative Office of the United States Courts has announced that the new fees shall take effect on October 17, 2005. Admin. Office of the U.S. Courts, Chapter 7 Bankruptcy Fees to Increase (June 8, 2005), *available at* www.uscourts.gov/newsroom/bankruptcyfees.html.

(d) Whenever any case or proceeding is dismissed in any bankruptcy court for want of jurisdiction, such court may order the payment of just costs.

(e) The clerk of the court may collect only the fees prescribed under this section.

(f)(1) Under the procedures prescribed by the Judicial Conference of the United States, the district court or the bankruptcy court may waive the filing fee in a case under chapter 7 of title 11 for an individual if the court determines that such individual has income less than 150 percent of the income official poverty line (as defined by the Office of Management and Budget, and revised annually in accordance with section 673(2) of the Omnibus Budget Reconciliation Act of 1981) applicable to a family of the size involved and is unable to pay that fee in installments. For purposes of this paragraph, the term "filing fee" means the filing fee required by subsection (a), or any other fee prescribed by the Judicial Conference under subsections (b) and (c) that is payable to the clerk upon the commencement of a case under chapter 7.

(2) The district court or the bankruptcy court may waive for such debtors other fees prescribed under subsections (b) and (c).

(3) This subsection does not restrict the district court or the bankruptcy court from waiving, in accordance with Judicial Conference policy, fees prescribed under this section for other debtors and creditors.

* * *

28 U.S.C. § 2075. Bankruptcy rules

The Supreme Court shall have the power to prescribe by general rules, the forms of process, writs, pleadings, and motions, and the practice and procedure in cases under title 11.

Such rules shall not abridge, enlarge, or modify any substantive right.

The Supreme Court shall transmit to Congress not later than May 1 of the year in which a rule prescribed under this section is to become effective a copy of the proposed rule. The rule shall take effect no earlier than December 1 of the year in which it is transmitted to congress unless otherwise provided by law. The bankruptcy rules promulgated under this section shall prescribe a form for the statement required under section 707(b)(2)(C) of title 11 and may provide general rules on the content of such statement.

A.3 Bankruptcy Abuse Prevention and Consumer Protection Act of 2005

Public Law Number 109-8, 119 Stat. 23 (April 20, 2005)

An Act

To amend title 11 of the United States Code, and for other purposes.

Be it enacted by the Senate and House of Representatives of the United States of America in Congress assembled,

SECTION 1. SHORT TITLE; REFERENCES; TABLE OF CONTENTS.

(a) SHORT TITLE.—This Act may be cited as the "Bankruptcy Abuse Prevention and Consumer Protection Act of 2005".

(b) TABLE OF CONTENTS.—The table of contents for this Act is as follows:

Sec. 446. Duties with respect to a debtor who is a plan administrator of an employee benefit plan.
Sec. 447. Appointment of committee of retired employees.

TITLE V—MUNICIPAL BANKRUPTCY PROVISIONS

Sec. 501. Petition and proceedings related to petition.
Sec. 502. Applicability of other sections to chapter 9.

TITLE VI—BANKRUPTCY DATA

Sec. 601. Improved bankruptcy statistics.
Sec. 602. Uniform rules for the collection of bankruptcy data.
Sec. 603. Audit procedures.
Sec. 604. Sense of Congress regarding availability of bankruptcy data.

TITLE VII—BANKRUPTCY TAX PROVISIONS

Sec. 701. Treatment of certain liens.
Sec. 702. Treatment of fuel tax claims.
Sec. 703. Notice of request for a determination of taxes.
Sec. 704. Rate of interest on tax claims.
Sec. 705. Priority of tax claims.
Sec. 706. Priority property taxes incurred.
Sec. 707. No discharge of fraudulent taxes in chapter 13.
Sec. 708. No discharge of fraudulent taxes in chapter 11.
Sec. 709. Stay of tax proceedings limited to prepetition taxes.
Sec. 710. Periodic payment of taxes in chapter 11 cases.
Sec. 711. Avoidance of statutory tax liens prohibited.
Sec. 712. Payment of taxes in the conduct of business.
Sec. 713. Tardily filed priority tax claims.
Sec. 714. Income tax returns prepared by tax authorities.
Sec. 715. Discharge of the estate's liability for unpaid taxes.
Sec. 716. Requirement to file tax returns to confirm chapter 13 plans.
Sec. 717. Standards for tax disclosure.
Sec. 718. Setoff of tax refunds.
Sec. 719. Special provisions related to the treatment of State and local taxes.
Sec. 720. Dismissal for failure to timely file tax returns.

TITLE VIII—ANCILLARY AND OTHER CROSS-BORDER CASES

Sec. 801. Amendment to add chapter 15 to title 11, United States Code.
Sec. 802. Other amendments to titles 11 and 28, United States Code.

TITLE IX—FINANCIAL CONTRACT PROVISIONS

Sec. 901. Treatment of certain agreements by conservators or receivers of insured depository institutions.
Sec. 902. Authority of the FDIC and NCUAB with respect to failed and failing institutions.
Sec. 903. Amendments relating to transfers of qualified financial contracts.
Sec. 904. Amendments relating to disaffirmance or repudiation of qualified financial contracts.
Sec. 905. Clarifying amendment relating to master agreements.
Sec. 906. Federal Deposit Insurance Corporation Improvement Act of 1991.
Sec. 907. Bankruptcy law amendments.
Sec. 908. Recordkeeping requirements.
Sec. 909. Exemptions from contemporaneous execution requirement.
Sec. 910. Damage measure.
Sec. 911. SIPC stay.

TITLE X—PROTECTION OF FAMILY FARMERS AND FAMILY FISHERMEN

Sec. 1001. Permanent reenactment of chapter 12.
Sec. 1002. Debt limit increase.
Sec. 1003. Certain claims owed to governmental units.
Sec. 1004. Definition of family farmer.
Sec. 1005. Elimination of requirement that family farmer and spouse receive over 50 percent of income from farming operation in year prior to bankruptcy.
Sec. 1006. Prohibition of retroactive assessment of disposable income.
Sec. 1007. Family fishermen.

TITLE XI—HEALTH CARE AND EMPLOYEE BENEFITS

Sec. 1101. Definitions.
Sec. 1102. Disposal of patient records.
Sec. 1103. Administrative expense claim for costs of closing a health care business and other administrative expenses.
Sec. 1104. Appointment of ombudsman to act as patient advocate.
Sec. 1105. Debtor in possession; duty of trustee to transfer patients.
Sec. 1106. Exclusion from program participation not subject to automatic stay.

TITLE XII—TECHNICAL AMENDMENTS

Sec. 1201. Definitions.
Sec. 1202. Adjustment of dollar amounts.
Sec. 1203. Extension of time.
Sec. 1204. Technical amendments.
Sec. 1205. Penalty for persons who negligently or fraudulently prepare bankruptcy petitions.
Sec. 1206. Limitation on compensation of professional persons.
Sec. 1207. Effect of conversion.
Sec. 1208. Allowance of administrative expenses.
Sec. 1209. Exceptions to discharge.
Sec. 1210. Effect of discharge.
Sec. 1211. Protection against discriminatory treatment.
Sec. 1212. Property of the estate.
Sec. 1213. Preferences.
Sec. 1214. Postpetition transactions.
Sec. 1215. Disposition of property of the estate.
Sec. 1216. General provisions.
Sec. 1217. Abandonment of railroad line.
Sec. 1218. Contents of plan.
Sec. 1219. Bankruptcy cases and proceedings.
Sec. 1220. Knowing disregard of bankruptcy law or rule.
Sec. 1221. Transfers made by nonprofit charitable corporations.
Sec. 1222. Protection of valid purchase money security interests.
Sec. 1223. Bankruptcy Judgeships.
Sec. 1224. Compensating trustees.
Sec. 1225. Amendment to section 362 of title 11, United States Code.
Sec. 1226. Judicial education.
Sec. 1227. Reclamation.
Sec. 1228. Providing requested tax documents to the court.
Sec. 1229. Encouraging creditworthiness.
Sec. 1230. Property no longer subject to redemption.
Sec. 1231. Trustees.
Sec. 1232. Bankruptcy forms.
Sec. 1233. Direct appeals of bankruptcy matters to courts of appeals.
Sec. 1234. Involuntary cases.
Sec. 1235. Federal election law fines and penalties as nondischargeable debt.

TITLE XIII—CONSUMER CREDIT DISCLOSURE

TITLE XIV—PREVENTING CORPORATE BANKRUPTCY ABUSE

TITLE XV—GENERAL EFFECTIVE DATE; APPLICATION OF AMENDMENTS

TITLE I—NEEDS-BASED BANKRUPTCY

SEC. 101. CONVERSION.

Section 706(c) of title 11, United States Code, is amended by inserting "or consents to" after "requests".

SEC. 102. DISMISSAL OR CONVERSION.

(a) IN GENERAL.—Section 707 of title 11, United States Code, is amended—

(1) by striking the section heading and inserting the following:

"§ 707. Dismissal of a case or conversion to a case under chapter 11 or 13"; and

(2) in subsection (b)—

(A) by inserting "(1)" after "(b)";

(B) in paragraph (1), as so redesignated by subparagraph (A) of this paragraph—

(i) in the first sentence—

(I) by striking "but not at the request or suggestion of" and inserting "trustee (or bankruptcy administrator, if any), or";

(II) by inserting ", or, with the debtor's consent, convert such a case to a case under chapter 11 or 13 of this title," after "consumer debts"; and

(III) by striking "a substantial abuse" and inserting "an abuse"; and

(ii) by striking the next to last sentence; and

(C) by adding at the end the following:

"(2)(A)(i) In considering under paragraph (1) whether the granting of relief would be an abuse of the provisions of this chapter, the court shall presume abuse exists if the debtor's current monthly income reduced by the amounts determined under clauses (ii), (iii), and (iv), and multiplied by 60 is not less than the lesser of—

"(I) 25 percent of the debtor's nonpriority unsecured claims in the case, or $6,000, whichever is greater; or

"(II) $10,000.

"(ii)(I) The debtor's monthly expenses shall be the debtor's applicable monthly expense amounts specified under the National Standards and Local Standards, and the debtor's actual monthly expenses for the categories specified as Other Necessary Expenses issued by the Internal Revenue Service for the area in which the debtor resides, as in effect on the date of the order for relief, for the debtor, the dependents of the debtor, and the spouse of the debtor in a joint case, if the spouse is not otherwise a dependent. Such expenses shall include reasonably necessary health insurance, disability insurance, and health savings account expenses for the debtor, the spouse of the debtor, or the dependents of the debtor. Notwithstanding any other provision of this clause, the monthly expenses of the debtor shall not include any payments for debts. In addition, the debtor's monthly expenses shall include the debtor's reasonably necessary expenses incurred to maintain the safety of the debtor and the family of the debtor from family violence as identified under section 309 of the Family Violence Prevention and Services Act, or other applicable Federal law. The expenses included in the debtor's monthly expenses described in the preceding sentence shall be kept confidential by the court. In addition, if it is demonstrated that it is reasonable and necessary, the debtor's monthly expenses may also include an additional allowance for food and clothing of up to 5 percent of the food and clothing categories as specified by the National Standards issued by the Internal Revenue Service.

"(II) In addition, the debtor's monthly expenses may include, if applicable, the continuation of actual expenses paid by the debtor that are reasonable and necessary for care and support of an elderly, chronically ill, or disabled household member or member of the debtor's immediate family (including parents, grandparents, siblings, children, and grandchildren of the debtor, the dependents of the debtor, and the spouse of the debtor in a joint case who is not a dependent) and who is unable to pay for such reasonable and necessary expenses.

"(III) In addition, for a debtor eligible for chapter 13, the debtor's monthly expenses may include the actual administrative expenses of administering a chapter 13 plan for the district in which the debtor resides, up to an amount of 10 percent of the projected plan payments, as determined under schedules issued by the Executive Office for United States Trustees.

"(IV) In addition, the debtor's monthly expenses may include the actual expenses for each dependent child less than 18 years of age, not to exceed $1,500 per year per child, to attend a private or public elementary or secondary school if the debtor provides documentation of such expenses and a detailed explanation of why such expenses are reasonable and necessary, and why such expenses are not already accounted for in the National Standards, Local Standards, or Other Necessary Expenses referred to in subclause (I).

"(V) In addition, the debtor's monthly expenses may include an allowance for housing and utilities, in excess of the allowance specified by the Local Standards for housing and utilities issued by the Internal Revenue Service, based on the actual expenses for home energy costs if the debtor provides documentation of such actual expenses and demonstrates that such actual expenses are reasonable and necessary.

"(iii) The debtor's average monthly payments on account of secured debts shall be calculated as the sum of—

"(I) the total of all amounts scheduled as contractually due to secured creditors in each month of the 60 months following the date of the petition; and

"(II) any additional payments to secured creditors necessary for the debtor, in filing a plan under chapter 13 of this title, to maintain possession of the debtor's primary residence, motor vehicle, or other property necessary for the support of the debtor and the debtor's dependents, that serves as collateral for secured debts;

divided by 60.

"(iv) The debtor's expenses for payment of all priority claims (including priority child support and alimony claims) shall be calculated as the total amount of debts entitled to priority, divided by 60.

"(B)(i) In any proceeding brought under this subsection, the presumption of abuse may only be rebutted by demonstrating special circumstances, such as a serious medical condition or a call or order to active duty in the Armed Forces, to the extent such special circumstances that justify additional expenses or adjustments of current monthly income for which there is no reasonable alternative.

"(ii) In order to establish special circumstances, the debtor shall be required to itemize each additional expense or adjustment of income and to provide—

"(I) documentation for such expense or adjustment to income; and

"(II) a detailed explanation of the special circumstances that make such expenses or adjustment to income necessary and reasonable.

"(iii) The debtor shall attest under oath to the accuracy of any information provided to demonstrate that additional expenses or adjustments to income are required.

"(iv) The presumption of abuse may only be rebutted if the additional expenses or adjustments to income referred to in clause (i) cause the product of the debtor's current monthly income reduced by the amounts determined under clauses (ii), (iii), and (iv) of subparagraph (A) when multiplied by 60 to be less than the lesser of—

"(I) 25 percent of the debtor's nonpriority unsecured claims, or $6,000, whichever is greater; or

"(II) $10,000.

"(C) As part of the schedule of current income and expenditures required under section 521, the debtor shall include a statement of the debtor's current monthly income, and the calculations that determine whether a presumption arises under subparagraph (A)(i), that show how each such amount is calculated.

"(D) Subparagraphs (A) through (C) shall not apply, and the court may not dismiss or convert a case based on any form of means testing, if the debtor is a disabled veteran (as defined in section 3741(1) of title 38), and the indebtedness occurred primarily during a period during which he or she was—

"(i) on active duty (as defined in section 101(d)(1) of title 10); or

"(ii) performing a homeland defense activity (as defined in section 901(1) of title 32).

"(3) In considering under paragraph (1) whether the granting of relief would be an abuse of the provisions of this chapter in a case in which the presumption in subparagraph (A)(i) of such paragraph does not arise or is rebutted, the court shall consider—

"(A) whether the debtor filed the petition in bad faith; or

"(B) the totality of the circumstances (including whether the debtor seeks to reject a personal services contract and the financial need for such rejection as sought by the debtor) of the debtor's financial situation demonstrates abuse.

"(4)(A) The court, on its own initiative or on the motion of a party in interest, in accordance with the procedures described in rule 9011 of the Federal Rules of Bankruptcy Procedure, may order the attorney for the debtor to reimburse the trustee for all reasonable costs in prosecuting a motion filed under section 707(b), including reasonable attorneys' fees, if—

"(i) a trustee files a motion for dismissal or conversion under this subsection; and

"(ii) the court—

"(I) grants such motion; and

"(II) finds that the action of the attorney for the debtor in filing a case under this chapter violated rule 9011 of the Federal Rules of Bankruptcy Procedure.

"(B) If the court finds that the attorney for the debtor violated rule 9011 of the Federal Rules of Bankruptcy Procedure, the court, on its own initiative or on the motion of a party in interest, in accordance with such procedures, may order—

"(i) the assessment of an appropriate civil penalty against the attorney for the debtor; and

"(ii) the payment of such civil penalty to the trustee, the United States trustee (or the bankruptcy administrator, if any).

"(C) The signature of an attorney on a petition, pleading, or written motion shall constitute a certification that the attorney has—

"(i) performed a reasonable investigation into the circumstances that gave rise to the petition, pleading, or written motion; and

"(ii) determined that the petition, pleading, or written motion—

"(I) is well grounded in fact; and

"(II) is warranted by existing law or a good faith argument for the extension, modification, or reversal of existing law and does not constitute an abuse under paragraph (1).

"(D) The signature of an attorney on the petition shall constitute a certification that the attorney has no knowledge after an inquiry that the information in the schedules filed with such petition is incorrect.

"(5)(A) Except as provided in subparagraph (B) and subject to paragraph (6), the court, on its own initiative or on the motion of a party in interest, in accordance with the procedures described in rule 9011 of the Federal Rules of Bankruptcy Procedure, may award a debtor all reasonable costs (including reasonable attorneys' fees) in contesting a motion filed by a party in interest (other than a trustee or United States trustee (or bankruptcy administrator, if any)) under this subsection if—

"(i) the court does not grant the motion; and

"(ii) the court finds that—

"(I) the position of the party that filed the motion violated rule 9011 of the Federal Rules of Bankruptcy Procedure; or

"(II) the attorney (if any) who filed the motion did not comply with the requirements of clauses (i) and (ii) of paragraph (4)(C), and the motion was made solely for the purpose of coercing a debtor into waiving a right guaranteed to the debtor under this title.

"(B) A small business that has a claim of an aggregate amount less than $1,000 shall not be subject to subparagraph (A)(ii)(I).

"(C) For purposes of this paragraph—

"(i) the term 'small business' means an unincorporated business, partnership, corporation, association, or organization that—

"(I) has fewer than 25 full-time employees as determined on the date on which the motion is filed; and

"(II) is engaged in commercial or business activity; and

"(ii) the number of employees of a wholly owned subsidiary of a corporation includes the employees of—

"(I) a parent corporation; and

"(II) any other subsidiary corporation of the parent corporation.

"(6) Only the judge or United States trustee (or bankruptcy administrator, if any) may file a motion under section 707(b), if the current monthly income of the debtor, or in a joint case, the debtor and the debtor's spouse, as of the date of the order for relief, when multiplied by 12, is equal to or less than—

"(A) in the case of a debtor in a household of 1 person, the median family income of the applicable State for 1 earner;

"(B) in the case of a debtor in a household of 2, 3, or 4 individuals, the highest median family income of the applicable State for a family of the same number or fewer individuals; or

"(C) in the case of a debtor in a household exceeding 4 individuals, the highest median family income of the applicable State for a family of 4 or fewer individuals, plus $525 per month for each individual in excess of 4.

"(7)(A) No judge, United States trustee (or bankruptcy administrator, if any), trustee, or other party in interest may file a motion under paragraph (2) if the current monthly income of the debtor, including a veteran (as that term is defined in section 101 of title 38), and the debtor's spouse combined, as of the date of the order for relief when multiplied by 12, is equal to or less than—

"(i) in the case of a debtor in a household of 1 person, the median family income of the applicable State for 1 earner;

"(ii) in the case of a debtor in a household of 2, 3, or 4 individuals, the highest median family income of the applicable State for a family of the same number or fewer individuals; or

"(iii) in the case of a debtor in a household exceeding 4 individuals, the highest median family income of the applicable State for a family of 4 or fewer individuals, plus $525 per month for each individual in excess of 4.

"(B) In a case that is not a joint case, current monthly income of the debtor's spouse shall not be considered for purposes of subparagraph (A) if—

"(i)(I) the debtor and the debtor's spouse are separated under applicable nonbankruptcy law; or

"(II) the debtor and the debtor's spouse are living separate and apart, other than for the purpose of evading subparagraph (A); and

"(ii) the debtor files a statement under penalty of perjury—

"(I) specifying that the debtor meets the requirement of subclause (I) or (II) of clause (i); and

"(II) disclosing the aggregate, or best estimate of the aggregate, amount of any cash or money payments received from the debtor's spouse attributed to the debtor's current monthly income.".

(b) DEFINITION.—Section 101 of title 11, United States Code, is amended by inserting after paragraph (10) the following:

"(10A) 'current monthly income'—

"(A) means the average monthly income from all sources that the debtor receives (or in a joint case the debtor and the debtor's spouse receive) without regard to whether such income is taxable income, derived during the 6- month period ending on—

"(i) the last day of the calendar month immediately preceding the date of the commencement of the case if the debtor files the schedule of current income required by section 521(a)(1)(B)(ii); or

"(ii) the date on which current income is determined by the court for purposes of this title if the debtor does not file the schedule of current income required by section 521(a)(1)(B)(ii); and

"(B) includes any amount paid by any entity other than the debtor (or in a joint case the debtor and the debtor's spouse), on a regular basis for the household expenses of the debtor or the debtor's dependents (and in a joint case the debtor's spouse if not otherwise a dependent), but excludes benefits received under the Social Security Act, payments to victims of war crimes or crimes against humanity on account of their status as victims of such crimes, and payments to victims of international terrorism (as defined in section 2331 of title 18) or domestic terrorism (as defined in section 2331 of title 18) on account of their status as victims of such terrorism;".

(c) UNITED STATES TRUSTEE AND BANKRUPTCY ADMINISTRATOR DUTIES.—Section 704 of title 11, United States Code, is amended—

(1) by inserting "(a)" before "The trustee shall—"; and

(2) by adding at the end the following:

"(b)(1) With respect to a debtor who is an individual in a case under this chapter—

"(A) the United States trustee (or the bankruptcy administrator, if any) shall review all materials filed by the debtor and, not later than 10 days after the date of the first meeting of creditors, file with the court a statement as to whether the debtor's case would be presumed to be an abuse under section 707(b); and

"(B) not later than 5 days after receiving a statement under subparagraph (A), the court shall provide a copy of the statement to all creditors.

"(2) The United States trustee (or bankruptcy administrator, if any) shall, not later than 30 days after the date of filing a statement under paragraph (1), either file a motion to dismiss or convert under section 707(b) or file a statement setting forth the reasons the United States trustee (or the bankruptcy administrator, if any) does not consider such a motion to be appropriate, if the United States trustee (or the bankruptcy administrator, if any) determines that the debtor's case should be presumed to be an abuse under section 707(b) and the product of the debtor's current monthly income, multiplied by 12 is not less than—

"(A) in the case of a debtor in a household of 1 person, the median family income of the applicable State for 1 earner; or

"(B) in the case of a debtor in a household of 2 or more individuals, the highest median family income of the applicable State for a family of the same number or fewer individuals.".

(d) NOTICE.—Section 342 of title 11, United States Code, is amended by adding at the end the following:

"(d) In a case under chapter 7 of this title in which the debtor is an individual and in which the presumption of abuse arises under section 707(b), the clerk shall give written notice to all creditors not later than 10 days after the date of the filing of the petition that the presumption of abuse has arisen.".

(e) NONLIMITATION OF INFORMATION.—Nothing in this title shall limit the ability of a creditor to provide information to a judge (except for information communicated ex parte, unless otherwise permitted by applicable law), United States trustee (or bankruptcy administrator, if any), or trustee.

(f) DISMISSAL FOR CERTAIN CRIMES.—Section 707 of title 11, United States Code, is amended by adding at the end the following:

"(c)(1) In this subsection—

"(A) the term 'crime of violence' has the meaning given such term in section 16 of title 18; and

"(B) the term 'drug trafficking crime' has the meaning given such term in section 924(c)(2) of title 18.

"(2) Except as provided in paragraph (3), after notice and a hearing, the court, on a motion by the victim of a crime of violence or a drug trafficking crime, may when it is in the best interest of the victim dismiss a voluntary case filed under this chapter by a debtor who is an individual if such individual was convicted of such crime.

"(3) The court may not dismiss a case under paragraph (2) if the debtor establishes by a preponderance of the evidence that the filing of a case under this chapter is necessary to satisfy a claim for a domestic support obligation.".

(g) CONFIRMATION OF PLAN.—Section 1325(a) of title 11, United States Code, is amended—

(1) in paragraph (5), by striking "and" at the end;

(2) in paragraph (6), by striking the period and inserting a semicolon; and

(3) by inserting after paragraph (6) the following:

"(7) the action of the debtor in filing the petition was in good faith;".

(h) APPLICABILITY OF MEANS TEST TO CHAPTER 13.—Section 1325(b) of title 11, United States Code, is amended—

(1) in paragraph (1)(B), by inserting "to unsecured creditors" after "to make payments"; and

(2) by striking paragraph (2) and inserting the following:

"(2) For purposes of this subsection, the term 'disposable income' means current monthly income received by the debtor (other than child support payments, foster care payments, or disability payments for a dependent child made in accordance with applicable nonbankruptcy law to the extent reasonably necessary to be expended for such child) less amounts reasonably necessary to be expended—

"(A)(i) for the maintenance or support of the debtor or a dependent of the debtor, or for a domestic support obligation, that first becomes payable after the date the petition is filed; and

"(ii) for charitable contributions (that meet the definition of 'charitable contribution' under section 548(d)(3) to a qualified religious or charitable entity or organization (as defined in section 548(d)(4)) in an amount not to exceed 15 percent of gross income of the debtor for the year in which the contributions are made; and

"(B) if the debtor is engaged in business, for the payment of expenditures necessary for the continuation, preservation, and operation of such business.

"(3) Amounts reasonably necessary to be expended under paragraph (2) shall be determined in accordance with subparagraphs (A) and (B) of section 707(b)(2), if the debtor has current monthly income, when multiplied by 12, greater than—

"(A) in the case of a debtor in a household of 1 person, the median family income of the applicable State for 1 earner;

"(B) in the case of a debtor in a household of 2, 3, or 4 individuals, the highest median family income of the applicable State for a family of the same number or fewer individuals; or

"(C) in the case of a debtor in a household exceeding 4 individuals, the highest median family income of the applicable State for a family of 4 or fewer individuals, plus $525 per month for each individual in excess of 4.".

(i) SPECIAL ALLOWANCE FOR HEALTH INSURANCE.—Section 1329(a) of title 11, United States Code, is amended—

(1) in paragraph (2) by striking "or" at the end;

(2) in paragraph (3) by striking the period at the end and inserting "; or"; and

(3) by adding at the end the following:

"(4) reduce amounts to be paid under the plan by the actual amount expended by the debtor to purchase health insurance for the debtor (and for any dependent of the debtor if such dependent does not otherwise have health insurance coverage) if the debtor documents the cost of such insurance and demonstrates that—

"(A) such expenses are reasonable and necessary;

"(B)(i) if the debtor previously paid for health insurance, the amount is not materially larger than the cost the debtor previously paid or the cost necessary to maintain the lapsed policy; or

"(ii) if the debtor did not have health insurance, the amount is not materially larger than the reasonable cost that would be incurred by a debtor who purchases health insurance, who has similar income, expenses, age, and health status, and who lives in the same geographical location with the same number of dependents who do not otherwise have health insurance coverage; and

"(C) the amount is not otherwise allowed for purposes of determining disposable income under section 1325(b) of this title; and upon request of any party in interest, files proof that a health insurance policy was purchased.".

(j) ADJUSTMENT OF DOLLAR AMOUNTS.—Section 104(b) of title 11, United States Code, is amended by striking "and 523(a)(2)(C)" each place it appears and inserting "523(a)(2)(C), 707(b), and 1325(b)(3)".

(k) DEFINITION OF "MEDIAN FAMILY INCOME".—Section 101 of title 11, United States Code, is amended by inserting after paragraph (39) the following:

"(39A) 'median family income' means for any year—

"(A) the median family income both calculated and reported by the Bureau of the Census in the then most recent year; and

"(B) if not so calculated and reported in the then current year, adjusted annually after such most recent year until the next year in which median family income is both calculated and reported by the Bureau of the Census, to reflect the percentage change in the

Consumer Price Index for All Urban Consumers during the period of years occurring after such most recent year and before such current year;''.

(k) CLERICAL AMENDMENT.—The table of sections for chapter 7 of title 11, United States Code, is amended by striking the item relating to section 707 and inserting the following:

''707. Dismissal of a case or conversion to a case under chapter 11 or 13.''.

SEC. 103. SENSE OF CONGRESS AND STUDY.

(a) SENSE OF CONGRESS.—It is the sense of Congress that the Secretary of the Treasury has the authority to alter the Internal Revenue Service standards established to set guidelines for repayment plans as needed to accommodate their use under section 707(b) of title 11, United States Code.

(b) STUDY.—

(1) IN GENERAL.—Not later than 2 years after the date of enactment of this Act, the Director of the Executive Office for United States Trustees shall submit a report to the Committee on the Judiciary of the Senate and the Committee on the Judiciary of the House of Representatives containing the findings of the Director regarding the utilization of Internal Revenue Service standards for determining—

(A) the current monthly expenses of a debtor under section 707(b) of title 11, United States Code; and

(B) the impact that the application of such standards has had on debtors and on the bankruptcy courts.

(2) RECOMMENDATION.—The report under paragraph (1) may include recommendations for amendments to title 11, United States Code, that are consistent with the findings of the Director under paragraph (1).

SEC. 104. NOTICE OF ALTERNATIVES.

Section 342(b) of title 11, United States Code, is amended to read as follows:

''(b) Before the commencement of a case under this title by an individual whose debts are primarily consumer debts, the clerk shall give to such individual written notice containing—

''(1) a brief description of—

''(A) chapters 7, 11, 12, and 13 and the general purpose, benefits, and costs of proceeding under each of those chapters; and

''(B) the types of services available from credit counseling agencies; and

''(2) statements specifying that—

''(A) a person who knowingly and fraudulently conceals assets or makes a false oath or statement under penalty of perjury in connection with a case under this title shall be subject to fine, imprisonment, or both; and

''(B) all information supplied by a debtor in connection with a case under this title is subject to examination by the Attorney General.''.

SEC. 105. DEBTOR FINANCIAL MANAGEMENT TRAINING TEST PROGRAM.

(a) DEVELOPMENT OF FINANCIAL MANAGEMENT AND TRAINING CURRICULUM AND MATERIALS.—The Director of the Executive Office for United States Trustees (in this section referred to as the ''Director'') shall consult with a wide range of individuals who are experts in the field of debtor education, including trustees who serve in cases under chapter 13 of title 11, United States Code, and who operate financial management education programs for debtors, and shall develop a financial management training curriculum and materials that can be used to educate debtors who are individuals on how to better manage their finances.

(b) TEST.—

(1) SELECTION OF DISTRICTS.—The Director shall select 6 judicial districts of the United States in which to test the effectiveness of the financial management training curriculum and materials developed under subsection (a).

(2) USE.—For an 18-month period beginning not later than 270 days after the date of the enactment of this Act, such curriculum and materials shall be, for the 6 judicial districts selected under paragraph (1), used as the instructional course concerning personal financial management for purposes of section 111 of title 11, United States Code.

(c) EVALUATION.—

(1) IN GENERAL.—During the 18-month period referred to in subsection (b), the Director shall evaluate the effectiveness of—

(A) the financial management training curriculum and materials developed under subsection (a); and

(B) a sample of existing consumer education programs such as those described in the Report of the National Bankruptcy Review Commission (October 20, 1997) that are representative of consumer education programs carried out by the credit industry, by trustees serving under chapter 13 of title 11, United States Code, and by consumer counseling groups.

(2) REPORT.—Not later than 3 months after concluding such evaluation, the Director shall submit a report to the Speaker of the House of Representatives and the President pro tempore of the Senate, for referral to the appropriate committees of the Congress, containing the findings of the Director regarding the effectiveness of such curriculum, such materials, and such programs and their costs.

SEC. 106. CREDIT COUNSELING.

(a) WHO MAY BE A DEBTOR.—Section 109 of title 11, United States Code, is amended by adding at the end the following:

"(h)(1) Subject to paragraphs (2) and (3), and notwithstanding any other provision of this section, an individual may not be a debtor under this title unless such individual has, during the 180-day period preceding the date of filing of the petition by such individual, received from an approved nonprofit budget and credit counseling agency described in section 111(a) an individual or group briefing (including a briefing conducted by telephone or on the Internet) that outlined the opportunities for available credit counseling and assisted such individual in performing a related budget analysis.

"(2)(A) Paragraph (1) shall not apply with respect to a debtor who resides in a district for which the United States trustee (or the bankruptcy administrator, if any) determines that the approved nonprofit budget and credit counseling agencies for such district are not reasonably able to provide adequate services to the additional individuals who would otherwise seek credit counseling from such agencies by reason of the requirements of paragraph (1).

"(B) The United States trustee (or the bankruptcy administrator, if any) who makes a determination described in subparagraph (A) shall review such determination not later than 1 year after the date of such determination, and not less frequently than annually thereafter. Notwithstanding the preceding sentence, a nonprofit budget and credit counseling agency may be disapproved by the United States trustee (or the bankruptcy administrator, if any) at any time.

"(3)(A) Subject to subparagraph (B), the requirements of paragraph (1) shall not apply with respect to a debtor who submits to the court a certification that—

"(i) describes exigent circumstances that merit a waiver of the requirements of paragraph (1);

"(ii) states that the debtor requested credit counseling services from an approved nonprofit budget and credit counseling agency, but was unable to obtain the services referred to in paragraph (1) during the 5-day period beginning on the date on which the debtor made that request; and

"(iii) is satisfactory to the court.

"(B) With respect to a debtor, an exemption under subparagraph (A) shall cease to apply to that debtor on the date on which the debtor meets the requirements of paragraph (1), but in no case may the exemption apply to that debtor after the date that is 30 days after the debtor files a petition, except that the court, for cause, may order an additional 15 days.

"(4) The requirements of paragraph (1) shall not apply with respect to a debtor whom the court determines, after notice and hearing, is unable to complete those requirements because of incapacity, disability, or active military duty in a military combat zone. For the purposes of this paragraph, incapacity means that the debtor is impaired by reason of mental illness or mental deficiency so that he is incapable of realizing and making rational decisions with respect to his financial responsibilities; and 'disability' means that the debtor is so physically impaired as to be unable, after reasonable effort, to participate in an in person, telephone, or Internet briefing required under paragraph (1).".

(b) CHAPTER 7 DISCHARGE.—Section 727(a) of title 11, United States Code, is amended—

(1) in paragraph (9), by striking "or" at the end;

(2) in paragraph (10), by striking the period and inserting "; or"; and

(3) by adding at the end the following:

"(11) after filing the petition, the debtor failed to complete an instructional course concerning personal financial management described in section 111, except that this paragraph shall not apply with respect to a debtor who is a person described in section 109(h)(4) or who resides in a district for which the United States trustee (or the bankruptcy administrator, if any) determines that the approved instructional courses are not adequate to service the additional individuals who would otherwise be required to complete such instructional courses under this section (The United States trustee (or the bankruptcy administrator, if any) who makes a determination described in this paragraph shall review such determination not later than 1 year after the date of such determination, and not less frequently than annually thereafter.).".

(c) CHAPTER 13 DISCHARGE.—Section 1328 of title 11, United States Code, is amended by adding at the end the following:

"(g)(1) The court shall not grant a discharge under this section to a debtor unless after filing a petition the debtor has completed an instructional course concerning personal financial management described in section 111.

"(2) Paragraph (1) shall not apply with respect to a debtor who is a person described in section 109(h)(4) or who resides in a district for which the United States trustee (or the bankruptcy administrator, if any) determines that the approved instructional courses are not adequate to service the additional individuals who would otherwise be required to complete such instructional course by reason of the requirements of paragraph (1).

"(3) The United States trustee (or the bankruptcy administrator, if any) who makes a determination described in paragraph (2) shall review such determination not later than 1 year after the date of such determination, and not less frequently than annually thereafter.".

(d) DEBTOR'S DUTIES.—Section 521 of title 11, United States Code, is amended—

(1) by inserting "(a)" before "The debtor shall—"; and

(2) by adding at the end the following:

"(b) In addition to the requirements under subsection (a), a debtor who is an individual shall file with the court—

"(1) a certificate from the approved nonprofit budget and credit counseling agency that provided the debtor services under section 109(h) describing the services provided to the debtor; and

"(2) a copy of the debt repayment plan, if any, developed under section 109(h) through the approved nonprofit budget and credit counseling agency referred to in paragraph (1).".

(e) GENERAL PROVISIONS.—

(1) IN GENERAL.—Chapter 1 of title 11, United States Code, is amended by adding at the end the following:

"§ 111. Nonprofit budget and credit counseling agencies; financial management instructional courses

"(a) The clerk shall maintain a publicly available list of—

"(1) nonprofit budget and credit counseling agencies that provide 1 or more services described in section 109(h) currently approved by the United States trustee (or the bankruptcy administrator, if any); and

"(2) instructional courses concerning personal financial management currently approved by the United States trustee (or the bankruptcy administrator, if any), as applicable.

"(b) The United States trustee (or bankruptcy administrator, if any) shall only approve a nonprofit budget and credit counseling agency or an instructional course concerning personal financial management as follows:

"(1) The United States trustee (or bankruptcy administrator, if any) shall have thoroughly reviewed the qualifications of the nonprofit budget and credit counseling agency or of the provider of the instructional course under the standards set forth in this section, and the services or instructional courses that will be offered by such agency or such provider, and may require such agency or such provider that has sought approval to provide information with respect to such review.

"(2) The United States trustee (or bankruptcy administrator, if any) shall have determined that such agency or such instructional course fully satisfies the applicable standards set forth in this section.

"(3) If a nonprofit budget and credit counseling agency or instructional course did not appear on the approved list for the district under subsection (a) immediately before approval under this section, approval under this subsection of such agency or such instructional course shall be for a probationary period not to exceed 6 months.

"(4) At the conclusion of the applicable probationary period under paragraph (3), the United States trustee (or bankruptcy administrator, if any) may only approve for an additional 1-year period, and for successive 1-year periods thereafter, an agency or instructional course that has demonstrated during the probationary or applicable subsequent period of approval that such agency or instructional course—

"(A) has met the standards set forth under this section during such period; and

"(B) can satisfy such standards in the future.

"(5) Not later than 30 days after any final decision under paragraph (4), an interested person may seek judicial review of such decision in the appropriate district court of the United States.

"(c)(1) The United States trustee (or the bankruptcy administrator, if any) shall only approve a nonprofit budget and credit counseling agency that demonstrates that it will provide qualified counselors, maintain adequate provision for safekeeping and payment of client funds, provide adequate counseling with respect to client credit problems, and deal responsibly and effectively with other matters relating to the quality, effectiveness, and financial security of the services it provides.

"(2) To be approved by the United States trustee (or the bankruptcy administrator, if any), a nonprofit budget and credit counseling agency shall, at a minimum—

"(A) have a board of directors the majority of which—

"(i) are not employed by such agency; and

"(ii) will not directly or indirectly benefit financially from the outcome of the counseling services provided by such agency;

"(B) if a fee is charged for counseling services, charge a reasonable fee, and provide services without regard to ability to pay the fee;

"(C) provide for safekeeping and payment of client funds, including an annual audit of the trust accounts and appropriate employee bonding;

"(D) provide full disclosures to a client, including funding sources, counselor qualifications, possible impact on credit reports, and any costs of such program that will be paid by such client and how such costs will be paid;

"(E) provide adequate counseling with respect to a client's credit problems that includes an analysis of such client's current financial condition, factors that caused such financial condition, and how such client can develop a plan to respond to the problems without incurring negative amortization of debt;

"(F) provide trained counselors who receive no commissions or bonuses based on the outcome of the counseling services provided by such agency, and who have adequate experience, and have been adequately trained to provide counseling services to individuals in financial difficulty, including the matters described in subparagraph (E);

"(G) demonstrate adequate experience and background in providing credit counseling; and

"(H) have adequate financial resources to provide continuing support services for budgeting plans over the life of any repayment plan.

"(d) The United States trustee (or the bankruptcy administrator, if any) shall only approve an instructional course concerning personal financial management—

"(1) for an initial probationary period under subsection (b)(3) if the course will provide at a minimum—

"(A) trained personnel with adequate experience and training in providing effective instruction and services;

"(B) learning materials and teaching methodologies designed to assist debtors in understanding personal financial management and that are consistent with stated objectives directly related to the goals of such instructional course;

"(C) adequate facilities situated in reasonably convenient locations at which such instructional course is offered, except that such facilities may include the provision of such instructional course by telephone or through the Internet, if such instructional course is effective;

"(D) the preparation and retention of reasonable records (which shall include the debtor's bankruptcy case number) to permit evaluation of the effectiveness of such instructional course, including any evaluation of satisfaction of instructional course requirements for each debtor attending such instructional course, which shall be available for inspection and evaluation by the Executive Office for United States Trustees, the United States trustee (or the bankruptcy administrator, if any), or the chief bankruptcy judge for the district in which such instructional course is offered; and

"(E) if a fee is charged for the instructional course, charge a reasonable fee, and provide services without regard to ability to pay the fee.

"(2) for any 1-year period if the provider thereof has demonstrated that the course meets the standards of paragraph (1) and, in addition—

"(A) has been effective in assisting a substantial number of debtors to understand personal financial management; and

"(B) is otherwise likely to increase substantially the debtor's understanding of personal financial management.

"(e) The district court may, at any time, investigate the qualifications of a nonprofit budget and credit counseling agency referred to in subsection (a), and request production of documents to ensure the integrity and effectiveness of such agency. The district court may, at any time, remove from the approved list under subsection (a) a nonprofit budget and credit counseling agency upon finding such agency does not meet the qualifications of subsection (b).

"(f) The United States trustee (or the bankruptcy administrator, if any) shall notify the clerk that a nonprofit budget and credit counseling agency or an instructional course is no longer approved, in which case the clerk shall remove it from the list maintained under subsection (a).

"(g)(1) No nonprofit budget and credit counseling agency may provide to a credit reporting agency information concerning whether a debtor has received or sought instruction concerning personal financial management from such agency.

"(2) A nonprofit budget and credit counseling agency that willfully or negligently fails to comply with any requirement under this title with respect to a debtor shall be liable for damages in an amount equal to the sum of—

"(A) any actual damages sustained by the debtor as a result of the violation; and

"(B) any court costs or reasonable attorneys' fees (as determined by the court) incurred in an action to recover those damages.".

(2) CLERICAL AMENDMENT.—The table of sections for chapter 1 of title 11, United States Code, is amended by adding at the end the following:

"111. Nonprofit budget and credit counseling agencies; financial management instructional courses.".

(f) LIMITATION.—Section 362 of title 11, United States Code, is amended by adding at the end the following:

"(i) If a case commenced under chapter 7, 11, or 13 is dismissed due to the creation of a debt repayment plan, for purposes of subsection (c)(3), any subsequent case commenced by the debtor under any such chapter shall not be presumed to be filed not in good faith.

"(j) On request of a party in interest, the court shall issue an order under subsection (c) confirming that the automatic stay has been terminated.".

SEC. 107. SCHEDULES OF REASONABLE AND NECESSARY EXPENSES.

For purposes of section 707(b) of title 11, United States Code, as amended by this Act, the Director of the Executive Office for United States Trustees shall, not later than 180 days after the date of enactment of this Act, issue schedules of reasonable and necessary administrative expenses of administering a chapter 13 plan for each judicial district of the United States.

TITLE II—ENHANCED CONSUMER PROTECTION

Subtitle A—Penalties for Abusive Creditor Practices

SEC. 201. PROMOTION OF ALTERNATIVE DISPUTE RESOLUTION.

(a) REDUCTION OF CLAIM.—Section 502 of title 11, United States Code, is amended by adding at the end the following:

"(k)(1) The court, on the motion of the debtor and after a hearing, may reduce a claim filed under this section based in whole on an unsecured consumer debt by not more than 20 percent of the claim, if—

"(A) the claim was filed by a creditor who unreasonably refused to negotiate a reasonable alternative repayment schedule proposed on behalf of the debtor by an approved nonprofit budget and credit counseling agency described in section 111;

"(B) the offer of the debtor under subparagraph (A)—

"(i) was made at least 60 days before the date of the filing of the petition; and

"(ii) provided for payment of at least 60 percent of the amount of the debt over a period not to exceed the repayment period of the loan, or a reasonable extension thereof; and

"(C) no part of the debt under the alternative repayment schedule is nondischargeable.

"(2) The debtor shall have the burden of proving, by clear and convincing evidence, that—

"(A) the creditor unreasonably refused to consider the debtor's proposal; and

"(B) the proposed alternative repayment schedule was made prior to expiration of the 60-day period specified in paragraph (1)(B)(i).".

(b) LIMITATION ON AVOIDABILITY.—Section 547 of title 11, United States Code, is amended by adding at the end the following:

"(h) The trustee may not avoid a transfer if such transfer was made as a part of an alternative repayment schedule between the debtor and any creditor of the debtor created by an approved nonprofit budget and credit counseling agency.".

SEC. 202. EFFECT OF DISCHARGE.

Section 524 of title 11, United States Code, is amended by adding at the end the following:

"(i) The willful failure of a creditor to credit payments received under a plan confirmed under this title, unless the order confirming the plan is revoked, the plan is in default, or the creditor has not received payments required to be made under the plan in the manner required by the plan (including crediting the amounts required under the plan), shall constitute a violation of an injunction under subsection (a)(2) if the act of the creditor to collect and failure to credit payments in the manner required by the plan caused material injury to the debtor.

"(j) Subsection (a)(2) does not operate as an injunction against an act by a creditor that is the holder of a secured claim, if—

"(1) such creditor retains a security interest in real property that is the principal residence of the debtor;

"(2) such act is in the ordinary course of business between the creditor and the debtor; and

"(3) such act is limited to seeking or obtaining periodic payments associated with a valid security interest in lieu of pursuit of in rem relief to enforce the lien.".

SEC. 203. DISCOURAGING ABUSE OF REAFFIRMATION AGREEMENT PRACTICES.

(a) IN GENERAL.—Section 524 of title 11, United States Code, as amended section 202, is amended—

(1) in subsection (c), by striking paragraph (2) and inserting the following:

"(2) the debtor received the disclosures described in subsection (k) at or before the time at which the debtor signed the agreement;"; and

(2) by adding at the end the following:

"(k)(1) The disclosures required under subsection (c)(2) shall consist of the disclosure statement described in paragraph (3), completed as required in that paragraph, together with the agreement specified in subsection (c), statement, declaration, motion and order described, respectively, in paragraphs (4) through (8), and shall be the only disclosures required in connection with entering into such agreement.

"(2) Disclosures made under paragraph (1) shall be made clearly and conspicuously and in writing. The terms 'Amount Reaffirmed' and 'Annual Percentage Rate' shall be disclosed more conspicuously than other terms, data or information provided in connection with this disclosure, except that the phrases 'Before agreeing to reaffirm a debt, review these important disclosures' and 'Summary of Reaffirmation Agreement' may be equally conspicuous. Disclosures may be made in a different order and may use terminology different from that set forth in paragraphs (2) through (8), except that the terms 'Amount Reaffirmed' and 'Annual Percentage Rate' must be used where indicated.

"(3) The disclosure statement required under this paragraph shall consist of the following:

"(A) The statement: 'Part A: Before agreeing to reaffirm a debt, review these important disclosures:';

"(B) Under the heading 'Summary of Reaffirmation Agreement', the statement: 'This Summary is made pursuant to the requirements of the Bankruptcy Code';

"(C) The 'Amount Reaffirmed', using that term, which shall be—

"(i) the total amount of debt that the debtor agrees to reaffirm by entering into an agreement of the kind specified in subsection (c), and "(ii) the total of any fees and costs accrued as of the date of the disclosure statement, related to such total amount.

"(D) In conjunction with the disclosure of the 'Amount Reaffirmed', the statements—

"(i) 'The amount of debt you have agreed to reaffirm'; and

"(ii) 'Your credit agreement may obligate you to pay additional amounts which may come due after the date of this disclosure. Consult your credit agreement.'.

"(E) The 'Annual Percentage Rate', using that term, which shall be disclosed as—

"(i) if, at the time the petition is filed, the debt is an extension of credit under an open end credit plan, as the terms 'credit' and 'open end credit plan' are defined in section 103 of the Truth in Lending Act, then—

"(I) the annual percentage rate determined under paragraphs (5) and (6) of section 127(b) of the Truth in Lending Act, as applicable, as disclosed to the debtor in the most recent periodic statement prior to entering into an agreement of the kind specified in subsection (c) or, if no such periodic statement has been given to the debtor during the prior 6 months, the annual percentage rate as it would have been so disclosed at the time the disclosure statement is given to the debtor, or to the extent this annual percentage rate is not readily available or not applicable, then

"(II) the simple interest rate applicable to the amount reaffirmed as of the date the disclosure statement is given to the debtor, or if different simple interest rates apply to different balances, the simple interest rate applicable to each such balance, identifying the amount of each such balance included in the amount reaffirmed, or

"(III) if the entity making the disclosure elects, to disclose the annual percentage rate under subclause (I) and the simple interest rate under subclause (II); or

"(ii) if, at the time the petition is filed, the debt is an extension of credit other than under an open end credit plan, as the terms 'credit' and 'open end credit plan' are defined in section 103 of the Truth in Lending Act, then—

"(I) the annual percentage rate under section 128(a)(4) of the Truth in Lending Act, as disclosed to the debtor in the most recent disclosure statement given to the debtor prior to the entering into an agreement of the kind specified in subsection (c) with respect to the debt, or, if no such disclosure statement was given to the debtor, the annual percentage rate as it would have been so disclosed at the time the disclosure statement is given to the debtor, or to the extent this annual percentage rate is not readily available or not applicable, then

"(II) the simple interest rate applicable to the amount reaffirmed as of the date the disclosure statement is given to the debtor, or if different simple interest rates apply to different balances, the simple interest rate applicable to each such balance, identifying the amount of such balance included in the amount reaffirmed, or

"(III) if the entity making the disclosure elects, to disclose the annual percentage rate under (I) and the simple interest rate under (II).

"(F) If the underlying debt transaction was disclosed as a variable rate transaction on the most recent disclosure given under the Truth in Lending Act, by stating 'The interest rate on your loan may be a variable interest rate which changes from time to time, so that the annual percentage rate disclosed here may be higher or lower.'.

"(G) If the debt is secured by a security interest which has not been waived in whole or in part or determined to be void by a final order of the court at the time of the disclosure, by disclosing that a security interest or lien in goods or property is asserted over some or all of the debts the debtor is reaffirming and listing the items and their original purchase price that are subject to the asserted security interest, or if not a purchase-money security interest then listing by items or types and the original amount of the loan.

"(H) At the election of the creditor, a statement of the repayment schedule using 1 or a combination of the following—

"(i) by making the statement: 'Your first payment in the amount of $_______ is due on _______ but the future payment amount may be different. Consult your reaffirmation agreement or credit agreement, as applicable.', and stating the amount of the first payment and the due date of that payment in the places provided;

"(ii) by making the statement: 'Your payment schedule will be:', and describing the repayment schedule with the number, amount, and due dates or period of payments scheduled to repay the debts reaffirmed to the extent then known by the disclosing party; or

"(iii) by describing the debtor's repayment obligations with reasonable specificity to the extent then known by the disclosing party.

"(I) The following statement: 'Note: When this disclosure refers to what a creditor 'may' do, it does not use the word 'may' to give the creditor specific permission. The word 'may' is used to tell you what might occur if the law permits the creditor to take the action. If you have questions about your reaffirming a debt or what the law requires, consult with the attorney who helped you negotiate this agreement reaffirming a debt. If you don't have an attorney helping you, the judge will explain the effect of your reaffirming a debt when the hearing on the reaffirmation agreement is held.".

"(J)(i) The following additional statements:

"Reaffirming a debt is a serious financial decision. The law requires you to take certain steps to make sure the decision is in your best interest. If these steps are not completed, the reaffirmation agreement is not effective, even though you have signed it.

"1. Read the disclosures in this Part A carefully. Consider the decision to reaffirm carefully. Then, if you want to reaffirm, sign the reaffirmation agreement in Part B (or you may use a separate agreement you and your creditor agree on).

"2. Complete and sign Part D and be sure you can afford to make the payments you are agreeing to make and have received a copy of the disclosure statement and a completed and signed reaffirmation agreement.

"3. If you were represented by an attorney during the negotiation of your reaffirmation agreement, the attorney must have signed the certification in Part C.

"4. If you were not represented by an attorney during the negotiation of your reaffirmation agreement, you must have completed and signed Part E.

"5. The original of this disclosure must be filed with the court by you or your creditor. If a separate reaffirmation agreement (other than the one in Part B) has been signed, it must be attached.

"6. If you were represented by an attorney during the negotiation of your reaffirmation agreement, your reaffirmation agreement becomes effective upon filing with the court unless the reaffirmation is presumed to be an undue hardship as explained in Part D.

"7. If you were not represented by an attorney during the negotiation of your reaffirmation agreement, it will not be effective unless the court approves it. The court will notify you of the hearing on your reaffirmation agreement. You must attend this hearing in bankruptcy court where the judge will review your reaffirmation agreement. The bankruptcy court must approve your reaffirmation agreement as consistent with your best interests, except that no court approval is required if your reaffirmation agreement is for a consumer debt secured by a mortgage, deed of trust, security deed, or other lien on your real property, like your home.

"Your right to rescind (cancel) your reaffirmation agreement. You may rescind (cancel) your reaffirmation agreement at any time before the bankruptcy court enters a discharge order, or before the expiration of the 60-day period that begins on the date your reaffirmation agreement is filed with the court, whichever occurs later. To rescind (cancel) your reaffirmation agreement, you must notify the creditor that your reaffirmation agreement is rescinded (or canceled).

"What are your obligations if you reaffirm the debt? A reaffirmed debt remains your personal legal obligation. It is not discharged in your bankruptcy case. That means that if you default on your reaffirmed debt after your bankruptcy case is over, your creditor may be able to take your property or your wages. Otherwise, your obligations will be determined by the reaffirmation agreement which may have changed the terms of the original agreement. For example, if you are reaffirming an open end credit agreement, the creditor may be permitted by that agreement or applicable law to change the terms of that agreement in the future under certain conditions.

"Are you required to enter into a reaffirmation agreement by any law? No, you are not required to reaffirm a debt by any law. Only agree to reaffirm a debt if it is in your best interest. Be sure you can afford the payments you agree to make.

"What if your creditor has a security interest or lien? Your bankruptcy discharge does not eliminate any lien on your property. A 'lien' is often referred to as a security interest, deed of trust, mortgage or security deed. Even if you do not reaffirm and your personal liability on the debt is discharged, because of the lien your creditor may still have the right to take the security property if you do not pay the debt or default on it. If the lien is on an item of personal property that is exempt under your State's law or that the trustee has abandoned, you may be able to redeem the item rather than reaffirm the debt. To redeem, you make a single payment to the creditor equal to the current value of the security property, as agreed by the parties or determined by the court.".

"(ii) In the case of a reaffirmation under subsection (m)(2), numbered paragraph 6 in the disclosures required by clause (i) of this subparagraph shall read as follows:

"6. If you were represented by an attorney during the negotiation of your reaffirmation agreement, your reaffirmation agreement becomes effective upon filing with the court.".

"(4) The form of such agreement required under this paragraph shall consist of the following:

" 'Part B: Reaffirmation Agreement. I (we) agree to reaffirm the debts arising under the credit agreement described below.

" 'Brief description of credit agreement:

" 'Description of any changes to the credit agreement made as part of this reaffirmation agreement:

" 'Signature:____________Date:

" 'Borrower:

" 'Co-borrower, if also reaffirming these debts:

" 'Accepted by creditor:

" 'Date of creditor acceptance:'.

"(5) The declaration shall consist of the following:

"(A) The following certification:

" 'Part C: Certification by Debtor's Attorney (If Any).

" 'I hereby certify that (1) this agreement represents a fully informed and voluntary agreement by the debtor; (2) this agreement does not impose an undue hardship on the debtor or any dependent of the debtor; and (3) I have fully advised the debtor of the legal effect and consequences of this agreement and any default under this agreement.

" 'Signature of Debtor's Attorney:____________Date:'.

"(B) If a presumption of undue hardship has been established with respect to such agreement, such certification shall state that in the opinion of the attorney, the debtor is able to make the payment.

"(C) In the case of a reaffirmation agreement under subsection (m)(2), subparagraph (B) is not applicable.

"(6)(A) The statement in support of such agreement, which the debtor shall sign and date prior to filing with the court, shall consist of the following:

" 'Part D: Debtor's Statement in Support of Reaffirmation Agreement.

" '1. I believe this reaffirmation agreement will not impose an undue hardship on my dependents or me. I can afford to make the payments on the reaffirmed debt because my monthly income (take home pay plus any other income received) is $_______, and my actual current monthly expenses including monthly payments on post-bankruptcy debt and other reaffirmation agreements total $_______, leaving $_______ to make the required payments on this reaffirmed debt. I understand that if my income less my monthly expenses does not leave enough to make the payments, this reaffirmation agreement is presumed to be an undue hardship on me and must be reviewed by the court. However, this presumption may be overcome if I explain to the satisfaction of the court how I can afford to make the payments here:______________.

"2. I received a copy of the Reaffirmation Disclosure Statement in Part A and a completed and signed reaffirmation agreement.".

"(B) Where the debtor is represented by an attorney and is reaffirming a debt owed to a creditor defined in section 19(b)(1)(A)(iv) of the Federal Reserve Act, the statement of support of the reaffirmation agreement, which the debtor shall sign and date prior to filing with the court, shall consist of the following:

" 'I believe this reaffirmation agreement is in my financial interest. I can afford to make the payments on the reaffirmed debt. I received a copy of the Reaffirmation Disclosure Statement in Part A and a completed and signed reaffirmation agreement.'.

"(7) The motion that may be used if approval of such agreement by the court is required in order for it to be effective, shall be signed and dated by the movant and shall consist of the following:

" 'Part E: Motion for Court Approval (To be completed only if the debtor is not represented by an attorney.). I (we), the debtor(s), affirm the following to be true and correct:

" 'I am not represented by an attorney in connection with this reaffirmation agreement.

" 'I believe this reaffirmation agreement is in my best interest based on the income and expenses I have disclosed in my Statement in Support of this reaffirmation agreement, and because (provide any additional relevant reasons the court should consider):

" 'Therefore, I ask the court for an order approving this reaffirmation agreement.'.

"(8) The court order, which may be used to approve such agreement, shall consist of the following:

" 'Court Order: The court grants the debtor's motion and approves the reaffirmation agreement described above.'.

"(*l*) Notwithstanding any other provision of this title the following shall apply:

"(1) A creditor may accept payments from a debtor before and after the filing of an agreement of the kind specified in subsection (c) with the court.

"(2) A creditor may accept payments from a debtor under such agreement that the creditor believes in good faith to be effective.

"(3) The requirements of subsections (c)(2) and (k) shall be satisfied if disclosures required under those subsections are given in good faith.

"(m)(1) Until 60 days after an agreement of the kind specified in subsection (c) is filed with the court (or such additional period as the court, after notice and a hearing and for cause, orders before the expiration of such period), it shall be presumed that such agreement is an undue hardship on the debtor if the debtor's monthly income less the debtor's monthly expenses as shown on the debtor's completed and signed statement in support of such agreement required under subsection (k)(6)(A) is less than the scheduled payments on the reaffirmed debt. This presumption shall be reviewed by the court. The presumption may be rebutted in writing by the debtor if the statement includes an explanation that identifies additional sources of funds to make the payments as agreed upon under the terms of such agreement. If the presumption is not rebutted to the satisfaction of the court, the court may disapprove such agreement. No agreement shall be disapproved without notice and a hearing to the debtor and creditor, and such hearing shall be concluded before the entry of the debtor's discharge.

"(2) This subsection does not apply to reaffirmation agreements where the creditor is a credit union, as defined in section 19(b)(1)(A)(iv) of the Federal Reserve Act.".

(b) LAW ENFORCEMENT.—

(1) IN GENERAL.—Chapter 9 of title 18, United States Code, is amended by adding at the end the following:

"§ 158. Designation of United States attorneys and agents of the Federal Bureau of Investigation to address abusive reaffirmations of debt and materially fraudulent statements in bankruptcy schedules

"(a) IN GENERAL.—The Attorney General of the United States shall designate the individuals described in subsection (b) to have primary responsibility in carrying out enforcement activities in addressing violations of section 152 or 157 relating to abusive reaffirmations of debt. In addition to addressing the violations referred to in the preceding sentence, the individuals described under subsection (b) shall address violations of section 152 or 157 relating to materially fraudulent statements in bankruptcy schedules that are intentionally false or intentionally misleading.

"(b) UNITED STATES ATTORNEYS AND AGENTS OF THE FEDERAL BUREAU OF INVESTIGATION.—The individuals referred to in subsection (a) are—

"(1) the United States attorney for each judicial district of the United States; and

"(2) an agent of the Federal Bureau of Investigation for each field office of the Federal Bureau of Investigation.

"(c) BANKRUPTCY INVESTIGATIONS.—Each United States attorney designated under this section shall, in addition to any other responsibilities, have primary responsibility for carrying out the duties of a United States attorney under section 3057.

"(d) BANKRUPTCY PROCEDURES.—The bankruptcy courts shall establish procedures for referring any case that may contain a materially fraudulent statement in a bankruptcy schedule to the individuals designated under this section.".

(2) CLERICAL AMENDMENT.—The table of sections for chapter 9 of title 18, United States Code, is amended by adding at the end the following:

"158. Designation of United States attorneys and agents of the Federal Bureau of Investigation to address abusive reaffirmations of debt and materially fraudulent statements in bankruptcy schedules.".

SEC. 204. PRESERVATION OF CLAIMS AND DEFENSES UPON SALE OF PREDATORY LOANS.

Section 363 of title 11, United States Code, is amended—

(1) by redesignating subsection (o) as subsection (p), and

(2) by inserting after subsection (n) the following:

"(*o*) Notwithstanding subsection (f), if a person purchases any interest in a consumer credit transaction that is subject to the Truth in Lending Act or any interest in a consumer credit contract (as defined in section 433.1 of title 16 of the Code of Federal Regulations (January 1, 2004), as amended from time to time), and if such interest is purchased through a sale under this section, then such person shall remain subject to all claims and defenses that are related to such consumer credit transaction or such consumer credit contract, to the same extent as such person would be subject to such claims and defenses of the consumer had such interest been purchased at a sale not under this section.".

SEC. 205. GAO STUDY AND REPORT ON REAFFIRMATION AGREEMENT PROCESS.

(a) STUDY.—The Comptroller General of the United States shall conduct a study of the reaffirmation agreement process that occurs under title 11 of the United States Code, to determine the overall treatment of consumers within the context of such process, and shall include in such study consideration of—

(1) the policies and activities of creditors with respect to reaffirmation agreements; and

(2) whether consumers are fully, fairly, and consistently informed of their rights pursuant to such title.

(b) REPORT TO THE CONGRESS.—Not later than 18 months after the date of the enactment of this Act, the Comptroller General shall submit to the President pro tempore of the Senate and the Speaker of the House of Representatives a report on the results of the study conducted under subsection (a), together with recommendations for legislation (if any) to address any abusive or coercive tactics found in connection with the reaffirmation agreement process that occurs under title 11 of the United States Code.

Subtitle B—Priority Child Support

SEC. 211. DEFINITION OF DOMESTIC SUPPORT OBLIGATION.

Section 101 of title 11, United States Code, is amended—

(1) by striking paragraph (12A); and

(2) by inserting after paragraph (14) the following:

"(14A) 'domestic support obligation' means a debt that accrues before, on, or after the date of the order for relief in a case under this title, including interest that accrues on that debt as provided under applicable nonbankruptcy law notwithstanding any other provision of this title, that is—

"(A) owed to or recoverable by—

"(i) a spouse, former spouse, or child of the debtor or such child's parent, legal guardian, or responsible relative; or

"(ii) a governmental unit;

"(B) in the nature of alimony, maintenance, or support (including assistance provided by a governmental unit) of such spouse, former spouse, or child of the debtor or such child's parent, without regard to whether such debt is expressly so designated;

"(C) established or subject to establishment before, on, or after the date of the order for relief in a case under this title, by reason of applicable provisions of—

"(i) a separation agreement, divorce decree, or property settlement agreement;

"(ii) an order of a court of record; or

"(iii) a determination made in accordance with applicable nonbankruptcy law by a governmental unit; and

"(D) not assigned to a nongovernmental entity, unless that obligation is assigned voluntarily by the spouse, former spouse, child of the debtor, or such child's parent, legal guardian, or responsible relative for the purpose of collecting the debt;".

SEC. 212. PRIORITIES FOR CLAIMS FOR DOMESTIC SUPPORT OBLIGATIONS.

Section 507(a) of title 11, United States Code, is amended—

(1) by striking paragraph (7);

(2) by redesignating paragraphs (1) through (6) as paragraphs (2) through (7), respectively;

(3) in paragraph (2), as so redesignated, by striking "First" and inserting "Second";

(4) in paragraph (3), as so redesignated, by striking "Second" and inserting "Third";

(5) in paragraph (4), as so redesignated—

(A) by striking "Third" and inserting "Fourth"; and

(B) by striking the semicolon at the end and inserting a period;

(6) in paragraph (5), as so redesignated, by striking "Fourth" and inserting "Fifth";

(7) in paragraph (6), as so redesignated, by striking "Fifth"

(8) in paragraph (7), as so redesignated, by striking "Sixth" and inserting "Seventh"; and

(9) by inserting before paragraph (2), as so redesignated, the following:

"(1) First:

"(A) Allowed unsecured claims for domestic support obligations that, as of the date of the filing of the petition in a case under this title, are owed to or recoverable by a spouse, former spouse, or child of the debtor, or such child's parent, legal guardian, or responsible relative, without regard to whether the claim is filed by such person or is filed by a governmental unit on behalf of such person, on the condition that funds received under this paragraph by a governmental unit under this title after the date of the filing of the petition shall be applied and distributed in accordance with applicable nonbankruptcy law.

"(B) Subject to claims under subparagraph (A), allowed unsecured claims for domestic support obligations that, as of the date of the filing of the petition, are assigned by a spouse, former spouse, child of the debtor, or such child's parent, legal guardian, or responsible relative to a governmental unit (unless such obligation is assigned voluntarily by the spouse, former spouse, child, parent, legal guardian, or responsible relative of the child for the purpose of collecting the debt) or are owed directly to or recoverable by a governmental unit under applicable nonbankruptcy law, on the condition that funds received under this paragraph by a governmental unit under this title after the date of the filing of the petition be applied and distributed in accordance with applicable nonbankruptcy law.

"(C) If a trustee is appointed or elected under section 701, 702, 703, 1104, 1202, or 1302, the administrative expenses of the trustee allowed under paragraphs (1)(A), (2), and (6) of section 503(b) shall be paid before payment of claims under subparagraphs (A) and (B), to the extent that the trustee administers assets that are otherwise available for the payment of such claims.".

SEC. 213. REQUIREMENTS TO OBTAIN CONFIRMATION AND DISCHARGE IN CASES INVOLVING DOMESTIC SUPPORT OBLIGATIONS.

Title 11, United States Code, is amended—

(1) in section 1129(a), by adding at the end the following:

"(14) If the debtor is required by a judicial or administrative order, or by statute, to pay a domestic support obligation, the debtor has paid all amounts payable under such order or such statute for such obligation that first become payable after the date of the filing of the petition.";

(2) in section 1208(c)—

(A) in paragraph (8), by striking "or" at the end;

(B) in paragraph (9), by striking the period at the end and inserting "; and"; and

(C) by adding at the end the following:

"(10) failure of the debtor to pay any domestic support obligation that first becomes payable after the date of the filing of the petition.";

(3) in section 1222(a)—

(A) in paragraph (2), by striking "and" at the end;

(B) in paragraph (3), by striking the period at the end and inserting "; and"; and

(C) by adding at the end the following:

"(4) notwithstanding any other provision of this section, a plan may provide for less than full payment of all amounts owed for a claim entitled to priority under section 507(a)(1)(B) only if the plan provides that all of the debtor's projected disposable income for a 5-year period beginning on the date that the first payment is due under the plan will be applied to make payments under the plan.";

(4) in section 1222(b)—

(A) in paragraph (10), by striking "and" at the end;

(B) by redesignating paragraph (11) as paragraph (12); and

(C) by inserting after paragraph (10) the following:

"(11) provide for the payment of interest accruing after the date of the filing of the petition on unsecured claims that are nondischargeable under section 1228(a), except that such interest may be paid only to the extent that the debtor has disposable income available to pay such interest after making provision for full payment of all allowed claims; and";

(5) in section 1225(a)—

(A) in paragraph (5), by striking "and" at the end;

(B) in paragraph (6), by striking the period at the end and inserting "; and"; and

(C) by adding at the end the following:

"(7) the debtor has paid all amounts that are required to be paid under a domestic support obligation and that first become payable after the date of the filing of the petition if the debtor is required by a judicial or administrative order, or by statute, to pay such domestic support obligation.";

(6) in section 1228(a), in the matter preceding paragraph (1), by inserting ", and in the case of a debtor who is required by a judicial or administrative order, or by statute, to pay a domestic support obligation, after such debtor certifies that all amounts payable under such order or such statute that are due on or before the date of the certification (including amounts due before the petition was filed, but only to the extent provided for by the plan) have been paid" after "completion by the debtor of all payments under the plan";

(7) in section 1307(c)—

(A) in paragraph (9), by striking "or" at the end;

(B) in paragraph (10), by striking the period at the end and inserting "; or"; and

(C) by adding at the end the following:

"(11) failure of the debtor to pay any domestic support obligation that first becomes payable after the date of the filing of the petition.";

(8) in section 1322(a)—

(A) in paragraph (2), by striking "and" at the end;

(B) in paragraph (3), by striking the period at the end and inserting "; and"; and

(C) by adding at the end the following:

"(4) notwithstanding any other provision of this section, a plan may provide for less than full payment of all amounts owed for a claim entitled to priority under section 507(a)(1)(B) only if the plan provides that all of the debtor's projected disposable income for a 5-year period beginning on the date that the first payment is due under the plan will be applied to make payments under the plan.";

(9) in section 1322(b)—

(A) in paragraph (9), by striking "; and" and inserting a semicolon;

(B) by redesignating paragraph (10) as paragraph (11); and

(C) inserting after paragraph (9) the following:

"(10) provide for the payment of interest accruing after the date of the filing of the petition on unsecured claims that are nondischargeable under section 1328(a), except that such interest may be paid only to the extent that the debtor has disposable income available to pay such interest after making provision for full payment of all allowed claims; and";

(10) in section 1325(a), as amended by section 102, by inserting after paragraph (7) the following:

"(8) the debtor has paid all amounts that are required to be paid under a domestic support obligation and that first become payable after the date of the filing of the petition if the debtor is required by a judicial or administrative order, or by statute, to pay such domestic support obligation; and";

(11) in section 1328(a), in the matter preceding paragraph (1), by inserting ", and in the case of a debtor who is required by a judicial or administrative order, or by statute, to pay a domestic support obligation, after such debtor certifies that all amounts payable under such order or such statute that are due on or before the date of the certification (including amounts due before the petition was filed, but only to the extent provided for by the plan) have been paid" after "completion by the debtor of all payments under the plan".

SEC. 214. EXCEPTIONS TO AUTOMATIC STAY IN DOMESTIC SUPPORT OBLIGATION PROCEEDINGS.

Section 362(b) of title 11, United States Code, is amended by striking paragraph (2) and inserting the following:

"(2) under subsection (a)—

"(A) of the commencement or continuation of a civil action or proceeding—

"(i) for the establishment of paternity;

"(ii) for the establishment or modification of an order for domestic support obligations;

"(iii) concerning child custody or visitation;

"(iv) for the dissolution of a marriage, except to the extent that such proceeding seeks to determine the division of property that is property of the estate; or

"(v) regarding domestic violence;

"(B) of the collection of a domestic support obligation from property that is not property of the estate;

"(C) with respect to the withholding of income that is property of the estate or property of the debtor for payment of a domestic support obligation under a judicial or administrative order or a statute;

"(D) of the withholding, suspension, or restriction of a driver's license, a professional or occupational license, or a recreational license, under State law, as specified in section 466(a)(16) of the Social Security Act;

"(E) of the reporting of overdue support owed by a parent to any consumer reporting agency as specified in section 466(a)(7) of the Social Security Act;

"(F) of the interception of a tax refund, as specified in sections 464 and 466(a)(3) of the Social Security Act or under an analogous State law; or

"(G) of the enforcement of a medical obligation, as specified under title IV of the Social Security Act;".

SEC. 215. NONDISCHARGEABILITY OF CERTAIN DEBTS FOR ALIMONY, MAINTENANCE, AND SUPPORT.

Section 523 of title 11, United States Code, is amended—

(1) in subsection (a)—

(A) by striking paragraph (5) and inserting the following:

"(5) for a domestic support obligation;"; and

(B) by striking paragraph (18);

(2) in subsection (c), by striking "(6), or (15)" each place it appears and inserting "or (6)"; and

(3) in paragraph (15), as added by Public Law 103-394 (108 Stat. 4133)—

(A) by inserting "to a spouse, former spouse, or child of the debtor and" before "not of the kind";

(B) by inserting "or" after "court of record,"; and

(C) by striking "unless—" and all that follows through the end of the paragraph and inserting a semicolon.

SEC. 216. CONTINUED LIABILITY OF PROPERTY.

Section 522 of title 11, United States Code, is amended—

(1) in subsection (c), by striking paragraph (1) and inserting the following:

"(1) a debt of a kind specified in paragraph (1) or (5) of section 523(a) (in which case, notwithstanding any provision of applicable nonbankruptcy law to the contrary, such property shall be liable for a debt of a kind specified in section 523(a)(5));";

(2) in subsection (f)(1)(A), by striking the dash and all that follows through the end of the subparagraph and inserting "of a kind that is specified in section 523(a)(5); or"; and

(3) in subsection (g)(2), by striking "subsection (f)(2)" and inserting "subsection (f)(1)(B)".

SEC. 217. PROTECTION OF DOMESTIC SUPPORT CLAIMS AGAINST PREFERENTIAL TRANSFER MOTIONS.

Section 547(c)(7) of title 11, United States Code, is amended to read as follows:

"(7) to the extent such transfer was a bona fide payment of a debt for a domestic support obligation;".

SEC. 218. DISPOSABLE INCOME DEFINED.

Section 1225(b)(2)(A) of title 11, United States Code, is amended by inserting "or for a domestic support obligation that first becomes payable after the date of the filing of the petition" after "dependent of the debtor".

SEC. 219. COLLECTION OF CHILD SUPPORT.

(a) DUTIES OF TRUSTEE UNDER CHAPTER 7.—Section 704 of title 11, United States Code, as amended by section 102, is amended—

(1) in subsection (a)—

(A) in paragraph (8), by striking "and" at the end;

(B) in paragraph (9), by striking the period and inserting a semicolon; and

(C) by adding at the end the following:

"(10) if with respect to the debtor there is a claim for a domestic support obligation, provide the applicable notice specified in subsection (c); and"; and

(2) by adding at the end the following:

"(c)(1) In a case described in subsection (a)(10) to which subsection (a)(10) applies, the trustee shall—

"(A)(i) provide written notice to the holder of the claim described in subsection (a)(10) of such claim and of the right of such holder to use the services of the State child support enforcement agency established under sections 464 and 466 of the Social Security Act for the State in which such holder resides, for assistance in collecting child support during and after the case under this title;

"(ii) include in the notice provided under clause (i) the address and telephone number of such State child support enforcement agency; and

"(iii) include in the notice provided under clause (i) an explanation of the rights of such holder to payment of such claim under this chapter;

"(B)(i) provide written notice to such State child support enforcement agency of such claim; and

"(ii) include in the notice provided under clause (i) the name, address, and telephone number of such holder; and

"(C) at such time as the debtor is granted a discharge under section 727, provide written notice to such holder and to such State child support enforcement agency of—

"(i) the granting of the discharge;

"(ii) the last recent known address of the debtor;

"(iii) the last recent known name and address of the debtor's employer; and

"(iv) the name of each creditor that holds a claim that—

"(I) is not discharged under paragraph (2), (4), or (14A) of section 523(a); or

"(II) was reaffirmed by the debtor under section 524(c).

"(2)(A) The holder of a claim described in subsection (a)(10) or the State child support enforcement agency of the State in which such holder resides may request from a creditor described in paragraph (1)(C)(iv) the last known address of the debtor.

"(B) Notwithstanding any other provision of law, a creditor that makes a disclosure of a last known address of a debtor in connection with a request made under subparagraph (A) shall not be liable by reason of making such disclosure.".

(b) DUTIES OF TRUSTEE UNDER CHAPTER 11.—Section 1106 of title 11, United States Code, is amended—

(1) in subsection (a)—

(A) in paragraph (6), by striking "and" at the end;

(B) in paragraph (7), by striking the period and inserting "; and"; and

(C) by adding at the end the following:

"(8) if with respect to the debtor there is a claim for a domestic support obligation, provide the applicable notice specified in subsection (c)."; and

(2) by adding at the end the following:

"(c)(1) In a case described in subsection (a)(8) to which subsection (a)(8) applies, the trustee shall—

"(A)(i) provide written notice to the holder of the claim described in subsection (a)(8) of such claim and of the right of such holder to use the services of the State child support enforcement agency established under sections 464 and 466 of the Social Security Act for the State in which such holder resides, for assistance in collecting child support during and after the case under this title; and

"(ii) include in the notice required by clause (i) the address and telephone number of such State child support enforcement agency;

"(B)(i) provide written notice to such State child support enforcement agency of such claim; and

"(ii) include in the notice required by clause (i) the name, address, and telephone number of such holder; and

"(C) at such time as the debtor is granted a discharge under section 1141, provide written notice to such holder and to such State child support enforcement agency of—

"(i) the granting of the discharge;

"(ii) the last recent known address of the debtor;

"(iii) the last recent known name and address of the debtor's employer; and

"(iv) the name of each creditor that holds a claim that—

"(I) is not discharged under paragraph (2), (4), or (14A) of section 523(a); or

"(II) was reaffirmed by the debtor under section 524(c).

"(2)(A) The holder of a claim described in subsection (a)(8) or the State child enforcement support agency of the State in which such holder resides may request from a creditor described in paragraph (1)(C)(iv) the last known address of the debtor.

"(B) Notwithstanding any other provision of law, a creditor that makes a disclosure of a last known address of a debtor in connection with a request made under subparagraph (A) shall not be liable by reason of making such disclosure.".

(c) DUTIES OF TRUSTEE UNDER CHAPTER 12.—Section 1202 of title 11, United States Code, is amended—

(1) in subsection (b)—

(A) in paragraph (4), by striking "and" at the end;

(B) in paragraph (5), by striking the period and inserting "; and"; and

(C) by adding at the end the following:

"(6) if with respect to the debtor there is a claim for a domestic support obligation, provide the applicable notice specified in subsection (c)."; and

(2) by adding at the end the following:

"(c)(1) In a case described in subsection (b)(6) to which subsection (b)(6) applies, the trustee shall—

"(A)(i) provide written notice to the holder of the claim described in subsection (b)(6) of such claim and of the right of such holder to use the services of the State child support enforcement agency established under sections 464 and 466 of the Social Security Act for the State in which such holder resides, for assistance in collecting child support during and after the case under this title; and

"(ii) include in the notice provided under clause (i) the address and telephone number of such State child support enforcement agency;

"(B)(i) provide written notice to such State child support enforcement agency of such claim; and

"(ii) include in the notice provided under clause (i) the name, address, and telephone number of such holder; and

"(C) at such time as the debtor is granted a discharge under section 1228, provide written notice to such holder and to such State child support enforcement agency of—

"(i) the granting of the discharge;

"(ii) the last recent known address of the debtor;

"(iii) the last recent known name and address of the debtor's employer; and

"(iv) the name of each creditor that holds a claim that—

"(I) is not discharged under paragraph (2), (4), or (14A) of section 523(a); or

"(II) was reaffirmed by the debtor under section 524(c).

"(2)(A) The holder of a claim described in subsection (b)(6) or the State child support enforcement agency of the State in which such holder resides may request from a creditor described in paragraph (1)(C)(iv) the last known address of the debtor.

"(B) Notwithstanding any other provision of law, a creditor that makes a disclosure of a last known address of a debtor in connection with a request made under subparagraph (A) shall not be liable by reason of making that disclosure.".

(d) DUTIES OF TRUSTEE UNDER CHAPTER 13.—Section 1302 of title 11, United States Code, is amended—

(1) in subsection (b)—

(A) in paragraph (4), by striking "and" at the end;

(B) in paragraph (5), by striking the period and inserting "; and"; and

(C) by adding at the end the following:

"(6) if with respect to the debtor there is a claim for a domestic support obligation, provide the applicable notice specified in subsection (d)."; and

(2) by adding at the end the following:

"(d)(1) In a case described in subsection (b)(6) to which subsection (b)(6) applies, the trustee shall—

"(A)(i) provide written notice to the holder of the claim described in subsection (b)(6) of such claim and of the right of such holder to use the services of the State child support enforcement agency established under sections 464 and 466 of the Social Security Act for the State in which such holder resides, for assistance in collecting child support during and after the case under this title; and

"(ii) include in the notice provided under clause (i) the address and telephone number of such State child support enforcement agency;

"(B)(i) provide written notice to such State child support enforcement agency of such claim; and

"(ii) include in the notice provided under clause (i) the name, address, and telephone number of such holder; and

"(C) at such time as the debtor is granted a discharge under section 1328, provide written notice to such holder and to such State child support enforcement agency of—

"(i) the granting of the discharge;

"(ii) the last recent known address of the debtor;

"(iii) the last recent known name and address of the debtor's employer; and

"(iv) the name of each creditor that holds a claim that—

"(I) is not discharged under paragraph (2) or (4) of section 523(a); or

"(II) was reaffirmed by the debtor under section 524(c).

"(2)(A) The holder of a claim described in subsection (b)(6) or the State child support enforcement agency of the State in which such holder resides may request from a creditor described in paragraph (1)(C)(iv) the last known address of the debtor.

"(B) Notwithstanding any other provision of law, a creditor that makes a disclosure of a last known address of a debtor in connection with a request made under subparagraph (A) shall not be liable by reason of making that disclosure.".

SEC. 220. NONDISCHARGEABILITY OF CERTAIN EDUCATIONAL BENEFITS AND LOANS.

Section 523(a) of title 11, United States Code, is amended by striking paragraph (8) and inserting the following:

"(8) unless excepting such debt from discharge under this paragraph would impose an undue hardship on the debtor and the debtor's dependents, for—

"(A)(i) an educational benefit overpayment or loan made, insured, or guaranteed by a governmental unit, or made under any program funded in whole or in part by a governmental unit or nonprofit institution; or "(ii) an obligation to repay funds received as an educational benefit, scholarship, or stipend; or

"(B) any other educational loan that is a qualified education loan, as defined in section 221(d)(1) of the Internal Revenue Code of 1986, incurred by a debtor who is an individual;".

Subtitle C—Other Consumer Protections

SEC. 221. AMENDMENTS TO DISCOURAGE ABUSIVE BANKRUPTCY FILINGS.

Section 110 of title 11, United States Code, is amended—

(1) in subsection (a)(1), by striking "or an employee of an attorney" and inserting "for the debtor or an employee of such attorney under the direct supervision of such attorney";

(2) in subsection (b)—

(A) in paragraph (1), by adding at the end the following: "If a bankruptcy petition preparer is not an individual, then an officer, principal, responsible person, or partner of the bankruptcy petition preparer shall be required to—

"(A) sign the document for filing; and

"(B) print on the document the name and address of that officer, principal, responsible person, or partner."; and

(B) by striking paragraph (2) and inserting the following:

"(2)(A) Before preparing any document for filing or accepting any fees from a debtor, the bankruptcy petition preparer shall provide to the debtor a written notice which shall be on an official form prescribed by the Judicial Conference of the United States in accordance with rule 9009 of the Federal Rules of Bankruptcy Procedure.

"(B) The notice under subparagraph (A)—

"(i) shall inform the debtor in simple language that a bankruptcy petition preparer is not an attorney and may not practice law or give legal advice;

"(ii) may contain a description of examples of legal advice that a bankruptcy petition preparer is not authorized to give, in addition to any advice that the preparer may not give by reason of subsection (e)(2); and

"(iii) shall—

"(I) be signed by the debtor and, under penalty of perjury, by the bankruptcy petition preparer; and

"(II) be filed with any document for filing.";

(3) in subsection (c)—

(A) in paragraph (2)—

(i) by striking "(2) For purposes" and inserting

"(2)(A) Subject to subparagraph (B), for purposes"; and

(ii) by adding at the end the following:

"(B) If a bankruptcy petition preparer is not an individual, the identifying number of the bankruptcy petition preparer shall be the Social Security account number of the officer, principal, responsible person, or partner of the bankruptcy petition preparer."; and

(B) by striking paragraph (3);

(4) in subsection (d)—

(A) by striking "(d)(1)" and inserting "(d)"; and

(B) by striking paragraph (2);

(5) in subsection (e)—

(A) by striking paragraph (2); and

(B) by adding at the end the following:

"(2)(A) A bankruptcy petition preparer may not offer a potential bankruptcy debtor any legal advice, including any legal advice described in subparagraph (B).

"(B) The legal advice referred to in subparagraph (A) includes advising the debtor—

"(i) whether—
"(I) to file a petition under this title; or
"(II) commencing a case under chapter 7, 11, 12, or 13 is appropriate;
"(ii) whether the debtor's debts will be discharged in a case under this title;
"(iii) whether the debtor will be able to retain the debtor's home, car, or other property after commencing a case under this title;
"(iv) concerning—
"(I) the tax consequences of a case brought under this title; or
"(II) the dischargeability of tax claims;
"(v) whether the debtor may or should promise to repay debts to a creditor or enter into a reaffirmation agreement with a creditor to reaffirm a debt;
"(vi) concerning how to characterize the nature of the debtor's interests in property or the debtor's debts; or
"(vii) concerning bankruptcy procedures and rights.";

(6) in subsection (f)—
(A) by striking "(f)(1)" and inserting "(f)"; and
(B) by striking paragraph (2);

(7) in subsection (g)—
(A) by striking "(g)(1)" and inserting "(g)"; and
(B) by striking paragraph (2);

(8) in subsection (h)—
(A) by redesignating paragraphs (1) through (4) as paragraphs (2) through (5), respectively;
(B) by inserting before paragraph (2), as so redesignated, the following:

"(1) The Supreme Court may promulgate rules under section 2075 of title 28, or the Judicial Conference of the United States may prescribe guidelines, for setting a maximum allowable fee chargeable by a bankruptcy petition preparer. A bankruptcy petition preparer shall notify the debtor of any such maximum amount before preparing any document for filing for a debtor or accepting any fee from the debtor.";

(C) in paragraph (2), as so redesignated—
(i) by striking "Within 10 days after the date of the filing of a petition, a bankruptcy petition preparer shall file a" and inserting "A";
(ii) by inserting "by the bankruptcy petition preparer shall be filed together with the petition," after "perjury"; and
(iii) by adding at the end the following: "If rules or guidelines setting a maximum fee for services have been promulgated or prescribed under paragraph (1), the declaration under this paragraph shall include a certification that the bankruptcy petition preparer complied with the notification requirement under paragraph (1).";

(D) by striking paragraph (3), as so redesignated, and inserting the following:

"(3)(A) The court shall disallow and order the immediate turnover to the bankruptcy trustee any fee referred to in paragraph (2) found to be in excess of the value of any services—
"(i) rendered by the bankruptcy petition preparer during the 12-month period immediately preceding the date of the filing of the petition; or
"(ii) found to be in violation of any rule or guideline promulgated or prescribed under paragraph (1).

"(B) All fees charged by a bankruptcy petition preparer may be forfeited in any case in which the bankruptcy petition preparer fails to comply with this subsection or subsection (b), (c), (d), (e), (f), or (g).

"(C) An individual may exempt any funds recovered under this paragraph under section 522(b)."; and

(E) in paragraph (4), as so redesignated, by striking "or the United States trustee" and inserting "the United States trustee (or the bankruptcy administrator, if any) or the court, on the initiative of the court,";

(9) in subsection (i)(1), by striking the matter preceding subparagraph (A) and inserting the following:

"(i)(1) If a bankruptcy petition preparer violates this section or commits any act that the court finds to be fraudulent, unfair, or deceptive, on the motion of the debtor, trustee, United States trustee (or the bankruptcy administrator, if any), and after notice and a hearing, the court shall order the bankruptcy petition preparer to pay to the debtor—";

(10) in subsection (j)—

(A) in paragraph (2)—

(i) in subparagraph (A)(i)(I), by striking "a violation of which subjects a person to criminal penalty";

(ii) in subparagraph (B)—

(I) by striking "or has not paid a penalty" and inserting "has not paid a penalty"; and

(II) by inserting "or failed to disgorge all fees ordered by the court" after "a penalty imposed under this section,";

(B) by redesignating paragraph (3) as paragraph (4); and

(C) by inserting after paragraph (2) the following:

"(3) The court, as part of its contempt power, may enjoin a bankruptcy petition preparer that has failed to comply with a previous order issued under this section. The injunction under this paragraph may be issued on the motion of the court, the trustee, or the United States trustee (or the bankruptcy administrator, if any)."; and

(11) by adding at the end the following:

"(*l*)(1) A bankruptcy petition preparer who fails to comply with any provision of subsection (b), (c), (d), (e), (f), (g), or (h) may be fined not more than $500 for each such failure.

"(2) The court shall triple the amount of a fine assessed under paragraph (1) in any case in which the court finds that a bankruptcy petition preparer—

"(A) advised the debtor to exclude assets or income that should have been included on applicable schedules;

"(B) advised the debtor to use a false Social Security account number;

"(C) failed to inform the debtor that the debtor was filing for relief under this title; or

"(D) prepared a document for filing in a manner that failed to disclose the identity of the bankruptcy petition preparer.

"(3) A debtor, trustee, creditor, or United States trustee (or the bankruptcy administrator, if any) may file a motion for an order imposing a fine on the bankruptcy petition preparer for any violation of this section.

"(4)(A) Fines imposed under this subsection in judicial districts served by United States trustees shall be paid to the United States trustee, who shall deposit an amount equal to such fines in a special account of the United States Trustee System Fund referred to in section 586(e)(2) of title 28. Amounts deposited under this subparagraph shall be available to fund the enforcement of this section on a national basis.

"(B) Fines imposed under this subsection in judicial districts served by bankruptcy administrators shall be deposited as offsetting receipts to the fund established under section 1931 of title 28, and shall remain available until expended to reimburse any appropriation for the amount paid out of such appropriation for expenses of the operation and maintenance of the courts of the United States.".

SEC. 222. SENSE OF CONGRESS.

It is the sense of Congress that States should develop curricula relating to the subject of personal finance, designed for use in elementary and secondary schools.

SEC. 223. ADDITIONAL AMENDMENTS TO TITLE 11, UNITED STATES CODE.

Section 507(a) of title 11, United States Code, as amended by section 212, is amended by inserting after paragraph (9) the following:

"(10) Tenth, allowed claims for death or personal injury resulting from the operation of a motor vehicle or vessel if such operation was unlawful because the debtor was intoxicated from using alcohol, a drug, or another substance.".

SEC. 224. PROTECTION OF RETIREMENT SAVINGS IN BANKRUPTCY.

(a) IN GENERAL.—Section 522 of title 11, United States Code, is amended—

(1) in subsection (b)—

(A) in paragraph (2)—

(i) in subparagraph (A), by striking "and" at the end;

(ii) in subparagraph (B), by striking the period at the end and inserting "; and";

(iii) by adding at the end the following:

"(C) retirement funds to the extent that those funds are in a fund or account that is exempt from taxation under section 401, 403, 408, 408A, 414, 457, or 501(a) of the Internal Revenue Code of 1986."; and

(iv) by striking "(2)(A) any property" and inserting:

"(3) Property listed in this paragraph is—

"(A) any property";

(B) by striking paragraph (1) and inserting:

"(2) Property listed in this paragraph is property that is specified under subsection (d), unless the State law that is applicable to the debtor under paragraph (3)(A) specifically does not so authorize.";

(C) by striking "(b) Notwithstanding" and inserting "(b)(1) Notwithstanding";

(D) by striking "paragraph (2)" each place it appears and inserting "paragraph (3)";

(E) by striking "paragraph (1)" each place it appears and inserting "paragraph (2)";

(F) by striking "Such property is—"; and

(G) by adding at the end the following:

"(4) For purposes of paragraph (3)(C) and subsection (d)(12), the following shall apply:

"(A) If the retirement funds are in a retirement fund that has received a favorable determination under section 7805 of the Internal Revenue Code of 1986, and that determination is in effect as of the date of the filing of the petition in a case under this title, those funds shall be presumed to be exempt from the estate.

"(B) If the retirement funds are in a retirement fund that has not received a favorable determination under such section 7805, those funds are exempt from the estate if the debtor demonstrates that—

"(i) no prior determination to the contrary has been made by a court or the Internal Revenue Service; and

"(ii)(I) the retirement fund is in substantial compliance with the applicable requirements of the Internal Revenue Code of 1986; or

"(II) the retirement fund fails to be in substantial compliance with the applicable requirements of the Internal Revenue Code of 1986 and the debtor is not materially responsible for that failure.

"(C) A direct transfer of retirement funds from 1 fund or account that is exempt from taxation under section 401, 403, 408, 408A, 414, 457, or 501(a) of the Internal Revenue Code of 1986, under section 401(a)(31) of the Internal Revenue Code of 1986, or otherwise, shall not cease to qualify for exemption under paragraph (3)(C) or subsection (d)(12) by reason of such direct transfer.

"(D)(i) Any distribution that qualifies as an eligible rollover distribution within the meaning of section 402(c) of the Internal Revenue Code of 1986 or that is described in clause (ii) shall not cease to qualify for exemption under paragraph (3)(C) or subsection (d)(12) by reason of such distribution.

"(ii) A distribution described in this clause is an amount that—

"(I) has been distributed from a fund or account that is exempt from taxation under section 401, 403, 408, 408A, 414, 457, or 501(a) of the Internal Revenue Code of 1986; and

"(II) to the extent allowed by law, is deposited in such a fund or account not later than 60 days after the distribution of such amount."; and

(2) in subsection (d)—

(A) in the matter preceding paragraph (1), by striking "subsection (b)(1)" and inserting "subsection (b)(2)"; and

(B) by adding at the end the following:

"(12) Retirement funds to the extent that those funds are in a fund or account that is exempt from taxation under section 401, 403, 408, 408A, 414, 457, or 501(a) of the Internal Revenue Code of 1986.".

(b) AUTOMATIC STAY.—Section 362(b) of title 11, United States Code, is amended—

(1) in paragraph (17), by striking "or" at the end;

(2) in paragraph (18), by striking the period and inserting a semicolon; and

(3) by inserting after paragraph (18) the following:

"(19) under subsection (a), of withholding of income from a debtor's wages and collection of amounts withheld, under the debtor's agreement authorizing that withholding and collection for the benefit of a pension, profit-sharing, stock bonus, or other plan established under section 401, 403, 408, 408A, 414, 457, or 501(c) of the Internal Revenue Code of 1986, that is sponsored by the employer of the debtor, or an affiliate, successor, or predecessor of such employer—

"(A) to the extent that the amounts withheld and collected are used solely for payments relating to a loan from a plan under section 408(b)(1) of the Employee Retirement Income Security Act of 1974 or is subject to section 72(p) of the Internal Revenue Code of 1986; or

"(B) a loan from a thrift savings plan permitted under subchapter III of chapter 84 of title 5, that satisfies the requirements of section 8433(g) of such title;

but nothing in this paragraph may be construed to provide that any loan made under a governmental plan under section 414(d), or a contract or account under section 403(b), of the Internal Revenue Code of 1986 constitutes a claim or a debt under this title;".

(c) EXCEPTIONS TO DISCHARGE.—Section 523(a) of title 11, United States Code, as amended by section 215, is amended by inserting after paragraph (17) the following:

"(18) owed to a pension, profit-sharing, stock bonus, or other plan established under section 401, 403, 408, 408A, 414, 457, or 501(c) of the Internal Revenue Code of 1986, under—

"(A) a loan permitted under section 408(b)(1) of the Employee Retirement Income Security Act of 1974, or subject to section 72(p) of the Internal Revenue Code of 1986; or

"(B) a loan from a thrift savings plan permitted under subchapter III of chapter 84 of title 5, that satisfies the requirements of section 8433(g) of such title;

but nothing in this paragraph may be construed to provide that any loan made under a governmental plan under section 414(d), or a contract or account under section 403(b), of the Internal Revenue Code of 1986 constitutes a claim or a debt under this title; or".

(d) PLAN CONTENTS.—Section 1322 of title 11, United States Code, is amended by adding at the end the following:

"(f) A plan may not materially alter the terms of a loan described in section 362(b)(19) and any amounts required to repay such loan shall not constitute 'disposable income' under section 1325.".

(e) ASSET LIMITATION.—

(1) LIMITATION.—Section 522 of title 11, United States Code, is amended by adding at the end the following:

"(n) For assets in individual retirement accounts described in section 408 or 408A of the Internal Revenue Code of 1986, other than a simplified employee pension under section 408(k) of such Code or a simple retirement account under section 408(p) of such Code, the aggregate value of such assets exempted under this section, without regard to amounts attributable to rollover contributions under section 402(c), 402(e)(6), 403(a)(4), 403(a)(5), and 403(b)(8) of the Internal Revenue Code of 1986, and earnings thereon, shall not exceed $1,000,000 in a case filed by a debtor who is an individual, except that such amount may be increased if the interests of justice so require.".

(2) ADJUSTMENT OF DOLLAR AMOUNTS.—Paragraphs (1) and (2) of section 104(b) of title 11, United States Code, are amended by inserting "522(n)," after "522(d),".

SEC. 225. PROTECTION OF EDUCATION SAVINGS IN BANKRUPTCY.

(a) EXCLUSIONS.—Section 541 of title 11, United States Code, is amended—

(1) in subsection (b)—

(A) in paragraph (4), by striking "or" at the end;

(B) by redesignating paragraph (5) as paragraph (9); and

(C) by inserting after paragraph (4) the following:

"(5) funds placed in an education individual retirement account (as defined in section 530(b)(1) of the Internal Revenue Code of 1986) not later than 365 days before the date of the filing of the petition in a case under this title, but—

"(A) only if the designated beneficiary of such account was a child, stepchild, grandchild, or stepgrandchild of the debtor for the taxable year for which funds were placed in such account;

"(B) only to the extent that such funds—

"(i) are not pledged or promised to any entity in connection with any extension of credit; and

"(ii) are not excess contributions (as described in section 4973(e) of the Internal Revenue Code of 1986); and

"(C) in the case of funds placed in all such accounts having the same designated beneficiary not earlier than 720 days nor later than 365 days before such date, only so much of such funds as does not exceed $5,000;

"(6) funds used to purchase a tuition credit or certificate or contributed to an account in accordance with section 529(b)(1)(A) of the Internal Revenue Code of 1986 under a qualified State tuition program (as defined in section 529(b)(1) of such Code) not later than 365 days before the date of the filing of the petition in a case under this title, but—

"(A) only if the designated beneficiary of the amounts paid or contributed to such tuition program was a child, stepchild, grandchild, or stepgrandchild of the debtor for the taxable year for which funds were paid or contributed;

"(B) with respect to the aggregate amount paid or contributed to such program having the same designated beneficiary, only so much of such amount as does not exceed the total contributions permitted under section 529(b)(7) of such Code with respect to such beneficiary, as adjusted beginning on the date of the filing of the petition in a case under this title by the annual increase or decrease (rounded to the nearest tenth of 1 percent) in the education expenditure category of the Consumer Price Index prepared by the Department of Labor; and

"(C) in the case of funds paid or contributed to such program having the same designated beneficiary not earlier than 720 days nor later than 365 days before such date, only so much of such funds as does not exceed $5,000;"; and

(2) by adding at the end the following:

"(e) In determining whether any of the relationships specified in paragraph (5)(A) or (6)(A) of subsection (b) exists, a legally adopted child of an individual (and a child who is a member of an individual's household, if placed with such individual by an authorized placement agency for legal adoption by such individual), or a foster child of an individual (if such child has as the child's principal place of abode the home of the debtor and is a member of the debtor's household) shall be treated as a child of such individual by blood.''.

(b) DEBTOR'S DUTIES.—Section 521 of title 11, United States Code, as amended by section 106, is amended by adding at the end the following:

''(c) In addition to meeting the requirements under subsection (a), a debtor shall file with the court a record of any interest that a debtor has in an education individual retirement account (as defined in section 530(b)(1) of the Internal Revenue Code of 1986) or under a qualified State tuition program (as defined in section 529(b)(1) of such Code).''.

SEC. 226. DEFINITIONS.

(a) DEFINITIONS.—Section 101 of title 11, United States Code, is amended—

(1) by inserting after paragraph (2) the following:

''(3) 'assisted person' means any person whose debts consist primarily of consumer debts and the value of whose nonexempt property is less than $150,000;'';

(2) by inserting after paragraph (4) the following:

''(4A) 'bankruptcy assistance' means any goods or services sold or otherwise provided to an assisted person with the express or implied purpose of providing information, advice, counsel, document preparation, or filing, or attendance at a creditors' meeting or appearing in a case or proceeding on behalf of another or providing legal representation with respect to a case or proceeding under this title;''; and

(3) by inserting after paragraph (12) the following:

''(12A) 'debt relief agency' means any person who provides any bankruptcy assistance to an assisted person in return for the payment of money or other valuable consideration, or who is a bankruptcy petition preparer under section 110, but does not include—

''(A) any person who is an officer, director, employee, or agent of a person who provides such assistance or of the bankruptcy petition preparer;

''(B) a nonprofit organization that is exempt from taxation under section 501(c)(3) of the Internal Revenue Code of 1986;

''(C) a creditor of such assisted person, to the extent that the creditor is assisting such assisted person to restructure any debt owed by such assisted person to the creditor;

''(D) a depository institution (as defined in section 3 of the Federal Deposit Insurance Act) or any Federal credit union or State credit union (as those terms are defined in section 101 of the Federal Credit Union Act), or any affiliate or subsidiary of such depository institution or credit union; or

''(E) an author, publisher, distributor, or seller of works subject to copyright protection under title 17, when acting in such capacity.''.

(b) CONFORMING AMENDMENT.—Section 104(b) of title 11, United States Code, is amended by inserting ''101(3),'' after ''sections'' each place it appears.

SEC. 227. RESTRICTIONS ON DEBT RELIEF AGENCIES.

(a) ENFORCEMENT.—Subchapter II of chapter 5 of title 11, United States Code, is amended by adding at the end the following:

''§ 526. Restrictions on debt relief agencies

''(a) A debt relief agency shall not—

''(1) fail to perform any service that such agency informed an assisted person or prospective assisted person it would provide in connection with a case or proceeding under this title;

''(2) make any statement, or counsel or advise any assisted person or prospective assisted person to make a statement in a document filed in a case or proceeding under this title, that is untrue and misleading, or that upon the exercise of reasonable care, should have been known by such agency to be untrue or misleading;

''(3) misrepresent to any assisted person or prospective assisted person, directly or indirectly, affirmatively or by material omission, with respect to—

"(A) the services that such agency will provide to such person; or

"(B) the benefits and risks that may result if such person becomes a debtor in a case under this title; or

"(4) advise an assisted person or prospective assisted person to incur more debt in contemplation of such person filing a case under this title or to pay an attorney or bankruptcy petition preparer fee or charge for services performed as part of preparing for or representing a debtor in a case under this title.

"(b) Any waiver by any assisted person of any protection or right provided under this section shall not be enforceable against the debtor by any Federal or State court or any other person, but may be enforced against a debt relief agency.

"(c)(1) Any contract for bankruptcy assistance between a debt relief agency and an assisted person that does not comply with the material requirements of this section, section 527, or section 528 shall be void and may not be enforced by any Federal or State court or by any other person, other than such assisted person.

"(2) Any debt relief agency shall be liable to an assisted person in the amount of any fees or charges in connection with providing bankruptcy assistance to such person that such debt relief agency has received, for actual damages, and for reasonable attorneys' fees and costs if such agency is found, after notice and a hearing, to have—

"(A) intentionally or negligently failed to comply with any provision of this section, section 527, or section 528 with respect to a case or proceeding under this title for such assisted person;

"(B) provided bankruptcy assistance to an assisted person in a case or proceeding under this title that is dismissed or converted to a case under another chapter of this title because of such agency's intentional or negligent failure to file any required document including those specified in section 521; or

"(C) intentionally or negligently disregarded the material requirements of this title or the Federal Rules of Bankruptcy Procedure applicable to such agency.

"(3) In addition to such other remedies as are provided under State law, whenever the chief law enforcement officer of a State, or an official or agency designated by a State, has reason to believe that any person has violated or is violating this section, the State—

"(A) may bring an action to enjoin such violation;

"(B) may bring an action on behalf of its residents to recover the actual damages of assisted persons arising from such violation, including any liability under paragraph (2); and

"(C) in the case of any successful action under subparagraph (A) or (B), shall be awarded the costs of the action and reasonable attorneys' fees as determined by the court.

"(4) The district courts of the United States for districts located in the State shall have concurrent jurisdiction of any action under subparagraph (A) or (B) of paragraph (3).

"(5) Notwithstanding any other provision of Federal law and in addition to any other remedy provided under Federal or State law, if the court, on its own motion or on the motion of the United States trustee or the debtor, finds that a person intentionally violated this section, or engaged in a clear and consistent pattern or practice of violating this section, the court may—

"(A) enjoin the violation of such section; or

"(B) impose an appropriate civil penalty against such person.

"(d) No provision of this section, section 527, or section 528 shall—

"(1) annul, alter, affect, or exempt any person subject to such sections from complying with any law of any State except to the extent that such law is inconsistent with those sections, and then only to the extent of the inconsistency; or

"(2) be deemed to limit or curtail the authority or ability—

"(A) of a State or subdivision or instrumentality thereof, to determine and enforce qualifications for the practice of law under the laws of that State; or

"(B) of a Federal court to determine and enforce the qualifications for the practice of law before that court.".

(b) CONFORMING AMENDMENT.—The table of sections for chapter 5 of title 11, United States Code, is amended by inserting after the item relating to section 525, the following:
"526. Restrictions on debt relief agencies.".

SEC. 228. DISCLOSURES.

(a) DISCLOSURES.—Subchapter II of chapter 5 of title 11, United States Code, as amended by section 227, is amended by adding at the end the following:

"§ 527. Disclosures

"(a) A debt relief agency providing bankruptcy assistance to an assisted person shall provide—

"(1) the written notice required under section 342(b)(1); and

"(2) to the extent not covered in the written notice described in paragraph (1), and not later than 3 business days after the first date on which a debt relief agency first offers to provide any bankruptcy assistance services to an assisted person, a clear and conspicuous written notice advising assisted persons that—

"(A) all information that the assisted person is required to provide with a petition and thereafter during a case under this title is required to be complete, accurate, and truthful;

"(B) all assets and all liabilities are required to be completely and accurately disclosed in the documents filed to commence the case, and the replacement value of each asset as defined in section 506 must be stated in those documents where requested after reasonable inquiry to establish such value;

"(C) current monthly income, the amounts specified in section 707(b)(2), and, in a case under chapter 13 of this title, disposable income (determined in accordance with section 707(b)(2)), are required to be stated after reasonable inquiry; and

"(D) information that an assisted person provides during their case may be audited pursuant to this title, and that failure to provide such information may result in dismissal of the case under this title or other sanction, including a criminal sanction.

"(b) A debt relief agency providing bankruptcy assistance to an assisted person shall provide each assisted person at the same time as the notices required under subsection (a)(1) the following statement, to the extent applicable, or one substantially similar. The statement shall be clear and conspicuous and shall be in a single document separate from other documents or notices provided to the assisted person:

"IMPORTANT INFORMATION ABOUT BANKRUPTCY ASSISTANCE SERVICES FROM AN ATTORNEY OR BANKRUPTCY PETITION PREPARER.

"If you decide to seek bankruptcy relief, you can represent yourself, you can hire an attorney to represent you, or you can get help in some localities from a bankruptcy petition preparer who is not an attorney. THE LAW REQUIRES AN ATTORNEY OR BANKRUPTCY PETITION PREPARER TO GIVE YOU A WRITTEN CONTRACT SPECIFYING WHAT THE ATTORNEY OR BANKRUPTCY PETITION PREPARER WILL DO FOR YOU AND HOW MUCH IT WILL COST. Ask to see the contract before you hire anyone.

"The following information helps you understand what must be done in a routine bankruptcy case to help you evaluate how much service you need. Although bankruptcy can be complex, many cases are routine.

"Before filing a bankruptcy case, either you or your attorney should analyze your eligibility for different forms of debt relief available under the Bankruptcy Code and which form of relief is most likely to be beneficial for you. Be sure you understand the relief you can obtain and its limitations. To file a bankruptcy case, documents called a Petition, Schedules and Statement of Financial Affairs, as well as in some cases a Statement of Intention need to be prepared correctly and filed with the bankruptcy court. You will have to pay a filing fee to the bankruptcy court. Once your case starts, you will have to attend the required first meeting of creditors where you may be questioned by a court official called a 'trustee' and by creditors.

" 'If you choose to file a chapter 7 case, you may be asked by a creditor to reaffirm a debt. You may want help deciding whether to do so. A creditor is not permitted to coerce you into reaffirming your debts.

" 'If you choose to file a chapter 13 case in which you repay your creditors what you can afford over 3 to 5 years, you may also want help with preparing your chapter 13 plan and with the confirmation hearing on your plan which will be before a bankruptcy judge.

" 'If you select another type of relief under the Bankruptcy Code other than chapter 7 or chapter 13, you will want to find out what should be done from someone familiar with that type of relief.

" 'Your bankruptcy case may also involve litigation. You are generally permitted to represent yourself in litigation in bankruptcy court, but only attorneys, not bankruptcy petition preparers, can give you legal advice.'.

"(c) Except to the extent the debt relief agency provides the required information itself after reasonably diligent inquiry of the assisted person or others so as to obtain such information reasonably accurately for inclusion on the petition, schedules or statement of financial affairs, a debt relief agency providing bankruptcy assistance to an assisted person, to the extent permitted by nonbankruptcy law, shall provide each assisted person at the time required for the notice required under subsection (a)(1) reasonably sufficient information (which shall be provided in a clear and conspicuous writing) to the assisted person on how to provide all the information the assisted person is required to provide under this title pursuant to section 521, including—

"(1) how to value assets at replacement value, determine current monthly income, the amounts specified in section 707(b)(2) and, in a chapter 13 case, how to determine disposable income in accordance with section 707(b)(2) and related calculations;

"(2) how to complete the list of creditors, including how to determine what amount is owed and what address for the creditor should be shown; and

"(3) how to determine what property is exempt and how to value exempt property at replacement value as defined in section 506.

"(d) A debt relief agency shall maintain a copy of the notices required under subsection (a) of this section for 2 years after the date on which the notice is given the assisted person.".

(b) CONFORMING AMENDMENT.—The table of sections for chapter 5 of title 11, United States Code, as amended by section 227, is amended by inserting after the item relating to section 526 the following:

"527. Disclosures.".

SEC. 229. REQUIREMENTS FOR DEBT RELIEF AGENCIES.

(a) ENFORCEMENT.—Subchapter II of chapter 5 of title 11, United States Code, as amended by sections 227 and 228, is amended by adding at the end the following:

"§ 528. Requirements for debt relief agencies

"(a) A debt relief agency shall—

"(1) not later than 5 business days after the first date on which such agency provides any bankruptcy assistance services to an assisted person, but prior to such assisted person's petition under this title being filed, execute a written contract with such assisted person that explains clearly and conspicuously—

"(A) the services such agency will provide to such assisted person; and

"(B) the fees or charges for such services, and the terms of payment;

"(2) provide the assisted person with a copy of the fully executed and completed contract;

"(3) clearly and conspicuously disclose in any advertisement of bankruptcy assistance services or of the benefits of bankruptcy directed to the general public (whether in general media, seminars or specific mailings, telephonic or electronic messages, or otherwise) that the services or benefits are with respect to bankruptcy relief under this title; and

"(4) clearly and conspicuously use the following statement in such advertisement: 'We are a debt relief agency. We help people file for bankruptcy relief under the Bankruptcy Code.' or a substantially similar statement.

"(b)(1) An advertisement of bankruptcy assistance services or of the benefits of bankruptcy directed to the general public includes—

"(A) descriptions of bankruptcy assistance in connection with a chapter 13 plan whether or not chapter 13 is specifically mentioned in such advertisement; and

"(B) statements such as 'federally supervised repayment plan' or 'Federal debt restructuring help' or other similar statements that could lead a reasonable consumer to believe that debt counseling was being offered when in fact the services were directed to providing bankruptcy assistance with a chapter 13 plan or other form of bankruptcy relief under this title.

"(2) An advertisement, directed to the general public, indicating that the debt relief agency provides assistance with respect to credit defaults, mortgage foreclosures, eviction proceedings, excessive debt, debt collection pressure, or inability to pay any consumer debt shall—

"(A) disclose clearly and conspicuously in such advertisement that the assistance may involve bankruptcy relief under this title; and

"(B) include the following statement: 'We are a debt relief agency. We help people file for bankruptcy relief under the Bankruptcy Code.' or a substantially similar statement.".

(b) CONFORMING AMENDMENT.—The table of sections for chapter 5 of title 11, United States Code, as amended by section 227 and 228, is amended by inserting after the item relating to section 527, the following:

"528. Requirements for debt relief agencies.".

SEC. 230. GAO STUDY.

(a) STUDY.—Not later than 270 days after the date of enactment of this Act, the Comptroller General of the United States shall conduct a study of the feasibility, effectiveness, and cost of requiring trustees appointed under title 11, United States Code, or the bankruptcy courts, to provide to the Office of Child Support Enforcement promptly after the commencement of cases by debtors who are individuals under such title, the names and social security account numbers of such debtors for the purposes of allowing such Office to determine whether such debtors have outstanding obligations for child support (as determined on the basis of information in the Federal Case Registry or other national database).

(b) REPORT.—Not later than 300 days after the date of enactment of this Act, the Comptroller General shall submit to the President pro tempore of the Senate and the Speaker of the House of Representatives a report containing the results of the study required by subsection (a).

SEC. 231. PROTECTION OF PERSONALLY IDENTIFIABLE INFORMATION.

(a) LIMITATION.—Section 363(b)(1) of title 11, United States Code, is amended by striking the period at the end and inserting the following:

", except that if the debtor in connection with offering a product or a service discloses to an individual a policy prohibiting the transfer of personally identifiable information about individuals to persons that are not affiliated with the debtor and if such policy is in effect on the date of the commencement of the case, then the trustee may not sell or lease personally identifiable information to any person unless—

"(A) such sale or such lease is consistent with such policy; or

"(B) after appointment of a consumer privacy ombudsman in accordance with section 332, and after notice and a hearing, the court approves such sale or such lease—

"(i) giving due consideration to the facts, circumstances, and conditions of such sale or such lease; and "(ii) finding that no showing was made that such sale or such lease would violate applicable nonbankruptcy law.".

(b) DEFINITION.—Section 101 of title 11, United States Code, is amended by inserting after paragraph (41) the following:

"(41A) 'personally identifiable information' means—

"(A) if provided by an individual to the debtor in connection with obtaining a product or a service from the debtor primarily for personal, family, or household purposes—

"(i) the first name (or initial) and last name of such individual, whether given at birth or time of adoption, or resulting from a lawful change of name;

"(ii) the geographical address of a physical place of residence of such individual;

"(iii) an electronic address (including an e-mail address) of such individual;

"(iv) a telephone number dedicated to contacting such individual at such physical place of residence;

"(v) a social security account number issued to such individual; or

"(vi) the account number of a credit card issued to such individual; or

"(B) if identified in connection with 1 or more of the items of information specified in subparagraph (A)—

"(i) a birth date, the number of a certificate of birth or adoption, or a place of birth; or

"(ii) any other information concerning an identified individual that, if disclosed, will result in contacting or identifying such individual physically or electronically;".

SEC. 232. CONSUMER PRIVACY OMBUDSMAN.

(a) CONSUMER PRIVACY OMBUDSMAN.—Title 11 of the United States Code is amended by inserting after section 331 the following:

"§ 332. Consumer privacy ombudsman

"(a) If a hearing is required under section 363(b)(1)(B), the court shall order the United States trustee to appoint, not later than 5 days before the commencement of the hearing, 1 disinterested person (other than the United States trustee) to serve as the consumer privacy ombudsman in the case and shall require that notice of such hearing be timely given to such ombudsman.

"(b) The consumer privacy ombudsman may appear and be heard at such hearing and shall provide to the court information to assist the court in its consideration of the facts, circumstances, and conditions of the proposed sale or lease of personally identifiable information under section 363(b)(1)(B). Such information may include presentation of—

"(1) the debtor's privacy policy;

"(2) the potential losses or gains of privacy to consumers if such sale or such lease is approved by the court;

"(3) the potential costs or benefits to consumers if such sale or such lease is approved by the court; and

"(4) the potential alternatives that would mitigate potential privacy losses or potential costs to consumers.

"(c) A consumer privacy ombudsman shall not disclose any personally identifiable information obtained by the ombudsman under this title.".

(b) COMPENSATION OF CONSUMER PRIVACY OMBUDSMAN.—Section 330(a)(1) of title 11, United States Code, is amended in the matter preceding subparagraph (A), by inserting "a consumer privacy ombudsman appointed under section 332," before "an examiner".

(c) CONFORMING AMENDMENT.—The table of sections for subchapter II of chapter 3 of title 11, United States Code, is amended by adding at the end the following:

"332. Consumer privacy ombudsman.".

SEC. 233. PROHIBITION ON DISCLOSURE OF NAME OF MINOR CHILDREN.

(a) PROHIBITION.—Title 11 of the United States Code, as amended by section 106, is amended by inserting after section 111 the following:

"§ 112. Prohibition on disclosure of name of minor children

"The debtor may be required to provide information regarding a minor child involved in matters under this title but may not be required to disclose in the public records in the case the name of such minor child. The debtor may be required to disclose the name of such minor child in a nonpublic record that is maintained by the court and made available by the court for examination by the United States trustee, the trustee, and the auditor (if any) serving under section 586(f) of title 28, in the case. The court, the United States trustee, the trustee, and such auditor shall not disclose the name of such minor child maintained in such nonpublic record.".

(b) CLERICAL AMENDMENT.—The table of sections for chapter 1 of title 11, United States Code, as amended by section 106, is amended by inserting after the item relating to section 111 the following:

"112. Prohibition on disclosure of name of minor children.".

(c) CONFORMING AMENDMENT.—Section 107(a) of title 11, United States Code, is amended by inserting "and subject to section 112" after "section".

SEC. 234. PROTECTION OF PERSONAL INFORMATION.

(a) RESTRICTION OF PUBLIC ACCESS TO CERTAIN INFORMATION CONTAINED IN BANKRUPTCY CASE FILES.—Section 107 of title 11, United States Code, is amended by adding at the end the following:

"(c)(1) The bankruptcy court, for cause, may protect an individual, with respect to the following types of information to the extent the court finds that disclosure of such information would create undue risk of identity theft or other unlawful injury to the individual or the individual's property:

"(A) Any means of identification (as defined in section 1028(d) of title 18) contained in a paper filed, or to be filed, in a case under this title.

"(B) Other information contained in a paper described in subparagraph (A).

"(2) Upon ex parte application demonstrating cause, the court shall provide access to information protected pursuant to paragraph (1) to an entity acting pursuant to the police or regulatory power of a domestic governmental unit.

"(3) The United States trustee, bankruptcy administrator, trustee, and any auditor serving under section 586(f) of title 28—

"(A) shall have full access to all information contained in any paper filed or submitted in a case under this title; and

"(B) shall not disclose information specifically protected by the court under this title.".

(b) SECURITY OF SOCIAL SECURITY ACCOUNT NUMBER OF DEBTOR IN NOTICE TO CREDITOR.—Section 342(c) of title 11, United States Code, is amended—

(1) by inserting "last 4 digits of the" before "taxpayer identification number"; and

(2) by adding at the end the following: "If the notice concerns an amendment that adds a creditor to the schedules of assets and liabilities, the debtor shall include the full taxpayer identification number in the notice sent to that creditor, but the debtor shall include only the last 4 digits of the taxpayer identification number in the copy of the notice filed with the court.".

(c) CONFORMING AMENDMENT—Section 107(a) of title 11, United States Code, is amended by striking "subsection (b)," and inserting "subsections (b) and (c),".

TITLE III—DISCOURAGING BANKRUPTCY ABUSE

SEC. 301. TECHNICAL AMENDMENTS.

Section 523(a)(17) of title 11, United States Code, is amended—
(1) by striking "by a court" and inserting "on a prisoner by any court";
(2) by striking "section 1915(b) or (f)" and inserting "subsection (b) or (f)(2) of section 1915"; and
(3) by inserting "(or a similar non-Federal law)" after "title 28" each place it appears.

SEC. 302. DISCOURAGING BAD FAITH REPEAT FILINGS.

Section 362(c) of title 11, United States Code, is amended—
(1) in paragraph (1), by striking "and" at the end;
(2) in paragraph (2), by striking the period at the end and inserting a semicolon; and
(3) by adding at the end the following:
"(3) if a single or joint case is filed by or against debtor who is an individual in a case under chapter 7, 11, or 13, and if a single or joint case of the debtor was pending within the preceding 1-year period but was dismissed, other than a case refiled under a chapter other than chapter 7 after dismissal under section 707(b)—
"(A) the stay under subsection (a) with respect to any action taken with respect to a debt or property securing such debt or with respect to any lease shall terminate with respect to the debtor on the 30th day after the filing of the later case;
"(B) on the motion of a party in interest for continuation of the automatic stay and upon notice and a hearing, the court may extend the stay in particular cases as to any or all creditors (subject to such conditions or limitations as the court may then impose) after notice and a hearing completed before the expiration of the 30-day period only if the party in interest demonstrates that the filing of the later case is in good faith as to the creditors to be stayed; and
"(C) for purposes of subparagraph (B), a case is presumptively filed not in good faith (but such presumption may be rebutted by clear and convincing evidence to the contrary)—
"(i) as to all creditors, if—
"(I) more than 1 previous case under any of chapters 7, 11, and 13 in which the individual was a debtor was pending within the preceding 1-year period;
"(II) a previous case under any of chapters 7, 11, and 13 in which the individual was a debtor was dismissed within such 1-year period, after the debtor failed to—
"(aa) file or amend the petition or other documents as required by this title or the court without substantial excuse (but mere inadvertence or negligence shall not be a substantial excuse unless the dismissal was caused by the negligence of the debtor's attorney);
"(bb) provide adequate protection as ordered by the court; or
"(cc) perform the terms of a plan confirmed by the court; or
"(III) there has not been a substantial change in the financial or personal affairs of the debtor since the dismissal of the next most previous case under chapter 7, 11, or 13 or any other reason to conclude that the later case will be concluded—
"(aa) if a case under chapter 7, with a discharge; or
"(bb) if a case under chapter 11 or 13, with a confirmed plan that will be fully performed; and
"(ii) as to any creditor that commenced an action under subsection (d) in a previous case in which the individual was a debtor if, as of the date of dismissal of such case, that action was still pending or had been resolved by terminating, conditioning, or limiting the stay as to actions of such creditor; and
"(4)(A)(i) if a single or joint case is filed by or against a debtor who is an individual under

this title, and if 2 or more single or joint cases of the debtor were pending within the previous year but were dismissed, other than a case refiled under section 707(b), the stay under subsection (a) shall not go into effect upon the filing of the later case; and

"(ii) on request of a party in interest, the court shall promptly enter an order confirming that no stay is in effect;

"(B) if, within 30 days after the filing of the later case, a party in interest requests the court may order the stay to take effect in the case as to any or all creditors (subject to such conditions or limitations as the court may impose), after notice and a hearing, only if the party in interest demonstrates that the filing of the later case is in good faith as to the creditors to be stayed;

"(C) a stay imposed under subparagraph (B) shall be effective on the date of the entry of the order allowing the stay to go into effect; and

"(D) for purposes of subparagraph (B), a case is presumptively filed not in good faith (but such presumption may be rebutted by clear and convincing evidence to the contrary)—

"(i) as to all creditors if—

"(I) 2 or more previous cases under this title in which the individual was a debtor were pending within the 1-year period;

"(II) a previous case under this title in which the individual was a debtor was dismissed within the time period stated in this paragraph after the debtor failed to file or amend the petition or other documents as required by this title or the court without substantial excuse (but mere inadvertence or negligence shall not be substantial excuse unless the dismissal was caused by the negligence of the debtor's attorney), failed to provide adequate protection as ordered by the court, or failed to perform the terms of a plan confirmed by the court; or

"(III) there has not been a substantial change in the financial or personal affairs of the debtor since the dismissal of the next most previous case under this title, or any other reason to conclude that the later case will not be concluded, if a case under chapter 7, with a discharge, and if a case under chapter 11 or 13, with a confirmed plan that will be fully performed; or

"(ii) as to any creditor that commenced an action under subsection (d) in a previous case in which the individual was a debtor if, as of the date of dismissal of such case, such action was still pending or had been resolved by terminating, conditioning, or limiting the stay as to such action of such creditor.".

SEC. 303. CURBING ABUSIVE FILINGS.

(a) IN GENERAL.—Section 362(d) of title 11, United States Code, is amended—

(1) in paragraph (2), by striking "or" at the end;

(2) in paragraph (3), by striking the period at the end and inserting "; or"; and

(3) by adding at the end the following:

"(4) with respect to a stay of an act against real property under subsection (a), by a creditor whose claim is secured by an interest in such real property, if the court finds that the filing of the petition was part of a scheme to delay, hinder, and defraud creditors that involved either—

"(A) transfer of all or part ownership of, or other interest in, such real property without the consent of the secured creditor or court approval; or

"(B) multiple bankruptcy filings affecting such real property.

If recorded in compliance with applicable State laws governing notices of interests or liens in real property, an order entered under paragraph (4) shall be binding in any other case under this title purporting to affect such real property filed not later than 2 years after the date of the entry of such order by the court, except that a debtor in a subsequent case under this title may move for relief from such order based upon changed circumstances or for good cause shown, after notice and a hearing. Any Federal, State, or local governmental unit that accepts notices of interests or liens in real property shall accept any certified copy of an order described in this subsection for indexing and recording.''.

(b) AUTOMATIC STAY.—Section 362(b) of title 11, United States Code, as amended by section 224, is amended by inserting after paragraph (19), the following:

"(20) under subsection (a), of any act to enforce any lien against or security interest in real property following entry of the order under subsection (d)(4) as to such real property in any prior case under this title, for a period of 2 years after the date of the entry of such an order, except that the debtor, in a subsequent case under this title, may move for relief from such order based upon changed circumstances or for other good cause shown, after notice and a hearing;

"(21) under subsection (a), of any act to enforce any lien against or security interest in real property—

"(A) if the debtor is ineligible under section 109(g) to be a debtor in a case under this title; or

"(B) if the case under this title was filed in violation of a bankruptcy court order in a prior case under this title prohibiting the debtor from being a debtor in another case under this title;''.

SEC. 304. DEBTOR RETENTION OF PERSONAL PROPERTY SECURITY.

Title 11, United States Code, is amended—

(1) in section 521(a), as so designated by section 106—

(A) in paragraph (4), by striking ", and'' at the end and inserting a semicolon;

(B) in paragraph (5), by striking the period at the end and inserting "; and''; and

(C) by adding at the end the following:

"(6) in a case under chapter 7 of this title in which the debtor is an individual, not retain possession of personal property as to which a creditor has an allowed claim for the purchase price secured in whole or in part by an interest in such personal property unless the debtor, not later than 45 days after the first meeting of creditors under section 341(a), either—

"(A) enters into an agreement with the creditor pursuant to section 524(c) with respect to the claim secured by such property; or

"(B) redeems such property from the security interest pursuant to section 722.

If the debtor fails to so act within the 45-day period referred to in paragraph (6), the stay under section 362(a) is terminated with respect to the personal property of the estate or of the debtor which is affected, such property shall no longer be property of the estate, and the creditor may take whatever action as to such property as is permitted by applicable nonbankruptcy law, unless the court determines on the motion of the trustee filed before the expiration of such 45-day period, and after notice and a hearing, that such property is of consequential value or benefit to the estate, orders appropriate adequate protection of the creditor's interest, and orders the debtor to deliver any collateral in the debtor's possession to the trustee.''; and

(2) in section 722, by inserting "in full at the time of redemption'' before the period at the end.

SEC. 305. RELIEF FROM THE AUTOMATIC STAY WHEN THE DEBTOR DOES NOT COMPLETE INTENDED SURRENDER OF CONSUMER DEBT COLLATERAL.

Title 11, United States Code, is amended—

(1) in section 362, as amended by section 106—

(A) in subsection (c), by striking "(e), and (f)'' and inserting "(e), (f), and (h)'';

(B) by redesignating subsection (h) as subsection (k) and transferring such subsection so as to insert it after subsection (j) as added by section 106; and

(C) by inserting after subsection (g) the following:

"(h)(1) In a case in which the debtor is an individual, the stay provided by subsection (a) is terminated with respect to personal property of the estate or of the debtor securing in whole or in part a claim, or subject to an unexpired lease, and such personal property shall no longer be property of the estate if the debtor fails within the applicable time set by section 521(a)(2)—

"(A) to file timely any statement of intention required under section 521(a)(2) with respect to such personal property or to indicate in such statement that the debtor will either surrender such personal property or retain it and, if retaining such personal property, either redeem such personal property pursuant to section 722, enter into an agreement of the kind specified in section 524(c) applicable to the debt secured by such personal property, or assume such unexpired lease pursuant to section 365(p) if the trustee does not do so, as applicable; and

"(B) to take timely the action specified in such statement, as it may be amended before expiration of the period for taking action, unless such statement specifies the debtor's intention to reaffirm such debt on the original contract terms and the creditor refuses to agree to the reaffirmation on such terms.

"(2) Paragraph (1) does not apply if the court determines, on the motion of the trustee filed before the expiration of the applicable time set by section 521(a)(2), after notice and a hearing, that such personal property is of consequential value or benefit to the estate, and orders appropriate adequate protection of the creditor's interest, and orders the debtor to deliver any collateral in the debtor's possession to the trustee. If the court does not so determine, the stay provided by subsection (a) shall terminate upon the conclusion of the hearing on the motion."; and

(2) in section 521, as amended by sections 106 and 225—

(A) in subsection (a)(2) by striking "consumer";

(B) in subsection (a)(2)(B)—

(i) by striking "forty-five days after the filing of a notice of intent under this section" and inserting "30 days after the first date set for the meeting of creditors under section 341(a)"; and

(ii) by striking "forty-five day" and inserting "30-day";

(C) in subsection (a)(2)(C) by inserting ", except as provided in section 362(h)" before the semicolon; and

(D) by adding at the end the following:

"(d) If the debtor fails timely to take the action specified in subsection (a)(6) of this section, or in paragraphs (1) and (2) of section 362(h), with respect to property which a lessor or bailor owns and has leased, rented, or bailed to the debtor or as to which a creditor holds a security interest not otherwise voidable under section 522(f), 544, 545, 547, 548, or 549, nothing in this title shall prevent or limit the operation of a provision in the underlying lease or agreement that has the effect of placing the debtor in default under such lease or agreement by reason of the occurrence, pendency, or existence of a proceeding under this title or the insolvency of the debtor. Nothing in this subsection shall be deemed to justify limiting such a provision in any other circumstance.".

SEC. 306. GIVING SECURED CREDITORS FAIR TREATMENT IN CHAPTER 13.

(a) IN GENERAL.—Section 1325(a)(5)(B)(i) of title 11, United States Code, is amended to read as follows:

"(i) the plan provides that—

"(I) the holder of such claim retain the lien securing such claim until the earlier of—

"(aa) the payment of the underlying debt determined under nonbankruptcy law; or

"(bb) discharge under section 1328; and

"(II) if the case under this chapter is dismissed or converted without completion of the plan, such lien shall also be retained by such holder to the extent recognized by applicable nonbankruptcy law; and".

(b) RESTORING THE FOUNDATION FOR SECURED CREDIT.—Section 1325(a) of title 11, United States Code, is amended by adding at the end the following:

"For purposes of paragraph (5), section 506 shall not apply to a claim described in that paragraph if the creditor has a purchase money security interest securing the debt that is the subject of the claim, the debt was incurred within the 910-day preceding the date of the filing of the petition, and the collateral for that debt consists of a motor vehicle (as defined in section 30102 of title 49) acquired for the personal use of the debtor, or if collateral for that debt consists of any other thing of value, if the debt was incurred during the 1-year period preceding that filing.".

(c) DEFINITIONS.—Section 101 of title 11, United States Code, is amended—

(1) by inserting after paragraph (13) the following:

"(13A) 'debtor's principal residence'—

"(A) means a residential structure, including incidental property, without regard to whether that structure is attached to real property; and

"(B) includes an individual condominium or cooperative unit, a mobile or manufactured home, or trailer;'; and

(2) by inserting after paragraph (27), the following:

"(27A) 'incidental property' means, with respect to a debtor's principal residence—

"(A) property commonly conveyed with a principal residence in the area where the real property is located;

"(B) all easements, rights, appurtenances, fixtures, rents, royalties, mineral rights, oil or gas rights or profits, water rights, escrow funds, or insurance proceeds; and

"(C) all replacements or additions;".

SEC. 307. DOMICILIARY REQUIREMENTS FOR EXEMPTIONS.

Section 522(b)(3) of title 11, United States Code, as so designated by section 106, is amended—

(1) in subparagraph (A)—

(A) by striking "180 days" and inserting "730 days"; and

(B) by striking ", or for a longer portion of such 180-day period than in any other place" and inserting "or if the debtor's domicile has not been located at a single State for such 730-day period, the place in which the debtor's domicile was located for 180 days immediately preceding the 730-day period or for a longer portion of such 180-day period than in any other place"; and

(2) by adding at the end the following:

"If the effect of the domiciliary requirement under subparagraph (A) is to render the debtor ineligible for any exemption, the debtor may elect to exempt property that is specified under subsection (d).".

SEC. 308. REDUCTION OF HOMESTEAD EXEMPTION FOR FRAUD.

Section 522 of title 11, United States Code, as amended by section 224, is amended—

(1) in subsection (b)(3)(A), as so designated by this Act, by inserting "subject to subsections (o) and (p)," before "any property"; and

(2) by adding at the end the following:

"(o) For purposes of subsection (b)(3)(A), and notwithstanding subsection (a), the value of an interest in—

"(1) real or personal property that the debtor or a dependent of the debtor uses as a residence;

"(2) a cooperative that owns property that the debtor or a dependent of the debtor uses as a residence;

"(3) a burial plot for the debtor or a dependent of the debtor; or

"(4) real or personal property that the debtor or a dependent of the debtor claims as a homestead;

shall be reduced to the extent that such value is attributable to any portion of any property that the debtor disposed of in the 10-year period ending on the date of the filing of the petition with the intent to hinder, delay, or defraud a creditor and that the debtor could not exempt, or that portion that the debtor could not exempt, under subsection (b), if on such date the debtor had held the property so disposed of.".

SEC. 309. PROTECTING SECURED CREDITORS IN CHAPTER 13 CASES.

(a) STOPPING ABUSIVE CONVERSIONS FROM CHAPTER 13.—Section 348(f)(1) of title 11, United States Code, is amended—

(1) in subparagraph (A), by striking "and" at the end;

(2) in subparagraph (B)—

(A) by striking "in the converted case, with allowed secured claims" and inserting "only in a case converted to a case under chapter 11 or 12, but not in a case converted to a case under chapter 7, with allowed secured claims in cases under chapters 11 and 12"; and

(B) by striking the period and inserting "; and"; and

(3) by adding at the end the following:

"(C) with respect to cases converted from chapter 13—

"(i) the claim of any creditor holding security as of the date of the petition shall continue to be secured by that security unless the full amount of such claim determined under applicable nonbankruptcy law has been paid in full as of the date of conversion, notwithstanding any valuation or determination of the amount of an allowed secured claim made for the purposes of the case under chapter 13; and

"(ii) unless a prebankruptcy default has been fully cured under the plan at the time of conversion, in any proceeding under this title or otherwise, the default shall have the effect given under applicable nonbankruptcy law.".

(b) GIVING DEBTORS THE ABILITY TO KEEP LEASED PERSONAL PROPERTY BY ASSUMPTION.—Section 365 of title 11, United States Code, is amended by adding at the end the following:

"(p)(1) If a lease of personal property is rejected or not timely assumed by the trustee under subsection (d), the leased property is no longer property of the estate and the stay under section 362(a) is automatically terminated.

"(2)(A) If the debtor in a case under chapter 7 is an individual, the debtor may notify the creditor in writing that the debtor desires to assume the lease. Upon being so notified, the creditor may, at its option, notify the debtor that it is willing to have the lease assumed by the debtor and may condition such assumption on cure of any outstanding default on terms set by the contract.

"(B) If, not later than 30 days after notice is provided under subparagraph (A), the debtor notifies the lessor in writing that the lease is assumed, the liability under the lease will be assumed by the debtor and not by the estate.

"(C) The stay under section 362 and the injunction under section 524(a)(2) shall not be violated by notification of the debtor and negotiation of cure under this subsection.

"(3) In a case under chapter 11 in which the debtor is an individual and in a case under chapter 13, if the debtor is the lessee with respect to personal property and the lease is not assumed in the plan confirmed by the court, the lease is deemed rejected as of the conclusion of the hearing on confirmation. If the lease is rejected, the stay under section 362 and any stay under section 1301 is automatically terminated with respect to the property subject to the lease.".

(c) ADEQUATE PROTECTION OF LESSORS AND PURCHASE MONEY SECURED CREDITORS.—

(1) CONFIRMATION OF PLAN.—Section 1325(a)(5)(B) of title 11, United States Code, as amended by section 306, is amended—

(A) in clause (i), by striking "and" at the end;

(B) in clause (ii), by striking "or" at the end and inserting "and"; and

(C) by adding at the end the following:

"(iii) if—

"(I) property to be distributed pursuant to this subsection is in the form of periodic payments, such payments shall be in equal monthly amounts; and

"(II) the holder of the claim is secured by personal property, the amount of such payments shall not be less than an amount sufficient to provide to the holder of such claim adequate protection during the period of the plan; or".

(2) PAYMENTS.—Section 1326(a) of title 11, United States Code, is amended to read as follows:

"(a)(1) Unless the court orders otherwise, the debtor shall commence making payments not later than 30 days after the date of the filing of the plan or the order for relief, whichever is earlier, in the amount—

"(A) proposed by the plan to the trustee;

"(B) scheduled in a lease of personal property directly to the lessor for that portion of the obligation that becomes due after the order for relief, reducing the payments under subparagraph (A) by the amount so paid and providing the trustee with evidence of such payment, including the amount and date of payment; and

"(C) that provides adequate protection directly to a creditor holding an allowed claim secured by personal property to the extent the claim is attributable to the purchase of such property by the debtor for that portion of the obligation that becomes due after the order for relief, reducing the payments under subparagraph (A) by the amount so paid and providing the trustee with evidence of such payment, including the amount and date of payment.

"(2) A payment made under paragraph (1)(A) shall be retained by the trustee until confirmation or denial of confirmation. If a plan is confirmed, the trustee shall distribute any such payment in accordance with the plan as soon as is practicable. If a plan is not confirmed, the trustee shall return any such payments not previously paid and not yet due and owing to creditors pursuant to paragraph (3) to the debtor, after deducting any unpaid claim allowed under section 503(b).

"(3) Subject to section 363, the court may, upon notice and a hearing, modify, increase, or reduce the payments required under this subsection pending confirmation of a plan.

"(4) Not later than 60 days after the date of filing of a case under this chapter, a debtor retaining possession of personal property subject to a lease or securing a claim attributable in whole or in part to the purchase price of such property shall provide the lessor or secured creditor reasonable evidence of the maintenance of any required insurance coverage with respect to the use or ownership of such property and continue to do so for so long as the debtor retains possession of such property.".

SEC. 310. LIMITATION ON LUXURY GOODS.

Section 523(a)(2)(C) of title 11, United States Code, is amended to read as follows:

"(C)(i) for purposes of subparagraph (A)—

"(I) consumer debts owed to a single creditor and aggregating more than $500 for luxury goods or services incurred by an individual debtor on or within 90 days before the order for relief under this title are presumed to be nondischargeable; and

"(II) cash advances aggregating more than $750 that are extensions of consumer credit under an open end credit plan obtained by an individual debtor on or within 70 days before the order for relief under this title, are presumed to be nondischargeable; and

"(ii) for purposes of this subparagraph—

"(I) the terms 'consumer', 'credit', and 'open end credit plan' have the same meanings as in section 103 of the Truth in Lending Act; and

"(II) the term 'luxury goods or services' does not include goods or services reasonably necessary for the support or maintenance of the debtor or a dependent of the debtor.".

SEC. 311. AUTOMATIC STAY.

(a) IN GENERAL.—Section 362(b) of title 11, United States Code, as amended by sections 224 and 303, is amended by inserting after paragraph (21), the following:

"(22) subject to subsection (l), under subsection (a)(3), of the continuation of any eviction, unlawful detainer action, or similar proceeding by a lessor against a debtor involving residential property in which the debtor resides as a tenant under a lease or rental agreement and with respect to which the lessor has obtained before the date of the filing of the bankruptcy petition, a judgment for possession of such property against the debtor;

"(23) subject to subsection (m), under subsection (a)(3), of an eviction action that seeks possession of the residential property in which the debtor resides as a tenant under a lease or rental agreement based on endangerment of such property or the illegal use of controlled substances on such property, but only if the lessor files with the court, and serves upon the debtor, a certification under penalty of perjury that such an eviction action has been filed, or that the debtor, during the 30-day period preceding the date of the filing of the certification, has endangered property or illegally used or allowed to be used a controlled substance on the property;

"(24) under subsection (a), of any transfer that is not avoidable under section 544 and that is not avoidable under section 549;".

(b) LIMITATIONS.—Section 362 of title 11, United States Code, as amended by sections 106 and 305, is amended by adding at the end the following:

"(*l*)(1) Except as otherwise provided in this subsection, subsection (b)(22) shall apply on the date that is 30 days after the date on which the bankruptcy petition is filed, if the debtor files with the petition and serves upon the lessor a certification under penalty of perjury that—

"(A) under nonbankruptcy law applicable in the jurisdiction, there are circumstances under which the debtor would be permitted to cure the entire monetary default that gave rise to the judgment for possession, after that judgment for possession was entered; and

"(B) the debtor (or an adult dependent of the debtor) has deposited with the clerk of the court, any rent that would become due during the 30-day period after the filing of the bankruptcy petition.

"(2) If, within the 30-day period after the filing of the bankruptcy petition, the debtor (or an adult dependent of the debtor) complies with paragraph (1) and files with the court and serves upon the lessor a further certification under penalty of perjury that the debtor (or an adult dependent of the debtor) has cured, under nonbankrupcty law applicable in the jurisdiction, the entire monetary default that gave rise to the judgment under which possession is sought by the lessor, subsection (b)(22) shall not apply, unless ordered to apply by the court under paragraph (3).

"(3)(A) If the lessor files an objection to any certification filed by the debtor under paragraph (1) or (2), and serves such objection upon the debtor, the court shall hold a hearing within 10 days after the filing and service of such objection to determine if the certification filed by the debtor under paragraph (1) or (2) is true.

"(B) If the court upholds the objection of the lessor filed under subparagraph (A)—

"(i) subsection (b)(22) shall apply immediately and relief from the stay provided under subsection (a)(3) shall not be required to enable the lessor to complete the process to recover full possession of the property; and

"(ii) the clerk of the court shall immediately serve upon the lessor and the debtor a certified copy of the court's order upholding the lessor's objection.

"(4) If a debtor, in accordance with paragraph (5), indicates on the petition that there was a judgment for possession of the residential rental property in which the debtor resides and does not file a certification under paragraph (1) or (2)—

"(A) subsection (b)(22) shall apply immediately upon failure to file such certification, and relief from the stay provided under subsection (a)(3) shall not be required to enable the lessor to complete the process to recover full possession of the property; and

"(B) the clerk of the court shall immediately serve upon the lessor and the debtor a certified copy of the docket indicating the absence of a filed certification and the applicability of the exception to the stay under subsection (b)(22).

"(5)(A) Where a judgment for possession of residential property in which the debtor resides as a tenant under a lease or rental agreement has been obtained by the lessor, the debtor shall so indicate on the bankruptcy petition and shall provide the name and address of the lessor that obtained that pre-petition judgment on the petition and on any certification filed under this subsection.

"(B) The form of certification filed with the petition, as specified in this subsection, shall provide for the debtor to certify, and the debtor shall certify—

"(i) whether a judgment for possession of residential rental housing in which the debtor resides has been obtained against the debtor before the date of the filing of the petition; and

"(ii) whether the debtor is claiming under paragraph (1) that under nonbankruptcy law applicable in the jurisdiction, there are circumstances under which the debtor would be permitted to cure the entire monetary default that gave rise to the judgment for possession, after that judgment of possession was entered, and has made the appropriate deposit with the court.

"(C) The standard forms (electronic and otherwise) used in a bankruptcy proceeding shall be amended to reflect the requirements of this subsection.

"(D) The clerk of the court shall arrange for the prompt transmittal of the rent deposited in accordance with paragraph (1)(B) to the lessor.

"(m)(1) Except as otherwise provided in this subsection, subsection (b)(23) shall apply on the date that is 15 days after the date on which the lessor files and serves a certification described in subsection (b)(23).

"(2)(A) If the debtor files with the court an objection to the truth or legal sufficiency of the certification described in subsection (b)(23) and serves such objection upon the lessor, subsection (b)(23) shall not apply, unless ordered to apply by the court under this subsection.

"(B) If the debtor files and serves the objection under subparagraph (A), the court shall hold a hearing within 10 days after the filing and service of such objection to determine if the situation giving rise to the lessor's certification under paragraph (1) existed or has been remedied.

"(C) If the debtor can demonstrate to the satisfaction of the court that the situation giving rise to the lessor's certification under paragraph (1) did not exist or has been remedied, the stay provided under subsection (a)(3) shall remain in effect until the termination of the stay under this section.

"(D) If the debtor cannot demonstrate to the satisfaction of the court that the situation giving rise to the lessor's certification under paragraph (1) did not exist or has been remedied—

"(i) relief from the stay provided under subsection (a)(3) shall not be required to enable the lessor to proceed with the eviction; and "(ii) the clerk of the court shall immediately serve upon the lessor and the debtor a certified copy of the court's order upholding the lessor's certification.

"(3) If the debtor fails to file, within 15 days, an objection under paragraph (2)(A)—

"(A) subsection (b)(23) shall apply immediately upon such failure and relief from the stay provided under subsection (a)(3) shall not be required to enable the lessor to complete the process to recover full possession of the property; and

"(B) the clerk of the court shall immediately serve upon the lessor and the debtor a certified copy of the docket indicating such failure.".

SEC. 312. EXTENSION OF PERIOD BETWEEN BANKRUPTCY DISCHARGES.

Title 11, United States Code, is amended—

(1) in section 727(a)(8), by striking "six" and inserting "8"; and

(2) in section 1328, by inserting after subsection (e) the following:

"(f) Notwithstanding subsections (a) and (b), the court shall not grant a discharge of all debts provided for in the plan or disallowed under section 502, if the debtor has received a discharge—

"(1) in a case filed under chapter 7, 11, or 12 of this title during the 4- year period preceding the date of the order for relief under this chapter, or

"(2) in a case filed under chapter 13 of this title during the 2-year period preceding the date of such order.".

SEC. 313. DEFINITION OF HOUSEHOLD GOODS AND ANTIQUES.

(a) DEFINITION.—Section 522(f) of title 11, United States Code, is amended by adding at the end the following:

"(4)(A) Subject to subparagraph (B), for purposes of paragraph (1)(B), the term 'household goods' means—

"(i) clothing;

"(ii) furniture;

"(iii) appliances;

"(iv) 1 radio;

"(v) 1 television;

"(vi) 1 VCR;

"(vii) linens;

"(viii) china;

"(ix) crockery;

"(x) kitchenware;

"(xi) educational materials and educational equipment primarily for the use of minor dependent children of the debtor;

"(xii) medical equipment and supplies;

"(xiii) furniture exclusively for the use of minor children, or elderly or disabled dependents of the debtor;

"(xiv) personal effects (including the toys and hobby equipment of minor dependent children and wedding rings) of the debtor and the dependents of the debtor; and

"(xv) 1 personal computer and related equipment.

"(B) The term 'household goods' does not include—

"(i) works of art (unless by or of the debtor, or any relative of the debtor);

"(ii) electronic entertainment equipment with a fair market value of more than $500 in the aggregate (except 1 television, 1 radio, and 1 VCR);

"(iii) items acquired as antiques with a fair market value of more than $500 in the aggregate;

"(iv) jewelry with a fair market value of more than $500 in the aggregate (except wedding rings); and "(v) a computer (except as otherwise provided for in this section), motor vehicle (including a tractor or lawn tractor), boat, or a motorized recreational device, conveyance, vehicle, watercraft, or aircraft.".

(b) STUDY.—Not later than 2 years after the date of enactment of this Act, the Director of the Executive Office for United States Trustees shall submit a report to the Committee on the Judiciary of the Senate and the Committee on the Judiciary of the House of Representatives containing its findings regarding utilization of the definition of household goods, as defined in section 522(f)(4) of title 11, United States Code, as added by subsection (a), with respect to the avoidance of nonpossessory, nonpurchase money security interests in household goods under section 522(f)(1)(B) of title 11, United States Code, and the impact such section 522(f)(4) has had on debtors and on the bankruptcy courts. Such report may include recommendations for amendments to such section 522(f)(4) consistent with the Director's findings.

SEC. 314. DEBT INCURRED TO PAY NONDISCHARGEABLE DEBTS.

(a) IN GENERAL.—Section 523(a) of title 11, United States Code, is amended by inserting after paragraph (14) the following:

"(14A) incurred to pay a tax to a governmental unit, other than the United States, that would be nondischargeable under paragraph (1);".

(b) DISCHARGE UNDER CHAPTER 13.—Section 1328(a) of title 11, United States Code, is amended by striking paragraphs (1) through (3) and inserting the following:

"(1) provided for under section 1322(b)(5);

"(2) of the kind specified in paragraph (2), (3), (4), (5), (8), or (9) of section 523(a);

"(3) for restitution, or a criminal fine, included in a sentence on the debtor's conviction of a crime; or

"(4) for restitution, or damages, awarded in a civil action against the debtor as a result of willful or malicious injury by the debtor that caused personal injury to an individual or the death of an individual.".

SEC. 315. GIVING CREDITORS FAIR NOTICE IN CHAPTERS 7 AND 13 CASES.

(a) NOTICE.—Section 342 of title 11, United States Code, as amended by section 102, is amended—

(1) in subsection (c)—

(A) by inserting "(1)" after "(c)";

(B) by striking ", but the failure of such notice to contain such information shall not invalidate the legal effect of such notice"; and

(C) by adding at the end the following:

"(2)(A) If, within the 90 days before the commencement of a voluntary case, a creditor supplies the debtor in at least 2 communications sent to the debtor with the current account number of the debtor and the address at which such creditor requests to receive correspondence, then any notice required by this title to be sent by the debtor to such creditor shall be sent to such address and shall include such account number.

"(B) If a creditor would be in violation of applicable nonbankruptcy law by sending any such communication within such 90-day period and if such creditor supplies the debtor in the last 2 communications with the current account number of the debtor and the address at which such creditor requests to receive correspondence, then any notice required by this title to be sent by the debtor to such creditor shall be sent to such address and shall include such account number."; and

(2) by adding at the end the following:

"(e)(1) In a case under chapter 7 or 13 of this title of a debtor who is an individual, a creditor at any time may both file with the court and serve on the debtor a notice of address to be used to provide notice in such case to such creditor.

"(2) Any notice in such case required to be provided to such creditor by the debtor or the court later than 5 days after the court and the debtor receive such creditor's notice of address, shall be provided to such address.

"(f)(1) An entity may file with any bankruptcy court a notice of address to be used by all the bankruptcy courts or by particular bankruptcy courts, as so specified by such entity at the time such notice is filed, to provide notice to such entity in all cases under chapters 7 and 13 pending in the courts with respect to which such notice is filed, in which such entity is a creditor.

"(2) In any case filed under chapter 7 or 13, any notice required to be provided by a court with respect to which a notice is filed under paragraph (1), to such entity later than 30 days after the filing of such notice under paragraph (1) shall be provided to such address unless with respect to a particular case a different address is specified in a notice filed and served in accordance with subsection (e).

"(3) A notice filed under paragraph (1) may be withdrawn by such entity.

"(g)(1) Notice provided to a creditor by the debtor or the court other than in accordance with this section (excluding this subsection) shall not be effective notice until such notice is brought to the attention of such creditor. If such creditor designates a person or an organizational subdivision of such creditor to be responsible for receiving notices under this title and establishes reasonable procedures so that such notices receivable by such creditor are to be delivered to such person or such subdivision, then a notice provided to such creditor other than in accordance with this section (excluding this subsection) shall not be considered to have been brought to the attention of such creditor until such notice is received by such person or such subdivision.

"(2) A monetary penalty may not be imposed on a creditor for a violation of a stay in effect under section 362(a) (including a monetary penalty imposed under section 362(k)) or for failure to comply with section 542 or 543 unless the conduct that is the basis of such violation or of such failure occurs after such creditor receives notice effective under this section of the order for relief.".

(b) DEBTOR'S DUTIES.—Section 521 of title 11, United States Code, as amended by sections 106, 225, and 305, is amended—

(1) in subsection (a), as so designated by section 106, by amending paragraph (1) to read as follows:

"(1) file—

"(A) a list of creditors; and

"(B) unless the court orders otherwise—

"(i) a schedule of assets and liabilities;

"(ii) a schedule of current income and current expenditures;

"(iii) a statement of the debtor's financial affairs and, if section 342(b) applies, a certificate—

"(I) of an attorney whose name is indicated on the petition as the attorney for the debtor, or a bankruptcy petition preparer signing the petition under section 110(b)(1), indicating that such attorney or the bankruptcy petition preparer delivered to the debtor the notice required by section 342(b); or

"(II) if no attorney is so indicated, and no bankruptcy petition preparer signed the petition, of the debtor that such notice was received and read by the debtor;

"(iv) copies of all payment advices or other evidence of payment received within 60 days before the date of the filing of the petition, by the debtor from any employer of the debtor;

"(v) a statement of the amount of monthly net income, itemized to show how the amount is calculated; and

"(vi) a statement disclosing any reasonably anticipated increase in income or expenditures over the 12-month period following the date of the filing of the petition;"; and

(2) by adding at the end the following:

"(e)(1) If the debtor in a case under chapter 7 or 13 is an individual and if a creditor files with the court at any time a request to receive a copy of the petition, schedules, and statement of financial affairs filed by the debtor, then the court shall make such petition, such schedules, and such statement available to such creditor.

"(2)(A) The debtor shall provide—

"(i) not later than 7 days before the date first set for the first meeting of creditors, to the trustee a copy of the Federal income tax return required under applicable law (or at the election of the debtor, a transcript of such return) for the most recent tax year ending immediately before the commencement of the case and for which a Federal income tax return was filed; and

"(ii) at the same time the debtor complies with clause (i), a copy of such return (or if elected under clause (i), such transcript) to any creditor that timely requests such copy.

"(B) If the debtor fails to comply with clause (i) or (ii) of subparagraph (A), the court shall dismiss the case unless the debtor demonstrates that the failure to so comply is due to circumstances beyond the control of the debtor.

"(C) If a creditor requests a copy of such tax return or such transcript and if the debtor fails to provide a copy of such tax return or such transcript to such creditor at the time the debtor provides such tax return or such transcript to the trustee, then the court shall dismiss the case unless the debtor demonstrates that the failure to provide a copy of such tax return or such transcript is due to circumstances beyond the control of the debtor.

"(3) If a creditor in a case under chapter 13 files with the court at any time a request to receive a copy of the plan filed by the debtor, then the court shall make available to such creditor a copy of the plan—

"(A) at a reasonable cost; and

"(B) not later than 5 days after such request is filed.

"(f) At the request of the court, the United States trustee, or any party in interest in a case under chapter 7, 11, or 13, a debtor who is an individual shall file with the court—

"(1) at the same time filed with the taxing authority, a copy of each Federal income tax return required under applicable law (or at the election of the debtor, a transcript of such tax return) with respect to each tax year of the debtor ending while the case is pending under such chapter;

"(2) at the same time filed with the taxing authority, each Federal income tax return required under applicable law (or at the election of the debtor, a transcript of such tax return) that had not been filed with such authority as of the date of the commencement of the case and that was subsequently filed for any tax year of the debtor ending in the 3-year period ending on the date of the commencement of the case;

"(3) a copy of each amendment to any Federal income tax return or transcript filed with the court under paragraph (1) or (2); and

"(4) in a case under chapter 13—

"(A) on the date that is either 90 days after the end of such tax year or 1 year after the date of the commencement of the case, whichever is later, if a plan is not confirmed before such later date; and

"(B) annually after the plan is confirmed and until the case is closed, not later than the date that is 45 days before the anniversary of the confirmation of the plan;

a statement, under penalty of perjury, of the income and expenditures of the debtor during the tax year of the debtor most recently concluded before such statement is filed under this paragraph, and of the monthly income of the debtor, that shows how income, expenditures, and monthly income are calculated.

"(g)(1) A statement referred to in subsection (f)(4) shall disclose—

"(A) the amount and sources of the income of the debtor;

"(B) the identity of any person responsible with the debtor for the support of any dependent of the debtor; and

"(C) the identity of any person who contributed, and the amount contributed, to the household in which the debtor resides.

"(2) The tax returns, amendments, and statement of income and expenditures described in subsections (e)(2)(A) and (f) shall be available to the United States trustee (or the bankruptcy administrator, if any), the trustee, and any party in interest for inspection and copying, subject to the requirements of section 315(c) of the Bankruptcy Abuse Prevention and Consumer Protection Act of 2005.

"(h) If requested by the United States trustee or by the trustee, the debtor shall provide—

"(1) a document that establishes the identity of the debtor, including a driver's license, passport, or other document that contains a photograph of the debtor; or

"(2) such other personal identifying information relating to the debtor that establishes the identity of the debtor.".

(c)(1) Not later than 180 days after the date of the enactment of this Act, the Director of the Administrative Office of the United States Courts shall establish procedures for safeguarding the confidentiality of any tax information required to be provided under this section.

(2) The procedures under paragraph (1) shall include restrictions on creditor access to tax information that is required to be provided under this section.

(3) Not later than 540 days after the date of enactment of this Act, the Director of the Administrative Office of the United States Courts shall prepare and submit to the President pro tempore of the Senate and the Speaker of the House of Representatives a report that—

(A) assesses the effectiveness of the procedures established under paragraph (1); and

(B) if appropriate, includes proposed legislation to—

(i) further protect the confidentiality of tax information; and

(ii) provide penalties for the improper use by any person of the tax information required to be provided under this section.

SEC. 316. DISMISSAL FOR FAILURE TO TIMELY FILE SCHEDULES OR PROVIDE REQUIRED INFORMATION.

Section 521 of title 11, United States Code, as amended by sections 106, 225, 305, and 315, is amended by adding at the end the following:

"(i)(1) Subject to paragraphs (2) and (4) and notwithstanding section 707(a), if an individual debtor in a voluntary case under chapter 7 or 13 fails to file all of the information required under subsection (a)(1) within 45 days after the date of the filing of the petition, the case shall be automatically dismissed effective on the 46th day after the date of the filing of the petition.

"(2) Subject to paragraph (4) and with respect to a case described in paragraph (1), any party in interest may request the court to enter an order dismissing the case. If requested, the court shall enter an order of dismissal not later than 5 days after such request.

"(3) Subject to paragraph (4) and upon request of the debtor made within 45 days after the date of the filing of the petition described in paragraph (1), the court may allow the debtor an additional period of not to exceed 45 days to file the information required under subsection (a)(1) if the court finds justification for extending the period for the filing.

"(4) Notwithstanding any other provision of this subsection, on the motion of the trustee filed before the expiration of the applicable period of time specified in paragraph (1), (2), or (3), and after notice and a hearing, the court may decline to dismiss the case if the court finds that the debtor attempted in good faith to file all the information required by subsection (a)(1)(B)(iv) and that the best interests of creditors would be served by administration of the case.".

SEC. 317. ADEQUATE TIME TO PREPARE FOR HEARING ON CONFIRMATION OF THE PLAN.

Section 1324 of title 11, United States Code, is amended—

(1) by striking "After" and inserting the following:

"(a) Except as provided in subsection (b) and after"; and

(2) by adding at the end the following:

"(b) The hearing on confirmation of the plan may be held not earlier than 20 days and not later than 45 days after the date of the meeting of creditors under section 341(a), unless the court determines that it would be in the best interests of the creditors and the estate to hold such hearing at an earlier date and there is no objection to such earlier date.".

SEC. 318. CHAPTER 13 PLANS TO HAVE A 5-YEAR DURATION IN CERTAIN CASES.

Title 11, United States Code, is amended—

(1) by amending section 1322(d) to read as follows:

"(d)(1) If the current monthly income of the debtor and the debtor's spouse combined, when multiplied by 12, is not less than—

"(A) in the case of a debtor in a household of 1 person, the median family income of the applicable State for 1 earner;

"(B) in the case of a debtor in a household of 2, 3, or 4 individuals, the highest median family income of the applicable State for a family of the same number or fewer individuals; or

"(C) in the case of a debtor in a household exceeding 4 individuals, the highest median family income of the applicable State for a family of 4 or fewer individuals, plus $525 per month for each individual in excess of 4, the plan may not provide for payments over a period that is longer than 5 years.

"(2) If the current monthly income of the debtor and the debtor's spouse combined, when multiplied by 12, is less than—

"(A) in the case of a debtor in a household of 1 person, the median family income of the applicable State for 1 earner;

"(B) in the case of a debtor in a household of 2, 3, or 4 individuals, the highest median family income of the applicable State for a family of the same number or fewer individuals; or

"(C) in the case of a debtor in a household exceeding 4 individuals, the highest median family income of the applicable State for a family of 4 or fewer individuals, plus $525 per month for each individual in excess of 4,

the plan may not provide for payments over a period that is longer than 3 years, unless the court, for cause, approves a longer period, but the court may not approve a period that is longer than 5 years.";

(2) in section 1325(b)(1)(B), by striking "three-year period" and inserting "applicable commitment period"; and

(3) in section 1325(b), as amended by section 102, by adding at the end the following:

"(4) For purposes of this subsection, the 'applicable commitment period'—

"(A) subject to subparagraph (B), shall be—

"(i) 3 years; or

"(ii) not less than 5 years, if the current monthly income of the debtor and the debtor's spouse combined, when multiplied by 12, is not less than—

"(I) in the case of a debtor in a household of 1 person, the median family income of the applicable State for 1 earner;

"(II) in the case of a debtor in a household of 2, 3, or 4 individuals, the highest median family income of the applicable State for a family of the same number or fewer individuals; or

"(III) in the case of a debtor in a household exceeding 4 individuals, the highest median family income of the applicable State for a family of 4 or fewer individuals, plus $525 per month for each individual in excess of 4; and

"(B) may be less than 3 or 5 years, whichever is applicable under subparagraph (A), but only if the plan provides for payment in full of all allowed unsecured claims over a shorter period."; and

(4) in section 1329(c), by striking "three years" and inserting "the applicable commitment period under section 1325(b)(1)(B)".

SEC. 319. SENSE OF CONGRESS REGARDING EXPANSION OF RULE 9011 OF THE FEDERAL RULES OF BANKRUPTCY PROCEDURE.

It is the sense of Congress that rule 9011 of the Federal Rules of Bankruptcy Procedure (11 U.S.C. App.) should be modified to include a requirement that all documents (including schedules), signed and unsigned, submitted to the court or to a trustee by debtors who represent themselves and debtors who are represented by attorneys be submitted only after the debtors or the debtors' attorneys have made reasonable inquiry to verify that the information contained in such documents is—

(1) well grounded in fact; and

(2) warranted by existing law or a good faith argument for the extension, modification, or reversal of existing law.

SEC. 320. PROMPT RELIEF FROM STAY IN INDIVIDUAL CASES.

Section 362(e) of title 11, United States Code, is amended—

(1) by inserting "(1)" after "(e)"; and

(2) by adding at the end the following:

"(2) Notwithstanding paragraph (1), in a case under chapter 7, 11, or 13 in which the debtor is an individual, the stay under subsection (a) shall terminate on the date that is 60 days after a request is made by a party in interest under subsection (d), unless—

"(A) a final decision is rendered by the court during the 60-day period beginning on the date of the request; or

"(B) such 60-day period is extended—

"(i) by agreement of all parties in interest; or

"(ii) by the court for such specific period of time as the court finds is required for good cause, as described in findings made by the court.".

SEC. 321. CHAPTER 11 CASES FILED BY INDIVIDUALS.

(a) PROPERTY OF THE ESTATE.—

(1) IN GENERAL.—Subchapter I of chapter 11 of title 11, United States Code, is amended by adding at the end the following:

"§ 1115. Property of the estate

"(a) In a case in which the debtor is an individual, property of the estate includes, in addition to the property specified in section 541—

"(1) all property of the kind specified in section 541 that the debtor acquires after the commencement of the case but before the case is closed, dismissed, or converted to a case under chapter 7, 12, or 13, whichever occurs first; and

"(2) earnings from services performed by the debtor after the commencement of the case but before the case is closed, dismissed, or converted to a case under chapter 7, 12, or 13, whichever occurs first.

"(b) Except as provided in section 1104 or a confirmed plan or order confirming a plan, the debtor shall remain in possession of all property of the estate.".

(2) CLERICAL AMENDMENT.—The table of sections for subchapter I of chapter 11 of title 11, United States Code, is amended by adding at the end the following:

"1115. Property of the estate.".

(b) CONTENTS OF PLAN.—Section 1123(a) of title 11, United States Code, is amended—

(1) in paragraph (6), by striking "and" at the end;

(2) in paragraph (7), by striking the period and inserting "; and"; and

(3) by adding at the end the following:

"(8) in a case in which the debtor is an individual, provide for the payment to creditors under the plan of all or such portion of earnings from personal services performed by the debtor after the commencement of the case or other future income of the debtor as is necessary for the execution of the plan.".

(c) CONFIRMATION OF PLAN.—

(1) REQUIREMENTS RELATING TO VALUE OF PROPERTY.—Section 1129(a) of title 11, United States Code, as amended by section 213, is amended by adding at the end the following:

"(15) In a case in which the debtor is an individual and in which the holder of an allowed unsecured claim objects to the confirmation of the plan—

"(A) the value, as of the effective date of the plan, of the property to be distributed under the plan on account of such claim is not less than the amount of such claim; or

"(B) the value of the property to be distributed under the plan is not less than the projected disposable income of the debtor (as defined in section 1325(b)(2)) to be received during the 5-year period beginning on the date that the first payment is due under the plan, or during the period for which the plan provides payments, whichever is longer.".

(2) REQUIREMENT RELATING TO INTERESTS IN PROPERTY.—Section 1129(b)(2)(B)(ii) of title 11, United States Code, is amended by inserting before the period at the end the following:

", except that in a case in which the debtor is an individual, the debtor may retain property included in the estate under section 1115, subject to the requirements of subsection (a)(14) of this section".

(d) EFFECT OF CONFIRMATION.—Section 1141(d) of title 11, United States Code, is amended—

(1) in paragraph (2), by striking "The confirmation of a plan does not discharge an individual debtor" and inserting "A discharge under this chapter does not discharge a debtor who is an individual"; and

(2) by adding at the end the following:

"(5) In a case in which the debtor is an individual—

"(A) unless after notice and a hearing the court orders otherwise for cause, confirmation of the plan does not discharge any debt provided for in the plan until the court grants a discharge on completion of all payments under the plan;

"(B) at any time after the confirmation of the plan, and after notice and a hearing, the court may grant a discharge to the debtor who has not completed payments under the plan if—

"(i) the value, as of the effective date of the plan, of property actually distributed under the plan on account of each allowed unsecured claim is not less than the amount that would have been paid on such claim if the estate of the debtor had been liquidated under chapter 7 on such date; and

"(ii) modification of the plan under section 1127 is not practicable; and".

(e) MODIFICATION OF PLAN.—Section 1127 of title 11, United States Code, is amended by adding at the end the following:

"(e) If the debtor is an individual, the plan may be modified at any time after confirmation of the plan but before the completion of payments under the plan, whether or not the plan has been substantially consummated, upon request of the debtor, the trustee, the United States trustee, or the holder of an allowed unsecured claim, to—

"(1) increase or reduce the amount of payments on claims of a particular class provided for by the plan;

"(2) extend or reduce the time period for such payments; or

"(3) alter the amount of the distribution to a creditor whose claim is provided for by the plan to the extent necessary to take account of any payment of such claim made other than under the plan.

"(f)(1) Sections 1121 through 1128 and the requirements of section 1129 apply to any modification under subsection (a).

"(2) The plan, as modified, shall become the plan only after there has been disclosure under section 1125 as the court may direct, notice and a hearing, and such modification is approved.".

SEC. 322. LIMITATIONS ON HOMESTEAD EXEMPTION.

(a) EXEMPTIONS.—Section 522 of title 11, United States Code, as amended by sections 224 and 308, is amended by adding at the end the following:

"(p)(1) Except as provided in paragraph (2) of this subsection and sections 544 and 548, as a result of electing under subsection (b)(3)(A) to exempt property under State or local law, a debtor may not exempt any amount of interest that was acquired by the debtor during the 1215-day period preceding the date of the filing of the petition that exceeds in the aggregate $125,000 in value in—

"(A) real or personal property that the debtor or a dependent of the debtor uses as a residence;

"(B) a cooperative that owns property that the debtor or a dependent of the debtor uses as a residence;

"(C) a burial plot for the debtor or a dependent of the debtor; or

"(D) real or personal property that the debtor or dependent of the debtor claims as a homestead.

"(2)(A) The limitation under paragraph (1) shall not apply to an exemption claimed under subsection (b)(3)(A) by a family farmer for the principal residence of such farmer.

"(B) For purposes of paragraph (1), any amount of such interest does not include any interest transferred from a debtor's previous principal residence (which was acquired prior to the beginning of such 1215-day period) into the debtor's current principal residence, if the debtor's previous and current residences are located in the same State.

"(q)(1) As a result of electing under subsection (b)(3)(A) to exempt property under State or local law, a debtor may not exempt any amount of an interest in property described in subparagraphs (A), (B), (C), and (D) of subsection (p)(1) which exceeds in the aggregate $125,000 if—

"(A) the court determines, after notice and a hearing, that the debtor has been convicted of a felony (as defined in section 3156 of title 18), which under the circumstances, demonstrates that the filing of the case was an abuse of the provisions of this title; or

"(B) the debtor owes a debt arising from—

"(i) any violation of the Federal securities laws (as defined in section 3(a)(47) of the Securities Exchange Act of 1934), any State securities laws, or any regulation or order issued under Federal securities laws or State securities laws;

"(ii) fraud, deceit, or manipulation in a fiduciary capacity or in connection with the purchase or sale of any security registered under section 12 or 15(d) of the Securities Exchange Act of 1934 or under section 6 of the Securities Act of 1933;

"(iii) any civil remedy under section 1964 of title 18; or

"(iv) any criminal act, intentional tort, or willful or reckless misconduct that caused serious physical injury or death to another individual in the preceding 5 years.

"(2) Paragraph (1) shall not apply to the extent the amount of an interest in property described in subparagraphs (A), (B), (C), and (D) of subsection (p)(1) is reasonably necessary for the support of the debtor and any dependent of the debtor.".

(b) ADJUSTMENT OF DOLLAR AMOUNTS.—Paragraphs (1) and (2) of section 104(b) of title 11, United States Code, as amended by section 224, are amended by inserting "522(p), 522(q)," after "522(n),".

SEC. 323. EXCLUDING EMPLOYEE BENEFIT PLAN PARTICIPANT CONTRIBUTIONS AND OTHER PROPERTY FROM THE ESTATE.

Section 541(b) of title 11, United States Code, as amended by section 225, is amended by adding after paragraph (6), as added by section 225(a)(1)(C), the following:

"(7) any amount—

"(A) withheld by an employer from the wages of employees for payment as contributions—

"(i) to—

"(I) an employee benefit plan that is subject to title I of the Employee Retirement Income Security Act of 1974 or under an employee benefit plan which is a governmental plan under section 414(d) of the Internal Revenue Code of 1986;

"(II) a deferred compensation plan under section 457 of the Internal Revenue Code of 1986; or

"(III) a tax-deferred annuity under section 403(b) of the Internal Revenue Code of 1986; except that such amount under this subparagraph shall not constitute disposable income as defined in section 1325(b)(2); or

"(ii) to a health insurance plan regulated by State law whether or not subject to such title; or

"(B) received by an employer from employees for payment as contributions—

"(i) to—

"(I) an employee benefit plan that is subject to title I of the Employee Retirement Income Security Act of 1974 or under an employee benefit plan which is a governmental plan under section 414(d) of the Internal Revenue Code of 1986;

"(II) a deferred compensation plan under section 457 of the Internal Revenue Code of 1986; or

"(III) a tax-deferred annuity under section 403(b) of the Internal Revenue Code of 1986; except that such amount under this subparagraph shall not constitute disposable income, as defined in section 1325(b)(2); or

"(ii) to a health insurance plan regulated by State law whether or not subject to such title;".

SEC. 324. EXCLUSIVE JURISDICTION IN MATTERS INVOLVING BANKRUPTCY PROFESSIONALS.

(a) IN GENERAL.—Section 1334 of title 28, United States Code, is amended—

(1) in subsection (b), by striking "Notwithstanding" and inserting "Except as provided in subsection (e)(2), and notwithstanding"; and

(2) by striking subsection (e) and inserting the following:

"(e) The district court in which a case under title 11 is commenced or is pending shall have exclusive jurisdiction—

"(1) of all the property, wherever located, of the debtor as of the commencement of such case, and of property of the estate; and

"(2) over all claims or causes of action that involve construction of section 327 of title 11, United States Code, or rules relating to disclosure requirements under section 327.".

(b) APPLICABILITY.—This section shall only apply to cases filed after the date of enactment of this Act.

SEC. 325. UNITED STATES TRUSTEE PROGRAM FILING FEE INCREASE.

(a) ACTIONS UNDER CHAPTER 7, 11, OR 13 OF TITLE 11, UNITED STATES CODE.—Section 1930(a) of title 28, United States Code, is amended—
(1) by striking paragraph (1) and inserting the following:
"(1) For a case commenced under—
"(A) chapter 7 of title 11, $200; and
"(B) chapter 13 of title 11, $150."; and
(2) in paragraph (3), by striking "$800" and inserting "$1000".

(b) UNITED STATES TRUSTEE SYSTEM FUND.—Section 589a(b) of title 28, United States Code, is amended—
(1) by striking paragraph (1) and inserting the following:
"(1)(A) 40.63 percent of the fees collected under section 1930(a)(1)(A) of this title; and
"(B) 70.00 percent of the fees collected under section 1930(a)(1)(B);";
(2) in paragraph (2), by striking "one-half" and inserting "75 percent"; and
(3) in paragraph (4), by striking "one-half" and inserting "100 percent".

(c) COLLECTION AND DEPOSIT OF MISCELLANEOUS BANKRUPTCY FEES.—Section 406(b) of the Judiciary Appropriations Act, 1990 (28 U.S.C. 1931 note) is amended by striking "pursuant to 28 U.S.C. section 1930(b)" and all that follows through "28 U.S.C. section 1931" and inserting "under section 1930(b) of title 28, United States Code, 31.25 of the fees collected under section 1930(a)(1)(A) of that title, 30.00 percent of the fees collected under section 1930(a)(1)(B) of that title, and 25 percent of the fees collected under section 1930(a)(3) of that title shall be deposited as offsetting receipts to the fund established under section 1931 of that title".

(d) SUNSET DATE.—The amendments made by subsections (b) and (c) shall be effective during the 2-year period beginning on the date of enactment of this Act.

(e) USE OF INCREASED RECEIPTS.—
(1) JUDGES' SALARIES AND BENEFITS.—The amount of fees collected under paragraphs (1) and (3) of section 1930(a) of title 28, United States Code, during the 5-year period beginning on the date of enactment of this Act, that is greater than the amount that would have been collected if the amendments made by subsection (a) had not taken effect shall be used, to the extent necessary, to pay the salaries and benefits of the judges appointed pursuant to section 1223 of this Act.
(2) REMAINDER.—Any amount described in paragraph (1), which is not used for the purpose described in paragraph (1), shall be deposited into the Treasury of the United States to the extent necessary to offset the decrease in governmental receipts resulting from the amendments made by subsections (b) and (c).

SEC. 326. SHARING OF COMPENSATION.

Section 504 of title 11, United States Code, is amended by adding at the end the following:

"(c) This section shall not apply with respect to sharing, or agreeing to share, compensation with a bona fide public service attorney referral program that operates in accordance with non-Federal law regulating attorney referral services and with rules of professional responsibility applicable to attorney acceptance of referrals.".

SEC. 327. FAIR VALUATION OF COLLATERAL.

Section 506(a) of title 11, United States Code, is amended by—
(1) inserting "(1)" after "(a)"; and
(2) by adding at the end the following:
"(2) If the debtor is an individual in a case under chapter 7 or 13, such value with respect to personal property securing an allowed claim shall be determined based on the

replacement value of such property as of the date of the filing of the petition without deduction for costs of sale or marketing. With respect to property acquired for personal, family, or household purposes, replacement value shall mean the price a retail merchant would charge for property of that kind considering the age and condition of the property at the time value is determined.''.

SEC. 328. DEFAULTS BASED ON NONMONETARY OBLIGATIONS.

(a) EXECUTORY CONTRACTS AND UNEXPIRED LEASES.—Section 365 of title 11, United States Code, is amended—

(1) in subsection (b)—

(A) in paragraph (1)(A), by striking the semicolon at the end and inserting the following: ''other than a default that is a breach of a provision relating to the satisfaction of any provision (other than a penalty rate or penalty provision) relating to a default arising from any failure to perform nonmonetary obligations under an unexpired lease of real property, if it is impossible for the trustee to cure such default by performing nonmonetary acts at and after the time of assumption, except that if such default arises from a failure to operate in accordance with a nonresidential real property lease, then such default shall be cured by performance at and after the time of assumption in accordance with such lease, and pecuniary losses resulting from such default shall be compensated in accordance with the provisions of this paragraph;''; and

(B) in paragraph (2)(D), by striking ''penalty rate or provision'' and inserting ''penalty rate or penalty provision'';

(2) in subsection (c)—

(A) in paragraph (2), by inserting ''or'' at the end;

(B) in paragraph (3), by striking ''; or'' at the end and inserting a period; and

(C) by striking paragraph (4);

(3) in subsection (d)—

(A) by striking paragraphs (5) through (9); and

(B) by redesignating paragraph (10) as paragraph (5); and

(4) in subsection (f)(1) by striking ''; except that'' and all that follows through the end of the paragraph and inserting a period.

(b) IMPAIRMENT OF CLAIMS OR INTERESTS.—Section 1124(2) of title 11, United States Code, is amended—

(1) in subparagraph (A), by inserting ''or of a kind that section 365(b)(2) expressly does not require to be cured'' before the semicolon at the end;

(2) in subparagraph (C), by striking ''and'' at the end;

(3) by redesignating subparagraph (D) as subparagraph (E); and

(4) by inserting after subparagraph (C) the following:

''(D) if such claim or such interest arises from any failure to perform a nonmonetary obligation, other than a default arising from failure to operate a nonresidential real property lease subject to section 365(b)(1)(A), compensates the holder of such claim or such interest (other than the debtor or an insider) for any actual pecuniary loss incurred by such holder as a result of such failure; and''.

SEC. 329. CLARIFICATION OF POSTPETITION WAGES AND BENEFITS.

Section 503(b)(1)(A) of title 11, United States Code, is amended to read as follows:

''(A) the actual, necessary costs and expenses of preserving the estate including—

''(i) wages, salaries, and commissions for services rendered after the commencement of the case; and

''(ii) wages and benefits awarded pursuant to a judicial proceeding or a proceeding of the National Labor Relations Board as back pay attributable to any period of time occurring after commencement of the case under this title, as a result of a violation of Federal or State law by the debtor, without regard to the time of the occurrence of unlawful conduct on which such award is based or to whether any services were rendered, if the court determines that payment of wages and benefits by reason of the operation of this clause will not substantially increase the probability of layoff or termination of current employees, or of nonpayment of domestic support obligations, during the case under this title;''.

SEC. 330. DELAY OF DISCHARGE DURING PENDENCY OF CERTAIN PROCEEDINGS.

(a) CHAPTER 7.—Section 727(a) of title 11, United States Code, as amended by section 106, is amended—

(1) in paragraph (10), by striking ''or'' at the end;

(2) in paragraph (11) by striking the period at the end and inserting ''; or''; and

(3) by inserting after paragraph (11) the following:

''(12) the court after notice and a hearing held not more than 10 days before the date of the entry of the order granting the discharge finds that there is reasonable cause to believe that—

''(A) section 522(q)(1) may be applicable to the debtor; and

''(B) there is pending any proceeding in which the debtor may be found guilty of a felony of the kind described in section 522(q)(1)(A) or liable for a debt of the kind described in section 522(q)(1)(B).''.

(b) CHAPTER 11.—Section 1141(d) of title 11, United States Code, as amended by section 321, is amended by adding at the end the following:

''(C) unless after notice and a hearing held not more than 10 days before the date of the entry of the order granting the discharge, the court finds that there is no reasonable cause to believe that—

''(i) section 522(q)(1) may be applicable to the debtor; and

''(ii) there is pending any proceeding in which the debtor may be found guilty of a felony of the kind described in section 522(q)(1)(A) or liable for a debt of the kind described in section 522(q)(1)(B).''.

(c) CHAPTER 12.—Section 1228 of title 11, United States Code, is amended—

(1) in subsection (a) by striking ''As'' and inserting ''Subject to subsection (d), as'',

(2) in subsection (b) by striking ''At'' and inserting ''Subject to subsection (d), at'', and

(3) by adding at the end the following:

''(f) The court may not grant a discharge under this chapter unless the court after notice and a hearing held not more than 10 days before the date of the entry of the order granting the discharge finds that there is no reasonable cause to believe that—

''(1) section 522(q)(1) may be applicable to the debtor; and

''(2) there is pending any proceeding in which the debtor may be found guilty of a felony of the kind described in section 522(q)(1)(A) or liable for a debt of the kind described in section 522(q)(1)(B).''.

(d) CHAPTER 13.—Section 1328 of title 11, United States Code, as amended by section 106, is amended—

(1) in subsection (a) by striking ''As'' and inserting ''Subject to subsection (d), as'',

(2) in subsection (b) by striking ''At'' and inserting ''Subject to subsection (d), at'', and

(3) by adding at the end the following:

''(h) The court may not grant a discharge under this chapter unless the court after notice and a hearing held not more than 10 days before the date of the entry of the order granting the discharge finds that there is no reasonable cause to believe that—

''(1) section 522(q)(1) may be applicable to the debtor; and

''(2) there is pending any proceeding in which the debtor may be found guilty of a felony of the kind described in section 522(q)(1)(A) or liable for a debt of the kind described in section 522(q)(1)(B).''.

SEC. 331. LIMITATION ON RETENTION BONUSES, SEVERANCE PAY, AND CERTAIN OTHER PAYMENTS.

Section 503 of title 11, United States Code, is amended by adding at the end the following:

"(c) Notwithstanding subsection (b), there shall neither be allowed, nor paid—

"(1) a transfer made to, or an obligation incurred for the benefit of, an insider of the debtor for the purpose of inducing such person to remain with the debtor's business, absent a finding by the court based on evidence in the record that—

"(A) the transfer or obligation is essential to retention of the person because the individual has a bona fide job offer from another business at the same or greater rate of compensation;

"(B) the services provided by the person are essential to the survival of the business; and

"(C) either—

"(i) the amount of the transfer made to, or obligation incurred for the benefit of, the person is not greater than an amount equal to 10 times the amount of the mean transfer or obligation of a similar kind given to nonmanagement employees for any purpose during the calendar year in which the transfer is made or the obligation is incurred; or

"(ii) if no such similar transfers were made to, or obligations were incurred for the benefit of, such nonmanagement employees during such calendar year, the amount of the transfer or obligation is not greater than an amount equal to 25 percent of the amount of any similar transfer or obligation made to or incurred for the benefit of such insider for any purpose during the calendar year before the year in which such transfer is made or obligation is incurred;

"(2) a severance payment to an insider of the debtor, unless—

"(A) the payment is part of a program that is generally applicable to all full-time employees; and

"(B) the amount of the payment is not greater than 10 times the amount of the mean severance pay given to nonmanagement employees during the calendar year in which the payment is made; or

"(3) other transfers or obligations that are outside the ordinary course of business and not justified by the facts and circumstances of the case, including transfers made to, or obligations incurred for the benefit of, officers, managers, or consultants hired after the date of the filing of the petition.".

SEC. 332. FRAUDULENT INVOLUNTARY BANKRUPTCY.

(a) SHORT TITLE.—This section may be cited as the "Involuntary Bankruptcy Improvement Act of 2005".

(b) INVOLUNTARY CASES.—Section 303 of title 11, United States Code, is amended by adding at the end the following:

"(*l*)(1) If—

"(A) the petition under this section is false or contains any materially false, fictitious, or fraudulent statement;

"(B) the debtor is an individual; and

"(C) the court dismisses such petition, the court, upon the motion of the debtor, shall seal all the records of the court relating to such petition, and all references to such petition.

"(2) If the debtor is an individual and the court dismisses a petition under this section, the court may enter an order prohibiting all consumer reporting agencies (as defined in section 603(f) of the Fair Credit Reporting Act (15 U.S.C. 1681a(f))) from making any consumer report (as defined in section 603(d) of that Act) that contains any information relating to such petition or to the case commenced by the filing of such petition.

"(3) Upon the expiration of the statute of limitations described in section 3282 of title 18, for a violation of section 152 or 157 of such title, the court, upon the motion of the debtor and for good cause, may expunge any records relating to a petition filed under this section.''.

(c) BANKRUPTCY FRAUD.—Section 157 of title 18, United States Code, is amended by inserting '', including a fraudulent involuntary bankruptcy petition under section 303 of such title'' after ''title 11''.

TITLE IV—GENERAL AND SMALL BUSINESS BANKRUPTCY PROVISIONS

Subtitle A—General Business Bankruptcy Provisions

SEC. 401. ADEQUATE PROTECTION FOR INVESTORS.

(a) DEFINITION.—Section 101 of title 11, United States Code, is amended by inserting after paragraph (48) the following:

''(48A) 'securities self regulatory organization' means either a securities association registered with the Securities and Exchange Commission under section 15A of the Securities Exchange Act of 1934 or a national securities exchange registered with the Securities and Exchange Commission under section 6 of the Securities Exchange Act of 1934;''.

(b) AUTOMATIC STAY.—Section 362(b) of title 11, United States Code, as amended by sections 224, 303, and 311, is amended by inserting after paragraph (24) the following:

''(25) under subsection (a), of—

''(A) the commencement or continuation of an investigation or action by a securities self regulatory organization to enforce such organization's regulatory power;

''(B) the enforcement of an order or decision, other than for monetary sanctions, obtained in an action by such securities self regulatory organization to enforce such organization's regulatory power; or

''(C) any act taken by such securities self regulatory organization to delist, delete, or refuse to permit quotation of any stock that does not meet applicable regulatory requirements;''.

SEC. 402. MEETINGS OF CREDITORS AND EQUITY SECURITY HOLDERS.

Section 341 of title 11, United States Code, is amended by adding at the end the following:

''(e) Notwithstanding subsections (a) and (b), the court, on the request of a party in interest and after notice and a hearing, for cause may order that the United States trustee not convene a meeting of creditors or equity security holders if the debtor has filed a plan as to which the debtor solicited acceptances prior to the commencement of the case.''.

SEC. 403. PROTECTION OF REFINANCE OF SECURITY INTEREST.

Subparagraphs (A), (B), and (C) of section 547(e)(2) of title 11, United States Code, are each amended by striking ''10'' each place it appears and inserting ''30''.

SEC. 404. EXECUTORY CONTRACTS AND UNEXPIRED LEASES.

(a) IN GENERAL.—Section 365(d)(4) of title 11, United States Code, is amended to read as follows:

''(4)(A) Subject to subparagraph (B), an unexpired lease of nonresidential real property under which the debtor is the lessee shall be deemed rejected, and the trustee shall immediately surrender that nonresidential real property to the lessor, if the trustee does not assume or reject the unexpired lease by the earlier of—

"(i) the date that is 120 days after the date of the order for relief; or

"(ii) the date of the entry of an order confirming a plan.

"(B)(i) The court may extend the period determined under subparagraph (A), prior to the expiration of the 120-day period, for 90 days on the motion of the trustee or lessor for cause.

"(ii) If the court grants an extension under clause (i), the court may grant a subsequent extension only upon prior written consent of the lessor in each instance.".

(b) EXCEPTION.—Section 365(f)(1) of title 11, United States Code, is amended by striking "subsection" the first place it appears and inserting "subsections (b) and".

SEC. 405. CREDITORS AND EQUITY SECURITY HOLDERS COMMITTEES.

(a) APPOINTMENT.—Section 1102(a) of title 11, United States Code, is amended by adding at the end the following:

"(4) On request of a party in interest and after notice and a hearing, the court may order the United States trustee to change the membership of a committee appointed under this subsection, if the court determines that the change is necessary to ensure adequate representation of creditors or equity security holders. The court may order the United States trustee to increase the number of members of a committee to include a creditor that is a small business concern (as described in section 3(a)(1) of the Small Business Act), if the court determines that the creditor holds claims (of the kind represented by the committee) the aggregate amount of which, in comparison to the annual gross revenue of that creditor, is disproportionately large.".

(b) INFORMATION.—Section 1102(b) of title 11, United States Code, is amended by adding at the end the following:

"(3) A committee appointed under subsection (a) shall—

"(A) provide access to information for creditors who—

"(i) hold claims of the kind represented by that committee; and

"(ii) are not appointed to the committee;

"(B) solicit and receive comments from the creditors described in subparagraph (A); and

"(C) be subject to a court order that compels any additional report or disclosure to be made to the creditors described in subparagraph (A).".

SEC. 406. AMENDMENT TO SECTION 546 OF TITLE 11, UNITED STATES CODE.

Section 546 of title 11, United States Code, is amended—

(1) by redesignating the second subsection (g) (as added by section 222(a) of Public Law 103-394) as subsection (h);

(2) in subsection (h), as so redesignated, by inserting "and subject to the prior rights of holders of security interests in such goods or the proceeds of such goods" after "consent of a creditor"; and

(3) by adding at the end the following:

"(i)(1) Notwithstanding paragraphs (2) and (3) of section 545, the trustee may not avoid a warehouseman's lien for storage, transportation, or other costs incidental to the storage and handling of goods.

"(2) The prohibition under paragraph (1) shall be applied in a manner consistent with any State statute applicable to such lien that is similar to section 7-209 of the Uniform Commercial Code, as in effect on the date of enactment of the Bankruptcy Abuse Prevention and Consumer Protection Act of 2005, or any successor to such section 7-209.".

SEC. 407. AMENDMENTS TO SECTION 330(a) OF TITLE 11, UNITED STATES CODE.

Section 330(a) of title 11, United States Code, is amended—

(1) in paragraph (3)—

(A) by striking "(A) In" and inserting "In"; and

(B) by inserting "to an examiner, trustee under chapter 11, or professional person" after "awarded"; and

(2) by adding at the end the following:

"(7) In determining the amount of reasonable compensation to be awarded to a trustee, the court shall treat such compensation as a commission, based on section 326.".

SEC. 408. POSTPETITION DISCLOSURE AND SOLICITATION.

Section 1125 of title 11, United States Code, is amended by adding at the end the following:

"(g) Notwithstanding subsection (b), an acceptance or rejection of the plan may be solicited from a holder of a claim or interest if such solicitation complies with applicable nonbankruptcy law and if such holder was solicited before the commencement of the case in a manner complying with applicable nonbankruptcy law.".

SEC. 409. PREFERENCES.

Section 547(c) of title 11, United States Code, is amended—

(1) by striking paragraph (2) and inserting the following:

"(2) to the extent that such transfer was in payment of a debt incurred by the debtor in the ordinary course of business or financial affairs of the debtor and the transferee, and such transfer was—

"(A) made in the ordinary course of business or financial affairs of the debtor and the transferee; or

"(B) made according to ordinary business terms;";

(2) in paragraph (8), by striking the period at the end and inserting "; or"; and

(3) by adding at the end the following:

"(9) if, in a case filed by a debtor whose debts are not primarily consumer debts, the aggregate value of all property that constitutes or is affected by such transfer is less than $5,000.".

SEC. 410. VENUE OF CERTAIN PROCEEDINGS.

Section 1409(b) of title 28, United States Code, is amended by inserting ", or a debt (excluding a consumer debt) against a noninsider of less than $10,000," after "$5,000". Section 1409(b) of title 28, United States Code, is further amended by striking "$5,000" and inserting "$15,000".

SEC. 411. PERIOD FOR FILING PLAN UNDER CHAPTER 11.

Section 1121(d) of title 11, United States Code, is amended—

(1) by striking "On" and inserting "(1) Subject to paragraph (2), on"; and

(2) by adding at the end the following:

"(2)(A) The 120-day period specified in paragraph (1) may not be extended beyond a date that is 18 months after the date of the order for relief under this chapter.

"(B) The 180-day period specified in paragraph (1) may not be extended beyond a date that is 20 months after the date of the order for relief under this chapter.".

SEC. 412. FEES ARISING FROM CERTAIN OWNERSHIP INTERESTS.

Section 523(a)(16) of title 11, United States Code, is amended—
(1) by striking "dwelling" the first place it appears;
(2) by striking "ownership or" and inserting "ownership,";
(3) by striking "housing" the first place it appears; and
(4) by striking "but only" and all that follows through "such period," and inserting "or a lot in a homeowners association, for as long as the debtor or the trustee has a legal, equitable, or possessory ownership interest in such unit, such corporation, or such lot,".

SEC. 413. CREDITOR REPRESENTATION AT FIRST MEETING OF CREDITORS.

Section 341(c) of title 11, United States Code, is amended by inserting at the end the following: "Notwithstanding any local court rule, provision of a State constitution, any otherwise applicable nonbankruptcy law, or any other requirement that representation at the meeting of creditors under subsection (a) be by an attorney, a creditor holding a consumer debt or any representative of the creditor (which may include an entity or an employee of an entity and may be a representative for more than 1 creditor) shall be permitted to appear at and participate in the meeting of creditors in a case under chapter 7 or 13, either alone or in conjunction with an attorney for the creditor. Nothing in this subsection shall be construed to require any creditor to be represented by an attorney at any meeting of creditors.".

SEC. 414. DEFINITION OF DISINTERESTED PERSON.

Section 101(14) of title 11, United States Code, is amended to read as follows:
"(14) 'disinterested person' means a person that—
"(A) is not a creditor, an equity security holder, or an insider;
"(B) is not and was not, within 2 years before the date of the filing of the petition, a director, officer, or employee of the debtor; and
"(C) does not have an interest materially adverse to the interest of the estate or of any class of creditors or equity security holders, by reason of any direct or indirect relationship to, connection with, or interest in, the debtor, or for any other reason;".

SEC. 415. FACTORS FOR COMPENSATION OF PROFESSIONAL PERSONS.

Section 330(a)(3) of title 11, United States Code, is amended—
(1) in subparagraph (D), by striking "and" at the end;
(2) by redesignating subparagraph (E) as subparagraph (F); and
(3) by inserting after subparagraph (D) the following:
"(E) with respect to a professional person, whether the person is board certified or otherwise has demonstrated skill and experience in the bankruptcy field; and".

SEC. 416. APPOINTMENT OF ELECTED TRUSTEE.

Section 1104(b) of title 11, United States Code, is amended—
(1) by inserting "(1)" after "(b)"; and
(2) by adding at the end the following:
"(2)(A) If an eligible, disinterested trustee is elected at a meeting of creditors under paragraph (1), the United States trustee shall file a report certifying that election.
"(B) Upon the filing of a report under subparagraph (A)—

"(i) the trustee elected under paragraph (1) shall be considered to have been selected and appointed for purposes of this section; and

"(ii) the service of any trustee appointed under subsection (d) shall terminate.

"(C) The court shall resolve any dispute arising out of an election described in subparagraph (A).".

SEC. 417. UTILITY SERVICE.

Section 366 of title 11, United States Code, is amended—

(1) in subsection (a), by striking "subsection (b)" and inserting "subsections (b) and (c)"; and

(2) by adding at the end the following:

"(c)(1)(A) For purposes of this subsection, the term 'assurance of payment' means—

"(i) a cash deposit;

"(ii) a letter of credit;

"(iii) a certificate of deposit;

"(iv) a surety bond;

"(v) a prepayment of utility consumption; or

"(vi) another form of security that is mutually agreed on between the utility and the debtor or the trustee.

"(B) For purposes of this subsection an administrative expense priority shall not constitute an assurance of payment.

"(2) Subject to paragraphs (3) and (4), with respect to a case filed under chapter 11, a utility referred to in subsection (a) may alter, refuse, or discontinue utility service, if during the 30-day period beginning on the date of the filing of the petition, the utility does not receive from the debtor or the trustee adequate assurance of payment for utility service that is satisfactory to the utility.

"(3)(A) On request of a party in interest and after notice and a hearing, the court may order modification of the amount of an assurance of payment under paragraph (2).

"(B) In making a determination under this paragraph whether an assurance of payment is adequate, the court may not consider—

"(i) the absence of security before the date of the filing of the petition;

"(ii) the payment by the debtor of charges for utility service in a timely manner before the date of the filing of the petition; or

"(iii) the availability of an administrative expense priority.

"(4) Notwithstanding any other provision of law, with respect to a case subject to this subsection, a utility may recover or set off against a security deposit provided to the utility by the debtor before the date of the filing of the petition without notice or order of the court.".

SEC. 418. BANKRUPTCY FEES.

Section 1930 of title 28, United States Code, is amended—

(1) in subsection (a), by striking "Notwithstanding section 1915 of this title, the" and inserting "The"; and

(2) by adding at the end the following:

"(f)(1) Under the procedures prescribed by the Judicial Conference of the United States, the district court or the bankruptcy court may waive the filing fee in a case under chapter 7 of title 11 for an individual if the court determines that such individual has income less than 150 percent of the income official poverty line (as defined by the Office of Management and Budget, and revised annually in accordance with section 673(2) of the Omnibus Budget Reconciliation Act of 1981) applicable to a family of the size involved and is unable to pay that fee in installments. For purposes of this paragraph, the term 'filing fee' means the filing fee required by subsection (a), or any other fee prescribed by the Judicial Conference under subsections (b) and (c) that is payable to the clerk upon the commencement of a case under chapter 7.

"(2) The district court or the bankruptcy court may waive for such debtors other fees prescribed under subsections (b) and (c).

"(3) This subsection does not restrict the district court or the bankruptcy court from waiving, in accordance with Judicial Conference policy, fees prescribed under this section for other debtors and creditors.".

SEC. 419. MORE COMPLETE INFORMATION REGARDING ASSETS OF THE ESTATE.

(a) IN GENERAL.—

(1) DISCLOSURE.—The Judicial Conference of the United States, in accordance with section 2075 of title 28 of the United States Code and after consideration of the views of the Director of the Executive Office for United States Trustees, shall propose amended Federal Rules of Bankruptcy Procedure and in accordance with rule 9009 of the Federal Rules of Bankruptcy Procedure shall prescribe official bankruptcy forms directing debtors under chapter 11 of title 11 of United States Code, to disclose the information described in paragraph (2) by filing and serving periodic financial and other reports designed to provide such information.

(2) INFORMATION.—The information referred to in paragraph (1) is the value, operations, and profitability of any closely held corporation, partnership, or of any other entity in which the debtor holds a substantial or controlling interest.

(b) PURPOSE.—The purpose of the rules and reports under subsection (a) shall be to assist parties in interest taking steps to ensure that the debtor's interest in any entity referred to in subsection (a)(2) is used for the payment of allowed claims against debtor.

Subtitle B—Small Business Bankruptcy Provisions

SEC. 431. FLEXIBLE RULES FOR DISCLOSURE STATEMENT AND PLAN.

Section 1125 of title 11, United States Code, is amended—

(1) in subsection (a)(1), by inserting before the semicolon "and in determining whether a disclosure statement provides adequate information, the court shall consider the complexity of the case, the benefit of additional information to creditors and other parties in interest, and the cost of providing additional information"; and

(2) by striking subsection (f), and inserting the following:

"(f) Notwithstanding subsection (b), in a small business case—

"(1) the court may determine that the plan itself provides adequate information and that a separate disclosure statement is not necessary;

"(2) the court may approve a disclosure statement submitted on standard forms approved by the court or adopted under section 2075 of title 28; and

"(3)(A) the court may conditionally approve a disclosure statement subject to final approval after notice and a hearing;

"(B) acceptances and rejections of a plan may be solicited based on a conditionally approved disclosure statement if the debtor provides adequate information to each holder of a claim or interest that is solicited, but a conditionally approved disclosure statement shall be mailed not later than 25 days before the date of the hearing on confirmation of the plan; and

"(C) the hearing on the disclosure statement may be combined with the hearing on confirmation of a plan.".

SEC. 432. DEFINITIONS.

(a) DEFINITIONS.—Section 101 of title 11, United States Code, is amended by striking paragraph (51C) and inserting the following:

"(51C) 'small business case' means a case filed under chapter 11 of this title in which the debtor is a small business debtor;

"(51D) 'small business debtor'—

"(A) subject to subparagraph (B), means a person engaged in commercial or business activities (including any affiliate of such person that is also a debtor under this title and excluding a person whose primary activity is the business of owning or operating real property or activities incidental thereto) that has aggregate noncontingent liquidated secured and unsecured debts as of the date of the petition or the date of the order for relief in an amount not more than $2,000,000 (excluding debts owed to 1 or more affiliates or insiders) for a case in which the United States trustee has not appointed under section 1102(a)(1) a committee of unsecured creditors or where the court has determined that the committee of unsecured creditors is not sufficiently active and representative to provide effective oversight of the debtor; and

"(B) does not include any member of a group of affiliated debtors that has aggregate noncontingent liquidated secured and unsecured debts in an amount greater than $2,000,000 (excluding debt owed to 1 or more affiliates or insiders);".

(b) CONFORMING AMENDMENT.—Section 1102(a)(3) of title 11, United States Code, is amended by inserting "debtor" after "small business".

(c) ADJUSTMENT OF DOLLAR AMOUNTS.—Section 104(b) of title 11, United States Code, as amended by section 226, is amended by inserting "101(51D)," after "101(3)," each place it appears.

SEC. 433. STANDARD FORM DISCLOSURE STATEMENT AND PLAN.

Within a reasonable period of time after the date of enactment of this Act, the Judicial Conference of the United States shall prescribe in accordance with rule 9009 of the Federal Rules of Bankruptcy Procedure official standard form disclosure statements and plans of reorganization for small business debtors (as defined in section 101 of title 11, United States Code, as amended by this Act), designed to achieve a practical balance between—

(1) the reasonable needs of the courts, the United States trustee, creditors, and other parties in interest for reasonably complete information; and

(2) economy and simplicity for debtors.

SEC. 434. UNIFORM NATIONAL REPORTING REQUIREMENTS.

(a) REPORTING REQUIRED.—

(1) IN GENERAL.—Chapter 3 of title 11, United States Code, is amended by inserting after section 307 the following:

"§ 308. Debtor reporting requirements

"(a) For purposes of this section, the term 'profitability' means, with respect to a debtor, the amount of money that the debtor has earned or lost during current and recent fiscal periods.

"(b) A small business debtor shall file periodic financial and other reports containing information including—

"(1) the debtor's profitability;

"(2) reasonable approximations of the debtor's projected cash receipts and cash disbursements over a reasonable period;

"(3) comparisons of actual cash receipts and disbursements with projections in prior reports;

"(4)(A) whether the debtor is—

"(i) in compliance in all material respects with postpetition requirements imposed by this title and the Federal Rules of Bankruptcy Procedure; and "(ii) timely filing tax returns and other required government filings and paying taxes and other administrative expenses when due;

"(B) if the debtor is not in compliance with the requirements referred to in subparagraph (A)(i) or filing tax returns and other required government filings and making the payments referred to in subparagraph (A)(ii), what the failures are and how, at what cost, and when the debtor intends to remedy such failures; and

"(C) such other matters as are in the best interests of the debtor and creditors, and in the public interest in fair and efficient procedures under chapter 11 of this title.".

(2) CLERICAL AMENDMENT.—The table of sections for chapter 3 of title 11, United States Code, is amended by inserting after the item relating to section 307 the following:

"308. Debtor reporting requirements.".

(b) EFFECTIVE DATE.—The amendments made by subsection (a) shall take effect 60 days after the date on which rules are prescribed under section 2075 of title 28, United States Code, to establish forms to be used to comply with section 308 of title 11, United States Code, as added by subsection (a).

SEC. 435. UNIFORM REPORTING RULES AND FORMS FOR SMALL BUSINESS CASES.

(a) PROPOSAL OF RULES AND FORMS.—The Judicial Conference of the United States shall propose in accordance with section 2073 of title 28 of the United States Code amended Federal Rules of Bankruptcy Procedure, and shall prescribe in accordance with rule 9009 of the Federal Rules of Bankruptcy Procedure official bankruptcy forms, directing small business debtors to file periodic financial and other reports containing information, including information relating to—

(1) the debtor's profitability;

(2) the debtor's cash receipts and disbursements; and

(3) whether the debtor is timely filing tax returns and paying taxes and other administrative expenses when due.

(b) PURPOSE.—The rules and forms proposed under subsection (a) shall be designed to achieve a practical balance among—

(1) the reasonable needs of the bankruptcy court, the United States trustee, creditors, and other parties in interest for reasonably complete information;

(2) a small business debtor's interest that required reports be easy and inexpensive to complete; and

(3) the interest of all parties that the required reports help such debtor to understand such debtor's financial condition and plan the such debtor's future.

SEC. 436. DUTIES IN SMALL BUSINESS CASES.

(a) DUTIES IN CHAPTER 11 CASES.—Subchapter I of chapter 11 of title 11, United States Code, as amended by section 321, is amended by adding at the end the following:

"§ 1116. Duties of trustee or debtor in possession in small business cases

"In a small business case, a trustee or the debtor in possession, in addition to the duties provided in this title and as otherwise required by law, shall—

"(1) append to the voluntary petition or, in an involuntary case, file not later than 7 days after the date of the order for relief—

"(A) its most recent balance sheet, statement of operations, cash-flow statement, and Federal income tax return; or

"(B) a statement made under penalty of perjury that no balance sheet, statement of operations, or cash-flow statement has been prepared and no Federal tax return has been filed;

"(2) attend, through its senior management personnel and counsel, meetings scheduled by the court or the United States trustee, including initial debtor interviews, scheduling conferences, and meetings of creditors convened under section 341 unless the court, after notice and a hearing, waives that requirement upon a finding of extraordinary and compelling circumstances;

"(3) timely file all schedules and statements of financial affairs, unless the court, after notice and a hearing, grants an extension, which shall not extend such time period to a date later than 30 days after the date of the order for relief, absent extraordinary and compelling circumstances;

"(4) file all postpetition financial and other reports required by the Federal Rules of Bankruptcy Procedure or by local rule of the district court;

"(5) subject to section 363(c)(2), maintain insurance customary and appropriate to the industry;

"(6)(A) timely file tax returns and other required government filings; and

"(B) subject to section 363(c)(2), timely pay all taxes entitled to administrative expense priority except those being contested by appropriate proceedings being diligently prosecuted; and

"(7) allow the United States trustee, or a designated representative of the United States trustee, to inspect the debtor's business premises, books, and records at reasonable times, after reasonable prior written notice, unless notice is waived by the debtor.".

(b) CLERICAL AMENDMENT.—The table of sections for chapter 11 of title 11, United States Code, as amended by section 321, is amended by inserting after the item relating to section 1115 the following:

"1116. Duties of trustee or debtor in possession in small business cases.".

SEC. 437. PLAN FILING AND CONFIRMATION DEADLINES.

Section 1121 of title 11, United States Code, is amended by striking subsection (e) and inserting the following:

"(e) In a small business case—

"(1) only the debtor may file a plan until after 180 days after the date of the order for relief, unless that period is—

"(A) extended as provided by this subsection, after notice and a hearing; or

"(B) the court, for cause, orders otherwise;

"(2) the plan and a disclosure statement (if any) shall be filed not later than 300 days after the date of the order for relief; and

"(3) the time periods specified in paragraphs (1) and (2), and the time fixed in section 1129(e) within which the plan shall be confirmed, may be extended only if—

"(A) the debtor, after providing notice to parties in interest (including the United States trustee), demonstrates by a preponderance of the evidence that it is more likely than not that the court will confirm a plan within a reasonable period of time;

"(B) a new deadline is imposed at the time the extension is granted; and

"(C) the order extending time is signed before the existing deadline has expired.".

SEC. 438. PLAN CONFIRMATION DEADLINE.

Section 1129 of title 11, United States Code, is amended by adding at the end the following:

"(e) In a small business case, the court shall confirm a plan that complies with the applicable provisions of this title and that is filed in accordance with section 1121(e) not later than 45 days after the plan is filed unless the time for confirmation is extended in accordance with section 1121(e)(3).".

SEC. 439. DUTIES OF THE UNITED STATES TRUSTEE.

Section 586(a) of title 28, United States Code, is amended—

(1) in paragraph (3)—

(A) in subparagraph (G), by striking "and" at the end;
(B) by redesignating subparagraph (H) as subparagraph (I); and
(C) by inserting after subparagraph (G) the following:
"(H) in small business cases (as defined in section 101 of title 11), performing the additional duties specified in title 11 pertaining to such cases; and";
(2) in paragraph (5), by striking "and" at the end;
(3) in paragraph (6), by striking the period at the end and inserting a semicolon; and
(4) by adding at the end the following:
"(7) in each of such small business cases—
"(A) conduct an initial debtor interview as soon as practicable after the date of the order for relief but before the first meeting scheduled under section 341(a) of title 11, at which time the United States trustee shall—
"(i) begin to investigate the debtor's viability;
"(ii) inquire about the debtor's business plan;
"(iii) explain the debtor's obligations to file monthly operating reports and other required reports;
"(iv) attempt to develop an agreed scheduling order; and
"(v) inform the debtor of other obligations;
"(B) if determined to be appropriate and advisable, visit the appropriate business premises of the debtor, ascertain the state of the debtor's books and records, and verify that the debtor has filed its tax returns; and
"(C) review and monitor diligently the debtor's activities, to identify as promptly as possible whether the debtor will be unable to confirm a plan; and
"(8) in any case in which the United States trustee finds material grounds for any relief under section 1112 of title 11, the United States trustee shall apply promptly after making that finding to the court for relief.".

SEC. 440. SCHEDULING CONFERENCES.

Section 105(d) of title 11, United States Code, is amended—
(1) in the matter preceding paragraph (1), by striking ", may"; and
(2) by striking paragraph (1) and inserting the following:
"(1) shall hold such status conferences as are necessary to further the expeditious and economical resolution of the case; and".

SEC. 441. SERIAL FILER PROVISIONS.

Section 362 of title 11, United States Code, as amended by sections 106, 305, and 311, is amended—
(1) in subsection (k), as so redesignated by section 305—
(A) by striking "An" and inserting "(1) Except as provided in paragraph (2), an"; and
(B) by adding at the end the following:
"(2) If such violation is based on an action taken by an entity in the good faith belief that subsection (h) applies to the debtor, the recovery under paragraph (1) of this subsection against such entity shall be limited to actual damages."; and
(2) by adding at the end the following:
"(n)(1) Except as provided in paragraph (2), subsection (a) does not apply in a case in which the debtor—
"(A) is a debtor in a small business case pending at the time the petition is filed;
"(B) was a debtor in a small business case that was dismissed for any reason by an order that became final in the 2-year period ending on the date of the order for relief entered with respect to the petition;
"(C) was a debtor in a small business case in which a plan was confirmed in the 2-year period ending on the date of the order for relief entered with respect to the petition; or

"(D) is an entity that has acquired substantially all of the assets or business of a small business debtor described in subparagraph (A), (B), or (C), unless such entity establishes by a preponderance of the evidence that such entity acquired substantially all of the assets or business of such small business debtor in good faith and not for the purpose of evading this paragraph.

"(2) Paragraph (1) does not apply—

"(A) to an involuntary case involving no collusion by the debtor with creditors; or

"(B) to the filing of a petition if—

"(i) the debtor proves by a preponderance of the evidence that the filing of the petition resulted from circumstances beyond the control of the debtor not foreseeable at the time the case then pending was filed; and

"(ii) it is more likely than not that the court will confirm a feasible plan, but not a liquidating plan, within a reasonable period of time.".

SEC. 442. EXPANDED GROUNDS FOR DISMISSAL OR CONVERSION AND APPOINTMENT OF TRUSTEE.

(a) EXPANDED GROUNDS FOR DISMISSAL OR CONVERSION.—Section 1112 of title 11, United States Code, is amended by striking subsection (b) and inserting the following:

"(b)(1) Except as provided in paragraph (2) of this subsection, subsection (c) of this section, and section 1104(a)(3), on request of a party in interest, and after notice and a hearing, absent unusual circumstances specifically identified by the court that establish that the requested conversion or dismissal is not in the best interests of creditors and the estate, the court shall convert a case under this chapter to a case under chapter 7 or dismiss a case under this chapter, whichever is in the best interests of creditors and the estate, if the movant establishes cause.

"(2) The relief provided in paragraph (1) shall not be granted absent unusual circumstances specifically identified by the court that establish that such relief is not in the best interests of creditors and the estate, if the debtor or another party in interest objects and establishes that—

"(A) there is a reasonable likelihood that a plan will be confirmed within the timeframes established in sections 1121(e) and 1129(e) of this title, or if such sections do not apply, within a reasonable period of time; and

"(B) the grounds for granting such relief include an act or omission of the debtor other than under paragraph (4)(A)—

"(i) for which there exists a reasonable justification for the act or omission; and

"(ii) that will be cured within a reasonable period of time fixed by the court.

"(3) The court shall commence the hearing on a motion under this subsection not later than 30 days after filing of the motion, and shall decide the motion not later than 15 days after commencement of such hearing, unless the movant expressly consents to a continuance for a specific period of time or compelling circumstances prevent the court from meeting the time limits established by this paragraph.

"(4) For purposes of this subsection, the term 'cause' includes—

"(A) substantial or continuing loss to or diminution of the estate and the absence of a reasonable likelihood of rehabilitation;

"(B) gross mismanagement of the estate;

"(C) failure to maintain appropriate insurance that poses a risk to the estate or to the public;

"(D) unauthorized use of cash collateral substantially harmful to 1 or more creditors;

"(E) failure to comply with an order of the court;

"(F) unexcused failure to satisfy timely any filing or reporting requirement established by this title or by any rule applicable to a case under this chapter;

"(G) failure to attend the meeting of creditors convened under section 341(a) or an examination ordered under rule 2004 of the Federal Rules of Bankruptcy Procedure without good cause shown by the debtor;

"(H) failure timely to provide information or attend meetings reasonably requested by the United States trustee (or the bankruptcy administrator, if any);

"(I) failure timely to pay taxes owed after the date of the order for relief or to file tax returns due after the date of the order for relief;

"(J) failure to file a disclosure statement, or to file or confirm a plan, within the time fixed by this title or by order of the court;

"(K) failure to pay any fees or charges required under chapter 123 of title 28;

"(L) revocation of an order of confirmation under section 1144;

"(M) inability to effectuate substantial consummation of a confirmed plan;

"(N) material default by the debtor with respect to a confirmed plan;

"(O) termination of a confirmed plan by reason of the occurrence of a condition specified in the plan; and

"(P) failure of the debtor to pay any domestic support obligation that first becomes payable after the date of the filing of the petition.".

(b) ADDITIONAL GROUNDS FOR APPOINTMENT OF TRUSTEE.—Section 1104(a) of title 11, United States Code, is amended—

(1) in paragraph (1), by striking "or" at the end;

(2) in paragraph (2), by striking the period at the end and inserting "; or"; and

(3) by adding at the end the following:

"(3) if grounds exist to convert or dismiss the case under section 1112, but the court determines that the appointment of a trustee or an examiner is in the best interests of creditors and the estate.".

SEC. 443. STUDY OF OPERATION OF TITLE 11, UNITED STATES CODE, WITH RESPECT TO SMALL BUSINESSES.

Not later than 2 years after the date of enactment of this Act, the Administrator of the Small Business Administration, in consultation with the Attorney General, the Director of the Executive Office for United States Trustees, and the Director of the Administrative Office of the United States Courts, shall—

(1) conduct a study to determine—

(A) the internal and external factors that cause small businesses, especially sole proprietorships, to become debtors in cases under title 11, United States Code, and that cause certain small businesses to successfully complete cases under chapter 11 of such title; and

(B) how Federal laws relating to bankruptcy may be made more effective and efficient in assisting small businesses to remain viable; and

(2) submit to the President pro tempore of the Senate and the Speaker of the House of Representatives a report summarizing that study.

SEC. 444. PAYMENT OF INTEREST.

Section 362(d)(3) of title 11, United States Code, is amended—

(1) by inserting "or 30 days after the court determines that the debtor is subject to this paragraph, whichever is later" after "90-day period)"; and

(2) by striking subparagraph (B) and inserting the following:

"(B) the debtor has commenced monthly payments that—

"(i) may, in the debtor's sole discretion, notwithstanding section 363(c)(2), be made from rents or other income generated before, on, or after the date of the commencement of the case by or from the property to each creditor whose claim is secured by such real estate (other than a claim secured by a judgment lien or by an unmatured statutory lien); and

"(ii) are in an amount equal to interest at the then applicable nondefault contract rate of interest on the value of the creditor's interest in the real estate; or".

SEC. 445. PRIORITY FOR ADMINISTRATIVE EXPENSES.

Section 503(b) of title 11, United States Code, is amended—
(1) in paragraph (5), by striking "and" at the end;
(2) in paragraph (6), by striking the period at the end and inserting a semicolon; and
(3) by adding at the end the following:
"(7) with respect to a nonresidential real property lease previously assumed under section 365, and subsequently rejected, a sum equal to all monetary obligations due, excluding those arising from or relating to a failure to operate or a penalty provision, for the period of 2 years following the later of the rejection date or the date of actual turnover of the premises, without reduction or setoff for any reason whatsoever except for sums actually received or to be received from an entity other than the debtor, and the claim for remaining sums due for the balance of the term of the lease shall be a claim under section 502(b)(6);".

SEC. 446. DUTIES WITH RESPECT TO A DEBTOR WHO IS A PLAN ADMINISTRATOR OF AN EMPLOYEE BENEFIT PLAN.

(a) IN GENERAL.—Section 521(a) of title 11, United States Code, as amended by sections 106 and 304, is amended—
(1) in paragraph (5), by striking "and" at the end;
(2) in paragraph (6), by striking the period at the end and inserting "; and"; and
(3) by adding after paragraph (6) the following:
"(7) unless a trustee is serving in the case, continue to perform the obligations required of the administrator (as defined in section 3 of the Employee Retirement Income Security Act of 1974) of an employee benefit plan if at the time of the commencement of the case the debtor (or any entity designated by the debtor) served as such administrator.".

(b) DUTIES OF TRUSTEES.—Section 704(a) of title 11, United States Code, as amended by sections 102 and 219, is amended—
(1) in paragraph (10), by striking "and" at the end; and
(2) by adding at the end the following:
"(11) if, at the time of the commencement of the case, the debtor (or any entity designated by the debtor) served as the administrator (as defined in section 3 of the Employee Retirement Income Security Act of 1974) of an employee benefit plan, continue to perform the obligations required of the administrator; and".

(c) CONFORMING AMENDMENT.—Section 1106(a)(1) of title 11, United States Code, is amended to read as follows:
"(1) perform the duties of the trustee, as specified in paragraphs (2), (5), (7), (8), (9), (10), and (11) of section 704;".

SEC. 447. APPOINTMENT OF COMMITTEE OF RETIRED EMPLOYEES.

Section 1114(d) of title 11, United States Code, is amended—
(1) by striking "appoint" and inserting "order the appointment of", and
(2) by adding at the end the following: "The United States trustee shall appoint any such committee.".

TITLE V—MUNICIPAL BANKRUPTCY PROVISIONS

SEC. 501. PETITION AND PROCEEDINGS RELATED TO PETITION.

(a) TECHNICAL AMENDMENT RELATING TO MUNICIPALITIES.—Section 921(d) of title 11, United States Code, is amended by inserting "notwithstanding section 301(b)" before the period at the end.

(b) CONFORMING AMENDMENT.—Section 301 of title 11, United States Code, is amended—

(1) by inserting "(a)" before "A voluntary"; and

(2) by striking the last sentence and inserting the following:

"(b) The commencement of a voluntary case under a chapter of this title constitutes an order for relief under such chapter.".

SEC. 502. APPLICABILITY OF OTHER SECTIONS TO CHAPTER 9.

Section 901(a) of title 11, United States Code, is amended—

(1) by inserting "555, 556," after "553,"; and

(2) by inserting "559, 560, 561, 562," after "557,".

TITLE VI—BANKRUPTCY DATA

SEC. 601. IMPROVED BANKRUPTCY STATISTICS.

(a) IN GENERAL.—Chapter 6 of title 28, United States Code, is amended by adding at the end the following:

"§ 159. Bankruptcy statistics

"(a) The clerk of the district court, or the clerk of the bankruptcy court if one is certified pursuant to section 156(b) of this title, shall collect statistics regarding debtors who are individuals with primarily consumer debts seeking relief under chapters 7, 11, and 13 of title 11. Those statistics shall be in a standardized format prescribed by the Director of the Administrative Office of the United States Courts (referred to in this section as the 'Director').

"(b) The Director shall—

"(1) compile the statistics referred to in subsection (a);

"(2) make the statistics available to the public; and

"(3) not later than July 1, 2008, and annually thereafter, prepare, and submit to Congress a report concerning the information collected under subsection (a) that contains an analysis of the information.

"(c) The compilation required under subsection (b) shall—

"(1) be itemized, by chapter, with respect to title 11;

"(2) be presented in the aggregate and for each district; and

"(3) include information concerning—

"(A) the total assets and total liabilities of the debtors described in subsection (a), and in each category of assets and liabilities, as reported in the schedules prescribed pursuant to section 2075 of this title and filed by debtors;

"(B) the current monthly income, average income, and average expenses of debtors as reported on the schedules and statements that each such debtor files under sections 521 and 1322 of title 11;

"(C) the aggregate amount of debt discharged in cases filed during the reporting period, determined as the difference between the total amount of debt and obligations of a debtor reported on the schedules and the amount of such debt reported in categories which are predominantly nondischargeable;

"(D) the average period of time between the date of the filing of the petition and the closing of the case for cases closed during the reporting period;

"(E) for cases closed during the reporting period—

"(i) the number of cases in which a reaffirmation agreement was filed; and

"(ii)(I) the total number of reaffirmation agreements filed;

"(II) of those cases in which a reaffirmation agreement was filed, the number of cases in which the debtor was not represented by an attorney; and

"(III) of those cases in which a reaffirmation agreement was filed, the number of cases in which the reaffirmation agreement was approved by the court;

"(F) with respect to cases filed under chapter 13 of title 11, for the reporting period—

"(i)(I) the number of cases in which a final order was entered determining the value of property securing a claim in an amount less than the amount of the claim; and

"(II) the number of final orders entered determining the value of property securing a claim;

"(ii) the number of cases dismissed, the number of cases dismissed for failure to make payments under the plan, the number of cases refiled after dismissal, and the number of cases in which the plan was completed, separately itemized with respect to the number of modifications made before completion of the plan, if any; and

"(iii) the number of cases in which the debtor filed another case during the 6-year period preceding the filing;

"(G) the number of cases in which creditors were fined for misconduct and any amount of punitive damages awarded by the court for creditor misconduct; and

"(H) the number of cases in which sanctions under rule 9011 of the Federal Rules of Bankruptcy Procedure were imposed against debtor's attorney or damages awarded under such Rule.".

(b) CLERICAL AMENDMENT.—The table of sections for chapter 6 of title 28, United States Code, is amended by adding at the end the following:

"159. Bankruptcy statistics.".

(c) EFFECTIVE DATE.—The amendments made by this section shall take effect 18 months after the date of enactment of this Act.

SEC. 602. UNIFORM RULES FOR THE COLLECTION OF BANKRUPTCY DATA.

(a) AMENDMENT.—Chapter 39 of title 28, United States Code, is amended by adding at the end the following:

"§ 589b. Bankruptcy data

"(a) RULES.—The Attorney General shall, within a reasonable time after the effective date of this section, issue rules requiring uniform forms for (and from time to time thereafter to appropriately modify and approve)—

"(1) final reports by trustees in cases under chapters 7, 12, and 13 of title 11; and

"(2) periodic reports by debtors in possession or trustees in cases under chapter 11 of title 11.

"(b) REPORTS.—Each report referred to in subsection (a) shall be designed (and the requirements as to place and manner of filing shall be established) so as to facilitate compilation of data and maximum possible access of the public, both by physical inspection at one or more central filing locations, and by electronic access through the Internet or other appropriate media.

"(c) REQUIRED INFORMATION.—The information required to be filed in the reports referred to in subsection (b) shall be that which is in the best interests of debtors and creditors, and in the public interest in reasonable and adequate information to evaluate the efficiency and practicality of the Federal bankruptcy system. In issuing rules proposing the forms referred to in subsection (a), the Attorney General shall strike the best achievable practical balance between—

"(1) the reasonable needs of the public for information about the operational results of the Federal bankruptcy system;

"(2) economy, simplicity, and lack of undue burden on persons with a duty to file reports; and

"(3) appropriate privacy concerns and safeguards.

"(d) FINAL REPORTS.—The uniform forms for final reports required under subsection (a) for use by trustees under chapters 7, 12, and 13 of title 11 shall, in addition to such other matters as are required by law or as the Attorney General in the discretion of the Attorney

General shall propose, include with respect to a case under such title—
"(1) information about the length of time the case was pending;
"(2) assets abandoned;
"(3) assets exempted;
"(4) receipts and disbursements of the estate;
"(5) expenses of administration, including for use under section 707(b), actual costs of administering cases under chapter 13 of title 11;
"(6) claims asserted;
"(7) claims allowed; and
"(8) distributions to claimants and claims discharged without payment,
in each case by appropriate category and, in cases under chapters 12 and 13 of title 11, date of confirmation of the plan, each modification thereto, and defaults by the debtor in performance under the plan.

"(e) PERIODIC REPORTS.—The uniform forms for periodic reports required under subsection (a) for use by trustees or debtors in possession under chapter 11 of title 11 shall, in addition to such other matters as are required by law or as the Attorney General in the discretion of the Attorney General shall propose, include—
"(1) information about the industry classification, published by the Department of Commerce, for the businesses conducted by the debtor;
"(2) length of time the case has been pending;
"(3) number of full-time employees as of the date of the order for relief and at the end of each reporting period since the case was filed;
"(4) cash receipts, cash disbursements and profitability of the debtor for the most recent period and cumulatively since the date of the order for relief;
"(5) compliance with title 11, whether or not tax returns and tax payments since the date of the order for relief have been timely filed and made;
"(6) all professional fees approved by the court in the case for the most recent period and cumulatively since the date of the order for relief (separately reported, for the professional fees incurred by or on behalf of the debtor, between those that would have been incurred absent a bankruptcy case and those not); and
"(7) plans of reorganization filed and confirmed and, with respect thereto, by class, the recoveries of the holders, expressed in aggregate dollar values and, in the case of claims, as a percentage of total claims of the class allowed.".

(b) CLERICAL AMENDMENT.—The table of sections for chapter 39 of title 28, United States Code, is amended by adding at the end the following:
"589b. Bankruptcy data.".

SEC. 603. AUDIT PROCEDURES.

(a) IN GENERAL.—
(1) ESTABLISHMENT OF PROCEDURES.—The Attorney General (in judicial districts served by United States trustees) and the Judicial Conference of the United States (in judicial districts served by bankruptcy administrators) shall establish procedures to determine the accuracy, veracity, and completeness of petitions, schedules, and other information that the debtor is required to provide under sections 521 and 1322 of title 11, United States Code, and, if applicable, section 111 of such title, in cases filed under chapter 7 or 13 of such title in which the debtor is an individual. Such audits shall be in accordance with generally accepted auditing standards and performed by independent certified public accountants or independent licensed public accountants, provided that the Attorney General and the Judicial Conference, as appropriate, may develop alternative auditing standards not later than 2 years after the date of enactment of this Act.
(2) PROCEDURES.—Those procedures required by paragraph (1) shall—
(A) establish a method of selecting appropriate qualified persons to contract to perform those audits;

(B) establish a method of randomly selecting cases to be audited, except that not less than 1 out of every 250 cases in each Federal judicial district shall be selected for audit;

(C) require audits of schedules of income and expenses that reflect greater than average variances from the statistical norm of the district in which the schedules were filed if those variances occur by reason of higher income or higher expenses than the statistical norm of the district in which the schedules were filed; and

(D) establish procedures for providing, not less frequently than annually, public information concerning the aggregate results of such audits including the percentage of cases, by district, in which a material misstatement of income or expenditures is reported.

(b) AMENDMENTS.—Section 586 of title 28, United States Code, is amended—

(1) in subsection (a), by striking paragraph (6) and inserting the following:

"(6) make such reports as the Attorney General directs, including the results of audits performed under section 603(a) of the Bankruptcy Abuse Prevention and Consumer Protection Act of 2005;"; and

(2) by adding at the end the following:

"(f)(1) The United States trustee for each district is authorized to contract with auditors to perform audits in cases designated by the United States trustee, in accordance with the procedures established under section 603(a) of the Bankruptcy Abuse Prevention and Consumer Protection Act of 2005.

"(2)(A) The report of each audit referred to in paragraph (1) shall be filed with the court and transmitted to the United States trustee. Each report shall clearly and conspicuously specify any material misstatement of income or expenditures or of assets identified by the person performing the audit. In any case in which a material misstatement of income or expenditures or of assets has been reported, the clerk of the district court (or the clerk of the bankruptcy court if one is certified under section 156(b) of this title) shall give notice of the misstatement to the creditors in the case.

"(B) If a material misstatement of income or expenditures or of assets is reported, the United States trustee shall—

"(i) report the material misstatement, if appropriate, to the United States Attorney pursuant to section 3057 of title 18; and

"(ii) if advisable, take appropriate action, including but not limited to commencing an adversary proceeding to revoke the debtor's discharge pursuant to section 727(d) of title 11.".

(c) AMENDMENTS TO SECTION 521 OF TITLE 11, U.S.C.—Section 521(a) of title 11, United States Code, as so designated by section 106, is amended in each of paragraphs (3) and (4) by inserting "or an auditor serving under section 586(f) of title 28" after "serving in the case".

(d) AMENDMENTS TO SECTION 727 OF TITLE 11, U.S.C.—Section 727(d) of title 11, United States Code, is amended—

(1) in paragraph (2), by striking "or" at the end;

(2) in paragraph (3), by striking the period at the end and inserting "; or"; and

(3) by adding at the end the following:

"(4) the debtor has failed to explain satisfactorily—

"(A) a material misstatement in an audit referred to in section 586(f) of title 28; or

"(B) a failure to make available for inspection all necessary accounts, papers, documents, financial records, files, and all other papers, things, or property belonging to the debtor that are requested for an audit referred to in section 586(f) of title 28.".

(e) EFFECTIVE DATE.—The amendments made by this section shall take effect 18 months after the date of enactment of this Act.

SEC. 604. SENSE OF CONGRESS REGARDING AVAILABILITY OF BANKRUPTCY DATA.

It is the sense of Congress that—

(1) the national policy of the United States should be that all data held by bankruptcy clerks

in electronic form, to the extent such data reflects only public records (as defined in section 107 of title 11, United States Code), should be released in a usable electronic form in bulk to the public, subject to such appropriate privacy concerns and safeguards as Congress and the Judicial Conference of the United States may determine; and

(2) there should be established a bankruptcy data system in which—

(A) a single set of data definitions and forms are used to collect data nationwide; and

(B) data for any particular bankruptcy case are aggregated in the same electronic record.

TITLE VII—BANKRUPTCY TAX PROVISIONS

SEC. 701. TREATMENT OF CERTAIN LIENS.

(a) TREATMENT OF CERTAIN LIENS.—Section 724 of title 11, United States Code, is amended—

(1) in subsection (b), in the matter preceding paragraph (1), by inserting "(other than to the extent that there is a properly perfected unavoidable tax lien arising in connection with an ad valorem tax on real or personal property of the estate)" after "under this title";

(2) in subsection (b)(2), by inserting "(except that such expenses, other than claims for wages, salaries, or commissions that arise after the date of the filing of the petition, shall be limited to expenses incurred under chapter 7 of this title and shall not include expenses incurred under chapter 11 of this title)" after "507(a)(1)"; and

(3) by adding at the end the following:

"(e) Before subordinating a tax lien on real or personal property of the estate, the trustee shall—

"(1) exhaust the unencumbered assets of the estate; and

"(2) in a manner consistent with section 506(c), recover from property securing an allowed secured claim the reasonable, necessary costs and expenses of preserving or disposing of such property.

"(f) Notwithstanding the exclusion of ad valorem tax liens under this section and subject to the requirements of subsection (e), the following may be paid from property of the estate which secures a tax lien, or the proceeds of such property:

"(1) Claims for wages, salaries, and commissions that are entitled to priority under section 507(a)(4).

"(2) Claims for contributions to an employee benefit plan entitled to priority under section 507(a)(5).".

(b) DETERMINATION OF TAX LIABILITY.—Section 505(a)(2) of title 11, United States Code, is amended—

(1) in subparagraph (A), by striking "or" at the end;

(2) in subparagraph (B), by striking the period at the end and inserting "; or"; and

(3) by adding at the end the following:

"(C) the amount or legality of any amount arising in connection with an ad valorem tax on real or personal property of the estate, if the applicable period for contesting or redetermining that amount under any law (other than a bankruptcy law) has expired.".

SEC. 702. TREATMENT OF FUEL TAX CLAIMS.

Section 501 of title 11, United States Code, is amended by adding at the end the following:

"(e) A claim arising from the liability of a debtor for fuel use tax assessed consistent with the requirements of section 31705 of title 49 may be filed by the base jurisdiction designated pursuant to the International Fuel Tax Agreement (as defined in section 31701 of title 49) and, if so filed, shall be allowed as a single claim.".

SEC. 703. NOTICE OF REQUEST FOR A DETERMINATION OF TAXES.

Section 505(b) of title 11, United States Code, is amended—

(1) in the first sentence, by inserting "at the address and in the manner designated in paragraph (1)" after "determination of such tax";
(2) by striking "(1) upon payment" and inserting "(A) upon payment";
(3) by striking "(A) such governmental unit" and inserting "(i) such governmental unit";
(4) by striking "(B) such governmental unit" and inserting "(ii) such governmental unit";
(5) by striking "(2) upon payment" and inserting "(B) upon payment";
(6) by striking "(3) upon payment" and inserting "(C) upon payment";
(7) by striking "(b)" and inserting "(2)"; and
(8) by inserting before paragraph (2), as so designated, the following:

"(b)(1)(A) The clerk shall maintain a list under which a Federal, State, or local governmental unit responsible for the collection of taxes within the district may—

"(i) designate an address for service of requests under this subsection; and

"(ii) describe where further information concerning additional requirements for filing such requests may be found.

"(B) If such governmental unit does not designate an address and provide such address to the clerk under subparagraph (A), any request made under this subsection may be served at the address for the filing of a tax return or protest with the appropriate taxing authority of such governmental unit.".

SEC. 704. RATE OF INTEREST ON TAX CLAIMS.

(a) IN GENERAL.—Subchapter I of chapter 5 of title 11, United States Code, is amended by adding at the end the following:

"§ 511. Rate of interest on tax claims

"(a) If any provision of this title requires the payment of interest on a tax claim or on an administrative expense tax, or the payment of interest to enable a creditor to receive the present value of the allowed amount of a tax claim, the rate of interest shall be the rate determined under applicable nonbankruptcy law.

"(b) In the case of taxes paid under a confirmed plan under this title, the rate of interest shall be determined as of the calendar month in which the plan is confirmed.".

(b) CLERICAL AMENDMENT.—The table of sections for subchapter I of chapter 5 of title 11, United States Code, is amended by adding at the end the following:

"511. Rate of interest on tax claims.".

SEC. 705. PRIORITY OF TAX CLAIMS.

Section 507(a)(8) of title 11, United States Code, is amended—

(1) in subparagraph (A)—

(A) in the matter preceding clause (i), by inserting "for a taxable year ending on or before the date of the filing of the petition" after "gross receipts";

(B) in clause (i), by striking "for a taxable year ending on or before the date of the filing of the petition"; and

(C) by striking clause (ii) and inserting the following:

"(ii) assessed within 240 days before the date of the filing of the petition, exclusive of—

"(I) any time during which an offer in compromise with respect to that tax was pending or in effect during that 240-day period, plus 30 days; and

"(II) any time during which a stay of proceedings against collections was in effect in a prior case under this title during that 240-day period, plus 90 days."; and

(2) by adding at the end the following:

"An otherwise applicable time period specified in this paragraph shall be suspended for any period during which a governmental unit is prohibited under applicable nonbankruptcy law from collecting a tax as a result of a request by the debtor for a hearing and an appeal of any collection action taken or proposed against the debtor, plus 90 days; plus any time during which the stay of proceedings was in effect in a prior case under this title or during which collection was precluded by the existence of 1 or more confirmed plans under this title, plus 90 days.''.

SEC. 706. PRIORITY PROPERTY TAXES INCURRED.

Section 507(a)(8)(B) of title 11, United States Code, is amended by striking ''assessed'' and inserting ''incurred''.

SEC. 707. NO DISCHARGE OF FRAUDULENT TAXES IN CHAPTER 13.

Section 1328(a)(2) of title 11, United States Code, as amended by section 314, is amended by striking ''paragraph'' and inserting ''section 507(a)(8)(C) or in paragraph (1)(B), (1)(C),''.

SEC. 708. NO DISCHARGE OF FRAUDULENT TAXES IN CHAPTER 11.

Section 1141(d) of title 11, United States Code, as amended by sections 321 and 330, is amended by adding at the end the following:

''(6) Notwithstanding paragraph (1), the confirmation of a plan does not discharge a debtor that is a corporation from any debt—

''(A) of a kind specified in paragraph (2)(A) or (2)(B) of section 523(a) that is owed to a domestic governmental unit, or owed to a person as the result of an action filed under subchapter III of chapter 37 of title 31 or any similar State statute; or

''(B) for a tax or customs duty with respect to which the debtor—

''(i) made a fraudulent return; or

''(ii) willfully attempted in any manner to evade or to defeat such tax or such customs duty.''.

SEC. 709. STAY OF TAX PROCEEDINGS LIMITED TO PREPETITION TAXES.

Section 362(a)(8) of title 11, United States Code, is amended by striking ''the debtor'' and inserting ''a corporate debtor's tax liability for a taxable period the bankruptcy court may determine or concerning the tax liability of a debtor who is an individual for a taxable period ending before the date of the order for relief under this title''.

SEC. 710. PERIODIC PAYMENT OF TAXES IN CHAPTER 11 CASES.

Section 1129(a)(9) of title 11, United States Code, is amended—

(1) in subparagraph (B), by striking ''and'' at the end;

(2) in subparagraph (C), by striking ''deferred cash payments,'' and all that follows through the end of the subparagraph, and inserting ''regular installment payments in cash—

''(i) of a total value, as of the effective date of the plan, equal to the allowed amount of such claim;

''(ii) over a period ending not later than 5 years after the date of the order for relief under section 301, 302, or 303; and

''(iii) in a manner not less favorable than the most favored nonpriority unsecured claim provided for by the plan (other than cash payments made to a class of creditors under section 1122(b)); and''; and

(3) by adding at the end the following:

"(D) with respect to a secured claim which would otherwise meet the description of an unsecured claim of a governmental unit under section 507(a)(8), but for the secured status of that claim, the holder of that claim will receive on account of that claim, cash payments, in the same manner and over the same period, as prescribed in subparagraph (C).".

SEC. 711. AVOIDANCE OF STATUTORY TAX LIENS PROHIBITED.

Section 545(2) of title 11, United States Code, is amended by inserting before the semicolon at the end the following: ", except in any case in which a purchaser is a purchaser described in section 6323 of the Internal Revenue Code of 1986, or in any other similar provision of State or local law".

SEC. 712. PAYMENT OF TAXES IN THE CONDUCT OF BUSINESS.

(a) PAYMENT OF TAXES REQUIRED.—Section 960 of title 28, United States Code, is amended—

(1) by inserting "(a)" before "Any"; and

(2) by adding at the end the following:

"(b) A tax under subsection (a) shall be paid on or before the due date of the tax under applicable nonbankruptcy law, unless—

"(1) the tax is a property tax secured by a lien against property that is abandoned under section 554 of title 11, within a reasonable period of time after the lien attaches, by the trustee in a case under title 11; or

"(2) payment of the tax is excused under a specific provision of title 11.

"(c) In a case pending under chapter 7 of title 11, payment of a tax may be deferred until final distribution is made under section 726 of title 11, if—

"(1) the tax was not incurred by a trustee duly appointed or elected under chapter 7 of title 11; or

"(2) before the due date of the tax, an order of the court makes a finding of probable insufficiency of funds of the estate to pay in full the administrative expenses allowed under section 503(b) of title 11 that have the same priority in distribution under section 726(b) of title 11 as the priority of that tax.".

(b) PAYMENT OF AD VALOREM TAXES REQUIRED.—Section 503(b)(1)(B)(i) of title 11, United States Code, is amended by inserting "whether secured or unsecured, including property taxes for which liability is in rem, in personam, or both," before "except".

(c) REQUEST FOR PAYMENT OF ADMINISTRATIVE EXPENSE TAXES ELIMINATED.—Section 503(b)(1) of title 11, United States Code, is amended—

(1) in subparagraph (B), by striking "and" at the end;

(2) in subparagraph (C), by adding "and" at the end; and

(3) by adding at the end the following:

"(D) notwithstanding the requirements of subsection (a), a governmental unit shall not be required to file a request for the payment of an expense described in subparagraph (B) or (C), as a condition of its being an allowed administrative expense;".

(d) PAYMENT OF TAXES AND FEES AS SECURED CLAIMS.—Section 506 of title 11, United States Code, is amended—

(1) in subsection (b), by inserting "or State statute" after "agreement"; and

(2) in subsection (c), by inserting ", including the payment of all ad valorem property taxes with respect to the property" before the period at the end.

SEC. 713. TARDILY FILED PRIORITY TAX CLAIMS.

Section 726(a)(1) of title 11, United States Code, is amended by striking "before the date on which the trustee commences distribution under this section;" and inserting the following: "on or before the earlier of—

"(A) the date that is 10 days after the mailing to creditors of the summary of the trustee's final report; or

"(B) the date on which the trustee commences final distribution under this section;".

SEC. 714. INCOME TAX RETURNS PREPARED BY TAX AUTHORITIES.

Section 523(a) of title 11, United States Code, as amended by sections 215 and 224, is amended—

(1) in paragraph (1)(B)—

(A) in the matter preceding clause (i), by inserting "or equivalent report or notice," after "a return,";

(B) in clause (i), by inserting "or given" after "filed"; and

(C) in clause (ii)—

(i) by inserting "or given" after "filed"; and

(ii) by inserting ", report, or notice" after "return"; and

(2) by adding at the end the following:

"For purposes of this subsection, the term 'return' means a return that satisfies the requirements of applicable nonbankruptcy law (including applicable filing requirements). Such term includes a return prepared pursuant to section 6020(a) of the Internal Revenue Code of 1986, or similar State or local law, or a written stipulation to a judgment or a final order entered by a nonbankruptcy tribunal, but does not include a return made pursuant to section 6020(b) of the Internal Revenue Code of 1986, or a similar State or local law.".

SEC. 715. DISCHARGE OF THE ESTATE'S LIABILITY FOR UNPAID TAXES.

Section 505(b)(2) of title 11, United States Code, as amended by section 703, is amended by inserting "the estate," after "misrepresentation,".

SEC. 716. REQUIREMENT TO FILE TAX RETURNS TO CONFIRM CHAPTER 13 PLANS.

(a) FILING OF PREPETITION TAX RETURNS REQUIRED FOR PLAN CONFIRMATION.—Section 1325(a) of title 11, United States Code, as amended by sections 102, 213, and 306, is amended by inserting after paragraph (8) the following:

"(9) the debtor has filed all applicable Federal, State, and local tax returns as required by section 1308.".

(b) ADDITIONAL TIME PERMITTED FOR FILING TAX RETURNS.—

(1) IN GENERAL.—Subchapter I of chapter 13 of title 11, United States Code, is amended by adding at the end the following:

"§ 1308. Filing of prepetition tax returns

"(a) Not later than the day before the date on which the meeting of the creditors is first scheduled to be held under section 341(a), if the debtor was required to file a tax return under applicable nonbankruptcy law, the debtor shall file with appropriate tax authorities all tax returns for all taxable periods ending during the 4-year period ending on the date of the filing of the petition.

"(b)(1) Subject to paragraph (2), if the tax returns required by subsection (a) have not been filed by the date on which the meeting of creditors is first scheduled to be held under section 341(a), the trustee may hold open that meeting for a reasonable period of time to allow the debtor an additional period of time to file any unfiled returns, but such additional period of time shall not extend beyond—

"(A) for any return that is past due as of the date of the filing of the petition, the date that is 120 days after the date of that meeting; or

"(B) for any return that is not past due as of the date of the filing of the petition, the later of—

"(i) the date that is 120 days after the date of that meeting; or

"(ii) the date on which the return is due under the last automatic extension of time for filing that return to which the debtor is entitled, and for which request is timely made, in accordance with applicable nonbankruptcy law.

"(2) After notice and a hearing, and order entered before the tolling of any applicable filing period determined under this subsection, if the debtor demonstrates by a preponderance of the evidence that the failure to file a return as required under this subsection is attributable to circumstances beyond the control of the debtor, the court may extend the filing period established by the trustee under this subsection for—

"(A) a period of not more than 30 days for returns described in paragraph (1); and

"(B) a period not to extend after the applicable extended due date for a return described in paragraph (2).

"(c) For purposes of this section, the term 'return' includes a return prepared pursuant to subsection (a) or (b) of section 6020 of the Internal Revenue Code of 1986, or a similar State or local law, or a written stipulation to a judgment or a final order entered by a nonbankruptcy tribunal.".

(2) CONFORMING AMENDMENT.—The table of sections for subchapter I of chapter 13 of title 11, United States Code, is amended by adding at the end the following:

"1308. Filing of prepetition tax returns.".

(c) DISMISSAL OR CONVERSION ON FAILURE TO COMPLY.—Section 1307 of title 11, United States Code, is amended—

(1) by redesignating subsections (e) and (f) as subsections (f) and (g), respectively; and

(2) by inserting after subsection (d) the following:

"(e) Upon the failure of the debtor to file a tax return under section 1308, on request of a party in interest or the United States trustee and after notice and a hearing, the court shall dismiss a case or convert a case under this chapter to a case under chapter 7 of this title, whichever is in the best interest of the creditors and the estate.".

(d) TIMELY FILED CLAIMS.—Section 502(b)(9) of title 11, United States Code, is amended by inserting before the period at the end the following: ", and except that in a case under chapter 13, a claim of a governmental unit for a tax with respect to a return filed under section 1308 shall be timely if the claim is filed on or before the date that is 60 days after the date on which such return was filed as required".

(e) RULES FOR OBJECTIONS TO CLAIMS AND TO CONFIRMATION.—It is the sense of Congress that the Judicial Conference of the United States should, as soon as practicable after the date of enactment of this Act, propose amended Federal Rules of Bankruptcy Procedure that provide—

(1) notwithstanding the provisions of Rule 3015(f), in cases under chapter 13 of title 11, United States Code, that an objection to the confirmation of a plan filed by a governmental unit on or before the date that is 60 days after the date on which the debtor files all tax returns required under sections 1308 and 1325(a)(7) of title 11, United States Code, shall be treated for all purposes as if such objection had been timely filed before such confirmation; and

(2) in addition to the provisions of Rule 3007, in a case under chapter 13 of title 11, United States Code, that no objection to a claim for a tax with respect to which a return is required to be filed under section 1308 of title 11, United States Code, shall be filed until such return has been filed as required.

SEC. 717. STANDARDS FOR TAX DISCLOSURE.

Section 1125(a)(1) of title 11, United States Code, is amended—

(1) by inserting "including a discussion of the potential material Federal tax consequences of the plan to the debtor, any successor to the debtor, and a hypothetical investor typical of the holders of claims or interests in the case," after "records,"; and

(2) by striking "a hypothetical reasonable investor typical of holders of claims or interests" and inserting "such a hypothetical investor".

SEC. 718. SETOFF OF TAX REFUNDS.

Section 362(b) of title 11, United States Code, as amended by sections 224, 303, 311, and 401, is amended by inserting after paragraph (25) the following:

"(26) under subsection (a), of the setoff under applicable nonbankruptcy law of an income tax refund, by a governmental unit, with respect to a taxable period that ended before the date of the order for relief against an income tax liability for a taxable period that also ended before the date of the order for relief, except that in any case in which the setoff of an income tax refund is not permitted under applicable nonbankruptcy law because of a pending action to determine the amount or legality of a tax liability, the governmental unit may hold the refund pending the resolution of the action, unless the court, on the motion of the trustee and after notice and a hearing, grants the taxing authority adequate protection (within the meaning of section 361) for the secured claim of such authority in the setoff under section 506(a);".

SEC. 719. SPECIAL PROVISIONS RELATED TO THE TREATMENT OF STATE AND LOCAL TAXES.

(a) IN GENERAL.—

(1) SPECIAL PROVISIONS.—Section 346 of title 11, United States Code, is amended to read as follows:

"§ 346. Special provisions related to the treatment of State and local taxes

"(a) Whenever the Internal Revenue Code of 1986 provides that a separate taxable estate or entity is created in a case concerning a debtor under this title, and the income, gain, loss, deductions, and credits of such estate shall be taxed to or claimed by the estate, a separate taxable estate is also created for purposes of any State and local law imposing a tax on or measured by income and such income, gain, loss, deductions, and credits shall be taxed to or claimed by the estate and may not be taxed to or claimed by the debtor. The preceding sentence shall not apply if the case is dismissed. The trustee shall make tax returns of income required under any such State or local law.

"(b) Whenever the Internal Revenue Code of 1986 provides that no separate taxable estate shall be created in a case concerning a debtor under this title, and the income, gain, loss, deductions, and credits of an estate shall be taxed to or claimed by the debtor, such income, gain, loss, deductions, and credits shall be taxed to or claimed by the debtor under a State or local law imposing a tax on or measured by income and may not be taxed to or claimed by the estate. The trustee shall make such tax returns of income of corporations and of partnerships as are required under any State or local law, but with respect to partnerships, shall make such returns only to the extent such returns are also required to be made under such Code. The estate shall be liable for any tax imposed on such corporation or partnership, but not for any tax imposed on partners or members.

"(c) With respect to a partnership or any entity treated as a partnership under a State or local law imposing a tax on or measured by income that is a debtor in a case under this title, any gain or loss resulting from a distribution of property from such partnership, or any distributive share of any income, gain, loss, deduction, or credit of a partner or member that is distributed, or considered distributed, from such partnership, after the commencement of the case, is gain, loss, income, deduction, or credit, as the case may be, of the partner or member, and if such partner or member is a debtor in a case under this title, shall be subject to tax in accordance with subsection (a) or (b).

"(d) For purposes of any State or local law imposing a tax on or measured by income, the taxable period of a debtor in a case under this title shall terminate only if and to the extent that the taxable period of such debtor terminates under the Internal Revenue Code of 1986.

"(e) The estate in any case described in subsection (a) shall use the same accounting method as the debtor used immediately before the commencement of the case, if such method of accounting complies with applicable nonbankruptcy tax law.

"(f) For purposes of any State or local law imposing a tax on or measured by income, a transfer of property from the debtor to the estate or from the estate to the debtor shall not be treated as a disposition for purposes of any provision assigning tax consequences to a disposition, except to the extent that such transfer is treated as a disposition under the Internal Revenue Code of 1986.

"(g) Whenever a tax is imposed pursuant to a State or local law imposing a tax on or measured by income pursuant to subsection (a) or (b), such tax shall be imposed at rates generally applicable to the same types of entities under such State or local law.

"(h) The trustee shall withhold from any payment of claims for wages, salaries, commissions, dividends, interest, or other payments, or collect, any amount required to be withheld or collected under applicable State or local tax law, and shall pay such withheld or collected amount to the appropriate governmental unit at the time and in the manner required by such tax law, and with the same priority as the claim from which such amount was withheld or collected was paid.

"(i)(1) To the extent that any State or local law imposing a tax on or measured by income provides for the carryover of any tax attribute from one taxable period to a subsequent taxable period, the estate shall succeed to such tax attribute in any case in which such estate is subject to tax under subsection (a).

"(2) After such a case is closed or dismissed, the debtor shall succeed to any tax attribute to which the estate succeeded under paragraph (1) to the extent consistent with the Internal Revenue Code of 1986.

"(3) The estate may carry back any loss or tax attribute to a taxable period of the debtor that ended before the date of the order for relief under this title to the extent that—

"(A) applicable State or local tax law provides for a carryback in the case of the debtor; and

"(B) the same or a similar tax attribute may be carried back by the estate to such a taxable period of the debtor under the Internal Revenue Code of 1986.

"(j)(1) For purposes of any State or local law imposing a tax on or measured by income, income is not realized by the estate, the debtor, or a successor to the debtor by reason of discharge of indebtedness in a case under this title, except to the extent, if any, that such income is subject to tax under the Internal Revenue Code of 1986.

"(2) Whenever the Internal Revenue Code of 1986 provides that the amount excluded from gross income in respect of the discharge of indebtedness in a case under this title shall be applied to reduce the tax attributes of the debtor or the estate, a similar reduction shall be made under any State or local law imposing a tax on or measured by income to the extent such State or local law recognizes such attributes. Such State or local law may also provide for the reduction of other attributes to the extent that the full amount of income from the discharge of indebtedness has not been applied.

"(k)(1) Except as provided in this section and section 505, the time and manner of filing tax returns and the items of income, gain, loss, deduction, and credit of any taxpayer shall be determined under applicable nonbankruptcy law.

"(2) For Federal tax purposes, the provisions of this section are subject to the Internal Revenue Code of 1986 and other applicable Federal nonbankruptcy law.".

(2) CLERICAL AMENDMENT.—The table of sections for chapter 3 of title 11, United States Code, is amended by striking the item relating to section 346 and inserting the following:

"346. Special provisions related to the treatment of State and local taxes.".

(b) CONFORMING AMENDMENTS.—Title 11 of the United States Code is amended—

(1) by striking section 728;

(2) in the table of sections for chapter 7 by striking the item relating to section 728;

(3) in section 1146—

(A) by striking subsections (a) and (b); and

(B) by redesignating subsections (c) and (d) as subsections (a) and (b), respectively; and
(4) in section 1231—
(A) by striking subsections (a) and (b); and
(B) by redesignating subsections (c) and (d) as subsections (a) and (b), respectively.

SEC. 720. DISMISSAL FOR FAILURE TO TIMELY FILE TAX RETURNS.

Section 521 of title 11, United States Code, as amended by sections 106, 225, 305, 315, and 316, is amended by adding at the end the following:

"(j)(1) Notwithstanding any other provision of this title, if the debtor fails to file a tax return that becomes due after the commencement of the case or to properly obtain an extension of the due date for filing such return, the taxing authority may request that the court enter an order converting or dismissing the case.

"(2) If the debtor does not file the required return or obtain the extension referred to in paragraph (1) within 90 days after a request is filed by the taxing authority under that paragraph, the court shall convert or dismiss the case, whichever is in the best interests of creditors and the estate.".

TITLE VIII—ANCILLARY AND OTHER CROSS-BORDER CASES

SEC. 801. AMENDMENT TO ADD CHAPTER 15 TO TITLE 11, UNITED STATES CODE.

(a) IN GENERAL.—Title 11, United States Code, is amended by inserting after chapter 13 the following:

"CHAPTER 15—ANCILLARY AND OTHER CROSS-BORDER CASES

"Sec.
"1501. Purpose and scope of application.

"SUBCHAPTER I—GENERAL PROVISIONS

"1502. Definitions.
"1503. International obligations of the United States.
"1504. Commencement of ancillary case.
"1505. Authorization to act in a foreign country.
"1506. Public policy exception.
"1507. Additional assistance.
"1508. Interpretation.

"SUBCHAPTER II—ACCESS OF FOREIGN REPRESENTATIVES AND CREDITORS TO THE COURT

"1509. Right of direct access.
"1510. Limited jurisdiction.
"1511. Commencement of case under section 301 or 303.
"1512. Participation of a foreign representative in a case under this title.
"1513. Access of foreign creditors to a case under this title.
"1514. Notification to foreign creditors concerning a case under this title.

"SUBCHAPTER III—RECOGNITION OF A FOREIGN PROCEEDING AND RELIEF

"1515. Application for recognition.
"1516. Presumptions concerning recognition.
"1517. Order granting recognition.
"1518. Subsequent information.
"1519. Relief that may be granted upon filing petition for recognition.

"§ 1501. Purpose and scope of application

"(a) The purpose of this chapter is to incorporate the Model Law on Cross-Border Insolvency so as to provide effective mechanisms for dealing with cases of cross-border insolvency with the objectives of—

"(1) cooperation between—

"(A) courts of the United States, United States trustees, trustees, examiners, debtors, and debtors in possession; and

"(B) the courts and other competent authorities of foreign countries involved in cross-border insolvency cases;

"(2) greater legal certainty for trade and investment;

"(3) fair and efficient administration of cross-border insolvencies that protects the interests of all creditors, and other interested entities, including the debtor;

"(4) protection and maximization of the value of the debtor's assets; and

"(5) facilitation of the rescue of financially troubled businesses, thereby protecting investment and preserving employment.

"(b) This chapter applies where—

"(1) assistance is sought in the United States by a foreign court or a foreign representative in connection with a foreign proceeding;

"(2) assistance is sought in a foreign country in connection with a case under this title;

"(3) a foreign proceeding and a case under this title with respect to the same debtor are pending concurrently; or

"(4) creditors or other interested persons in a foreign country have an interest in requesting the commencement of, or participating in, a case or proceeding under this title.

"(c) This chapter does not apply to—

"(1) a proceeding concerning an entity, other than a foreign insurance company, identified by exclusion in section 109(b);

"(2) an individual, or to an individual and such individual's spouse, who have debts within the limits specified in section 109(e) and who are citizens of the United States or aliens lawfully admitted for permanent residence in the United States; or

"(3) an entity subject to a proceeding under the Securities Investor Protection Act of 1970, a stockbroker subject to subchapter III of chapter 7 of this title, or a commodity broker subject to subchapter IV of chapter 7 of this title.

"(d) The court may not grant relief under this chapter with respect to any deposit, escrow, trust fund, or other security required or permitted under any applicable State insurance law or regulation for the benefit of claim holders in the United States.

"SUBCHAPTER I—GENERAL PROVISIONS

"§ 1502. Definitions

"For the purposes of this chapter, the term—

"(1) 'debtor' means an entity that is the subject of a foreign proceeding;

"(2) 'establishment' means any place of operations where the debtor carries out a nontransitory economic activity;

"(3) 'foreign court' means a judicial or other authority competent to control or supervise a foreign proceeding;

"(4) 'foreign main proceeding' means a foreign proceeding pending in the country where the debtor has the center of its main interests;

"(5) 'foreign nonmain proceeding' means a foreign proceeding, other than a foreign main proceeding, pending in a country where the debtor has an establishment;

"(6) 'trustee' includes a trustee, a debtor in possession in a case under any chapter of this title, or a debtor under chapter 9 of this title;

"(7) 'recognition' means the entry of an order granting recognition of a foreign main proceeding or foreign nonmain proceeding under this chapter; and

"(8) 'within the territorial jurisdiction of the United States', when used with reference to property of a debtor, refers to tangible property located within the territory of the United States and intangible property deemed under applicable nonbankruptcy law to be located within that territory, including any property subject to attachment or garnishment that may properly be seized or garnished by an action in a Federal or State court in the United States.

"§ 1503. International obligations of the United States

"To the extent that this chapter conflicts with an obligation of the United States arising out of any treaty or other form of agreement to which it is a party with one or more other countries, the requirements of the treaty or agreement prevail.

"§ 1504. Commencement of ancillary case

"A case under this chapter is commenced by the filing of a petition for recognition of a foreign proceeding under section 1515.

"§ 1505. Authorization to act in a foreign country

"A trustee or another entity (including an examiner) may be authorized by the court to act in a foreign country on behalf of an estate created under section 541. An entity authorized to act under this section may act in any way permitted by the applicable foreign law.

"§ 1506. Public policy exception

"Nothing in this chapter prevents the court from refusing to take an action governed by this chapter if the action would be manifestly contrary to the public policy of the United States.

"§ 1507. Additional assistance

"(a) Subject to the specific limitations stated elsewhere in this chapter the court, if recognition is granted, may provide additional assistance to a foreign representative under this title or under other laws of the United States.

"(b) In determining whether to provide additional assistance under this title or under other laws of the United States, the court shall consider whether such additional assistance, consistent with the principles of comity, will reasonably assure—

"(1) just treatment of all holders of claims against or interests in the debtor's property;

"(2) protection of claim holders in the United States against prejudice and inconvenience in the processing of claims in such foreign proceeding;

"(3) prevention of preferential or fraudulent dispositions of property of the debtor;

"(4) distribution of proceeds of the debtor's property substantially in accordance with the order prescribed by this title; and

"(5) if appropriate, the provision of an opportunity for a fresh start for the individual that such foreign proceeding concerns.

"§ 1508. Interpretation

"In interpreting this chapter, the court shall consider its international origin, and the need to promote an application of this chapter that is consistent with the application of similar statutes adopted by foreign jurisdictions.

"SUBCHAPTER II—ACCESS OF FOREIGN REPRESENTATIVES AND CREDITORS TO THE COURT

"§ 1509. Right of direct access

"(a) A foreign representative may commence a case under section 1504 by filing directly with the court a petition for recognition of a foreign proceeding under section 1515.

"(b) If the court grants recognition under section 1517, and subject to any limitations that the court may impose consistent with the policy of this chapter—

"(1) the foreign representative has the capacity to sue and be sued in a court in the United States;

"(2) the foreign representative may apply directly to a court in the United States for appropriate relief in that court; and

"(3) a court in the United States shall grant comity or cooperation to the foreign representative.

"(c) A request for comity or cooperation by a foreign representative in a court in the United States other than the court which granted recognition shall be accompanied by a certified copy of an order granting recognition under section 1517.

"(d) If the court denies recognition under this chapter, the court may issue any appropriate order necessary to prevent the foreign representative from obtaining comity or cooperation from courts in the United States.

"(e) Whether or not the court grants recognition, and subject to sections 306 and 1510, a foreign representative is subject to applicable nonbankruptcy law.

"(f) Notwithstanding any other provision of this section, the failure of a foreign representative to commence a case or to obtain recognition under this chapter does not affect any right the foreign representative may have to sue in a court in the United States to collect or recover a claim which is the property of the debtor.

"§ 1510. Limited jurisdiction

"The sole fact that a foreign representative files a petition under section 1515 does not subject the foreign representative to the jurisdiction of any court in the United States for any other purpose.

"§ 1511. Commencement of case under section 301 or 303

"(a) Upon recognition, a foreign representative may commence—

"(1) an involuntary case under section 303; or

"(2) a voluntary case under section 301 or 302, if the foreign proceeding is a foreign main proceeding.

"(b) The petition commencing a case under subsection (a) must be accompanied by a certified copy of an order granting recognition. The court where the petition for recognition has been filed must be advised of the foreign representative's intent to commence a case under subsection (a) prior to such commencement.

"§ 1512. Participation of a foreign representative in a case under this title

"Upon recognition of a foreign proceeding, the foreign representative in the recognized proceeding is entitled to participate as a party in interest in a case regarding the debtor under this title.

"§ 1513. Access of foreign creditors to a case under this title

"(a) Foreign creditors have the same rights regarding the commencement of, and participation in, a case under this title as domestic creditors.

"(b)(1) Subsection (a) does not change or codify present law as to the priority of claims under section 507 or 726, except that the claim of a foreign creditor under those sections shall not be given a lower priority than that of general unsecured claims without priority solely because the holder of such claim is a foreign creditor.

"(2)(A) Subsection (a) and paragraph (1) do not change or codify present law as to the allowability of foreign revenue claims or other foreign public law claims in a proceeding under this title.

"(B) Allowance and priority as to a foreign tax claim or other foreign public law claim shall be governed by any applicable tax treaty of the United States, under the conditions and circumstances specified therein.

"§ 1514. Notification to foreign creditors concerning a case under this title

"(a) Whenever in a case under this title notice is to be given to creditors generally or to any class or category of creditors, such notice shall also be given to the known creditors generally, or to creditors in the notified class or category, that do not have addresses in the United States. The court may order that appropriate steps be taken with a view to notifying any creditor whose address is not yet known.

"(b) Such notification to creditors with foreign addresses described in subsection (a) shall be given individually, unless the court considers that, under the circumstances, some other form of notification would be more appropriate. No letter or other formality is required.

"(c) When a notification of commencement of a case is to be given to foreign creditors, such notification shall—

"(1) indicate the time period for filing proofs of claim and specify the place for filing such proofs of claim;

"(2) indicate whether secured creditors need to file proofs of claim; and

"(3) contain any other information required to be included in such notification to creditors under this title and the orders of the court.

"(d) Any rule of procedure or order of the court as to notice or the filing of a proof of claim shall provide such additional time to creditors with foreign addresses as is reasonable under the circumstances.

"SUBCHAPTER III—RECOGNITION OF A FOREIGN PROCEEDING AND RELIEF

"§ 1515. Application for recognition

"(a) A foreign representative applies to the court for recognition of a foreign proceeding in which the foreign representative has been appointed by filing a petition for recognition.

"(b) A petition for recognition shall be accompanied by—

"(1) a certified copy of the decision commencing such foreign proceeding and appointing the foreign representative;

"(2) a certificate from the foreign court affirming the existence of such foreign proceeding and of the appointment of the foreign representative; or

"(3) in the absence of evidence referred to in paragraphs (1) and (2), any other evidence acceptable to the court of the existence of such foreign proceeding and of the appointment of the foreign representative.

"(c) A petition for recognition shall also be accompanied by a statement identifying all foreign proceedings with respect to the debtor that are known to the foreign representative.

"(d) The documents referred to in paragraphs (1) and (2) of subsection (b) shall be translated into English. The court may require a translation into English of additional documents.

"§ 1516. Presumptions concerning recognition

"(a) If the decision or certificate referred to in section 1515(b) indicates that the foreign proceeding is a foreign proceeding and that the person or body is a foreign representative, the court is entitled to so presume.

"(b) The court is entitled to presume that documents submitted in support of the petition for recognition are authentic, whether or not they have been legalized.

"(c) In the absence of evidence to the contrary, the debtor's registered office, or habitual residence in the case of an individual, is presumed to be the center of the debtor's main interests.

"§ 1517. Order granting recognition

"(a) Subject to section 1506, after notice and a hearing, an order recognizing a foreign proceeding shall be entered if—

"(1) such foreign proceeding for which recognition is sought is a foreign main proceeding or foreign nonmain proceeding within the meaning of section 1502;

"(2) the foreign representative applying for recognition is a person or body; and

"(3) the petition meets the requirements of section 1515.

"(b) Such foreign proceeding shall be recognized—

"(1) as a foreign main proceeding if it is pending in the country where the debtor has the center of its main interests; or

"(2) as a foreign nonmain proceeding if the debtor has an establishment within the meaning of section 1502 in the foreign country where the proceeding is pending.

"(c) A petition for recognition of a foreign proceeding shall be decided upon at the earliest possible time. Entry of an order recognizing a foreign proceeding constitutes recognition under this chapter.

"(d) The provisions of this subchapter do not prevent modification or termination of recognition if it is shown that the grounds for granting it were fully or partially lacking or have ceased to exist, but in considering such action the court shall give due weight to possible prejudice to parties that have relied upon the order granting recognition. A case under this chapter may be closed in the manner prescribed under section 350.

"§ 1518. Subsequent information

"From the time of filing the petition for recognition of a foreign proceeding, the foreign representative shall file with the court promptly a notice of change of status concerning—

"(1) any substantial change in the status of such foreign proceeding or the status of the foreign representative's appointment; and

"(2) any other foreign proceeding regarding the debtor that becomes known to the foreign representative.

"§ 1519. Relief that may be granted upon filing petition for recognition

"(a) From the time of filing a petition for recognition until the court rules on the petition, the court may, at the request of the foreign representative, where relief is urgently needed to protect the assets of the debtor or the interests of the creditors, grant relief of a provisional nature, including—

"(1) staying execution against the debtor's assets;

"(2) entrusting the administration or realization of all or part of the debtor's assets located in the United States to the foreign representative or another person authorized by the court, including an examiner, in order to protect and preserve the value of assets that, by their nature or because of other circumstances, are perishable, susceptible to devaluation or otherwise in jeopardy; and

"(3) any relief referred to in paragraph (3), (4), or (7) of section 1521(a).

"(b) Unless extended under section 1521(a)(6), the relief granted under this section terminates when the petition for recognition is granted.

"(c) It is a ground for denial of relief under this section that such relief would interfere with the administration of a foreign main proceeding.

"(d) The court may not enjoin a police or regulatory act of a governmental unit, including a criminal action or proceeding, under this section.

"(e) The standards, procedures, and limitations applicable to an injunction shall apply to relief under this section.

"(f) The exercise of rights not subject to the stay arising under section 362(a) pursuant to paragraph (6), (7), (17), or (27) of section 362(b) or pursuant to section 362(n) shall not be stayed by any order of a court or administrative agency in any proceeding under this chapter.

"§ 1520. Effects of recognition of a foreign main proceeding

"(a) Upon recognition of a foreign proceeding that is a foreign main proceeding—

"(1) sections 361 and 362 apply with respect to the debtor and the property of the debtor that is within the territorial jurisdiction of the United States;

"(2) sections 363, 549, and 552 apply to a transfer of an interest of the debtor in property that is within the territorial jurisdiction of the United States to the same extent that the sections would apply to property of an estate;

"(3) unless the court orders otherwise, the foreign representative may operate the debtor's business and may exercise the rights and powers of a trustee under and to the extent provided by sections 363 and 552; and

"(4) section 552 applies to property of the debtor that is within the territorial jurisdiction of the United States.

"(b) Subsection (a) does not affect the right to commence an individual action or proceeding in a foreign country to the extent necessary to preserve a claim against the debtor.

"(c) Subsection (a) does not affect the right of a foreign representative or an entity to file a petition commencing a case under this title or the right of any party to file claims or take other proper actions in such a case.

"§ 1521. Relief that may be granted upon recognition

"(a) Upon recognition of a foreign proceeding, whether main or nonmain, where necessary to effectuate the purpose of this chapter and to protect the assets of the debtor or the interests of the creditors, the court may, at the request of the foreign representative, grant any appropriate relief, including—

"(1) staying the commencement or continuation of an individual action or proceeding concerning the debtor's assets, rights, obligations or liabilities to the extent they have not been stayed under section 1520(a);

"(2) staying execution against the debtor's assets to the extent it has not been stayed under section 1520(a);

"(3) suspending the right to transfer, encumber or otherwise dispose of any assets of the debtor to the extent this right has not been suspended under section 1520(a);

"(4) providing for the examination of witnesses, the taking of evidence or the delivery of information concerning the debtor's assets, affairs, rights, obligations or liabilities;

"(5) entrusting the administration or realization of all or part of the debtor's assets within the territorial jurisdiction of the United States to the foreign representative or another person, including an examiner, authorized by the court;

"(6) extending relief granted under section 1519(a); and

"(7) granting any additional relief that may be available to a trustee, except for relief available under sections 522, 544, 545, 547, 548, 550, and 724(a).

"(b) Upon recognition of a foreign proceeding, whether main or nonmain, the court may, at the request of the foreign representative, entrust the distribution of all or part of the debtor's assets located in the United States to the foreign representative or another person, including an examiner, authorized by the court, provided that the court is satisfied that the interests of creditors in the United States are sufficiently protected.

"(c) In granting relief under this section to a representative of a foreign nonmain proceeding, the court must be satisfied that the relief relates to assets that, under the law of the United States, should be administered in the foreign nonmain proceeding or concerns information required in that proceeding.

"(d) The court may not enjoin a police or regulatory act of a governmental unit, including a criminal action or proceeding, under this section.

"(e) The standards, procedures, and limitations applicable to an injunction shall apply to relief under paragraphs (1), (2), (3), and (6) of subsection (a).

"(f) The exercise of rights not subject to the stay arising under section 362(a) pursuant to paragraph (6), (7), (17), or (27) of section 362(b) or pursuant to section 362(n) shall not be stayed by any order of a court or administrative agency in any proceeding under this chapter.

"§ 1522. Protection of creditors and other interested persons

"(a) The court may grant relief under section 1519 or 1521, or may modify or terminate relief under subsection (c), only if the interests of the creditors and other interested entities, including the debtor, are sufficiently protected.

NEW 2005 Revised Edition!

The National Consumer Law Center Guide to

SURVIVING DEBT

(425 pages)

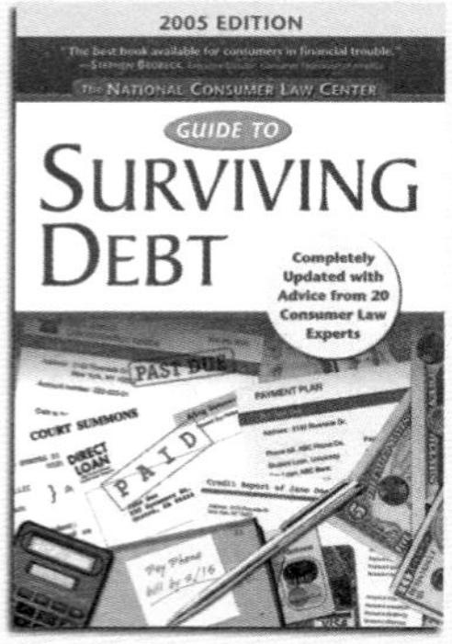

"A gold mine on topics like how to handle collectors, which debts to pay first, and how collection lawsuits work."
— U.S. News and World Report

New and expanded advice from 20 consumer law experts on:

- Dealing with debt collectors
- Your credit report
- Which debts to pay first
- When to refinance
- Saving your home or car
- Income tax collections
- Credit card debt
- Student loans and loan consolidation
- How to find effective credit counseling agencies
- Your bankruptcy rights, and much more.

"Outstanding manual. Seldom is such useful, authoritative information available for so small a price!"
— Booklist, Magazine of the American Library Assn.

THE PRACTICE OF CONSUMER LAW

Seeking Economic Justice

With CD-Rom (328 pages)

A practical volume to get you started or help you stay on track in a consumer law practice:

- Opening a private consumer law practice: choosing a specialty, fee agreements, networking with others, how to market yourself
- Making even small consumer claims cost-effective
- Sample consumer law pleadings, client retainer forms, co-counseling agreements, checklists and interview questionnaires, discovery, and trial documents
- Consumer law remedies in individual suits and defense tactics

- How to take an out-of-state deposition
- Challenging 13 types of abusive businesses
- Biographies of over 100 consumer law attorneys, describing the nature of their practice and more.

Order securely online at www.consumerlaw.org

National Consumer Law Center
77 Summer Street • 10th Floor • Boston MA 02110 • (617) 542-9595 • Fax (617) 542-8028 • www.consumerlaw.org

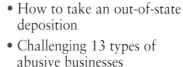

NO POSTAGE NECESSARY IF MAILED IN THE UNITED STATES

BUSINESS REPLY MAIL
FIRST-CLASS MAIL PERMIT NO. 1639 BOSTON, MA

POSTAGE WILL BE PAID BY ADDRESSEE

National Consumer Law Center
Publications Department
77 Summer Street, 10th Floor
Boston, MA 02110-9828

"(b) The court may subject relief granted under section 1519 or 1521, or the operation of the debtor's business under section 1520(a)(3), to conditions it considers appropriate, including the giving of security or the filing of a bond.

"(c) The court may, at the request of the foreign representative or an entity affected by relief granted under section 1519 or 1521, or at its own motion, modify or terminate such relief.

"(d) Section 1104(d) shall apply to the appointment of an examiner under this chapter. Any examiner shall comply with the qualification requirements imposed on a trustee by section 322.

"§ 1523. Actions to avoid acts detrimental to creditors

"(a) Upon recognition of a foreign proceeding, the foreign representative has standing in a case concerning the debtor pending under another chapter of this title to initiate actions under sections 522, 544, 545, 547, 548, 550, 553, and 724(a).

"(b) When a foreign proceeding is a foreign nonmain proceeding, the court must be satisfied that an action under subsection (a) relates to assets that, under United States law, should be administered in the foreign nonmain proceeding.

"§ 1524. Intervention by a foreign representative

"Upon recognition of a foreign proceeding, the foreign representative may intervene in any proceedings in a State or Federal court in the United States in which the debtor is a party.

"SUBCHAPTER IV—COOPERATION WITH FOREIGN COURTS AND FOREIGN REPRESENTATIVES

"§ 1525. Cooperation and direct communication between the court and foreign courts or foreign representatives

"(a) Consistent with section 1501, the court shall cooperate to the maximum extent possible with a foreign court or a foreign representative, either directly or through the trustee.

"(b) The court is entitled to communicate directly with, or to request information or assistance directly from, a foreign court or a foreign representative, subject to the rights of a party in interest to notice and participation.

"§ 1526. Cooperation and direct communication between the trustee and foreign courts or foreign representatives

"(a) Consistent with section 1501, the trustee or other person, including an examiner, authorized by the court, shall, subject to the supervision of the court, cooperate to the maximum extent possible with a foreign court or a foreign representative.

"(b) The trustee or other person, including an examiner, authorized by the court is entitled, subject to the supervision of the court, to communicate directly with a foreign court or a foreign representative.

"§ 1527. Forms of cooperation

"Cooperation referred to in sections 1525 and 1526 may be implemented by any appropriate means, including—

"(1) appointment of a person or body, including an examiner, to act at the direction of the court;

"(2) communication of information by any means considered appropriate by the court;

"(3) coordination of the administration and supervision of the debtor's assets and affairs;

"(4) approval or implementation of agreements concerning the coordination of proceedings; and

"(5) coordination of concurrent proceedings regarding the same debtor.

"SUBCHAPTER V—CONCURRENT PROCEEDINGS

"§ 1528. Commencement of a case under this title after recognition of a foreign main proceeding

"After recognition of a foreign main proceeding, a case under another chapter of this title may be commenced only if the debtor has assets in the United States. The effects of such case shall be restricted to the assets of the debtor that are within the territorial jurisdiction of the United States and, to the extent necessary to implement cooperation and coordination under sections 1525, 1526, and 1527, to other assets of the debtor that are within the jurisdiction of the court under sections 541(a) of this title, and 1334(e) of title 28, to the extent that such other assets are not subject to the jurisdiction and control of a foreign proceeding that has been recognized under this chapter.

"§ 1529. Coordination of a case under this title and a foreign proceeding

"If a foreign proceeding and a case under another chapter of this title are pending concurrently regarding the same debtor, the court shall seek cooperation and coordination under sections 1525, 1526, and 1527, and the following shall apply:

"(1) If the case in the United States pending at the time the petition for recognition of such foreign proceeding is filed—

"(A) any relief granted under section 1519 or 1521 must be consistent with the relief granted in the case in the United States; and

"(B) section 1520 does not apply even if such foreign proceeding is recognized as a foreign main proceeding.

"(2) If a case in the United States under this title commences after recognition, or after the date of the filing of the petition for recognition, of such foreign proceeding—

"(A) any relief in effect under section 1519 or 1521 shall be reviewed by the court and shall be modified or terminated if inconsistent with the case in the United States; and

"(B) if such foreign proceeding is a foreign main proceeding, the stay and suspension referred to in section 1520(a) shall be modified or terminated if inconsistent with the relief granted in the case in the United States.

"(3) In granting, extending, or modifying relief granted to a representative of a foreign nonmain proceeding, the court must be satisfied that the relief relates to assets that, under the laws of the United States, should be administered in the foreign nonmain proceeding or concerns information required in that proceeding.

"(4) In achieving cooperation and coordination under sections 1528 and 1529, the court may grant any of the relief authorized under section 305.

"§ 1530. Coordination of more than 1 foreign proceeding

"In matters referred to in section 1501, with respect to more than 1 foreign proceeding regarding the debtor, the court shall seek cooperation and coordination under sections 1525, 1526, and 1527, and the following shall apply:

"(1) Any relief granted under section 1519 or 1521 to a representative of a foreign nonmain proceeding after recognition of a foreign main proceeding must be consistent with the foreign main proceeding.

"(2) If a foreign main proceeding is recognized after recognition, or after the filing of a petition for recognition, of a foreign nonmain proceeding, any relief in effect under section 1519 or 1521 shall be reviewed by the court and shall be modified or terminated if inconsistent with the foreign main proceeding.

"(3) If, after recognition of a foreign nonmain proceeding, another foreign nonmain proceeding is recognized, the court shall grant, modify, or terminate relief for the purpose of facilitating coordination of the proceedings.

"§ 1531. Presumption of insolvency based on recognition of a foreign main proceeding

"In the absence of evidence to the contrary, recognition of a foreign main proceeding is, for the purpose of commencing a proceeding under section 303, proof that the debtor is generally not paying its debts as such debts become due.

"§ 1532. Rule of payment in concurrent proceedings

"Without prejudice to secured claims or rights in rem, a creditor who has received payment with respect to its claim in a foreign proceeding pursuant to a law relating to insolvency may not receive a payment for the same claim in a case under any other chapter of this title regarding the debtor, so long as the payment to other creditors of the same class is proportionately less than the payment the creditor has already received.".

(b) CLERICAL AMENDMENT.—The table of chapters for title 11, United States Code, is amended by inserting after the item relating to chapter 13 the following:

"15. Ancillary and Other Cross-Border Cases ....1501".

SEC. 802. OTHER AMENDMENTS TO TITLES 11 AND 28, UNITED STATES CODE.

(a) APPLICABILITY OF CHAPTERS.—Section 103 of title 11, United States Code, is amended—

(1) in subsection (a), by inserting before the period the following: ", and this chapter, sections 307, 362(n), 555 through 557, and 559 through 562 apply in a case under chapter 15"; and

(2) by adding at the end the following:

"(k) Chapter 15 applies only in a case under such chapter, except that—

"(1) sections 1505, 1513, and 1514 apply in all cases under this title; and

"(2) section 1509 applies whether or not a case under this title is pending.".

(b) DEFINITIONS.—Section 101 of title 11, United States Code, is amended by striking paragraphs (23) and (24) and inserting the following:

"(23) 'foreign proceeding' means a collective judicial or administrative proceeding in a foreign country, including an interim proceeding, under a law relating to insolvency or adjustment of debt in which proceeding the assets and affairs of the debtor are subject to control or supervision by a foreign court, for the purpose of reorganization or liquidation;

"(24) 'foreign representative' means a person or body, including a person or body appointed on an interim basis, authorized in a foreign proceeding to administer the reorganization or the liquidation of the debtor's assets or affairs or to act as a representative of such foreign proceeding;".

(c) AMENDMENTS TO TITLE 28, UNITED STATES CODE.—

(1) PROCEDURES.—Section 157(b)(2) of title 28, United States Code, is amended—

(A) in subparagraph (N), by striking "and" at the end;

(B) in subparagraph (O), by striking the period at the end and inserting "; and"; and

(C) by adding at the end the following:

"(P) recognition of foreign proceedings and other matters under chapter 15 of title 11.".

(2) BANKRUPTCY CASES AND PROCEEDINGS.—Section 1334(c) of title 28, United States Code, is amended by striking "Nothing in" and inserting "Except with respect to a case under chapter 15 of title 11, nothing in".

(3) DUTIES OF TRUSTEES.—Section 586(a)(3) of title 28, United States Code, is amended by striking "or 13" and inserting "13, or 15".

(4) VENUE OF CASES ANCILLARY TO FOREIGN PROCEEDINGS.—Section 1410 of title 28, United States Code, is amended to read as follows:

"§ 1410. Venue of cases ancillary to foreign proceedings

"A case under chapter 15 of title 11 may be commenced in the district court of the United States for the district—

"(1) in which the debtor has its principal place of business or principal assets in the United States;

"(2) if the debtor does not have a place of business or assets in the United States, in which there is pending against the debtor an action or proceeding in a Federal or State court; or

"(3) in a case other than those specified in paragraph (1) or (2), in which venue will be consistent with the interests of justice and the convenience of the parties, having regard to the relief sought by the foreign representative.".

(d) OTHER SECTIONS OF TITLE 11.—Title 11 of the United States Code is amended—

(1) in section 109(b), by striking paragraph (3) and inserting the following:

"(3)(A) a foreign insurance company, engaged in such business in the United States; or

"(B) a foreign bank, savings bank, cooperative bank, savings and loan association, building and loan association, or credit union, that has a branch or agency (as defined in section 1(b) of the International Banking Act of 1978 in the United States.";

(2) in section 303, by striking subsection (k);

(3) by striking section 304;

(4) in the table of sections for chapter 3 by striking the item relating to section 304;

(5) in section 306 by striking ", 304," each place it appears;

(6) in section 305(a) by striking paragraph (2) and inserting the following:

"(2)(A) a petition under section 1515 for recognition of a foreign proceeding has been granted; and

"(B) the purposes of chapter 15 of this title would be best served by such dismissal or suspension.'; and

(7) in section 508—

(A) by striking subsection (a); and

(B) in subsection (b), by striking "(b)".

TITLE IX—FINANCIAL CONTRACT PROVISIONS

SEC. 901. TREATMENT OF CERTAIN AGREEMENTS BY CONSERVATORS OR RECEIVERS OF INSURED DEPOSITORY INSTITUTIONS.

(a) DEFINITION OF QUALIFIED FINANCIAL CONTRACT.—

(1) FDIC-INSURED DEPOSITORY INSTITUTIONS.—Section 11(e)(8)(D) of the Federal Deposit Insurance Act (12 U.S.C. 1821(e)(8)(D)) is amended—

(A) by striking "subsection—" and inserting "subsection, the following definitions shall apply:"; and

(B) in clause (i), by inserting ", resolution, or order" after "any similar agreement that the Corporation determines by regulation".

(2) INSURED CREDIT UNIONS.—Section 207(c)(8)(D) of the Federal Credit Union Act (12 U.S.C. 1787(c)(8)(D)) is amended—

(A) by striking "subsection—" and inserting "subsection, the following definitions shall apply:"; and

(B) in clause (i), by inserting ", resolution, or order" after "any similar agreement that the Board determines by regulation".

(b) DEFINITION OF SECURITIES CONTRACT.—

(1) FDIC-INSURED DEPOSITORY INSTITUTIONS.—Section 11(e)(8)(D)(ii) of the Federal Deposit Insurance Act (12 U.S.C. 1821(e)(8)(D)(ii)) is amended to read as follows:

"(ii) SECURITIES CONTRACT.—The term 'securities contract'—

"(I) means a contract for the purchase, sale, or loan of a security, a certificate of deposit, a mortgage loan, or any interest in a mortgage loan, a group or index of securities, certificates of deposit, or mortgage loans or interests therein (including any interest therein or based on the value thereof) or any option on any of the foregoing, including any option to purchase or sell any such security, certificate of deposit, mortgage loan, interest, group or index, or option, and including any repurchase or reverse repurchase transaction on any such security, certificate of deposit, mortgage loan, interest, group or index, or option;

"(II) does not include any purchase, sale, or repurchase obligation under a participation in a commercial mortgage loan unless the Corporation determines by regulation, resolution, or order to include any such agreement within the meaning of such term;

"(III) means any option entered into on a national securities exchange relating to foreign currencies;

"(IV) means the guarantee by or to any securities clearing agency of any settlement of cash, securities, certificates of deposit, mortgage loans or interests therein, group or index of securities, certificates of deposit, or mortgage loans or interests therein (including any interest therein or based on the value thereof) or option on any of the foregoing, including any option to purchase or sell any such security, certificate of deposit, mortgage loan, interest, group or index, or option;

"(V) means any margin loan;

"(VI) means any other agreement or transaction that is similar to any agreement or transaction referred to in this clause;

"(VII) means any combination of the agreements or transactions referred to in this clause;

"(VIII) means any option to enter into any agreement or transaction referred to in this clause;

"(IX) means a master agreement that provides for an agreement or transaction referred to in subclause (I), (III), (IV), (V), (VI), (VII), or (VIII), together with all supplements to any such master agreement, without regard to whether the master agreement provides for an agreement or transaction that is not a securities contract under this clause, except that the master agreement shall be considered to be a securities contract under this clause only with respect to each agreement or transaction under the master agreement that is referred to in subclause (I), (III), (IV), (V), (VI), (VII), or (VIII); and

"(X) means any security agreement or arrangement or other credit enhancement related to any agreement or transaction referred to in this clause, including any guarantee or reimbursement obligation in connection with any agreement or transaction referred to in this clause.".

(2) INSURED CREDIT UNIONS.—Section 207(c)(8)(D)(ii) of the Federal Credit Union Act (12 U.S.C. 1787(c)(8)(D)(ii)) is amended to read as follows:

"(ii) SECURITIES CONTRACT.—The term 'securities contract'—

"(I) means a contract for the purchase, sale, or loan of a security, a certificate of deposit, a mortgage loan, or any interest in a mortgage loan, a group or index of securities, certificates of deposit, or mortgage loans or interests therein (including any interest therein or based on the value thereof) or any option on any of the foregoing, including any option to purchase or sell any such security, certificate of deposit, mortgage loan, interest, group or index, or option, and including any repurchase or reverse repurchase transaction on any such security, certificate of deposit, mortgage loan, interest, group or index, or option;

"(II) does not include any purchase, sale, or repurchase obligation under a participation in a commercial mortgage loan unless the Board determines by regulation, resolution, or order to include any such agreement within the meaning of such term;

"(III) means any option entered into on a national securities exchange relating to foreign currencies;

"(IV) means the guarantee by or to any securities clearing agency of any settlement of cash, securities, certificates of deposit, mortgage loans or interests therein, group or index of securities, certificates of deposit, or mortgage loans or interests therein (including any interest therein or based on the value thereof) or option on any of the foregoing, including any option to purchase or sell any such security, certificate of deposit, mortgage loan, interest, group or index, or option;

"(V) means any margin loan;

"(VI) means any other agreement or transaction that is similar to any agreement or transaction referred to in this clause;

"(VII) means any combination of the agreements or transactions referred to in this clause;

"(VIII) means any option to enter into any agreement or transaction referred to in this clause;

"(IX) means a master agreement that provides for an agreement or transaction referred to in subclause (I), (III), (IV), (V), (VI), (VII), or (VIII), together with all supplements to any such master agreement, without regard to whether the master agreement provides for an agreement or transaction that is not a securities contract under this clause, except that the master agreement shall be considered to be a securities contract under this clause only with respect to each agreement or transaction under the master agreement that is referred to in subclause (I), (III), (IV), (V), (VI), (VII), or (VIII); and

"(X) means any security agreement or arrangement or other credit enhancement related to any agreement or transaction referred to in this clause, including any guarantee or reimbursement obligation in connection with any agreement or transaction referred to in this clause.".

(c) DEFINITION OF COMMODITY CONTRACT.—

(1) FDIC-INSURED DEPOSITORY INSTITUTIONS.—Section 11(e)(8)(D)(iii) of the Federal Deposit Insurance Act (12 U.S.C. 1821(e)(8)(D)(iii)) is amended to read as follows:

"(iii) COMMODITY CONTRACT.—The term 'commodity contract' means—

"(I) with respect to a futures commission merchant, a contract for the purchase or sale of a commodity for future delivery on, or subject to the rules of, a contract market or board of trade;

"(II) with respect to a foreign futures commission merchant, a foreign future;

"(III) with respect to a leverage transaction merchant, a leverage transaction;

"(IV) with respect to a clearing organization, a contract for the purchase or sale of a commodity for future delivery on, or subject to the rules of, a contract market or board of trade that is cleared by such clearing organization, or commodity option traded on, or subject to the rules of, a contract market or board of trade that is cleared by such clearing organization;

"(V) with respect to a commodity options dealer, a commodity option;

"(VI) any other agreement or transaction that is similar to any agreement or transaction referred to in this clause;

"(VII) any combination of the agreements or transactions referred to in this clause;

"(VIII) any option to enter into any agreement or transaction referred to in this clause;

"(IX) a master agreement that provides for an agreement or transaction referred to in subclause (I), (II), (III), (IV), (V), (VI), (VII), or (VIII), together with all supplements to any such master agreement, without regard to whether the master agreement provides for an agreement or transaction that is not a commodity contract under this clause, except that the master agreement shall be considered to be a commodity contract under this clause only with respect to each agreement or transaction under the master agreement that is referred to in subclause (I), (II), (III), (IV), (V), (VI), (VII), or (VIII); or

"(X) any security agreement or arrangement or other credit enhancement related to any agreement or transaction referred to in this clause, including any guarantee or reimbursement obligation in connection with any agreement or transaction referred to in this clause.".

(2) INSURED CREDIT UNIONS.—Section 207(c)(8)(D)(iii) of the Federal Credit Union Act (12 U.S.C. 1787(c)(8)(D)(iii)) is amended to read as follows:

"(iii) COMMODITY CONTRACT.—The term 'commodity contract' means—

"(I) with respect to a futures commission merchant, a contract for the purchase or sale of a commodity for future delivery on, or subject to the rules of, a contract market or board of trade;

"(II) with respect to a foreign futures commission merchant, a foreign future;

"(III) with respect to a leverage transaction merchant, a leverage transaction;

"(IV) with respect to a clearing organization, a contract for the purchase or sale of a commodity for future delivery on, or subject to the rules of, a contract market or board of trade that is cleared by such clearing organization, or commodity option traded on, or subject to the rules of, a contract market or board of trade that is cleared by such clearing organization;

"(V) with respect to a commodity options dealer, a commodity option;

"(VI) any other agreement or transaction that is similar to any agreement or transaction referred to in this clause;

"(VII) any combination of the agreements or transactions referred to in this clause;

"(VIII) any option to enter into any agreement or transaction referred to in this clause;

"(IX) a master agreement that provides for an agreement or transaction referred to in subclause (I), (II), (III), (IV), (V), (VI), (VII), or (VIII), together with all supplements to any such master agreement, without regard to whether the master agreement provides for an agreement or transaction that is not a commodity contract under this clause, except that the master agreement shall be considered to be a commodity contract under this clause only with respect to each agreement or transaction under the master agreement that is referred to in subclause (I), (II), (III), (IV), (V), (VI), (VII), or (VIII); or

"(X) any security agreement or arrangement or other credit enhancement related to any agreement or transaction referred to in this clause, including any guarantee or reimbursement obligation in connection with any agreement or transaction referred to in this clause.".

(d) DEFINITION OF FORWARD CONTRACT.—

(1) FDIC-INSURED DEPOSITORY INSTITUTIONS.—Section 11(e)(8)(D)(iv) of the Federal Deposit Insurance Act (12 U.S.C. 1821(e)(8)(D)(iv)) is amended to read as follows:

"(iv) FORWARD CONTRACT.—The term 'forward contract' means—

"(I) a contract (other than a commodity contract) for the purchase, sale, or transfer of a commodity or any similar good, article, service, right, or interest which is presently or in the future becomes the subject of dealing in the forward contract trade, or product or byproduct thereof, with a maturity date more than 2 days after the date the contract is entered into, including, a repurchase transaction, reverse repurchase transaction, consignment, lease, swap, hedge transaction, deposit, loan, option, allocated transaction, unallocated transaction, or any other similar agreement;

"(II) any combination of agreements or transactions referred to in subclauses (I) and (III);

"(III) any option to enter into any agreement or transaction referred to in subclause (I) or (II);

"(IV) a master agreement that provides for an agreement or transaction referred to in subclauses (I), (II), or (III), together with all supplements to any such master agreement, without regard to whether the master agreement provides for an agreement or transaction that is not a forward contract under this clause, except that the master agreement shall be considered to be a forward contract under this clause only with respect to each agreement or transaction under the master agreement that is referred to in subclause (I), (II), or (III); or

"(V) any security agreement or arrangement or other credit enhancement related to any agreement or transaction referred to in subclause (I), (II), (III), or (IV), including any guarantee or reimbursement obligation in connection with any agreement or transaction referred to in any such subclause.".

(2) INSURED CREDIT UNIONS.—Section 207(c)(8)(D)(iv) of the Federal Credit Union Act (12 U.S.C. 1787(c)(8)(D)(iv)) is amended to read as follows:

"(iv) FORWARD CONTRACT.—The term 'forward contract' means—

"(I) a contract (other than a commodity contract) for the purchase, sale, or transfer of a commodity or any similar good, article, service, right, or interest which is presently or in the future becomes the subject of dealing in the forward contract trade, or product or byproduct thereof, with a maturity date more than 2 days after the date the contract is entered into, including, a repurchase transaction, reverse repurchase transaction, consignment, lease, swap, hedge transaction, deposit, loan, option, allocated transaction, unallocated transaction, or any other similar agreement;

"(II) any combination of agreements or transactions referred to in subclauses (I) and (III);

"(III) any option to enter into any agreement or transaction referred to in subclause (I) or (II);

"(IV) a master agreement that provides for an agreement or transaction referred to in subclauses (I), (II), or (III), together with all supplements to any such master agreement, without regard to whether the master agreement provides for an agreement or transaction that is not a forward contract under this clause, except that the master agreement shall be considered to be a forward contract under this clause only with respect to each agreement or transaction under the master agreement that is referred to in subclause (I), (II), or (III); or

"(V) any security agreement or arrangement or other credit enhancement related to any agreement or transaction referred to in subclause (I), (II), (III), or (IV), including any guarantee or reimbursement obligation in connection with any agreement or transaction referred to in any such subclause.".

(e) DEFINITION OF REPURCHASE AGREEMENT.—

(1) FDIC-INSURED DEPOSITORY INSTITUTIONS.—Section 11(e)(8)(D)(v) of the Federal Deposit Insurance Act (12 U.S.C. 1821(e)(8)(D)(v)) is amended to read as follows:

"(v) REPURCHASE AGREEMENT.—The term 'repurchase agreement' (which definition also applies to a reverse repurchase agreement)—

"(I) means an agreement, including related terms, which provides for the transfer of one or more certificates of deposit, mortgage-related securities (as such term is defined in the Securities Exchange Act of 1934), mortgage loans, interests in mortgage-related securities or mortgage loans, eligible bankers' acceptances, qualified foreign government securities or securities that are direct obligations of, or that are fully guaranteed by, the United States or any agency of the United States against the transfer of funds by the transferee of such certificates of deposit, eligible bankers' acceptances, securities, mortgage loans, or interests with a simultaneous agreement by such transferee to transfer to the transferor thereof certificates of deposit, eligible bankers' acceptances, securities, mortgage loans, or interests as described above, at a date certain not later than 1 year after such transfers or on demand, against the transfer of funds, or any other similar agreement;

"(II) does not include any repurchase obligation under a participation in a commercial mortgage loan unless the Corporation determines by regulation, resolution, or order to include any such participation within the meaning of such term;

"(III) means any combination of agreements or transactions referred to in subclauses (I) and (IV);

"(IV) means any option to enter into any agreement or transaction referred to in subclause (I) or (III);

"(V) means a master agreement that provides for an agreement or transaction referred to in subclause (I), (III), or (IV), together with all supplements to any such master agreement, without regard to whether the master agreement provides for an agreement or transaction that is not a repurchase agreement under this clause, except that the master agreement shall be considered to be a repurchase agreement under this subclause only with respect to each agreement or transaction under the master agreement that is referred to in subclause (I), (III), or (IV); and

"(VI) means any security agreement or arrangement or other credit enhancement related to any agreement or transaction referred to in subclause (I), (III), (IV), or (V), including any guarantee or reimbursement obligation in connection with any agreement or transaction referred to in any such subclause.

For purposes of this clause, the term 'qualified foreign government security' means a security that is a direct obligation of, or that is fully guaranteed by, the central government of a member of the Organization for Economic Cooperation and Development (as determined by regulation or order adopted by the appropriate Federal banking authority).".

(2) INSURED CREDIT UNIONS.—Section 207(c)(8)(D)(v) of the Federal Credit Union Act (12 U.S.C. 1787(c)(8)(D)(v)) is amended to read as follows:

"(v) REPURCHASE AGREEMENT.—The term 'repurchase agreement' (which definition also applies to a reverse repurchase agreement)—

"(I) means an agreement, including related terms, which provides for the transfer of one or more certificates of deposit, mortgage-related securities (as such term is defined in the Securities Exchange Act of 1934), mortgage loans, interests in mortgage-related securities or mortgage loans, eligible bankers' acceptances, qualified foreign government securities or securities that are direct obligations of, or that are fully guaranteed by, the United States or any agency of the United States against the transfer of funds by the transferee of such certificates of deposit, eligible bankers' acceptances, securities, mortgage loans, or interests with a simultaneous agreement by such transferee to transfer to the transferor thereof certificates of deposit, eligible bankers' acceptances, securities, mortgage loans, or interests as described above, at a date certain not later than 1 year after such transfers or on demand, against the transfer of funds, or any other similar agreement;

"(II) does not include any repurchase obligation under a participation in a commercial mortgage loan unless the Board determines by regulation, resolution, or order to include any such participation within the meaning of such term;

"(III) means any combination of agreements or transactions referred to in subclauses (I) and (IV);

"(IV) means any option to enter into any agreement or transaction referred to in subclause (I) or (III);

"(V) means a master agreement that provides for an agreement or transaction referred to in subclause (I), (III), or (IV), together with all supplements to any such master agreement, without regard to whether the master agreement provides for an agreement or transaction that is not a repurchase agreement under this clause, except that the master agreement shall be considered to be a repurchase agreement under this subclause only with respect to each agreement or transaction under the master agreement that is referred to in subclause (I), (III), or (IV); and

"(VI) means any security agreement or arrangement or other credit enhancement related to any agreement or transaction referred to in subclause (I), (III), (IV), or (V), including any guarantee or reimbursement obligation in connection with any agreement or transaction referred to in any such subclause.

For purposes of this clause, the term "qualified foreign government security" means a security that is a direct obligation of, or that is fully guaranteed by, the central government of a member of the Organization for Economic Cooperation and Development (as determined by regulation or order adopted by the appropriate Federal banking authority).".

(f) DEFINITION OF SWAP AGREEMENT.—

(1) FDIC-INSURED DEPOSITORY INSTITUTIONS.—Section 11(e)(8)(D)(vi) of the Federal Deposit Insurance Act (12 U.S.C. 1821(e)(8)(D)(vi)) is amended to read as follows:

"(vi) SWAP AGREEMENT.—The term 'swap agreement' means—

"(I) any agreement, including the terms and conditions incorporated by reference in any such agreement, which is an interest rate swap, option, future, or forward agreement, including a rate floor, rate cap, rate collar, cross-currency rate swap, and basis swap; a spot, same day-tomorrow, tomorrow-next, forward, or other foreign exchange or precious metals agreement; a currency swap, option, future, or forward agreement; an equity index or equity swap, option, future, or forward agreement; a debt index or debt swap, option, future, or forward agreement; a total return, credit spread or credit swap, option, future, or forward agreement; a commodity index or commodity swap, option, future, or forward-agreement; or a weather swap, weather derivative, or weather option;

"(II) any agreement or transaction that is similar to any other agreement or transaction referred to in this clause and that is of a type that has been, is presently, or in the future becomes, the subject of recurrent dealings in the swap markets (including terms and conditions incorporated by reference in such agreement) and that is a forward, swap, future, or option on one or more rates, currencies, commodities, equity securities or other equity instruments, debt securities or other debt instruments, quantitative measures associated with an occurrence, extent of an occurrence, or contingency associated with a financial, commercial, or economic consequence, or economic or financial indices or measures of economic or financial risk or value;

"(III) any combination of agreements or transactions referred to in this clause;

"(IV) any option to enter into any agreement or transaction referred to in this clause;

"(V) a master agreement that provides for an agreement or transaction referred to in subclause (I), (II), (III), or (IV), together with all supplements to any such master agreement, without regard to whether the master agreement contains an agreement or transaction that is not a swap agreement under this clause, except that the master agreement shall be considered to be a swap agreement under this clause only with respect to each agreement or transaction under the master agreement that is referred to in subclause (I), (II), (III), or (IV); and

"(VI) any security agreement or arrangement or other credit enhancement related to any agreements or transactions referred to in subclause (I), (II), (III), (IV), or (V), including any guarantee or reimbursement obligation in connection with any agreement or transaction referred to in any such subclause.

Such term is applicable for purposes of this subsection only and shall not be construed or applied so as to challenge or affect the characterization, definition, or treatment of any swap agreement under any other statute, regulation, or rule, including the Securities Act of 1933, the Securities Exchange Act of 1934, the Public Utility Holding Company Act of 1935, the Trust Indenture Act of 1939, the Investment Company Act of 1940, the Investment Advisers Act of 1940, the Securities Investor Protection Act of 1970, the Commodity Exchange Act, the Gramm-Leach-Bliley Act, and the Legal Certainty for Bank Products Act of 2000.'.

(2) INSURED CREDIT UNIONS.—Section 207(c)(8)(D) of the Federal Credit Union Act (12 U.S.C. 1787(c)(8)(D)) is amended by adding at the end the following new clause:

"(vi) SWAP AGREEMENT.—The term 'swap agreement' means—

"(I) any agreement, including the terms and conditions incorporated by reference in any such agreement, which is an interest rate swap, option, future, or forward agreement, including a rate floor, rate cap, rate collar, cross-currency rate swap, and basis swap; a spot, same day-tomorrow, tomorrow-next, forward, or other foreign exchange or precious metals agreement; a currency swap, option, future, or forward agreement; an equity index or equity swap, option, future, or forward agreement; a debt index or debt swap, option, future, or forward agreement; a total return, credit spread or credit swap, option, future, or forward agreement; a commodity index or commodity swap, option, future, or forward agreement; or a weather swap, weather derivative, or weather option;

"(II) any agreement or transaction that is similar to any other agreement or transaction referred to in this clause and that is of a type that has been, is presently, or in the future becomes, the subject of recurrent dealings in the swap markets (including terms and conditions incorporated by reference in such agreement) and that is a forward, swap, future, or option on one or more rates, currencies, commodities, equity securities or other equity instruments, debt securities or other debt instruments, quantitative measures associated with an occurrence, extent of an occurrence, or contingency associated with a financial, commercial, or economic consequence, or economic or financial indices or measures of economic or financial risk or value;

"(III) any combination of agreements or transactions referred to in this clause;

"(IV) any option to enter into any agreement or transaction referred to in this clause;

"(V) a master agreement that provides for an agreement or transaction referred to in subclause (I), (II), (III), or (IV), together with all supplements to any such master agreement, without regard to whether the master agreement contains an agreement or transaction that is not a swap agreement under this clause, except that the master agreement shall be considered to be a swap agreement under this clause only with respect to each agreement or transaction under the master agreement that is referred to in subclause (I), (II), (III), or (IV); and

"(VI) any security agreement or arrangement or other credit enhancement related to any agreements or transactions referred to in subclause (I), (II), (III), (IV), or (V), including any guarantee or reimbursement obligation in connection with any agreement or transaction referred to in any such subclause.

Such term is applicable for purposes of this subsection only and shall not be construed or applied so as to challenge or affect the characterization, definition, or treatment of any swap agreement under any other statute, regulation, or rule, including the Securities Act of 1933, the Securities Exchange Act of 1934, the Public Utility Holding Company Act of 1935, the Trust Indenture Act of 1939, the Investment Company Act of 1940, the Investment Advisers Act of 1940, the Securities Investor Protection Act of 1970, the Commodity Exchange Act, the Gramm-Leach-Bliley Act, and the Legal Certainty for Bank Products Act of 2000.'.

(g) DEFINITION OF TRANSFER.—

(1) FDIC-INSURED DEPOSITORY INSTITUTIONS.—Section 11(e)(8)(D)(viii) of the Federal Deposit Insurance Act (12 U.S.C. 1821(e)(8)(D)(viii)) is amended to read as follows:

"(viii) TRANSFER.—The term 'transfer' means every mode, direct or indirect, absolute or conditional, voluntary or involuntary, of disposing of or parting with property or with an interest in property, including retention of title as a security interest and foreclosure of the depository institution's equity of redemption.".

(2) INSURED CREDIT UNIONS.—Section 207(c)(8)(D) of the Federal Credit Union Act (12 U.S.C. 1787(c)(8)(D)) (as amended by subsection (f) of this section) is amended by adding at the end the following new clause:

"(viii) TRANSFER.—The term 'transfer' means every mode, direct or indirect, absolute or conditional, voluntary or involuntary, of disposing of or parting with property or with an interest in property, including retention of title as a security interest and foreclosure of the depository institution's equity of redemption.".

(h) TREATMENT OF QUALIFIED FINANCIAL CONTRACTS.—

(1) FDIC-INSURED DEPOSITORY INSTITUTIONS.—Section 11(e)(8) of the Federal Deposit Insurance Act (12 U.S.C. 1821(e)(8)) is amended—

(A) in subparagraph (A)—

(i) by striking "paragraph (10)" and inserting "paragraphs (9) and (10)";

(ii) in clause (i), by striking "to cause the termination or liquidation" and inserting "such person has to cause the termination, liquidation, or acceleration"; and

(iii) by striking clause (ii) and inserting the following new clause:

"(ii) any right under any security agreement or arrangement or other credit enhancement related to one or more qualified financial contracts described in clause (i);"; and

(B) in subparagraph (E), by striking clause (ii) and inserting the following:

"(ii) any right under any security agreement or arrangement or other credit enhancement related to one or more qualified financial contracts described in clause (i);".

(2) INSURED CREDIT UNIONS.—Section 207(c)(8) of the Federal Credit Union Act (12 U.S.C. 1787(c)(8)) is amended—

(A) in subparagraph (A)—

(i) by striking "paragraph (12)" and inserting "paragraphs (9) and (10)";

(ii) in clause (i), by striking "to cause the termination or liquidation" and inserting "such person has to cause the termination, liquidation, or acceleration"; and

(iii) by striking clause (ii) and inserting the following new clause:

"(ii) any right under any security agreement or arrangement or other credit enhancement related to 1 or more qualified financial contracts described in clause (i);"; and

(B) in subparagraph (E), by striking clause (ii) and inserting the following new clause:

"(ii) any right under any security agreement or arrangement or other credit enhancement related to 1 or more qualified financial contracts described in clause (i);".

(i) AVOIDANCE OF TRANSFERS.—

(1) FDIC-INSURED DEPOSITORY INSTITUTIONS.—Section 11(e)(8)(C)(i) of the Federal Deposit Insurance Act (12 U.S.C. 1821(e)(8)(C)(i)) is amended by inserting "section 5242 of the Revised Statutes of the United States or any other Federal or State law relating to the avoidance of preferential or fraudulent transfers," before "the Corporation".

(2) INSURED CREDIT UNIONS.—Section 207(c)(8)(C)(i) of the Federal Credit Union Act (12 U.S.C. 1787(c)(8)(C)(i)) is amended by inserting "section 5242 of the Revised Statutes of the United States or any other Federal or State law relating to the avoidance of preferential or fraudulent transfers," before "the Board".

SEC. 902. AUTHORITY OF THE FDIC AND NCUAB WITH RESPECT TO FAILED AND FAILING INSTITUTIONS.

(a) FEDERAL DEPOSIT INSURANCE CORPORATION.—

(1) IN GENERAL.—Section 11(e)(8) of the Federal Deposit Insurance Act (12 U.S.C. 1821(e)(8)) is amended—

(A) in subparagraph (E), by striking "other than paragraph (12) of this subsection, subsection (d)(9)" and inserting "other than subsections (d)(9) and (e)(10)"; and

(B) by adding at the end the following new subparagraphs:

"(F) CLARIFICATION.—No provision of law shall be construed as limiting the right or power of the Corporation, or authorizing any court or agency to limit or delay, in any manner, the right or power of the Corporation to transfer any qualified financial contract in accordance with paragraphs (9) and (10) of this subsection or to disaffirm or repudiate any such contract in accordance with subsection (e)(1) of this section.

"(G) WALKAWAY CLAUSES NOT EFFECTIVE.—

"(i) IN GENERAL.—Notwithstanding the provisions of subparagraphs (A) and (E), and sections 403 and 404 of the Federal Deposit Insurance Corporation Improvement Act of 1991, no walkaway clause shall be enforceable in a qualified financial contract of an insured depository institution in default.

"(ii) WALKAWAY CLAUSE DEFINED.—For purposes of this subparagraph, the term 'walkaway clause' means a provision in a qualified financial contract that, after calculation of a value of a party's position or an amount due to or from 1 of the parties in accordance with its terms upon termination, liquidation, or acceleration of the qualified financial contract, either does not create a payment obligation of a party or extinguishes a payment obligation of a party in whole or in part solely because of such party's status as a nondefaulting party.''.

(2) TECHNICAL AND CONFORMING AMENDMENT.—Section 11(e)(12)(A) of the Federal Deposit Insurance Act (12 U.S.C. 1821(e)(12)(A)) is amended by inserting ''or the exercise of rights or powers by'' after ''the appointment of''.

(b) NATIONAL CREDIT UNION ADMINISTRATION BOARD.—

(1) IN GENERAL.—Section 207(c)(8) of the Federal Credit Union Act (12 U.S.C. 1787(c)(8)) is amended—

(A) in subparagraph (E) (as amended by section 901(h)), by striking ''other than paragraph (12) of this subsection, subsection (b)(9)'' and inserting ''other than subsections (b)(9) and (c)(10)''; and

(B) by adding at the end the following new subparagraphs:

''(F) CLARIFICATION.—No provision of law shall be construed as limiting the right or power of the Board, or authorizing any court or agency to limit or delay, in any manner, the right or power of the Board to transfer any qualified financial contract in accordance with paragraphs (9) and (10) of this subsection or to disaffirm or repudiate any such contract in accordance with subsection (c)(1) of this section.

''(G) WALKAWAY CLAUSES NOT EFFECTIVE.—

''(i) IN GENERAL.—Notwithstanding the provisions of subparagraphs (A) and (E), and sections 403 and 404 of the Federal Deposit Insurance Corporation Improvement Act of 1991, no walkaway clause shall be enforceable in a qualified financial contract of an insured credit union in default.

''(ii) WALKAWAY CLAUSE DEFINED.—For purposes of this subparagraph, the term 'walkaway clause' means a provision in a qualified financial contract that, after calculation of a value of a party's position or an amount due to or from 1 of the parties in accordance with its terms upon termination, liquidation, or acceleration of the qualified financial contract, either does not create a payment obligation of a party or extinguishes a payment obligation of a party in whole or in part solely because of such party's status as a nondefaulting party.''.

(2) TECHNICAL AND CONFORMING AMENDMENT.—Section 207(c)(12)(A) of the Federal Credit Union Act (12 U.S.C. 1787(c)(12)(A)) is amended by inserting ''or the exercise of rights or powers by'' after ''the appointment of''.

SEC. 903. AMENDMENTS RELATING TO TRANSFERS OF QUALIFIED FINANCIAL CONTRACTS.

(a) FDIC-INSURED DEPOSITORY INSTITUTIONS.—

(1) TRANSFERS OF QUALIFIED FINANCIAL CONTRACTS TO FINANCIAL INSTITUTIONS.—Section 11(e)(9) of the Federal Deposit Insurance Act (12 U.S.C. 1821(e)(9)) is amended to read as follows:

''(9) TRANSFER OF QUALIFIED FINANCIAL CONTRACTS.—

''(A) IN GENERAL.—In making any transfer of assets or liabilities of a depository institution in default which includes any qualified financial contract, the conservator or receiver for such depository institution shall either—

''(i) transfer to one financial institution, other than a financial institution for which a conservator, receiver, trustee in bankruptcy, or other legal custodian has been appointed or which is otherwise the subject of a bankruptcy or insolvency proceeding—

''(I) all qualified financial contracts between any person or any affiliate of such person and the depository institution in default;

''(II) all claims of such person or any affiliate of such person against such depository institution under any such contract (other than any claim which, under the terms of any such contract, is subordinated to the claims of general unsecured creditors of such institution);

"(III) all claims of such depository institution against such person or any affiliate of such person under any such contract; and

"(IV) all property securing or any other credit enhancement for any contract described in subclause (I) or any claim described in subclause (II) or (III) under any such contract; or

"(ii) transfer none of the qualified financial contracts, claims, property or other credit enhancement referred to in clause (i) (with respect to such person and any affiliate of such person).

"(B) TRANSFER TO FOREIGN BANK, FOREIGN FINANCIAL INSTITUTION, OR BRANCH OR AGENCY OF A FOREIGN BANK OR FINANCIAL INSTITUTION.—In transferring any qualified financial contracts and related claims and property under subparagraph (A)(i), the conservator or receiver for the depository institution shall not make such transfer to a foreign bank, financial institution organized under the laws of a foreign country, or a branch or agency of a foreign bank or financial institution unless, under the law applicable to such bank, financial institution, branch or agency, to the qualified financial contracts, and to any netting contract, any security agreement or arrangement or other credit enhancement related to one or more qualified financial contracts, the contractual rights of the parties to such qualified financial contracts, netting contracts, security agreements or arrangements, or other credit enhancements are enforceable substantially to the same extent as permitted under this section.

"(C) TRANSFER OF CONTRACTS SUBJECT TO THE RULES OF A CLEARING ORGANIZATION.—In the event that a conservator or receiver transfers any qualified financial contract and related claims, property, and credit enhancements pursuant to subparagraph (A)(i) and such contract is cleared by or subject to the rules of a clearing organization, the clearing organization shall not be required to accept the transferee as a member by virtue of the transfer.

"(D) DEFINITIONS.—For purposes of this paragraph, the term 'financial institution' means a broker or dealer, a depository institution, a futures commission merchant, or any other institution, as determined by the Corporation by regulation to be a financial institution, and the term 'clearing organization' has the same meaning as in section 402 of the Federal Deposit Insurance Corporation Improvement Act of 1991.".

(2) NOTICE TO QUALIFIED FINANCIAL CONTRACT COUNTERPARTIES.—Section 11(e)(10)(A) of the Federal Deposit Insurance Act (12 U.S.C. 1821(e)(10)(A)) is amended in the material immediately following clause (ii) by striking "the conservator" and all that follows through the period and inserting the following: "the conservator or receiver shall notify any person who is a party to any such contract of such transfer by 5:00 p.m. (eastern time) on the business day following the date of the appointment of the receiver in the case of a receivership, or the business day following such transfer in the case of a conservatorship.".

(3) RIGHTS AGAINST RECEIVER AND CONSERVATOR AND TREATMENT OF BRIDGE BANKS.—Section 11(e)(10) of the Federal Deposit Insurance Act (12 U.S.C. 1821(e)(10)) is amended—

(A) by redesignating subparagraph (B) as subparagraph (D); and

(B) by inserting after subparagraph (A) the following new subparagraphs:

"(B) CERTAIN RIGHTS NOT ENFORCEABLE.—

"(i) RECEIVERSHIP.—A person who is a party to a qualified financial contract with an insured depository institution may not exercise any right that such person has to terminate, liquidate, or net such contract under paragraph (8)(A) of this subsection or section 403 or 404 of the Federal Deposit Insurance Corporation Improvement Act of 1991, solely by reason of or incidental to the appointment of a receiver for the depository institution (or the insolvency or financial condition of the depository institution for which the receiver has been appointed)—

"(I) until 5:00 p.m. (eastern time) on the business day following the date of the appointment of the receiver; or

"(II) after the person has received notice that the contract has been transferred pursuant to paragraph (9)(A).

"(ii) CONSERVATORSHIP.—A person who is a party to a qualified financial contract with an insured depository institution may not exercise any right that such person has to terminate, liquidate, or net such contract under paragraph (8)(E) of this subsection or section 403 or 404 of the Federal Deposit Insurance Corporation Improvement Act of 1991, solely by reason of or incidental to the appointment of a conservator for the depository institution (or the insolvency or financial condition of the depository institution for which the conservator has been appointed).

"(iii) NOTICE.—For purposes of this paragraph, the Corporation as receiver or conservator of an insured depository institution shall be deemed to have notified a person who is a party to a qualified financial contract with such depository institution if the Corporation has taken steps reasonably calculated to provide notice to such person by the time specified in subparagraph (A).

"(C) TREATMENT OF BRIDGE BANKS.—The following institutions shall not be considered to be a financial institution for which a conservator, receiver, trustee in bankruptcy, or other legal custodian has been appointed or which is otherwise the subject of a bankruptcy or insolvency proceeding for purposes of paragraph (9):

"(i) A bridge bank.

"(ii) A depository institution organized by the Corporation, for which a conservator is appointed either—

"(I) immediately upon the organization of the institution; or

"(II) at the time of a purchase and assumption transaction between the depository institution and the Corporation as receiver for a depository institution in default.".

(b) INSURED CREDIT UNIONS.—

(1) TRANSFERS OF QUALIFIED FINANCIAL CONTRACTS TO FINANCIAL INSTITUTIONS.—Section 207(c)(9) of the Federal Credit Union Act (12 U.S.C. 1787(c)(9)) is amended to read as follows:

"(9) TRANSFER OF QUALIFIED FINANCIAL CONTRACTS.—

"(A) IN GENERAL.—In making any transfer of assets or liabilities of a credit union in default which includes any qualified financial contract, the conservator or liquidating agent for such credit union shall either—

"(i) transfer to 1 financial institution, other than a financial institution for which a conservator, receiver, trustee in bankruptcy, or other legal custodian has been appointed or which is otherwise the subject of a bankruptcy or insolvency proceeding—

"(I) all qualified financial contracts between any person or any affiliate of such person and the credit union in default;

"(II) all claims of such person or any affiliate of such person against such credit union under any such contract (other than any claim which, under the terms of any such contract, is subordinated to the claims of general unsecured creditors of such credit union);

"(III) all claims of such credit union against such person or any affiliate of such person under any such contract; and

"(IV) all property securing or any other credit enhancement for any contract described in subclause (I) or any claim described in subclause (II) or (III) under any such contract; or

"(ii) transfer none of the qualified financial contracts, claims, property or other credit enhancement referred to in clause (i) (with respect to such person and any affiliate of such person).

"(B) TRANSFER TO FOREIGN BANK, FOREIGN FINANCIAL INSTITUTION, OR BRANCH OR AGENCY OF A FOREIGN BANK OR FINANCIAL INSTITU-

TION.—In transferring any qualified financial contracts and related claims and property under subparagraph (A)(i), the conservator or liquidating agent for the credit union shall not make such transfer to a foreign bank, financial institution organized under the laws of a foreign country, or a branch or agency of a foreign bank or financial institution unless, under the law applicable to such bank, financial institution, branch or agency, to the qualified financial contracts, and to any netting contract, any security agreement or arrangement or other credit enhancement related to 1 or more qualified financial contracts, the contractual rights of the parties to such qualified financial contracts, netting contracts, security agreements or arrangements, or other credit enhancements are enforceable substantially to the same extent as permitted under this section.

"(C) TRANSFER OF CONTRACTS SUBJECT TO THE RULES OF A CLEARING ORGANIZATION.—In the event that a conservator or liquidating agent transfers any qualified financial contract and related claims, property, and credit enhancements pursuant to subparagraph (A)(i) and such contract is cleared by or subject to the rules of a clearing organization, the clearing organization shall not be required to accept the transferee as a member by virtue of the transfer.

"(D) DEFINITIONS.—For purposes of this paragraph—

"(i) the term 'financial institution' means a broker or dealer, a depository institution, a futures commission merchant, a credit union, or any other institution, as determined by the Board by regulation to be a financial institution; and

"(ii) the term 'clearing organization' has the same meaning as in section 402 of the Federal Deposit Insurance Corporation Improvement Act of 1991.".

(2) NOTICE TO QUALIFIED FINANCIAL CONTRACT COUNTERPARTIES.—Section 207(c)(10)(A) of the Federal Credit Union Act (12 U.S.C. 1787(c)(10)(A)) is amended in the material immediately following clause (ii) by striking "the conservator" and all that follows through the period and inserting the following: "the conservator or liquidating agent shall notify any person who is a party to any such contract of such transfer by 5:00 p.m. (eastern time) on the business day following the date of the appointment of the liquidating agent in the case of a liquidation, or the business day following such transfer in the case of a conservatorship.".

(3) RIGHTS AGAINST LIQUIDATING AGENT AND CONSERVATOR AND TREATMENT OF BRIDGE BANKS.—Section 207(c)(10) of the Federal Credit Union Act (12 U.S.C. 1787(c)(10)) is amended—

(A) by redesignating subparagraph (B) as subparagraph (D); and

(B) by inserting after subparagraph (A) the following new subparagraphs:

"(B) CERTAIN RIGHTS NOT ENFORCEABLE.—

"(i) LIQUIDATION.—A person who is a party to a qualified financial contract with an insured credit union may not exercise any right that such person has to terminate, liquidate, or net such contract under paragraph (8)(A) of this subsection or section 403 or 404 of the Federal Deposit Insurance Corporation Improvement Act of 1991, solely by reason of or incidental to the appointment of a liquidating agent for the credit union institution (or the insolvency or financial condition of the credit union for which the liquidating agent has been appointed)—

"(I) until 5:00 p.m. (eastern time) on the business day following the date of the appointment of the liquidating agent; or

"(II) after the person has received notice that the contract has been transferred pursuant to paragraph (9)(A).

"(ii) CONSERVATORSHIP.—A person who is a party to a qualified financial contract with an insured credit union may not exercise any right that such person has to terminate, liquidate, or net such contract under paragraph (8)(E) of this subsection or section 403 or 404 of the Federal Deposit Insurance Corporation Improvement Act of 1991, solely by reason of or incidental to the appointment of a conservator for the credit union or the insolvency or financial condition of the credit union for which the conservator has been appointed).

"(iii) NOTICE.—For purposes of this paragraph, the Board as conservator or liquidating agent of an insured credit union shall be deemed to have notified a person who is a party to a qualified financial contract with such credit union if the Board has taken steps reasonably calculated to provide notice to such person by the time specified in subparagraph (A).

"(C) TREATMENT OF BRIDGE BANKS.—The following institutions shall not be considered to be a financial institution for which a conservator, receiver, trustee in bankruptcy, or other legal custodian has been appointed or which is otherwise the subject of a bankruptcy or insolvency proceeding for purposes of paragraph (9):

"(i) A bridge bank.

"(ii) A credit union organized by the Board, for which a conservator is appointed either—

"(I) immediately upon the organization of the credit union; or

"(II) at the time of a purchase and assumption transaction between the credit union and the Board as receiver for a credit union in default.".

SEC. 904. AMENDMENTS RELATING TO DISAFFIRMANCE OR REPUDIATION OF QUALIFIED FINANCIAL CONTRACTS.

(a) FDIC-INSURED DEPOSITORY INSTITUTIONS.—Section 11(e) of the Federal Deposit Insurance Act (12 U.S.C. 1821(e)) is amended—

(1) by redesignating paragraphs (11) through (15) as paragraphs (12) through (16), respectively;

(2) by inserting after paragraph (10) the following new paragraph:

"(11) DISAFFIRMANCE OR REPUDIATION OF QUALIFIED FINANCIAL CONTRACTS.—In exercising the rights of disaffirmance or repudiation of a conservator or receiver with respect to any qualified financial contract to which an insured depository institution is a party, the conservator or receiver for such institution shall either—

"(A) disaffirm or repudiate all qualified financial contracts between—

"(i) any person or any affiliate of such person; and

"(ii) the depository institution in default; or

"(B) disaffirm or repudiate none of the qualified financial contracts referred to in subparagraph (A) (with respect to such person or any affiliate of such person).'; and

(3) by adding at the end the following new paragraph:

"(17) SAVINGS CLAUSE.—The meanings of terms used in this subsection are applicable for purposes of this subsection only, and shall not be construed or applied so as to challenge or affect the characterization, definition, or treatment of any similar terms under any other statute, regulation, or rule, including the Gramm-Leach-Bliley Act, the Legal Certainty for Bank Products Act of 2000, the securities laws (as that term is defined in section 3(a)(47) of the Securities Exchange Act of 1934), and the Commodity Exchange Act.".

(b) INSURED CREDIT UNIONS.—Section 207(c) of the Federal Credit Union Act (12 U.S.C. 1787(c)) is amended—

(1) by redesignating paragraphs (11), (12), and (13) as paragraphs (12), (13), and (14), respectively;

(2) by inserting after paragraph (10) the following new paragraph:

"(11) DISAFFIRMANCE OR REPUDIATION OF QUALIFIED FINANCIAL CONTRACTS.—In exercising the rights of disaffirmance or repudiation of a conservator or liquidating agent with respect to any qualified financial contract to which an insured credit union is a party, the conservator or liquidating agent for such credit union shall either—

"(A) disaffirm or repudiate all qualified financial contracts between—

"(i) any person or any affiliate of such person; and

"(ii) the credit union in default; or

"(B) disaffirm or repudiate none of the qualified financial contracts referred to in subparagraph (A) (with respect to such person or any affiliate of such person).'; and

(3) by adding at the end the following new paragraph:

"(15) SAVINGS CLAUSE.—The meanings of terms used in this subsection are applicable for purposes of this subsection only, and shall not be construed or applied so as to challenge or affect the characterization, definition, or treatment of any similar terms under any other statute, regulation, or rule, including the Gramm-Leach-Bliley Act, the Legal Certainty for Bank Products Act of 2000, the securities laws (as that term is defined in section (a)(47) of the Securities Exchange Act of 1934), and the Commodity Exchange Act.".

SEC. 905. CLARIFYING AMENDMENT RELATING TO MASTER AGREEMENTS.

(a) FDIC-INSURED DEPOSITORY INSTITUTIONS.—Section 11(e)(8)(D)(vii) of the Federal Deposit Insurance Act (12 U.S.C. 1821(e)(8)(D)(vii)) is amended to read as follows:

"(vii) TREATMENT OF MASTER AGREEMENT AS ONE AGREEMENT.—Any master agreement for any contract or agreement described in any preceding clause of this subparagraph (or any master agreement for such master agreement or agreements), together with all supplements to such master agreement, shall be treated as a single agreement and a single qualified financial contract. If a master agreement contains provisions relating to agreements or transactions that are not themselves qualified financial contracts, the master agreement shall be deemed to be a qualified financial contract only with respect to those transactions that are themselves qualified financial contracts.".

(b) INSURED CREDIT UNIONS.—Section 207(c)(8)(D) of the Federal Credit Union Act (12 U.S.C. 1787(c)(8)(D)) is amended by inserting after clause (vi) (as added by section 901(f)) the following new clause:

"(vii) TREATMENT OF MASTER AGREEMENT AS ONE AGREEMENT.—Any master agreement for any contract or agreement described in any preceding clause of this subparagraph (or any master agreement for such master agreement or agreements), together with all supplements to such master agreement, shall be treated as a single agreement and a single qualified financial contract. If a master agreement contains provisions relating to agreements or transactions that are not themselves qualified financial contracts, the master agreement shall be deemed to be a qualified financial contract only with respect to those transactions that are themselves qualified financial contracts.".

SEC. 906. FEDERAL DEPOSIT INSURANCE CORPORATION IMPROVEMENT ACT OF 1991.

(a) DEFINITIONS.—Section 402 of the Federal Deposit Insurance Corporation Improvement Act of 1991 (12 U.S.C. 4402) is amended—

(1) in paragraph (2)—

(A) in subparagraph (A)(ii), by inserting before the semicolon ", or is exempt from such registration by order of the Securities and Exchange Commission"; and

(B) in subparagraph (B), by inserting before the period ", that has been granted an exemption under section 4(c)(1) of the Commodity Exchange Act, or that is a multilateral clearing organization (as defined in section 408 of this Act)";

(2) in paragraph (6)—

(A) by redesignating subparagraphs (B) through (D) as subparagraphs (C) through (E), respectively;

(B) by inserting after subparagraph (A) the following new subparagraph:

"(B) an uninsured national bank or an uninsured State bank that is a member of the Federal Reserve System, if the national bank or State member bank is not eligible to make application to become an insured bank under section 5 of the Federal Deposit Insurance Act;"; and

(C) by amending subparagraph (C), so redesignated, to read as follows:

"(C) a branch or agency of a foreign bank, a foreign bank and any branch or agency of the foreign bank, or the foreign bank that established the branch or agency, as those terms are defined in section 1(b) of the International Banking Act of 1978;";

(3) in paragraph (11), by inserting before the period "and any other clearing organization with which such clearing organization has a netting contract";

(4) by amending paragraph (14)(A)(i) to read as follows:

"(i) means a contract or agreement between 2 or more financial institutions, clearing organizations, or members that provides for netting present or future payment obligations or payment entitlements (including liquidation or close out values relating to such obligations or entitlements) among the parties to the agreement; and"; and

(5) by adding at the end the following new paragraph:

"(15) PAYMENT.—The term 'payment' means a payment of United States dollars, another currency, or a composite currency, and a noncash delivery, including a payment or delivery to liquidate an unmatured obligation.".

(b) ENFORCEABILITY OF BILATERAL NETTING CONTRACTS.—Section 403 of the Federal Deposit Insurance Corporation Improvement Act of 1991 (12 U.S.C. 4403) is amended—

(1) by striking subsection (a) and inserting the following:

"(a) GENERAL RULE.—Notwithstanding any other provision of State or Federal law (other than paragraphs (8)(E), (8)(F), and (10)(B) of section 11(e) of the Federal Deposit Insurance Act, paragraphs (8)(E), (8)(F), and (10)(B) of section 207(c) of the Federal Credit Union Act, or any order authorized under section 5(b)(2) of the Securities Investor Protection Act of 1970), the covered contractual payment obligations and the covered contractual payment entitlements between any 2 financial institutions shall be netted in accordance with, and subject to the conditions of, the terms of any applicable netting contract (except as provided in section 561(b)(2) of title 11, United States Code)."; and

(2) by adding at the end the following new subsection:

"(f) ENFORCEABILITY OF SECURITY AGREEMENTS.—The provisions of any security agreement or arrangement or other credit enhancement related to one or more netting contracts between any 2 financial institutions shall be enforceable in accordance with their terms (except as provided in section 561(b)(2) of title 11, United States Code), and shall not be stayed, avoided, or otherwise limited by any State or Federal law (other than paragraphs (8)(E), (8)(F), and (10)(B) of section 11(e) of the Federal Deposit Insurance Act, paragraphs (8)(E), (8)(F), and (10)(B) of section 207(c) of the Federal Credit Union Act, and section 5(b)(2) of the Securities Investor Protection Act of 1970).".

(c) ENFORCEABILITY OF CLEARING ORGANIZATION NETTING CONTRACTS.—Section 404 of the Federal Deposit Insurance Corporation Improvement Act of 1991 (12 U.S.C. 4404) is amended—

(1) by striking subsection (a) and inserting the following:

"(a) GENERAL RULE.—Notwithstanding any other provision of State or Federal law (other than paragraphs (8)(E), (8)(F), and (10)(B) of section 11(e) of the Federal Deposit Insurance Act, paragraphs (8)(E), (8)(F), and (10)(B) of section 207(c) of the Federal Credit Union Act, and any order authorized under section 5(b)(2) of the Securities Investor Protection Act of 1970), the covered contractual payment obligations and the covered contractual payment entitlements of a member of a clearing organization to and from all other members of a clearing organization shall be netted in accordance with and subject to the conditions of any applicable netting contract (except as provided in section 561(b)(2) of title 11, United States Code)."; and

(2) by adding at the end the following new subsection:

"(h) ENFORCEABILITY OF SECURITY AGREEMENTS.—The provisions of any security agreement or arrangement or other credit enhancement related to one or more netting contracts between any 2 members of a clearing organization shall be enforceable in accordance with their terms (except as provided in section 561(b)(2) of title 11, United States Code), and shall not be stayed, avoided, or otherwise limited by any State or Federal law (other than paragraphs (8)(E), (8)(F), and (10)(B) of section 11(e) of the Federal Deposit Insurance Act, paragraphs (8)(E), (8)(F), and (10)(B) of section 207(c) of the Federal Credit Union Act, and section 5(b)(2) of the Securities Investor Protection Act of 1970).".

(d) ENFORCEABILITY OF CONTRACTS WITH UNINSURED NATIONAL BANKS, UNINSURED FEDERAL BRANCHES AND AGENCIES, CERTAIN UNINSURED STATE MEMBER BANKS, AND EDGE ACT CORPORATIONS.—The Federal Deposit Insurance Corporation Improvement Act of 1991 (12 U.S.C. 4401 et seq.) is amended—

(1) by redesignating section 407 as section 407A; and

(2) by inserting after section 406 the following new section:

"SEC. 407. TREATMENT OF CONTRACTS WITH UNINSURED NATIONAL BANKS, UNINSURED FEDERAL BRANCHES AND AGENCIES, CERTAIN UNINSURED STATE MEMBER BANKS, AND EDGE ACT CORPORATIONS.

"(a) IN GENERAL.—Notwithstanding any other provision of law, paragraphs (8), (9), (10), and (11) of section 11(e) of the Federal Deposit Insurance Act shall apply to an uninsured national bank or uninsured Federal branch or Federal agency, a corporation chartered under section 25A of the Federal Reserve Act, or an uninsured State member bank which operates, or operates as, a multilateral clearing organization pursuant to section 409 of this Act, except that for such purpose—

"(1) any reference to the 'Corporation as receiver' or 'the receiver or the Corporation' shall refer to the receiver appointed by the Comptroller of the Currency in the case of an uninsured national bank or uninsured Federal branch or agency, or to the receiver appointed by the Board of Governors of the Federal Reserve System in the case of a corporation chartered under section 25A of the Federal Reserve Act or an uninsured State member bank;

"(2) any reference to the 'Corporation' (other than in section 11(e)(8)(D) of such Act), the 'Corporation, whether acting as such or as conservator or receiver', a 'receiver', or a 'conservator' shall refer to the receiver or conservator appointed by the Comptroller of the Currency in the case of an uninsured national bank or uninsured Federal branch or agency, or to the receiver or conservator appointed by the Board of Governors of the Federal Reserve System in the case of a corporation chartered under section 25A of the Federal Reserve Act or an uninsured State member bank; and

"(3) any reference to an 'insured depository institution' or 'depository institution' shall refer to an uninsured national bank, an uninsured Federal branch or Federal agency, a corporation chartered under section 25A of the Federal Reserve Act, or an uninsured State member bank which operates, or operates as, a multilateral clearing organization pursuant to section 409 of this Act.

"(b) LIABILITY.—The liability of a receiver or conservator of an uninsured national bank, uninsured Federal branch or agency, a corporation chartered under section 25A of the Federal Reserve Act, or an uninsured State member bank which operates, or operates as, a multilateral clearing organization pursuant to section 409 of this Act, shall be determined in the same manner and subject to the same limitations that apply to receivers and conservators of insured depository institutions under section 11(e) of the Federal Deposit Insurance Act.

"(c) REGULATORY AUTHORITY.—

"(1) IN GENERAL.—The Comptroller of the Currency in the case of an uninsured national bank or uninsured Federal branch or agency and the Board of Governors of the Federal Reserve System in the case of a corporation chartered under section 25A of the Federal Reserve Act, or an uninsured State member bank that operates, or operates as, a multilateral clearing organization pursuant to section 409 of this Act, in consultation with the Federal Deposit Insurance Corporation, may each promulgate regulations solely to implement this section.

"(2) SPECIFIC REQUIREMENT.—In promulgating regulations, limited solely to implementing paragraphs (8), (9), (10), and (11) of section 11(e) of the Federal Deposit Insurance Act, the Comptroller of the Currency and the Board of Governors of the Federal Reserve System each shall ensure that the regulations generally are consistent with the regulations and policies of the Federal Deposit Insurance Corporation adopted pursuant to the Federal Deposit Insurance Act.

"(d) DEFINITIONS.—For purposes of this section, the terms 'Federal branch', 'Federal agency', and 'foreign bank' have the same meanings as in section 1(b) of the International Banking Act of 1978.".

SEC. 907. BANKRUPTCY LAW AMENDMENTS.

(a) DEFINITIONS OF FORWARD CONTRACT, REPURCHASE AGREEMENT, SECURITIES CLEARING AGENCY, SWAP AGREEMENT, COMMODITY CONTRACT, AND SECURITIES CONTRACT.—Title 11, United States Code, is amended—

(1) in section 101—

(A) in paragraph (25)—

(i) by striking "means a contract" and inserting "means—

"(A) a contract";

(ii) by striking ", or any combination thereof or option thereon;" and inserting ", or any other similar agreement;"; and

(iii) by adding at the end the following:

"(B) any combination of agreements or transactions referred to in subparagraphs (A) and (C);

"(C) any option to enter into an agreement or transaction referred to in subparagraph (A) or (B);

"(D) a master agreement that provides for an agreement or transaction referred to in subparagraph (A), (B), or (C), together with all supplements to any such master agreement, without regard to whether such master agreement provides for an agreement or transaction that is not a forward contract under this paragraph, except that such master agreement shall be considered to be a forward contract under this paragraph only with respect to each agreement or transaction under such master agreement that is referred to in subparagraph (A), (B), or (C); or

"(E) any security agreement or arrangement, or other credit enhancement related to any agreement or transaction referred to in subparagraph (A), (B), (C), or (D), including any guarantee or reimbursement obligation by or to a forward contract merchant or financial participant in connection with any agreement or transaction referred to in any such subparagraph, but not to exceed the damages in connection with any such agreement or transaction, measured in accordance with section 562;";

(B) in paragraph (46), by striking "on any day during the period beginning 90 days before the date of" and inserting "at any time before";

(C) by amending paragraph (47) to read as follows:

"(47) 'repurchase agreement' (which definition also applies to a reverse repurchase agreement)—

"(A) means—

"(i) an agreement, including related terms, which provides for the transfer of one or more certificates of deposit, mortgage related securities (as defined in section 3 of the Securities Exchange Act of 1934), mortgage loans, interests in mortgage related securities or mortgage loans, eligible bankers' acceptances, qualified foreign government securities (defined as a security that is a direct obligation of, or that is fully guaranteed by, the central government of a member of the Organization for Economic Cooperation and Development), or securities that are direct obligations of, or that are fully guaranteed by, the United States or any agency of the United States against the transfer of funds by the transferee of such certificates of deposit, eligible bankers' acceptances, securities, mortgage loans, or interests, with a simultaneous agreement by such transferee to transfer to the transferor thereof certificates of deposit, eligible bankers' acceptance, securities, mortgage loans, or interests of the kind described in this clause, at a date certain not later than 1 year after such transferor on demand, against the transfer of funds;

"(ii) any combination of agreements or transactions referred to in clauses (i) and (iii);

"(iii) an option to enter into an agreement or transaction referred to in clause (i) or (ii);

"(iv) a master agreement that provides for an agreement or transaction referred to in clause (i), (ii), or (iii), together with all supplements to any such master agreement, without regard to whether such master agreement provides for an agreement or transaction that is not a repurchase agreement under this paragraph, except that such master agreement shall be considered to be a repurchase agreement under this paragraph only with respect to each agreement or transaction under the master agreement that is referred to in clause (i), (ii), or (iii); or

"(v) any security agreement or arrangement or other credit enhancement related to any agreement or transaction referred to in clause (i), (ii), (iii), or (iv), including any guarantee or reimbursement obligation by or to a repo participant or financial participant in connection with any agreement or transaction referred to in any such clause, but not to exceed the damages in connection with any such agreement or transaction, measured in accordance with section 562 of this title; and

"(B) does not include a repurchase obligation under a participation in a commercial mortgage loan;";

(D) in paragraph (48), by inserting ", or exempt from such registration under such section pursuant to an order of the Securities and Exchange Commission," after "1934"; and

(E) by amending paragraph (53B) to read as follows:

"(53B) 'swap agreement'—

"(A) means—

"(i) any agreement, including the terms and conditions incorporated by reference in such agreement, which is—

"(I) an interest rate swap, option, future, or forward agreement, including a rate floor, rate cap, rate collar, cross-currency rate swap, and basis swap;

"(II) a spot, same day-tomorrow, tomorrow-next, forward, or other foreign exchange or precious metals agreement;

"(III) a currency swap, option, future, or forward agreement;

"(IV) an equity index or equity swap, option, future, or forward agreement;

"(V) a debt index or debt swap, option, future, or forward agreement;

"(VI) a total return, credit spread or credit swap, option, future, or forward agreement;

"(VII) a commodity index or a commodity swap, option, future, or forward agreement; or

"(VIII) a weather swap, weather derivative, or weather option;

"(ii) any agreement or transaction that is similar to any other agreement or transaction referred to in this paragraph and that—

"(I) is of a type that has been, is presently, or in the future becomes, the subject of recurrent dealings in the swap markets (including terms and conditions incorporated by reference therein); and

"(II) is a forward, swap, future, or option on one or more rates, currencies, commodities, equity securities, or other equity instruments, debt securities or other debt instruments, quantitative measures associated with an occurrence, extent of an occurrence, or contingency associated with a financial, commercial, or economic consequence, or economic or financial indices or measures of economic or financial risk or value;

"(iii) any combination of agreements or transactions referred to in this subparagraph;

"(iv) any option to enter into an agreement or transaction referred to in this subparagraph;

"(v) a master agreement that provides for an agreement or transaction referred to in clause (i), (ii), (iii), or (iv), together with all supplements to any such master agreement, and without regard to whether the master agreement contains an agreement or transaction that is not a swap agreement under this paragraph, except that the master agreement shall be considered to be a swap agreement under this paragraph only with respect to each agreement or transaction under the master agreement that is referred to in clause (i), (ii), (iii), or (iv); or

"(vi) any security agreement or arrangement or other credit enhancement related to any agreements or transactions referred to in clause (i) through (v), including any guarantee or reimbursement obligation by or to a swap participant or financial participant in connection with any agreement or transaction referred to in any such clause, but not to exceed the damages in connection with any such agreement or transaction, measured in accordance with section 562; and

"(B) is applicable for purposes of this title only, and shall not be construed or applied so as to challenge or affect the characterization, definition, or treatment of any swap agreement under any other statute, regulation, or rule, including the Securities Act of 1933, the Securities Exchange Act of 1934, the Public Utility Holding Company Act of 1935, the Trust Indenture Act of 1939, the Investment Company Act of 1940, the Investment Advisers Act of 1940, the Securities Investor Protection Act of 1970, the Commodity Exchange Act, the Gramm-Leach-Bliley Act, and the Legal Certainty for Bank Products Act of 2000;";

(2) in section 741(7), by striking paragraph (7) and inserting the following:

"(7) 'securities contract'—

"(A) means—

"(i) a contract for the purchase, sale, or loan of a security, a certificate of deposit, a mortgage loan or any interest in a mortgage loan, a group or index of securities, certificates of deposit, or mortgage loans or interests therein (including an interest therein or based on the value thereof), or option on any of the foregoing, including an option to purchase or sell any such security, certificate of deposit, mortgage loan, interest, group or index, or option, and including any repurchase or reverse repurchase transaction on any such security, certificate of deposit, mortgage loan, interest, group or index, or option;

"(ii) any option entered into on a national securities exchange relating to foreign currencies;

"(iii) the guarantee by or to any securities clearing agency of a settlement of cash, securities, certificates of deposit, mortgage loans or interests therein, group or index of securities, or mortgage loans or interests therein (including any interest therein or based on the value thereof), or option on any of the foregoing, including an option to purchase or sell any such security, certificate of deposit, mortgage loan, interest, group or index, or option;

"(iv) any margin loan;

"(v) any other agreement or transaction that is similar to an agreement or transaction referred to in this subparagraph;

"(vi) any combination of the agreements or transactions referred to in this subparagraph;

"(vii) any option to enter into any agreement or transaction referred to in this subparagraph;

"(viii) a master agreement that provides for an agreement or transaction referred to in clause (i), (ii), (iii), (iv), (v), (vi), or (vii), together with all supplements to any such master agreement, without regard to whether the master agreement provides for an agreement or transaction that is not a securities contract under this subparagraph, except that such master agreement shall be considered to be a securities contract under this subparagraph only with respect to each agreement or transaction under such master agreement that is referred to in clause (i), (ii), (iii), (iv), (v), (vi), or (vii); or

"(ix) any security agreement or arrangement or other credit enhancement related to any agreement or transaction referred to in this subparagraph, including any guarantee or reimbursement obligation by or to a stockbroker, securities clearing agency, financial institution, or financial participant in connection with any agreement or transaction referred to in this subparagraph, but not to exceed the damages in connection with any such agreement or transaction, measured in accordance with section 562; and

"(B) does not include any purchase, sale, or repurchase obligation under a participation in a commercial mortgage loan;"; and

(3) in section 761(4)—

(A) by striking "or" at the end of subparagraph (D); and

(B) by adding at the end the following:

"(F) any other agreement or transaction that is similar to an agreement or transaction referred to in this paragraph;

"(G) any combination of the agreements or transactions referred to in this paragraph;

"(H) any option to enter into an agreement or transaction referred to in this paragraph;

"(I) a master agreement that provides for an agreement or transaction referred to in subparagraph (A), (B), (C), (D), (E), (F), (G), or (H), together with all supplements to such master agreement, without regard to whether the master agreement provides for an agreement or transaction that is not a commodity contract under this paragraph, except that the master agreement shall be considered to be a commodity contract under this paragraph only with respect to each agreement or transaction under the master agreement that is referred to in subparagraph (A), (B), (C), (D), (E), (F), (G), or (H); or

"(J) any security agreement or arrangement or other credit enhancement related to any agreement or transaction referred to in this paragraph, including any guarantee or reimbursement obligation by or to a commodity broker or financial participant in connection with any agreement or transaction referred to in this paragraph, but not to exceed the damages in connection with any such agreement or transaction, measured in accordance with section 562;".

(b) DEFINITIONS OF FINANCIAL INSTITUTION, FINANCIAL PARTICIPANT, AND FORWARD CONTRACT MERCHANT.—Section 101 of title 11, United States Code, is amended—

(1) by striking paragraph (22) and inserting the following:

"(22) 'financial institution' means—

"(A) a Federal reserve bank, or an entity (domestic or foreign) that is a commercial or savings bank, industrial savings bank, savings and loan association, trust company, federally-insured credit union, or receiver, liquidating agent, or conservator for such entity and, when any such Federal reserve bank, receiver, liquidating agent, conservator or entity is acting as agent or custodian for a customer in connection with a securities contract (as defined in section 741) such customer; or

"(B) in connection with a securities contract (as defined in section 741) an investment company registered under the Investment Company Act of 1940;";

(2) by inserting after paragraph (22) the following:

"(22A) 'financial participant' means—

"(A) an entity that, at the time it enters into a securities contract, commodity contract, swap agreement, repurchase agreement, or forward contract, or at the time of the date of the filing of the petition, has one or more agreements or transactions described in paragraph (1), (2), (3), (4), (5), or (6) of section 561(a) with the debtor or any other entity (other than an affiliate) of a total gross dollar value of not less than $1,000,000,000 in notional or actual principal amount outstanding on any day during the previous 15-month period, or has gross mark-to-market positions of not less than $100,000,000 (aggregated across counterparties) in one or more such agreements or transactions with the debtor or any other entity (otherthan an affiliate) on any day during the previous 15-month period; or

"(B) a clearing organization (as defined in section 402 of the Federal Deposit Insurance Corporation Improvement Act of 1991);"; and

(3) by striking paragraph (26) and inserting the following:

"(26) 'forward contract merchant' means a Federal reserve bank, or an entity the business of which consists in whole or in part of entering into forward contracts as or with merchants in a commodity (as defined in section 761) or any similar good, article, service, right, or interest which is presently or in the future becomes the subject of dealing in the forward contract trade;".

(c) DEFINITION OF MASTER NETTING AGREEMENT AND MASTER NETTING AGREEMENT PARTICIPANT.—Section 101 of title 11, United States Code, is amended by inserting after paragraph (38) the following new paragraphs:

"(38A) 'master netting agreement'—

"(A) means an agreement providing for the exercise of rights, including rights of netting, setoff, liquidation, termination, acceleration, or close out, under or in connection with one or more contracts that are described in any one or more of paragraphs (1) through (5) of section 561(a), or any security agreement or arrangement or other credit enhancement related to one or more of the foregoing, including any guarantee or reimbursement obligation related to 1 or more of the foregoing; and

"(B) if the agreement contains provisions relating to agreements or transactions that are not contracts described in paragraphs (1) through (5) of section 561(a), shall be deemed to be a master netting agreement only with respect to those agreements or transactions that are described in any one or more of paragraphs (1) through (5) of section 561(a);

"(38B) 'master netting agreement participant' means an entity that, at any time before the date of the filing of the petition, is a party to an outstanding master netting agreement with the debtor;".

(d) SWAP AGREEMENTS, SECURITIES CONTRACTS, COMMODITY CONTRACTS, FORWARD CONTRACTS, REPURCHASE AGREEMENTS, AND MASTER NETTING AGREEMENTS UNDER THE AUTOMATIC-STAY.—

(1) IN GENERAL.—Section 362(b) of title 11, United States Code, as amended by sections 224, 303, 311, 401, and 718, is amended—

(A) in paragraph (6), by inserting ", pledged to, under the control of," after "held by";

(B) in paragraph (7), by inserting ", pledged to, under the control of," after "held by";

(C) by striking paragraph (17) and inserting the following:

"(17) under subsection (a), of the setoff by a swap participant or financial participant of a mutual debt and claim under or in connection with one or more swap agreements that constitutes the setoff of a claim against the debtor for any payment or other transfer of property due from the debtor under or in connection with any swap agreement against any payment due to the debtor from the swap participant or financial participant under or in connection with any swap agreement or against cash, securities, or other property held by, pledged to, under the control of, or due from such swap participant or financial participant to margin, guarantee, secure, or settle any swap agreement;"; and

(D) by inserting after paragraph (26) the following:

"(27) under subsection (a), of the setoff by a master netting agreement participant of a mutual debt and claim under or in connection with one or more master netting agreements or any contract or agreement subject to such agreements that constitutes the setoff of a claim against the debtor for any payment or other transfer of property due from the debtor under or in connection with such agreements or any contract or agreement subject to such agreements against any payment due to the debtor from such master netting agreement participant under or in connection with such agreements or any contract or agreement subject to such agreements or against cash, securities, or other property held by, pledged to, under the control of, or due from such master netting agreement participant to margin, guarantee, secure, or settle such agreements or any contract or agreement subject to such agreements, to the extent that such participant is eligible to exercise such offset rights under paragraph (6), (7), or (17) for each individual contract covered by the master netting agreement in issue; and".

(2) LIMITATION.—Section 362 of title 11, United States Code, as amended by sections 106, 305, 311, and 441, is amended by adding at the end the following:

"(*o*) The exercise of rights not subject to the stay arising under subsection (a) pursuant to paragraph (6), (7), (17), or (27) of subsection (b) shall not be stayed by any order of a court or administrative agency in any proceeding under this title.".

(e) LIMITATION OF AVOIDANCE POWERS UNDER MASTER NETTING AGREEMENT.—Section 546 of title 11, United States Code, is amended—

(1) in subsection (g) (as added by section 103 of Public Law 101-311)—

(A) by striking "under a swap agreement";

(B) by striking "in connection with a swap agreement" and inserting "under or in connection with any swap agreement"; and

(C) by inserting "or financial participant" after "swap participant"; and

(2) by adding at the end the following:

"(j) Notwithstanding sections 544, 545, 547, 548(a)(1)(B), and 548(b) the trustee may not avoid a transfer made by or to a master netting agreement participant under or in connection with any master netting agreement or any individual contract covered thereby that is made before the commencement of the case, except under section 548(a)(1)(A) and except to the extent that the trustee could otherwise avoid such a transfer made under an individual contract covered by such master netting agreement.".

(f) FRAUDULENT TRANSFERS OF MASTER NETTING AGREEMENTS.—Section 548(d)(2) of title 11, United States Code, is amended—

(1) in subparagraph (C), by striking "and" at the end;

(2) in subparagraph (D), by striking the period and inserting "; and"; and

(3) by adding at the end the following new subparagraph:

"(E) a master netting agreement participant that receives a transfer in connection with a master netting agreement or any individual contract covered thereby takes for value to the extent of such transfer, except that, with respect to a transfer under any individual contract covered thereby, to the extent that such master netting agreement participant otherwise did not take (or is otherwise not deemed to have taken) such transfer for value.".

(g) TERMINATION OR ACCELERATION OF SECURITIES CONTRACTS.—

Section 555 of title 11, United States Code, is amended—

(1) by amending the section heading to read as follows:

"§ 555. Contractual right to liquidate, terminate, or accelerate a securities contract"; and

(2) in the first sentence, by striking "liquidation" and inserting "liquidation, termination, or acceleration".

(h) TERMINATION OR ACCELERATION OF COMMODITIES OR FORWARD CONTRACTS.—Section 556 of title 11, United States Code, is amended—

(1) by amending the section heading to read as follows:

"§ 556. Contractual right to liquidate, terminate, or accelerate a commodities contract or forward contract";

(2) in the first sentence, by striking "liquidation" and inserting "liquidation, termination, or acceleration"; and

(3) in the second sentence, by striking "As used" and all that follows through "right," and inserting "As used in this section, the term 'contractual right' includes a right set forth in a rule or bylaw of a derivatives clearing organization (as defined in the Commodity Exchange Act), a multilateral clearing organization (as defined in the Federal Deposit Insurance Corporation Improvement Act of 1991), a national securities exchange, a national securities association, a securities clearing agency, a contract market designated under the Commodity Exchange Act, a derivatives transaction execution facility registered under the Commodity Exchange Act, or a board of trade (as defined in the

Commodity Exchange Act) or in a resolution of the governing board thereof and a right,''.

(i) TERMINATION OR ACCELERATION OF REPURCHASE AGREEMENTS.—Section 559 of title 11, United States Code, is amended—

(1) by amending the section heading to read as follows:

"§ 559. Contractual right to liquidate, terminate, or accelerate a repurchase agreement";

(2) in the first sentence, by striking ''liquidation'' and inserting ''liquidation, termination, or acceleration''; and

(3) in the third sentence, by striking ''As used'' and all that follows through ''right,'' and inserting ''As used in this section, the term 'contractual right' includes a right set forth in a rule or bylaw of a derivatives clearing organization (as defined in the Commodity Exchange Act), a multilateral clearing organization (as defined in the Federal Deposit Insurance Corporation Improvement Act of 1991), a national securities exchange, a national securities association, a securities clearing agency, a contract market designated under the Commodity Exchange Act, a derivatives transaction execution facility registered under the Commodity Exchange Act, or a board of trade (as defined in the Commodity Exchange Act) or in a resolution of the governing board thereof and a right,''.

(j) LIQUIDATION, TERMINATION, OR ACCELERATION OF SWAP AGREEMENTS.—Section 560 of title 11, United States Code, is amended—

(1) by amending the section heading to read as follows:

"§ 560. Contractual right to liquidate, terminate, or accelerate a swap agreement";

(2) in the first sentence, by striking ''termination of a swap agreement'' and inserting ''liquidation, termination, or acceleration of one or more swap agreements'';

(3) by striking ''in connection with any swap agreement'' and inserting ''in connection with the termination, liquidation, or acceleration of one or more swap agreements''; and

(4) in the second sentence, by striking ''As used'' and all that follows through ''right,'' and inserting ''As used in this section, the term 'contractual right' includes a right set forth in a rule or bylaw of a derivatives clearing organization (as defined in the Commodity Exchange Act), a multilateral clearing organization (as defined in the Federal Deposit Insurance Corporation Improvement Act of 1991), a national securities exchange, a national securities association, a securities clearing agency, a contract market designated under the Commodity Exchange Act, a derivatives transaction execution facility registered under the Commodity Exchange Act, or a board of trade (as defined in the Commodity Exchange Act) or in a resolution of the governing board thereof and a right,''.

(k) LIQUIDATION, TERMINATION, ACCELERATION, OR OFFSET UNDER A MASTER NETTING AGREEMENT AND ACROSS CONTRACTS.—

(1) IN GENERAL.—Title 11, United States Code, is amended by inserting after section 560 the following:

"§ 561. Contractual right to terminate, liquidate, accelerate, or offset under a master netting agreement and across contracts; proceedings under chapter 15

''(a) Subject to subsection (b), the exercise of any contractual right, because of a condition of the kind specified in section 365(e)(1), to cause the termination, liquidation, or acceleration of or to offset or net termination values, payment amounts, or other transfer obligations arising under or in connection with one or more (or the termination, liquidation, or acceleration of one or more)—

''(1) securities contracts, as defined in section 741(7);

''(2) commodity contracts, as defined in section 761(4);

''(3) forward contracts;

''(4) repurchase agreements;

''(5) swap agreements; or

''(6) master netting agreements,

shall not be stayed, avoided, or otherwise limited by operation of any provision of this title or by any order of a court or administrative agency in any proceeding under this title.

''(b)(1) A party may exercise a contractual right described in subsection (a) to terminate, liquidate, or accelerate only to the extent that such party could exercise such a right under section 555, 556, 559, or 560 for each individual contract covered by the master netting agreement in issue.

"(2) If a debtor is a commodity broker subject to subchapter IV of chapter 7—

"(A) a party may not net or offset an obligation to the debtor arising under, or in connection with, a commodity contract traded on or subject to the rules of a contract market designated under the Commodity Exchange Act or a derivatives transaction execution facility registered under the Commodity Exchange Act against any claim arising under, or in connection with, other instruments, contracts, or agreements listed in subsection (a) except to the extent that the party has positive net equity in the commodity accounts at the debtor, as calculated under such subchapter; and

"(B) another commodity broker may not net or offset an obligation to the debtor arising under, or in connection with, a commodity contract entered into or held on behalf of a customer of the debtor and traded on or subject to the rules of a contract market designated under the Commodity Exchange Act or a derivatives transaction execution facility registered under the Commodity Exchange Act against any claim arising under, or in connection with, other instruments, contracts, or agreements listed in subsection (a).

"(3) No provision of subparagraph (A) or (B) of paragraph (2) shall prohibit the offset of claims and obligations that arise under—

"(A) a cross-margining agreement or similar arrangement that has been approved by the Commodity Futures Trading Commission or submitted to the Commodity Futures Trading Commission under paragraph (1) or (2) of section 5c(c) of the Commodity Exchange Act and has not been abrogated or rendered ineffective by the Commodity Futures Trading Commission; or

"(B) any other netting agreement between a clearing organization (as defined in section 761) and another entity that has been approved by the Commodity Futures Trading Commission.

"(c) As used in this section, the term 'contractual right' includes a right set forth in a rule or bylaw of a derivatives clearing organization (as defined in the Commodity Exchange Act), a multilateral clearing organization (as defined in the Federal Deposit Insurance Corporation Improvement Act of 1991), a national securities exchange, a national securities association, a securities clearing agency, a contract market designated under the Commodity Exchange Act, a derivatives transaction execution facility registered under the Commodity Exchange Act, or a board of trade (as defined in the Commodity Exchange Act) or in a resolution of the governing board thereof, and a right, whether or not evidenced in writing, arising under common law, under law merchant, or by reason of normal business practice.

"(d) Any provisions of this title relating to securities contracts, commodity contracts, forward contracts, repurchase agreements, swap agreements, or master netting agreements shall apply in a case under chapter 15, so that enforcement of contractual provisions of such contracts and agreements in accordance with their terms will not be stayed or otherwise limited by operation of any provision of this title or by order of a court in any case under this title, and to limit avoidance powers to the same extent as in a proceeding under chapter 7 or 11 of this title (such enforcement not to be limited based on the presence or absence of assets of the debtor in the United States).".

(2) CONFORMING AMENDMENT.—The table of sections for chapter 5 of title 11, United States Code, is amended by inserting after the item relating to section 560 the following:

"561. Contractual right to terminate, liquidate, accelerate, or offset under a master netting agreement and across contracts; proceedings under chapter 15.".

(l) COMMODITY BROKER LIQUIDATIONS.—Title 11, United States Code, is amended by inserting after section 766 the following:

"§ 767. Commodity broker liquidation and forward contract merchants, commodity brokers, stockbrokers, financial institutions, financial participants, securities clearing agencies, swap participants, repo participants, and master netting agreement participants

"Notwithstanding any other provision of this title, the exercise of rights by a forward contract merchant, commodity broker, stockbroker, financial institution, financial participant, securities clearing agency, swap participant, repo participant, or master netting agreement participant under this title shall not affect the priority of any unsecured claim it may have after the exercise of such rights.".

(m) STOCKBROKER LIQUIDATIONS.—Title 11, United States Code, is amended by inserting after section 752 the following:

"§ 753. Stockbroker liquidation and forward contract merchants, commodity brokers, stockbrokers, financial institutions, financial participants, securities clearing agencies, swap participants, repo participants, and master netting agreement participants

"Notwithstanding any other provision of this title, the exercise of rights by a forward contract merchant, commodity broker, stockbroker, financial institution, financial participant, securities clearing agency, swap participant, repo participant, or master netting agreement participant under this title shall not affect the priority of any unsecured claim it may have after the exercise of such rights.".

(n) SETOFF.—Section 553 of title 11, United States Code, is amended—

(1) in subsection (a)(2)(B)(ii), by inserting before the semicolon the following: "(except for a setoff of a kind described in section 362(b)(6), 362(b)(7), 362(b)(17), 362(b)(27), 555, 556, 559, 560, or 561)";

(2) in subsection (a)(3)(C), by inserting before the period the following: "(except for a setoff of a kind described in section 362(b)(6), 362(b)(7), 362(b)(17), 362(b)(27), 555, 556, 559, 560, or 561)"; and

(3) in subsection (b)(1), by striking "362(b)(14)," and inserting "362(b)(17), 362(b)(27), 555, 556, 559, 560, 561,".

(o) SECURITIES CONTRACTS, COMMODITY CONTRACTS, AND FORWARD CONTRACTS.—Title 11, United States Code, is amended—

(1) in section 362(b)(6), by striking "financial institutions," each place such term appears and inserting "financial institution, financial participant,";

(2) in sections 362(b)(7) and 546(f), by inserting "or financial participant" after "repo participant" each place such term appears;

(3) in section 546(e), by inserting "financial participant," after "financial institution,";

(4) in section 548(d)(2)(B), by inserting "financial participant," after "financial institution,";

(5) in section 548(d)(2)(C), by inserting "or financial participant" after "repo participant";

(6) in section 548(d)(2)(D), by inserting "or financial participant" after "swap participant";

(7) in section 555—

  (A) by inserting "financial participant," after "financial institution,"; and

  (B) by striking the second sentence and inserting the following: "As used in this section, the term 'contractual right' includes a right set forth in a rule or bylaw of a derivatives clearing organization (as defined in the Commodity Exchange Act), a multilateral clearing organization (as defined in the Federal Deposit Insurance Corporation Improvement Act of 1991), a national securities exchange, a national securities association, a securities clearing agency, a contract market designated under the Commodity Exchange Act, a derivatives transaction execution facility registered under the Commodity Exchange Act, or a board of trade (as defined in the Commodity Exchange Act), or in a resolution of the governing board thereof, and a right, whether or not in writing, arising under common law, under law merchant, or by reason of normal business practice.";

(8) in section 556, by inserting ", financial participant," after "commodity broker";

(9) in section 559, by inserting "or financial participant" after "repo participant" each place such term appears; and

(10) in section 560, by inserting "or financial participant" after "swap participant".

(p) CONFORMING AMENDMENTS.—Title 11, United States Code, is amended—

(1) in the table of sections for chapter 5—

(A) by amending the items relating to sections 555 and 556 to read as follows:
"555. Contractual right to liquidate, terminate, or accelerate a securities contract.
"556. Contractual right to liquidate, terminate, or accelerate a commodities contract or forward contract.";
and
(B) by amending the items relating to sections 559 and 560 to read as follows:
"559. Contractual right to liquidate, terminate, or accelerate a repurchase agreement.
"560. Contractual right to liquidate, terminate, or accelerate a swap agreement.";
and
(2) in the table of sections for chapter 7—
(A) by inserting after the item relating to section 766 the following:
"767. Commodity broker liquidation and forward contract merchants, commodity brokers, stockbrokers, financial institutions, financial participants, securities clearing agencies, swap participants, repo participants, and master netting agreement participants.";
and
(B) by inserting after the item relating to section 752 the following:
"753. Stockbroker liquidation and forward contract merchants, commodity brokers, stockbrokers, financial institutions, financial participants, securities clearing agencies, swap participants, repo participants, and master netting agreement participants.".

SEC. 908. RECORDKEEPING REQUIREMENTS.

(a) FDIC-INSURED DEPOSITORY INSTITUTIONS.—Section 11(e)(8) of the Federal Deposit Insurance Act (12 U.S.C. 1821(e)(8)) is amended by adding at the end the following new subparagraph:

"(H) RECORDKEEPING REQUIREMENTS.—The Corporation, in consultation with the appropriate Federal banking agencies, may prescribe regulations requiring more detailed recordkeeping by any insured depository institution with respect to qualified financial contracts (including market valuations) only if such insured depository institution is in a troubled condition (as such term is defined by the Corporation pursuant to section 32).".

(b) INSURED CREDIT UNIONS.—Section 207(c)(8) of the Federal Credit Union Act (12 U.S.C. 1787(c)(8)) is amended by adding at the end the following new subparagraph:

"(H) RECORDKEEPING REQUIREMENTS.—The Board, in consultation with the appropriate Federal banking agencies, may prescribe regulations requiring more detailed recordkeeping by any insured credit union with respect to qualified financial contracts (including market valuations) only if such insured credit union is in a troubled condition (as such term is defined by the Board pursuant to section 212).".

SEC. 909. EXEMPTIONS FROM CONTEMPORANEOUS EXECUTION REQUIREMENT.

Section 13(e)(2) of the Federal Deposit Insurance Act (12 U.S.C. 1823(e)(2)) is amended to read as follows:

"(2) EXEMPTIONS FROM CONTEMPORANEOUS EXECUTION REQUIREMENT.—An agreement to provide for the lawful collateralization of—

"(A) deposits of, or other credit extension by, a Federal, State, or local governmental entity, or of any depositor referred to in section 11(a)(2), including an agreement to provide collateral in lieu of a surety bond;
"(B) bankruptcy estate funds pursuant to section 345(b)(2) of title 11, United States Code;
"(C) extensions of credit, including any overdraft, from a Federal reserve bank or Federal home loan bank; or
"(D) one or more qualified financial contracts, as defined in section 11(e)(8)(D),

shall not be deemed invalid pursuant to paragraph (1)(B) solely because such agreement was not executed contemporaneously with the acquisition of the collateral or because of pledges, delivery, or substitution of the collateral made in accordance with such agreement.''.

SEC. 910. DAMAGE MEASURE.

(a) IN GENERAL.—Title 11, United States Code, is amended—

(1) by inserting after section 561, as added by section 907, the following:

"§ 562. Timing of damage measurement in connection with swap agreements, securities contracts, forward contracts, commodity contracts, repurchase agreements, and master netting agreements

"(a) If the trustee rejects a swap agreement, securities contract (as defined in section 741), forward contract, commodity contract (as defined in section 761), repurchase agreement, or master netting agreement pursuant to section 365(a), or if a forward contract merchant, stockbroker, financial institution, securities clearing agency, repo participant, financial participant, master netting agreement participant, or swap participant liquidates, terminates, or accelerates such contract or agreement, damages shall be measured as of the earlier of—

"(1) the date of such rejection; or

"(2) the date or dates of such liquidation, termination, or acceleration.

"(b) If there are not any commercially reasonable determinants of value as of any date referred to in paragraph (1) or (2) of subsection (a), damages shall be measured as of the earliest subsequent date or dates on which there are commercially reasonable determinants of value.

"(c) For the purposes of subsection (b), if damages are not measured as of the date or dates of rejection, liquidation, termination, or acceleration, and the forward contract merchant, stockbroker, financial institution, securities clearing agency, repo participant, financial participant, master netting agreement participant, or swap participant or the trustee objects to the timing of the measurement of damages—

"(1) the trustee, in the case of an objection by a forward contract merchant, stockbroker, financial institution, securities clearing agency, repo participant, financial participant, master netting agreement participant, or swap participant; or

"(2) the forward contract merchant, stockbroker, financial institution, securities clearing agency, repo participant, financial participant, master netting agreement participant, or swap participant, in the case of an objection by the trustee,

has the burden of proving that there were no commercially reasonable determinants of value as of such date or dates.''; and

(2) in the table of sections for chapter 5, by inserting after the item relating to section 561 (as added by section 907) the following new item:

"562. Timing of damage measure in connection with swap agreements, securities contracts, forward contracts, commodity contracts, repurchase agreements, or master netting agreements.''.

(b) CLAIMS ARISING FROM REJECTION.—Section 502(g) of title 11, United States Code, is amended—

(1) by inserting "(1)" after "(g)"; and

(2) by adding at the end the following:

"(2) A claim for damages calculated in accordance with section 562 shall be allowed under subsection (a), (b), or (c), or disallowed under subsection (d) or (e), as if such claim had arisen before the date of the filing of the petition.''.

SEC. 911. SIPC STAY.

Section 5(b)(2) of the Securities Investor Protection Act of 1970 (15 U.S.C. 78eee(b)(2)) is amended by adding at the end the following new subparagraph:

"(C) EXCEPTION FROM STAY.—

"(i) Notwithstanding section 362 of title 11, United States Code, neither the filing of an application under subsection (a)(3) nor any order or decree obtained by SIPC from the court shall operate as a stay of any contractual rights of a creditor to liquidate, terminate, or accelerate a securities contract, commodity contract, forward contract, repurchase agreement, swap agreement, or master netting agreement, as those terms are defined in sections 101, 741, and 761 of title 11, United States Code, to offset or net termination values, payment amounts, or other transfer obligations arising under or in connection with one or more of such contracts or agreements, or to foreclose on any cash collateral pledged by the debtor, whether or not with respect to one or more of such contracts or agreements.

"(ii) Notwithstanding clause (i), such application, order, or decree may operate as a stay of the foreclosure on, or disposition of, securities collateral pledged by the debtor, whether or not with respect to one or more of such contracts or agreements, securities sold by the debtor under a repurchase agreement, or securities lent under a securities lending agreement.

"(iii) As used in this subparagraph, the term 'contractual right' includes a right set forth in a rule or bylaw of a national securities exchange, a national securities association, or a securities clearing agency, a right set forth in a bylaw of a clearing organization or contract market or in a resolution of the governing board thereof, and a right, whether or not in writing, arising under common law, under law merchant, or by reason of normal business practice.".

TITLE X—PROTECTION OF FAMILY FARMERS AND FAMILY FISHERMEN

SEC. 1001. PERMANENT REENACTMENT OF CHAPTER 12.

(a) REENACTMENT.—

(1) IN GENERAL.—Chapter 12 of title 11, United States Code, as reenacted by section 149 of division C of the Omnibus Consolidated and Emergency Supplemental Appropriations Act, 1999 (Public Law 105-277), and as in effect on June 30, 2005, is hereby reenacted.

(2) EFFECTIVE DATE OF REENACTMENT.—Paragraph (1) shall take effect on July 1, 2005.

(b) AMENDMENTS.—Chapter 12 of title 11, United States Code, as reenacted by subsection (a), is amended by this Act.

(c) CONFORMING AMENDMENT.—Section 302 of the Bankruptcy Judges, United States Trustees, and Family Farmer Bankruptcy Act of 1986 (28 U.S.C. 581 note) is amended by striking subsection (f).

SEC. 1002. DEBT LIMIT INCREASE.

Section 104(b) of title 11, United States Code, as amended by section 226, is amended by inserting "101(18)," after "101(3)," each place it appears.

SEC. 1003. CERTAIN CLAIMS OWED TO GOVERNMENTAL UNITS.

(a) CONTENTS OF PLAN.—Section 1222(a)(2) of title 11, United States Code, as amended by section 213, is amended to read as follows:

"(2) provide for the full payment, in deferred cash payments, of all claims entitled to priority under section 507, unless—

"(A) the claim is a claim owed to a governmental unit that arises as a result of the sale, transfer, exchange, or other disposition of any farm asset used in the debtor's farming operation, in which case the claim shall be treated as an unsecured claim that is not entitled to priority under section 507, but the debt shall be treated in such manner only if the debtor receives a discharge; or

"(B) the holder of a particular claim agrees to a different treatment of that claim;".

(b) SPECIAL NOTICE PROVISIONS.—Section 1231(b) of title 11, United States Code, as so designated by section 719, is amended by striking "a State or local governmental unit" and inserting "any governmental unit".

(c) EFFECTIVE DATE; APPLICATION OF AMENDMENTS.—This section and the amendments made by this section shall take effect on the date of the enactment of this Act and shall not apply with respect to cases commenced under title 11 of the United States Code before such date.

SEC. 1004. DEFINITION OF FAMILY FARMER.

Section 101(18) of title 11, United States Code, is amended—

(1) in subparagraph (A)—

(A) by striking "$1,500,000" and inserting "$3,237,000"; and

(B) by striking "80" and inserting "50"; and

(2) in subparagraph (B)(ii)—

(A) by striking "$1,500,000" and inserting "$3,237,000"; and

(B) by striking "80" and inserting "50".

SEC. 1005. ELIMINATION OF REQUIREMENT THAT FAMILY FARMER AND SPOUSE RECEIVE OVER 50 PERCENT OF INCOME FROM FARMING OPERATION IN YEAR PRIOR TO BANKRUPTCY.

Section 101(18)(A) of title 11, United States Code, is amended by striking "for the taxable year preceding the taxable year" and inserting the following:

"for—

"(i) the taxable year preceding; or

"(ii) each of the 2d and 3d taxable years preceding; the taxable year".

SEC. 1006. PROHIBITION OF RETROACTIVE ASSESSMENT OF DISPOSABLE INCOME.

(a) CONFIRMATION OF PLAN.—Section 1225(b)(1) of title 11, United States Code, is amended—

(1) in subparagraph (A) by striking "or" at the end;

(2) in subparagraph (B) by striking the period at the end and inserting "; or"; and

(3) by adding at the end the following:

"(C) the value of the property to be distributed under the plan in the 3-year period, or such longer period as the court may approve under section 1222(c), beginning on the date that the first distribution is due under the plan is not less than the debtor's projected disposable income for such period.".

(b) MODIFICATION OF PLAN.—Section 1229 of title 11, United States Code, is amended by adding at the end the following:

"(d) A plan may not be modified under this section—

"(1) to increase the amount of any payment due before the plan as modified becomes the plan;

"(2) by anyone except the debtor, based on an increase in the debtor's disposable income, to increase the amount of payments to unsecured creditors required for a particular month so that the aggregate of such payments exceeds the debtor's disposable income for such month; or

"(3) in the last year of the plan by anyone except the debtor, to require payments that would leave the debtor with insufficient funds to carry on the farming operation after the plan is completed.".

SEC. 1007. FAMILY FISHERMEN.

(a) DEFINITIONS.—Section 101 of title 11, United States Code, is amended—

(1) by inserting after paragraph (7) the following:

"(7A) 'commercial fishing operation' means—

"(A) the catching or harvesting of fish, shrimp, lobsters, urchins, seaweed, shellfish, or other aquatic species or products of such species; or

"(B) for purposes of section 109 and chapter 12, aquaculture activities consisting of raising for market any species or product described in subparagraph (A);

"(7B) 'commercial fishing vessel' means a vessel used by a family fisherman to carry out a commercial fishing operation;"; and

(2) by inserting after paragraph (19) the following:

"(19A) 'family fisherman' means—

"(A) an individual or individual and spouse engaged in a commercial fishing operation—

"(i) whose aggregate debts do not exceed $1,500,000 and not less than 80 percent of whose aggregate noncontingent, liquidated debts (excluding a debt for the principal residence of such individual or such individual and spouse, unless such debt arises out of a commercial fishing operation), on the date the case is filed, arise out of a commercial fishing operation owned or operated by such individual or such individual and spouse; and

"(ii) who receive from such commercial fishing operation more than 50 percent of such individual's or such individual's and spouse's gross income for the taxable year preceding the taxable year in which the case concerning such individual or such individual and spouse was filed; or

"(B) a corporation or partnership—

"(i) in which more than 50 percent of the outstanding stock or equity is held by—

"(I) 1 family that conducts the commercial fishing operation; or

"(II) 1 family and the relatives of the members of such family, and such family or such relatives conduct the commercial fishing operation; and

"(ii)(I) more than 80 percent of the value of its assets consists of assets related to the commercial fishing operation;

"(II) its aggregate debts do not exceed $1,500,000 and not less than 80 percent of its aggregate noncontingent, liquidated debts (excluding a debt for 1 dwelling which is owned by such corporation or partnership and which a shareholder or partner maintains as a principal residence, unless such debt arises out of a commercial fishing operation), on the date the case is filed, arise out of a commercial fishing operation owned or operated by such corporation or such partnership; and

"(III) if such corporation issues stock, such stock is not publicly traded;

"(19B) 'family fisherman with regular annual income' means a family fisherman whose annual income is sufficiently stable and regular to enable such family fisherman to make payments under a plan under chapter 12 of this title;".

(b) WHO MAY BE A DEBTOR.—Section 109(f) of title 11, United States Code, is amended by inserting "or family fisherman" after "family farmer".

(c) CHAPTER 12.—Chapter 12 of title 11, United States Code, is amended—

(1) in the chapter heading, by inserting "**OR FISHERMAN**" after "**FAMILY FARMER**";

(2) in section 1203, by inserting "or commercial fishing operation" after "farm"; and

(3) in section 1206, by striking "if the property is farmland or farm equipment" and inserting "if the property is farmland, farm equipment, or property used to carry out a commercial fishing operation (including a commercial fishing vessel)".

(d) CLERICAL AMENDMENT.—In the table of chapters for title 11, United States Code, the item relating to chapter 12, is amended to read as follows:

"12. Adjustments of Debts of Family Farmer or Family Fisherman with Regular Annual Income ....1201".

(e) APPLICABILITY.—Nothing in this section shall change, affect, or amend the Fishery Conservation and Management Act of 1976 (16 U.S.C. 1801 et seq.).

TITLE XI—HEALTH CARE AND EMPLOYEE BENEFITS

SEC. 1101. DEFINITIONS.

(a) HEALTH CARE BUSINESS DEFINED.—Section 101 of title 11, United States Code, as amended by section 306, is amended—

(1) by redesignating paragraph (27A) as paragraph (27B); and

(2) by inserting after paragraph (27) the following:

"(27A) 'health care business'—

"(A) means any public or private entity (without regard to whether that entity is organized for profit or not for profit) that is primarily engaged in offering to the general public facilities and services for—

"(i) the diagnosis or treatment of injury, deformity, or disease; and

"(ii) surgical, drug treatment, psychiatric, or obstetric care; and

"(B) includes—

"(i) any—

"(I) general or specialized hospital;

"(II) ancillary ambulatory, emergency, or surgical treatment facility;

"(III) hospice;

"(IV) home health agency; and

"(V) other health care institution that is similar to an entity referred to in subclause (I), (II), (III), or (IV); and

"(ii) any long-term care facility, including any—

"(I) skilled nursing facility;

"(II) intermediate care facility;

"(III) assisted living facility;

"(IV) home for the aged;

"(V) domiciliary care facility; and

"(VI) health care institution that is related to a facility referred to in subclause (I), (II), (III), (IV), or (V), if that institution is primarily engaged in offering room, board, laundry, or personal assistance with activities of daily living and incidentals to activities of daily living;".

(b) PATIENT AND PATIENT RECORDS DEFINED.—Section 101 of title 11, United States Code, is amended by inserting after paragraph (40) the following:

"(40A) 'patient' means any individual who obtains or receives services from a health care business;

"(40B) 'patient records' means any written document relating to a patient or a record recorded in a magnetic, optical, or other form of electronic medium;".

(c) RULE OF CONSTRUCTION.—The amendments made by subsection (a) of this section shall not affect the interpretation of section 109(b) of title 11, United States Code.

SEC. 1102. DISPOSAL OF PATIENT RECORDS.

(a) IN GENERAL.—Subchapter III of chapter 3 of title 11, United States Code, is amended by adding at the end the following:

"§ 351. Disposal of patient records

"If a health care business commences a case under chapter 7, 9, or 11, and the trustee does not have a sufficient amount of funds to pay for the storage of patient records in the manner required under applicable Federal or State law, the following requirements shall apply:

"(1) The trustee shall—

"(A) promptly publish notice, in 1 or more appropriate newspapers, that if patient records are not claimed by the patient or an insurance provider (if applicable law permits the insurance provider to make that claim) by the date that is 365 days after the date of that notification, the trustee will destroy the patient records; and

"(B) during the first 180 days of the 365-day period described in subparagraph (A), promptly attempt to notify directly each patient that is the subject of the patient records and appropriate insurance carrier concerning the patient records by mailing to the most recent known address of that patient, or a family member or contact person for that patient, and to the appropriate insurance carrier an appropriate notice regarding the claiming or disposing of patient records.

"(2) If, after providing the notification under paragraph (1), patient records are not claimed during the 365-day period described under that paragraph, the trustee shall mail, by certified mail, at the end of such 365- day period a written request to each appropriate Federal agency to request permission from that agency to deposit the patient records with that agency, except that no Federal agency is required to accept patient records under this paragraph.

"(3) If, following the 365-day period described in paragraph (2) and after providing the notification under paragraph (1), patient records are not claimed by a patient or insurance provider, or request is not granted by a Federal agency to deposit such records with that agency, the trustee shall destroy those records by—

"(A) if the records are written, shredding or burning the records; or

"(B) if the records are magnetic, optical, or other electronic records, by otherwise destroying those records so that those records cannot be retrieved.".

(b) CLERICAL AMENDMENT.—The table of sections for subchapter III of chapter 3 of title 11, United States Code, is amended by adding at the end the following:

"351. Disposal of patient records.".

SEC. 1103. ADMINISTRATIVE EXPENSE CLAIM FOR COSTS OF CLOSING A HEALTH CARE BUSINESS AND OTHER ADMINISTRATIVE EXPENSES.

Section 503(b) of title 11, United States Code, as amended by section 445, is amended by adding at the end the following:

"(8) the actual, necessary costs and expenses of closing a health care business incurred by a trustee or by a Federal agency (as defined in section 551(1) of title 5) or a department or agency of a State or political subdivision thereof, including any cost or expense incurred—

"(A) in disposing of patient records in accordance with section 351; or

"(B) in connection with transferring patients from the health care business that is in the process of being closed to another health care business; and".

SEC. 1104. APPOINTMENT OF OMBUDSMAN TO ACT AS PATIENT ADVOCATE.

(a) OMBUDSMAN TO ACT AS PATIENT ADVOCATE.—

(1) APPOINTMENT OF OMBUDSMAN.—Title 11, United States Code, as amended by

section 232, is amended by inserting after section 332 the following:

"§ 333. Appointment of patient care ombudsman

"(a)(1) If the debtor in a case under chapter 7, 9, or 11 is a health care business, the court shall order, not later than 30 days after the commencement of the case, the appointment of an ombudsman to monitor the quality of patient care and to represent the interests of the patients of the health care business unless the court finds that the appointment of such ombudsman is not necessary for the protection of patients under the specific facts of the case.

"(2)(A) If the court orders the appointment of an ombudsman under paragraph (1), the United States trustee shall appoint 1 disinterested person (other than the United States trustee) to serve as such ombudsman.

"(B) If the debtor is a health care business that provides long-term care, then the United States trustee may appoint the State Long-Term Care Ombudsman appointed under the Older Americans Act of 1965 for the State in which the case is pending to serve as the ombudsman required by paragraph (1).

"(C) If the United States trustee does not appoint a State Long-Term Care Ombudsman under subparagraph (B), the court shall notify the State Long-Term Care Ombudsman appointed under the Older Americans Act of 1965 for the State in which the case is pending, of the name and address of the person who is appointed under subparagraph (A).

"(b) An ombudsman appointed under subsection (a) shall—

"(1) monitor the quality of patient care provided to patients of the debtor, to the extent necessary under the circumstances, including interviewing patients and physicians;

"(2) not later than 60 days after the date of appointment, and not less frequently than at 60-day intervals thereafter, report to the court after notice to the parties in interest, at a hearing or in writing, regarding the quality of patient care provided to patients of the debtor; and

"(3) if such ombudsman determines that the quality of patient care provided to patients of the debtor is declining significantly or is otherwise being materially compromised, file with the court a motion or a written report, with notice to the parties in interest immediately upon making such determination.

"(c)(1) An ombudsman appointed under subsection (a) shall maintain any information obtained by such ombudsman under this section that relates to patients (including information relating to patient records) as confidential information. Such ombudsman may not review confidential patient records unless the court approves such review in advance and imposes restrictions on such ombudsman to protect the confidentiality of such records.

"(2) An ombudsman appointed under subsection (a)(2)(B) shall have access to patient records consistent with authority of such ombudsman under the Older Americans Act of 1965 and under non-Federal laws governing the State Long-Term Care Ombudsman program.".

(2) CLERICAL AMENDMENT.—The table of sections for subchapter II of chapter 3 of title 11, United States Code, as amended by section 232, is amended by adding at the end the following:

"333. Appointment of ombudsman.".

(b) COMPENSATION OF OMBUDSMAN.—Section 330(a)(1) of title 11, United States Code, is amended—

(1) in the matter preceding subparagraph (A), by inserting "an ombudsman appointed under section 333, or" before "a professional person"; and

(2) in subparagraph (A), by inserting "ombudsman," before "professional person".

SEC. 1105. DEBTOR IN POSSESSION; DUTY OF TRUSTEE TO TRANSFER PATIENTS.

(a) IN GENERAL.—Section 704(a) of title 11, United States Code, as amended by sections 102, 219, and 446, is amended by adding at the end the following:

"(12) use all reasonable and best efforts to transfer patients from a health care business that is in the process of being closed to an appropriate health care business that—

"(A) is in the vicinity of the health care business that is closing;

"(B) provides the patient with services that are substantially similar to those provided by the health care business that is in the process of being closed; and

"(C) maintains a reasonable quality of care.".

(b) CONFORMING AMENDMENT.—Section 1106(a)(1) of title 11, United States Code, as amended by section 446, is amended by striking "and (11)" and inserting "(11), and (12)".

SEC. 1106. EXCLUSION FROM PROGRAM PARTICIPATION NOT SUBJECT TO AUTOMATIC STAY.

Section 362(b) of title 11, United States Code, is amended by inserting after paragraph (27), as amended by sections 224, 303, 311, 401, 718, and 907, the following:

"(28) under subsection (a), of the exclusion by the Secretary of Health and Human Services of the debtor from participation in the medicare program or any other Federal health care program (as defined in section 1128B(f) of the Social Security Act pursuant to title XI or XVIII of such Act).".

TITLE XII—TECHNICAL AMENDMENTS

SEC. 1201. DEFINITIONS.

Section 101 of title 11, United States Code, as amended by this Act, is further amended—

(1) by striking "In this title—" and inserting "In this title the following definitions shall apply:";

(2) in each paragraph (other than paragraph (54A)), by inserting "The term" after the paragraph designation;

(3) in paragraph (35)(B), by striking "paragraphs (21B) and (33)(A)" and inserting "paragraphs (23) and (35)";

(4) in each of paragraphs (35A), (38), and (54A), by striking "; and" at the end and inserting a period;

(5) in paragraph (51B)—

(A) by inserting "who is not a family farmer" after "debtor" the first place it appears; and

(B) by striking "thereto having aggregate" and all that follows through the end of the paragraph and inserting a semicolon;

(6) by striking paragraph (54) and inserting the following:

"(54) The term 'transfer' means—

"(A) the creation of a lien;

"(B) the retention of title as a security interest;

"(C) the foreclosure of a debtor's equity of redemption; or

"(D) each mode, direct or indirect, absolute or conditional, voluntary or involuntary, of disposing of or parting with—

"(i) property; or

"(ii) an interest in property;";

(7) in paragraph (54A)—

(A) by striking "the term" and inserting "The term"; and

(B) by indenting the left margin of paragraph (54A) 2 ems to the right; and

(8) in each of paragraphs (1) through (35), in each of paragraphs (36), (37), (38A), (38B) and (39A), and in each of paragraphs (40) through (55), by striking the semicolon at the end and inserting a period.

SEC. 1202. ADJUSTMENT OF DOLLAR AMOUNTS.

Section 104(b) of title 11, United States Code, as amended by this Act, is further amended—

(1) by inserting "101(19A)," after "101(18)," each place it appears;

(2) by inserting "522(f)(3) and 522(f)(4)," after "522(d)," each place it appears;

(3) by inserting "541(b), 547(c)(9)," after "523(a)(2)(C)," each place it appears;

(4) in paragraph (1), by striking "and 1325(b)(3)" and inserting "1322(d), 1325(b), and 1326(b)(3) of this title and section 1409(b) of title 28"; and

(5) in paragraph (2), by striking "and 1325(b)(3) of this title" and inserting "1322(d), 1325(b), and 1326(b)(3) of this title and section 1409(b) of title 28".

SEC. 1203. EXTENSION OF TIME.

Section 108(c)(2) of title 11, United States Code, is amended by striking "922" and all that follows through "or", and inserting "922, 1201, or".

SEC. 1204. TECHNICAL AMENDMENTS.

Title 11, United States Code, is amended—

(1) in section 109(b)(2), by striking "subsection (c) or (d) of"; and

(2) in section 552(b)(1), by striking "product" each place it appears and inserting "products".

SEC. 1205. PENALTY FOR PERSONS WHO NEGLIGENTLY OR FRAUDULENTLY PREPARE BANKRUPTCY PETITIONS.

Section 110(j)(4) of title 11, United States Code, as so redesignated by section 221, is amended by striking "attorney's" and inserting "attorneys".

SEC. 1206. LIMITATION ON COMPENSATION OF PROFESSIONAL PERSONS.

Section 328(a) of title 11, United States Code, is amended by inserting "on a fixed or percentage fee basis," after "hourly basis,".

SEC. 1207. EFFECT OF CONVERSION.

Section 348(f)(2) of title 11, United States Code, is amended by inserting "of the estate" after "property" the first place it appears.

SEC. 1208. ALLOWANCE OF ADMINISTRATIVE EXPENSES.

Section 503(b)(4) of title 11, United States Code, is amended by inserting "subparagraph (A), (B), (C), (D), or (E) of" before "paragraph (3)".

SEC. 1209. EXCEPTIONS TO DISCHARGE.

Section 523 of title 11, United States Code, as amended by sections 215 and 314, is amended—

(1) by transferring paragraph (15), as added by section 304(e) of Public Law 103-394 (108 Stat. 4133), so as to insert such paragraph after subsection (a)(14A);
(2) in subsection (a)(9), by striking "motor vehicle" and inserting "motor vehicle, vessel, or aircraft"; and
(3) in subsection (e), by striking "a insured" and inserting "an insured".

SEC. 1210. EFFECT OF DISCHARGE.

Section 524(a)(3) of title 11, United States Code, is amended by striking "section 523" and all that follows through "or that" and inserting "section 523, 1228(a)(1), or 1328(a)(1), or that".

SEC. 1211. PROTECTION AGAINST DISCRIMINATORY TREATMENT.

Section 525(c) of title 11, United States Code, is amended—
(1) in paragraph (1), by inserting "student" before "grant" the second place it appears; and
(2) in paragraph (2), by striking "the program operated under part B, D, or E of" and inserting "any program operated under".

SEC. 1212. PROPERTY OF THE ESTATE.

Section 541(b)(4)(B)(ii) of title 11, United States Code, is amended by inserting "365 or" before "542".

SEC. 1213. PREFERENCES.

(a) IN GENERAL.—Section 547 of title 11, United States Code, as amended by section 201, is amended—
(1) in subsection (b), by striking "subsection (c)" and inserting "subsections (c) and (i)"; and
(2) by adding at the end the following:
"(i) If the trustee avoids under subsection (b) a transfer made between 90 days and 1 year before the date of the filing of the petition, by the debtor to an entity that is not an insider for the benefit of a creditor that is an insider, such transfer shall be considered to be avoided under this section only with respect to the creditor that is an insider.".

(b) APPLICABILITY.—The amendments made by this section shall apply to any case that is pending or commenced on or after the date of enactment of this Act.

SEC. 1214. POSTPETITION TRANSACTIONS.

Section 549(c) of title 11, United States Code, is amended—
(1) by inserting "an interest in" after "transfer of" each place it appears;
(2) by striking "such property" and inserting "such real property"; and
(3) by striking "the interest" and inserting "such interest".

SEC. 1215. DISPOSITION OF PROPERTY OF THE ESTATE.

Section 726(b) of title 11, United States Code, is amended by striking "1009,".

SEC. 1216. GENERAL PROVISIONS.

Section 901(a) of title 11, United States Code, is amended by inserting "1123(d)," after "1123(b),".

SEC. 1217. ABANDONMENT OF RAILROAD LINE.

Section 1170(e)(1) of title 11, United States Code, is amended by striking "section 11347" and inserting "section 11326(a)".

SEC. 1218. CONTENTS OF PLAN.

Section 1172(c)(1) of title 11, United States Code, is amended by striking "section 11347" and inserting "section 11326(a)".

SEC. 1219. BANKRUPTCY CASES AND PROCEEDINGS.

Section 1334(d) of title 28, United States Code, is amended—
(1) by striking "made under this subsection" and inserting "made under subsection (c)"; and
(2) by striking "This subsection" and inserting "Subsection (c) and this subsection".

SEC. 1220. KNOWING DISREGARD OF BANKRUPTCY LAW OR RULE.

Section 156(a) of title 18, United States Code, is amended—
(1) in the first undesignated paragraph—
(A) by inserting "(1) the term" before "bankruptcy"; and
(B) by striking the period at the end and inserting "; and"; and
(2) in the second undesignated paragraph—
(A) by inserting "(2) the term" before "document"; and
(B) by striking "this title" and inserting "title 11".

SEC. 1221. TRANSFERS MADE BY NONPROFIT CHARITABLE CORPORATIONS.

(a) SALE OF PROPERTY OF ESTATE.—Section 363(d) of title 11, United States Code, is amended by striking "only" and all that follows through the end of the subsection and inserting
"only—
"(1) in accordance with applicable nonbankruptcy law that governs the transfer of property by a corporation or trust that is not a moneyed, business, or commercial corporation or trust; and
"(2) to the extent not inconsistent with any relief granted under subsection (c), (d), (e), or (f) of section 362.".

(b) CONFIRMATION OF PLAN OF REORGANIZATION.—Section 1129(a) of title 11, United States Code, as amended by sections 213 and 321, is amended by adding at the end the following:
"(16) All transfers of property of the plan shall be made in accordance with any applicable provisions of nonbankruptcy law that govern the transfer of property by a corporation or trust that is not a moneyed, business, or commercial corporation or trust.".

(c) TRANSFER OF PROPERTY.—Section 541 of title 11, United States Code, as amended by section 225, is amended by adding at the end the following:

"(f) Notwithstanding any other provision of this title, property that is held by a debtor that is a corporation described in section 501(c)(3) of the Internal Revenue Code of 1986 and exempt from tax under section 501(a) of such Code may be transferred to an entity that is not such a corporation, but only under the same conditions as would apply if the debtor had not filed a case under this title.".

(d) APPLICABILITY.—The amendments made by this section shall apply to a case pending under title 11, United States Code, on the date of enactment of this Act, or filed under that title on or after that date of enactment, except that the court shall not confirm a plan under chapter 11 of title 11, United States Code, without considering whether this section would substantially affect the rights of a party in interest who first acquired rights with respect to the debtor after the date of the filing of the petition. The parties who may appear and be heard in a proceeding under this section include the attorney general of the State in which the debtor is incorporated, was formed, or does business.

(e) RULE OF CONSTRUCTION.—Nothing in this section shall be construed to require the court in which a case under chapter 11 of title 11, United States Code, is pending to remand or refer any proceeding, issue, or controversy to any other court or to require the approval of any other court for the transfer of property.

SEC. 1222. PROTECTION OF VALID PURCHASE MONEY SECURITY INTERESTS.

Section 547(c)(3)(B) of title 11, United States Code, is amended by striking "20" and inserting "30".

SEC. 1223. BANKRUPTCY JUDGESHIPS.

(a) SHORT TITLE.—This section may be cited as the "Bankruptcy Judgeship Act of 2005".

(b) TEMPORARY JUDGESHIPS.—

(1) APPOINTMENTS.—The following bankruptcy judges shall be appointed in the manner prescribed in section 152(a)(1) of title 28, United States Code, for the appointment of bankruptcy judges provided for in section 152(a)(2) of such title:

(A) One additional bankruptcy judge for the eastern district of California.
(B) Three additional bankruptcy judges for the central district of California.
(C) Four additional bankruptcy judges for the district of Delaware.
(D) Two additional bankruptcy judges for the southern district of Florida.
(E) One additional bankruptcy judge for the southern district of Georgia.
(F) Three additional bankruptcy judges for the district of Maryland.
(G) One additional bankruptcy judge for the eastern district of Michigan.
(H) One additional bankruptcy judge for the southern district of Mississippi.
(I) One additional bankruptcy judge for the district of New Jersey.
(J) One additional bankruptcy judge for the eastern district of New York.
(K) One additional bankruptcy judge for the northern district of New York.
(L) One additional bankruptcy judge for the southern district of New York.
(M) One additional bankruptcy judge for the eastern district of North Carolina.
(N) One additional bankruptcy judge for the eastern district of Pennsylvania.
(O) One additional bankruptcy judge for the middle district of Pennsylvania.
(P) One additional bankruptcy judge for the district of Puerto Rico.
(Q) One additional bankruptcy judge for the western district of Tennessee.
(R) One additional bankruptcy judge for the eastern district of Virginia.
(S) One additional bankruptcy judge for the district of South Carolina.
(T) One additional bankruptcy judge for the district of Nevada.

(2) VACANCIES.—

(A) DISTRICTS WITH SINGLE APPOINTMENTS.—Except as provided in subparagraphs (B), (C), (D), and (E), the first vacancy occurring in the office of bankruptcy judge in each of the judicial districts set forth in paragraph (1)—

(i) occurring 5 years or more after the appointment date of the bankruptcy judge appointed under paragraph (1) to such office; and

(ii) resulting from the death, retirement, resignation, or removal of a bankruptcy judge;

shall not be filled.

(B) CENTRAL DISTRICT OF CALIFORNIA.—The 1st, 2d, and 3d vacancies in the office of bankruptcy judge in the central district of California—

(i) occurring 5 years or more after the respective 1st, 2d, and 3d appointment dates of the bankruptcy judges appointed under paragraph (1)(B); and

(ii) resulting from the death, retirement, resignation, or removal of a bankruptcy judge; shall not be filled.

(C) DISTRICT OF DELAWARE.—The 1st, 2d, 3d, and 4th vacancies in the office of bankruptcy judge in the district of Delaware—

(i) occurring 5 years or more after the respective 1st, 2d, 3d, and 4th appointment dates of the bankruptcy judges appointed under paragraph (1)(F); and

(ii) resulting from the death, retirement, resignation, or removal of a bankruptcy judge; shall not be filled.

(D) SOUTHERN DISTRICT OF FLORIDA.—The 1st and 2d vacancies in the office of bankruptcy judge in the southern district of Florida—

(i) occurring 5 years or more after the respective 1st and 2d appointment dates of the bankruptcy judges appointed under paragraph (1)(D); and

(ii) resulting from the death, retirement, resignation, or removal of a bankruptcy judge; shall not be filled.

(E) DISTRICT OF MARYLAND.—The 1st, 2d, and 3d vacancies in the office of bankruptcy judge in the district of Maryland—

(i) occurring 5 years or more after the respective 1st, 2d, and 3d appointment dates of the bankruptcy judges appointed under paragraph (1)(F); and

(ii) resulting from the death, retirement, resignation, or removal of a bankruptcy judge; shall not be filled.

(c) EXTENSIONS.—

(1) IN GENERAL.—The temporary office of bankruptcy judges authorized for the northern district of Alabama, the district of Delaware, the district of Puerto Rico, and the eastern district of Tennessee under paragraphs (1), (3), (7), and (9) of section 3(a) of the Bankruptcy Judgeship Act of 1992 (28 U.S.C. 152 note) are extended until the first vacancy occurring in the office of a bankruptcy judge in the applicable district resulting from the death, retirement, resignation, or removal of a bankruptcy judge and occurring 5 years after the date of the enactment of this Act.

(2) APPLICABILITY OF OTHER PROVISIONS.—All other provisions of section 3 of the Bankruptcy Judgeship Act of 1992 (28 U.S.C. 152 note) remain applicable to the temporary office of bankruptcy judges referred to in this subsection.

(d) TECHNICAL AMENDMENTS.—Section 152(a) of title 28, United States Code, is amended—

(1) in paragraph (1), by striking the first sentence and inserting the following: "Each bankruptcy judge to be appointed for a judicial district, as provided in paragraph (2), shall be appointed by the court of appeals of the United States for the circuit in which such district is located."; and

(2) in paragraph (2)—

(A) in the item relating to the middle district of Georgia, by striking "2" and inserting "3"; and

(B) in the collective item relating to the middle and southern districts of Georgia, by striking "Middle and Southern . . . . . . 1".

(e) EFFECTIVE DATE.—The amendments made by this section shall take effect on the date of the enactment of this Act.

SEC. 1224. COMPENSATING TRUSTEES.

Section 1326 of title 11, United States Code, is amended—

(1) in subsection (b)—

(A) in paragraph (1), by striking "and";

(B) in paragraph (2), by striking the period at the end and inserting "; and"; and

(C) by adding at the end the following:

"(3) if a chapter 7 trustee has been allowed compensation due to the conversion or dismissal of the debtor's prior case pursuant to section 707(b), and some portion of that compensation remains unpaid in a case converted to this chapter or in the case dismissed under section 707(b) and refiled under this chapter, the amount of any such unpaid compensation, which shall be paid monthly—

"(A) by prorating such amount over the remaining duration of the plan; and

"(B) by monthly payments not to exceed the greater of—

"(i) $25; or

"(ii) the amount payable to unsecured nonpriority creditors, as provided by the plan, multiplied by 5 percent, and the result divided by the number of months in the plan."; and

(2) by adding at the end the following:

"(d) Notwithstanding any other provision of this title—

"(1) compensation referred to in subsection (b)(3) is payable and may be collected by the trustee under that paragraph, even if such amount has been discharged in a prior case under this title; and

"(2) such compensation is payable in a case under this chapter only to the extent permitted by subsection (b)(3).".

SEC. 1225. AMENDMENT TO SECTION 362 OF TITLE 11, UNITED STATES CODE.

Section 362(b)(18) of title 11, United States Code, is amended to read as follows:

"(18) under subsection (a) of the creation or perfection of a statutory lien for an ad valorem property tax, or a special tax or special assessment on real property whether or not ad valorem, imposed by a governmental unit, if such tax or assessment comes due after the date of the filing of the petition;".

SEC. 1226. JUDICIAL EDUCATION.

The Director of the Federal Judicial Center, in consultation with the Director of the Executive Office for United States Trustees, shall develop materials and conduct such training as may be useful to courts in implementing this Act and the amendments made by this Act, including the requirements relating to the means test under section 707(b), and reaffirmation agreements under section 524, of title 11 of the United States Code, as amended by this Act.

SEC. 1227. RECLAMATION.

(a) RIGHTS AND POWERS OF THE TRUSTEE.—Section 546(c) of title 11, United States Code, is amended to read as follows:

"(c)(1) Except as provided in subsection (d) of this section and in section 507(c), and subject to the prior rights of a holder of a security interest in such goods or the proceeds thereof, the rights and powers of the trustee under sections 544(a), 545, 547, and 549 are subject to the right of a seller of goods that has sold goods to the debtor, in the ordinary course of such seller's business, to reclaim such goods if the debtor has received such goods while insolvent, within 45 days before the date of the commencement of a case under this title, but such seller may not reclaim such goods unless such seller demands in writing reclamation of such goods—

"(A) not later than 45 days after the date of receipt of such goods by the debtor; or

"(B) not later than 20 days after the date of commencement of the case, if the 45-day period expires after the commencement of the case.

"(2) If a seller of goods fails to provide notice in the manner described in paragraph (1), the seller still may assert the rights contained in section 503(b)(9).".

(b) ADMINISTRATIVE EXPENSES.—Section 503(b) of title 11, United States Code, as amended by sections 445 and 1103, is amended by adding at the end the following:

"(9) the value of any goods received by the debtor within 20 days before the date of commencement of a case under this title in which the goods have been sold to the debtor in the ordinary course of such debtor's business.".

SEC. 1228. PROVIDING REQUESTED TAX DOCUMENTS TO THE COURT.

(a) CHAPTER 7 CASES.—The court shall not grant a discharge in the case of an individual who is a debtor in a case under chapter 7 of title 11, United States Code, unless requested tax documents have been provided to the court.

(b) CHAPTER 11 AND CHAPTER 13 CASES.—The court shall not confirm a plan of reorganization in the case of an individual under chapter 11 or 13 of title 11, United States Code, unless requested tax documents have been filed with the court.

(c) DOCUMENT RETENTION.—The court shall destroy documents submitted in support of a bankruptcy claim not sooner than 3 years after the date of the conclusion of a case filed by an individual under chapter 7, 11, or 13 of title 11, United States Code. In the event of a pending audit or enforcement action, the court may extend the time for destruction of such requested tax documents.

SEC. 1229. ENCOURAGING CREDITWORTHINESS.

(a) SENSE OF THE CONGRESS.—It is the sense of the Congress that—

(1) certain lenders may sometimes offer credit to consumers indiscriminately, without taking steps to ensure that consumers are capable of repaying the resulting debt, and in a manner which may encourage certain consumers to accumulate additional debt; and

(2) resulting consumer debt may increasingly be a major contributing factor to consumer insolvency.

(b) STUDY REQUIRED.—The Board of Governors of the Federal Reserve System (hereafter in this section referred to as the "Board") shall conduct a study of—

(1) consumer credit industry practices of soliciting and extending credit—

(A) indiscriminately;

(B) without taking steps to ensure that consumers are capable of repaying the resulting debt; and

(C) in a manner that encourages consumers to accumulate additional debt; and

(2) the effects of such practices on consumer debt and insolvency.

(c) REPORT AND REGULATIONS.—Not later than 12 months after the date of enactment of this Act, the Board—

(1) shall make public a report on its findings with respect to the indiscriminate solicitation and extension of credit by the credit industry;

(2) may issue regulations that would require additional disclosures to consumers; and

(3) may take any other actions, consistent with its existing statutory authority, that the Board finds necessary to ensure responsible industrywide practices and to prevent resulting consumer debt and insolvency.

SEC. 1230. PROPERTY NO LONGER SUBJECT TO REDEMPTION.

Section 541(b) of title 11, United States Code, as amended by sections 225 and 323, is amended by adding after paragraph (7), as added by section 323, the following:

"(8) subject to subchapter III of chapter 5, any interest of the debtor in property where the debtor pledged or sold tangible personal property (other than securities or written or printed evidences of indebtedness or title) as collateral for a loan or advance of money given by a person licensed under law to make such loans or advances, where—

"(A) the tangible personal property is in the possession of the pledgee or transferee;

"(B) the debtor has no obligation to repay the money, redeem the collateral, or buy back the property at a stipulated price; and

"(C) neither the debtor nor the trustee have exercised any right to redeem provided under the contract or State law, in a timely manner as provided under State law and section 108(b); or".

SEC. 1231. TRUSTEES.

(a) SUSPENSION AND TERMINATION OF PANEL TRUSTEES AND STANDING TRUSTEES.—Section 586(d) of title 28, United States Code, is amended—

(1) by inserting "(1)" after "(d)"; and

(2) by adding at the end the following:

"(2) A trustee whose appointment under subsection (a)(1) or under subsection (b) is terminated or who ceases to be assigned to cases filed under title 11, United States Code, may obtain judicial review of the final agency decision by commencing an action in the district court of the United States for the district for which the panel to which the trustee is appointed under subsection (a)(1), or in the district court of the United States for the district in which the trustee is appointed under subsection (b) resides, after first exhausting all available administrative remedies, which if the trustee so elects, shall also include an administrative hearing on the record. Unless the trustee elects to have an administrative hearing on the record, the trustee shall be deemed to have exhausted all administrative remedies for purposes of this paragraph if the agency fails to make a final agency decision within 90 days after the trustee requests administrative remedies. The Attorney General shall prescribe procedures to implement this paragraph. The decision of the agency shall be affirmed by the district court unless it is unreasonable and without cause based on the administrative record before the agency.".

(b) EXPENSES OF STANDING TRUSTEES.—Section 586(e) of title 28, United States Code, is amended by adding at the end the following:

"(3) After first exhausting all available administrative remedies, an individual appointed under subsection (b) may obtain judicial review of final agency action to deny a claim of actual, necessary expenses under this subsection by commencing an action in the district court of the United States for the district where the individual resides. The decision of the agency shall be affirmed by the district court unless it is unreasonable and without cause based upon the administrative record before the agency.

"(4) The Attorney General shall prescribe procedures to implement this subsection.".

SEC. 1232. BANKRUPTCY FORMS.

Section 2075 of title 28, United States Code, is amended by adding at the end the following:

"The bankruptcy rules promulgated under this section shall prescribe a form for the statement required under section 707(b)(2)(C) of title 11 and may provide general rules on the content of such statement.".

SEC. 1233. DIRECT APPEALS OF BANKRUPTCY MATTERS TO COURTS OF APPEALS.

(a) APPEALS.—Section 158 of title 28, United States Code, is amended—

(1) in subsection (c)(1), by striking "Subject to subsection (b)," and inserting "Subject to subsections (b) and (d)(2),"; and

(2) in subsection (d)—

(A) by inserting "(1)" after "(d)"; and

(B) by adding at the end the following:

"(2)(A) The appropriate court of appeals shall have jurisdiction of appeals described in the first sentence of subsection (a) if the bankruptcy court, the district court, or the bankruptcy appellate panel involved, acting on its own motion or on the request of a party to the judgment, order, or decree described in such first sentence, or all the appellants and appellees (if any) acting jointly, certify that—

"(i) the judgment, order, or decree involves a question of law as to which there is no controlling decision of the court of appeals for the circuit or of the Supreme Court of the United States, or involves a matter of public importance;

"(ii) the judgment, order, or decree involves a question of law requiring resolution of conflicting decisions; or

"(iii) an immediate appeal from the judgment, order, or decree may materially advance the progress of the case or proceeding in which the appeal is taken;

and if the court of appeals authorizes the direct appeal of the judgment, order, or decree.

"(B) If the bankruptcy court, the district court, or the bankruptcy appellate panel—

"(i) on its own motion or on the request of a party, determines that a circumstance specified in clause (i), (ii), or (iii) of subparagraph (A) exists; or

"(ii) receives a request made by a majority of the appellants and a majority of appellees (if any) to make the certification described in subparagraph (A); then the bankruptcy court, the district court, or the bankruptcy appellate panel shall make the certification described in subparagraph (A).

"(C) The parties may supplement the certification with a short statement of the basis for the certification.

"(D) An appeal under this paragraph does not stay any proceeding of the bankruptcy court, the district court, or the bankruptcy appellate panel from which the appeal is taken, unless the respective bankruptcy court, district court, or bankruptcy appellate panel, or the court of appeals in which the appeal in pending, issues a stay of such proceeding pending the appeal.

"(E) Any request under subparagraph (B) for certification shall be made not later than 60 days after the entry of the judgment, order, or decree.".

(b) PROCEDURAL RULES.—

(1) TEMPORARY APPLICATION.—A provision of this subsection shall apply to appeals under section 158(d)(2) of title 28, United States Code, until a rule of practice and procedure relating to such provision and such appeals is promulgated or amended under chapter 131 of such title.

(2) CERTIFICATION.—A district court, a bankruptcy court, or a bankruptcy appellate panel may make a certification under section 158(d)(2) of title 28, United States Code, only with respect to matters pending in the respective bankruptcy court, district court, or bankruptcy appellate panel.

(3) PROCEDURE.—Subject to any other provision of this subsection, an appeal authorized by the court of appeals under section 158(d)(2)(A) of title 28, United States Code, shall be taken in the manner prescribed in subdivisions (a)(1), (b), (c), and (d) of rule 5 of the Federal Rules of Appellate Procedure. For purposes of subdivision (a)(1) of rule 5—

(A) a reference in such subdivision to a district court shall be deemed to include a reference to a bankruptcy court and a bankruptcy appellate panel, as appropriate; and

(B) a reference in such subdivision to the parties requesting permission to appeal to be served with the petition shall be deemed to include a reference to the parties to the judgment, order, or decree from which the appeal is taken.

(4) FILING OF PETITION WITH ATTACHMENT.—A petition requesting permission to appeal, that is based on a certification made under subparagraph (A) or (B) of section 158(d)(2) shall—

(A) be filed with the circuit clerk not later than 10 days after the certification is entered on the docket of the bankruptcy court, the district court, or the bankruptcy appellate panel from which the appeal is taken; and

(B) have attached a copy of such certification.

(5) REFERENCES IN RULE 5.—For purposes of rule 5 of the Federal Rules of Appellate Procedure—

(A) a reference in such rule to a district court shall be deemed to include a reference to a bankruptcy court and to a bankruptcy appellate panel; and

(B) a reference in such rule to a district clerk shall be deemed to include a reference to a clerk of a bankruptcy court and to a clerk of a bankruptcy appellate panel.

(6) APPLICATION OF RULES.—The Federal Rules of Appellate Procedure shall apply in the courts of appeals with respect to appeals authorized under section 158(d)(2)(A), to the extent relevant and as if such appeals were taken from final judgments, orders, or decrees of the district courts or bankruptcy appellate panels exercising appellate jurisdiction under subsection (a) or (b) of section 158 of title 28, United States Code.

SEC. 1234. INVOLUNTARY CASES.

(a) AMENDMENTS.—Section 303 of title 11, United States Code, is amended—

(1) in subsection (b)(1), by—

(A) inserting "as to liability or amount" after "bona fide dispute"; and

(B) striking "if such claims" and inserting "if such noncontingent, undisputed claims"; and

(2) in subsection (h)(1), by inserting "as to liability or amount" before the semicolon at the end.

(b) EFFECTIVE DATE; APPLICATION OF AMENDMENTS.—This section and the amendments made by this section shall take effect on the date of the enactment of this Act and shall apply with respect to cases commenced under title 11 of the United States Code before, on, and after such date.

SEC. 1235. FEDERAL ELECTION LAW FINES AND PENALTIES AS NONDISCHARGEABLE DEBT.

Section 523(a) of title 11, United States Code, as amended by section 314, is amended by inserting after paragraph (14A) the following:

"(14B) incurred to pay fines or penalties imposed under Federal election law;".

TITLE XIII—CONSUMER CREDIT DISCLOSURE

SEC. 1301. ENHANCED DISCLOSURES UNDER AN OPEN END CREDIT PLAN.

(a) MINIMUM PAYMENT DISCLOSURES.—Section 127(b) of the Truth in Lending Act (15 U.S.C. 1637(b)) is amended by adding at the end the following:

"(11)(A) In the case of an open end credit plan that requires a minimum monthly payment of not more than 4 percent of the balance on which finance charges are accruing, the following statement, located on the front of the billing statement, disclosed clearly and conspicuously: 'Minimum Payment Warning: Making only the minimum payment will increase the interest you pay and the time it takes to repay your balance. For example, making only the typical 2% minimum monthly payment on a balance of $1,000 at an interest rate of 17% would take 88 months to repay the balance in full. For an estimate of the time it would take to repay your balance, making only minimum payments, call this toll-free number: ______________.' (the blank space to be filled in by the creditor).

"(B) In the case of an open end credit plan that requires a minimum monthly payment of more than 4 percent of the balance on which finance charges are accruing, the following statement, in a prominent location on the front of the billing statement, disclosed clearly and conspicuously: 'Minimum Payment Warning: Making only the required minimum payment will increase the interest you pay and the time it takes to repay your balance. Making a typical 5% minimum monthly payment on a balance of $300 at an interest rate of 17% would take 24 months to repay the balance in full. For an estimate of the time it would take to repay your balance, making only minimum monthly payments, call this toll-free number: ______________.' (the blank space to be filled in by the creditor).

"(C) Notwithstanding subparagraphs (A) and (B), in the case of a creditor with respect to which compliance with this title is enforced by the Federal Trade Commission, the following statement, in a prominent location on the front of the billing statement, disclosed clearly and conspicuously: 'Minimum Payment Warning: Making only the required minimum payment will increase the interest you pay and the time it takes to repay your balance. For example, making only the typical 5% minimum monthly payment on a balance of $300 at an interest rate of 17% would take 24 months to repay the balance in full. For an estimate of the time it would take to repay your balance, making only minimum monthly payments, call the Federal Trade Commission at this toll-free number: ______________.' (the blank space to be filled in by the creditor). A creditor who is subject to this subparagraph shall not be subject to subparagraph (A) or (B).

"(D) Notwithstanding subparagraph (A), (B), or (C), in complying with any such subparagraph, a creditor may substitute an example based on an interest rate that is greater than 17 percent. Any creditor that is subject to subparagraph (B) may elect to provide the disclosure required under subparagraph (A) in lieu of the disclosure required under subparagraph (B).

"(E) The Board shall, by rule, periodically recalculate, as necessary, the interest rate and repayment period under subparagraphs (A), (B), and (C).

"(F)(i) The toll-free telephone number disclosed by a creditor or the Federal Trade Commission under subparagraph (A), (B), or (G), as appropriate, may be a toll-free telephone number established and maintained by the creditor or the Federal Trade Commission, as appropriate, or may be a toll-free telephone number established and maintained by a third party for use by the creditor or multiple creditors or the Federal Trade Commission, as appropriate. The toll-free telephone number may connect consumers to an automated device through which consumers may obtain information described in subparagraph (A), (B), or (C), by inputting information using a touch-tone telephone or similar device, if consumers whose telephones are not equipped to use such automated device are provided the opportunity to be connected to an individual from whom the information described in subparagraph (A), (B), or (C), as applicable, may be obtained. A person that receives a request for information described in subparagraph (A), (B), or (C) from an obligor through the toll-free telephone number disclosed under subparagraph (A), (B), or (C), as applicable, shall disclose in response to such request only the information set forth in the table promulgated by the Board under subparagraph (H)(i).

"(ii)(I) The Board shall establish and maintain for a period not to exceed 24 months following the effective date of the Bankruptcy Abuse Prevention and Consumer Protection Act of 2005, a toll-free telephone number, or provide a toll-free telephone number established and maintained by a third party, for use by creditors that are depository institutions (as defined in section 3 of the Federal Deposit Insurance Act), including a Federal credit union or State credit union (as defined in section 101 of the Federal Credit Union Act), with total assets not exceeding $250,000,000. The toll-free telephone number may connect consumers to an automated device through which consumers may obtain information described in subparagraph (A) or (B), as applicable, by inputting information using a touch-tone telephone or similar device, if consumers whose telephones are not equipped to use such automated device are provided the opportunity to be connected to an individual from whom the information described in subparagraph (A) or (B), as applicable, may be obtained. A person that receives a request for information described in subparagraph (A) or (B) from an obligor through the toll-free telephone number disclosed under subparagraph (A) or (B), as applicable, shall disclose in response to such request only the information set forth in the table promulgated by the Board under subparagraph (H)(i). The dollar amount contained in this subclause shall be adjusted according to an indexing mechanism established by the Board.

"(II) Not later than 6 months prior to the expiration of the 24-month period referenced in subclause (I), the Board shall submit to the Committee on Banking, Housing, and Urban Affairs of the Senate and the Committee on Financial Services of the House of Representatives a report on the program described in subclause (I).

"(G) The Federal Trade Commission shall establish and maintain a toll-free number for the purpose of providing to consumers the information required to be disclosed under subparagraph (C).

"(H) The Board shall—

"(i) establish a detailed table illustrating the approximate number of months that it would take to repay an outstanding balance if a consumer pays only the required minimum monthly payments and if no other advances are made, which table shall clearly present standardized information to be used to disclose the information required to be disclosed under subparagraph (A), (B), or (C), as applicable;

"(ii) establish the table required under clause (i) by assuming—

"(I) a significant number of different annual percentage rates;

"(II) a significant number of different account balances;

"(III) a significant number of different minimum payment amounts; and

"(IV) that only minimum monthly payments are made and no additional extensions of credit are obtained; and

"(iii) promulgate regulations that provide instructional guidance regarding the manner in which the information contained in the table established under clause (i) should be used in responding to the request of an obligor for any information required to be disclosed under subparagraph (A), (B), or (C).

"(I) The disclosure requirements of this paragraph do not apply to any charge card account, the primary purpose of which is to require payment of charges in full each month.

"(J) A creditor that maintains a toll-free telephone number for the purpose of providing customers with the actual number of months that it will take to repay the customer's outstanding balance is not subject to the requirements of subparagraph (A) or (B).

"(K) A creditor that maintains a toll-free telephone number for the purpose of providing customers with the actual number of months that it will take to repay an outstanding balance shall include the following statement on each billing statement: 'Making only the minimum payment will increase the interest you pay and the time it takes to repay your balance. For more information, call this toll-free number:______________ .".

(b) REGULATORY IMPLEMENTATION.—

(1) IN GENERAL.—The Board of Governors of the Federal Reserve System (hereafter in this title referred to as the "Board") shall promulgate regulations implementing the requirements of section 127(b)(11) of the Truth in Lending Act, as added by subsection (a) of this section.

(2) EFFECTIVE DATE.—Section 127(b)(11) of the Truth in Lending Act, as added by subsection (a) of this section, and the regulations issued under paragraph (1) of this subsection shall not take effect until the later of—

(A) 18 months after the date of enactment of this Act; or

(B) 12 months after the publication of such final regulations by the Board.

(c) STUDY OF FINANCIAL DISCLOSURES.—

(1) IN GENERAL.—The Board may conduct a study to determine the types of information available to potential borrowers from consumer credit lending institutions regarding factors qualifying potential borrowers for credit, repayment requirements, and the consequences of default.

(2) FACTORS FOR CONSIDERATION.—In conducting a study under paragraph (1), the Board should, in consultation with the other Federal banking agencies (as defined in section 3 of the Federal Deposit Insurance Act), the National Credit Union Administration, and the Federal Trade Commission, consider the extent to which—

(A) consumers, in establishing new credit arrangements, are aware of their existing payment obligations, the need to consider those obligations in deciding to take on new credit, and how taking on excessive credit can result in financial difficulty;

(B) minimum periodic payment features offered in connection with open end credit plans impact consumer default rates;

(C) consumers make only the required minimum payment under open end credit plans;

(D) consumers are aware that making only required minimum payments will increase the cost and repayment period of an open end credit obligation; and

(E) the availability of low minimum payment options is a cause of consumers experiencing financial difficulty.

(3) REPORT TO CONGRESS.—Findings of the Board in connection with any study conducted under this subsection shall be submitted to Congress. Such report shall also include recommendations for legislative initiatives, if any, of the Board, based on its findings.

SEC. 1302. ENHANCED DISCLOSURE FOR CREDIT EXTENSIONS SECURED BY A DWELLING.

(a) OPEN END CREDIT EXTENSIONS.—

(1) CREDIT APPLICATIONS.—Section 127A(a)(13) of the Truth in Lending Act (15 U.S.C. 1637a(a)(13)) is amended—

(A) by striking "CONSULTATION OF TAX ADVISER.—A statement that the" and inserting the following: "TAX DEDUCTIBILITY.—A statement that—

"(A) the"; and

(B) by striking the period at the end and inserting the following: "; and

"(B) in any case in which the extension of credit exceeds the fair market value (as defined under the Internal Revenue Code of 1986) of the dwelling, the interest on the portion of the credit extension that is greater than the fair market value of the dwelling is not tax deductible for Federal income tax purposes.".

(2) CREDIT ADVERTISEMENTS.—Section 147(b) of the Truth in Lending Act (15 U.S.C. 1665b(b)) is amended—

(A) by striking "If any" and inserting the following:

"(1) IN GENERAL.—If any"; and

(B) by adding at the end the following:

"(2) CREDIT IN EXCESS OF FAIR MARKET VALUE.—Each advertisement described in subsection (a) that relates to an extension of credit that may exceed the fair market value of the dwelling, and which advertisement is disseminated in paper form to the public or through the Internet, as opposed to by radio or television, shall include a clear and conspicuous statement that—

"(A) the interest on the portion of the credit extension that is greater than the fair market value of the dwelling is not tax deductible for Federal income tax purposes; and

"(B) the consumer should consult a tax adviser for further information regarding the deductibility of interest and charges.".

(b) NON-OPEN END CREDIT EXTENSIONS.—

(1) CREDIT APPLICATIONS.—Section 128 of the Truth in Lending Act (15 U.S.C. 1638) is amended—

(A) in subsection (a), by adding at the end the following:

"(15) In the case of a consumer credit transaction that is secured by the principal dwelling of the consumer, in which the extension of credit may exceed the fair market value of the dwelling, a clear and conspicuous statement that—

"(A) the interest on the portion of the credit extension that is greater than the fair market value of the dwelling is not tax deductible for Federal income tax purposes; and

"(B) the consumer should consult a tax adviser for further information regarding the deductibility of interest and charges."; and

(B) in subsection (b), by adding at the end the following:

"(3) In the case of a credit transaction described in paragraph (15) of subsection (a), disclosures required by that paragraph shall be made to the consumer at the time of application for such extension of credit.".

(2) CREDIT ADVERTISEMENTS.—Section 144 of the Truth in Lending Act (15 U.S.C. 1664) is amended by adding at the end the following:

"(e) Each advertisement to which this section applies that relates to a consumer credit transaction that is secured by the principal dwelling of a consumer in which the extension of credit may exceed the fair market value of the dwelling, and which advertisement is disseminated in paper form to the public or through the Internet, as opposed to by radio or television, shall clearly and conspicuously state that—

"(1) the interest on the portion of the credit extension that is greater than the fair market value of the dwelling is not tax deductible for Federal income tax purposes; and

"(2) the consumer should consult a tax adviser for further information regarding the deductibility of interest and charges.".

(c) REGULATORY IMPLEMENTATION.—

(1) IN GENERAL.—The Board shall promulgate regulations implementing the amendments made by this section.

(2) EFFECTIVE DATE.—Regulations issued under paragraph (1) shall not take effect until the later of—

(A) 12 months after the date of enactment of this Act; or

(B) 12 months after the date of publication of such final regulations by the Board.

SEC. 1303. DISCLOSURES RELATED TO "INTRODUCTORY RATES".

(a) INTRODUCTORY RATE DISCLOSURES.—Section 127(c) of the Truth in Lending Act (15 U.S.C. 1637(c)) is amended by adding at the end the following:

"(6) ADDITIONAL NOTICE CONCERNING 'INTRODUCTORY RATES'.—

"(A) IN GENERAL.—Except as provided in subparagraph (B), an application or solicitation to open a credit card account and all promotional materials accompanying such application or solicitation for which a disclosure is required under paragraph (1), and that offers a temporary annual percentage rate of interest, shall—

"(i) use the term 'introductory' in immediate proximity to each listing of the temporary annual percentage rate applicable to such account, which term shall appear clearly and conspicuously;

"(ii) if the annual percentage rate of interest that will apply after the end of the temporary rate period will be a fixed rate, state in a clear and conspicuous manner in a prominent location closely proximate to the first listing of the temporary annual percentage rate (other than a listing of the temporary annual percentage rate in the tabular format described in section 122(c)), the time period in which the introductory period will end and the annual percentage rate that will apply after the end of the introductory period; and

"(iii) if the annual percentage rate that will apply after the end of the temporary rate period will vary in accordance with an index, state in a clear and conspicuous manner in a prominent location closely proximate to the first listing of the temporary annual percentage rate (other than a listing in the tabular format prescribed by section 122(c)), the time period in which the introductory period will end and the rate that will apply after that, based on an annual percentage rate that was in effect within 60 days before the date of mailing the application or solicitation.

"(B) EXCEPTION.—Clauses (ii) and (iii) of subparagraph (A) do not apply with respect to any listing of a temporary annual percentage rate on an envelope or other enclosure in which an application or solicitation to open a credit card account is mailed.

"(C) CONDITIONS FOR INTRODUCTORY RATES.—An application or solicitation to open a credit card account for which a disclosure is required under paragraph (1), and that offers a temporary annual percentage rate of interest shall, if that rate of interest is revocable under any circumstance or upon any event, clearly and conspicuously disclose, in a prominent manner on or with such application or solicitation—

"(i) a general description of the circumstances that may result in the revocation of the temporary annual percentage rate; and

"(ii) if the annual percentage rate that will apply upon the revocation of the temporary annual percentage rate—

"(I) will be a fixed rate, the annual percentage rate that will apply upon the revocation of the temporary annual percentage rate; or

"(II) will vary in accordance with an index, the rate that will apply after the temporary rate, based on an annual percentage rate that was in effect within 60 days before the date of mailing the application or solicitation.

"(D) DEFINITIONS.—In this paragraph—

"(i) the terms 'temporary annual percentage rate of interest' and 'temporary annual percentage rate' mean any rate of interest applicable to a credit card account for an introductory period of less than 1 year, if that rate is less than an annual percentage rate that was in effect within 60 days before the date of mailing the application or solicitation; and

"(ii) the term 'introductory period' means the maximum time period for which the temporary annual percentage rate may be applicable.

"(E) RELATION TO OTHER DISCLOSURE REQUIREMENTS.—Nothing in this paragraph may be construed to supersede subsection (a) of section 122, or any disclosure required by paragraph (1) or any other provision of this subsection.".

(b) REGULATORY IMPLEMENTATION.—

(1) IN GENERAL.—The Board shall promulgate regulations implementing the requirements of section 127(c)(6) of the Truth in Lending Act, as added by this section.

(2) EFFECTIVE DATE.—Section 127(c)(6) of the Truth in Lending Act, as added by this section, and regulations issued under paragraph (1) of this subsection shall not take effect until the later of—

(A) 12 months after the date of enactment of this Act; or

(B) 12 months after the date of publication of such final regulations by the Board.

SEC. 1304. INTERNET-BASED CREDIT CARD SOLICITATIONS.

(a) INTERNET-BASED SOLICITATIONS.—Section 127(c) of the Truth in Lending Act (15 U.S.C. 1637(c)) is amended by adding at the end the following:

"(7) INTERNET-BASED SOLICITATIONS.—

"(A) IN GENERAL.—In any solicitation to open a credit card account for any person under an open end consumer credit plan using the Internet or other interactive computer service, the person making the solicitation shall clearly and conspicuously disclose—

"(i) the information described in subparagraphs (A) and (B) of paragraph (1); and

"(ii) the information described in paragraph (6).

"(B) FORM OF DISCLOSURE.—The disclosures required by subparagraph (A) shall be—

"(i) readily accessible to consumers in close proximity to the solicitation to open a credit card account; and

"(ii) updated regularly to reflect the current policies, terms, and fee amounts applicable to the credit card account.

"(C) DEFINITIONS.—For purposes of this paragraph—

"(i) the term 'Internet' means the international computer network of both Federal and non-Federal interoperable packet switched data networks; and

"(ii) the term 'interactive computer service' means any information service, system, or access software provider that provides or enables computer access by multiple users to a computer server, including specifically a service or system that provides access to the Internet and such systems operated or services offered by libraries or educational institutions.''.

(b) REGULATORY IMPLEMENTATION.—

(1) IN GENERAL.—The Board shall promulgate regulations implementing the requirements of section 127(c)(7) of the Truth in Lending Act, as added by this section.

(2) EFFECTIVE DATE.—The amendment made by subsection (a) and the regulations issued under paragraph (1) of this subsection shall not take effect until the later of—

(A) 12 months after the date of enactment of this Act; or

(B) 12 months after the date of publication of such final regulations by the Board.

SEC. 1305. DISCLOSURES RELATED TO LATE PAYMENT DEADLINES AND PENALTIES.

(a) DISCLOSURES RELATED TO LATE PAYMENT DEADLINES AND PENALTIES.—Section 127(b) of the Truth in Lending Act (15 U.S.C. 1637(b)) is amended by adding at the end the following:

''(12) If a late payment fee is to be imposed due to the failure of the obligor to make payment on or before a required payment due date, the following shall be stated clearly and conspicuously on the billing statement:

''(A) The date on which that payment is due or, if different, the earliest date on which a late payment fee may be charged.

''(B) The amount of the late payment fee to be imposed if payment is made after such date.''.

(b) REGULATORY IMPLEMENTATION.—

(1) IN GENERAL.—The Board shall promulgate regulations implementing the requirements of section 127(b)(12) of the Truth in Lending Act, as added by this section.

(2) EFFECTIVE DATE.—The amendment made by subsection (a) and regulations issued under paragraph (1) of this subsection shall not take effect until the later of—

(A) 12 months after the date of enactment of this Act; or

(B) 12 months after the date of publication of such final regulations by the Board.

SEC. 1306. PROHIBITION ON CERTAIN ACTIONS FOR FAILURE TO INCUR FINANCE CHARGES.

(a) PROHIBITION ON CERTAIN ACTIONS FOR FAILURE TO INCUR FINANCE CHARGES.—Section 127 of the Truth in Lending Act (15 U.S.C. 1637) is amended by adding at the end the following:

''(h) PROHIBITION ON CERTAIN ACTIONS FOR FAILURE TO INCUR FINANCE CHARGES.—A creditor of an account under an open end consumer credit plan may not terminate an account prior to its expiration date solely because the consumer has not incurred finance charges on the account. Nothing in this subsection shall prohibit a creditor from terminating an account for inactivity in 3 or more consecutive months.''.

(b) REGULATORY IMPLEMENTATION.—

(1) IN GENERAL.—The Board shall promulgate regulations implementing the requirements of section 127(h) of the Truth in Lending Act, as added by this section.

(2) EFFECTIVE DATE.—The amendment made by subsection (a) and regulations issued under paragraph (1) of this subsection shall not take effect until the later of—

(A) 12 months after the date of enactment of this Act; or

(B) 12 months after the date of publication of such final regulations by the Board.

SEC. 1307. DUAL USE DEBIT CARD.

(a) REPORT.—The Board may conduct a study of, and present to Congress a report containing its analysis of, consumer protections under existing law to limit the liability of consumers for unauthorized use of a debit card or similar access device. Such report, if submitted, shall include recommendations for legislative initiatives, if any, of the Board, based on its findings.

(b) CONSIDERATIONS.—In preparing a report under subsection (a), the Board may include—

(1) the extent to which section 909 of the Electronic Fund Transfer Act (15 U.S.C. 1693g), as in effect at the time of the report, and the implementing regulations promulgated by the Board to carry out that section provide adequate unauthorized use liability protection for consumers;

(2) the extent to which any voluntary industry rules have enhanced or may enhance the level of protection afforded consumers in connection with such unauthorized use liability; and

(3) whether amendments to the Electronic Fund Transfer Act (15 U.S.C. 1693 et seq.), or revisions to regulations promulgated by the Board to carry out that Act, are necessary to further address adequate protection for consumers concerning unauthorized use liability.

SEC. 1308. STUDY OF BANKRUPTCY IMPACT OF CREDIT EXTENDED TO DEPENDENT STUDENTS.

(a) STUDY.—

(1) IN GENERAL.—The Board shall conduct a study regarding the impact that the extension of credit described in paragraph (2) has on the rate of cases filed under title 11 of the United States Code.

(2) EXTENSION OF CREDIT.—The extension of credit described in this paragraph is the extension of credit to individuals who are—

(A) claimed as dependents for purposes of the Internal Revenue Code of 1986; and

(B) enrolled within 1 year of successfully completing all required secondary education requirements and on a full-time basis, in postsecondary educational institutions.

(b) REPORT.—Not later than 1 year after the date of enactment of this Act, the Board shall submit to the Senate and the House of Representatives a report summarizing the results of the study conducted under subsection (a).

SEC. 1309. CLARIFICATION OF CLEAR AND CONSPICUOUS.

(a) REGULATIONS.—Not later than 6 months after the date of enactment of this Act, the Board, in consultation with the other Federal banking agencies (as defined in section 3 of the Federal Deposit Insurance Act), the National Credit Union Administration Board, and the Federal Trade Commission, shall promulgate regulations to provide guidance regarding the meaning of the term "clear and conspicuous", as used in subparagraphs (A), (B), and (C) of section 127(b)(11) and clauses (ii) and (iii) of section 127(c)(6)(A) of the Truth in Lending Act.

(b) EXAMPLES.—Regulations promulgated under subsection (a) shall include examples of clear and conspicuous model disclosures for the purposes of disclosures required by the provisions of the Truth in Lending Act referred to in subsection (a).

(c) STANDARDS.—In promulgating regulations under this section, the Board shall ensure that the clear and conspicuous standard required for disclosures made under the provisions of the Truth in Lending Act referred to in subsection (a) can be implemented in a manner which results in disclosures which are reasonably understandable and designed to call attention to the nature and significance of the information in the notice.

TITLE XIV—PREVENTING CORPORATE BANKRUPTCY ABUSE

SEC. 1401. EMPLOYEE WAGE AND BENEFIT PRIORITIES.

Section 507(a) of title 11, United States Code, as amended by section 212, is amended—

(1) in paragraph (4) by striking "90" and inserting "180", and

(2) in paragraphs (4) and (5) by striking "$4,000" and inserting "$10,000".

SEC. 1402. FRAUDULENT TRANSFERS AND OBLIGATIONS.

Section 548 of title 11, United States Code, is amended—
(1) in subsections (a) and (b) by striking "one year" and inserting "2 years",
(2) in subsection (a)—
(A) by inserting "(including any transfer to or for the benefit of an insider under an employment contract)" after "transfer" the 1st place it appears, and
(B) by inserting "(including any obligation to or for the benefit of an insider under an employment contract)" after "obligation" the 1st place it appears, and
(3) in subsection (a)(1)(B)(ii)—
(A) in subclause (II) by striking "or" at the end,
(B) in subclause (III) by striking the period at the end and inserting "; or", and
(C) by adding at the end the following:
"(IV) made such transfer to or for the benefit of an insider, or incurred such obligation to or for the benefit of an insider, under an employment contract and not in the ordinary course of business.".
(4) by adding at the end the following:
"(e)(1) In addition to any transfer that the trustee may otherwise avoid, the trustee may avoid any transfer of an interest of the debtor in property that was made on or within 10 years before the date of the filing of the petition, if—
"(A) such transfer was made to a self-settled trust or similar device;
"(B) such transfer was by the debtor;
"(C) the debtor is a beneficiary of such trust or similar device; and
"(D) the debtor made such transfer with actual intent to hinder, delay, or defraud any entity to which the debtor was or became, on or after the date that such transfer was made, indebted.
"(2) For the purposes of this subsection, a transfer includes a transfer made in anticipation of any money judgment, settlement, civil penalty, equitable order, or criminal fine incurred by, or which the debtor believed would be incurred by—
"(A) any violation of the securities laws (as defined in section 3(a)(47) of the Securities Exchange Act of 1934 (15 U.S.C. 78c(a)(47))), any State securities laws, or any regulation or order issued under Federal securities laws or State securities laws; or
"(B) fraud, deceit, or manipulation in a fiduciary capacity or in connection with the purchase or sale of any security registered under section 12 or 15(d) of the Securities Exchange Act of 1934 (15 U.S.C. 78l and 78o(d)) or under section 6 of the Securities Act of 1933 (15 U.S.C. 77f).".

SEC. 1403. PAYMENT OF INSURANCE BENEFITS TO RETIRED EMPLOYEES.

Section 1114 of title 11, United States Code, is amended—
(1) by redesignating subsection (l) as subsection (m), and
(2) by inserting after subsection (k) the following:
"(*l*) If the debtor, during the 180-day period ending on the date of the filing of the petition—
"(1) modified retiree benefits; and
"(2) was insolvent on the date such benefits were modified; the court, on motion of a party in interest, and after notice and a hearing, shall issue an order reinstating as of the date the modification was made, such benefits as in effect immediately before such date unless the court finds that the balance of the equities clearly favors such modification.".

SEC. 1404. DEBTS NONDISCHARGEABLE IF INCURRED IN VIOLATION OF SECURITIES FRAUD LAWS.

(a) PREPETITION AND POSTPETITION EFFECT.—Section 523(a)(19)(B) of title 11, United States Code, is amended by inserting ", before, on, or after the date on which the petition was filed," after "results".

(b) EFFECTIVE DATE UPON ENACTMENT OF SARBANES-OXLEY ACT.—The amendment made by subsection (a) is effective beginning July 30, 2002.

SEC. 1405. APPOINTMENT OF TRUSTEE IN CASES OF SUSPECTED FRAUD.

Section 1104 of title 11, United States Code, is amended by adding at the end the following:

"(e) The United States trustee shall move for the appointment of a trustee under subsection (a) if there are reasonable grounds to suspect that current members of the governing body of the debtor, the debtor's chief executive or chief financial officer, or members of the governing body who selected the debtor's chief executive or chief financial officer, participated in actual fraud, dishonesty, or criminal conduct in the management of the debtor or the debtor's public financial reporting.".

SEC. 1406. EFFECTIVE DATE; APPLICATION OF AMENDMENTS.

(a) EFFECTIVE DATE.—Except as provided in subsection (b), this title and the amendments made by this title shall take effect on the date of the enactment of this Act.

(b) APPLICATION OF AMENDMENTS.—

(1) IN GENERAL.—cept as provided in paragraph (2), the amendments made by this title shall apply only with respect to cases commenced under title 11 of the United States Code on or after the date of the enactment of this Act.

(2) AVOIDANCE PERIOD.—The amendment made by section 1402(1) shall apply only with respect to cases commenced under title 11 of the United States Code more than 1 year after the date of the enactment of this Act.

TITLE XV—GENERAL EFFECTIVE DATE; APPLICATION OF AMENDMENTS

SEC. 1501. EFFECTIVE DATE; APPLICATION OF AMENDMENTS.

(a) EFFECTIVE DATE.—Except as otherwise provided in this Act, this Act and the amendments made by this Act shall take effect 180 days after the date of enactment of this Act.

(b) APPLICATION OF AMENDMENTS.—

(1) IN GENERAL.—Except as otherwise provided in this Act and paragraph (2), the amendments made by this Act shall not apply with respect to cases commenced under title 11, United States Code, before the effective date of this Act.

(2) CERTAIN LIMITATIONS APPLICABLE TO DEBTORS.—The amendments made by sections 308, 322, and 330 shall apply with respect to cases commenced under title 11, United States Code, on or after the date of the enactment of this Act.

SEC. 1502. TECHNICAL CORRECTIONS.

(a) CONFORMING AMENDMENTS TO TITLE 11 OF THE UNITED STATES CODE.—Title 11 of the United States Code, as amended by the preceding provisions of this Act, is amended—

(1) in section 507—

(A) in subsection (a)—

(i) in paragraph (5)(B)(ii) by striking "paragraph (3)" and inserting "paragraph (4)"; and

(ii) in paragraph (8)(D) by striking "paragraph (3)" and inserting "paragraph (4)";

(B) in subsection (b) by striking "subsection (a)(1)" and inserting "subsection (a)(2)"; and

(C) in subsection (d) by striking "subsection (a)(3)" and inserting "subsection (a)(1)";

(2) in section 523(a)(1)(A) by striking "507(a)(2)" and inserting "507(a)(3)";

(3) in section 752(a) by striking "507(a)(1)" and inserting "507(a)(2)";

(4) in section 766—

(A) in subsection (h) by striking "507(a)(1)" and inserting "507(a)(2)"; and

(B) in subsection (i) by striking "507(a)(1)" each place it appears and inserting "507(a)(2)";

(5) in section 901(a) by striking "507(a)(1)" and inserting "507(a)(2)";

(6) in section 943(b)(5) by striking "507(a)(1)" and inserting "507(a)(2)";

(7) in section 1123(a)(1) by striking "507(a)(1), 507(a)(2)" and inserting "507(a)(2), 507(a)(3)";

(8) in section 1129(a)(9)—

(A) in subparagraph (A) by striking "507(a)(1) or 507(a)(2)" and inserting "507(a)(2) or 507(a)(3)"; and

(B) in subparagraph (B) by striking "507(a)(3)" and inserting "507(a)(1)";

(9) in section 1226(b)(1) by striking "507(a)(1)" and inserting "507(a)(2)"; and

(10) in section 1326(b)(1) by striking "507(a)(1)" and inserting "507(a)(2)".

(b) RELATED CONFORMING AMENDMENT.—Section 6(e) of the Securities Investor Protection Act of 1970 (15 U.S.C. 78fff(e)) is amended by striking "507(a)(1)" and inserting "507(a)(2)".

A.4 Selected Legislative History of the Bankruptcy Abuse Prevention and Consumer Protection Act of 2005

109th CONGRESS 1st Session
House of Representatives
Rept. 109-31

BANKRUPTCY ABUSE PREVENTION AND CONSUMER PROTECTION ACT OF 2005
REPORT
of the
COMMITTEE ON THE JUDICIARY
HOUSE OF REPRESENTATIVES
to accompany
S. 256
together with
DISSENTING, ADDITIONAL DISSENTING, AND ADDITIONAL MINORITY VIEWS
APRIL 8, 2005-

* * *

Consumer Creditor Bankruptcy Protections.

Needs-Based Reforms. Chapter 7 is a form of bankruptcy relief by which an individual debtor receives an immediate unconditional discharge of personal liability for certain debts in exchange for relinquishing his or her nonexempt assets to a bankruptcy trustee for liquidation and distribution to creditors.[41] This "unconditional discharge" in chapter 7 contrasts with the "conditional discharge" provisions of chapter 13, under which a debtor commits to repay some portion of his or her financial obligations in exchange for retaining nonexempt assets and receiving a broader discharge of debt than is available under chapter 7. Allowing consumer debtors in financial distress to choose voluntarily an "unconditional discharge" has been a part of American bankruptcy law since the enactment of the Bankruptcy Act of 1898.[42]

The concept of needs-based bankruptcy relief has long been debated in the United States. President Herbert Hoover, for instance, recommended to Congress in 1932, "The discretion of the courts in granting or refusing discharges should be broadened, and they should be authorized to postpone discharges for a time and require bankrupts, during the period of suspension, to make some satisfaction out of after-acquired property as a condition to the granting of a

41 Under the Bankruptcy Code, only an individual may obtain a chapter 7 discharge. Thus, a corporation is not eligible to receive a discharge under chapter 7. 11 U.S.C. § 727(a)(1).

42 Bankruptcy Act of 1898, 30 Stat. 544 (1898) (repealed 1978). The rationale of an unconditional discharge was explained by Congress more than 100 years ago:

> [W]hen an honest man is hopelessly down financially, nothing is gained for the public by keeping him down, but, on the contrary, the public good will be promoted by having his assets distributed ratably as far as they will go among his creditors and letting him start anew.

H.R. Rep. No. 55-65, at 43 (1897).

full discharge."[43] In 1938, chapter XIII (the predecessor to chapter 13 of the Bankruptcy Code) was enacted as a purely voluntary form of bankruptcy relief that allowed a debtor to propose a plan to repay creditors out of future earnings.[44]

Over the ensuing years, there continued to be repeated expressions of support for and opposition to means-testing bankruptcy reform.[45] In 1967, various organizations testifying before Congress in support of such reform included the American Bar Association, the American Bankers Association, the Chamber of Commerce of the United States, CUNA, the National Federation of Independent Businesses, and the American Industrial Bankers Association.[46] The Commission on the Bankruptcy Laws of the United States, while supporting the concept that repayment plans should be "fostered," nevertheless concluded in 1973 that "forced participation by a debtor in a plan requiring contributions out of future income has so little prospect for success that it should not be adopted as a feature of the bankruptcy system."[47] The Bankruptcy Reform Act of 1978[48] retained the principle that a debtor's decision to choose relief premised on repayment to creditors should be "completely voluntary."[49]

Although the Bankruptcy Code as originally enacted in 1978 provided that a chapter 7 case could only be dismissed for "cause," the Code was amended in 1984 to permit the court to dismiss a chapter 7 case for "substantial abuse."[50] This provision, codified in section 707(b) of the Bankruptcy Code,[51] was added "as part of a package of consumer credit amendments designed to reduce perceived abuses in the use of chapter 7."[52] It was intended to respond "to concerns that some debtors who could easily pay their creditors might resort to chapter 7 to avoid their obligations."[53] In 1986, section 707(b) was further amended to allow a United States trustee (a Department of Justice official) to move for dismissal.[54]

The utility of section 707(b) is limited for several reasons. Under current law, neither the court nor the United States trustee is required to file a motion to dismiss a chapter 7 case for substantial abuse under section 707(b). In addition, other parties in interest, such as chapter 7 trustees and creditors, are prohibited from filing such motions. In fact, section 707(b) specifies that a motion under that provision may not even be made "at the request or suggestion of any party in interest."[55] The standard for dismissal—substantial abuse—is inherently vague, which has lead to its disparate interpretation and application by the bankruptcy bench.[56] Some courts, for example, hold that a debtor's ability to repay a significant portion of his or her debts out of future income constitutes substantial abuse and therefore is cause for dismissal;[57] others do not.[58] A further reason militating against filing section 707(b) motions is that the Bankruptcy Code codifies a presumption that favors granting a debtor a discharge.[59]

Over the course of its hearings since the 105th Congress, the Committee received testimony explaining that if needs-based reforms and other measures were implemented, the rate of repayment to creditors would increase as more debtors were shifted into chapter 13 (a form of bankruptcy relief where the debtor commits to repay a portion or all of his debts in exchange for receiving a broad discharge of debt) as opposed to chapter 7 (a form of bankruptcy relief where the debtor receives an immediate discharge of per-

43 President's Special Message to the Congress on Reform of Judicial Procedure, 69 Pub. Papers 83, 90 (Feb. 29, 1932).

44 Chandler Act of 1938, 52 Stat. 840 (1938).

45 *See, e.g.*, Report of the Commission on the Bankruptcy Laws of the United States—July 1973, H.R. Doc. No. 93 137, pt. I, at 158 (1973) (observing that "proposals have been made to Congress from time to time that a debtor able to obtain relief under chapter XIII [predecessor of chapter 13] should be denied relief in straight bankruptcy").

46 *Hearings on H.R. 1057 and H.R. 5771 Before the Subcomm. No. 4 of the House Comm. on the Judiciary*, 90th Cong. (1967).

47 *See, e.g.*, Report of the Commission on the Bankruptcy Laws of the United States—July 1973, H.R. Doc. No. 93-137, pt. I, at 159 (1973).

48 Pub. L. No. 95-598, 92 Stat. 2549 (1978).

49 H.R. Rep. No. 95-595, at 120 (1977) (observing that "[t]he thirteenth amendment prohibits involuntary servitude" and suggesting that "a mandatory chapter 13, by forcing an individual to work for creditors, would violate this prohibition").

50 Bankruptcy Amendments and Federal Judgeship Act of 1984, Pub. L. No. 98-353, § 312, 98 Stat. 333, 335 (1984).

51 11 U.S.C. § 707(b).

52 6 Lawrence P. King et al., Collier on Bankruptcy § 707.LH[2], at 707–30 (15th ed. rev. 2002).

53 *Id.* at § 707.04.

54 Bankruptcy Judges, United States Trustees, and Family Farmer Bankruptcy Act of 1986, Pub. L. No. 99-554, § 219, 100 Stat. 3088, 3101 (1986).]

55 11 U.S.C. § 707(b).

56 *See, e.g.*, David White, *Disorder in the Court: Section 707(b) of the Bankruptcy Code*, 1995-96 Ann. Survey of Bankr. L. 333, 355 (1996) (noting that the courts "have taken divergent views in an attempt to define the term" and have resorted to "a variety of methods" in applying it to specific cases); Robert C. Furr & Marc P. Barmat, *11 U.S.C. Section 707(b)—The U.S. Trustee's Weapon Against Abuse*, Nat'l Ass'n Bankr. Trustees (NABTalk) 11, 14 (Winter 2002–03).

57 *See, e.g.*, *Zolg v. Kelly* (*In re* Kelly), 841 F.2d 908, 913-14 (9th Cir. 1988) (observing that the "principal factor to be considered in determining substantial abuse is the debtor's ability to repay debts for which a discharge is sought").

58 *See, e.g.*, *In re* Braley, 103 B.R. 758 (Bankr. E.D. Va. 1989), *aff'd*, 110 B.R. 211 (E.D. Va. 1990). Notwithstanding the fact that the debtors in Braley had disposable monthly income of nearly $2,700, the bankruptcy court did not dismiss the case for substantial abuse. *Id.* at 760. The court concluded, "Based upon this legislative history, we are persuaded that no future income tests exists [sic] in 707(b) and if it did, as a finding of fact, the Braley family has insufficient future income to merit barring the door in light of the circumstances of this Navy family." *Id.* at 762.

59 Section 707(b) of the Bankruptcy Code mandates that "[t]here shall be a presumption in favor of granting the relief requested by the debtor." 11 U.S.C. § 707(b).

sonal liability on certain debts in exchange for turning over his or her nonexempt assets to the bankruptcy trustee for distribution to creditors).

Needs-based reforms would amend section 707(b) of the Bankruptcy Code to permit a court, on its own motion, or on motion of the United States trustee, private trustee, bankruptcy administrator, or other party in interest (including a creditor), to dismiss a chapter 7 case for abuse if it was filed by an individual debtor whose debts are primarily consumer debts. Alternatively, the chapter 7 case could be converted to a case under chapter 11 or chapter 13 on consent of the debtor.

In addition, these reforms contemplate replacing the current law's presumption in favor of the debtor with a mandatory presumption of abuse that would arise under certain conditions. As amended, section 707(b) of the Bankruptcy Code would require a court to presume that abuse exists if the amount of the debtor's remaining income, after certain expenses and other specified amounts are deducted from the debtor's current monthly income (a defined term)[60] when multiplied by 60, exceeds the lower of the following: (1) 25 percent of the debtor's nonpriority unsecured claims, or $6000 (whichever is greater); or (2) $10,000. Section 102 mandates that the debtor's expenses include reasonably necessary expenditures for health insurance, disability insurance, and health savings accounts for the debtor, the debtor's spouse, and dependents of the debtor. In addition, the debtor's expenses must include those incurred to maintain the safety of the debtor and the debtor's family from family violence as identified in section 309 of the Family Violence Prevention and Services Act or other applicable law. In addition to other specified expenses,[61] the debtor's monthly expenses—exclusive of any payments for debts (unless otherwise permitted)—must be the applicable monthly amounts set forth in the Internal Revenue Service Financial Analysis Handbook[62] as Necessary Expenses[63] under the National[64] and Local Standards[65] categories and

60 Section 102(b) of the bill defines "current monthly income" as the average monthly income from all sources that the debtor receives (or, in a joint case, the debtor and the debtor's spouse receive), without regard to whether it is taxable income, in the six-month period preceding the bankruptcy filing. It includes any amount paid on a regular basis by any entity (other than the debtor or, in a joint case, the debtor and the debtor's spouse) to the household expenses of the debtor or the debtor's dependents and, in a joint case, the debtor's spouse, if not otherwise a dependent. It excludes Social Security Act benefits and payments to victims of war crimes or crimes against humanity on account of their status as victims of such crimes. It also excludes payments to victims of international terrorism or domestic terrorism (as defined in 18 U.S.C. § 2331) on account of their status as victims of such terrorism.

61 Under section 102(a), a debtor's monthly expenses may also include:

- an additional five percent of the food and clothing expense allowances under the Internal Revenue Service National Standards expenses category, if demonstrated to be reasonable and necessary;
- the debtor's average monthly payments on account of secured debts, including any additional payments to secured creditors that a chapter 13 debtor must make to retain possession of a debtor's primary residence, motor vehicle, or other property necessary for the support of the debtor and the debtor's dependents that collateralizes such debts;
- claims and expenses entitled to priority under section 507 of the Bankruptcy Code, such as child support and alimony;
- the continuation of actual expenses paid by the debtor that are reasonable and necessary for the care and support of an elderly, chronically ill, or disabled household member or member of the debtor's immediate family who is otherwise unable to pay such expenses;
- housing and utility expenses in excess of those specified by the Internal Revenue Service, under certain circumstances;
- the actual administrative expenses (including reasonable attorneys' fees) of administering a chapter 13 plan for the district in which the debtor resides up to ten percent of projected plan payments, as determined under schedules issued by the Executive Office for United States Trustees; and
- the actual expenses for each dependent child under the age of 18 years up to $1,500 per year per child to attend a private elementary or secondary school, under certain circumstances.

62 Internal Revenue Service, Internal Revenue Manual—Financial Analysis Handbook pt. 5.15.1 (rev. May 1, 2004).

63 The Internal Revenue Manual defines the term "necessary expenses" as expenses:

> that are necessary to provide for a taxpayer's and his or her family's health and welfare and/or production of income. The expenses must be reasonable. The total necessary expenses establish the minimum a taxpayer and family need to live.

Id. at pt. 5.15.1.7.

64 The Internal Revenue Manual's "National Standards" establish standards for five types of expenses: food (includes all meals, home and away), housekeeping supplies (includes laundry and cleaning supplies; other household products such as cleaning and toilet tissue, paper towels and napkins; lawn and garden supplies; postage and stationary), apparel and services (includes shoes and clothing, laundry and dry cleaning, and shoe repair), personal care products and services (includes hair care products, haircuts, oral hygiene products, electric personal care appliances), and miscellaneous (a discretionary allowance of $100 for one person and $25 for each additional person in a taxpayer's family). Except for miscellaneous expenses, these expense standards are derived from Bureau of Labor Statistics Consumer Expenditure Survey and are stratified by income and household size. *Id.* at pt. 5.15.1.8.

65 "Local Standards," under the Internal Revenue Manual, establish expense standards for housing (e.g., mortgage or rent, property taxes, interest, parking, necessary maintenance and repair, homeowner's or renter's insurance, and homeowner dues and condominium fees) and transportation expenditures (e.g., vehicle insurance, vehicle payment, maintenance, fuel, state and local registration, parking fees, tolls, driver's license fees, and public transportation). Utilities (e.g., gas, electricity, water, fuel, oil, bottled gas, wood and other fuels, trash and garbage collection, septic cleaning, and telephone) are included under the housing expense category. Housing standards are established for each county within a state. Transportation standards are determined on a regional basis. *Id.* at pt. 5.15.1.9.

the debtor's actual monthly expenditures for items categorized as Other Necessary Expenses.[66]

The means test permits the mandatory presumption of abuse to be rebutted only if: (1) the debtor demonstrates special circumstances justifying any additional expense or adjustment to the debtor's current monthly income for which there is no reasonable alternative; and (2) such additional expense or income adjustment caused the debtor's current monthly income (reduced by various amounts) when multiplied by 60 to be less than the lesser of either: (i) 25 percent of the debtor's nonpriority unsecured claims, or $6,000 (whichever is greater), or (ii) $10,000.[67] Special circumstances include such factors as whether the debtor has a serious medical condition or is on active duty in the Armed Services to the extent these factors justify adjustment to income or expenses.

Where the mandatory presumption of abuse does not apply or has been rebutted, the court, in order to determine whether the granting of relief under chapter 7 would constitute an abuse, must consider: (1) whether the debtor filed the chapter 7 case in bad faith; or (2) whether the totality of circumstances of the debtor's financial situation (including whether the debtor seeks to reject a personal services contract and the financial need for such rejection) demonstrates abuse.

Should a court grant a section 707(b) motion made by a trustee and find that the action of the debtor's counsel in filing the chapter 7 case violated Federal Rule of Bankruptcy Procedure 9011,[68] S. 256 authorizes the court to order the attorney to reimburse the trustee for all reasonable costs in prosecuting the motion, including reasonable attorneys' fees. In addition, the court may assess an appropriate civil penalty.[69]

Two types of "safe harbors" apply to the means test. One provides that only a judge, United States trustee, bankruptcy administrator, or private trustee may file a motion to dismiss a chapter 7 case under section 707(b) of the Bankruptcy Code if the debtor's income (or in a joint case, the income of debtor and the debtor's spouse) does not exceed the state median family income for a family of equal or lesser size (adjusted for larger sized families), or the state median family income for one earner in the case of a one-person household. The second safe harbor provides that no motion under section 707(b)(2) (dismissal based on a chapter 7 debtor's ability to repay) may be filed by a judge, United States trustee, bankruptcy administrator, private trustee, or other party in interest if the debtor (including the circumstance where the debtor is a veteran) and the debtor's spouse combined have income that does not exceed the state median family income for a family of equal or lesser size (adjusted for larger sized families), or the state median family income for one earner in the case of a one-person household.[70] In addition, the bill includes a safe harbor from the bill's needs-based test for a disabled veteran whose indebtedness occurred primarily during a period when the individual was on active duty (as defined in 10 U.S.C. § 101(d)(1)) or performing a homeland defense activity (as defined in 32 U.S.C. 901(1)).

Other Reforms Dealing with Abuse. S. 256 contains various reforms tailored to remedy certain types of fraud and abuse within the present bankruptcy system. For example, the bill substantially limits a debtor's ability to file successive bankruptcy cases. It also addresses abusive practices by consumer debtors who, for example, knowingly load up with credit card purchases or recklessly obtain cash advances and then file for bankruptcy relief. In addition, S. 256 prevents the discharge of debts based on fraud, embezzlement, and malicious injury in a chapter 13 case. Other abuse reforms include a provision authorizing the court to dismiss a chapter 7 case filed by an individual debtor convicted of a crime of violence or a drug trafficking crime on motion of the victim, under certain circumstances. And, the court, as a

66 The Internal Revenue Manual does not establish monetary amounts with regard to necessary expenses that it characterizes as "Other Expenses." Rather, it provides a non-exclusive list of these expenses, that must otherwise satisfy the "necessary expense test," described in note 63 *supra*. The list includes expenditures for certain accounting and legal fees, child care, dependent care for an elderly or disabled person, health care, taxes, court-ordered payments, life insurance, involuntary deductions (e.g., union dues, uniforms, work shoes), charitable contributions, and certain education expenses. *Id.* at pt. 5.15.1.10.

67 The debtor must itemize and provide documentation of each additional expense or income adjustment as well as explain the special circumstances that make such expense or income adjustment reasonable and necessary. In addition, the debtor must attest under oath to the accuracy of any information provided to demonstrate that such additional expenses or adjustments to income are required.

68 Fed. R. Bankr. P. 9011. This rule is the bankruptcy analog to Federal Rule of Civil Procedure 11, which authorizes a court to impose sanctions against an attorney or party who commences a frivolous actions or files other inappropriate documents in violation of this Rule's requirements.

69 Section 102(a) of S. 256 specifies that the signature of an attorney on a bankruptcy petition, pleading, or written motion constitutes a certification that the attorney has: (1) performed a reasonable investigation into the circumstances giving rise to such petition, pleading or motion; and (2) determined that the document is well grounded in fact and warranted by existing law or a good faith argument for the extension, modification, or reversal of existing law; and does not constitute an abuse under section 707(b)(1) of the Bankruptcy Code. Pursuant to section 102(a), the signature of an attorney on a bankruptcy petition constitutes a certification that the attorney has no knowledge after an inquiry that the information in the schedules filed with such petition is incorrect.

70 In a case that is not a joint case, current monthly income of the debtor's spouse is not considered if the debtor and the debtor's spouse are separated under applicable nonbankruptcy law or the debtor and the debtor's spouse are living separate and apart (other than for the purpose of evading this provision) and the debtor files a statement under penalty of perjury containing certain specified information.

condition of confirming a chapter 13 plan, must find that the debtor filed the chapter 13 case in good faith. The bill also restricts the so-called "mansion loophole." Under current bankruptcy law, debtors living in certain states can shield from their creditors virtually all of the equity in their homes. In light of this, some debtors actually relocate to these states just to take advantage of their "mansion loophole" laws. S. 256 closes this loophole for abuse by requiring a debtor to be a domiciliary in the state for at least two years before he or she can claim that state's homestead exemption; the current requirement can be as little as 91 days.[71] The bill further reduces the opportunity for abuse by requiring a debtor to own the homestead for at least 40 months before he or she can use state exemption law; current law imposes no such requirement.[72] S. 256 prevents securities law violators and others who have engaged in criminal conduct from shielding their homestead assets from those whom they have defrauded or injured. If a debtor was convicted of a felony, violated a securities law, or committed a criminal act, intentional tort, or engaged in reckless misconduct that caused serious physical injury or death, the bill overrides state homestead exemption law and caps the debtor's homestead exemption at $125,000. To the extent a debtor's homestead exemption was obtained through the fraudulent conversion of nonexempt assets (e.g., cash) during the ten-year period preceding the filing of the bankruptcy case, S. 256 requires such exemption to be reduced by the amount attributable to the debtor's fraud.

S. 256 also authorizes a trustee to avoid any transfer of property that a debtor made to a self-settled trust (of which the debtor is a beneficiary) within the ten-year period preceding the filing of the debtor's bankruptcy case if the debtor made the transfer with actual intent to hinder, delay, or defraud a creditor of the debtor.

Protections for Creditors—In General. S. 256 includes provisions intended to provide greater protections for creditors, while ensuring that the claims of those creditors entitled to priority treatment, such as spousal and child support claimants, are not adversely impacted. These include provisions: (1) ensuring that creditors receive proper and timely notice of important events and proceedings in a bankruptcy case; (2) prohibiting abusive serial filings and extending the period between successive discharges; and (3) implementing various provisions designed to improve the accuracy of the information contained in debtors' schedules, statements of financial affairs. They also clarify that creditors holding consumer debts may participate without counsel at the section 341 meeting of creditors (which provides an opportunity for creditors to examine the debtor under oath).

Enforcement of Family Support Obligations. S. 256 accords domestic and child support claimants a broad spectrum of special protections. The legislation creates a uniform and expanded definition of domestic support obligations to include debts that accrue both before or after a bankruptcy case is filed. It gives the highest payment priority for these debts (current law only accords them a seventh-level priority),[73] with allowance for the payment of trustee administrative expenses, under certain conditions. In addition, the bill mandates that a debtor must be current on postpetition domestic support obligations to confirm a chapter 11, chapter 12 (family farmer) or chapter 13 plan of reorganization. To facilitate the domestic support collection efforts by governmental units, the legislation creates various exceptions to automatic stay provisions of the Bankruptcy Code (which enjoin many forms of creditor collection activities). It also broadens the categories of nondischargeable family support obligations with the result that these debts will not be extinguished at the end of the bankruptcy process. The legislation, in addition, mandates that spousal and child support claimants as well as state child support agencies receive specified information and notices relevant to pending bankruptcy cases.

Protections for Secured Creditors. S. 256's protections for secured creditors include a prohibition against bifurcating a secured debt incurred within the 910-day period preceding the filing of a bankruptcy case if the debt is secured by a purchase money security interest in a motor vehicle acquired for the debtor's personal use. Where the collateral consists of any other type of property having value, S. 256 prohibits bifurcation of specified secured debts if incurred during the one-year period preceding the filing of the bankruptcy case. The bill clarifies current law to specify that the value of a claim secured by personal property is the replacement value of such property without deduction for the secured creditor's costs of sale or marketing. In addition, the bill terminates the automatic stay with respect to personal property if the debtor does not timely reaffirm the underlying obligation or redeem the property.[74] S. 256 also specifies that a secured claimant retains its lien in a chapter 13 case until the underlying debt is paid or the debtor receives a discharge.

Protections for Lessors. With respect to the interests of lessors, S. 256 requires chapter 13 debtors to remain current on their personal property leases and to provide proof of adequate insurance. The bill specifies that a lessor may condition assumption of a personal property lease on cure of any outstanding default and it provides that a lessor is not required to permit such assumption. The bill also addresses

71 *See* 11 U.S.C. § 522(b)(2)(2)(A).

72 If the debtor owns the homestead for less than 40 months, the provision imposes a $125,000 homestead cap. In effect, this provision overrides state exemption law authorizing a homestead exemption in excess of this amount and allows such law to control if it authorizes a homestead exemption in a lesser amount.

73 11 U.S.C. § 507(a)(7).

74 Redemption is a method by which a chapter 7 debtor can retain certain types of personal property by paying the holder of a lien on such property the allowed amount of the holder's secured lien. 11 U.S.C. § 722.

a problem faced by thousands of large and small residential landlords across the nation whose tenants file for bankruptcy relief solely for the purpose of staying pending eviction proceedings so that they can live "rent free."

Consumer Debtor Bankruptcy Protections. The bill's consumer protections include provisions strengthening professionalism standards for attorneys and others who assist consumer debtors with their bankruptcy cases. S. 256 mandates that certain services and specified notices be given to consumers by professionals and others who provide bankruptcy assistance. To ensure compliance with these provisions, the bill institutes various enforcement mechanisms.

In addition, S. 256 amends the Truth in Lending Act to require certain credit card solicitations, monthly billing statements, and related materials to include important disclosures and explanatory statements regarding introductory interest rates and minimum payments, among other matters. These additional disclosures are intended to give debtors important information to enable them to better manage their financial affairs.

S. 256 contains provisions to help debtors better understand their rights and obligations with respect to reaffirmation agreements. To enforce these protections, the bill requires the Attorney General to designate a United States Attorney for each judicial district and a FBI agent for each field office to have primary law enforcement responsibility regarding abusive reaffirmation practices, among other matters.

The legislation also expands a debtor's ability to exempt certain tax-qualified retirement accounts and pensions. It creates a new provision that allows a consumer debtor to exempt certain education IRAs and state tuition plans for his or her child's postsecondary education from the claims of creditors.

Most importantly, S. 256 requires debtors to participate in credit counseling programs before filing for bankruptcy relief (unless special circumstances do not permit such participation). The legislation's credit counseling provisions are intended to give consumers in financial distress an opportunity to learn about the consequences of bankruptcy—such as the potentially devastating effect it can have on their credit rating[75]—before they decide to file for bankruptcy relief. The bill also requires debtors, after they file for bankruptcy relief, to receive financial management training that will provide them with guidance about how to manage their finances, so that they can avoid future financial difficulties. The mandatory credit counseling and financial management training requirements do not apply if the debtor is unable to complete these requirements because of incapacity or disability, or because he or she is on active duty in a military combat zone.

75 Under current law, for example, a bankruptcy filing may be reported on a consumer's credit report for ten years. 15 U.S.C. § 1681c (2002).

Other debtor protections include expanded notice requirements for consumers. Under the bill, individuals with primarily consumer debts must receive notice of alternatives to bankruptcy relief before they file for bankruptcy and it requires them to be informed of other matters pertaining to the integrity of the bankruptcy system. The legislation also permits certain filing fees and related charges to be waived, in appropriate cases, for individuals who lack the ability to pay these costs.

* * *

SECTION-BY-SECTION ANALYSIS AND DISCUSSION

Sec. 1. Short Title; References; Table of Contents. The short title of this measure is the Bankruptcy Abuse Prevention and Consumer Protection Act of 2005 (the "Act").

TITLE I. NEEDS-BASED BANKRUPTCY

Sec. 101. Conversion. Under current law, section 706(c) of the Bankruptcy Code provides that a court may not convert a chapter 7 case unless the debtor requests such conversion. Section 101 of the Act amends this provision to allow a chapter 7 case to be converted to a case under chapter 12 or chapter 13 on request or consent of the debtor.

Section 102. Dismissal or Conversion. Section 102 implements needs-based debt relief, the legislation's principal consumer bankruptcy reform. Under section 707(b) of the Bankruptcy Code, a chapter 7 case filed by a debtor who is an individual may be dismissed for substantial abuse only on motion of the court or the United States trustee. It specifically prohibits such dismissal at the suggestion of any party in interest.

Section 102 of the Act revises current law in several significant respects. First, it amends section 707(b) of the Bankruptcy Code to permit—in addition to the court and the United States trustee—a trustee, bankruptcy administrator, or a party in interest to seek dismissal or conversion of a chapter 7 case to one under chapter 11 or 13 on consent of the debtor, under certain circumstances. In addition, section 102 of the Act changes the current standard for dismissal from "substantial abuse" to "abuse." Section 102 of the Act also amends Bankruptcy Code section 707(b) to mandate a presumption of abuse if the debtor's current monthly income (reduced by certain specified amounts) when multiplied by 60 is not less than the lesser of 25 percent of the debtor's nonpriority unsecured claims or $6,000 (whichever is greater), or $10,000.

To determine whether the presumption of abuse applies under section 707(b) of the Bankruptcy Code, section 102(a) of the Act specifies certain monthly expense amounts that are to be deducted from the debtor's "current monthly income" (a defined term). These expense items include:

- the applicable monthly expenses for the debtor as well as for the debtor's dependents and spouse in a joint case (if the spouse is not otherwise a dependent) specified under the Internal Revenue Service's National Standards (with provision for an additional five percent for food and clothing if the debtor can demonstrate that such additional amount is reasonable and necessary) and the IRS Local Standards;
- the actual monthly expenses for the debtor, the debtor's dependents, and the debtor's spouse in a joint case (if the spouse is not otherwise a dependent) for the categories specified by the Internal Revenue Service as Other Necessary Expenses;
- reasonably necessary expenses incurred to maintain the safety of the debtor and the debtor's family from family violence as specified in section 309 of the Family Violence Prevention and Services Act or other applicable Federal law, with provision for the confidentiality of these expenses; reasonably necessary expenses for health insurance, disability insurance, and health savings account expenditures for the debtor, the debtor's spouse, and dependents of the debtor;
- the debtor's average monthly payments on account of secured debts and priority claims as explained below; and
- if the debtor is eligible to be a debtor under chapter 13, the actual administrative expenses of administering a chapter 13 plan for the district in which the debtor resides, up to 10 percent of projected plan payments, as determined under schedules issued by the Executive Office for United States Trustees.

With respect to secured debts, Section 102(a)(2)(C) of the Act specifies that the debtor's average monthly payments on account of secured debts is calculated as the sum of the following divided by 60: (1) all amounts scheduled as contractually due to secured creditors for each month of the 60-month period following filing of the case; and (2) any additional payments necessary, in filing a plan under chapter 13, to maintain possession of the debtor's primary residence, motor vehicle or other property necessary for the support of the debtor and the debtor's dependents, that serves as collateral for secured debts.

With respect to priority claims, section 102(a)(2)(C) of the Act specifies that the debtor's expenses for payment of such claims (including child support and alimony claims) is calculated as the total of such debts divided by 60.

The provision permits a debtor, if applicable, to deduct from current monthly income the continuation of actual expenses paid by the debtor that are reasonable and necessary for the care and support of an elderly, chronically ill, or disabled household member or member of the debtor's immediate family (providing such individual is unable to pay for these expenses).

Under section 102, a debtor may also deduct the actual expenses for each dependent child of a debtor to attend a private or public elementary or secondary school up to $1,500 per child if the debtor: (1) documents such expenses, and (2) provides a detailed explanation of why such expenses are reasonable and necessary. In addition, the debtor must explain why such expenses are not already accounted for under any of the Internal Revenue Service National and Local Standards, and Other Expenses categories.

Other expenses that a debtor may claim include additional housing and utilities allowances based on the debtor's actual home energy expenses if the debtor documents such expenses and demonstrates that they are reasonable and necessary.

While the Act replaces the current law's presumption in favor of granting relief requested by a chapter 7 debtor with a presumption of abuse (if applicable under the income and expense analysis previously described), it does provide that this presumption may be rebutted under certain circumstances. Section 102(a)(2)(C) of the Act amends Bankruptcy Code section 707(b) to provide that the presumption of abuse may be rebutted only if: (1) the debtor demonstrates special circumstances, such as a serious medical condition or a call or order to active duty in the Armed Forces, to the extent such special circumstances justify additional expenses or adjustments of current monthly income for which there is no reasonable alternative; and (2) the additional expenses or adjustments cause the product of the debtor's current monthly income (reduced by the specified expenses) when multiplied by 60 to be less than the lesser of 25 percent of the debtor's nonpriority unsecured claims, or $6,000 (whichever is greater); or $10,000. In addition, the debtor must itemize and document each additional expense or income adjustment as well as provide a detailed explanation of the special circumstances that make such expense or adjustment necessary and reasonable. Further, the debtor must attest under oath to the accuracy of any information provided to demonstrate that such additional expense or adjustment to income is required.

To implement these needs-based reforms, the Act requires the debtor to file, as part of the schedules of current income and current expenditures, a statement of current monthly income. This statement must show: (1) the calculations that determine whether a presumption of abuse arises under section 707(b) (as amended), and (2) how each amount is calculated.

An exception to the needs-based test applies with respect to a debtor who is a disabled veteran whose indebtedness occurred primarily during a period when the individual was on active duty (as defined in 10 U.S.C. § 101(d)(1)) or performing a homeland defense activity (as defined in 32 U.S.C. 901(1)).

In a case where the presumption of abuse does not apply or has been rebutted, section 102(a)(2)(C) of the Act amends Bankruptcy Code section 707(b) to require a court to consider whether: (1) the debtor filed the chapter 7 case in bad faith; or (2) the totality of the circumstances of the debtor's financial situation demonstrates abuse, including whether the debtor wants to reject a personal services contract and the debtor's financial need for such rejection.

Under section 102(a)(2)(C) of the Act, a court may on its own initiative or on motion of a party in interest in accordance with rule 9011 of the Federal Rules of Bankruptcy Procedure, order a debtor's attorney to reimburse the trustee for all reasonable costs incurred in prosecuting a section 707(b) motion if: (1) a trustee files such motion; (2) the motion is granted; and (3) the court finds that the action of the debtor's attorney in filing the case under chapter 7 violated rule 9011. If the court determines that the debtor's attorney violated rule 9011, it may on its own initiative or on motion of a party in interest in accordance with such rule, order the assessment of an appropriate civil penalty against debtor's counsel and the payment of such penalty to the trustee, United States trustee, or bankruptcy administrator. This provision clarifies that a motion for costs or the imposition of a civil penalty must be made by a party in interest or by the court itself in accordance with rule 9011.

Section 102(a)(2)(C) of the Act provides that the signature of an attorney on a petition, pleading or written motion shall constitute a certification that the attorney has: (1) performed a reasonable investigation into the circumstances that gave rise to such document; and (2) determined that such document is well-grounded in fact and warranted by existing law or a good faith argument for the extension, modification, or reversal of existing law and does not constitute an abuse under section 707(b)(1). In addition, such attorney's signature on the petition constitutes a certification that the attorney has no knowledge after an inquiry that the information in the schedules filed with the petition is incorrect.

Section 102(a)(2)(C) of the Act amends section 707(b) of the Bankruptcy Code to permit a court on its own initiative or motion by a party in interest in accordance with rule 9011 of the Federal Rules of Bankruptcy Procedure to award a debtor reasonable costs (including reasonable attorneys' fees) in contesting a section 707(b) motion filed by a party in interest (other than a trustee, United States trustee or bankruptcy administrator) if the court: (1) does not grant the section 707(b) motion; and (2) finds that either the movant violated rule 9011, or the attorney (if any) who filed the motion did not comply with section 707(b)(4)(C) and such was made solely for the purpose of coercing a debtor into waiving a right guaranteed under the Bankruptcy Code to such debtor. An exception applies with respect to a movant that is a "small business" with a claim in an aggregate amount of less than $1,000. A small business, for purposes of this provision, is defined as an unincorporated business, partnership, corporation, association or organization that engages in commercial or business activities and employs less than 25 full-time employees. The number of employees of a wholly owned subsidiary includes the employees of the parent and any other subsidiary corporation of the parent. Section 102(a)(2)(C) of the Act clarifies that the motion for costs must be made by a party in interest or by the court. The use of the phraseology in this provision, "in accordance with rule 9011 of the Federal Rules of Bankruptcy Procedure," is intended to indicate that the procedures for the motion of a party in interest or a court acting on its own initiative are the procedures outlined in rule 9011(c).

The Act includes two "safe harbors" with respect to its needs-based reforms. One safe harbor allows only a judge, United States trustee, or bankruptcy administrator to file a section 707(b) motion (based on the debtor's ability to repay, bad faith, or the totality of the circumstances) if the chapter 7 debtor's current monthly income (or in a joint case, the income of the debtor and the debtor's spouse) falls below the state median family income for a family of equal or lesser size (adjusted for larger sized families), or the state median family income for one earner in the case of a one-person household.

The Act's second safe harbor only pertains to a motion under section 707(b)(2), that is, a motion to dismiss based on a debtor's ability to repay. It does not allow a judge, United States trustee, bankruptcy administrator or party in interest to file such motion if the income of the debtor (including a veteran, as that term is defined in 38 U.S.C. § 101) and the debtor's spouse is less than certain monetary thresholds. This provision does not consider the nonfiling spouse's income if the debtor and the debtor's spouse are separated under applicable nonbankruptcy law, or the debtor and the debtor's spouse are living separate and apart, other than for the purpose of evading section 707(b)(2). The debtor must file a statement under penalty of perjury specifying that he or she meets one of these criteria. In addition, the statement must disclose the aggregate (or best estimate) of the amount of any cash or money payments received from the debtor's spouse attributed to the debtor's current monthly income.

Section 102(b) of the Act amends section 101 of the Bankruptcy Code to define "current monthly income" as the average monthly income that the debtor receives (or in a joint case, the debtor and debtor's spouse receive) from all sources, without regard to whether it is taxable income, in a specified six-month period preceding the filing of the bankruptcy case. The Act specifies that the six-month period is determined as ending on the last day of the calendar month immediately preceding the filing of the bankruptcy case, if the debtor files the statement of current income required by Bankruptcy Code section 521. If the debtor does not file such schedule, the court determines the date on which current income is calculated.

"Current monthly income" includes any amount paid by any entity other than the debtor (or, in a joint case, the debtor and the debtor's spouse if not otherwise a dependent) on a regular basis for the household expenses of the debtor or the debtor's dependents (and, the debtor's spouse in a joint case, if not otherwise a dependent). It excludes Social Security Act benefits and payments to victims of war crimes or crimes against humanity on account of their status as victims of such crimes. In addition, the Act provides that current monthly income does not include payments to victims of international or domestic terrorism as defined in section 2331 of title 18 of the United States Code on account of their status as victims of such terrorism.

Section 102(c) of the Act amends section 704 of the Bankruptcy Code to require the United States trustee or bankruptcy administrator in a chapter 7 case where the debtor is an individual to: (1) review all materials filed by the debtor; and (2) file a statement with the court (within ten days following the meeting of creditors held pursuant to section 341 of the Bankruptcy Code) as to whether or not the debtor's case should be presumed to be an abuse under section 707(b). The court must provide a copy of such statement to all creditors within five days after its filing. Within 30 days of the filing of such statement, the United States trustee or bankruptcy administrator must file either: (1) a motion under section 707(b); or (2) a statement setting forth the reasons why such motion is not appropriate in any case where the debtor's filing should be presumed to be an abuse and the debtor's current monthly income exceeds certain monetary thresholds.

In a chapter 7 case where the presumption of abuse applies under section 707(b), section 102(d) of the Act amends Bankruptcy Code section 342 to require the clerk to provide written notice to all creditors within ten days after commencement of the case stating that the presumption of abuse applies in such case.

Section 102(e) of the Act provides that nothing in the Bankruptcy Code limits the ability of a creditor to give information to a judge (except for information communicated ex parte, unless otherwise permitted by applicable law), United States trustee, bankruptcy administrator, or trustee.

Section 102(f) of the Act adds a provision to Bankruptcy Code section 707 to permit the court to dismiss a chapter 7 case filed by a debtor who is an individual on motion by a victim of a crime of violence (as defined in section 16 of title 18 of the United States Code) or a drug trafficking crime (as defined in section 924(c)(2) of title 18 of the United States Code). The case may be dismissed if the debtor was convicted of such crime and dismissal is in the best interest of the victim, unless the debtor establishes by a preponderance of the evidence that the filing of the case is necessary to satisfy a claim for a domestic support obligation.

Section 102(g) of the Act amends section 1325(a) of the Bankruptcy Code to require the court, as a condition of confirming a chapter 13 plan, to find that the debtor's action in filing the case was in good faith.

Section 102(h) of the Act amends section 1325(b)(1) of the Bankruptcy Code to specify that the court must find, in confirming a chapter 13 plan to which there has been an objection, that the debtor's disposable income will be paid to unsecured creditors. It also amends section 1325(b)(2)'s definition of disposable income. As defined under this provision, the term means income received by the debtor (other than child support payments, foster care payments, or certain disability payments for a dependent child) less amounts reasonably necessary to be expended for: (1) the maintenance or support of the debtor or the debtor's dependent; (2) a domestic support obligation that first becomes due after the case is filed; (3) charitable contributions (as defined in Bankruptcy Code section 548(d)(3)) to a qualified religious or charitable entity or organization (as defined in Bankruptcy Code section 548(d)(4)) in an amount that does not exceed 15 percent of the debtor's gross income for the year in which the contributions are made; and (4) if the debtor is engaged in business, the payment of expenditures necessary for the continuation, preservation, and operation of the business. Section 1325(b)(3) provides that the amounts reasonably necessary to be expended under section 1325(b)(2) are determined in accordance with section 707(b)(2)(A) and (B) if the debtor's income exceeds certain monetary thresholds.

Section 102(i) of the Act amends Bankruptcy Code section 1329(a) to require the amounts paid under a confirmed chapter 13 plan to be reduced by the actual amount expended by the debtor to purchase health insurance for the debtor and the debtor's dependents (if those dependents do not otherwise have such insurance) if the debtor documents the cost of such insurance and demonstrates such expense is reasonable and necessary, and the amount is not otherwise allowed for purposes of determining disposable income under section 1325(b). If the debtor previously paid for health insurance, the debtor must demonstrate that the amount is not materially greater than the amount the debtor previously paid. If the debtor did not previously have such insurance, the amount may not be not materially larger than the reasonable cost that would be incurred by a debtor with similar characteristics. Upon request of any party in interest, the debtor must file proof that a health insurance policy was purchased.

Section 102(j) of the Act amends section 104 of the Bankruptcy Code to provide for the periodic adjustment of monetary amounts specified in sections 707(b) and 1325(b)(3) of the Bankruptcy Code, as amended by this Act.

Section 102(k) adds to section 101 of the Bankruptcy Code a definition of "median family income."

Sec. 103. Sense of Congress and Study. Section 103(a) of the Act expresses the sense of Congress that the Secretary of the Treasury has the authority to alter the Internal Revenue Service expense standards to set guidelines for repayment plans as needed to accommodate their use under section 707(b) of the Bankruptcy Code, as amended. Section 103(b) requires the Executive Office for United States Trustees to submit a report within two years from the date of the Act's enactment regarding the utilization of the Internal Revenue Service expense standards for determining the current monthly expenses of a debtor under section 707(b) and the impact that the application of these standards has had on debtors and the bankruptcy courts. The report may include recommendations for amendments to the Bankruptcy Code that are consistent with the report's findings.

Sec. 104. Notice of Alternatives. Section 104 of the Act amends section 342(b) of the Bankruptcy Code to require the clerk, before the commencement of a bankruptcy case by an individual whose debts are primarily consumer debts, to supply such individual with a written notice containing: (1) a brief description of chapters 7, 11, 12, and 13 and the general purpose, benefits, and costs of proceeding under each of these chapters; (2) the types of services available from credit counseling agencies; (3) a statement advising that a person who knowingly and fraudulently conceals assets or makes a false oath or statement under penalty of perjury in connection with a bankruptcy case shall be subject to fine, imprisonment, or both; and (4) a statement warning that all information supplied by a debtor in connection with the case is subject to examination by the Attorney General.

Sec. 105. Debtor Financial Management Training Test Program. Section 105 of the Act requires the Director of the Executive Office for United States Trustees to: (1) consult with a wide range of debtor education experts who operate financial management education programs; and (2) develop a financial management training curriculum and materials that can be used to teach individual debtors how to manage their finances better. The Director must select six judicial districts to test the effectiveness of the financial management training curriculum and materials for an 18-month period beginning not later than 270 days after the Act's enactment date. For these six districts, the curricula and materials must be used as the instructional personal financial management course required under Bankruptcy Code section 111. Over the period of the study, the Director must evaluate the effectiveness of the curriculum and materials as well as consider a sample of existing consumer education programs (such as those described in the Report of the National Bankruptcy Review Commission) that are representative of consumer education programs sponsored by the credit industry, chapter 13 trustees, and consumer counseling groups. Not later than three months after concluding such evaluation, the Director must submit to Congress a report with findings regarding the effectiveness and cost of the curricula, materials, and programs.

Sec. 106. Credit Counseling. Section 106(a) of the Act amends section 109 of the Bankruptcy Code to require an individual—as a condition of eligibility for bankruptcy relief—to receive credit counseling within the 180-day period preceding the filing of a bankruptcy case by such individual. The credit counseling must be provided by an approved nonprofit budget and credit counseling agency consisting of either an individual or group briefing (which may be conducted telephonically or via the Internet) that outlined opportunities for available credit counseling and assisted the individual in performing a budget analysis. This requirement does not apply to a debtor who resides in a district where the United States trustee or bankruptcy administrator has determined that approved nonprofit budget and credit counseling agencies in that district are not reasonably able to provide adequate services to such individuals. Although such determination must be reviewed annually, the United States trustee or bankruptcy administrator may disapprove a nonprofit budget and credit counseling agency at any time.

A debtor may be temporarily exempted from this requirement if he or she submits to the court a certification that: (1) describes exigent circumstances meriting a waiver of this requirement; (2) states that the debtor requested credit counseling services from an approved nonprofit budget and credit counseling agency, but was unable to obtain such services within the five-day period beginning on the date the debtor made the request; and (3) is satisfactory to the court. This exemption terminates when the debtor meets the requirements for credit counseling participation, but not longer than 30 days after the case is filed, unless the court, for cause, extends this period up to an additional 15 days.

In addition, the mandatory credit counseling requirement does not apply to a debtor whom the court determines, after notice and a hearing, is unable to complete this requirement because of incapacity, disability, or active military duty in a military combat zone. Incapacity, under this provision, means the debtor is impaired by reason of mental illness or mental deficiency so that the debtor is incapable of realizing and making rational decisions with respect to his or her financial responsibilities. Disability, under this provision, means the debtor is so physically impaired as to be unable, after reasonable effort, to receive credit counseling whether by participating in person, or via telephone or Internet briefing.

Section 106(b) of the Act amends section 727(a) of the Bankruptcy Code to deny a discharge to a chapter 7 debtor who fails to complete a personal financial management instructional course. This provision, however, does not apply if the debtor resides in a district where the United States trustee or bankruptcy administrator has determined that the approved instructional courses in that district are not adequate. Such determination must be reviewed annually by the United States trustee or bankruptcy administrator. In addition, it does not apply to a debtor whom the court determines, after notice and a hearing, is unable to complete this requirement because of incapacity, disability, or active military duty in a military combat zone.

Section 106(c) of the Act amends section 1328 of the Bankruptcy Code to deny a discharge to a chapter 13 debtor who fails to complete a personal financial management instructional course. This requirement does not apply if the debtor resides in a district where the United States trustee or bankruptcy administrator has determined that the approved instructional courses in that district are not adequate. Such determination must be reviewed annually by the United States trustee or bankruptcy administrator. In addition, it does not apply to a debtor whom the court determines, after notice and a hearing, is unable to complete this requirement because of incapacity, disability, or active military duty in a military combat zone.

Section 106(d) of the Act amends section 521 of the Bankruptcy Code to require a debtor who is an individual to file with the court: (1) a certificate from an approved nonprofit budget and credit counseling agency describing the services it provided the debtor pursuant to section 109(h); and (2) a copy of the repayment plan, if any, that was developed by the agency pursuant to section 109(h).

Section 106(e) of the Act adds section 111 to the Bankruptcy Code requiring the clerk to maintain a publicly available list of approved: (1) credit counseling agencies that provide the services described in section 109(h) of the Bankruptcy Code; and (2) personal financial management instructional courses. Section 106(e) further provides that the United States trustee or bankruptcy administrator may only approve an agency or course provider under this provision pursuant to certain specified criteria. These include, for example, if a fee is charged for such services by the agency or course provider, the fee must be reasonable and such services must be provided without regard to ability to pay the fee. If such agency or provider course is approved, the approval may only be for a probationary period of up to six months. At the conclusion of the probationary period, the United States trustee or bankruptcy administrator may only approve such agency or instructional course for an additional one-year period and, thereafter for successive one-year periods, which has demonstrated during such period that it met the standards set forth in this provision and can satisfy such standards in the future.

Within 30 days after any final decision occurring after the expiration of the initial probationary period or after any subsequent period, an interested person may seek judicial review of such decision in the appropriate United States district court. In addition, the district court, at any time, may investigate the qualifications of a credit counseling agency and request the production of documents to ensure the agency's integrity and effectiveness. The district court may remove a credit counseling agency that does not meet the specified qualifications from the approved list. The United States trustee or bankruptcy administrator must notify the clerk that a credit counseling agency or instructional course is no longer approved and the clerk must remove such entity from the approved list.

Section 106(e) prohibits a credit counseling agency from providing information to a credit reporting agency as to whether an individual debtor has received or sought personal financial management instruction. A credit counseling agency that willfully or negligently fails to comply with any requirement under the Bankruptcy Code with respect to a debtor shall be liable to the debtor for damages in an amount equal to: (1) actual damages sustained by the debtor as a result of the violation; and (2) any court costs or reasonable attorneys' fees incurred in an action to recover such damages.

Section 106(f) of the Act amends section 362 of the Bankruptcy Code to provide that if a chapter 7, 11, or 13 case is dismissed due to the creation of a debt repayment plan, the presumption that a case was not filed in good faith under section 362(c)(3) shall not apply to any subsequent bankruptcy case commenced by the debtor. It also provides that the court, on request of a party in interest, must issue an order under section 362(c) confirming that the automatic stay has terminated.

Sec. 107. Schedules of Reasonable and Necessary Expenses. For purposes of section 707(b) of the Bankruptcy Code, section 107 of the Act requires the Director of the Executive Office for United States Trustees to issue schedules of reasonable and necessary administrative expenses (including reasonable attorneys' fees) relating to the administration of a chapter 13 plan for each judicial district not later than 180 days after the date of enactment of the Act.

TITLE II. ENHANCED CONSUMER PROTECTION

Subtitle A. Penalties for Abusive Creditor Practices

Sec. 201. Promotion of Alternative Dispute Resolution. Subsection (a) of section 201 of the Act amends section 502 of the Bankruptcy Code to permit the court, after a hearing on motion of the debtor, to reduce a claim based in whole on an unsecured consumer debt by up to 20 percent if: (1) the claim was filed by a creditor who unreasonably refused to negotiate a reasonable alternative repayment schedule proposed by an approved credit counseling agency on behalf of the debtor; (2) the debtor's offer was made at least 60 days before the filing of the case; (3) the offer provided for payment of at least 60 percent of the debt over a period not exceeding the loan's repayment period or a reasonable extension thereof; and (4) no part of the debt is nondischargeable. The debtor has the burden of proving by clear and convincing evidence that: (1) the creditor unreasonably refused to consider the debtor's proposal; and (2) the proposed alternative repayment schedule was made prior to the expiration of the 60-day period. Section 201(b) amends section 547 of the Bankruptcy Code to prohibit the avoidance as a preferential transfer a payment by a debtor to a creditor pursuant to an alternative repayment plan created by an approved credit counseling agency.

Sec. 202. Effect of Discharge. Section 202 of the Act amends section 524 of the Bankruptcy Code in two respects. First, it provides that the willful failure of a creditor to credit payments received under a confirmed chapter 11, 12, or 13 plan constitutes a violation of the discharge injunction if the creditor's action to collect and failure to credit payments in the manner required by the plan caused material injury to the debtor. This provision does not apply if the order confirming the plan is revoked, the plan is in default, or the creditor has not received payments required to be made under the plan in the manner prescribed by the plan. Second, section 202 amends section 524 of the Bankruptcy Code to provide that the discharge injunction does not apply to a creditor having a claim secured by an interest in real property that is the debtor's principal residence if the creditor communicates with the debtor in the ordinary course of business between the creditor and the debtor and such communication is limited to seeking or obtaining periodic payments associated with a valid security interest in lieu of the pursuit of in rem relief to enforce the lien.

Sec. 203. Discouraging Abuse of Reaffirmation Agreement Practices. Section 203 of the Act effectuates a comprehensive overhaul of the law applicable to reaffirmation agreements. Subsection (a) amends section 524 of the Bankruptcy Code to mandate that certain specified disclosures be provided to a debtor at or before the time he or she signs a reaffirmation agreement. These specified disclosures, which are the only disclosures required in connection with a reaffirmation agreement, must be in writing and be made clearly and conspicuously. In addition, the disclosure must include certain advisories and explanations. At the election of the creditor, the disclosure statement may include a repayment schedule. If the debtor is represented by counsel, section 203(a) mandates that the attorney file a certification stating that the agreement represents a fully informed and voluntary agreement by the debtor, that the agreement does not impose an undue hardship on the debtor or any dependent of the debtor, and that the attorney fully advised the debtor of the legal effect and consequences of such agreement as well as of any default thereunder. In those instances where the presumption of undue hardship applies, the attorney must also certify that the debtor is able to make the payments required under the reaffirmation agreement. Further, the debtor must submit a statement setting forth the debtor's monthly income and actual current monthly expenditures. If the debtor is represented by counsel and the debt being reaffirmed is owed to a credit union, a modified version of this statement must be used.

Notwithstanding any other provision of the Bankruptcy Code, section 203(a) permits a creditor to accept payments from a debtor: (1) before and after the filing of a reaffirmation agreement with the court; or (2) pursuant to a reaffirmation agreement that the creditor believes in good faith to be effective. It further provides that the requirements specified in subsections (c)(2) and (k) of section 524 are satisfied if the disclosures required by these provisions are given in good faith.

Where the amount of the scheduled payments due on the reaffirmed debt (as disclosed in the debtor's statement) exceeds the debtor's available income, it is presumed for 60 days from the date on which the reaffirmation agreement is filed with the court that the agreement presents an undue hardship. The court must review such presumption, which can be rebutted by the debtor by a written statement explaining the additional sources of funds that would enable the debtor to make the required payments on the reaffirmed debt. If the presumption is not rebutted to the satisfaction of the court, the court may disapprove the reaffirmation agreement. No reaffirmation agreement may be disapproved without notice and hearing to the debtor and creditor. The hearing must be concluded before the entry of the debtor's discharge. The requirements set forth in this paragraph do not apply to reaffirmation agreements if the creditor is a credit union.

Section 203(b) amends title 18 of the United States Code to require the Attorney General to designate a United States Attorney for each judicial district and to appoint a Federal Bureau of Investigation agent for each field office to have primary law enforcement responsibilities for violations of sections 152 and 157 of title 18 with respect to abusive reaffirmation agreements and materially fraudulent statements in bankruptcy schedules that are intentionally false or misleading. In addition, section 203(b) provides that the designated United States Attorney has primary responsibility with respect to bankruptcy investigations under section 3057 of title 18. Section 203(b) further provides that the bankruptcy courts must establish procedures for referring any case in which a materially fraudulent bankruptcy schedule has been filed.

Sec. 204. Preservation of Claims and Defenses Upon Sale of Predatory Loans. Section 204 of the Act adds a provision to section 363 of the Bankruptcy Code with respect to sales of any interest in a consumer transaction that is subject to the Truth in Lending Act or any interest in a consumer credit contract (as defined in section 433.1 of title 16 of the Code of Federal Regulations). It provides that the purchaser of such interest remains subject to all claims and defenses that are related to such assets to the same extent as that person would be subject to if the sale was not conducted under section 363.

Sec. 205. GAO Study and Report on Reaffirmation Agreement Process. Section 205 of the Act directs the Comptroller General of the United States to report to Congress on how consumers are treated in connection with the reaffirmation agreement process. This report must include: (1) the policies and activities of creditors with respect to reaffirmation agreements; and (2) whether such consumers are fully, fairly, and consistently informed of their rights under the Bankruptcy Code. The report, which must be completed not later than 18 months after the date of enactment of this Act, may include recommendations for legislation to address any abusive or coercive tactics found in connection with the reaffirmation process.

Subtitle B. Priority Child Support

Sec. 211. Definition of Domestic Support Obligation. Section 211 of the Act amends section 101 of the Bankruptcy Code to define a domestic support obligation as a debt that accrues before, on, or after the date of the order for relief and that it includes interest that accrues pursuant to applicable nonbankruptcy law. As defined in the Act, the term includes a debt owed to or recoverable by: (1) a spouse, former spouse, or child of the debtor, or such child's parent, legal guardian, or responsible relative; or (2) a governmental unit. To qualify as a domestic support obligation, the debt must be in the nature of alimony, maintenance, or support (including assistance provided by a governmental unit), without regard to whether such debt is expressly so designated. It must be established or subject to establishment before, on, or after the date of the order of relief pursuant to: (1) a separation agreement, divorce decree, or property settlement agreement; (2) an order of a court of record; or (3) a determination made in accordance with applicable nonbankruptcy law by a governmental unit. It does not apply to a debt assigned to a nongovernmental entity, unless it was assigned voluntarily by the spouse, former spouse, child, or parent solely for the purpose of collecting the debt.

Sec. 212. Priorities for Claims for Domestic Support Obligations. Section 212 of the Act amends section 507(a) of the Bankruptcy Code to accord first priority in payment to allowed unsecured claims for domestic support obligations that, as of the petition date, are owed to or recoverable by a spouse, former spouse, or child of the debtor, or the parent, legal guardian, or responsible relative of such child, without regard to whether such claim is filed by the claimant or by a governmental unit on behalf of such claimant, on the condition that funds received by such unit under this provision be applied and distributed in accordance with nonbankruptcy law. Subject to these claims, section 212 accords the same payment priority to allowed unsecured claims for domestic support obligations that, as of the petition date, were assigned by a spouse, former spouse, child of the debtor, or such child's parent, legal guardian, or responsible relative to a governmental unit (unless the claimant assigned the claim voluntarily for the purpose of collecting the debt), or are owed directly to or recoverable by a governmental unit under applicable nonbankruptcy law, on the condition that funds received by such unit under this provision be applied and distributed in accordance with nonbankruptcy law. Where a trustee administers assets that may be available for payment of domestic support obligations under section 507(a)(1) (as amended), administrative expenses of the trustee allowed under section 503(b)(1)(A), (2) and (6) of the Bankruptcy Code must be paid before such claims to the extent the trustee administers assets that are otherwise available for the payment of these claims.

Sec. 213. Requirements To Obtain Confirmation and Discharge in Cases Involving Domestic Support Obligations. With respect to chapter 11 cases, section 213(1) adds a condition for confirmation of a plan. It amends section 1129(a) of the Bankruptcy Code to provide that if a chapter 11 debtor is required by judicial or administrative order or statute to pay a domestic support obligation, then the debtor must pay all amounts payable under such order or statute that became payable postpetition as a prerequisite for confirmation.

With respect to chapter 12 cases, section 213(2) of the Act amends section 1208(c) of the Bankruptcy Code to provide that the failure of a debtor to pay any domestic support obligation that first becomes payable postpetition is cause for conversion or dismissal of the case. Section 213(3) amends Bankruptcy Code section 1222(a) to permit a chapter 12 debtor to propose a plan paying less than full payment of all amounts owed for a claim entitled to priority under Bankruptcy Code section 507(a)(1)(B) if all of the debtor's projected disposable income for a five-year period is applied to make payments under the plan. Section 213(4) of the Act amends Bankruptcy Code section 1222(b) to permit a chapter 12 debtor to propose a plan that pays postpetition interest on claims that are nondischargeable under Section 1228(a), but only to the extent that the debtor has disposable income available to pay such interest after payment of all allowed claims in full. Section 213(5) amends Bankruptcy Code section 1225(a) to provide that if a chapter 12 debtor is required by judicial or administrative order or statute to pay a domestic support obligation, then the debtor must pay such obligations pursuant to such order or statute that became payable postpetition as a condition of confirmation. Section 213(6) amends Bankruptcy Code section 1228(a) to condition the granting of a chapter 12 discharge upon the debtor's payment of certain postpetition domestic support obligations.

With respect to chapter 13 cases, section 213(7) of the Act amends Bankruptcy Code section 1307(c) to provide that the failure of a debtor to pay any domestic support obligation that first becomes payable postpetition is cause for conversion or dismissal of the debtor's case. Section 213(8) amends Bankruptcy Code section 1322(a) to permit a chapter 13 debtor to propose a plan paying less than the full amount of a claim entitled to priority under Bankruptcy Code section 507(a)(1)(B) if the plan provides that all of the debtor's projected disposable income over a five-year period will be applied to make payments under the plan. Section 213(9) amends Bankruptcy Code section 1322(b) to permit a chapter 13 debtor to propose a plan that pays postpetition interest on nondischargeable debts under section 1328(a), but only to the extent that the debtor has disposable income available to pay such interest after payment in full of all allowed claims. Section 213(10) amends Bankruptcy Code section 1325(a) to provide that if a chapter 13 debtor is required by judicial or administrative order or statute to pay a domestic support obligation, then the debtor must pay all such obligations pursuant to such order or statute that became payable postpetition as a condition of confirmation. Section 213(11) amends Bankruptcy Code section 1328(a) to condition the granting of a chapter 13 discharge on the debtor's payment of certain postpetition domestic support obligations.

Sec. 214. Exceptions To Automatic Stay in Domestic Support Proceedings. Under current law, section 362(b)(2) of the Bankruptcy Code excepts from the automatic stay the commencement or continuation of an action or proceeding: (1) for the establishment of paternity; or (2) the establishment or modification of an order for alimony, maintenance or support. It also permits the collection of such obligations from property that is not property of the estate. Section 214 makes several revisions to Bankruptcy Code section 362(b)(2). First, it replaces the reference to "alimony, maintenance or support" with "domestic support obligations." Second, it adds to section 362(b)(2) actions or proceedings concerning: (1) child custody or visitation; (2) the dissolution of a marriage (except to the extent such proceeding seeks division of property that is property of the estate); and (3) domestic violence. Third, it permits the withholding of income that is property of the estate or property of the debtor for payment of a domestic support obligation under a judicial or administrative order as well as the withholding, suspension, or restriction of a driver's license, or a professional, occupational or recreational license under state law, pursuant to section 466(a)(16) of the Social Security Act. Fourth, it authorizes the reporting of overdue support owed by a parent to any consumer reporting agency pursuant to section 466(a)(7) of the Social Security Act. Fifth, it permits the interception of tax refunds as authorized by sections 464 and 466(a)(3) of the Social Security Act or analogous state law. Sixth, it allows medical obligations, as specified under title IV of the Social Security Act, to be enforced notwithstanding the automatic stay.

Sec. 215. Nondischargeability of Certain Debts for Alimony, Maintenance, and Support. Section 215 of the Act amends Bankruptcy Code section 523(a)(5) to provide that a "domestic support obligation" (as defined in section 211 of the Act) is nondischargeable and eliminates Bankruptcy Code section 523(a)(18). Section 215(2) amends Bankruptcy Code section 523(c) to delete the reference to section 523(a)(15) in that provision. Section 215(3) amends section 523(a)(15) to provide that obligations to a spouse, former spouse, or a child of the debtor (not otherwise described in section 523(a)(5)) incurred in connection with a divorce or separation or related action are nondischargeable irrespective of the debtor's inability to pay such debts.

Sec. 216. Continued Liability of Property. Section 216(1) of the Act amends section 522(c) of the Bankruptcy Code to make exempt property liable for nondischargeable domestic support obligations notwithstanding any contrary provision of applicable nonbankruptcy law. Section 216(2) and (3) make conforming amendments to sections 522(f)(1)(A) and 522(g)(2) of the Bankruptcy Code.

Sec. 217. Protection of Domestic Support Claims Against Preferential Transfer Motions. Section 217 of the Act makes a conforming amendment to Bankruptcy Code section 547(c)(7) to provide that a bona fide payment of a debt for a domestic support obligation may not be avoided as a preferential transfer.

Sec. 218. Disposable Income Defined. Section 218 of the Act amends section 1225(b)(2)(A) of the Bankruptcy Code to provide that disposable income in a chapter 12 case does not include payments for postpetition domestic support obligations.

Sec. 219. Collection of Child Support. Section 219 amends sections 704, 1106, 1202, and 1302 of the Bankruptcy Code to require trustees in chapter 7, 11, 12, and 13 cases to provide certain notices to child support claimants and governmental enforcement agencies. In addition, the Act conforms internal statutory cross references to Bankruptcy Code section 523(a)(14A) and deletes the reference to Bankruptcy Code section 523(a)(14) with respect to chapter 13, as this provision is inapplicable to that chapter.

Section 219(a) requires a chapter 7 trustee to provide written notice to a domestic support claimant of the right to use the services of a state child support enforcement agency established under sections 464 and 466 of the Social Security Act in the state where the claimant resides for assistance in collecting child support during and after the bankruptcy case. The notice must include the agency's address and telephone number as well as explain the claimant's right to payment under the applicable chapter of the Bankruptcy Code. In addition, the trustee must provide written notice to the claimant and the agency of such claim and include the name, address, and telephone number of the child support claimant. At the time the debtor is granted a discharge, the trustee must notify both the child support claimant and the agency that the debtor was granted a discharge as well as supply them with the debtor's last known address, the last known name and address of the debtor's employer, and the name of each creditor holding a debt that is not discharged under section 523(a)(2), (4) or (14A) or holding a debt that was reaffirmed pursuant to Bankruptcy Code section 524. A claimant or agency may request the debtor's last known address from a creditor holding a debt that is not discharged under section 523(a)(2), (4) or (14A) or that is reaffirmed pursuant to section 524 of the Bankruptcy Code. A creditor who discloses such information, however, is not liable to the debtor or any other person by reason of such disclosure. Subsections (b), (c), and (d) of section 219 of the Act impose comparable requirements for chapter 11, 12, and 13 trustees.

Sec. 220. Nondischargeability of Certain Educational Benefits and Loans. Section 220 of the Act amends section 523(a)(8) of the Bankruptcy Code to provide that a debt for a qualified education loan (as defined in section 221(e)(1) of the Internal Revenue Code) is nondischargeable, unless excepting such debt from discharge would impose an undue hardship on the debtor and the debtor's dependents.

Subtitle C. Other Consumer Protections

Sec. 221. Amendments To Discourage Abusive Bankruptcy Filings. Section 221 of the Act makes a series of amendments to section 110 of the Bankruptcy Code. First, section 221 clarifies that the definition of a bankruptcy petition preparer does not include an attorney for a debtor or an employee of an attorney under the direct supervision of such attorney. Second, it amends subsections (b) and (c) of section 110 to provide that if a bankruptcy petition preparer is not an individual, then an officer, principal, responsible person, or partner of the preparer must sign certain documents filed in connection with the bankruptcy case as well as state the person's name and address on such documents. Third, it requires a bankruptcy petition preparer to give the debtor written notice (as prescribed by the Judicial Conference of the United States) explaining that the preparer is not an attorney and may not practice law or give legal advice. The notice may include examples of legal advice that a preparer may not provide. Such notice must be signed by the preparer under penalty of perjury and the debtor and be filed with any document for filing. Fourth, the petition preparer is prohibited from giving legal advice, including with respect to certain specified items. Fifth, it permits the Supreme Court to promulgate rules or the Judicial Conference of the United States to issue guidelines for setting the maximum fees that a bankruptcy petition preparer may charge for services. Sixth, section 221 requires the preparer to notify the debtor of such maximum fees. Seventh, it specifies that the bankruptcy petition preparer must certify that it complied with this notification requirement. Eighth, it requires the court to order the turnover of any fees in excess of the value of the services rendered by the preparer within the 12-month period preceding the bankruptcy filing. Ninth, section 221 provides that all fees charged by a preparer may be forfeited if the preparer fails to comply with certain requirements specified in Bankruptcy Code section 110, as amended by this provision. Tenth, it allows a debtor to exempt fees recovered under this provision pursuant to Bankruptcy Code section 522(b). Eleventh, it specifically authorizes the court to enjoin a bankruptcy petition preparer who has violated a court order issued under section 110. Twelfth, it generally revises section 110's penalty provisions and requires such penalties to be paid into a special fund of the United States trustee for the purpose of funding the enforcement of section 110 on a national basis. With respect to Bankruptcy Administrator districts, the funds are to be deposited as offsetting receipts pursuant to section 1931 of title 28 of the United States Code.

Sec. 222. Sense of Congress. Section 222 of the Act expresses the sense of Congress that the states should develop personal finance curricula for use in elementary and secondary schools.

Sec. 223. Additional Amendments to Title 11, United States Code. Section 223 of the Act amends section 507(a) of the Bankruptcy Code to accord a tenth-level priority to claims for death or personal injuries resulting from the debtor's operation of a motor vehicle or vessel while intoxicated.

Sec. 224. Protection of Retirement Savings in Bankruptcy. The intent of section 224 is to expand the protection for tax-favored retirement plans or arrangements that may not be already protected under Bankruptcy Code section 541(c)(2) pursuant to *Patterson v. Shumate*,[84] or other state or Federal law. Subsection (a) of section 224 of the Act amends section 522 of the Bankruptcy Code to permit a debtor to exempt certain retirement funds to the extent those monies are in a fund or account that is exempt from taxation under section 401, 403, 408, 408A, 414, 457, or 501(a) of the Internal Revenue Code and that have received a favorable determination pursuant to Internal Revenue Code section 7805 that is in effect as of the date of the commencement of the case. If the retirement monies are in a retirement fund that has not received a favorable determination, those monies are exempt if the debtor demonstrates that no prior unfavorable determination has been made by a court or the Internal Revenue Service, and the retirement fund is in substantial compliance with the applicable requirements of the Internal Revenue Code. If the retirement fund fails to be in substantial compliance with applicable requirements of the Internal Revenue Code, the debtor may claim the retirement funds as exempt if he or she is not materially responsible for such failure. This section also applies to certain direct transfers and rollover distributions. In addition, this provision ensures that the specified retirement funds are exempt under state as well as Federal law.

Section 224(b) amends section 362(b) of the Bankruptcy Code to except from the automatic stay the withholding of income from a debtor's wages pursuant to an agreement authorizing such withholding for the benefit of a pension, profit-sharing, stock bonus, or other employer-sponsored plan established under Internal Revenue Code section 401, 403, 408, 408A, 414, 457, or 501(c) to the extent that the amounts withheld are used solely to repay a loan from a plan as authorized by section 408(b)(1) of the Employee Retirement Income Security Act of 1974 or subject to Internal Revenue Code section 72(p) or with respect to a loan from certain thrift savings plans. Section 224(b) further provides that this exception may not be used to cause any loan made

84 504 U.S. 753 (1992).

under a governmental plan under section 414(d) or a contract or account under section 403(b) of the Internal Revenue Code to be construed to be a claim or debt within the meaning of the Bankruptcy Code.

Section 224(c) amends Bankruptcy Code section 523(a) to except from discharge any amount owed by the debtor to a pension, profit-sharing, stock bonus, or other plan established under Internal Revenue Code section 401, 403, 408, 408A, 414, 457, or 501(c) under a loan authorized under section 408(b)(1) of the Employee Retirement Income Security Act of 1974 or subject to Internal Revenue Code section 72(p) or with respect to a loan from certain thrift savings plans. Section 224(c) further provides that this exception to discharge may not be used to cause any loan made under a governmental plan under section 414(d) or a contract or account under section 403(b) of the Internal Revenue Code to be construed to be a claim or debt within the meaning of the Bankruptcy Code.

Section 224(d) amends Bankruptcy Code section 1322 to provide that a chapter 13 plan may not materially alter the terms of a loan described in section 362(b)(19) and that any amounts required to repay such loan shall not constitute "disposable income" under section 1325 of the Bankruptcy Code.

Section 224(e) amends section 522 of the Bankruptcy Code to impose a $1 million cap (periodically adjusted pursuant to section 104 of the Bankruptcy Code to reflect changes in the Consumer Price Index) on the value of the debtor's interest in an individual retirement account established under either section 408 or 408A of the Internal Revenue Code (other than a simplified employee pension account under section 408(k) or a simple retirement account under section 408(p) of the Internal Revenue Code) that a debtor may claim as exempt property. This limit applies without regard to amounts attributable to rollover contributions made pursuant to section 402(c), 402(e)(6), 403(a)(4), 403(a)(5), or 403(b)(8) of the Internal Revenue Code and earnings thereon. The cap may be increased if required in the interests of justice.

Sec. 225. Protection of Education Savings in Bankruptcy. Subsection (a) of section 225 of the Act amends section 541 of the Bankruptcy Code to provide that funds placed not later than 365 days before the filing of the bankruptcy case in an education individual retirement account are not property of the estate if certain criteria are met. First, the designated beneficiary of such account must be a child, stepchild, grandchild or step-grandchild of the debtor for the taxable year during which funds were placed in the account. A legally adopted child or a foster child, under certain circumstances, may also qualify as a designated beneficiary. Second, such funds may not be pledged or promised to an entity in connection with any extension of credit and they may not be excess contributions (as described in section 4973(e) of the Internal Revenue Code). Funds deposited between 720 days and 365 days before the filing date are protected to the extent they do not exceed $5,000. Similar criteria apply with respect to funds used to purchase a tuition credit or certificate or to funds contributed to a qualified state tuition plan under section 529(b)(1)(A) of the Internal Revenue Code. Section 225(b) amends Bankruptcy Code section 521 to require a debtor to file with the court a record of any interest that the debtor has in an education individual retirement account or qualified state tuition program.

Sec. 226. Definitions. Subsection (a) of section 226 of the Act amends section 101 of the Bankruptcy Code to add certain definitions with respect to debt relief agencies. Section 226(a)(1) defines an "assisted person" as a person whose debts consist primarily of consumer debts and whose nonexempt assets are less than $150,000. Section 226(a)(2) defines "bankruptcy assistance" as any goods or services sold or otherwise provided to an assisted person with the express or implied purpose of giving information, advice, or counsel; preparing documents for filing; or attending a meeting of creditors pursuant to section 341; appearing in a case or proceeding on behalf of a person; or providing legal representation in a case or proceeding under the Bankruptcy Code. Section 226(a)(3) defines a "debt relief agency" as any person (including a bankruptcy petition preparer) who provides bankruptcy assistance to an assisted person in return for the payment of money or other valuable consideration. The definition specifically excludes certain entities. First, it does not apply to a person who is an officer, director, employee, or agent of a person who provides bankruptcy assistance or of a bankruptcy petition preparer. Second, it is not applicable to a nonprofit organization exemption from taxation under section 501(c)(3) of the Internal Revenue Code. Third, it is inapplicable to a creditor who assisted such person to the extent the assistance pertained to the restructuring of any debt owed by the person to the creditor. Fourth, the definition does not apply to a depository institution (as defined in section 3 of the Federal Deposit Insurance Act), or any Federal or state credit union (as defined in section 101 of the Federal Credit Union Act), as well as any affiliate or subsidiary of such depository institution or credit union. Fifth, an author, publisher, distributor, or seller of works subject to copyright protection under title 17 of the United States Code when acting in such capacity is not within the ambit of this definition.

Section 226(b) amends section 104(B)(1) of the Bankruptcy Code to permit the monetary amount set forth in the definition of an "assisted person" to be automatically adjusted to reflect the change in the Consumer Price Index.

Sec. 227. Restrictions on Debt Relief Agencies. Section 227 of the Act creates a new provision in the Bankruptcy Code intended to proscribe certain activities of a debt relief agency. It prohibits such agency from: (1) failing to perform any service that it informed an assisted person it would provide; (2) advising an assisted person to make an untrue and misleading statement (or that upon the exercise of reasonable care, should have been known to be untrue or misleading) in a document filed in a bankruptcy case; (3) misrepresenting the services it provides and the benefits and risks of bankruptcy; and (4) advising an assisted person or prospective assisted person to incur additional debt in contemplation of filing for bankruptcy relief or for the purpose of paying fees for services rendered by an attorney or petition preparer in connection with the bankruptcy case. Any waiver by an assisted person of the protections under this provision are unenforceable, except against a debt relief agency.

In addition, section 227 imposes penalties for the violation of section 526, 527 or 528 of the Bankruptcy Code. First, any contract between a debt relief agency and an assisted person that does not comply with these provisions is void and may not be enforced by any state or Federal court or by any person, except an assisted person. Second, a debt relief agency is liable to an assisted person, under certain circumstances, for any fees or charges paid by such person to the agency, actual damages, and reasonable attorneys' fees and costs. The chief law enforcement officer of a state who has reason to believe that a person has violated or is violating section 526 may seek to have such violation enjoined and recover actual damages. Third, section 227 provides that the United States district court has concurrent jurisdiction of certain actions under section 526. Fourth, section 227 provides that sections 526, 527 and 528 preempt inconsistent state law. In addition, it provides that these provisions do not limit or curtail the authority of a Federal court, a state, or a subdivision or instrumentality of a state, to determine and enforce qualifications for the practice of law before the Federal court or under the laws of that state.

Sec. 228. Disclosures. Section 228 of the Act requires a debt relief agency to provide certain specified written notices to an assisted person. These include the notice required under section 342(b)(1) (as amended by this Act) as well as a notice advising that: (1) all information the assisted person provides in connection with the case must be complete, accurate and truthful; (2) all assets and liabilities must be completely and accurately disclosed in the documents filed to commence the case, including the replacement value of each asset (if required) after reasonable inquiry to establish such value; (3) current monthly income, monthly expenses and, in a chapter 13 case, disposable income, must be stated after reasonable inquiry; and (4) the information an assisted person provides may be audited and that the failure to provide such information may result in dismissal of the case or other sanction including, in some instances, criminal sanctions. In addition, the agency must supply certain specified advisories and explanations regarding the bankruptcy process. Further, this provision requires the agency to advise an assisted person (to the extent permitted under nonbankruptcy law) concerning asset valuation, the calculation of disposable income, and the determination of exempt property.

Sec. 229. Requirements for Debt Relief Agencies. Section 229 adds a provision to the Bankruptcy Code requiring a debt relief agency—not later than five business days after the first date on which it provides any bankruptcy assistance services to an assisted person (but prior to such assisted person's bankruptcy petition being filed)—to execute a written contract with the assisted person. The contract must specify clearly and conspicuously the services the agency will provide, the basis on which fees will be charged for such services, and the terms of payment. The assisted person must be given a copy of the fully executed and completed. The debt relief agency must include certain specified mandatory statements in any advertisement of bankruptcy assistance services or regarding the benefits of bankruptcy that is directed to the general public whether through the general media, seminars, specific mailings, telephonic or electronic messages, or otherwise.

Sec. 230. GAO Study. Section 230 of the Act directs the Comptroller General of the United States to study and prepare a report on the feasibility, efficacy and cost of requiring trustees to supply certain specified information about a debtor's bankruptcy case to the Office of Child Support Enforcement for the purpose of determining whether a debtor has outstanding child support obligations.

Sec. 231. Protection of Personally Identifiable Information. Section 231 of the Act clarifies that it applies to personally identifiable information and does not preempt applicable nonbankruptcy law. In addition, the provision specifies that court approval must be preceded by the appointment of a privacy ombudsman to effectuate the intent of this provision.

Subsection (a) amends Bankruptcy Code section 363(b)(1) to provide that if a debtor, in connection with offering a product or service, discloses to an individual a policy prohibiting the transfer of personally identifiable information to persons unaffiliated with the debtor, and the policy is in effect at the time of the bankruptcy filing, then the trustee may not sell or lease such information unless either of the following conditions is satisfied: (1) the sale is consistent with such policy; or (2) the court, after appointment of a consumer privacy ombudsman (pursuant to section 332 of the Bankruptcy Code, as amended) and notice and hearing, the court approves the sale or lease upon due consideration of the facts, circumstances, and conditions of the sale or lease.

Section 231(b) amends Bankruptcy Code section 101 to add a definition of "personally identifiable information." The term applies to information provided by an individual to the debtor in connection with obtaining a product or service from the debtor primarily for personal, family, or household purposes. It includes the individual's: (1) first name or initial and last name (whether given at birth or adoption or legally changed); (2) physical home address; (3) electronic address, including an e-mail address; (4) home telephone number; (5) Social Security account number; or (vi) credit card account number. The term also includes information if it is identified in connection with the above items: (1) an individual's birth date, birth or adoption certificate number, or place of birth; or (2) any other information concerning an identified individual that, if disclosed, will result in the physical or electronic contacting or identification of that person.

Sec. 232. Consumer Privacy Ombudsman. Section 232 implements the preceding provision of the Act with respect to the appointment and responsibilities of a consumer privacy ombudsman. It provides that if a hearing is required under section 363(b)(1)(B) (as amended), the court must order the United States trustee to appoint a disinterested person to serve as the consumer privacy ombudsman and to provide timely notice of the hearing to such person. It permits the ombudsman to appear and be heard at such hearing. The ombudsman must provide the court with information to assist its consideration of the facts, circumstances and conditions of the proposed sale or lease of personally identifiable information. The information may include a presentation of the debtor's privacy policy, potential losses or gains of privacy to consumers if the sale or lease is approved, potential costs or benefits to consumers if the sale or lease is approved, and possible alternatives that would mitigate potential privacy losses or costs to consumers. Section 232 prohibits the ombudsman from disclosing any personally identifiable information obtained in the case by such individual. In addition, the provision amends Bankruptcy Code section 330(a)(1) to permit an ombudsman to be compensated.

Sec. 233. Prohibition on Disclosure of Name of Minor Children. Section 233 of the Act adds a new provision to the Bankruptcy Code (section 112) specifying that a debtor may be required to provide information regarding his or her minor child in connection with the bankruptcy case, but such debtor may not be required to disclose the child's name in the public records. It provides, however, that the debtor may be required to disclose this information in a nonpublic record maintained by the court, which may be available for inspection by the United States trustee, trustee or an auditor, if any. Section 233 prohibits the court, United States trustee, trustee, or auditor from disclosing such minor child's name.

Sec. 234. Protection of Personal Information. Bankruptcy Code section 107, with certain exceptions, provides that all papers filed in a bankruptcy case are public records. Exceptions include trade secrets, confidential research, and scandalous or defamatory matter. Section 234(a) adds a new provision to section 107 that permits a bankruptcy court to prohibit the disclosure of certain types of information concerning an individual to the extent the court finds that disclosure of such information would create undue risk of identity theft or other unlawful injury to the individual or the individual's property. The protected information includes any means of identification as defined in 18 U.S.C. § 1028(d) that is contained in a document filed in a bankruptcy case. The bankruptcy court must provide access to information protected under this new provision to an entity acting pursuant to the police or regulatory power of a domestic governmental unit upon ex parte application demonstrating cause. The provision also provides that the United States trustee, bankruptcy administrator, trustee, and any auditor serving pursuant to section 586(f) of title 28 of the United States Code shall have access to all information contained in a bankruptcy case and that such persons shall not disclose information specifically protected by the court. Section 234(b) amends Bankruptcy Code section 342(c), which requires a debtor to disclose in any notice required by the debtor to be given to a creditor to include the debtor's taxpayer identification number. Section 234(b) requires the debtor only to supply the last four digits of the taxpayer identification number. If, however, the notice concerns an amendment that adds a creditor to the schedules of assets or liabilities, the debtor must include the full taxpayer identification number in the notice sent to such creditor. The notice filed with the court must only include the last four digits of such notice.

TITLE III. DISCOURAGING BANKRUPTCY ABUSE

Sec. 301. Technical Amendments. Section 301 of the Act makes a clarifying amendment to section 523(a)(17) of the Bankruptcy Code concerning the dischargeability of court fees incurred by prisoners. Section 523(a)(17) was added to the Bankruptcy Code by the Omnibus Consolidated Rescissions and Appropriations Act of 1996[85] to except from discharge the filing fees and related costs and expenses assessed by a court in a civil case or appeal. As the result of a drafting error, however, this provision might be construed to apply to filing fees, costs or expenses incurred by any debtor, not solely by those who are prisoners. The amendment eliminates this ambiguity and makes other conforming changes to narrow its application in accordance with its original intent.

Sec. 302. Discouraging Bad Faith Repeat Filings. Section 302 of the Act amends section 362(c) of the Bankruptcy Code to terminate the automatic stay within 30 days in a chapter 7, 11, or 13 case filed by or against an individual if such individual was a debtor in a previously dismissed case pending within the preceding one-year period. The provision does not apply to a case refiled under a chapter other than chapter 7 after dismissal of the prior chapter 7 case pursuant to section 707(b) of the Bankruptcy Code. Upon motion of a party in interest, the court may continue the automatic stay after notice and a hearing completed prior to

85 Pub. L. No. 104-134, § 804(b) (1996).

the expiration of the 30-day period if such party demonstrates that the latter case was filed in good faith as to the creditors who are stayed by the filing.

For purposes of this provision, a case is presumptively not filed in good faith as to all creditors (but such presumption may be rebutted by clear and convincing evidence) if: (1) more than one bankruptcy case under chapter 7, 11 or 13 was previously filed by the debtor within the preceding one-year period; (2) the prior chapter 7, 11, or 13 case was dismissed within the preceding year for the debtor's failure to (a) file or amend without substantial excuse a document required under the Bankruptcy Code or court order, (b) provide adequate protection ordered by the court, or (c) perform the terms of a confirmed plan; or (3) there has been no substantial change in the debtor's financial or personal affairs since the dismissal of the prior case, or there is no reason to conclude that the pending case will conclude either with a discharge (if a chapter 7 case) or confirmation (if a chapter 11 or 13 case). In addition, section 302 provides that a case is presumptively deemed not to be filed in good faith as to any creditor who obtained relief from the automatic stay in the prior case or sought such relief in the prior case and such action was pending at the time of the prior case's dismissal. The presumption may be rebutted by clear and convincing evidence. A similar presumption applies if two or more bankruptcy cases were pending in the one-year preceding the filing of the pending case.

Sec. 303. Curbing Abusive Filings. Section 303 of the Act is intended to reduce abusive filings. Subsection (a) amends Bankruptcy Code section 362(d) to add a new ground for relief from the automatic stay. Under this provision, cause for relief from the automatic stay may be established for a creditor whose claim is secured by an interest in real property, if the court finds that the filing of the bankruptcy case was part of a scheme to delay, hinder and defraud creditors that involved either: (1) a transfer of all or part of an ownership interest in real property without such creditor's consent or without court approval; or (2) multiple bankruptcy filings affecting the real property. If recorded in compliance with applicable state law governing notice of an interest in or a lien on real property, an order entered under this provision is binding in any other bankruptcy case for two years from the date of entry of such order. A debtor in a subsequent case may move for relief based upon changed circumstances or for good cause shown after notice and a hearing. Section 303(a) further provides that any federal, state or local governmental unit that accepts a notice of interest or a lien in real property, must accept a certified copy of an order entered under this provision.

Section 303(b) amends Bankruptcy Code section 362(b) to except from the automatic stay an act to enforce any lien against or security interest in real property within two years following the entry of an order entered under section 362(d)(4). A debtor, in a subsequent case, may move for relief from such order based upon changed circumstances or for other good cause shown after notice and a hearing. Section 303(b) also provides that the automatic stay does not apply in a case where the debtor: (1) is ineligible to be a debtor in a bankruptcy case pursuant to section 109(g) of the Bankruptcy Code; or (2) filed the bankruptcy case in violation of an order issued in a prior bankruptcy case prohibiting the debtor from being a debtor in a subsequent bankruptcy case.

Sec. 304. Debtor Retention of Personal Property Security. Section 304(1) of the Act amends section 521(a) of the Bankruptcy Code to provide that an individual who is a chapter 7 debtor may not retain possession of personal property securing, in whole or in part, a purchase money security interest unless the debtor, within 45 days after the first meeting of creditors, enters into a reaffirmation agreement with the creditor, or redeems the property. If the debtor fails to so act within the prescribed period, the property is not subject to the automatic stay and is no longer property of the estate. An exception applies if the court: (1) determines on motion of the trustee filed before the expiration of the 45-day period that the property has consequential value or would benefit the bankruptcy estate; (2) orders adequate protection of the creditor's interest; and (3) directs the debtor to deliver any collateral in the debtor's possession. Section 304(2) amends section 722 to clarify that a chapter 7 debtor must pay the redemption value in full at the time of redemption.

Sec. 305. Relief from the Automatic Stay When the Debtor Does Not Complete Intended Surrender of Consumer Debt Collateral. Paragraph (1) of section 305 of the Act amends Bankruptcy Code section 362 to terminate the automatic stay with respect to personal property of the estate or of the debtor in a chapter 7, 11, or 13 case (where the debtor is an individual) that secures a claim (in whole or in part) or is subject to an unexpired lease if the debtor fails to: (1) file timely a statement of intention as required by section 521(a)(2) of the Bankruptcy Code with respect to such property; or (2) indicate in such statement whether the property will be surrendered or retained, and if retained, whether the debtor will redeem the property or reaffirm the debt, or assume an unexpired lease, if the trustee does not. Likewise, the automatic stay is terminated if the debtor fails to take the action specified in the statement of intention in a timely manner, unless the statement specifies reaffirmation and the creditor refuses to enter into the reaffirmation agreement on the original contract terms. In addition to terminating the automatic stay, this provision renders such property to be no longer property of the estate. An exception pertains where the court determines, on the motion of the trustee made prior to the expiration of the applicable time period under section 521(a)(2), and after notice and a hearing, that such property is of consequential value or benefit to the estate, orders adequate protection of the creditor's interest, and directs the debtor to deliver any collateral in the debtor's possession.

Section 305(2) amends section 521 of the Bankruptcy Code to make the requirement to file a statement of intention applicable to all secured debts, not just secured consumer debts. In addition, it requires the debtor to effectuate his or her stated intention within 30 days from the first date set for the meeting of creditors. If the debtor fails to timely undertake certain specified actions with respect to property that a lessor or bailor owns and has leased, rented or bailed to the debtor or in which a creditor has a security interest (not otherwise avoidable under section 522(f), 544, 545, 547, 548 or 549 of the Bankruptcy Code), then nothing in the Bankruptcy Code shall prevent or limit the operation of a provision in a lease or agreement that places the debtor in default by reason of the debtor's bankruptcy or insolvency.

Sec. 306. Giving Secured Creditors Fair Treatment in Chapter 13. Subsection (a) of section 306 of the Act amends Bankruptcy Code section 1325(a)(5)(B)(i) to require—as a condition of confirmation—that a chapter 13 plan provide that a secured creditor retain its lien until the earlier of when the underlying debt is paid or the debtor receives a discharge. If the case is dismissed or converted prior to completion of the plan, the secured creditor is entitled to retain its lien to the extent recognized under applicable nonbankruptcy law.

Section 306(b) adds a new paragraph to section 1325(a) of the Bankruptcy Code specifying that Bankruptcy Code section 506 does not apply to a debt incurred within the two and one-half year period preceding the filing of the bankruptcy case if the debt is secured by a purchase money security interest in a motor vehicle acquired for the personal use of the debtor within 910 days preceding the filing of the petition. Where the collateral consists of any other type of property having value, section 306(b) provides that section 506 of the Bankruptcy Code does not apply if the debt was incurred during the one-year period preceding the filing of the bankruptcy case.

Section 306(c)(1) amends section 101 of the Bankruptcy Code to define the term "debtor's principal residence" as a residential structure (including incidental property) without regard to whether or not such structure is attached to real property. The term includes an individual condominium or cooperative unit as well as a mobile or manufactured home, or a trailer.

Section 306(c)(2) amends section 101 of the Bankruptcy Code to define the term "incidental property" as property commonly conveyed with a principal residence in the area where the real property is located. The term includes all easements, rights, appurtenances, fixtures, rents, royalties, mineral rights, oil or gas rights or profits, water rights, escrow funds, and insurance proceeds. Further, the term encompasses all replacements and additions.

Sec. 307. Domiciliary Requirements for Exemptions. Section 307 of the Act amends section 522(b)(2)(A) of the Bankruptcy Code to extend the time that a debtor must be domiciled in a state from 180 days to 730 days before he or she may claim that state's exemptions. If the debtor's domicile has not been located in a single state for the 730-day period, then the state where the debtor was domiciled in the 180-day period preceding the 730-day period (or the longer portion of such 180-day period) controls. If the effect of this provision is to render the debtor ineligible for any exemption, the debtor may elect to exempt property of the kind described in the Federal exemption notwithstanding the state has opted out of the Federal exemption allowances.

Sec. 308. Reduction of Homestead Exemption for Fraud. Section 308 amends section 522 of the Bankruptcy Code to reduce the value of a debtor's interest in the following property that may be claimed as exempt under certain circumstances: (i) real or personal property that the debtor or a dependent of the debtor uses as a residence, (ii) a cooperative that owns property that the debtor or a dependent of the debtor uses as a residence, (iii) a burial plot, or (iv) real or personal property that the debtor or dependent of the debtor claims as a homestead. Where nonexempt property is converted to the above-specified exempt property within the ten-year period preceding the filing of the bankruptcy case, the exemption must be reduced to the extent such value was acquired with the intent to hinder, delay or defraud a creditor.

Sec. 309. Protecting Secured Creditors in Chapter 13 Cases. Section 309(a) of the Act amends Bankruptcy Code section 348(f)(1)(B) to provide that valuations of property and allowed secured claims in a chapter 13 case only apply if the case is subsequently converted to one under chapter 11 or 12. If the chapter 13 case is converted to one under chapter 7, then the creditor holding security as of the petition date shall continue to be secured unless its claim was paid in full as of the conversion date. In addition, unless a prebankruptcy default has been fully cured at the time of conversion, then the default in any bankruptcy proceeding shall have the effect given under applicable nonbankruptcy law.

Section 309(b) amends section 365 of the Bankruptcy Code to provide that if a lease of personal property is rejected or not assumed by the trustee in a timely manner, such property is no longer property of the estate and the automatic stay under Bankruptcy Code section 362 with respect to such property is terminated. With regard to a chapter 7 case in which the debtor is an individual, the debtor may notify the creditor in writing of his or her desire to assume the lease. Upon being so notified, the creditor may, at its option, inform the debtor that it is willing to have the lease assumed and condition such assumption on cure of any outstanding default on terms set by the contract. If within 30 days after such notice the debtor gives written notice to the lessor that the lease is assumed, the debtor (not the bankruptcy estate) assumes the liability under the lease.

Section 309(b) provides that the automatic stay of section 362 and the discharge injunction of section 524 are not violated if the creditor notifies the debtor and negotiates a cure under section 365(p)(2) (as amended). In a chapter 11 or 13 case where the debtor is an individual lessee with respect to a personal property lease and the lease is not assumed in the confirmed plan, the lease is deemed rejected as of the conclusion of the confirmation hearing. If the lease is rejected, the automatic stay under section 362 as well as the chapter 13 codebtor stay under section 1301 are automatically terminated with respect to such property.

Section 309(c)(1) amends Bankruptcy Code section 1325(a)(5)(B) to require that periodic payments pursuant to a chapter 13 plan with respect to a secured claim be made in equal monthly installments. Where the claim is secured by personal property, the amount of such payments shall not be less than the amount sufficient to provide adequate protection to the holder of such claim. Section 309(c)(2) amends section 1326(a) of the Bankruptcy Code to require a chapter 13 debtor to commence making payments within 30 days after the filing of the plan or the order for relief, whichever is earlier. The amount of such payment must be the amount proposed in the plan, scheduled in a personal property lease for that portion of the obligation that becomes due postpetition (which amount shall reduce the payment required to be made to such lessor pursuant to the plan), and provides adequate protection directly to a creditor holding an allowed claim secured by personal property to the extent the claim is attributable to the purchase of such property (which amount shall reduce the payment required to be made to such secured creditor pursuant to the plan). Payments made pursuant to a plan must be retained by the chapter 13 trustee until confirmation or denial of confirmation. Section 309(c)(2) provides that if the plan is confirmed, the trustee must distribute payments received from the debtor as soon as practicable in accordance with the plan. If the plan is not confirmed, the trustee must return to the debtor payments not yet due and owing to creditors. Pending confirmation and subject to section 363, the court, after notice and a hearing, may modify the payments required under this provision. Section 309(c)(2) requires the debtor, within 60 days following the filing of the bankruptcy case, to provide reasonable evidence of any required insurance coverage with respect to the use or ownership of leased personal property or property securing, in whole or in part, a purchase money security interest.

Sec. 310. Limitation on Luxury Goods. Section 310 amends section 523(a)(2)(C) of the Bankruptcy Code. Under current law, consumer debts owed to a single creditor that, in the aggregate, exceed $1,075 for luxury goods or services incurred within 60 days before the commencement of the case are presumed to be nondischargeable. As amended, the presumption applies if the aggregate amount of consumer debts for luxury goods or services is more than $500 for luxury goods or services incurred by an individual debtor within 90 days before the order for relief. With respect to cash advances, current law provides that cash advances aggregating more than $1,075 that are extensions of consumer credit under an open-end credit plan obtained by an individual debtor within 60 days before the case is filed are presumed to be nondischargeable. As amended, section 523(a)(2)(C) presumes that cash advances aggregating more than $750 and that are incurred within 70 days are nondischargeable. The term, "luxury goods or services," does not include goods or services reasonably necessary for the support or maintenance of the debtor or a dependent of the debtor. In addition, "an extension of consumer credit under an open-end credit plan" has the same meaning as this term has under the Consumer Credit Protection Act.

Sec. 311. Automatic Stay. Section 311 of the Act amends section 362(b) of the Bankruptcy Code to except from the automatic stay a judgment of eviction with respect to a residential leasehold under certain circumstances. It is the intent of this provision to create an exception to the automatic stay of section 362(a)(3) to permit the recovery of possession by rental housing providers of their property in certain circumstances where a judgment for possession has been obtained against a debtor/resident before the filing of the petition for bankruptcy. Section 311 is intended to apply to manufactured housing communities, where tenants own their own homes and pay monthly rent to community owners for the land upon which their home sits. Tenants who fail to pay rent for the land beneath their homes located in manufactured housing communities would no longer be able to avoid their rental obligations under the protection of the automatic stay. It is also the intent of this section to permit eviction actions based on illegal use of controlled substances or endangering property in certain circumstances.

Section 311 gives tenants a reasonable amount of time after filing the petition to cure the default giving rise to the judgment for possession as long as there are circumstances in which applicable nonbankruptcy law allows a default to be cured after a judgment has been obtained. Where nonbankruptcy law applicable in the jurisdiction does not permit a tenant to cure a monetary default after the judgment for possession has been obtained, the automatic stay of section 362(a)(3) does not operate to limit action by a rental housing provider to proceed with, or a marshal, sheriff, or similar local officer to execute, the judgment for possession. Where the debtor claims that applicable law permits a tenant to cure after the judgment for possession has been obtained, the automatic stay operates only where the debtor files a certification with the bankruptcy petition asserting that applicable law permits such action and that the debtor or an adult dependent of the debtor has paid to the court all rent that will come due during the 30 days following the filing of the petition. If, within thirty days following the filing of the petition, the debtor or an adult dependent of the debtor certifies that the entire monetary default that gave rise to the judgment for possession has been cured, the automatic stay remains in effect. If a lessor has filed or wishes to file an eviction action based on the use of illegal controlled substances or property endangerment, the section allows the lessor in certain cases to file a certification of such circumstance with the court and obtain an exception to the stay.

For both the judgment based on monetary default and the controlled substance or endangerment exceptions, the section provides an opportunity for challenge by either the lessor or the tenant to certifications filed by the other party and a timely hearing for the court to resolve any disputed facts and rule on the factual or legal sufficiency of the certifications. Where the court finds for the lessor, the clerk shall immediately serve upon the parties a copy of the court's order confirming that an exception to the automatic stay is applicable. Where the court finds for the tenant, the stay shall remain in effect. It is the intent of this section that the clerk's certified copy of the docket or order shall be sufficient evidence that the exception under paragraph 22 or paragraph 23 is applicable for a marshal, sheriff, or similar local officer to proceed immediately to execute the judgment for possession if applicable law otherwise permits such action, or for an eviction action for use of illegal controlled substances or property endangerment to proceed. This section does not provide any new right to either landlords or tenants relating to evictions or defenses to eviction under otherwise applicable law.

Section 311 also excepts from the automatic stay a transfer that is not avoidable under Bankruptcy Code section 544 and that is not avoidable under Bankruptcy Code section 549. This amendment responds to a 1997 Ninth Circuit case in which two purchase money lenders (without knowledge that the debtor had recently filed an undisclosed chapter 11 case that was later converted to chapter 7), funded the debtor's acquisition of an apartment complex and recorded their purchase-money deed of trust immediately following recordation of the deed to the debtors.[86]

Sec. 312. Extension of Period Between Bankruptcy Discharges. Section 312 of the Act amends section 727(a)(8) of the Bankruptcy Code to extend the period before which a chapter 7 debtor may receive a subsequent chapter 7 discharge from six to eight years. It also amends section 1328 to prohibit the issuance of a discharge in a subsequent chapter 13 case if the debtor received a discharge in a prior chapter 7, 11, or 12 case within four years preceding the filing of the subsequent chapter 13 case. In addition, it prohibits the issuance of a discharge in a subsequent chapter 13 case if the debtor received a discharge in a chapter 13 case filed during the two-year period preceding the date of the filing of the subsequent chapter 13 case.

Sec. 313. Definition of Household Goods and Antiques. Subsection (a) of section 313 of the Act amends section 522(f) of the Bankruptcy Code to codify a modified version of the Federal Trade Commission's definition of "household goods" for purposes of the avoidance of a nonpossessory, nonpurchase money lien in such property. It also specifies various items that are expressly not household goods. Section 313 specifies a monetary threshold for the exclusions pertaining to electronic entertainment equipment, antiques, and jewelry. In addition, it provides that works of art are not household goods, unless by or of the debtor or by any relative of the debtor. Section 313(b) requires the Director of the Executive Office for United States Trustees to prepare a report containing findings with respect to the use of this definition. The report may include recommendations for amendments to the definition of "household goods" as codified in section 522(f)(4).

Sec. 314. Debt Incurred To Pay Nondischargeable Debts. Subsection (a) of section 314 of the Act amends section 523(a) of the Bankruptcy Code to make a debt incurred to pay a nondischargeable tax owed to a governmental unit (other than a tax owed to the United States) nondischargeable. Section 314(b) amends section 1328(a) of the Bankruptcy Code to make the following additional debts nondischargeable in a chapter 13 case: (1) debts for money, property, services, or extensions of credit obtained through fraud or by a false statement in writing under section 523(a)(2)(A) and (B) of the Bankruptcy Code; (2) consumer debts owed to a single creditor that aggregate to more than $500 for luxury goods or services incurred by an individual debtor within 90 days before the filing of the bankruptcy case, and cash advances aggregating more than $750 that are

86 *Thompson v. Margen* (*In re* McConville), 110 F.3d 47 (9th Cir.), *cert. denied*, 522 U.S. 966 (1997). The bankruptcy trustee sought to avoid the lien created by the lenders' deed of trust by asserting that the deed was an unauthorized, postpetition transfer under Bankruptcy Code section 549(a). The lenders claimed that the voluntary transfer to them was a transfer of real property to good faith purchasers for value, which thereby excepted it, under Bankruptcy Code section 549(c) from avoidance. The bankruptcy court held that the postpetition recordation of the lenders' deed of trust was without authorization under the Bankruptcy Code or by the court and was therefore avoidable under section 549(a) and that the lenders did not qualify under the section 549(c) exception as good faith purchasers of real property for value. The District Court subsequently affirmed the bankruptcy court's ruling granting the trustee the authority to avoid the lenders' lien. *McConville v. David Margen and Lawton Associates* (*In re* McConville), No. C 94-3308, 1994 U.S. Dist. LEXIS 18095 (N.D. Cal. Dec. 14, 1994). On appeal, the lower court's decision in *McConville* was initially affirmed. *Thompson v. Margen* (*In re* McConville), 84 F.3d 340 (9th Cir. 1996). The Ninth Circuit, however, subsequently issued an amended opinion, also affirming the lower court, *Thompson v. Margen* (*In re* McConville), 97 F.3d 316 (9th Cir. 1996), and finally issued an opinion withdrawing its prior opinion and deciding the case on other grounds. It held that by obtaining secured credit from the lenders after filing but before the appointment of a trustee, the debtors violated their fiduciary responsibility to their creditors. *Thompson v. Margen* (*In re* McConville), 110 F.3d 47 (9th Cir. 1997).

extensions of consumer credit obtained by a debtor under an open-end credit plan within 70 days before the order for relief under section 523(a)(2)(C) (as amended); (3) pursuant to section 523(a)(3) of the Bankruptcy Code, debts that require a timely request for a dischargeability determination, if the creditor lacks notice or does not have actual knowledge of the case in time to make such request; (4) debts resulting from fraud or defalcation by the debtor acting as a fiduciary under section 523(a)(4) of the Bankruptcy Code; and (5) debts for restitution or damages, awarded in a civil action against the debtor as a result of willful or malicious conduct by the debtor that caused personal injury to an individual or the death of an individual.

Sec. 315. Giving Creditors Fair Notice in Chapters 7 and 13 Cases. Section 315 of the Act amends several provisions of the Bankruptcy Code. Subsection (a) amends Bankruptcy Code section 342(c) to delete the provision specifying that the failure of a notice to include certain information required to be given by a debtor to a creditor does not invalidate the notice's legal effect. It adds a provision requiring a debtor to send any notice he or she must provide under the Bankruptcy Code to the address stated by the creditor and to include in such notice the current account number, if within 90 days prior to the date that the debtor filed for bankruptcy relief the creditor in at least two communications sent to the debtor set forth such address and account number. If the creditor would be in violation of applicable nonbankruptcy law by sending any such communication during this time period, then the debtor must send the notice to the address provided by the creditor stated in the last two communications containing the creditor's address and such notice shall include the current account number. Section 315(a) also permits a creditor in a chapter 7 or 13 case (where the debtor is an individual) to file with the court and serve on the debtor the address to be used to notify such creditor in that case. Five days after receipt of such notice, the court and the debtor, respectively, must use the address so specified to provide notice to such creditor.

In addition, section 315(a) specifies that an entity may file a notice with the court stating an address to be used generally by all bankruptcy courts for chapter 7 and 13 cases, or by particular bankruptcy courts, as specified by such entity. This address must be used by the court to supply notice in such cases within 30 days following the filing of such notice where the entity is a creditor. Notice given other than as provided in section 342 is not effective until it has been brought to the creditor's attention. If the creditor has designated a person or organizational subdivision to be responsible for receiving notices concerning bankruptcy cases and has established reasonable procedures so that these notices will be delivered to such person or subdivision, a notice will not be considered to have been brought to the attention of such creditor until it has been received by such person or subdivision. This provision also prohibits the imposition of any monetary penalty for violation of the automatic stay or for the failure to comply with the Bankruptcy Code sections 542 and 543 unless the creditor has received effective notice under section 342.

Section 315(b) amends section 521 to specify additional duties of a debtor. This provision requires the debtor to file a certificate executed by the debtor's attorney or bankruptcy petition preparer stating that the attorney or preparer supplied the debtor with the notice required under Bankruptcy Code section 342(b). If the debtor is not represented by counsel and did not use the services of a bankruptcy petition preparer, then the debtor must sign a certificate stating that he or she obtained and read such notice. In addition, the debtor must file: (1) copies of all payment advices or other evidence of payment, if any, from any employer within 60 days preceding the bankruptcy filing; (2) a statement of the amount of monthly net income, itemized to show how such amount is calculated; and (3) a statement disclosing any reasonably anticipated increase in income or expenditures in the 12-month period following the date of filing. Upon request of a creditor, section 315(b) of the Act requires the court to make the petition, schedules, and statement of financial affairs of an individual who is a chapter 7 or 13 debtor available to such creditor.

In addition, section 315(b) requires such debtor to provide the trustee not later than seven days before the date first set for the meeting of creditors a copy of his or her Federal income tax return or transcript (at the election of the debtor) for the latest taxable period ending prior to the filing of the bankruptcy case for which a tax return was filed. Should the debtor fail to comply with this requirement, the case must be dismissed unless the debtor demonstrates that such failure was due to circumstances beyond the debtor's control. Upon request, the debtor must provide a copy of the tax return or transcript to the requesting creditor at the time the debtor supplies the return or transcript to the trustee. A creditor in a chapter 13 case may, at any time, file a notice with the court requesting a copy of the plan. The court must supply a copy of the chapter 13 plan at a reasonable cost not later than 5 days after such request. In addition, the Act clarifies that this provision applies to Federal income tax returns.

During the pendency of a chapter 7, 11 or 13 case, the debtor must file with the court, at the request of the judge, United States trustee, or any party in interest, at the time filed with the taxing authority, copies of any Federal income tax returns (or transcripts thereof) that were not filed for the three-year period preceding the date on which the order for relief was entered. In addition, the debtor must file copies of any amendments to such tax returns.

In a chapter 13 case, the debtor must file a statement, under penalty of perjury, of income and expenditures in the preceding tax year and monthly income showing how the amounts were calculated. The statement must be filed on the date that is the later of 90 days after the close of the debtor's tax year or one year after the order for relief, unless a plan has been confirmed. Thereafter, the statement must be filed on or before the date that is 45 days before the anniversary date of the plan's confirmation, until the case is closed. The statement must disclose the amount and sources of the debtor's income, the identity of any person responsible with the debtor for the support of the debtor's dependents, the identity of any person who contributed to the debtor's household expenses, and the amount of any such contributions.

Section 315(b)(2) mandates that the tax returns, amendments thereto, and the statement of income and expenditures of an individual who is a chapter 7 or chapter 13 debtor be made available to the United States trustee or bankruptcy administrator, the trustee, and any party in interest for inspection and copying, subject to procedures established by the Director of the Administrative Office for United States Courts within 180 days from the date of enactment of this Act. The procedures must safeguard the confidentiality of any tax information required under this provision and include restrictions on creditor access to such information. In addition, the Director must, within 540 days from the Act's enactment date, prepare and submit to Congress a report that assesses the effectiveness of such procedures and, if appropriate, includes recommendations for legislation to further protect the confidentiality of such tax information and to impose penalties for its improper use. If requested by the United States trustee or trustee, the debtor must provide a document establishing the debtor's identity, which may include a driver's license, passport, or other document containing a photograph of the debtor, and such other personal identifying information relating to the debtor.

Sec. 316. Dismissal for Failure To Timely File Schedules or Provide Required Information. Section 316 of the Act amends section 521 of the Bankruptcy Code to provide that if an individual debtor in a voluntary chapter 7 or chapter 13 case fails to file all of the information required under section 521(a)(1) within 45 days of the date on which the case is filed, the case must be automatically dismissed, effective on the 46th day. The 45-day period may be extended for an additional 45-day period providing the debtor requests such extension prior to the expiration of the original 45-day period and the court finds justification for such extension. Upon request of a party in interest, the court must enter an order of dismissal within 5 days of such request. Section 316 provides that a court may decline to dismiss the case if: (1) the trustee files a motion before the stated time periods; (2) the court finds, after notice and a hearing, that the debtor in good faith attempted to file all the information required under section 521(a)(1)(B)(iv); and (3) the court finds that the best interests of creditors would be served by continued administration of the case.

Sec. 317. Adequate Time To Prepare for Hearing on Confirmation of the Plan. Section 317 of the Act amends section 1324 of the Bankruptcy Code to require the chapter 13 confirmation hearing to be held not earlier than 20 days following the first date set for the meeting of creditors and not later than 45 days from this date, unless the court determines that it would be in the best interests of creditors and the estate to hold such hearing at an earlier date and there is no objection to such earlier date.

Sec. 318. Chapter 13 Plans To Have a 5-Year Duration in Certain Cases. Paragraph (1) of section 318 of the Act amends Bankruptcy Code sections 1322(d) and 1325(b) to specify that a chapter 13 plan may not provide for payments over a period that is not less than five years if the current monthly income of the debtor and the debtor's spouse combined exceeds certain monetary thresholds. If the current monthly income of the debtor and the debtor's spouse fall below these thresholds, then the duration of the plan may not be longer than three years, unless the court, for cause, approves a longer period up to five years. The applicable commitment period may be less if the plan provides for payment in full of all allowed unsecured claims over a shorter period. Section 318(2), (3), and (4) make conforming amendments to sections 1325(b) and 1329(c) of the Bankruptcy Code.

Sec. 319. Sense of Congress Regarding Expansion of Rule 9011 of the Federal Rules of Bankruptcy Procedure. Section 319 of the Act expresses a sense of the Congress that Federal Rule of Bankruptcy Procedure 9011 be modified to require that all documents (including schedules), whether signed or unsigned, supplied to the court or the trustee by a debtor may be submitted only after the debtor or the debtor's attorney has made reasonable inquiry to verify that the information contained in such documents is well-grounded in fact and warranted by existing law or a good faith argument for the extension, modification, or reversal of existing law.

Sec. 320. Prompt Relief from Stay in Individual Cases. Section 320 of the Act amends section 362(e) of the Bankruptcy Code to terminate the automatic stay in a chapter 7, 11, or 13 case of an individual debtor within 60 days following a request for relief from the stay, unless the bankruptcy court renders a final decision prior to the expiration of the 60-day time period, such period is extended pursuant to agreement of all parties in interest, or a specific extension of time is required for good cause as described in findings made by the court.

Sec. 321. Chapter 11 Cases Filed by Individuals. Section 321(a) of the Act creates a new provision under chapter 11 of the Bankruptcy Code specifying that property of the estate of an individual debtor includes, in addition to that identified in section 541 of the Bankruptcy Code, all property of the kind described in section 541 that the debtor acquires after commencement of the case, but before the case is closed, dismissed or converted to a case under chapter 7, 12, or 13 (whichever occurs first). In addition, it includes earnings from services performed by the debtor after commencement of the case, but before the case is closed, dismissed or converted to a case under chapter 7, 12, or 13. Except as provided in section 1104 of the Bankruptcy Code or the order confirming a chapter 11 plan, section 321(a) provides that the debtor remains in possession of all property of the estate.

Section 321(b) amends Bankruptcy Code section 1123 to require the chapter 11 plan of an individual debtor to provide for the payment to creditors of all or such portion of the debtor's earnings from personal services performed after commencement of the case or other future income that is necessary for the plan's execution.

Section 321(c) amends Bankruptcy Code section 1129(a) to include an additional requirement for confirmation in a chapter 11 case of an individual debtor upon objection to confirmation by a holder of an allowed unsecured claim. In such instance, the value of property to be distributed under the plan on account of such claim, as of the plan's effective date, must not be less than the amount of such claim; or be not less than the debtor's projected disposable income (as defined in section 1325(b)(2)) to be received during the five-year period beginning on the date that the first payment is due under the plan or during the plan's term, whichever is longer. Section 321(c) also amends section 1129(b)(2)(B)(ii) of the Bankruptcy Code to provide that an individual chapter 11 debtor may retain property included in the estate under section 1115 (as added by the Act), subject to section 1129(a)(14).

Section 321(d)(1) amends Bankruptcy Code section 1141(d) to provide that a discharge under chapter 11 does not discharge a debtor who is an individual from any debt excepted from discharge under Bankruptcy Code section 523. Section 321(d)(2) of the Act provides that in a chapter 11 individual debtor is not discharged until all plan payments have been made. The court may grant a hardship discharge if the value of property actually distributed under the plan—as of the plan's effective date—is not less than the amount that would have been available for distribution if the case was liquidated under chapter 7 on such date, and modification of the plan is not practicable.

Section 321(e) of the Act amends section 1127 to permit a plan in a chapter 11 case of an individual debtor to be modified postconfirmation for the purpose of increasing or reducing the amount of payments, extending or reducing the time period for such payments, or altering the amount of distribution to a creditor whose claim is provided for by the plan. Such modification may be made at any time on request of the debtor, trustee, United States trustee, or holder of an allowed unsecured claim. The provision specifies that sections 1121 through 1129 apply to such modification. In addition, it provides that the modified plan shall become the confirmed plan only if: (1) there has been disclosure pursuant to section 1125 (as the court directs); (2) notice and a hearing; and (3) such modification is approved.

Sec. 322. Limitations on Homestead Exemption. Section 322(a) amends section 522 of the Bankruptcy Code to impose an aggregate monetary limitation of $125,000, subject to Bankruptcy Code sections 544 and 548, on the value of property that the debtor may claim as exempt under State or local law pursuant to section 522(b)(3)(A) under certain circumstances. The monetary cap applies if the debtor acquired such property within the 1,215-day period preceding the filing of the petition and the property consists of any of the following: (1) real or personal property of the debtor or that a dependent of the debtor uses as a residence; (2) an interest in a cooperative that owns property, which the debtor or the debtor's dependent uses as a residence; (3) a burial plot for the debtor or the debtor's dependent; or (4) real or personal property that the debtor or dependent of the debtor claims as a homestead. This limitation does not apply to a principal residence claimed as exempt by a family farmer. In addition, the limitation does not apply to any interest transferred from a debtor's principal residence (which was acquired prior to the beginning of the specified time period) to the debtor's current principal residence, if both the previous and current residences are located in the same State.

Section 322(a) further amends section 522 to add a provision that does not allow a debtor to exempt any amount of an interest in property described in the preceding paragraph in excess of $125,000 if any of the following applies:

1. The court determines, after notice and a hearing, that the debtor has been convicted of a felony (as defined in section 3156 of title 18), which under the circumstance demonstrates that the filing of the case was an abuse of the provisions of the Bankruptcy Code; or
2. debtor owes a debt arising from:
   a. any violation of the Federal securities laws defined in section 3(a)(47) of the Securities and Exchange Act of 1934, any state securities laws, or any regulation or order issued under Federal securities laws or state securities laws;
   b. fraud, deceit, or manipulation in a fiduciary capacity or in connection with the purchase or sale of any security registered under section 12 or 15(d) of the Securities Exchange Act of 1934, or under section 6 of the Securities Act of 1933;
   c. any civil remedy under section 1964 of title 18 of the United States Code; or
   d. any criminal act, intentional tort, or willful or reckless misconduct that caused serious physical injury or death to another individual in the preceding five years.

An exception to the monetary limit applies to the extent the value of the homestead property is reasonably necessary for the support of the debtor and any dependent of the debtor. The monetary limitation set forth in section 322(a) is subject to automatic adjustment pursuant to section 104 of the Bankruptcy Code.

Sec. 323. Excluding Employee Benefit Plan Participant Contributions and Other Property from the Estate. Section 323 of the Act amends section 541(b) of the Bankruptcy Code to exclude as property of the estate funds withheld or received by an employer from its employees' wages for payment as contributions to specified employee retirement plans, deferred compensation plans, and tax-deferred annuities. Such contributions do not constitute disposable income as defined in section 1325(b)(2) of the Bankruptcy Code. Section 323 also excludes as property of the estate funds withheld by an employer from the wages of its employees for payment as contributions to health insurance plans regulated by State law.

Sec. 324. Exclusive Jurisdiction in Matters Involving Bankruptcy Professionals. Section 324 of the Act amends section 1334 of title 28 of the United State Code to give a district court exclusive jurisdiction of all claims or causes of action involving the construction of section 327 of the Bankruptcy Code or rules relating to disclosure requirements under such provision.

Sec. 325. United States Trustee Program Filing Fee Increase. Section 325(a) of the Act amends section 1930(a) of title 28 of the United States Code to increase the chapter 7 filing fee from $155 to $200 and decrease the chapter 13 filing fee from $155 to $150. It also increases the chapter 11 filing fee from $800 to $1,000. Subsection 325(b) amends section 589a of title 28 of the United States Code to reallocate the percentage of certain filing fees collected for the United States Trustee Fund. Subsection 325(c) amends section 406(b) of the Judiciary Appropriations Act of 1990 to reallocate the percentage of certain filing fees collected under section 1930 of title 28 of the United States Code to fund the operation and maintenance of the Federal court system. Section 325(d) provides that the amendments made by subsections (b) and (c) are effective for the two-year period beginning on the Act's date of enactment. Section 325(e)(1) mandates that the amount of fees collected under 28 U.S.C. § 1930(a)(1) (chapter 7 filing fees) and 28 U.S.C. 1930(a)(3) (chapter 11 filing fees) that is greater than the amount that would have been collected if these provisions were not amended by section 325 be allocated to the extent necessary to pay for the salaries and benefits of judges appointed pursuant to section 1223 of this Act. Section 325(e)(2) provides that any amount of fees in excess of that used to pay the salaries and benefits of judges appointed pursuant to section 1223 be deposited in the Treasury to the extent necessary to offset the decrease in governmental receipts resulting from the amendments made by section 325(b) (United States Trustee Fund) and section 325(c) (federal court system fund).

Sec. 326. Sharing of Compensation. Section 326 amends Bankruptcy Code section 504 to create a limited exception to the prohibition against fee sharing. The provision allows the sharing of compensation with bona fide public service attorney referral programs that operate in accordance with non-federal law regulating attorney referral services and with rules of professional responsibility applicable to attorney acceptance of referrals.

Sec. 327. Fair Valuation of Collateral. Section 327 of the Act amends section 506(a) of the Bankruptcy Code to provide that the value of an allowed claim secured by personal property that is an asset in an individual debtor's chapter 7 or 13 case is determined based on the replacement value of such property as of the filing date of the bankruptcy case without deduction for selling or marketing costs. With respect to property acquired for personal, family, or household purposes, replacement value is the price a retail merchant would charge for property of that kind considering the age and condition of the property at the time its value is determined.

Sec. 328. Defaults Based on Nonmonetary Obligations. Subsection (a)(1) of section 328 of the Act amends section 365(b) to provide that a trustee does not have to cure a default that is a breach of a provision (other than a penalty rate or penalty provision) relating to a default arising from any failure to perform a nonmonetary obligation under an unexpired lease of real property, if it is impossible for the trustee to cure the default by performing such nonmonetary act at and after the time of assumption. If the default arises from a failure to operate in accordance with a nonresidential real property lease, the default must be cured by performance at and after the time of assumption in accordance with the lease. Pecuniary losses resulting from such default must be compensated pursuant to section 365(b)(1). In addition, section 328(a)(1) amends section 365(b)(2)(D) to clarify that it applies to penalty provisions. Section 328(a)(2) through (4) make technical revisions to section 365(c), (d) and (f) by deleting language that is no longer effective pursuant to the Rail Safety Enforcement and Review Act.[87]

Section 328(b) amends section 1124(2)(A) of the Bankruptcy Code to clarify that a claim is not impaired if section 365(b)(2) (as amended by this Act) expressly does not require a default with respect to such claim to be cured. In addition, it provides that any claim or interest that arises from the failure to perform a nonmonetary obligation (other than a default arising from the failure to operate a nonresidential real property lease subject to section 365(b)(1)(A)), is impaired unless the holder of such claim or interest (other than the debtor or an insider) is compensated for any actual pecuniary loss incurred by the holder as a result of such failure.

Sec. 329. Clarification of Postpetition Wages and Benefits. Section 329 amends Bankruptcy Code section 503(b)(1)(A) to accord administrative expense status to certain back pay

87 Pub. L. No. 102-365, 106 Stat. 972 (1992).

awards. This provision applies to a back pay award attributable to any period of time occurring postpetition as a result of a violation of Federal or state law by the debtor pursuant to an action brought in a court or before the National Labor Relations Board, providing the bankruptcy court determines that the award will not substantially increase the probability of layoff or termination of current employees or of nonpayment of domestic support obligations.

Sec. 330. Delay of Discharge During Pendency of Certain Proceedings. Section 330(a) of the Act amends section 727(a) of the Bankruptcy Code to require the court to withhold the entry of a debtor's discharge order if the court, after notice and a hearing, finds that there is reasonable cause to believe that there is a pending proceeding in which the debtor may be found guilty of a felony of the kind described in Bankruptcy Code section 522(q)(1) or liable for a debt of the kind described in Bankruptcy Code section 522(q)(2). Subsections (b), (c), and (d) make comparable revisions to the discharge provisions under chapter 11, 12, and 13, respectively.

Sec. 331. Limitation on Retention Bonuses, Severance Pay, and Certain Other Payments. Section 331 amends Bankruptcy Code section 503 to prohibit the allowance or payment of certain transfers or obligations, unless otherwise authorized by the court. It applies to transfers made to or obligations incurred for the benefit of an insider of the debtor for the purpose of inducing such person to remain with the debtor's business, unless the court makes certain specified findings. In addition, it prohibits a severance payment to an insider of a debtor, unless it satisfies certain criteria. Further, it prohibits the payment of other transfers or obligations that are outside the ordinary course of business and not justified by the facts and circumstances of the case, including transfers made to, or obligations incurred for the benefit of, officers, mangers, or consultants hired after the date of the filing of the petition.

Sec. 332. Fraudulent Involuntary Bankruptcy. Bankruptcy Code section 303 permits a creditor to force an individual or business into bankruptcy by filing an involuntary bankruptcy petition against such entity. Before an order for relief is entered in the case, the court must make certain findings that support granting such relief (e.g., the debtor is generally not paying debts as they become due; or a custodian was appointed within the 120-day period preceding the filing of the petition). If such findings are not made, the court may dismiss the case. As with most documents filed in connection with a bankruptcy case, the filing of an involuntary bankruptcy petition is a matter of public record and is open for examination by any entity.[88] In addition, the Fair Credit Reporting Act[89] permits credit reporting agencies to note the involuntary bankruptcy filing on a person's credit report for up to ten years.[90] Although the Fair Credit Reporting Act permits a consumer to have his or her credit report revised to reflect the fact, for instance, that the involuntary bankruptcy case was dismissed prior to the entry of an order for relief, the report may, nevertheless, still refer to the filing of the case.[91]

Unfortunately, tax protesters and other extremists, in addition to other forms of obstreperous litigation (such as filing false liens), are now resorting to filing fraudulent involuntary bankruptcy petitions against public officials and other innocent parties. In 2002, for example, one tax protester filed fraudulent involuntary bankruptcy petitions against 36 local public officials in Wisconsin,[92] some of whom did not find out about the petitions until "they attempted to use a credit card or execute some other financial transaction."[93] These fraudulent involuntary petition filings were subsequently dismissed by the bankruptcy court, which found that they were filed in bad faith without legal basis and were commenced "for the sole purpose of harassment of the named public officials."[94] Nevertheless, "[d]espite the fact that the [fraudulent involuntary bankruptcy] petitions are often dismissed," as one State assistant attorney general observed, "the filings continue to cause financial problems for the victims."[95] The devastating effect of a fraudulent involuntary bankruptcy filing on an innocent person's credit rating is illustrated by what occurred in Wisconsin and its aftermath. Although the bankruptcy court in dismissing these cases also directed all credit reporting agencies to expunge any record of these filings from the officials' credit reports,[96] the bankruptcy petition filings nevertheless "caused some officials' credit cards to be

88 11 U.S.C. § 107(a).

89 15 U.S.C. § 1681.

90 15 U.S.C. § 1681c(a)(1).

91 *See, e.g.*, 15 U.S.C. § 1681i (2000); Letter from Ronald G. Isaac, Attorney, Federal Trade Commission—Division of Financial Practices/Bureau of Consumer Protection, to Anonymous (Nov. 5, 1999), available at *http://www.ftc.gov/os/statutes/frca/anon.htm*.

92 *See In re* Kenealy, No. 02-26100-MDM (Bankr. E.D. Wis. May 21, 2002). Involuntary petitions "were filed against all but one of the County Board supervisors," the county corporation counsel, county sheriff, clerk of courts, and county circuit judge. Jeff Cole, *Paperwork Used for Revenge; Protester's Bogus Bankruptcy Petitions Temporarily Disrupt Officials' Credit*, Milwaukee J. Sentinel, June 6, 2002, at 1B. The protester also filed numerous liens in the amount of $15 million against these individuals as well. Jeff Cole, *Man Charged with Filing False Documents; Town of Fredonia Protester's Case is 5th Brought by State*, Milwaukee J. Sentinel, May 21, 2002, at 1B.

93 Jeff Cole, *Paperwork Used for Revenge; Protester's Bogus Bankruptcy Petitions Temporarily Disrupt Officials' Credit*, Milwaukee J. Sentinel, June 6, 2002, at 1B.

94 *In re* Kenealy, No. 02-26100-MDM (Bankr. E.D. Wis. May 21, 2002).

95 Roy Korte, Terrorism: A Law Enforcement Perspective, Anti-Defamation League (2002), *available at http://www.adl.org/learn/columns/roy5%5korte.asp*.

96 *In re* Kenealy, No. 02-26100-MDM (Bankr. E.D. Wis. May 21, 2002).

canceled, almost caused the sale of one supervisor's house to be stopped, and caused continuing credit problems for other officials."[97]

Section 332 responds to these concerns by permitting the court to seal and subsequently expunge all records pertaining to a fraudulent involuntary petition. Section 332(a) sets forth the short title of the section as the "Involuntary Bankruptcy Improvement Act of 2005." Section 332(b) amends Bankruptcy Code section 303 to permit the court, upon motion of the debtor, to seal all court records pertaining to an involuntary bankruptcy petition if: (1) the petition is false or contains any materially false, fictitious, or fraudulent statement; (2) the debtor is an individual; and (3) the court dismisses the petition. The provision further permits the court, if the debtor is an individual, to prohibit any consumer reporting agency from making any consumer report that contains any information relating to such petition or to the case commenced by the filing of such petition. It further provides that upon the expiration of the statute of limitations described in 18 U.S.C. § 3282 for a violation of 18 U.S.C. § 152 (concerning crimes for concealment of assets, false oaths and claims, and bribery) and 18 U.S.C. § 157 (bankruptcy fraud), the court may, upon motion of the debtor and for good cause, expunge any records pertaining to such petition. Section 332(c) amends section 157 of title 18 to make it a criminal offense to file a fraudulent involuntary bankruptcy petition. Section 332 is similar to legislation considered by the House in the 108th Congress.[98]

TITLE IV. GENERAL AND SMALL BUSINESS BANKRUPTCY PROVISIONS

Subtitle A. General Business Bankruptcy Provisions

Sec. 401. Adequate Protection for Investors. Subsection (a) of section 401 of the Act amends section 101 of the Bankruptcy Code to define "securities self regulatory organization" as a securities association or national securities exchange registered with the Securities and Exchange Commission. Section 401(b) amends section 362 of the Bankruptcy Code to except from the automatic stay certain enforcement actions by a securities self regulatory organization.

Sec. 402. Meetings of Creditors and Equity Security Holders. Section 402 amends section 341 of the Bankruptcy Code to permit a court, on request of a party in interest and after notice and a hearing, to order the United States trustee not to convene a meeting of creditors or equity security holders if a debtor has filed a plan for which the debtor solicited acceptances prior to the commencement of the case.

Sec. 403. Protection of Refinance of Security Interest. Section 403 amends section 547(e)(2) of the Bankruptcy Code to increase the perfection period from ten to 30 days for the purpose of determining whether a transfer is an avoidable preference.

Sec. 404. Executory Contracts and Unexpired Leases. Subsection (a) of section 404 of the Act amends section 365(d)(4) of the Bankruptcy Code to establish a firm, bright line deadline by which an unexpired lease of nonresidential real property must be assumed or rejected. If such lease is not assumed or rejected by such deadline, then such lease shall be deemed rejected, and the trustee shall immediately surrender such property to the lessor. Section 404(a) permits a bankruptcy trustee to assume or reject a lease on a date which is the earlier of the date of confirmation of a plan or the date which is 120 days after the date of the order for relief. An extension of time may be granted, within the 120 day period, for an additional 90 days, for cause, upon motion of the trustee or lessor. Any subsequent extension can only be granted by the judge upon the prior written consent of the lessor either by the lessor's motion for an extension or on motion of the trustee, provided that the trustee has the prior written approval of the lessor. This provision is designed to remove the bankruptcy judge's discretion to grant extensions of the time for the retail debtor to decide whether to assume or reject a lease after a maximum possible period of 210 days from the time of entry of the order of relief. Beyond that maximum period, the judge has no authority to grant further time unless the lessor has agreed in writing to the extension.

Section 404(b) amends section 365(f)(1) to assure that section 365(f) does not override any part of section 365(b). Thus, section 404(b) makes a trustee's authority to assign an executory contract or unexpired lease subject not only to section 365(c), but also to section 365(b), which is given full effect. Therefore, for example, assumption or assignment of a lease of real property in a shopping center must be subject to the provisions of the lease, such as use clauses.

Sec. 405. Creditors and Equity Security Holders Committees. Subsection (a) of section 405 of the Act amends section 1102(a)(2) of the Bankruptcy Code to permit, after notice and a hearing, a court, on request of a party in interest, to order a change in a committee's membership if necessary to ensure adequate representation of creditors or equity security holders in a chapter 11 case. It specifies that the court may direct the United States trustee to increase the membership of a committee for the purpose of including a small business concern if the court determines that such creditor's

97 Jeff Cole, *"Paper Terrorist" Gets Five Years in Prison*, Milwaukee J. Sentinel, Jan. 18, 2003, at 1B.

98 H.R. 1529, 108th Cong. (2003). The bill was ordered favorably reported without amendment by the House Judiciary Committee, H.R. Rep. No. 108-110 (2003), and passed by voice vote by the House. 149 Cong. Rec. H5104 (daily ed. June 10, 2003). The principal difference between this legislation and section 332 of the Act is that the bill would have permitted the court to expunge the case upon dismissal of the fraudulent involuntary petition.

claim is of the kind represented by the committee and that, in the aggregate, is disproportionately large when compared to the creditor's annual gross revenue.

Section 405(b) requires the committee to give creditors having claims of the kind represented by the committee access to information. In addition, the committee must solicit and receive comments from these creditors and, pursuant to court order, make additional reports or disclosures available to them.

Sec. 406. Amendment to Section 546 of Title 11, United States Code. Section 406 of the Act corrects an erroneous subsection designation in section 546 of the Bankruptcy Code. It redesignates the second subsection (g) as subsection (i). In addition, section 406 amends section 546(i) (as redesignated) to subject that provision to the prior rights of security interest holders. Further, section 406 adds a new provision to section 546 that prohibits a trustee from avoiding a warehouse lien for storage, transportation, or other costs incidental to the storage and handling of goods. It specifies that this prohibition must be applied in a manner consistent with any applicable state statute that is similar to section 7-209 of the Uniform Commercial Code.

Sec. 407. Amendments to Section 330(a) of Title 11, United States Code. Section 407 amends section 330(a)(3) of the Bankruptcy Code to clarify that this provision applies to examiners, chapter 11 trustees, and professional persons. This section also amends section 330(a) to add a provision that requires a court, in determining the amount of reasonable compensation to award to a trustee, to treat such compensation as a commission pursuant to section 326 of the Bankruptcy Code.

Sec. 408. Postpetition Disclosure and Solicitation. Section 408 amends section 1125 of the Bankruptcy Code to permit an acceptance or rejection of a chapter 11 plan to be solicited from the holder of a claim or interest if the holder was solicited before the commencement of the case in a manner that complied with applicable nonbankruptcy law.

Sec. 409. Preferences. Section 409 amends section 547(c)(2) of the Bankruptcy Code to provide that a trustee may not avoid a transfer to the extent such transfer was in payment of a debt incurred by the debtor in the ordinary course of the business or financial affairs of the debtor and the transferee and such transfer was made either: (1) in the ordinary course of the debtor's and the transferee's business or financial affairs; or (2) in accordance with ordinary business terms. Present law requires the recipient of a preferential transfer to establish both of these grounds in order to sustain a defense to a preferential transfer proceeding. In a case in which the debts are not primarily consumer debts, section 409 provides that a transfer may not be avoided if the aggregate amount of all property constituting or affected by the transfer is less than $5,000.

Sec. 410. Venue of Certain Proceedings. Section 1409(b) of title 28 of the United States Code provides that a proceeding to recover a money judgment of, or property worth less than, certain specified amounts must be commenced in the district where the defendant resides. Section 410 amends section 1409(b) to provide that a proceeding to recover a debt (excluding a consumer debt) against a noninsider of the debtor that is less than $10,000 must be commenced in the district where the defendant resides. In addition, section 410 increases the $5,000 threshold for a consumer debt[99] to $15,000.

Sec. 411. Period for Filing Plan under Chapter 11. Section 411 amends section 1121(d) of the Bankruptcy Code to mandate that a debtor's exclusive period for filing a plan may not be extended beyond a date that is 18 months after the order for relief in the chapter 11 case. In addition, it provides that the debtor's exclusive period for obtaining acceptances of the plan may not be extended beyond 20 months after the order for relief.

Sec. 412. Fees Arising from Certain Ownership Interests. Section 412 amends section 523(a)(16) of the Bankruptcy Code to broaden the protections accorded to community associations with respect to fees or assessments arising from the debtor's interest in a condominium, cooperative, or homeowners' association. Irrespective of whether or not the debtor physically occupies such property, fees or assessments that accrue during the period the debtor or the trustee has a legal, equitable, or possessory ownership interest in such property are nondischargeable.

Sec. 413. Creditor Representation at First Meeting of Creditors. Section 413 amends section 341(c) of the Bankruptcy Code to permit a creditor holding a consumer debt or any representative of such creditor, notwithstanding any local court rule, provision of a state constitution, or any otherwise applicable nonbankruptcy law, or any other requirement that such creditor must be represented by counsel, to appear at and participate in a section 341 meeting of creditors in chapter 7 and chapter 13 cases either alone or in conjunction with an attorney. In addition, the provision clarifies that it cannot be construed to require a creditor to be represented by counsel at any meeting of creditors.

Sec. 414. Definition of Disinterested Person. Section 414 amends section 101(14) of the Bankruptcy Code to eliminate the requirement that an investment banker be a disinterested person.

Sec. 415. Factors for Compensation of Professional Persons. Section 415 amends section 330(a)(3) of the Bankruptcy Code to permit the court to consider, in awarding compensation to a professional person, whether such person

99 A consumer debt is defined as a "debt incurred by an individual primarily for a personal, family, or household purpose." 11 U.S.C. § 101(8).

is board certified or otherwise has demonstrated skill and experience in the practice of bankruptcy law.

Sec. 416. Appointment of Elected Trustee. Section 416 of the Act amends section 1104(b) of the Bankruptcy Code to clarify the procedure for the election of a trustee in a chapter 11 case. Section 1104(b) permits creditors to elect an eligible, disinterested person to serve as the trustee in the case, provided certain conditions are met. Section 416 amends this provision to require the United States trustee to file a report certifying the election of a chapter 11 trustee. Upon the filing of the report, the elected trustee is deemed to be selected and appointed for purposes of section 1104 and the service of any prior trustee appointed in the case is terminated. Section 416 also clarifies that the court shall resolve any dispute arising out of a chapter 11 trustee election.

Sec. 417. Utility Service. Section 417 amends section 366 of the Bankruptcy Code to provide that assurance of payment, for purposes of this provision, includes a cash deposit, letter of credit, certificate of deposit, surety bond, prepayment of utility consumption, or other form of security that is mutually agreed upon by the debtor or trustee and the utility. It also specifies that an administrative expense priority does not constitute an assurance of payment. With respect to chapter 11 cases, section 417 permits a utility to alter, refuse or discontinue service if it does not receive adequate assurance of payment that is satisfactory to the utility within 30 days of the filing of the petition. The court, upon request of a party in interest, may modify the amount of this payment after notice and a hearing. In determining the adequacy of such payment, a court may not consider: (1) the absence of security before the case was filed; (2) the debtor's timely payment of utility service charges before the case was filed; or (3) the availability of an administrative expense priority. Notwithstanding any other provision of law, section 417 permits a utility to recover or set off against a security deposit provided prepetition by the debtor to the utility without notice or court order.

Sec. 418. Bankruptcy Fees. Section 418 of the Act amends section 1930 of title 28 of the United States Code to permit a district court or a bankruptcy court, pursuant to procedures prescribed by the Judicial Conference of the United States, to waive the chapter 7 filing fee for an individual and certain other fees under subsections (b) and (c) of section 1930 if such individual's income is less than 150 percent of the official poverty level (as defined by the Office of Management and Budget) and the individual is unable to pay such fee in installments. Section 418 also clarifies that section 1930, as amended, does not prevent a district or bankruptcy court from waiving other fees for creditors and debtors, if in accordance with Judicial Conference policy.

Sec. 419. More Complete Information Regarding Assets of the Estate. Section 419 of the Act directs the Judicial Conference of the United States, after consideration of the views of the Director of the Executive Office for United States Trustees, to propose official rules and forms directing chapter 11 debtors to disclose information concerning the value, operations, and profitability of any closely held corporation, partnership, or other entity in which the debtor holds a substantial or controlling interest. Section 419 is intended to ensure that the debtor's interest in any of these entities is used for the payment of allowed claims against debtor.

Subtitle B. Small Business Bankruptcy Provisions

Sec. 431. Flexible Rules for Disclosure Statement and Plan. Section 431 of the Act amends section 1125 of the Bankruptcy Code to streamline the disclosure statement process and to provide for more flexibility. Section 431(1) amends section 1125(a)(1) of the Bankruptcy Code to require a bankruptcy court, in determining whether a disclosure statement supplies adequate information, to consider the complexity of the case, the benefit of additional information to creditors and other parties in interest, and the cost of providing such additional information. With regard to a small business case, section 431(2) amends section 1125(f) to permit the court to dispense with a disclosure statement if the plan itself supplies adequate information. In addition, it provides that the court may approve a disclosure statement submitted on standard forms approved by the court or adopted under section 2075 of title 28 of the United States Code. Further, section 431(2) provides that the court may conditionally approve a disclosure statement, subject to final approval after notice and a hearing, and allow the debtor to solicit acceptances of the plan based on such disclosure statement. The hearing on the disclosure statement may be combined with the confirmation hearing.

Sec. 432. Definitions. Section 432 of the Act amends section 101 of the Bankruptcy Code to define a "small business case" as a chapter 11 case in which the debtor is a small business debtor. Section 432, in turn, defines a "small business debtor" as a person engaged in commercial or business activities (including an affiliate of such person that is also a debtor, but excluding a person whose primary activity is the business of owning or operating real property or activities incidental thereto) having aggregate noncontingent, liquidated secured and unsecured debts of not more than $2 million (excluding debts owed to affiliates or insiders of the debtor) as of the date of the petition or the order for relief. This monetary definition applies only in a case where the United States trustee has not appointed a creditors' committee or where the court has determined that the creditors' committee is not sufficiently active and representative to provide effective oversight of the debtor. It does not apply to any member of a group of affiliated debtors that has aggregate noncontingent, liquidated secured and unsecured debts in excess of $2 million (excluding debts owed to one or more affiliates or insiders). This provision also requires this monetary figure to be periodically adjusted for inflation pursuant to section 104 of the Bankruptcy Code.

Sec. 433. Standard Form Disclosure Statement and Plan. Section 433 of the Act directs the Judicial Conference of the United States to propose for adoption standard form disclosure statements and reorganization plans for small business debtors. The provision requires the forms to achieve a practical balance between the needs of the court, case administrators, and other parties in interest to have reasonably complete information as well as the debtor's need for economy and simplicity.

Sec. 434. Uniform National Reporting Requirements. Subsection (a) of section 434 of the Act adds a provision to the Bankruptcy Code mandating additional reporting requirements for small business debtors. It requires a small business debtor to file periodic financial reports and other documents containing the following information with respect to the debtor's business operations: (1) profitability; (2) reasonable approximations of projected cash receipts and disbursements; (3) comparisons of actual cash receipts and disbursements with projections in prior reports; (4) whether the debtor is complying with postpetition requirements pursuant to the Bankruptcy Code and Federal Rules of Bankruptcy Procedure; (5) whether the debtor is timely filing tax returns and other government filings; and (6) whether the debtor is paying taxes and other administrative expenses when due. In addition, the debtor must report on such other matters that are in the best interests of the debtor and the creditors and in the public interest. If the debtor is not in compliance with any postpetition requirements pursuant to the Bankruptcy Code and Federal Rules of Bankruptcy Procedure, or is not filing tax returns or other required governmental filings, paying taxes and other administrative expenses when due, the debtor must report: (1) what the failures are, (2) how they will be cured; (3) the cost of their cure; and (4) when they will be cured. Section 434(b) specifies that the effective date of this provision is 60 days after the date on which the rules required under this provision are promulgated.

Sec. 435. Uniform Reporting Rules and Forms for Small Business Cases. Subsection (a) of section 435 of the Act directs the Judicial Conference of the United States to propose official rules and forms with respect to the periodic financial reports and other information that a small business debtor must file concerning its profitability, cash receipts and disbursements, filing of its tax returns, and payment of its taxes and other administrative expenses.

Section 435(b) requires the rules and forms to achieve a practical balance between the need for reasonably complete information by the bankruptcy court, United States trustee, creditors and other parties in interest, and the small business debtor's interest in having such forms be easy and inexpensive to complete. The forms should also be designed to help the small business debtor better understand its financial condition and plan its future.

Sec. 436. Duties in Small Business Cases. Section 436 of the Act is intended to implement greater administrative oversight and controls over small business chapter 11. The provision requires a chapter 11 trustee or debtor to:

1. file with a voluntary petition (or in an involuntary case, within seven days from the date of the order for relief) the debtor's most recent financial statements (including a balance sheet, statement of operations, cash flow statement, and Federal income tax return) or a statement explaining why such information is not available;
2. attend, through its senior management personnel and counsel, meetings scheduled by the bankruptcy court or the United States trustee (including the initial debtor interview and meeting of creditors pursuant to section 341 of the Bankruptcy Code), unless the court waives this requirement after notice and a hearing upon a finding of extraordinary and compelling circumstances;
3. timely file all requisite schedules and the statement of financial affairs, unless the court, after notice and a hearing, grants an extension of up to 30 days from the order of relief, absent extraordinary and compelling circumstances;
4. file all postpetition financial and other reports required by the Federal Rules of Bankruptcy Procedure or by local rule of the district court;
5. maintain insurance that is customary and appropriate for the industry, subject to section 363(c)(2);
6. timely file tax returns and other required government filings;
7. timely pay all administrative expense taxes (except for certain contested claims), subject to section 363(c)(2); and
8. permit the United States trustee to inspect the debtor's business premises, books, and records at reasonable hours after appropriate prior written notice, unless notice is waived by the debtor.

Sec. 437. Plan Filing and Confirmation Deadlines. Section 437 of the Act amends section 1121(e) of the Bankruptcy Code with respect to the period of time within which a small business debtor must file and confirm a plan of reorganization. This provision provides that a small business debtor's exclusive period to file a plan is 180 days from the date of the order for relief, unless the period is extended after notice and a hearing, or the court, for cause, orders otherwise. It further provides that a small business debtor must file a plan and any disclosure statement not later than 300 days after the order for relief. These time periods and the time fixed in section 1129(e) may be extended only if: (1) the debtor, after providing notice to parties in interest, demonstrates by a preponderance of the evidence that it is more likely than not that the court will confirm a plan within a reasonable period of time; (2) a new deadline is imposed at the time the extension is granted; and (3) the order granting such extension is signed before the expiration of the existing deadline.

Sec. 438. Plan Confirmation Deadline. Section 438 of the Act amends Bankruptcy Code section 1129 to require the court to confirm a plan not later than 45 days after it is filed if the plan complies with the applicable provisions of the Bankruptcy Code, unless this period is extended pursuant to section 1121(e)(3).

Sec. 439. Duties of the United States Trustee. Section 439 of the Act amends section 586(a) of title 28 of the United States Code to require the United States trustee to perform the following additional duties with respect to small business debtors:

1. conduct an initial debtor interview before the meeting of creditors for the purpose of (a) investigating the debtor's viability, (b) inquiring about the debtor's business plan, (c) explaining the debtor's obligation to file monthly operating reports, (d) attempting to obtain an agreed scheduling order setting various time frames (such as the date for filing a plan and effecting confirmation), and (e) informing the debtor of other obligations;
2. if determined to be appropriate and advisable, inspect the debtor's business premises for the purpose of reviewing the debtor's books and records and verifying that the debtor has filed its tax returns;
3. review and monitor diligently the debtor's activities to determine as promptly as possible whether the debtor will be unable to confirm a plan; and
4. promptly apply to the court for relief in any case in which the United States trustee finds material grounds for dismissal or conversion of the case.

Sec. 440. Scheduling Conferences. Section 440 amends section 105(d) of the Bankruptcy Code to mandate that a bankruptcy court hold status conferences as are necessary to further the expeditious and economical resolution of a bankruptcy case.

Sec. 441. Serial Filer Provisions. Paragraph (1) of section 441 of the Act amends section 362 of the Bankruptcy Code to provide that a court may award only actual damages for a violation of the automatic stay committed by an entity in the good faith belief that subsection (h) of section 362 (as amended) applies to the debtor. Section 441(2) adds a new subsection to section 362 of the Bankruptcy Code specifying that the automatic stay does not apply where the chapter 11 debtor: (1) is a debtor in a small business case pending at the time the subsequent case is filed; (2) was a debtor in a small business case dismissed for any reason pursuant to an order that became final in the two-year period ending on the date of the order for relief entered in the pending case; (3) was a debtor in small business case in which a plan was confirmed in the two-year period ending on the date of the order for relief entered in the pending case; or (4) is an entity that has acquired substantially all of the assets or business of a small business debtor described in the preceding paragraphs, unless such entity establishes by a preponderance of the evidence that it acquired the assets or business in good faith and not for the purpose of evading this provision.

An exception to this provision applies to a chapter 11 case that is commenced involuntarily and involves no collusion between the debtor and the petitioning creditors. Also, it does not apply if the debtor proves by a preponderance of the evidence that: (1) the filing of the subsequent case resulted from circumstances beyond the debtor's control and which were not foreseeable at the time the prior case was filed; and (2) it is more likely than not that the court will confirm a feasible plan of reorganization (but not a liquidating plan) within a reasonable time.

Sec. 442. Expanded Grounds for Dismissal or Conversion and Appointment of Trustee. Subsection (a) of section 442 of the Act amends section 1112(b) of the Bankruptcy Code to mandate that the court convert or dismiss a chapter 11 case, whichever is in the best interests of creditors and the estate, if the movant establishes cause, absent unusual circumstances. In this regard, the court must specify the circumstances that support the court's finding that conversion or dismissal is not in the best interests of creditors and the estate.

In addition, the provision specifies an exception to the provision's mandatory requirement applies if: (1) the debtor or a party in interest objects and establishes that there is a reasonable likelihood that a plan will be confirmed within the time periods set forth in sections 1121(e) and 1129(e), or if these provisions are inapplicable, within a reasonable period of time; (2) the grounds for granting such relief include an act or omission of the debtor for which there exists a reasonable justification for such act or omission; and (3) such act or omission will be cured within a reasonable period of time.

The court must commence the hearing on a section 1112(b) motion within 30 days of its filing and decide the motion not later than 15 days after commencement of the hearing unless the movant expressly consents to a continuance for a specified period of time or compelling circumstances prevent the court from meeting these time limits. Section 442 provides that the term "cause" under section 1112(b), as amended by this provision, includes the following:

1. substantial or continuing loss to or diminution of the estate and the absence of a reasonable likelihood of rehabilitation;
2. gross mismanagement of the estate;
3. failure to maintain appropriate insurance that poses a material risk to the estate or the public;

4. unauthorized use of cash collateral that is harmful to one or more creditors;
5. failure to comply with a court order;
6. unexcused failure to timely satisfy any filing or reporting requirement under the Bankruptcy Code or applicable rule;
7. failure to attend the section 341 meeting of creditors or an examination pursuant to rule 2004 of the Federal Rules of Bankruptcy Procedure, without good cause shown by the debtor;
8. failure to timely provide information or to attend meetings reasonably requested by the United States trustee or bankruptcy administrator;
9. failure to timely pay taxes owed after the order for relief or to file tax returns due postpetition;
10. failure to file a disclosure statement or to confirm a plan within the time fixed by the Bankruptcy Code or pursuant to court order;
11. failure to pay any requisite fees or charges under chapter 123 of title 28 of the United States Code;
12. revocation of a confirmation order;
13. inability to effectuate substantial consummation of a confirmed plan;
14. material default by the debtor with respect to a confirmed plan;
15. termination of a plan by reason of the occurrence of a condition specified in the plan; and
16. the debtor's failure to pay any domestic support obligation that first becomes payable postpetition.

Section 442(b) creates an additional ground for the appointment of a chapter 11 trustee or examiner under section 1104(a). It provides that should the bankruptcy court determine cause exists to convert or dismiss a chapter 11 case, it may appoint a trustee or examiner if it is in the best interests of creditors and the bankruptcy estate.

Section 442(b) is designed to benefit creditors when a chapter 11 case would otherwise be dismissed or converted to a chapter 7 case pursuant to section 1112 of the Bankruptcy Code. Section 442(b) allows the court to appoint a chapter 11 trustee or examiner, as an alternative to dismissing or converting the case to chapter 7, if in the best interest of creditors and the bankruptcy estate. Section 442(b) is not intended to ease the standards for appointing chapter 11 trustees. Practice under Chapter X of the Bankruptcy Act of 1898 demonstrated that routine appointment of trustees deters the use of reorganization statutes and increases the likelihood that by the time a company resorts to bankruptcy relief, it must liquidate. It is therefore important for section 442(b) to be used only for cases that would otherwise be dismissed or converted to chapter 7, and not as an alternative method for attaining the appointment of a chapter 11 trustee.

Sec. 443. Study of Operation of Title 11, United States Code, with Respect to Small Businesses. Section 443 of the Act directs the Administrator of the Small Business Administration, in consultation with the Attorney General, the Director of the Executive Office for United States Trustees, and the Director of the Administrative Office of the United States Courts, to conduct a study to determine: (1) the internal and external factors that cause small businesses (particularly sole proprietorships) to seek bankruptcy relief and the factors that cause small businesses to successfully complete their chapter 11 cases; and (2) how the bankruptcy laws may be made more effective and efficient in assisting small business to remain viable.

Sec. 444. Payment of Interest. Paragraph (1) of section 444 of the Act amends section 362(d)(3) of the Bankruptcy Code to require a court to grant relief from the automatic stay within 30 days after it determines that a single asset real estate debtor is subject to this provision. Section 444(2) amends section 362(d)(3)(B) to specify that relief from the automatic stay shall be granted unless the single asset real estate debtor has commenced making monthly payments to each creditor secured by the debtor's real property (other than a claim secured by a judgment lien or unmatured statutory lien) in an amount equal to the interest at the then applicable nondefault contract rate of interest on the value of the creditor's interest in the real estate. It allows a debtor in its sole discretion to make the requisite interest payments out of rents or other proceeds generated by the real property, notwithstanding section 363(c)(2).

Sec. 445. Priority for Administrative Expenses. Section 445 of the Act amends section 503(b) of the Bankruptcy Code to add a new administrative expense priority for a nonresidential real property lease that is assumed under section 365 and then subsequently rejected. The amount of the priority is the sum of all monetary obligations due under the lease (excluding penalties and obligations arising from or relating to a failure to operate) for the two-year period following the rejection date or actual turnover of the premises (whichever is later), without reduction or setoff for any reason, except for sums actually received or to be received from a nondebtor. Any remaining sums due for the balance of the term of the lease are treated as a claim under section 502(b)(6) of the Bankruptcy Code.

Sec. 446. Duties with Respect to a Debtor Who Is a Plan Administrator of an Employee Benefit Plan. Subsection (a) of section 446 of the Act amends Bankruptcy Code section 521(a) to require a debtor, unless a trustee is serving in the case, to serve as the administrator (as defined in the Employee Retirement Income Security Act of 1974) of an employee benefit plan if the debtor served in such capacity at the time the case was filed. Section 446(b) amends Bankruptcy Code section 704 to require the chapter 7 trustee to perform the obligations of such administrator in a case where the debtor or an entity designated by the debtor was required to perform such obligations. Section 446(c) amends Bankruptcy Code section 1106(a) to require a chapter 11 trustee to perform these obligations.

Sec. 447. Appointment of Committee of Retired Employees. This provision amends section 1114(d) of the Bankruptcy Code to clarify that it is the responsibility of the United States trustee to appoint members to a committee of retired employees.

TITLE V. MUNICIPAL BANKRUPTCY PROVISIONS

Sec. 501. Petition and Proceedings Related to Petition. Section 501 amends sections 921(d) and 301 of the Bankruptcy Code to clarify that the court must enter the order for relief in a chapter 9 case.

Sec. 502. Applicability of Other Sections to Chapter 9. Section 502 of the of the Act amends section 901 of the Bankruptcy Code to make the following sections applicable to chapter 9 cases:

1. section 555 (contractual right to liquidate, terminate or accelerate a securities contract);
2. section 556 (contractual right to liquidate, terminate or accelerate a commodities or forward contract);
3. section 559 (contractual right to liquidate, terminate or accelerate a repurchase agreement);
4. section 560 (contractual right to liquidate, terminate or accelerate a swap agreement);
5. section 561 (contractual right to liquidate, terminate, accelerate, or offset under a master netting agreement and across contracts); and
6. section 562 (damage measure in connection with swap agreements, securities contracts, forward contracts, commodity contracts, repurchase agreements, or master netting agreement).

TITLE VI. BANKRUPTCY DATA

Sec. 601. Improved Bankruptcy Statistics. This provision amends chapter 6 of title 28 of the United States Code to require the clerk for each district (or the bankruptcy court clerk if one has been certified pursuant to section 156(b) of title 28 of the United States Code) to collect certain statistics for chapter 7, 11, and 13 cases in a standardized format prescribed by the Director of the Administrative Office of the United States Courts and to make this information available to the public. Not later than July 1, 2008, the Director must submit a report to Congress concerning the statistical information collected and then must report annually thereafter. The statistics must be itemized by chapter of the Bankruptcy Code and be presented in the aggregate for each district. The specific categories of information that must be gathered include the following:

1. scheduled total assets and liabilities of debtors who are individuals with primarily consumer debts under chapters 7, 11 and 13 by category;
2. such debtors' current monthly income, average income, and average expenses;
3. the aggregate amount of debts discharged during the reporting period based on the difference between the total amount of scheduled debts and by categories that are predominantly nondischargeable;
4. the average time between the filing of the bankruptcy case and the closing of the case;
5. the number of cases in which reaffirmation agreements were filed, the total number of reaffirmation agreements filed, the number of cases in which the debtor was pro se and a reaffirmation agreement was filed, and the number of cases in which the reaffirmation agreement was approved by the court;
6. for chapter 13 cases, information on the number of: (a) final orders determining the value of secured property in an amount less than the amount of the secured claim, (b) final orders that determined the value of property securing a claim, (c) cases dismissed, (d) cases dismissed for failure to make payments under the plan, (e) cases refiled after dismissal, (f) cases in which the plan was completed (separately itemized with respect to the number of modifications made before completion of the plan, and (g) cases in which the debtor had previously sought bankruptcy relief within the six years preceding the filing of the present case;
7. the number of cases in which creditors were fined for misconduct and the amount of any punitive damages awarded for creditor misconduct; and
8. the number of cases in which sanctions under rule 9011 of the Federal Rules of Bankruptcy Procedure were imposed against a debtor's counsel and the damages awarded under this rule.

Section 601 provides that the amendments in this provision take effect 18 months after the date of enactment of this Act.

Sec. 602. Uniform Rules for the Collection of Bankruptcy Data. Section 602 of the Act amends chapter 39 of title 28 of the United States Code to require the Attorney General to promulgate rules mandating the establishment of uniform forms for final reports in chapter 7, 12 and 13 cases and periodic reports in chapter 11 cases. This provision also specifies that these reports be designed to facilitate compilation of data and to provide maximum public access by physical inspection at one or more central filing locations and by electronic access through the Internet or other appropriate media. The information should enable an evaluation of the efficiency and practicality of the bankruptcy system. In issuing rules, the Attorney General must consider: (1) the reasonable needs of the public for information about the Federal bankruptcy system; (2) the economy, simplicity, and lack of undue burden on persons obligated to file the reports; and (3) appropriate privacy concerns and safeguards.

Section 602 provides that final reports by trustees in chapter 7, 12, and 13 cases include the following information: (1) the length of time the case was pending; (2) assets abandoned; (3) assets exempted; (4) receipts and disbursements of the estate; (5) administrative expenses, including those associated with section 707(b) of the Bankruptcy Code, and the actual costs of administering chapter 13 cases; (6) claims asserted; (7) claims allowed; and (8) distributions to claimants and claims discharged without payment. With regard to chapter 11 cases, section 602 provides that periodic reports include the following information regarding:

1. the industry classification for businesses conducted by the debtor, as published by the Department of Commerce;
2. the length of time that the case was pending;
3. the number of full-time employees as of the date of the order for relief and at the end of each reporting period;
4. cash receipts, cash disbursements, and profitability of the debtor for the most recent period and cumulatively from the date of the order for relief;
5. the debtor's compliance with the Bankruptcy Code, including whether tax returns have been filed and taxes have been paid;
6. professional fees approved by the court for the most recent period and cumulatively from the date of the order for relief; and
7. plans filed and confirmed, including the aggregate recoveries of holders by class and as a percentage of total claims of an allowed class.

Sec. 603. Audit Procedures. Subsection (a)(1) of section 603 of the Act requires the Attorney General (for judicial districts served by United States trustees) and the Judicial Conference of the United States (for judicial districts served by bankruptcy administrators) to establish procedures to determine the accuracy, veracity, and completeness of petitions, schedules and other information filed by debtors pursuant to sections 111, 521 and 1322 of the Bankruptcy Code. Section 603(a)(1) requires the audits to be conducted in accordance with generally accepted auditing standards and performed by independent certified public accountants or independent licensed public accountants. It permits the Attorney General and the Judicial Conference to develop alternative auditing standards not later than two years after the date of enactment of this Act. Section 603(a)(2) requires these procedures to: (1) establish a method of selecting appropriate qualified contractors to perform these audits; (2) establish a method of randomly selecting cases for audit, and that a minimum of at least one case out of every 250 cases be selected for audit; (3) require audits in cases where the schedules of income and expenses reflect greater than average variances from the statistical norm for the district if they occur by reason of higher income or higher expenses than the statistical norm in which the schedules were filed; and (4) require the aggregate results of such audits, including the percentage of cases by district in which a material misstatement of income or expenditures is reported, to be made available to the public on an annual basis.

Section 603(b) amends section 586 of title 28 of the United States Code to require the United States trustee to submit reports as directed by the Attorney General, including the results of audits performed under section 603(a). In addition, it authorizes the United States trustee to contract with auditors to perform the audits specified in this provision. Further, it requires the report of each audit to be filed with the court and transmitted to the United States trustee. The report must specify material misstatements of income, expenditures or assets. In a case where a material misstatement has been reported, the clerk must provide notice of such misstatement to creditors and the United States trustee must report it to the United States Attorney, if appropriate, for possible criminal prosecution. If advisable, the United States trustee must also take appropriate action, such as revoking the debtor's discharge.

Section 603(c) amends section 521 of the Bankruptcy Code to make it a duty of the debtor to cooperate with an auditor. Section 603(d) amends section 727 of the Bankruptcy Code to add, as a ground for revocation of a chapter 7 discharge the debtor's failure to: (a) satisfactorily explain a material misstatement discovered as the result of an audit pursuant to this provision; or (b) make available for inspection all necessary documents or property belonging to the debtor that are requested in connection with such audit. Section 603(e) provides that the amendments made by this provision take effect 18 months after the Act's date of enactment.

Sec. 604. Sense of Congress Regarding Availability of Bankruptcy Data. Section 604 expresses a sense of the Congress that it is a national policy of the United States that all data collected by bankruptcy clerks in electronic form (to the extent such data relates to public records pursuant to section 107 of the Bankruptcy Code) should be made available to the public in a useable electronic form in bulk, subject to appropriate privacy concerns and safeguards as determined by the Judicial Conference of the United States. It also states that a uniform bankruptcy data system should be established that uses a single set of data definitions and forms to collect such data and that data for any particular bankruptcy case should be aggregated in electronic format.

TITLE VII. BANKRUPTCY TAX PROVISIONS

Sec. 701. Treatment of Certain Tax Liens. Subsection (a) of section 701 of the Act makes several amendments to section 724 of the Bankruptcy Code to provide greater protection for holders of tax liens on real or personal property of the estate, particularly holders of *ad valorem* tax liens. Many school boards obtain liens on real property to ensure collection of unpaid *ad valorem* taxes. Under current law, local governments are sometimes unable to collect these taxes despite the presence of a lien because they may be subordinated to certain claims and expenses as a result of section 724. Pursuant to section 701(a), subordination of *ad valorem* tax liens is still possible under section 724(b), but limited to the payment of: (1) claims for wages, salaries, and commissions entitled to priority under section 507(a)(4); and (2) claims for contributions to employee benefit plans entitled to priority under section 507(a)(5). Section 701(a) will also protect the holders of these tax liens as well as Federal tax liens from erosion of their claims' status by expenses incurred under chapter 11 of the Bankruptcy Code. Before a tax lien on real or personal property may be subordinated pursuant to section 724, the chapter 7 trustee must exhaust all other unencumbered estate assets and, consistent with section 506, recover reasonably necessary costs and expenses of preserving or disposing of such property.

Section 701(b) amends section 505(a)(2) of the Bankruptcy Code to prevent a bankruptcy court from determining the amount or legality of an *ad valorem* tax on real or personal property if the applicable period for contesting or redetermining the amount of the claim under nonbankruptcy law has expired.

Sec. 702. Treatment of Fuel Tax Claims. Section 702 of the Act amends section 501 of the Bankruptcy Code to simplify the process for filing of claims by states for certain fuel taxes. Rather than requiring each state to file a claim for these taxes (as is the case under current law), section 702 permits the designated "base jurisdiction" under the International Fuel Tax Agreement to file a claim on behalf of all states, which would then be allowed as a single claim.

Sec. 703. Notice of Request for a Determination of Taxes. Under current law, a trustee or debtor in possession may request a governmental unit to determine administrative tax liabilities in order to receive a discharge of those liabilities. There are no requirements as to the content or form of such notice to the government. Section 703 of the Act amends section 505(b) of the Bankruptcy Code to require the clerk of each district to maintain a list of addresses designated by governmental units for service of section 505 requests. In addition, the list may also include information concerning filing requirements specified by such governmental units. If a governmental entity does not designate an address and provide that address to the bankruptcy court clerk, any request made under section 505(b) of the Bankruptcy Code may be served at the address for the filing of a tax return or protest of the appropriate taxing authority of that governmental unit.

Sec. 704. Rate of Interest on Tax Claims. Under current law, there is no uniform rate of interest applicable to tax claims. As a result, varying standards have been used to determine the applicable rate. Section 704 of the Act amends the Bankruptcy Code to add section 511 for the purpose of simplifying the interest rate calculation. It provides that for all tax claims (federal, state, and local), including administrative expense taxes, the interest rate shall be determined in accordance with applicable nonbankruptcy law. With respect to taxes paid under a confirmed plan, the rate of interest is determined as of the calendar month in which the plan is confirmed.

Sec. 705. Priority of Tax Claims. Under current law, a tax claim is entitled to be treated as a priority claim if it arises within certain specified time periods. In the case of income taxes, a priority arises, among other time periods, if the tax return was due within three years of the filing of the bankruptcy petition or if the assessment of the tax was made within 240 days of the filing of the petition. The 240-day period is tolled during the time that an offer in compromise is pending (plus 30 days). Though the statute is silent, the Supreme Court in *Young v. United States*, 535 U.S. 93 (2002) held that the three-year period is tolled during the pendency of a previous bankruptcy case. Section 705 amends section 507(a)(8) of the Bankruptcy Code to codify the rule tolling priority periods during the pendency of a previous bankruptcy case during that three-year or 240-day period together with an additional 90 days. It also includes tolling provisions to adjust for the collection due process rights provided by the Internal Revenue Service Restructuring and Reform Act of 1998. During any period in which the government is prohibited from collecting a tax as a result of a request by the debtor for a hearing and an appeal of any collection action taken against the debtor, the priority is tolled, plus 90 days. Also, during any time in which there was a stay of proceedings in a prior bankruptcy case or collection of an income tax was precluded by a confirmed bankruptcy plan, the priority is tolled, plus 90 days.

Sec. 706. Priority Property Taxes Incurred. Under current law, many provisions of the Bankruptcy Code are keyed to the word "assessed." While this term has an accepted meaning in the Federal system, it is not used in many state and local statutes and has created some confusion. To eliminate this problem with respect to real property taxes, section 706 amends section 507(a)(8)(B) of the Bankruptcy Code by replacing the word "assessed" with "incurred."

Sec. 707. No Discharge of Fraudulent Taxes in Chapter 13. Under current law, a debtor's ability to discharge tax debts varies depending on whether the debtor is in chapter 7 or chapter 13. In a chapter 7 case, taxes that are not dischargeable include taxes from a return due within three years of the petition date, taxes assessed within 240 days, or taxes related to an unfiled return or false return. Chapter 13, on the other hand, allows these obligations to be discharged. Section 707 of the Act amends Bankruptcy Code section 1328(a)(2) to prohibit the discharge of tax claims described in section 523(a)(1)(B) and (C) as well as claims for a tax required to be collected or withheld and for which the debtor is liable in whatever capacity pursuant to section 507(a)(8)(C).

Sec. 708. No Discharge of Fraudulent Taxes in Chapter 11. Under current law, the confirmation of a chapter 11 plan discharges a corporate debtor from most debts. Section 708 amends section 1141(d) of the Bankruptcy Code to except from discharge in a corporate chapter 11 case a debt specified in subsections 523(a)(2)(A) or (B) of the Bankruptcy Code owed to a domestic governmental unit. In addition, it excepts from discharge a debt owed to a person as the result of an action filed under subchapter III of chapter 37 of title 31 of the United States Code or any similar state statute. Section 708 excepts from discharge a debt for a tax or customs duty with respect to which the debtor made a fraudulent tax return or willfully attempted in any manner to evade or defeat such tax.

Sec. 709. Stay of Tax Proceedings Limited to Prepetition Taxes. Under current law, the filing of a petition for relief under the Bankruptcy Code activates an automatic stay that enjoins the commencement or continuation of a case in the United States Tax Court. This rule was arguably extended in *Halpern v. Commissioner*,[100] which held that the tax court did not have jurisdiction to hear a case involving a postpetition year. To address this issue, section 709 of the Act amends section 362(a)(8) of the Bankruptcy Code to specify that the automatic stay is limited to an individual debtor's prepetition taxes (taxes incurred before entering bankruptcy). The amendment clarifies that the automatic stay does not apply to an individual debtor's postpetition taxes. In addition, section 709 provides that the stay applies to both prepetition and postpetition tax liabilities of a corporation so long as it is a liability that the bankruptcy court may determine.

Sec. 710. Periodic Payment of Taxes in Chapter 11 Cases. Section 710 of the Act amends section 1129(a)(9) of the Bankruptcy Code to provide that the allowed amount of priority tax claims (as of the plan's effective date) must be paid in regular cash installments within five years from the entry of the order for relief. The manner of payment may not be less favorable than that accorded the most favored nonpriority unsecured claim provided for by the plan (other than cash payments made to a class of creditors under section 1122(b)). In addition, it requires the same payment treatment to be accorded to a secured claim that would otherwise meet the description of an unsecured claim under section 507(a)(8).

Sec. 711. Avoidance of Statutory Liens Prohibited. The Internal Revenue Code gives special protections to certain purchasers of securities and motor vehicles notwithstanding the existence of a filed tax lien. Section 711 of the Act amends section 545(2) of the Bankruptcy Code to prevent that provision's special protections from being used to avoid an otherwise valid lien. Specifically, it prevents the avoidance of unperfected liens against a bona fide purchaser, if the purchaser qualifies as such under section 6323 of the Internal Revenue Code or a similar provision under state or local law.

Sec. 712. Payment of Taxes in the Conduct of Business. Although current law generally requires trustees and receivers to pay taxes in the ordinary course of the debtor's business, the payment of administrative expenses must first be authorized by the court. Section 712(a) of the Act amends section 960 of title 28 of the United States Code to clarify that postpetition taxes in the ordinary course of business must be paid on or before when such tax is due under applicable nonbankruptcy law, with certain exceptions. This requirement does not apply if the obligation is a property tax secured by a lien against property that is abandoned under section 554 within a reasonable time after the lien attaches. In addition, the requirement does not pertain where the payment is excused under the Bankruptcy Code. With respect to chapter 7 cases, section 712(a) provides that the payment of a tax claim may be deferred until final distribution pursuant to section 726 if the tax was not incurred by a chapter 7 trustee or if the court, prior to the due date of the tax, finds that the estate has insufficient funds to pay all administrative expenses in full. Section 712(b) amends section 503(b)(1)(B)(i) of the Bankruptcy Code to clarify that this provision applies to secured as well as unsecured tax claims, including property taxes based on liability that is *in rem*, *in personam* or both. Section 712(c) amends section 503(b)(1) to exempt a governmental unit from the requirement to file a request for payment of an administrative expense. Section 712(d)(1) amends section 506(b) to provide that to the extent that an allowed claim is oversecured, the holder is entitled to interest and any reasonable fees, costs, or charges provided for under state law. Section 712(d)(2), in turn, amends section 506(c) to permit a trustee to recover from a secured creditor the payment of all *ad valorem* property taxes.

Sec. 713. Tardily Filed Priority Tax Claims. Section 713 of the Act amends section 726(a)(1) of the Bankruptcy Code to require a claim under section 507 that is not timely filed pursuant to section 501 to be entitled to a distribution if such claim is filed the earlier of the date that is ten days following the mailing to creditors of the summary of the trustee's final report or before the trustee commences final distribution.

Sec. 714. Income Tax Returns Prepared by Tax Authorities. Section 714 of the Act amends section 523(a) of the Bankruptcy Code to provide that a return prepared pursuant to section 6020(a) of the Internal Revenue Code, or similar State or local law, constitutes filing a return (and the debt can be discharged), but that a return filed on behalf of a

100 96 T.C. 895 (1991).

taxpayer pursuant to section 6020(b) of the Internal Revenue Code, or similar State or local law, does not constitute filing a return (and the debt cannot be discharged).

Sec. 715. Discharge of the Estate's Liability for Unpaid Taxes. Under the Bankruptcy Code, a trustee or debtor in possession may request a prompt audit to determine post-petition tax liabilities incurred by the bankruptcy estate. If the government does not make a determination or request an extension of time to audit, then the trustee or debtor in possession is discharged from any such tax liability. Several court cases have held that while this protects the debtor and the trustee, it does not necessarily protect the estate. Section 715 of the Act amends section 505(b) of the Bankruptcy Code to clarify that the estate is also protected if the government does not make a determination or request an extension of time to audit the debtor's tax returns. Therefore, if the government does not make a determination of post-petition tax liabilities or request extension of time to audit, then the estate's liability for unpaid taxes is discharged.

Sec. 716. Requirement to File Tax Returns to Confirm Chapter 13 Plans. Under current law, a debtor may enjoy the benefits of chapter 13 even if delinquent in the filing of tax returns. Section 716 of the Act responds to this problem. Subsection (a) amends section 1325(a) of the Bankruptcy Code to require a chapter 13 debtor to file all applicable Federal, state, and local tax returns as a condition of confirmation as required by section 1308 (as added by section 716(b)). Section 716(b) adds section 1308 to chapter 13 to require a chapter 13 debtor to be current on the filing of tax returns for the four-year period preceding the filing of the case. If the returns are not filed by the date on which the meeting of creditors is first scheduled, the trustee may hold open that meeting for a reasonable period of time to allow the debtor to file any unfiled returns. The additional period of time may not extend beyond 120 days after the date of the meeting of the creditors or beyond the date on which the return is due under the last automatic extension of time for filing. The debtor, however, may obtain an extension of time from the court if the debtor demonstrates by a preponderance of the evidence that the failure to file was attributable to circumstances beyond the debtor's control.

Section 716(c) amends section 1307 of the Bankruptcy Code to provide that if a chapter 13 debtor fails to file a tax return as required by section 1308, the court must dismiss the case or convert it to one under chapter 7 (whichever is in the best interests of creditors and the estate) on request of a party in interest or the United States trustee after notice and a hearing.

Section 716(d) amends section 502(b)(9) of the Bankruptcy Code to provide that in a chapter 13 case, a governmental unit's tax claim based on a return filed under section 1308 shall be deemed to be timely filed if the claim is filed within 60 days from the date on which such return is filed. Section 716(e) states the sense of the Congress that the Judicial Conference of the United States should propose for adoption official rules with respect an objection by a governmental unit to confirmation of a chapter 13 plan when such claim pertains to a tax return filed pursuant to section 1308.

Sec. 717. Standards for Tax Disclosure. Before creditors and stockholders may be solicited to vote on a chapter 11 plan, the plan proponent must file a disclosure statement that provides adequate information to holders of claims and interests so they can make a decision as to whether or not to vote in favor of the plan. As the tax consequences of a plan can have a significant impact on the debtor's reorganization prospects, section 717 amends section 1125(a) of the Bankruptcy Code to require that a chapter 11 disclosure statement discuss the plan's potential material Federal tax consequences to the debtor, any successor to the debtor, and to a hypothetical investor that is representative of the claimants and interest holders in the case.

Sec. 718. Setoff of Tax Refunds. Under current law, the filing of a bankruptcy petition automatically stays the setoff of a prepetition tax refund against a prepetition tax obligation unless the bankruptcy court approves the setoff. Interest and penalties that may continue to accrue may also be nondischargeable pursuant to section 523(a)(1) of the Bankruptcy Code and cause individual debtors undue hardship. Section 718 of the Act amends section 362(b) of the Bankruptcy Code to create an exception to the automatic stay whereby such setoff could occur without court order unless it would not be permitted under applicable nonbankruptcy law because of a pending action to determine the amount or legality of the tax liability. In that circumstance, the governmental authority may hold the refund pending resolution of the action, unless the court, on motion of the trustee and after notice and a hearing, grants the taxing authority adequate protection pursuant to section 361.

Sec. 719. Special Provisions Related to the Treatment of State and Local Taxes. Section 719 of the Act conforms state and local income tax administrative issues to the Internal Revenue Code. For example, under Federal law, a bankruptcy petitioner filing on March 5 has two tax years (January 1 to March 4, and March 5 to December 31). Under the Bankruptcy Code, however, state and local tax years are divided differently (January 1 to March 5, and March 6 to December 31). Section 719 requires the states to follow the Federal convention. It conforms state and local tax administration to the Internal Revenue Code in the following areas: division of tax liabilities and responsibilities between the estate and the debtor, tax consequences with respect to partnerships and transfers of property, and the taxable period of a debtor. Section 719 does not conform state and local tax rates to Federal tax rates.

Sec. 720. Dismissal for Failure to Timely File Tax Returns. Under existing law, there is no definitive rule with respect to whether a bankruptcy court may dismiss a bankruptcy case if the debtor fails to file returns for taxes incurred postpetition. Section 720 of the Act amends section 521 of the Bankruptcy Code to allow a taxing authority to request that the court dismiss or convert a bankruptcy case if the debtor fails to file a postpetition tax return or obtain an extension. If the debtor does not file the required return or obtain the extension within 90 days from the time of the request by the taxing authority to file the return, the court must convert or dismiss the case, whichever is in the best interest of creditors and the estate.

TITLE VIII. ANCILLARY AND OTHER CROSS-BORDER CASES

Title VIII of the Act adds a new chapter to the Bankruptcy Code for transnational bankruptcy cases. It incorporates the Model Law on Cross-Border Insolvency to encourage cooperation between the United States and foreign countries with respect to transnational insolvency cases. Title VIII is intended to provide greater legal certainty for trade and investment as well as to provide for the fair and efficient administration of cross-border insolvencies, which protects the interests of creditors and other interested parties, including the debtor. In addition, it serves to protect and maximize the value of the debtor's assets.

Sec. 801. Amendment to Add Chapter 15 to Title 11, United States Code. Section 801 introduces chapter 15 to the Bankruptcy Code, which is the Model Law on Cross-Border Insolvency ("Model Law") promulgated by the United Nations Commission on International Trade Law ("UNCITRAL") at its Thirtieth Session on May 12–30, 1997.[101] Cases brought under chapter 15 are intended to be ancillary to cases brought in a debtor's home country, unless a full United States bankruptcy case is brought under another chapter. Even if a full case is brought, the court may decide under section 305 to stay or dismiss the United States case under the other chapter and limit the United States' role to an ancillary case under this chapter.[102] If the full case is not dismissed, it will be subject to the provisions of this chapter governing cooperation, communication and coordination with the foreign courts and representatives. In any case, an order granting recognition is required as a prerequisite to the use of sections 301 and 303 by a foreign representative.

Sec. 1501. Purpose and scope of application. Section 1501 combines the Preamble to the Model Law (subsection (1)) with its article 1 (subsections (2) and (3)).[103] It largely tracks the language of the Model Law with appropriate United States references. However, it adds in subsection (3) an exclusion of certain natural persons who may be considered ordinary consumers. Although the consumer exclusion is not in the text of the Model Law, the discussions at UNCITRAL recognized that such exclusion would be necessary in countries like the United States where there are special provisions for consumer debtors in the insolvency laws.[104]

The reference to section 109(e) essentially defines "consumer debtors" for purposes of the exclusion by incorporating the debt limitations of that section, but not its requirement of regular income. The exclusion adds a requirement that the debtor or debtor couple be citizens or long-term legal residents of the United States. This ensures that residents of other countries will not be able to manipulate this exclusion to avoid recognition of foreign proceedings in their home countries or elsewhere.

The first exclusion in subsection (c) constitutes, for the United States, the exclusion provided in article 1, subsection (2), of the Model Law.[105] Foreign representatives of foreign proceedings which are excluded from the scope of chapter 15 may seek comity from courts other than the bankruptcy court since the limitations of section 1509(b)(2) and (3) would not apply to them.

The reference to section 109(b) interpolates into chapter 15 the entities governed by specialized insolvency regimes under United States law which are currently excluded from liquidation proceedings under title 11. Section 1501 contains an exception to the section 109(b) exclusions so that foreign proceedings of foreign insurance companies are eligible for recognition and relief under chapter 15 as they had been under section 304. However, section 1501(d) has the effect of leaving to State regulation any deposit, escrow, trust fund or the like posted by a foreign insurer under State law.

Sec. 1502. Definitions. "Debtor" is given a special definition for this chapter. This definition does not come from the Model Law, but is necessary to eliminate the need to refer repeatedly to "the same debtor as in the foreign proceeding." With certain exceptions, the term "person" used in the Model Law has been replaced with "entity," which is defined broadly in section 101(15) to include natural persons and various legal entities, thus matching the intended breadth of the term "person" in the Model Law. The exceptions include contexts in which a natural person is intended and those in which the Model Law language already refers to both persons and entities other than per-

101 The text of the Model Law and the Report of UNCITRAL on its adoption are found at U.N.G.A., 52d Sess., Supp. No. 17 (A/52/17) ("Report"). That Report and the Guide to Enactment of the UNCITRAL Model Law on Cross-Border Insolvency, U.N. Gen. Ass., UNCITRAL 30th Sess. U.N. Doc. A/CN.9/442 (1997) ("Guide"), which was discussed in the negotiations leading to the Model Law and published by UNCITRAL as an aid to enacting countries, should be consulted for guidance as to the meaning and purpose of its provisions. The development of the provisions in the negotiations at UNCITRAL, in which the United States was an active participant, is recounted in the interim reports of the Working Group that are cited in the Report.

102 *See* section 1529 and commentary.

103 Guide at 16–19.

104 *See id.* at 18, ¶ 60; 19 ¶ 66.

105 *Id.* at 17.

sons. The definition of "trustee" for this chapter ensures that debtors in possession and debtors, as well as trustees, are included in the term.[106]

The definition of "within the territorial jurisdiction of the United States" in subsection (7) is not taken from the Model Law. It has been added because the United States, like some other countries, asserts insolvency jurisdiction over property outside its territorial limits under appropriate circumstances. Thus a limiting phrase is useful where the Model Law and this chapter intend to refer only to property within the territory of the enacting state. In addition, a definition of "recognition" supplements the Model Law definitions and merely simplifies drafting of various other sections of chapter 15.

Two key definitions of "foreign proceeding" and "foreign representative," are found in sections 101(23) and (24), which have been amended consistent with Model Law article 2.[107] The definitions of "establishment," "foreign court," "foreign main proceeding," and "foreign non-main proceeding" have been taken from Model Law article 2, with only minor language variations necessary to comport with United States terminology. Additionally, defined terms have been placed in alphabetical order.[108] In order to be recognized as a foreign non-main proceeding, the debtor must at least have an establishment in that foreign country.[109]

Sec. 1503. International obligations of the United States. This section is taken exactly from the Model Law with only minor adaptations of terminology.[110] Although this section makes an international obligation prevail over chapter 15, the courts will attempt to read the Model Law and the international obligation so as not to conflict, especially if the international obligation addresses a subject matter less directly related than the Model Law to a case before the court.

Sec. 1504. Commencement of ancillary case. Article 4 of the Model Law is designed for designation of the competent court which will exercise jurisdiction under the Model Law. In United States law, section 1334(a) of title 28 gives exclusive jurisdiction to the district courts in a "case" under this title.[111] Therefore, since the competent court has been determined in title 28, this section instead provides that a petition for recognition commences a "case," an approach that also invokes a number of other useful procedural provisions. In addition, a new subsection (P) to section 157 of title 28 makes cases under this chapter part of the core jurisdiction of bankruptcy courts if referred by the district courts, thus completing the designation of the competent court. Finally, the particular bankruptcy court that will rule on the petition is determined pursuant to a revised section 1410 of title 28 governing venue and transfer.[112]

The title "ancillary" in the title of this section and in the title of this chapter emphasizes the United States policy in favor of a general rule that countries other than the home country of the debtor, where a main proceeding would be brought, should usually act through ancillary proceedings in aid of the main proceedings, in preference to a system of full bankruptcies (often called "secondary" proceedings) in each state where assets are found. Under the Model Law, notwithstanding the recognition of a foreign main proceeding, full bankruptcy cases are permitted in each country (see sections 1528 and 1529). In the United States, the court will have the power to suspend or dismiss such cases where appropriate under section 305.

Sec. 1505. Authorization to act in a foreign country. The language in this section varies from the wording of article 5 of the Model Law as necessary to comport with United States law and terminology. The slight alteration to the language in the last sentence is meant to emphasize that the identification of the trustee or other entity entitled to act is under United States law, while the scope of actions that may be taken by the trustee or other entity under foreign law is limited by the foreign law.[113]

The related amendment to section 586(a)(3) of title 28 makes acting pursuant to authorization under this section an additional power of a trustee or debtor in possession. While the Model Law automatically authorizes an administrator to act abroad, this section requires all trustees and debtors to obtain court approval before acting abroad. That requirement is a change from the language of the Model Law, but one that is purely internal to United States law.[114] Its main purpose is to ensure that the court has knowledge and control of possibly expensive activities, but it will have the collateral benefit of providing further assurance to foreign courts that the United States debtor or representative is under judicial authority and supervision. This requirement means that the first-day orders in reorganization cases should include authorization to act under this section where appropriate.

---

106 *See* section 1505.

107 Guide at 19-21, ¶¶ 67–68.

108 *See* Guide at 19, (Model Law) 21 ¶ 75 (concerning establishment); 21 ¶ 74 (concerning foreign court); 21 ¶¶ 72, 73 and 75 (concerning foreign main and non-main proceedings).

109 *See id.* at 21, ¶ 75.

110 *See id.* at 22, Art. 3.

111 *See id.* at 23, Art. 4.

112 New section 1410 of title 28 provides as follows:

> A case under chapter 15 of title 11 may be commenced in the district court for the district——
>
> (1) in which the debtor has its principal place of business or principal assets in the United States;
>
> (2) if the debtor does not have a place of business or assets in the United States, in which there is pending against the debtor an action or proceeding or enforcement of judgment in a Federal or State court; or
>
> (3) in a case other than those specified in paragraph (1) or (2), in which venue will be consistent with the interests of justice and the convenience of the parties having regard to the relief sought by the foreign representative.

113 *See* Guide at 24.

114 *See id.* at 24, Art. 5.

This section also contemplates the designation of an examiner or other natural person to act for the estate in one or more foreign countries where appropriate. One instance might be a case in which the designated person had a special expertise relevant to that assignment. Another might be where the foreign court would be more comfortable with a designated person than with an entity like a debtor in possession. Either are to be recognized under the Model Law.[115]

Sec. 1506. Public policy exception. This provision follows the Model Law article 5 exactly, is standard in UNCITRAL texts, and has been narrowly interpreted on a consistent basis in courts around the world. The word "manifestly" in international usage restricts the public policy exception to the most fundamental policies of the United States.[116]

Sec. 1507. Additional assistance. Subsection (1) follows the language of Model Law article 7.[117] Subsection (2) makes the authority for additional relief (beyond that permitted under sections 1519–1521, below) subject to the conditions for relief heretofore specified in United States law under section 304, which is repealed. This section is intended to permit the further development of international cooperation begun under section 304, but is not to be the basis for denying or limiting relief otherwise available under this chapter. The additional assistance is made conditional upon the court's consideration of the factors set forth in the current subsection 304(c) in a context of a reasonable balancing of interests following current case law. The references to "estate" in section 304 have been changed to refer to the debtor's property, because many foreign systems do not create an estate in insolvency proceedings of the sort recognized under this chapter. Although the case law construing section 304 makes it clear that comity is the central consideration, its physical placement as one of six factors in subsection (c) of section 304 is misleading, since those factors are essentially elements of the grounds for granting comity. Therefore, in subsection (2) of this section, comity is raised to the introductory language to make it clear that it is the central concept to be addressed.[118]

Sec. 1508. Interpretation. This provision follows conceptually Model Law article 8 and is a standard one in recent UNCITRAL treaties and model laws. Changes to the language were made to express the concepts more clearly in United States vernacular.[119] Interpretation of this chapter on a uniform basis will be aided by reference to the Guide and the Reports cited therein, which explain the reasons for the terms used and often cite their origins as well. Uniform interpretation will also be aided by reference to CLOUT, the UNCITRAL Case Law On Uniform Texts, which is a service of UNCITRAL. CLOUT receives reports from national reporters all over the world concerning court decisions interpreting treaties, model laws, and other text promulgated by UNCITRAL. Not only are these sources persuasive, but they advance the crucial goal of uniformity of interpretation. To the extent that the United States courts rely on these sources, their decisions will more likely be regarded as persuasive elsewhere.

Sec. 1509. Right of direct access. This section implements the purpose of article 9 of the Model Law, enabling a foreign representative to commence a case under this chapter by filing a petition directly with the court without preliminary formalities that may delay or prevent relief. It varies the language to fit United States procedural requirements and it imposes recognition of the foreign proceeding as a condition to further rights and duties of the foreign representative. If recognition is granted, the foreign representative will have full capacity under United States law (subsection (b)(1)), may request such relief in a state or Federal court other than the bankruptcy court (subsection (b)(2)), and shall be granted comity or cooperation by such non-bankruptcy court (subsection (b)(3) and (c)). Subsections (b)(2), (b)(3), and (c) make it clear that chapter 15 is intended to be the exclusive door to ancillary assistance to foreign proceedings. The goal is to concentrate control of these questions in one court. That goal is important in a Federal system like that of the United States with many different courts, state and federal, that may have pending actions involving the debtor or the debtor's property. This section, therefore, completes for the United States the work of article 4 of the Model Law ("competent court") as well as article 9.[120]

Although a petition under current section 304 is the proper method for achieving deference by a United States court to a foreign insolvency proceeding under present law, some cases in state and Federal courts under current law have granted comity suspension or dismissal of cases involving foreign proceedings without requiring a section 304 petition or even referring to the requirements of that section. Even if the result is correct in a particular case, the procedure is undesirable, because there is room for abuse of comity. Parties would be free to avoid the requirements of this chapter and the expert scrutiny of the bankruptcy court by applying directly to a state or Federal court unfamiliar with the statutory requirements. Such an application could be made after denial of a petition under this chapter. This section concentrates the recognition and deference process in one United States court, ensures against abuse, and empowers a court that will be fully informed of the current status of all foreign proceedings involving the debtor.[121]

115 *See id.* at 23–24, ¶ 82.
116 *See id.* at 25.
117 *Id.* at 26.
118 *Id.*
119 *Id.* at 26, ¶ 91.
120 *See id.* at 23, Art. 4, ¶¶ 79–83; 27 Art. 9, ¶ 93.
121 *See id.* at 27, Art. 9; 34–35, Art. 15 and ¶¶ 116–119; 39–40, Art. 18, ¶¶ 133–134; *see also* sections 1515(3), 1518.

Subsection (d) has been added to ensure that a foreign representative cannot seek relief in courts in the United States after being denied recognition by the court under this chapter. Subsection (e) makes activities in the United States by a foreign representative subject to applicable United States law, just as 28 U.S.C. section 959 does for a domestic trustee in bankruptcy.[122] Subsection (f) provides a limited exception to the prior recognition requirement so that collection of a claim which is property of the debtor, for example an account receivable, by a foreign representative may proceed without commencement of a case or recognition under this chapter.

Sec. 1510. Limited jurisdiction. Section 1510, article 10 of the Model Law, is modeled on section 306 of the Bankruptcy Code. Although the language referring to conditional relief in section 306 is not included, the court has the power under section 1522 to attach appropriate conditions to any relief it may grant. Nevertheless, the authority in section 1522 is not intended to permit the imposition of jurisdiction over the foreign representative beyond the boundaries of the case under this chapter and any related actions the foreign representative may take, such as commencing a case under another chapter of this title.

Sec. 1511. Commencement of Case Under Section 301 or 303. This section reflects the intent of article 11 of the Model Law, but adds language that conforms to United States law or that is otherwise necessary in the United States given its many bankruptcy court districts and the importance of full information and coordination among them.[123] Article 11 does not distinguish between voluntary and involuntary proceedings, but seems to have implicitly assumed an involuntary proceeding.[124] Subsection 1(a)(2) goes farther and permits a voluntary filing, with its much simpler requirements, if the foreign proceeding that has been recognized is a main proceeding.

Sec. 1512. Participation of a foreign representative in a case under this title. This section tracks article 12 of the Model Law with a slight alteration to tie into United States procedural terminology.[125] The effect of this section is to make the recognized foreign representative a party in interest in any pending or later commenced United States bankruptcy case.[126] Throughout this chapter, the word "case" has been substituted for the word "proceeding" in the Model Law when referring to cases under the United States Bankruptcy Code, to conform to United States usage.

Sec. 1513. Access of foreign creditors to a case under this title. This section mandates nondiscriminatory or "national" treatment for foreign creditors, except as provided in subsection (b) and section 1514. It follows the intent of Model Law article 13, but the language required alteration to fit into the Bankruptcy Code.[127] The law as to priority for foreign claims that fit within a class given priority treatment under section 507 (for example, foreign employees or spouses) is unsettled. This section permits the continued development of case law on that subject and its general principle of national treatment should be an important factor to be considered. At a minimum, under this section, foreign claims must receive the treatment given to general unsecured claims without priority, unless they are in a class of claims in which domestic creditors would also be subordinated.[128] The Model Law allows for an exception to the policy of nondiscrimination as to foreign revenue and other public law claims.[129] Such claims (such as tax and Social Security claims) have been traditionally denied enforcement in the United States, inside and outside of bankruptcy. The Bankruptcy Code is silent on this point, so the rule is purely a matter of traditional case law. It is not clear if this policy should be maintained or modified, so this section leaves this question to developing case law. It also allows the Department of the Treasury to negotiate reciprocal arrangements with our tax treaty partners in this regard, although it does not mandate any restriction of the evolution of case law pending such negotiations.

Sec. 1514. Notification of foreign creditors concerning a case under title 11. This section ensures that foreign creditors receive proper notice of cases in the United States.[130] As "foreign creditor" is not a defined term, foreign addresses are used as the distinguishing factor. The Federal Rules of Bankruptcy Procedure ("Rules") should be amended to conform to the requirements of this section, including a special form for initial notice to such creditors. In particular, the Rules must provide additional time for such creditors to file proofs of claim where appropriate and require the court to make specific orders in that regard in proper circumstances. The notice must specify that secured claims must be asserted, because in many countries such claims are not affected by an insolvency proceeding and need not be filed.[131] If a foreign creditor has made an appropriate request for notice, it will receive notices in every instance where notices would be sent to other creditors who have made such requests. Subsection (d) replaces the reference to "a reasonable time period" in Model Law article 14(3)(a).[132] It makes clear that the Rules, local rules, and court orders must make appropriate adjustments in time periods and bar dates

122 *Id.* at 27, ¶ 93.
123 *See id.* at 28, Art. 11.
124 *Id.* at 38, ¶¶ 97–99.
125 *Id.* at 29, Art. 12.
126 *Id.* at 29, ¶¶ 10–102.
127 *Id.* at 30, ¶ 103.
128 *See id.* at 30, ¶ 104.
129 *See id.* at 31, ¶ 105.
130 *See* Model Law, Art. 14; Guide at 31-32, ¶¶ 106-109.
131 Guide at 33, ¶ 111.
132 *Id.* at 31, Art. 14(3)(a).

so that foreign creditors have a reasonable time within which to receive notice or take an action.

Sec. 1515. Application for recognition of a foreign proceeding. This section follows article 15 of the Model Law with minor changes.[133] The Rules will require amendment to provide forms for some or all of the documents mentioned in this section, to make necessary additions to Rules 1000 and 2002 to facilitate appropriate notices of the hearing on the petition for recognition, and to require filing of lists of creditors and other interested persons who should receive notices. Throughout the Model Law, the question of notice procedure is left to the law of the enacting state.[134]

Sec. 1516. Presumptions concerning recognition. This section follows article 16 of the Model Law with minor changes.[135] Although sections 1515 and 1516 are designed to make recognition as simple and expedient as possible, the court may hear proof on any element stated. The ultimate burden as to each element is on the foreign representative, although the court is entitled to shift the burden to the extent indicated in section 1516. The word "proof" in subsection (3) has been changed to "evidence" to make it clearer using United States terminology that the ultimate burden is on the foreign representative.[136] "Registered office" is the term used in the Model Law to refer to the place of incorporation or the equivalent for an entity that is not a natural person.[137] The presumption that the place of the registered office is also the center of the debtor's main interest is included for speed and convenience of proof where there is no serious controversy.

Sec. 1517. Order granting recognition. This section closely tracks article 17 of the Model Law, with a few exceptions.[138] The decision to grant recognition is not dependent upon any findings about the nature of the foreign proceedings of the sort previously mandated by section 304(c) of the Bankruptcy Code. The requirements of this section, which incorporates the definitions in section 1502 and sections 101(23) and (24), are all that must be fulfilled to attain recognition. Reciprocity was specifically suggested as a requirement for recognition on more than one occasion in the negotiations that resulted in the Model Law. It was rejected by overwhelming consensus each time. The United States was one of the leading countries opposing the inclusion of a reciprocity requirement.[139] In this regard, the Model Law conforms to section 304, which has no such requirement.

The drafters of the Model Law understood that only a main proceeding or a non-main proceeding meeting the standards of section 1502 (that is, one brought where the debtor has an establishment) were entitled to recognition under this section. The Model Law has been slightly modified to make this point clear by referring to the section 1502 definition of main and non-main proceedings, as well as to the general definition of a foreign proceeding in section 101(23). A petition under section 1515 must show that proceeding is a main or a qualifying non-main proceeding in order to obtain recognition under this section.

Consistent with the position of various civil law representatives in the drafting of the Model Law, recognition creates a status with the effects set forth in section 1520, so those effects are not viewed as orders to be modified, as are orders granting relief under sections 1519 and 1521. Subsection (4) states the grounds for modifying or terminating recognition. On the other hand, the effects of recognition (found in section 1520 and including an automatic stay) are subject to modification under section 362(d), made applicable by section 1520(2), which permits relief from the automatic stay of section 1520 for cause.

Paragraph 1(d) of section 17 of the Model Law has been omitted as an unnecessary requirement for United States purposes, because a petition submitted to the wrong court will be dismissed or transferred under other provisions of United States law.[140] The reference to section 350 refers to the routine closing of a case that has been completed and will invoke requirements including a final report from the foreign representative in such form as the Rules may provide or a court may order.[141]

Sec. 1518. Subsequent information. This section follows the Model Law, except to eliminate the word "same," which is rendered unnecessary by the definition of "debtor" in section 1502, and to provide for a formal document to be filed with the court.[142] Judges in several jurisdictions, including the United States, have reported a need for a requirement of complete and candid reports to the court of all proceedings, worldwide, involving the debtor. This section will ensure that such information is provided to the court on a timely basis. Any failure to comply with this section will be subject to the sanctions available to the court for violations of the statute. The section leaves to the Rules the form of the required notice and related questions of notice to parties in interest, the time for filing, and the like.

Sec. 1519. Relief may be granted upon petition for recognition of a foreign proceeding. This section generally follows article 19 of the Model Law.[143] The bankruptcy court will have jurisdiction to grant emergency relief under Rule 7065 pending a hearing on the petition for recognition. This

133 *Id.* at 33.
134 *See id.* at 36, ¶ 121.
135 *Id.* at 36
136 *Id.* at 36, Art. 16(3).
137 *Id.*
138 *Id.* at 37.
139 Report of the Working Group on Insolvency Law on the Work of Its Twentieth Session (Vienna, 7–18 Oct. 1996), at 6, ¶¶ 16–20.
140 Guide at 37, Art. 17(1)(d).
141 *Id.*
142 *Id.* at 39–40, ¶¶ 133, 134.
143 *Id.* at 40.

section does not expand or reduce the scope of section 105 as determined by cases under section 105 nor does it modify the sweep of sections 555 to 560. Subsection (d) precludes injunctive relief against police and regulatory action under section 1519, leaving section 105 as the only avenue for such relief. Subsection (e) makes clear that this section contemplates injunctive relief and that such relief is subject to specific rules and a body of jurisprudence. Subsection (f) was added to complement amendments to the Bankruptcy Code provisions dealing with financial contracts.

Sec. 1520. Effects of recognition of a foreign main proceeding. In general, this chapter sets forth all the relief that is available as a matter of right based upon recognition hereunder, although additional assistance may be provided under section 1507 and this chapter has no effect on any relief currently available under section 105. The stay created by article 20 of the Model Law is imported to chapter 15 from existing provisions of the Code. Subsection (a)(1) combines subsections 1(a) and (b) of article 20 of the Model Law, because section 362 imposes the restrictions required by those two subsections as well as additional restrictions.[144]

Subsections (a)(2) and (4) apply the Bankruptcy Code sections that impose the restrictions called for by subsection 1(c) of the Model Law. In both cases, the provisions are broader and more complete than those contemplated by the Model Law, but include all the restraints the Model Law provisions would impose.[145] As the foreign proceeding may or may not create an "estate" similar to that created in cases under this title, the restraints are applicable to actions against the debtor under section 362(a) and with respect to the property of the debtor under the remaining sections. The only property covered by this section is property within the territorial jurisdiction of the United States as defined in section 1502. To achieve effects on property of the debtor which is not within the territorial jurisdiction of the United States, the foreign representative would have to commence a case under another chapter of this title.

By applying sections 361 and 362, subsection (a) makes applicable the United States exceptions and limitations to the restraints imposed on creditors, debtors, and other in a case under this title, as stated in article 20(2) of the Model Law.[146] It also introduces the concept of adequate protection provided in sections 362 and 363. These exceptions and limitations include those set forth in sections 362(b), (c) and (d). As a result, the court has the power to terminate the stay pursuant to section 362(d), for cause, including a failure of adequate protection.[147]

Subsection (a)(2), by its reference to sections 363 and 552 adds to the powers of a foreign representative of a foreign main proceeding an automatic right to operate the debtor's business and exercise the power of a trustee under sections 363 and 542, unless the court orders otherwise. A foreign representative of a foreign main proceeding may need to continue a business operation to maintain value and granting that authority automatically will eliminate the risk of delay. If the court is uncomfortable about this authority in a particular situation, it can "order otherwise" as part of the order granting recognition.

Two special exceptions to the automatic stay are embodied in subsections (b) and (c). To preserve a claim in certain foreign countries, it may be necessary to commence an action. Subsection (b) permits the commencement of such an action, but would not allow for its further prosecution. Subsection (c) provides that there is no stay of the commencement of a full United States bankruptcy case. This essentially provides an escape hatch through which any entity, including the foreign representative, can flee into a full case. The full case, however, will remain subject to subchapters IV and V on cooperation and coordination of proceedings and to section 305 providing for stay or dismissal. Section 108 of the Bankruptcy Code provides the tolling protection intended by Model Law article 20(3), so no exception is necessary for claims that might be extinguished under United States law.[148]

Sec. 1521. Relief that may be granted upon recognition of a foreign proceeding. This section follows article 21 of the Model Law, with detailed changes to conform to United States law.[149] The exceptions in subsection (a)(7) relate to avoiding powers. The foreign representative's status as to such powers is governed by section 1523 below. The avoiding power in section 549 and the exceptions to that power are covered by section 1520(a)(2). The word "adequately" in the Model Law, articles 21(2) and 22(1), has been changed to "sufficiently" in sections 1521(b) and 1522(a) to avoid confusion with a very specialized legal term in United States bankruptcy, "adequate protection."[150] Subsection (c) is designed to limit relief to assets having some direct connection with a non-main proceeding, for example where they were part of an operating division in the jurisdiction of the non-main proceeding when they were fraudulently conveyed and then brought to the United States.[151] Subsections (d), (e) and (f) are identical to those same subsections of section 1519. This section does not expand or reduce the scope of relief currently available in ancillary cases under sections 105 and 304 nor does it modify the sweep of sections 555 through 560.

Sec. 1522. Protection of creditors and other interested persons. This section follows article 22 of the Model Law with changes for United States usage and references to

144 *Id.* at 42, Art. 20 1(a), (b).
145 *Id.* at 42, 45.
146 *Id.* at 42, Art. 20(2); 44, ¶ 148, 150.
147 *Id.* at 42, Art. 20(3); 44–45, ¶ 151 152.
148 *Id.*
149 *Id.* at 45–46, Art. 21.
150 *Id.* at 46, Art. 21(2); 47, Art. 22(1).
151 *See id.* at 46–47, ¶ 158, 160.

relevant Bankruptcy Code sections.[152] It gives the bankruptcy court broad latitude to mold relief to meet specific circumstances, including appropriate responses if it is shown that the foreign proceeding is seriously and unjustifiably injuring United States creditors. For a response to a showing that the conditions necessary to recognition did not actually exist or have ceased to exist, see section 1517. Concerning the change of "adequately" in the Model Law to "sufficiently" in this section, see section 1521. Subsection (d) is new and simply makes clear that Bankruptcy Code section 1104(d) shall apply to the appointment of an examiner appointed in a case under chapter 15 and such examiner shall be subject to certain duties and bonding requirements based on those imposed on trustees and examiners under other chapters of this title.

Sec. 1523. Actions to avoid acts detrimental to creditors. This section follows article 23 of the Model Law, with wording to fit it within procedure under this title.[153] It confers standing on a recognized foreign representative to assert an avoidance action but only in a pending case under another chapter of this title. The Model Law is not clear about whether it would grant standing in a recognized foreign proceeding if no full case were pending. This limitation reflects concerns raised by the United States delegation during the UNCITRAL debates that a simple grant of standing to bring avoidance actions neglects to address very difficult choice of law and forum issues. This limited grant of standing in section 1523 does not create or establish any legal right of avoidance nor does it create or imply any legal rules with respect to the choice of applicable law as to the avoidance of any transfer of obligation.[154] The courts will determine the nature and extent of any such action and what national law may be applicable to such action.

Sec. 1524. Intervention by a foreign representative. The wording is the same as the Model Law, except for a few clarifying words.[155] This section gives the foreign representative whose foreign proceeding has been recognized the right to intervene in United States cases, state or federal, where the debtor is a party. Recognition being an act under Federal bankruptcy law, it must take effect in state as well as Federal courts. This section does not require substituting the foreign representative for the debtor, although that result may be appropriate in some circumstances.

Sec. 1525. Cooperation and direct communication between the court and foreign courts or foreign representatives. The wording of this provision is nearly identical to that of the Model Law.[156] The right of courts to communicate with other courts in worldwide insolvency cases is of central importance. This section authorizes courts to do so. This right must be exercised, however, with due regard to the rights of the parties. Guidelines for such communications are left to the Federal rules of bankruptcy procedure.

Sec. 1526 Cooperation and direct communication between the trustee and foreign courts or foreign representatives. This section closely tracks the Model Law.[157] The language in Model Law article 26 concerning the trustee's function was eliminated as unnecessary because it is always implied under United States law. The section authorizes the trustee, including a debtor in possession, to cooperate with other proceedings.

Sec. 1527. Forms of cooperation. This section is identical to the Model Law.[158] United States bankruptcy courts already engage in most of the forms of cooperation described here, but they now have explicit statutory authorization for acts like the approval of protocols of the sort used in cases.[159]

Sec. 1528. Commencement of a case under title 11 after recognition of a foreign main proceeding. This section follows the Model Law, with specifics of United States law replacing the general clause at the end of the section to cover assets normally included within the jurisdiction of the United States courts in bankruptcy cases, except where assets are subject to the jurisdiction of another recognized proceeding.[160] In a full bankruptcy case, the United States bankruptcy court generally has jurisdiction over assets outside the United States. Here that jurisdiction is limited where those assets are controlled by another recognized proceeding, if it is a main proceeding.

The court may use section 305 of this title to dismiss, stay, or limit a case as necessary to promote cooperation and coordination in a cross-border case. In addition, although the jurisdictional limitation applies only to United States bankruptcy cases commenced after recognition of a foreign proceeding, the court has ample authority under the next section and section 305 to exercise its discretion to dismiss, stay, or limit a United States case filed after a petition for recognition of a foreign main proceeding has been filed but before it has been approved, if recognition is ultimately granted.

Sec. 1529. Coordination of a case under title 11 and a foreign proceeding. This section follows the Model Law almost exactly, but subsection (4) adds a reference to section 305 to make it clear the bankruptcy court may continue to use that section, as under present law, to dismiss or suspend a United States case as part of coordination and cooperation with foreign proceedings.[161] This provision is consistent

152 *Id.* at 47.
153 *Id.* at 48–49.
154 *See id.* at 49, ¶ 166.
155 *Id.* at 49.
156 *Id.* at 50.
157 *Id.* at 51.
158 Guide at 51, 53.
159 *See e.g., In re* Maxwell Communication Corp., 93 F.2d 1036 (2d Cir. 1996).
160 Guide at 54–55.
161 *Id.* at 55–56.

with United States policy to act ancillary to a foreign main proceeding whenever possible.

Sec. 1530. Coordination of more than one foreign proceeding. This section follows article 30 of the Model Law exactly.[162] It ensures that a foreign main proceeding will be given primacy in the United States, consistent with the overall approach of the United States favoring assistance to foreign main proceedings.

Sec. 1531. Presumption of insolvency based on recognition of a foreign main proceeding. This section follows the Model Law exactly, inserting a reference to the standard for an involuntary case under this title.[163] Where an insolvency proceeding has begun in the home country of the debtor, and in the absence of contrary evidence, the foreign representative should not have to make a new showing that the debtor is in the sort of financial distress requiring a collective judicial remedy. The word "proof" in this provision here means "presumption." The presumption does not arise for any purpose outside this section.

Sec. 1532. Rule of payment in concurrent proceeding. This section follows the Model Law exactly and is very similar to prior section 508(a), which is repealed. The Model Law language is somewhat clearer and broader than the equivalent language of prior section 508(a).[164]

Sec. 802. Other Amendments to Titles 11 and 28, United States Code. Section 802(a) amends section 103 of the Bankruptcy Code to clarify the provisions of the Code that apply to chapter 15 and to specify which portions of chapter 15 apply in cases under other chapters of title 11. Section 802(b) amends the Bankruptcy Code's definitions of foreign proceeding and foreign representative in section 101. The new definitions are nearly identical to those contained in the Model Law but add to the phrase "under a law relating to insolvency" the words "or debt adjustment." This addition emphasizes that the scope of the Model Law and chapter 15 is not limited to proceedings involving only debtors which are technically insolvent, but broadly includes all proceedings involving debtors in severe financial distress, so long as those proceedings also meet the other criteria of section 101(24).[165]

Section 802(c) amends section 157(b)(2) of title 28 to provide that proceedings under chapter 15 will be core proceedings while other amendments to title 28 provide that the United States trustee's standing extends to cases under chapter 15 and that the United States trustee's duties include acting in chapter 15 cases. Although the United States will continue to assert worldwide jurisdiction over property of a domestic or foreign debtor in a full bankruptcy case under chapters 7 and 13 of this title, subject to deference to foreign proceedings under chapter 15 and section 305, the situation is different in a case commenced under chapter 15. There the United States is acting solely in an ancillary position, so jurisdiction over property is limited to that stated in chapter 15.

Section 802(d) amends section 109 of the Bankruptcy Code to permit recognition of foreign proceedings involving foreign insurance companies and involving foreign banks which do not have a branch or agency in the United States (as defined in 12 U.S.C. 3101). While a foreign bank not subject to United States regulation will be eligible for chapter 15 as a consequence of the amendment to section 109, section 303 prohibits the commencement of a full involuntary case against such a foreign bank unless the bank is a debtor in a foreign proceeding.

While section 304 is repealed and replaced by chapter 15, access to the jurisprudence which developed under section 304 is preserved in the context of new section 1507. On deciding whether to grant the additional assistance contemplated by section 1507, the court must consider the same factors specified in former section 304. The venue provisions for cases ancillary to foreign proceedings have been amended to provide a hierarchy of choices beginning with principal place of business in the United States, if any. If there is no principal place of business in the United States, but there is litigation against a debtor, then the district in which the litigation is pending would be the appropriate venue. In any other case, venue must be determined with reference to the interests of justice and the convenience of the parties.

TITLE IX. FINANCIAL CONTRACT PROVISIONS

Sec. 901. Treatment of Certain Agreements by Conservators of Receivers of Insured Depository Institutions. Subsections (a) through (f) of section 901 of the Act amend the definitions of "qualified financial contract," "securities contract," "commodity contract," "forward contract," "repurchase agreement" and "swap agreement" contained in the Federal Deposit Insurance Act (FDIA) and the Federal Credit Union Act (FCUA) to make them consistent with the definitions in the Bankruptcy Code and to reflect the enactment of the Commodity Futures Modernization Act of 2000 (CFMA). It is intended that the legislative history and case law surrounding those terms, to the date of this amendment, be incorporated into the legislative history of the FDIA and the FCUA.

Subsection (b) amends the definition of "securities contract" expressly to encompass margin loans, to clarify the coverage of securities options and to clarify the coverage of repurchase and reverse repurchase transactions. The inclusion of "margin loans" in the definition is intended to encompass only those loans commonly known in the securities industry as "margin loans," such as credit permitted in a margin account under the Federal Reserve Board's Regu-

162 *Id.* at 57.
163 *Id.* at 58.
164 *Id.* at 59.
165 *Id.* at 51–52, 71.

lation T (whether or not effected in that account) or arrangements where a financial intermediary—a stockbroker, financial institution, financial participant, or securities agency—extends credit in connection with the purchase, sale, carrying, or trading of securities. "Margin loans" do not include, however, other loans that happen to be secured by securities collateral. The reference in subsection (b) to a "guarantee by or to any securities clearing agency" is intended to cover other arrangements, such as novation, that have an effect similar to a guarantee. The reference to a "loan" of a security in the definition is intended to apply to loans of securities, whether or not for a "permitted purpose" under margin regulations. The reference to "repurchase and reverse repurchase transactions" is intended to eliminate any inquiry under the qualified financial contract provisions of the FDIA or FCUA as to whether a repurchase or reverse repurchase transaction is a purchase and sale transaction or a secured financing. Repurchase and reverse repurchase transactions meeting certain criteria are already covered under the definition of "repurchase agreement" in the FDIA (and a regulation of the Federal Deposit Insurance Corporation (FDIC)). Repurchase and reverse repurchase transactions on all securities (including, for example, equity securities, asset-backed securities, corporate bonds and commercial paper) are included under the definition of "securities contract." Subsection (b) also specifies that purchase, sale and repurchase obligations under a participation in a commercial mortgage loan do not constitute "securities contracts." While a contract for the purchase, sale or repurchase of a participation may constitute a "securities contract," the purchase, sale or repurchase obligation embedded in a participation agreement does not make that agreement a "securities contract."

A number of terms used in the qualified financial contract provisions, but not defined therein, are intended to have the meanings set forth in the analogous provisions of the Bankruptcy Code or Federal Deposit Insurance Corporation Improvement Act ("FDICIA"), such as, for example, "securities clearing agency." The term "person," however, is not intended to be so interpreted. Instead, "person" is intended to have the meaning set forth in section 1 of title 1 of the United States Code.

Section 901(c) amends with respect the definition of "commodity contract" in section 11(e)(8)(D)(iii) of the FDIA and in section 207(c)(8)(D)(iii) of the FCUA. Section 901(d) amends section 11(e)(8)(D)(iv) of the FDIA and section 207(c)(8)(D)(iv) of the FCUA with respect to the definition of a "forward contract."

Subsection (e) amends the definition of "repurchase agreement" in the FDIA and the FCUA to codify the substance of the FDIC's 1995 regulation defining repurchase agreement to include those on qualified foreign government securities.[166] The term "qualified foreign government securities" is defined to include those that are direct obligations of, or fully guaranteed by, central governments of members of the Organization for Economic Cooperation and Development (OECD), as determined by rule, of the appropriate Federal banking agency. Subsection (e) reflects developments in the repurchase agreement markets, which increasingly use foreign government securities as the underlying asset. The securities are limited to those issued by or guaranteed by full members of the OECD, as well as countries that have concluded special lending arrangements with the International Monetary Fund associated with the Fund's General Arrangements to Borrow.

Subsection (e) also amends the definition of "repurchase agreement" to include those on mortgage-related securities, mortgage loans and interests therein, and expressly to include principal and interest-only U.S. government and agency securities as securities that can be the subject of a "repurchase agreement." The reference in the definition to United States government- and agency-issued or fully guaranteed securities is intended to include obligations issued or guaranteed by Fannie Mae and the Federal Home Loan Mortgage Corporation (Freddie Mac) as well as all obligations eligible for purchase by Federal Reserve banks under the similar language of section 14(b) of the Federal Reserve Act. This amendment is not intended to affect the status of repos involving securities or commodities as securities contracts, commodity contracts, or forward contracts, and their consequent eligibility for similar treatment under the qualified financial contract provisions. In particular, an agreement for the sale and repurchase of a security would continue to be a securities contract as defined in the FDIA or FCUA, even if not a "repurchase agreement" as defined in the FDIA or FCUA. Similarly, an agreement for the sale and repurchase of a commodity, even though not a "repurchase agreement" as defined in the FDIA or FCUA, would continue to be a forward contract for purposes of the FDIA or FCUA.

Subsection (e), like subsection (b) for "securities contracts," specifies that repurchase obligations under a participation in a commercial mortgage loan do not make the participation agreement a "repurchase agreement." Such repurchase obligations embedded in participations in commercial loans (such as recourse obligations) do not constitute a "repurchase agreement." A repurchase agreement involving the transfer of participations in commercial mortgage loans with a simultaneous agreement to repurchase the participation on demand or at a date certain one year or less after such transfer, however, would constitute a "repurchase agreement" as well as a "securities contract."

Section 901(f) of the Act amends the definition of "swap agreement" to include an "interest rate swap, option, future, or forward agreement, including a rate floor, rate cap, rate collar, cross-currency rate swap, and basis swap; a spot, same day-tomorrow, tomorrow-next, forward, or other foreign exchange or precious metals agreement; a currency

166 *See* 12 C.F.R. § 360.5.

swap, option, future, or forward agreement; an equity index or equity swap, option, future, or forward agreement; a debt index or debt swap, option, future, or forward agreement; a total return, credit spread or credit swap, option, future, or forward agreement; a commodity index or commodity swap, option, future, or forward agreement; or a weather swap, weather derivative, or weather option." As amended, the definition of "swap agreement" will update the statutory definition and achieve contractual netting across economically similar transactions that are the subject of recurring dealings in the swap agreements.

The definition of "swap agreement" originally was intended to provide sufficient flexibility to avoid the need to amend the definition as the nature and uses of swap transactions matured. To that end, the phrase "or any other similar agreement" was included in the definition. (The phrase "or any similar agreement" has been added to the definitions of "forward contract," "commodity contract," "repurchase agreement" and "securities contract" for the same reason.) To clarify this, subsection (f) expands the definition of "swap agreement" to include "any agreement or transaction that is similar to any other agreement or transaction referred to in [section 11(e)(8)(D)(vi) of the FDIA] and is of a type that has been, is presently, or in the future becomes, the subject of recurrent dealings in the swap markets . . . and that is a forward, swap, future, or option on one or more rates, currencies, commodities, equity securities or other equity instruments, debt securities or other debt instruments, quantitative measures associated with an occurrence, extent of an occurrence, or contingency associated with a financial, commercial, or economic consequence, or economic or financial indices or measures of economic or financial risk or value."

The definition of "swap agreement," however, should not be interpreted to permit parties to document non-swaps as swap transactions. Traditional commercial arrangements, such as supply agreements, or other non-financial market transactions, such as commercial, residential or consumer loans, cannot be treated as "swaps" under the FDIA, the FCUA, or the Bankruptcy Code simply because the parties purport to document or label the transactions as "swap agreements." In addition, these definitions apply only for purposes of the FDIA, the FCUA, and the Bankruptcy Code. These definitions, and the characterization of a certain transaction as a "swap agreement," are not intended to affect the characterization, definition, or treatment of any instruments under any other statute, regulation, or rule including, but not limited to, the statutes, regulations or rules enumerated in subsection (f). Similarly, Section 17 and a new paragraph of Section 11(e) of the FDIA provide that the definitions of "securities contract," "repurchase agreement," "forward contract," and "commodity contract," and the characterization of certain transactions as such a contract or agreement, are not intended to affect the characterization, definition, or treatment of any instruments under any other statute, regulation, or rule including, but not limited to, the statutes, regulations or rules enumerated in subsection (f).

The definition also includes any security agreement or arrangement, or other credit enhancement, related to a swap agreement, including any guarantee or reimbursement obligation related to a swap agreement. This ensures that any such agreement, arrangement or enhancement is itself deemed to be a swap agreement, and therefore eligible for treatment as such for purposes of termination, liquidation, acceleration, offset and netting under the FDIA, FCUA, and the Bankruptcy Code. Similar changes are made in the definitions of "forward contract," "commodity contract," "repurchase agreement" and "securities contract."

The use of the term "forward" in the definition of "swap agreement" is not intended to refer only to transactions that fall within the definition of "forward contract." Instead, a "forward" transaction could be a "swap agreement" even if not a "forward contract."

Section 901(g) amends the definition of "transfer" in the FDIA and FCUA, which is a key term used in both, to ensure that it is broadly construed to encompass dispositions of property or interests in property. The definition tracks the Bankruptcy Code's definition of this term in Bankruptcy Code section 101.

Section 901(h) makes clarifying technical changes to conform the receivership and conservatorship provisions of the FDIA and the FCUA. It also clarifies that the FDIA and the FCUA expressly protect rights under security agreements, arrangements or other credit enhancements related to one or more qualified financial contracts (QFCs). An example of a security arrangement is a right of setoff, and examples of other credit enhancements are letters of credit, guarantees, reimbursement obligations and other similar agreements.

Section 901(i) of the Act clarifies that no provision of Federal or state law relating to the avoidance of preferential or fraudulent transfers (including the anti-preference provision of the National Bank Act) can be invoked to avoid a transfer made in connection with any QFC of an insured depository institution in conservatorship or receivership, absent actual fraudulent intent on the part of the transferee.

Sec. 902. Authority of the FDIC and NCUAB with Respect to Failed and Failing Institutions. Section 902 of the Act provides that no provision of law, including FDICIA, shall be construed to limit the power of the FDIC or the NCUAB to transfer or to repudiate any QFC in accordance with its powers under the FDIA or FCUA, respectively. As discussed below, there has been some uncertainty regarding whether or not FDICIA limits the authority of the FDIC or the NCUAB to transfer or to repudiate QFCs of an insolvent financial institution. Section 902, as well as other provisions in the Act, clarify that FDICIA does not limit the transfer powers of the FDIC or the NCUAB with respect to QFCs. Section 902 denies enforcement to "walkaway" clauses in

QFCs. A walkaway clause is defined as a provision that, after calculation of a value of a party's position or an amount due to or from one of the parties upon termination, liquidation or acceleration of the QFC, either does not create a payment obligation of a party or extinguishes a payment obligation of a party in whole or in part solely because of such party's status as a non-defaulting party.

Sec. 903. Amendments Relating to Transfers of Qualified Financial Contracts. Section 903 of the Act amends the FDIA and the FCUA to expand the transfer authority of the FDIC and the NCUAB, respectively to permit transfers of QFCs to "financial institutions" as defined in FDICIA or in regulations. This provision will allow the FDIC and NCUAB to transfer QFCs to a non-depository financial institution provided the institution is not subject to bankruptcy or insolvency proceedings.

The new FDIA and FCUA provisions specify that when the FDIC and NCUAB transfer QFCs that are cleared on or subject to the rules of a particular clearing organization, the transfer will not require the clearing organization to accept the transferee as a member of the organization. This provision gives the FDIC and NCUAB flexibility in resolving QFCs cleared on or subject to the rules of a clearing organization, while preserving the ability of such organizations to enforce appropriate risk reducing membership requirements. The amendment does not require the clearing organization to accept for clearing any QFCs from the transferee, except on the terms and conditions applicable to other parties permitted to clear through that clearing organization. "Clearing organization" is defined to mean a "clearing organization" within the meaning of FDICIA (as amended both by the CFMA and by Section 906 of the Act).

The new FDIA and FCUA provisions also permit transfers to an eligible financial institution that is a non-U.S. person, or the branch or agency of a non-U.S. person or a U.S. financial institution that is not an FDIC-insured institution if, following the transfer, the contractual rights of the parties would be enforceable substantially to the same extent as under the FDIA and the FCUA. It is expected that neither the FDIC nor the NCUAB would transfer QFCs to such a financial institution if there were an impending change of law that would impair the enforceability of the parties' contractual rights.

Section 903 amends the notification requirements following a transfer of the QFCs of a failed depository institution to require the FDIC and NCUAB to notify any party to a transferred QFC of such transfer by 5:00 p.m. (Eastern Time) on the business day following the date of the appointment of the FDIC acting as receiver or following the date of such transfer by the FDIC or NCUAB acting as a conservator. This amendment is consistent with the policy statement on QFCs issued by the FDIC on December 12, 1989.

Section 903 amends the FDIA to clarify the relationship between the FDIA and FDICIA. There has been some uncertainty whether FDICIA permits counterparties to terminate or liquidate a QFC before the expiration of the time period provided by the FDIA during which the FDIC may repudiate or transfer a QFC in a conservatorship or receivership. Subsection (c) provides that a party may not terminate a QFC based solely on the appointment of the FDIC as receiver until 5:00 p.m. (Eastern Time) on the business day following the appointment of the receiver or after the person has received notice of a transfer under FDIA section 11(d)(9), or based solely on the appointment of the FDIC as conservator, notwithstanding the provisions of FDICIA. This provides the FDIC with an opportunity to undertake an orderly resolution of the insured depository institution. Section 903 makes a similar change to the FCUA.

Section 903 also prohibits the enforcement of rights of termination or liquidation that arise solely because of the insolvency of the institution or are based on the "financial condition" of the depository institution in receivership or conservatorship. For example, termination based on a cross-default provision in a QFC that is triggered upon a default under another contract could be rendered ineffective if such other default was caused by an acceleration of amounts due under that other contract, and such acceleration was based solely on the appointment of a conservator or receiver for that depository institution. Similarly, a provision in a QFC permitting termination of the QFC based solely on a downgraded credit rating of a party will not be enforceable in an FDIC or NCUAB receivership or conservatorship because the provision is based solely on the financial condition of the depository institution in default. However, any payment, delivery or other performance-based default, or breach of a representation or covenant putting in question the enforceability of the agreement, will not be deemed to be based solely on financial condition for purposes of this provision. The amendment is not intended to prevent counterparties from taking all actions permitted and recovering all damages authorized upon repudiation of any QFC by a conservator or receiver, or from taking actions based upon a receivership or other financial condition-triggered default in the absence of a transfer (as contemplated in Section 11(e)(10) of the FDIA). The amendment allows the FDIC or NCUAB to meet its obligation to provide notice to parties to transferred QFCs by taking steps reasonably calculated to provide notice to such parties by the required time. This is consistent with the existing policy statement on QFCs issued by the FDIC on December 12, 1989.

Finally, the amendment permits the FDIC or NCUAB to transfer QFCs of a failed depository institution to a bridge bank or a depository institution organized by the FDIC or NCUAB for which a conservator is appointed either (i) immediately upon the organization of such institution or (ii) at the time of a purchase and assumption transaction between the FDIC or NCUAB and the institution. This provision clarifies that such institutions are not to be considered financial institutions that are ineligible to receive such transfers under FDIA section 11(e)(9). This is consistent with the existing policy statement on QFCs issued by the FDIC on December 12, 1989.

Sec. 904. Amendments Relating to Disaffirmance or Repudiation of Qualified Financial Contracts. Section 904 of the Act limits the disaffirmance and repudiation authority of the FDIC and NCUAB with respect to QFCs so that such authority is consistent with their transfer authority under FDIA section 11(e)(9) or FCUA section 207(c). This ensures that no disaffirmance, repudiation or transfer authority of the FDIC or NCUAB may be exercised to "cherry-pick" or otherwise treat independently all the QFCs between a depository institution in default and a person or any affiliate of such person. The FDIC has announced that its policy is not to repudiate or disaffirm QFCs selectively. This unified treatment is fundamental to the reduction of systemic risk.

Sec. 905. Clarifying Amendment Relating to Master Agreements. Section 905 of the Act specifies that a master agreement for one or more securities contracts, commodity contracts, forward contracts, repurchase agreements or swap agreements will be treated as a single QFC under the FDIA or the FCUA (but only with respect to the underlying agreements are themselves QFCs). This provision ensures that cross-product netting pursuant to a master agreement, or pursuant to an umbrella agreement for separate master agreements between the same parties, each of which is used to document one or more qualified financial contracts, will be enforceable under the FDIA and the FCUA. Cross-product netting permits a wide variety of financial transactions between two parties to be netted, thereby maximizing the present and potential future risk-reducing benefits of the netting arrangement between the parties. Express recognition of the enforceability of such cross-product master agreements furthers the policy of increasing legal certainty and reducing systemic risks in the case of an insolvency of a large financial participant.

Sec. 906. Federal Deposit Insurance Corporation Improvement Act of 1991. Subsection (a)(1) of section 906 of the Act amends the definition of "clearing organization" in section 402 of the FDICIA to include clearinghouses that are subject to exemptions pursuant to orders of the Securities and Exchange Commission or the Commodity Futures Trading Commission and to include multilateral clearing organizations (the definition of which was added to FDICIA by the CFMA).

FDICIA provides that a netting arrangement will be enforced pursuant to its terms, notwithstanding the failure of a party to the agreement. The current netting provisions of FDICIA, however, limit this protection to "financial institutions," which include depository institutions. Section 906(a)(2) amends the FDICIA definition of covered institutions to include (i) uninsured national and State member banks, irrespective of their eligibility for deposit insurance and (ii) foreign banks (including the foreign bank and its branches or agencies as a combined group, or only the foreign bank parent of a branch or agency). The latter change will extend the protections of FDICIA to ensure that U.S. financial organizations participating in netting agreements with foreign banks are covered by the Act, thereby enhancing the safety and soundness of these arrangements. It is intended that a non-defaulting foreign bank and its branches and agencies be considered to be a single financial institution for purposes of the bilateral netting provisions of FDICIA (except to the extent that the non-defaulting foreign bank and its branches and agencies on the one hand, and the defaulting financial institution, on the other, have entered into agreements that clearly evidence an intention that the non-defaulting foreign bank and its branches and agencies be treated as separate financial institutions for purposes of the bilateral netting provisions of FDICIA).

Subsection (a)(3) amends the FDICIA to provide that, for purposes of FDICIA, two or more clearing organizations that enter into a netting contract are considered "members" of each other. This assures the enforceability of netting arrangements involving two or more clearing organizations and a member common to all such organizations, thus reducing systemic risk in the event of the failure of such a member. Under the current FDICIA provisions, the enforceability of such arrangements depends on a case-by-case determination that clearing organizations could be regarded as members of each other for purposes of FDICIA.

Section 906(a)(4) of the Act amends the FDICIA definition of netting contract and the general rules applicable to netting contracts. The current FDICIA provisions require that the netting agreement must be governed by the law of the United States or a State to receive the protections of FDICIA. Many of these agreements, however, particularly netting arrangements covering positions taken in foreign exchange dealings, are governed by the laws of a foreign country. This subsection broadens the definition of "netting contract" to include those agreements governed by foreign law, and preserves the FDICIA requirement that a netting contract not be invalid under, or precluded by, Federal law.

Section 906(b) and (c) establish two exceptions to FDICIA's protection of the enforceability of the provisions of netting contracts between financial institutions and among clearing organization members. First, the termination provisions of netting contracts will not be enforceable based solely on (i) the appointment of a conservator for an insolvent depository institution under the FDIA or FCUA, or (ii) the appointment of a receiver or liquidating agent for such institution under the FDIA or FCUA, if such receiver or liquidating agent transfers or repudiates QFCs in accordance with the FDIA or FCUA and gives notice of a transfer by 5:00 p.m. on the business day following such appointment. This change is made to confirm the FDIC's and FCUA's flexibility to transfer or repudiate the QFCs of an insolvent depository institution in accordance with the terms of the

FDIA or FCUA. This modification also provides important legal certainty regarding the treatment of QFCs under the FDIA and FCUA, because the current relationship between these statutes and FDICIA is unclear.

The second exception provides that FDICIA does not override a stay order under SIPA with respect to foreclosure on securities (but not cash) collateral of a debtor (section 911 of the Act makes a conforming change to SIPA). There is also an exception relating to insolvent commodity brokers. Subsections (b) and (c) also clarify that a security agreement or other credit enhancement related to a netting contract is enforceable to the same extent as the underlying netting contract.

Section 906(d) of the Act adds a new section 407 to FDICIA. This new section provides that, notwithstanding any other law, QFCs with uninsured national banks, uninsured Federal branches or agencies, or Edge Act corporations, or uninsured State member banks that operate, or operate as, a multilateral clearing organization and that are placed in receivership or conservatorship will be treated in the same manner as if the contract were with an insured national bank or insured Federal branch for which a receiver or conservator was appointed. This provision will ensure that parties to QFCs with these institutions will have the same rights and obligations as parties entering into the same agreements with insured depository institutions. The new section also specifically limits the powers of a receiver or conservator for such an institution to those contained in 12 U.S.C. § 1821(e)(8), (9), (10), and (11), which address QFCs.

While the amendment would apply the same rules that apply to insured institutions, the provision would not change the rules that apply to insured institutions. Nothing in this section would amend the International Banking Act, the Federal Deposit Insurance Act, the National Bank Act, or other statutory provisions with respect to receiverships of insured national banks or Federal branches.

Sec. 907. Bankruptcy Law Amendments. Section 907 of the Act makes a series of amendments to the Bankruptcy Code. Subsection (a)(1) amends the Bankruptcy Code definitions of "repurchase agreement" and "swap agreement" to conform with the amendments to the FDIA contained in sections 901(e) and (f) of the Act.

In connection with the definition of "repurchase agreement," the term "qualified foreign government securities" is defined to include securities that are direct obligations of, or fully guaranteed by, central governments of members of the Organization for Economic Cooperation and Development (OECD). This language reflects developments in the repurchase agreement markets, which increasingly use foreign government securities as the underlying asset. The securities are limited to those issued by or guaranteed by full members of the OECD, as well as countries that have concluded special lending arrangements with the International Monetary Fund associated with the Fund's General Arrangements to Borrow.

Subsection (a)(1) also amends the definition of "repurchase agreement" to include those on mortgage-related securities, mortgage loans and interests therein, and to include principal and interest-only U.S. government and agency securities as securities that can be the subject of a "repurchase agreement." The reference in the definition to United States government- and agency-issued or fully guaranteed securities is intended to include obligations issued or guaranteed by Fannie Mae and the Federal Home Loan Mortgage Corporation (Freddie Mac) as well as all obligations eligible for purchase by Federal Reserve banks under the similar language of section 14(b) of the Federal Reserve Act.

This amendment is not intended to affect the status of repos involving securities or commodities as securities contracts, commodity contracts, or forward contracts, and their consequent eligibility for similar treatment under other provisions of the Bankruptcy Code. In particular, an agreement for the sale and repurchase of a security would continue to be a securities contract as defined in the Bankruptcy Code and thus also would be subject to the Bankruptcy Code provisions pertaining to securities contracts, even if not a "repurchase agreement" as defined in the Bankruptcy Code. Similarly, an agreement for the sale and repurchase of a commodity, even though not a "repurchase agreement" as defined in the Bankruptcy Code, would continue to be a forward contract for purposes of the Bankruptcy Code and would be subject to the Bankruptcy Code provisions pertaining to forward contracts.

Subsection (a)(1) specifies that repurchase obligations under a participation in a commercial mortgage loan do not make the participation agreement a "repurchase agreement." These repurchase obligations embedded in participations in commercial loans (such as recourse obligations) do not constitute a "repurchase agreement." However, a repurchase agreement involving the transfer of participations in commercial mortgage loans with a simultaneous agreement to repurchase the participation on demand or at a date certain one year or less after such transfer would constitute a "repurchase agreement" (as well as a "securities contract").

The definition of "swap agreement" is amended to include an "interest rate swap, option, future, or forward agreement, including a rate floor, rate cap, rate collar, cross-currency rate swap, and basis swap; a spot, same day-tomorrow, tomorrow-next, forward, or other foreign exchange or precious metals agreement; a currency swap, option, future, or forward agreement; an equity index or equity swap, option, future, or forward agreement; a debt index or debt swap, option, future, or forward agreement; a total return, credit spread or credit swap, option, future, or forward agreement; a commodity index or commodity swap, option, future, or forward agreement; or a weather swap, weather derivative, or weather option." As amended, the definition of "swap agreement" will update the statutory definition and achieve contractual netting across economically similar transactions.

The definition of "swap agreement" originally was intended to provide sufficient flexibility to avoid the need to amend the definition as the nature and uses of swap transactions matured. To that end, the phrase "or any other similar agreement" was included in the definition. (The phrase "or any similar agreement" has been added to the definitions of "forward contract," "commodity contract," "repurchase agreement," and "securities contract" for the same reason.) To clarify this, subsection (a)(1) expands the definition of "swap agreement" to include "any agreement or transaction that is similar to any other agreement or transaction referred to in [Section 101(53B) of the Bankruptcy Code] and that is of a type that has been, is presently, or in the future becomes, the subject of recurrent dealings in the swap markets" and [that] is a forward, swap, future, or option on one or more rates, currencies, commodities, equity securities or other equity instruments, debt securities or other debt instruments, quantitative measures associated with an occurrence, extent of an occurrence, or contingency associated with a financial, commercial, or economic consequence, or economic or financial indices or measures of economic or financial risk or value."

The definition of "swap agreement" in this subsection should not be interpreted to permit parties to document non-swaps as swap transactions. Traditional commercial arrangements, such as supply agreements, or other non-financial market transactions, such as commercial, residential or consumer loans, cannot be treated as "swaps" under the FDIA, the FCUA, or the Bankruptcy Code because the parties purport to document or label the transactions as "swap agreements." These definitions, and the characterization of a certain transaction as a "swap agreement," are not intended to affect the characterization, definition, or treatment of any instruments under any other statute, regulation, or rule including, but not limited to, the statutes, regulations or rules enumerated in subsection (a)(1)(C). Similarly, the definitions of "securities contract," "repurchase agreement," and "commodity contract" and the characterization of certain transactions as such a contract or agreement, are not intended to affect the characterization, definition, or treatment of any instrument under any other statute, regulation, or rule including, but not limited to, the statutes, regulations or rules enumerated in subsection (f).

The definition also includes any security agreement or arrangement, or other credit enhancement, related to a swap agreement, including any guarantee or reimbursement obligation related to a swap agreement. This ensures that any such agreement, arrangement or enhancement is itself deemed to be a swap agreement, and therefore eligible for treatment as such for purposes of termination, liquidation, acceleration, offset and netting under the Bankruptcy Code, the FDIA and the FCUA. Similar changes are made in the definitions of "forward contract," "commodity contract," "repurchase agreement," and "securities contract." An example of a security arrangement is a right of setoff; examples of other credit enhancements are letters of credit and other similar agreements. A security agreement or arrangement or guarantee or reimbursement obligation related to a "swap agreement," "forward contract," "commodity contract," "repurchase agreement" or "securities contract" will be such an agreement or contract only to the extent of the damages in connection with such agreement measured in accordance with Section 562 of the Bankruptcy Code (added by the Act). This limitation does not affect, however, the other provisions of the Bankruptcy Code (including Section 362(b)) relating to security arrangements in connection with agreements or contracts that otherwise qualify as "swap agreements," "forward contracts," "commodity contracts," "repurchase agreements" or "securities contracts."

The use of the term "forward" in the definition of "swap agreement" is not intended to refer only to transactions that fall within the definition of "forward contract." Instead, a "forward" transaction could be a "swap agreement" even if not a "forward contract."

Subsections (a)(2) and (a)(3) amend the Bankruptcy Code definitions of "securities contract" and "commodity contract," respectively, to conform them to the definitions in the FDIA.

Subsection (a)(2), like the amendments to the FDIA and the FCUA, amends the definition of "securities contract" expressly to encompass margin loans, to clarify the coverage of securities options and to clarify the coverage of repurchase and reverse repurchase transactions. The inclusion of "margin loans" in the definition is intended to encompass only those loans commonly known in the securities industry as "margin loans," such as credit permitted in a margin account under the Federal Reserve Board's Regulation T (whether or not effected in that account) or arrangements where a financial intermediary—a stockbroker, financial institution, financial participant, or securities clearing agency—extends credit in connection with the purchase, sale, carrying, or trading of securities. "Margin loans" do not include, however, other loans that happen to be secured by securities collateral. The reference in subsection (b) to a "guarantee" by or to a "securities clearing agency" is intended to cover other arrangements, such as novation, that have an effect similar to a guarantee. The reference to a "loan" of a security in the definition is intended to apply to loans of securities, whether or not for a "permitted purpose" under margin regulations. The reference to "repurchase and reverse repurchase transactions" is intended to eliminate any inquiry under section 555 and related provisions as to whether a repurchase or reverse repurchase transaction is a purchase and sale transaction or a secured financing. Repurchase and reverse repurchase transactions meeting certain criteria are already covered under the definition of "repurchase agreement" in the Bankruptcy Code. Repurchase and reverse repurchase transactions on all securities (including, for example, equity securities, asset-backed securities, corporate bonds and commercial paper) are included under the definition of "securities contract." A repurchase or reverse repurchase transaction which is a "securities contract" but not a "repurchase agreement" would thus be subject to the "counterparty limitations" contained in section 555 of the Bankruptcy Code (i.e., only stockbrokers, financial institutions, securities clearing agencies and financial participants can avail themselves of section 555 and related provisions).

Subsection (a)(2) also specifies that purchase, sale and repurchase obligations under a participation in a commercial mortgage loan do not constitute "securities contracts." While a contract for the purchase, sale or repurchase of a participation may constitute a "securities contract," the purchase, sale or repurchase obligation embedded in a participation agreement does not make that agreement a "securities contract." Section 907(a) clarifies the reference to guarantee or reimbursement obligation.

Section 907(b) amends the Bankruptcy Code definitions of "financial institution" and "forward contract merchant." The definition for "financial institution" includes Federal Reserve Banks and the receivers or conservators of insolvent depository institutions. With respect to securities contracts, the definition of "financial institution" expressly includes investment companies registered under the Investment Company Act of 1940.

Subsection (b) also adds a new definition of "financial participant" to limit the potential impact of insolvencies upon other major market participants. This definition will allow such market participants to close-out and net agreements with insolvent entities under sections 362(b)(6), 555, and 556 even if the creditor could not qualify as, for example, a commodity broker. Sections 362(b)(6), 555 and 556 preserve the limitations of the right to close-out and net such contracts, in most cases, to entities who qualify under the Bankruptcy Code's counterparty limitations. However, where the counterparty has transactions with a total gross dollar value of at least $1 billion in notional or actual principal amount outstanding on any day during the previous 15-month period, or has gross mark-to-market positions of at least $100 million (aggregated across counterparties) in one or more agreements or transactions on any day during the previous 15-month period, sections 362(b)(6), 555 and 556 and corresponding amendments would permit it to exercise netting and related rights irrespective of its inability otherwise to satisfy those counterparty limitations. This change will help prevent systemic impact upon the markets from a single failure, and is derived from threshold tests contained in Regulation EE promulgated by the Federal Reserve Board in implementing the netting provisions of the Federal Deposit Insurance Corporation Improvement Act. It is intended that the 15-month period be measured with reference to the 15 months preceding the filing of a petition by or against the debtor.

"Financial participant" is also defined to include "clearing organizations" within the meaning of FDICIA (as amended by the CFMA and Section 906 of the Act). This amendment, together with the inclusion of "financial participants" as eligible counterparties in connection with "commodity contracts," "forward contracts" and "securities contracts" and the amendments made in other Sections of the Act to include "financial participants" as counterparties eligible for the protections in respect of "swap agreements" and "repurchase agreements," take into account the CFMA and will allow clearing organizations to benefit from the protections of all of the provisions of the Bankruptcy Code relating to these contracts and agreements. This will further the goal of promoting the clearing of derivatives and other transactions as a way to reduce systemic risk. The definition of "financial participant" (as with the other provisions of the Bankruptcy Code relating to "securities contracts," "forward contracts," "commodity contracts," "repurchase agreements" and "swap agreements") is not mutually exclusive, i.e., an entity that qualifies as a "financial participant" could also be a "swap participant," "repo participant," "forward contract merchant," "commodity broker," "stockbroker," "securities clearing agency" and/or "financial institution."

Section 907(c) of the Act adds to the Bankruptcy Code new definitions for the terms "master netting agreement" and "master netting agreement participant." The definition of "master netting agreement" is designed to protect the termination and close-out netting provisions of cross-product master agreements between parties. Such an agreement may be used: (i) to document a wide variety of securities contracts, commodity contracts, forward contracts, repurchase agreements and swap agreements, or (ii) as an umbrella agreement for separate master agreements between the same parties, each of which is used to document a discrete type of transaction. The definition includes security agreements or arrangements or other credit enhancements related to one or more such agreements and clarifies that a master netting agreement will be treated as such even if it documents transactions that are not within the enumerated categories of qualifying transactions (but the provisions of the Bankruptcy Code relating to master netting agreements and the other categories of transactions will not apply to such other transactions). A "master netting agreement participant" is any entity that is a party to an outstanding master netting agreement with a debtor before the filing of a bankruptcy petition.

Subsection (d) amends section 362(b) of the Bankruptcy Code to protect enforcement, free from the automatic stay, of setoff or netting provisions in swap agreements and in master netting agreements and security agreements or arrangements related to one or more swap agreements or master netting agreements. This provision parallels the other provisions of the Bankruptcy Code that protect netting provisions of securities contracts, commodity contracts, forward contracts, and repurchase agreements. Because the relevant definitions include related security agreements, the references to "setoff" in these provisions, as well as in section 362(b)(6) and (7) of the Bankruptcy Code, are intended to refer also to rights to foreclose on, and to set off against obligations to return, collateral securing swap agreements, master netting agreements, repurchase agreements, securities contracts, commodity contracts, or forward contracts. Collateral may be pledged to cover the cost of replacing the defaulted transactions in the relevant market, as well as other costs and expenses incurred or estimated to be incurred for the purpose of hedging or reducing the risks arising out of such termination. Enforcement of these agreements and arrangements free from the automatic stay is consistent with the policy goal of minimizing systemic risk.

Subsection (d) also clarifies that the provisions protecting setoff and foreclosure in relation to securities contracts, commodity contracts, forward contracts, repurchase agreements, swap agreements, and master netting agreements free from the automatic stay apply to collateral pledged by the debtor but that cannot technically be "held by" the creditor, such as receivables and book-entry securities, and to collateral that has been repledged by the creditor and securities re-sold pursuant to repurchase agreements.

Subsections (e) and (f) of section 907 of the Act amend sections 546 and 548(d) of the Bankruptcy Code to provide that transfers made under or in connection with a master netting agreement may not be avoided by a trustee except where such transfer is made with actual intent to hinder, delay or defraud and not taken in good faith. This amendment provides the same protections for a transfer made under, or in connection with, a master netting agreement as currently is provided for margin payments, settlement payments and other transfers received by commodity brokers, forward contract merchants, stockbrokers, financial institutions, securities clearing agencies, repo participants, and swap participants under sections 546 and 548(d), except to the extent the trustee could otherwise avoid such a transfer made under an individual contract covered by such master netting agreement.

Subsections (g), (h), (i), and (j) of section 907 clarify that the provisions of the Bankruptcy Code that protect: (i) rights of liquidation under securities contracts, commodity contracts, forward contracts and repurchase agreements also protect rights of termination or acceleration under such contracts, and (ii) rights to terminate under swap agreements also protect rights of liquidation and acceleration.

Section 907(k) of the Act adds a new section 561 to the Bankruptcy Code to protect the contractual right of a master netting agreement participant to enforce any rights of termination, liquidation, acceleration, offset or netting under a master netting agreement. These rights include rights arising: (i) from the rules of a derivatives clearing organization, multilateral clearing organization, securities clearing agency, securities exchange, securities association, contract market, derivatives transaction execution facility or board of trade; (ii) under common law, law merchant; or (iii) by reason of normal business practice. This reflects the enactment of the CFMA and the current treatment of rights under swap agreements under section 560 of the Bankruptcy Code. Similar changes to reflect the enactment of the CFMA have been made to the definition of "contractual right" for purposes of Sections 555, 556, 559, and 560 of the Bankruptcy Code.

Subsections (b)(2)(A) and (b)(2)(B) of new Section 561 limit the exercise of contractual rights to net or to offset obligations where the debtor is a commodity broker and one leg of the obligations sought to be netted relates to commodity contracts traded on or subject to the rules of a contract market designated under the Commodity Exchange Act or a derivatives transaction execution facility registered under the Commodity Exchange Act. Under subsection (b)(2)(A) netting or offsetting is not permitted in these circumstances if the party seeking to net or to offset has no positive net equity in the commodity accounts at the debtor. Subsection (b)(2)(B) applies only if the debtor is a commodity broker, acting on behalf of its own customer, and is in turn a customer of another commodity broker. In that case, the latter commodity broker may not net or offset obligations under such commodity contracts with other claims against its customer, the debtor. Subsections (b)(2)(A) and (b)(2)(B) limit the depletion of assets available for distribution to customers of commodity brokers. Subsection (b)(2)(C) provides an exception to subsections (b)(2)(A) and (b)(2)(B) for cross-margining and other similar arrangements approved by, or submitted to and not rendered ineffective by, the Commodity Futures Trading Commission, as well as certain other netting arrangements.

For the purposes of Bankruptcy Code sections 555, 556, 559, 560, and 561, it is intended that the normal business practice in the event of a default of a party based on bankruptcy or insolvency is to terminate, liquidate or accelerate securities contracts, commodity contracts, forward contracts, repurchase agreements, swap agreements and master netting agreements with the bankrupt or insolvent party. The protection of netting and offset rights in sections 560 and 561 is in addition to the protections afforded in sections 362(b)(6), (b)(7), (b)(17), and (b)(28) of the Bankruptcy Code.

Under the Act, the termination, liquidation or acceleration rights of a master netting agreement participant are subject to limitations contained in other provisions of the Bankruptcy Code relating to securities contracts and repurchase agreements. In particular, if a securities contract or repurchase agreement is documented under a master netting agreement, a party's termination, liquidation and acceleration rights would be subject to the provisions of the Bankruptcy Code relating to orders authorized under the provisions of SIPA or any statute administered by the SEC. In addition, the netting rights of a party to a master netting agreement would be subject to any contractual terms between the parties limiting or waiving netting or set off rights. Similarly, a waiver by a bank or a counterparty of netting or set off rights in connection with QFCs would be enforceable under the FDIA.

New section 561 of the Bankruptcy Code clarifies that the provisions of the Bankruptcy Code related to securities contracts, commodity contracts, forward contracts, repurchase agreements, swap agreements and master netting agreements apply in a proceeding ancillary to a foreign insolvency proceeding under new section 304 of the Bankruptcy Code.

Subsections (l) and (m) of section 907 of the Act clarify that the exercise of termination and netting rights will not otherwise affect the priority of the creditor's claim after the exercise of netting, foreclosure and related rights.

Subsection (n) amends section 553 of the Bankruptcy Code to clarify that the acquisition by a creditor of setoff rights in connection with swap agreements, repurchase agreements, securities contracts, forward contracts, commodity contracts and master netting agreements cannot be avoided as a preference. This subsection also adds setoff of the kinds described in sections 555, 556, 559, 560, and 561 of the Bankruptcy Code to the types of setoff excepted from section 553(b).

Section 907(o), as well as other subsections of the Act, adds references to "financial participant" in all the provisions of the Bankruptcy Code relating to securities, forward and commodity contracts and repurchase and swap agreements.

Sec. 908. Recordkeeping Requirements. Section 908 of the Act amends section 11(e)(8) of the Federal Deposit Insurance Act to explicitly authorize the FDIC, in consultation with appropriate Federal banking agencies, to prescribe regulations on recordkeeping by any insured depository institution with respect to QFCs only if the insured financial institution is in a troubled condition (as such term is defined in the FDIA).

Sec. 909. Exemptions from Contemporaneous Execution Requirement. Section 909 of the Act amends FDIA section 13(e)(2) to provide that an agreement for the collateralization of governmental deposits, bankruptcy estate funds, Federal Reserve Bank or Federal Home Loan Bank extensions of credit or one or more QFCs shall not be deemed invalid solely because such agreement was not entered into contemporaneously with the acquisition of the collateral or because of pledges, delivery or substitution of the collateral made in accordance with such agreement.

The amendment codifies portions of policy statements issued by the FDIC regarding the application of section 13(e), which codifies the "D'Oench Duhme" doctrine. With respect to QFCs, this codification recognizes that QFCs often are subject to collateral and other security arrangements that may require posting and return of collateral on an ongoing basis based on the mark-to-market values of the collateralized transactions. The codification of only portions of the existing FDIC policy statements on these and related issues should not give rise to any negative implication regarding the continued validity of these policy statements.

Sec. 910. Damage Measure. Section 910 of the Act adds a new section 562 to the Bankruptcy Code providing that damages under any swap agreement, securities contract, forward contract, commodity contract, repurchase agreement or master netting agreement will be calculated as of the earlier of: (i) the date of rejection of such agreement by a trustee, or (ii) the date or dates of liquidation, termination or acceleration of such contract or agreement.

Section 562 provides an exception to the rules in (i) and (ii) if there are no commercially reasonable determinants of value as of such date or dates, in which case damages are to be measured as of the earliest subsequent date or dates on which there are commercially reasonable determinants of value. Although it is expected that in most circumstances damages would be measured as of the date or dates of either rejection or liquidation, termination or acceleration, in certain unusual circumstances, such as dysfunctional markets or liquidation of very large portfolios, there may be no commercially reasonable determinants of value for liquidating any such agreements or contracts or for liquidating all such agreements and contracts in a large portfolio on a single day. It is expected that measuring damages as of a date or dates before the date of liquidation, termination, or acceleration will occur only in very unusual circumstances.

The party determining damages is given limited discretion to determine the dates as of which damages are to be measured. Its actions are circumscribed unless there are no "commercially reasonable" determinants of value for it to measure damages on the date or dates of either rejection or liquidation, termination or acceleration. The references to "commercially reasonable" are intended to reflect existing state law standards relating to a creditor's actions in determining damages. New section 562 provides that if damages are not measured as of either the date of rejection or the date or dates of liquidation, termination or acceleration and the trustee challenges the timing of the measurement of damages by the non-defaulting party determining the damages, then the non-defaulting party, rather than the trustee, has the burden of proving the absence of any commercially reasonable determinants of value.

New section 562 is not intended to have any impact on the determination under the Bankruptcy Code of the timing of damages for contracts and agreements other than those specified in section 562. Also, section 562 does not apply to proceedings under the FDIA, and it is not intended that Section 562 have any impact on the interpretation of the provisions of the FDIA relating to timing of damages in respect of QFCs or other contracts.

Sec. 911. SIPC Stay. Section 911 of the Act amends SIPA to provide that an order or decree issued pursuant to SIPA shall not operate as a stay of any right of liquidation, termination, acceleration, offset or netting under one or more securities contracts, commodity contracts, forward contracts, repurchase agreements, swap agreements or master netting agreements (as defined in the Bankruptcy Code and including rights of foreclosure on collateral), except that such order or decree may stay any right to foreclose on or dispose of securities (but not cash) collateral pledged by the debtor or sold by the debtor under a repurchase agreement or lent by the debtor under a securities lending agreement. A corresponding amendment to FDICIA is made by section 906. A creditor that was stayed in exercising rights against such securities would be entitled to post-insolvency interest to the extent of the value of such securities.

TITLE X. PROTECTION OF FAMILY FARMERS AND FAMILY FISHERMEN

Sec. 1001. Permanent Reenactment of Chapter 12. Chapter 12 is a specialized form of bankruptcy relief available only to a "family farmer with regular annual income,"[167] a defined term.[168] This form of bankruptcy relief permits eligible family farmers, under the supervision of a bankruptcy trustee,[169] to reorganize their debts pursuant to a repayment plan.[170] The special attributes of chapter 12 make it better suited to meet the particularized needs of family farmers in financial distress than other forms of bankruptcy relief, such as chapter 11[171] and chapter 13.[172]

Chapter 12 was enacted on a temporary 7-year basis as part of the Bankruptcy Judges, United States Trustees, and Family Farmer Bankruptcy Act of 1986[173] in response to the farm financial crisis of the early- to mid-1980's.[174] It was subsequently reenacted and extended on several occasions. The most recent extension, authorized as part of the Farm Security and Rural Investment Act of 2002, provides that chapter remains in effect until December 31, 2002.[175]

Section 1001(a) of the Act reenacts chapter 12 of the Bankruptcy Code and provides that such reenactment takes effect as of July 1, 2005. Section 1001(b) makes a conforming amendment to section 302 of the Bankruptcy Judges, United States Trustees, and Family Farmer Bankruptcy Act of 1986. As a result of this provision, chapter 12 becomes a permanent form of relief under the Bankruptcy Code.

Sec. 1002. Debt Limit Increase. Section 1002 of the Act amends section 104(b) of the Bankruptcy Code to provide for periodic adjustments for inflation of the debt eligibility limit for family farmers.

Sec. 1003. Certain Claims Owed to Governmental Units. Subsection (a) of section 1003 of the Act amends section 1222(a) of the Bankruptcy Code to add an exception with respect to payments to a governmental unit for a debt entitled to priority under section 507 if such debt arises from the sale, transfer, exchange, or other disposition of an asset used in the debtor's farming operation, but only if the debtor receives a discharge. Section 1003(b) amends section 1231(b) of the Bankruptcy Code to have it apply to any governmental unit. Subsection (c) provides that section 1003 becomes effective on the date of enactment of this Act and applies to cases commenced after such effective date.

Sec. 1004. Definition of Family Farmer. Section 1004 of the Act amends the definition of "family farmer" in section 101(18) of the Bankruptcy Code to increase the debt eligibility limit from $1,500,000 to $3,237,000. It also reduces the percentage of the farmer's liabilities that must arise out of the debtor's farming operation for eligibility purposes from 80 percent to 50 percent.

Sec. 1005. Elimination of Requirement that Family Farmer and Spouse Receive over 50 Percent of Income from Farming Operation in Year Prior to Bankruptcy. Section 1005 of the Act amends the Bankruptcy Code's definition of "family farmer" with respect to the determination of the farmer's income. Current law provides that a debtor, in order to be eligible to be a family farmer, must derive a specified percentage of his or her income from farming activities for the taxable year preceding the commencement of the bank-

---

167 11 U.S.C. § 109(f).

168 11 U.S.C. § 101(19).

169 11 U.S.C. § 1202.

170 11 U.S.C. § 1222.

171 For example, chapter 12 is typically less complex and expensive than chapter 11, a form of bankruptcy relief generally utilized to effectuate large corporate reorganizations.

172 Chapter 13, a form of bankruptcy relief for individuals seeking to reorganize their debts, limits its eligibility to debtors with debts in lower amounts than permitted for eligibility purposes under chapter 12. *Cf.* 11 U.S.C. § 109(e), 101(18).

173 Pub. L. No. 99-554, § 255, 100 Stat. 3088, 3105 (1986).

174 *See* U.S. Dept. of Agriculture, Info. Bull. No. 724-09, Issues in Agricultural and Rural Finance: Do Farmers Need a Separate Chapter in the Bankruptcy Code? (Oct. 1997).

> As one of the principal proponents of this legislation explained:
>
> I doubt there will be anything that we do that will have such an immediate impact in the grassroots of our country with respect to the situation that exists in most of the heartland, and that is in the agricultural sector. . . .
>
> You know, William Jennings Bryan in his famous speech, the Cross of Gold, almost 60 years ago [sic], stated these words: "Destroy our cities and they will spring up again as if by magic; but destroy our farms, and the grass will grow in every city in our country."
>
> This legislation will hopefully stem the tide that we have seen so recently in the massive bankruptcies in the family farm area.
>
> 132 Cong. Rec. 28,147 (1986) (statement of Rep. Mike Synar (D-Okla.)).

175 Pub. L. No. 107-171, § 10814 (2002).

ruptcy case. Section 1005 adjusts the threshold percentage to be met during either: (1) the taxable year preceding the filing of the bankruptcy case; or (2) the taxable year in the second and third taxable years preceding the filing of the bankruptcy case.

Sec. 1006. Prohibition of Retroactive Assessment of Disposable Income. Section 1006 of the Act amends the Bankruptcy Code in two respects concerning chapter 12 plans. Section 1006(a) amends Bankruptcy Code section 1225(b) to permit the court to confirm a plan even if the distribution proposed under the plan equal or exceed the debtor's projected disposable income for that period, providing the plan otherwise satisfies the requirements for confirmation. Section 1006(b) amends Bankruptcy Code section 1229 to restrict the bases for modifying a confirmed chapter 12 plan. Specifically, Section 1006(b) to provide that a confirmed chapter 12 plan may not be modified to increase the amount of payments due prior to the date of the order modifying the confirmation of the plan. Where the modification is based on an increase in the debtor's disposable income, the plan may not be modified to require payments to unsecured creditors in any particular month in an amount greater than the debtor's disposable income for that month, unless the debtor proposes such a modification. Section 1006(b) further provides that a modification of a plan shall not require payments that would leave the debtor with insufficient funds to carry on the farming operation after the plan is completed, unless the debtor proposes such a modification.

Sec. 1007. Family Fishermen. Subsection (a) of section 1007 of the Act amends Bankruptcy Code section 101 to add definitions of "commercial fishing operation," "commercial fishing vessel," "family fisherman" and "family fisherman with regular annual income." The definition of "commercial fishing operation" includes the catching or harvesting of fish, shrimp, lobsters, urchins, seaweed, shellfish, or other aquatic species or products. The term "commercial fishing vessel" is defined as a vessel used by a fisher to "carry out a commercial fishing operation." The term "family fisherman" is defined as an individual engaged in a commercial fishing operation, with an aggregate debt limit of $1.5 million. The definition specifies that at least 80 percent of those debts must be derived from a commercial fishing operation. The percentage of income that must be derived from such operation is specified to be more than 50 percent of the individual's gross income for the taxable year preceding the taxable year in which the case was filed. Similar provisions are included for corporations and partnerships. The term "family fisherman with regular annual income" is defined as a family fisherman whose annual income is sufficiently stable and regular to enable such person to make payments under a chapter 12 plan. Section 1007(b) amends Bankruptcy Code section 109 to provide that a family fisherman is eligible to be a debtor under chapter 12. Section 1007(c) amends the heading of chapter 12 to include a reference to family fisherman and makes conforming revisions to Sections 1203 and 1206.

TITLE XI. HEALTH CARE AND EMPLOYEE BENEFITS

Sec. 1101. Definitions. Subsection (a) of section 1101 of the Act amends section 101 of the Bankruptcy Code to add a definition of "health care business." The definition includes any public or private entity (without regard to whether that entity is for or not for profit) that is primarily engaged in offering to the general public facilities and services for the diagnosis or treatment of injury, deformity or disease; and surgical, drug treatment, psychiatric or obstetric care. It also includes the following entities: (1) a general or specialized hospital; (2) an ancillary ambulatory, emergency, or surgical treatment facility; (3) a hospice; (d) a home health agency; (e) other health care institution that is similar to an entity referred to in (a) through (d); and other long-term care facility. These include a skilled nursing facility, intermediate care facility, assisted living facility, home for the aged, domiciliary care facility, or health care institution that is related to an aforementioned facility. Section 1101(b) amends Bankruptcy Code section 101 to add a definition of "patient." The term means an individual who obtains or receives services from a health care business. Section 1101(c) amends section 101 of the Bankruptcy Code to add a definition of "patient records." The term means any written document relating to a patient or record recorded in a magnetic, optical, or other form of electronic medium. Section 1101(d) specifies that the amendments effectuated by new section 101(27A) do not affect the interpretation of section 109(b).

Sec. 1102. Disposal of Patient Records. Section 1102 of the Act adds a provision to the Bankruptcy Code specifying requirements for the disposal of patient records in a chapter 7, 9, or 11 case of a health care business where the trustee lacks sufficient funds to pay for the storage of such records in accordance with applicable Federal or state law. The requirements chiefly consist of providing notice to the affected patients and specifying the method of disposal for unclaimed records. They are intended to protect the privacy and confidentiality of a patient's medical records when they are in the custody of a health care business in bankruptcy. The provision specifies the following requirements:

1. The trustee shall: (a) publish notice in one or more appropriate newspapers stating that if the records are not claimed by the patient or an insurance provider (if permitted under applicable law) within 365 days of the date of such notice, then the trustee will destroy such records; and (b) during the first 180 days of such 365-day period, attempt to directly notify by mail each patient and appropriate insurance carrier of the claiming or disposing of such records.
2. If after providing such notice patient records are not

claimed within the specified period, the trustee shall, upon the expiration of such period, send a request by certified mail to each appropriate Federal agency to request permission from such agency to deposit the records with the agency.

3. If after providing the notice as set forth above, patient records are not claimed, the trustee shall destroy such records as follows: (a) by shredding or burning, if the records are written; or (b) by destroying the records so that their information cannot be retrieved, if the records are magnetic, optical or electronic.

It is anticipated that if the estate of the debtor lacks the funds to pay for the costs and expenses related to the above, the trustee may recover such costs and expenses under section 506(c) of the Bankruptcy Code.

Sec. 1103. Administrative Expense Claim for Costs of Closing a Health Care Business and Other Administrative Expenses. Section 1103 of the Act amends section 503(b) of the Bankruptcy Code to provide that the actual, necessary costs and expenses of closing a health care business (including the disposal of patient records or transferral of patients) incurred by a trustee, Federal agency, or a department or agency of a state are allowed administrative expenses.

Sec. 1104. Appointment of Ombudsman to Act as Patient Advocate. Section 1104 of the Act adds a provision to the Bankruptcy Code requiring the court to order the appointment of an ombudsman to monitor the quality of patient care within 30 days after commencement of a chapter 7, 9, or 11 health care business bankruptcy case, unless the court finds that such appointment is not necessary for the protection of patients under the specific facts of the case. The ombudsman must be a disinterested person. If the health care business is a long-term care facility, a person who is serving as a State Long-Term Care Ombudsman of the Older Americans Act of 1965 may be appointed as the ombudsman in such case. The ombudsman must: (1) monitor the quality of patient care to the extent necessary under the circumstances, including interviewing patients and physicians; (2) report to the court, not less than 60 days from the date of appointment and then every 60 days thereafter, at a hearing or in writing regarding the quality of patient care at the health care business involved; and (3) notify the court by motion or written report (with notice to appropriate parties in interest) if the ombudsman determines that the quality of patient care is declining significantly or is otherwise being materially compromised. The provision requires the ombudsman to maintain any information obtained that relates to patients (including patient records) as confidential. Section 1104(b) amends section 330(a)(1) of the Bankruptcy Code to authorize the payment of reasonable compensation to an ombudsman.

Sec. 1105. Debtor in Possession; Duty of Trustee to Transfer Patients. Section 1105 of the Act amends section 704(a) of the Bankruptcy Code to require a trustee or debtor in possession to use all reasonable and best efforts to transfer patients from a health care business that is in the process of being closed to an appropriate health care business. The transferee health care business should be in the vicinity of the transferor health care business, provide the patient with services that are substantially similar to those provided by the transferor health care business, and maintain a reasonable quality of care.

Sec. 1106. Exclusion from Program Participation Not Subject to Automatic Stay. Section 1106 amends section 362(b) of the Bankruptcy Code to except from the automatic stay the exclusion by the Secretary of Health and Human Services of a debtor from participation in the medicare program or other specified Federal health care programs.

TITLE XII. TECHNICAL AMENDMENTS

Sec. 1201. Definitions. Section 1201 of the Act amends the definitions contained in section 101 of the Bankruptcy Code. Paragraphs (1), (2), (4), and (7) of section 1201 make technical changes to section 101 to convert each definition into a sentence (thereby facilitating future amendments to the separate paragraphs) and to redesignate the definitions in correct and completely numerical sequence. Paragraph (3) of section 1101 makes necessary and conforming amendments to cross references to the newly redesignated definitions.

Paragraph (5) of section 1201 concerns single asset real estate debtors. A single asset real estate chapter 11 case presents special concerns. As the name implies, the principal asset in this type of case consists of some form of real estate, such as undeveloped land. Typically, the form of ownership of a single asset real estate debtor is a corporation or limited partnership. The largest creditor in a single asset real estate case is typically the secured lender who advanced the funds to the debtor to acquire the real property. Often, a single asset real estate debtor resorts to filing for bankruptcy relief for the sole purpose of staying an impending foreclosure proceeding or sale commenced by the secured lender. Foreclosure actions are filed when the debtor lacks sufficient cash flow to service the debt and maintain the property. Taxing authorities may also have liens against the property. Based on the nature of its principal asset, a single asset real estate debtor often has few, if any, unsecured creditors. If unsecured creditors exist, they may have only nominal claims against the single asset real estate debtor. Depending on the nature and ownership of any business operating on the debtor's real property, the debtor may have few, if any, employees. Accordingly, there may be little interest on behalf of unsecured creditors in a single asset real estate case to serve on a creditors' committee.

In 1994, the Bankruptcy Code was amended to accord special treatment for single asset real estate debtors. It defined this type of debtor as a bankruptcy estate comprised of a single piece of real property or project, other than residential real property with fewer than four residential units. The property or project must generate substantially all of the debtor's gross income. A debtor that conducts substantial business on the property beyond that relating to its operation is excluded from this definition. In addition, the definition fixed a monetary cap. To qualify as a single asset real estate debtor, the debtor could not have noncontingent, liquidated secured debts in excess of $4 million. Subparagraph (5)(A) amends the definition of "single asset real estate" to exclude family farmers from this definition. Paragraph (5)(B) amends section 101(51B) of the Bankruptcy Code to eliminate the $4 million debt limitation on single asset real estate. The present $4 million cap prevents the use of the expedited relief procedure in many commercial property reorganizations, and effectively provides an opportunity for a number of debtors to abusively file for bankruptcy in order to obtain the protection of the automatic stay against their creditors. As a result of this amendment, creditors in more cases will be able to obtain the expedited relief from the automatic stay which is made available under section 362(d)(3) of the Bankruptcy Code.

Paragraph (6) of section 1201, together with section 1214, respond to a 1997 Ninth Circuit case, in which two purchase money lenders (without knowledge that the debtor had recently filed an undisclosed chapter 11 case that was subsequently converted to chapter 7), funded the debtor's acquisition of an apartment complex and recorded their purchase-money deed of trust immediately following recordation of the deed to the debtors.[176] Specifically, it amends the definition of "transfer" in section 101(54) of the Bankruptcy Code to include the "creation of a lien." This amendment gives expression to a widely held understanding since the enactment of the Bankruptcy Reform Act of 1978,[177] that is, a transfer includes the creation of a lien.

Sec. 1202. Adjustment of Dollar Amounts. Bankruptcy Code section 104 provides for the periodic automatic adjustment of certain dollar amounts specified in the Code to reflect the change in the Consumer Price Index. Section 1202 amends Bankruptcy Code section 104(b) to add a reference to certain other monetary amounts specified in the Bankruptcy Code section. These include: (1) section 522(f)(3) (pertaining to the avoidance of certain liens on implements and other personal property valued at less than $5,000); (2) section 101(19A) (definition of family fisherman); (3) section 522(f)(4) (definition of household goods); (4) section 541(b) (property items, such as certain educational individual retirement accounts and tuition credit or certificate programs, that do not constitute property of the bankruptcy estate); (5) section 547(c)(9) (limits the avoidance of a preferential transfer, under certain circumstances); (6) section 1322(d) (concerning the applicability of the needs-based test to chapter 13 debtors with above median incomes); (7) section 1325(b) (determination of disposable income for chapter 13 debtors with above median incomes); and (8) section 1326(b)(3) (payments to a chapter 7 trustee in a chapter 13 case). In addition, the provision adds a reference to section 1409(b) of title 28 of the United States Code, which pertains to the venue of proceedings to recover a money judgment or property.

Sec. 1203. Extension of Time. Section 1203 of the Act makes a technical amendment to correct a reference error described in amendment notes contained in the United States Code. As specified in the amendment note relating to subsection (c)(2) of section 108 of the Bankruptcy Code, the amendment made by section 257(b)(2)(B) of Public Law 99-554 could not be executed as stated.

Sec. 1204. Technical Amendments. Section 1204 of the Act makes technical amendments to Bankruptcy Code sections 109(b)(2) (to strike an statutory cross reference), 541(b)(2) (to add "or" to the end of this provision), and 522(b)(1) (to replace "product" with "products").

Sec. 1205. Penalty for Persons Who Negligently or Fraudulently Prepare Bankruptcy Petitions. Section 1205 of the Act amends section 110(j)(4) of the Bankruptcy Code to change the reference to attorneys from the singular possessive to the plural possessive.

Sec. 1206. Limitation on Compensation of Professional Persons. Section 328(a) of the Bankruptcy Code provides that a trustee or a creditors' and equity security holders' committee may, with court approval, obtain the services of a professional person on any reasonable terms and conditions of employment, including on a retainer, on an hourly basis, or on a contingent fee basis. Section 1206 of the Act amends section 328(a) to include compensation "on a fixed or percentage fee basis" in addition to the other specified forms of reimbursement.

Sec. 1207. Effect of Conversion. Section 1207 of the Act makes a technical correction in section 348(f)(2) of the Bankruptcy Code to clarify that the first reference to property, like the subsequent reference to property, is a reference to property of the estate.

Sec. 1208. Allowance of Administrative Expenses. Section 1208 of the Act amends section 503(b)(4) of the Bankruptcy Code to limit the types of compensable professional services rendered by an attorney or accountant that can qualify as administrative expenses in a bankruptcy case. Expenses for attorneys or accountants incurred by individual members of creditors' or equity security holders' committees are not recoverable, but expenses incurred for such professional services incurred by such committees themselves would be.

176 *Thompson v. Margen* (*In re* McConville), 110 F.3d 47 (9th Cir.), *cert. denied*, 522 U.S. 966 (1997).

177 Pub. L. No. 95-598, 92 Stat. 2549 (1978).

Sec. 1209. Exceptions to Discharge. Section 1209 of the Act amends section 523(a) of the Bankruptcy Code to correct a technical error in the placement of paragraph (15), which was added to section 523 by section 304(e)(1) of the Bankruptcy Reform Act of 1994. Section 1209 also amends section 523(a)(9), which makes nondischargeable any debt resulting from death or personal injury arising from the debtor's unlawful operation of a motor vehicle while intoxicated, to add "watercraft, or aircraft" after "motor vehicle." Neither additional term should be defined or included as a "motor vehicle" in section 523(a)(9) and each is intended to comprise unpowered as well as motor-powered craft. Congress previously made the policy judgment that the equities of persons injured by drunk drivers outweigh the responsible debtor's interest in a fresh start, and here clarifies that the policy applies not only on land but also on the water and in the air. Viewed from a practical standpoint, this provision closes a loophole that gives intoxicated watercraft and aircraft operators preferred treatment over intoxicated motor vehicle drivers and denies victims of alcohol and drug related boat and plane accidents the same rights accorded to automobile accident victims under current law. Finally, this section corrects a grammatical error in section 523(e).

Sec. 1210. Effect of Discharge. Section 1210 of the Act makes technical amendments to correct errors in section 524(a)(3) of the Bankruptcy Code caused by section 257(o)(2) of Public Law 99-554 and section 501(d)(14)(A) of Public Law 103-394.[178]

Sec. 1211. Protection Against Discriminatory Treatment. Section 1211 of the Act conforms a reference to its antecedent reference in section 525(c) of the Bankruptcy Code. The omission of "student" before "grant" in the second place it appears in section 525(c) made possible the interpretation that a broader limitation on lender discretion was intended, so that no loan could be denied because of a prior bankruptcy if the lending institution was in the business of making student loans. Section 1211 is intended to make clear that lenders involved in making government guaranteed or insured student loans are not barred by this Bankruptcy Code provision from denying other types of loans based on an applicant's bankruptcy history; only student loans and grants, therefore, cannot be denied under section 525(c) because of a prior bankruptcy.

Sec. 1212. Property of the Estate. Production payments are royalties tied to the production of a certain volume or value of oil or gas, determined without regard to production costs. They typically would be paid by an oil or gas operator to the owner of the underlying property on which the oil or gas is found. Under section 541(b)(4)(B)(ii) of the Bankruptcy Code, added by the Bankruptcy Reform Act of 1994, production payments are generally excluded from the debtor's estate, provided they could be included only by virtue of section 542 of the Bankruptcy Code, which relates generally to the obligation of those holding property which belongs in the estate to turn it over to the trustee. Section 1212 of the Act adds to this proviso a reference to section 365 of the Bankruptcy Code, which authorizes the trustee to assume or reject an executory contract or unexpired lease. It thereby clarifies the original Congressional intent to generally exclude production payments from the debtor's estate.

Sec. 1213. Preferences. Section 547 of the Bankruptcy Code authorizes a trustee to avoid a preferential payment made to a creditor by a debtor within 90 days of filing, whether the creditor is an insider or an outsider. To address the concern that a corporate insider (such as an officer or director who is a creditor of his or her own corporation) has an unfair advantage over outside creditors, section 547 also authorizes a trustee to avoid a preferential payment made to an insider creditor between 90 days and one year before filing. Several recent cases, including *DePrizio*,[179] allowed the trustee to "reach-back" and avoid a transfer to a noninsider creditor made within the 90-day to one-year time frame if an insider benefitted from the transfer in some way. This had the effect of discouraging lenders from obtaining loan guarantees, lest transfers to the lender be vulnerable to recapture by reason of the debtor's insider relationship with the loan guarantor. Section 202 of the Bankruptcy Reform Act of 1994 addressed the *DePrizio* problem by inserting a new section 550(c) into the Bankruptcy Code to prevent avoidance or recovery from a noninsider creditor during the 90-day to one-year period even though the transfer to the noninsider benefitted an insider creditor. The 1994 amendments, however, failed to make a corresponding amendment to section 547, which deals with the avoidance of preferential transfers. As a result, a trustee could still utilize section 547 to avoid a preferential lien given to a noninsider bank, more than 90 days but less than one year before bankruptcy, if the transfer benefitted an insider guarantor of the debtor's debt. Accordingly, section 1213 of the Act makes a perfecting amendment to section 547 to provide that if the trustee avoids a transfer given by the debtor to a noninsider for the benefit of an insider creditor between 90 days and one year before filing, that avoidance is valid only with respect to the insider creditor. Thus both the previous amendment to section 550 and the perfecting amendment to section 547 protect the noninsider from the avoiding powers of the trustee exercised with respect to transfers made during the 90-day to one year pre-filing period. This provision is intended to apply to any case, including any adversary proceeding, that is pending or commenced on or after the date of enactment of this Act.

178 For a description of these errors, see the appropriate footnote and amendment notes in the United States Code.

179 *Levit v. Ingersoll Rand Fin. Corp.*, 874 F.2d 1186 (7th Cir. 1989); *see also Ray v. City Bank and Trust Co.* (*In re* C-L Cartage Co.), 899 F.2d 1490 (6th Cir. 1990); *Manufacturers Hanover Leasing Corp. v. Lowrey* (*In re* Robinson Bros. Drilling, Inc.), 892 F.2d 850 (10th Cir. 1989).

Sec. 1214. Postpetition Transactions. Section 1214 of the Act amends section 549(c) of the Bankruptcy Code to clarify its application to an interest in real property. This amendment should be construed in conjunction with section 1201 of the Act.[180]

Sec. 1215. Disposition of Property of the Estate. Section 1215 of the Act amends section 726(b) of the Bankruptcy Code to strike an erroneous reference.[181]

Sec. 1216. General Provisions. Section 1216 of the Act amends section 901(a) of the Bankruptcy Code to correct an omission in a list of sections applicable to cases under chapter 9 of title 11 of the United States Code.

Sec. 1217. Abandonment of Railroad Line. Section 1217 of the Act amends section 1170(e)(1) of the Bankruptcy Code to reflect the fact that section 11347 of title 49 of the United States Code was repealed by section 102(a) of Public Law 104-88 and that provisions comparable to section 11347 appear in section 11326(a) of title 49 of the United States Code.

Sec. 1218. Contents of Plan. Section 1218 of the Act amends section 1172(c)(1) of the Bankruptcy Code to reflect the fact that section 11347 of title 49 of the United States Code was repealed by section 102(a) of Public Law 104-88 and that provisions comparable to section 11347 appear in section 11326(a) of title 49 of the United States Code.

Sec. 1219. Bankruptcy Cases and Proceedings. Section 1219 of the Act amends section 1334(d) of title 28 of the United States Code to make clarifying references.[182]

Sec. 1220. Knowing Disregard of Bankruptcy Law or Rule. Section 1220 of the Act amends section 156(a) of title 18 of the United States Code to make stylistic changes and correct a reference to the Bankruptcy Code.

Sec. 1221. Transfers Made by Nonprofit Charitable Corporations. Section 1221 of the Act amends section 363(d) of the Bankruptcy Code to restrict the authority of a trustee to use, sell, or lease property by a nonprofit corporation or trust. First, the use, sell or lease of such property must be in accordance with applicable nonbankruptcy law and to the extent it is not inconsistent with any relief granted under certain specified provisions of section 362 of the Bankruptcy Code concerning the applicability of the automatic stay. Second, section 1221 imposes similar restrictions with regard to plan confirmation requirements for chapter 11 cases. Third, it amends section 541 of the Bankruptcy Code to provide that any property of a bankruptcy estate in which the debtor is a nonprofit corporation (as described in certain provisions of the Internal Revenue Code) may not be transferred to an entity that is not such a corporation, but only under the same conditions that would apply if the debtor was not in bankruptcy. The amendments made by this section apply to cases pending on the date of enactment or to cases filed after such date. Section 1221 provides that a court may not confirm a plan without considering whether this provision would substantially affect the rights of a party in interest who first acquired rights with respect to the debtor postpetition. Nothing in this provision may be construed to require the court to remand or refer any proceeding, issue, or controversy to any other court or to require the approval of any other court for the transfer of property.

Sec. 1222. Protection of Valid Purchase Money Security Interests. Section 1222 of the Act extends the applicable perfection period for a security interest in property of the debtor in section 547(c)(3)(B) of the Bankruptcy Code from 20 to 30 days.

Sec. 1223. Bankruptcy Judgeships. The substantial increase in bankruptcy case filings clearly creates a need for additional bankruptcy judgeships. In the 105th Congress, the House responded to this need by passing H.R. 1596, which would have created additional permanent and temporary bankruptcy judgeships and extended an existing temporary position. Section 1223 extends four existing temporary judgeships and authorizes 28 additional bankruptcy judgeships. In determining the official duty stations of bankruptcy judges and places of holding court pursuant to section 152(b)(1) of title 28 of the United States Code regarding the additional judgeships authorized in this section, the Judicial Conference should consider the convenience of the parties, the district's geography, and factors that would facilitate better administration of cases, such as may be presented in the Eastern District of California with respect to Bakersfield, for example.

Sec. 1224. Compensating Trustees. Section 1224 of the Act amends section 1326 of the Bankruptcy Code to provide that if a chapter 7 trustee has been allowed compensation as a result of the conversion or dismissal of the debtor's prior case pursuant to section 707(b) and some portion of that compensation remains unpaid, the amount of any such unpaid compensation must be repaid in the debtor's subsequent chapter 13 case. This payment must be prorated over the term of the plan and paid on a monthly basis. The amount of the monthly payment may not exceed the greater of $25 or the amount payable to unsecured nonpriority creditors as provided by the plan, multiplied by five percent and the result divided by the number of months of the plan.

Sec. 1225. Amendment to Section 362 of Titile11, United States Code. Section 1225 of the Act amends section 362(b) of the Bankruptcy Code to except from the automatic stay the creation or perfection of a statutory lien for an *ad valorem* property tax or for a special tax or special assess-

180 *See supra* notes 86 and 176 and accompanying text.

181 For a description of the error, see the appropriate footnote and amendment notes in the United States Code.

182 For a description of the errors, see the appropriate footnote and amendment notes in the United States Code.

ment on real property (whether or not *ad valorem*) that is imposed by a governmental unit, if such tax or assessment becomes due after the filing of the petition.

Sec. 1226. Judicial Education. Section 1226 of the Act requires the Director of the Federal Judicial Center, in consultation with the Director of the Executive Office for United States Trustees, to develop materials and conduct training as may be useful to the courts in implementing this Act, including the needs-based reforms under section 707(b) (as amended by this Act) and amendments pertaining to reaffirmation agreements.

Sec. 1227. Reclamation. Section 1227 of the Act amends section 546(c) of the Bankruptcy Code to provide that the rights of a trustee under sections 544(a), 545, 547, and 549 are subject to the rights of a seller of goods to reclaim goods sold in the ordinary course of business to the debtor if: (1) the debtor, while insolvent, received these goods not later than 45 days prior to the commencement of the case, and (2) written demand for reclamation of the goods is made not later than 45 days after receipt of such goods by the debtor or not later than 20 days after the commencement of the case, if the 45-day period expires after the commencement of the case. If the seller fails to provide notice in the manner provided in this provision, the seller may still assert the rights set forth in section 503(b)(7) of the Bankruptcy Code. Section 1227(b) amends Bankruptcy Code section 503(b) to provide that the value of any goods received by a debtor not later than within 20 days prior to the commencement of a bankruptcy case in which the goods have been sold to the debtor in the ordinary course of the debtor's business is an allowed administrative expense.

Sec. 1228. Providing Requested Tax Documents to the Court. Subsection (a) of section 1228 of the Act provides that the court may not grant a discharge to an individual in a case under chapter 7 unless requested tax documents have been provided to the court. Section 1228(b) similarly provides that the court may not confirm a chapter 11 or 13 plan unless requested tax documents have been filed with the court. Section 1228(c) directs the court to destroy documents submitted in support of a bankruptcy claim not sooner than three years after the date of the conclusion of a bankruptcy case filed by an individual debtor under chapter 7, 11, or 13. In the event of a pending audit or enforcement action, the court may extend the time for destruction of such requested tax documents.

Sec. 1229. Encouraging Creditworthiness. Subsection (a) of section 1229 of the Act expresses the sense of the Congress that certain lenders may sometimes offer credit to consumers indiscriminately and that resulting consumer debt may be a major contributing factor leading to consumer insolvency. Section 1229(b) directs the Board of Governors of the Federal Reserve to study certain consumer credit industry solicitation and credit granting practices as well as the effect of such practices on consumer debt and insolvency. The specified practices involve the solicitation and extension of credit on an indiscriminate basis that encourages consumers to accumulate additional debt and where the lender fails to ensure that the consumer borrower is capable of repaying the debt. Section 1229(c) requires the study described in subsection (b) to be prepared within 12 months from the date of the Act's enactment. This provision authorizes the Board to issue regulations requiring additional disclosures to consumers and permits it to undertake any other actions consistent with its statutory authority, which are necessary to ensure responsible industry practices and to prevent resulting consumer debt and insolvency.

Sec. 1230. Property No Longer Subject to Redemption. Section 1230 of the Act amends section 541(b) of the Bankruptcy Code to provide that, under certain circumstances, an interest of the debtor in tangible personal property (other than securities, or written or printed evidences of indebtedness or title) that the debtor pledged or sold as collateral for a loan or advance of money given by a person licensed under law to make such loan or advance is not property of the estate. Subject to subchapter III of chapter 5 of the Bankruptcy Code, the provision applies where: (1) the property is in the possession of the pledgee or transferee; (2) the debtor has no obligation to repay the money, redeem the collateral, or buy back the property at a stipulated price; and (3) neither the debtor nor the trustee have exercised any right to redeem provided under the contract or State law in a timely manner as provided under state law and section 108(b) of the Bankruptcy Code.

Sec. 1231. Trustees. Section 1231 of the Act establishes a series of procedural protections for chapter 7 and chapter 13 trustees concerning final agency decisions relating to trustee appointments and future case assignments. Section 1231(a) amends section 586(d) of title 28 of the United States Code to allow a chapter 7 or chapter 13 trustee to obtain judicial review of such decisions by commencing an action in the United States district court after the trustee exhausts all available administrative remedies. Unless the trustee elects to have an administrative hearing on the record, the trustee is deemed to have exhausted all administrative remedies under this provision if the agency fails to make a final agency decision within 90 days after the trustee requests an administrative remedy. The provision requires the Attorney General to promulgate procedures to implement this provision. It further provides that the agency's decision must be affirmed by the district court unless it is unreasonable and without cause based on the administrative record before the agency.

Section 1231(b) amends section 586(e) of title 28 of the United States Code to permit a chapter 13 trustee to obtain judicial review of certain final agency actions relating to claims for actual, necessary expenses under section 586(e). The trustee may commence an action in the United States district court where the trustee resides. The agency's decision must be affirmed by the district court unless it is unreasonable and without cause based on the administrative record before the agency. It directs the Attorney General to prescribe procedures to implement this provision.

Sec. 1232. Bankruptcy Forms. Section 1232 of the Act amends section 2075 of title 28 of the United States Code to a form to be prescribed for the statement specified under section 707(b)(2)(C) of the Bankruptcy Code and to promulgate general rules on the content of such statement.

Sec. 1233. Direct Appeals of Bankruptcy Matters to Courts of Appeals. Under current law, appeals from decisions rendered by the bankruptcy court are either heard by the district court or a bankruptcy appellate panel. In addition to the time and cost factors attendant to the present appellate system, decisions rendered by a district court as well as a bankruptcy appellate panel are generally not binding and lack stare decisis value.

To address these problems, section 1233 of the Act amends section 158(d) of title 28 to establish a procedure to facilitate appeals of certain decisions, judgments, orders and decrees of the bankruptcy courts to the circuit courts of appeals by means of a two-step certification process. The first step is a certification by the bankruptcy court, district court, or bankruptcy appellate panel (acting on its own motion or on the request of a party, or the appellants and appellees acting jointly). Such certification must be issued by the lower court if: (1) the bankruptcy court, district court, or bankruptcy appellate panel determines that one or more of certain specified standards are met; or (2) a majority in number of the appellants and a majority in number of the appellees request certification and represent that one or more of the standards are met. The second step is authorization by the circuit court of appeals. Jurisdiction for the direct appeal would exist in the circuit court of appeals only if the court of appeals authorizes the direct appeal.

This procedure is intended to be used to settle unresolved questions of law where there is a need to establish clear binding precedent at the court of appeals level, where the matter is one of public importance, where there is a need to resolve conflicting decisions on a question of law, or where an immediate appeal may materially advance the progress of the case or proceeding. The courts of appeals are encouraged to authorize direct appeals in these circumstances. While fact-intensive issues may occasionally offer grounds for certification even when binding precedent already exists on the general legal issue in question, it is anticipated that this procedure will rarely be used in that circumstance or in an attempt to bring to the circuit courts of appeals matters that can appropriately be resolved initially by district court judges or bankruptcy appellate panels.

Sec. 1234. Involuntary Cases. Section 1234 of the Act amends the Bankruptcy Code's criteria for commencing an involuntary bankruptcy case. Current law renders a creditor ineligible if its claim is contingent as to liability or the subject of a bona fide dispute. This provision amends section 303(b)(1) to specify that a creditor would be ineligible to file an involuntary petition if the creditor's claim was the subject of a bona fide dispute as to liability or amount. It further provides that the claims needed to meet the monetary threshold must be undisputed. The provision makes a conforming revision to section 303(h)(1). Section 1234 becomes effective on the date of enactment of this Act and applies to cases commenced before, on, and after such date.

Sec. 1235. Federal Election Law Fines and Penalties as Nondischargeable Debt. Section 1235 of the Act amends section 523(a) of the Bankruptcy Code to make debts incurred to pay fines or penalties imposed under Federal election law nondischargeable.

TITLE XIII. CONSUMER CREDIT DISCLOSURE

Sec. 1301. Enhanced Disclosures under an Open End Credit Plan. Section 1301 of the Act amends section 127(b) of the Truth in Lending Act to mandate the inclusion of certain specified disclosures in billing statements with respect to various open end credit plans. In general, these statements must contain an example of the time it would take to repay a stated balance at a specified interest rate. In addition, they must warn the borrower that making only the minimum payment will increase the amount of interest that must be paid and the time it takes to repay the balance. Further, a toll-free telephone number must be provided where the borrower can obtain an estimate of the time it would take to repay the balance if only minimum payments are made. With respect to a creditor whose compliance with title 15 of the United States Code is enforced by the Federal Trade Commission (FTC), the billing statement must advise the borrower to contact the FTC at a toll-free telephone number to obtain an estimate of the time it would take to repay the borrower's balance. Section 1301(a) permits the creditor to substitute an example based on a higher interest rate. As necessary, the provision requires the Board of Governors of the Federal Reserve System ("Board"), to periodically recalculate by rule the interest rate and repayment periods specified in Section 1301(a). With respect to the toll-free telephone number, section 1301(a) permits a third party to establish and maintain it. Under certain circumstances, the toll-free number may connect callers to an automated device.

For a period not to exceed 24 months from the effective date of the Act, the Board is required to establish and maintain a toll-free telephone number (or provide a toll-free telephone number established and maintained by a third party) for use by creditors that are depository institutions (as defined in section 3 of the Federal Deposit Insurance Act), including a Federal or state credit union (as defined in section 101 of the Federal Credit Union Act), with total assets not exceeding $250 million. Not later than six months prior to the expiration of the 24-month period, the Board must submit a report on this program to the Committee on Banking, Housing, and Urban Affairs of the Senate, and the Committee on Financial Services of the House of Representatives. In addition, section 1301(a) requires the Board to establish a detailed table illustrating the approximate number of months that it would take to repay an outstanding balance if a consumer pays only the required minimum month payments and if no other advances are made. The table should reflect a significant number of different annual percentage rates, and account balances, minimum payment amounts. The Board must also promulgate regulations providing instructional guidance regarding the manner in which the information contained in the tables should be used to respond to a request by an obligor under this provision. Section 1301(a) provides that the disclosure requirements of this provision are inapplicable to any charge card account where the primary purpose of which is to require payment of charges in full each month.

Section 1301(b)(1) requires the Federal Reserve Board to promulgate regulations implementing section 1301(a)'s amendments to section 127. Section 1301(b)(2) specifies that the effective date of the amendments under subsection (a) and the regulations required under this provision shall not take effect until the later of 18 months after the date of enactment of this Act or 12 months after the publication of final regulations by the Board.

Section 1301(c) authorizes the Federal Reserve Board to conduct a study to determine the types of information available to potential borrowers from consumer credit lending institutions regarding factors qualifying potential borrowers for credit, repayment requirements, and the consequences of default. The provision specifies the factors that should be considered. The study's findings must be submitted to Congress and include recommendations for legislative initiatives, based on the Board's findings.

Sec. 1302. Enhanced Disclosure for Credit Extensions Secured by a Dwelling. Subsection (a)(1) of section 1302 of the Act amends section 127A(a)(13) of the Truth in Lending Act to require a statement in any case in which the extension of credit exceeds the fair market value of a dwelling specifying that the interest on the portion of the credit extension that is greater than the fair market value of the dwelling is not tax deductible for Federal income tax purposes. Section 1302(a)(2) amends section 147(b) of the Truth in Lending Act to require an advertisement relating to an extension of credit that may exceed the fair market value of a dwelling and such advertisement is disseminated in paper form to the public or through the Internet (as opposed to dissemination by radio or television) to include a specified statement. The statement must disclose that the interest on the portion of the credit extension that is greater than the fair market value of the dwelling is not tax deductible for Federal income tax purposes and that the consumer should consult a tax advisor for further information regarding the deductibility of interest and charges.

With respect to non-open end credit extensions, section 1302(b)(1) amends section 128 of the Truth in Lending Act to require that a consumer receive a specified statement at the time he or she applies for credit with respect to a consumer credit transaction secured by the consumer's principal dwelling and where the credit extension may exceed the fair market value of the dwelling. The statement must disclose that the interest on the portion of the credit extension that exceeds the dwelling's fair market value is not tax deductible for Federal income tax purposes and that the consumer should consult a tax advisor for further information regarding the deductibility of interest and charges. Section 1302(b)(2) requires certain advertisements disseminated in paper form to the public or through the Internet that relate to a consumer credit transaction secured by a consumer's principal dwelling where the extension of credit may exceed the dwelling's fair market value to contain specified statements. These statements advise that the interest on the portion of the credit extension that is greater than the fair market value of the dwelling is not tax deductible for Federal income tax purposes and that the consumer should consult a tax advisor for further information regarding the deductibility of interest and charges.

Section 1302(c)(1) requires the Federal Reserve Board to promulgate regulations implementing the amendments effectuated by this provision. Section 1302(c)(2) provides that these regulations shall not take effect until the later of 12 months following the Act's enactment date or 12 months after the date of publication of such final regulations by the Board.

Sec. 1303. Disclosures Related to "Introductory Rates." Subsection (a) of section 1303 of the Act amends section 127(c) of the Truth in Lending Act by adding a provision to specify further requirements for applications, solicitations and related materials that are subject to section 127(c)(1). With respect to an application or solicitation to open a credit card account and all promotional materials accompanying such application or solicitation involving an "introductory rate" offer, such materials must do the following if they offer a temporary annual percentage rate of interest:

1. the term "introductory" in immediate proximity to each listing of the temporary annual percentage interest rate applicable to such account;
2. if the annual percentage interest rate that will apply after the end of the temporary rate period will be a fixed rate, the time period in which the introductory period will end and the annual percentage rate that will apply after the end of the introductory period must be clearly and conspicuously stated in a prominent location closely proximate to the first listing of the temporary annual percentage rate;

3. if the annual percentage rate that will apply after the end of the temporary rate period will vary in accordance with an index, the time period in which the introductory period will end and the rate that will apply after that, based on an annual percentage rate that was in effect 60 days before the date of mailing of the application or solicitation must be clearly and conspicuously stated in a prominent location closely proximate to the first listing of the temporary annual percentage rate.

The second and third provisions described above do not apply to any listing of a temporary annual percentage rate on an envelope or other enclosure in which an application or solicitation to open a credit card account is mailed. With respect to an application or solicitation to open a credit card account for which disclosure is required pursuant to section 127(c)(1) of the Truth in Lending Act, section 1303(a) specifies that certain statements be made if the rate of interest is revocable under any circumstance or upon any event. The statements must clearly and conspicuously appear in a prominent manner on or with the application or solicitation. The disclosures include a general description of the circumstances that may result in the revocation of the temporary annual percentage rate and an explanation of the type of interest rate that will apply upon revocation of the temporary rate.

To implement this provision, section 1303(b) amends section 127(c) of the Truth in Lending Act to define various relevant terms and requires the Board to promulgate regulations. The provision does not become effective until the earlier of 12 months after the Act's enactment date or 12 months after the date of publication of such final regulations.

Sec. 1304. Internet-Based Credit Card Solicitations. Subsection (a) of section 1304 of the Act amends section 127(c) of the Truth in Lending Act to require any solicitation to open a credit card account for an open end consumer credit plan through the Internet or other interactive computer service to clearly and conspicuously include the disclosures required under section 127(c)(1)(A) and (B). It also specifies that the disclosure required pursuant to section 127(c)(1)(A) be readily accessible to consumers in close proximity to the solicitation and be updated regularly to reflect current policies, terms, and fee amounts applicable to the credit card account. Section 1304(a) defines terms relevant to the Internet.

Section 1304(b) requires the Federal Reserve Board to promulgate regulations implementing this provision. It also provides that the amendments effectuated by section 1304 do not take effect until the later of 12 months after the Act's enactment date or 12 months after the date of publication of such regulations.

Sec. 1305. Disclosures Related to Late Payment Deadlines and Penalties. Subsection (a) of section 1305 of the Act amends section 127(b) of the Truth in Lending Act to provide that if a late payment fee is to be imposed due to the obligor's failure to make payment on or before a required payment due date, the billing statement must specify the date on which that payment is due (or if different the earliest date on which a late payment fee may be charged) and the amount of the late payment fee to be imposed if payment is made after such date.

Section 1305(b) requires the Federal Reserve Board to promulgate regulations implementing this provision. The amendments effectuated by this provision and the regulations promulgated thereunder shall not take effect until the later of 12 months after the Act's enactment date or 12 months after the date of publication of the regulations.

Sec. 1306. Prohibition on Certain Actions for Failure to Incur Finance Charges. Subsection (a) of section 1306 of the Act amends section 127 of the Truth in Lending Act to add a provision prohibiting a creditor of an open end consumer credit plan from terminating an account prior to its expiration date solely because the consumer has not incurred finance charges on the account. The provision does not prevent the creditor from terminating such account for inactivity for three or more consecutive months.

Section 1306(b) requires the Federal Reserve Board to promulgate regulations implementing the amendments effectuated by section 1306(a) and provides that they do not become effective until the later of 12 months after the Act's enactment date or 12 months after the date of publication of such final regulations.

Sec. 1307. Dual Use Debit Card. Subsection (a) of section 1307 of the act provides that the Federal Reserve Board may conduct a study and submit a report to Congress containing its analysis of consumer protections under existing law to limit the liability of consumers for unauthorized use of a debit card or similar access device. The report must include recommendations for legislative initiatives, if any, based on its findings.

Section 1307(b) provides that the Federal Reserve Board, in preparing its report, may include analysis of section 909 of the Electronic Fund Transfer Act to the extent this provision is in effect at the time of the report and the implementing regulations. In addition, the analysis may pertain to whether any voluntary industry rules have enhanced or may enhance the level of protection afforded consumers in connection with such unauthorized use liability and whether amendments to the Electronic Fund Transfer Act or implementing regulations are necessary to further address adequate protection for consumers concerning unauthorized use liability.

Sec. 1308. Study of Bankruptcy Impact of Credit Extended to Dependent Students. Section 1308 of the Act directs the Board of Governors of the Federal Reserve to study the impact that the extension of credit to dependents (defined under the Internal Revenue Code of 1986) who are enrolled in postsecondary educational institutions has on the rate of bankruptcy cases filed. The report must be submitted to the Senate and House of Representatives no later than one year from the Act's enactment date.

Sec. 1309. Clarification of Clear and Conspicuous. Subsection (a) of section 1309 of the Act requires the Board (in consultation with other Federal banking agencies, the National Credit Union Administration Board, and the Federal Trade Commission) to promulgate regulations not later than six months after the Act's enactment date to provide guidance on the meaning of the term "clear and conspicuous" as it is used in section 127(b)(11)(A), (B) and (C) and section 127(c)(6)(A)(ii) and (iii) of the Truth in Lending Act.

Section 1309(b) provides that regulations promulgated under section 1309(a) shall include examples of clear and conspicuous model disclosures for the purpose of disclosures required under the Truth in Lending Act provisions set forth therein.

Section 1309(c) requires the Federal Reserve Board, in promulgating regulations under this provision, to ensure that the clear and conspicuous standard required for disclosures made under the Truth in Lending Act provisions set forth in section 1309(a) can be implemented in a manner that results in disclosures which are reasonably understandable and designed to call attention to the nature and significance of the information in the notice.

TITLE XIV. PREVENTING CORPORATE BANKRUPTCY ABUSE

Sec. 1401. Employee Wage and Benefit Priorities. Section 1401 of the Act amends Bankruptcy Code section 507(a) to provide heightened protections for employees by increasing the monetary cap on wage and employee benefit claims entitled to priority under the Bankruptcy Code from $4,650 to $10,000 and lengthens the reachback period for wage claims from 90 days to 180 days. As few employees will continue working without pay for an extended period, the principal effect of extending the time period to 180 days is that a greater portion of unpaid vacation, severance, and sick leave pay will be entitled to priority payment.

Sec. 1402. Fraudulent Transfers and Obligations. Section 1402 of the Act amends section 548 of the Bankruptcy Code to enhance the recovery of avoidable transfers and excessive prepetition compensation, such as bonuses, paid to insiders of a debtor. It effectuates two changes to current law that would make it easier for a trustee to avoid pre-petition transfers. First, section 1402(1) extends the one-year reachback period for fraudulent transfers to two years. Second, section 1402(2) amends Bankruptcy Code section 548(a) to clarify that it permits the recovery of any transfer to or an obligation incurred for the benefit of an insider under an employment contract, under certain conditions. In addition, section 1402 adds a new provision to section 548 authorizing a bankruptcy trustee to avoid any transfer of an interest of the debtor in property that was made on or within the ten-year period preceding the filing of the debtor's bankruptcy case if: (a) the transfer was made to a self-settled trust or similar device; (b) the transfer was made by the debtor; (c) the debtor is a beneficiary of such trust or similar device; and (d) the debtor made such transfer with actual intent to hinder, delay, or defraud any entity to which the debtor was or became, on or after the date of such transfer, indebted. For purposes of this provision, a transfer includes a transfer made in anticipation of any money judgment, criminal fine, or similar obligation or which the debtor believed would be incurred as a result of: (1) a violation of Federal or state securities laws, regulations, or orders; or (2) fraud, deceit, or manipulation in fiduciary capacity or in connection with the purchase or sale of a security under specified provisions of the Federal securities laws.

Sec. 1403. Payment of Insurance Benefits to Retired Employees. Current bankruptcy law prevents a chapter 11 debtor from unilaterally modifying certain retiree benefits, such as health insurance, during the pendency of the bankruptcy case unless an authorized retiree representative is appointed and agrees to the modification, or the court authorizes the modification. Section 1403 amends Bankruptcy Code section 1114 to prevent debtors from evading these requirements by terminating retiree benefit plans on the eve of bankruptcy. The amendment would require retroactive reinstatement of retiree benefits that were modified within 180 days before the debtor filed for bankruptcy protection, unless the court finds that the balance of the equities clearly favors the modification.

Sec. 1404. Debts Nondischargeable If Incurred in Violation of Securities Fraud Laws. Bankruptcy Code section 523(a)(19) makes certain debts nondischargeable that result from the violation of Federal securities law, state securities law, or any regulation or order issued under such Federal or state securities law nondischargeable. Section 1404 amends Bankruptcy Code section 523(a)(19)(B) to provide that it applies to such debts that result before, on, or after the date on which the petition was filed from any judgment, order, consent order, decree, settlement agreement, or from any court or administrative order for damages or for other specified payments owed by the debtor. Section 1404 is effective as of July 30, 2002.

Sec. 1405. Appointment of Trustee in Cases of Suspected Fraud. Section 1405 amends Bankruptcy Code section 1104 to require the United States trustee to move for the appointment of a trustee if there are reasonable grounds to suspect that current members of a chapter 11 debtor's governing body, chief executive officer, chief financial officer, or members of the debtor's governing body who selected the debtor's chief executive officer or chief financial officer participated in actual fraud, dishonesty, or criminal conduct in the management of the debtor or the debtor's public financial reporting.

Sec. 1406. Effective Date; Application of Amendments. Section 1406 provides that title XIV, with the exception of one provision, takes effect on the date of enactment of this Act and the amendments apply only to cases commenced after such date. The exception applies to section 1402(1) of the Act, which applies only to cases commenced under the Bankruptcy Code more than one year after the date of enactment of this Act.

TITLE XV. GENERAL EFFECTIVE DATE; APPLICATION OF AMENDMENTS

Sec. 1501. Effective Date; Application of Amendments. Subsection (a) of section 1501 of the Act provides that the Act shall take effect 180 days after the date of enactment, unless otherwise specified in this Act. Section 1501(b) provides that the amendments made by this Act shall not apply to cases commenced under the Bankruptcy Code before the Act's effective date, unless otherwise specified in this Act. The provision specifies that the amendments made by sections 308, 322 and 330 shall apply to cases commenced on or after the date of enactment of this Act.

Sec. 1502. Technical Corrections. In light of the renumbering of a paragraph in Bankruptcy Code section 507 as effectuated by section 212 of this Act, section 1502 corrects various cross-references in the Bankruptcy Code to reflect such renumbering.

* * *

Appendix B Interim Bankruptcy Rules

On August 22, 2005, the Judicial Conference of the United States released proposed amendments to the Bankruptcy Rules, and urged courts to adopt them as interim rules. This Appendix reprints the cover memoranda from the Chair and from the Reporter of the Advisory Committee on Bankruptcy Rules of the Judicial Conference of the United States, and then reprints a red-lined version of all the proposed amendments to the Rules, marked to show changes from the existing Rules, along with Committee Notes about the proposed changes. The amendments and notes are also found on the CD-Rom accompanying this volume. At the same time, new and amended Official Forms were released, and these are found in Appx. D, *infra*.

The Judicial Conference states: "The Interim Rules are expected to apply to bankruptcy cases from October 17, 2005, until final rules are promulgated and effective under the regular Rules Enabling Act process. The Advisory Committee and Committee on Rules of Practice and Procedure expect to publish for public comment proposed new and amended Federal Rules of Bankruptcy Procedure—based substantially on the Interim Rules modified as appropriate after considering comments from the bench and bar as a result of the use of the Interim Rules—and any additional revisions to the Official Forms in August 2006."

COMMITTEE ON RULES OF PRACTICE AND PROCEDURE
OF THE
JUDICIAL CONFERENCE OF THE UNITED STATES
WASHINGTON, D.C. 20544

DAVID F. LEVI
CHAIR

PETER G. McCABE
SECRETARY

CHAIRS OF ADVISORY COMMITTEES

SAMUEL A. ALITO, JR.
APPELLATE RULES

THOMAS S. ZILLY
BANKRUPTCY RULES

LEE H. ROSENTHAL
CIVIL RULES

SUSAN C. BUCKLEW
CRIMINAL RULES

JERRY E. SMITH
EVIDENCE RULES

August 22,2005

MEMORANDUM TO ALL: Chief Judges, United States District Courts Judges, United States Bankruptcy Courts

On April 20, 2005 the Bankruptcy Abuse Prevention and Consumer Protection Act of 2005 (the Act) was enacted into law. Most provisions of the Act are effective October 17, 2005. Several of its provisions were effective upon enactment, while other provisions have individualized effective dates. Since the enactment of the Act, the Advisory Committee on Bankruptcy Rules has been engaged in an intensive effort to review the new Act and determine the necessary changes to the rules to implement the Act by the effective date. The general effective date of 180 days after enactment has not provided sufficient time to promulgate National Rules and Official Forms under the Rules Enabling Act, 28 U.S.C. §§ 2071–2077. This is normally a three-year process.

As a result, the Advisory Committee on Bankruptcy Rules has prepared Interim Rules and Official Forms designed to implement the substantive and procedural changes mandated by the Act. These Interim Rules and Official Forms have been approved by the Advisory Committee on Bankruptcy Rules and the Standing Committee on Rules of Practice and Procedure of the Judicial Conference of the United States. The Advisory Committee and the Standing Rules Committee recommend and urge all local courts to adopt the Interim Rules. Widespread adoption of the Interim Rules will provide uniform procedures for implementing the Act and at the same time supply a valuable base of experience for the ongoing work of the Advisory Committee. The Official Forms have also been approved by the Judicial Conference of the United States, and pursuant to Bankruptcy Rule 9009, the Official Forms must be observed and used with alterations as may be appropriate. Please note that two sections of the means testing forms are under study and subject to revision.

The Interim Rules have been drafted so they are integrated into, and are consistent with, the Federal Rules of Bankruptcy Procedure, and are highlighted by underlining and strikeouts. The Committee Notes that follow the rules explain the purpose of the particular Interim Rule. With the Federal Rules of Bankruptcy Procedure, they apply as one set of rules for cases and proceedings governed by the Act. For cases and proceedings not governed by the Act, the Federal

Rules of Bankruptcy Procedure and the local rules of court will continue to apply. The Interim Rules, Official Forms with explanatory Committee Notes, memorandum prepared by the Committee's Reporter summarizing the Interim Rules and amended and new Official Forms, and a draft court order adopting the Interim Rules can be found on the internet at <www.uscourts.gov/rules>.

The Advisory Committee intends to continue to carefully study the new Act with the goal to publish proposed National Rules no later than August 2006 with final adoption and an effective date of December 1, 2008. We anticipate the National Rules will be substantially in the form of the Interim Rules modified after considering input from the bench and bar as a result of the use of the Interim Rules.

In emphasizing the temporary nature of the Interim Rules, the Committee seeks comments from the bench and bar relating to the use of the Interim Rules and Official Forms. Comments should be directed to:

Peter G. McCabe, Secretary
Committee on Rules of Practice and Procedure
Thurgood Marshall Federal Judiciary Building
Washington, D.C. 20544

To allow for early comments on the Interim Rules and Official Forms you may also send comments electronically via the internet at <www.uscourts.gov/rules>.

David F. Levi
Chair, Committee on Rules of
Practice and Procedure

Thomas S. Zilly
Chair, Advisory Committee on
Federal Rules of Bankruptcy Procedure

cc: District Court Executives
Clerks, United States District Courts
Clerks, United States Bankruptcy Courts

COMMITTEE ON RULES OF PRACTICE AND PROCEDURE
OF THE
JUDICIAL CONFERENCE OF THE UNITED STATES
WASHINGTON, D.C. 20544

DAVID F. LEVI
CHAIR

PETER G. McCABE
SECRETARY

CHAIRS OF ADVISORY COMMITTEES

SAMUEL A. ALITO, JR.
APPELLATE RULES

THOMAS S. ZILLY
BANKRUPTCY RULES

LEE H. ROSENTHAL
CIVIL RULES

SUSAN C. BUCKLEW
CRIMINAL RULES

JERRY E. SMITH
EVIDENCE RULES

MEMORANDUM TO: Advisory Committee on Bankruptcy Rules

FROM: Professor Jeffrey W. Morris, Reporter, Advisory Committee on Bankruptcy Rules

DATE: August 5, 2005

RE: Proposed Interim Bankruptcy Rules and Amended and New Official Forms

INTERIM RULES AMENDMENTS AND RULES ADDITIONS TO IMPLEMENT CHANGES MADE BY THE 2005 BANKRUPTCY REFORM LEGISLATION

The Bankruptcy Abuse Prevention and Consumer Protection Act of 2005 (the "Act") exceeds 500 pages in length and touches on nearly every aspect of bankruptcy cases. It introduces the concept of a means test as a requirement of eligibility for chapter 7 relief, adds an entirely new chapter to the Code (chapter 15 governing cross border insolvencies), and creates new categories of debtors and cases (health care businesses and small business cases), among other things. Many of these provisions necessitate the amendment or creation of bankruptcy rules and forms.

The provisions of the Act generally are effective on October 17, 2005. Several of its provisions were effective upon the enactment date, April 20, 2005, while several others have individualized effective dates. Most importantly, however, the general effective date of 180 days after enactment does not provide sufficient time to promulgate rules under the Rules Enabling Act to implement the statutory changes. Thus, the attached proposed rules and forms are offered for adoption through standing or general orders by each of the district courts. For the sake of clarity, these rules are titled "Interim Rules and Forms" to denote that they are expected to apply to bankruptcy cases only from October 17, 2005, until final rules and forms are promulgated and effective under the regular Rules Enabling Act process.

Adoption of these Interim Rules and Forms will bridge the gap between the Act's effective date and the promulgation of rules by the Supreme Court through the regular Rules Enabling Act process. In the meantime, the Advisory Committee on Bankruptcy Rules and the Committee on the Rules of Practice and Procedure will be moving forward with the study and preparation for publication of proposed rules and forms to implement the changes to the Bankruptcy Code contained in the Act. These proposals likely will include all of the attached Interim Rules and Forms, either in their current form, or as the Committees might revise them prior to further publication. Other proposed amendments will also be included in the package of proposals that will be published for comment, most likely in August 2006. The Committees hope and expect that practice under these proposed rules will generate commentary on the rules that will guide them in the process of the proposal of amendments under the Rules Enabling Act.

The amendments and additions are broken out into five categories of rules amendments: consumer; business; health care; cross border; and appeals. Several rules are amended by more than one category of the Interim Rules, and each amendment is described within each category. A total of thirty-five rules either are added to or amended by these Interim Rules. There are seven new rules. Among the Consumer Rules, Rule 5008 is new. New rules included in the Health Care Rules are Rules 1021, 2007.2, 2015.1, 2015.2, and 6011. The Cross Border rules include new Rule 5012.

A number of the amendments are relatively brief and technical in nature. Others are more extensive because they implement entirely new concepts added to the Code by the Act. Those amendments that are designated as technical are those that simply update the rule to adopt new terminology or definitions included in the Act, or that adopt a deadline set out in the statute. The designation of a particular rule as "technical" appears immediately after the boldface identification of the rule. "Conforming" amendments contain lengthier changes, but they only add or delete language necessary to conform the rules to the amendments to the Code. The following is a brief description of the Interim Rules set out by the separate categories.

CONSUMER RULES

Rule 1006 is amended to implement the provisions in the Act that, for the first time on a nationwide basis, authorize the courts to waive the payment of filing fees by debtors. The amendment directs the debtor to use the Official Form for requesting a fee waiver. The amendment also permits the court to allow the payment of the filing fee in installments even if the debtor has made a payment to an attorney in connection with the case.

Rule 1007 (conforming) is amended to reflect the expanded obligations of debtors to file a variety of documents and materials by the Act. The amendments address the filing of current monthly income statements and other forms to implement the means test imposed by the 2005 bankruptcy reform legislation. There are also changes to require debtors to file additional materials such as payment advices and education income retirement accounts, as well as certificates for the completion of credit counseling and financial management programs mandated by the legislation. **This rule is also otherwise amended by the Business and Cross Border Rules.**

Rule 1009 (technical) is amended to correct a cross reference to the Bankruptcy Code due to the restructuring of § 521 of the Code by the Act.

Rule 1017 (conforming) is amended to implement the amendments to § 707(b) of the Code by the Act that permit parties in interest to move to dismiss the chapter 7 case of an individual whose debts are primarily consumer debts as abusive. The amendments to subdivision (e) of the rule preserve the time limits already in place for § 707 motions. The rule also requires that a motion filed under § 707(b)(3) state with particularity the circumstances that present the alleged abuse.

Rule 1019 (conforming) is amended because the Act is likely to lead to more conversions of cases to and from chapters 7 and 13. The amendments preserve deadlines for motions to dismiss a case under § 707(b) upon conversion of a case from chapter 13 to chapter 7.

Rule 2002 (conforming) is amended to reflect the 2005 revisions to § 704 of the Bankruptcy Code in the Act requiring the court to provide a copy to all creditors of a statement by the United States trustee as to whether the debtor's case would be presumed to be an abuse under § 707(b) not later than five days after receiving it. **This rule is also otherwise amended by the Business and Cross Border Rules.**

Rule 3002 (conforming) is amended to conform to changes in the Code made by the Act. Under § 502(b)(9), governmental units asserting claims based on tax returns filed under § 1308 during a chapter 13 case have a different time period for filing proofs of those claims. Paragraph (c)(1) is amended to conform to § 502(b)(9). **This rule is also otherwise amended by the Business Rules.**

Rule 4002 is amended to implement the provisions of the Act that expand the obligation of debtors to provide additional evidence of personal identity, current income, and recent Federal income tax returns or tax transcripts. Amendments to the rule had been published for comment in August 2004, and this amendment carries forward from that proposed amendment the debtor's obligation to provide evidence of financial accounts existing at the time of the commencement of the case.

Rule 4003 (conforming) is amended to reflect the Act's addition of § 522(q) to the Bankruptcy Code. Section 522(q) imposes a $125,000 limit on a state homestead exemption if the debtor has been convicted of a felony or owes a debt arising from certain causes of action. Other revised provisions of the Bankruptcy Code, such as § 727(a)(12) and § 1328(h), suggest that the court may consider issues relating to § 522 late in the case, and thus the 30-day period for objections would not be appropriate for this provision. Thus, a new subdivision (b)(2) is added to provide a separate time limit for this provision.

Rule 4004 (conforming) is amended to implement several provisions added to the Bankruptcy Code by the Act. The amendments address the postponement of the court's entry of a discharge pending the debtor's completion of a financial management program as well as the need to postpone the discharge to consider whether the debtor has committed a felony or owes a debt arising from certain causes of action within a particular time frame.

Rule 4006 (conforming) is amended to reflect the Act's revision of the Bankruptcy Code that requires individual debtors to complete a course in personal financial management as a condition to the entry of a discharge. If the debtor fails to complete the course, no discharge will be entered, but the case may be closed. The amended rule provides notice to parties in interest, including the debtor, that no discharge was entered.

Rule 4007 (conforming) is amended because the Act expands the exceptions to discharge upon completion of a chapter 13 plan. Subdivision (c) extends to chapter 13 the same time limits applicable to other chapters of the Code with respect to the two exceptions to discharge that have been added to § 1328(a) and that are within § 523(c). Subdivision (d) is amended to establish a deadline for filing a complaint in a chapter 13 case only for § 523(a)(6), rather than for all of the categories of claims under § 523(c).

Rule 4008 (conforming) is amended to reflect the Act's addition of §§ 524(k)(6)(A) and 524(m) to the Bankruptcy Code. The provisions require that a debtor file a signed statement in support of a reaffirmation, and authorize a court to review the agreements if, based on the assertions on the statement, the agreement is presumed to be an undue hardship. The rule revision requires that an accompanying statement show the total income and expense figures from schedules I and J and an explanation of any discrepancies. This will allow the court to evaluate the reaffirmation for undue hardship as § 524(m) requires.

Rule 5008 is new. The 2005 revisions to § 342 of the Bankruptcy Code require that clerks give written notice to all creditors not later than 10 days after the date of the filing of the petition that a presumption of abuse has arisen under § 707(b). A statement filed by the debtor will be the source of the clerk's information about the presumption of abuse. This rule enables the clerk to meet its obligation to send the notice within the statutory time period set forth in § 342. In the event that the court receives the debtor's statement after the clerk has sent the first notice, and the debtor's statement indicates a presumption of abuse, this rule requires that the clerk send a second notice.

BUSINESS RULES

Rule 1007 (technical) is amended to recognize the limitation on the extension of the time to file schedules and statements when the debtor is a small business debtor. Section 1116(3), added to the Bankruptcy Code by the Act in 2005, establishes a specific standard for the courts to apply in the event that the debtor in possession or the trustee seeks an extension for the filing of these forms for a period beyond 30 days after the order for relief. **This rule is also otherwise amended by the Consumer and Cross Border Rules.**

Rule 1020 is essentially a new rule that reflects the change in the definition of a small business debtor made by the Act. The former rule is deleted, and the new rule provides a procedure for informing the parties, the United States trustee, and the court of whether the debtor is a small business debtor. It also provides procedures for bringing to the court disputes regarding the proper characterization of the debtor. Because it is important to resolve such disputes early in the case, a time limit for objecting to the debtor's self-designation is imposed. Rule 9006(b)(1), which governs enlargement of time, is applicable to the time limits set forth in this rule. Subdivision (c), which relates the presence and activity of a committee of unsecured creditors, is designed to be consistent with the Code's definition of "small business debtor."

Rule 2002 is amended in several respects to implement amendments made to the Bankruptcy Code by the Act. Subdivision (b) is amended to require that notice of a hearing on the approval of a plan to serve as a disclosure statement be given in a small business case in chapter 11. Subdivision (p)(1) is added to the rule to give the court flexibility to direct that notice by other means shall supplement notice by mail, or to enlarge the notice period, for creditors with foreign addresses now required by § 1514(d) of the Code. This portion of the rule recognizes that the court has discretion to establish procedures to determine, on its own initiative, whether relief under subdivision (p) is appropriate, but that the court is not required to establish such procedures and may decide to act only on request of a party in interest. Subdivision (p)(2) is added to the rule to grant creditors with a foreign address to which notices are mailed at least 30 days notice of, the time within which to file proofs of claims if notice is mailed to the foreign address, unless the court orders otherwise. If cause exists, such as likely delays in the delivery of notices in particular locations, the court may extend the notice period for creditors with foreign addresses. The court also may shorten the additional notice time if circumstances so warrant. **This rule is also otherwise amended by the Consumer Rules and the Cross Border Rules.**

Rule 2003 (technical) is amended to implement the Act's amendment to § 341(e) of the Bankruptcy Code. The amendment to the rule authorizes the court, on request of a party in interest and after notice and a hearing, to order that a meeting of creditors not be convened if the debtor had solicited acceptances of a plan prior to the commencement of the case. The amended rule recognizes that a meeting of creditors may not be held in those cases.

Rule 2007.1 (conforming) is amended to reflect the change in the manner of the election and appointment of trustees in chapter 11 cases. The 2005 amendments to the Bankruptcy Code reduce somewhat the role of the United States trustee in the appointment process, so the amendments to Rule 2007.1 limit that role and require the elected trustee to file an affidavit setting forth information regarding that person's connections with creditors and others with an interest in the case.

Rule 3002 is amended to implement § 1514(d) which was added to the Bankruptcy Code by the Act. Subdivision (c)(6) gives the court discretion to extend the time for filing a proof of claim for a creditor who received notice of the time to file the claim at a foreign address, if the court finds that the notice was not sufficient, under the particular circumstances, to give the foreign creditor a reasonable time to file a proof of claim.

Rule 3003 (technical) is amended to implement § 1514(d), which was added to the Code by the Act in 2005, by making the new Rule 3002(c)(6) applicable in chapter 9 and chapter 11 cases.

Rule 3016 is amended to recognize that, in 2005, the Act added § 1125(f)(1) to the Code to provide that the plan proponent in a small business case need not file a disclosure statement if the plan itself includes adequate information and the court finds that a separate disclosure statement is unnecessary. If the plan is intended to provide adequate information in a small business case, it may be conditionally approved as a disclosure statement under Rule 3017.1 and is subject to all other rules applicable to disclosure statements in small business cases.

Rule 3017.1 (technical) is amended to implement the Act's amendment to the Bankruptcy Code that permits the court in a small business chapter 11 case to conditionally approve a plan intended to provide adequate information. The plan is then treated as a disclosure statement under this rule.

Rule 3019 (conforming) is amended because the Act added to the Bankruptcy Code a provision for the modification of plans filed by individual debtors in chapter 11 cases. The rule is amended to establish the procedure for filing and objecting to a proposed modification of a confirmed plan.

Rule 5003 (technical) is amended to implement the addition of § 505(b)(1) to the Code by the Act in 2005. That section allows taxing authorities to designate addresses to use for the service of a request under that subsection.

Rule 6004 (conforming) is amended to implement sections 332 and 363(b)(1)(B), which the Act added to the Code in 2005. Those sections require the appointment of a consumer privacy ombudsman in certain circumstances when a debtor proposes to sell personally identifiable information.

Rule 9006 (technical) is amended to recognize that extensions of time for filing schedules and a statement of financial affairs by small business debtors cannot be extended beyond the time set in § 1116(3) of the Code as added by the Act in 2005. This amendment operates in tandem with the amendment to Rule 1007(c) to recognize this restriction on expanding the time to file these documents in small business cases.

HEALTH CARE RULES

Rule 1021 is new. It is added to the rules to implement § 101(27A) of the Code, added by the Act in 2005. That section defines health care businesses, and the rule authorizes parties in interest to seek an order identifying a debtor as a health care business. The debtor, in a voluntary case and the petitioning creditors in an involuntary case will make the health care business identification on the petition. If a party in interest disagrees with the determination by the debtor or petitioning creditors that the debtor is not a health care business, the party can move for an order designating the debtor as a health care business.

Rule 2007.2 (conforming) is new. It is added to the rules to govern the appointment of a health care ombudsman in the first 30 days of all health care business cases unless the court finds that the appointment is not necessary for the protection of patients. This is a new obligation created by § 333 of the Code added by the Act in 2005. The rule recognizes this obligation and provides that any party in interest that believes that the appointment of a health care ombudsman is unnecessary in the case must file its objection to the appointment within the first twenty days of the case. That entity also must notify other interested parties that the objection has been filed. The court will then consider the objection and determine whether to order the United States trustee to make the appointment. In the absence of any timely objections, the court will enter an order directing the United States trustee to appoint the ombudsman. The rule also permits parties in interest to file motions either to appoint or terminate the appointment of these ombudsmen, and it sets forth the procedure for approving the appointment.

Rule 2015.1 is new. It is added to implement § 333(b) and (c) added to the Code in 2005 by the Act. The rule requires ten days notice of reports to be made by the health care ombudsman and sets out the entities to whom the notice must be given. The rule permits the notice to relate to a single report or to periodic reports to be given throughout the course of the case. That is, the notice may serve as notice of all reports to be given by the ombudsman at specified intervals during the case. Interested parties will then be able to review the written reports or attend the hearings at which oral reports might be given. The Rule also implements § 333(c)(1) added to the Code in 2005 by the Act. The statute requires court approval of the ombudsman's review of the patient records with the imposition of appropriate restrictions to protect the confidentiality of the records. The rule requires the ombudsman to notify the United States trustee, the patient, and any family member or contact person whose name and address have been given to the trustee or the debtor that the ombudsman is seeking access to otherwise confidential patient records. This provides an opportunity for the patient and United States trustee to appear and be heard on the matter and should assist the court in reaching its decision both as to access to the records and appropriate restrictions on that access to ensure continued confidentiality. A notice given under the rule is expressly made subject to applicable nonbankruptcy laws governing patient privacy.

Rule 2015.2 (conforming) is new. It is added to implement § 704(a)(12) which was added to the Code in 2005 by the Act. That section authorizes the trustee to relocate patients when a health care business debtor's facility is being closed. The statute permits the trustee to take this action without the need for any order from the court, but the notice required by this rule will enable patients who contend that the trustee's actions violate § 704(a)(12) to have those issues resolved. A notice given under the rule is expressly made subject to applicable nonbankruptcy laws governing patient privacy.

Rule 6011 is new. It is added to implement 5 351(1) which was added to the Code in 2005 by the Act. That provision requires the trustee to notify patients that their patient records will be destroyed if they remain unclaimed for one year after the publication of a notice in an appropriate newspaper. The statute also requires that individualized notice be sent to each patient and every family member and other contact person to whom the debtor is providing information about the patient's health. Subdivisions (a) and (b) establish minimum requirements for notices to patients, their family members, and contact persons to ensure that sufficient information is provided to these persons regarding the trustee's intent to dispose of patient records. Subdivision (c) directs the trustee to maintain proof of compliance with § 351(1)(B), but it prohibits filing the proof of compliance unless the court orders the trustee to file it under seal because the proof of compliance may contain patient names that should or must remain confidential. Subdivision (d) requires the trustee to file a report with the court regarding the destruction of patient records. This certification is intended to ensure that the trustee properly completed the destruction process. Again, notices under this rule are expressly made subject to applicable nonbankruptcy laws governing patient privacy.

CROSS BORDER RULES

Rule 1007 is amended to require that any entity filing a petition for recognition to commence a case under chapter 15 of the Code file a list of entities with whom the debtor is engaged in litigation in the United States. This chapter was added to the Code by the Act. The recognition of a foreign proceeding makes § 362 of the Code operative in the case, so the amendment to the rule requires the entity filing a petition for recognition to file a list of parties to pending litigation with the debtor. These entities can them be notified prior to the imposition of the automatic stay that the petitioner has sought relief under chapter 15. **This rule is also otherwise amended by the Consumer and Business Rules.**

Rule 1010 (conforming) is amended to implement the changes to the Bankruptcy Code made by the Act. It repealed § 304 of the Code and replaced it with chapter 15 governing both ancillary and cross-border cases. Under that chapter, a foreign representative commences a case by filing a petition for recognition of a pending foreign proceeding. This amendment requires service of the summons and petition on the debtor and any entity against whom the representative is seeking provisional relief. The rule also provides that the court may direct that service be made on additional entities as appropriate.

Rule 1011 (technical) is amended to reflect the 2005 enactment of the Act which repealed § 304 of the Code and added chapter 15 to the Code. Section 304 covered cases "ancillary to foreign proceedings", while chapter 15 of the Code governs cross-border insolvencies and introduces the concept of a petition for recognition of a foreign proceeding. The amendment implements this new terminology.

Rule 2002 is amended by adding subdivision (q) to the rule to require that notice be given to the debtor and entities against whom provisional relief is sought of a hearing on a petition for recognition of a foreign proceeding. There is no need at this stage of the proceedings to provide notice to all creditors. If the foreign representative should take action to commence a case under another chapter of the Code, the rules governing those proceedings will operate to provide that notice is given to all creditors. **This rule is also otherwise amended by the Business and Consumer Rules.**

Rule 2015 (conforming) is amended by inserting a new subdivision (d) to implement the 2005 enactment of § 1518 of the Code as a part of the Act. That section directs the foreign representative to make reports to the court, and the rule sets the time for the filing of those reports. Former subdivision (d) is renumbered as subdivision (e). **This rule is also amended by the Business Rules.**

Rule 5012 (conforming) is new. It is added to implement § 1525 of the Code which was added by the Act. The rule provides an opportunity for parties in the case to take appropriate action prior to the communication between courts to establish procedures for the manner of the communication and the right to participate in the communication.

DIRECT APPEAL RULES

Rule 8001 is amended to implement the direct appeal provisions that the Act added in 2005. The Act amended 28 U.S.C. § 158 to authorize appeals directly to the courts of appeals upon certification either by the bankruptcy or district court or the bankruptcy appellate panel. Certification is also available to the parties either on request to the court, or if all of the parties agree. The rule sets out the procedure for obtaining a certification, whether by the court on its own initiative, or upon request of a party. The rule also provides that review by the court of appeals, which is at its discretion, requires that a party file a timely notice of appeal.

Rule 8003 is amended to implement the direct appeal provisions that the Act added in 2005. It provides that a certification by the lower court or the allowance of leave to appeal by the court of appeals is deemed to satisfy the requirement for leave to appeal even if no motion for leave to appeal has been filed.

TABLE OF CONTENTS

PROPOSED AMENDMENTS TO THE FEDERAL RULES OF BANKRUPTCY PROCEDURE

PROPOSED AMENDMENTS TO THE FEDERAL RULES OF BANKRUPTCY PROCEDURE

Rule 1006. Filing Fee

(a) GENERAL REQUIREMENT. Every petition shall be accompanied by the filing fee except as provided in subdivisions (b) and (c) of this rule. For the purpose of this rule, "filing fee" means the filing fee prescribed by 28 U.S.C. § 1930(a)(1)–(a)(5) and any other fee prescribed by the Judicial Conference of the United States under 28 U.S.C. § 1930(b) that is payable to the clerk upon the commencement of a case under the Code.

(b) PAYMENT OF FILING FEE IN INSTALLMENTS

(1) *Application ~~for Permission~~ to Pay Filing Fee in Installments.* A voluntary petition by an individual shall be accepted for filing if accompanied by the debtor's signed application, prepared as prescribed by the appropriate Official Form, stating that the debtor is unable to pay the filing fee except in installments. ~~The application shall state the proposed terms of the installment payments and that the applicant has neither paid any money nor transferred any property to an attorney for services in connection with the case.~~

* * * * *

(3) *Postponement of Attorney's Fees.* ~~The filing fee~~ All installments of the filing fee must be paid in full before the debtor or chapter 13 trustee may make further payments ~~pay an~~ to an attorney or any other person who renders service to the debtor in connection with the case.

(c) WAIVER OF FILING FEE. A voluntary chapter 7 petition filed by an individual shall be accepted for filing if accompanied by the debtor's application requesting a waiver under 28 U.S.C. § 1930(f), prepared as prescribed by the appropriate Official Form.

COMMITTEE NOTE

Subdivision (a) is amended to include a reference to new subdivision (c), which deals with fee waivers under 28 U.S.C. § 1930(f) which was added in 2005.

Subdivision (b)(1) is amended to delete the sentence requiring a disclosure that the debtor has not paid an attorney or other person in connection with the case. Inability to pay the filing fee in installments is one of the requirements for a fee waiver under the 2005 revisions to 28 U.S.C. § 1930(f). If the attorney payment prohibition were retained, payment of an attorney's fee would render many debtors ineligible for installment payment and thus enhance their eligibility for the fee waiver. The deletion of this prohibition from the rule, which was not statutorily required, ensures that debtors who have the financial ability to pay the fee in installments will do so rather than requesting a waiver.

Subdivision (b)(3) is amended in conformance with the changes to (b)(1) to reflect the 2005 amendments. The change is meant to clarify that (b)(3) refers to payments made after the debtor has filed the bankruptcy case and after the debtor has received permission to pay the fee in installments. Otherwise, the subdivision may conflict with intent and effect of the amendments to subdivision (b)(1).

Rule 1007. Lists, Schedules, ~~and~~ Statements, and Other Documents; Time Limits

(a) LIST OF CREDITORS AND EQUITY SECURITY HOLDERS, AND CORPORATE OWNERSHIP STATEMENT.

* * * * *

(4) *Chapter 15 Case.* Unless the court orders otherwise, a foreign representative filing a petition for recognition under chapter 15 shall file with the petition a list containing the name and address of all administrators in foreign proceedings of the debtor, all parties to any litigation in which the debtor is a party and that is pending in the United States at the time of the filing of the petition, and all entities against whom provisional relief is being sought under § 1519 of the Code.

~~(4)~~(5) *Extension of Time.* Any extension of time for the filing of lists required by this subdivision may be granted only on motion for cause shown and on notice to the United States trustee and to any trustee, committee elected ~~pursuant to~~under § 705 or appointed ~~pursuant to~~under § 1102 of the Code, or other party as the court may direct.

(b) SCHEDULES, ~~AND~~ STATEMENTS, AND OTHER DOCUMENTS REQUIRED.

(1) Except in a chapter 9 municipality case, the debtor, unless the court orders otherwise, shall file the following schedules, statements, and other documents, prepared as prescribed by the appropriate Official Forms, if any:

(A) schedules of assets and liabilities~~,~~;

(B) a schedule of current income and expenditures~~,~~;

(C) a schedule of executory contracts and unexpired leases~~, and~~;

(D) a statement of financial affairs~~, prepared as prescribed by the appropriate Official Forms,~~;

(E) copies of all payment advices or other evidence of payment, if any, with all but the last four digits of the debtor's social security number redacted, received by the debtor from an employer within 60 days before the filing of the petition; and

(F) a record of any interest that the debtor has in an account or program of the type specified in § 521(c) of the Code.

(2) An individual debtor in a chapter 7 case shall file a statement of intention as required by § 521(a)~~521(2)~~ of the Code, prepared as prescribed by the appropriate Official Form. A copy of the statement of intention shall be served on the trustee and the creditors named in the statement on or before the filing of the statement.

(3) Unless the United States trustee has determined that the credit counseling requirement of § 109 does not apply in the district, an individual debtor must file the certificate and debt repayment plan, if any, required by § 521(b), a certification under § 109(h)(3), or a request for a determination by the court under § 109(h)(4).

(4) Unless § 707(b)(2)(D) applies, an individual debtor in a chapter 7 case with primarily consumer debts shall file a statement of current monthly income prepared as prescribed by the appropriate Official Form, and, if the debtor has current monthly income greater than the applicable median family income for the applicable state and household size, the calculations in accordance with § 707(b), prepared as prescribed by the appropriate Official Form.

(5) An individual debtor in a chapter 11 case shall file a statement of current monthly income, prepared as prescribed by the appropriate Official Form.

(6) A debtor in a chapter 13 case shall file a statement of current monthly income, prepared as prescribed by the appropriate Official Form, and, if the debtor has current monthly income greater than the median family income for the applicable state and family size, a calculation of disposable income in accordance with § 1325(b)(3), prepared as prescribed by the appropriate Official Form.

(7) An individual debtor in a chapter 7 or chapter 13 case shall file a statement regarding completion of a course in personal financial management, prepared as prescribed by the appropriate Official Form.

(c) TIME LIMITS.* In a voluntary case, the schedules, ~~and~~ statements, and other documents required by subdivision (b)(1), (4), (5), and (6)~~, other than the statement of intention,~~ shall be filed

* Includes amendments that take effect on December 1, 2005.

with the petition~~, or~~ within 15 days thereafter, except as otherwise provided in subdivisions (d), (e), (f), and (h) of this rule. In an involuntary case the list in subdivision (a)(2), and the schedules, ~~and~~ statements, and other documents required by subdivision (b)(1)~~, other than the statement of intention,~~ shall be filed by the debtor within 15 days after entry of the order for relief. The documents required by subdivision (b)(3) shall be filed with the petition in a voluntary case. The statement required by subdivision (b)(7) shall be filed by the debtor within 45 days after the first date set for the meeting of creditors under § 341 of the Code in a chapter 7 case, and no later than the last payment made by the debtor as required by the plan or the filing of a motion for entry of a discharge under § 1328(b) in a chapter 13 case. Lists, schedules, ~~and~~ statements, and other documents filed prior to the conversion of a case to another chapter shall be deemed filed in the converted case unless the court directs otherwise. Except as provided in § 1116(3) of the Code, any ~~Any~~ extension of time for the filing of the schedules, ~~and~~ statements, and other documents may be granted only on motion for cause shown and on notice to the United States trustee and to any committee elected under § 705 or appointed under § 1102 of the Code, trustee, examiner, or other party as the court may direct. Notice of an extension shall be given to the United States trustee and to any committee, trustee, or other party as the court may direct.

* * * * *

COMMITTEE NOTE

The title of this rule is expanded to refer to "documents" in conformity with the 2005 amendments to § 521 and related provisions of the Bankruptcy Code that include a wider range of documentary requirements.

Subdivision (a) is amended to require that any foreign representative filing a petition for recognition to commence a case under chapter 15, which was added to the Code in 2005, file a list of entities with whom the debtor is engaged in litigation in the United States. The foreign representative filing the petition for recognition also must list any entities against whom provisional relief is being sought as well as all administrators in foreign proceedings of the debtor. This should ensure that the entities most interested in the case, or their representatives, will receive notice of the petition under Rule 2002(q).

Subdivision (b)(1) addresses schedules, statements, and other documents that the debtor must file unless the court orders otherwise and other than in a case under Chapter 9. This subdivision is amended to include documentary requirements added by the 2005 amendments to § 521 that apply to the same group of debtors and have the same time limits as the existing requirements of (b)(1). Consistent with the E-Government Act of 2002, Pub. L. No. 107-347, 116 Stat. 2921 (2002), the payment advices should be redacted before they are filed.

Subdivision (b)(2) is amended to conform the renumbering of the subsections of § 521.

Subdivisions (b)(3) through (b)(7) are new. They implement the 2005 amendments to the Bankruptcy Code. Subdivision (b)(3) provides a procedure for filing documents relating to the nonprofit credit counseling requirement provided by the 2005 amendments to § 109.

Subdivision (b)(4) addresses the filing of information about current monthly income, as defined in § 101, for certain chapter 7 debtors and, if required, additional calculations of expenses required by the 2005 revisions to § 707(b).

Subdivision (b)(5) addresses the filing of information about current monthly income, as defined in § 101, for individual chapter 11 debtors. The 2005 amendments to § 1129(a)(15) condition plan confirmation for individual debtors on the commitment of disposable income as defined in § 1325(b)(2), which is based on current monthly income.

Subdivision (b)(6) addresses the filing of information about current monthly income, as defined in § 101, for chapter 13 debtors and, if required, additional calculations of expenses. These changes are necessary because the 2005 amendments to § 1325 require that determinations of disposable income start with current monthly income.

Subdivision (b)(7) reflects the 2005 amendments to §§ 727 and 1328 that condition the receipt of a discharge on the completion of a personal financial management course, with certain exceptions.

Subdivision (c) is amended to include time limits for the filing requirements added to subdivision (b) due to the 2005 amendments to the Bankruptcy Code, and to make conforming amendments. Separate time limits are provided for the documentation of credit counseling and for the statement of the completion of the financial management course.

Subdivision (c) of the rule is also amended to recognize the limitation on the extension of time to file schedules and statements when the debtor is a small business debtor. Section 1116(3), added to the Bankruptcy Code in 2005, establishes a specific standard for courts to apply in the event that the debtor in possession or the trustee seeks an extension for filing these forms for a period beyond 30 days after the order for relief.

Rule 1009. Amendments of Voluntary Petitions, Lists, Schedules and Statements

* * * * *

(b) STATEMENT OF INTENTION. The statement of intention may be amended by the debtor at any time before the expiration of the period provided in § 521(a) ~~521(2)(B)~~ of the Code. The debtor shall give notice of the amendment to the trustee and to any entity affected thereby.

* * * * *

COMMITTEE NOTE

Subdivision (b) is amended to conform to the 2005 amendments to § 521 of the Bankruptcy Code.

Rule 1010. Service of Involuntary Petition and Summons; Petition ~~Commencing Ancillary Case~~ For Recognition of a Foreign Nonmain Proceeding

On the filing of an involuntary petition or a petition ~~commencing a case ancillary to~~ for recognition of a foreign nonmain proceeding the clerk shall forthwith issue a summons for service. When an involuntary petition is filed, service shall be made on the debtor. When a petition ~~commencing an ancillary case~~ for recognition of a foreign nonmain proceeding is filed, service shall be made on the ~~parties against whom relief is sought pursuant to § 304(b)~~ debtor, any entity against whom provisional relief is sought under § 1519 of the Code, and on any other parties as the court may direct. The summons shall be served with a copy of the petition in the manner provided for service of a summons and complaint by Rule 7004(a) or (b). If service cannot be so made, the court may order that the summons and petition be served by mailing copies to the party's last known address, and by at least one publication in a manner and form directed by the court. The summons and petition may be served on the party anywhere. Rule 7004(e) and Rule 4(*l*) F.R.Civ.P. apply when service is made or attempted under this rule.

COMMITTEE NOTE

This rule is amended to implement the 2005 amendments to the Bankruptcy Code, which repealed § 304 of the Code and replaced it with chapter 15 governing ancillary and other cross-boarder cases. Under chapter 15, a foreign representative commences a case by filing a petition for recognition of a pending foreign nonmain proceeding. The amendment requires service of the summons and petition on the debtor and any entity against whom the representative is seeking provisional relief. Until the court enters a recognition order under § 1517, no stay is in effect unless the court enters some form of provisional relief under § 1519. Thus, there is no need to serve all creditors of the debtor upon filing the petition for recognition. Only those entities against whom specific provisional relief is sought need to be served. The court may direct that service be made on additional entities as appropriate.

This rule does not apply to a petition for recognition of a foreign main proceeding.

Rule 1011. Responsive Pleading or Motion in Involuntary and ~~Ancillary~~ Cross-Border Cases

(a) WHO MAY CONTEST PETITION. The debtor named in an involuntary petition or a party in interest to a petition ~~commencing a case ancillary to a~~ for recognition of a foreign proceeding may contest the petition. In the case of a petition against a partnership under Rule 1004, a nonpetitioning general partner, or a person who is alleged to be a general partner but denies the allegation, may contest the petition.

* * * * *

COMMITTEE NOTE

The rule is amended to reflect the 2005 amendments to the Bankruptcy Code, which repealed § 304 of the Code and added chapter 15. Section 304 covered cases ancillary to foreign proceedings, while chapter 15 of the code governs ancillary and other cross-border cases and introduces the concept of a petition for recognition of a foreign proceeding.

Rule 1017. Dismissal or Conversion of Case; Suspension

* * * * *

(e) DISMISSAL OF AN INDIVIDUAL DEBTOR'S CHAPTER 7 CASE OR CONVERSION TO A CASE UNDER CHAPTER 11 or 13 FOR ~~SUBSTANTIAL~~ ABUSE. The court may dismiss or, with the debtor's consent, convert an individual debtor's case for ~~substantial~~ abuse under § 707(b) only on motion ~~by the United States trustee or on the court's own motion~~ and after a hearing on notice to the debtor, the trustee, the United States trustee, and any other entities as the court directs.

(1) Except as otherwise provided in § 704(b)(2), a ~~A~~ motion to dismiss a case for ~~substantial~~ abuse under § 707(b) or (c) may be filed ~~by the United States trustee~~ only within 60 days after the first date set for the meeting of creditors under § 341(a), unless, on request filed ~~by the United States trustee~~ before the time has expired, the court for cause extends the time for filing the motion to dismiss. The ~~United States trustee~~ party filing the motion shall set forth in the motion all matters to be considered ~~submitted to the court for its consideration~~ at the hearing. A motion to dismiss under § 707(b)(1) and (3) shall state with particularity the circumstances alleged to constitute abuse.

* * * * *

COMMITTEE NOTE

Subdivisions (e) and (e)(1) are amended to implement the 2005 revisions to § 707 of the Bankruptcy Code. These revisions permit conversion of a chapter 7 case to a case under chapter 11 or 13, change the basis for dismissal or conversion from "substantial abuse" to "abuse," authorize parties other than the United States trustee to bring motions under § 707(b) under certain circumstances, and add § 707(c) to create an explicit ground for dismissal based on the request of a victim of a crime of violence or drug trafficking. The conforming amendments to subdivision (e) preserve the time limits already in place for § 707 motions, except to the extent that §704(b)(2) sets the deadline for the United States Trustee to act. In contrast to the grounds for a motion to dismiss under § 707(b)(2), which are quite specific, the grounds under § 707(b)(1) and (3) are very general. Subdivision (e) therefore requires that motions to dismiss under §§ 707(b)(1) and (3) state with particularity the circumstances alleged to constitute abuse to enable the debtor to respond.

Rule 1019. Conversion of Chapter 11 Reorganization Case, Chapter 12 Family Farmer's Debt Adjustment Case, or Chapter 13 Individual's Debt Adjustment Case to a Chapter 7 Liquidation Case

* * * * *

(2) NEW FILING PERIODS. A new time period for filing ~~claims,~~ a motion under § 707(b) or (c), a claim, a complaint objecting to discharge, or a complaint to obtain a determination of dischargeability of any debt shall commence under ~~pursuant to~~ Rules 1017, 3002, 4004, or 4007, provided that a new time period shall not commence if a chapter 7 case had been converted to a chapter 11, 12, or 13 case and thereafter reconverted to a chapter 7 case and the time for filing ~~claims,~~ a motion under § 707(b) or (c), a claim, a complaint objecting to discharge, or a complaint to obtain a determination of the dischargeability of any debt, or any extension thereof, expired in the original chapter 7 case.

* * * * *

COMMITTEE NOTE

Subdivision (2) is amended to provide a new filing period for motions under § 707(b) and (c) of the Code when a case is converted to chapter 7.

Rule 1020. ~~Election to be Considered a Small Business in a Chapter 11 Reorganization Case~~ Small Business Chapter 11 Reorganization Case

~~In a chapter 11 reorganization case, a debtor that is a small business may elect to be considered a small business by filing a written statement of election not later than 60 days after the date of the order for relief.~~

(a) SMALL BUSINESS DEBTOR DESIGNATION. In a voluntary chapter 11 case, the debtor shall state in the petition whether the debtor is a small business debtor. In an involuntary chapter 11 case, the debtor shall file within 15 days after entry of the order for relief a statement as to whether the debtor is a small business debtor. Except as provided in subdivision (c), the status of the case with respect to whether it is a small business case shall be in accordance with the debtor's statement under this subdivision, unless and until the court enters an order finding that the debtor's statement is incorrect.

(b) OBJECTING TO DESIGNATION. Except as provided in subdivision (c), the United States trustee or a party in interest may file an objection to the debtor's statement under subdivision (a) not later than 30 days after the conclusion of the meeting of creditors held under § 341(a) of the Code, or within 30 days after any amendment to the statement, whichever is later.

(c) APPOINTMENT OF COMMITTEE OF UNSECURED CREDITORS. If the United States trustee has appointed a committee of unsecured creditors under § 1102(a)(1), the case shall proceed as a small business case only if, and from the time when, the court enters an order determining that the committee has not been sufficiently active and representative to provide effective oversight of the debtor and that the debtor satisfies all the other requirements for being a small business. A request for a determination under this subdivision may be filed by the United States trustee or a party in interest only within a reasonable time after the failure of the committee to be sufficiently active and representative. The debtor may file a request for a determination at any time as to whether the committee has been sufficiently active and representative.

(d)PROCEDURE FOR OBJECTION OR DETERMINATION. Any objection or request for a determination under this rule shall be governed by Rule 9014 and served on the debtor, the debtor's attorney, the United States trustee, the trustee, any committee appointed under § 1102 or its authorized agent, or, if no committee of unsecured creditors has been appointed under § 1102, on the creditors included on the list filed under Rule 1007(d), and on such other entities as the court may direct.

COMMITTEE NOTE

Under the Bankruptcy Code, as amended in 2005, there are no provisions permitting or requiring a small business debtor to elect to be treated as a small business. Therefore, there is no longer any need for a rule on elections to be considered a small business.

The 2005 amendments to the Code include several provisions relating to small business cases under chapter 11. Section 101 of the Code includes definitions of "small business debtor" and "small business case." The purpose of the new language in this rule is to provide a procedure for informing the parties, the United States trustee, and the court of whether the debtor is a small business debtor, and to provide procedures for resolving disputes regarding the proper characterization of the debtor. Because it is important to resolve such disputes early in the case, a time limit for objecting to the debtor's self-designation is imposed. Rule 9006(b)(1), which governs enlargement of time, is applicable to the time limits set forth in this rule.

An important factor in determining whether the debtor is a small business debtor is whether the United States trustee has appointed a committee of unsecured creditors under § 1102 of the Code, and whether such a committee is sufficiently active and representative. Subdivision (c), relating to the appointment and activity of a committee of unsecured creditors, is designed to be consistent with the Code's definition of "small business debtor."

Rule 1021. Health Care Business Case

(a) HEALTH CARE BUSINESS DESIGNATION. Unless the court orders otherwise, if a petition in a case under chapter 7, chapter 9, or chapter 11 states that the debtor is a health care business, the case shall proceed as a case in which the debtor is a health care business.

(b) MOTION. The United States trustee or a party in interest may file a motion for a determination as to whether the debtor is a health care business. The motion shall be transmitted to the United States trustee and served on the debtor, the trustee, any committee elected under § 705 or appointed under § 1102 of the Code or its authorized agent, or, if the case is a chapter 9 municipality case or a chapter 11 reorganization case and no committee of unsecured creditors has been appointed under § 1102, on the creditors included on the list filed under Rule 1007(d), and such other entities as the court may direct. The motion shall be governed by Rule 9014.

COMMITTEE NOTE

Section 101(27A) of the Code, added in 2005, defines health care business. This rule provides procedures for identifying the debtor as a health care business. The debtor in a voluntary case, or petitioning creditors in an involuntary case, will usually make the identification by checking the appropriate box on the petition. If a party in interest or the United States trustee disagrees with the determination by the debtor or the petitioning creditors as to whether the debtor is a health care business, this rule provides procedures for resolving the dispute.

Rule 2002. Notices to Creditors, Equity Security Holders, Administrators in Foreign Proceedings, Persons Against Whom Provisional Relief is Sought in Ancillary and Other Cross-Border Cases, United States, and United States Trustee

(a) TWENTY-DAY NOTICES TO PARTIES IN INTEREST. Except as provided in subdivisions (h), (i), ~~and *(l)*~~ *(l)*, (p), and (q) of this rule, the clerk, or some other person as the court may direct, shall give the debtor, the trustee, all creditors and indenture trustees at least 20 days' notice by mail of:

* * * * *

(b) TWENTY-FIVE-DAY NOTICES TO PARTIES IN INTEREST. Except as provided in subdivision *(l)* of this rule, the clerk, or some other person as the court may direct, shall give the debtor, the trustee, all creditors and indenture trustees not less than 25 days notice by mail of (1) the time fixed for filing objections and the hearing to consider approval of a disclosure statement or, under § 1125(f), to make a final determination whether the plan provides adequate information so that a separate disclosure statement is not necessary; and (2) the time fixed for filing objections and the hearing to consider confirmation of a chapter 9, chapter 11, or chapter 13 plan.

(c) CONTENTS OF NOTICE.

(1) *Proposed Use, Sale, or Lease of Property.* Subject to Rule 6004 the notice of a proposed use, sale, or lease of property required by subdivision (a)(2) of this rule shall include the time and place of any public sale, the terms and conditions of any private sale and the time fixed for filing objections. The notice of a proposed use, sale, or lease of property, including real estate, is sufficient if it generally describes the property. The notice of a proposed sale or lease of personally identifiable information under § 363(b)(1)(A) or (B) of the Code shall state whether the sale is consistent with a policy prohibiting the transfer of the information.

* * * * *

(f) OTHER NOTICES. Except as provided in subdivision (*l*) of this rule, the clerk, or some other person as the court may direct, shall give the debtor, all creditors, and indenture trustees notice by mail of: (1) the order for relief; (2) the dismissal or the conversion of the case to another chapter, or the suspension of proceedings under § 305; (3) the time allowed for filing claims pursuant to Rule 3002; (4) the time fixed for filing a complaint objecting to the debtor's discharge pursuant to § 727 of the Code as provided in Rule 4004; (5) the time fixed for filing a complaint to determine the dischargeability of a debt pursuant to § 523 of the Code as provided in Rule 4007; (6) the waiver, denial, or revocation of a discharge as provided in Rule 4006; (7) entry of an order confirming a chapter 9, 11, or 12 plan; ~~and~~ (8) a summary of the trustee's final report in a chapter 7 case if the net proceeds realized exceed $1,500; (9) a notice under Rule 5008 regarding the presumption of abuse; and (10) a statement under § 704(b)(1) as to whether the debtor's case would be presumed to be an abuse under § 707(b). Notice of the time fixed for accepting or rejecting a plan pursuant to Rule 3017(c) shall be given in accordance with Rule 3017(d).

* * * * *

(p) NOTICE TO A FOREIGN CREDITOR.

(1) If, at the request of a party in interest or the United States trustee, or on its own initiative, the court finds that a notice mailed within the time prescribed by these rules would not be sufficient to give a creditor with a foreign address to which notices under these rules are mailed reasonable notice under the circumstances, the court may order that the notice be supplemented with notice by other means or that the time prescribed for the notice by mail be enlarged.

(2) Unless the court for cause orders otherwise, a creditor with a foreign address to which notices under this rule are mailed shall be given at least 30 days' notice of the time fixed for filing a proof of claim under Rule 3002(c) or Rule 3003(c).

(q) NOTICE OF PETITION FOR RECOGNITION OF FOREIGN PROCEEDING AND OF COURT'S INTENTION TO COMMUNICATE WITH FOREIGN COURTS AND FOREIGN REPRESENTATIVES.

(1) *Notice of Petition for Recognition.* The clerk, or some other person as the court may direct, shall forthwith give the debtor, all administrators in foreign proceedings of the debtor, all entities against whom provisional relief is being sought under § 1519 of the Code, all parties to any litigation in which the debtor is a party and that is pending in the United State at the time of the filing of the petition, and such other entities as the court may direct, at least 20 days' notice by mail of the hearing on the petition for recognition of a foreign proceeding. The notice shall state whether the petition seeks recognition as a foreign main proceeding or a foreign nonmain proceeding.

(2) *Notice of Court's Intention to Communicate with Foreign Courts and Foreign Representatives.* The clerk, or some other person as the court may direct, shall give the debtor, all administrators in foreign proceedings of the debtor, all entities against whom provisional relief is being sought under § 1519 of the Code, all parties to any litigation in which the debtor is a party and that is pending in the United States at the time of the filing of the petition, and such other entities as the court may direct, notice by mail of the court's intention to communicate with a foreign court or foreign representative as prescribed by Rule 5012.

COMMITTEE NOTE

Subdivision (b) is amended to provide for 25 days' notice of the time for the court to make a final determination whether the plan in a small business case can serve as a disclosure statement. Conditional approval of a disclosure statement in a small business case is governed by Rule 3017.1 and does not require 25 days' notice. The court may consider this matter in a hearing combined with the confirmation hearing in a small business case.

Subdivision (c)(1) is amended to require that a trustee leasing or selling personally identifiable information under § 363(b)(1)(A) or(B) of the Code, as amended in 2005, include in the notice of the lease or sale transaction a statement as to whether the lease or sale is consistent with a policy prohibiting the transfer of the information.

Section 1514(d) of the Code, added in 2005, requires that such additional time as is reasonable under the circumstances be given to creditors with foreign addresses with respect to notices and the filing of a proof of claim. Thus, subdivision (p)(1) is added to the rule to give the court flexibility to direct that notice by other means shall supplement notice by mail, or to enlarge the notice period, for creditors with foreign addresses. If cause exists, such as likely delays in the delivery of mailed notices in particular locations, the court may order that notice also be given by email, facsimile, or private courier. Alternatively, the court may enlarge the notice period for a creditor with a foreign address. It is expected that in most situations involving foreign creditors, fairness will not require any additional notice or extension of the notice period. This rule recognizes that the court has discretion to establish procedures to determine, on its own initiative, whether relief under subdivision (p) is appropriate, but that the court is not required to establish such procedures and may decide to act only on request of a party in interest.

Subdivisions (f)(9) and (10) are new. They reflect the 2005 amendments to §§ 342(d) and 704(b) of the Bankruptcy Code. Section 342(d) requires the clerk to give notice to creditors shortly after the commencement of the case as to whether a presumption of abuse exists. Subdivision (f)(9) adds this notice to the list of notices that the clerk must give. Subdivision (f)(10) implements the amendment to § 704(b) which requires the court to provide a copy to all creditors of a statement by the United States trustee or bankruptcy administrator as to whether the debtor's case would be presumed to be an abuse under § 707(b) not later than five days after receiving it.

Subdivision (p)(2) is added to the rule to grant creditors with a foreign address to which notices are mailed at least 30 days' notice of the time within which to file proofs of claims if notice is mailed to the foreign address, unless the court orders otherwise. If cause exists, such as likely delays in the delivery of notices in particular locations, the court may extend the notice period for creditors with foreign addresses. The court may also shorten the additional notice time if circumstances so warrant. For example, if the court in a chapter 11 case determines that supplementing the notice to a foreign creditor with notice by electronic means, such as email or facsimile, would give the creditor reasonable notice, the court may order that the creditor be given only 20 days' notice in accordance with Rule 2002(a)(7).

Subdivision (q) is added to require that notice of the hearing on the petition for recognition of a foreign proceeding be given to the debtor, all administrators in foreign proceedings of the debtor, entities against whom provisional relief is sought, and entities with whom the debtor is engaged in litigation at the time of the commencement of the case. There is no need at this stage of the proceedings to provide notice to all creditors. If the foreign representative should take action to commence a case under another chapter of the Code, the rules governing those proceedings will operate to provide that notice is given to all creditors.

The rule also requires notice of the court's intention to communicate with a foreign court or foreign representative under Rule 5012.

Rule 2003. Meeting of Creditors or Equity Security Holders

(a) DATE AND PLACE. Except as provided in § 341(e) of the Code, in ~~In~~ a chapter 7 liquidation or a chapter 11 reorganization case, the United States trustee shall call a meeting of creditors to be held no fewer than 20 and no more than 40 days after the order of relief. In a chapter 12 family farmer debt adjustment case, the United States trustee shall call a meeting of creditors to be held no fewer than 20 and no more than 35 days after the order for relief. In a chapter 13 individual's debt adjustment case, the United States trustee shall call a meeting of creditors to be held no fewer than 20 and no more than 50 days after the order for relief. If there is an appeal from or a motion to vacate the order for relief, or if there is a motion to dismiss the case, the United States trustee may set a later date for the meeting. The meeting may be held at a regular place for holding court or at any other place designated by the United States trustee within the district convenient for the parties in interest. If the United States trustee designates a place for the meeting which is not regularly staffed by the United States trustee or an assistant who may preside at the meeting, the meeting may be held not more than 60 days after the order for relief.

* * * * *

COMMITTEE NOTE

If the debtor has solicited acceptances to a plan before commencement of the case, § 341(e), which was added to the Bankruptcy Code in 2005, authorizes the court, on request of a party in interest and after notice and a hearing, to order that a meeting of creditors not be convened. The rule is amended to recognize that a meeting of creditors might not be held in those cases.

Rule 2007.1. Appointment of Trustee or Examiner in a Chapter 11 Reorganization Case

* * * * *

(b) ELECTION OF TRUSTEE.

* * * * *

(3) *Report of Election and Resolution of Disputes.*

(A) Report of Undisputed Election. If no dispute arises out of the election ~~is not disputed~~, the United States trustee shall promptly file a report ~~of~~ certifying the election, including the name and address of the person elected and a statement that the election is undisputed. The report shall be accompanied by a verified statement of the person elected setting forth the person's connections with the debtor, creditors, any other party in interest, their respective attorneys and accountants, the United States trustee, or any person employed in the office of the United States trustee. ~~The United States trustee shall file with the report an application for approval of the appointment in accordance with subdivision (c) of this rule. The report constitutes appointment of the elected person to serve as trustee, subject to court approval, as of the date of entry of the order approving the appointment.~~

(B) Dispute Arising Out of an ~~Disputed~~ Election. If a dispute arises out of an ~~the~~ election ~~is disputed~~, the United States trustee shall promptly file a report stating that the election is disputed, informing the court of the nature of the dispute, and listing the name and address of any candidate elected under any alternative presented by the dispute. The report shall be accompanied by a verified statement by each candidate elected under each alternative presented by the dispute, setting forth the person's connections with the debtor, creditors, any other party in interest, their respective attorneys and accountants, the United States trustee, ~~and~~ or any person employed in the office of the United States trustee. Not later than the date on which the report of the disputed election is filed, the United States trustee shall mail a copy of the report and each verified statement to any party in interest that has made a request to convene a meeting under § 1104(b) or to receive a copy of the report, and to any committee appointed under § 1102 of the Code. ~~Unless a motion for the resolution of the dispute is filed not later than 10 days after the United States trustee files the report, any person appointed by the United States trustee under § 1104(d) and approved in accordance with subdivision (c) of this rule shall serve as trustee. If a motion for the resolution of the dispute is timely filed, and the court determines the result of the election and approves the person elected, the report will constitute appointment of the elected person as of the date of entry of the order approving the appointment.~~

(c) APPROVAL OF APPOINTMENT. An order approving the appointment of a trustee ~~elected under § 1104(b) or appointed under § 1104(d),~~ or ~~the appointment of~~ an examiner under § 1104(d) of the Code, shall be made on application of the United States trustee. The application shall state the name of the person appointed and, to the best of the applicant's knowledge, all the person's connections with the debtor, creditors, any other parties in interest, their respective attorneys and accountants, the United States trustee, ~~and~~ or persons employed in the office of the United

States trustee. ~~Unless the person has been elected under § 1104(b), the~~ The application shall state the names of the parties in interest with whom the United States trustee consulted regarding the appointment. The application shall be accompanied by a verified statement of the person appointed setting forth the person's connections with the debtor, creditors, any other party in interest, their respective attorneys and accountants, the United States trustee, ~~and~~ or any person employed in the office of the United States trustee.

COMMITTEE NOTE

Under § 1104(b)(2) of the Code, as amended in 2005, if an eligible, disinterested person is elected to serve as trustee in a chapter 11 case, the United States trustee is directed to file a report certifying the election. The person elected does not have to be appointed to the position. Rather, the filing of the report certifying the election itself constitutes the appointment. The section further provides that in the event of a dispute in the election of a trustee, the court must resolve the matter. The rule is amended to be consistent with § 1104(b)(2).

When the United States trustee files a report certifying the election of a trustee, the person elected must provide a verified statement, similar to the statement required of professional persons under Rule 2014, disclosing connections with parties in interest and certain other persons connected with the case. Although court approval of the person elected is not required, the disclosure of the person's connections will enable parties in interest to determine whether the person is disinterested.

Rule 2007.2. Appointment of Patient Care Ombudsman in a Health Care Business Case

(a) ORDER TO APPOINT PATIENT CARE OMBUDSMAN. In a chapter 7, chapter 9, or chapter 11 case in which the debtor is a health care business, the court shall order the appointment of a patient care ombudsman under § 333 of the Code, unless the court, on motion of the United States trustee or a party in interest filed not later than 20 days after the commencement of the case or within another time fixed by the court, finds that the appointment of a patient care ombudsman is not necessary for the protection of patients under the specific circumstances of the case.

(b) MOTION FOR ORDER TO APPOINT OMBUDSMAN. If the court has ordered that the appointment of an ombudsman is not necessary, or has ordered the termination of the appointment of an ombudsman, the court, on motion of the United States trustee or a party in interest, may order the appointment at any time during the case if the court finds that the appointment of an ombudsman has become necessary to protect patients.

(c) APPOINTMENT OF OMBUDSMAN. If a patient care ombudsman is appointed under § 333, the United States trustee shall promptly file a notice of the appointment, including the name and address of the person appointed. Unless the person appointed is a State Long-Term Care Ombudsman, the notice shall be accompanied by a verified statement of the person appointed setting forth the person's connections with the debtor, creditors, patients, any other party in interest, their respective attorneys and accountants, the United States trustee, and any person employed in the office of the United States trustee.

(d) TERMINATION OF APPOINTMENT. On motion of the United States trustee or a party in interest, the court may terminate the appointment of a patient care ombudsman if the court finds that the appointment is not necessary for the protection of patients.

(e) MOTION. A motion under this rule shall be governed by Rule 9014. The motion shall be transmitted to the United States trustee and served on the debtor, the trustee, any committee elected under § 705 or appointed under § 1102 of the Code or its authorized agent, or, if the case is a chapter 9 municipality case or a chapter 11 reorganization case and no committee of unsecured creditors has been appointed under § 1102, on the creditors included on the list filed under Rule 1007(d), and such other entities as the court may direct.

COMMITTEE NOTE

Section 333 of the Code, added in 2005, requires the court to order the appointment of a health care ombudsman within the first 30 days of a health care business case, unless the court finds that the appointment is not necessary for the protection of patients. The rule recognizes this requirement and provides a procedure by which a party may obtain a court order finding that the appointment of a patient care ombudsman is unnecessary. In the absence of a timely motion under subdivision (a) of this rule, the court will enter an order directing the United States trustee to appoint the ombudsman.

Subdivision (b) recognizes that, despite a previous order finding that a patient care ombudsman is not necessary, circumstances of the case may change or newly discovered evidence may demonstrate the necessity of an ombudsman to protect the interests of patients. In that event, a party may move the court for an order directing the appointment of an ombudsman.

When the appointment of a patient care ombudsman is ordered, the United States trustee is required to appoint a disinterested person to serve in that capacity. Court approval of the appointment is not required, but subdivision (c) requires the person appointed, if not a State Long-Term Care Ombudsman, to file a verified statement similar to the statement filed by profession persons under Rule 2014 so that parties in interest will have information relevant to disinterestedness. If a party believes that the person appointed is not disinterested, it may file a motion asking the court to find that the person is not eligible to serve.

Subdivision (d) permits parties in interest to move for the termination of the appointment of a patient care ombudsman. If the movant can show that there no longer is any need for the ombudsman, the court may order the termination of the appointment.

Rule 2015. Duty to Keep Records, Make Reports, and Give Notice of Case or Change of Status

* * * * *

(d) FOREIGN REPRESENTATIVE. In a case in which the court has granted recognition of a foreign proceeding under chapter 15, the foreign representative shall file any notice required under § 1518 of the Code within 15 days after the date when the representative becomes aware of the subsequent information.

~~(d)~~(e) TRANSMISSION OF REPORTS. In a chapter 11 case the court may direct that copies or summaries of annual reports and copies or summaries of other reports shall be mailed to the creditors, equity security holders, and indenture trustees. The court may also direct the publication of summaries of any such reports. A copy of every report or summary mailed or published pursuant to this subdivision shall be transmitted to the United States trustee.

COMMITTEE NOTE

The rule is amended to fix the time for the filing of notices under § 1519 which was added to the Code in 2005. Former subdivision (d) is renumbered as subdivision (e).

Rule 2015.1. Patient Care Ombudsman

(a) REPORTS. Unless the court orders otherwise, a patient care ombudsman, at least 10 days before making a report under § 333(b)(2) of the Code, shall give notice that the report will be made to the court. The notice shall be transmitted to the United States trustee, posted conspicuously at the health care facility that is the subject of the report, and served on the debtor, the trustee, all patients, and any committee elected under § 705 or appointed under § 1102 of the Code or its authorized agent, or, if the case is a chapter 9 municipality case or a chapter 11 reorganization case and no committee of unsecured creditors has been appointed under § 1102, on the creditors included on the list filed under Rule 1007(d), and such other entities as the court may direct. The notice shall state the date and time when the report will be made, the manner in which the report will be made, and, if the report is in writing, the name, address, telephone number, email address, and website, if any, of the person from whom a copy of the report may be obtained at the debtor's expense.

(b) AUTHORIZATION TO REVIEW CONFIDENTIAL PATIENT RECORDS. A motion by a health care ombudsman under § 333(c) to review confidential patient records shall be governed by Rule 9014, served on the patient and any family member or other contact person whose name and address has been given to the trustee or the debtor for the purpose of providing information regarding the patient's health care, and transmitted to the United States trustee subject to applicable nonbankruptcy law relating to patient privacy. Unless the court orders otherwise, a hearing on the motion may be commenced no earlier than 15 days after service of the motion.

COMMITTEE NOTE

This rule is new. It implements § 333, added to the Code in 2005. Subdivision (a) is designed to give parties in interest, including patients or their representatives, sufficient notice so that they will be able to review written reports or attend hearings at which reports are made. The rule permits a notice to relate to a single report or to periodic reports to be given during the case. For example, the ombudsman may give notice that reports will be made at specified intervals or dates during the case.

Subdivision (a) of the rule requires that the notice be posted conspicuously at the health care facility in a place where it will be seen by patients and their families or others visiting the patient. This may require posting in common areas and patient rooms within the facility. Because health care facilities and the patients they serve can vary greatly, the locations of the posted notice should be tailored to the specific facility that is the subject of the report.

Subdivision (b) requires the ombudsman to notify the patient and the United States trustee that the ombudsman is seeking access to confidential patient records so that they will be able to appear and be heard on the matter. This procedure should assist the court in reaching its decision both as to access to the records and appropriate restrictions on that access to ensure continued confidentiality. Notices given under this rule are subject to provisions under applicable federal and state law that relate to the protection of patients' privacy, such as the Health Insurance Portability and Accountability Act of 1996, Pub. L. No. 104-191 (HIPAA).

Rule 2015.2. Transfer of Patient in Health Care Business Case

Unless the court orders otherwise, if the debtor is a health care business, the trustee may not transfer a patient to another health care business under § 704(a)(12) of the Code unless the trustee gives at least 10 days' notice of the transfer to the patient care ombudsman, if any, and to the patient and any family member or other contact person whose name and address has been given to the trustee or the debtor for the purpose of providing information regarding the patient's health care subject to applicable nonbankruptcy law relating to patient privacy.

COMMITTEE NOTE

This rule is new. Section 704(a)(12), added to the Code in 2005, authorizes the trustee to relocate patients when a health care business debtor's facility is in the process of being closed. The Code permits the trustee to take this action without the need for any court order, but the notice required by this rule will enable a patient care ombudsman appointed under § 333, or a patient who contends that the trustee's actions violate § 704(a)(12), to have those issues resolved before the patient is transferred.

The rule also permits the court to enter an order dispensing with or altering the notice requirement in proper circumstances. The facility could be closed immediately, or very quickly, such that 10 days' notice would not be possible in some instances. In that event, the court may shorten the time required for notice.

Notices given under this rule are subject to provisions under applicable federal and state law that relate to the protection of patients' privacy, such as the Health Insurance Portability and Accountability Act of 1996, Pub. L. No. 104-191 (HIPAA).

Rule 3002. Filing Proof of Claim or Interest

* * * * *

(c) TIME FOR FILING. In a chapter 7 liquidation, chapter 12 family farmer's debt adjustment, or chapter 13 individual's debt adjustment case, a proof of claim is timely filed if it is filed not later than 90 days after the first date set for the meeting of creditors called under § 341(a) of the Code, except as follows:

(1) A proof of claim filed by a governmental unit, other than for a claim resulting from a tax return filed under § 1308, is timely filed if it is filed not later than 180 days after the date of the order for relief. On motion of a governmental unit before the expiration of such period and for cause shown, the court may extend the time for filing of a claim by the governmental unit. A proof of claim filed by a governmental unit for a claim resulting from a tax return filed under § 1308 is timely filed if it is filed not later than 180 days after the date of the order for relief or 60 days after the date of the filing of the tax return, whichever is later.

* * * * *

(6) If notice of the time for filing a proof of claim has been mailed to a creditor at a foreign address, on motion filed by the creditor before or after the expiration of the time, the court may extend the time by not more than 60 days if the court finds that the notice was not sufficient under the circumstances to give the creditor a reasonable time to file a proof of claim.

COMMITTEE NOTE

Subdivision (c)(1) is amended to reflect the addition of § 1308 to the Bankruptcy Code in 2005. This provision requires that chapter 13 debtors file tax returns during the pendency of the case, and imposes bankruptcy-related consequences if debtors fail to do so. Subdivision (c)(1) provides additional time for governmental units to file a proof of claim for tax obligations with respect to tax returns filed during the pendency of a chapter 13 case.

Paragraph (c)(6) is added to give the court discretion to extend the time for filing a proof of claim for a creditor who received notice of the time to file the claim at a foreign address, if the court finds that the notice was not sufficient, under the particular circumstances, to give the foreign creditor a reasonable time to file a proof of claim. This amendment is designed to comply with § 1514(d), which was added to the Code in 2005 and requires that the rules and orders of the court provide such additional time as is reasonable under the circumstances for foreign creditors to file claims in cases under all chapters of the Code.

Rule 3003. Filing Proof of Claim or Equity Security Interest in Chapter 9 Municipality or Chapter 11 Reorganization Cases

* * * * *

(c) FILING PROOF OF CLAIM.

(1) *Who May File.* Any creditor or indenture trustee may file a proof of claim within the time prescribed by subdivision (c)(3) of this rule.

(2) *Who Must File.* Any creditor or equity security holder whose claim or interest is not scheduled or scheduled as disputed, contingent, or unliquidated shall file a proof of claim or interest within the time prescribed by subdivision (c)(3) of this rule; any creditor who fails to do so shall not be treated as a creditor with respect to such claim for the purpose of voting and distribution.

(3) *Time for Filing.* The court shall fix and for cause shown may extend the time within which proofs of claim or interest may be filed. Notwithstanding the expiration of such time, a proof of claim may be filed to the extent and under the conditions stated in Rule 3002(c)(2), (c)(3), ~~and~~ (c)(4), and (c)(6).

(4) *Effect of Filing Claim or Interest.* A proof of claim or interest executed and filed in accordance with this subdivision shall supersede any scheduling of that claim or interest pursuant to § 521(a)(1) of the Code.

(5) *Filing by Indenture Trustee.* An indenture trustee may file a claim on behalf of all known or unknown holders of securities issued pursuant to the trust instrument under which it is trustee.

* * * * *

COMMITTEE NOTE

The rule is amended to implement § 1514(d), which was added to the Code in 2005, by making the new Rule 3002(c)(6) applicable in chapter 9 and chapter 11 cases. Section 1514(d)requires that creditors with foreign addresses be provided such additional time as is reasonable under the circumstances to file proofs of claims.

Rule 3016. Filing of Plan and Disclosure Statement in Chapter 9 Municipality or Chapter 11 Reorganization Cases

* * * * *

(b) DISCLOSURE STATEMENT. In a chapter 9 or 11 case, a disclosure statement under § 1125 or evidence showing compliance with § 1126(b) of the Code shall be filed with the plan or within a time fixed by the court, unless the plan is intended to provide adequate information under § 1125(f)(1). If the plan is intended to provide adequate information under § 1125(f)(1), it shall be so designated and Rule 3017.1 shall apply as if the plan is a disclosure statement.

* * * * *

COMMITTEE NOTE

Subdivision (b) is amended to recognize that, in 2005, § 1125(f)(1) was added to the Code to provide that the plan proponent in a small business case need not file a disclosure statement if the plan itself includes adequate information and the court finds that a separate disclosure statement is unnecessary. If the plan is intended to provide adequate information in a small business case, it may be conditionally approved as a disclosure statement under Rule 3017.1 and is subject to all other rules applicable to disclosure statements in small business cases.

Rule 3017.1. Court Consideration of Disclosure Statement in a Small Business Case

(a) CONDITIONAL APPROVAL OF DISCLOSURE STATEMENT. ~~If the debtor is~~ In a small business case ~~and has made a timely election to be considered a small business in a chapter 11 case~~, the court may, on application of the plan proponent or on its own initiative, conditionally approve a disclosure statement filed in accordance with Rule 3016~~(b)~~. On or before conditional approval of the disclosure statement, the court shall:

(1) fix a time within which the holders of claims and interests may accept or reject the plan;

(2) fix a time for filing objections to the disclosure statement;

(3) fix a date for the hearing on final approval of the disclosure statement to be held if a timely objection is filed; and

(4) fix a date for the hearing on confirmation.

(b) APPLICATION OF RULE 3017. Rule 3017(a), (b), (c), and (e) do not apply to a conditionally approved disclosure statement. Rule 3017(d) applies to a conditionally approved disclosure statement, except that conditional approval is considered approval of the disclosure statement for the purpose of applying Rule 3017(d).

(c) FINAL APPROVAL.

(1) *Notice.* Notice of the time fixed for filing objections and the hearing to consider final approval of the disclosure statement shall be given in accordance with Rule 2002 and may be combined with notice of the hearing on confirmation of the plan.

(2) *Objections.* Objections to the disclosure statement shall be filed, transmitted to the United States trustee, and served on the

debtor, the trustee, any committee appointed under the Code and any other entity designated by the court at any time before final approval of the disclosure statement or by an earlier date as the court may fix.

(3) *Hearing*. If a timely objection to the disclosure statement is filed, the court shall hold a hearing to consider final approval before or combined with the hearing on confirmation of the plan.

COMMITTEE NOTE

Section 101 of the Code, as amended in 2005, defines a "small business case" and "small business debtor," and eliminates any need to elect that status. Therefore, the reference in the rule to an election is deleted.

As provided in the amendment to Rule 3016(b), a plan intended to provide adequate information in a small business case under § 1125(f)(1) may be conditionally approved and is otherwise treated as a disclosure statement under this rule.

Rule 3019. Modification of Accepted Plan Before or After Confirmation in a Chapter 9 Municipality or Chapter 11 Reorganization Case

(a) In a chapter 9 or chapter 11 case, after a plan has been accepted and before its confirmation, the proponent may file a modification of the plan. If the court finds after hearing on notice to the trustee, any committee appointed under the Code, and any other entity designated by the court that the proposed modification does not adversely change the treatment of the claim of any creditor or the interest of any equity security holder who has not accepted in writing the modification, it shall be deemed accepted by all creditors and equity security holders who have previously accepted the plan.

(b) If the debtor is an individual, a request to modify the plan under § 1127(e) of the Code shall identify the proponent and shall be filed together with the proposed modification. The clerk, or some other person as the court may direct, shall give the debtor, the trustee, and all creditors not less than 20 days' notice by mail of the time fixed for filing objections and, if an objection is filed, the hearing to consider the proposed modification, unless the court orders otherwise with respect to creditors who are not affected by the proposed modification. A copy of the notice shall be transmitted to the United States trustee. A copy of the proposed modification shall be included with the notice. Any objection to the proposed modification shall be filed and served on the debtor, the proponent of the modification, the trustee, and any other entity designated by the court, and shall be transmitted to the United States trustee. An objection to a proposed modification is governed by Rule 9014.

COMMITTEE NOTE

Section 1127 was amended in 2005 to provide for modification of a confirmed plan in a chapter 11 case of an individual debtor. The rule is amended to establish the procedure for filing and objecting to a proposed modification of a confirmed plan.

Rule 4002. Duties of Debtor

(a) IN GENERAL. In addition to performing other duties prescribed by the Code and rules, the debtor shall:

(1) attend and submit to an examination at the times ordered by the court;

(2) attend the hearing on a complaint objecting to discharge and testify, if called as a witness;

(3) inform the trustee immediately in writing as to the location of real property in which the debtor has an interest and the name and address of every person holding money or property subject to the debtor's withdrawal or order if a schedule of property has not yet been filed pursuant to Rule 1007;

(4) cooperate with the trustee in the preparation of an inventory, the examination of proofs of claim, and the administration of the estate; and

(5) file a statement of any change of the debtor's address.

(b) INDIVIDUAL DEBTOR'S DUTY TO PROVIDE DOCUMENTATION.

(1) *Personal Identification*. Every individual debtor shall bring to the meeting of creditors under § 341:

(A) a picture identification issued by a governmental unit, or other personal identifying information that establishes the debtor's identity; and

(B) evidence of social security number(s), or a written statement that such documentation does not exist.

(2) *Financial Information*. Every individual debtor shall bring to the meeting of creditors under § 341 and make available to the trustee the following documents or copies of them, or provide a written statement that the documentation does not exist or is not in the debtor's possession:

(A) evidence of current income such as the most recent pay stub;

(B) unless the trustee or the United States trustee instructs otherwise, statements for each of the debtor's depository and investment accounts, including checking, savings, and money market accounts, mutual funds and brokerage accounts for the time period that includes the date of the filing of the petition; and

(C) documentation of monthly expenses claimed by the debtor when required by § 707(b)(2)(A) or (B).

(3) *Tax Return*. At least 7 days before the first date set for the meeting of creditors under § 341, the debtor shall provide to the trustee a copy of the debtor's Federal income tax return for the most recent tax year ending immediately before the commencement of the case and for which a return was filed, including any attachments, or a transcript of the tax return, or provide a written statement that the documentation does not exist.

(4) *Tax Returns Provided to Creditors*. If a creditor, at least 15 days before the first date set for the meeting of creditors under § 341, requests a copy of the debtor's tax return that is to be provided to the trustee under subdivision (b)(3), the debtor shall provide to the requesting creditor a copy of the return, including any attachments, or a transcript of the tax return, or provide a written statement that the documentation does not exist at least 7 days before the first date set for the meeting of creditors under § 341.

(5) The debtor's obligation to provide tax returns under Rule 4002(b)(3) and (b)(4) is subject to procedures for safeguarding the confidentiality of tax information established by the Director of the Administrative office of the United States Courts.

COMMITTEE NOTE

The rule is amended to implement the directives of § 521(a)(1)(B)(iv) and (e)(2) of the Code, which were added by the

2005 amendments. These Code amendments expressly require the debtor to file with the court, or provide to the trustee, specific documents. The amendments to the rule implement these obligations and establish a time frame for creditors to make requests for a copy of the debtor's Federal income tax return. The rule also requires the debtor to provide documentation in support of claimed expenses under § 707(b)(2)(A) and (B).

Subdivision (b) is also amended to require the debtor to cooperate with the trustee by providing materials and documents necessary to assist the trustee in performance of the trustee's duties. Nothing in the rule, however, is intended to limit or restrict the debtor's duties under § 521, or to limit the access of the Attorney General to any information provided by the debtor in the case. The rule does not require that the debtor create documents or obtain documents from third parties; rather, the debtor's obligation is to bring to the meeting of creditors under § 341 the documents which the debtor possesses. Any written statement that the debtor provides indicating either that documents do not exist or are not in the debtor's possession must be verified or contain an unsworn declaration as required under Rule 1008.

Because the amendment implements the debtor's duty to cooperate with the trustee, the materials provided to the trustee would not be made available to any other party in interest at the § 341 meeting of creditors other than the Attorney General. Some of the documents may contain otherwise private information that should not be disseminated. For example, pay stubs and financial account statements might include the social security numbers of the debtor and the debtor's spouse and dependents, as well as the names of the debtor's children. The debtor should redact all but the last four digits of all social security numbers and the names of any minors when they appear in these documents. This type of information would not usually be needed by creditors and others who may be attending the meeting. If a creditor perceives a need to review specific documents or other evidence, the creditor may proceed under Rule 2004.

Tax information produced under this rule is subject to procedures for safeguarding confidentiality established by the Director of the Administrative Office of the United States Courts.

Rule 4003. Exemptions

* * * * *

(b) OBJECTING TO A CLAIM OF EXEMPTIONS.

(1) Except as provided in paragraph (2), a ~~A~~ party in interest may file an objection to the list of property claimed as exempt ~~only~~ within 30 days after the meeting of creditors held under § 341(a) is concluded or within 30 days after any amendment to the list or supplemental schedules is filed, whichever is later. The court may, for cause, extend the time for filing objections if, before the time to object expires, a party in interest files a request for an extension.

(2) An objection to a claim of exemption based on § 522(q) shall be filed before the closing of the case. If an exemption is first claimed after a case is reopened, an objection shall be filed before the reopened case is closed.

(3) Copies of the objections shall be delivered or mailed to the trustee, the person filing the list, and the attorney for that person.

* * * * *

COMMITTEE NOTE

Subdivision (b) is amended to reflect the 2005 addition of subsection (q) to § 522 of the Bankruptcy Code. Section 522(q) imposes a $125,000 limit on a state homestead exemption if the debtor has been convicted of a felony or owes a debt arising from certain causes of action. Other revised provisions of the Bankruptcy Code, such as § 727(a)(12) and § 1328(h), suggest that the court may consider issues relating to § 522 late in the case, and the 30-day period for objections would not be appropriate for this provision. A new subdivision (b)(2) is added to provide a separate time limit for this provision.

Rule 4004. Grant or Denial of Discharge

* * * * *

(c) GRANT OF DISCHARGE.

(1)

* * * * *

(F) a motion to extend the time for filing a motion to dismiss the case under Rule 1017(e)~~(1)~~ is pending, ~~or~~

(G) the debtor has not paid in full the filing fee prescribed by 28 U.S.C. § 1930(a) and any other fee prescribed by the Judicial Conference of the United States under 28 U.S.C. § 1930(b) that is payable to the clerk upon the commencement of a case under the Code, unless the court has waived the fees under 28 U.S.C. § 1930(f);

(H) the debtor has not filed with the court a statement regarding completion of a course in personal financial management as required by Rule 1007(b)(7);

(I) a motion to delay or postpone discharge under § 727(a)(12) is pending; or

(J) a presumption that a reaffirmation agreement is an undue hardship has arisen under § 524(m).

COMMITTEE NOTE

Subdivision (c)(1)(G) is amended to reflect the fee waiver provision added in 2005 to 28 U.S.C. § 1930.

Subdivision (c)(1)(H) is new. It reflects the 2005 additions to the Bankruptcy Code of §§ 727(a)(11) and 1328(g), which require that individual debtors complete a course in personal financial management as a condition to the entry of a discharge. Including this requirement in the rule helps prevent the inadvertent entry of a discharge when the debtor has not complied with this requirement. If a debtor fails to file the required statement regarding a personal financial management course, the clerk will close the bankruptcy case without the entry of a discharge.

Subdivision (c)(1)(I) is new. It reflects the 2005 addition to the Bankruptcy Code of § 727(a)(12). This provision is linked to § 522(q). Section 522(q) limits the availability of the homestead exemption for individuals who have been convicted of a felony or who owe a debt arising from certain causes of action within a particular time frame. The existence of reasonable cause to believe that § 522(q) may be applicable to the debtor constitutes grounds for withholding the discharge.

Subdivision (c)(1)(J) is new. It reflects the 2005 revisions to § 524 of the Bankruptcy Code that alter the requirements for approval of reaffirmation agreements. Section 524(m) sets forth circumstances under which a reaffirmation agreement is presumed to be an undue hardship. This triggers an obligation to review the presumption and may require notice and a hearing. Subdivision (c)(1)(J) has been added to prevent the discharge from being entered until the court approves or disapproves the reaffirmation agreement in accordance with § 524(m).

Rule 4006. Notice of No Discharge

If an order is entered denying or revoking a discharge or if a waiver of discharge is filed, the clerk, after the order becomes final or the waiver is filed, or, in the case of an individual, if the case is closed without the entry of an order of discharge, shall promptly give notice thereof to all ~~creditors~~ parties in interest in the manner provided in Rule 2002.

COMMITTEE NOTE

Rule 4006 is amended to reflect the 2005 revisions to the Bankruptcy Code requiring that individual debtors complete a course in personal financial management as a condition to the entry of a discharge. If the debtor fails to complete the course, no discharge will be entered, but the case may be closed. The amended rule provides notice to parties in interest, including the debtor, that no discharge was entered.

Rule 4007. Determination of Dischargeability of a Debt

* * * * *

(c) TIME FOR FILING COMPLAINT UNDER § 523(c) IN A CHAPTER 7 LIQUIDATION, CHAPTER 11 REORGANIZATION, ~~OR~~ CHAPTER 12 FAMILY FARMER'S DEBT ADJUSTMENT CASE, OR CHAPTER 13 INDIVIDUAL'S DEBT ADJUSTMENT CASE; NOTICE OF TIME FIXED. Except as provided in subdivision (d), a ~~A~~ complaint to determine the dischargeability of a debt under § 523(c) shall be filed no later than 60 days after the first date set for the meeting of creditors under § 341(a). The court shall give all creditors no less than 30 days' notice of the time so fixed in the manner provided in Rule 2002. On motion of any party in interest, after hearing on notice, the court may for cause extend the time fixed under this subdivision. The motion shall be filed before the time has expired.

(d) TIME FOR FILING COMPLAINT UNDER § ~~523(c)~~ 523(a)(6) IN CHAPTER 13 INDIVIDUAL'S DEBT ADJUSTMENT CASE; NOTICE OF TIME FIXED. On motion by a debtor for a discharge under § 1328(b), the court shall enter an order fixing the time to file a complaint to determine the dischargeability of any debt under § ~~523(c)~~ 523(a)(6) and shall give no less than 30 days' notice of the time fixed to all creditors in the manner provided in Rule 2002. On motion of any party in interest after hearing on notice the court may for cause extend the time fixed under this subdivision. The motion shall be filed before the time has expired.

* * * * *

COMMITTEE NOTE

Subdivision (c) is amended to reflect the 2005 amendments to § 1328(a) of the Bankruptcy Code. This revision expands the exceptions to discharge upon completion of a chapter 13 plan. Subdivision (c) extends to chapter 13 the same time limits applicable to other chapters of the Code with respect to the two exceptions to discharge that have been added to § 1328(a) and that are within § 523(c).

The amendment to subdivision (d) reflects the 2005 amendments to § 1328(a) that expands the exceptions to discharge upon completion of a chapter 13 plan, including two out of three of the provisions that fall within § 523(c). However, the 2005 revisions to § 1328(a) do not include a reference to § 523(a)(6), which is the third provision to which § 523(c) refers. Thus, the need for subdivision (d) is now limited to that provision.

Rule 4008. Discharge and Reaffirmation Hearing

Not more than 30 days following the entry of an order granting or denying a discharge, or confirming a plan in a chapter 11 reorganization case concerning an individual debtor and on not less than 10 days notice to the debtor and the trustee, the court may hold a hearing as provided in § 524(d) of the Code. A motion by the debtor for approval of a reaffirmation agreement shall be filed before or at the hearing. The debtor's statement required under § 524(k) shall be accompanied by a statement of the total income and total expense amounts stated on schedules I and J. If there is a difference between the income and expense amounts stated on schedules I and J and the statement required under § 524(k), the accompanying statement shall include an explanation of any difference.

COMMITTEE NOTE

Rule 4008 is amended to reflect the 2005 addition of §§ 524(k)(6)(A) and 524(m) to the Bankruptcy Code. These provisions require that a debtor file a signed statement in support of a reaffirmation agreement, and authorize a court to review the agreement if, based on the assertions on the statement, the agreement is presumed to be an undue hardship. The rule revision requires that an accompanying statement show the total income and expense amounts stated on schedules I and J and an explanation of any discrepancies. This will allow the court to evaluate the reaffirmation for undue hardship as § 524(m) requires. A corresponding change has been made to Rule 4004(c) to prevent the entry of a discharge until the court has approved or disapproved the reaffirmation agreement in accordance with § 524(m).

Rule 5003. Records Kept By the Clerk

* * * * *

(e) REGISTER OF MAILING ADDRESSES OF FEDERAL AND STATE GOVERNMENTAL UNITS AND CERTAIN TAXING AUTHORITIES. The United States or the state or territory in which the court is located may file a statement designating its mailing address. The United States, state, territory, or local governmental unit responsible for the collection of taxes within the district in which the case is pending may file a statement designating an address for service of requests under § 505(b) of the Code, and the designation shall describe where further information concerning additional requirements for filing such requests may be found. The clerk shall keep, in the form and manner as the Director of the Administrative Office of the United States Courts may prescribe, a register that includes ~~these~~ the mailing addresses designated under this subdivision, but the clerk is not required to include in the register more than one mailing address for each department, agency, or instrumentality of the United States or the state or territory. If more than one address for a department, agency, or instrumentality is included in the register, the clerk shall also include information that would enable a user of the register to determine the circumstances when each address is applicable, and mailing notice to only one applicable address is sufficient to provide effective notice. The clerk shall update the register annually, effective January 2 of each year. The mailing address in the register is conclusively presumed to be a proper address for the governmental unit, but the failure to use that mailing address does not invalidate any notice that is otherwise effective under applicable law.

* * * * *

COMMITTEE NOTE

The rule is amended to implement the addition of § 505(b)(1) to the Code in 2005, which allows taxing authorities to designate addresses to use for the service of a request under that subsection.

Rule 5008. Notice Regarding Presumption of Abuse in Chapter 7 Cases Of Individual Debtors

In a chapter 7 case of an individual with primarily consumer debts in which a presumption of abuse has arisen under § 707(b), the clerk shall give to creditors notice of the presumption of abuse in accordance with Rule 2002 within 10 days after the date of the filing of the petition. If the debtor has not filed a statement indicating whether a presumption of abuse has arisen, the clerk shall give notice to creditors within 10 days after the date of the filing of the petition that the debtor has not filed the statement and that further notice will be given if a later filed statement indicates that a presumption of abuse has arisen. If a debtor later files a statement indicating that a presumption of abuse has arisen, the clerk shall give notice to creditors of the presumption of abuse as promptly as practicable.

COMMITTEE NOTE

This rule is new. The 2005 revisions to § 342 of the Bankruptcy Code require that clerks give written notice to all creditors not later than 10 days after the date of the filing of the petition that a presumption of abuse has arisen under § 707(b). A statement filed by the debtor will be the source of the clerk's information about the presumption of abuse. This rule enables the clerk to meet its obligation to send the notice within the statutory time period set forth in § 342. In the event that the court receives the debtor's statement after the clerk has sent the first notice, and the debtor's statement indicates a presumption of abuse, this rule requires that the clerk send a second notice.

Rule 5012. Communication and Cooperation With Foreign Courts and Foreign Representatives

Except for communications for scheduling and administrative purposes, the court in any case commenced by a foreign representative shall give at least 20 days' notice of its intent to communicate with a foreign court or a foreign representative. The notice shall identify the subject of the anticipated communication and shall be given in the manner provided by Rule 2002(q). Any entity that wishes to participate in the communication shall notify the court of its intention not later than 5 days before the scheduled communication.

COMMITTEE NOTE

This rule is new. It implements § 1525 which was added to the Code in 2005. The rule provides an opportunity for parties in the case to take appropriate action prior to the communication between courts or between the court and a foreign representative to establish procedures for the manner of the communication and the right to participate in the communication. Participation in the communication includes both active and passive participation. Parties wishing to participate must notify the court at least 5 days before the hearing so that ample time exists to make arrangements necessary to permit the participation.

Rule 6004. Use, Sale, or Lease of Property

* * * * *

(g) SALE OF PERSONALLY IDENTIFIABLE INFORMATION.

(1) *Motion.* A motion for authority to sell or lease personally identifiable information under § 363(b)(1)(B) shall include a request for an order directing the United States trustee to appoint a consumer privacy ombudsman under § 332. The motion shall be governed by Rule 9014 and shall be served on any committee elected under § 705 or appointed under § 1102 of the Code, or if the case is a chapter 11 reorganization case and no committee of unsecured creditors has been appointed under § 1102, on the creditors included on the list of creditors filed under Rule 1007(d), and on such other entities as the court may direct. The motion shall be transmitted to the United States trustee.

(2) *Appointment.* If a consumer privacy ombudsman is appointed under § 332, no later than 5 days before the hearing on the motion under § 363(b)(1)(B), the United States trustee shall file a notice of the appointment, including the name and address of the person appointed. The United States trustee's notice shall be accompanied by a verified statement of the person appointed setting forth the person's connections with the debtor, creditors, any other party in interest, their respective attorneys and accountants, the United States trustee, or any person employed in the office of the United States trustee.

~~(g)~~(h) STAY OF ORDER AUTHORIZING USE, SALE, OR LEASE OF PROPERTY. An order authorizing the use, sale, or lease of property other than cash collateral is stayed until the expiration of 10 days after entry of the order, unless the court orders otherwise.

COMMITTEE NOTE

This rule is amended to implement §§ 332 and 363(b)(1)(B), which were added to the Code in 2005.

Rule 6011. Disposal of Patient Records in Health Care Business Case

(a) NOTICE BY PUBLICATION UNDER § 351(1)(A). A notice regarding the claiming or disposing of patient records under § 351(1)(A) shall not identify patients by name or other identifying information, but shall:

(1) identify with particularity the health care facility whose patient records the trustee proposes to destroy;

(2) state the name, address, telephone number, email address, and website, if any, of a person from whom information about the patient records may be obtained and how those records may be claimed; and

(3) state the date by which the patient records must be claimed, and that if they are not so claimed the records will be destroyed.

(b) NOTICE BY MAIL UNDER § 351(1)(B). Subject to applicable nonbankruptcy law relating to patient privacy, a notice regarding the claiming or disposing of patient records under § 351(1)(B) shall, in addition to including the information in subdivision (a), direct that a patient's family member or other representative who receives the notice inform the patient of the notice, and be mailed to the patient and any family member or other contact person whose name and address have been given to the trustee or the debtor for the purpose of providing information regarding the patient's health care, and to insurance companies known to have provided health care insurance to the patient.

(c) PROOF OF COMPLIANCE WITH NOTICE REQUIREMENT. Unless the court orders the trustee to file proof of compliance with § 351(1)(B) under seal, the trustee shall not file, but shall maintain, the proof of compliance for a reasonable time.

(d) REPORT OF DESTRUCTION OF RECORDS. The trustee shall file, not later than 30 days after the destruction of patient records under § 351(3), a report certifying that the unclaimed records have been destroyed and explaining the method used to effect the destruction. The report shall not identify patients by name or other identifying information.

COMMITTEE NOTE

This rule is new. This rule implements § 351(1), which was added to the Code in 2005. That provision requires the trustee to notify patients that their patient records will be destroyed if they remain unclaimed for one year after the publication of a notice in an appropriate newspaper. The Code provision also requires that individualized notice be sent to each patient and to the patient's family member or other contact person.

The variety of health care businesses and the range of current and former patients present the need for flexibility in the creation and publication of the notices that will be given. Nevertheless, there are some matters that must be included in any notice being given to patients, their family members, and contact persons to ensure that sufficient information is provided to these persons regarding the trustee's intent to dispose of patient records. Subdivision (a) of the rule lists the minimum requirements for notices given under § 351(1)(A), and subdivision (b) governs the form of notices under § 351(1)(B). Notices given under this rules are subject to provisions under applicable federal and state law that relate to the protection of patients' privacy, such as the Health Insurance Portability and Accountability Act of 1996, Pub. L. No. 104-191 (HIPAA).

Subdivision (c) directs the trustee to maintain proof of compliance with § 351(1)(B), but it prohibits filing the proof of compliance unless the court orders the trustee to file it under seal because the proof of compliance may contain patient names that should or must remain confidential.

Subdivision (d) requires the trustee to file a report with the court regarding the destruction of patient records. This certification is intended to ensure that the trustee properly completed the destruction process. However, because the report will be filed with the court and ordinarily will be available to the public under § 107, the names, addresses, and other identifying information of the patient shall not be included in the report to protect the patient privacy.

Rule 8001. Manner of Taking Appeal; Voluntary Dismissal; Certification to Court of Appeals

* * * * *

(f) CERTIFICATION FOR DIRECT APPEAL TO COURT OF APPEALS

(1) *Timely Appeal Required.* A certification of a judgment, order, or decree of a bankruptcy court to a court of appeals under 28 U.S.C. § 158(d)(2) shall not be treated as a certification entered on the docket within the meaning of § 1233(b)(4)(A) of Public Law No. 109-8 until a timely appeal has been taken in the manner required by subdivisions (a) and (b) of this rule and the notice of appeal has become effective under Rule 2002.

(2) *Court Where Made.* A certification that a circumstance specified in 28 U.S.C. § 158(d)(2)(A)(i)–(iii) exists shall be filed in the court in which a matter is pending for purposes of 28 U.S.C. § 158(d)(2) and this rule. A matter is pending in a bankruptcy court until the docketing of the appeal of a final judgment, order, or decree in accordance with Rule 8007(b) or the grant of leave to appeal an interlocutory judgment, order, or decree under 28 U.S.C. § 158(a). A matter is pending in a district court or bankruptcy appellate panel after an appeal of an interlocutory judgment, order, or decree has been docketed in accordance with Rule 8007(b) or leave to appeal has been granted under 28 U.S.C. § 158(a).

(A) *Certification by Court on Request or Court's Own Initiative.*

(i) *Before Docketing or Grant of Leave to Appeal.* Only a bankruptcy court may make a certification on request or on its own initiative while the matter is pending in bankruptcy court.

(ii) *After Docketing or Grant of Leave to Appeal.* Only the district court or bankruptcy appellate panel involved may make a certification on request of the parties or on its own initiative while the matter is pending in the district court or bankruptcy appellate panel.

(B) *Certification by All Appellants and Appellees Acting Jointly.* A certification by all the appellants and appellees, if any, acting jointly may be made by filing the appropriate Official Form with the clerk of the court in which the matter is pending. The certification may be accompanied by a short statement of the basis for the certification, which may include the information listed in subdivision (f)(3)(C) of this rule.

(3) *Request for Certification; Filing; Service; Contents.*

(A) A request for certification shall be filed, within the time specified by 28 U.S.C. § 158(d)(2), with the clerk of the court in which the matter is pending.

(B) Notice of the filing of a request for certification shall be served in the manner required for service of a notice of appeal under Rule 8004.

(C) A request for certification shall include the following:

(i) the facts necessary to understand the question presented;

(ii) the question itself;

(iii) the relief sought;

(iv) the reasons why the appeal should be allowed and is authorized by statute or rule, including why a circumstance specified in 28 U.S.C. § 158(d)(2)(A)(i)–(iii) exists; and

(v) an attached copy of the judgment, order, or decree complained of and any related opinion or memorandum.

(D) A party may file a response to a request for certification or a cross-request within 10 days after the notice of the request is served, or another time fixed by the court.

(E) The request, cross request, and any response shall not be governed by Rule 9014 and shall be submitted without oral argument unless the court otherwise directs.

(F) A certification of an appeal under 28 U.S.C. § 158(d)(2) shall be made in a separate document served on the parties.

(4) *Certification on Court's Own Initiative.*

(A) A certification of an appeal on the court's own initiative under 28 U.S.C. § 158(d)(2) shall be made in a separate document served on the parties in the manner required for service of a notice of appeal under Rule 8004. The certification shall be accompanied by an opinion or memorandum that contains the information required by subdivision (f)(3)(C)(i)–(iv) of this rule.

(B) A party may file a supplementary short statement of the basis for certification within 10 days after the certification.

COMMITTEE NOTE

Subdivision (f) is added to the rule to implement the 2005 amendments to 28 U.S.C. § 158(d). That section authorizes appeals directly to the court of appeals, with that court's consent, upon certification that a ground for the appeal exists under § 158(d)(2)(A)(i)–(iii). Certification can be made by the court on its own initiative or in response to a request of a party. Certification also can be made by all of the appellants and appellees. An uncodified provision in Public Law No. 109-8, § 1233(b)(4), requires that, not later than 10 days after a certification is entered on the docket, there must be filed with the circuit clerk a petition requesting permission to appeal. Given the short time limit to file the petition with the circuit clerk, subdivision (f)(1) provides that entry of a certification on the docket does not occur until an effective appeal is taken under Rule 8003(a) or (b).

The rule adopts a bright-line test for identifying the court in which a matter is pending. Under subdivision (f)(2), the bright-line chosen is the "docketing" under Rule 8007(b) of an appeal of a final judgment, order or decree, or the granting of leave to appeal an interlocutory judgment, order or decree, whichever is earlier.

To ensure that parties are aware of a certification, the rule requires either that it be made on the Official Form (if being made by all of the parties to the appeal) or on a separate document (whether the certification is made on the court's own initiative or in response to a request by a party). This is particularly important because the rule adopts the bankruptcy practice established by Rule 8001(a) and (b) of requiring a notice of appeal in every instance, including interlocutory orders, of appeals from bankruptcy court orders, judgments, and decrees. Because this requirement is satisfied by filing the notice of appeal that takes the appeal to the district court or bankruptcy appellate panel in the first instance, the rule does not require a separate notice of appeal if a certification occurs after a district court or bankruptcy appellate panel decision.

Rule 8003. Leave to Appeal

* * * * *

(d) If leave to appeal is required by 28 U.S.C. § 158(a) and has not earlier been granted, the authorization of a direct appeal by a court of appeals under 28 U.S.C. § 158(d)(2) shall be deemed to satisfy the requirement for leave to appeal.

COMMITTEE NOTE

The rule is amended to add subdivision (d) to solve the jurisdictional problem that could otherwise ensue when a district court or bankruptcy appellate panel has not granted leave to appeal under 28 U.S.C. § 158(a)(3). If the court of appeals accepts the appeal, the requirement of leave to appeal is deemed satisfied. However, if the court of appeals does not authorize a direct appeal, the question of whether to grant leave to appeal remains a matter to be resolved by the district court or the bankruptcy appellate panel.

Rule 9006. Time

* * * * *

(b) ENLARGEMENT.

(1) In General. Except as provided in paragraphs (2) and (3) of this subdivision, when an act is required or allowed to be done at or within a specified period by these rules or by a notice given thereunder or by order of court, the court for cause shown may at any time in its discretion (1) with or without motion or notice order the period enlarged if the request therefor is made before the expiration of the period originally prescribed or as extended by a previous order or (2) on motion made after the expiration of the specified period permit the act to be done where the failure to act was the result of excusable neglect.

(2) Enlargement Not Permitted. The court may not enlarge the time for taking action under Rules 1007(d), 2003(a) and (d), 7052, 9023, and 9024.

(3) Enlargement Limited. The court may enlarge the time for taking action under Rules 1006(b)(2), 1007(c) with respect to the time to file schedules and statements in a small business case, 1017(e), 3002(c), 4003(b), 4004(a), 4007(c), 8002 and 9033, only to the extent and under the conditions stated in those rules.

* * * * *

COMMITTEE NOTE

Section 1116(3) of the Code, as amended in 2005, places specific limits on the time for filing schedules and a statement of affairs in small business cases. The rule is amended to recognize that extensions of time for filing these documents are governed by Rule 1007(c), which is amended to recognize restrictions on expanding the time to file these documents in small business cases.

Rule 9009. Forms

The Official Forms prescribed by the Judicial Conference of the United States shall be observed and used with alterations as may be appropriate. Forms may be combined and their contents rearranged to permit economies in their use. The Director of the Administrative Office of the United States Courts may issue additional forms for use under the Code. The forms shall be construed to be consistent with these rules and the Code. References in the Official Forms to these rules shall include the Interim Rules approved by the Committee on Rules of Practice and Procedure to implement Public Law No. 109-8.

COMMITTEE NOTE

The Official Forms refer to the Federal Rules of Bankruptcy Procedure. This rule is amended so that the references to rules in the Official Forms includes the Interim Rules that implement the provisions of the Bankruptcy Abuse Prevention and Consumer Protection Act of 2005 (Public Law Number 109-8).

Appendix C Bankruptcy Fees

C.1 Initial Filing Fees

Bankruptcy filing fees have been amended by Public Law No. 109-13, 119 Stat. 231 (enacted May 11, 2005). The Administrative Office of the United States Courts has announced that the new fees will take effect on October 17, 2005. As of that date the fees for chapter 7, 12, and 13 filings will be:

Chapter 7 Filing Fees	
Filing fee	$220
Administrative fee	$39
Trustee fee	$15
TOTAL	**$274**
Chapter 12 Filing Fees	
Filing fee	$200
Administrative fee	$30
TOTAL	**$230**
Chapter 13 Filing Fees	
Filing fee	$150
Administrative fee	$39
TOTAL	**$189**

C.2 Bankruptcy Court Miscellaneous Fee Schedule

The fee schedule is issued by the Judicial Conference of the United States in accordance with 28 U.S.C. § 1930(b). It became effective January 1, 2005. This schedule may also be found on the CD-Rom accompanying this volume.

Following are fees to be charged for services provided by the bankruptcy courts. No fees are to be charged for services rendered on behalf of the United States, with the exception of those specifically prescribed in items 1, 3, and 5, or to bankruptcy administrators appointed under Public Law No. 99-554, § 302(d)(3)(I). No fees under this schedule shall be charged to federal agencies or programs which are funded from judiciary appropriations, including, but not limited to, agencies, organizations, and individuals providing services authorized by the Criminal Justice Act, 18 U.S.C. § 3006A.

(1) For reproducing any record or paper, $.50 per page. This fee shall apply to paper copies made from either: (1) original documents; or (2) microfiche or microfilm reproductions of the original records. This fee shall apply to services rendered on behalf of the United States if the record or paper requested is available through electronic access.

(2) For certification of any document or paper, whether the certification is made directly on the document or by separate instrument, $9. For exemplification of any document or paper, twice the amount of the charge for certification.

(3) For reproduction of recordings of proceedings, regardless of the medium, $26, including the cost of materials. This fee shall apply to services rendered on behalf of the United States, if the reproduction of the recording is available electronically.

(4) For amendments to a debtor's schedules of creditors, lists of creditors, matrix, or mailing lists, $26 for each amendment, provided the bankruptcy judge may, for good cause, waive the charge in any case. No fee is required when the nature of the amendment is to change the address of a creditor or an attorney for a creditor listed on the schedules or to add the name and address of an attorney for a listed creditor.

(5) For every search of the records of the bankruptcy court conducted by the clerk of the bankruptcy court or a deputy clerk, $26 per name or item searched. This fee shall apply to services rendered on behalf of the United States if the information requested is available through electronic access.

(6) For filing a complaint, a fee shall be collected in the same amount as the filing fee prescribed in 28 U.S.C. § 1914(a) for instituting any civil action other than a writ of habeas corpus. If the United States, other than a United States trustee acting as a trustee in a case under title 11, or a debtor is the plaintiff, no fee is required. If a trustee or debtor in possession is the plaintiff, the fee should be payable only from the estate and to the extent there is any estate realized. If a child support creditor or its representative is the plaintiff, and if such plaintiff files the form required by § 304(g) of the Bankruptcy Reform Act of 1994, no fee is required.

(7) For filing or indexing any document not in a case or proceeding for which a filing fee has been paid, $39.

(8) In all cases filed under title 11, the clerk shall collect from the debtor or the petitioner a miscellaneous administrative fee of $39. This fee may be paid in installments in the same manner that the filing fee may be paid in installments, consistent with the procedure set forth in Federal Rule of Bankruptcy Procedure 1006.

(9) Upon the filing of a petition under chapter 7 of the Bankruptcy Code, the petitioner shall pay $15 to the clerk of the court for payment to trustees serving in cases as provided in 11 U.S.C. § 330(b)(2). An application to pay the fee in installments may be filed in the manner set forth in Federal Rule of Bankruptcy Procedure 1006(b).

(10) Upon the filing of a motion to convert a case to chapter 7 of the Bankruptcy Code, the movant shall pay $15 to the clerk of court for payment to trustees serving in cases as provided in 11 U.S.C. § 330(b)(2). Upon the filing of a notice of conversion pursuant to section 1208(a) or section 1307(a) of the Code, $15 shall be paid to the clerk of the court for payment to trustees serving in cases as provided in 11 U.S.C. § 330(b)(2). If the trustee serving in the case before the conversion is the movant, the fee shall be payable only from the estate that exists prior to conversion.

(11) For filing a motion to reopen a Bankruptcy Code case, a fee shall be collected in the same amount as the filing fee prescribed by 28 U.S.C. § 1930(a) for commencing a new case on the date of reopening, unless the reopening is to correct an administrative error or for actions related to the debtor's discharge. The court may waive this fee under appropriate circumstances or may defer payment of the fee from trustees pending discovery of additional assets. If payment is deferred, the fee shall be waived if no additional assets are discovered.

(12) For each microfiche sheet of film or microfilm jacket copy of any court record, where available, $5.

(13) For retrieval of a record from a Federal Records Center, National Archives, or other storage location removed from the place of business of the court, $45.

(14) For a check paid into the court which is returned for lack of funds, $45.

(15) For docketing a proceeding on appeal or review from a final judgment of a bankruptcy judge pursuant to 28 U.S.C. § 158(a) and (b), the fee shall be the same amount as the fee for docketing a case on appeal or review to the appellate court as required by Item 1 of the Courts of Appeals Miscellaneous Fee Schedule. A separate fee shall be paid by each party filing a notice of appeal in the bankruptcy court, but parties filing a joint notice of appeal in the bankruptcy court are required to pay only one fee. If a trustee or debtor in possession is the appellant, the fee should be payable only from the estate and to the extent there is any estate realized.

(16) For filing a petition ancillary to a foreign proceeding under 11 U.S.C. § 304, the fee shall be the same amount as the fee for a case commenced under chapter 11 of title 11 as required by 28 U.S.C. § 1930(a)(3).

(17) The court may charge and collect fees commensurate with the cost of providing copies of the local rules of court. The court may also distribute copies of the local rules without charge.

(18) The clerk shall assess a charge for the handling of registry funds deposited with the court, to be assessed from interest earnings and in accordance with the detailed fee schedule issued by the Director of the Administrative Office of the United States Courts.

(19) When a joint case filed under § 302 of title 11 is divided into two separate cases at the request of the debtor(s), a fee shall be charged equal to the current filing fee for the chapter under which the joint case was commenced.

(20) For filing a motion to terminate, annul, modify, or condition the automatic stay provided under § 362(a)

of title 11, a motion to compel abandonment of property of the estate pursuant to Rule 6007(b) of the Federal Rules of Bankruptcy Procedure, or a motion to withdraw the reference of a case or proceeding under 28 U.S.C. § 157(d), $150. No fee is required for a motion for relief from the codebtor stay or for a stipulation for court approval of an agreement for relief from a stay. If a child support creditor or its representative is the movant, and if such movant files the form required by § 304(g) of the Bankruptcy Reform Act of 1994, no fee is required.

(21) For docketing a cross appeal from a bankruptcy court determination, the fee shall be the same amount as the fee for docketing a case on appeal or review to the appellate court as required by Item 1 of the Courts of Appeals Miscellaneous Fee Schedule. If a trustee or debtor in possession is the appellant, the fee should be payable only from the estate and to the extent there is any estate realized.

Appendix D New and Amended Official Bankruptcy Forms

D.1 Introduction

On August 11, 2005, the Executive Committee of the Judicial Conference of the United States approved nine new and thirty-three amended Official Forms. Form 6D was further revised on August 31 and two sections of the means testing forms, as of September 7, 2005, are still under study and subject to revision. Consequently, practitioners should continue to check for any announced changes to the Official Forms, which should be posted at www.uscourts.gov/rules/index.html. Practitioners should also check whether any alterations have been made to the Official Forms by the local courts in which they practice.

This Appendix reprints all the new Official Forms and all amended Official Forms relevant to consumer bankruptcies, current through September 7, 2005. The forms may also be found in PDF format on the CD-Rom accompanying this volume. More importantly, *Bankruptcy Forms* software, also found on the CD-Rom, allows practitioners to complete many of these Official Forms on their word processor, utilizing either Microsoft Word or WordPerfect.

This Appendix also reprints portions of an August 5, 2005 Memorandum from the Reporter of the Advisory Committee on Bankruptcy Rules which provides an overview of the changes made to the Official Forms. The Appendix also reprints the Committee Notes to each of the individual forms which describe the changes in more detail. Appendix G, *infra*, includes ten new sample pleadings specifically drafted to meet the requirements of the 2005 Act, and Appendix H, *infra*, contains a detailed questionnaire that, when completed, will gather the information needed by the practitioner to complete the new Official Forms. Information regarding the electronic filing of the Official Forms may be found on the CD-Rom accompanying this volume.

Blank Official Forms Table of Contents

	Schedule G—Executory Contracts and Unexpired Leases [*amended*]
	Schedule H—Codebtors [*amended*]
	Schedule I—Current Income of Individual Debtor(s) [*amended*]
	Schedule J—Current Expenditures of Individual Debtor(s) [*amended*]
	Declaration Concerning Debtor's Schedules [*amended*]
Official Form 7	Statement of Financial Affairs [*amended*]
Official Form 8	Chapter 7 Individual Debtor's Statement of Intention [*amended*]
Official Form 9	Notice of Bankruptcy Case, Meeting of Creditors, and Deadlines
	9A—Chapter 7 Individual or Joint Debtor No Asset Case [*amended*]
	9B—Chapter 7 Corporation/Partnership No Asset Case [*amended but not reprinted herein*]
	9C—Chapter 7 Individual or Joint Debtor Asset Case [*amended*]
	9D—Chapter 7 Corporation/Partnership Asset Case [*amended but not reprinted herein*]
	9E(Alt.)—Chapter 11 Individual or Joint Debtor Case [*amended but not reprinted herein*]
	9F—Chapter 11 Corporation/Partnership Case [*amended but not reprinted herein*]
	9F(Alt.)—Chapter 11 Corporation/Partnership Case [*amended but not reprinted herein*]
	9G—Chapter 12 Individual or Joint Debtor Family Farmer Case [*amended*]
	9H—Chapter 12 Corporation/Partnership Family Farmer Case [*amended*]
	9I—Chapter 13 Case [*amended*]
Official Form 10	Proof of Claim [*amended*]
Official Form 16A	Caption (Full) [*amended*]
Official Form 16B	Caption (Short Title) [*not amended and thus not reprinted herein*]
Official Form 16D	Caption for Use in Adversary Proceeding [*not amended and thus not reprinted herein*]
Official Form 17	Notice of Appeal [*not amended and thus not reprinted herein*]
Official Form 18	Discharge of Debtor in a Chapter 7 Case [*amended*]
Official Form 19A	Declaration and Signature of Non-Attorney Bankruptcy Petition Preparer (11 U.S.C. § 110) [*amended; replaces former Official Form 19*]
Official Form 19B	Notice to Debtor by Non-Attorney Bankruptcy Petition Preparer [*new*]
Official Form 20A	Notice of Motion or Objection [*not amended and thus not reprinted herein*]
Official Form 20B	Notice of Objection to Claim [*not amended and thus not reprinted herein*]
Official Form 21	Statement of Social Security Number [*not amended and thus not reprinted herein*]
Official Form 22A	Statement of Current Monthly Income and Means Test Calculation: For Use in Chapter 7 [*new*]
Official Form 22A (Alt.)	Statement of Current Monthly Income and Means Test Calculation: For Use in Chapter 7 (If IRS Separates Its Housing Allowance) [*new*]
Official Form 22B	Statement of Current Monthly Income: For Use in Chapter 11 [*new*]
Official Form 22C	Statement of Current Monthly Income and Disposable Income Calculation: For Use in Chapter 13 [*new*]
Official Form 22C (Alt.)	Statement of Current Monthly Income and Disposable Income Calculation: For Use in Chapter 13 (If IRS Separates Its Housing Allowance) [*new*]
Official Form 23	Debtor's Certification of Completion of Instructional Course Concerning Personal Financial Management [*new*]
Official Form 24	Certification to Court of Appeals By All Parties [*new*]

D.2 Memorandum Concerning Proposed Official Bankruptcy Forms

COMMITTEE ON RULES OF PRACTICE AND PROCEDURE
OF THE
JUDICIAL CONFERENCE OF THE UNITED STATES
WASHINGTON, D.C. 20544

DAVID F. LEVI
CHAIR

PETER G. McCABE
SECRETARY

CHAIRS OF ADVISORY COMMITTEES

SAMUEL A. ALITO, JR.
APPELLATE RULES

THOMAS S. ZILLY
BANKRUPTCY RULES

LEE H. ROSENTHAL
CIVIL RULES

SUSAN C. BUCKLEW
CRIMINAL RULES

JERRY E. SMITH
EVIDENCE RULES

MEMORANDUM TO: Advisory Committee on Bankruptcy Rules

FROM: Professor Jeffrey W. Morris, Reporter, Advisory Committee on Bankruptcy Rules

DATE: August 5, 2005

RE: Proposed Interim Bankruptcy Rules and Amended and New Official Forms

* * *

The Bankruptcy Abuse Prevention and Consumer Protection Act of 2005 (the "Act") is the most substantial amendments of the bankruptcy laws since the enactment of the Bankruptcy Code in 1978. The amendments introduce the concept of a means test as a requirement of eligibility for chapter 7 relief, add an entirely new chapter to the Code (chapter 15 governing ancillary and other cross border insolvencies), and create new categories of debtors and cases (health care businesses and small business cases), among other things. Many of these provisions necessitate the amendment or creation of bankruptcy rules and forms.

The Advisory Committee on the Bankruptcy Rules conducted a careful review of the Act to identify the need to amend the existing Official Forms or to propose new forms. As a result of that study, the Advisory Committee recommends the adoption of nine new Official Forms and amendments to thirty-three of the existing Official Forms. The forms to implement the means test, to permit the waiver of filing fees and to pay the filing fee in installments, and to assist the Administrative Office to compile statistical information as required by 28 U.S.C. § 191 include the extensive changes or additions that required the Committee to make significant policy decisions regarding the Act and Rules.

Much like the amendments and additions to the Bankruptcy Rules, most of the changes to the Official Forms are either technical or conforming changes. The technical changes are minor changes required to implement a specific provision of the Act. For example, the Act extends the time between chapter 7 discharges from six years to eight years. A number of forms require debtors to provide their names for six years, and technical amendments change each of those references to eight years. An example of a conforming amendment is the change made to Official Form B6C (Schedule C—Property Claimed as Exempt) to implement the amendment to § 522(b)(3)(A) that requires that the debtor's domicile to have been in the same state for the 730 days prior to the filing of the petition. Previously, the domicile requirement was only the greater part of the 180 days before the filing of the petition. Similarly, question 3 on the Statement of Financial Affairs asks the debtor to set out payments made to creditors in the 90 days prior to the commencement of the case, but it directs the debtor to exclude from the list those payments to a particular creditor that in the aggregate total $600 or less. The form is amended to limit that question to debtors with primarily consumer debts, and the question is expanded to direct debtors whose debts are primarily business debts to exclude payments to a particular creditor that in the aggregate exceed $5,000.

Many Official Forms vary according to the chapter or the nature of the debtor. Official Form 9 is the Notice of § 341 Meeting, and there are separate notices for each chapter. Within chapters, the same notice may differ if the case is proceeding as a no asset case or if there appear to be assets that will lead to a distribution to creditors. Consequently, global changes in the form are made for each of the chapters and for each type of debtor.

The most significant addition to the Official Forms is the means test form. There are separate versions of the form for use by individual debtors in cases under chapters 7, 11, and 13 because the Act applies the means test slightly differently in each chapter. See Official Forms 22A, 22A(Alt.), 22B, 22C, and 22C(Alt.). The test also requires the use of census bureau data and data from the Internal Revenue Service, as well as other data supplied by and unique to the debtor completing the form. The Act sometimes fails to resolve potential conflicts, and the Committee has worked closely with the Executive Office of United States Trustees to propose a form that will gather all of the necessary information in a way that is manageable for debtors and effective for the United States Trustee Program to perform its duties regarding the means test. One matter remains unresolved. The Internal Revenue Service expense allowances for housing are not broken down in a manner consistent with the means test included in the Act. The Service is considering providing that breakdown so that the means test form can be streamlined, and a favorable decision on the issue could be forthcoming prior to the effective date of the Act. In the meantime, however, the Advisory Committee has approved alternative means test forms, and the form that assumes the need to break down the expenses separately from the IRS allowances would be removed from the list of Official Forms whenever the Service provides the expense breakdown. The United States Trustee Program supports the adoption of the means test forms.

A form that is amended to conform to the Act, but that includes a significant change from the existing form, is Official Form 3. The form is the Application to Pay Filing Fee in Installments as well as an order granting the application. The Act amends 28 U.S.C. § 1930 to authorize the courts to waive the filing fee for certain debtors which caused the Advisory Committee to propose an amendment to Rule 1006, the rule governing applications for the payment of filing fees in installments. Consequently, the attached forms include proposed Official Forms 3A and 3B. Form 3A is an amended version of current Official Form 3. It is amended to conform to the newly proposed rule, and it no longer bars the debtor from seeking to pay the fee in installments if the debtor has made any payments to an attorney or other person in connection with the case. Form 3B is the form for use when the debtor is seeking a waiver of the fee. This form is derived in part from the form used in pilot districts that permitted fee waivers from 1994 to 1997.

Official Form 6 is amended to assist the Administrative Office of the United States Courts to meet its obligation under 28 U.S.C. § 159 to compile data as to the amount of debt being discharged in bankruptcy cases. That provision, added by the Act, requires changes to the schedules of assets and liabilities and the summary of the schedules so that the Administrative Office can effectively mine the data from the forms. The summary of the schedules in the proposed Official Form directs the debtor to provide the information necessary to make the statistical analysis required of the Administrative Office.

Each new or amended Official Form is attached. The Committee Note to each Form provides a brief description of the reason for the change.

[Note: The Housing and Utilities question on Forms 22A, 22A(Alt.), Form 22C, and Form 22C(Alt.) is under further study because the IRS has not formally amended its Housing Allowance to separate housing acquisition costs from the total housing allowance. In addition, Question 1 on Forms 22C and 22C(Alt.) is under further study to determine if both spouses should be required to complete the form in chapter 13 cases.

Working drafts of these forms are provided for information of the bench, bar, and public, and to enable software companies to begin work on revising their products to incorporate the Interim Bankruptcy Rules and Official Forms. Final versions of Forms 22A, 22A(Alt.), Form 22C, and Form 22C(Alt.) will be posted by September 9, 2005.]

* * *

D.3 Advisory Committee on Bankruptcy Rules Notes to New and Amended Official Bankruptcy Forms

Form 1

The form is amended to implement amendments to the Bankruptcy Code contained in the Bankruptcy Abuse Prevention and Consumer Protection Act of 2005, Pub. L. No. 109-8, 119 Stat. 23 (April 20, 2005). The period for which the debtor must provide all names used and information about any prior bankruptcy cases is now eight years to match the required time between the granting of discharges to the same debtor in § 727(a)(8) of the Code as amended in 2005. The box indicating the debtor's selection of a chapter under which to file the case been amended to delete "Sec. 304—Case ancillary to foreign proceeding" and replace it with "Chapter 15 Petition for Recognition of a Foreign Main Proceeding" and "Chapter 15 Petition for Recognition of a Foreign Nonmain Proceeding" reflecting the 2005 repeal of § 304 and enactment of chapter 15 of Code. A statement of venue to be used in a chapter 15 case also has been added.

The section of the form labeled "Type of Debtor" has been revised and subtitled "Form of Organization." This section is revised to make it clear that a limited liability corporation ("LLC") and limited liability partnership ("LLP") should identify itself as a "corporation." A new section titled "Nature of Business" has been created that includes both existing check boxes that identify certain types of debtors for which the Bankruptcy Code provides special treatment, such as stockbrokers and railroads, and a new checkbox for a "health care business" for which the 2005 amendments to the Code include specific requirements. This section of the form also contains checkboxes for single asset real estate debtors and nonprofit organizations which will be used by trustees and creditors and by the Director of the Administrative Office of the United States Courts in preparing statistical reports and analyses. The statistical section of the form also is amended to provide more detail concerning the number of creditors in a case. A check box also has been added for a debtor to indicate that the debtor is applying for a waiver of the filing fee, to implement the 2005 enactment of 28 U.S.C. § 1930(f) authorizing the bankruptcy court to waive the filing fee in certain circumstances.

Although the 2005 Act eliminated an eligible debtor's option to elect to be treated as a "small business" in a chapter 11 case, new provisions for such debtors added to the Code in 2005 make it desirable to identify eligible debtors at the outset of the case. Accordingly, the section of the form labeled "Chapter 11 Small Business" has been revised and renamed "Chapter 11 Debtors" for this purpose. Chapter 11 debtors that meet the definition of "small business debtor" in § 101 of the Code are directed to identify themselves in this section of the form. In addition, chapter 11 debtors whose aggregate noncontingent debts owed to non-insiders or affiliates are less than $2 million are directed to identify themselves in this section.

A space is provided for individuals to certify that they have received budget and credit counseling prior to filing, as required by § 109(h) which was added to the Code in 2005, or to request a waiver of the requirement. Space also is provided for a debtor who is a tenant of residential real property to state whether the debtor's landlord has a judgment against the debtor for possession of the premises, whether under applicable nonbankruptcy law the debtor would be permitted to cure the monetary default, and whether the debtor has made the appropriate deposit with the court. This addition to the form implements § 362(l) which was added to the Code in 2005.

The signature sections and the declaration under penalty of perjury by an individual debtor concerning the notice received about bankruptcy relief, the declaration under penalty of perjury by a bankruptcy petition preparer, and the declaration and certification by an attorney all are amended to include new material mandated by the 2005 Act. A signature section also is provided for a representative of a foreign proceeding.

Form 3A

The form is amended to direct the debtor to state that, until the filing fee is paid in full, the debtor will not make any additional payment or transfer any additional property to an attorney or any other person for services in connection with the case. The declaration and certification by a non-attorney bankruptcy petition preparer in the form are amended to include material mandated by § 110 of the Code as amended by the Bankruptcy Abuse Prevention and Consumer Protection Act of 2005, Pub. L. No. 109-8, 119 Stat. 23 (April 20, 2005). The certification by a non-attorney bankruptcy petition preparer is re-named a declaration and also is revised to include material mandated by § 110 of the Code as amended in 2005. The order is amended to provide space for the court to set forth a payment schedule other than the one proposed by the debtor.

Form 3B

This form is new. 28 U.S.C. § 1930(f), enacted as part of the Bankruptcy Abuse and Consumer Protection Act of 2005, Pub. L. No. 109-8, 119 Stat. 23 (April 20, 2005), provides that "under procedures prescribed by the Judicial Conference of the United States, the district court or the bankruptcy court may waive the filing fee in a case under chapter 7 of title 11 for an individual if the court determines that such individual has income less than 150 percent of the income official poverty line . . . applicable to a family of the size involved and is unable to pay that fee in installments." To implement this provision, Rule 1006 is amended to add a new subdivision (c). Official Form 3B is the form referenced in that subdivision, and is to be used by individual chapter 7 debtors when applying for a waiver of the filing fee. A corresponding standard order also is included.

Form 6

The forms of the Schedules of Assets and Liabilities are amended to implement the provisions of the Bankruptcy Abuse Prevention and Consumer Protection Act of 2005, Pub. L. No. 109-8, 119 Stat. 23, (April 20, 2005). An amendment that directs the debtor to avoid disclosing the name of any minor child occurs in several of the schedules in conformity with § 112 which was added to the Code in 2005. Section 112 provides for the debtor to provide the name of any minor child confidentially to the court, should the trustee need the information to evaluate properly the information filed by the debtor.

The "Statistical Summary of Certain Liabilities" is added to collect information needed to prepare statistical reports required under 28 U.S.C. § 159, which was enacted as part of the 2005 Act.

Schedules A, B, C, and D are amended to delete the word "market" from the columns in which the debtor reports the value of various kinds of property. Amendments to § 506 of the Code enacted in 2005 specify that "replacement value" must be used in connection with certain property. The schedules no longer specify "market" value and permit the debtor to choose the appropriate one, whether that be replacement, market, or some other value. Valuation of property, generally, is the subject of extensive provisions in the Code, and the deletion of the word "market" from the determinations of value to be made by the debtor on the schedules is intended to remove any inference about choice of valuation standard. This deletion simply indicates that the form takes no position on the which Code provision or valuation standard may be applicable in any instance.

The following paragraphs describe changes that are specific to each schedule.

Schedule B—Personal Property is amended to require the debtor to list any interests in an education IRA, as § 541(b)(5), added to the Code in 2005, makes special provision for them. The schedule also is amended to require the debtor to disclose the existence of any customer lists or other compilations containing personally identifiable information provided by an individual to the debtor in connection with obtaining a product or service from the debtor for personal, family, or household purposes. This amendment implements § 332, which was added to the Code in 2005.

Schedule C—Property Claimed as Exempt is amended to delete descriptive information concerning the length of domicile required for the debtor to qualify to claim certain exemptions. Any summary of the amendments enacted in 2005 to § 522 of the Code concerning these requirements might inadvertently cause the debtor to lose important rights. Accordingly, the form now directs the debtor to indicate whether exemptions are being claimed under § 522(b)(2) or § 522(b)(3) and whether the debtor claims a homestead exemption that exceeds $125,000.

Schedule E—Creditors Holding Unsecured Priority Claims is amended to implement the changes in priority to which a claim may be entitled under 11 U.S.C. § 507 as amended by the 2005 Act and to add the new priority included in the Reform Act for claims for death or personal injury while the debtor was intoxicated. "Subtotal" and "Total" boxes have been added to the column labeled "Amount Entitled to Priority" to assist the individual debtor to complete the Means Test form.

Schedule G—Executory Contracts and Unexpired Leases is amended by deleting the note to the debtor advising that parties listed on this schedule may not receive notice of the filing of the bankruptcy case unless they also are listed on one of the schedules of liabilities. The better practice is for all parties to transactions with the debtor to receive notice of the filing of the case, and an amendment Rule 1007 requiring the debtor to provide a mailing list that includes these parties is scheduled to take effect December 1, 2005.

Schedule H—Codebtors is amended to add specifics about community property jurisdictions in connection with the requirement to provide the name of any spouse of a debtor who resides or resided in a community property jurisdiction. This amendment also mirrors amendments made in 1997 to Official Form 7, the Statement of Financial Affairs and will assure that these codebtors receive notice of the filing of the bankruptcy case. The form also is amended to extend from six years to eight years the time period for which this information is reported pursuant to the 2005 amendments to § 727(a)(8) of the Code.

Schedule I—Current Income of Individual Debtor(s) is amended to require the income of a nondebtor spouse to be reported in cases filed under chapters 7 and 11. Line numbers have been added to assist the debtor in calculating and reporting totals. A new subtotal line for income from sources other than as an employee and a new "total monthly income" line provide for this form to be used in conjunction with Schedule J to satisfy the requirements of § 521(a)(l)(B)(v), which was added to the Code in 2005. The form also has been revised to provide the statement concerning any anticipated increase or decrease in income required in § 521(a)(l)(B)(vi), which also was added to the Code in 2005.

Schedule J—Current Expenditures of Individual Debtor(s). A direction has been added to require the debtor to report any increase or decrease in expenses anticipated to occur within the year following the filing of the document, as required by § 521(a)(l)(B)(vi), which was added to the Code in 2005. The form also is amended to provide, in conjunction with Schedule I, a statement of monthly net income, itemized to show how the amount is calculated, as required by § 522(a)(l)(B)(v), which was added to the Code in 2005.

Declaration Concerning Debtor's Schedules—The declaration by a non-attorney bankruptcy petition preparer is amended to include material mandated by § 110 of the Code as amended in 2005.

Form 7

The form is amended in several ways to reflect changes in the Bankruptcy Code made by the Bankruptcy Abuse Prevention and Consumer Protection Act of 2005, Pub. L. No. 109-8, 119 Stat. 23 (April 20, 2005). A new sentence in the introduction advises the debtor not to disclose the name and address of any minor child.

The definition of "in business" is amended in the introductory section and in Question 1 and Question 18 to clarify that various part-time activities can result in the debtor being "in business" for purposes of the form.

Question 1 is amended to specify that, in addition to the income from the debtor's primary employment, the debtor must include income from part-time activities either as an employee or from self-employment. The debtor now also will report the source of all income from employment or operation of a business, even if there is only one source, in order to assist the trustee in reviewing the pay stubs, etc., filed by the debtor in the case.

Question 3 is amended to accommodate amendments to § 547(c) of the Code enacted in 2005 which exempt from recovery by the trustee payments by a debtor for a domestic support obligation or as part of an alternative repayment schedule negotiated by an approved nonprofit budgeting and credit counseling agency. In addition, Question 3 now requires a debtor with primarily non-consumer debts to report only those transfers that aggregate more than $5,000 to any creditor in the 90-day period prior to the filing of the petition, as a result of the addition of § 547(c)(9) to the Code in 2005.

In Question 10, the extension of the reachback period for transfers from one year to two years reflects the 2005 amendment to § 548(a)(1) of the Code to permit a trustee to avoid a fraudulent transfer made by the debtor within two years of the date of the filing of the petition. Question 10 also is amended to implement new § 548(e) added to the Code in 2005 to require the debtor to disclose all transfers to any self-settled asset protection trust within the ten years before the filing of the petition.

Question 15 is amended to extend from two years to three years the preterition time period for which the debtor must disclose the addresses of all premises occupied by the debtor. This information will assist the trustee, the United States trustee, and the court to ascertain whether any homestead exemption asserted by the debtor is properly claimed under § 522(v)(3)(A) as amended, and §§ 522(p) and (q) as added to the Code in 2005.

The form also is amended to extend from six years to eight years the period before the filing of the petition concerning which the debtor is required to disclose the name of the debtor's spouse or of any former spouse who resides or resided with the debtor in a community property state. In addition, the certification by a non-attorney bankruptcy petition preparer is renamed a "declaration" and is amended to include material mandated by 11 U.S.C. § 110 as amended by the 2005 Act.

Form 8

The form is amended to conform to § 521(a)(6), which was added to the Code by the Bankruptcy Abuse Prevention and Consumer Protection Act of 2005, Pub. L. No. 109-8, 119 Stat. 23 (April 20, 2005), by adding a section covering personal property subject to an unexpired lease and an option labeled "lease will be assumed pursuant to 11 U.S.C. § 362(h)(1)(A)" to the choices a debtor may make. The certification by a non-attorney bankruptcy petition preparer in the form is renamed a "declaration" and is amended to include material mandated by the 2005 amendments to § 110 of the Code.

Form 9

The form is amended in a variety of way to implement the provisions of the Bankruptcy Abuse Prevention and Consumer Protection Act of 2005, Pub. L. No. 109-8, 119 Stat. 23 (April 20, 2005). All versions of the form are amended to advise creditors to consult an attorney concerning what rights they may have in the specific case. All versions of the form are also amended to provide information about filing claims to creditors with foreign addresses and to advise those creditors to consult a lawyer familiar with United States bankruptcy law regarding any questions they may have about their rights in a particular case. These amendments implement § 1514, which was added to the Code in 2005.

Forms 9A and 9C are amended to include a box in which the clerk can notify creditors in a chapter 7 case filed by an individual with primarily consumer debts whether the presumption of abuse has arisen under § 707(b) of the Code as amended in 2005. Under § 342(d) of the Code, the clerk has a duty to notify creditors concerning the presumption within ten days of the filing of the petition. If cases in which the debtor does not file Official Form 22A with the petition, the forms provide for the clerk to state that insufficient information has been filed, and to inform creditors that if later-filed information indicates that the presumption arises, creditors will be sent another notice.

In cases involving serial filers (debtors who have filed more than one case within a specified period), the automatic stay provided by § 362(a) of the Code as amended in 2005 may not apply or may be limited in duration, unless the stay is extended or imposed by court order. The form contains a general statement alerting debtors to this possibility.

Section 1514, added to the Code in 2005, also requires that a secured creditor with a foreign address be advised whether the creditor is required to file a proof of claim, and Forms 9B, 9D, 9E, 9E (Alt.), 9F, 9F (Alt.), 9G, 9H, and 9I are amended to include general information addressing that question. Forms 9E, 9E (Alt.), 9F, and 9F (Alt.) also are amended to inform creditors that in a case in which the debtor has filed a plan for which it has solicited acceptances before filing the case, the court may, after notice and a hearing, order that the United States trustee not convene a meeting of creditors.

Forms 9E and 9E Alt. are amended to state that, unless the court orders otherwise, an individual chapter 11 debtor's discharge is not effective until completion of all payments under the plan, as provided in § 1141(d)(5) which was added to the Code in 2005. Forms 9F and 9F (Alt.) are amended to include a deadline to file a complaint to determine the dischargeability of a debt, in conformity with § 1141(d)(6) which was added to the Code in 2005.

Form 9I is amended to include a deadline to file a complaint to determine the dischargeability of certain debts. This amendment implements 2005 amendment to § 1328(a)(1) of the Code.

Form 10

The form is amended to conform to changes in the priority afforded the claims of certain creditors in § 507(a) of the Code as amended by the Bankruptcy Abuse Prevention and Consumer Protection Act of 2005, Pub. L. No. 109-8, 119 Stat. 23 (April 20, 2005).

Form 16A

The form is amended to require that the title of the case include all names used by the debtor within the last eight years in conformity with § 727(a)(8) as amended by the Bankruptcy Abuse Prevention and Consumer Protection Act of 2005, Pub. L. No. 109-8, 119 Stat. 23 (April 20, 2005), extending from six years to eight years the period during which a debtor is barred from receiving successive discharges.

Form 18

The form is amended to require that the title of the case include all names used by the debtor within the eight years prior to the filing of the petition in the case in conformity with § 727(a)(8) as amended by the Bankruptcy Abuse Prevention and Consumer Protection Act of 2005, Pub. L. No. 109-8, 119 Stat. 23 (April 20, 2005), extending from six years to eight years the period during which a debtor is barred from receiving successive discharges. The explanation part of the form is amended to include additional types of debts that are not discharged under § 523(a) as amended in 2005 and to revise certain terminology in conformity with provisions of the 2005 Act.

Form 19A

The certification by a non-attorney bankruptcy petition preparer in this form is renamed a "declaration" and is amended to include material mandated by amendments to § 110 of the Code in the Bankruptcy Abuse Prevention and Consumer Protection Act of 2005, Pub. L. No. 109-8, 119 Stat. 23 (April 20, 2005).

Form 19B

This form is new. It contains the notice a non-attorney bankruptcy petition preparer is required to give to a debtor under § 110 of the Code as amended by the Bankruptcy Abuse Prevention and Consumer Protection Act of 2005, Pub. L. No. 109-8, 119 Stat. 23 (April 20, 2005). The notice states, in language mandated in the 2005 Act, that the bankruptcy petition preparer is not an attorney and must not give legal advice. The form includes examples of advice a bankruptcy petition preparer may not give that are take from § 110(e)(2), which also was added to the Code in 2005. The notice must be signed by the debtor and by the bankruptcy petition preparer and filed with any document for filing prepared by the bankruptcy petition preparer.

Forms 22A, 22B, & 23C

A. Overview

One of the changes in bankruptcy practice introduced by the Bankruptcy Abuse Prevention and Consumer Protection Act of 2005 is a definition of "current monthly income," set out in § 101(10A) of the Code. Certain individual debtors in Chapter 7, all individual debtors in Chapter 11, and all Chapter 13 debtors are required to calculate their income under this definition. Certain Chapter 7 and 13 debtors are further required to calculate deductions from current monthly income allowed under the means test of § 707(b)(2)(A). Chapter 7 debtors subject to the means test may, as a result of these calculations, be subject to a presumption of abuse. The means test deductions are used in Chapter 13 to calculate disposable income under § 1325(b)(2) and (3). To comply with the reporting and calculation requirements involving current monthly income and the means test, three separate forms have been provided—one for Chapter 7, one for Chapter 11, and one for Chapter 13. This note first describes the "current monthly income" calculation that is common to all three of the forms, next describes the means test deductions employed in the Chapter 7 and 13 forms, and finally addresses particular issues that are unique to each of the separate forms.

B. Calculation of current monthly income

Current monthly income ("CMI"), as defined in § 101(10A), has different purposes in each of the three chapters in which it is used, but basic computation is the same. CMI is a monthly average of defined "income" received in the six calendar months prior to the bankruptcy filing by the debtor and, in a joint case, the debtor's spouse. The "income" to be included in this average is (1) income from all sources, whether or not taxable, and (2) any amount paid by an entity other than the debtor (or the debtor's spouse in a joint case) on a regular basis for the household expenses of the debtor, the debtor's dependents, and (in a joint case) the debtor's spouse if not otherwise a dependent. However, the income to be averaged is defined as not including "benefits received under the Social Security Act" and certain payments received by victims of terrorism, war crimes, and crimes against humanity.

The forms address the calculation of CMI, in each chapter, by a series of line entries, divided into columns providing for separate entries by the debtor and the debtor's spouse. The calculation line entries are set out in Part II of the Chapter 7 form, and Part I of the forms for Chapter 11 and Chapter 13. These line entries for calculating CMI are introduced by a set of instructions and check boxes indicating when the "debtor's spouse" column is required to be completed. The instructions also direct the required averaging of the income reported on the line entries.

The line entries specify several common types of income and then include a "catch-all" line for other types. The specific entry lines address gross wages; business and rental income; interest, dividends, and royalties; pension and retirement income; and regular contributions to the debtor's household expenses. Gross wages (before taxes) are required to be entered. Consistent with usage in the Internal Revenue Manual and the American Community Survey of the Census Bureau, business and rental income is defined as gross receipts less ordinary and necessary expenses. Unemployment compensation is given special treatment. Because the federal government provides funding for state unemployment compensation under the Social Security Act, there may be a dispute about whether unemployment compensation is a "benefit received under the Social Security Act." The forms take no position on the merits of this argument, but give debtors the option of making the argument by reporting unemployment compensation separately from their current monthly income. The separate reporting allows parties in interest to determine the materiality of an exclusion of unemployment compensation and to challenge it. The forms provide instruction for proper totaling of the income lines.

C. Means test deductions from current monthly income

Deductions from CMI are set out in § 707(b)(2)(A)(ii)—(iv). The forms for Chapter 7 and Chapter 13 have identical sections (Parts V and III, respectively) for calculating these deductions. The calculations are divided into subparts reflecting three different kinds of allowed deductions.

1. Deductions under IRS standards

Subpart A deals with deductions from CMI, set out in § 707(b)(2)(A)(ii), for "the debtor's applicable monthly expense amounts specified under the National Standards and Local Standards, and the debtor's actual monthly expenses for the categories specified as Other Necessary Expenses issued by the Internal Revenue Service for the area in which the debtor resides." The forms provide entry lines for each of the specified expense deductions under the IRS standards, and instructions on the entry lines identify the web pages where the relevant IRS allowances can be found. As with all of the deductions in § 707(b)(2)(A)(ii), deductions under the IRS standards are subject to the proviso that they not include "any payments for debts."

The IRS National Standards provide a single allowance for food, clothing, household supplies, personal care, and miscellany, depending on income and household size. The forms contain an entry line for the applicable allowance.

The IRS Local Standards provide separate deductions for housing and utilities and for transportation, with different amounts for different areas of the country, depending on the debtor's family size and number of the number of the debtor's vehicles. Each of the amounts specified by the IRS in the Local Standards are treated by the IRS as a cap on actual expenses, but because § 707(b)(2)(A)(ii) provides for deduction in the "amounts specified under the . . . Local Standards," the forms treat these amounts as allowed deductions.

[For use with the alternate versions of the Chapter 7 and 13 forms: The Local Standards for housing and utilities separate this expense category into a utilities/maintenance component and a mortgage/rental expense component. The utilities/maintenance component is a simple allowance, covering a variety of expenses involved in the operation of a residence. The mortgage/rental expense component covers the cost of acquiring the residence; for homeowners with mortgages, the mortgage/rental expense thus involves debt payment, since the cost of a mortgage is part of the allowance. Accordingly, the form requires debtors to deduct from allowance for mortgage/rental expense the average monthly mortgage payment (principal and interest), up to the full amount of the IRS mortgage/rental expense. This average payment is as reported on the separate line of the form for deductions of secured debt, pursuant to § 707(b)(2)(a)(iii).]

[For use with the original versions of the Chapter 7 and 13 forms: The Local Standards for housing and utilities provide a single expense allowance covering both the cost of acquiring housing (rent or mortgage payments) and the cost of utilities, insurance and maintenance connected with the housing. Because this allowance includes debt payment, the form directs debtors to deduct any portion of the allowance that includes payments on debts secured by their homes. The proper manner of calculating this deduction from the housing and utilities allowance will have to be determined by judicial decisions.]

The Local Standards for transportation separate this expense category into a vehicle operation/public transportation component and a component for ownership/lease expense. The amount of the vehicle operation/public transportation allowance depends on the number of vehicles the debtor operates, with debtors who do not operate vehicles being given a public transportation expense. The instruction for this line item makes it clear that every debtor is thus entitled to some transportation expense allowance. No debt payment is involved in this allowance. However, for debtors with debt secured by the vehicles that they operate, the ownership/lease expense does involve debt payment. Accordingly, the form requires debtors to reduce the allowance for ownership/lease expense by the average monthly loan payment amount (principal and interest), up to the full amount of the IRS ownership/lease expense amount. This average payment is as reported on the separate line of the form for deductions of secured debt, pursuant to § 707(b)(2)(a)(iii).

The IRS does not set out allowances for "Other Necessary Expenses." Rather, it sets out a number of categories for such expenses, and describes the nature of the expenses that may be deducted in each of these categories. Section 707(b)(2)(a)(ii) allows a deduction for the debtor's actual expenses in these specified categories, subject to its requirement that payment of debt not be included. Several of the IRS categories deal with debt repayment and so are not included in the forms. Several other categories deal with expense items that are more expansively addressed by specific statutory allowances. The remaining IRS categories are set out in individual line entries. Instructions on the individual entry lines reflect limitations imposed by the IRS and the need to avoid inclusion of items deducted elsewhere on the forms.

The forms call for a subtotal of the deductions allowed under the IRS standards.

2. Additional statutory expense deductions

In addition to the IRS expense deductions, subclauses (I), (II), (IV), and (V) of § 707(b)(2)(A)(ii) allow six special expense deductions. Each of these additional expense items is set out on a separate line entry in Subpart B, introduced by an instruction that there should not be double counting of any expense already included in the IRS deductions. Contributions to tax-exempt charities provide another statutory expense deduction. Specifically, § 1325(b)(2)(A)(ii) expressly allows a deduction from CMI for such contributions (up to 15% of the debtor's gross income), and § 707(b)(l) provides that in considering whether a Chapter 7 filing is an abuse, the court may not take into consideration "whether a debtor . . . continues to make [tax-exempt] charitable contributions." Accordingly, Subpart B also includes an entry line for charitable contributions. Again, the forms call for the additional statutory expense deductions to be subtotaled.

3. Deductions for payment of debt

Subpart C of the forms deals with deductions from CMI for payment of secured and priority debt, as well as a deduction for an administrative fees that would be incurred if the debtor paid debts through a Chapter 13 plan. In accord with § 707(b)(2)(A)(iii), the deduction for secured debt is divided into two entry lines-one for payments that are contractually due during the 60 months following the bankruptcy filing, the other for amounts needed to retain necessary collateral securing debts in default. In each situation, the instructions for the entry lines require dividing the total payment amount by 60, as the statute directs. Priority debt, deductible pursuant to § 707(b)(2)(A)(iv), is treated on a single entry line, also requiring division by 60. The defined deduction for the expenses of administering a Chapter 13 plan is allowed by § 707(b)(2)(A)(ii)(III) only for debtors eligible for Chapter 13. The forms treat this deduction in an entry line that requires the eligible debtor to state the amount of the prospective Chapter 13 plan payment and multiply that payment amount by the percentage fee established for the debtor's district by the Executive Office for United States Trustees. The forms refer debtors to a website that will set out this percentage fee. An entry line is provided for subtotaling the debt payment deductions.

4. Total deductions

Finally, the forms direct that the subtotals from Subparts A, By and C be added together to arrive at the total of allowed deductions from CMI.

5. Additional claimed deductions

The forms do not provide for deductions from CMI for expenses in categories that are not specifically identified as "Other Necessary Expenses" in the Internal Revenue Manual. However, debtors may wish to claim expenses that do not fall within the categories listed as "Other Necessary Expenses" in the forms. The forms provide sections (Part VII in the Chapter 7 form and Part V in the Chapter 13 form) for such expenses to be identified and totaled. Although expenses listed in these sections are not deducted from CMI for purposes of the forms' calculations, the listing provides a basis for debtors to assert that these expenses should be deducted from CMI under § 707(b)(2)(A)(ii)(I), and that the results of the forms' calculation are therefore inaccurate.

D. The Chapter-specific forms

1. Chapter 7

The Chapter 7 form has several unique aspects. The form includes, in the upper right comer of the first page, a check box requiring the debtor to state whether or not a presumption of abuse exists as a result of the calculations required by the form. This check box is intended to give clerks of court a conspicuous indication of the cases for which they will be required to provide notice of a presumption of abuse pursuant to § 342(d).

Part I of the form implements the provision of § 707(b)(2)(D) that excludes certain disabled veterans from any form of means testing, making it unnecessary to compute the CMI of such veterans. Debtors who declare under penalty of perjury that they are disabled veterans within the statutory definition are directed to verify their declaration in Part VII, to check the "no presumption" box at the beginning of the form, and to disregard the remaining parts of the form.

Part II of the form is the computation of current monthly income ("CMI") as defined in § 101(10A). Section 707(b)(2) eliminates standing to assert the means test's presumption of abuse if the debtor's annualized CMI does not exceed a defined median state in-come. For this purpose, the CMI of the debtor's spouse is added to the debtor's CMI even if the debtor's spouse is not a joint debtor, unless the debtor declares under penalty of perjury that the spouses are legally separated or living separately other than for purposes of evading the means test. Accordingly, the calculation of CMI in Part II directs a computation of the CMI of the debtor's spouse in all cases of married debtors where the debtor is unable to make the specified declaration or where the debtors are filing jointly, and the CMI of both spouses in these cases is added for purposes of determining standing under § 707(b)(7).

Part III of the form provides for the comparison of the debtor's CMI for purposes of § 707(b)(7) to the applicable state median income. It then directs debtors whose income does not exceed the applicable median to verify the form and check the "no presumption" box at the beginning of the form, but not to complete the remaining parts of the form. Debtors whose CMI does exceed the applicable state median are required to complete the remaining parts of the form.

Part IV of the form provides for an adjustment to the CMI of a married debtor, not filing jointly, whose spouse's CMI was included with the debtor's for purposes of determining standing to assert the means test presumption. The means test itself does not charge a married debtor in a non-joint case with the income of the non-filing spouse, but rather only with contributions made by that spouse to the household expenses of the debtor and the debtor's dependents, as provided in the definition of CMI in § 101(10A). Accordingly, Part IV calls for the combined CMI total of Part II to be reduced by the amount of the non-filing spouse's income that was not contributed to the household expenses of the debtor or the debtor's dependents.

Part V of the form provides for a calculation of allowed deductions from the debtor's CMI, as described above.

Part VI provides for a determination of whether the debtor's CMI, less the allowed deductions, gives rise to a presumption of abuse under § 707(b)(2)(A). Depending on the outcome of this determination, the debtor is directed to check the appropriate box at the beginning of the form and to sign the verification in Part VIII. Part VII allows the debtor to claim additional deductions, as discussed above.

2. Chapter 11

The Chapter 11 form is the simplest of the three, since the means-test deductions of § 707(b)(2) are not employed in determining the extent of an individual Chapter 11 debtor's disposable income. Rather, § 1129(a)(15) requires payments of disposable income "as defined in section 1325(b)(2)," and that paragraph allows calculation of disposable income under judicially-determined standards, rather than pursuant to the means test deductions, specified for higher income Chapter 13 debtors by § 1325(b)(3). However, § 1325(b)(2) does require that CMI be used as the starting point in the judicial determination of disposable income, and so the Chapter 11 form requires this calculation (in Part I of the form), as described above, together with a verification (in Part II).

3. Chapter 13

Like the Chapter 7 form, the form for Chapter 13 debtors contains a number of special provisions. Because § 1325(b)(3) employs the means test deductions for debtors whose CMI exceeds the applicable state median income, the upper right corner of the first page includes check boxes requiring the debtor to state whether § 1325(b)(3) applies, thus quickly informing standing trustees and other interested parties of the need to consider these deductions.

Part I of the form is the calculation of CMI, as described above.

Part II of the form compares the debtor's CMI to the applicable state median, allowing the determination of the applicability of the means-test deductions required by § 1325(b)(3).

Part III provides for calculation of the means-test deductions provided in § 707(b)(2), described above, as incorporated by § 1325(b)(3) for debtors with CMI above the applicable state median.

Part IV provides for three adjustments required by special provisions affecting disposable income. First, § 1325(b)(2) itself excludes from CMI in the determination of disposable income certain "child support payments, foster care payments, [and] disability payments for a dependent child." Because payments of this kind are included in the definition of CMI in § 101(10A), a line entry for deduction of these payments is provided. Second, a line entry is provided for deduction of contributions by the debtor to certain retirement plans, listed in § 541(b)(7)(B), since that provision states that such contributions "shall not constitute disposable income, as defined in section 1325(b)." Third, the same line entry also allows a deduction from disposable income for payments on loans from retirement accounts that are excepted from the automatic stay by § 362(b)(19), since § 1322(f) provides that for a "loan described in section 362(b)(19) . . . any amounts required to repay such loan shall not constitute 'disposable income' under section 1325."

The Chapter 13 form does not provide a deduction from disposable income for the Chapter 13 debtor's anticipated attorney fees. There is no specific statutory allowance for such a deduction, and none appears necessary. Section 1325(b)(1)(B) requires that disposable income contributed to a Chapter 13 plan be used to pay "unsecured creditors." A debtor's attorney who has not taken a security interest in the debtor's property is an unsecured creditor who may be paid from disposable income.

Part V of the form allows the debtor to claim additional deductions, as described above, and Part VI is the verification.

Form 23

The form is new. Sections 727(a)(11) and 1328(g)(1), which were added to the Code by the Bankruptcy Abuse Prevention and Consumer Protection Act of 2005, Pub. L. No. 109-8, 119 Stat. 23 (April 20, 2005), require the debtor to complete an instructional course concerning personal financial management as a condition for receiving a discharge. The completed form, when filed by the debtor, will signal the clerk that this condition has been satisfied.

Form 24

This form is new. Rule 8001, as amended in 2005, requires that any certification of an appeal bankruptcy court judgment, order, or decree directly to the United States Court of Appeals by all the appellants and appellees (if any) acting jointly be filed on this form.

D.4 Blank New and Amended Official Bankruptcy Forms

(Official Form 1) (10/05)

United States Bankruptcy Court **____________ District of ____________**	**Voluntary Petition**

Name of Debtor (if individual, enter Last, First, Middle):	Name of Joint Debtor (Spouse) (Last, First, Middle):
All Other Names used by the Debtor in the last 8 years (include married, maiden, and trade names):	All Other Names used by the Joint Debtor in the last 8 years (include married, maiden, and trade names):
Last four digits of Soc. Sec./Complete EIN or other Tax I.D. No. (if more than one, state all):	Last four digits of Soc. Sec./Complete EIN or other Tax I.D. No. (if more than one, state all):
Street Address of Debtor (No. & Street, City, and State): ZIPCODE	Street Address of Joint Debtor (No. & Street, City, and State): ZIPCODE
County of Residence or of the Principal Place of Business:	County of Residence or of the Principal Place of Business:
Mailing Address of Debtor (if different from street address): ZIPCODE	Mailing Address of Joint Debtor (if different from street address): ZIPCODE

Location of Principal Assets of Business Debtor (if different from street address above):
ZIPCODE

Type of Debtor (Form of Organization)
(Check **one** box.)

- ☐ Individual (includes Joint Debtors)
- ☐ Corporation (includes LLC and LLP)
- ☐ Partnership
- ☐ Other (If debtor is not one of the above entities, check this box and provide the information requested below.)

State type of entity: ____________

Nature of Business
(Check **all** applicable boxes.)

- ☐ Health Care Business
- ☐ Single Asset Real Estate as defined in 11 U.S.C. § 101 (51B)
- ☐ Railroad
- ☐ Stockbroker
- ☐ Commodity Broker
- ☐ Clearing Bank
- ☐ Nonprofit Organization qualified under 15 U.S.C. § 501(c)(3)

Chapter of Bankruptcy Code Under Which the Petition is Filed (Check one box)

- ☐ Chapter 7
- ☐ Chapter 9
- ☐ Chapter 11
- ☐ Chapter 12
- ☐ Chapter 13
- ☐ Chapter 15 Petition for Recognition of a Foreign Main Proceeding
- ☐ Chapter 15 Petition for Recognition of a Foreign Nonmain Proceeding

Nature of Debts (Check one box)

- ☐ Consumer/Non-Business
- ☐ Business

Filing Fee (Check one box)

- ☐ Full Filing Fee attached
- ☐ Filing Fee to be paid in installments (Applicable to individuals only) Must attach signed application for the court's consideration certifying that the debtor is unable to pay fee except in installments. Rule 1006(b). See Official Form 3A.
- ☐ Filing Fee waiver requested (Applicable to chapter 7 individuals only). Must attach signed application for the court's consideration. See Official Form 3B.

Chapter 11 Debtors

Check one box:

- ☐ Debtor is a small business debtor as defined in 11 U.S.C. § 101(51D).
- ☐ Debtor is not a small business debtor as defined in 11 U.S.C. § 101(51D).

Check if:

- ☐ Debtor's aggregate noncontingent liquidated debts owed to non-insiders or affliates are less than $2 million.

Statistical/Administrative Information

- ☐ Debtor estimates that funds will be available for distribution to unsecured creditors.
- ☐ Debtor estimates that, after any exempt property is excluded and administrative expenses paid, there will be no funds available for distribution to unsecured creditors.

THIS SPACE IS FOR COURT USE ONLY

Estimated Number of Creditors

1-49	50-99	100-199	200-999	1,000-5,000	5,001-10,000	10,001-25,000	25,001-50,000	50,001-100,000	OVER 100,000
☐	☐	☐	☐	☐	☐	☐	☐	☐	☐

Estimated Assets

$0 to $50,000	$50,001 to $100,000	$100,001 to $500,000	$500,001 to $1 million	$1,000,001 to $10 million	$10,000,001 to $50 million	$50,000,001 to $100 million	More than $100 million
☐	☐	☐	☐	☐	☐	☐	☐

Estimated Debts

$0 to $50,000	$50,001 to $100,000	$100,001 to $500,000	$500,001 to $1 million	$1,000,001 to $10 million	$10,000,001 to $50 million	$50,000,001 to $100 million	More than $100 million
☐	☐	☐	☐	☐	☐	☐	☐

(Official Form 1) (10/05)

FORM B1, Page 2

Voluntary Petition *(This page must be completed and filed in every case)*	Name of Debtor(s):	
Prior Bankruptcy Case Filed Within Last 8 Years (If more than one, attach additional sheet)		
Location Where Filed:	Case Number:	Date Filed:
Pending Bankruptcy Case Filed by any Spouse, Partner or Affiliate of this Debtor (If more than one, attach additional sheet)		
Name of Debtor:	Case Number:	Date Filed:
District:	Relationship:	Judge:

Exhibit A

(To be completed if debtor is required to file periodic reports (e.g., forms 10K and 10Q) with the Securities and Exchange Commission pursuant to Section 13 or 15(d) of the Securities Exchange Act of 1934 and is requesting relief under chapter 11.)

☐ Exhibit A is attached and made a part of this petition.

Exhibit B

(To be completed if debtor is an individual whose debts are primarily consumer debts.)

I, the attorney for the petitioner named in the foregoing petition, declare that I have informed the petitioner that [he or she] may proceed under chapter 7, 11, 12, or 13 of title 11, United States Code, and have explained the relief available under each such chapter.
I further certify that I delivered to the debtor the notice required by § 342(b) of the Bankruptcy Code.

X ______________________________

Signature of Attorney for Debtor(s) Date

Exhibit C

Does the debtor own or have possession of any property that poses or is alleged to pose a threat of imminent and identifiable harm to public health or safety?

☐ Yes, and Exhibit C is attached and made a part of this petition.

☐ No

Certification Concerning Debt Counseling by Individual/Joint Debtor(s)

☐ I/we have received approved budget and credit counseling during the 180-day period preceding the filing of this petition.

☐ I/we request a waiver of the requirement to obtain budget and credit counseling prior to filing based on exigent circumstances. (Must attach certification describing.)

Information Regarding the Debtor (Check the Applicable Boxes)

Venue (Check any applicable box)

☐ Debtor has been domiciled or has had a residence, principal place of business, or principal assets in this District for 180 days immediately preceding the date of this petition or for a longer part of such 180 days than in any other District.

☐ There is a bankruptcy case concerning debtor's affiliate, general partner, or partnership pending in this District.

☐ Debtor is a debtor in a foreign proceeding and has its principal place of business or principal assets in the United States in this District, or has no principal place of business or assets in the United States but is a defendant in an action or proceeding [in a federal or state court] in this District, or the interests of the parties will be served in regard to the relief sought in this District.

Statement by a Debtor Who Resides as a Tenant of Residential Property

Check all applicable boxes.

☐ Landlord has a judgment aganist the debtor for possession of debtor's residence. (If box checked, complete the following.)

____

(Name of landlord that obtained judgment)

____

(Address of landlord)

☐ Debtor claims that under applicable nonbankruptcy law, there are circumstances under which the debtor would be permitted to cure the entire monetary default that gave rise to the judgment for possession, after the judgment for possession was entered, and

☐ Debtor has included in this petition the deposit with the court of any rent that would become due during the 30-day period after the filing of the petition.

(Official Form 1) (10/05) **FORM B1,** Page 3

Voluntary Petition
(This page must be completed and filed in every case)

Name of Debtor(s):

Signatures

Signature(s) of Debtor(s) (Individual/Joint)

I declare under penalty of perjury that the information provided in this petition is true and correct.
[If petitioner is an individual whose debts are primarily consumer debts and has chosen to file under chapter 7] I am aware that I may proceed under chapter 7, 11, 12 or 13 of title 11, United States Code, understand the relief available under each such chapter, and choose to proceed under chapter 7.
[If no attorney represents me and no bankruptcy petition preparer signs the petition] I have obtained and read the notice required by § 342(b) of the Bankruptcy Code.

I request relief in accordance with the chapter of title 11, United States Code, specified in this petition.

X______________________________
Signature of Debtor

X______________________________
Signature of Joint Debtor

____
Telephone Number (If not represented by attorney)

____
Date

Signature of a Foreign Representative of a Recognized Foreign Proceedings

I declare under penalty of perjury that the information provided in this petition is true and correct, that I am the foreign representative of a debtor in a foreign main proceeding, and that I am authorized to file this petition. A certified copy of the order granting recognition is attached.

X______________________________
(Signature of Foreign Representative)

____
(Printed Name of Foreign Representative)

____
(Date)

Signature of Attorney

X______________________________
Signature of Attorney for Debtor(s)

____
Printed Name of Attorney for Debtor(s)

____
Firm Name

____
Address

____

____
Telephone Number

____
Date

Signature of Debtor (Corporation/Partnership)

I declare under penalty of perjury that the information provided in this petition is true and correct, and that I have been authorized to file this petition on behalf of the debtor.

The debtor requests relief in accordance with the chapter of title 11, United States Code, specified in this petition.

X______________________________
Signature of Authorized Individual

____
Printed Name of Authorized Individual

____
Title of Authorized Individual

____
Date

Signature of Non-Attorney Bankruptcy Petition Preparer

I declare under penalty of perjury that: (1) I am a bankruptcy petition preparer as defined in 11 U.S.C. § 110; (2) I prepared this document for compensation and have provided the debtor with a copy of this document and the notices and information required under 11 U.S.C. §§ 110(b), 110(h), and 342(b); and, (3) if rules or guidelines have been promulgated pursuant to 11 U.S.C. § 110(h) setting a maximum fee for services chargeable by bankruptcy petition preparers, I have given the debtor notice of the maximum amount before preparing any document for filing for a debtor or accepting any fee from the debtor, as required in that section.Official Form 19B is attached.

____
Printed Name and title, if any, of Bankruptcy Petition Preparer

____
Social Security number (If the bankrutpcy petition preparer is not an individual, state the Social Security number of the officer, principal, responsible person or partner of the bankruptcy petition preparer.)(Required by 11 U.S.C. § 110.)

____
Address

____

X______________________________

Signature of Bankruptcy Petition Preparer or officer, principal, responsible person,or partner whose social security number is provided above.

Names and Social Security numbers of all other individuals who prepared or assisted in preparing this document unless the bankruptcy petition preparer is not an individual:

If more than one person prepared this document, attach additional sheets conforming to the appropriate official form for each person.

A bankruptcy petition preparer's failure to comply with the provisions of title 11 and the Federal Rules of Bankruptcy Procedure may result in fines or imprisonment or both 11 U.S.C. §110; 18 U.S.C. §156.

Form 3A
(10/05)

United States Bankruptcy Court

_______________ District Of _______________

In re _______________________________________,
Debtor

Case No. __________________

Chapter ___________

APPLICATION TO PAY FILING FEE IN INSTALLMENTS

1. In accordance with Fed. R. Bankr. P. 1006, I apply for permission to pay the filing fee amounting to $____________ in installments.

2. I am unable to pay the filing fee except in installments.

3. Until the filing fee is paid in full, I will not make any additional payment or transfer any additional property to an attorney or any other person for services in connection with this case.

4. I propose the following terms for the payment of the Filing Fee.*

$ __________________ Check one ☐ With the filing of the petition, or
☐ On or before ____________

$ __________________ on or before ___________________________________

$ __________________ on or before ___________________________________

$ __________________ on or before ___________________________________

* The number of installments proposed shall not exceed four (4), and the final installment shall be payable not later than 120 days after filing the petition. For cause shown, the court may extend the time of any installment, provided the last installment is paid not later than 180 days after filing the petition. Fed. R. Bankr. P. 1006(b)(2).

5. I understand that if I fail to pay any installment when due, my bankruptcy case may be dismissed and I may not receive a discharge of my debts.

____
Signature of Attorney Date

____
Name of Attorney

____
Signature of Debtor Date
(In a joint case, both spouses must sign.)

____
Signature of Joint Debtor (if any) Date

DECLARATION AND SIGNATURE OF NON-ATTORNEY BANKRUPTCY PETITION (See 11 U.S.C. § 110)

I declare under penalty of perjury that: (1) I am a bankruptcy petition preparer as defined in 11 U.S.C. § 110; (2) I prepared this document for compensation and have provided the debtor with a copy of this document and the notices and information required under 11 U.S.C. §§ 110(b), 110(h), and 342(b); (3) if rules or guidelines have been promulgated pursuant to 11 U.S.C. § 110(h) setting a maximum fee for services chargeable by bankruptcy petition preparers, I have given the debtor notice of the maximum amount before preparing any document for filing for a debtor or accepting any fee from the debtor, as required under that section; and (4) I will not accept any additional money or other property from the debtor before the filing fee is paid in full.

____
Printed or Typed Name and Title, if any, of Bankruptcy Petition Preparer

____
Social Security No. (Required by 11 U.S.C. § 110.)

If the bankruptcy petition preparer is not an individual, state the name, title (if any), address, and social security number of the officer, principal, responsible person, or partner who signs the document.

____

____
Address

x______________________________________
Signature of Bankruptcy Petition Preparer

____
Date

Names and Social Security numbers of all other individuals who prepared or assisted in preparing this document, unless the bankruptcy petition preparer is not an individual:

If more than one person prepared this document, attach additional signed sheets conforming to the appropriate Official Form for each person. A bankruptcy petition preparer's failure to comply with the provisions of title 11 and the Federal Rules of Bankruptcy Procedure may result in fines or imprisonment or both. 11 U.S.C. § 110; 18 U.S.C. § 156.

Form 3A Contd.
(10/05)

United States Bankruptcy Court
_______________ District Of _______________

In re ____,
Debtor

Case No. __________________

Chapter ___________

ORDER APPROVING PAYMENT OF FILING FEE IN INSTALLMENTS

☐ IT IS ORDERED that the debtor(s) may pay the filing fee in installments on the terms proposed in the foregoing application.

☐ IT IS ORDERED that the debtor(s) shall pay the filing fee according to the following terms:

$ __________________ Check one ☐ With the filing of the petition, or
☐ On or before _____________

$ __________________ on or before ___________________________________

$ __________________ on or before ___________________________________

$ __________________ on or before ___________________________________

☐ IT IS FURTHER ORDERED that until the filing fee is paid in full the debtor(s) shall not make any additional payment or transfer any additional property to an attorney or any other person for services in connection with this case.

BY THE COURT

Date: ___________________

____
United States Bankruptcy Judge

Form B3B
(10/05)

APPLICATION FOR WAIVER OF THE CHAPTER 7 FILING FEE FOR INDIVIDUALS WHO CANNOT PAY THE FILING FEE IN FULL OR IN INSTALLMENTS

The court fee for filing a case under chapter 7 of the Bankruptcy Code is $274.

If you cannot afford to pay the full fee at the time of filing, you may apply to pay the fee in installments. A form, which is available from the bankruptcy clerk's office, must be completed to make that application. If your application to pay in installments is approved, you will be permitted to file your petition, completing payment of the fee over the course of four to six months.

If you cannot afford to pay the fee either in full at the time of filing or in installments, then you may request a waiver of the filing fee by completing this application and filing it with the Clerk of Court. A judge will decide whether you have to pay the fee. By law, the judge may waive the fee only if your income is less than 150 percent of the official poverty line applicable to your family size and you are unable to pay the fee in installments. You may obtain information about the poverty guidelines at www.uscourts.gov or in the bankruptcy clerk's office.

Required information. Complete all items in the application, and attach requested schedules. Then sign the application on the last page. If you and your spouse are filing a joint bankruptcy petition, you both must provide information as requested and sign the application.

Form B3B
(10/05)

In re: ____________________ Case No. ____________________
Debtor(s) (if known)

APPLICATION FOR WAIVER OF THE CHAPTER 7 FILING FEE
FOR INDIVIDUALS WHO CANNOT PAY THE FILING FEE IN FULL OR IN INSTALLMENTS

Part A. Family Size and Income

1. Including yourself, your spouse, and dependents you have listed or will list on Schedule I (Current Income of Individual Debtors(s)), how many people are in your family? (Do not include your spouse if you are separated AND are not filing a joint petition.) __________

2. Restate the following information that you provided, or will provide, on Line 16 of Schedule I. Attach a completed copy of Schedule I, if it is available.

   Total Combined Monthly Income (Line 16 of Schedule I): $__________

3. State the monthly net income, if any, of dependents included in Question 1 above. Do not include any income already reported in Item 2. If none, enter $0.

   $__________

4. Add the "Total Combined Monthly Income" reported in Question 2 to your dependents' monthly net income from Question 3.

   $__________

5. Do you expect the amount in Question 4 to increase or decrease by more than 10% during the next 6 months? Yes ___ No ___

   If yes, explain.

Part B: Monthly Expenses

6. EITHER (a) attach a completed copy of Schedule J (Schedule of Monthly Expenses), and state your total monthly expenses reported on Line 18 of that Schedule, OR (b) if you have not yet completed Schedule J, provide an estimate of your total monthly expenses.

   $ __________

7. Do you expect the amount in Question 6 to increase or decrease by more than 10% during the next 6 months? Yes ___ No ___
   If yes, explain.

Part C. Real and Personal Property

EITHER (1) attach completed copies of Schedules A (Real Property) and Schedule B (Personal Property), OR (2) if you have not yet completed those schedules, answer the following questions.

8. State the amount of cash you have on hand: $ __________

9. State below any money you have in savings, checking, or other accounts in a bank or other financial institution.

Bank or Other Financial Institution:	Type of Account such as savings, checking, CD:	Amount:
____________________	____________________	$ __________
____________________	____________________	$ __________

Form B3B Cont.
(10/05)

10. State below the assets owned by you. **Do not list ordinary household furnishings and clothing**.

Home	Address: __________________________ __________________________	Value: $ __________ Amount owed on mortgages and liens: $ __________
Other real estate	Address: __________________________ __________________________	Value: $ __________ Amount owed on mortgages and liens: $ __________
Motor vehicle	Model/Year: __________________ __________________________	Value: $ __________ Amount owed: $ __________
Motor vehicle	Model/Year: __________________ __________________________	Value: $ __________ Amount owed: $ __________
Other	Description__________________ __________________________	Value: $ __________ Amount owed: $ __________

11. State below any person, business, organization, or governmental unit that owes you money and the amount that is owed.

Name of Person, Business, or Organization that Owes You Money	Amount Owed
______________________________	$ __________
______________________________	$ __________

Part D. Additional Information.

12. Have you paid an **attorney** any money for services in connection with this case, including the completion of this form, the bankruptcy petition, or schedules? Yes ___ No ___
If yes, how much have you paid? $ ___________

13. Have you promised to pay or do you anticipate paying an **attorney** in connection with your bankruptcy case? Yes ___ No ___
If yes, how much have you promised to pay or do you anticipate paying? $ ___________

14. Have you paid **anyone other than an attorney** (such as a bankruptcy petition preparer, paralegal, typing service, or another person) any money for services in connection with this case, including the completion of this form, the bankruptcy petition, or schedules? Yes ___ No ___
If yes, how much have you paid? $ ___________

15. Have you promised to pay or do you anticipate paying **anyone other than an attorney** (such as a bankruptcy petition preparer, paralegal, typing service, or another person) any money for services in connection with this case, including the completion of this form, the bankruptcy petition, or schedules?
Yes ___ No ___
If yes, how much have you promised to pay or do you anticipate paying? $ ___________

16. Has anyone paid an attorney or other person or service in connection with this case, on your behalf?
Yes ___ No ___

If yes, explain.

Form B3B Cont.
(10/05)

17. Have you previously filed for bankruptcy relief during the past eight years? Yes ___ No ___

Case Number (if known)	Year filed	Location of filing	Did you obtain a discharge? (if known)
________________	______	____________	Yes ____ No ____ Don't know ____
________________	______	____________	Yes ____ No ____ Don't know ____

18. Please provide any other information that helps to explain why you are unable to pay the filing fee in installments.

19. I (we) declare under penalty of perjury that I (we) cannot currently afford to pay the filing fee in full or in installments and that the foregoing information is true and correct.

Executed on: ________________ ____________________________
Date Signature of Debtor

________________ ____________________________
Date Signature of Co-debtor

DECLARATION AND SIGNATURE OF BANKRUPTCY PETITION PREPARER (See 11 U.S.C. § 110)

I declare under penalty of perjury that: (1) I am a bankruptcy petition preparer as defined in 11 U.S.C. § 110; (2) I prepared this document for compensation and have provided the debtor with a copy of this document and the notices and information required under 11 U.S.C. §§ 110(b), 110(h), and 342(b); and (3) if rules or guidelines have been promulgated pursuant to 11 U.S.C. § 110(h) setting a maximum fee for services chargeable by bankruptcy petition preparers, I have given the debtor notice of the maximum amount before preparing any document for filing for a debtor or accepting any fee from the debtor, as required under that section.

____ ____________________
Printed or Typed Name and Title, if any, of Bankruptcy Petition Preparer Social Security No. (Required by 11 U.S.C. §110.)

If the bankruptcy petition preparer is not an individual, state the name, title (if any), address, and social security number of the officer, principal, responsible person, or partner who signs the document.

____

____
Address

x______________________________________ ________________
Signature of Bankruptcy Petition Preparer Date

Names and Social Security numbers of all other individuals who prepared or assisted in preparing this document, unless the bankruptcy petition preparer is not an individual:

If more than one person prepared this document, attach additional signed sheets conforming to the appropriate Official Form for each person.
A bankruptcy petition preparer's failure to comply with the provisions of title 11 and the Federal Rules of Bankruptcy Procedure may result in fines or imprisonment or both. 11 U.S.C. § 110; 18 U.S.C. § 156.

Form B3B
(10/05)

United State Bankruptcy Court
_________ District of __________

In re: ____________________ Case No. ____________________
Debtor(s)

ORDER ON DEBTOR'S APPLICATION FOR WAIVER OF THE CHAPTER 7 FILING FEE

Upon consideration of the debtor's "Application for Waiver of the Chapter 7 Filing Fee," the court orders that the application be:

[ ] GRANTED.

This order is subject to being vacated at a later time if developments in the administration of the bankruptcy case demonstrate that the waiver was unwarranted.

[ ] DENIED.

The debtor shall pay the chapter 7 filing fee according to the following terms:

$ __________ on or before __________

$ __________ on or before __________

$ __________ on or before __________

$ __________ on or before __________

Until the filing fee is paid in full, the debtor shall not make any additional payment or transfer any additional property to an attorney or any other person for services in connection with this case.

IF THE DEBTOR FAILS TO TIMELY PAY THE FILING FEE IN FULL OR TO TIMELY MAKE INSTALLMENT PAYMENTS, THE COURT MAY DISMISS THE DEBTOR'S CHAPTER 7 CASE.

[ ] SCHEDULED FOR HEARING.

A hearing to consider the debtor's "Application for Waiver of the Chapter 7 Filing Fee" shall be held on __________________ at ________ am/pm at ____.
(address of courthouse)

IF THE DEBTOR FAILS TO APPEAR AT THE SCHEDULED HEARING, THE COURT MAY DEEM SUCH FAILURE TO BE THE DEBTOR'S CONSENT TO THE ENTRY OF AN ORDER DENYING THE FEE WAIVER APPLICATION BY DEFAULT.

BY THE COURT:

DATE: __________

____
United States Bankruptcy Judge

Form B6
(10/05)

FORM 6. SCHEDULES

Summary of Schedules
Statistical Summary of Certain Liabilities

Schedule A - Real Property
Schedule B - Personal Property
Schedule C - Property Claimed as Exempt
Schedule D - Creditors Holding Secured Claims
Schedule E - Creditors Holding Unsecured Priority Claims
Schedule F - Creditors Holding Unsecured Nonpriority Claims
Schedule G - Executory Contracts and Unexpired Leases
Schedule H - Codebtors
Schedule I - Current Income of Individual Debtor(s)
Schedule J - Current Expenditures of Individual Debtor(s)

Unsworn Declaration under Penalty of Perjury

GENERAL INSTRUCTIONS: The first page of the debtor's schedules and the first page of any amendments thereto must contain a caption as in Form 16B. Subsequent pages should be identified with the debtor's name and case number. If the schedules are filed with the petition, the case number should be left blank

Schedules D, E, and F have been designed for the listing of each claim only once. Even when a claim is secured only in part or entitled to priority only in part, it still should be listed only once. A claim which is secured in whole or it part should be listed on Schedule D only, and a claim which is entitled to priority in whole or in part should be listed on Schedule E only. Do not list the same claim twice. If a creditor has more than one claim, such as claims arising from separate transactions, each claim should be scheduled separately.

Review the specific instructions for each schedule before completing the schedule.

Form 6-Summary
(10/05)

United States Bankruptcy Court

_______________ District Of _______________

In re ______________________________, Case No. ________________
Debtor

Chapter __________

SUMMARY OF SCHEDULES

Indicate as to each schedule whether that schedule is attached and state the number of pages in each. Report the totals from Schedules A, B, D, E, F, I, and J in the boxes provided. Add the amounts from Schedules A and B to determine the total amount of the debtor's assets. Add the amounts of all claims from Schedules D, E, and F to determine the total amount of the debtor's liabilities. Individual debtors must also complete the "Statistical Summary of Certain Liabilities."

AMOUNTS SCHEDULED

NAME OF SCHEDULE	ATTACHED (YES/NO)	NO. OF SHEETS	ASSETS	LIABILITIES	OTHER
A - Real Property			$		
B - Personal Property			$		
C - Property Claimed as Exempt					
D - Creditors Holding Secured Claims				$	
E - Creditors Holding Unsecured Priority Claims				$	
F - Creditors Holding Unsecured Nonpriority Claims				$	
G - Executory Contracts and Unexpired Leases					
H - Codebtors					
I - Current Income of Individual Debtor(s)					$
J - Current Expenditures of Individual Debtors(s)					$
TOTAL			$	$	

Form 6-Summ2
(10/05)

United States Bankruptcy Court

________________ District Of ________________

In re ____,
Debtor

Case No. ____________________

Chapter ____________

STATISTICAL SUMMARY OF CERTAIN LIABILITIES (28 U.S.C. § 159) [Individual Debtors Only]

Summarize the following types of liabilities, as reported in the Schedules, and total them.

Type of Liability	**Amount**
Domestic Support Obligations (from Schedule E)	$
Taxes and Certain Other Debts Owed to Governmental Units (from Schedule E)	$
Claims for Death or Personal Injury While Debtor Was Intoxicated (from Schedule E)	$
Student Loan Obligations (from Schedule F)	$
Domestic Support, Separation Agreement, and Divorce Decree Obligations Not Reported on Schedule E	$
Obligations to Pension or Profit-Sharing, and Other Similar Obligations (from Schedule F)	$
TOTAL	$

The foregoing information is for statistical purposes only under 28 U.S.C § 159.

Form B6A
(10/05)

In re ______________________________________, Case No. ______________________
Debtor (If known)

SCHEDULE A - REAL PROPERTY

Except as directed below, list all real property in which the debtor has any legal, equitable, or future interest, including all property owned as a co-tenant, community property, or in which the debtor has a life estate. Include any property in which the debtor holds rights and powers exercisable for the debtor's own benefit. If the debtor is married, state whether husband, wife, or both own the property by placing an "H," "W," "J," or "C" in the column labeled "Husband, Wife, Joint, or Community." If the debtor holds no interest in real property, write "None" under "Description and Location of Property."

Do not include interests in executory contracts and unexpired leases on this schedule. List them in Schedule G - Executory Contracts and Unexpired Leases.

If an entity claims to have a lien or hold a secured interest in any property, state the amount of the secured claim. See Schedule D. If no entity claims to hold a secured interest in the property, write "None" in the column labeled "Amount of Secured Claim."

If the debtor is an individual or if a joint petition is filed, state the amount of any exemption claimed in the property only in Schedule C - Property Claimed as Exempt.

DESCRIPTION AND LOCATION OF PROPERTY	NATURE OF DEBTOR'S INTEREST IN PROPERTY	HUSBAND, WIFE, JOINT, OR COMMUNITY	CURRENT VALUE OF DEBTOR'S INTEREST IN PROPERTY, WITHOUT DEDUCTING ANY SECURED CLAIM OR EXEMPTION	AMOUNT OF SECURED CLAIM
		Total➤		

(Report also on Summary of Schedules.)

Form B6B
(10/05)

In re ____, Case No. ___________________________
Debtor (If known)

SCHEDULE B - PERSONAL PROPERTY

Except as directed below, list all personal property of the debtor of whatever kind. If the debtor has no property in one or more of the categories, place an "x" in the appropriate position in the column labeled "None." If additional space is needed in any category, attach a separate sheet properly identified with the case name, case number, and the number of the category. If the debtor is married, state whether husband, wife, or both own the property by placing an "H," "W," "J," or "C" in the column labeled "Husband, Wife, Joint, or Community." If the debtor is an individual or a joint petition is filed, state the amount of any exemptions claimed only in Schedule C - Property Claimed as Exempt.

Do not list interests in executory contracts and unexpired leases on this schedule. List them in Schedule G - Executory Contracts and Unexpired Leases.

If the property is being held for the debtor by someone else, state that person's name and address under "Description and Location of Property." In providing the information requested in this schedule, do not include the name or address of a minor child. Simply state "a minor child."

TYPE OF PROPERTY	NONE	DESCRIPTION AND LOCATION OF PROPERTY	HUSBAND, WIFE, JOINT, OR COMMUNITY	CURRENT VALUE OF DEBTOR'S INTEREST IN PROPERTY, WITH-OUT DEDUCTING ANY SECURED CLAIM OR EXEMPTION
1. Cash on hand.				
2. Checking, savings or other financial accounts, certificates of deposit, or shares in banks, savings and loan, thrift, building and loan, and homestead associations, or credit unions, brokerage houses, or cooperatives.				
3. Security deposits with public utilities, telephone companies, landlords, and others.				
4. Household goods and furnishings, including audio, video, and computer equipment.				
5. Books; pictures and other art objects; antiques; stamp, coin, record, tape, compact disc, and other collections or collectibles.				
6. Wearing apparel.				
7. Furs and jewelry.				
8. Firearms and sports, photographic, and other hobby equipment.				
9. Interests in insurance policies. Name insurance company of each policy and itemize surrender or refund value of each.				
10. Annuities. Itemize and name each issuer.				
11. Interests in an education IRA as defined in 26 U.S.C. § 530(b)(1) or under a qualified State tuition plan as defined in 26 U.S.C. § 529(b)(1). Give particulars. (File separately the record(s) of any such interest(s). 11 U.S.C. § 521(c); Rule 1007(b)).				

Form B6B-Cont.
(10/05)

In re ______________________________________, Case No. ______________________
Debtor (If known)

SCHEDULE B - PERSONAL PROPERTY
(Continuation Sheet)

TYPE OF PROPERTY	N O N E	DESCRIPTION AND LOCATION OF PROPERTY	HUSBAND, WIFE, JOINT, OR COMMUNITY	CURRENT VALUE OF DEBTOR'S INTEREST IN PROPERTY, WITH-OUT DEDUCTING ANY SECURED CLAIM OR EXEMPTION
12. Interests in IRA, ERISA, Keogh, or other pension or profit sharing plans. Give particulars.				
13. Stock and interests in incorporated and unincorporated businesses. Itemize.				
14. Interests in partnerships or joint ventures. Itemize.				
15. Government and corporate bonds and other negotiable and non-negotiable instruments.				
16. Accounts receivable.				
17. Alimony, maintenance, support, and property settlements to which the debtor is or may be entitled. Give particulars.				
18. Other liquidated debts owed to debtor including tax refunds. Give particulars.				
19. Equitable or future interests, life estates, and rights or powers exercisable for the benefit of the debtor other than those listed in Schedule A – Real Property.				
20. Contingent and noncontingent interests in estate of a decedent, death benefit plan, life insurance policy, or trust.				
21. Other contingent and unliquidated claims of every nature, including tax refunds, counterclaims of the debtor, and rights to setoff claims. Give estimated value of each.				

Form B6B-cont.
(10/05)

In re ____, Case No. ______________________
Debtor (If known)

SCHEDULE B -PERSONAL PROPERTY

(Continuation Sheet)

TYPE OF PROPERTY	NONE	DESCRIPTION AND LOCATION OF PROPERTY	HUSBAND, WIFE, JOINT, OR COMMUNITY	CURRENT VALUE OF DEBTOR'S INTEREST IN PROPERTY, WITH-OUT DEDUCTING ANY SECURED CLAIM OR EXEMPTION
22. Patents, copyrights, and other intellectual property. Give particulars.				
23. Licenses, franchises, and other general intangibles. Give particulars.				
24. Customer lists or other compilations containing personally identifiable information (as defined in 11 U.S.C. § 101(41A)) provided to the debtor by individuals in connection with obtaining a product or service from the debtor primarily for personal, family, or household purposes.				
25. Automobiles, trucks, trailers, and other vehicles and accessories.				
26. Boats, motors, and accessories.				
27. Aircraft and accessories.				
28. Office equipment, furnishings, and supplies.				
29. Machinery, fixtures, equipment, and supplies used in business.				
30. Inventory.				
31. Animals.				
32. Crops - growing or harvested. Give particulars.				
33. Farming equipment and implements.				
34. Farm supplies, chemicals, and feed.				
35. Other personal property of any kind not already listed. Itemize.				

__________continuation sheets attached Total➤ $

(Include amounts from any continuation sheets attached. Report total also on Summary of Schedules.)

Form B6C
(10/05)

In re ____,
Debtor

Case No. ________________________
(If known)

SCHEDULE C - PROPERTY CLAIMED AS EXEMPT

Debtor claims the exemptions to which debtor is entitled under:
(Check one box)
☐ 11 U.S.C. § 522(b)(2)
☐ 11 U.S.C. § 522(b)(3)

☐ Check if debtor claims a homestead exemption that exceeds $125,000.

DESCRIPTION OF PROPERTY	SPECIFY LAW PROVIDING EACH EXEMPTION	VALUE OF CLAIMED EXEMPTION	CURRENT VALUE OF PROPERTY WITHOUT DEDUCTING EXEMPTION

Form B6D
(10/05) **In re** ____________________________, **Case No.** ____________________________
Debtor **(If known)**

SCHEDULE D – CREDITORS HOLDING SECURED CLAIMS

State the name, mailing address, including zip code, and last four digits of any account number of all entities holding claims secured by property of the debtor as of the date of filing of the petition. The complete account number of any account the debtor has with the creditor is useful to the trustee and the creditor and may be provided if the debtor chooses to do so. List creditors holding all types of secured interests such as judgment liens, garnishments, statutory liens, mortgages, deeds of trust, and other security interests.

List creditors in alphabetical order to the extent practicable. If a minor child is a creditor, indicate that by stating "a minor child" and do not disclose the child's name. See 11 U.S.C. § 112; Fed. R. Bankr. P. 1007(m). If all secured creditors will not fit on this page, use the continuation sheet provided.

If any entity other than a spouse in a joint case may be jointly liable on a claim, place an "X" in the column labeled "Codebtor," include the entity on the appropriate schedule of creditors, and complete Schedule H – Codebtors. If a joint petition is filed, state whether husband, wife, both of them, or the marital community may be liable on each claim by placing an "H," "W," "J," or "C" in the column labeled "Husband, Wife, Joint, or Community."

If the claim is contingent, place an "X" in the column labeled "Contingent." If the claim is unliquidated, place an "X" in the column labeled "Unliquidated." If the claim is disputed, place an "X" in the column labeled "Disputed." (You may need to place an "X" in more than one of these three columns.)

Report the total of all claims listed on this schedule in the box labeled "Total" on the last sheet of the completed schedule. Report this total also on the Summary of Schedules.

☐ Check this box if debtor has no creditors holding secured claims to report on this Schedule D.

CREDITOR'S NAME AND MAILING ADDRESS INCLUDING ZIP CODE AND A ACCOUNT NUMBER (*See Instructions Above*)	CODEBTOR	HUSBAND, WIFE, JOINT, OR COMMUNITY	DATE CLAIM WAS INCURRED, NATURE OF LIEN , AND DESCRIPTION AND VALUE OF PROPERTY SUBJECT TO LIEN	CONTINGENT	UNLIQUIDATED	DISPUTED	AMOUNT OF CLAIM WITHOUT DEDUCTING VALUE OF COLLATERAL	UNSECURED PORTION, IF ANY
ACCOUNT NO.			VALUE $					
ACCOUNT NO.			VALUE $					
ACCOUNT NO.			VALUE $					
ACCOUNT NO.			VALUE $					
_____continuation sheets attached			Subtotal ► (Total of this page)				$	
			Total ► (Use only on last page)				$	

(Report total also on Summary of Schedules)

Form B6D – Cont.
(10/05)
In re ______________________________________, **Case No.** ______________________________________
Debtor **(If known)**

SCHEDULE D – CREDITORS HOLDING SECURED CLAIMS

(Continuation Sheet)

CREDITOR'S NAME AND MAILING ADDRESS INCLUDING ZIP CODE AND A ACCOUNT NUMBER (*See Instructions Above*)	CODEBTOR	HUSBAND, WIFE, JOINT, OR COMMUNITY	DATE CLAIM WAS INCURRED, NATURE OF LIEN , AND DESCRIPTION AND VALUE OF PROPERTY SUBJECT TO LIEN	CONTINGENT	UNLIQUIDATED	DISPUTED	AMOUNT OF CLAIM WITHOUT DEDUCTING VALUE OF COLLATERAL	UNSECURED PORTION, IF ANY
ACCOUNT NO.			VALUE $					
ACCOUNT NO.			VALUE $					
ACCOUNT NO.			VALUE $					
ACCOUNT NO.			VALUE $					
ACCOUNT NO.			VALUE $					
Sheet no.___of___continuation sheets attached to Schedule of Creditors Holding Secured Claims			Subtotal ► (Total of this page)				$	
			Total ► (Use only on last page)				$	

Form B6E
(10/05)

In re ______________________________, Debtor

Case No. ______________________ (if known)

SCHEDULE E - CREDITORS HOLDING UNSECURED PRIORITY CLAIMS

A complete list of claims entitled to priority, listed separately by type of priority, is to be set forth on the sheets provided. Only holders of unsecured claims entitled to priority should be listed in this schedule. In the boxes provided on the attached sheets, state the name, mailing address, including zip code, and last four digits of the account number, if any, of all entities holding priority claims against the debtor or the property of the debtor, as of the date of the filing of the petition. Use a separate continuation sheet for each type of priority and label each with the type of priority.

The complete account number of any account the debtor has with the creditor is useful to the trustee and the creditor and may be provided if the debtor chooses to do so. If a minor child is a creditor, indicate that by stating "a minor child" and do not disclose the child's name. See 11 U.S.C. § 112; Fed.R.Bankr.P. 1007(m).

If any entity other than a spouse in a joint case may be jointly liable on a claim, place an "X" in the column labeled "Codebtor," include the entity on the appropriate schedule of creditors, and complete Schedule H-Codebtors. If a joint petition is filed, state whether husband, wife, both of them or the marital community may be liable on each claim by placing an "H,""W,""J," or "C" in the column labeled "Husband, Wife, Joint, or Community." If the claim is contingent, place an "X" in the column labeled "Contingent." If the claim is unliquidated, place an "X" in the column labeled "Unliquidated." If the claim is disputed, place an "X" in the column labeled "Disputed." (You may need to place an "X" in more than one of these three columns.)

Report the total of claims listed on each sheet in the box labeled "Subtotal" on each sheet. Report the total of all claims listed on this Schedule E in the box labeled "Total" on the last sheet of the completed schedule. Report this total also on the Summary of Schedules.

Report the total of amounts entitled to priority listed on each sheet in the box labeled "Subtotal" on each sheet. Report the total of all amounts entitled to priority listed on this Schedule E in the box labeled "Total" on the last sheet of the completed schedule. If applicable, also report this total on the Means Test form.

☐ Check this box if debtor has no creditors holding unsecured priority claims to report on this Schedule E.

TYPES OF PRIORITY CLAIMS (Check the appropriate box(es) below if claims in that category are listed on the attached sheets)

☐ **Domestic Support Obligations**

Claims for domestic support that are owed to or recoverable by a spouse, former spouse, or child of the debtor, or the parent, legal guardian, or responsible relative of such a child, or a governmental unit to whom such a domestic support claim has been assigned to the extent provided in 11 U.S.C. § 507(a)(1).

☐ **Extensions of credit in an involuntary case**

Claims arising in the ordinary course of the debtor's business or financial affairs after the commencement of the case but before the earlier of the appointment of a trustee or the order for relief. 11 U.S.C. § 507(a)(3).

☐ **Wages, salaries, and commissions**

Wages, salaries, and commissions, including vacation, severance, and sick leave pay owing to employees and commissions owing to qualifying independent sales representatives up to $10,000* per person earned within 180 days immediately preceding the filing of the original petition, or the cessation of business, whichever occurred first, to the extent provided in 11 U.S.C. § 507(a)(4).

☐ **Contributions to employee benefit plans**

Money owed to employee benefit plans for services rendered within 180 days immediately preceding the filing of the original petition, or the cessation of business, whichever occurred first, to the extent provided in 11 U.S.C. § 507(a)(5).

Form B6E Contd.
(10/05)

In re ____ , Case No.______________________
Debtor (if known)

☐ **Certain farmers and fishermen**

Claims of certain farmers and fishermen, up to $4,925* per farmer or fisherman, against the debtor, as provided in 11 U.S.C. § 507(a)(6).

☐ **Deposits by individuals**

Claims of individuals up to $2,225* for deposits for the purchase, lease, or rental of property or services for personal, family, or household use, that were not delivered or provided. 11 U.S.C. § 507(a)(7).

☐ **Taxes and Certain Other Debts Owed to Governmental Units**

Taxes, customs duties, and penalties owing to federal, state, and local governmental units as set forth in 11 U.S.C. § 507(a)(8).

☐ **Commitments to Maintain the Capital of an Insured Depository Institution**

Claims based on commitments to the FDIC, RTC, Director of the Office of Thrift Supervision, Comptroller of the Currency, or Board of Governors of the Federal Reserve System, or their predecessors or successors, to maintain the capital of an insured depository institution. 11 U.S.C. § 507 (a)(9).

☐ **Claims for Death or Personal Injury While Debtor Was Intoxicated**

Claims for death or personal injury resulting from the operation of a motor vehicle or vessel while the debtor was intoxicated from using alcohol, a drug, or another substance. 11 U.S.C. § 507(a)(10).

* Amounts are subject to adjustment on April 1, 2007, and every three years thereafter with respect to cases commenced on or after the date of adjustment.

____ continuation sheets attached

Form B6E - Cont.
(10/05)

In re ______________________________, Case No. ______________________
Debtor (If known)

SCHEDULE E - CREDITORS HOLDING UNSECURED PRIORITY CLAIMS

(Continuation Sheet)

____
TYPE OF PRIORITY

CREDITOR'S NAME, MAILING ADDRESS INCLUDING ZIP CODE, AND ACCOUNT NUMBER (See instructions.)	CODEBTOR	HUSBAND, WIFE, JOINT, OR COMMUNITY	DATE CLAIM WAS INCURRED AND CONSIDERATION FOR CLAIM	CONTINGENT	UNLIQUIDATED	DISPUTED	AMOUNT OF CLAIM	AMOUNT ENTITLED TO PRIORITY
Account No.								
Account No.								
Account No.								
Account No.								
Account No.								

Sheet no. ___ of ___ sheets attached to Schedule of Creditors Holding Priority Claims

Subtotal➤ (Total of this page)	$	$
Total➤ (Use only on last page of the completed Schedule E. (Report total also on Summary of Schedules)	$	$

In re ______________________________, **Case No.** ______________________

Debtor **(If known)**

SCHEDULE F- CREDITORS HOLDING UNSECURED NONPRIORITY CLAIMS

State the name, mailing address, including zip code, and last four digits of any account number, of all entities holding unsecured claims without priority against the debtor or the property of the debtor, as of the date of filing of the petition. The complete account number of any account the debtor has with the creditor is useful to the trustee and the creditor and may be provided if the debtor chooses to do so. If a minor child is a creditor, indicate that by stating "a minor child" and do not disclose the child's name. See 11 U.S.C. § 112; Fed.R.Bankr.P. 1007(m). Do not include claims listed in Schedules D and E. If all creditors will not fit on this page, use the continuation sheet provided.

If any entity other than a spouse in a joint case may be jointly liable on a claim, place an "X" in the column labeled "Codebtor," include the entity on the appropriate schedule of creditors, and complete Schedule H - Codebtors. If a joint petition is filed, state whether husband, wife, both of them, or the marital community maybe liable on each claim by placing an "H," "W," "J," or "C" in the column labeled "Husband, Wife, Joint, or Community."

If the claim is contingent, place an "X" in the column labeled "Contingent." If the claim is unliquidated, place an "X" in the column labeled "Unliquidated." If the claim is disputed, place an "X" in the column labeled "Disputed." (You may need to place an "X" in more than one of these three columns.)

Report the total of all claims listed on this schedule in the box labeled "Total" on the last sheet of the completed schedule. Report this total also on the Summary of Schedules.

☐ Check this box if debtor has no creditors holding unsecured claims to report on this Schedule F.

CREDITOR'S NAME, MAILING ADDRESS INCLUDING ZIP CODE, AND ACCOUNT NUMBER (See instructions above.)	CODEBTOR	HUSBAND, WIFE, JOINT, OR COMMUNITY	DATE CLAIM WAS INCURRED AND CONSIDERATION FOR CLAIM. IF CLAIM IS SUBJECT TO SETOFF, SO STATE.	CONTINGENT	UNLIQUIDATED	DISPUTED	AMOUNT OF CLAIM WITHOUT DEDUCTING VALUE OF COLLATERAL
ACCOUNT NO.							
ACCOUNT NO.							
ACCOUNT NO.							
ACCOUNT NO.							

Subtotal➤ $

_____continuation sheets attached

Total➤ $
(Use only on last page of the completed Schedule F.)
(Report also on Summary of Schedules.)

In re ______________________________, **Case No.** ______________________________
Debtor **(If known)**

SCHEDULE F - CREDITORS HOLDING UNSECURED NONPRIORITY CLAIMS

(Continuation Sheet)

CREDITOR'S NAME, MAILING ADDRESS INCLUDING ZIP CODE, AND ACCOUNT NUMBER (See instructions above.)	CODEBTOR	HUSBAND, WIFE, JOINT, OR COMMUNITY	DATE CLAIM WAS INCURRED AND CONSIDERATION FOR CLAIM. IF CLAIM IS SUBJECT TO SETOFF, SO STATE.	CONTINGENT	UNLIQUIDATED	DISPUTED	AMOUNT OF CLAIM WITHOUT DEDUCTING VALUE OF COLLATERAL
ACCOUNT NO.							
ACCOUNT NO.							
ACCOUNT NO.							
ACCOUNT NO.							
ACCOUNT NO.							

Sheet no.___of___sheets attached to Schedule of Creditors Holding Unsecured Nonpriority Claims

Subtotal➤ $

Total➤ $
(Use only on last page of the completed Schedule F.)
(Report also on Summary of Schedules.)

Form B6G
(10/05)

In re ____ , Case No.__________________

Debtor (if known)

SCHEDULE G - EXECUTORY CONTRACTS AND UNEXPIRED LEASES

Describe all executory contracts of any nature and all unexpired leases of real or personal property. Include any timeshare interests. State nature of debtor's interest in contract, i.e., "Purchaser," "Agent," etc. State whether debtor is the lessor or lessee of a lease. Provide the names and complete mailing addresses of all other parties to each lease or contract described. If a minor child is a party to one of the leases or contracts, indicate that by stating "a minor child" and do not disclose the child's name. See 11 U.S.C. § 112; Fed.R. Bankr. P. 1007(m).

☐ Check this box if debtor has no executory contracts or unexpired leases.

NAME AND MAILING ADDRESS, INCLUDING ZIP CODE, OF OTHER PARTIES TO LEASE OR CONTRACT.	DESCRIPTION OF CONTRACT OR LEASE AND NATURE OF DEBTOR'S INTEREST. STATE WHETHER LEASE IS FOR NONRESIDENTIAL REAL PROPERTY. STATE CONTRACT NUMBER OF ANY GOVERNMENT CONTRACT.

Form B6H
(10/05)

In re ____ ,
Debtor

Case No. ________________________________
(if known)

SCHEDULE H - CODEBTORS

Provide the information requested concerning any person or entity, other than a spouse in a joint case, that is also liable on any debts listed by debtor in the schedules of creditors. Include all guarantors and co-signers. If the debtor resides or resided in a community property state, commonwealth, or territory (including Alaska, Arizona, California, Idaho, Louisiana, Nevada, New Mexico, Puerto Rico, Texas, Washington, or Wisconsin) within the eight year period immediately preceding the commencement of the case, identify the name of the debtor's spouse and of any former spouse who resides or resided with the debtor in the community property state, commonwealth, or territory. Include all names used by the nondebtor spouse during the eight years immediately preceding the commencement of this case. If a minor child is a codebtor or a creditor, indicate that by stating "a minor child" and do not disclose the child's name. See 11 U.S.C. § 112; Fed. Bankr. P. 1007(m).

☐ Check this box if debtor has no codebtors.

NAME AND ADDRESS OF CODEBTOR	NAME AND ADDRESS OF CREDITOR

Form B6I
(10/05)

In re ____ , Case No.________________________________
Debtor (if known)

SCHEDULE I - CURRENT INCOME OF INDIVIDUAL DEBTOR(S)

The column labeled "Spouse" must be completed in all cases filed by joint debtors and by a married debtor in a chapter 7, 11, 12, or 13 case whether or not a joint petition is filed, unless the spouses are separated and a joint petition is not filed. Do not state the name of any minor child.

Debtor's Marital Status:	DEPENDENTS OF DEBTOR AND SPOUSE	
	RELATIONSHIP:	AGE:

Employment:	DEBTOR	SPOUSE
Occupation		
Name of Employer		
How long employed		
Address of Employer		

INCOME: (Estimate of average monthly income)	DEBTOR	SPOUSE
1. Current monthly gross wages, salary, and commissions (Prorate if not paid monthly.)	$__________	$__________
2. Estimate monthly overtime	$__________	$__________
3. SUBTOTAL	$__________	$__________
4. LESS PAYROLL DEDUCTIONS		
a. Payroll taxes and social security	$__________	$__________
b. Insurance	$__________	$__________
c. Union dues	$__________	$__________
d. Other (Specify): ____________________	$__________	$__________
5. SUBTOTAL OF PAYROLL DEDUCTIONS	$__________	$__________
6. TOTAL NET MONTHLY TAKE HOME PAY	$__________	$__________
7. Regular income from operation of business or profession or firm. (Attach detailed statement)	$__________	$__________
8. Income from real property	$__________	$__________
9. Interest and dividends	$__________	$__________
10. Alimony, maintenance or support payments payable to the debtor for the debtor's use or that of dependents listed above.	$__________	$__________
11. Social security or government assistance (Specify):____________________	$__________	$__________
12. Pension or retirement income	$__________	$__________
13. Other monthly income (Specify):____________________ ____________________	$__________	$__________
	$__________	$__________
14. SUBTOTAL OF LINES 7 THROUGH 13	$__________	$__________
15. TOTAL MONTHLY INCOME (Add amounts shown on lines 6 and 14)	$__________	$__________
16. TOTAL COMBINED MONTHLY INCOME: $__________		

(Report also on Summary of Schedules.)

17. Describe any increase or decrease in income reasonably anticipated to occur within the year following the filing of this document:

____

____

Form B6J
(10/05)

In re ____ , Case No.____________________________

Debtor (if known)

SCHEDULE J - CURRENT EXPENDITURES OF INDIVIDUAL DEBTOR(S)

Complete this schedule by estimating the average monthly expenses of the debtor and the debtor's family. Pro rate any payments made bi-weekly, quarterly, semi-annually, or annually to show monthly rate.

Check this box if a joint petition is filed and debtor's spouse maintains a separate household. Complete a separate schedule of expenditures labeled "Spouse."

1. Rent or home mortgage payment (include lot rented for mobile home) $ ____________
   - a. Are real estate taxes included? Yes ________ No ________
   - b. Is property insurance included? Yes ________ No ________
2. Utilities: a. Electricity and heating fuel $ ____________
   - b. Water and sewer $ ____________
   - c. Telephone $ ____________
   - d. Other ________________________________ $ ____________
3. Home maintenance (repairs and upkeep) $ ____________
4. Food $ ____________
5. Clothing $ ____________
6. Laundry and dry cleaning $ ____________
7. Medical and dental expenses $ ____________
8. Transportation (not including car payments) $ ____________
9. Recreation, clubs and entertainment, newspapers, magazines, etc. $ ____________
10. Charitable contributions $ ____________
11. Insurance (not deducted from wages or included in home mortgage payments)
    - a. Homeowner's or renter's $ ____________
    - b. Life $ ____________
    - c. Health $ ____________
    - d. Auto $ ____________
    - e. Other ________________________________ $ ____________
12. Taxes (not deducted from wages or included in home mortgage payments) (Specify) ________________________________ $ ____________
13. Installment payments: (In chapter 11, 12, and 13 cases, do not list payments to be included in the plan)
    - a. Auto $ ____________
    - b. Other ________________________________ $ ____________
    - c. Other ________________________________ $ ____________
14. Alimony, maintenance, and support paid to others $ ____________
15. Payments for support of additional dependents not living at your home $ ____________
16. Regular expenses from operation of business, profession, or farm (attach detailed statement) $ ____________
17. Other ________________________________ $ ____________
18. TOTAL MONTHLY EXPENSES (Report also on Summary of Schedules) $ ____________
19. Describe any increase or decrease in expenditures reasonably anticipated to occur within the year following the filing of this document:
    ____
20. STATEMENT OF MONTHLY NET INCOME
    - a. Total monthly income from Line 16 of Schedule I $ ____________
    - b. Total monthly expenses from Line 18 above $ ____________
    - c. Monthly net income (a. minus b.) $ ____________

Official Form 6-Decl.
(10/05)

In re ______________________________ , Case No. ______________________

Debtor (If known)

DECLARATION CONCERNING DEBTOR'S SCHEDULES

DECLARATION UNDER PENALTY OF PERJURY BY INDIVIDUAL DEBTOR

I declare under penalty of perjury that I have read the foregoing summary and schedules, consisting of ____________________
(Total shown on summary page plus 1.)
sheets, and that they are true and correct to the best of my knowledge, information, and belief.

Date ______________________ Signature: ______________________________
Debtor

Date ______________________ Signature: ______________________________
(Joint Debtor, if any)

[If joint case, both spouses must sign.]

DECLARATION AND SIGNATURE OF NON-ATTORNEY BANKRUPTCY PETITION PREPARER (See 11 U.S.C. § 110)

I declare under penalty of perjury that: (1) I am a bankruptcy petition preparer as defined in 11 U.S.C. § 110; (2) I prepared this document for compensation and have provided the debtor with a copy of this document and the notices and information required under 11 U.S.C. §§ 110(b), 110(h) and 342(b); and, (3) if rules or guidelines have been promulgated pursuant to 11 U.S.C. § 110(h) setting a maximum fee for services chargeable by bankruptcy petition preparers, I have given the debtor notice of the maximum amount before preparing any document for filing for a debtor or accepting any fee from the debtor, as required by that section.

______________________________ ______________________
Printed or Typed Name of Bankruptcy Petition Preparer Social Security No.
(Required by 11 U.S.C. § 110.)

If the bankruptcy petition preparer is not an individual, state the name, title (if any), address, and social security number of the officer, principal, responsible person, or partner who signs this document.

____

____
Address

X ______________________________ ______________
Signature of Bankruptcy Petition Preparer Date

Names and Social Security numbers of all other individuals who prepared or assisted in preparing this document, unless the bankruptcy petition preparer is not an individual:

If more than one person prepared this document, attach additional signed sheets conforming to the appropriate Official Form for each person.

A bankruptcy petition preparer's failure to comply with the provisions of title 11 and the Federal Rules of Bankruptcy Procedure may result in fines or imprisonment or both. 11 U.S.C. § 110; 18 U.S.C. § 156.

DECLARATION UNDER PENALTY OF PERJURY ON BEHALF OF A CORPORATION OR PARTNERSHIP

I, the ______________________ [the president or other officer or an authorized agent of the corporation or a member or an authorized agent of the partnership] of the ______________________ [corporation or partnership] named as debtor in this case, declare under penalty of perjury that I have read the foregoing summary and schedules, consisting of ______________________ sheets, and that they are true and correct to the best of my knowledge, information, and belief. *(Total shown on summary page plus 1.)*

Date ______________________

Signature: ______________________________

____
[Print or type name of individual signing on behalf of debtor.]

[An individual signing on behalf of a partnership or corporation must indicate position or relationship to debtor.]

Penalty for making a false statement or concealing property: Fine of up to $500,000 or imprisonment for up to 5 years or both. 18 U.S.C. §§ 152 and 3571.

Official Form 7
(10/05)

UNITED STATES BANKRUPTCY COURT

______________________________ DISTRICT OF ______________________________

In re: ________________________________, Case No. ________________________________
Debtor (if known)

STATEMENT OF FINANCIAL AFFAIRS

This statement is to be completed by every debtor. Spouses filing a joint petition may file a single statement on which the information for both spouses is combined. If the case is filed under chapter 12 or chapter 13, a married debtor must furnish information for both spouses whether or not a joint petition is filed, unless the spouses are separated and a joint petition is not filed. An individual debtor engaged in business as a sole proprietor, partner, family farmer, or self-employed professional, should provide the information requested on this statement concerning all such activities as well as the individual's personal affairs. Do not include the name or address of a minor child in this statement. Indicate payments, transfers and the like to minor children by stating "a minor child." See 11 U.S.C. § 112; Fed. R. Bankr. P. 1007(m).

Questions 1 - 18 are to be completed by all debtors. Debtors that are or have been in business, as defined below, also must complete Questions 19 - 25. **If the answer to an applicable question is "None," mark the box labeled "None."** If additional space is needed for the answer to any question, use and attach a separate sheet properly identified with the case name, case number (if known), and the number of the question.

DEFINITIONS

"In business." A debtor is "in business" for the purpose of this form if the debtor is a corporation or partnership. An individual debtor is "in business" for the purpose of this form if the debtor is or has been, within six years immediately preceding the filing of this bankruptcy case, any of the following: an officer, director, managing executive, or owner of 5 percent or more of the voting or equity securities of a corporation; a partner, other than a limited partner, of a partnership; a sole proprietor or self-employed full-time or part-time. An individual debtor also may be "in business" for the purpose of this form if the debtor engages in a trade, business, or other activity, other than as an employee, to supplement income from the debtor's primary employment.

"Insider." The term "insider" includes but is not limited to: relatives of the debtor; general partners of the debtor and their relatives; corporations of which the debtor is an officer, director, or person in control; officers, directors, and any owner of 5 percent or more of the voting or equity securities of a corporate debtor and their relatives; affiliates of the debtor and insiders of such affiliates; any managing agent of the debtor. 11 U.S.C. § 101.

---

1. **Income from employment or operation of business**

None ☐

State the gross amount of income the debtor has received from employment, trade, or profession, or from operation of the debtor's business, including part-time activities either as an employee or in independent trade or business, from the beginning of this calendar year to the date this case was commenced. State also the gross amounts received during the **two years** immediately preceding this calendar year. (A debtor that maintains, or has maintained, financial records on the basis of a fiscal rather than a calendar year may report fiscal year income. Identify the beginning and ending dates of the debtor's fiscal year.) If a joint petition is filed, state income for each spouse separately. (Married debtors filing under chapter 12 or chapter 13 must state income of both spouses whether or not a joint petition is filed, unless the spouses are separated and a joint petition is not filed.)

AMOUNT	SOURCE

2. Income other than from employment or operation of business

None ☐

State the amount of income received by the debtor other than from employment, trade, profession, operation of the debtor's business during the **two years** immediately preceding the commencement of this case. Give particulars. If a joint petition is filed, state income for each spouse separately. (Married debtors filing under chapter 12 or chapter 13 must state income for each spouse whether or not a joint petition is filed, unless the spouses are separated and a joint petition is not filed.)

AMOUNT	SOURCE

---

3. Payments to creditors

Complete a. or b., as appropriate, and c.

None ☐

a. *Individual or joint debtor(s) with primarily consumer debts:* List all payments on loans, installment purchases of goods or services, and other debts to any creditor made within **90 days** immediately preceding the commencement of this case if the aggregate value of all property that constitutes or is affected by such transfer is not less than $600. Indicate with an asterisk (*) any payments that were made to a creditor on account of a domestic support obligation or as part of an alternative repayment schedule under a plan by an approved nonprofit budgeting and creditor counseling agency. (Married debtors filing under chapter 12 or chapter 13 must include payments by either or both spouses whether or not a joint petition is filed, unless the spouses are separated and a joint petition is not filed.)

NAME AND ADDRESS OF CREDITOR	DATES OF PAYMENTS	AMOUNT PAID	AMOUNT STILL OWING

None ☐

b. *Debtor whose debts are not primarily consumer debts:* List each payment or other transfer to any creditor made within **90** days immediately preceding the commencement of the case if the aggregate value of all property that constitutes or is affected by such transfer is not less than $5,000. (Married debtors filing under chapter 12 or chapter 13 must include payments and other transfers by either or both spouses whether or not a joint petition is filed, unless the spouses are separated and a joint petition is not filed.)

NAME AND ADDRESS OF CREDITOR	DATES OF PAYMENTS/ TRANSFERS	AMOUNT PAID OR VALUE OF TRANSFERS	AMOUNT STILL OWING

None ☐

c. *All debtors:* List all payments made within **one year** immediately preceding the commencement of this case to or for the benefit of creditors who are or were insiders. (Married debtors filing under chapter 12 or chapter 13 must include payments by either or both spouses whether or not a joint petition is filed, unless the spouses are separated and a joint petition is not filed.)

NAME AND ADDRESS OF CREDITOR AND RELATIONSHIP TO DEBTOR	DATE OF PAYMENT	AMOUNT PAID	AMOUNT STILL OWING

---

4. Suits and administrative proceedings, executions, garnishments and attachments

None ☐

a. List all suits and administrative proceedings to which the debtor is or was a party within **one year** immediately preceding the filing of this bankruptcy case. (Married debtors filing under chapter 12 or chapter 13 must include information concerning either or both spouses whether or not a joint petition is filed, unless the spouses are separated and a joint petition is not filed.)

CAPTION OF SUIT AND CASE NUMBER	NATURE OF PROCEEDING	COURT OR AGENCY AND LOCATION	STATUS OR DISPOSITION

None ☐

b. Describe all property that has been attached, garnished or seized under any legal or equitable process within **one year** immediately preceding the commencement of this case. (Married debtors filing under chapter 12 or chapter 13 must include information concerning property of either or both spouses whether or not a joint petition is filed, unless the spouses are separated and a joint petition is not filed.)

NAME AND ADDRESS OF PERSON FOR WHOSE BENEFIT PROPERTY WAS SEIZED	DATE OF SEIZURE	DESCRIPTION AND VALUE OF PROPERTY

5. Repossessions, foreclosures and returns

None ☐

List all property that has been repossessed by a creditor, sold at a foreclosure sale, transferred through a deed in lieu of foreclosure or returned to the seller, within **one year** immediately preceding the commencement of this case. (Married debtors filing under chapter 12 or chapter 13 must include information concerning property of either or both spouses whether or not a joint petition is filed, unless the spouses are separated and a joint petition is not filed.)

NAME AND ADDRESS OF CREDITOR OR SELLER	DATE OF REPOSSESSION, FORECLOSURE SALE, TRANSFER OR RETURN	DESCRIPTION AND VALUE OF PROPERTY

6. Assignments and receiverships

None ☐

a. Describe any assignment of property for the benefit of creditors made within **120 days** immediately preceding the commencement of this case. (Married debtors filing under chapter 12 or chapter 13 must include any assignment by either or both spouses whether or not a joint petition is filed, unless the spouses are separated and a joint petition is not filed.)

NAME AND ADDRESS OF ASSIGNEE	DATE OF ASSIGNMENT	TERMS OF ASSIGNMENT OR SETTLEMENT

None ☐

b. List all property which has been in the hands of a custodian, receiver, or court-appointed official within **one year** immediately preceding the commencement of this case. (Married debtors filing under chapter 12 or chapter 13 must include information concerning property of either or both spouses whether or not a joint petition is filed, unless the spouses are separated and a joint petition is not filed.)

NAME AND ADDRESS OF CUSTODIAN	NAME AND LOCATION OF COURT CASE TITLE & NUMBER	DATE OF ORDER	DESCRIPTION AND VALUE Of PROPERTY

7. Gifts

None ☐

List all gifts or charitable contributions made within **one year** immediately preceding the commencement of this case except ordinary and usual gifts to family members aggregating less than $200 in value per individual family member and charitable contributions aggregating less than $100 per recipient. (Married debtors filing under chapter 12 or chapter 13 must include gifts or contributions by either or both spouses whether or not a joint petition is filed, unless the spouses are separated and a joint petition is not filed.)

NAME AND ADDRESS OF PERSON OR ORGANIZATION	RELATIONSHIP TO DEBTOR, IF ANY	DATE OF GIFT	DESCRIPTION AND VALUE OF GIFT

8. Losses

None ☐

List all losses from fire, theft, other casualty or gambling within **one year** immediately preceding the commencement of this case **or since the commencement of this case**. (Married debtors filing under chapter 12 or chapter 13 must include losses by either or both spouses whether or not a joint petition is filed, unless the spouses are separated and a joint petition is not filed.)

DESCRIPTION AND VALUE OF PROPERTY	DESCRIPTION OF CIRCUMSTANCES AND, IF LOSS WAS COVERED IN WHOLE OR IN PART BY INSURANCE, GIVE PARTICULARS	DATE OF LOSS

9. Payments related to debt counseling or bankruptcy

None ☐

List all payments made or property transferred by or on behalf of the debtor to any persons, including attorneys, for consultation concerning debt consolidation, relief under the bankruptcy law or preparation of a petition in bankruptcy within **one year** immediately preceding the commencement of this case.

NAME AND ADDRESS OF PAYEE	DATE OF PAYMENT, NAME OF PAYER IF OTHER THAN DEBTOR	AMOUNT OF MONEY OR DESCRIPTION AND VALUE OF PROPERTY

10. Other transfers

5

None ☐ a. List all other property, other than property transferred in the ordinary course of the business or financial affairs of the debtor, transferred either absolutely or as security within **two years** immediately preceding the commencement of this case. (Married debtors filing under chapter 12 or chapter 13 must include transfers by either or both spouses whether or not a joint petition is filed, unless the spouses are separated and a joint petition is not filed.)

NAME AND ADDRESS OF TRANSFEREE, RELATIONSHIP TO DEBTOR	DATE	DESCRIBE PROPERTY TRANSFERRED AND VALUE RECEIVED

None ☐ b. List all property transferred by the debtor within **ten years** immediately preceding the commencement of this case to a self-settled trust or similar device of which the debtor is a beneficiary.

NAME OF TRUST OR OTHER DEVICE	DATE(S) OF TRANSFER(S)	AMOUNT OF MONEY OR DESCRIPTION AND VALUE OF PROPERTY OR DEBTOR'S INTEREST IN PROPERTY

11. **Closed financial accounts**

None ☐ List all financial accounts and instruments held in the name of the debtor or for the benefit of the debtor which were closed, sold, or otherwise transferred within **one year** immediately preceding the commencement of this case. Include checking, savings, or other financial accounts, certificates of deposit, or other instruments; shares and share accounts held in banks, credit unions, pension funds, cooperatives, associations, brokerage houses and other financial institutions. (Married debtors filing under chapter 12 or chapter 13 must include information concerning accounts or instruments held by or for either or both spouses whether or not a joint petition is filed, unless the spouses are separated and a joint petition is not filed.)

NAME AND ADDRESS OF INSTITUTION	TYPE OF ACCOUNT, LAST FOUR DIGITS OF ACCOUNT NUMBER, AND AMOUNT OF FINAL BALANCE	AMOUNT AND DATE OF SALE OR CLOSING

12. **Safe deposit boxes**

None ☐ List each safe deposit or other box or depository in which the debtor has or had securities, cash, or other valuables within **one year** immediately preceding the commencement of this case. (Married debtors filing under chapter 12 or chapter 13 must include boxes or depositories of either or both spouses whether or not a joint petition is filed, unless the spouses are separated and a joint petition is not filed.)

NAME AND ADDRESS OF BANK OR OTHER DEPOSITORY	NAMES AND ADDRESSES OF THOSE WITH ACCESS TO BOX OR DEPOSITORY	DESCRIPTION OF CONTENTS	DATE OF TRANSFER OR SURRENDER, IF ANY

13. **Setoffs**

None List all setoffs made by any creditor, including a bank, against a debt or deposit of the debtor within **90 days** preceding

☐ the commencement of this case. (Married debtors filing under chapter 12 or chapter 13 must include information concerning either or both spouses whether or not a joint petition is filed, unless the spouses are separated and a joint petition is not filed.)

NAME AND ADDRESS OF CREDITOR	DATE OF SETOFF	AMOUNT OF SETOFF

---

14. Property held for another person

None ☐ List all property owned by another person that the debtor holds or controls.

NAME AND ADDRESS OF OWNER	DESCRIPTION AND VALUE OF PROPERTY PROPERTY	LOCATION OF

---

15. Prior address of debtor

None ☐ If debtor has moved within **three years** immediately preceding the commencement of this case, list all premises which the debtor occupied during that period and vacated prior to the commencement of this case. If a joint petition is filed, report also any separate address of either spouse.

ADDRESS	NAME USED	DATES OF OCCUPANCY

---

16. Spouses and Former Spouses

None ☐ If the debtor resides or resided in a community property state, commonwealth, or territory (including Alaska, Arizona, California, Idaho, Louisiana, Nevada, New Mexico, Puerto Rico, Texas, Washington, or Wisconsin) within **eight years** immediately preceding the commencement of the case, identify the name of the debtor's spouse and of any former spouse who resides or resided with the debtor in the community property state.

NAME

17. Environmental Information.

For the purpose of this question, the following definitions apply:

"Environmental Law" means any federal, state, or local statute or regulation regulating pollution, contamination, releases of hazardous or toxic substances, wastes or material into the air, land, soil, surface water, groundwater, or other medium, including, but not limited to, statutes or regulations regulating the cleanup of these substances, wastes, or material.

"Site" means any location, facility, or property as defined under any Environmental Law, whether or not presently or formerly owned or operated by the debtor, including, but not limited to, disposal sites.

"Hazardous Material" means anything defined as a hazardous waste, hazardous substance, toxic substance, hazardous material, pollutant, or contaminant or similar term under an Environmental Law.

None ☐

a. List the name and address of every site for which the debtor has received notice in writing by a governmental unit that it may be liable or potentially liable under or in violation of an Environmental Law. Indicate the governmental unit, the date of the notice, and, if known, the Environmental Law:

SITE NAME AND ADDRESS	NAME AND ADDRESS OF GOVERNMENTAL UNIT	DATE OF NOTICE	ENVIRONMENTAL LAW

None ☐

b. List the name and address of every site for which the debtor provided notice to a governmental unit of a release of Hazardous Material. Indicate the governmental unit to which the notice was sent and the date of the notice.

SITE NAME AND ADDRESS	NAME AND ADDRESS OF GOVERNMENTAL UNIT	DATE OF NOTICE	ENVIRONMENTAL LAW

None ☐

c. List all judicial or administrative proceedings, including settlements or orders, under any Environmental Law with respect to which the debtor is or was a party. Indicate the name and address of the governmental unit that is or was a party to the proceeding, and the docket number.

NAME AND ADDRESS OF GOVERNMENTAL UNIT	DOCKET NUMBER	STATUS OR DISPOSITION

---

18 . Nature, location and name of business

None ☐

a. *If the debtor is an individual,* list the names, addresses, taxpayer identification numbers, nature of the businesses, and beginning and ending dates of all businesses in which the debtor was an officer, director, partner, or managing executive of a corporation, partner in a partnership, sole proprietor, or was self-employed in a trade, profession, or other activity either full- or part-time within **six years** immediately preceding the commencement of this case, or in which the debtor owned 5 percent or more of the voting or equity securities within **six years** immediately preceding the commencement of this case.

If the debtor is a partnership, list the names, addresses, taxpayer identification numbers, nature of the businesses, and beginning and ending dates of all businesses in which the debtor was a partner or owned 5 percent or more of the voting or equity securities, within **six years** immediately preceding the commencement of this case.

If the debtor is a corporation, list the names, addresses, taxpayer identification numbers, nature of the businesses, and beginning and ending dates of all businesses in which the debtor was a partner or owned 5 percent or more of the voting or equity securities within **six years** immediately preceding the commencement of this case.

NAME	LAST FOUR DIGITS OF SOC. SEC. NO./ COMPLETE EIN OR OTHER TAXPAYER I.D. NO.	ADDRESS	NATURE OF BUSINESS	BEGINNING AND ENDING DATES

None ☐ b. Identify any business listed in response to subdivision a., above, that is "single asset real estate" as defined in 11 U.S.C. § 101.

NAME	ADDRESS

The following questions are to be completed by every debtor that is a corporation or partnership and by any individual debtor who is or has been, within **six years** immediately preceding the commencement of this case, any of the following: an officer, director, managing executive, or owner of more than 5 percent of the voting or equity securities of a corporation; a partner, other than a limited partner, of a partnership, a sole proprietor, or self-employed in a trade, profession, or other activity, either full- or part-time.

(An individual or joint debtor should complete this portion of the statement ***only*** *if the debtor is or has been in business, as defined above, within six years immediately preceding the commencement of this case. A debtor who has not been in business within those six years should go directly to the signature page.)*

19. **Books, records and financial statements**

None ☐ a. List all bookkeepers and accountants who within **two years** immediately preceding the filing of this bankruptcy case kept or supervised the keeping of books of account and records of the debtor.

NAME AND ADDRESS	DATES SERVICES RENDERED

None ☐ b. List all firms or individuals who within **two years** immediately preceding the filing of this bankruptcy case have audited the books of account and records, or prepared a financial statement of the debtor.

NAME	ADDRESS	DATES SERVICES RENDERED

None ☐ c. List all firms or individuals who at the time of the commencement of this case were in possession of the books of account and records of the debtor. If any of the books of account and records are not available, explain.

NAME	ADDRESS

None d. List all financial institutions, creditors and other parties, including mercantile and trade agencies, to whom a

☐ financial statement was issued by the debtor within **two years** immediately preceding the commencement of this case.

NAME AND ADDRESS DATE ISSUED

---

20. Inventories

None ☐ a. List the dates of the last two inventories taken of your property, the name of the person who supervised the taking of each inventory, and the dollar amount and basis of each inventory.

DATE OF INVENTORY	INVENTORY SUPERVISOR	DOLLAR AMOUNT OF INVENTORY (Specify cost, market or other basis)

None ☐ b. List the name and address of the person having possession of the records of each of the inventories reported in a., above.

DATE OF INVENTORY	NAME AND ADDRESSES OF CUSTODIAN OF INVENTORY RECORDS

---

21 . Current Partners, Officers, Directors and Shareholders

None ☐ a. If the debtor is a partnership, list the nature and percentage of partnership interest of each member of the partnership.

NAME AND ADDRESS	NATURE OF INTEREST	PERCENTAGE OF INTEREST

None ☐ b. If the debtor is a corporation, list all officers and directors of the corporation, and each stockholder who directly or indirectly owns, controls, or holds 5 percent or more of the voting or equity securities of the corporation.

NAME AND ADDRESS	TITLE	NATURE AND PERCENTAGE OF STOCK OWNERSHIP

---

22 . Former partners, officers, directors and shareholders

None ☐ a. If the debtor is a partnership, list each member who withdrew from the partnership within **one year** immediately preceding the commencement of this case.

NAME	ADDRESS	DATE OF WITHDRAWAL

10

None ☐ b. If the debtor is a corporation, list all officers, or directors whose relationship with the corporation terminated within **one year** immediately preceding the commencement of this case.

NAME AND ADDRESS	TITLE	DATE OF TERMINATION

23 . Withdrawals from a partnership or distributions by a corporation

None ☐ If the debtor is a partnership or corporation, list all withdrawals or distributions credited or given to an insider, including compensation in any form, bonuses, loans, stock redemptions, options exercised and any other perquisite during **one year** immediately preceding the commencement of this case.

NAME & ADDRESS OF RECIPIENT, RELATIONSHIP TO DEBTOR	DATE AND PURPOSE OF WITHDRAWAL	AMOUNT OF MONEY OR DESCRIPTION AND VALUE OF PROPERTY

24. Tax Consolidation Group.

None ☐ If the debtor is a corporation, list the name and federal taxpayer identification number of the parent corporation of any consolidated group for tax purposes of which the debtor has been a member at any time within **six years** immediately preceding the commencement of the case.

NAME OF PARENT CORPORATION	TAXPAYER IDENTIFICATION NUMBER (EIN)

25. Pension Funds.

None ☐ If the debtor is not an individual, list the name and federal taxpayer identification number of any pension fund to which the debtor, as an employer, has been responsible for contributing at any time within **six years** immediately preceding the commencement of the case.

NAME OF PENSION FUND	TAXPAYER IDENTIFICATION NUMBER (EIN)

* * * * * *

11

[If completed by an individual or individual and spouse]

I declare under penalty of perjury that I have read the answers contained in the foregoing statement of financial affairs and any attachments thereto and that they are true and correct.

Date ____________________ Signature of Debtor ______________________________

Date ____________________ Signature of Joint Debtor (if any) ______________________________

[If completed on behalf of a partnership or corporation]

I, declare under penalty of perjury that I have read the answers contained in the foregoing statement of financial affairs and any attachments thereto and that they are true and correct to the best of my knowledge, information and belief.

Date ____________________ Signature ______________________________

____
Print Name and Title

[An individual signing on behalf of a partnership or corporation must indicate position or relationship to debtor.]

____ continuation sheets attached

Penalty for making a false statement: Fine of up to $500,000 or imprisonment for up to 5 years, or both. 18 U.S.C. §§ 152 and 3571

DECLARATION AND SIGNATURE OF NON-ATTORNEY BANKRUPTCY PETITION PREPARER (See 11 U.S.C. § 110)

I declare under penalty of perjury that: (1) I am a bankruptcy petition preparer as defined in 11 U.S.C. § 110; (2) I prepared this document for compensation and have provided the debtor with a copy of this document and the notices and information required under 11 U.S.C. §§ 110(b), 110(h), and 342(b); and, (3) if rules or guidelines have been promulgated pursuant to 11 U.S.C. § 110(h) setting a maximum fee for services chargeable by bankruptcy petition preparers, I have given the debtor notice of the maximum amount before preparing any document for filing for a debtor or accepting any fee from the debtor, as required by that section.

______________________________ ____________________
Printed or Typed Name and Title, if any, of Bankruptcy Petition Preparer Social Security No.(Required by 11 U.S.C. § 110.)

If the bankruptcy petition preparer is not an individual, state the name, title (if any), address, and social security number of the officer, principal, responsible person, or partner who signs this document.

____

____
Address

X ______________________________ ____________________
Signature of Bankruptcy Petition Preparer Date

Names and Social Security numbers of all other individuals who prepared or assisted in preparing this document if the bankruptcy petition preparer is not an individual:

If more than one person prepared this document, attach additional signed sheets conforming to the appropriate Official Form for each person.

A bankruptcy petition preparer's failure to comply with the provisions of title 11 and the Federal Rules of Bankruptcy Procedure may result in fines or imprisonment or both. 18 U.S.C. § 156.

Form 8
(10/05)

United States Bankruptcy Court

_______________ District Of _______________

In re ______________________________,
Debtor

Case No. __________________
Chapter 7

CHAPTER 7 INDIVIDUAL DEBTOR'S STATEMENT OF INTENTION

☐ I have filed a schedule of assets and liabilities which includes consumer debts secured by property of the estate.
☐ I have filed a schedule of executory contracts and unexpired leases which includes personal property subject to an unexpired lease.
☐ I intend to do the following with respect to the property of the estate which secures those debts or is subject to a lease:

Description of Secured Property	Creditor's Name	Property will be Surrendered	Property is claimed as exempt	Property will be redeemed pursuant to 11 U.S.C. § 722	Debt will be reaffirmed pursuant to 11 U.S.C. § 524(c)

Description of Leased Property	Lessor's Name	Lease will be assumed pursuant to 11 U.S.C. § 362(h)(1)(A)

Date: ________________

____
Signature of Debtor

DECLARATION OF NON-ATTORNEY BANKRUPTCY PETITION PREPARER (See 11 U.S.C. § 110)

I declare under penalty of perjury that: (1) I am a bankruptcy petition preparer as defined in 11 U.S.C. § 110; (2) I prepared this document for compensation and have provided the debtor with a copy of this document and the notices and information required under 11 U.S.C. §§ 110(b), 110(h), and 342(b); and, (3) if rules or guidelines have been promulgated pursuant to 11 U.S.C. § 110(h) setting a maximum fee for services chargeable by bankruptcy petition preparers, I have given the debtor notice of the maximum amount before preparing any document for filing for a debtor or accepting any fee from the debtor, as required in that section.

_______________________________ _______________
Printed or Typed Name of Bankruptcy Petition Preparer Social Security No. (Required under 11 U.S.C. § 110.)

If the bankruptcy petition preparer is not an individual, state the name, title (if any), address, and social security number of the officer, principal, responsible person or partner who signs this document.

____

____
Address

X_______________________________ _______________
Signature of Bankruptcy Petition Preparer Date

Names and Social Security Numbers of all other individuals who prepared or assisted in preparing this document unless the bankruptcy petition preparer is not an individual:

If more than one person prepared this document, attach additional signed sheets conforming to the appropriate Official Form for each person.

A bankruptcy petition preparer's failure to comply with the provisions of title 11 and the Federal Rules of Bankruptcy Procedure may result in fines or imprisonment or both. 11 U.S.C. § 110; 18 U.S.C. § 156.

FORM B9A (Chapter 7 Individual or Joint Debtor No Asset Case (10/05))

UNITED STATES BANKRUPTCY COURT______________ **District of**________________________

Notice of
Chapter 7 Bankruptcy Case, Meeting of Creditors, & Deadlines

[A chapter 7 bankruptcy case concerning the debtor(s) listed below was filed on ________________(date).]
or [A bankruptcy case concerning the debtor(s) listed below was originally filed under chapter_______________on
____________________(date) and was converted to a case under chapter 7 on____________________.]

You may be a creditor of the debtor. **This notice lists important deadlines.** You may want to consult an attorney to protect your rights. All documents filed in the case may be inspected at the bankruptcy clerk's office at the address listed below. NOTE: The staff of the bankruptcy clerk's office cannot give legal advice.

See Reverse Side for Important Explanations

Debtor(s) (name(s) and address):	Case Number:
	Last four digits of Social Security No./Complete EIN or other Taxpayer ID No.
All other names used by the Debtor(s) in the last 8 years (include married, maiden, and trade names):	Bankruptcy Trustee (name and address):
Attorney for Debtor(s) (name and address): Telephone number:	Telephone number:

Meeting of Creditors

Date: / / Time: ( ) A. M. ( ) P. M. Location:

Presumption of Abuse under 11 U.S.C. § 707(b)

See "Presumption of Abuse" on the reverse side.

Depending on the documents filed with the petition, one of the following statements will appear.

The presumption of abuse does not arise.
Or
The presumption of abuse arises.
Or
Insufficient information has been filed to date to permit the clerk to make any determination concerning the presumption of abuse. If more complete information, when filed, shows that the presumption has arisen, creditors will be notified.

Deadlines:

Papers must be *received* by the bankruptcy clerk's office by the following deadlines:

Deadline to File a Complaint Objecting to Discharge of the Debtor or to Determine Dischargeability of Certain Debts:

Deadline to Object to Exemptions:

Thirty (30) days after the *conclusion* of the meeting of creditors.

Creditors May Not Take Certain Actions:

In most instances, the filing of the bankruptcy case automatically stays certain collection and other actions against the debtor and the debtor's property. Under certain circumstances, the stay may be limited to 30 days or not exist at all, although the debtor can request the court to extend or impose a stay. If you attempt to collect a debt or take other action in violation of the Bankruptcy Code, you may be penalized. Consult a lawyer to determine your rights in this case.

Please Do Not File A Proof of Claim Unless You Receive a Notice To Do So.

Foreign Creditors

A creditor to whom this notice is sent at a foreign address should read the information under "Do Not File a Proof of Claim at This Time" on the reverse side.

Address of the Bankruptcy Clerk's Office:	**For the Court:**
Telephone number:	Clerk of the Bankruptcy Court:
Hours Open:	Date:

EXPLANATIONS **Form B9A (10/05)**

Filing of Chapter 7 Bankruptcy Case	A bankruptcy case under Chapter 7 of the Bankruptcy Code (title 11, United States Code) has been filed in this court by or against the debtor(s) listed on the front side, and an order for relief has been entered.
Legal Advice	The staff of the bankruptcy clerk's office cannot give legal advice. Consult a lawyer to determine your rights in this case.
Creditors Generally May Not Take Certain Actions	Prohibited collection actions are listed in Bankruptcy Code § 362. Common examples of prohibited actions include contacting the debtor by telephone, mail, or otherwise to demand repayment; taking actions to collect money or obtain property from the debtor; repossessing the debtor's property; starting or continuing lawsuits or foreclosures; and garnishing or deducting from the debtor's wages. Under certain circumstances, the stay may be limited to 30 days or not exist at all, although the debtor can request the court to extend or impose a stay.
Presumption of Abuse	If the presumption of abuse arises, creditors may have the right to file a motion to dismiss the case under § 707(b) of the Bankruptcy Code. The debtor may rebut the presumption by showing special circumstances.
Meeting of Creditors	A meeting of creditors is scheduled for the date, time, and location listed on the front side. *The debtor (both spouses in a joint case) must be present at the meeting to be questioned under oath by the trustee and by creditors.* Creditors are welcome to attend, but are not required to do so. The meeting may be continued and concluded at a later date without further notice.
Do Not File a Proof of Claim at This Time	There does not appear to be any property available to the trustee to pay creditors. *You therefore should not file a proof of claim at this time.* If it later appears that assets are available to pay creditors, you will be sent another notice telling you that you may file a proof of claim, and telling you the deadline for filing your proof of claim. If this notice is mailed to a creditor at a foreign address, the creditor may file a motion requesting the court to extend the deadline.
Discharge of Debts	The debtor is seeking a discharge of most debts, which may include your debt. A discharge means that you may never try to collect the debt from the debtor. If you believe that the debtor is not entitled to receive a discharge under Bankruptcy Code § 727 (a) *or* that a debt owed to you is not dischargeable under Bankruptcy Code § 523 (a) (2), (4), or (6), you must start a lawsuit by filing a complaint in the bankruptcy clerk's office by the "Deadline to File a Complaint Objecting to Discharge of the Debtor or to Determine Dischargeability of Certain Debts" listed on the front side. The bankruptcy clerk's office must receive the complaint and any required filing fee by that Deadline.
Exempt Property	The debtor is permitted by law to keep certain property as exempt. Exempt property will not be sold and distributed to creditors. The debtor must file a list of all property claimed as exempt. You may inspect that list at the bankruptcy clerk's office. If you believe that an exemption claimed by the debtor is not authorized by law, you may file an objection to that exemption. The bankruptcy clerk's office must receive the objections by the "Deadline to Object to Exemptions" listed on the front side.
Bankruptcy Clerk's Office	Any paper that you file in this bankruptcy case should be filed at the bankruptcy clerk's office at the address listed on the front side. You may inspect all papers filed, including the list of the debtor's property and debts and the list of the property claimed as exempt, at the bankruptcy clerk's office.
Foreign Creditors	Consult a lawyer familiar with United States bankruptcy law if you have any questions regarding your rights in this case.

Refer To Other Side For Important Deadlines and Notices

FORM B9C (Chapter 7 Individual or Joint Debtor Asset Case (10/05))

UNITED STATES BANKRUPTCY COURT_______________ **District of**_________________________

Notice of
Chapter 7 Bankruptcy Case, Meeting of Creditors, & Deadlines

[A chapter 7 bankruptcy case concerning the debtor(s) listed below was filed on ____________________(date).]
or [A bankruptcy case concerning the debtor(s) listed below was originally filed under chapter________________on
______________________(date) and was converted to a case under chapter 7 on____________________.]

You may be a creditor of the debtor. **This notice lists important deadlines.** You may want to consult an attorney to protect your rights. All documents filed in the case may be inspected at the bankruptcy clerk's office at the address listed below. NOTE: The staff of the bankruptcy clerk's office cannot give legal advice.

See Reverse Side for Important Explanations

Debtor(s) (name(s) and address):	Case Number: Last four digits of Social Security No./Complete EIN or other Taxpayer ID No.:
All other names used by the Debtor(s) in the last 8 years (include married, maiden, and trade names):	Bankruptcy Trustee (name and address):
Attorney for Debtor(s) (name and address): Telephone number:	Telephone number:

Meeting of Creditors

Date: / / Time: ( ) A. M. Location:
( ) P. M.

Presumption of Abuse under 11 U.S.C. § 707(b)
See "Presumption of Abuse" on the reverse side.

Depending on the documents filed with the petition, one of the following statements will appear.

The presumption of abuse does not arise.
Or
The presumption of abuse arises.
Or
Insufficient information has been filed to date to permit the clerk to make any determination concerning the presumption of abuse. If more complete information, when filed, shows that the presumption has arisen, creditors will be notified.

Deadlines:
Papers must be *received* by the bankruptcy clerk's office by the following deadlines:

Deadline to File a Proof of Claim:
For all creditors (except a governmental unit): For a governmental unit:

Foreign Creditors:
A creditor to whom this notice is sent at a foreign address should read the information under "Claims" on the reverse side.

Deadline to File a Complaint Objecting to Discharge of the Debtor or to Determine Dischargeability of Certain Debts:

Deadline to Object to Exemptions:
Thirty (30) days after the *conclusion* of the meeting of creditors.

Creditors May Not Take Certain Actions:
In most instances, the filing of the bankruptcy case automatically stays certain collection and other actions against the debtor and the debtor's property. Under certain circumstances, the stay may be limited to 30 days or not exist at all, although the debtor can request the court to extend or impose a stay. If you attempt to collect a debt or take other action in violation of the Bankruptcy Code, you may be penalized. Consult a lawyer to determine your rights in this case.

Address of the Bankruptcy Clerk's Office: Telephone number:	**For the Court:** Clerk of the Bankruptcy Court:
Hours Open:	Date:

EXPLANATIONS **Form B9C (10/05)**

Filing of Chapter 7 Bankruptcy Case	A bankruptcy case under Chapter 7 of the Bankruptcy Code (title 11, United States Code) has been filed in this court by or against the debtor(s) listed on the front side, and an order for relief has been entered.
Legal Advice	The staff of the bankruptcy clerk's office cannot give legal advice. Consult a lawyer to determine your rights in this case.
Creditors Generally May Not Take Certain Actions	Prohibited collection actions are listed in Bankruptcy Code § 362. Common examples of prohibited actions include contacting the debtor by telephone, mail, or otherwise to demand repayment; taking actions to collect money or obtain property from the debtor; repossessing the debtor's property; starting or continuing lawsuits or foreclosures; and garnishing or deducting from the debtor's wages. Under certain circumstances, the stay may be limited to 30 days or not exist at all, although the debtor can request the court to extend or impose a stay.
Meeting of Creditors	A meeting of creditors is scheduled for the date, time, and location listed on the front side. *The debtor (both spouses in a joint case) must be present at the meeting to be questioned under oath by the trustee and by creditors.* Creditors are welcome to attend, but are not required to do so. The meeting may be continued and concluded at a later date without further notice.
Claims	A Proof of Claim is a signed statement describing a creditor's claim. If a Proof of Claim form is not included with this notice, you can obtain one at any bankruptcy clerk's office. A secured creditor retains rights in its collateral regardless of whether that creditor files a Proof of Claim. If you do not file a Proof of Claim by the "Deadline to File a Proof of Claim" listed on the front side, you might not be paid any money on your claim from other assets in the bankruptcy case. To be paid you must file a Proof of Claim even if your claim is listed in the schedules filed by the debtor. Filing a Proof of Claim submits the creditor to the jurisdiction of the bankruptcy court, with consequences a lawyer can explain. For example, a secured creditor who files a Proof of Claim may surrender important nonmonetary rights, including the right to a jury trial. **Filing Deadline for a Foreign Creditor:** The deadlines for filing claims set forth on the front of this notice apply to all creditors. If this notice has been mailed to a creditor at a foreign address, the creditor may file a motion requesting the court to extend the deadline.
Discharge of Debts	The debtor is seeking a discharge of most debts, which may include your debt. A discharge means that you may never try to collect the debt from the debtor. If you believe that the debtor is not entitled to receive a discharge under Bankruptcy Code § 727 (a) *or* that a debt owed to you is not dischargeable under Bankruptcy Code § 523 (a) (2), (4), or (6), you must start a lawsuit by filing a complaint in the bankruptcy clerk's office by the "Deadline to File a Complaint Objecting to Discharge of the Debtor or to Determine Dischargeability of Certain Debts" listed on the front side. The bankruptcy clerk's office must receive the complaint and any required filing fee by that Deadline.
Exempt Property	The debtor is permitted by law to keep certain property as exempt. Exempt property will not be sold and distributed to creditors. The debtor must file a list of all property claimed as exempt. You may inspect that list at the bankruptcy clerk's office. If you believe that an exemption claimed by the debtor is not authorized by law, you may file an objection to that exemption. The bankruptcy clerk's office must receive the objections by the "Deadline to Object to Exemptions" listed on the front side.
Presumption of Abuse	If the presumption of abuse arises, creditors may have the right to file a motion to dismiss the case under § 707(b) of the Bankruptcy Code. The debtor may rebut the presumption by showing special circumstances.
Bankruptcy Clerk's Office	Any paper that you file in this bankruptcy case should be filed at the bankruptcy clerk's office at the address listed on the front side. You may inspect all papers filed, including the list of the debtor's property and debts and the list of the property claimed as exempt, at the bankruptcy clerk's office.
Liquidation of the Debtor's Property and Payment of Creditors' Claims	The bankruptcy trustee listed on the front of this notice will collect and sell the debtor's property that is not exempt. If the trustee can collect enough money, creditors may be paid some or all of the debts owed to them, in the order specified by the Bankruptcy Code. To make sure you receive any share of that money, you must file a Proof of Claim, as described above.
Foreign Creditors	Consult a lawyer familiar with United States bankruptcy law if you have any questions regarding your rights in this case.

Refer To Other Side For Important Deadlines and Notices

FORM B9G (Chapter 12 Individual or Joint Debtor Family Farmer (10/05))

UNITED STATES BANKRUPTCY COURT______________ **District of**______________________

Notice of
Chapter 12 Bankruptcy Case, Meeting of Creditors, & Deadlines

[The debtor(s) listed below filed a chapter 12 bankruptcy case on ____________________(date).]
or [A bankruptcy case concerning the debtor(s) listed below was originally filed under chapter________________on
____________________ (date) and was converted to a case under chapter 12 on__________________.]

You may be a creditor of the debtor. **This notice lists important deadlines.** You may want to consult an attorney to protect your rights. All documents filed in the case may be inspected at the bankruptcy clerk's office at the address listed below.
NOTE: The staff of the bankruptcy clerk's office cannot give legal advice.

See Reverse Side for Important Explanations

Debtor(s) (name(s) and address): Telephone number:	Case Number: Last four digits of Social Security No./Complete EIN or other Taxpayer ID No.:
All other names used by the Debtor(s) in the last 8 years (include married, maiden, and trade names): Attorney for Debtor(s) (name and address): Telephone number:	Bankruptcy Trustee (name and address): Telephone number:

Meeting of Creditors

Date: / / Time: ( ) A. M. ( ) P. M. Location:

Deadlines:

Papers must be *received* by the bankruptcy clerk's office by the following deadlines:

Deadline to File a Proof of Claim:

For all creditors(except a governmental unit): For a governmental unit:

Foreign Creditors

A creditor to whom this notice is sent at a foreign address should read the information under "Claims" on the reverse side.

Deadline to File a Complaint to Determine Dischargeability of Certain Debts:

Deadline to Object to Exemptions:

Thirty (30) days after the *conclusion* of the meeting of creditors.

Filing of Plan, Hearing on Confirmation of Plan

[The debtor has filed a plan. The plan or a summary of the plan is enclosed. The hearing on confirmation will be held:
Date:____________________Time:__________________Location:______________________________]
or [The debtor has filed a plan. The plan or a summary of the plan and notice of confirmation hearing will be sent separately.]
or [The debtor has not filed a plan as of this date. You will be sent separate notice of the hearing on confirmation of the plan.]

Creditors May Not Take Certain Actions:

In most instances, the filing of the bankruptcy case automatically stays certain collection and other actions against the debtor, the debtor's property, and certain codebtors. Under certain circumstances, the stay may be limited to 30 days or not exist at all, although the debtor can request the court to extend or impose a stay. If you attempt to collect a debt or take other action in violation of the Bankruptcy Code, you may be penalized. Consult a lawyer to determine your rights in this case.

Address of the Bankruptcy Clerk's Office: **Telephone number:**	**For the Court:** Clerk of the Bankruptcy Court:
Hours Open:	Date:

EXPLANATIONS **Form B9G (10/05)**

Filing of Chapter 12 Bankruptcy Case	A bankruptcy case under Chapter 12 of the Bankruptcy Code (title 11, United States Code) has been filed in this court by the debtor(s) listed on the front side, and an order for relief has been entered. Chapter 12 allows family farmers to adjust their debts pursuant to a plan. A plan is not effective unless confirmed by the court. You may object to confirmation of the plan and appear at the confirmation hearing. A copy or summary of the plan [is included with this notice] *or* [will be sent to you later], and [the confirmation hearing will be held on the date indicated on the front of this notice] *or* [you will be sent notice of the confirmation hearing]. The debtor will remain in possession of the debtor's property and may continue to operate the debtor's business unless the court orders otherwise.
Legal Advice	The staff of the bankruptcy clerk's office cannot give legal advice. Consult a lawyer to determine your rights in this case.
Creditors Generally May Not Take Certain Actions	Prohibited collection actions against the debtor and certain codebtors are listed in Bankruptcy Code § 362 and § 1201. Common examples of prohibited actions include contacting the debtor by telephone, mail, or otherwise to demand repayment; taking actions to collect money or obtain property from the debtor; repossessing the debtor's property; starting or continuing lawsuits or foreclosures; and garnishing or deducting from the debtor's wages. Under certain circumstances, the stay may be limited in duration or not exist at all, although the debtor may have the right to request the court to extend or impose a stay.
Meeting of Creditors	A meeting of creditors is scheduled for the date, time, and location listed on the front side. *The debtor (both spouses in a joint case) must be present at the meeting to be questioned under oath by the trustee and by creditors.* Creditors are welcome to attend, but are not required to do so. The meeting may be continued and concluded at a later date without further notice.
Claims	A Proof of Claim is a signed statement describing a creditor's claim. If a Proof of Claim form is not included with this notice, you can obtain one at any bankruptcy clerk's office. A secured creditor retains rights in its collateral regardless of whether that creditor files a Proof of Claim. If you do not file a Proof of Claim by the "Deadline to File a Proof of Claim" listed on the front side, you might not be paid any money on your claim from other assets in the bankruptcy case. To be paid you must file a Proof of Claim even if your claim is listed in the schedules filed by the debtor. Filing a Proof of Claim submits the creditor to the jurisdiction of the bankruptcy court, with consequences a lawyer can explain. For example, a secured creditor who files a Proof of Claim may surrender important nonmonetary rights, including the right to a jury trial. **Filing Deadline for a Foreign Creditor:** The deadlines for filing claims set forth on the front of this notice apply to all creditors. If this notice has been mailed to a creditor at a foreign address, the creditor may file a motion requesting the court to extend the deadline.
Discharge of Debts	The debtor is seeking a discharge of most debts, which may include your debt. A discharge means that you may never try to collect the debt from the debtor. If you believe that a debt owed to you is not dischargeable under Bankruptcy Code § 523 (a) (2), (4), or (6), you must start a lawsuit by filing a complaint in the bankruptcy clerk's office by the "Deadline to File a Complaint to Determine Dischargeability of Certain Debts" listed on the front side. The bankruptcy clerk's office must receive the complaint and any required filing fee by that Deadline.
Exempt Property	The debtor is permitted by law to keep certain property as exempt. Exempt property will not be sold and distributed to creditors, even if the debtor's case is converted to chapter 7. The debtor must file a list of all property claimed as exempt. You may inspect that list at the bankruptcy clerk's office. If you believe that an exemption claimed by the debtor is not authorized by law, you may file an objection to that exemption. The bankruptcy clerk's office must receive the objection by the "Deadline to Object to Exemptions" listed on the front side.
Bankruptcy Clerk's Office	Any paper that you file in this bankruptcy case should be filed at the bankruptcy clerk's office at the address listed on the front side. You may inspect all papers filed, including the list of the debtor's property and debts and the list of the property claimed as exempt, at the bankruptcy clerk's office.
Foreign Creditors	Consult a lawyer familiar with United States bankruptcy law if you have any questions regarding your rights in this case.

Refer To Other Side For Important Deadlines and Notices

FORM B9H (Chapter 12 Corporation/Partnership Family Farmer (10/05))

UNITED STATES BANKRUPTCY COURT________________ **District of**____________________________

Notice of
Chapter 12 Bankruptcy Case, Meeting of Creditors, & Deadlines

[The debtor [corporation] *or* [partnership] listed below filed a chapter 12 bankruptcy case on ____________________ (date).]
or [A bankruptcy case concerning the debtor [corporation] *or* [partnership] listed below was originally filed under chapter________________ on ______________________ (date) and was converted to a case under chapter 12 on______________________.]

You may be a creditor of the debtor. **This notice lists important deadlines.** You may want to consult an attorney to protect your rights. All documents filed in the case may be inspected at the bankruptcy clerk's office at the address listed below. NOTE: The staff of the bankruptcy clerk's office cannot give legal advice.

See Reverse Side for Important Explanations

Debtor(s) (name(s) and address): Telephone number:	Case Number:\ Last four digits of Social Security No./Complete EIN or other Taxpayer ID No.:
All other names used by the Debtor(s) in the last 8 years (include trade names): Attorney for Debtor(s) (name and address): Telephone number:	Bankruptcy Trustee (name and address): Telephone number:

Meeting of Creditors

Date: / / Time: ( ) A. M. Location:
( ) P. M.

Deadlines:

Papers must be *received* by the bankruptcy clerk's office by the following deadlines:

Deadline to File a Proof of Claim:

For all creditors(except a governmental unit): For a governmental unit:

Foreign Creditors

A creditor to whom this notice is sent at a foreign address should read the information under "Claims" on the reverse side.

Deadline to File a Complaint to Determine Dischargeability of Certain Debts:

Filing of Plan, Hearing on Confirmation of Plan

[The debtor has filed a plan. The plan or a summary of the plan is enclosed. The hearing on confirmation will be held:
Date:____________________Time:____________________Location:____________________________________]
or [The debtor has filed a plan. The plan or a summary of the plan and notice of confirmation hearing will be sent separately.]
or [The debtor has not filed a plan as of this date. You will be sent separate notice of the hearing on confirmation of the plan.]

Creditors May Not Take Certain Actions:

In most instances, the filing of the bankruptcy case automatically stays certain collection and other actions against the debtor and the debtor's property. Under certain circumstances, the stay may be limited to 30 days or not exist at all, although the debtor can request the court to extend or impose a stay. If you attempt to collect a debt or take other action in violation of the Bankruptcy Code, you may be penalized. Consult a lawyer to determine your rights in this case.

Address of the Bankruptcy Clerk's Office: **Telephone number:**	**For the Court:** Clerk of the Bankruptcy Court:
Hours Open:	Date:

EXPLANATIONS **Form B9H (10/05)**

Filing of Chapter 12 Bankruptcy Case	A bankruptcy case under Chapter 12 of the Bankruptcy Code (title 11, United States Code) has been filed in this court by the debtor listed on the front side, and an order for relief has been entered. Chapter 12 allows family farmers to adjust their debts pursuant to a plan. A plan is not effective unless confirmed by the court. You may object to confirmation of the plan and appear at the confirmation hearing. A copy or summary of the plan [is included with this notice] *or* [will be sent to you later], and [the confirmation hearing will be held on the date indicated on the front of this notice] *or* [you will be sent notice of the confirmation hearing]. The debtor will remain in possession of the debtor's property and may continue to operate the debtor's business unless the court orders otherwise.
Legal Advice	The staff of the bankruptcy clerk's office cannot give legal advice. Consult a lawyer to determine your rights in this case.
Creditors Generally May Not Take Certain Actions	Prohibited collection actions against the debtor and certain codebtors are listed in Bankruptcy Code § 362 and § 1201. Common examples of prohibited actions include contacting the debtor by telephone, mail, or otherwise to demand repayment; taking actions to collect money or obtain property from the debtor; repossessing the debtor's property; and starting or continuing lawsuits or foreclosures. Under certain circumstances, the stay may be limited in duration or not exist at all, although the debtor may have the right to request the court to extend or impose a stay.
Meeting of Creditors	A meeting of creditors is scheduled for the date, time, and location listed on the front side. *The debtor's representative must be present at the meeting to be questioned under oath by the trustee and by creditors.* Creditors are welcome to attend, but are not required to do so. The meeting may be continued and concluded at a later date without further notice.
Claims	A Proof of Claim is a signed statement describing a creditor's claim. If a Proof of Claim form is not included with this notice, you can obtain one at any bankruptcy clerk's office. A secured creditor retains rights in its collateral regardless of whether that creditor files a Proof of Claim. If you do not file a Proof of Claim by the "Deadline to File a Proof of Claim" listed on the front side, you might not be paid any money on your claim from other assets in the bankruptcy case. To be paid you must file a Proof of Claim even if your claim is listed in the schedules filed by the debtor. Filing a Proof of Claim submits the creditor to the jurisdiction of the bankruptcy court, with consequences a lawyer can explain. For example, a secured creditor who files a Proof of Claim may surrender important nonmonetary rights, including the right to a jury trial. **Filing Deadline for a Foreign Creditor:** The deadlines for filing claims set forth on the front of this notice apply to all creditors. If this notice has been mailed to a creditor at a foreign address, the creditor may file a motion requesting the court to extend the deadline.
Discharge of Debts	The debtor is seeking a discharge of most debts, which may include your debt. A discharge means that you may never try to collect the debt from the debtor. If you believe that a debt owed to you is not dischargeable under Bankruptcy Code § 523 (a) (2), (4), or (6), you must start a lawsuit by filing a complaint in the bankruptcy clerk's office by the "Deadline to File a Complaint to Determine Dischargeability of Certain Debts" listed on the front side. The bankruptcy clerk's office must receive the complaint and any required filing fee by that Deadline.
Bankruptcy Clerk's Office	Any paper that you file in this bankruptcy case should be filed at the bankruptcy clerk's office at the address listed on the front side. You may inspect all papers filed, including the list of the debtor's property and debts and the list of the property claimed as exempt, at the bankruptcy clerk's office.
Foreign Creditors	Consult a lawyer familiar with United States bankruptcy law if you have any questions regarding your rights in this case.

Refer To Other Side For Important Deadlines and Notices

FORM B9I (Chapter 13 Case (10/05))

UNITED STATES BANKRUPTCY COURT ______________ **District of** ______________________

Notice of
Chapter 13 Bankruptcy Case, Meeting of Creditors, & Deadlines

[The debtor(s) listed below filed a chapter 13 bankruptcy case on __________________ (date).]
or [A bankruptcy case concerning the debtor(s) listed below was originally filed under chapter ______________
on ____________________ (date) and was converted to a case under chapter 13 on ____________________.]

You may be a creditor of the debtor. **This notice lists important deadlines.** You may want to consult an attorney to protect your rights. All documents filed in the case may be inspected at the bankruptcy clerk's office at the address listed below.
NOTE: The staff of the bankruptcy clerk's office cannot give legal advice.

See Reverse Side for Important Explanations

Debtor(s) (name(s) and address): Telephone number:	Case Number: Last four digits of Social Security No./Complete EIN or other Taxpayer ID No.:
All other names used by the Debtor(s) in the last 8 years (include married, maiden, and trade names):	Bankruptcy Trustee (name and address): Telephone number:
Attorney for Debtor(s) (name and address): Telephone number:	

Meeting of Creditors

Date: / / Time: ( ) A. M. ( ) P. M. Location:

Deadlines:

Papers must be *received* by the bankruptcy clerk's office by the following deadlines:

Deadline to File a Proof of Claim:

For all creditors(except a governmental unit): For a governmental unit:

Foreign Creditors

A creditor to whom this notice is sent at a foreign address should read the information under "Claims" on the reverse side.

Deadline to File a Complaint to Determine Dischargeability of Certain Debts:

Deadline to Object to Exemptions:

Thirty (30) days after the *conclusion* of the meeting of creditors.

Filing of Plan, Hearing on Confirmation of Plan

[The debtor has filed a plan. The plan or a summary of the plan is enclosed. The hearing on confirmation will be held:
Date:____________________Time:__________________Location:______________________________]
or [The debtor has filed a plan. The plan or a summary of the plan and notice of confirmation hearing will be sent separately.]
or [The debtor has not filed a plan as of this date. You will be sent separate notice of the hearing on confirmation of the plan.]

Creditors May Not Take Certain Actions:

In most instances, the filing of the bankruptcy case automatically stays certain collection and other actions against the debtor, the debtor's property, and certain codebtors. Under certain circumstances, the stay may be limited to 30 days or not exist at all, although the debtor can request the court to extend or impose a stay. If you attempt to collect a debt or take other action in violation of the Bankruptcy Code, you may be penalized. Consult a lawyer to determine your rights in this case.

Address of the Bankruptcy Clerk's Office: **Telephone number:**	**For the Court:** Clerk of the Bankruptcy Court:
Hours Open:	Date:

EXPLANATIONS **Form B9I (10/05)**

Filing of Chapter 13 Bankruptcy Case	A bankruptcy case under Chapter 13 of the Bankruptcy Code (title 11, United States Code) has been filed in this court by the debtor(s) listed on the front side, and an order for relief has been entered. Chapter 13 allows an individual with regular income and debts below a specified amount to adjust debts pursuant to a plan. A plan is not effective unless confirmed by the bankruptcy court. You may object to confirmation of the plan and appear at the confirmation hearing. A copy or summary of the plan [is included with this notice] *or* [will be sent to you later], and [the confirmation hearing will be held on the date indicated on the front of this notice] *or* [you will be sent notice of the confirmation hearing]. The debtor will remain in possession of the debtor's property and may continue to operate the debtor's business, if any, unless the court orders otherwise.
Legal Advice	The staff of the bankruptcy clerk's office cannot give legal advice. Consult a lawyer to determine your rights in this case.
Creditors Generally May Not Take Certain Actions	Prohibited collection actions against the debtor and certain codebtors are listed in Bankruptcy Code § 362 and § 1301. Common examples of prohibited actions include contacting the debtor by telephone, mail, or otherwise to demand repayment; taking actions to collect money or obtain property from the debtor; repossessing the debtor's property; starting or continuing lawsuits or foreclosures; and garnishing or deducting from the debtor's wages. Under certain circumstances, the stay may be limited to 30 days or not exist at all, although the debtor can request the court to exceed or impose a stay.
Meeting of Creditors	A meeting of creditors is scheduled for the date, time, and location listed on the front side. *The debtor (both spouses in a joint case) must be present at the meeting to be questioned under oath by the trustee and by creditors.* Creditors are welcome to attend, but are not required to do so. The meeting may be continued and concluded at a later date without further notice
Claims	A Proof of Claim is a signed statement describing a creditor's claim. If a Proof of Claim form is not included with this notice, you can obtain one at any bankruptcy clerk's office. A secured creditor retains rights in its collateral regardless of whether that creditor files a Proof of Claim. If you do not file a Proof of Claim by the "Deadline to File a Proof of Claim" listed on the front side, you might not be paid any money on your claim from other assets in the bankruptcy case. To be paid you must file a Proof of Claim even if your claim is listed in the schedules filed by the debtor. Filing a Proof of Claim submits the creditor to the jurisdiction of the bankruptcy court, with consequences a lawyer can explain. For example, a secured creditor who files a Proof of Claim may surrender important nonmonetary rights, including the right to a jury trial. **Filing Deadline for a Foreign Creditor:** The deadlines for filing claims set forth on the front of this notice apply to all creditors. If this notice has been mailed to a creditor at a foreign address, the creditor may file a motion requesting the court to extend the deadline.
Discharge of Debts	The debtor is seeking a discharge of most debts, which may include your debt. A discharge means that you may never try to collect the debt from the debtor. If you believe that a debt owed to you is not dischargeable under Bankruptcy Code § 523 (a) (2) or (4), you must start a lawsuit by filing a complaint in the bankruptcy clerk's office by the "Deadline to File a Complaint to Determine Dischargeability of Certain Debts" listed on the front side. The bankruptcy clerk's office must receive the complaint and any required filing fee by that deadline.
Exempt Property	The debtor is permitted by law to keep certain property as exempt. Exempt property will not be sold and distributed to creditors, even if the debtor's case is converted to chapter 7. The debtor must file a list of all property claimed as exempt. You may inspect that list at the bankruptcy clerk's office. If you believe that an exemption claimed by the debtor is not authorized by law, you may file an objection to that exemption. The bankruptcy clerk's office must receive the objection by the "Deadline to Object to Exemptions" listed on the front side.
Bankruptcy Clerk's Office	Any paper that you file in this bankruptcy case should be filed at the bankruptcy clerk's office at the address listed on the front side. You may inspect all papers filed, including the list of the debtor's property and debts and the list of the property claimed as exempt, at the bankruptcy clerk's office.
Foreign Creditors	Consult a lawyer familiar with United States bankruptcy law if you have any questions regarding your rights in this case.

Refer To Other Side For Important Deadlines and Notices

FORM B10 (Official Form 10) (10/05)

UNITED STATES BANKRUPTCY COURT ________________ DISTRICT OF ________________

PROOF OF CLAIM

Name of Debtor

Case Number

NOTE: This form should not be used to make a claim for an administrative expense arising after the commencement of the case. A "request" for payment of an administrative expense may be filed pursuant to 11 U.S.C. § 503.

Name of Creditor (The person or other entity to whom the debtor owes money or property):

Name and address where notices should be sent:

Telephone number:

☐ Check box if you are aware that anyone else has filed a proof of claim relating to your claim. Attach copy of statement giving particulars.

☐ Check box if you have never received any notices from the bankruptcy court in this case.

☐ Check box if the address differs from the address on the envelope sent to you by the court.

THIS SPACE IS FOR COURT USE ONLY

Last four digits of account or other number by which creditor identifies debtor:

Check here if this claim ☐ replaces ☐ amends a previously filed claim, dated:__________

1. Basis for Claim

☐ Goods sold
☐ Services performed
☐ Money loaned
☐ Personal injury/wrongful death
☐ Taxes
☐ Other ______________________

☐ Retiree benefits as defined in 11 U.S.C. § 1114(a)
☐ Wages, salaries, and compensation (fill out below)
Last four digits of your SS #: _______
Unpaid compensation for services performed
from ________________ to ________________
(date) (date)

2. Date debt was incurred:

3. If court judgment, date obtained:

4. Classification of Claim. Check the appropriate box or boxes that best describe your claim and state the amount of the claim at the time case filed. See reverse side for important explanations.

Unsecured Nonpriority Claim $______________

☐ Check this box if: a) there is no collateral or lien securing your claim, or b) your claim exceeds the value of the property securing it, or if c) none or only part of your claim is entitled to priority.

Unsecured Priority Claim

☐ Check this box if you have an unsecured claim, all or part of which is entitled to priority.

Amount entitled to priority $__________

Specify the priority of the claim:

☐ Domestic support obligations under 11 U.S.C. § 507(a)(1)(A) or (a)(1)(B)

☐ Wages, salaries, or commissions (up to $10,000),* earned within 180 days before filing of the bankruptcy petition or cessation of the debtor's business, whichever is earlier - 11 U.S.C. § 507(a)(4).

☐ Contributions to an employee benefit plan - 11 U.S.C. § 507(a)(5).

Secured Claim

☐ Check this box if your claim is secured by collateral (including a right of setoff).

Brief Description of Collateral:
☐ Real Estate ☐ Motor Vehicle ☐ Other________

Value of Collateral: $________________

Amount of arrearage and other charges at time case filed included in secured claim, if any: $______________

☐ Up to $2,225* of deposits toward purchase, lease, or rental of property or services for personal, family, or household use - 11 U.S.C. § 507(a)(7).

☐ Taxes or penalties owed to governmental units - 11 U.S.C. § 507(a)(8).

☐ Other - Specify applicable paragraph of 11 U.S.C. § 507(a)(____).

**Amounts are subject to adjustment on 4/1/07 and every 3 years thereafter with respect to cases commenced on or after the date of adjustment.*

5. Total Amount of Claim at Time Case Filed: $__________ __________ __________ __________
(unsecured) (secured) (priority) (Total)

☐ Check this box if claim includes interest or other charges in addition to the principal amount of the claim. Attach itemized statement of all interest or additional charges.

6. Credits: The amount of all payments on this claim has been credited and deducted for the purpose of making this proof of claim.

7. Supporting Documents: *Attach copies of supporting documents,* such as promissory notes, purchase orders, invoices, itemized statements of running accounts, contracts, court judgments, mortgages, security agreements, and evidence of perfection of lien. DO NOT SEND ORIGINAL DOCUMENTS. If the documents are not available, explain. If the documents are voluminous, attach a summary.

8. Date-Stamped Copy: To receive an acknowledgment of the filing of your claim, enclose a stamped, self-addressed envelope and copy of this proof of claim.

THIS SPACE IS FOR COURT USE ONLY

Date

Sign and print the name and title, if any, of the creditor or other person authorized to file this claim (attach copy of power of attorney, if any):

Penalty for presenting fraudulent claim: Fine of up to $500,000 or imprisonment for up to 5 years, or both. 18 U.S.C. §§ 152 and 3571.

FORM B10 (Official Form 10) (10/05)

INSTRUCTIONS FOR PROOF OF CLAIM FORM

The instructions and definitions below are general explanations of the law. In particular types of cases or circumstances, such as bankruptcy cases that are not filed voluntarily by a debtor, there may be exceptions to these general rules.

— DEFINITIONS —

Debtor

The person, corporation, or other entity that has filed a bankruptcy case is called the debtor.

Creditor

A creditor is any person, corporation, or other entity to whom the debtor owed a debt on the date that the bankruptcy case was filed.

Proof of Claim

A form telling the bankruptcy court how much the debtor owed a creditor at the time the bankruptcy case was filed (the amount of the creditor's claim). This form must be filed with the clerk of the bankruptcy court where the bankruptcy case was filed.

Secured Claim

A claim is a secured claim to the extent that the creditor has a lien on property of the debtor (collateral) that gives the creditor the right to be paid from that property before creditors who do not have liens on the property.

Examples of liens are a mortgage on real estate and a security interest in a car, truck, boat, television set, or other item of property. A lien may have been obtained through a court proceeding before the bankruptcy case began; in some states a court judgment is a lien. In addition, to the extent a creditor also owes money to the debtor (has a right of setoff), the creditor's claim may be a secured claim. (See also *Unsecured Claim.*)

Unsecured Claim

If a claim is not a secured claim it is an unsecured claim. A claim may be partly secured and partly unsecured if the property on which a creditor has a lien is not worth enough to pay the creditor in full.

Unsecured Priority Claim

Certain types of unsecured claims are given priority, so they are to be paid in bankruptcy cases before most other unsecured claims (if there is sufficient money or property available to pay these claims). The most common types of priority claims are listed on the proof of claim form. Unsecured claims that are not specifically given priority status by the bankruptcy laws are classified as *Unsecured Nonpriority Claims.*

Items to be completed in Proof of Claim form (if not already filled in)

Court, Name of Debtor, and Case Number:

Fill in the name of the federal judicial district where the bankruptcy case was filed (for example, Central District of California), the name of the debtor in the bankruptcy case, and the bankruptcy case number. If you received a notice of the case from the court, all of this information is near the top of the notice.

Information about Creditor:

Complete the section giving the name, address, and telephone number of the creditor to whom the debtor owes money or property, and the debtor's account number, if any. If anyone else has already filed a proof of claim relating to this debt, if you never received notices from the bankruptcy court about this case, if your address differs from that to which the court sent notice, or if this proof of claim replaces or changes a proof of claim that was already filed, check the appropriate box on the form.

1. Basis for Claim:

Check the type of debt for which the proof of claim is being filed. If the type of debt is not listed, check "Other" and briefly describe the type of debt. If you were an employee of the debtor, fill in your social security number and the dates of work for which you were not paid.

2. Date Debt Incurred:

Fill in the date when the debt first was owed by the debtor.

3. Court Judgments:

If you have a court judgment for this debt, state the date the court entered the judgment.

4. Classification of Claim

Secured Claim:

Check the appropriate place if the claim is a secured claim. You must state the type and value of property that is collateral for the claim, attach copies of the documentation of your lien, and state the amount past due on the claim as of the date the bankruptcy case was filed. A claim may be partly secured and partly unsecured. (See DEFINITIONS, above).

Unsecured Priority Claim:

Check the appropriate place if you have an unsecured priority claim, and state the amount entitled to priority. (See DEFINITIONS, above). A claim may be partly priority and partly nonpriority if, for example, the claim is for more than the amount given priority by the law. Check the appropriate place to specify the type of priority claim.

Unsecured Nonpriority Claim:

Check the appropriate place if you have an unsecured nonpriority claim, sometimes referred to as a "general unsecured claim". (See DEFINITIONS, above.) If your claim is partly secured and partly unsecured, state here the amount that is unsecured. If part of your claim is entitled to priority, state here the amount **not** entitled to priority.

5. Total Amount of Claim at Time Case Filed:

Fill in the total amount of the entire claim. If interest or other charges in addition to the principal amount of the claim are included, check the appropriate place on the form and attach an itemization of the interest and charges.

6. Credits:

By signing this proof of claim, you are stating under oath that in calculating the amount of your claim you have given the debtor credit for all payments received from the debtor.

7. Supporting Documents:

You must attach to this proof of claim form copies of documents that show the debtor owes the debt claimed or, if the documents are too lengthy, a summary of those documents. If documents are not available, you must attach an explanation of why they are not available.

Form 16A
(10/05)

Form 16A. CAPTION (FULL)

United States Bankruptcy Court

_______________ District Of _______________

In re ____, *[Set forth here all names including married, maiden, and trade names used by debtor within last 8 years.]* Debtor	)	Case No. ________________
Address ____ ____	)	Chapter ___________
Last four digits of Social Security No(s).: ______________ ____	)	
Employer's Tax Identification No(s). *[if any]:* __________ ____	)	

[Designation of Character of Paper]

Form 18
(10/05)

United States Bankruptcy Court

______________ District Of ______________

In re ____________________________________,
[Set forth here all names including married, maiden, and trade names used by debtor within last 8 years.]
Debtor

Case No. ______________

Address ____________________________________
____

Chapter 7

Last four digits of Social Security No(s).: ____________________
____
Employer's Tax Identification No(s). *[if any]*:____________________
____

DISCHARGE OF DEBTOR

It appearing that the debtor is entitled to a discharge, **IT IS ORDERED:** The debtor is granted a discharge under section 727 of title 11, United States Code, (the Bankruptcy Code).

Dated: ____________________

BY THE COURT

____
United States Bankruptcy Judge

SEE THE BACK OF THIS ORDER FOR IMPORTANT INFORMATION.

Official Form 18 - Contd.
(10/05)

EXPLANATION OF BANKRUPTCY DISCHARGE IN A CHAPTER 7 CASE

This court order grants a discharge to the person named as the debtor. It is not a dismissal of the case and it does not determine how much money, if any, the trustee will pay to creditors.

Collection of Discharged Debts Prohibited

The discharge prohibits any attempt to collect from the debtor a debt that has been discharged. For example, a creditor is not permitted to contact a debtor by mail, phone, or otherwise, to file or continue a lawsuit, to attach wages or other property, or to take any other action to collect a discharged debt from the debtor. *[In a case involving community property:* There are also special rules that protect certain community property owned by the debtor's spouse, even if that spouse did not file a bankruptcy case.] A creditor who violates this order can be required to pay damages and attorney's fees to the debtor.

However, a creditor may have the right to enforce a valid lien, such as a mortgage or security interest, against the debtor's property after the bankruptcy, if that lien was not avoided or eliminated in the bankruptcy case. Also, a debtor may voluntarily pay any debt that has been discharged.

Debts That are Discharged

The chapter 7 discharge order eliminates a debtor's legal obligation to pay a debt that is discharged. Most, but not all, types of debts are discharged if the debt existed on the date the bankruptcy case was filed. (If this case was begun under a different chapter of the Bankruptcy Code and converted to chapter 7, the discharge applies to debts owed when the bankruptcy case was converted.)

Debts that are Not Discharged.

Some of the common types of debts which are not discharged in a chapter 7 bankruptcy case are:

a. Debts for most taxes;

b. Debts incurred to pay nondischargeable taxes;

c. Debts that are domestic support obligations;

d. Debts for most student loans;

e. Debts for most fines, penalties, forfeitures, or criminal restitution obligations;

f. Debts for personal injuries or death caused by the debtor's operation of a motor vehicle, vessel, or aircraft while intoxicated;

g. Some debts which were not properly listed by the debtor;

h. Debts that the bankruptcy court specifically has decided or will decide in this bankruptcy case are not discharged;

i. Debts for which the debtor has given up the discharge protections by signing a reaffirmation agreement in compliance with the Bankruptcy Code requirements for reaffirmation of debts.

j. Debts owed to certain pension, profit sharing, stock bonus, other retirement plans, or to the Thrift Savings Plan for federal employees for certain types of loans from these plans.

This information is only a general summary of the bankruptcy discharge. There are exceptions to these general rules. Because the law is complicated, you may want to consult an attorney to determine the exact effect of the discharge in this case.

Form 19A
(10/05)

United States Bankruptcy Court

_______________ District Of _______________

In re ______________________,
Debtor

Case No. ____________________

Chapter ____________

DECLARATION AND SIGNATURE OF NON-ATTORNEY BANKRUPTCY PETITION PREPARER (11 U.S.C. § 110)

I declare under penalty of perjury that:

(1) I am a bankruptcy petition preparer as defined in 11 U.S.C. § 110;
(2) I prepared the accompanying document for compensation and have provided the debtor with a copy of that document and the notices and information required under 11 U.S.C. §§ 110(b), 110(h), and 342 (b); and
(3) if rules or guidelines have been promulgated pursuant to 11 U.S.C. § 110(h) setting a maximum fee for services chargeable by bankruptcy petition preparers, I have given the debtor notice of the maximum amount before preparing any document for filing for a debtor or accepting any fee from the debtor, as required by that section.

____
Printed or Typed Name of Bankruptcy Petition Preparer

If the bankruptcy petition preparer is not an individual, state the name, address, and social security number of the officer, principal, responsible person or partner who signs this document.

____
Social Security No.

____

____
Address

X ____ ____________
Signature of Bankruptcy Petition Preparer Date

Names and Social Security numbers of all other individuals who prepared or assisted in preparing this document, unless the bankruptcy petition preparer is not an individual:

If more than one person prepared this document, attach additional signed sheets conforming to the appropriate Official Form for each person.

A bankruptcy petition preparer's failure to comply with the provisions of title 11 and the Federal Rules of Bankruptcy Procedure may result in fines or imprisonment or both. 11 U.S.C. § 110; 18 U.S.C. § 156.

Form 19B
(10/05)

United States Bankruptcy Court

_______________ District Of _______________

In re ________________________________,
Debtor

Case No. ________________

Chapter _____________

NOTICE TO DEBTOR BY NON-ATTORNEY BANKRUPTCY PETITION PREPARER

[Must be filed with any document prepared by a bankruptcy petition preparer.]

I am a bankruptcy petition preparer. I am not an attorney and may not practice law or give legal advice. Before preparing any document for filing as defined in § 110(a)(2) of the Bankruptcy Code or accepting any fees, I am required by law to provide you with this notice concerning bankruptcy petition preparers. Under the law, § 110 of the Bankruptcy Code (11 U.S.C. § 110), I am forbidden to offer you any legal advice, including advice about any of the following:

- whether to file a petition under the Bankruptcy Code (11 U.S.C. § 101 et seq.);
- whether commencing a case under chapter 7, 11, 12, or 13 is appropriate;
- whether your debts will be eliminated or discharged in a case under the Bankruptcy Code;
- whether you will be able to retain your home, car, or other property after commencing a case under the Bankruptcy Code;
- concerning the tax consequences of a case brought under the Bankruptcy Code;
- concerning the dischargeability of tax claims;
- whether you may or should promise to repay debts to a creditor or enter into a reaffirmation agreement with a creditor to reaffirm a debt;
- concerning how to characterize the nature of your interests in property or your debts; or
- concerning bankruptcy procedures and rights.

[The notice may provide additional examples of legal advice that a bankruptcy petition preparer is not authorized to give.]

In addition, under 11 U.S.C. § 110(h), the Supreme Court or the Judicial Conference of the United States may promulgate rules or guidelines setting a maximum allowable fee chargeable by a bankruptcy petition preparer. As required by law, I have notified you of the maximum amount, if any, before preparing any document for filing or accepting any fee from you.

____
Signature of Debtor Date
[In a joint case, both spouses must sign.]

____
Joint Debtor (if any) Date

Form 19B Cont.
(10/05)

DECLARATION AND SIGNATURE OF NON-ATTORNEY BANKRUPTCY PETITION PREPARER (*See* 11 U.S.C. § 110)

I declare under penalty of perjury that: (1) I am a bankruptcy petition preparer as defined in 11 U.S.C. § 110; (2) I prepared this document for compensation and have provided the debtor with a copy of this document and the notices and information required under 11 U.S.C. §§ 110(b), 110(h), and 342(b); and (3) if rules or guidelines have been promulgated pursuant to 11 U.S.C. § 110(h) setting a maximum fee for services chargeable by bankruptcy petition preparers, I have given the debtor notice of the maximum amount before preparing any document for filing for a debtor or accepting any fee from the debtor, as required by that section.

______________________________________ ____________________
Printed or Typed Name and Title, if any, of Bankruptcy Petition Preparer

Social Security No. (Required by 11 U.S.C. § 110.)

If the bankruptcy petition preparer is not an individual, state the name, title (if any), address, and social security number of the officer, principal, responsible person, or partner who signs this document.

____

____
Address

X __________________________________ ______________________
Signature of Bankruptcy Petition Preparer

Date

Names and Social Security numbers of all other individuals who prepared or assisted in preparing this document, unless the bankruptcy petition preparer is not an individual:

If more than one person prepared this document, attach additional signed sheets conforming to the appropriate Official Form for each person.

A bankruptcy petition preparer's failure to comply with the provisions of title 11 and the Federal Rules of Bankruptcy Procedure may result in fines or imprisonment or both. 11 U.S.C. § 110; 18 U.S.C. § 156.

Form B22A (Chapter 7) (10/05)

In re ______________________________
Debtor(s)

Case Number: ____________________
(If known)

Check the box as directed in Parts I, III, and VI of this statement.
☐ **Presumption arises**
☐ **Presumption does not arise**

STATEMENT OF CURRENT MONTHLY INCOME AND MEANS TEST CALCULATION

FOR USE IN CHAPTER 7

In addition to Schedules I and J, this statement must be completed by every individual Chapter 7 debtor, whether or not filing jointly, whose debts are primarily consumer debts. Joint debtors may complete one statement only.

Part I. EXCLUSION FOR DISABLED VETERANS

1	If you are a disabled veteran described in the Veteran's Declaration in this Part I, (1) check the box at the beginning of the Veteran's Declaration, (2) check the "Presumption does not arise" box at the top of this statement, and (3) complete the verification in Part VIII. Do not complete any of the remaining parts of this statement. ☐ **Veteran's Declaration.** By checking this box, I declare under penalty of perjury that I am a disabled veteran (as defined in 38 U.S.C. § 3741(1)) whose indebtedness occurred primarily during a period in which I was on active duty (as defined in 10 U.S.C. § 101(d)(1)) or while I was performing a homeland defense activity (as defined in 32 U.S.C. §901(1)).

Part II. CALCULATION OF MONTHLY INCOME FOR § 707(b)(7) EXCLUSION

2	**Marital/filing status.** Check the box that applies and complete the balance of this part of this statement as directed. a. ☐ Unmarried. **Complete only Column A ("Debtor's Income") for Lines 3-11.** b. ☐ Married, not filing jointly, with declaration of separate households. By checking this box, debtor declares under penalty of perjury: "My spouse and I are legally separated under applicable non-bankruptcy law or my spouse and I are living apart other than for the purpose of evading the requirements of § 707(b)(2)(A) of the Bankruptcy Code." **Complete only Column A ("Debtor's Income") for Lines 3-11.** c. ☐ Married, not filing jointly, without the declaration of separate households set out in Line 2.b above. **Complete both Column A ("Debtor's Income") and Column B (Spouse's Income) for Lines 3-11.** d. ☐ Married, filing jointly. **Complete both Column A ("Debtor's Income") and Column B ("Spouse's Income") for Lines 3-11.**		
	All figures must reflect average monthly income for the six calendar months prior to filing the bankruptcy case, ending on the last day of the month before the filing. If you received different amounts of income during these six months, you must total the amounts received during the six months, divide this total by six, and enter the result on the appropriate line.	**Column A Debtor's Income**	**Column B Spouse's Income**
3	**Gross wages, salary, tips, bonuses, overtime, commissions.**	$	$
4	**Income from the operation of a business, profession, or farm.** Subtract Line b from Line a and enter the difference on Line 4. Do not enter a number less than zero. **Do not include any part of the business expenses entered on Line b as a deduction in Part V.** a. Gross receipts — $ b. Ordinary and necessary business expenses — $ c. Business income — Subtract Line b from Line a	$	$
5	**Rent and other real property income.** Subtract Line b from Line a and enter the difference on Line 5. Do not enter a number less than zero. **Do not include any part of the operating expenses entered on Line b as a deduction in Part V.** a. Gross receipts — $ b. Ordinary and necessary operating expenses — $ c. Rental income — Subtract Line b from Line a	$	$
6	**Interest, dividends, and royalties.**	$	$
7	**Pension and retirement income.**	$	$
8	**Regular contributions to the household expenses of the debtor or the debtor's dependents, including child or spousal support.** Do not include contributions from the debtor's spouse if Column B is completed.	$	$

9	**Unemployment compensation.** Enter the amount in Column A and, if applicable, Column B. However, if you contend that unemployment compensation received by you or your spouse was a benefit under the Social Security Act, do not list the amount of such compensation in Column A or B, but instead state the amount in the space below: Unemployment compensation claimed to be a benefit under the Social Security Act — Debtor $ ________ Spouse $ ________	$	$
10	**Income from all other sources.** If necessary, list additional sources on a separate page. **Do not include** any benefits received under the Social Security Act or payments received as a victim of a war crime, crime against humanity, or as a victim of international or domestic terrorism. Specify source and amount. a. ________ $ b. ________ $ Total and enter on Line 10	$	$
11	**Subtotal of Current Monthly Income for § 707(b)(7).** Add Lines 3 thru 10 in Column A, and, if Column B is completed, add Lines 3 through 10 in Column B. Enter the total(s).	$	$
12	**Total Current Monthly Income for § 707(b)(7).** If Column B has been completed, add Line 11, Column A to Line 11, Column B, and enter the total. If Column B has not been completed, enter the amount from Line 11, Column A.	$	

Part III. APPLICATION OF § 707(b)(7) EXCLUSION

13	**Annualized Current Monthly Income for § 707(b)(7).** Multiply the amount from Line 12 by the number 12 and enter the result.	$
14	**Applicable median family income.** Enter the median family income for the applicable state and household size. (This information is available by family size at www.usdoj.gov/ust/ or from the clerk of the bankruptcy court.) a. Enter debtor's state of residence: ________ b. Enter debtor's household size: ________	$
15	**Application of Section 707(b)(7).** Check the applicable box and proceed as directed. ☐ **The amount on Line 13 is less than or equal to the amount on Line 14.** Check the "Presumption does not arise" box at the top of page 1 of this statement, and complete Part VIII; do not complete Parts IV, V, VI, or VII. ☐ **The amount on Line 13 is more than the amount on Line 14.** Complete the remaining parts of this statement.	

Complete Parts IV, V, VI, and VII of this statement only if required. (See Line 15.)

Part IV. CALCULATION OF CURRENT MONTHLY INCOME FOR § 707(b)(2)

16	**Enter the amount from Line 12.**	$
17	**Marital adjustment.** If you checked the box at Line 2.c, enter the amount of the income listed in Line 11, Column B that was NOT regularly contributed to the household expenses of the debtor or the debtor's dependents. If you did not check box at Line 2.c, enter zero.	$
18	**Current monthly income for § 707(b)(2).** Subtract Line 17 from Line 16 and enter the result.	$

Part V. CALCULATION OF DEDUCTIONS ALLOWED UNDER § 707(b)(2)

Subpart A: Deductions under Standards of the Internal Revenue Service (IRS)

19	**National Standards: food, clothing, household supplies, personal care, and miscellaneous.** Enter "Total" amount from IRS National Standards for Allowable Living Expenses for the applicable family size and income level. (This information is available at www.usdoj.gov/ust/ or from the clerk of the bankruptcy court.)	$

20	~~**Local Standards: housing and utilities.** Enter the amount of the IRS Housing and Utilities Standards allowance for your county and family size (this information is available at www.usdoj.gov/ust/ or from the clerk of the bankruptcy court), adjusted to deduct any portion of the allowance that includes payments on debts secured by your home, listed in Line 41.~~ **(Under revision)**		$
21	**Local Standards: transportation; vehicle operation/public transportation expense.** You are entitled to an expense allowance in this category regardless of whether you pay the expenses of operating a vehicle and regardless of whether you use public transportation. Check the number of vehicles for which you pay the operating expenses or for which the operating expenses are included as a contribution to your household expenses in Line 8. ☐ 0 ☐ 1 ☐ 2 or more. Enter the amount from IRS Transportation Standards, Operating Costs & Public Transportation Costs for the applicable number of vehicles in the applicable Metropolitan Statistical Area or Census Region. (This information is available at www.usdoj.gov/ust/ or from the clerk of the bankruptcy court.)		$
22	**Local Standards: transportation ownership/lease expense; Vehicle 1.** Check the number of vehicles for which you claim an ownership/lease expense. (You may not claim an ownership/lease expense for more than two vehicles.) ☐ 1 ☐ 2 or more. Enter, in Line a below, the amount of the IRS Transportation Standards, Ownership Costs, First Car (available at www.usdoj.gov/ust/ or from the clerk of the bankruptcy court); enter in Line b the total of the Average Monthly Payments for any debts secured by Vehicle 1, as stated in Line 41; subtract Line b from Line a and enter the result in Line 22. **Do not enter an amount less than zero.**		
	a. IRS Transportation Standards, Ownership Costs, First Car	$	
	b. Average Monthly Payment for any debts secured by Vehicle 1, as stated in Line 41	$	
	c. Net ownership/lease expense for Vehicle 1	Subtract Line b from Line a.	$
23	**Local Standards: transportation ownership/lease expense; Vehicle 2.** Complete this Line only if you checked the "2 or more" Box in Line 23. Enter, in Line a below, the amount of the IRS Transportation Standards, Ownership Costs, Second Car (available at www.usdoj.gov/ust/ or from the clerk of the bankruptcy court); enter in Line b the total of the Average Monthly Payments for any debts secured by Vehicle 2, as stated in Line 41; subtract Line b from Line a and enter the result in Line 23. **Do not enter an amount less than zero.**		
	a. IRS Transportation Standards, Ownership Costs, Second Car	$	
	b. Average Monthly Payments for debts secured by Vehicle 2, if any, as stated in Line 41	$	
	c. Net ownership/lease expense for Vehicle 2	Subtract Line b from Line a.	$
24	**Other Necessary Expenses: taxes.** Enter the total average monthly expense that you actually incur for all federal, state, and local taxes, other than real estate and sales taxes, such as income taxes, self employment taxes, social security taxes, and Medicare taxes. **Do not include real estate or sales taxes.**		
25	**Other Necessary Expenses: mandatory payroll deductions.** Enter the total average monthly payroll deductions that are required for your employment, such as mandatory retirement contributions, union dues, and uniform costs. **Do not include discretionary amounts, such as non-mandatory 401(k) contributions.**		$
26	**Other Necessary Expenses: life insurance.** Enter average monthly premiums that you actually pay for term life insurance for yourself. **Do not include premiums for insurance on your dependents, for whole life, or for any other form of insurance.**		$
27	**Other Necessary Expenses: court-ordered payments.** Enter the total monthly amount that you are required to pay pursuant to court order, such as spousal or child support payments. **Do not include payments on past due support obligations included in Line 43.**		$
28	**Other Necessary Expenses: education for employment or for a physically or mentally challenged child.** Enter the total monthly amount that you actually expend for education that is a condition of employment and for education that is required for a physically or mentally challenged dependent child for whom no public education providing similar services is available.		$
29	**Other Necessary Expenses: childcare.** Enter the average monthly amount that you actually expend on childcare. **Do not include payments made for children's education.**		$
30	**Other Necessary Expenses: health care.** Enter the average monthly amount that you actually expend on health care expenses that are not reimbursed by insurance or paid by a health savings account. **Do not include payments for health insurance listed in Line 33.**		$

31	**Other Necessary Expenses: telecommunication services.** Enter the average monthly expenses that you actually pay for cell phones, pagers, call waiting, caller identification, special long distance, or internet services necessary for the health and welfare of you or your dependents. **Do not include any amount previously deducted.**	$
32	**Total Expenses Allowed under IRS Standards.** Enter the total of Lines 19 through 31	$
	Subpart B: Additional Expense Deductions under § 707(b) **Note: Do not include any expenses that you have listed in Lines 19-31**	
33	**Health Insurance, Disability Insurance, and Health Savings Account Expenses.** List the average monthly amounts that you actually expend in each of the following categories and enter the total. a. Health Insurance — $ b. Disability Insurance — $ c. Health Savings Account — $ Total: Add Lines a, b and c	$
34	**Continued contributions to the care of household or family members.** Enter the actual monthly expenses that you will continue to pay for the reasonable and necessary care and support of an elderly, chronically ill, or disabled member of your household or member of your immediate family who is unable to pay for such expenses.	$
35	**Protection against family violence.** Enter any average monthly expenses that you actually incurred to maintain the safety of your family under the Family Violence Prevention and Services Act or other applicable federal law.	$
36	**Home energy costs in excess of the allowance specified by the IRS Local Standards.** Enter the average monthly amount by which your home energy costs exceed the allowance in the IRS Local Standards for Housing and Utilities. **You must provide your case trustee with documentation demonstrating that the additional amount claimed is reasonable and necessary**.	$
37	**Education expenses for dependent children less than 18.** Enter the average monthly expenses that you actually incur, not to exceed $125 per child, in providing elementary and secondary education for your dependent children less than 18 years of age. **You must provide your case trustee with documentation demonstrating that the amount claimed is reasonable and necessary and not already accounted for in the IRS Standards**.	$
38	**Additional food and clothing expense.** Enter the average monthly amount by which your food and clothing expenses exceed the combined allowances for food and apparel in the IRS National Standards, not to exceed five percent of those combined allowances. (This information is available at www.usdoj.gov/ust/ or from the clerk of the bankruptcy court.) **You must provide your case trustee with documentation demonstrating that the additional amount claimed is reasonable and necessary**.	$
39	**Continued charitable contributions.** Enter the amount that you will continue to contribute in the form of cash or financial instruments to a charitable organization as defined in 26 U.S.C. § 170(c)(1)-(2).	$
40	**Total Additional Expense Deductions under § 707(b).** Enter the total of Lines 33 through 39	$
	Subpart C: Deductions for Debt Payment	
41	**Future payments on secured claims.** For each of your debts that is secured by an interest in property that you own, list the name of creditor, identify the property securing the debt, and state the Average Monthly Payment. The Average Monthly Payment is the total of all amounts contractually due to each Secured Creditor in the 60 months following the filing of the bankruptcy case, divided by 60. If necessary, list additional entries on a separate page. **Do not include items you have previously deducted, such as insurance and taxes.**	$

Line 33:

a.	Health Insurance	$
b.	Disability Insurance	$
c.	Health Savings Account	$
		Total: Add Lines a, b and c

Line 41:

	Name of Creditor	Property Securing the Debt	60-month Average Payment
a.			$
b.			$
c.			$
			Total: Add Lines a, b and c

42	**Past due payments on secured claims.** If any of the debts listed in Line 41 are in default, and the property securing the debt is necessary for your support or the support of your dependents, you may include in your deductions 1/60th of the amount that you must pay the creditor as a result of the default (the "cure amount") in order to maintain possession of the property. List any such amounts in the following chart and enter the total. If necessary, list additional entries on a separate page.	

	Name of Creditor	Property Securing the Debt in Default	1/60th of the Cure Amount
a.			$
b.			$
c.			$
			Total: Add Lines a, b and c

Line 42 total: $

43	**Payments on priority claims.** Enter the total amount of all priority claims (including priority child support and alimony claims), divided by 60.	$
44	**Chapter 13 administrative expenses.** If you are eligible to file a case under Chapter 13, complete the following chart, multiply the amount in Line a by the amount in Line b, and enter the resulting administrative expense.	

a.	Projected average monthly Chapter 13 plan payment.	$
b.	Current multiplier for your district as determined under schedules issued by the Executive Office for United States Trustees. (This information is available at www.usdoj.gov/ust/ or from the clerk of the bankruptcy court.)	x
c.	Average monthly administrative expense of Chapter 13 case	Total: Multiply Lines a and b

Line 44 total: $

45	**Total Deductions for Debt Payment.** Enter the total of Lines 41 through 44.	$

Subpart D: Total Deductions Allowed under § 707(b)(2)

46	**Total of all deductions allowed under § 707(b)(2).** Enter the total of Lines 32, 40, and 45.	$

Part VI. DETERMINATION OF § 707(b)(2) PRESUMPTION

47	**Enter the amount from Line 18 (Current monthly income for § 707(b)(2))**	$
48	**Enter the amount from Line 46 (Total of all deductions allowed under § 707(b)(2))**	$
49	**Monthly disposable income under § 707(b)(2).** Subtract Line 48 from Line 47 and enter the result	$
50	**60-month disposable income under § 707(b)(2).** Multiply the amount in Line 49 by the number 60 and enter the result.	$

51 **Initial presumption determination.** Check the applicable box and proceed as directed.

☐ **The amount on Line 50 is less than $6,000** Check the "Presumption does not arise" box at the top of page 1 of this statement, and complete the verification in Part VII. Do not complete the remainder of Part VI.

☐ **The amount set forth on Line 50 is more than $10,000.** Check the "Presumption arises" box at the top of page 1 of this statement, and complete the verification in Part VII. Do not complete the remainder of Part VI.

☐ **The amount on Line 50 is at least $6,000, but not more than $10,000.** Complete the remainder of Part VI (Lines 52 through 54).

52	**Enter the amount of your total non-priority unsecured debt**	$
53	**Threshold debt payment amount.** Multiply the amount in Line 52 by the number 0.25 and enter the result.	$

54 **Secondary presumption determination.** Check the applicable box and proceed as directed.

☐ **The amount on Line 50 is less than the amount on Line 53.** Check the "Presumption does not arise" box at the top of page 1 of this statement, and complete the verification in Part VIII.

☐ **The amount on Line 50 is equal to or greater than the amount on Line 53.** Check the "Presumption arises" box at the top of page 1 of this statement, and complete the verification in Part VIII. You may also complete Part VII.

Part VII: ADDITIONAL EXPENSE CLAIMS

55 **Other Expenses.** List and describe any monthly expenses, not otherwise stated in this form, that are required for the health and welfare of you and your family and that you contend should be an additional deduction from your current monthly income under § 707(b)(2)(A)(ii)(I). If necessary, list additional sources on a separate page. All figures should reflect your average monthly expense for each item. Total the expenses.

	Expense Description	Monthly Amount
a.		$
b.		$
c.		$
	Total: Add Lines a, b, and c	$

Part VIII: VERIFICATION

56 I declare under penalty of perjury that the information provided in this statement is true and correct. *(If this a joint case, both debtors must sign.)*

Date: ____________________ Signature: ____________________
(Debtor)

Date: ____________________ Signature: ____________________
(Joint Debtor, if any)

Form B22A(Alt.) (Chapter 7) (10/05)

In re ______________________________
Debtor(s)

Case Number: ____________________
(If known)

Check the box as directed in Parts I, III, and VI of this statement.
☐ **Presumption arises**
☐ **Presumption does not arise**

STATEMENT OF CURRENT MONTHLY INCOME AND MEANS TEST CALCULATION

FOR USE IN CHAPTER 7 (IF IRS SEPARATES ITS HOUSING ALLOWANCE)

In addition to Schedules I and J, this statement must be completed by every individual Chapter 7 debtor, whether or not filing jointly, whose debts are primarily consumer debts. Joint debtors may complete one statement only.

Part I. EXCLUSION FOR DISABLED VETERANS

1	If you are a disabled veteran described in the Veteran's Declaration in this Part I, (1) check the box at the beginning of the Veteran's Declaration, (2) check the "Presumption does not arise" box at the top of this statement, and (3) complete the verification in Part VIII. Do not complete any of the remaining parts of this statement. ☐ **Veteran's Declaration.** By checking this box, I declare under penalty of perjury that I am a disabled veteran (as defined in 38 U.S.C. § 3741(1)) whose indebtedness occurred primarily during a period in which I was on active duty (as defined in 10 U.S.C. § 101(d)(1)) or while I was performing a homeland defense activity (as defined in 32 U.S.C. §901(1)).

Part II. CALCULATION OF MONTHLY INCOME FOR § 707(b)(7) EXCLUSION

2	**Marital/filing status.** Check the box that applies and complete the balance of this part of this statement as directed. a. ☐ Unmarried. **Complete only Column A ("Debtor's Income") for Lines 3-11.** b. ☐ Married, not filing jointly, with declaration of separate households. By checking this box, debtor declares under penalty of perjury: "My spouse and I are legally separated under applicable non-bankruptcy law or my spouse and I are living apart other than for the purpose of evading the requirements of § 707(b)(2)(A) of the Bankruptcy Code." **Complete only Column A ("Debtor's Income") for Lines 3-11.** c. ☐ Married, not filing jointly, without the declaration of separate households set out in Line 2.b above. **Complete both Column A ("Debtor's Income") and Column B (Spouse's Income) for Lines 3-11.** d. ☐ Married, filing jointly. **Complete both Column A ("Debtor's Income") and Column B ("Spouse's Income") for Lines 3-11.**		
	All figures must reflect average monthly income for the six calendar months prior to filing the bankruptcy case, ending on the last day of the month before the filing. If you received different amounts of income during these six months, you must total the amounts received during the six months, divide this total by six, and enter the result on the appropriate line.	**Column A Debtor's Income**	**Column B Spouse's Income**
3	**Gross wages, salary, tips, bonuses, overtime, commissions.**	$	$
4	**Income from the operation of a business, profession, or farm**. Subtract Line b from Line a and enter the difference on Line 4. Do not enter a number less than zero. **Do not include any part of the business expenses entered on Line b as a deduction in Part V.** a. Gross receipts — $ b. Ordinary and necessary business expenses — $ c. Business income — Subtract Line b from Line a	$	$
5	**Rent and other real property income.** Subtract Line b from Line a and enter the difference on Line 5. Do not enter a number less than zero. **Do not include any part of the operating expenses entered on Line b as a deduction in Part V.** a. Gross receipts — $ b. Ordinary and necessary operating expenses — $ c. Rental income — Subtract Line b from Line a	$	$
6	**Interest, dividends, and royalties.**	$	$
7	**Pension and retirement income.**	$	$
8	**Regular contributions to the household expenses of the debtor or the debtor's dependents, including child or spousal support.** Do not include contributions from the debtor's spouse if Column B is completed.	$	$

9	**Unemployment compensation.** Enter the amount in Column A and, if applicable, Column B. However, if you contend that unemployment compensation received by you or your spouse was a benefit under the Social Security Act, do not list the amount of such compensation in Column A or B, but instead state the amount in the space below: Unemployment compensation claimed to be a benefit under the Social Security Act | Debtor $ ______ | Spouse $ ______	$	$
10	**Income from all other sources.** If necessary, list additional sources on a separate page. **Do not include** any benefits received under the Social Security Act or payments received as a victim of a war crime, crime against humanity, or as a victim of international or domestic terrorism. Specify source and amount. a. ______ $ b. ______ $ Total and enter on Line 10	$	$
11	**Subtotal of Current Monthly Income for § 707(b)(7).** Add Lines 3 thru 10 in Column A, and, if Column B is completed, add Lines 3 through 10 in Column B. Enter the total(s).	$	$
12	**Total Current Monthly Income for § 707(b)(7).** If Column B has been completed, add Line 11, Column A to Line 11, Column B, and enter the total. If Column B has not been completed, enter the amount from Line 11, Column A.	$	

Part III. APPLICATION OF § 707(b)(7) EXCLUSION

13	**Annualized Current Monthly Income for § 707(b)(7).** Multiply the amount from Line 12 by the number 12 and enter the result.	$
14	**Applicable median family income.** Enter the median family income for the applicable state and household size. (This information is available by family size at www.usdoj.gov/ust/ or from the clerk of the bankruptcy court.) a. Enter debtor's state of residence: ______ b. Enter debtor's household size: ______	$
15	**Application of Section 707(b)(7).** Check the applicable box and proceed as directed. ☐ **The amount on Line 13 is less than or equal to the amount on Line 14.** Check the "Presumption does not arise" box at the top of page 1 of this statement, and complete Part VIII; do not complete Parts IV, V, VI, or VII. ☐ **The amount on Line 13 is more than the amount on Line 14.** Complete the remaining parts of this statement.	

Complete Parts IV, V, VI, and VII of this statement only if required. (See Line 15.)

Part IV. CALCULATION OF CURRENT MONTHLY INCOME FOR § 707(b)(2)

16	**Enter the amount from Line 12.**	$
17	**Marital adjustment.** If you checked the box at Line 2.c, enter the amount of the income listed in Line 11, Column B that was NOT regularly contributed to the household expenses of the debtor or the debtor's dependents. If you did not check box at Line 2.c, enter zero.	$
18	**Current monthly income for § 707(b)(2).** Subtract Line 17 from Line 16 and enter the result.	$

Part V. CALCULATION OF DEDUCTIONS ALLOWED UNDER § 707(b)(2)

Subpart A: Deductions under Standards of the Internal Revenue Service (IRS)

19	**National Standards: food, clothing, household supplies, personal care, and miscellaneous.** Enter "Total" amount from IRS National Standards for Allowable Living Expenses for the applicable family size and income level. (This information is available at www.usdoj.gov/ust/ or from the clerk of the bankruptcy court.)	$
20	**Local Standards: housing and utilities; utilities/maintenance expense.** Enter the amount of the IRS Housing and Utilities Standards; Utilities/Maintenance Expense for the applicable county and family size. (This information is available at www.usdoj.gov/ust/ or from the clerk of the bankruptcy court).	$

21 ~~**Local Standards: housing and utilities; mortgage/rental expense.** Enter, in Line a below, the amount of the IRS Housing and Utilities Standards; Mortgage/Rental Expense for your county and family size (available at www.usdoj.gov/ust/ or from the clerk of the bankruptcy court); enter on Line b the total of the Average Monthly Payments for any debts secured by your home, as stated in Line 42; subtract Line b from Line a and enter the result in Line 21. **Do not enter an amount less than zero.**~~

(Under revision)

a.	IRS Housing and Utilities Standards; Mortgage/Rental Expense	$
b.	Average Monthly Payment for any debts secured by your home, if any, as stated in Line 42	$
c.	Net mortgage/rental expense	Subtract Line b from Line a.

22 **Local Standards: transportation; vehicle operation/public transportation expense.** You are entitled to an expense allowance in this category regardless of whether you pay the expenses of operating a vehicle and regardless of whether you use public transportation.

Check the number of vehicles for which you pay the operating expenses or for which the operating expenses are included as a contribution to your household expenses in Line 8.

☐ 0 ☐ 1 ☐ 2 or more.

Enter the amount from IRS Transportation Standards, Operating Costs & Public Transportation Costs for the applicable number of vehicles in the applicable Metropolitan Statistical Area or Census Region. (This information is available at www.usdoj.gov/ust/ or from the clerk of the bankruptcy court.) $

23 **Local Standards: transportation ownership/lease expense; Vehicle 1.** Check the number of vehicles for which you claim an ownership/lease expense. (You may not claim an ownership/lease expense for more than two vehicles.)

☐ 1 ☐ 2 or more.

Enter, in Line a below, the amount of the IRS Transportation Standards, Ownership Costs, First Car (available at www.usdoj.gov/ust/ or from the clerk of the bankruptcy court); enter in Line b the total of the Average Monthly Payments for any debts secured by Vehicle 1, as stated in Line 42; subtract Line b from Line a and enter the result in Line 23. **Do not enter an amount less than zero.**

a.	IRS Transportation Standards, Ownership Costs, First Car	$
b.	Average Monthly Payment for any debts secured by Vehicle 1, as stated in Line 42	$
c.	Net ownership/lease expense for Vehicle 1	Subtract Line b from Line a.

$

24 **Local Standards: transportation ownership/lease expense; Vehicle 2.** Complete this Line only if you checked the "2 or more" Box in Line 23.

Enter, in Line a below, the amount of the IRS Transportation Standards, Ownership Costs, Second Car (available at www.usdoj.gov/ust/ or from the clerk of the bankruptcy court); enter in Line b the total of the Average Monthly Payments for any debts secured by Vehicle 2, as stated in Line 42; subtract Line b from Line a and enter the result in Line 24. **Do not enter an amount less than zero.**

a.	IRS Transportation Standards, Ownership Costs, Second Car	$
b.	Average Monthly Payment for any debts secured by Vehicle 2, as stated in Line 42	$
c.	Net ownership/lease expense for Vehicle 2	Subtract Line b from Line a.

$

25 **Other Necessary Expenses: taxes.** Enter the total average monthly expense that you actually incur for all federal, state, and local taxes, other than real estate and sales taxes, such as income taxes, self employment taxes, social security taxes, and Medicare taxes. **Do not include real estate or sales taxes.**

26 **Other Necessary Expenses: mandatory payroll deductions.** Enter the total average monthly payroll deductions that are required for your employment, such as mandatory retirement contributions, union dues, and uniform costs. **Do not include discretionary amounts, such as non-mandatory 401(k) contributions.** $

27 **Other Necessary Expenses: life insurance.** Enter average monthly premiums that you actually pay for term life insurance for yourself. **Do not include premiums for insurance on your dependents, for whole life or for any other form of insurance.** $

28 **Other Necessary Expenses: court-ordered payments.** Enter the total monthly amount that you are required to pay pursuant to court order, such as spousal or child support payments. **Do not include payments on past due support obligations included in Line 44.** $

29	**Other Necessary Expenses: education for employment or for a physically or mentally challenged child.** Enter the total monthly amount that you actually expend for education that is a condition of employment and for education that is required for a physically or mentally challenged dependent child for whom no public education providing similar services is available.	$
30	**Other Necessary Expenses: childcare.** Enter the average monthly amount that you actually expend on childcare. **Do not include payments made for children's education.**	$
31	**Other Necessary Expenses: health care.** Enter the average monthly amount that you actually expend on health care expenses that are not reimbursed by insurance or paid by a health savings account. **Do not include payments for health insurance listed in Line 34.**	$
32	**Other Necessary Expenses: telecommunication services.** Enter the average monthly expenses that you actually pay for cell phones, pagers, call waiting, caller identification, special long distance, or internet services necessary for the health and welfare of you or your dependents. **Do not include any amount previously deducted.**	$
33	**Total Expenses Allowed under IRS Standards.** Enter the total of Lines 19 through 32.	$
	Subpart B: Additional Expense Deductions under § 707(b) **Note: Do not include any expenses that you have listed in Lines 19-32**	
34	**Health Insurance, Disability Insurance, and Health Savings Account Expenses.** List the average monthly amounts that you actually expend in each of the following categories and enter the total. a. Health Insurance $ b. Disability Insurance $ c. Health Savings Account $ Total: Add Lines a, b, and c	$
35	**Continued contributions to the care of household or family members.** Enter the actual monthly expenses that you will continue to pay for the reasonable and necessary care and support of an elderly, chronically ill, or disabled member of your household or member of your immediate family who is unable to pay for such expenses.	$
36	**Protection against family violence.** Enter any average monthly expenses that you actually incurred to maintain the safety of your family under the Family Violence Prevention and Services Act or other applicable federal law.	$
37	**Home energy costs in excess of the allowance specified by the IRS Local Standards.** Enter the average monthly amount by which your home energy costs exceed the allowance in the IRS Local Standards for Housing and Utilities. **You must provide your case trustee with documentation demonstrating that the additional amount claimed is reasonable and necessary**.	$
38	**Education expenses for dependent children less than 18.** Enter the average monthly expenses that you actually incur, not to exceed $125 per child, in providing elementary and secondary education for your dependent children less than 18 years of age. **You must provide your case trustee with documentation demonstrating that the amount claimed is reasonable and necessary and not already accounted for in the IRS Standards**.	$
39	**Additional food and clothing expense.** Enter the average monthly amount by which your food and clothing expenses exceed the combined allowances for food and apparel in the IRS National Standards, not to exceed five percent of those combined allowances. (This information is available at www.usdoj.gov/ust/ or from the clerk of the bankruptcy court.) **You must provide your case trustee with documentation demonstrating that the additional amount claimed is reasonable and necessary**.	$
40	**Continued charitable contributions.** Enter the amount that you will continue to contribute in the form of cash or financial instruments to a charitable organization as defined in 26 U.S.C. § 170(c)(1)-(2).	$
41	**Total Additional Expense Deductions under § 707(b).** Enter the total of Lines 34 through 40	$

Subpart C: Deductions for Debt Payment

42 **Future payments on secured claims.** For each of your debts that is secured by an interest in property that you own, list the name of creditor, identify the property securing the debt, and state the Average Monthly Payment. The Average Monthly Payment is the total of all amounts contractually due to each Secured Creditor in the 60 months following the filing of the bankruptcy case, divided by 60. If necessary, list additional entries on a separate page. **Do not include items you have previously deducted, such as insurance and taxes.**

	Name of Creditor	Property Securing the Debt	60-month Average Payment
a.			$
b.			$
c.			$
			Total: Add Lines a, b, and c.

$

43 **Past due payments on secured claims.** If any of the debts listed in Line 42 are in default, and the property securing the debt is necessary for your support or the support of your dependents, you may include in your deductions 1/60th of the amount that you must pay the creditor as a result of the default (the "cure amount") in order to maintain possession of the property. List any such amounts in the following chart and enter the total. If necessary, list additional entries on a separate page.

	Name of Creditor	Property Securing the Debt in Default	1/60th of the Cure Amount
a.			$
b.			$
c.			$
			Total: Add Lines a, b, and c

$

44 **Payments on priority claims.** Enter the total amount of all priority claims (including priority child support and alimony claims), divided by 60. $

45 **Chapter 13 administrative expenses.** If you are eligible to file a case under Chapter 13, complete the following chart, multiply the amount in Line a by the amount in Line b, and enter the resulting administrative expense.

a.	Projected average monthly Chapter 13 plan payment.	$
b.	Current multiplier for your district as determined under schedules issued by the Executive Office for United States Trustees. (This information is available at www.usdoj.gov/ust/ or from the clerk of the bankruptcy court.)	x
c.	Average monthly administrative expense of Chapter 13 case	Total: Multiply Lines a and b

$

46 **Total Deductions for Debt Payment.** Enter the total of Lines 42 through 45. $

Subpart D: Total Deductions Allowed under § 707(b)(2)

47 **Total of all deductions allowed under § 707(b)(2).** Enter the total of Lines 33, 41, and 46. $

Part VI. DETERMINATION OF § 707(b)(2) PRESUMPTION

48	**Enter the amount from Line 18 (Current monthly income for § 707(b)(2))**	$
49	**Enter the amount from Line 47 (Total of all deductions allowed under § 707(b)(2))**	$
50	**Monthly disposable income under § 707(b)(2).** Subtract Line 49 from Line 48 and enter the result	$
51	**60-month disposable income under § 707(b)(2).** Multiply the amount in Line 50 by the number 60 and enter the result.	$

52	**Initial presumption determination.** Check the applicable box and proceed as directed. ☐ **The amount on Line 51 is less than $6,000** Check the "Presumption does not arise" box at the top of page 1 of this statement, and complete the verification in Part VII. Do not complete the remainder of Part VI. ☐ **The amount set forth on Line 51 is more than $10,000**. Check the "Presumption arises" box at the top of page 1 of this statement, and complete the verification in Part VII. Do not complete the remainder of Part VI. ☐ **The amount on Line 51 is at least $6,000, but not more than $10,000.** Complete the remainder of Part VI (Lines 53 through 55).
53	**Enter the amount of your total non-priority unsecured debt** — $
54	**Threshold debt payment amount.** Multiply the amount in Line 53 by the number 0.25 and enter the result. — $
55	**Secondary presumption determination.** Check the applicable box and proceed as directed. ☐ **The amount on Line 51 is less than the amount on Line 54.** Check the "Presumption does not arise" box at the top of page 1 of this statement, and complete the verification in Part VIII. ☐ **The amount on Line 51 is equal to or greater than the amount on Line 54.** Check the "Presumption arises" box at the top of page 1 of this statement, and complete the verification in Part VIII. You may also complete Part VII.

Part VII: ADDITIONAL EXPENSE CLAIMS

56 **Other Expenses.** List and describe any monthly expenses, not otherwise stated in this form, that are required for the health and welfare of you and your family and that you contend should be an additional deduction from your current monthly income under § 707(b)(2)(A)(ii)(I). If necessary, list additional sources on a separate page. All figures should reflect your average monthly expense for each item. Total the expenses.

	Expense Description	Monthly Amount
a.		$
b.		$
c.		$
	Total: Add Lines a, b, and c	$

Part VIII: VERIFICATION

57 I declare under penalty of perjury that the information provided in this statement is true and correct. *(If this a joint case, both debtors must sign.)*

Date: ______________________ Signature: ______________________ (Debtor)

Date: ______________________ Signature: ______________________ (Joint Debtor, if any)

Form B22B (Chapter 11) (10/05)

In re ______________________________
Debtor(s)

Case Number: __________________
(If known)

STATEMENT OF CURRENT MONTHLY INCOME

FOR USE IN CHAPTER 11

In addition to Schedules I and J, this statement must be completed by every individual Chapter 11 debtor, whether or not filing jointly. Joint debtors may complete one statement only.

Part I. CALCULATION OF CURRENT MONTHLY INCOME

1	**Marital/filing status.** Check the box that applies and complete the balance of this part of this statement as directed. a. ☐ Unmarried. **Complete only Column A ("Debtor's Income") for Lines 2-10.** b. ☐ Married, not filing jointly. **Complete only Column A ("Debtor's Income") for Lines 2-10.** c. ☐ Married, filing jointly. **Complete both Column A ("Debtor's Income") and Column B ("Spouse's Income") for Lines 2-10.**		
	All figures must reflect average monthly income for the six calendar months prior to filing the bankruptcy case, ending on the last day of the month before the filing. If you received different amounts of income during these six months, you must total the amounts received during the six months, divide this total by six, and enter the result on the appropriate line.	**Column A Debtor's Income**	**Column B Spouse's Income**
2	**Gross wages, salary, tips, bonuses, overtime, commissions.**	$	$
3	**Net income from the operation of a business, profession, or farm.** Subtract Line b from Line a and enter the difference on Line 3. Do not enter a number less than zero. a. Gross receipts — $ b. Ordinary and necessary business expenses — $ c. Business income — Subtract Line b from Line a	$	$
4	**Net rental and other real property income.** Subtract Line b from Line a and enter the difference on Line 4. Do not enter a number less than zero. a. Gross receipts — $ b. Ordinary and necessary operating expenses — $ c. Rental income — Subtract Line b from Line a	$	$
5	**Interest, dividends, and royalties.**	$	$
6	**Pension and retirement income.**	$	$
7	**Regular contributions to the household expenses of the debtor or the debtor's dependents, including child or spousal support.** Do not include contributions from the debtor's spouse if Column B is completed.	$	$
8	**Unemployment compensation.** Enter the amount in Column A and, if applicable, Column B. However, if you contend that unemployment compensation received by you or your spouse was a benefit under the Social Security Act, do not list the amount of such compensation in Column A or B, but instead state the amount in the space below: Unemployment compensation claimed to be a benefit under the Social Security Act — Debtor $ ________ — Spouse $ ________	$	$
9	**Income from all other sources**. If necessary, list additional sources on a separate page. **Do not include** any benefits received under the Social Security Act or payments received as a victim of a war crime, crime against humanity, or as a victim of international or domestic terrorism. Specify source and amount. a. ________ $ b. ________ $ Total and enter on Line 9	$	$
10	**Subtotal of current monthly income.** Add Lines 2 thru 9 in Column A, and, if Column B is completed, add Lines 2 through 9 in Column B. Enter the total(s).	$	$
11	**Total current monthly income.** If Column B has been completed, add Line 10, Column A to Line 10, Column B, and enter the total. If Column B has not been completed, enter the		

	amount from Line 10, Column A.	$

Part II: VERIFICATION	
12	I declare under penalty of perjury that the information provided in this statement is true and correct. *(If this a joint case, both debtors must sign.)* Date: ________________ Signature: ________________ (Debtor) Date: ________________ Signature: ________________ (Joint Debtor, if any)

Form B22C (Chapter 13) (10/05)

In re ______________________________
Debtor(s)

Case Number: ____________________
(If known)

Check the box as directed in Part II, Line 14 of this statement.
☐ **Disposable income determined under § 1325(b)(3)**
☐ **Disposable income not determined under § 1325(b)(3)**

STATEMENT OF CURRENT MONTHLY INCOME AND DISPOSABLE INCOME CALCULATION

FOR USE IN CHAPTER 13

In addition to Schedules I and J, this statement must be completed by every individual Chapter 13 debtor, whether or not filing jointly. Joint debtors may complete one statement only.

Part I. CALCULATION OF CURRENT MONTHLY INCOME

1	**Marital/filing status.** Check the box that applies and complete the balance of this part of this statement as directed. a. ☐ Unmarried. **Complete only Column A ("Debtor's Income") for Lines 2-10.** b. ☐ ~~Married, not filing jointly. **Complete only Column A ("Debtor's Income") for Lines 2-10.**~~ **(Under Revision)** c. ☐ Married, filing jointly. **Complete both Column A ("Debtor's Income") and Column B ("Spouse's Income") for Lines 2-10.**		
	All figures must reflect average monthly income for the six calendar months prior to filing the bankruptcy case, ending on the last day of the month before the filing. If you received different amounts of income during these six months, you must total the amounts received during the six months, divide this total by six, and enter the result on the appropriate line.	**Column A Debtor's Income**	**Column B Spouse's Income**
2	**Gross wages, salary, tips, bonuses, overtime, commissions.**	$	$
3	**Income from the operation of a business, profession, or farm.** Subtract Line b from Line a and enter the difference on Line 3. Do not enter a number less than zero. **Do not include any part of the business expenses entered on Line b as a deduction in Part III.** a. Gross receipts — $ b. Ordinary and necessary business expenses — $ c. Business income — Subtract Line b from Line a	$	$
4	**Rent and other real property income.** Subtract Line b from Line a and enter the difference on Line 4. Do not enter a number less than zero. **Do not include any part of the operating expenses entered on Line b as a deduction in Part III.** a. Gross receipts — $ b. Ordinary and necessary operating expenses — $ c. Rental income — Subtract Line b from Line a	$	$
5	**Interest, dividends, and royalties.**	$	$
6	**Pension and retirement income.**	$	$
7	**Regular contributions to the household expenses of the debtor or the debtor's dependents, including child or spousal support**. Do not include contributions from the debtor's spouse if Column B is completed.	$	$
8	**Unemployment compensation.** Enter the amount in Column A and, if applicable, Column B. However, if you contend that unemployment compensation received by you or your spouse was a benefit under the Social Security Act, do not list the amount of such compensation in Column A or B, but instead state the amount in the space below: Unemployment compensation claimed to be a benefit under the Social Security Act — Debtor $ ________ — Spouse $ ________	$	$
9	**Income from all other sources.** Specify source and amount. If necessary, list additional sources on a separate page. Total and enter on Line 9. **Do not include** any benefits received under the Social Security Act or payments received as a victim of a war crime, crime against humanity, or as a victim of international or domestic terrorism. a. ____________ $ b. ____________ $	$	$
10	**Subtotal of current monthly income.** Add Lines 2 thru 9 in Column A, and, if Column B is completed, add Lines 2 through 9 in Column B. Enter the total(s).	$	$

11	**Total current monthly income.** If Column B has been completed, add Line 10, Column A to Line 10, Column B, and enter the total. If Column B has not been completed, enter the amount from Line 10, Column A.	$

	Part II. APPLICATION OF § 1325(b)(3)	
12	**Annualized current monthly income.** Multiply the amount from Line 11 by the number 12 and enter the result.	$
13	**Applicable median family income.** Enter the median family income for applicable state and household size. (This information is available by family size at www.usdoj.gov/ust/ or from the clerk of the bankruptcy court.) a. Enter debtor's state of residence: ______________ b. Enter debtor's household size: __________	$
14	**Application of § 1325(b)(3).** Check the applicable box and proceed as directed. ☐ **The amount on Line 12 is less than or equal to the amount on Line 13.** Check the box at the top of page 1 of this statement that states "Disposable income not determined under § 1325(b)(3)" and complete Part VI of this statement; do not complete Parts III, IV, or V. ☐ **The amount on Line 12 is more than the amount on Line 13.** Check the box at the top of page 1 of this statement that states "Disposable income determined under § 1325(b)(3)" and complete the remaining parts of this statement.	

Complete Parts III, IV, and V of this statement only if required. (See Line 14.)

	Part III. CALCULATION OF DEDUCTIONS ALLOWED UNDER § 707(b)(2)	
	Subpart A: Deductions under Standards of the Internal Revenue Service (IRS)	
15	**National Standards: food, clothing, household supplies, personal care, and miscellaneous.** Enter the "Total" amount from IRS National Standards for Allowable Living Expenses for the applicable family size and income level. (This information is available at www.usdoj.gov/ust/ or from the clerk of the bankruptcy court.)	$
16	~~**Local Standards: housing and utilities.** Enter the amount of the IRS Housing and Utilities Standards allowance for your county and family size (this information is available at www.usdoj.gov/ust/ or from the clerk of the bankruptcy court), adjusted to deduct any portion of the allowance that includes payments on debts secured by your home, listed in Line 37.~~ **(Under revision)**	$
17	**Local Standards: transportation; vehicle operation/public transportation expense.** You are entitled to an expense allowance in this category regardless of whether you pay the expenses of operating a vehicle and regardless of whether you use public transportation. Check the number of vehicles for which you pay the operating expenses or for which the operating expenses are included as a contribution to your household expenses in Line 7. ☐ 0 ☐ 1 ☐ 2 or more. Enter the amount from IRS Transportation Standards, Operating Costs & Public Transportation Costs for the applicable number of vehicles in the applicable Metropolitan Statistical Area or Census Region. (This information is available at www.usdoj.gov/ust/ or from the clerk of the bankruptcy court.)	$
18	**Local Standards: transportation ownership/lease expense; Vehicle 1.** Check the number of vehicles for which you claim an ownership/lease expense. (You may not claim an ownership/lease expense for more than two vehicles.) ☐ 1 ☐ 2 or more. Enter, in Line a below, the amount of the IRS Transportation Standards, Ownership Costs, First Car (available at www.usdoj.gov/ust/ or from the clerk of the bankruptcy court); enter in Line b the total of the Average Monthly Payments for any debts secured by Vehicle 1, as stated in Line 37; subtract Line b from Line a and enter the result in Line 18. **Do not enter an amount less than zero.** a. | IRS Transportation Standards, Ownership Costs, First Car | $ b. | Average Monthly Payment for any debts secured by Vehicle 1, as stated in Line 37 | $ c. | Net ownership/lease expense for Vehicle 1 | Subtract Line b from Line a.	$

19	**Local Standards: transportation ownership/lease expense; Vehicle 2.** Complete this Line only if you checked the "2 or more" Box in Line 18. Enter, in Line a below, the amount of the IRS Transportation Standards, Ownership Costs, Second Car (available at www.usdoj.gov/ust/ or from the clerk of the bankruptcy court); enter in Line b the total of the Average Monthly Payments for any debts secured by Vehicle 2, as stated in Line 37; subtract Line b from Line a and enter the result in Line 19. **Do not enter an amount less than zero.** a. | IRS Transportation Standards, Ownership Costs, Second Car | $ b. | Average Monthly Payment for any debts secured by Vehicle 2, as stated in Line 37 | $ c. | Net ownership/lease expense for Vehicle 2 | Subtract Line b from Line a.	$
20	**Other Necessary Expenses: taxes.** Enter the total average monthly expense that you actually incur for all federal, state and local taxes, other than real estate and sales taxes, such as income taxes, self employment taxes, social security taxes, and Medicare taxes. **Do not include real estate or sales taxes.**	$
21	**Other Necessary Expenses: mandatory payroll deductions.** Enter the total average monthly payroll deductions that are required for your employment, such as mandatory retirement contributions, union dues, and uniform costs. **Do not include discretionary amounts, such as non-mandatory 401(k) contributions.**	$
22	**Other Necessary Expenses: life insurance.** Enter average monthly premiums that you actually pay for term life insurance for yourself. **Do not include premiums for insurance on your dependents, for whole life, or for any other form of insurance.**	$
23	**Other Necessary Expenses: court-ordered payments.** Enter the total monthly amount that you are required to pay pursuant to court order, such as spousal or child support payments. **Do not include payments on past due support obligations included in Line 39.**	$
24	**Other Necessary Expenses: education for employment or for a physically or mentally challenged child.** Enter the total monthly amount that you actually expend for education that is a condition of employment and for education that is required for a physically or mentally challenged dependent child for whom no public education providing similar services is available.	
25	**Other Necessary Expenses: childcare.** Enter the average monthly amount that you actually expend on childcare. **Do not include payments made for children's education.**	$
26	**Other Necessary Expenses: health care.** Enter the average monthly amount that you actually expend on health care expenses that are not reimbursed by insurance or paid by a health savings account. **Do not include payments for health insurance listed in Line 29.**	$
27	**Other Necessary Expenses: telecommunication services.** Enter the average monthly expenses that you actually pay for cell phones, pagers, call waiting, caller identification, special long distance, or internet services necessary for the health and welfare of you or your dependents. **Do not include any amount previously deducted.**	$
28	**Total Expenses Allowed under IRS Standards.** Enter the total of Lines 15 through 27	$
	Subpart B: Additional Expense Deductions under § 707(b) **Note: Do not include any expenses that you have listed in Lines 15-27**	
29	**Health Insurance, Disability Insurance, and Health Savings Account Expenses.** List the average monthly amounts that you actually expend in each of the following categories and enter the total. a. | Health Insurance | $ b. | Disability Insurance | $ c. | Health Savings Account | $ Total: Add Lines a, b, and c	$
30	**Continued contributions to the care of household or family members.** Enter the actual monthly expenses that you will continue to pay for the reasonable and necessary care and support of an elderly, chronically ill, or disabled member of your household or member of your immediate family who is unable to pay for such expenses. **Do not include payments listed in Line 24.**	$
31	**Protection against family violence.** Enter any average monthly expenses that you actually incurred to maintain the safety of your family under the Family Violence Prevention and Services Act or other applicable federal law.	$
32	**Home energy costs in excess of the allowance specified by the IRS Local Standards.** Enter the average monthly amount by which your home energy costs exceed the allowance in the IRS Local Standards for Housing and Utilities. **You must provide your case trustee with documentation demonstrating that the additional amount claimed is reasonable and necessary.**	$

33	**Education expenses for dependent children under 18.** Enter the average monthly expenses that you actually incur, not to exceed $125 per child, in providing elementary and secondary education for your dependent children less than 18 years of age. **You must provide your case trustee with documentation demonstrating that the amount claimed is reasonable and necessary and not already accounted for in the IRS Standards.**	$
34	**Additional food and clothing expense.** Enter the average monthly amount by which your food and clothing expenses exceed the combined allowances for food and apparel in the IRS National Standards, not to exceed five percent of those combined allowances. (This information is available at www.usdoj.gov/ust/ or from the clerk of the bankruptcy court.) **You must provide your case trustee with documentation demonstrating that the additional amount claimed is reasonable and necessary.**	$
35	**Continued charitable contributions.** Enter the amount that you will continue to contribute in the form of cash or financial instruments to a charitable organization as defined in 26 U.S.C. § 170(c)(1)-(2).	$
36	**Total Additional Expense Deductions under § 707(b).** Enter the total of Lines 29 through 35.	$

Subpart C: Deductions for Debt Payment

37	**Future payments on secured claims.** For each of your debts that is secured by an interest in property that you own, list the name of creditor, identify the property securing the debt, and state the Average Monthly Payment. The Average Monthly Payment is the total of all amounts contractually due to each Secured Creditor in the 60 months following the filing of the bankruptcy case, divided by 60. If necessary, list additional entries on a separate page. **Do not include items you have previously deducted, such as insurance and real estate taxes.**	$

	Name of Creditor	Property Securing the Debt	60-month Average Payment
a.			$
b.			$
c.			$
			Total: Add Lines a, b, and c

38	**Past due payments on secured claims.** If any of the debts listed in Line 37 are in default, and the property securing the debt is necessary for your support or the support of your dependents, you may include in your deductions 1/60th of the amount that you must pay the creditor as a result of the default (the "cure amount") in order to maintain possession of the property. List any such amounts in the following chart and enter the total. If necessary, list additional entries on a separate page.	$

	Name of Creditor	Property Securing the Debt in Default	1/60th of the Cure Amount
a.			$
b.			$
c.			$
			Total: Add Lines a, b, and c

39	**Payments on priority claims.** Enter the total amount of all priority claims (including priority child support and alimony claims), divided by 60.	$
40	**Chapter 13 administrative expenses.** Multiply the amount in Line a by the amount in Line b, and enter the resulting administrative expense.	$

a.	Projected average monthly Chapter 13 plan payment.	$
b.	Current multiplier for your district as determined under schedules issued by the Executive Office for United States Trustees. (This information is available at www.usdoj.gov/ust/ or from the clerk of the bankruptcy court.)	x
c.	Average monthly administrative expense of Chapter 13 case	Total: Multiply Lines a and b

41	**Total Deductions for Debt Payment.** Enter the total of Lines 37 through 40.	$

Subpart D: Total Deductions Allowed under § 707(b)(2)

42	**Total of all deductions allowed under § 707(b)(2).** Enter the total of Lines 28, 36, and 41.	$

Part IV. DETERMINATION OF DISPOSABLE INCOME UNDER § 1325(b)(2)

43	**Total current monthly income.** Enter the amount from Line 11.	$
44	**Support income.** Enter the monthly average of any child support payments, foster care payments, or disability payments for a dependent child, included in Line 7, that you received in accordance with applicable nonbankruptcy law, to the extent reasonably necessary to be expended for such child.	$
45	**Qualified retirement deductions.** Enter the monthly average of (a) all contributions or wage deductions made to qualified retirement plans, as specified in § 541(b)(7) and (b) all repayments of loans from retirement plans, as specified in § 362(b)(19).	$
46	**Total of all deductions allowed under § 707(b)(2).** Enter the amount from Line 42.	$
47	**Total adjustments to determine disposable income.** Add the amounts on Lines 44, 45, and 46 and enter the result.	$
48	**Monthly Disposable Income Under § 1325(b)(2).** Subtract Line 47 from Line 43 and enter the result.	$

Part V: ADDITIONAL EXPENSE CLAIMS

49 **Other Expenses.** List and describe any monthly expenses, not otherwise stated in this form, that are required for the health and welfare of you and your family and that you contend should be an additional deduction from your current monthly income under § 707(b)(2)(A)(ii)(I). If necessary, list additional sources on a separate page. All figures should reflect your average monthly expense for each item. Total the expenses.

	Expense Description	Monthly Amount
a.		$
b.		$
c.		$
	Total: Add Lines a, b, and c	$

Part VI: VERIFICATION

50 I declare under penalty of perjury that the information provided in this statement is true and correct. *(If this a joint case, both debtors must sign.)*

Date: ____________________ Signature: ____________________
(Debtor)

Date: ____________________ Signature: ____________________
(Joint Debtor, if any)

Form B22C(Alt.) (Chapter 13) (10/05)

In re ______________________
Debtor(s)

Case Number: ______________________
(If known)

Check the box as directed in Part II, Line 14 of this statement.
☐ **Disposable income determined under § 1325(b)(3)**
☐ **Disposable income not determined under § 1325(b)(3)**

STATEMENT OF CURRENT MONTHLY INCOME AND DISPOSABLE INCOME CALCULATION

FOR USE IN CHAPTER 13 (IF IRS SEPARATES ITS HOUSING ALLOWANCE)

In addition to Schedules I and J, this statement must be completed by every individual Chapter 13 debtor, whether or not filing jointly. Joint debtors may complete one statement only.

Part I. CALCULATION OF CURRENT MONTHLY INCOME

1	**Marital/filing status.** Check the box that applies and complete the balance of this part of this statement as directed. a. ☐ Unmarried. **Complete only Column A ("Debtor's Income") for Lines 2-10.** b. ☐ ~~Married, not filing jointly.~~ ~~**Complete only Column A ("Debtor's Income") for Lines 2-10.**~~ **(Under revision)** c. ☐ Married, filing jointly. **Complete both Column A ("Debtor's Income") and Column B ("Spouse's Income") for Lines 2-10.**		
	All figures must reflect average monthly income for the six calendar months prior to filing the bankruptcy case, ending on the last day of the month before the filing. If you received different amounts of income during these six months, you must total the amounts received during the six months, divide this total by six, and enter the result on the appropriate line.	**Column A Debtor's Income**	**Column B Spouse's Income**
2	**Gross wages, salary, tips, bonuses, overtime, commissions.**	$	$
3	**Income from the operation of a business, profession, or farm.** Subtract Line b from Line a and enter the difference on Line 3. Do not enter a number less than zero. **Do not include any part of the business expenses entered on Line b as a deduction in Part III.** a. Gross receipts — $ b. Ordinary and necessary business expenses — $ c. Business income — Subtract Line b from Line a	$	$
4	**Rent and other real property income.** Subtract Line b from Line a and enter the difference on Line 4. Do not enter a number less than zero. **Do not include any part of the operating expenses entered on Line b as a deduction in Part III.** a. Gross receipts — $ b. Ordinary and necessary operating expenses — $ c. Rental income — Subtract Line b from Line a	$	$
5	**Interest, dividends, and royalties.**	$	$
6	**Pension and retirement income.**	$	$
7	**Regular contributions to the household expenses of the debtor or the debtor's dependents, including child or spousal support.** Do not include contributions from the debtor's spouse if Column B is completed.	$	$
8	**Unemployment compensation.** Enter the amount in Column A and, if applicable, Column B. However, if you contend that unemployment compensation received by you or your spouse was a benefit under the Social Security Act, do not list the amount of such compensation in Column A or B, but instead state the amount in the space below: Unemployment compensation claimed to be a benefit under the Social Security Act — Debtor $ ________ — Spouse $ ________	$	$
9	**Income from all other sources.** Specify source and amount. If necessary, list additional sources on a separate page. Total and enter on Line 9. **Do not include** any benefits received under the Social Security Act or payments received as a victim of a war crime, crime against humanity, or as a victim of international or domestic terrorism. a. ________ $ b. ________ $	$	$
10	**Subtotal of current monthly income.** Add Lines 2 thru 9 in Column A, and, if Column B is completed, add Lines 2 through 9 in Column B. Enter the total(s).	$	$

11	**Total current monthly income.** If Column B has been completed, add Line 10, Column A to Line 10, Column B, and enter the total. If Column B has not been completed, enter the amount from Line 10, Column A.	$

	Part II. APPLICATION OF § 1325(b)(3)	
12	**Annualized current monthly income.** Multiply the amount from Line 11 by the number 12 and enter the result.	$
13	**Applicable median family income.** Enter the median family income for applicable state and household size. (This information is available by family size at www.usdoj.gov/ust/ or from the clerk of the bankruptcy court.) a. Enter debtor's state of residence: ______________ b. Enter debtor's household size: __________	$
14	**Application of § 1325(b)(3).** Check the applicable box and proceed as directed. ☐ **The amount on Line 12 is less than or equal to the amount on Line 13.** Check the box at the top of page 1 of this statement that states "Disposable income not determined under § 1325(b)(3)" and complete Part VI of this statement; do not complete Parts III, IV, or V. ☐ **The amount on Line 12 is more than the amount on Line 13.** Check the box at the top of page 1 of this statement that states "Disposable income determined under § 1325(b)(3)" and complete the remaining parts of this statement.	

Complete Parts III, IV, and V of this statement only if required. (See Line 14.)

	Part III. CALCULATION OF DEDUCTIONS ALLOWED UNDER § 707(b)(2)	
	Subpart A: Deductions under Standards of the Internal Revenue Service (IRS)	
15	**National Standards: food, clothing, household supplies, personal care, and miscellaneous.** Enter the "Total" amount from IRS National Standards for Allowable Living Expenses for the applicable family size and income level. (This information is available at www.usdoj.gov/ust/ or from the clerk of the bankruptcy court.)	$
16	~~**Local Standards: housing and utilities; utilities/maintenance expense.** Enter the amount of the IRS Housing and Utilities Standards; Utilities/Maintenance Expense for the applicable county and family size. (This information is available at www.usdoj.gov/ust/ or from the clerk of the bankruptcy court).~~ **(Under revision)**	$
17	**Local Standards: housing and utilities; mortgage/rental expense.** Enter, in Line a below, the amount of the IRS Housing and Utilities Standards; Mortgage/Rental Expense for your county and family size (available at www.usdoj.gov/ust/ or from the clerk of the bankruptcy court); enter on Line b the total of the Average Monthly Payments for any debts secured by your home, as stated in Line 38; subtract Line b from Line a and enter the result in Line 17. **Do not enter an amount less than zero.** a. IRS Housing and Utilities Standards; Mortgage/Rental Expense — $ b. Average Monthly Payment for any debts secured by your home, if any, as stated in Line 38 — $ c. Net mortgage/rental expense — Subtract Line b from Line a.	
18	**Local Standards: transportation; vehicle operation/public transportation expense.** You are entitled to an expense allowance in this category regardless of whether you pay the expenses of operating a vehicle and regardless of whether you use public transportation. Check the number of vehicles for which you pay the operating expenses or for which the operating expenses are included as a contribution to your household expenses in Line 7. ☐ 0 ☐ 1 ☐ 2 or more. Enter the amount from IRS Transportation Standards, Operating Costs & Public Transportation Costs for the applicable number of vehicles in the applicable Metropolitan Statistical Area or Census Region. (This information is available at www.usdoj.gov/ust/ or from the clerk of the bankruptcy court.)	$

<table>
<tr><td>19</td><td>Local Standards: transportation ownership/lease expense; Vehicle 1. Check the number of vehicles for which you claim an ownership/lease expense. (You may not claim an ownership/lease expense for more than two vehicles.) ☐ 1 ☐ 2 or more.
Enter, in Line a below, the amount of the IRS Transportation Standards, Ownership Costs, First Car (available at www.usdoj.gov/ust/ or from the clerk of the bankruptcy court); enter in Line b the total of the Average Monthly Payments for any debts secured by Vehicle 1, as stated in Line 38; subtract Line b from Line a and enter the result in Line 19. Do not enter an amount less than zero.
<table>
<tr><td>a.</td><td>IRS Transportation Standards, Ownership Costs, First Car</td><td>$</td></tr>
<tr><td>b.</td><td>Average Monthly Payment for any debts secured by Vehicle 1, as stated in Line 38</td><td>$</td></tr>
<tr><td>c.</td><td>Net ownership/lease expense for Vehicle 1</td><td>Subtract Line b from Line a.</td></tr>
</table></td><td>$</td></tr>
<tr><td>20</td><td>Local Standards: transportation ownership/lease expense; Vehicle 2. Complete this Line only if you checked the "2 or more" Box in Line 20.
Enter, in Line a below, the amount of the IRS Transportation Standards, Ownership Costs, Second Car (available at www.usdoj.gov/ust/ or from the clerk of the bankruptcy court); enter in Line b the total of the Average Monthly Payments for any debts secured by Vehicle 2, as stated in Line 38; subtract Line b from Line a and enter the result in Line 20. Do not enter an amount less than zero.
<table>
<tr><td>a.</td><td>IRS Transportation Standards, Ownership Costs, Second Car</td><td>$</td></tr>
<tr><td>b.</td><td>Average Monthly Payment for any debts secured by Vehicle 2, as stated in Line 38</td><td>$</td></tr>
<tr><td>c.</td><td>Net ownership/lease expense for Vehicle 2</td><td>Subtract Line b from Line a.</td></tr>
</table></td><td>$</td></tr>
<tr><td>21</td><td>Other Necessary Expenses: taxes. Enter the total average monthly expense that you actually incur for all federal, state, and local taxes, other than real estate and sales taxes, such as income taxes, self employment taxes, social security taxes, and Medicare taxes. Do not include real estate or sales taxes.</td><td>$</td></tr>
<tr><td>22</td><td>Other Necessary Expenses: mandatory payroll deductions. Enter the total average monthly payroll deductions that are required for your employment, such as mandatory retirement contributions, union dues, and uniform costs. Do not include discretionary amounts, such as non-mandatory 401(k) contributions.</td><td>$</td></tr>
<tr><td>23</td><td>Other Necessary Expenses: life insurance. Enter average monthly premiums that you actually pay for term life insurance for yourself. Do not include premiums for insurance on your dependents, for whole life or for any other form of insurance.</td><td>$</td></tr>
<tr><td>24</td><td>Other Necessary Expenses: court-ordered payments. Enter the total monthly amount that you are required to pay pursuant to court order, such as spousal or child support payments. Do not include payments on past due support obligations included in Line 40.</td><td>$</td></tr>
<tr><td>25</td><td>Other Necessary Expenses: education for employment or for a physically or mentally challenged child. Enter the total monthly amount that you actually expend for education that is a condition of employment and for education that is required for a physically or mentally challenged dependent child for whom no public education providing similar services is available.</td><td></td></tr>
<tr><td>26</td><td>Other Necessary Expenses: childcare. Enter the average monthly amount that you actually expend on childcare. Do not include payments made for children's education.</td><td>$</td></tr>
<tr><td>27</td><td>Other Necessary Expenses: health care. Enter the average monthly amount that you actually expend on health care expenses that are not reimbursed by insurance or paid by a health savings account. Do not include payments for health insurance listed in Line 30.</td><td>$</td></tr>
<tr><td>28</td><td>Other Necessary Expenses: telecommunication services. Enter the average monthly expenses that you actually pay for cell phones, pagers, call waiting, caller identification, special long distance, or internet services necessary for the health and welfare of you or your dependents. Do not include any amount previously deducted.</td><td>$</td></tr>
<tr><td>29</td><td>Total Expenses Allowed under IRS Standards. Enter the total of Lines 15 through 28</td><td>$</td></tr>
</table>

Subpart B: Additional Expense Deductions under § 707(b)

Note: Do not include any expenses that you have listed in Lines 15-28

30	**Health Insurance, Disability Insurance, and Health Savings Account Expenses.** List the average monthly amounts that you actually expend in each of the following categories and enter the total. a. Health Insurance $ b. Disability Insurance $ c. Health Savings Account $ Total: Add Lines a, b, and c	$
31	**Continued contributions to the care of household or family members.** Enter the actual monthly expenses that you will continue to pay for the reasonable and necessary care and support of an elderly, chronically ill, or disabled member of your household or member of your immediate family who is unable to pay for such expenses. **Do not include payments listed in Line 25.**	$
32	**Protection against family violence.** Enter any average monthly expenses that you actually incurred to maintain the safety of your family under the Family Violence Prevention and Services Act or other applicable federal law.	$
33	**Home energy costs in excess of the allowance specified by the IRS Local Standards.** Enter the average monthly amount by which your home energy costs exceed the allowance in the IRS Local Standards for Housing and Utilities. **You must provide your case trustee with documentation demonstrating that the additional amount claimed is reasonable and necessary**.	$
34	**Education expenses for dependent children under 18.** Enter the average monthly expenses that you actually incur, not to exceed $125 per child, in providing elementary and secondary education for your dependent children less than 18 years of age. **You must provide your case trustee with documentation demonstrating that the amount claimed is reasonable and necessary and not already accounted for in the IRS Standards**.	$
35	**Additional food and clothing expense.** Enter the average monthly amount by which your food and clothing expenses exceed the combined allowances for food and apparel in the IRS National Standards, not to exceed five percent of those combined allowances. (This information is available at www.usdoj.gov/ust/ or from the clerk of the bankruptcy court.) **You must provide your case trustee with documentation demonstrating that the additional amount claimed is reasonable and necessary**.	$
36	**Continued charitable contributions.** Enter the amount that you will continue to contribute in the form of cash or financial instruments to a charitable organization as defined in 26 U.S.C. § 170(c)(1)-(2).	$
37	**Total Additional Expense Deductions under § 707(b).** Enter the total of Lines 30 through 36.	$

Subpart C: Deductions for Debt Payment

38	**Future payments on secured claims.** For each of your debts that is secured by an interest in property that you own, list the name of creditor, identify the property securing the debt, and state the Average Monthly Payment. The Average Monthly Payment is the total of all amounts contractually due to each Secured Creditor in the 60 months following the filing of the bankruptcy case, divided by 60. If necessary, list additional entries on a separate page. **Do not include items you have previously deducted, such as insurance and real estate taxes.**	

	Name of Creditor	Property Securing the Debt	60-month Average Payment
a.			$
b.			$
c.			$
			Total: Add Lines a, b, and c — $

39	**Past due payments on secured claims.** If any of the debts listed in Line 38 are in default, and the property securing the debt is necessary for your support or the support of your dependents, you may include in your deductions 1/60th of the amount that you must pay the creditor as a result of the default (the "cure amount") in order to maintain possession of the property. List any such amounts in the following chart and enter the total. If necessary, list additional entries on a separate page.	

	Name of Creditor	Property Securing the Debt in Default	1/60th of the Cure Amount
a.			$
b.			$
c.			$
			Total: Add Lines a, b, and c — $

40	**Payments on priority claims.** Enter the total amount of all priority claims (including priority child support and alimony claims), divided by 60.	$
41	**Chapter 13 administrative expenses.** Multiply the amount in Line a by the amount in Line b, and enter the resulting administrative expense. a. Projected average monthly Chapter 13 plan payment. — $ b. Current multiplier for your district as determined under schedules issued by the Executive Office for United States Trustees. (This information is available at www.usdoj.gov/ust/ or from the clerk of the bankruptcy court.) — x c. Average monthly administrative expense of Chapter 13 case — Total: Multiply Lines a and b	$
42	**Total Deductions for Debt Payment.** Enter the total of Lines 38 through 41.	$
	Subpart D: Total Deductions Allowed under § 707(b)(2)	
43	**Total of all deductions allowed under § 707(b)(2).** Enter the total of Lines 29, 37, and 42.	$

Part IV. DETERMINATION OF DISPOSABLE INCOME UNDER § 1325(b)(2)

44	**Total current monthly income.** Enter the amount from Line 11.	$
45	**Support income.** Enter the monthly average of any child support payments, foster care payments, or disability payments for a dependent child, included in Line 7, that you received in accordance with applicable nonbankruptcy law, to the extent reasonably necessary to be expended for such child.	$
46	**Qualified retirement deductions.** Enter the monthly average of (a) all contributions or wage deductions made to qualified retirement plans, as specified in § 541(b)(7) and (b) all repayments of loans from retirement plans, as specified in § 362(b)(19).	$
47	**Total of all deductions allowed under § 707(b)(2).** Enter the amount from Line 43.	$
48	**Total adjustments to determine disposable income.** Add the amounts on Lines 45, 46, and 47 and enter the result.	$
49	**Monthly Disposable Income Under § 1325(b)(2).** Subtract Line 48 from Line 44 and enter the result.	$

Part V: ADDITIONAL EXPENSE CLAIMS

50 **Other Expenses.** List and describe any monthly expenses, not otherwise stated in this form, that are required for the health and welfare of you and your family and that you contend should be an additional deduction from your current monthly income under § 707(b)(2)(A)(ii)(I). If necessary, list additional sources on a separate page. All figures should reflect your average monthly expense for each item. Total the expenses.

	Expense Description	Monthly Amount
a.		$
b.		$
c.		$
	Total: Add Lines a, b, and c	$

Part VI: VERIFICATION

51 I declare under penalty of perjury that the information provided in this statement is true and correct. *(If this a joint case, both debtors must sign.)*

Date: ____________________ Signature: ____________________ (Debtor)

Date: ____________________ Signature: ____________________ (Joint Debtor, if any)

Form 23
(10/05)

United States Bankruptcy Court

_______________ District Of _______________

In re ______________________________________,
Debtor

Case No. ___________________

Chapter ___________

DEBTOR'S CERTIFICATION OF COMPLETION OF INSTRUCTIONAL COURSE CONCERNING PERSONAL FINANCIAL MANAGEMENT

[Complete one of the following statements.]

☐ I/We, ____. the debtor(s) in the above-
(Printed Name(s) of Debtor and Joint Debtor, if any)
styled case hereby certify that on ___________________ I/we completed an instructional
(Date)
course in personal financial management provided by ________________________________,
(Name of Provider)
an approved personal financial management instruction provider. If the provider furnished a document attesting to the completion of the personal financial management instructional course, a copy of that document is attached.

☐ I/We, ____, the debtor(s) in the above-styled
(Printed Names of Debtor and Joint Debtor, if any)
case, hereby certify that no personal financial management course is required because:
[Check the appropriate box.]

☐ I am/We are incapacitated or disabled, as defined in 11 U.S.C. § 109(h);

☐ I am/We are on active military duty in a military combat zone; or

☐ I/We reside in a district in which the United States trustee (or bankruptcy administrator) has determined that the approved instructional courses are not adequate at this time to serve the additional individuals who would otherwise be required to complete such courses.

Signature of Debtor: ____

Date: ___________________

Signature of Joint Debtor: ___________________________________

Date: ___________________

Form 24
(10/05)

[Caption as described in Fed. R. Bankr. P. 7010 or 9004(b), as applicable.]

CERTIFICATION TO COURT OF APPEALS BY ALL PARTIES

A notice of appeal having been filed in the above-styled matter on _________*[Date]*, ___________________, ________________________, and ______________________, *[Names of all the appellants and all the appellees, if any]*, who are all the appellants [and all the appellees] hereby certify to the court under 28 U.S.C. § 158(d)(2)(A) that a circumstance specified in 28 U.S.C. § 158(d)(2) exists as stated below.

Leave to appeal in this matter [_] is [_] is not required under 28 U.S.C. § 158(a).

[If from a final judgment, order, or decree] This certification arises in an appeal from a final judgment, order, or decree of the United States Bankruptcy Court for the _________ District of __________ entered on ___________*[Date]*.

[If from an interlocutory order or decree] This certification arises in an appeal from an interlocutory order or decree, and the parties hereby request leave to appeal as required by 28 U.S.C. § 158(a).

[The certification shall contain one or more of the following statements, as is appropriate to the circumstances.]

The judgment, order, or decree involves a question of law as to which there is no controlling decision of the court of appeals for this circuit or of the Supreme Court of the United States, or involves a matter of public importance.

Or

The judgment, order, or decree involves a question of law requiring resolution of conflicting decisions.

Or

An immediate appeal from the judgment, order, or decree may materially advance the progress of the case or proceeding in which the appeal is taken.

Form 24, Cont'd. Page 2

[The parties may include or attach the information specified in Rule 8001(f)(3)(C).]

Signed: *[If there are more than two signatories, all must sign and provide the information requested below. Attach additional signed sheets if needed.]*

____
Attorney for Appellant (or Appellant, if not represented by an attorney)

____
Printed Name of Signer

____
____
Address

____
Telephone No.

____
Date

____
Attorney for Appellant (or Appellant if not represented by an attorney)

____
Printed Name of Signer

____
____
Address

____
Telephone No.

____
Date

Appendix E

Practice Aids

E.1 Date Calculator

The 2005 amendments to the Bankruptcy Code have added several new time periods for events occurring pre-petition that could determine fundamental aspects of a bankruptcy case, such as the availability of the automatic stay, the ability to claim exemptions, and the right to a discharge. In some cases, these time periods may affect the debtor's decision when to file bankruptcy.

The CD-Rom accompanying this volume contains a Date Calculator, a tool that can assist attorneys in approximating the dates of these various time periods, based on a projected filing date. Enter a filing date in the Calculator on the CD-Rom, and the Calculator automatically lists twenty-one key look-back dates, before or after which dates specified events must or must not have occurred. A sample page is listed below.

Disclaimer: This program is not intended to be a substitute for an attorney's exercise of independent judgment and analysis in advising a client. Moreover, the method for counting how days are calculated for a particular look-back period may depend upon the precise wording of a statute and its construction by the courts. Thus, attorneys are advised to review the statutory language before independently determining the date in question.

Date Calculator

Enter Projected Filing Date: December 15, 2005

Pre-Petition Time Period	Code Provision	Date
60 days	Payment advices received from employer within 60 days of petition; § 521(a)(1)(B)(iv)	Oct. 16, 2005
60 days	Creditor unreasonably refused to negotiate alternative repayment schedule made at least 60 days before petition; § 502(k)	Oct. 16, 2005
70 days	Cash advances more than $750 within 70 days of petition presumed nondischargeable; § 523(a)(2)(C)(i)(II)	Oct. 6, 2005
90 days	Luxury goods debts incurred within 90 days of petition presumed nondischargeable; § 523(a)(2)(C)(i)(I)	Sept. 16, 2005
180 days	Credit counseling briefing during 180-day period before petition; § 109(h)(1)	June 18, 2005
1 year	Cramdown prohibited on purchase money loan secured by non-auto collateral incurred within 1 year of petition; § 1325(a)	Dec. 15, 2004
1 year	Automatic stay exceptions based on prior cases filed within 1 year of petition; § 362(c)(i)	Dec. 15, 2004
365 days	Funds placed in education IRA within 365 days of petition excluded from estate; § 541(b)(5)	Dec. 15, 2004
720 days	Funds up to $5,000 placed in education IRA between 720 and 365 days before petition excluded from estate; § 541(b)(5)(C)	Dec. 26, 2003
365 days	Funds used to purchase state tuition credit within 365 days of petition excluded from estate; § 541(b)(6)	Dec. 15, 2004
720 days	Funds up to $5,000 used to purchase state tuition credit between 720 and 365 days before petition excluded from estate; § 541(b)(6)(C)	Dec. 26, 2003
2 years	Real property automatic stay exception within 2 years of entry of *in rem* order in prior case; § 362(c)(i)	Dec. 15, 2003
2 years	No discharge in chapter 13 case if prior discharge entered in chapter 13 case filed within 2 years of order for relief; § 1328(f)(1)	Dec. 15, 2003
730 days	Location of debtor's domicile during 730-day period before petition used for determining exemptions; § 522(b)(3)(A)	Dec. 16, 2003
910 days (730 + 180)	Location of debtor's domicile during 180-day period (or greater portion of 180 days) preceding 730-day period used for determining exemptions, if domicile not in single state for first 730 days; § 522(b)(3)(A)	June 19, 2003
910 days	Cramdown prohibited on purchase money auto loan incurred within 910 days of petition; § 1325(a)	June 19, 2003
1215 days	Homestead interest limited to $125,000 exemption if interest acquired during 1215-day period before petition; § 522(p)(1)	Aug. 18, 2002
4 years	No discharge in chapter 13 case if prior discharge entered in chapter 7, 11, or 12 case filed within 4 years of order for relief; § 1328(f)(1)	Dec. 15, 2001
5 years	Homestead interest limited to $125,000 exemption based on criminal act, intentional tort, willful or reckless misconduct that caused serious physical injury or death within 5 years of petition; § 522(q)(1)	Dec. 15, 2000
8 years	No discharge in chapter 7 case if prior chapter 7 discharge entered in case filed within 8 years of petition; § 727(a)(8)	Dec. 15, 1997
10 years	Homestead interest not exempt to extent attributable to non-exempt property disposed of with the intent to hinder, delay or defraud a creditor within 10 years of petition; § 522(*o*)	Dec. 15, 1995

E.2 Obtaining Tax Returns or Transcripts from the Internal Revenue Service

The 2005 amendments to the Bankruptcy Code require the debtor to provide tax returns or transcripts in certain situations. This section provides forms to request this information from the Internal Revenue Service (I.R.S.) Typically it is quicker and easier to obtain tax transcripts rather than tax returns, and the tax information provided in transcripts will generally cause less invasion of the debtor's privacy.

There are several different types of tax transcripts. Section 521, as amended in 2005, provides that a transcript of a return may be filed or provided at the election of the debtor, but does not specify which type of transcript is to be used. Due primarily to privacy concerns, in most cases the preferred transcript will be the simplest, the MFTRA-X. Other transcripts, such as the IMF MCC SPECIFIC or the TXMOD, contain more information.

Transcripts can be requested from the national Priority Hotline at (866) 860-4259. Request the transcript of choice (usually the MFTRA-X) for the relevant tax years. The I.R.S. representative will ask you to send them a completed Form 8821 or Form 2848 via facsimile (both forms are reprinted *infra* and may also be found on the CD-Rom accompanying this volume). If you are not representing the debtor in matters before the I.R.S., you would not typically submit Form 2848. A power of attorney is not required for the debtor to authorize the disclosure of tax return information through Form 8821.

The I.R.S. representative will also request a cover letter stating the type of transcript, the tax years, the type of tax, and the client's Social Security Number and address. The cover letter can request that the I.R.S. send the transcripts via facsimile in response to the request, but the I.R.S. may mail them in any event. Another alternative is to contact a local I.R.S. office to see if it will send transcripts via facsimile upon request.

Transcripts can also be obtained by the debtor by using Form 4506-T (reprinted *infra* and also found on the CD-Rom accompanying this volume), which is mailed or sent via facsimile to the regional I.R.S. offices listed in the form's instructions. To obtain the MFTRA-X transcript, the debtor should check the box on line 6c, which is designated as "Record of Account." The debtor may request on line 5 that the transcript be mailed to the attorney for the debtor.

The debtor can request a copy of the actual return instead of a transcript by using Form 4506 (reprinted *infra* and also found on the CD-Rom accompanying this volume). In general it is faster and simpler to request the transcript instead of the return.

Forms Reproduced in This Appendix

Form 8821 Tax Information Authorization

Form 2848 Power of Attorney and Declaration of Representative

Form 4506 Request for Copy of Tax Return

Form 4506-T Request for Transcript of Tax Return

Form **8821**
(Rev. April 2004)
Department of the Treasury
Internal Revenue Service

Tax Information Authorization

▶ **Do not use this form to request a copy or transcript of your tax return. Instead, use Form 4506 or Form 4506-T.**

OMB No. 1545-1165

For IRS Use Only
Received by:
Name ____________
Telephone ( )
Function ____________
Date / /

1 Taxpayer information. Taxpayer(s) must sign and date this form on line 7.

Taxpayer name(s) and address (type or print)	Social security number(s)	Employer identification number
	Daytime telephone number ( )	Plan number (if applicable)

2 Appointee. If you wish to name more than one appointee, attach a list to this form.

Name and address

CAF No. ....
Telephone No. ....
Fax No. ....
Check if new: Address ☐ Telephone No. ☐ Fax No. ☐

3 Tax matters. The appointee is authorized to inspect and/or receive confidential tax information in any office of the IRS for the tax matters listed on this line. Do not use Form 8821 to request copies of tax returns.

(a) Type of Tax (Income, Employment, Excise, etc.) or Civil Penalty	(b) Tax Form Number (1040, 941, 720, etc.)	(c) Year(s) or Period(s) (see the instructions for line 3)	(d) Specific Tax Matters (see instr.)

4 Specific use not recorded on Centralized Authorization File (CAF). If the tax information authorization is for a specific use not recorded on CAF, check this box. See the instructions on page 3. If you check this box, skip lines 5 and 6 . ▶ ☐

5 Disclosure of tax information (you **must** check a box on line 5a or 5b unless the box on line 4 is checked):

a If you want copies of tax information, notices, and other written communications sent to the appointee on an ongoing basis, check this box . . . . ▶ ☐

b If you do not want any copies of notices or communications sent to your appointee, check this box . . . . . ▶ ☐

6 Retention/revocation of tax information authorizations. This tax information authorization automatically revokes all prior authorizations for the same tax matters you listed on line 3 above unless you checked the box on line 4. If you do not want to revoke a prior tax information authorization, you **must** attach a copy of any authorizations you want to remain in effect **and** check this box . . . . ▶ ☐

To revoke this tax information authorization, see the instructions on page 3.

7 Signature of taxpayer(s). If a tax matter applies to a joint return, **either** husband or wife must sign. If signed by a corporate officer, partner, guardian, executor, receiver, administrator, trustee, or party other than the taxpayer, I certify that I have the authority to execute this form with respect to the tax matters/periods on line 3 above.

▶ **IF NOT SIGNED AND DATED, THIS TAX INFORMATION AUTHORIZATION WILL BE RETURNED.**

Signature ____________ Date ______

Print Name ____________ Title (if applicable)

☐ ☐ ☐ ☐ ☐ PIN number for electronic signature

Signature ____________ Date ______

Print Name ____________ Title (if applicable)

☐ ☐ ☐ ☐ ☐ PIN number for electronic signature

For Privacy Act and Paperwork Reduction Act Notice, see page 4. Cat. No. 11596P Form **8821** (Rev. 4-2004)

General Instructions

Section references are to the Internal Revenue Code unless otherwise noted.

What's New

Authorization to file Form 8821 electronically. Your appointee may be able to file Form 8821 with the IRS electronically. PIN number boxes have been added to the taxpayer's signature section. Entering a PIN number will give your appointee authority to file Form 8821 electronically using the PIN number as the electronic signature. You can use any five digits other than all zeroes as a PIN number. You may use the same PIN number that you used on other filings with the IRS. See **Where To File** on page 3 if completing Form 8821 only for this purpose.

Purpose of Form

Form 8821 authorizes any individual, corporation, firm, organization, or partnership you designate to inspect and/or receive your confidential information in any office of the IRS for the type of tax and the years or periods you list on Form 8821. You may file your own tax information authorization without using Form 8821, but it must include all the information that is requested on Form 8821.

Form 8821 does not authorize your appointee to advocate your position with respect to the Federal tax laws; to execute waivers, consents, or closing agreements; or to otherwise represent you before the IRS. If you want to authorize an individual to represent you, use Form 2848, Power of Attorney and Declaration of Representative.

Use Form 4506, Request for Copy of Tax Return, to get a copy of your tax return.

Use new Form 4506-T, Request for Transcript of Tax Return, to order: (a) transcript of tax account information and (b) Form W-2 and Form 1099 series information.

Use Form 56, Notice Concerning Fiduciary Relationship, to notify the IRS of the existence of a fiduciary relationship. A fiduciary (trustee, executor, administrator, receiver, or guardian) stands in the position of a taxpayer and acts as the taxpayer. Therefore, a fiduciary does not act as an appointee and should not file Form 8821. If a fiduciary wishes to authorize an appointee to inspect and/or receive confidential tax information on behalf of the fiduciary, Form 8821 must be filed and signed by the fiduciary acting in the position of the taxpayer.

When To File

Form 8821 must be received by the IRS within 60 days of the date it was signed and dated by the taxpayer.

Where To File Chart

IF you live in . . .	THEN use this address . . .	Fax Number*
Alabama, Arkansas, Connecticut, Delaware, District of Columbia, Florida, Georgia, Illinois, Indiana, Kentucky, Louisiana, Maine, Maryland, Massachusetts, Michigan, Mississippi, New Hampshire, New Jersey, New York, North Carolina, Ohio, Pennsylvania, Rhode Island, South Carolina, Tennessee, Vermont, Virginia, or West Virginia	Internal Revenue Service Memphis Accounts Management Center Stop 8423 5333 Getwell Road Memphis, TN 38118	901-546-4115
Alaska, Arizona, California, Colorado, Hawaii, Idaho, Iowa, Kansas, Minnesota, Missouri, Montana, Nebraska, Nevada, New Mexico, North Dakota, Oklahoma, Oregon, South Dakota, Texas, Utah, Washington, Wisconsin, or Wyoming	Internal Revenue Service Ogden Accounts Management Center 1973 N. Rulon White Blvd. Mail Stop 6737 Ogden, UT 84404	801-620-4249
All APO and FPO addresses, American Samoa, nonpermanent residents of Guam or the Virgin Islands**, Puerto Rico (or if excluding income under Internal Revenue Code section 933), a foreign country: U.S. citizens and those filing Form 2555, 2555-EZ, or 4563.	Internal Revenue Service Philadelphia Accounts Management Center DPSW 312 11601 Roosevelt Blvd. Philadelphia, PA 19255	215-516-1017

*These numbers may change without notice.

**Permanent residents of Guam should use Department of Taxation, Government of Guam, P.O. Box 23607, GMF, GU 96921; permanent residents of the Virgin Islands should use: V.I. Bureau of Internal Revenue, 9601 Estate Thomas Charlotte Amaile, St. Thomas, V.I. 00802.

Where To File

Generally, mail or fax Form 8821 directly to the IRS. See the **Where To File Chart** on page 2. Exceptions are listed below.

- If Form 8821 is for a specific tax matter, mail or fax it to the office handling that matter. For more information, see the instructions for line 4.
- If you complete Form 8821 only for the purpose of electronic signature authorization, do not file Form 8821 with the IRS. Instead, give it to your appointee, who will retain the document.

Revocation of an Existing Tax Information Authorization

If you want to revoke an existing tax information authorization and do not want to name a new appointee, send a copy of the previously executed tax information authorization to the IRS, using the **Where To File Chart** on page 2. The copy of the tax information authorization must have a current signature of the taxpayer under the original signature on line 7. Write "REVOKE" across the top of Form 8821. If you do not have a copy of the tax information authorization you want to revoke, send a statement to the IRS. The statement of revocation must indicate that the authority of the tax information authorization is revoked, list the tax matters, must be signed and dated by the taxpayer, and list the name and address of each recognized appointee whose authority is revoked.

To revoke a specific use tax information authorization, send the tax information authorization or statement of revocation to the IRS office handling your case, using the above instructions.

Taxpayer Identification Numbers (TINs)

TINs are used to identify taxpayer information with corresponding tax returns. It is important that you furnish correct names, social security numbers (SSNs), individual taxpayer identification numbers (ITINs), or employer identification numbers (EINs) so that the IRS can respond to your request.

Partnership Items

Sections 6221–6234 authorize a Tax Matters Partner to perform certain acts on behalf of an affected partnership. Rules governing the use of Form 8821 do not replace any provisions of these sections.

Specific Instructions

Line 1. Taxpayer Information

Individuals. Enter your name, TIN, and your street address in the space provided. Do not enter your appointee's address or post office box. If a joint return is used, also enter your spouse's name and TIN. Also enter your EIN if applicable.

Corporations, partnerships, or associations. Enter the name, EIN, and business address.

Employee plan. Enter the plan name, EIN of the plan sponsor, three-digit plan number, and business address of the plan sponsor.

Trust. Enter the name, title, and address of the trustee, and the name and EIN of the trust.

Estate. Enter the name, title, and address of the decedent's executor/personal representative, and the name and identification number of the estate. The identification number for an estate includes both the EIN, if the estate has one, and the decedent's TIN.

Line 2. Appointee

Enter your appointee's full name. Use the identical full name on all submissions and correspondence. Enter the nine-digit CAF number for each appointee. If an appointee has a CAF number for any previously filed Form 8821 or power of attorney (Form 2848), use that number. If a CAF number has not been assigned, enter "NONE," and the IRS will issue one directly to your appointee. The IRS does not assign CAF numbers to requests for employee plans and exempt organizations.

If you want to name more than one appointee, indicate so on this line and attach a list of appointees to Form 8821.

Check the appropriate box to indicate if either the address, telephone number, or fax number is new since a CAF number was assigned.

Line 3. Tax Matters

Enter the type of tax, the tax form number, the years or periods, and the specific tax matter. Enter "Not applicable," in any of the columns that do not apply.

For example, you may list "Income tax, Form 1040" for calendar year "2003" and "Excise tax, Form 720" for the "1st, 2nd, 3rd, and 4th quarters of 2003." For multiple years, you may list "2001 through (thru or a dash (—)) 2003" for an income tax return; for quarterly returns, list "1st, 2nd, 3rd, and 4th quarters of 2001 through 2002" (or 2nd 2002 — 3rd 2003). For fiscal years, enter the ending year and month, using the YYYYMM format. Do not use a general reference such as "All years,""All periods," or "All taxes." Any tax information authorization with a general reference will be returned.

You may list any tax years or periods that have already ended as of the date you sign the tax information authorization. Also, you may include on a tax information authorization future tax periods that end no later than 3 years after the date the tax information authorization is received by the IRS. The 3 future periods are determined starting after December 31 of the year the tax information authorization is received by the IRS. You must enter the type of tax, the tax form number, and the future year(s) or period(s). If the matter relates to estate tax, enter the date of the decedent's death instead of the year or period.

In **column (d),** enter any specific information you want the IRS to provide. Examples of column (d) information are: lien information, a balance due amount, a specific tax schedule, or a tax liability.

For requests regarding Form 8802, Application for United States Residency Certification, enter "Form 8802" in column (d) and check the specific use box on line 4. Also, enter the appointee's information as instructed on Form 8802.

Line 4. Specific Use Not Recorded on CAF

Generally, the IRS records all tax information authorizations on the CAF system. However, authorizations relating to a specific issue are not recorded.

Check the box on line 4 if Form 8821 is filed for any of the following reasons: (a) requests to disclose information to loan companies or educational institutions, (b) requests to disclose information to Federal or state agency investigators for background checks, (c) application for EIN, or (d) claims filed on Form 843, Claim for Refund and Request for Abatement. If you check the box on line 4, your appointee should mail or fax Form 8821 to the IRS office handling the matter. Otherwise, your appointee should bring a copy of Form 8821 to each appointment to inspect or receive information. A specific-use tax information authorization will not revoke any prior tax information authorizations.

Line 6. Retention/Revocation of Tax Information Authorizations

Check the box on this line and attach a copy of the tax information authorization you do not want to revoke. The filing of Form 8821 will not revoke any Form 2848 that is in effect.

Line 7. Signature of Taxpayer(s)

Individuals. You must sign and date the authorization. Either husband or wife must sign if Form 8821 applies to a joint return.

Corporations. Generally, Form 8821 can be signed by: (a) an officer having legal authority to bind the corporation, (b) any person designated by the board of directors or other governing body, (c) any officer or employee on written request by any principal officer and attested to by the secretary or other officer, and (d) any other person authorized to access information under section 6103(e).

Partnerships. Generally, Form 8821 can be signed by any person who was a member of the partnership during any part of the tax period covered by Form 8821. See **Partnership Items** on page 3.

All others. See section 6103(e) if the taxpayer has died, is insolvent, is a dissolved corporation, or if a trustee, guardian, executor, receiver, or administrator is acting for the taxpayer.

Privacy Act and Paperwork Reduction Act Notice

We ask for the information on this form to carry out the Internal Revenue laws of the United States. Form 8821 is provided by the IRS for your convenience and its use is voluntary. If you designate an appointee to inspect and/or receive confidential tax information, you are required by section 6103(c) to provide the information requested on Form 8821. Under section 6109, you must disclose your social security number (SSN), employer identification number (EIN), or individual taxpayer identification number (ITIN). If you do not provide all the information requested on this form, we may not be able to honor the authorization.

Routine uses of this information include giving it to the Department of Justice for civil and criminal litigation, and to cities, states, and the District of Columbia for use in administering their tax laws. We may also give this information to other countries pursuant to tax treaties. We may also disclose this information to Federal and state agencies to enforce Federal nontax criminal laws and to combat terrorism. The authority to disclose information to combat terrorism expired on December 31, 2003. Legislation is pending that would reinstate this authority.

You are not required to provide the information requested on a form that is subject to the Paperwork Reduction Act unless the form displays a valid OMB control number. Books or records relating to a form or its instructions must be retained as long as their contents may become material in the administration of any Internal Revenue law.

The time needed to complete and file this form will vary depending on individual circumstances. The estimated average time is: **Recordkeeping,** 6 min.; **Learning about the law or the form,** 12 min.; **Preparing the form,** 24 min.; **Copying and sending the form to the IRS,** 20 min.

If you have comments concerning the accuracy of these time estimates or suggestions for making Form 8821 simpler, we would be happy to hear from you. You can write to the Tax Products Coordinating Committee, Western Area Distribution Center, Rancho Cordova, CA 95743-0001. **Do not** send Form 8821 to this address. Instead, see the **Where To File Chart** on page 2.

Form **2848** (Rev. March 2004) Department of the Treasury Internal Revenue Service

Power of Attorney and Declaration of Representative

▶ Type or print. ▶ See the separate instructions.

OMB No. 1545-0150

For IRS Use Only

Received by:

Name ______

Telephone ______

Function ______

Date / /

Part I **Power of Attorney**

Caution: *Form 2848 will not be honored for any purpose other than representation before the IRS.*

1 **Taxpayer information.** Taxpayer(s) must sign and date this form on page 2, line 9.

Taxpayer name(s) and address	Social security number(s)	Employer identification number
	Daytime telephone number ( )	Plan number (if applicable)

hereby appoint(s) the following representative(s) as attorney(s)-in-fact:

2 **Representative(s)** must sign and date this form on page 2, Part II.

Name and address	CAF No. ______ Telephone No. ______ Fax No. ______ Check if new: Address ☐ Telephone No. ☐ Fax No. ☐
Name and address	CAF No. ______ Telephone No. ______ Fax No. ______ Check if new: Address ☐ Telephone No. ☐ Fax No. ☐
Name and address	CAF No. ______ Telephone No. ______ Fax No. ______ Check if new: Address ☐ Telephone No. ☐ Fax No. ☐

to represent the taxpayer(s) before the Internal Revenue Service for the following tax matters:

3 **Tax matters**

Type of Tax (Income, Employment, Excise, etc.) or Civil Penalty (see the instructions for line 3)	Tax Form Number (1040, 941, 720, etc.)	Year(s) or Period(s) (see the instructions for line 3)

4 **Specific use not recorded on Centralized Authorization File (CAF).** If the power of attorney is for a specific use not recorded on CAF, check this box. See the instructions for **Line 4. Specific uses not recorded on CAF.** . . . . ▶ ☐

5 **Acts authorized.** The representatives are authorized to receive and inspect confidential tax information and to perform any and all acts that I (we) can perform with respect to the tax matters described on line 3, for example, the authority to sign any agreements, consents, or other documents. The authority does not include the power to receive refund checks (see line 6 below), the power to substitute another representative, the power to sign certain returns, or the power to execute a request for disclosure of tax returns or return information to a third party. See the line 5 instructions for more information.

Exceptions. An unenrolled return preparer cannot sign any document for a taxpayer and may only represent taxpayers in limited situations. See **Unenrolled Return Preparer** on page 2 of the instructions. An enrolled actuary may only represent taxpayers to the extent provided in section 10.3(d) of Circular 230. See the line 5 instructions for restrictions on tax matters partners.

List any specific additions or deletions to the acts otherwise authorized in this power of attorney: ______

______

______

______

6 **Receipt of refund checks.** If you want to authorize a representative named on line 2 to receive, **BUT NOT TO ENDORSE OR CASH**, refund checks, initial here ______ and list the name of that representative below.

Name of representative to receive refund check(s) ▶

For Privacy Act and Paperwork Reduction Notice, see page 4 of the instructions. Cat. No. 11980J Form **2848** (Rev. 3-2004)

7 Notices and communications. Original notices and other written communications will be sent to you and a copy to the first representative listed on line 2.

a If you also want the second representative listed to receive a copy of notices and communications, check this box . . ▶ ☐

b If you do not want any notices or communications sent to your representative(s), check this box . . . . ▶ ☐

8 Retention/revocation of prior power(s) of attorney. The filing of this power of attorney automatically revokes all earlier power(s) of attorney on file with the Internal Revenue Service for the same tax matters and years or periods covered by this document. If you **do not** want to revoke a prior power of attorney, check here. . . . . ▶ ☐

YOU MUST ATTACH A COPY OF ANY POWER OF ATTORNEY YOU WANT TO REMAIN IN EFFECT.

9 Signature of taxpayer(s). If a tax matter concerns a joint return, **both** husband and wife must sign if joint representation is requested, otherwise, see the instructions. If signed by a corporate officer, partner, guardian, tax matters partner, executor, receiver, administrator, or trustee on behalf of the taxpayer, I certify that I have the authority to execute this form on behalf of the taxpayer.

▶ **IF NOT SIGNED AND DATED, THIS POWER OF ATTORNEY WILL BE RETURNED.**

Signature	Date	Title (if applicable)

Print Name	PIN Number ☐☐☐☐☐	Print name of taxpayer from line 1 if other than individual

Signature	Date	Title (if applicable)

Print Name	PIN Number ☐☐☐☐☐

Part II Declaration of Representative

Caution: *Students with a special order to represent taxpayers in Qualified Low Income Taxpayer Clinics or the Student Tax Clinic Program, see the instructions for Part II.*

Under penalties of perjury, I declare that:

- I am not currently under suspension or disbarment from practice before the Internal Revenue Service;
- I am aware of regulations contained in Treasury Department Circular No. 230 (31 CFR, Part 10), as amended, concerning the practice of attorneys, certified public accountants, enrolled agents, enrolled actuaries, and others;
- I am authorized to represent the taxpayer(s) identified in Part I for the tax matter(s) specified there; and
- I am one of the following:

a Attorney—a member in good standing of the bar of the highest court of the jurisdiction shown below.

b Certified Public Accountant—duly qualified to practice as a certified public accountant in the jurisdiction shown below.

c Enrolled Agent—enrolled as an agent under the requirements of Treasury Department Circular No. 230.

d Officer—a bona fide officer of the taxpayer's organization.

e Full-Time Employee—a full-time employee of the taxpayer.

f Family Member—a member of the taxpayer's immediate family (i.e., spouse, parent, child, brother, or sister).

g Enrolled Actuary—enrolled as an actuary by the Joint Board for the Enrollment of Actuaries under 29 U.S.C. 1242 (the authority to practice before the Service is limited by section 10.3(d) of Treasury Department Circular No. 230).

h Unenrolled Return Preparer—the authority to practice before the Internal Revenue Service is limited by Treasury Department Circular No. 230, section 10.7(c)(1)(viii). You must have prepared the return in question and the return must be under examination by the IRS. See **Unenrolled Return Preparer** on page 2 of the instructions.

▶ **IF THIS DECLARATION OF REPRESENTATIVE IS NOT SIGNED AND DATED, THE POWER OF ATTORNEY WILL BE RETURNED.** See the Part II instructions.

Designation—Insert above letter **(a–h)**	Jurisdiction (state) or identification	Signature	Date

Form **4506**

(Rev. July 2005)

Department of the Treasury
Internal Revenue Service

Request for Copy of Tax Return

▶ **Do not sign this form unless all applicable lines have been completed. Read the instructions on page 2.**

▶ **Request may be rejected if the form is incomplete, illegible, or any required line was blank at the time of signature.**

OMB No. 1545-0429

Tip: You may be able to get your tax return or return information from other sources. If you had your tax return completed by a paid preparer, they should be able to provide you a copy of the return. The IRS can provide a **Tax Return Transcript** for many returns free of charge. The transcript provides most of the line entries from the tax return and usually contains the information that a third party (such as a mortgage company) requires. See **Form 4506-T,** Request for Transcript of Tax Return, or you can call 1-800-829-1040 to order a transcript.

1a Name shown on tax return. If a joint return, enter the name shown first.	**1b First social security number on tax return or employer identification number (see instructions)**
2a If a joint return, enter spouse's name shown on tax return	**2b Second social security number if joint tax return**

3 Current name, address (including apt., room, or suite no.), city, state, and ZIP code

4 Previous address shown on the last return filed if different from line 3

5 If the tax return is to be mailed to a third party (such as a mortgage company), enter the third party's name, address, and telephone number. The IRS has no control over what the third party does with the tax return.

Caution: *If a third party requires you to complete Form 4506,* ***do not*** *sign Form 4506 if lines 6 and 7 are blank.*

6 **Tax return requested** (Form 1040, 1120, 941, etc.) and all attachments as originally submitted to the IRS, including Form(s) W-2, schedules, or amended returns. Copies of Forms 1040, 1040A, and 1040EZ are generally available for 7 years from filing before they are destroyed by law. Other returns may be available for a longer period of time. Enter only one return number. If you need more than one type of return, you must complete another Form 4506. ▶ ____________

Note. *If the copies must be certified for court or administrative proceedings, check here* . . . . ☐

7 **Year or period requested.** Enter the ending date of the year or period, using the mm/dd/yyyy format. If you are requesting more than eight years or periods, you must attach another Form 4506.

___/___/___ ___/___/___ ___/___/___ ___/___/___

___/___/___ ___/___/___ ___/___/___ ___/___/___

8 **Fee.** There is a $39 fee for each return requested. **Full payment must be included with your request or it will be rejected. Make your check or money order payable to "United States Treasury." Enter your SSN or EIN and "Form 4506 request" on your check or money order.**

a	Cost for each return	$ 39.00
b	Number of returns requested on line 7	
c	Total cost. Multiply line 8a by line 8b	$

9 If we cannot find the tax return, we will refund the fee. If the refund should go to the third party listed on line 5, check here . . ☐

Signature of taxpayer(s). I declare that I am either the taxpayer whose name is shown on line 1a or 2a, or a person authorized to obtain the tax return requested. If the request applies to a joint return, **either** husband or wife must sign. If signed by a corporate officer, partner, guardian, tax matters partner, executor, receiver, administrator, trustee, or party other than the taxpayer, I certify that I have the authority to execute Form 4506 on behalf of the taxpayer.

Telephone number of taxpayer on line 1a or 2a
(   )

Sign Here

▶ **Signature** (see instructions) Date

▶ **Title** (if line 1a above is a corporation, partnership, estate, or trust)

▶ **Spouse's** signature Date

For Privacy Act and Paperwork Reduction Act Notice, see page 2. Cat. No. 41721E Form **4506** (Rev. 7-2005)

General Instructions

Section references are to the Internal Revenue Code.

Purpose of form. Use Form 4506 to request a copy of your tax return. You can also designate a third party to receive the tax return. See line 5.

How long will it take? It may take up to 60 calendar days for us to process your request.

Tip. Use Form 4506-T, Request for Transcript of Tax Return, to request tax return transcripts, tax account information, W-2 information, 1099 information, verification of non-filing, and record of account.

Where to file. Attach payment and mail Form 4506 to the address below for the state you lived in when that return was filed. There are two address charts: one for individual returns (Form 1040 series) and one for all other returns.

Note. *If you are requesting more than one return and the chart below shows two different service centers, mail your request to the service center based on the address of your most recent return.*

Chart for individual returns (Form 1040 series)

If you filed an individual return and lived in:	Mail to the Internal Revenue Service at:
District of Columbia, Maine, Maryland, Massachusetts, New Hampshire, New York, Vermont	RAIVS Team 310 Lowell St. Stop 679 Andover, MA 01810
Alabama, Delaware, Florida, Georgia, North Carolina, Rhode Island, South Carolina, Virginia	RAIVS Team 4800 Buford Hwy. Stop 91 Chamblee, GA 30341
Arkansas, Kansas, Kentucky, Louisiana, Mississippi, Oklahoma, Tennessee, Texas, West Virginia	RAIVS Team 3651 South Interregional Hwy. Stop 6716 Austin, TX 78741
Alaska, Arizona, California, Colorado, Hawaii, Idaho, Montana, Nebraska, Nevada, New Mexico, Oregon, South Dakota, Utah, Washington, Wyoming	RAIVS Team Stop 38101 Fresno, CA 93888
Connecticut, Illinois, Indiana, Iowa, Michigan, Minnesota, Missouri, North Dakota, Ohio, Wisconsin	RAIVS Team Stop B41-6700 Kansas City, MO 64999
New Jersey, Pennsylvania, a foreign country, or A.P.O. or F.P.O. address	RAIVS Team DP SE 135 Philadelphia, PA 19255-0695

Chart for all other returns

If you lived in or your business was in:	Mail to the Internal Revenue Service at:
Alabama, Alaska, Arizona, Arkansas, California, Colorado, Florida, Georgia, Hawaii, Idaho, Iowa, Kansas, Louisiana, Minnesota, Mississippi, Missouri, Montana, Nebraska, Nevada, New Mexico, North Dakota, Oklahoma, Oregon, South Dakota, Tennessee, Texas, Utah, Washington, Wyoming	RAIVS Team Mail Stop 6734 Ogden, UT 84409
Connecticut, Delaware, District of Columbia, Illinois, Indiana, Kentucky, Maine, Maryland, Massachusetts, Michigan, New Hampshire, New Jersey, New York, North Carolina, Ohio, Pennsylvania, Rhode Island, South Carolina, Vermont, Virginia, West Virginia, Wisconsin	RAIVS Team P.O. Box 145500 Stop 2800F Cincinnati, OH 45250

Line 1b. Enter your employer identification number (EIN) if you are requesting a copy of a business return. Otherwise, enter the first social security number (SSN) shown on the return. For example, if you are requesting Form 1040 that includes Schedule C (Form 1040), enter your SSN.

Signature and date. Form 4506 must be signed and dated by the taxpayer listed on line 1a or 2a. If you completed line 5 requesting the return be sent to a third party, the IRS must receive Form 4506 within 60 days of the date signed by the taxpayer or it will be rejected.

Individuals. Copies of jointly filed tax returns may be furnished to either spouse. Only one signature is required. Sign Form 4506 exactly as your name appeared on the original return. If you changed your name, also sign your current name.

Corporations. Generally, Form 4506 can be signed by: (1) an officer having legal authority to bind the corporation, (2) any person designated by the board of directors or other governing body, or (3) any officer or employee on written request by any principal officer and attested to by the secretary or other officer.

Partnerships. Generally, Form 4506 can be signed by any person who was a member of the partnership during any part of the tax period requested on line 7.

All others. See section 6103(e) if the taxpayer has died, is insolvent, is a dissolved corporation, or if a trustee, guardian, executor, receiver, or administrator is acting for the taxpayer.

Documentation. For entities other than individuals, you must attach the authorization document. For example, this could be the letter from the principal officer authorizing an employee of the corporation or the Letters Testamentary authorizing an individual to act for an estate.

Signature by a representative. A representative can sign Form 4506 for a taxpayer only if this authority has been specifically delegated to the representative on Form 2848, line 5. Form 2848 showing the delegation must be attached to Form 4506.

Privacy Act and Paperwork Reduction Act Notice. We ask for the information on this form to establish your right to gain access to the requested return(s) under the Internal Revenue Code. We need this information to properly identify the return(s) and respond to your request. Sections 6103 and 6109 require you to provide this information, including your SSN or EIN, to process your request. If you do not provide this information, we may not be able to process your request. Providing false or fraudulent information may subject you to penalties.

Routine uses of this information include giving it to the Department of Justice for civil and criminal litigation, and cities, states, and the District of Columbia for use in administering their tax laws. We may also disclose this information to other countries under a tax treaty, to federal and state agencies to enforce federal nontax criminal laws, or to federal law enforcement and intelligence agencies to combat terrorism.

You are not required to provide the information requested on a form that is subject to the Paperwork Reduction Act unless the form displays a valid OMB control number. Books or records relating to a form or its instructions must be retained as long as their contents may become material in the administration of any Internal Revenue law. Generally, tax returns and return information are confidential, as required by section 6103.

The time needed to complete and file Form 4506 will vary depending on individual circumstances. The estimated average time is: **Learning about the law or the form,** 10 min.; **Preparing the form,** 16 min.; and **Copying, assembling, and sending the form to the IRS,** 20 min.

If you have comments concerning the accuracy of these time estimates or suggestions for making Form 4506 simpler, we would be happy to hear from you. You can write to Internal Revenue Service, Tax Products Coordinating Committee, SE:W:CAR:MP:T:T:SP, 1111 Constitution Ave. NW, IR-6406, Washington, DC 20224. Do not send the form to this address. Instead, see *Where to file* on this page.

Form **4506-T** (January 2004)

Department of the Treasury
Internal Revenue Service

Request for Transcript of Tax Return

► **Do not sign this form unless all applicable parts have been completed. Read the instructions on page 2.**

► **Request may be rejected if the form is incomplete, illegible, or any required part was blank at the time of signature.**

OMB No. 1545-1872

TIP: Use new Form 4506-T to order a transcript or other return information free of charge. See the product list below. You can also call 1-800-829-1040 to order a transcript. If you need a copy of your return, use **Form 4506,** Request for Copy of Tax Return. There is a fee to get a copy of your return.

1a Name shown on tax return. If a joint return, enter the name shown first.

1b First social security number on tax return or employer identification number (see instructions)

2a If a joint return, enter spouse's name shown on tax return

2b Second social security number if joint tax return

3 Current name, address (including apt., room, or suite no.), city, state, and ZIP code

4 Address, (including apt., room, or suite no.), city, state, and ZIP code shown on the last return filed if different from line 3

5 If the transcript or tax information is to be mailed to a third party (such as a mortgage company), enter the third party's name, address, and telephone number. The IRS has no control over what the third party does with the tax information.

CAUTION: *Lines 6 and 7 must be completed if the third party requires you to complete Form 4506-T.* ***Do not*** *sign Form 4506-T if the third party requests that you sign Form 4506-T and lines 6 and 7 are blank.*

6 Product requested. Most requests will be processed within 10 business days. If the product requested relates to information from a return filed more than 4 years ago, it may take up to 30 days. Enter the return number here and check the box below. ► ____________

a **Return Transcript,** which includes most of the line items of a tax return as filed with the IRS. Transcripts are generally available for the following returns: Form 1040 series, Form 1065, Form 1120, Form 1120A, Form 1120H, Form 1120L, and Form 1120S. Return transcripts are available for the current year and returns processed during the prior 3 processing years . . . . ☐

b **Account Transcript,** which contains information on the financial status of the account, such as payments made on the account, penalty assessments, and adjustments made by you or the IRS after the return was filed. Return information is limited to items such as tax liability and estimated tax payments. Account transcripts are available for most returns . . . . ☐

c **Record of Account,** which is a combination of line item information and later adjustments to the account. Available for current year and 3 prior tax years . . . . ☐

d **Verification of Nonfiling,** which is proof from the IRS that you did not file a return for the year . . . . ☐

e **Form W-2, Form 1099 series, Form 1098 series, or Form 5498 series transcript.** The IRS can provide a transcript that includes data from these information returns. State or local information is not included with the Form W-2 information. The IRS may be able to provide this transcrpit information for up to 10 years. Information for the current year is generally not available until the year after it is filed with the IRS. For example, W-2 information for 2003, filed in 2004, will not be available from the IRS until 2005. If you need W-2 information for retirement purposes, you should contact the Social Security Administration at 1-800-772-1213 . . . . ☐

CAUTION: *If you need a copy of Form W-2 or Form 1099, you should first contact the payer. To get a copy of the Form W-2 or Form 1099 filed with your return, you must use Form 4506 and request a copy of your return, which includes all attachments.*

7 Year or period requested. Enter the ending date of the year or period, using the mm/dd/yyyy format. If you are requesting more than four years or periods, you must attach another Form 4506-T.

___/___/______ ___/___/______ ___/___/______ ___/___/______

Signature of taxpayer(s). I declare that I am either the taxpayer whose name is shown on line 1a or 2a, or a person authorized to obtain the tax information requested. If the request applies to a joint return, **either** husband or wife must sign. If signed by a corporate officer, partner, guardian, tax matters partner, executor, receiver, administrator, trustee, or party other than the taxpayer, I certify that I have the authority to execute Form 4506-T on behalf of the taxpayer.

Sign Here

Telephone number of taxpayer on line 1a or 2a ( )

Signature (see instructions) Date

Title (if line 1a above is a corporation, partnership, estate, or trust)

Spouse's signature Date

For Privacy Act and Paperwork Reduction Act Notice, see page 2. Cat. No. 37667N Form **4506-T** (1-2004)

A Change To Note

- **New Form 4506-T**, Request for Transcript of Tax Return, is used to request tax return transcripts, tax account transcripts, W-2 information, 1099 information, verification of non-filing, and a record of account. **Form 4506,** Request for Copy of Tax Return, is now used only to request copies of tax returns.

Instructions

Purpose of form. Use Form 4506-T to request tax return information. You can also designate a third party to receive the information. See line 5.

Where to file. Mail or fax Form 4506-T to the address below for the state you lived in when that return was filed. There are two address charts: one for individual transcripts (Form 1040 series) and one for all other transcripts.

Note: *If you are requesting more than one transcript or other product and the chart below shows two different service centers, mail your request to the service center based on the address of your most recent return.*

Chart for individual transcripts (Form 1040 series)

If you lived in and filed an individual return:	Mail or fax to the Internal Revenue Service at:
Maine, Massachusetts, New Hampshire, New York, Vermont	RAIVS Team 310 Lowell St. Stop 679 Andover, MA 01810 978-691-6859
Alabama, Florida, Georgia, Mississippi, North Carolina, South Carolina, West Virginia, Rhode Island	RAIVS Team 4800 Buford Hwy. Stop 91 Chamblee, GA 30341 678-530-5326
Arkansas, Colorado, Kentucky, Louisiana, New Mexico, Oklahoma, Tennessee, Texas	RAIVS Team 3651 South Interregional Hwy. Stop 6716 Austin, TX 78741 512-460-2272
Alaska, Arizona, California, Hawaii, Idaho, Montana, Nevada, Oregon, Utah, Washington, Wyoming	RAIVS Team Stop 38101 Fresno, CA 93888 559-253-4992
Delaware, Illinois, Indiana, Iowa, Kansas, Michigan, Minnesota, Missouri, Nebraska, North Dakota, South Dakota, Wisconsin	RAIVS Team Stop B41-6700 Kansas City, MO 64999 816-823-7667
Ohio, Virginia	RAIVS Team 5333 Getwell Rd. Stop 2826 Memphis, TN 38118 901-546-4175
Connecticut, District of Columbia, Maryland, New Jersey, Pennsylvania, a foreign country, or A.P.O. or F.P.O. address	RAIVS Team DP SE 135 Philadelphia, PA 19255-0695 215-516-2931

Chart for all other transcripts

If you lived in:	Mail to the Internal Revenue Service at:
Alabama, Alaska, Arizona, Arkansas, California, Colorado, Florida, Georgia, Hawaii, Idaho, Iowa, Kansas, Louisiana, Minnesota, Mississippi, Missouri, Montana, Nebraska, Nevada, New Mexico, North Dakota, Oklahoma, Oregon, South Dakota, Tennessee, Texas, Utah, Washington, Wyoming	RAIVS Team Mail Stop 6734 Ogden, UT 84201 801-620-6922
Connecticut, Delaware, District of Columbia, Illinois, Indiana, Kentucky, Maine, Maryland, Massachusetts, Michigan, New Hampshire, New Jersey, New York, North Carolina, Ohio, Pennsylvania, Rhode Island, South Carolina, Vermont, Virginia, West Virginia, Wisconsin	RAIVS Team P.O. Box 145500 Stop 2800F Cincinnati, OH 45250 859-669-3592

Line 1b. Enter your employer identification number if your request relates to a business return. Otherwise, enter the first social security number (SSN) shown on the return. For example, if you are requesting Form 1040 that includes Schedule C (Form 1040), enter your SSN.

Signature and date. Form 4506-T must be signed and dated by the taxpayer listed on line 1a or 2a. If you completed line 5 requesting the information be sent to a third party, the IRS must receive Form 4506-T within 60 days of the date signed by the taxpayer or it will be rejected.

Individuals. Transcripts of jointly filed tax returns may be furnished to either spouse. Only one signature is required. Sign Form 4506-T exactly as your name appeared on the original return. If you changed your name, also sign your current name.

Corporations. Generally, Form 4506-T can be signed by: (1) an officer having legal authority to bind the corporation, (2) any person designated by the board of directors or other governing body, or (3) any officer or employee on written request by any principal officer and attested to by the secretary or other officer.

Partnerships. Generally, Form 4506-T can be signed by any person who was a member of the partnership during any part of the tax period requested on line 7.

All others. See section 6103(e) if the taxpayer has died, is insolvent, is a dissolved corporation, or if a trustee, guardian, executor, receiver, or administrator is acting for the taxpayer.

Documentation. For entities other than individuals, you must attach the authorization document. For example, this could be the letter from the principal officer authorizing an employee of the corporation or the Letters Testamentary authorizing an individual to act for an estate.

Privacy Act and Paperwork Reduction Act Notice. We ask for the information on this form to establish your right to gain access to the requested tax information under the Internal Revenue Code. We need this information to properly identify the tax information and respond to your request. Sections 6103 and 6109 require you to provide this information, including your SSN or EIN. If you do not provide this information, we may not be able to process your request. Providing false or fraudulent information may subject you to penalties.

Routine uses of this information include giving it to the Department of Justice for civil and criminal litigation, and cities, states, and the District of Columbia for use in administering their tax laws. We may also disclose this information to Federal and state agencies to enforce Federal nontax criminal laws and to combat terrorism.

You are not required to provide the information requested on a form that is subject to the Paperwork Reduction Act unless the form displays a valid OMB control number. Books or records relating to a form or its instructions must be retained as long as their contents may become material in the administration of any Internal Revenue law. Generally, tax returns and return information are confidential, as required by section 6103.

The time needed to complete and file Form 4506-T will vary depending on individual circumstances. The estimated average time is: **Learning about the law or the form,** 10 min.; **Preparing the form,** 11 min.; and **Copying, assembling, and sending the form to the IRS,** 20 min.

If you have comments concerning the accuracy of these time estimates or suggestions for making Form 4506-T simpler, we would be happy to hear from you. You can write to the Tax Products Coordinating Committee, Western Area Distribution Center, Rancho Cordova, CA 95743-0001. **Do not** send the form to this address. Instead, see **Where to file** on this page.

Appendix F Means Test Data

F.1 Median Income by State

Debtors with incomes below their state's median family income will not be subjected to the "means test" formula to determine whether a debtor is presumed ineligible for a chapter 7 discharge. The following table provides the median family income data published by the Executive Office of the United States Trustee for the year 2004. The Executive Office of the United States Trustee states that the 2004 median income data should be used for completing Official Bankruptcy Forms 22A and 22C until the data is adjusted in early 2006. This table is also available at www.usdoj.gov/ust/bapcpa/meanstesting.htm and on the CD-Rom accompanying this volume.

One-person households are based on one-wage-earner figures and, if the household has more than four family members, the highest median income for a family of four should be used plus $6300 per year for each additional family member (this figure will be adjusted for inflation every three years under section 104(b) of the Code).

Census Bureau Median Family Income By Family Size
(in 2004 inflation-adjusted dollars)

The following link provides the median family income data published for the year 2004, reproduced in a format designed for ease of use in completing Bankruptcy Forms B22A and B22C. **The 2004 median income data should be used for completing Bankruptcy Forms B22A and B22C until the data is adjusted in early 2006.**

		FAMILY SIZE		
STATE	1 EARNER	2 PEOPLE	3 PEOPLE	4 PEOPLE *
ALABAMA	$32,762	$39,755	$48,957	$54,338
ALASKA	$43,709	$59,980	$68,140	$76,369
ARIZONA	$35,648	$46,429	$51,348	$58,187
ARKANSAS	$28,949	$37,178	$41,231	$49,790
CALIFORNIA	$42,012	$53,506	$59,633	$68,310
COLORADO	$40,044	$54,187	$58,565	$66,664
CONNECTICUT	$52,530	$61,374	$76,506	$88,276
DELAWARE	$38,944	$51,955	$61,508	$72,003
DISTRICT OF COLUMBIA	$38,349	$62,167	$62,167	$62,167
FLORIDA	$35,883	$44,831	$49,612	$59,798
GEORGIA	$34,396	$45,775	$49,855	$58,060
HAWAII	$45,513	$54,534	$64,554	$75,785
IDAHO	$32,531	$42,990	$47,288	$55,914
ILLINOIS	$41,602	$51,572	$62,178	$70,357
INDIANA	$35,373	$46,603	$50,804	$63,276
IOWA	$35,321	$46,518	$54,099	$61,951
KANSAS	$36,556	$48,610	$54,537	$59,498
KENTUCKY	$32,172	$37,932	$46,383	$55,001
LOUISIANA	$30,646	$38,017	$45,732	$51,402
MAINE	$36,527	$46,340	$52,432	$64,083

** Add $6,300 for each individual in excess of 4.*

		FAMILY SIZE		
STATE	1 EARNER	2 PEOPLE	3 PEOPLE	4 PEOPLE *
MARYLAND	$46,624	$58,556	$70,043	$85,554
MASSACHUSETTS	$47,176	$55,291	$71,416	$85,157
MICHIGAN	$40,504	$47,444	$60,431	$68,563
MINNESOTA	$40,650	$54,598	$64,851	$73,498
MISSISSIPPI	$28,288	$35,729	$37,794	$49,893
MISSOURI	$35,493	$44,631	$49,925	$62,265
MONTANA	$30,603	$41,984	$44,732	$50,666
NEBRASKA	$35,868	$45,541	$54,248	$59,979
NEVADA	$37,243	$50,387	$51,645	$52,750
NEW HAMPSHIRE	$50,411	$57,784	$68,360	$82,134
NEW JERSEY	$52,493	$58,547	$75,470	$88,401
NEW MEXICO	$30,614	$39,876	$41,420	$47,256
NEW YORK	$39,463	$48,492	$57,430	$67,564
NORTH CAROLINA	$32,411	$42,105	$49,206	$55,117
NORTH DAKOTA	$32,769	$45,821	$53,580	$58,298
OHIO	$36,109	$44,734	$55,390	$62,991
OKLAHOMA	$31,375	$41,058	$47,703	$49,881
OREGON	$36,299	$47,080	$52,842	$59,202
PENNSYLVANIA	$38,931	$44,361	$58,986	$66,569
RHODE ISLAND	$40,463	$51,334	$57,967	$69,029
SOUTH CAROLINA	$32,378	$43,263	$48,557	$59,694
SOUTH DAKOTA	$32,083	$42,014	$51,678	$59,479
TENNESSEE	$33,031	$41,468	$49,017	$55,907
TEXAS	$33,280	$46,454	$48,755	$56,246
UTAH	$41,103	$45,374	$51,219	$57,916
VERMONT	$37,298	$49,503	$59,259	$65,833
VIRGINIA	$41,779	$54,604	$61,106	$71,948
WASHINGTON	$42,452	$52,272	$57,773	$70,857
WEST VIRGINIA	$32,599	$35,183	$45,629	$51,795
WISCONSIN	$37,873	$48,281	$58,135	$67,869
WYOMING	$38,518	$50,957	$52,181	$62,014

** Add $6,300 for each individual in excess of 4.*

COMMONWEALTH OR U.S. TERRITORY		FAMILY SIZE		
	1 EARNER	2 PEOPLE	3 PEOPLE	4 PEOPLE *
GUAM	$31,514	$37,679	$42,938	$51,961
NORTHERN MARIANA ISLANDS	$21,162	$21,162	$24,621	$36,213
PUERTO RICO	$17,513	$17,513	$19,263	$22,738
VIRGIN ISLANDS	$25,003	$30,052	$32,041	$35,105

** Add $6,300 for each individual in excess of 4.*

F.2 Internal Revenue Service Standards as to Allowable Expenses

F.2.1 Internal Revenue Manual (IRM) Provisions Regarding Allowable Expenses

Reprinted from www.irs.gov/irm/index.html.

Part 5, Collecting Process
Chapter 15. Financial Analysis
Section 1. Financial Analysis Handbook

5.15.1 Financial Analysis Handbook

* * *

* * *

5.15.1.7 (05-01-2004) Allowable Expense Overview

1. Allowable expenses include those expenses that meet the necessary expense test. *The necessary expense test is defined as expenses that are necessary to provide for a taxpayer's and his or her family's health and welfare and/or production of income*. The expenses must be reasonable. The total necessary expenses establish the minimum a taxpayer and family needs to live.
2. There are three types of necessary expenses:
    - National Standards
    - Local Standards
    - Other Expenses
3. National Standards: These establish standards for reasonable amounts for five necessary expenses. Four of them come from the Bureau of Labor Statistics (BLS) Consumer Expenditure Survey: food, housekeeping supplies, apparel and services, and personal care products and services. The fifth category, miscellaneous, is a discretionary amount established by the Service. It is $100 for one person and $25 for each additional person in the taxpayer's household.

    Note:

    All five standards are included in one total national standard expense.

4. Local Standards: These establish standards for two necessary expenses: housing and transportation. Taxpayers will be allowed the local standard or the amount actually paid, whichever is less.
    A. Housing - Standards are established for each county within a state. When deciding if a deviation is appropriate, consider the cost of moving to a new residence; the increased cost of transportation to work and school that will result from moving to lower-cost housing and the tax consequences. The tax consequence is the difference between the benefit the taxpayer currently derives from the interest and property tax deductions on Schedule A to the benefit the taxpayer would derive without the same or adjusted expense.
    B. Transportation - The transportation standards consist of nationwide figures for loan or lease payments referred to as ownership cost, and additional amounts for operating costs broken down by Census Region and Metropolitan Statistical Area. Operating costs were derived from BLS data. If a taxpayer has a car payment, the allowable ownership cost added to the allowable operating cost equals the allowable transportation expense. If a taxpayer has no car payment only the operating cost portion of the transportation standard is used to figure the allowable transportation expense. Under ownership costs, separate caps are provided for the first car and second car. If the taxpayer does not own a car a standard public transportation amount is allowed.
5. Other - Other expenses may be allowed if they meet the necessary expense test. The amount allowed must be reasonable considering the taxpayer's individual facts and circumstances.
6. Conditional expenses. These expenses do not meet the necessary expenses test. However, they are allowable if the tax liability, including projected accruals, can be fully paid within five years.
7. National local expense standards are guidelines. If it is determined a standard amount is inadequate to provide for a specific taxpayer's basic living expenses, allow a deviation. Require the taxpayer to provide reasonable substantiation and document the case file.
8. Generally, the total number of persons allowed for national standard expenses should be the same as those allowed as dependents on the taxpayer's current year income tax return. Verify exemptions claimed on taxpayer's income tax return meet the dependency requirements of the IRC. There may be reasonable exceptions. Fully document the reasons for any exceptions. For example, foster children or children for whom adoption is pending.
9. A deviation from the local standard is not allowed merely because it is inconvenient for the taxpayer to dispose of valued assets.
10. Revenue officers should consider the length of the payments. Although it may be appropriate to allow for payments made on the secured debts that meet the necessary expense test, if the debt will be fully repaid in one year only allow those payments for one year.

5.15.1.8 (05-01-2004)
National Standards

1. National standards include the following expenses:
    A. Apparel and services. Includes shoes and clothing, laundry and dry cleaning, and shoe repair.
    B. Food. Includes all meals, home and away.
    C. Housekeeping supplies. Includes laundry and cleaning supplies; other household products such as cleaning and toilet tissue, paper towels and napkins; lawn and garden supplies; postage and stationary; and other miscellaneous household supplies.
    D. Personal care products and services. Includes hair care products, haircuts and beautician services, oral hygiene products and articles, shaving needs, cosmetics, perfume, bath preparations, deodorants, feminine hygiene products, electric personal care appliances, personal care services, and repair of personal care appliances.
    E. Miscellaneous. A discretionary allowance of $100 for one person and $25 for each additional person in a taxpayer's family.
2. Allow taxpayers the total national standard amount for their income level.

    Example: *The taxpayer's expenses are: housekeeping supplies - $150, clothing - $150, food - $600, miscellaneous - $400 (Total Expenses - $1,300). The taxpayer is allowed the national standard of $1,100.*

3. A taxpayer that claims more than the total allowed by the national standards must substantiate and justify each separate expense of the total national standard amounts.

   Example: *A taxpayer may claim a higher food expense than allowed. Justification would be based on prescribed or required dietary needs.*

5.15.1.9 (05-01-2004)
Local Standards

1. Local standards include the following expenses:
   A. Housing and Utilities. The utilities include gas, electricity, water, fuel, oil, bottled gas, trash and garbage collection, wood and other fuels, septic cleaning, and telephone. Housing expenses include: mortgage or rent, property taxes, interest, parking, necessary maintenance and repair, homeowner's or renter's insurance, homeowner dues and condominium fees. Usually, this is considered necessary only for the place of residence. Any other housing expenses should be allowed only if, based on a taxpayer's individual facts and circumstances, disallowance will cause the taxpayer economic hardship.
   B. Transportation. Vehicle insurance, vehicle payment (lease or purchase), maintenance, fuel, state and local registration, required inspection, parking fees, tolls, driver's license, public transportation. Transportation costs not required to produce income or ensure the health and welfare of the family are not considered necessary. Consider availability of public transportation if car payments (purchase or lease) will prevent the tax liability from being paid in part or full. Public transportation costs could be an option if it does not significantly increase commuting time and inconvenience the taxpayer.

   Note:

   If the taxpayer has no car payment, or no car, question how the taxpayer travels to and from work, grocer, medical care, etc. The taxpayer is only allowed the operating cost or the cost of transportation.

5.15.1.10 (05-01-2004)
Other Expenses

1. Other expenses may be considered if they meet the necessary expense test - they must provide for the health and welfare of the taxpayer and/or his or her family or they must be for the production of income. This is determined based on the facts and circumstances of each case.
2. If other expenses are determined to be necessary and, therefore allowable, document the reasons for the decision in your history.
3. The amount allowed for necessary or conditional expenses depends on the taxpayer's ability to full pay the liability within five years and on the taxpayer's individual facts and circumstances. If the liability can be paid within 5 years, it may be appropriate to allow the taxpayer the excessive necessary and conditional expenses. If the taxpayer cannot pay within 5 years, it may be appropriate to allow the taxpayer the excessive necessary and conditional expenses for up to one year in order to modify or eliminate the expense. *(See IRM 5.14, Installment Agreements)*

Expense Item	Expense is Necessary if:	Notes/Tips
Accounting and legal fees.	Representation before the Service is needed or meets the necessary expense tests. Amount must be reasonable.	Disallow any other accounting or legal fees. Disallow costs not related to solving current liability.
Charitable contributions *(Donations to tax exempt organizations)*	If it is a condition of employment or meets the necessary expense tests. Example: A minister is required to tithe according to his employment contract.	Disallow any other charitable contributions that are not considered necessary. Example: Review the employment contract.

Child Care*(Baby-sitting, day care, nursery and preschool)*	It meets the necessary expense test. Only reasonable amounts are allowed.	Cost of child care can vary greatly. Do not allow unusually large child care expense if more reasonable alternatives are available. Consider the age of the child and if both parents work.
Court-Ordered Payments*(Alimony, child support, including orders made by the state, and other court ordered payments)*	If court ordered and being paid, they are allowable. If payments are not being made, do not allow the expense. Child support payments for natural children or legally adopted dependents may be allowed.	Review the court order.
Dependent Care*(For the care of the elderly, invalid, or handicapped.)*	If there is no alternative to the taxpayer paying the expense.	
Education	It is required for a physically or mentally challenged child and no public education providing similar services is available. Also allowed only for the taxpayer and only if required as condition of employment.	**Example:** An attorney must take so many education credits each year or they will not be accredited and could eventually lose their license to practice before the State Bar. A teacher could lose their position or in some States their pay is commensurate with their education credits.
Health Care	Required for the health and welfare of the family. Elective surgery would not be allowed such as plastic surgery or elective dental work. The taxpayer must provide proof of excessive out of pocket medical expenses.	To determine monthly expenses, the total out of pocket expenses would be divided by 12. The Schedule A may also be used to determine the yearly expense. Ensure that the amount used is out of pocket after insurance claims are paid. Substantiate that payments are being made.
Involuntary Deductions	If it is a requirement of the job; i.e. union dues, uniforms, work shoes.	To determine monthly expenses, the total out of pocket expenses would be divided by 12.
Life Insurance	If it is a term policy on the life of the taxpayer only.	If there are whole life policies, these should be reviewed as an asset for borrowing against or liquidating. Life insurance used as an investment is not a necessary expense.
Secured or legally perfected debts	If it meets the necessary expense test.	Taxpayer must substantiate that the payments are being made.
Unsecured Debts	If the taxpayer substantiates and justifies the expense, the minimum payment may be allowed. The necessary expense test of health and welfare and/or production of income must be met. Except	Examples of unsecured debts which may be necessary expenses include: Payments required for the production of income such as payments to suppliers and payments on

	for payments required for the production of income, payments on unsecured debts will not be allowed if the tax liability, including projected accruals, can be paid in full within 90 days.	lines of credit needed for business and payment of debts incurred in order to pay a federal tax liability.
Taxes	It is for current federal, FICA, Medicare, state and local taxes.	Current taxes are allowed regardless of whether the taxpayer made them in the past or not. Delinquent state and local taxes are allowable depending on the priority of the FTL and/or Service agreement with the state and local taxing agencies.
Optional Telephones and Telephone Services *(Cell phone, pager, Call waiting, caller identification or long distance)*	It must meet the necessary expense test.	
Student Loans	If it is secured by the federal government and only for the taxpayer's education.	Taxpayer must substantiate that the payments are being made.
Internet Provider/E-mail	If it meets the necessary expense test - generally for production of income.	
Repayment of loans made for payment of Federal Taxes	If the loan is secured by the taxpayer's assets when those assets are of reasonable value and are necessary to provide for the health and welfare of the family.	

5.15.1.11 (05-01-2004)
Determining Individual Income

1. For purposes of determining the taxpayers' ability to pay, total household income must first be determined. Refer to Section 5.1.15.1.4, Shared Expenses for a complete explanation of determining proportionate income and expense calculations. If the taxpayer refuses to provide total household income, allocate 50% (or an appropriate percentage based on the number of household individuals) of household expenses to the taxpayer.
2. Income consists of the following:
   A. Wages - Wages include salary, tips, meal allowance, parking allowance or any other money or compensation received by the taxpayer as an employee for services rendered. This includes the taxpayer and spouse.

   Note:

   Use the following formulas to calculate gross monthly wages or salaries:
   If paid weekly, multiply weekly gross wages by 4.3.
   If paid bi-weekly (every 2 weeks), multiply bi-weekly gross wages by 2.17.
   If income is sporadic or seasonal, use the annual income figure from the W-2 or the 1040 and divide by 12 to determine the average monthly income.

   B. Interest and Dividends. Includes any interest or dividends that the taxpayer receives or that is credited to an account and can be withdrawn by the taxpayer and used for household expenses. The annual total should be divided by 12 to determine the average monthly income Look for brokerage accounts for dividends from publicly traded corporations and look for undisclosed bank accounts for interest payers.

Note:

If the interest bearing accounts are used as an asset, and the taxpayer will be withdrawing the funds from the account to reduce the tax liability, the dividends or interest would not be used in the income stream.

C. Net Income from Self-Employment or Schedule C. The amount the taxpayer earned after paying ordinary and necessary business expenses. This amount may be determined from an analysis of the Form 433-B or the Schedule C from the most current Form 1040. If the net business is a loss, enter " zero" . Do not enter a negative number.

Note:

If the 433-B is used or the taxpayer provides their own income and expense statement, it must reflect a sufficient time frame to accurately determine the monthly average that could be expected for the entire year.

D. Net Rental Income. The amount earned after paying ordinary and necessary monthly rental expenses. If it is a loss, enter a "zero" . Do not enter a negative number.
E. Pensions. Includes social security, IRA, profit sharing plans, etc. Pensions could be used as an asset or as part of the income stream. Refer to IRM 5.15.1.13, Business Expenses.
F. Child Support. Include the actual amount received in addition to other debts or bills the spouse is paying. For example, the court order assigns $200 a week for support but also requires all medical bills to be paid. In determining total expense, adjust the expense accordingly.
G. Alimony. Includes the assigned payments made by the non-resident spouse. However, consider if other bills are being paid, such as the mortgage, and adjust the expense accordingly.
H. Other. This could include payments from a trust account, royalties, renting a room, gambling winnings, sale of property, etc. Tax return information could include various sources of income.

5.15.1.12 (05-01-2004)
Business Entities

1. Businesses and individuals both have the same type assets. For example, cash is the same for a corporation or an individual. However, some assets that are unique to businesses can be more complex or difficult to determine actual value. Many businesses employ accounting firms to maintain records and books or use over the counter software programs. Because of the complexity of business entities, acquiring and reviewing these records are very important in determining the true value of an asset. The statements you should secure from business entities are described below.
2. Income Statement. Income Statement or Profit and Loss Statement is a financial statement that shows revenue, expenses and profit during a given accounting period, usually either a quarter or a year. Along with the balance sheet, the income statement is a tool used to assess the health and prospects of a company. The income statement shows revenue and expenses, including operating expenses, depreciation, income taxes and extraordinary items. Using the income statement, a taxpayer or revenue officer can quickly figure cash flow, profit margins and other important indicators of how the business is doing.
3. Balance Sheet. A firm's balance sheet is a snapshot of its financial picture on a given day. A balance sheet shows the financial position of a company by indicating the resources that it owns, the debts that it owes and the amount of the owner's equity in the business. One side of the balance sheet totals up assets, moving from most liquid (cash) to least liquid (plant and equipment or goodwill). The other side of the balance sheet lists liabilities in order of immediacy. Remember that assets must equal liabilities plus shareholders equity. The balance sheet, along with the

income statement, is an important tool for analyzing the financial health of a company. Using the balance sheet, compare current assets and current liabilities to assess equity; and consider hidden value in assets.

A. Assets are any item of value owned by a business. A firm's assets are listed on its balance sheet, where they are set off against its liabilities. Assets may include factories, land, inventories, off-shore accounts, vehicles and other items. However, not all assets are created equal. Some assets, such as cash, are easy to value and liquidate. In addition to cash, there are assets called cash equivalents.

B. Cash Equivalents are short term, highly liquid investments (three months maturity or less) that are made with idle cash. These can be included as equivalents of cash for cash flow purposes. Others, such as buildings and farmland, are quite real too, and somewhat more difficult to value accurately. These kinds of assets are collectively known as tangible assets. Intangible assets, such as goodwill, also can be important to the success of the enterprise. Goodwill, for instance, could include a valued brand gained in an acquisition (a famous brand, such as Coca-Cola, doesn't normally show up on balance sheet otherwise). Other examples of intangible assets are patents, franchises, licenses and customer lists.

C. In general, firms are required to carry assets on their books at cost less depreciation. This conservative principle means that the balance sheets of most companies understate the true value of their holdings.

D. Liabilities are the opposite of assets. A liability is a debt, an obligation to pay. Thus, short-term debt (less than 1 year to maturity), long-term debt and certain other obligations appear as liabilities on a company's balance sheet.

E. Consult local revenue agents with questions about adjusting the financial information for a particular item.

5.15.1.13 (05-01-2004)
Business Expenses

1. The IRC permits a taxpayer entity to reduce its income by deducting expenses paid to earn that income. Often these expenses help to identify assets to pay the tax liability.
2. Deductions may not necessarily be allowed as an expense in determining the ability to pay-- only actual cash expenses are used. If the taxpayer submits their own income and expense statement, the non-cash expenses should be removed from the analysis.

    Example: *The taxpayer takes a 10K deduction for depreciation - this amount would not be allowed as an expense.*

3. Substantiation and verification is required for cash expenses.
4. In analyzing and verifying the business income and expenses or deductions, real or potential assets may be identified. The following charts provide an explanation of the income or expense item and other considerations for identifying assets or other considerations.
5. Compensation of Officers. This amount represents compensation paid to corporate officers during the taxable year.

Expense	Assets/Other Considerations
The compensation paid to the officers in the form of cash.	Compensation is not always in the form of cash. Corporate officers may have compensation packages that includes: • Stocks and stock options • Insurance • Automobiles or air planes • Townhouses or condos located in vacation areas.

Tip: Often the officers are also shareholders or close relatives of the shareholders. Make certain:

- The benefits provided during the year are not for personal gain
- The compensation is not excessive for the corporation's ability to pay or the

local economy

- The corporation is not inflating the officers' salaries to reduce the net gain

Reminder: If a revenue officer encounters the commingling of corporate and individual assets and/or income, coordinate with local Counsel and consider pursuing alter ego or transferee assessments. Since sufficient detail is not always present on Schedule E, obtain it from the representative or taxpayer.

6. Bad Debt. Bad debts are amounts owed to the corporation but uncollectible.

Expense	Asset/Other Considerations
Bad debts are never an expense item.	This deduction represents the amount that remains uncollected after the corporation exhausts all avenues to collect the debt. Determine the relationship between the debtor and the corporation. For example: • Loans to officers or shareholders that were not repaid. • Absence of a note or security agreement that proves the existence of the loan to the officer or shareholder. • The corporation chooses not to pursue the debtor because of a close relationship. For example, a loan made to an officer or shareholder's child. • The corporation did not attempt to collect the debt. • The debtor is insolvent and unable to pay the debt.

Tip: This section is critical if the case is a defunct or bankrupt corporation. Bad debt may have caused the corporation to become insolvent. Determining the next action would depend on how the bad debt was incurred.
Example: *A supplier files bankruptcy leaving the taxpayer with an unmanageable bad debt and subsequent bankruptcy or taxpayer transferred assets to a relative and then claimed bankruptcy. In the first example, do not pursue; in the second example, review IRC § 6901, Transferred Assets, and proceed accordingly.*

7. Taxes and Licenses. This represents deductible taxes and license fees paid on assets by the corporation.

Expense	Assets/Other Considerations
Determine the type of taxes and licenses included and for which assets they are paid.	They can represent any asset deemed taxable by local, county and state taxing authorities. For example: • Land and buildings • Machinery and equipment • Vehicles • Taxi or Liquor License

Tip: Ask the taxpayer the location of the assets. Contact or research city, county and state offices to verify the location, description, valuation and other pertinent data for possible enforced collection against the assets. If you locate an asset being used by a shareholder, officer or employee without proper compensation, get the full details. Consider an alter ego or transferee relationship.

8. Interest. Interest deduction represents any interest paid or payable on corporate debt secured by an asset.

Expense	Asset/Other Considerations
Interest may be loans of cash to purchase real estate, machinery, or equipment.	Make certain that the interest deduction is not on any asset used by the corporate shareholders or officers for personal gain. For example: • Interest payments to corporate officers on loans they made to the corporation. This is potentially preferential treatment of creditors if other priority debt is not paid, e.g., taxes. • Interest payments to corporate officers on the capital investment they made to the corporation, again a preferential treatment. • Interest payment for personal debts of the corporate officers or other subsidiaries. • Interest payments on nonexistent loans to corporate officers.

Tip: Revenue officers that encounter these arrangements, should consider the possibility of corporate assets being dissipated. Pursue the beneficiary of this arrangement with a transferee or alter ego assessment.

9. Depreciation. Depreciation is a method to deduct the purchase price or basis of an asset over its useful life.

Expense	Asset/Other Consideration
Depreciation is never an expense item.	Form 4562, Depreciation and Amortization, is used to list the basis and depreciation of assets for tax purposes. Ask for the depreciation work papers or schedules for the prior, current and subsequent years. Comparing one year to another can help determine the true value of the assets. The disappearance of an asset from one year's depreciation schedule could mean the asset was: • Discarded, sold, traded-in or exchanged. • Fully depreciated for tax purposes. There should be either an asset or proceeds from the disposition of the asset.

Tip: The true value of an asset is not necessarily shown on the Form 4562 or the depreciation work papers. Although the asset may have been fully depreciated, it may have some market value.

10. Depletion. Depletion is similar to depreciation, but applies to assets such as oil, gas, coal or gemstones. Since the asset is removed from the ground, the depletion allowance is computed to account for this removal from the source.

Expense	Asset/Other Considerations
Depletion is never an expense item.	Depletion discloses the availability of an asset or a right to an asset. Identify the source of the asset and: • Locate the source of the depletion. • Gather the necessary information to levy on the proceeds generated from the depletion deduction.

	For example, name and address of the payor.

Tip: The right to the asset can be sold. The best customer will be the payor or company removing the item from the ground.

11. Pension, Profit Sharing Plans and Employee Benefit Programs. Generally, pensions, profit-sharing plans and employee benefits programs indicate a retirement account for the employees and corporate officers.

Expense	Asset/Other Considerations
Determine the corporation's interest in the plans.	Some corporations use investment firms for these accounts. Other corporations maintain and operate their own plans. Refer to the IRM for details on the possibility of pursuing collection action on this asset. For example: • The sole beneficiaries for these accounts are the officers or shareholders whose funds may be used to offset the tax liability or the Trust Fund Recovery Penalty assessment. • The deposits are to hide corporate assets under the officers' or shareholders' names. • The deposits can be borrowed against to pay the outstanding tax liability.

Tip: Get the specific details on the owners and share amounts for each contributor and check with an employee plans specialist before proceeding.

12. Other deductions. Other deductions represent the cumulative total of all deductions that do not have a line entry on the return.

Expense	Asset/Other Considerations
Review schedule of other expenses in order to verify necessary business expenses.	This may disclose assets not previously identified. Clarify questionable or excessive deductions. Be alert to expenses made for the personal gain of the officers or shareholders. For example: • Bonuses • Excessive travel and related expenses • Luxury vehicles • Boats • Real property not related to business use

TIP: Commingling of personal and business expenses may lead to an alter ego or transferee assessment. Duplicate expenses should be eliminated.

13. Net Operating Loss (NOL) Deduction. The net operating loss is not an "out-of-pocket" expense but an artificial amount based upon tax law.

Expense	Asset/Other Considerations
NOL is never considered an expense.	This discloses that the corporation may be able to make a larger payment on the tax liability.

TIP: Do not let the accountant or the corporation reduce its ability to pay by this amount. This represents a "paper loss" only and not a real reduction in value.

5.15.1.14 (05-01-2004)
Determining Business Income

1. Income represents the return in money from a business, labor or capital investment: gains, profits, salary, and wages.
2. Gross Receipts or Sales.

Income	Other Considerations
Gross receipts represent money received by the corporation for the goods sold or services rendered. This figure is the total before any expenses are reported.	Gross receipts may be deposited in an operating account at regular intervals, such as daily, weekly, or any other time based on business practices.

TIP: Comparing the prior, current and subsequent years' gross receipts gives revenue officers a good idea of the cash flow. This is helpful when projecting future cash flow and considering an installment agreement.

3. Dividends.

Income	Other Considerations
Dividends represent receivables or money received by the corporation.	These funds may be investment or security accounts; or, they may be reinvested in the entity paying them. This amount may not reflect an entire year's earnings.

TIP: Determine the length of time needed to earn the amounts reported. A revenue officer may determine that an amount initially thought to be nominal, is in fact worth pursuing. Review bank statements, Forms 1099, and brokerage statements.

4. Interest.

Income	Other Considerations
Interest income represents money received from bank accounts or investments.	The reported interest income discloses the source that generated the income. Examples include cash, savings account and bonds. These interest amounts may be credited to the account on which they were paid; deposited after receipt; or, used to purchase additional investments.

TIP:A revenue officer may determine that an amount initially thought to be nominal, is in fact worth pursuing. The amount could have been earned over a short period of time, while the corporation was looking for somewhere to invest its money. Ask if the sources of interest are still available to pay or reduce the tax liability. If the taxpayer says "no " , then ask what happened to the funds and when did it happen. If the taxpayer says "yes" , ask where they are located and when can they pay.

5. Gross Rents.

Income	Other Considerations
Gross rents represent payments received for the use of corporate assets and may be in the form of monies, services, assets, bartering or any combination of these.	Establish how payments are made to determine which assets are available and the location and value of assets. For example, the corporation leases space to other businesses.

TIP: Gross rents disclose the existence of an asset. Determine the asset and the payor, then levy on the receivable or seize the asset if necessary.

6. Gross Royalties.

Income	Other Considerations
Similar to gross rents but is normally earned on assets such as recordings, films, or mineral rights.	Royalty income can lead to an account receivable that can be levied or the right to that receivable that can be sold.

TIP: For recordings look for a production company; for films look for a distributor; and for minerals, look for a site or buyer of rights.

7. Capital Gain Net Income.

Income	Other Considerations
Represents the net of the short-term and long-term gains and losses reported on Schedule D, Capital Gains and Losses.	Schedule D discloses proceeds from the sale of an asset and may indicate the taxpayer disposed of an asset. Determine what was sold; to whom it was sold; what happened to the money; was the asset replaced and where is it.

TIP: It is not unusual for someone who sells stock to own other stock and reinvest the sale proceeds into more stock. If land was sold, it could be a portion of a larger parcel still held by the taxpayer. Identify the asset and payor to determine possible levy sources.

There may be a fraudulent conveyance if assets are sold for a nominal amount to a friend or relative to prevent IRS collection action.

8. Net Gain (or Loss).

Income	Other Considerations
Form 4797, Sale of Business Property, is used to report the gain or loss generated from the sale of business assets.	This form would include assets that were partially or fully depreciated and then sold.

TIP: If the funds generated from the sale are still available, apply the funds to the tax liability. If the funds generated from the sale are not available, determine what happened to them.

9. Other Income.

Income	Other Considerations
Other income represents items that do not fit into one of the specific categories on Form 1120. For example: • A construction company may have income from scrap construction materials. • A legal firm may have referral fees. • A Medical Professional Corporation may have expert witness fees for serving at a trial.	The other income sources can disclose a wide spectrum of items depending on the nature of the business. Request an explanation of the amount shown and then proceed according to the findings.

F.2.2 National Standards for Allowable Living Expenses

Effective January 1, 2005.

Applicable to all states except Alaska and Hawaii. *See* §§ F.2.3, F.2.4, *infra*. Reprinted from www.irs.gov/businesses/small/article/0,,id=104627,00.html.

One Person National Standards Based on Gross Monthly Income								
Item	**less than $833**	**$833 to $1,249**	**$1,250 to $1,666**	**$1,667 to $2,499**	**$2,500 to $3,333**	**$3,334 to $4,166**	**$4,167 to $5,833**	**$5,834 and over**
Food	197	215	231	258	300	339	369	543
Housekeeping supplies	19	20	25	26	29	36	37	51
Apparel & services	60	61	70	75	100	124	134	207
Personal care products & services	19	24	26	27	40	42	43	44
Miscellaneous	108	108	108	108	108	108	108	108
Total	**$403**	**$428**	**$460**	**$494**	**$577**	**$649**	**$691**	**$953**

Two Persons National Standards Based on Gross Monthly Income								
Item	**less than $833**	**$833 to $1,249**	**$1,250 to $1,666**	**$1,667 to $2,499**	**$2,500 to $3,333**	**$3,334 to $4,166**	**$4,167 to $5,833**	**$5,834 and over**
Food	336	337	338	424	439	487	559	691
Housekeeping supplies	36	37	38	48	52	53	107	108
Apparel & services	81	88	91	95	125	132	164	276
Personal care products & services	33	34	35	43	44	51	56	71
Miscellaneous	134	134	134	134	134	134	134	134
Total	**$620**	**$630**	**$636**	**$744**	**$794**	**$857**	**$1,020**	**$1,280**

Three Persons National Standards Based on Gross Monthly Income								
Item	**less than $833**	**$833 to $1,249**	**$1,250 to $1,666**	**$1,667 to $2,499**	**$2,500 to $3,333**	**$3,334 to $4,166**	**$4,167 to $5,833**	**$5,834 and over**
Food	467	468	469	470	490	546	622	778
Housekeeping supplies	41	42	43	49	53	55	108	109
Apparel & services	132	144	157	158	159	188	204	303
Personal care products & services	34	36	37	44	45	52	61	79
Miscellaneous	161	161	161	161	161	161	161	161
Total	**$835**	**$851**	**$867**	**$882**	**$908**	**$1,002**	**$1,156**	**$1,430**

Four Persons National Standards Based on Gross Monthly Income								
Item	**less than $833**	**$833 to $1,249**	**$1,250 to $1,666**	**$1,667 to $2,499**	**$2,500 to $3,333**	**$3,334 to $4,166**	**$4,167 to $5,833**	**$5,834 and over**
Food	468	525	526	527	528	640	722	868
Housekeeping supplies	42	43	44	50	54	61	109	110
Apparel & services	146	169	170	171	174	189	217	317
Personal care products & services	37	42	43	45	46	53	62	81
Miscellaneous	188	188	188	188	188	188	188	188
Total	**$881**	**$967**	**$971**	**$981**	**$990**	**$1,131**	**$1,298**	**$1,564**

More than Four Persons National Standards Based on Gross Monthly Income								
Item	**less than $833**	**$833 to $1,249**	**$1,250 to $1,666**	**$1,667 to $2,499**	**$2,500 to $3,333**	**$3,334 to $4,166**	**$4,167 to $5,833**	**$5,834 and over**
For each additional person, add to four person total allowance:	$134	$145	$155	$166	$177	$188	$199	$209

F.2.3 Standards for Allowable Living Expenses—Alaska

Effective January 1, 2005.

Reprinted from www.irs.gov/businesses/small/article/0,,id=104935,00.html.

One Person National Standards for Alaska
Based on Gross Monthly Income

Item	less than $833	$833 to $1,249	$1,250 to $1,666	$1,667 to $2,499	$2,500 to $3,333	$3,334 to $4,166	$4,167 to $5,833	$5,834 and over
Food	229	249	268	299	348	393	428	630
Housekeeping supplies	22	23	29	30	34	42	43	59
Apparel & services	70	71	81	87	116	144	155	240
Personal care products & services	22	28	30	31	46	49	50	51
Miscellaneous	125	125	125	125	125	125	125	125
Total	**$468**	**$496**	**$533**	**$572**	**$669**	**$753**	**$801**	**$1,105**

Two Persons National Standards for Alaska
Based on Gross Monthly Income

Item	less than $833	$833 to $1,249	$1,250 to $1,666	$1,667 to $2,499	$2,500 to $3,333	$3,334 to $4,166	$4,167 to $5,833	$5,834 and over
Food	390	391	392	492	509	565	648	802
Housekeeping supplies	42	43	44	56	60	61	124	125
Apparel & services	94	102	106	110	145	153	190	320
Personal care products & services	38	39	41	50	51	59	65	82
Miscellaneous	155	155	155	155	155	155	155	155
Total	**$719**	**$730**	**$738**	**$863**	**$920**	**$993**	**$1,182**	**$1,484**

Three Persons National Standards for Alaska Based on Gross Monthly Income								
Item	**less than $833**	**$833 to $1,249**	**$1,250 to $1,666**	**$1,667 to $2,499**	**$2,500 to $3,333**	**$3,334 to $4,166**	**$4,167 to $5,833**	**$5,834 and over**
Food	542	543	544	545	568	633	722	902
Housekeeping supplies	48	49	50	57	61	64	125	126
Apparel & services	153	167	182	183	184	218	237	351
Personal care products & services	39	42	43	51	52	60	71	92
Miscellaneous	187	187	187	187	187	187	187	187
Total	**$969**	**$988**	**$1,006**	**$1,023**	**$1,052**	**$1,162**	**$1,342**	**$1,658**

Four Persons National Standards for Alaska Based on Gross Monthly Income								
Item	**less than $833**	**$833 to $1,249**	**$1,250 to $1,666**	**$1,667 to $2,499**	**$2,500 to $3,333**	**$3,334 to $4,166**	**$4,167 to $5,833**	**$5,834 and over**
Food	543	609	610	611	612	742	838	1,007
Housekeeping supplies	49	50	51	58	63	71	126	128
Apparel & services	169	196	197	198	202	219	252	368
Personal care products & services	43	49	50	52	53	61	72	94
Miscellaneous	218	218	218	218	218	218	218	218
Total	**$1,022**	**$1,122**	**$1,126**	**$1,137**	**$1,148**	**$1,311**	**$1,506**	**$1,815**

More than Four Persons National Standards for Alaska Based on Gross Monthly Income								
Item	**less than $833**	**$833 to $1,249**	**$1,250 to $1,666**	**$1,667 to $2,499**	**$2,500 to $3,333**	**$3,334 to $4,166**	**$4,167 to $5,833**	**$5,834 and over**
For each additional person, add to four person total allowance:	$155	$168	$180	$193	$205	$218	$231	$242

F.2.4 Standards for Allowable Living Expenses—Hawaii

Effective January 1, 2005.

Reprinted from www.irs.gov/businesses/small/article/0,,id=104937,00.html.

One Person National Standards for Hawaii Based on Gross Monthly Income								
Item	**less than $833**	**$833 to $1,249**	**$1,250 to $1,666**	**$1,667 to $2,499**	**$2,500 to $3,333**	**$3,334 to $4,166**	**$4,167 to $5,833**	**$5,834 and over**
Food	199	217	233	261	303	342	373	548
Housekeeping supplies	19	20	25	26	29	36	37	52
Apparel & services	61	62	71	76	101	125	135	209
Personal care products & services	19	24	26	27	40	42	43	44
Miscellaneous	109	109	109	109	109	109	109	109
Total	**$407**	**$432**	**$464**	**$499**	**$582**	**$654**	**$697**	**$962**

Two Persons National Standards for Hawaii Based on Gross Monthly Income								
Item	**less than $833**	**$833 to $1,249**	**$1,250 to $1,666**	**$1,667 to $2,499**	**$2,500 to $3,333**	**$3,334 to $4,166**	**$4,167 to $5,833**	**$5,834 and over**
Food	339	340	341	428	443	492	565	698
Housekeeping supplies	36	37	38	48	53	54	108	109
Apparel & services	82	89	92	96	126	133	166	279
Personal care products & services	33	34	35	43	44	52	57	72
Miscellaneous	135	135	135	135	135	135	135	135
Total	**$625**	**$635**	**$641**	**$750**	**$801**	**$866**	**$1,031**	**$1,293**

Three Persons National Standards for Hawaii
Based on Gross Monthly Income

Item	less than $833	$833 to $1,249	$1,250 to $1,666	$1,667 to $2,499	$2,500 to $3,333	$3,334 to $4,166	$4,167 to $5,833	$5,834 and over
Food	472	473	474	475	495	551	628	786
Housekeeping supplies	41	42	43	49	54	56	109	110
Apparel & services	133	145	159	160	161	190	206	306
Personal care products & services	34	36	37	44	45	53	62	80
Miscellaneous	163	163	163	163	163	163	163	163
Total	**$843**	**$859**	**$876**	**$891**	**$918**	**$1,013**	**$1,168**	**$1,445**

Four Persons National Standards for Hawaii
Based on Gross Monthly Income

Item	less than $833	$833 to $1,249	$1,250 to $1,666	$1,667 to $2,499	$2,500 to $3,333	$3,334 to $4,166	$4,167 to $5,833	$5,834 and over
Food	473	530	531	532	533	646	729	877
Housekeeping supplies	42	43	44	51	55	62	110	111
Apparel & services	147	171	172	173	176	191	219	320
Personal care products & services	37	42	43	45	46	54	63	82
Miscellaneous	190	190	190	190	190	190	190	190
Total	**$889**	**$976**	**$980**	**$991**	**$1,000**	**$1,143**	**$1,311**	**$1,580**

More than Four Persons National Standards for Hawaii
Based on Gross Monthly Income

Item	less than $833	$833 to $1,249	$1,250 to $1,666	$1,667 to $2,499	$2,500 to $3,333	$3,334 to $4,166	$4,167 to $5,833	$5,834 and over
For each additional person, add to four person total allowance:	$135	$146	$157	$168	$179	$190	$201	$211

F.2.5 Housing and Utilities Allowable Living Expenses—Puerto Rico

Effective Jan.1, 2005.

Reprinted from http://www.irs.gov/businesses/small/article/0,,id=132322,00.html.

Maximum Monthly Allowance			
County	Family of 2 or less	Family of 3	Family of 4 or more
Adjuntas Municipio	542	638	733
Aguada Municipio	572	673	774
Aguadilla Municipio	662	779	896
Aguas Buenas Municipio	657	773	890
Aibonito Municipio	637	749	862
Añasco Municipio	536	630	725
Arecibo Municipio	631	743	854
Arroyo Municipio	507	597	686
Barceloneta Municipio	572	673	774
Barranquitas Municipio	581	683	785
Bayamón Municipio	757	890	1,024
Cabo Rojo Municipio	596	701	806
Caguas Municipio	712	837	963
Camuy Municipio	583	686	789
Canóvanas Municipio	654	769	884
Carolina Municipio	760	894	1,028
Cataño Municipio	870	1,024	1,178
Cayey Municipio	679	799	919
Ceiba Municipio	582	685	788
Ciales Municipio	551	648	745
Cidra Municipio	690	812	934
Coamo Municipio	553	651	749
Comerío Municipio	617	726	835
Corozal Municipio	590	694	798
Culebra Municipio	562	661	760
Dorado Municipio	812	956	1,099
Fajardo Municipio	629	740	851
Florida Municipio	596	701	806
Guánica Municipio	557	655	754
Guayama Municipio	612	719	827
Guayanilla Municipio	607	714	821
Guaynabo Municipio	1,118	1,315	1,513
Gurabo Municipio	747	878	1,010
Hatillo Municipio	612	719	827
Hormigueros Municipio	582	685	788

Humacao Municipio	640	753	865
Isabela Municipio	557	655	754
Jayuya Municipio	533	627	721
Juana Díaz Municipio	551	649	746
Juncos Municipio	664	781	898
Lajas Municipio	555	653	751
Lares Municipio	552	650	747
Las Marías Municipio	515	606	697
Las Piedras Municipio	616	725	834
Loíza Municipio	633	745	857
Luquillo Municipio	632	744	855
Manatí Municipio	629	740	851
Maricao Municipio	481	566	651
Maunabo Municipio	564	663	763
Mayagüez Municipio	673	792	911
Moca Municipio	592	696	801
Morovis Municipio	554	652	750
Naguabo Municipio	598	704	810
Naranjito Municipio	598	704	810
Orocovis Municipio	564	663	763
Patillas Municipio	563	662	761
Peñuelas Municipio	507	597	686
Ponce Municipio	631	743	854
Quebradillas Municipio	598	704	810
Rincón Municipio	611	718	826
Río Grande Municipio	658	775	891
Sabana Grande Municipio	558	657	755
Salinas Municipio	541	637	732
San Germán Municipio	554	652	750
San Juan Municipio	877	1,032	1,186
San Lorenzo Municipio	611	718	826
San Sebastián Municipio	566	666	766
Santa Isabel Municipio	578	680	782
Toa Alta Municipio	795	936	1,076
Toa Baja Municipio	728	856	985
Trujillo Alto Municipio	812	956	1,099
Utuado Municipio	539	634	730
Vega Alta Municipio	620	729	839
Vega Baja Municipio	681	801	921
Vieques Municipio	608	715	822
Villalba Municipio	581	683	785
Yabucoa Municipio	625	735	845
Yauco Municipio	596	701	806

F.2.6 Allowable Living Expenses for Transportation

Reprinted from www.irs.gov/businesses/small/article/0,,id=104623,00.html.

Ownership Costs			
National		**First Car**	**Second Car**
		$475	$338
Operating Costs & Public Transportation Costs			
Region	**No Car**	**One Car**	**Two Cars**
Northeast Region	$230	$298	$393
New York	$302	$384	$479
Philadelphia	$236	$298	$392
Boston	$259	$284	$380
Pittsburgh	$161	$286	$380
Midwest Region	$194	$251	$345
Chicago	$257	$329	$422
Detroit	$312	$376	$469
Milwaukee	$212	$247	$341
Minneapolis-St. Paul	$276	$303	$397
Cleveland	$198	$293	$387
Cincinnati	$222	$272	$365
St. Louis	$203	$287	$383
Kansas City	$246	$291	$384
South Region	$197	$242	$336
Washington, D.C.	$289	$313	$407
Baltimore	$225	$240	$334
Atlanta	$283	$258	$351
Miami	$284	$344	$439
Tampa	$255	$265	$359
Dallas-Ft. Worth	$309	$332	$425
Houston	$281	$367	$462
West Region	$246	$305	$399
Los Angeles	$275	$353	$448
San Francisco	$317	$373	$466
San Diego	$311	$318	$415
Portland	$189	$246	$339
Seattle	$258	$335	$427
Honolulu	$295	$314	$409
Anchorage	$312	$336	$431
Phoenix	$273	$326	$420
Denver	$302	$351	$442

* Does not include personal property taxes. (effective January 1, 2005)

For Use with Allowable Transportation Expenses Table

The Operating Costs and Public Transportation Costs sections of the Transportation Standards are provided by Census Region and Metropolitan Statistical Area (MSA). The following table lists the states that comprise each Census Region. Once the taxpayer's Census Region has been ascertained, to determine if an MSA standard is applicable, use the definitions below to see if the taxpayer lives within an MSA (MSAs are defined by county and city, where applicable). If the taxpayer does not reside in an MSA, use the regional standard.

Northeast Census Region		
Maine, New Hampshire, Vermont, Massachusetts, Rhode Island, Connecticut, Pennsylvania, New York, New Jersey		
MSA	**COUNTIES**	
New York	*in NY:*	Bronx, Dutchess, Kings, Nassau, New York, Orange, Putnam, Queens, Richmond, Rockland, Suffolk, Westchester
	in NJ:	Bergen, Essex, Hudson, Hunterdon, Mercer, Middlesex, Monmouth, Morris, Ocean, Passaic, Somerset, Sussex, Union, Warren
	in CT:	Fairfield, Litchfield, Middlesex, New Haven
	in PA:	Pike
Philadelphia	*in PA:*	Bucks, Chester, Delaware, Montgomery, Philadelphia
	in NJ:	Atlantic, Burlington, Camden, Cape May, Cumberland, Gloucester, Salem
	in DE:	New Castle
	in MD:	Cecil
Boston	*in MA:*	Bristol, Essex, Hampden, Middlesex, Norfolk, Plymouth, Suffolk, Worcester
	in NH:	Hillsborough, Merrimack, Rockingham, Strafford
	in CT:	Windham
	in ME:	York
Pittsburgh	*in PA:*	Allegheny, Beaver, Butler, Fayette, Washington, Westmoreland

Midwest Census Region		
North Dakota, South Dakota, Nebraska, Kansas, Missouri, Illinois, Indiana, Ohio, Michigan, Wisconsin, Minnesota, Iowa		
MSA	**COUNTIES (unless otherwise specified)**	
Chicago	*in IL:*	Cook, DeKalb, DuPage, Grundy, Kane, Kankakee, Kendall, Lake, McHenry, Will
	in IN:	Lake, Porter
	in WI:	Kenosha
Detroit	*in MI:*	Genesee, Lapeer, Lenawee, Livingston, Macomb, Monroe, Oakland, St. Clair, Washtenaw, Wayne
Milwaukee	*in WI:*	Milwaukee, Ozaukee, Racine, Washington, Waukesha
Minneapolis-St. Paul	*in MN:*	Anoka, Carver, Chisago, Dakota, Hennepin, Isanti, Ramsey, Scott, Sherburne, Washington, Wright
	in WI:	Pierce, St. Croix
Cleveland	*in OH:*	Ashtabula, Cuyahoga, Geauga, Lake, Lorain, Medina, Portage, Summit
Cincinnati	*in OH:*	Brown, Butler, Clermont, Hamilton, Warren
	in KY:	Boone, Campbell, Gallatin, Grant, Kenton, Pendleton
	in IN:	Dearborn, Ohio
St. Louis	*in MO:*	Crawford, Franklin, Jefferson, Lincoln, St. Charles, St. Louis, Warren, St. Louis city
	in IL:	Clinton, Jersey, Madison, Monroe, St.Clair
Kansas City	*in MO:*	Cass, Clay, Clinton, Jackson, Lafayette, Platte, Ray
	in KS:	Johnson, Leavenworth, Miami, Wyandotte

South Census Region		
Texas, Oklahoma, Arkansas, Louisiana, Mississippi, Tennessee, Kentucky, West Virginia, Virginia, Maryland, District of Columbia, Delaware, North Carolina, South Carolina, Georgia, Florida, Alabama		
MSA	**COUNTIES (unless otherwise specified)**	
Washington, D.C.	*in DC:*	District of Columbia
	in MD:	Calvert, Charles, Frederick, Montgomery, Prince George's, Washington
	in VA:	Arlington, Clarke, Culpepper, Fairfax, Fauquier, King George, Loudoun, Prince William, Spotsylvania, Stafford, Warren, Alexandria city, Fairfax city, Falls Church city, Fredericksburg city, Manassas city, Manassas Park city
	in WV:	Berkeley, Jefferson
Baltimore	*in MD:*	Anne Arundel, Baltimore, Carroll, Harford, Howard, Queen Anne's, Baltimore city
Atlanta	*in GA:*	Barrow, Bartow, Carroll, Cherokee, Clayton, Cobb, Coweta, DeKalb, Douglas, Fayette, Forsyth, Fulton, Gwinnett, Henry, Newton, Paulding, Pickens, Rockdale, Spalding, Walton
Miami	*in FL:*	Broward, Miami-Dade
Tampa	*in FL:*	Hernando, Hillsborough, Pasco, Pinellas
Dallas-Ft. Worth	*in TX:*	Collin, Dallas, Denton, Ellis, Henderson, Hood, Hunt, Johnson, Kaufman, Parker, Rockwall, Tarrant
Houston	*in TX:*	Brazoria, Chambers, Fort Bend, Galveston, Harris, Liberty, Montgomery, Waller

West Census Region:		
New Mexico, Arizona, Colorado, Wyoming, Montana, Nevada, Utah, Washington, Oregon, Idaho, California, Alaska, Hawaii		
MSA	**COUNTIES (unless otherwise specified)**	
Los Angeles	*in CA:*	Los Angeles, Orange, Riverside, San Bernadino, Ventura
San Francisco	*in CA:*	Alameda, Contra Costa, Marin, Napa, San Francisco, San Mateo, Santa Clara, Santa Cruz, Solano, Sonoma
San Diego	*in CA:*	San Diego
Portland	*in OR:*	Clackamas, Columbia, Marion, Multnomah, Polk, Washington, Yamhill
	in WA:	Clark
Seattle	*in WA:*	Island, King, Kitsap, Pierce, Snohomish, Thurston
Honolulu	*in HI:*	Honolulu
Anchorage	*in AK:*	Anchorage borough
Phoenix	*in AZ:*	Maricopa, Pinal
Denver	*in CO:*	Adams, Arapahoe, Boulder, Denver, Douglas, Jefferson, Weld

Appendix G

Sample Bankruptcy Pleadings Pertaining Specifically to the 2005 Amendments

This appendix and the CD-Rom accompanying this volume contain ten sample pleadings drafted to respond to changes in bankruptcy practice necessitated by the 2005 amendments to the Bankruptcy Code. NCLC's *Consumer Bankruptcy Law and Practice* (7th ed. 2004) contains 154 other sample pleadings and forms that were drafted prior to the enactment of the 2005 amendments. While these pleadings are still generally applicable, care must be taken to review them in light of the 2005 changes.

All captions have been deleted in favor of reference to Official Form 16A, the revised version of which appears in Appendix D, *supra*. These pleadings are also found in both Adobe Acrobat (PDF) format and Microsoft Word format on the CD-Rom accompanying this volume. These pleadings should be edited using your word-processing program in order to fit the particulars of an actual case.

Pleadings and Other Forms Contained in This Appendix

Form 1 Debtor's Certification in Support of Waiver of Credit Counseling Requirement Based on Exigent Circumstances

[*Caption: Official Form 16A*]

Debtor's Certification in Support of Waiver of Credit Counseling Requirement[1]

I/We, [*name of debtor and joint debtor, if any*], the Debtor(s) in the above-styled case, hereby declare under penalty of perjury that:

1. On [*date*], we filed a petition under chapter 13 of the Bankruptcy Code.

2. Because a foreclosure sale of our home was scheduled for the day following the filing of the petition, we were unable to delay the filing of the petition. [*Insert description of other exigent circumstances.*]

3. Prior to the filing of the petition, we requested credit counseling services from an approved agency, [*name of agency*], but were unable to obtain the services during the five-day period following the request.

4. We intend to obtain a credit counseling briefing within thirty days of the filing of the petition.

Date: [*signature*]
Debtor

Date: [*signature*]
Joint Debtor

Form 2 Debtor's Statement of Special Circumstances to Rebut Presumption of Abuse Under § 707(b)(2)[2]

[*Caption: Official Form 16A*]

Debtor's Statement of Special Circumstances

I, [*name of debtor*], the Debtor in the above-styled case, hereby declares under penalty of perjury that the following is true and correct:[3]

1. On [*date*], I filed a petition under chapter 7 of the Bankruptcy Code, and indicated on the Statement of Current Monthly Income and Means Test Calculation that my current monthly income is $3250.

2. This amount was determined by taking the monthly average of all income I received during the six-month period ending on the last day of the month before my bankruptcy filing.

3. For the first three months of this six-month period, I worked at the local General Motors plant as an assembler earning approximately $30 per hour with overtime. In the fourth month, General Motors unexpectedly closed the local plant and I was laid off from my job. For the remaining three months of the six-month period, I received only $1500 per month as severance pay.

4. Given the current market for manufacturing jobs in the Baltimore area and the fact there are no longer any local auto industry jobs after the General Motors plant closing, I was fortunate to find my current job. However, I am now earning only $1800 per month, and my new job requires a much longer commute.

5. The Statement of Current Monthly Income and Means Test Calculation that I filed therefore incorrectly shows that I have an extra $1450 per month that I am not actually receiving.

6. I also listed on the Statement of Current Monthly Income and Means Test Calculation, based on the IRS Transportation Standards, Operating Costs and Public Transportation Costs, an amount of $240 per month for my vehicle operation expense.

7. My new job requires me to travel an additional 120 miles every workday, for a total of 150 miles per workday. With the current cost of gas averaging $2.60 per gallon, I am spending approximately $500 per month on gas alone.

8. Once again, the Statement of Current Monthly Income and Means Test Calculation incorrectly shows that I have at least $260 in extra available income per month to pay unsecured creditors when that amount is actually being paid for my transportation to work.

Date: [*signature*]
Debtor

Form 3 Motion for Exemption from Credit Counseling and Financial Education Requirement Based on Incapacity, Disability, or Active Military Duty

[*Caption: Official Form 16A*]

Motion to Exempt Debtor from Credit Counseling and Financial Education Requirement

Debtor hereby requests that this Court, pursuant to 11 U.S.C. § 109(h)(4), exempt her (1) from the requirement under § 109(h)(1) that she receive budget and credit counseling, (2) the requirement under 11 U.S.C. § 521(b) that she file a certificate from an approved budget and credit counseling agency, and (3) the requirement under 11 U.S.C. § 727(a)(11) that she complete a course on personal financial management. In support of this motion, the Debtor states as follows:

---

1 Although § 109(h)(3)(A) refers to this certification as relating to a "waiver" or "exemption" from the requirements of § 109(h)(1), the certification provides only a deferral of the requirements as the debtor must still obtain counseling within thirty days of the petition date. The court may, for cause, extend this period by an additional fifteen days.

2 To rebut a presumption of abuse arising under the means test, § 707(b)(2)(B)(i) states that the debtor must demonstrate that "special circumstances" exist that "justify additional expenses or adjustments of current monthly income for which there is no reasonable alternative." To establish special circumstances, the debtor must itemize each additional expense or adjustment of income and provide, accompanied by an oath as to the accuracy of any information provided, (1) documentation for such expense or adjustment to income and (2) a detailed explanation of the special circumstances that make such expenses or adjustment to income necessary and reasonable. This form may be submitted to the trustee or United States Trustee by debtor's counsel in an attempt to convince them not to file a motion to dismiss under § 707(b), or it may be attached to the response filed by the debtor if a motion to dismiss is filed.

3 The oath requirement under § 707(b)(2)(B)(iii) applies only when the statement is used in a court proceeding, and need not be included if used informally before a proceeding.

[*Alternative A—Disability*]

1. The Debtor is a seventy-three-year-old disabled individual who filed bankruptcy pursuant to chapter 7 of the Bankruptcy Code on [*date*].

2. Due to a stroke suffered by the Debtor after filing bankruptcy, the Debtor is currently hospitalized, unable to travel, and has difficulty communicating. Upon release from the hospital, it is expected that she will be transferred to a nursing home.

3. The Debtor's physical problems prevent her from participating in an in-person, telephone, or Internet credit counseling session, or a financial management course.

[*Alternative B—Incapacity*]

1. The Debtor is an eighty-year-old disabled individual who filed bankruptcy pursuant to chapter 7 of the Bankruptcy Code on [*date*].

2. The Debtor suffers from advanced dementia, which has caused her to have loss of memory and difficulty performing complex tasks. This dementia renders the Debtor incapacitated with respect to her financial responsibilities, which is the reason why the petition in this matter was filed by her representative pursuant to Bankruptcy Rule 1004.1.

3. The Debtor's condition prevents her from participating in an in-person, telephone, or Internet credit counseling session, or a financial management course.

[*Alternative C—Active Military Duty*]

1. The Debtor filed bankruptcy pursuant to chapter 7 of the Bankruptcy Code on [*date*].

2. Shortly after filing the petition, the Debtor was called to active military duty and is currently serving in Iraq.

WHEREFORE, the Debtor requests that this motion be approved, and that the Debtor be exempted from the credit counseling and financial education requirements pursuant to 11 U.S.C. § 109(h)(4).

Date: [*signature*]
Attorney for Debtor

Form 4 Motion to Excuse Filing of Lost or Unavailable Payment Advices[4]

[*Caption: Official Form 16A*]

Motion to Excuse Complete Filing of Payment Advices

Debtor, by his counsel, hereby moves that he be excused from filing all of the payment advices received from his employer within sixty days of the petition. In support of this motion, Debtor states:

1. Debtor filed a voluntary petition under chapter 7 of the Bankruptcy Code on [*date*].

2. At the time the petition was filed, Debtor was able to locate pay stubs from his employer covering the period thirty days before the petition date. These pay stubs are attached as Exhibit A.

3. Despite the Debtor's best efforts, he has been unable to find all of his pay stubs for the entire sixty-day prepetition period. The Debtor believes that the missing pay stubs have been lost or destroyed.

4. The Debtor requested that his employer provide copies of the missing pay stubs, but the employer has refused to provide them.

5. The Debtor was employed by the same employer for the entire sixty-day prepetition period. Included with the pay stubs attached as Exhibit A is the last pay stub received by the Debtor before filing this bankruptcy. This pay stub is for the period ending [*date*], and it includes a year-to-date total of all income received by the Debtor prior to filing the petition.

6. This Court has authority pursuant to § 521(a)(1)(B) to modify the filing requirements under that section.

WHEREFORE, the Debtor requests that he be permitted to file this case without submitting all payment advices required by 11 U.S.C. § 521(a)(1)(B)(iv).

Date: [*signature*]
Attorney for Debtor

4 Section 521(a)(1)(B)(iv) requires the debtor to file with the petition all payment advices or other evidence of payment received by the debtor from an employer within sixty days of petition, unless the court orders otherwise. This form may used if the debtor is unable to produce all of the payment advices received during this period.

Form 5 Motion and Order for Additional Time to File Documents and Information Required Under § 521(a)(1)[5]

[*Caption: Official Form 16A*]

Motion for Additional Time to Comply with Requirements Under Section 521(a)(1)

Debtor, [*name of debtor*], by his attorney, respectfully represents:

1. Debtor filed a voluntary petition under chapter 13 of the Bankruptcy Code on April 6, 2006.

2. Debtor's petition was prepared and filed in an expedited manner to stop a pending foreclosure sale of the Debtor's home scheduled for April 7, 2006. The Debtor was therefore unable to gather all the necessary documents for completing the chapter 13 schedules, statement of affairs, plan and other information and documents required under § 521(a)(1) when the petition was filed.

3. Debtor filed a Motion for Extension of Time to File Chapter 13 Schedules, Statement of Affairs and Chapter 13 Plan, and an extension of time was granted until May 11, 2006.

4. On April 23, 2006, Debtor was hospitalized following an automobile accident. Debtor is currently recovering from surgery and is not expected to be released from the hospital until May 15, 2006.

5. During the next few weeks, Debtor will have little ability or opportunity to take the steps necessary to complete the chapter 13 statement and plan on time.

5 This form may be used to seek an additional forty-five-day period to file the information required under § 521(a)(1). An extension of time under § 521(i)(3) may be granted on motion for cause shown, which must be filed within forty-five days after the filing of the petition. The granting of this motion will prevent the case from being "automatically dismissed" under § 521(i)(1) if the information required by § 521(a)(1) is not filed within forty-five days of the petition.

6. It is requested that the Court grant the Debtor an additional period of forty-five days, pursuant to 11 U.S.C. § 521(i)(3) and Rule 1007(c) of the Federal Rules of Bankruptcy Procedure, so that the Debtor may assist counsel in submitting the necessary forms and information.

7. This motion is not made for the purposes of delay and no creditor will suffer any prejudice if Debtor is granted an additional extension of time.

WHEREFORE, Debtor requests that this Court grant him an extension of time until July 5, 2006, in which to file his chapter 13 schedules, statement of affairs, chapter 13 plan, and all other information and forms required by 11 U.S.C. § 521(a)(1).

Date: [*signature*]
Attorney for Debtor

[*Caption: Official Form 16A*]

Order

AND NOW, this [*date*] day of [*month*], 2006, upon consideration of Debtor's Motion for Additional Time to Comply with Requirements Under Section 521(a)(1), it is hereby ORDERED and DECREED that said Motion is GRANTED. Debtor shall have until July 5, 2006 to file his chapter 13 schedules, statement of affairs, chapter 13 plan, and all other information and forms required by 11 U.S.C. § 521(a)(1).

Date: [*signature*]
United States Bankruptcy Judge

Form 6 Motion to Invoke Automatic Stay in Case Filed After Two Prior Dismissals Within Year of Filing[6]

[*Caption: Official Form 16A*]

Motion to Invoke Automatic Stay

The Debtor hereby moves this Court, pursuant to § 362(c)(3)(B), for an order invoking the automatic stay provided under § 362(a) as to all creditors. In support of this motion, the Debtor states as follows:

1. The Debtor filed a petition in this matter under chapter 13 on October 18, 2005.

2. The Debtor had previously filed a chapter 13 case which was dismissed on September 15, 2004 because the Debtor had failed to file the schedules, statement of affairs, and plan. Three days after the petition had been filed in that case, the Debtor's daughter had been seriously injured in an auto accident. In caring for her daughter, the Debtor was unable to gather all the necessary documents for her attorney to complete the required documents for filing.[7]

3. After the condition of the Debtor's daughter had stabilized, she filed a second chapter 13 case on November 23, 2004, and her plan in that case was confirmed on January 12, 2004. However, this case was voluntarily dismissed by the Debtor on July 7, 2004, because the Debtor, though no fault of her own, had been laid off from her job and was therefore unable to maintain payments under her chapter 13 plan.

4. The Debtor has now been called back to work and she does not anticipate any further job interruptions.

5. The petition in this case has been filed in good faith. The Debtor believes that the chapter 13 plan she has submitted will be confirmed and that she will be able to fully perform under the terms of the plan.

6. The Debtor's two prior chapter 13 cases dismissed on September 15, 2004 and July 7, 2004 were the only previous cases by the debtor that were pending during the preceding year.[8]

7. The Debtor's prior chapter 13 cases were not dismissed because the Debtor failed to provide adequate protection ordered by the court.

8. The Debtor's prior chapter 13 cases were not dismissed at a time when there had been a motion for relief that was pending before the court or resolved with an order terminating, conditioning, or limiting the stay.

WHEREFORE, the Debtor requests that this Court invoke the automatic stay under § 362(a) as to all creditors for the duration of this chapter 13 proceeding, or until such time as the stay is terminated under § 362(c)(1) or (c)(2), or a motion for relief is granted under § 362(d).

Date: [*signature*]
Attorney for Debtor

Form 7 Motion for Continuation of Automatic Stay in Case Filed After Prior Dismissal Within Year of Filing[9]

[*Caption: Official Form 16A*]

Motion for Continuation of Automatic Stay

The Debtor hereby moves this Court, pursuant to § 362(c)(3)(B), for an order continuing the automatic stay provided under § 362(a) as to all creditors. In support of this motion, the Debtor states as follows:

1. The Debtor filed a petition under chapter 13 on October 18, 2005.

2. The Debtor had previously filed a chapter 13 case which was dismissed on January 15, 2005. This case was dismissed because

6 Section 362(c)(4) provides that the automatic stay does not take effect in a case if the debtor has had two or more prior cases dismissed within the preceding one-year period. The stay may be invoked pursuant § 362(c)(4)(B), if the debtor files a motion within thirty days of the petition date and demonstrates that the later case has been filed in good faith.

7 Paragraphs 2 through 5 are intended to demonstrate that the case was filed in good faith based on changed circumstances, and to rebut the presumption arising under § 362(c)(4)(D)(i) that the case was filed in bad faith because a prior case had been dismissed due to the debtor's failure to file without substantial excuse any required documents, or to perform the terms of a confirmed plan.

8 Paragraphs 5 through 8 are intended to establish that other grounds for the creation of a bad faith presumption under § 362(c)(4)(D)(i) and (ii) do not apply.

9 Section 362(c)(3) provides for the termination of the automatic stay thirty days after the petition is filed if the debtor has had a case dismissed within the preceding one-year period. The stay may be extended beyond the thirty-day period pursuant § 362(c)(3)(B), if the debtor files a motion within the thirty-day period before the expiration of the stay and demonstrates that the later case has been filed in good faith.

the Debtor, though no fault of her own, had been laid off from her job and was therefore unable to maintain payments under her chapter 13 plan.[10]

3. The Debtor has now obtained new employment in a permanent position and is being paid at a higher salary than she was receiving at her previous job.

4. The petition in this case has been filed in good faith. The Debtor believes that the chapter 13 plan she has submitted will be confirmed and that she will be able to fully perform under the terms of the plan.

5. The Debtor's prior chapter 13 case, dismissed on January 15, 2005, was the only previous case by the Debtor that was pending during the preceding year.[11]

6. The Debtor's prior chapter 13 case was not dismissed because the Debtor failed to file or amend her petition or any required documents, or to provide adequate protection ordered by the court.

7. The Debtor's prior chapter 13 case was not dismissed at a time when there had been a motion for relief that was pending before the court or resolved with an order terminating, conditioning, or limiting the stay.

WHEREFORE, the Debtor requests that this Court continue the automatic stay under § 362(a) as to all creditors for the duration of this chapter 13 proceeding, or until such time as the stay is terminated under § 362(c)(1) or (c)(2), or a motion for relief is granted under § 362(d).

Date: [*signature*]
Attorney for Debtor

Form 8 Debtor's Certification in Support of Extension of Automatic Stay As to Pending Eviction Action[12]

[*Caption: Official Form 16A*]

Debtor's Certification in Support of Extension of Automatic Stay Pursuant to Section 362(*l*)(2)

I, [*name of debtor*], the Debtor in the above-styled case, hereby declares under penalty of perjury that:

1. On [*date*], I filed a petition under chapter 13 of the Bankruptcy Code, and indicated on the petition that [*name of landlord*] had obtained a judgment for possession of my residence.

2. At the time of the filing of the petition, I certified that there were circumstances under which I would be permitted under applicable nonbankruptcy law to cure the entire monetary default that gave rise to the judgment for possession. I also deposited with the clerk of the court the sum of [*amount*], which was the rent that would come due during the thirty-day period following the filing of the petition.

3. I have cured under applicable nonbankruptcy law, within the thirty-day period after the filing of the petition, the entire monetary default that gave rise to the judgment for possession by paying to [*landlord*] the sum of [*amount*].

Date: [*signature*]
Debtor

Form 9 Motion for Relief from *In Rem* Order Entered in Prior Case[13]

[*Caption: Official Form 16A*]

Motion for Relief from *In Rem* Order

The Debtor hereby moves this Court, pursuant to § 362(d)(4), for relief from the Order entered in Case No. [*case number*] prohibiting the application of the automatic stay as to the Debtor's property, and for an order invoking the automatic stay provided under § 362(a) as to that property. In support of this motion, the Debtor states as follows:

1. The Debtor filed a petition in this matter under chapter 13 on January 18, 2006.

2. In June 2005, National Mortgage (hereinafter National), the servicer of the Debtor's home mortgage, initiated foreclosure proceedings against the Debtor's property.

3. Prior to this time, the Debtor had spent countless hours with National's collection and legal departments attempting to resolve a long-standing dispute with National over whether payments she had made to a former servicer just prior to the transfer of servicing to National had been properly credited to her account. Although the Debtor had provided proof that these payments had been accepted by the former servicer, National continued to treat the account as if it were in default.

4. In response to the legal advertisement listing her home for foreclosure, the Debtor was contacted by Foreclosure Rescue Co., (hereinafter Rescue). Rescue initially left a note in her mailbox stating that it could "make [the Debtor] a loan to stop the foreclosure." An agent for Rescue later came to the Debtor's home and

---

10 Paragraphs 2 through 4 are intended to demonstrate that the case was filed in good faith based on changed circumstances, and to rebut the presumption arising under § 362(c)(3)(C)(i) that the case was filed in bad faith because the prior case had been dismissed due to the debtor's failure to perform the terms of a confirmed plan.

11 Paragraphs 5 through 7 are intended to establish that other grounds for the creation of a bad faith presumption under § 362(c)(3)(C)(i) do not apply.

12 Section 362(*l*)(1) provides that the stay exception under § 362(b)(22) will not apply until thirty days after the case is filed if the debtor files as part of the petition, and serves on the landlord, an initial certification that (1) circumstances exist because of which the debtor would be permitted under applicable nonbankruptcy law to cure the entire monetary default that gave rise to the judgment for possession, and (2) the debtor, or an adult dependent of the debtor, has deposited with the clerk any rent that would become due during the thirty-day period after the filing of the petition. This second certification is filed in order have the stay remain in force beyond the thirty-day period following the petition date.

13 Sections 362(b)(20) and 362(d)(4) create an exception from the stay for the enforcement of a security interest in real property following the entry of an order in a prior bankruptcy case prohibiting the application of the automatic stay as to that property. Unless relief from the order is granted in a subsequent case, the *in rem* order shall remain in effect for a period of two years after entry. Section 362(d)(4) provides that the debtor may move in a subsequent case for relief from an *in rem* order based upon changed circumstances or for good cause shown, after notice and a hearing.

stated that he was a mortgage broker and that Rescue could help the Debtor avoid foreclosure by providing her with a low-interest mortgage.

5. The Rescue agent then visited the Debtor's home several times in the weeks prior to the scheduled foreclosure to complete what the Debtor believed was an application for mortgage refinancing. The Debtor paid the sum of $750 to Rescue and provided information about her financial situation for the loan application.

6. The Debtor was also asked to sign several documents and advised the Rescue agent that she had difficulty reading documents. The Rescue agent told her not to worry about reading the documents because they were all part of the loan application and would help her to save her home.

7. One week prior to the foreclosure sale, the Debtor was advised by Rescue that although it had not yet found a replacement mortgage, Rescue had negotiated a cancellation of the sale with National. The Debtor then paid an additional sum of $350 to Rescue which she was told would cover the cost of a home appraisal.

8. Approximately two months later, the Debtor received notice from National that it had reinstituted foreclosure proceedings. She then contacted Rescue and was told that it could no longer assist her.

9. Included with the documents Rescue had the Debtor sign was a deed conveying a partial interest in her home to Chuck Buyer. Rescue then prepared and filed with this Court a chapter 7 bankruptcy petition in the name of Mr. Buyer (Case No. [*case number*]). Rescue also arranged for a copy of the petition to be sent National the day before the originally scheduled foreclosure sale, and advised National of the application of the automatic stay.

10. The Debtor had no knowledge of the conveyance to Mr. Buyer or that Rescue had arranged for him file a bankruptcy petition relating to her property.

11. On October 25, 2005, National obtained an order from this Court in the case filed by Mr. Buyer, Case No. [*case number*], pursuant to 11 U.S.C. § 362(b)(20) and § 362(d)(4), prohibiting the application of the automatic stay as to the Debtor's property located at [*address*]. The Order was recorded at the land records office for [*county name*] County on October 26, 2005.

12. The petition in this case has been filed in good faith. The Debtor believes that the chapter 13 plan she has submitted will be confirmed and that she will be able to fully perform under the terms of the plan.

13. The Debtor will seek a determination as part of the claims process as to the amount owed to National for any prepetition arrears. The Debtor's plan provides for the payment of this amount and the curing of any default on the mortgage.

14. The Debtor will also attempt in an adversary proceeding to recover all monies paid to Rescue and obtain an order voiding the partial transfer of her property to Mr. Buyer.

15. The Debtor's residence is and at all times relevant to this case has been an asset included in the Debtor's bankruptcy estate.

16. The Debtor has substantial equity in her property and National has been afforded adequate protection of its interest.

WHEREFORE, the Debtor requests that this Court vacate the Order entered in Case No. [*case number*], and invoke the automatic stay under § 362(a) as to National and the property located at [*address*] for the duration of this chapter 13 proceeding, or until such time as the stay is terminated under § 362(c)(1) or (c)(2), or a motion for relief is granted under § 362(d).

Date: [*signature*]
Attorney for Debtor

Form 10 Objection to Claim Seeking Reduction of Claim Amount Based on Creditor's Refusal to Negotiate Repayment Plan

[*Caption: Official Form 16A*]

Objection to Claim Seeking Reduction of Claim Amount Pursuant to Section 502(k)

Debtors, by counsel, object to Proof of Claim Number Six, filed by [*claimant*] in the amount of $4508.00 and seek a reduction of the claim amount pursuant to 11 U.S.C. § 502(k). In support of this Motion, the Debtors state:

1. On [*date*], [*claimant*] filed a Proof of Claim in the amount of $4508.00 on an unsecured credit card debt owed by the Debtors.

2. Prior to filing bankruptcy, the Debtors sought the assistance of the nonprofit budget and credit counseling agency, [*name of agency*], which is an approved agency pursuant to 11 U.S.C. § 111.

3. On [*date at least sixty days before filing*], [*agency*] proposed an alternative repayment schedule to [*claimant*] on behalf of the Debtors.

4. This repayment schedule provided for payments to be made by the Debtors in the amount of $76.50 per month for a period of three years.

5. The total amount proposed to be paid by the Debtors to the [*claimant*] under this repayment schedule was $2754, which was more than 60% of the amount of the debt owed to the [*claimant*].

6. Based on the Debtors' income and expenses at the time this offer was made, the payment amount represented the Debtors' best effort to reasonably repay the debt.

7. [*Claimant*] failed to respond to this offer of a reasonable repayment schedule made by the Debtors through [*agency*].

8. On information and belief, a substantial portion of the amount claimed to be owed to the [*claimant*] represents penalty interest fees, late fees, overlimit fees, and other charges.[14]

WHEREFORE, based on this Court's authority under 11 U.S.C. § 502(k), the Debtors respectfully request that this Court reduce the claim amount by 20%, disallow the Proof of Claim filed by [*claimant*] to the extent that it seeks payment in an amount greater than $3606.40, award attorney fees pursuant to 11 U.S.C. § 105 for the prosecution of this objection, and order such other and further relief as is just and proper.

Date: [*signature*]
Attorney for Debtor

14 Although this allegation is not required, it may assist the court in finding that the creditor unreasonably refused to negotiate the repayment plan.

Appendix H Bankruptcy Questionnaire Reflecting New 2005 Requirements[1]

Bankruptcy is a right provided by law to people who are deeply in debt and in need of a fresh start. Bankruptcy will discharge many of your debts and you will not have to pay them, except, in some cases, secured debts for the purchase of particular merchandise or debts on which you gave a mortgage or put up other property as collateral.

The law allows you to keep some money and most types of necessary property in bankruptcy. To receive this protection, it is necessary that you list all items asked for in the following questions: if you do not list an item, that item will not be protected in bankruptcy. You must also list *everyone* to whom you owe money. If you leave out one of your creditors, you may have to pay the money to that creditor or you may lose your right to bankruptcy. It may also be considered a crime if you intentionally give false information or leave out information. If you have any questions about whether you can keep certain property or whether you should list a debt, write that question down and remember to ask the lawyer. We know this questionnaire is long. Preparing your bankruptcy papers properly takes a lot of time and a lot of information. If we work together on this, we can protect your family from great hardship and give you the new start the law intends you to have.

There is a filing fee of $274.00 which must be paid to the court in chapter 7 cases ($189.00 if your case is filed under chapter 13). If you do not have the money at the time you file, the court may allow you up to four months to pay the fee in installments. If you are unable to pay the filing fee even in installments, you may request that the court waive the filing fee. Some of the information requested on this questionnaire will be needed to prepare a request to waive the filing fee. If you do not request a filing fee waiver or the court does not approve your request, you must pay the filing fee to get a discharge.

You must also receive budget and credit counseling from an approved credit counseling agency at least 180 days before your case is filed. It is usually a good idea for you to meet with us before you receive the credit counseling. We can provide you with a list of approved credit counseling agencies. You should fill out this questionnaire before meeting with the credit counseling agency and refer to it as needed.

After your case is filed, you will need to attend a meeting with the bankruptcy trustee and you may have to appear at a court hearing. Before the court will give you a discharge, you must also complete an approved course in personal finances. This course will take approximately two hours to complete. We will give you a list of organizations that provide approved courses. In a chapter 7 case, you should sign up for the course soon after your case is filed. If you file a chapter 13 case, we will discuss with you later when you should take the course.

(1) Fill out *every* question on all of the pages. Wherever you are given a choice of YES or NO on these forms, check either YES or NO, whichever is correct. Please fill out these pages as well as you can. We will help with any questions you don't understand.

(2) Write clearly or typewrite your answers. We *must* be able to read them.

(3) Wherever the name of a person or firm is asked for, give the *full address. Make the address accurate.* Your discharge from each debt depends upon your giving a complete and correct address.

(4) If you do not know the exact amount you owe, fill in a *HIGH* estimate. Do *not* leave the amount blank and do not say "don't know."

(5) Wherever you need more room, turn the page over and put the information on the back together with the number of the question.

(6) List *every creditor and everybody* that has had anything to do with your debts, including cosigners. Please include accurate account numbers. If a bill you owe has been sent to a collection agency or any attorney, list *both* the person you originally owed *and* the collection agency or any attorney, giving the *full* address of each. If the collection agency has an attorney, list the person you originally owed, the collection agency, and the attorney, giving the full address of each.

---

1 This questionnaire updates the questionnaire found in Appendix H of NCLC's Consumer Bankruptcy Law and Practice (7th ed. 2004) to reflect the new requirements contained in the 2005 bankruptcy amendments. The original questionnaire was based in part on a form developed by New Haven Legal Assistance. This questionnaire is also available in Microsoft Word and Adobe Acrobat (PDF) format on the CD-Rom accompanying this volume. Use the PDF format if you wish to reprint the questionnaire, and the Word format if you want to edit the document using your word-processing program.

(7) Whenever a question asks you to be prepared to give details, gather all papers concerning the matter, including bills and collection letters, and bring them with you when you return this form. In any event, be sure to bring with you the following items (unless they don't apply to you):

(a) Picture identification card and Social Security card or other document containing your social security number;
(b) Deeds and mortgages on your house or other real estate;
(c) Any insurance policies;
(d) Any papers relating to past bankruptcies and Wage Earner Plans (Chapter 13);
(e) Copies of tax returns for past two years, and copies of your pay check stubs for the last sixty days (and you should keep all pay stubs you receive while your bankruptcy case is pending);
(f) Copies of your last several bank statements and copies of statements from any other deposit accounts, such as a credit union or brokerage account, including IRAs, 401(k)s, and other pension accounts (and you should keep the first bank statement you receive after your case is filed as we may need to provide it to the trustee);
(g) Legal papers, lawsuits, eviction notices, divorce papers, separation agreements, alimony orders, and child support orders;
(h) Any appraisals or tax assessment papers;
(i) Any other papers you have concerning any of your debts; and
(j) Any lease or installment sale ("lease purchase" or "rent-to-own") agreements for housing (apartment, house, mobile home) or other property (cars, televisions, etc.) that you have signed and that are still in effect or not fully paid.

Complete All Questions. If you and your spouse are not living together, and there is no possibility that your spouse will file bankruptcy along with you, you don't have to answer the questions about your spouse.

1. Name and Residence Information:

A. Your full name: ______________________________

Your spouse's full name: ______________________________

B. Your Social Security Number: ______________________________

Your spouse's Social Security Number: ______________________________

C. Your date of birth and age: ______________________________

Your spouse's date of birth and age: ______________________________

D. List any other names used by you or your spouse (including maiden name), or other ways you have signed your names to papers and checks during the last eight years:

____

____

____

____

E. Current Address: ______________________________

(Street)

____

(City) (County) (Zip Code)

F. Telephone Number: ______________________________

G. List all addresses you have had in the last three years, the dates when you lived there, and the name you used while living there. If you and your spouse are filing bankruptcy together, list addresses for each for the last three years (include street, town, and zip code).

Addresses	*Date Moved In*	*Date Moved Out*	*Name Used*

2. Prior Bankruptcy: Have you ever been involved before in a bankruptcy (chapter 7, 11, 12, or 13)? YES___ NO___. If YES, bring *all* papers from the case(s) to our office.

What Chapter?	*Date Case Filed*	*Did You Get a Discharge?*	*If Yes, List Date of Discharge*	*If Dismissed, List Date and Reason Why Dismissed*

3. Other Bankruptcies: Have there been any other bankruptcies filed by someone other than you or your spouse to stop a foreclosure on your home? YES _____ NO _____. If YES, give details: ______________________________

____

____

4. Occupation and Income:

A. Usual type of work: ______________________________

B. Name and address of current employer: ______________________________

____

C. Spouse's usual type of work: ______________________________

D. Name and address of spouse's current employer: ______________________________

____

E. How long have you been at your current job?: __________________ Your spouse? __________________

F. List all income received in the last six months by you and your spouse (do not list your spouse's income if you are not filing bankruptcy together and you are legally separated):
(Bring a copy with you to our office of all pay stubs or other records from your employer of all pay received within the past sixty days.)

	Income Received (Give gross income)	*Source* (Names and addresses of employers or specify social security, welfare, unemployment, self-employment, investments, etc.)	*By Whom* (Self or spouse)
1 month ago:			
2 months ago:			
3 months ago:			
4 months ago:			
5 months ago:			
6 months ago:			

List all income received so far this year and in the last two years by you or your spouse:

	Income Received (Give gross income as reported on tax returns)	*Source* (Names and addresses of employers or specify social security, welfare, unemployment, self-employment, investments, etc.)	*By Whom* (Self or spouse)
So far this year:			
Last year:			
Year before last:			

G. Have you or your spouse been in business by yourself or with others during the last six years? YES ____ NO ____. If yes, give the dates, name of the business, its address, and the names of others in business with you or your spouse. ____________________

H. Are there any debts from your former business? YES ___ NO ___. If YES, list them in questions 32 and 33 and give details here:____________________

I. (1) If you employed anyone (such as regular employees, cleaning people, gardeners, babysitters), do you still owe them wages? YES ___ NO ___. If YES, give name and address of employee, dates worked, amount owed, and work done. ____________________

(2) Has anyone given you money to purchase property or services that you were unable to provide? YES ___ NO ___. If YES, give details: ____________________

J. Have you ever been on welfare within the past two years? YES ___ NO ___. Has anyone in your immediate family? YES ___ NO ___. If YES to either question, specify the persons, dates, amounts received, and places (if state welfare, name the state, if local welfare, name the city or county).

____

K. Have you ever received or been told you have received more money from the government than you were supposed to (such as social security, welfare, unemployment compensation, food stamps, etc.)?
YES ___ NO ___. If YES, give details:

L. Do you have any vacation time that is due you from your employer? YES _____ NO _____. If YES, how much is due? ____________

M. Do you have an IRA (including Roth or education IRA) or any other pension plan? YES ____ NO _____. If YES, give details: ____________

N. Have you paid or contributed any funds to a tax-exempt tuition program, or purchased any tuition credits or certificates? YES _____ NO _____. If YES, give details: ____________

O. Are you the beneficiary of a trust or future interest? YES _____ NO _____. If YES, give details: ____________

P. Do you expect to receive more than a small amount of money or property at any time in the near future by way of gift or life insurance proceeds? YES _____ NO _____. If YES, give details: ____________

Q. (1) Do you expect to inherit any money or property in the near future? YES ___ NO ___. If YES, give details: ____________

(2) Has anyone died and left you anything (including insurance benefits)? YES ___ NO ___. If YES, give details: ____________

5. Taxes: (***Bring a copy of your W-2 forms and any tax returns you have filed within the past year with you to our office.***)

A. Have you received any tax refunds this year? YES ___ NO ___. State $ __________ Federal $ __________

B. What income tax refunds do you expect to receive this year? State $ __________ Federal $ __________

C. Does this amount include an Earned Income Credit? YES _____ NO _____.

D. Have you already filed for the refund? YES _____ NO _____.

E. When do you expect to receive the tax refund? ____________

F. Do you know if anyone intends to take or intercept your tax refund? YES __ NO __. If YES, give details. ____________

G. Did you sign an agreement or refund anticipation loan with a tax preparer to get your refund early? YES _____ NO _____.

H. (1) Is any other person (such as your spouse) entitled to part of your refund? YES ___ NO ___.

(2) Have you filed income tax returns every year for the last seven years? YES ___ NO ___.

(3) Do you have copies of your income tax returns filed in the last four years? YES ____ NO ____. If NO, state the years for which you do not have copies: ____________

(4) Do you owe any taxes to the United States? YES ___ NO ___. If YES, give the name and address of the department or agency to which the tax is owing, the kind of tax that is owing, and the years for which the tax is owing: ____________

(5) Do you owe any taxes to any states? YES _____ NO _____. If YES, give the name of the state and the department or agency therein, the address of the department or agency, the kind of tax that is owing, and the years for which the tax is owing: ____________

(6) Do you owe any taxes to a county, district, or city? YES _____ NO _____. If YES, give the name of the county, district, or city, the kind of tax that is owing, and the years for which the tax is owing: ____________

(7) Besides taxes, do you owe any other money to any branch of the United States Government (e.g., FHA, VA, repossessions or loans, withholding taxes [if you were in business], or money owed Small Business Administration)? YES _____ NO _____. If YES, give the name of the branch, its address, the amount owing, and why it is owed: ____________

6. Debts Repaid:

A. If you have made any payments totaling more than $600 to a creditor within the last ninety days, give the name of the creditor and the dates and amount of the payments:

Creditor's Name & Address	*Is the Creditor a Relative?*	*Payment Dates*	*Amount of Payment*

Please make sure to bring any payment books you have with you.

B. Have you made any payments within the last year to creditors who are or were insiders (relatives or business partners)? YES _____ NO _____. If YES, give details:

____

____

____

C. (1) Have you ever had a student loan or cosigned for someone else's student loan? YES ___ NO ___.
If YES to either question, please state:
(2) Who lent you the money? ____
(3) What school was the loan for? ____
(4) Did the student finish the course of study at the school? YES _____ NO _____. If NO, why not?
____
(6) Who is trying to collect the debt? ____
(7) How much have you paid on the debt (include any tax refund intercepts)? ________________
(8) Has anyone else made payments on the debt? YES ____ NO _____. How much? $________________

7. Suits: (*Bring in all papers relating to any suits or criminal cases.*)

A. Have you ever been sued by any person, company, or organization? YES ___ NO ____. If YES, state:

Case Name	*Case No.*	*Name and Address of Court*	*Type of Case*	*Result of Case*

B. Have any court suits resulted in a lien being placed on your property? YES _____ NO _____.

C. Have you ever sued any person, company, or organization? YES ____ NO ____. If yes, state:

Case Name	*Case No.*	*Name and Address of Court*	*Type of Case*	*Result of Case*

D. Do you have any criminal charges or convictions? YES ____ NO ____. If yes, state:

Case No.	*Name of Court*	*Charges*	*Result of Case*	*Do You Owe Fines, Restitution, or Any Other Money?*

E. Have you been involved in any administrative agency cases (unemployment compensation, worker's compensation, etc.) in the past 12 months? YES ____ NO ____. If yes, state:

Case Name	*Case No.*	*Agency's Name and Address*	*Type of Case*	*Result of Case*

F. Do you have any possible reason for suing someone for damage to your property or for injuries to yourself or other members of your family? YES _____ NO _____. If YES, who could you sue, how much money is involved, and why could you sue? ____

____

____

8. Garnishment, Attachment, and Sheriff's Sale:

A. Have you ever had any property listed for or sold at a foreclosure, tax sale, or sheriff's sale, or levied upon? YES _____ NO _____. If YES, bring any papers concerning those actions to the office and state:

What Property Was Sold or Listed for Sale	*Value of Property*	*Date*	*Name and Address of Creditor*

B. Has money from your pay check or bank account been garnished, or taken or frozen by a creditor, including your bank or credit union, because of a debt? YES ____ NO ____. If YES, give the following:

Name and Address of Creditor Who Received the Money	*Amount Taken*	*Dates*

9. Repossessions and Returns:

A. Have you had any property or merchandise repossessed during the last year? YES ____ NO ____. If YES, bring all papers including all letters telling you of the repossession or sale.

Description of Property	*Month & Year of Repossession*	*Who Repossessed Item (Name, Address)*	*Value of Property When Repossessed*

B. Have you voluntarily returned any property or merchandise to the seller in the past year? YES _____ NO _____. If YES, state:

Description of Property	*Month & Year of Return to Seller*	*Seller's Name and Address*	*Value of Property at Time of Return*

10. Property of Yours Held by Someone Else:

A. Does any other person have any of your property? (This includes any check you may have given to a payday lender or check cashing service.) YES _____ NO _____. If YES, list the following:

Type of Property	*Value*	*Being Held By (Name and Address)*	*Why Is This Person Holding the Property?*

B. Have you given or made an assignment of any of your property for the benefit of your creditors or any settlements with your creditors within the past two years? YES _____ NO _____. If YES, give the name and address of the creditor and the terms and conditions under which you gave the property to the creditor or made an agreement with the creditor: ____

____

____

C. Is any of your property in the hands of a court-appointed person (a receiver), or in the hands of a person who is holding it for your benefit and use (a trustee)? If YES, give details:

____

____

D. Is any of your property in the possession of a pawnbroker, storage company or repairman? YES_____ NO _____. If YES, describe and give its value: ____

____

____

____

11. Gifts and Transfers:

A. Have you made sales of property, mortgages, gifts, or transfers of any substantial property or cash within the last four years? YES _____ NO _____. If YES, give the following:

Name of Person Who Received Property	*Description of Property*	*Month and Year of Gift or Sale*	*Was Sale or Gift to a Relative?*

B. Have you used any money from the sale or transfer of any property within the past ten years to purchase or improve your current home, or to pay down the mortgage? YES _____ NO _____ . If YES, give the following:

Description of Property Sold or Transferred	*Month and Year of Sale or Transfer*	*Amount You Got from Sale or Transfer*	*How Much of This Amount Was Used to Buy or Improve Your Home?*

12. Losses:

A. Did you lose any substantial amount of money as a result of fire, theft, or gambling during the last year? YES _____ NO _____. If YES, state the following:

What Caused the Loss?	*Value of the Money or Property That Was Lost*	*Date of the Loss*

B. Did insurance pay for any part of the loss? YES__ NO__. If YES, what was date of payment? ______________ How much was paid? $ ________________

13. Payments or Transfers to Attorney or Debt Consultants:

A. Give the date, name, and address of any attorney or bankruptcy consultant (petition preparer, typing service, document preparation service, independent paralegal) you have consulted during the past year:

____

____

B. Give the reason for which you consulted the attorney or bankruptcy consultant:

____

C. How much have you paid the attorney or bankruptcy consultant? $ _______________

D. Did you promise to pay money to the attorney or bankruptcy consultant? YES _____ NO _____. If YES, give the amount and terms of the agreement: ______________________________

____

____

E. Give the name and address of any credit counseling agency or debt settlement company you have consulted during the past year and the date when you consulted them: ______________________________

____

F. Did the agency have you sign up for a plan to repay or settle your debts? YES _____ NO _____. If YES, give the amount and terms of the plan (*and bring a copy of the plan with you to our office*): ______________

____

G. How much have you paid the agency or company? $ _____________

H. Have you consulted anyone else about your debts in the past year? YES _____ NO _____. If YES, give name, address, and amount(s) paid for the service: ______________________________

____

____

I. Did any of your debts result from a refinancing or a consolidation loan? YES ___ NO ___. If YES, which ones?

____

____

Please be sure to bring all papers for these loans with you.

14. Closed Bank Accounts:
Have you or your spouse had your name on any bank account (such as savings, checking, certificates of deposit) during the past 12 months that is now closed? YES __ NO __. If YES, state:

Bank's Name and Address	*Acct. No.*	*Type of Account (Savings/Checking)*	*Names of Others on Account*	*Date Closed*	*Final Balance*

15. Safe Deposit Boxes:
Have you or your spouse had a safe deposit box during the last year? YES _____ NO _____.
If YES, list the name and address of the bank, the name and address of everyone who had access to the box, the contents of the box and, if you no longer have the box, the date it was closed:

____
____
____

16. Property Held for Another Person: Do you have any money, property, furniture, etc. that belongs to another person or that you are holding for the benefit of someone else (in trust)? YES ____ NO____. If YES, what is the property, who owns it, and what is it worth? Include name and address of the owners:

Type of Property	*Value*	*Owned By*	*Address*	*Relative? (Yes or No)*

At what address are you keeping this property? ______________________________

17. Leases: Have you had an auto lease, rent-to-own, or rental-purchase transaction in the past four years?
YES _____ NO ______. If YES, give details: ______________________________
____
____
____

18. Cooperatives: Are you a member of any type of cooperative (housing, food, agricultural, etc.)? If YES, give details:
____
____
____

19. Alimony, Child Support, and Property Settlements:

A. Have you had any previous marriages? YES __ NO __. If YES, what is the name of your former spouse?
____
Please be sure that any debts from prior marriages which were never paid are listed with your other debts.

B. Does anybody owe you any money or child support? YES _____ NO _____.
Who? ________________________ How much? $____________________

C. Have you ever been ordered to pay child support? YES ____ NO ____.
Alimony? YES ____ NO ____.
Property Settlement? YES ____ NO ____.
If yes to any question, state:
(1) To whom do you make the payments? ______________________________
(2) Are you behind in your payments? ______________________________
(3) Are the persons you are required to support this way on welfare? ______________________________
(4) Do you have any family court hearings coming up? If YES, explain and give dates:
____
____

D. Do you expect to be involved in a property settlement with your spouse or former spouse in the near future?
YES _____ NO _____.

20. Accidents and Driver's License:

A. Have you been involved in a vehicle accident in the last four years? YES ____ NO ____.

B. Has your vehicle been involved in an accident in the last four years? YES ____ NO ____.

C. Have your children ever injured anyone else or their property? YES ____ NO ____.

D. Have you ever lost your driver's license? YES ____ NO ____. If YES, give details:

____

____

____

21. Cosigners and Debts Incurred for Other People:

A. Were there any cosigners for you on any of the debts you have listed in these forms? YES _____ NO _____. If YES, give the cosigner's name and address, and which debts were cosigned:

____

B. Have you ever been the cosigner on someone else's loan or debt which hasn't been paid off? YES _____ NO _____. If YES, list the following for each debt:

Creditor's Name and Address	*Date of Debt*	*Amount Owing*	*Name and Address of Person You Cosigned For*

C. Have you borrowed any money for someone else's benefit? YES _____ NO _____. If YES, list the following unless you are sure that loan or debt has been paid:

Creditor's Name and Address	*Collection Agent or Attorneys*	*Date of Debt and Which Spouse Owes*	*For What*	*Current Amount of Claim*

D. If you put up any of your property as collateral on a debt you cosigned, list the following:

Creditor	*Type of Property*	*How Much the Property Is Worth Now*

22. Credit Card and Finance Company Debts:

A. Have you obtained cash advances of more than $750 in the last seventy days or used any credit card to purchase more than $500 worth of goods or services in the last ninety days? YES ______ NO ______. If YES, give details: ____

____

____

B. Have you ever gone over your credit limit on any credit cards? YES _____ NO _____. If YES, give details:____

____

____

C. If any of your debts listed on this form are owed to finance companies, did you sign an agreement that listed some of your property (such as a second television or VCR) and stated that the property would be security or collateral for the loan? YES _____ NO _____. If YES, which ones? ______________________

____

____

D. Do you owe money on a payday loan, auto title loan, or for a check cashing service? YES ___ NO ___. If YES, give details:

____

____

23. Evictions:

A. Has your current landlord sued you or brought an eviction suit against you? YES ____ NO ____. If YES, state:

Case Name	*Case No.*	*Name and Address of Court*	*Reason for Suit or Eviction*	*Result of Case (Eviction Judgment?) or Date of Hearing*

B. Does your current landlord have an eviction judgment or order against you? YES ____ NO ____. If YES, and the eviction is based on your nonpayment of rent, list the following:

Regular Rent Payment (Specify Monthly, Weekly, Other)	*When Are Rent Payments Due?*	*Back Rent You Owe*

C. Is your landlord planning to bring an eviction suit against you? YES ____ NO ____. If YES, give details and state if your landlord is claiming that you have damaged the property or used illegal drugs on the property:

____

____

24. Secured Debts: (*Answer Every Question*). Do you owe any money for any property or goods which can be repossessed or foreclosed if you fail to make payments? YES ____ NO ____. Have you agreed with any creditor that it can take any of your possessions from you, such as your car or your furniture, if you don't keep up with your payments? YES ____ NO ____. Do you have any mortgages or liens on your property? YES _____ NO _____. For all these debts, give the following information, including the full name and address of the creditor AND the attorney or collection agency.

Names and Addresses of Creditor, Collection Agency, & Attorney	*Acct. No.*	*Date & Purpose of Debt*	*What Property Is Collateral or Subject to Lien?*	*Current Value of Property*	*Original Amount Owed*	*Current Balance*	*Monthly Payment & No. of Payments Behind*	*Who Owes? (Which Spouse? Co-signers?)*

If the collateral is a home or a car, do you have insurance on the property? YES ____ NO ____.

Is any of the collateral located somewhere other than your home? YES ____ NO ____. If YES, describe: ______

Do you dispute any of these debts? YES ___ NO ___. If yes, which ones? ______

Do you have an FHA, FmHA (Rural Housing), or VA Mortgage? ______

25. Unsecured Debts: List all creditors, including creditors who have judgments or whose claims you dispute. Anyone who you think may have a claim against you must be listed even if the claim is old. ***For each debt, please give all information requested. If a collection agency or an attorney is involved, list it and the person or company you originally owed.***

Creditor's Name and Address	*Name and Address of Collection Agency and Attorney, If Any*	*Account No.*	*Date of Debt*	*What Is Debt For?*	*Current Amount of Claim*	*Which Spouse Owes?*	*Any Co-signers?*

Do you dispute any of these debts? YES ____ NO ____. If YES, which ones? ______________________________

____

____

Now review all the debts you have listed on this page and the last. Have you forgotten any:

medical bills?	mail order bills?	schools?	condominium assessments?	utility or telephone bills?
credit card bills?	judgments?	student loans?	traffic tickets or parking tickets?	loans from relatives?
store charges?	loan companies?	welfare debts?	criminal restitution debts?	money owed to creditors who repossessed your property?
cable T.V. bills?	debts you cosigned?	back rent?	bills for goods or services?	loans on your pension?
payday loans?	provided to your dependents?		bills owed to old landlords?	

26. Asset Listing:

(If you are married and living with your spouse, designate any items listed below that are not jointly owned.)

A. REAL PROPERTY (Home):

(1) Do you own real estate that you use as your home? YES _____ NO _____. Describe and give the location of this property (house, mobile home, condominium, cooperative, land, etc.) in which you hold an interest:

____

____

____

(2) Co-owners: ______________________________

(3) Purchase price: ______________ Date purchased: ______________

(4) Original mortgage amount: ______________ Downpayment amount: ______________

(5) Have you used any funds that you did not borrow to purchase or improve your home? YES __ NO __. If YES, list the amounts and give details: ______________________________

____

(6) If not purchased, state when and how you became the owner (inheritance, gift, etc.): ______________

(7) Present value of your house: ______________________________

(8) Outstanding mortgage balance: ______________________________

(9) Are there any other mortgages? YES ____ NO ____. If YES, give the name and address of each company:

____

____

(10) Is any mortgage insured by the FHA, VA, or a private mortgage insurance company? YES ____ NO ____. If YES, give details: ______________________________

____

B. REAL PROPERTY (Other Real Estate):

(1) Do you own other real estate? YES _____ NO _____. Describe and give the location of all real property (lot, house, condominium, cooperative, land, burial plot, etc.) in which you hold an interest:

____

____

____

(2) Co-owners: ______________________________

(3) Outstanding mortgage balance: ______________________________

(4) Name of mortgage company: ______________________________

(5) Purchase price: ______________ Year purchased: ______________

(6) Present value of your house: ______________________________

(7) Are there any other mortgages? YES __ NO __. If YES, give the name and address of each company:

____

____

(8) Is any mortgage insured by the FHA, VA, or a private mortgage insurance company? YES ____ NO ____. If YES, give details: ______________________________

____

C. PERSONAL PROPERTY:

(1) Cash on hand: $______________________________

(2) Do you have any deposits of money in banks, savings and loan associations, or credit unions? If YES, list the name and address of the bank, savings and loan association, or credit union, and the amount:

____

____

(3) Have you given a security deposit to any landlord, utility, or anyone else? YES ____ NO _____. If YES, list the name and address of the person or company and the amount:

____

____

(4) List your major property items such as stove, refrigerator, TV, sewing machine, furniture, guns, etc., giving approximate age and value (what you could get for it if you sold it). (These goods usually can be protected, but you must list them to protect them.)

Item	*Approximate Age*	*Value (What You Could Get for It If You Sold It)*

____
____
____
____
____
____
____
____
____
____
____
____
____

If any of the above items are being financed through a company, list the item and the name and address of the company below: ____
____
____
____

(5) Give an estimate of the value (what you could get for it if you sold it) of the following:
All your furniture not already listed: $________ All your clothing: $________ All minor appliances not already listed: $______ All your household goods not already listed (dishes, utensils, food, etc.): $_______

(6) List each item of jewelry that you own, and an estimate of its value (what you could get for it if you sold it):
____

D. CARS, MOBILE HOMES, TRAILERS AND BOATS:
Do you have any cars, trucks, mobile homes, boats, trailers, or motorcycles? YES _____ NO _____. If YES, give the year, make, model, value, who is financing it, and amount owed:
____
____
____

E. OTHER PROPERTY:
Do you own any life insurance policies? YES _____ NO _____.
If YES, list insurance company's name and address: ____
____
How long have you had each policy? ____
Cash surrender value: ____
Do you have any other insurance, including credit insurance? YES _____ NO _____. If YES, describe:
____
____
Do you expect to receive any money from any insurance in the near future? YES _____ NO _____. If YES, give details: ____
____
Do you own any stocks? YES _____ NO _____. Value: $________________
Do you own any bonds (including U.S. Savings Bonds)? YES ____ NO ____. Value: $____________________
Do you own any machinery, tools, or fixtures used in your business or work? YES ____ NO ____. If YES, list and state what you could sell it for: ____
____
____
Do you have any animals or pets? YES _____ NO _____. If YES, describe and give value (what you could sell them for): ____
____

Do you have any right to receive commissions or other payments from any previous job you have held?
YES _____ NO _____. Does anyone owe you any money? YES _____ NO _____. If YES to either, state names, addresses and amounts owed: ____
____
____

Do you have any books, prints or pictures, stamps or coins, or sports equipment of substantial value?
YES _____ NO _____. If YES, describe and estimate their value: ________________________________
____
____
____

Do you have any stock in trade (inventory)? YES ____ NO ____. If YES, describe and estimate the value:
____
____

Do you own anything else not mentioned above? YES _____ NO _____. If YES, describe and state its value (what you could sell it for): ____
____
____
____

Does any of the property that you own or possess pose a threat of harm to public health or safety?
YES _____ NO _____.
Is the threat imminent? YES _____ NO _____.
Has anyone ever alleged that any of the property that you own or possess poses a threat of imminent harm to public health or safety? YES _____ NO _____.
Was the threat alleged to be imminent? YES _____ NO _____.
Give details regarding any threat or alleged threat to public health or safety, including identification of property and nature of potential harm or alleged harm. ____
____
____
____

27. Budget Information:

A. Do you currently receive your pay or other income (check one):

	YOU	YOUR SPOUSE
WEEKLY	________	________
EVERY 2 WEEKS	________	________
MONTHLY	________	________
OTHER	________	________

B. What is the gross amount received in wages or other income (before taxes or other deductions)?

YOU	YOUR SPOUSE
________	________

C. What deductions, if any, are taken out?

	YOU	YOUR SPOUSE
Taxes	________	________
Insurance	________	________
Union dues	________	________
Other (identify: ______________)	________	________

D. What is the usual amount of your check (take-home pay)?

YOU	YOUR SPOUSE
________	________

E. Is your job subject to seasonal or other changes?

YOU	YES _____	NO _____
YOUR SPOUSE	YES _____	NO _____

F. What was your gross income (reported on W-2 form and tax return) for last year?

YOU	YOUR SPOUSE
__________	__________

G. If you receive alimony, maintenance, or support, what is the amount you get on a regular basis?

YOU	YOUR SPOUSE
__________	__________

H. List all dependents of you and your spouse.

	NAME	AGE	RELATIONSHIP
YOU			
YOUR SPOUSE			

I. List all members of your household.

NAME	AGE	RELATIONSHIP

J. Do you expect your income to increase or decrease more than 10% in the next year? YES ____ NO _____.

K. Do you expect to have any increase or decrease in expenses (like medical bills) in the near future? YES____ NO_____. If YES, describe: ____

____

____

L. Do you, your spouse, or your dependents receive income from any source other than jobs, alimony, maintenance, or support listed above (such as public assistance, unemployment compensation, social security, SSI, pension, etc.)? YES _____ NO _____. If YES, list:

Source of Income	*To Whom Payable*	*Amount per Month*

M. Do you, your spouse, or your dependents receive any regular contributions to your household expenses from any source not listed above? YES _____ NO _____. If YES, list:

Source of Contribution	*To Whom Payable*	*Amount per Month*

N. Is your family eligible for food stamps? YES _____ NO _____.
If YES, how much in food stamps do you receive per month? $________________________

O. Monthly Expenses. (Give realistic estimates. If your expenses add up to more than the income you have listed, or less than your income, be prepared to explain why.)

What are your average monthly expenses for (if you and your spouse are not filing bankruptcy together, list separately any regular monthly contribution your spouse makes to the following household expenses):

	Average Monthly Expenses	Spouse's Contribution
Rent or mortgage	______	______
Are real estate taxes included? ___		
Is property tax included? ___		
Condo or homeowners association fees	______	______
Trash pickup	______	______
Electricity	______	______
Heat	______	______
Water	______	______
Telephone		
Basic	______	______
Optional	______	______
Other utilities (internet, cable T.V., etc.)	______	______
	______	______
Home maintenance (repairs and upkeep)	______	______
Food (cash you spend on food)	______	______
Amount of food stamps you spend	______	______
Clothing	______	______
Laundry and cleaning	______	______
Medications	______	______
Other medical and dental expenses	______	______
Public transportation	______	______
Automobile upkeep	______	______
Gasoline and oil	______	______
Newspapers, magazines, school books	______	______
Recreation	______	______
Charitable contributions	______	______
Club and union dues (not deducted from wages)	______	______
Insurance (not deducted from wages)		
Homeowner's or renter's	______	______
Life	______	______
Health	______	______
Auto	______	______
Other ______	______	______
Taxes (not deducted from wages or included in mortgage payment)	______	______
Installment payments		
Vehicle	______	______
Other ______	______	______
Other ______	______	______
Alimony, maintenance or support payments	______	______
Other payments for support of dependents	______	______
Expenses for operating your business	______	______
Other expenses (list types of expenses) (e.g., home maintenance, security system, school)		
Identify: ______	______	______
______	______	______

P. Do you have any monthly expenses not listed above that you pay for the care and support of an elderly, chronically ill, or disabled member of your household or your immediate family? YES____ NO_____. If YES, describe: ____

____

____

Q. Do you have any monthly expenses not listed above that you pay to keep your family safe from domestic violence? YES____ NO_____. If YES, describe: ____

____

____

R. Do you pay any expenses for your dependent children under the age of eighteen to attend a private or public elementary or secondary school? YES____ NO_____. If YES, describe: __________________________

____

____

Appendix I

Bankruptcy Client Handout Reflecting the 2005 Amendments

This appendix contains a client handout answering common bankruptcy questions, updated to include the bankruptcy changes going into effect October 17, 2005.[1] The National Consumer Law Center provides copyright permission for individuals and organizations to copy or adapt this handout for distribution without charge to consumers. No permission is granted to include this material in other publications for sale.

To facilitate adaptation of the handout, it is also found in both Microsoft Word and Adobe Acrobat (PDF) format on the CD-Rom accompanying this volume. Copy it into a word-processing program and edit it to meet individual needs.

NCLC's *Consumer Bankruptcy Law and Practice* (7th ed. 2004) contains four client handouts. The handout, *infra*, replaces the one found in Appendix I.2 of that volume. The other handouts found in that volume in Appendices I.3–I.5 are not included in this appendix, and have not been adapted to reflect the 2005 amendments.

NCLC has also produced other resources for clients. The *NCLC Guide to Surviving Debt* is NCLC's most popular book, and a new edition was released in early 2005. (Because the book was written prior to passage of the 2005 amendments, the bankruptcy chapter has not been updated to reflect those changes.)

The *NCLC Guide to Surviving Debt* provides precise, practical advice on how to deal with an overwhelming debt load, including such topics as:

- Bankruptcy rights;
- Dealing with debt collectors;
- What consumers need to know about their credit rating;
- Which debts to pay first;
- Refinancing do's and don'ts;
- Saving a home from foreclosure;
- Automobile repossessions;
- Evictions and utility shutoffs;
- Credit card debt;
- Student loans.

A number of bankruptcy practitioners and credit counselors purchase bulk-discounted quantities of this book to distribute to clients, by calling (617) 542-9595. Consumers can also purchase individual copies by calling the same telephone number or by ordering securely on-line at www.consumerlaw.org.

A large number of additional consumer education brochures are found on the CD-Rom accompanying this volume, and are also available free of charge at www.consumerlaw.org.

---

1 The original version of this handout, which has now been updated, was adapted (1) from a pamphlet prepared by Legal Services, Inc., under a grant from the Pennsylvania Law Coordination Center, and (2) from National Consumer Law Center, *NCLC Guide to Surviving Debt*.

Answers to Common Bankruptcy Questions

A decision to file for bankruptcy should be made only after determining that bankruptcy is the best way to deal with your financial problems. This brochure can not explain every aspect of the bankruptcy process. If you still have questions after reading it, you should speak with an attorney familiar with bankruptcy or a paralegal working for an attorney.

What Is Bankruptcy?

Bankruptcy is a legal proceeding in which a person who can not pay his or her bills can get a fresh financial start. The right to file for bankruptcy is provided by federal law, and all bankruptcy cases are handled in federal court. Filing bankruptcy immediately stops all of your creditors from seeking to collect debts from you, at least until your debts are sorted out according to the law.

What Can Bankruptcy Do for Me?

Bankruptcy may make it possible for you to:

- Eliminate the legal obligation to pay most or all of your debts. This is called a "discharge" of debts. It is designed to give you a fresh financial start.
- Stop foreclosure on your house or mobile home and allow you an opportunity to catch up on missed payments. (Bankruptcy does not, however, automatically eliminate mortgages and other liens on your property without payment.)
- Prevent repossession of a car or other property, or force the creditor to return property even after it has been repossessed.
- Stop wage garnishment, debt collection harassment, and similar creditor actions to collect a debt.
- Restore or prevent termination of utility service.
- Allow you to challenge the claims of creditors who have committed fraud or who are otherwise trying to collect more than you really owe.

What Bankruptcy Can Not Do

Bankruptcy can not, however, cure every financial problem. Nor is it the right step for every individual. In bankruptcy, it is usually *not* possible to:

- Eliminate certain rights of "secured" creditors. A "secured" creditor has taken a mortgage or other lien on property as collateral for the loan. Common examples are car loans and home mortgages. You *can* force secured creditors to take payments over time in the bankruptcy process and bankruptcy *can* eliminate your obligation to pay any additional money if your property is taken. Nevertheless, you generally can not keep the collateral unless you continue to pay the debt.
- Discharge types of debts singled out by the bankruptcy law for special treatment, such as child support, alimony, certain other debts related to divorce, most student loans, court restitution orders, criminal fines, and some taxes.
- Protect cosigners on your debts. When a relative or friend has co-signed a loan, and the consumer discharges the loan in bankruptcy, the cosigner may still have to repay all or part of the loan.
- Discharge debts that arise after bankruptcy has been filed.

What Different Types of Bankruptcy Cases Should I Consider?

There are four types of bankruptcy cases provided under the law:

- *Chapter 7* is known as "straight" bankruptcy or "liquidation." It requires a debtor to give up property which exceeds certain limits called "exemptions," so the property can be sold to pay creditors.
- *Chapter 11*, known as "reorganization," is used by businesses and a few individual debtors whose debts are very large.
- *Chapter 12* is reserved for family farmers and fishermen.
- *Chapter 13* is called "debt adjustment." It requires a debtor to file a plan to pay debts (or parts of debts) from current income.

Most people filing bankruptcy will want to file under either chapter 7 or chapter 13. Either type of case may be filed individually or by a married couple filing jointly.

If your income is above the median income for a family the size of your household in your state, you may have to file a chapter 13 case (the national median family income for a family of 4 in 2004 was approximately $63,012—your state's figures may be higher or lower). A higher-income consumer must fill out "means test" forms requiring detailed information about income and expenses. If, under standards in the law, the consumer is found to have a certain amount left over that could be paid to unsecured creditors, the bankruptcy court may decide that the consumer can not file a chapter 7 case, unless there are special extenuating circumstances.

Chapter 7 (Straight Bankruptcy)

In a bankruptcy case under chapter 7, you file a petition asking the court to discharge your debts. The basic idea in a chapter 7 bankruptcy is to wipe out (discharge) your debts in exchange for your giving up property, except for "exempt" property which the law allows you to keep. In most cases, all of your property will be exempt. But property which is not exempt is sold, with the money distributed to creditors.

If you want to keep property like a home or a car and are behind on the payments on a mortgage or car loan, a chapter 7 case probably will not be the right choice for you. That is because chapter 7 bankruptcy does not eliminate the right of mortgage holders or car loan creditors to take your property to cover your debt.

Chapter 13 (Reorganization)

In a chapter 13 case you file a "plan" showing how you will pay off some of your past-due and current debts over three to five years. The most important thing about a chapter 13 case is that it will allow you to keep valuable property—especially your home and car—which might otherwise be lost, if you can make the payments which the bankruptcy law requires to be made to your creditors. In most cases, these payments will be at least as much as your regular monthly payments on your mortgage or car loan, with some extra payment to get caught up on the amount you have fallen behind.

You should consider filing a chapter 13 plan if you

(1) own your home and are in danger of losing it because of money problems;

(2) are behind on debt payments, but can catch up if given some time;

(3) have valuable property which is not exempt, but you can afford to pay creditors from your income over time.

You will need to have enough income in chapter 13 to pay for your necessities and to keep up with the required payments as they come due.

What Does It Cost to File for Bankruptcy?

It now costs $274 to file for bankruptcy under chapter 7 and $189 to file for bankruptcy under chapter 13, whether for one person or a married couple. The court may allow you to pay this filing fee in installments if you can not pay all at once. If you are unable to pay the filing fee in installments, you may request that the court waive the filing fee. If you hire an attorney you will also have to pay the attorney's fees you agree to.

What Must I Do Before Filing Bankruptcy?

You must receive budget and credit counseling from an approved credit counseling agency within 180 days before your bankruptcy case is filed. The agency will review possible options available to you in credit counseling and assist you in reviewing your budget. Different agencies provide the counseling in-person, by telephone, or over the Internet. If you decide to file bankruptcy, you will need to file with the bankruptcy forms in your case a certificate from the agency stating that you received the counseling.

If you decide to go ahead with bankruptcy, you should be very careful in choosing an agency for the required counseling. It is extremely difficult to sort out the good counseling agencies from the bad ones. Many agencies are legitimate, but many are simply rip-offs. And being an "approved" agency for bankruptcy counseling is no guarantee that the agency is good. It is also important to understand that even good agencies won't be able to help you much if you're already too deep in financial trouble.

Some of the approved agencies offer debt management plans (also called DMPs). This is a plan to repay some or all of your debts in which you send the counseling agency a monthly payment that it then distributes to your creditors. Debt management plans can be helpful for some consumers. For others, they are a terrible idea. The problem is that many counseling agencies will pressure you into a debt management plan as a way of avoiding bankruptcy whether it makes sense for you or not. It is important to keep in mind these important points:

- Bankruptcy is not necessarily to be avoided at all costs. In many cases, bankruptcy may actually be the best choice for you.
- If you sign up for a debt management plan that you can't afford, you may end up in bankruptcy anyway (and a copy of the plan must also be filed in your bankruptcy case).
- There are approved agencies for bankruptcy counseling that do not offer debt management plans.

It is usually a good idea for you to meet with an attorney before you receive the required credit counseling. Unlike a credit counselor, who can not give legal advice, an attorney can provide counseling on whether bankruptcy is the best option. If bankruptcy is not the right answer for you, a good attorney will offer a range of other suggestions. The attorney can also provide you with a list of approved credit counseling agencies, or you can check the website for the United States Trustee Program office at www.usdoj.gov/ust.

What Property Can I Keep?

[*Note to the Attorney: This answer is accurate for states that permit the federal exemptions. For states which have opted out of federal exemptions, the answer must be adapted to indicate that the debtor's exemptions are those specified by state law.*]

In a chapter 7 case, you can keep all property which the law says is "exempt" from the claims of creditors. You can choose between your exemptions under your state law or under federal law. In many cases, the federal exemptions are better.

Federal exemptions include:

- $18,450 in equity in your home;
- $2950 in equity in your car;
- $475 per item in any household goods up to a total of $9850;
- $1850 in things you need for your job (tools, books, etc.);
- $975 in any property, plus part of the unused exemption in your home, up to $9250;
- Your right to receive certain benefits such as social security, unemployment compensation, veteran's benefits, public assistance, and pensions—regardless of the amount.

The amounts of the exemptions are doubled when a married couple files together.

In determining whether property is exempt, you must keep a few things in mind. The value of property is not the amount you paid for it, but what it is worth now. Especially for furniture and cars, this may be a lot less than what you paid or what it would cost to buy a replacement.

You also only need to look at your equity in property. This means that you count your exemptions against the full value minus any money that you owe on mortgages or liens. For example, if you own a $50,000 house with a $40,000 mortgage, you count your exemptions against the $10,000 which is your equity if you sell it.

While your exemptions allow you to keep property even in a chapter 7 case, your exemptions do not make any difference to the right of a mortgage holder or car loan creditor to take the property to cover the debt if you are behind. In a chapter 13 case, you can keep all of your property if your plan meets the requirements of the bankruptcy law. In most cases you will have to pay the mortgages or liens as you would if you didn't file bankruptcy.

What Will Happen to My Home and Car If I File Bankruptcy?

In most cases you will not lose your home or car during your bankruptcy case as long as your equity in the property is fully exempt. Even if your property is not fully exempt, you will be able to keep it, if you pay its non-exempt value to creditors in chapter 13.

However, some of your creditors may have a "security interest" in your home, automobile or other personal property. This means that you gave that creditor a mortgage on the home or put your other property up as collateral for the debt. Bankruptcy does not make these security interests go away. If you don't make your payments on that debt, the creditor may be able to take and sell the home or the property, during or after the bankruptcy case.

There are several ways that you can keep collateral or mortgaged property after you file bankruptcy. You can agree to keep making your payments on the debt until it is paid in full. Or you can pay the creditor the amount that the property you want to keep is worth. In some cases involving fraud or other improper conduct by the creditor, you may be able to challenge the debt. If you put up your household goods as collateral for a loan (other than a loan to purchase the goods), you can usually keep your property without making any more payments on that debt.

Can I Own Anything After Bankruptcy?

Yes! Many people believe they can not own anything for a period of time after filing for bankruptcy. This is not true. You can keep your exempt property and anything you obtain after the bankruptcy is filed. However, if you receive an inheritance, a property settlement, or life insurance benefits within 180 days after filing for bankruptcy, that money or property may have to be paid to your creditors if the property or money is not exempt.

Will Bankruptcy Wipe Out All My Debts?

Yes, with some exceptions. Bankruptcy will not normally wipe out:

(1) money owed for child support or alimony, fines, and some taxes;
(2) debts not listed on your bankruptcy petition;
(3) loans you got by knowingly giving false information to a creditor, who reasonably relied on it in making you the loan;
(4) debts resulting from "willful and malicious" harm;
(5) most student loans, except if the court decides that payment would be an undue hardship;
(6) mortgages and other liens which are not paid in the bankruptcy case (but bankruptcy will wipe out your obligation to pay any additional money if the property is sold by the creditor).

Will I Have to Go to Court?

In most bankruptcy cases, you only have to go to a proceeding called the "meeting of creditors" to meet with the bankruptcy trustee and any creditor who chooses to come. Most of the time, this meeting will be a short and simple procedure where you are asked a few questions about your bankruptcy forms and your financial situation.

Occasionally, if complications arise, or if you choose to dispute a debt, you may have to appear before a judge at a hearing. If you need to go to court, you will receive notice of the court date and time from the court and/or from your attorney.

What Else Must I Do to Complete My Case?

After your case is filed, you must complete an approved course in personal finances. This course will take approximately two hours to complete. Your attorney can give you a list of organizations that provide approved courses, or you can check the website for the United States Trustee Program office at www.usdoj.gov/ust. In a chapter 7 case, you should sign up for the course soon after your case is filed. If you file a chapter 13 case, you should ask your attorney when you should take the course.

Will Bankruptcy Affect My Credit?

There is no clear answer to this question. Unfortunately, if you are behind on your bills, your credit may already be bad. Bankruptcy will probably not make things any worse.

The fact that you've filed a bankruptcy can appear on your credit record for ten years. But because bankruptcy wipes out your old debts, you are likely to be in a better position to pay your current bills, and you may be able to get new credit.

What Else Should I Know?

Utility services—Public utilities, such as the electric company, can not refuse or cut off service because you have filed for bankruptcy. However, the utility can require a deposit for future service and you do have to pay bills which arise after bankruptcy is filed.

Discrimination—An employer or government agency can not discriminate against you because you have filed for bankruptcy.

Driver's license—If you lost your license solely because you couldn't pay court-ordered damages caused in an accident, bankruptcy will allow you to get your license back.

Co-signers—If someone has co-signed a loan with you and you file for bankruptcy, the co-signer may have to pay your debt. If you file a chapter 13, you may be able to protect co-signers, depending upon the terms of your chapter 13 plan.

How Do I Find a Bankruptcy Attorney?

As with any area of the law, it is important to carefully select an attorney who will respond to your personal situation. The attorney should not be too busy to meet you individually and to answer questions as necessary.

The best way to find a trustworthy bankruptcy attorney is to seek recommendations from family, friends or other members of the community, especially any attorney you know and respect. You should carefully read retainers and other documents the attorney asks you to sign. You should not hire an attorney unless he or she agrees to represent you throughout the case.

In bankruptcy, as in all areas of life, remember that the person advertising the cheapest rate is not necessarily the best. Many of the best bankruptcy lawyers do not advertise at all.

Document preparation services also known as "typing services" or "paralegal services" involve non-lawyers who offer to prepare bankruptcy forms for a fee. Problems with these services often arise because non-lawyers can not offer advice on difficult bankruptcy cases and they offer no services once a bankruptcy case has begun. There are also many shady operators in this field, who give bad advice and defraud consumers.

When first meeting a bankruptcy attorney, you should be prepared to answer the following questions:

- What types of debt are causing you the most trouble?
- What are your significant assets?
- How did your debts arise and are they secured?
- Is any action about to occur to foreclose or repossess property or to shut off utility service?
- What are your goals in filing the case?

Can I File Bankruptcy Without an Attorney?

Although it may be possible for some people to file a bankruptcy case without an attorney, it is not a step to be taken lightly. The process is difficult and you may lose property or other rights if you do not know the law. It takes patience and careful preparation. Chapter 7 (straight bankruptcy) cases are easier. Very few people have been able to successfully file chapter 13 (debt adjustment) cases on their own.

> Remember: The law often changes. Each case is different. This pamphlet is meant to give you general information and not to give you specific legal advice.

Quick Reference to the Consumer Credit and Sales Legal Practice Series

References are to sections in *all* manuals in NCLC's Consumer Credit and Sales Legal Practice Series. References followed by "S" appear only in a Supplement.

Readers should also consider another search option available at ***www.consumerlaw.org/keyword***. There, users can search all sixteen NCLC manuals for a case name, party name, statutory or regulatory citation, or *any* other word, phrase, or combination of terms. The search engine provides the title, page number and context of every occurrence of that word or phrase within each of the NCLC manuals. Further search instructions and tips are provided on the web site.

The Quick Reference to the Consumer Credit and Sales Legal Practice Series pinpoints where to find specific topics analyzed in the NCLC manuals. References are to individual manual or supplement sections. (The Quick Reference contains no references to this 2005 Special Guide.) For more information on these volumes, see *What Your Library Should Contain* at the beginning of this volume, or go to www.consumerlaw.org.

This Quick Reference is a speedy means to locate key terms in the appropriate NCLC manual. More detailed indexes are found at the end of the individual NCLC volumes. Both the detailed contents pages and the detailed indexes for each manual are also available on NCLC's web site, www.consumerlaw.org.

NCLC *strongly recommends,* when searching for PLEADINGS on a particular subject, that users refer to the *Index Guide* accompanying *Consumer Law Pleadings on CD-Rom*, and *not* to this *Quick Reference*. Another option is to search for pleadings directly on the *Consumer Law Pleadings* CD-Rom or on the *Consumer Law in a Box* CD-Rom, using the finding tools that are provided on the CD-Roms themselves.

The finding tools found on *Consumer Law in a Box* are also an effective means to find statutes, regulations, agency interpretations, legislative history, and other primary source material found on NCLC's CD-Roms. Other search options are detailed at page vii, *supra*.

Abbreviations

AUS	=	Access to Utility Service (3d ed. 2004)
Auto	=	Automobile Fraud (2d ed. 2003 and 2005 Supp.)
Arbit	=	Consumer Arbitration Agreements (4th ed. 2004)
CBPL	=	Consumer Banking and Payments Law (3d ed. 2005)
Bankr	=	Consumer Bankruptcy Law and Practice (7th ed. 2004)
CCA	=	Consumer Class Actions: A Practical Litigation Guide (5th ed. 2002 and 2005 Supp.)
CLP	=	Consumer Law Pleadings, Numbers One Through Ten (2004)
COC	=	The Cost of Credit (3d ed. 2005)
CD	=	Credit Discrimination (4th ed. 2005)
FCR	=	Fair Credit Reporting (5th ed. 2002 and 2005 Supp.)
FDC	=	Fair Debt Collection (5th ed. 2004 and 2005 Supp.)
Repo	=	Repossessions and Foreclosures (5th ed. 2002 and 2004 Supp.)
Stud	=	Student Loan Law (2d ed. 2002 and 2004 Supp.)
TIL	=	Truth in Lending (5th ed. 2003 and 2004 Supp.)
UDAP	=	Unfair and Deceptive Acts and Practices (6th ed. 2004)
Warr	=	Consumer Warranty Law (2d ed. 2001 and 2005 Supp.)

References are to sections in *all* manuals in NCLC's Consumer Credit and Sales Legal Practice Series

References are to sections in *all* manuals in NCLC's Consumer Credit and Sales Legal Practice Series

References are to sections in *all* manuals in NCLC's Consumer Credit and Sales Legal Practice Series

References are to sections in *all* manuals in NCLC's Consumer Credit and Sales Legal Practice Series

References are to sections in *all* manuals in NCLC's Consumer Credit and Sales Legal Practice Series

References are to sections in *all* manuals in NCLC's Consumer Credit and Sales Legal Practice Series

About the Companion CD-Rom

CD-Rom Supersedes All Prior CD-Roms

This CD-Rom supersedes the CD-Rom accompanying *Consumer Bankruptcy Law and Practice* (7th ed. 2004) and all other editions and supplements. Discard all prior CDs and disks. This 2005 CD-Rom contains everything found on all earlier CDs and disks and contains much additional and updated material.

What Is on the CD-Rom

For a detailed listing of the CD's contents, see the CD-Rom Contents section following this book's table of contents. Highlights and new additions include:

- A red-lined Bankruptcy Code and Title 28 showing the 2005 changes, the 2005 Act, and selected legislative history;
- Interim bankruptcy rules and other rule changes;
- Law Disks' *Bankruptcy Forms*, updated with the new and amended Official Forms, which allows completion of the petition, schedules, and certain other forms on a word processor:[1]
  - The Petition;
  - Applications and Orders for Filing Fee Waivers and to Pay Filing Fee in Installments;
  - The Official Form 6 Schedules, as amended;
  - The Official Form 7 Statement of Financial Affairs;
  - The Individual Debtor's Statement of Intention;
  - Means Test Forms;
  - Attorney Compensation Disclosure Form;
  - The Proof of Claim Form, with current amendments; and
  - Captions and Social Security Number Form;
- All new and amended Official Forms with Committee Notes;
- Sample pleadings pertaining specifically to the 2005 changes, and 150 other bankruptcy pleadings;
- A number of other blank official forms and forms promulgated by the Administrative Office of the U.S. Courts, all up-to-date;
- A date calculator to provide specific dates corresponding to key look-back events relevant to the 2005 changes;
- Means testing data required by the 2005 changes, including median income by state and IRS standards as to allowable living expenses; and
- A bankruptcy questionnaire to facilitate debtor representation, client handouts answering common bankruptcy questions and numerous other consumer education brochures, updated for 2005.

How to Use the CD-Rom

The CD's pop-up menu quickly allows you to use the CD—just place the CD into its drive and click on the "Start NCLC CD" button that will pop up in the middle of the screen. You can also access the CD by clicking on a desktop icon that you can create using the pop-up menu.[2] For detailed installation instructions, see *One-Time Installation* below.

All the CD-Rom's information is available in PDF (Acrobat) format, making the information:

- Highly readable (identical to the printed pages in the book);
- Easily navigated (with bookmarks, "buttons," and Internet-style forward and backward searches);
- Easy to locate with keyword searches and other quick-search techniques across the whole CD-Rom; and
- Easy to paste into a word processor.

While much of the material is also found on the CD-Rom in word processing format, we strongly recommend you use the material in PDF format—not only because it is easiest to use, contains the most features, and includes more material, but also because you can easily switch back to a word processing format when you prefer.

Acrobat Reader 5.0.5 and 7.0.1 come free of charge with the CD-Rom. **We strongly recommend that new Acrobat users read the Acrobat tutorial on the Home Page. It takes two minutes and will really pay off.**

1 *Bankruptcy Forms* is for attorneys only, and does NOT include required statements for non-attorney "bankruptcy petition preparers."

2 Alternatively, click on the D:\Start.pdf file on "My Computer" or open that file in Acrobat—always assuming "D:" is the CD-Rom drive on your computer.

How to Find Documents in Word Processing Format

Most pleadings and other practice aids are also available in Microsoft Word format to make them more easily adaptable for individual use. (Current versions of WordPerfect are able to convert the Word documents upon opening them.) The CD-Rom offers several ways to find those word processing documents. One option is simply to browse to the folder on the CD-Rom containing all the word processing files and open the desired document from your standard word processing program, such as Word or WordPerfect. All word processing documents are in the D:\WP_Files folder, if "D:" is the CD-Rom drive,[3] and are further organized by book title. Documents that appear in the book are named after the corresponding appendix; other documents have descriptive file names.

Another option is to navigate the CD in PDF format, and, when a particular document is on the screen, click on the corresponding bookmark for the "Word version of . . ." This will automatically run Word, WordPerfect for Windows, *or any other word processor* that is associated with the ".DOC" extension, and then open the word processing file that corresponds to the Acrobat document.[4]

How to Use Law Disks' *Bankruptcy Forms*

This CD makes it easier than ever before to use Law Disks' *Bankruptcy Forms*. Just click on the Bankruptcy Forms Software button, and then click on the button for the form you wish to fill out, either in Word or Corel WordPerfect. Save the resulting file under a new name and print it out. There is no need to install the software to your hard drive.

Links are provided for information about specific local bankruptcy rules available on the Internet. In addition, a button provides information on electronic filing of bankruptcy forms.

Restricted Technical Support for Law Disks' *Bankruptcy Forms*

Bankruptcy Forms *is provided as a public service and as a bonus, so that law offices can file the basic bankruptcy forms using their word processors. This version of* Bankruptcy Forms *is unsupported software, which means: you may use the program, for your own use, without paying any additional charge. However, because you have received a working* Bankruptcy Forms *program at nominal cost,* **there is no technical support provided**.

This software allows insertion on most word processors of required information directly into the forms. Technical support should not be necessary. Please do not call NCLC with technical questions. If you feel you need technical support, you can purchase it from Law Disks, 734 Franklin Ave., Garden City, NY 11530, Tel. and FAX (516) 741-5740, support@lawdisks.com. For more information, visit Law Disks' web site at www.lawdisks.com or open the file "LawDisks" in the LAWDISKS subdirectory of this CD-Rom.

3 The CD-Rom drive could be any letter following "D:" depending on your computer's configuration.

4 For instructions on how to associate WordPerfect to the ".DOC" extension, go to the CD-Rom's home page and click on "How to Use/Help," then "Word Files."

Important Information Before Opening the CD-Rom Package

Before opening the CD-Rom package, please read this information. Opening the package constitutes acceptance of the following described terms. In addition, the *book* is not returnable once the seal to the *CD-Rom* has been broken.

The CD-Rom is copyrighted and all rights are reserved by the National Consumer Law Center, Inc. No copyright is claimed to the text of statutes, regulations, excerpts from court opinions, or any part of an original work prepared by a United States Government employee. *Bankruptcy Forms* is copyrighted 1991–2005 by Law Disks, all rights reserved. *Bankruptcy Forms* is the property of Law Disks.

You may not commercially distribute the CD-Rom or otherwise reproduce, publish, distribute or use the disk in any manner that may infringe on any copyright or other proprietary right of the National Consumer Law Center or Law Disks. Nor may you otherwise transfer the disk or this agreement to any other party unless that party agrees to accept the terms and conditions of this agreement. You may use the disk on only one computer and by one user at a time.

The CD-Rom is warranted to be free of defects in materials and faulty workmanship under normal use for a period of ninety days after purchase. If a defect is discovered in the disk during this warranty period, a replacement disk can be obtained at no charge by sending the defective disk, postage prepaid, with information identifying the purchaser, to National Consumer Law Center, Publications Department, 77 Summer Street, 10th Floor, Boston, MA 02110. After the ninety-day period, a replacement will be available on the same terms, but will also require a $20 prepayment.

The National Consumer Law Center makes no other warranty or representation, either express or implied, with respect to this disk, its quality, performance, merchantability, or fitness for a particular purpose. In no event will the National Consumer Law Center be liable for direct, indirect, special, incidental, or consequential damages arising out of the use or inability to use the disk. The exclusion of implied warranties is not effective in some states, and thus this exclusion may not apply to you.

Except as stated above, *Bankruptcy Forms* is sold AS IS, THERE ARE NO WARRANTIES, THERE IS NO WARRANTY OF MERCHANTABILITY, NOR ANY WARRANTY OF FITNESS FOR ANY PARTICULAR PURPOSE. ALL LIABILITY RESULTING FROM HOW THE USER FILLS IN THE FORM IS DISCLAIMED.

Some states do not allow the disclaimer of implied warranties, so this disclaimer may not apply to you. *Bankruptcy Forms* is an electronic form. Law Disks and NCLC have no control over how you fill in the form, and have no attorney-client relationship with you or with your clients. Using *Bankruptcy Forms* will be considered acceptance of the conditions above.

System Requirements

Use of this CD-Rom requires a Windows-based PC with a CD-Rom drive. (Macintosh users report success using NCLC CDs, but the CD has been tested only on Windows-based PCs.) The CD-Rom's features are optimized with Acrobat Reader 5 or later. Acrobat Reader versions 5.0.5 and 7.0.1 are included free on this CD-Rom, and either will work with this CD-Rom as long as it is compatible with your version of Windows. Acrobat Reader 5 is compatible with Windows 95/98/Me/NT/2000/XP, while Acrobat Reader 7.0.1 is compatible with Windows 98SE/Me/NT/2000/XP. If you already have Acrobat Reader 6.0, we *highly* recommend you download and install the 6.0.1 update from Adobe's web site at www.adobe.com because a bug in version 6.0 interferes with optimum use of this CD-Rom. See the *Acrobat 6 Problem* button on the home page for details. The Microsoft Word versions of pleadings and practice aids can be used with any reasonably current word processor (1995 or later).

One-Time Installation

When the CD-Rom is inserted in its drive, a menu will pop up automatically. (Please be patient if you have a slow CD-Rom drive; this will only take a few moments.) If you do not already have Acrobat Reader 5.0.5 or 7.0.1, first click the "Install Acrobat Reader" button. Do not reboot, but then click on the "Make Shortcut Icon" button. (You need not make another shortcut icon if you already have done so for another NCLC CD.) Then reboot and follow the *How to Use the CD-Rom* instructions above.

[*Note*: If the pop-up menu fails to appear, go to "My Computer," right-click "D:" if that is the CD-Rom drive, and select "Open." Then double-click on "Read_Me.txt" for alternate installation and use instructions.]